BEHAVIOR MODIFICATION

Handbook of
Assessment, Intervention,
and Evaluation

Eileen D. Gambrill

BEHAVIOR MODIFICATION

Handbook of
Assessment, Intervention,
and Evaluation

Jossey-Bass Publishers
San Francisco • Washington • London • 1977

BEHAVIOR MODIFICATION
Handbook of Assessment, Intervention, and Evaluation
by Eileen D. Gambrill

The Jossey-Bass
Behavioral Science Series

THE AUTHOR

Eileen D. Gambrill is associate professor of social welfare at the University of California, Berkeley. She received the Ph.D. in social work and psychology from the University of Michigan in 1965 and then spent a year on a clinical postdoctoral fellowship to study behavior therapy with Joseph Wolpe. In 1966-67 she was assistant professor in the Department of Social Work and lecturer in the Department of Psychology at the University of Wisconsin, Madison, and from 1967-1970 she taught in the School of Social Work at the University of Michigan. While at Michigan, she was associate project director of a grant to explore the utilization of behavioral methods in social welfare; articles published in *Behavior Therapy* and *Social Work* (1970 and 1971) describe this endeavor. She joined the faculty at the University of California, Berkeley, in 1970.

Gambrill's special research interests while at the University of California have included decision making in foster care, social skills training, and developing and evaluating procedures for training paraprofessionals in behavioral procedures. In relation to these special interest areas, Gambrill has published *Decision Making in Foster Care: A Training Manual* (with Ted J. Stein, 1976), a series of articles in *Public Welfare* (with Kermit T. Wiltse and Ted J. Stein, 1974-75), and *It's Up to You: Developing Assertive Social Skills* (with Cheryl A. Richey, 1976). In addition, she has been editor of the Newsletter of the Association for Advancement of Behavior Therapy for the past three years and is currently on the editorial board of *Behavior Therapy*.

To the memory of my parents
Irene and William Gambrill

Preface

Behavior modification is a mode of therapy and a way of understanding individuals that differs from, yet has parallels to, other therapeutic approaches. It focuses on the interaction between the individual and his environment, including both internal and external events. The number of people interested in this field has grown rapidly over the past decade. An almost overwhelming quantity of material is now available on the various assessment, intervention, and evaluation techniques that give this mode of therapy its distinctive quality. To date, however, no one source has offered information about the vast range of applications while also focusing specifically on how to apply behavioral procedures. In preparing this handbook, it has been my desire to include—in one volume—as much information as possible, yet to keep this information within a framework most useful to those professionals who are currently using—or wish to use—behavior modification methods in their work.

To achieve this goal, three elements are emphasized throughout the handbook—*assessment, intervention,* and *evaluation.* A number of chapters deal extensively with the steps involved in assessment, and every chapter that addresses a special problem area presents additional information on assessment methods. Intervention and evaluation procedures are likewise stressed, for successful application of a behavioral model of practice requires becoming aware of the many intervention possibilities that exist. Selecting those plans that have a high probability of success and that are also agreeable to the client and learning how to evaluate what is happening—even with initially vague presenting problems—is a critical aspect of behavior therapy.

Although my primary intent has been to show, in a step-by-step manner, how to use behavioral methods in practice, several other concerns have been influential in compiling this handbook. By presenting a wide variety of techniques, I hope to reach several groups of professionals—not only those who are currently practicing behavior modification or some other method, and who wish to expand their range, but also those who are just beginning their practices and could benefit from a compendium of information about this field. Since the book describes many aspects of behavioral practice that have often been neglected—such as the concern for client involvement—professionals will recognize continuities between their current methods and behavioral procedures. Thus, no matter what the orientation of the practitioner is, the material presented in this volume can prove useful. Social workers, psychologists, psychiatrists, and counselors who work in open settings (such as family service agencies, community mental health centers, and child guidance centers) will be able to view the ways in which behavioral methods have been used with numerous problems and will also be able to begin to employ these methods in practice.

As an outgrowth of my concern to reach as many professionals as possible, I have tried to give a realistic view of what the field of behavior modification actually is. There are a surprising number of misconceptions and stereotypes about behavioral methods. Contrary to the image presented in much of the popular literature and in movies such as *Clockwork Orange*, clients are very much involved in the behavior modification process—in the selection both of procedures and of objectives. In addition, the thoughts and feelings of clients, as well as external events, are considered. Stereotypes have the disadvantage of making any approach appear more limited than it really is, and the same is true of this field. There is a great diversity of ways to assess a problem, deal with it, and evaluate the results, and one of the strengths of behavior modification is its adaptability to specific circumstances.

Further, the everyday realities of clinical practice often do not mesh with what is put forth as *ideal*. Practitioners often have to work within limitations of time, what data or data-gathering means are available, equipment at one's disposal, what the client is comfortable with, and so on. To be able to recognize what is practical is vital if the practitioner is to employ behavioral methods with a reasonable assurance of success. That is why I have included a range of procedures related to each problem area. If sophisticated equipment is not available to the professional, other options are available. If a client is unwilling to undertake a certain approach to achieve desired outcomes, there are other methods that may be effective.

Above all, my intent in preparing this handbook has been to help practitioners become informed consumers of the behavioral literature. As behavioral methods continue to be practiced, as more and more data become available on the effectiveness of specific techniques, certain precepts about the field will change. Some procedures will be modified; controlled experimental work will introduce other procedures. Readers are encouraged to keep up with the ever-changing literature, and this book should provide a good base on which to start the keeping-up process. Numerous journals found in the reference section have published, and continue to publish, important articles in the field. Those devoted especially to behavioral methods include *Behaviour Research and Therapy, Journal of Behavior Therapy and Experimental Psychiatry, Journal of Applied Behavior Analysis, Behavior Therapy, Behavior Modification,* and *Cognitive Behavior Modification.* In addition, many relevant articles will be found scattered in other journals.

Six themes woven throughout this handbook underscore

my orientation and what I have tried to accomplish: (1) *The self-management aspects of behavioral procedures*—that is, the extent to which the client learns how to create changes in his or her own environment. Self-management can mean learning how to regulate anxiety, learning new social behaviors that allow one to expand his range of social interactions, or learning negotiation skills that allow, for example, a teenager to remain with her parents rather than be removed from home. (2) The importance of taking into account *internal events, such as thoughts, as well as external events.* What we say to ourselves—various misconceptions or unrealistic expectations (whether negative or positive), for example—may profoundly influence how we behave. (3) *The need for multiform assessment and intervention*, in which many possible factors related to a problem area are identified and intervention procedures selected accordingly. It is necessary to identify the factors related to a presenting problem, the way in which significant others may or may not contribute to the problem area, the assets of the client and his significant others, and so forth. Then, given selected objectives, the possible intervention procedures can be decided on. (4) *The advantages and ethics of being accountable*—that is, determining the effectiveness of certain procedures in any given situation. Examples are offered on how presenting problems can be more clearly identified during assessment and on how behavior, feelings, or thoughts related to these can be identified and monitored to see if they are, in fact, changing. (5) *The careful search for client assets* during assessment so that they can be usefully employed in change efforts. The behavioral perspective encourages viewing clients in terms of their assets instead of their deficits, so that change efforts can build on existing skills. (6) *Involving the client in the change process to the greatest extent possible.* Such involvement includes designing a clear counselor-client contract that identifies the responsibilities and expectations of each party. It also includes assuring the conditions for informed consent in selecting both change procedures and objectives. This is an ethical stance that also helps clients learn to make decisions for themselves.

The coverage in this handbook is based on the following criteria: the extent of the empirical literature supporting various methods, the degree to which the client may be comfortable with various methods, the frequency with which a problem is posed in open settings (in contrast to residential settings), the degree to which the method offers useful self-management skills to the client, and the ease with which the procedure can be arranged. Thus, in choosing between a method that induces discomfort and one that does not but seems to be as effective, I have opted to describe the latter. Likewise, I have chosen to emphasize procedures that do not require special apparatus. Case examples are included throughout the book to illustrate assessment, intervention, and evaluation methods.

Chapter One takes an overall look at the behavioral model of practice and discusses various misconceptions about behavioral methods. Basic behavioral principles are discussed in Chapter Two, and important features of behavioral practice in Chapter Three. Such features include understanding the client's view of the problem, forming a more helpful conceptualization of the problem, and securing client involvement. Chapters Four through Seven are devoted to assessment, particularly to areas that cause difficulty for those new to a behavioral approach—such as determining ways to define behaviors, thoughts, or feelings so that these can be readily monitored by the client or counselor. Attention is also paid to defining specific objectives so that progress can be evaluated and to identifying reinforcers and significant others to use in change programs.

Chapter Eight focuses on factors to consider in selecting intervention plans, describes a variety of ways to evaluate the effectiveness of intervention procedures, and discusses ways to ensure that changes will be maintained. Chapters Nine through Twenty-One describe the application of behavioral procedures to special populations and problem areas, such as parent-child and marital interaction; dysfunctional anger and anxiety reactions; social skill deficits; alcohol and drug problems; and use of behavioral methods in education settings, with health-related problems, with severe behavior disturbances, and with sexual problems. Assessment information relevant to each area is presented in these chapters, and a behavioral view of the problem or interaction area offered. For example, differences between happily married and unhappy couples are discussed in Chapter

Ten, and descriptive studies of the differences between de-pressed and nondepressed individuals are described in Chapter Fourteen. Also presented in each chapter are a variety of behav-ioral procedures designed to alter specific reactions, guidelines for selecting procedures, and the advantages and disadvantages of each. Chapter Twenty-Two discusses ethical issues, and Chap-ter Twenty-Three highlights a number of topics that will be of special concern in the future, such as increasing accountability and preventive efforts.

In keeping with my primary intent, I have focused on the use of behavioral principles in practice. Competence in generic interviewing skills, such as achieving rapport with clients, is assumed; however, interviewing skills that are uniquely relevant to use of behavioral methods are described. Since it is likely that no new intervention approach can be learned simply by reading and practice by oneself, I strongly encourage readers to seek supervision in the use of new procedures.

In addition to the primary audience mentioned earlier, this book should also be useful in graduate courses in profes-sional schools where behavioral methods are taught, such as in schools of social work, psychology departments, psychiatry training programs, and counselor training programs. The mate-rial it contains complements currently available books that describe the empirical literature related to given methods but do not discuss how to employ behavioral procedures in practice.

It pleases me to offer a special acknowledgment to Edwin J. Thomas of the University of Michigan School of Social Work for his early vision of the potential value of behavioral princi-ples to the field of social work and for his encouragement of students to develop or continue their interest in this area. A spe-cial note of thanks is also due Joseph Wolpe at Temple Univer-sity for what he has contributed to the field of behavior therapy and for his openness to having his work viewed week after week by a budding behavioral therapist. A third note of thanks goes to Kermit T. Wiltse of the School of Social Welfare, University of California, Berkeley, for his pragmatic approach to social problems, which is so very compatible with a behavioral view. The contribution of doctoral students over the years who have established an interest in behavioral methods is gratefully acknowledged, as are the efforts of all those persons who have contributed to the increasingly rich supply of information concerning behavioral methods and whose work I have utilized so liberally in this handbook.

Berkeley, California   Eileen D. Gambrill
March 1977

Contents

Contents

Therapy (Rational Restructuring) • Thought Stopping
• Coping Skills That Emphasize the Role of Affective
Reactions • Role of Problem-Solving Skills •
Learning How to Handle Anger

BEHAVIOR MODIFICATION

Handbook of
Assessment, Intervention,
and Evaluation

1

Assumptions about why people behave as they do and about how change can be brought about influence what information is considered necessary about problems as well as the intervention processes selected. Thus, the assumptions of counselors concerning why people behave in certain ways and how they can change is more than a personal matter—these assumptions affect the type of help clients receive. A bewildering and diverse array of theories of change are now available and they compete for attention and adherents. However, in spite of these many options there are few well-controlled studies that compare the effectiveness of different methods with selected populations (see, for example, Paul, 1966; Sloane, Staples, Cristol, Yorkston, and Whipple, 1975).

Overview of
Behavior Modification

Most frameworks tend to emphasize either inner events or outer events, although some stress the importance of both. Traditional psychoanalytic theory, for example, stresses inner events, the remembered experience, and the long past occurrence. Traditional Rogerian theory assumes that each person contains within himself the direction for his own development and that it is the role of the counselor to bring this more clearly into the client's awareness. Forms of encounter and group therapy assume that experiencing ourselves in relation to others, seeing ourselves through the eyes of others, will help us change. Existential views stress the need for choice, the responsibility of each person to choose among the many alternatives that life poses.

Many change efforts are now guided by some form of psychoanalytic framework. Inherent in this framework is the assumption that observable behavioral problems are only the outward signs of some underlying process, which must be altered to bring about any lasting change. A focus of change efforts on the behavior itself, according to this model, would not succeed, because no change has supposedly been brought about in underlying causative factors. Other aspects of this common orientation include an emphasis on verbal reports concerning early histories, the tendency to label client problems and efforts to alter inner processes by verbal means. In contrast, in more recent years there has been a growing interest in a mode of understanding and influencing behavior that rests far more on the identification of factors external to the person, on factors existing in the personal environment of the subject. This mode of therapy and of understanding stresses the relationship of the individual to his environment. This relationship is posited to be an interactive one, in which there is mutual influence between the individual and environmental events, in ways discoverable by systematic study of these interactions. This stance offers another way to view the world and, as with all new views, if it is embraced some old beliefs will be abandoned, some questioned, and others bolstered. Seeing the world a bit differently can be an interesting pursuit in and of itself. But, more importantly, hopefully it will offer new skills to use in helping people attain their goals.

Characteristics of a Behavioral Model

This behavioral model contains many assumptions that differ from the psychodynamic model and that influence the kind of information required about a client and that direct the kinds of techniques used to modify behavior. Behavior modification may be seen as having a number of essential characteristics, each playing a vital role in understanding and altering behavior.

Assessment and Intervention Informed by Behavioral Principles. The data base on which behavior modification itself rests consists of the theoretical and empirical literature within social learning theory that has been generated over the past fifty years. Behavioral intervention does not rest so much on theories devised to account for observed relationships between behavior and environmental conditions, as on the empirical relationships that have been found to hold over a wide range of animal species, behaviors, and situations. Today we know far more than we did thirty years ago about how our behavior is affected by its relationship with the environment. We know that various relationships between behavior and the environment result in certain rates and patterns of behavior, and these principles of behavior form the basis of contingency management—the rearrangement of relationships between behavior and environmental events so that desirable behaviors increase and undesirable ones decrease. Behavior modification is the use and evaluation of these principles in applied settings. Certainly, in practice, hypothetical extensions of knowledge are made and it would be untrue to say that the application of behavioral principles is totally empirically based. However, it is accurate to say that those who employ behavioral methods draw from the empirical and theoretical literature within the field of social learning. This body of work and theory is used for devising assessment and intervention procedures, procedures that are modified by continual concern for evaluation of their effectiveness. Practice in this field is thus informed and guided by these principles.

Emphasis on Identification of Current Controlling Conditions. The behavioral model emphasizes the *relationship* between behavior and the *current* antecedent and consequent events that affect behavior. This is in contrast to an account that may merely place a label on the behavior. A teacher, for example, may say, "Ralph is aggressive." If pressed to explain what she means by the word *aggressive*, she may say that Ralph hits other children and talks out in class. Often descriptive accounts are also accepted as explanatory, that is, as inferring causation. If the teacher is asked why Ralph behaves this way, and answers, "Because he is aggressive," she is employing a descriptive term as a pseudoexplanatory term (Staats and Staats, 1963). The difficulty here, if choice of intervention method is at issue, is that one may think that the means are now at hand to select an intervention method; however, no information has been added concerning the determinants of the behavior that would aid in deciding on intervention.

The behavioral model entails the identification of the events that occasion and maintain behavior. These may be located inside a person—for example, anticipation of consequences (Bandura, 1969) and self-reinforcement—or in the external environment. In the example already used, let us assume that both peer and teacher attention followed Ralph's hitting other children and talking out, whereas appropriate behaviors were ignored. A functional relationship may then be inferred between these behaviors and such attention. We are in a much different situation now regarding implications for intervention, because the maintaining conditions for the behaviors have been tentatively identified. Attention is directed toward identification of the ways in which environments related to problematic behaviors are deviant, rather than toward deviant behavior.

The past is considered to be reflected in the present, and information about a person's past may provide valuable information as to available resources or unusual social histories that may be related to presenting problems. However, such information about a past condition need not imply some continuing difficulty stemming from that event. Conditions sustaining the present behavior may be quite different from those present when the behavior was established.

Deemphasis on Labeling. Practitioners working within many interpersonal helping modes, including the behavioral one, have come to distrust psychiatric and other diagnostic labels. These categories are very difficult to define explicitly (they seldom include explicit reference to behavior), they are used inconsistently, and the labels do not indicate any treatment modality (Kanfer and Saslow, 1969). This lack of emphasis on the use of "diagnostic" labels removes the possibility of using these in an explanatory sense and so of beclouding attempts to move from assessment to intervention. Iatrogenic (physician-induced) effects may result from the labeling process. That is, as a result of labeling, other people as well as the client may prompt behaviors compatible with the label. If Ralph's teacher writes in his record that he is "aggressive," his next teacher, who may read this, may react in a different manner toward him. She may provoke behaviors that are congruent with the label, because she expects them to occur. Also, if Ralph is told that he is "aggressive" often enough, this may increase the frequency of cues he presents to himself via the label and so increase undesirable behavior.

The classification of behavior into categories (labeling) is itself viewed as a behavior that varies from culture to culture, from person to person, and from time to time, dependent on maintaining conditions within a given environment (Szasz, 1961). It is of particular relevance to examine the historical development of the label *mentally ill*, because this label is still widely used and its attachment to an individual may have many undesirable effects. Sarbin (1967) points out that the label *illness* was first used as a metaphor, and later reified into a mythical entity. The "as if . . ." at first attached to a description—for example, "It is *as if* she were sick"—was later dropped, leaving the statement, "She is sick." The same transition is illustrated for the term *mental illness*. "Contemporary users of the mental-illness concept are guilty of illicitly shifting from metaphor to myth. Instead of maintaining the metaphorical rhetoric, 'it is as if there were states of mind,' and 'it is as if some *states of the mind* could be characterized as sickness,' the contemporary mentalist conducts much of his work as if he believes that minds are   real   entities and that, like bodies, they can be sick or healthy. . . . One outcome of the exclusive verbal preoccupation with psychic states is the neglect and avoidance of events in the social systems that might be antecedent to instances of misconduct illicitly and arbitrarily called *symptoms*" (Sarbin, 1967, pp. 450-451).

Emphasis on Observable, Countable Responses. Traditionally, practitioners have concerned themselves with many classes of events that are unobservable, such as thoughts, feelings, states, and moods, with no attempt to identify referents for these that are observable and countable either by the individual himself or by someone else. Trying to change uncount-

able entities presents many difficulties. It may prevent determination of the conditions that maintain the behavior. If the
behavior is only vaguely described—for example, if the teacher
does not identify the behaviors to which she refers when she
says, "Ralph is aggressive"—it will be difficult to locate the
events related to these behaviors. Lack of specification may
therefore prohibit effective intervention, because if the maintaining conditions are not isolated, intervention may be mis-
directed. Also, obtaining a baseline regarding the behavior is
impossible. That is, we will not know how often the behavior
occurred prior to intervention and so will have difficulty in
accurately assessing the effects of any change methods introduced. Within a behavioral model, the behaviors, thoughts, or
feelings selected for change must be countable and observable,
either by the client or, preferably, by someone else, in addition
to being relevant to presenting problems. For example, a client
with low self-esteem could count the number of positive and
negative self-statements that occurred each day. The goals of
intervention are clearly stated and a written agreement is
entered into between the counselor and client. This precludes
the pursuit of hidden objectives. The counselor is *not* free to
pursue whatever objectives he feels would be helpful to the
client. Because objectives are clearly stated, the client is in a
better position to question the counselor if actions are recommended or areas are explored that seem to bear no relation to
goals.

     Emphasis on Positive, not Punitive Change Methods. The
behavioral model emphasizes increasing desirable behaviors,
thoughts, or feelings through use of positive methods. Clients
are encouraged to "catch" others doing something good, rather
than to try to "catch" them doing something bad, and the same
applies to their own behavior. This emphasis is made not only
because people find the use of positive methods more pleasant,
but also because positive methods are usually more effective.
The most extensive accumulation of data indicating that punishment is often *not* an effective way to change behavior has been
generated within a behavioral perspective (see, for example,
Azrin and Holz, 1966). Only in special situations would presen-

tation of aversive events be recommended; for example, if a behavior is very dangerous to the client, or where the rate of inappropriate behavior is so high that it is difficult or impossible to increase desirable behaviors without first decreasing undesirable ones.

Emphasis on Measurement of Effects. Those who utilize a behavioral model display a concern for collecting quantitative data regarding the effects of intervention. Obtaining such data is less problematic in the behavioral model, compared with other models, because behaviors are identified in observable, countable terms. The frequency, magnitude, or duration of a behavior, thought, or feeling before intervention is compared with the frequency, magnitude, or duration after change efforts. Evaluation is integrally related to case management in that it provides feedback for both clients and practitioners as to what is working and to what degree. Clients themselves often gather the data needed for evaluation.

Rejection of Special Causative Factors Related to "Problematic" Behavior. Within many traditional theories of psychopathology, processes are inferred to exist that are not inferred when "normal" behavior is considered (Ullman and Krasner, 1969). In the behavioral model, no such distinction is made concerning the controlling conditions of behavior labeled as *normal* and behavior labeled as *abnormal*. All behavior is considered to be governed by the same principles of behavior, although certainly there are varied social histories that may result in a wide range of diverse behavior.

The Role of Thoughts and Feelings

Thoughts are taken into account both in understanding behavior as well as in the development of procedures to alter behavior; in fact, the major experimental work supporting the importance of cognitive factors lies within social learning research (see, for example, Bandura, 1969). The emphasis given to cognitive processes is highlighted by Bandura's (in press) recent proposal that changes achieved by various intervention methods are effective to the extent that they alter the level and strength of expectations of personal efficacy (the conviction that one can successfully execute the behavior required to produce a given outcome). This is contrasted with outcome expectancy, which is defined "as a person's estimate that a given behavior will lead to certain outcomes" (p. 5). "Outcome and efficacy expectations are differentiated because individuals can believe that a particular course of action will produce certain outcomes, but such information does not influence their behavior, because they entertain serious doubts about whether they can perform the necessary activities" (p. 5). Expectations of personal mastery thus affect both the display as well as the persistence of coping behavior. What we anticipate influences our behavior, and awareness of the relationship between behavior and its consequences facilitates learning (Bandura, 1969). What clients think in anticipation of, during, or following problematic reactions is important to identify in order to select effective intervention procedures. However, within a behavioral approach, one does not depend solely on altered awareness to induce and maintain changes in behavior, thoughts, or feelings. It is considered important to complement awareness or new attitudes with environmental supports as well as by the establishment of needed skills.

Many behavioral methods rely heavily on cognitive factors, including, for example, the stress inoculation methods described in Chapter Twelve. Thoughts are also of concern when a client has misconceptions about his behavior or environment. As in many approaches, these must be challenged, their role in maintaining difficulties identified, and more accurate conceptions developed. And careful attention must be devoted during change efforts to creating client expectations that will facilitate change.

Problematic emotional reactions are often of concern to clients, and feelings may serve as antecedents for emotional reactions, thoughts, or behavior. Some of the oldest methods employed within a behavioral framework were concerned with altering problematic feelings, such as anxiety (see, for example, Wolpe, 1958). Clients acquire skills that allow them to influence feelings such as tension, anger, and depression (see, for example,

Chapter Twelve). However, an emphasis solely on changing feelings to remedy problems is rejected. There is a recognition of the degree to which *both* thoughts and feelings are influenced by what happens in our environment based on an extensive experimental literature in both laboratory and applied settings (see, for example, Bandura, 1969; Kanfer and Phillips, 1969). Achieving a change in feeling may not rectify a lack of needed skills, change faulty thought patterns, or arrange incentives in the natural environment that may be required to support such changes. Feelings are considered to be by-products of the relationships between behavior and the environment (Skinner, 1971). That is, rather than a feeling causing a certain behavior, the feeling itself is considered to be a product of what we have experienced. Feelings serve as clues to relationships between behavior and environment. Devoting sole attention to feelings and attitudes as causative agents often results in ignoring important environmental factors that influence behavior.

The Question of Symptom Substitution

According to psychoanalytic theory, presenting problems are merely the surface manifestations of underlying difficulties, and it is these to which attention must be devoted for change to take place that is not accompanied by an increase in other problem behavior. Because the behavioral model of change does not accept this particular version of the medical model, it is not expected that remedying presenting problems will be accompanied by an increase in other problems.

The occurrence or nonoccurrence of symptom substitution is an empirical question. That is, has it been found to take place or not? As Bandura (1969) notes, the symptom substitution hypothesis cannot be adequately tested, because it fails to specify exactly what constitutes a symptom, when such substitution should take place, the social conditions that most facilitate its occurrence, and the form that it will take. Thus, even if continued examination of a client's behavior were to be made year after year following treatment, no reliable criteria are available to distinguish between substitute behaviors, the development of new undesirable behaviors that have nothing to do with those previously under treatment, or the persistence of old, undesirable behaviors that simply had not been noticed before until even more unadaptive behavior was eliminated.

Because of the strong emphasis within traditional analytic theory on the issue of symptom substitution, many studies in the behavioral literature have attempted to determine whether symptom substitution has occurred, even though, as noted, this is a difficult undertaking because of the definitional problems of the concept of a symptom (see, for example, Paul, 1968). It is now well demonstrated that symptom substitution does not occur if important related antecedent and maintaining conditions are addressed. In fact, the decrease of a presenting problem is more typically followed by positive changes in how a person feels and thinks about himself and others (see, for example, Wahler and Pollio, 1968), as well as by an increase in the positive feelings of significant others. For example, elimination of bed wetting that has been a problem for many months or years is usually a great relief to a parent, and enables the parent to respond more positively toward his or her child. Developing social skills in an adult woman who complains that she has few friends offers her ways to increase her range of pleasurable events. Removal of presenting problems, given adequate intervention, thus usually leads to positive changes rather than to the occurrence of other problems.

The caveat in the last sentence is "given adequate intervention." Assessment should include a careful search for factors to which a problem might be related. Unlike the analytic approach, this search is mainly within the current environment and recent past. Drinking behavior, for example, may be related to a variety of inter- and intrapersonal factors such as lack of assertive behavior and marital discord. If such factors are not located and modified during intervention, a recurrence of drinking or, more probably, a failure to change drinking patterns may occur. Behavioral intervention, then, is not focused solely on the presenting problem or "symptom."

Misconceptions About Behavioral Methods

There are a number of beliefs about behavioral methods that are inaccurate. The terminology of the approach has facilitated the development of some of these myths, particularly terms such as *behavior modification*, which seems to connote a cold, mechanistic, inhumane approach to interpersonal helping. Also, writers in this area have sometimes neglected to describe components of their procedures that are important in all interpersonal helping endeavors, such as respect and regard for clients, the importance of putting clients at ease, and the concern for client rights. Reservations about employing a behavioral perspective may be caused by acceptance of some of these beliefs.

"Behavior Modification Makes Heavy Use of Aversive Control." As behavioral methods have become more popular, there has been increasing mislabeling of change attempts as *behavioral*. Some people consider the term *behavior modification* to refer to any attempt to alter behavior, including chemotherapy, brain surgery, and electroshock therapy procedures, which have nothing to do with the systematic application of behavioral principles. The belief that aversive control is emphasized within a behavioral model has been fostered by media presentations such as the movie *Clockwork Orange*, which has incorrectly been construed to depict behavior modification methods. The movie certainly depicts an attempt to change behavior, but it does not appropriately employ behavioral methods. It shows no use of positive reinforcement for alternative behaviors nor careful planning for the maintenance of desirable behaviors in the natural environment, nor was the client a participant in selection of objectives. This demonstrates the disadvantage of the popular term for the behavioral model of intervention, *behavior modification*. People have been trying to alter the behavior of their fellows since the beginning of time, but only in select instances could we say that a behavior modification procedure was used.

"Behavioral Methods Make Use of Bribery." Some people

object to the emphasis within the behavioral approach on the use of positive events, on the grounds that this is bribery. The term *bribery*, however, refers to giving someone something for carrying out an unethical action. Thus, the use of positive reinforcers, to increase desirable behaviors could not accurately be considered bribery. Strangely enough, there is often a willingness to punish undesirable behaviors, but an unwillingness to offer positive incentives to increase behaviors that "the person should do anyway." This is usually coupled with a failure to recognize external incentives for one's own behavior. For example, a teacher may say that she teaches because she loves it. However, it is somewhat doubtful if most teachers would continue working without pay.

"People Become Dependent on External Incentives." A concern is sometimes raised that if positive incentives are offered for appropriate behavior, the person will become dependent on them. The term *dependency* may refer either to continued expectations of reinforcement for performance or to loss of intrinsic interest in the activity after external reinforcers are offered. Incentives that are not already part of the natural environment are avoided when possible. If it is necessary to introduce artificial reinforcers such as tokens or points, a part of the total program is arranging their removal and maintaining behavior under natural conditions. There is conflicting evidence that the introduction of external reinforcers will undermine intrinsic interest (see, for example, Feingold and Mahoney, 1975). Usually, external reinforcers are not introduced when intrinsic ones are present.

"Other Interpersonal Helping Skills Must be Discarded." It is sometimes thought that available interpersonal helping skills must be discarded if a behavioral model of intervention is adopted. This is not true. The ability to place people at ease during interviews, to develop rapport, to be a careful observer of clients in order to catch possible contradictions between verbal and nonverbal behavior, and to perceive emotional changes in clients are all important within a behavioral framework. Exposure to a wide range of clients and the appreciation for the diverse environmental stresses that may affect people

that this cultivates makes it more likely that relevant areas will be explored. The ability to recognize biases and the skills that have been developed for being careful not to impose these on clients are invaluable here too.

"Behavior Modification Dehumanizes People." Central to the objection that behavioral modification dehumanizes people is the belief that there is no room within a behavioral approach for self-direction, the belief that, within a behavioral framework, people are considered to be pawns of their environment. In fact, however, the roles of thoughts and feelings are recognized and a stress placed on offering the client skills that will enable greater influence over his environment (see, for example, Watson and Tharp, 1972; Thoreson and Mahoney, 1974). It is believed that the best way to guard against or alter unwanted influence is to recognize that one is being influenced and a goal of many behavioral programs is to offer clients an understanding of basic behavioral principles and change methods to use these in their daily lives. Many writers in the field, such as Skinner (1953, 1971), have advocated wide distribution of information about the principles of behavior so people can recognize ways in which their behavior is influenced by the environment and so be in a more informed position to alter it. The belief that behavior modification dehumanizes people also seems related to the view that behavioral methods impose control where none exists (Skinner, 1953). This view fails to recognize the influence processes that are already present. Denying the influence of behavioral principles no more negates their effects than would the law of gravity be suspended if we did not believe this (unless, of course, we quickly started to rise).

One source of the belief that behavioral methods impose objectives on people more so than other helping methods stems from the mislabeling of some efforts as *behavioral.* Another source of such statements seems to stem from the incorrect belief that behavioral methods are all-powerful, that anyone who is familiar with them can readily employ them to create change without the awareness or willingness of others. It is, fortunately, *not* an easy matter to change someone's behavior without their awareness, and if a person does not wish to have their behavior altered, it is impossible to do so unless one has access to important controlling variables in the environment. The client is an active participant in the selection of objectives within a behavioral model of intervention. Recognition of the role that environmental conditions play in maintaining problematic behaviors, and the rejection of the traditional medical model of illness, prevents the imposition of invidious labels on clients.

All helping endeavors contain social influence factors (Bandura, 1969). Clients become familiar with the counselor's view of the world and may begin using it to explain their own world. Counselor behavior within the interview influences the client's behavior even in very nondirective helping approaches (see, for example, Truax, 1966). This source of influence is well recognized within a behavioral approach, which encourages the counselor to be careful not to unduly influence the client in the selection of objectives and to make biases clear if they exist. Nonrecognition of such influences allows their use in an unsystematic or undercover way. These characteristics of a behavioral approach are well within a view of concerned helping as enhancing awareness of external influence and offering skills in expanding one's range of influence.

"Use of Behavioral Methods Will not be Challenging." Some seem to believe that use of a behavioral model, although it might be helpful to clients, will not require imagination and creativity. However, as with all methods of interpersonal helping, knowledge as well as creativity are needed. Both assessment and intervention procedures are tailored for each client. Assessment requires a range of skills as well as creativity to discover relevant maintaining conditions and antecedents and to determine alternative behaviors, thoughts, or feelings to be increased. Because behavioral methods do not rely on insight or awareness alone in achieving change, the client must be helped to arrange his environment so that he will learn to provide incentives to maintain behavior, and needed skills must be established. Evaluation offers concrete feedback that can be usefully employed in case management. Of course, the only way to discover whether a behavioral framework can be useful and challenging to employ is to become familiar with this and try it out.

"There Is Really Nothing New About the Behavioral Approach." An easy way to discount anything new is to say that one already does it. Now, the principles of behavior do affect everyone. However, this does not mean that they are employed in a systematic way to alter behavior, thoughts, or feelings. It is the *systematicness* with which behavioral principles are applied in relation to identified objectives and the concern for evaluation of change efforts that characterize a behavioral approach. Random or occasional, unevaluated use of positive incentives to change vaguely defined or even well-defined behaviors is not a behavioral approach.

"Behavior Modification Only Deals with Superficial Problems." Over the years, particularly within the last decade, behavioral methods have been applied to the total range of clinical problems, as is illustrated in this book. The belief that behavioral modification is superficial, like some other misconceptions, results from a lack of familiarity with the breadth of behavioral efforts.

"Behavior Modification Teaches People How to Manipulate Each Other." Behavior modification, if effective, offers clients ways to influence their environment, a large part of which may be other people, but does not teach them to manipulate this environment in an insidious or unfair way. A good example of this is assertion training, in which clients are encouraged to express positive and negative feelings in a way that does not injure themselves or others (Alberti and Emmons, 1974). Clients are encouraged to involve significant others in change efforts and to pursue reciprocally pleasing changes in which no one gains at the other's expense; rather, both gain.

There may be situations when an ethical argument could be made for showing one group how to change the behavior of another group without the awareness of the latter. For example, students aged twelve to fifteen have been taught how to increase their teachers' positive statements and to decrease their negative statements (Graubard, Rosenberg, and Miller, 1971). It could be said that such an endeavor is unfair to the teachers. However, if students have no other way to alter the teachers' behavior, it could also be argued that it is unethical to withhold such skills from them. Ethical issues involved in behavior change are discussed more fully in Chapter Twenty-Two.

"The Use of Behavioral Methods Implies Acceptance of a Specific Value System." Technology itself does not offer guidelines as to how it should be employed. The fact that we can now split atoms and generate enormous energy sources does not inform us as to what to do with this capability. The same is true with the principles of behavior—the discovery of systematic relationships between behavior and the environment does not inform us as to how this knowledge should be employed. No particular value system is implied by a technology of behavior change; like any other knowledge, it can be employed for humanitarian purposes or for purposes that serve only the interests of a few to the detriment of many.

"The Counselor-Client Relationship is Unimportant Within a Behavioral Framework." It is often mistakenly assumed that the relationship between the counselor and the client is unimportant when employing behavioral methods. This is not the case. The empathy and warmth of the counselor increase the probability that clients will share important information, because they will be more comfortable and more willing to carry out agreed-on assignments that are essential for treatment effects. However, these relationship factors are not considered the sole or main effective ingredient in achieving desired outcomes. Rather, they are viewed as the interpersonal context within which intervention is most likely to be successful. It should also be noted that in work with some clients, such as autistic children or severely psychotic patients, there is initially no possibility for establishing a relationship. One advantage of behavioral methods is that they can be employed without the necessity of establishing a relationship.

"Behavioral Methods Impose Control Where None Exists." Some view the use of behavioral methods as imposing control where none exists. This view fails to recognize the influence of environmental factors already present. Functional relationships affect our behavior whether or not we wish to accord them recognition. It is true that preexisting contingencies (associations between our behavior and the environment) may not be

"planned." Use of behavioral principles to increase appropriate behaviors entails their systematic use, in contrast with the haphazard manner in which contingencies may have been arranged. It is sometimes said that the contingencies that already exist are "more natural," meaning that no one has systematically arranged them to attain given ends. This lack of planning may be precisely why the client seeks aid with problems in living. The accidental arrangement of contingencies is just as "controlling" in terms of influencing behavior as are planned contingencies. As Skinner (1953) has noted, the problems raised by the possible control of behavior cannot be avoided by refusing to recognize the possibility of control and its implications.

Summary

The behavioral model of intervention entails the systematic application of behavioral principles. There is an emphasis on the current relationship between behavior and the environment, and people are considered to both influence and be influenced by the environment. The focus is placed on the presenting problem as well as on factors that appear to be related to it. There is a concern with identifying problems in observable terms, and an emphasis on positive methods of change and on evaluation of change efforts. The role of thoughts and feelings is considered, as well as that of overt behavior. Special causative factors related to problematic behavior are rejected, as is the use of labels.

A variety of misconceptions are held about behavioral methods, including the belief that heavy use is made of aversive control and bribery and that other helping skills, such as those involved in establishing a relationship, must be discarded. Other misconceptions that do not accurately describe the behavioral enterprise include the following: that it is based solely on theory; that it imposes objectives on people and dehumanizes them; that it only deals with superficial problems; that it teaches people how to manipulate each other, and allows them to become dependent on external incentives; that symptom substitution will occur; and that it implies acceptance of a specific value system.

2

Effective application of a behavioral framework requires a firm understanding of basic behavioral principles. This chapter offers only an overview of these principles, and the reader is urged to consult sources that offer more extensive elaborations (see, for example, Ferster, Culbertson, and Boren, 1975), and, for more advanced material, Bandura (1969) or Kanfer and Phillips (1969).

Operant Behavior: The Importance of Consequences

Operant behavior is defined by the way it changes the environment (Ferster, Culbertson, and Boren, 1975). It is behavior that is maintained by its consequences. The term *operant*

Some Basic Terminology and Concepts

refers to a class of behaviors all of which have an identical effect on the environment. Thus a child may find that he can succeed in gaining his mother's attention in a certain situation by starting to yell, by punching her on the leg, or by biting his brother. The consequences of behavior increase or decrease its future probability. That is, depending on what happens after we engage in certain behaviors, we may be more or less likely to engage in similar behaviors on similar occasions in the future. If a teen-ager steals a car, has a great ride, and receives lots of admiration from his friends for his "feat," he is more likely to repeat this behavior on future occasions. Or, if a mother finds that she can remove the whining of a child by giving him what he is asking for, she may be more inclined to do so on later occasions, since she has successfully altered her environment (removed an annoying event) as a result of her behavior.

Verbal behavior acquires an influence over our actions because on past occasions it has been followed by certain consequences. If a parent has followed through with promises in the past, and says to her seven-year-old, "Put your toys away now and you can go out and play for an hour before supper," he is more likely to put his toys away. Verbal behavior often consists of promises or threats of certain consequences given certain behaviors, and we will act on verbal statements to the extent that they have in the past accurately described what actually happens. Behavior may be established or maintained by either positive or negative reinforcement.

Positive Reinforcement. The term *positive reinforcement* refers to a procedure in which some event is presented following a behavior that results in an increase in the future likelihood of that behavior. The definition involves *two* important factors. The first refers to a procedure (a behavior is followed by the presentation of an event) and the second refers to an *effect on behavior* (that is, the probability is increased that the behavior will be displayed again). For example, if we do a favor for a friend and she thanks us, we may be more likely to do her another favor in the future. The teen-ager described earlier is more likely to steal cars on future occasions. (Note that the term *positive reinforcement* refers to a procedure, whereas the term *positive reinforcer* refers to an event that, when presented contingent on some behavior, increases the future likelihood of that behavior.)

Most reinforcers that influence us are *conditioned or secondary reinforcers*, in contrast to *primary reinforcers*, such as food and physical contact, which function as reinforcers without any prior learning history. Money and approval do not affect us at birth, but come to do so via our social history, through being paired with things that are already reinforcing. If a mother's smile is repeatedly associated with food and physical contact, the smile will become a conditioned reinforcer for an infant, and may then increase behavior that it follows. For example, if the mother asks the child to do something and, when it is accomplished, smiles and presents approving words, this may increase compliant behavior. An event may also assume positive functions by being associated with the removal of negative events. Some events, such as approval and money, are occasions on which many behaviors may be reinforced. They are associated with the reduction of a variety of states of deprivation and are known as *generalized reinforcers*, reinforcers capable of maintaining a wide range of behaviors independent of particular states of deprivation (Holland and Skinner, 1961). "A generalized reinforcer, such as money, which leads to such a variety of performances controlled by different kinds of deprivations, is likely to remain effective under almost all conditions. It is difficult to imagine an individual so satiated in every area of deprivation that money would not be an effective occasion for some behavior. Generalized reinforcers are very important in verbal behavior and education. Reinforcement by generalized reinforcers is likely to be a prominent feature wherever human behavior is social" (Ferster, Culbertson, and Boren, 1975, p. 309). Attention and affection "are conditioned reinforcers which maintain behavior because they are discriminative stimuli for future behavior in other chains of performances leading ultimately to other reinforcers. The approval of one's friends, for example, makes possible their acceptance and issuance of invitations for social occasions, their continued association which in turn makes possible cooperative behaviors, their lending and borrowing of money, and so forth" (Ferster, Culbertson, and Boren, 1975, p. 381).

Because of different learning histories, an event that functions as a positive reinforcer for one person may not do so for another. Each of us has a unique reinforcer profile: that list of events that function as positive reinforcers. Also, an event that functions as a reinforcer in one situation may not do so in another. Significant others, such as parents, spouses, or teachers, often assume that what is reinforcing for them should also be reinforcing for those with whom they interact (their significant others). This may not be so. Such events could, however, be developed as reinforcers. For example, teacher approval could be established as a reinforcer by pairing it with events or items that already function as a reinforcer.

A number of factors influence the effectiveness of positive reinforcement, and are therefore important to consider in planning intervention programs and for understanding why certain problematic behaviors occur or appropriate behaviors fail to occur. These factors include the *amount* of reinforcement; the *time interval* between the behavior and the reinforcing event; the *schedule* of reinforcement; and the *frequency* of reinforcement. The amount of reinforcement (for example, fifty cents, one dollar, five dollars) is not as important as the frequency of reinforcement. A reinforcer should follow desirable behaviors immediately, because if it does not, it may follow some other behavior, an increase in which may occur instead. It takes a while for positive reinforcement to create a change in behavior, in contrast with aversive control, which may have an immediate effect. This is probably why many people employ punishment rather than positive means of influence. It should be noted that these relationships can be altered by cognitive factors. For example, the importance of immediacy of reinforcement may be eliminated through cognitions by which the person views consequences in the aggregate rather than in terms of immediate effect (Baum, 1973). "People process and synthesize feedback information from sequences of events over long intervals about the situational circumstances and the patterns and rates of actions that are necessary to produce given outcomes ... the same consequences can increase, reduce or have no effect upon behavior depending upon whether individuals are led to believe that the consequences signify correct responses, incorrect responses, or occur noncontingently ([see] Dulany, 1968)" (Bandura, in press, pp. 4-5).

Effective use of positive reinforcement. Requisites for the use of positive reinforcement include identification of an observable, countable behavior, selection of some event that will function as a reinforcer, arrangement for the behavior to take place, and arrangement for the reinforcer to follow the behavior. There are a number of ways behavior may be prompted, including the use of verbal instructions, presentation of a cue associated with the availability of reinforcement, display of an appropriate model, or physical guidance (Bandura, 1969). There are a number of ways consequences may be potentiated (made more potent), including increasing the state of deprivation related to a reinforcing consequence, presenting the reinforcer immediately, lowering response requirements to attain the reinforcer, or linking a consequence to some other important consequence. Conversely, decreasing deprivation or increasing delay of reinforcement or response requirements and breaking links between the reinforcing consequence and other important ones will decrease the potency of reinforcing consequences.

To establish new behaviors or increase behaviors, reinforcement should be provided immediately, frequently, in small amounts, and consistently. Unless consequences follow desirable behaviors closely in time, some other behavior that happens to occur may be reinforced, one that may be undesirable. Delayed reinforcement is not as effective as immediate reinforcement, although delays may be "bridged" by cognitive activities. For example, if a mother tells her child that, because he broke a plate, his father will spank him when he comes home from work, this interim may be filled with anticipated unpleasant events. Unfortunately, the father's arrival will become a feared event. Or, if the child is very young, no connection may be made between the later event and the earlier misdeed. Tokens may be employed to "bridge" delays in access to back up reinforcers.

For reinforcement to contact behavior, the behavior must occur. Many people make the mistake of waiting for a low-frequency behavior to occur before they reinforce it, rather than selecting the closest approximation to the final behavior, reinforcing this, then moving on to the next approximation, and so forth. Selecting small steps to reinforce makes frequent reinforcement possible, because the behaviors occur often. Errors usually made include selecting steps that are too big for the client, that is, they do not allow frequent reinforcement. The more frequently behavior is reinforced, the more rapidly new behaviors can be established. Frequent reinforcement is especially important during the acquisition of new behaviors. With some behaviors, such as those related to the development of academic skills, feedback should always occur. Errors are usually made in selecting a frequency of reinforcement that is not high enough. Reinforcement should encourage task completion, rather than time spent on a task. Increasing time spent in a task such as cleaning or studying may not necessarily result in an increase in task completion.

To maintain behavior, it should be reinforced intermittently. Positive reinforcement is usually combined with an extinction procedure for undesirable behaviors. Whenever possible, "natural" rather than artificial reinforcers should be used, and behaviors reinforced that will continue to be supported in the natural environment (Ayllon and Azrin, 1968b). Either reinforcer exposure, in which a person observes another person utilizing a reinforcer, or reinforcer sampling, in which the reinforcer is sampled in the situation in which it is used, can be employed to prime (increase the use of) a reinforcer (Ayllon and Azrin, 1968a, 1968b). Behavior may be prompted by a variety of procedures, including verbal instructions, physical guidance, model presentation of someone performing the desired behaviors, requiring the person to perform the initial portions of a behavior (Ayllon and Azrin, 1968b) or presentation of other cues for the behavior. Relationships between behavior and reinforcers can be highlighted by verbally describing the contingency before it is put into effect, as well as when it occurs. If an attempt to employ positive reinforcement fails, a number of factors may be responsible that relate directly to a violation of one or more of the requisites for use of the procedure. The event employed as a reinforcer may not fill this function. Behavior may not be reinforced frequently enough. Perhaps the behavior is not specified, so it cannot be consistently followed with a positive consequence. Perhaps the reinforcer is delayed too long, or is not presented consistently following the behavior. The behavior may only occur infrequently, thus providing minimal opportunity to follow it with a positive event. Prompting may be necessary, to remind the client to perform the behavior. Or an easier approximation may have to be selected for reinforcement that occurs more frequently. Punishment may be mixed with positive reinforcement, thus diluting the effects of positive events. Insufficient time may have been allowed for positive effects to occur. Unless someone is monitoring the performance (that is, counting its frequency), so that the frequency of the behavior is known before efforts to change it (a baseline exists), there is no accurate way to know whether there is a decrease, increase, or no change at all in the behavior. The latter two points apply to the possible effects of all procedures.

Schedules of Reinforcement. Some behavior is followed by the same reinforcer on every occasion (a continuous schedule of reinforcement). If your favorite coffee shop is always open at 9 A.M. on Tuesdays, walking to get some coffee at that time will always be reinforced. Most behavior is maintained on some intermittent schedule of reinforcement; that is, a consequence does not follow every instance of our behavior. Only on some occasions when one pulls a slot machine handle will a jackpot appear. The schedule on which behavior is reinforced is important, because it can have a great effect on the frequency with which a behavior occurs, as well as on the ease with which it can be decreased. Continuous reinforcement schedules provide for the fastest acquisition of behavior and for the most rapid decrease of behavior when reinforcement is no longer provided. Thus, if one's goal is to establish a behavior, continuous reinforcement will bring about the most rapid increase. Maintenance of behavior in the natural environment, in which only periodic reinforcement usually occurs, requires shifting to an intermittent schedule after behavior stabilizes. "The greatest source of intermittent reinforcement in human behavior occurs in social situations. There the behavior of one person has its effect in the action of a second. For example, someone asks a person standing at the window whether the taxi has arrived yet. The performance whose reinforcement schedule is being analyzed is 'Has the taxi come?' The reinforcement for this verbal performance is a reply from the person at the window. Whether the person at the window replies depends upon all the variables which might influence his behavior. He may be disinclined to reply for many reasons: he may be preoccupied with concerns completely unrelated to the speaker; he may be disinclined to answer because he has just had an argument with the speaker; he may be hard of hearing. Whatever the conditions governing the behavior of the person at the window, the result is that the behavior of the speaker may go unreinforced on one or more occasions" (Ferster, Culbertson, and Boren, 1975, p. 319).

Intermittent schedules are of two main types, known as *ratio* and *interval*. In ratio schedules, either a fixed or variable number of behaviors are required before some consequence occurs. Such schedules usually produce high performance rates. An example of a *fixed*-ratio schedule is piecework production in a factory. Each type of intermittent schedule produces a distinct pattern of behavior (Ferster, Culbertson, and Boren, 1975). In a fixed-ratio schedule, a pause in responding typically occurs after reinforcement, followed by a fairly steady rate of behavior until the next reinforcer occurs. Pulling the lever on a slot machine offers an example of a *variable*-ratio schedule. This schedule generates behaviors that have a high stable rate and are very difficult to decelerate. In fixed-ratio schedules, the higher the ratio, the higher the rate at which behavior will occur (one reinforcement for every ten behaviors is a higher ratio than one reinforcement for every five). And, with a variable-ratio schedule, the higher the average ratio (the average number of behaviors required before a consequence follows) the higher the rate of behavior. Parents who reinforce undesirable behaviors on high ratio schedules of reinforcement ensure a high rate of this behavior, one that is difficult to decrease. A special history is required to develop well-maintained behavior on large fixed- or variable-ratio schedules, many small and intermediate schedules must first be used to achieve a performance on a large fixed-ratio schedule (Ferster, Culbertson, and Boren, 1975). Behaviors expected of a person may not occur, because this process of approximating larger ratios is not carried out. For example, children in a classroom differ in terms of how much output they have been required to display prior to reinforcement. If the teacher requires the same output for all children, those who are not accustomed to this will not perform. The teacher may label them *lazy* or *unmotivated*, not realizing that she herself must arrange the motivating conditions for their behavior by offering them facilitating schedules of reinforcement. Thus a disinterest in initiating an activity may be caused by too thin a schedule of reinforcement for the behavior. Thus behavior can be maintained on very high ratio schedules (much behavior is required for a reinforcer) by gradually increasing the response requirement for reinforcement. However, if response requirements are increased too rapidly, performance will rapidly decrease. Transition from a variable-ratio schedule of reinforcement, in which small outputs are sometimes reinforced, to a large fixed-ratio schedule may disrupt behavior. Perhaps this accounts in part for depression and lower output when a person is promoted from a job where tasks are reinforced on a variable schedule to one where behavior is reinforced only after a high set number of behaviors.

In interval schedules, behavior is reinforced only after a fixed or variable amount of time has passed. The first behavior that occurs *after* a certain time interval passes is reinforced. Behaviors that occur prior to this are not reinforced. Waiting for a bus that only arrives on the hour is an example of a fixed-interval schedule. A pause following reinforcement also occurs in fixed-interval schedules, but it is shorter than the pauses in fixed-ratio schedules. In contrast with fixed-ratio schedules, fixed-interval schedules have what is known as a *recuperative* feature: Reinforcement may occur after a single response. This will provide some reinforcement, even though an individual has a low inclination to respond and is responsible for the maintenance of behavior on interval schedules under a variety of reinforcement frequencies. Fixed-ratio strain, or abulia (lack of behavior), is a unique property of ratio scheduling. "The salesman usually sells his product in proportion to the number of calls he makes, rather than to the passage of time. A clear effect of a ratio schedule of reinforcement is in the piecework pay of the factory worker. This is a fixed-ratio schedule of reinforcement where the employee is paid directly as a function of the amount of behavior he emits. It is well known that this type of incentive produces a high rate of activity compared with any other pay system. Like all forms of ratio reinforcement, however, both the salesman and the pieceworker may be disinclined to work if too much behavior is required per reinforcement (fixed-ratio strain)" (Ferster, Culbertson, and Boren, 1975, p. 444). An example of a behavior on a variable-interval schedule would be a child's request for an ice-cream cone, when the mother only buys one when she thinks enough time (which is variable) has passed since the child last had one. Variable-interval schedules create behavior that occurs at a lower rate and that is also difficult to decelerate. A lower rate results, because reinforcement is not dependent on the output of behavior. Many conditions that are secondary to the *actual* schedule of reinforcement in effect may influence rate of behavior in interval schedules (Ferster, Culbertson, and Boren, 1975). In certain conditions where behavior is very strong, for example, such as waiting for an ambulance, there may be a fairly steady output of pacing or looking in spite of the fact that it (the reinforcer) is not due to arrive for a set period of time. Thus, in ratio schedules, it is the number of behaviors that affects the availability of reinforcement, whereas in interval schedules, it is the passage of time, in addition to a behavior occurring. In ratio schedules, the probability of reinforcement increases only with response output, not with the passage of time. Interval schedules differentially reinforce low rates of behavior, whereas ratio schedules differentially reinforce high rates of behavior.

Reinforcement may be contingent on a low rate of behavior. For example, a teacher may answer a question only if a student asks one per day. Or, a high rate of behavior may be reinforced. Some reinforcers are on a limited hold; that is, they are available only until a certain time. For example, driving to a restaurant will only be reinforced if you arrive before closing time.

Note that when a *variable* schedule is used, it is more difficult to decrease behavior. Parents who try to decrease behavior by no longer reinforcing it often do this only for a period of time. That is, they provide periodic reinforcement, which will create behavior that is difficult to decrease. Even an occasional reinforcer can maintain behavior.

Scheduling of reinforcement is often related to presenting problems. Perhaps a husband becomes less consistent in offering attention and approval to his wife after taking on a new job, which encourages an increase in "nagging" behavior. Difficulty getting to work may reflect a pause pattern in responding, which occurs in fixed-ratio schedules where a certain response output is required for reinforcement. A writer, for example, may have difficulty initiating a new task right after one has been completed.

Many changes, such as obtaining a promotion at work, require a large amount of behavior, rendering adult behavior especially liable to disruption. Certain times, such as adolescence and retirement, entail large changes in schedules of reinforcement, which in part account for some of the behavioral alterations seen during these stages.

> [In adolescence] the social environment requires more instances of sustained speech. Social contacts become more difficult as the adolescent's friends become more mobile and the opportunities to be with them require more behavior on his part. Relationships with the opposite sex require courtship behaviors in which substantial amounts of behavior may be required before the reinforcer occurs. Heretofore, a girl could be approached casually and a relationship maintained by a simple interchange. With adolescence, the boy needs to arrange a date in advance, have money for certain kinds of activities, be prepared to converse under arbitrary conditions, dress in particular ways and, in general, court the lady. 'By the same token, the girl will have to prepare herself in manner of dress, make-up, and grooming, and to arrange conditions so that there is some likelihood that she will find herself in the company of the opposite sex.... The sudden changes in the child's environment that occur at adolescence may disrupt the newly emerging behaviors. The important dimension of the schedule to be analyzed here is how the transition from one schedule of reinforcement to another may occur and how this transition might weaken behavior. [Ferster, Culbertson, and Boren, 1971, p. 417]

Behaviors that are maintained on "thin schedules" of reinforcement are especially likely to be disrupted by a punishment that would otherwise have little effect. Emotional states are more likely to disrupt behavior maintained on fixed-ratio schedules, where there are long pauses after reinforcement for the emotional state to increase, than with behaviors on variable-ratio schedules, in which small behavioral requirements are occasionally reinforced (Ferster, Culbertson, and Boren, 1975). A further influence of schedules is shown by the effects of preceding schedules on later ones.

Negative Reinforcement. Behavior can be established and maintained by removing unpleasant events following its performance. Thus, we will not only tend to repeat behaviors that result in pleasurable consequences, but also to repeat those that get rid of annoying or painful events. Let us say the sun is shining in your eyes and you pull down a shade, which removes the glare. Your behavior is maintained by negative reinforcement, getting rid of something annoying. Or, let us say a child is nagging his mother to buy him a candy bar, repeating over and over, "Buy me a candy bar." The mother may find this unpleasant and finally may buy him one, resulting in removal of nagging. Her behavior succeeds in removing an unpleasant event. In both positive and negative reinforcement, behavior results in a change in the environment, but in the former instance, something is presented, while in the latter, something is removed. Both procedures *increase* the future probability of behavior and both involve contingencies (that is, relationships between behavior and the environment). On the next occasion when the mother is present, her son might ask for a cookie and, since he received one in the past, might persist in asking. The mother, because he was quiet after she gave him one in the past, will be more likely to again give him a cookie. The definition of negative reinforcement includes two parts, the description of a procedure (the removal of some event contingent on a behavior) and a behavioral effect (a subsequent increase in the future probability of the behavior). As with positive reinforcers, the classification of an event as a negative reinforcer depends on its effects on behavior. We cannot tell for sure whether an event will function as a negative reinforcer until we arrange its removal following a behavior and see whether there is a future increase in behavior. Just as there are a variety of positive reinforcers, there are a variety of types of negative reinforcers, including social ones (disapproval, criticism), material ones (shock), undesired activities (cleaning), and negative self-statements. Most are conditioned reinforcers. Just as what functions as a positive reinforcer varies from person to person, depending on the person's social history, what functions as a negative reinforcer also varies.

Much of our everyday behavior is maintained by negative reinforcement. Many people use this to influence others. That is, they present unpleasant events to a person until they perform some desired behavior, at which time the event is removed, as illustrated in the example of the child asking for a cookie. Natural contingencies involving negative reinforcement (for example, moving out of the sun on a hot day) differ in important ways from socially imposed ones—for example, a parent's request to a child to "pick up your toys," which carries an implied threat of an unpleasant event if the child does not comply (Ferster, Culbertson, and Boren, 1975). Natural contingencies usually allow a range of behavior that will remove an unpleasant event. For example, you may run, walk, skip, hop, cover yourself, use an umbrella, and so forth to decrease the heat of the sun. This is not true with socially arranged contingencies. Also, behavior under natural negative reinforcing contingencies benefits the person, whereas the controller is the beneficiary in social contingencies. The same factors that are important with positive reinforcement are important with negative reinforcement: the immediacy of reinforcement; the amount of reinforcement, that is, the amount of negative stimulation removed contingent upon behavior; the schedule of reinforcement; and the frequency of reinforcement.

Negative reinforcement can be used to establish avoidance or escape behavior. Avoidance behavior is maintained by the removal of anticipated unpleasant events, for example, not starting a conversation with someone because of fear of rejection, whereas escape behavior is maintained by the removal of some negative event already present—for example, terminating a conversation with someone who annoys you. When using this approach in applied settings, it is important that the person be able to eliminate the aversive event that is present through performance of a desirable behavior. For example, a mother may send a child to her room for making a request in a nasty way, and inform her that she can come out when she is ready to speak to her mother politely.

Effective use of negative reinforcement. Requisites include specification of an observable, countable behavior, selection of some event that will function as a negative reinforcer, presentation of this event, and arrangement for the consistent removal of this event after a behavior. Optionally, termination of the aversive event should be under the control of the client. If possible, positive reinforcement should be used instead. Positive reinforcement of desirable behavior should always be blended with use of negative reinforcement to avoid undesirable emotional effects and to reinforce specific alternative behaviors. Failure of an attempt to employ negative reinforcement may result from not satisfying one of the requirements for effective use of punishment, failure to remove the aversive event immediately after the behavior or failure to specify a behavior. (See also last two points mentioned in discussion of positive reinforcement.)

Superstitious Conditioning. Some behaviors may be maintained by *adventitious reinforcement*; that is, the accidental pairing of behavior with some consequence. For example, carrying a rabbit's foot may be followed by an absence of a feared event, thus increasing the tendency to carry this around. Or a complex ritual may be maintained by avoidance of some imagined consequence. Such reinforcement is especially possible when the avoidance of unwanted events is concerned as revealed in the following conversation:

> *A:* "Why do you carry that ladder around?"
> *B:* "To keep the lions away."
> *A:* "That's crazy, there aren't any lions around here."
> *B:* "See!"

Operant Extinction. Consequences may also decrease behavior. If our behavior is followed by an annoying event (punishment), or by the removal of a positive reinforcer (response cost), or is no longer followed by reinforcing events (operant extinction), it will decrease in frequency. If a child's request for a cookie results in a slap from his mother (an aversive event), or if she consistently ignores his requests (no longer attends to these—operant extinction), he will eventually make fewer requests. If someone is caught speeding and receives a fine (response cost), he or she may be less likely to speed during the next few days. Thus, what happens after behavior may make it more or less likely on future occasions.

Behavior that is no longer followed by reinforcing consequences will decrease. In operant extinction, there is no longer any contingency between the behavior and the reinforcer that followed it in the past. The schedule of reinforcement, in effect, influences how rapid this decrease will be. If a continuous reinforcement schedule has been in effect and an extinction procedure is applied, there may be an initial increase in the frequency and intensity of the behavior. However, this will be followed by a rapid decrease. For example, if a child's request has typically been granted and then such behavior is consistently ignored, he or she may shout even louder, and more frequently at first. The decrease is more gradual if behavior has been maintained on an intermittent schedule of reinforcement, and an initial increase in the behavior is less likely. The initial increase that may sometimes occur when an extinction procedure is employed may be very annoying to significant others. This can be avoided if positive reinforcement is provided for alternative behaviors. This mix of positive reinforcement for desirable behaviors and extinction of undesired behaviors is known as *differential reinforcement of other behavior*. Extinction alone is rarely employed, because of the mentioned temporary increase in problem behavior, the unpleasant emotional effects caused by withdrawal of reinforcement, and its failure to increase desirable alternative behaviors.

Note that the behavior must occur without being reinforced for an extinction procedure to be in effect. And there must be a resultant decrease in behavior over the long term. Often it is not possible to withhold reinforcement following a behavior, and other procedures must be employed. One can only be certain that the reinforcer maintaining a behavior has been identified after it is no longer provided and a subsequent decrease in behavior is observed.

Effective use of operant extinction. The requisites for *operant extinction* include identification of an observable, countable behavior; identification of the reinforcer(s) maintaining the behavior; and *consistently* withholding reinforcement following the behavior. Only if reinforcers are consistently withheld will the procedure be effective, because, if they are not, the behavior will be placed on an intermittent schedule of reinforcement, which will increase the durability of the behavior. Optimally, extinction is combined with the positive reinforcement of desirable behaviors. This will avoid the initial acceleration of undesirable behavior, increase a specific other desirable behavior, and avoid emotional effects that accompany extinction. The response *must occur* without being reinforced for an extinction procedure to be in effect. Thus extinction alone would not be recommended for behaviors that are very aversive to others or dangerous. For such behaviors, one may choose to positively reinforce desirable alternatives and to use aversive consequences such as a "time out" following undesirable behaviors. This would also be necessary when the reinforcer for the behavior cannot be identified. Disadvantages of extinction when used alone include an initial acceleration of behavior that may be aversive to others; no specific desirable responses may be accelerated—in fact, some other undesirable response may occur; and undesirable emotional effects may result. Failure of an attempt to use operant extinction may result from not consistently withholding the reinforcer; or perhaps one reinforcer was withheld, but there are other more powerful reinforcers still in effect. Even when extinction is combined with positive reinforcement for desirable behaviors, it may take a few days to see a change in behavior.

Punishment. Punishment involves the presentation of an aversive event after a behavior, followed by the subsequent decrease in that behavior (Azrin and Holz, 1966). The definition includes two factors, the description of a procedure and an effect on behavior. Determination of whether an event is a punishing one requires arranging a contingency and seeing if there is a *de*crease in behavior. Punishment and negative reinforcement are closely related, because, in order to arrange for negative reinforcement of a behavior, some negative event must be presented that can be removed contingent on behavior. This event is presented after some immediately preceding behavior (or its lack), and functions as a punishing event for that behavior. For example, failure to take the garbage out may result in being nagged, which is terminated after this task is performed. Note that punishment can be used without identifying the reinforcer maintaining the behavior.

Punishment is widely used in everyday life to influence the behavior of others. The mother who slaps her child, the supervisor who tells you that your reports are bad, the teacher who sends a child to the principal's office—all hope that they will change behavior. Their hopes are often not only for a decrease in certain behavior, but also for an increase in others. The supervisor hopes to decrease bad report writing and increase good report writing. The mother hopes to decrease rude backtalk and to increase polite verbal behavior in her child. However, often desirable alternatives are not identified and reinforced. Rather, people attempt to prod others into doing things by punishing behavior and removing this contingent on desired behavior. A mother may stop nagging her daughter to do the dishes when the daughter finally gets up and does them. Whenever a power differential exists between two people—for example, between parents and children, or between teachers and students—it is possible to coerce behavior out of the less powerful by threatening some aversive event or the withdrawal of some privilege for failure to comply (Michael, 1972). There is usually something readily at hand to remove. The threat is removed contingent on completion of the task. Use of punishment is probably encouraged by its immediate effects or a lack of knowledge about how to change behavior via positive control, or a low tolerance level for undesirable behaviors.

There are many disadvantages of employing punishment alone to change behavior (Azrin and Holz, 1966). For example, the person delivering the punishing stimulus serves as a model for undesirable behaviors, that is, hitting or yelling. In addition, avoidance responses may develop—for example, if a parent makes heavy use of punishment, he or she may be avoided as much as possible by his or her child and thus become less effective in influencing behavior via positive means. Neutral cues that are present when punishment is delivered may acquire secondary aversive properties by being paired with the punishing events. At a future time, these cues may evoke emotional responses, resulting in avoidance behavior. By punishing behaviors in children that are required at a later time, such as sexual behavior, situational contexts with sexual stimuli may be avoided and so cause future problems. If punishment is intense, other behaviors may be affected. That is, the rate of a variety of behaviors, including desirable ones, may be decreased.

Negative events may increase the frequency of behavior under certain circumstances. If the negative event is a cue for a positive reinforcer to follow, the behavior will increase (Azrin and Holz, 1966). For example, if a mother only provides physical affection to her child after she severely beats her, the inappropriate behaviors occasioning the beating may increase. (Since in these instances, there is no decrease in behavior, these relationships between behavior and its consequences cannot accurately be called *punishment* procedures.) The discomfort involved in punishment is unpleasant for the offender, and permission to use punishment allows one to do so from anger (Foxx and Azrin, 1972). Punishment only teaches what not to do (Thorndike, 1932) and leaves the development of desirable behaviors to chance. It does not eliminate the reinforcement for inappropriate behavior. Neither does it undo any damage caused by the inappropriate behavior (Foxx and Azrin, 1972). In addition, if behavior is punished in a situation that differs from those where a response suppression is hoped for, the client may be able to discriminate between these different situations and no response decrease may occur (Bucher and Lovaas, 1968). Aversive events should be differentiated from punishment. There are many types of aversive events, including withholding of reinforcement, removal of a positive reinforcer, and presentation of an aversive event.

Many of the same variables that influence the effects of reinforcement also influence the effectiveness of punishment, including the immediacy with which a negative event follows behavior, the intensity of this event and the schedule of punishment. Behavior reduction is directly related to the proportion of responses that are punished. Punishment is more effective if initially introduced at an intense level than if it is introduced at moderate or mild levels. Also, if punishment is mild, habituation to the punishing stimuli may occur, resulting in a decrease in the effect of the punishing stimuli.

If behavior is still being reinforced, the effects of punishment will be influenced by the schedule of reinforcement that is in effect. For example, tantrums may still be reinforced by parental attention delivered on a variable-ratio schedule. This will decrease the effects of punishment. However, if an alternative way is provided to obtain the event that is reinforcing a problematic behavior (such as parental approval), punishment can be very effective in decreasing behavior.

Deprivation will decrease the effects of punishment. If a person is deprived of a reinforcer, for example, social approval, punishment of behaviors that result in this will not be as effective. Punishment will be ineffective if escape from the contingency is possible. If a mother tells her son that because he was late for dinner he will receive no dinner that evening, and if he is free to go across the street and have dinner with a friend, her words will have little impact.

If possible, given the many disadvantages of punishment, its use is avoided unless the advantages outweigh the disadvantages. If a behavior is dangerous, such as with some self-injurious behavior, a procedure that can reduce this immediately has a high priority. Punishment, however, should always be combined with positive reinforcement of desirable behavior.

Large changes in reinforcement or punishment schedule or amount are usually accompanied by emotional reactions or a disruption in ongoing behavior (Millenson, 1967). If a teacher suddenly severely criticizes a child, he may have difficulty continuing any tasks in which he was involved. Similarly, if a person gets a call while ironing that he has just won a $5000 trip for his jingle about Crispy Cracky cereals, it is unlikely that he will continue ironing. Just as a large change in the amount of a reinforcer or punishing event can alter behavior, so can a drastic change in the schedule of reinforcement. This, too, is likely to create emotional effects in which behavior is disrupted, such as when a companion who supported most of another person's behavior dies.

The procedure of overcorrection is a mild punishment procedure, in which the person is required to correct the consequences of misbehavior by restoring the situation to an improved state or to practice correct behaviors contingent on misbehavior (Foxx and Azrin, 1972). This procedure seems to be applicable in a wide range of situations, produces strong immediate effects, and is more acceptable to those who carry out change efforts, because of its mildness. As with any punishment procedure, it should always be combined with positive reinforcement of desirable behaviors. Overcorrection has been found to produce positive side effects on topographically dissimilar behaviors (Epstein, Doke, Sajwaj, Sorrell, and Rimmer, 1974).

Effective use of punishment. Requisites for the use of *punishment* include identification of some observable, countable behavior; selection of an event that will function as a punishing stimulus; and arrangement for the consistent presentation of this immediately following the behavior. With some behaviors, such as head banging, it may not be possible to gain control over the sources of reinforcement for the behavior, and so operant extinction cannot be employed. Also, the frequency of the behavior may be so high that it interferes with the performance of desirable behaviors, and so these cannot be reinforced. Contingent application of aversive stimuli can be employed to reduce this high frequency, so that alternative behaviors can be reinforced. This procedure should always be combined with positive reinforcement of desirable alternatives. Positive reinforcement of alternative behaviors enables their establishment in situations in which the punished behaviors typically occurred. Unauthorized escape from the contingency must be prevented and, if possible, every instance of the undesired behavior should be followed by the punishing event. Intermittent punishment makes the probability of reinforcement for the behavior more likely, although if the behavior has already been considerably reduced, such a schedule may be as effective as a continuous one (Clark, Rowbury, Baer, and Baer, 1973). It is important to make sure that the punishing event is not associated with the delivery of positive reinforcement. It is much more effective to punish the early components in a chain of misbehavior than later components. These early components are more easily disrupted, and this prohibits reinforcement of the misbehavior that would occur if the behavior was completed. Sources of support for the undesirable behavior should be removed; otherwise, the effects of punishment will be diluted by continued reinforcement of the behavior. Care must be taken not to allow habituation to the aversive event through its gradual rather than high-intensity introduction or through its extended use. It may not be possible to deliver the punishing event following a behavior, in which case a conditioned event such as saying "No" or "Stop that" may be employed (Azrin and Holz, 1966). Pairing of such verbal cues with punishment will permit the influence of the behavior by the verbal cue alone. Informing the person of the reasons why he should not engage in the behavior is sometimes helpful. For example, restrictions placed on a child's behavior are more effective when the punitive agent is not around or when children have been informed of the reasons for the restrictions (Parke, 1969). Decreasing the degree of motivation in relation to the punished behavior is also important. Other procedures are available for decreasing behavior and are less objectionable, including the differential reinforcement of other behavior or positive reinforcement combined with time out. There are many disadvantages of punishment when used alone, as previously described.

If an attempt to employ punishment fails, the event being used as an aversive event may not in fact have this function, or sources of positive reinforcement for the behavior may still be present. Perhaps alternative routes to obtain positive reinforcement have not been provided, or escape from the contingency was possible, or one of the other requisites for the effective use of punishment may not have been satisfied.

Response Cost: Removal of a Positive Reinforcer Following Behavior. Response cost involves the contingent removal of a positive reinforcer. Like operant extinction and the use of punishment, response cost, by definition, results in a decrease in behavior. Unlike extinction, this procedure involves a contingency (relationship) between behavior and its consequences, that is, some reinforcer that is already being sampled, such as watching television; some opportunity or privilege that is normally available, such as use of the car on the weekend; or some reinforcer that has been accumulated, such as money, is removed. An example of the use of response cost would be removal of opportunity to visit a friend contingent on stealing (Wetzel, 1966) or being fined ten points for not completing a chore. Unlike punishment, it does not involve the presentation of an aversive event. For this reason, the disadvantages listed under punishment are not usually associated with response cost, making the procedure more desirable. One cannot be sure that removal of an event will entail a response cost until it is taken away contingent on behavior and a decrease in frequency occurs. Some amount of reinforcement must first be offered, so that there is something to withdraw. Response cost is often employed as a part of token or point programs, because tokens or points can easily be deducted from a person's account. Removal of tangible items is often difficult (such as trying to take a candy bar back from a child) and entails attention to the person that actually might support inappropriate behavior.

Effective use of response cost. In order to effectively use *response cost*, an observable, countable behavior must be selected; a positive reinforcer to be removed identified; and the consistent removal of this event following the response arranged. Response cost should be used together with positive reinforcement of desirable behaviors. The cost should be arranged beforehand—for example, how many points will be lost contingent on certain misbehaviors (how much television time will be lost as a result of misbehavior). The loss should be in accord with the severity of the behavior, and should be consistently and immediately applied, and the contingency verbally described. A variety of possibilities arise if an attempt to use response cost fails. The event being removed may not be an important reinforcer or perhaps too little positive reinforcement is provided for alternative behaviors. (See also the possibilities listed in the discussion of punishment.)

Time Out. When a person is removed from one environment (the "time-in" environment) to another that is less reinforcing, contingent on some behavior, this is called *time out*. This procedure is often employed with young children. Time-out contingencies may involve a variety of components, including: (1) removal of positive reinforcers (if the environment from which one was removed entailed their sampling); (2) reinforcement of desirable behavior, because the time-out period is terminated only after inappropriate behavior has stopped; (3) isolation itself may be unpleasant, and so a punishment contingency involving the presentation of aversive events might also be involved; (4) operant extinction since inappropriate behaviors, if maintained in part by social attention, will no longer be reinforced during the time out, nor will appropriate behavior (Sherman and Baer, 1969; Azrin and Holz, 1966). Unlike extinction, no reinforcement is available for any behavior during the time-out period.

Time out is very effective in decreasing behavior of children, especially when alternative desirable behaviors are reinforced. One advantage of time out is that, like punishment, it is not necessary to identify the reinforcer maintaining the behavior. Because it is often difficult to identify what event(s) is maintaining a behavior, it is important to have available procedures, such as response cost, punishment, and time out, that do not require this. Time out will not be effective if the inappropriate behavior can be reinforced during time out, as is true of self-stimulatory behavior, such as rocking, which appears to be intrinsically reinforcing (Lovaas and Newsom, 1976).

Effective use of time out. Requisites for time out include selecting an observable countable behavior, selection of a time-out area that does not contain positive reinforcers, and arranging the consistent removal of the person to this area contingent on the behavior. The most common way in which time out is employed is to remove a child from a reinforcing environment contingent on selected undesirable behaviors, for a brief period of time—for example, two to five minutes. The briefest time out that is effective should be selected, in order to decrease time away from situations allowing reinforcement of appropriate behavior and to decrease the possibility of a disrupting effect on all behaviors. A warning of the imminent use of time out if the behavior does not change should be employed, and a verbalized reason offered, such as, "You hit your brother and so will have to spend two minutes in time out." Ideally, the person himself determines the length of time out by stipulating that he must stay in time out until he is ready to behave appropriately. Whether this will work must be tested out in each case. It may result in time-out periods that are so brief they are not effective. Time out will not be effective if few reinforcers are available outside of time out. Advantages of time out include being able to carry out the procedure relatively unemotionally (compared to use of punishment), and allowing each person to calm down during the period of separation (Gelfand and Hartmann, 1975). Thus interpersonal friction is less. Also, the procedure requires only a brief removal from situations allowing reinforcement of desirable behavior. Time out can, however, create emotional behavior such as crying, screaming, or physical attacks. Places such as the bathroom have been used in the home. Time out may be arranged in the very room in which the problematic behavior occurs, if an enclosure can be provided that permits temporary isolation. For example, Pendergrass (1972) employed an isolation booth constructed in the playroom situation by attaching a plywood panel to two cabinet doors, which produced a triangular, open-topped enclosure at the side of the room. It is important that the room employed for time out not contain reinforcers; if it does, to be placed there would not be unpleasant. Required conditions for termination of the time-out period must be clearly identified and should be described to the person (for example, that time out will be extended if inappropriate behavior, such as yelling during time out, occurs).

A rapid reduction in behavior is not only of import when the behavior is self-injurious, but also when it is very aversive to significant others, such as teachers and parents. When this is the case, time out, combined with the reinforcement of desirable behaviors, may be chosen in preference to differential reinforcement where operant extinction is employed, because the latter procedure will be slower, and mediators may lose patience and abandon the entire enterprise. Also, in some instances, differential reinforcement may not be effective. Wahler (1969a) for example, attempted to employ this procedure to change the behavior of children; however, no changes occurred over a month's time. When time out was combined with positive reinforcement of desirable behaviors, a rapid change in behavior occurred. Patterson (1971a) recommends the introduction of positive reinforcement for desirable behaviors prior to the use of time out, so that the overall amount of positive reinforcement offered will be increased.

If a time-out procedure is not effective, the following possibilities should be scanned: The time-out area offers reinforcers; time out is not consistently enforced; the process of enforcing the time out is a positive experience in that attention is offered, rather than being carried out in a matter-of-fact way; time-out periods are too long, thus not allowing opportunity for positive reinforcement of appropriate behaviors; time out is not immediately enforced following inappropriate behavior; desirable behaviors are not reinforced; or time-out periods may be ended even though inappropriate behavior is occurring.

Antecedents. Just as what happens after our behavior may increase or decrease its probability, antecedent events also influence its occurrence. We are more likely to perform behavior in situations in which we have previously been reinforced for that behavior, and less likely to perform the behavior in situations in which it has been punished or not been reinforced. Suppose Mr. Smith typically adjourns to the livingroom and reads the paper after dinner and that earlier in their marriage his wife attempted to initiate a conversation with him at this time, but was lucky to receive a "humm" or rattle of the paper following such attempts. She probably no longer tries to initiate conversations with him during this time, since her behavior has not been reinforced in this situation. Her husband reading the paper in the living room after dinner is a cue that her verbal behavior will not be reinforced. If her attempts are successful when he stops reading the paper, the latter is a cue (a discriminative event) for initiating a conversation. Thus antecedent events attain an influencing role over behavior through their association with reinforcing events. An antecedent event that facilitates a behavior is called a *discriminative stimulus* (S^D). Those that signal a probability of not being reinforced are called *S deltas* (S^Δ). Thus a discrimination is established by reinforcing a behavior in one situation and not in another; that is, by differential reinforcement. Establishing appropriate discriminations is a critical aspect of developing effective repertoires. Most of our behavior consists of *discriminated operants*, that is, behaviors that occur only in certain situations. Situational factors that are not directly related to whether or not our behavior is reinforced, but that are usually present (props), may also affect behavior if these change radically (Goldiamond and Dyrud, 1967).

It is not uncommon for school social workers to hear the following comment from a parent: "I cannot understand why he is so well behaved in school, because he is a devil at home." It is likely that the child is reinforced for tantrum behavior at home, whereas at school this behavior is not reinforced. The mother becomes a cue for tantrums, because she reinforces such behavior, whereas the teacher is an S^Δ for tantrums, because she does not. Behaviors can be increased by presenting stimuli associated with their reinforcement or by removing events associated with their failure to be reinforced. Removal of a discriminative event for a behavior or presentation of an S^Δ will decrease associated behaviors. Stimulus control involves the rearrangement of antecedent events so as to increase desired behaviors and decrease undesired ones. A discrimination may be established without the occurrence of errors and with minimal disruption of behavior by starting out with large differences between two or more stimuli that are easily distinguishable. This is known as *errorless discrimination learning* or *fading*, and avoids intermittent reinforcement, because all behaviors are reinforced.

Inappropriate or inadequate discriminations are often of concern in presenting problems. Examples of such discrimination include failure of a "keep-out" sign to occasion avoidance behavior, or assumption by a wife that various behaviors of her husband indicate disapproval, when in fact he is thinking about work-related problems. Consequences provided to others may have discriminative effects on observers' behavior (Bandura, 1969). For example, watching someone else receive positive consequences for on-task behavior may increase the frequency of an observer's own on-task behavior.

Effective use of antecedent events (stimulus control). Requisites for effective use of antecedents include identification of a specific, observable, countable behavior to be increased and decreased; identification of readily discriminable cues related to each; presentation of cues for appropriate behaviors; elimination or suppression of cues for undesirable behaviors; reinforcement for appropriate behavior; operant extinction of inappropriate behaviors; and fading of any artificial procedural components as desirable behaviors increase. Since new behaviors are most easily established in novel stimulus situations, the introduction of such events may be deliberately arranged. Verbal, written, or tape-recorded instructions may be used as prompts for appropriate behaviors. Their use can substantially increase the probability of desirable behaviors. Modeling cues may also be employed to cue behaviors. Stimulus control procedures are especially useful when behaviors exist, but occur in the wrong situations, or do not occur frequently enough in some contexts. These procedures can often be usefully blended with rearrangement of contingencies (see, for example, Ayllon and Azrin, 1964).

Chaining. Only by artificial isolation do we select one behavior for study. Each of our behaviors is part of a sequence involving various behaviors, antecedents, and consequences. A behavior may be a reinforcer for a preceding one and a cue for a behavior that follows. Heroin use, for example, includes a series of behaviors and their related antecedents and consequences. Chains of behavior are easier to interrupt in the early stages of the chain, which are further removed from the final reinforcer. Conversely, influence by the reinforcer is greatest near the end of a chain of behavior, which accounts for the effectiveness of response priming, in which the client is placed in the context in which she will be reinforced for a given behavior (O'Brien, Azrin, and Henson, 1969). Chains of behavior are most easily established starting from the end of the chain, because of this proximity to reinforcement.

Shaping. Just as it is important to know how to increase or decrease behaviors that are already present, it is also important to be able to establish new ones. For example, it may be necessary to teach a child complex skills, such as how to dress himself, or to teach an adult how to initiate and maintain social exchanges. Shaping can be used to establish new behaviors, taking advantage of the normal variability in behavior, selecting variations that are closest to the desired behavior to reinforce and ignoring others. Thus, in shaping, two procedures are employed: positive reinforcement for successive approximations and operant extinction for other behaviors. This procedure may have to be employed when verbal instructions and model presentation cannot be relied on alone. Some conditioned reinforcer is established first in order to allow immediate reinforcement of behavior. For example, a clicker may first be paired with some reinforcer such as food, or tokens or points established as a reinforcer. When an approximation occurs, the clicker can be immediately sounded as a signal that reinforcement is available.

Shaping requires clear identification of desired objectives as well as of approximations to these objectives and the closest current approximation that will be reinforced; prompting of the desired initial performance requirement and immediate reinforcement of this by an event that is nondistracting and nonsatiating; determination of when to reinforce only a closer approximation; and knowing how to rectify "backsliding" toward more distant approximations. In addition, reinforcement for behaviors that are not approximations to desired behaviors must be withheld. Part of the "art" involved in shaping is immediately reinforcing approximations to correct behavior. Establishing specific criteria for reinforcement for each step of the shaping program aids identification of the behavior to be reinforced. Requirements for reinforcement are established so that they can be easily met, thus allowing frequent reinforcement of correct approximations. Long intervals without reinforcement should be avoided, because this places many behaviors on an extinction schedule and will reduce needed quantities and variabilities of behavior. With children, a recommendation has been made that reinforcement should be earned for 80 percent or more of attempts to perform correct behavior (Gelfand and Hartmann, 1975). Unearned reinforcers that are awarded for minimal efforts or even no effort may be needed, to encourage the person to keep working. This should be used sparingly. Prompts for appropriate behavior, which may include verbal instructions, physical guidance or modeling cues, and praise for desired behaviors, should be included, as well as descriptions of contingencies. Prompts are removed as soon as possible so behavior will occur without reminders. Additional reinforcement may be provided for close approximations, for example, three tokens rather than one. Sufficient reinforcement should be provided for each approximation; however, reinforcement should then await a closer approximation. Common errors in trying to shape behavior include failure to carefully define objectives and intermediate steps so it is not clear what to reinforce and what not to reinforce; setting a performance requirement that is too difficult; failure to identify an item that can be offered immediately; and giving too much or too little reinforcement for approximations. If an approximation is reinforced too often, this will decrease the variability of behavior that will encourage a closer approximation; if too few reinforcers are given, behavior may drift back to more distant behavior. Multiple types and sources of reinforcement will help to maintain the effectiveness of the reinforcement procedure.

If a shaping attempt fails, these points should be reviewed in relation to the procedure used, as well as additional points noted in the discussions of positive reinforcement and operant extinction. Verbal instructions and manual guidance may be needed, or they may have been included when no longer necessary, thus preventing the person from carrying out more of the involved chain of behavior by himself. Perhaps a difficult way of performing an approximation has been reinforced that makes the next steps difficult, such as trying to insert legs into pants while standing rather than sitting (Gelfand and Hartmann, 1975). Temporary periods of a lack of progress may occur where it is necessary to reinforce an earlier approximation, enrich verbal prompts, use physical guidance, or reduce the performance requirements for the next behavior to be reinforced. If behavior ceases entirely, even when no new requirements have been introduced, an approximation that was stabilized can be selected for reinforcement, and after this again stabilizes, criteria for new behaviors can be introduced, in smaller steps. Perhaps the person has become satiated or fatigued. If so, an early response performed successfully can be reinforced and the training session ended. It is possible that an optimal learning environment has not been selected, and thus there is a high frequency of undesirable behaviors. For example, other people may be around, which may distract the person's attention.

Gardner, Brust, and Watson (1970) have developed a scale to assess a trainer's proficiency with shaping procedures. This includes four major categories. The category of shaping includes the following items: obtaining the subject's attention; determining the operant level (the closest approximation); demonstrating the desired behavior; starting with the correct step; using the proper sequence of steps; proceeding to the next step appropriately; and returning to an earlier step when necessary. Rewarding includes the following ten items: finding an effective reinforcer; giving the reinforcer immediately following the approximation; giving verbal reinforcement enthusiastically; offering the verbal reinforcer together with the material reinforcer; offering the physical reinforcer (such as a hug) enthusiastically; offering physical reinforcement together with the material reinforcer (for example, hugging a child and offering him a bite of food); employing praise to establish chains of behavior (so material reinforcement can be faded out); altering the reinforcer as necessary (for example, if satiation occurs); withholding reinforcement correctly; and offering reinforcement correctly. Items included under the category of communicating are giving the correct emphasis to important words when giving instructions; using correct verbal instructions (so different trainers will use the same ones); using the person's name before the instruction; offering the correct gesture (to supplement verbally expressed information); using physical prompts effectively; and fading physical prompts and gestures as soon as possible. The final category, rapport and miscellaneous, includes getting acquainted with the person before training; showing adequate patience during training, interacting with the subject in a respectful manner; ignoring inappropriate behavior; preparing the training room correctly before training (having needed props and removing distractions); and training for one task at a time. Some of the components mentioned are more or less important dependent on the characteristics of the person being trained. If a retarded child is involved, use of modeling gestures and prompts, for example, may be more necessary than if one is shaping behavior in a nonretarded child who may be more responsive to verbal instructions alone. The gradual introduction of a client to fear-inducing events can be conceptualized as a shaping process in which approach to such events is gradually reinforced.

Model Presentation. Another way to establish new behaviors is to have the person observe someone else perform a behavior. A child could be asked to watch another child dress himself, or an adult could watch a videotape of another person initiating and maintaining conversations. Model presentation is more efficient than shaping, because an entire sequence of behaviors can be presented and the person requested to imitate it, instead of waiting for each approximation to occur before reinforcing it. Requisites for use of modeling include identification of observable, countable behaviors to be increased; presentation of an appropriate model; arranging for the observer to attend to the model's behavior; ability of the observer to imitate the behavior and to retain the behavioral components; and reinforcement for the observer imitating the behavior (Bandura, 1969). Drawing the client's attention to response components to be learned through verbal prompts will facilitate observational learning.

Watching a model may have other effects in addition to establishing new behaviors (Bandura, 1969). Behaviors that already exist may be increased or decreased, depending on the consequences that follow the model's behavior. That is, models may inhibit or disinhibit behavior. If a student observes another classmate get caught cheating, he may be less likely to cheat himself; or, conversely, if he sees a fellow student get away with this behavior, he may be more likely to cheat. If the model's behavior is followed by punishing consequences, we are less likely to perform that behavior, whereas if his behavior is followed by positive consequences, we are more likely to perform the behavior. Emotional responses can also be vicariously (simply through watching others) conditioned or extinguished. A child's fear of thunderstorms may be related to his mother's display of fear on such occasions. Watching a model approach a feared object increases the probability that someone who is anxious in the presence of such objects will also approach these (see, for example, Bandura, Blanchard, and Ritter, 1969). Watching someone else may also facilitate behaviors, that is, function as a cue for a behavior not subject to inhibitory processes. For example, smoking may increase when one is around others who also smoke.

The observer must see some relationship between what happens to the model and what might happen to him or her if he or she performed the behavior. Models differ in the extent to which their behavior is likely to be influential. Prestige, similarity of the model to the observer, and power of the model are characteristics that facilitate modeling effects. These variables increase attention, because of their role as a signal for positive events following modeled behaviors. A variety of procedures may be employed to enhance response production, including self-instructions, verbal instructions, or role playing during which behaviors are practiced. If an attempt to employ model presentation fails, the procedure used should be checked to make sure the requisites for the use of model presentation have been satisfied. Perhaps the client does not possess component responses. Perhaps these will have to be individually shaped or individually established through model presentation before they can all be put together in a longer chain of behavior. Attention of the client to the model may not have been arranged. Or perhaps no incentives have been provided for imitation of the model.

Deprivation and Satiation. Deprivation of a reinforcer increases the likelihood of all behaviors that may result in its acquisition. If a child is deprived of social contacts, he is more likely to engage in behaviors that will result in such contacts. Deprivation thus functions as a "potentiating" factor (Goldiamond and Dyrud, 1967). As noted by Ferster, Culbertson, and Boren (1975), the aversive event in negative reinforcement is functionally equivalent to deprivation in positive reinforcement. On the other hand, if someone has been satiated, behavior maintained by this event will no longer function as a reinforcer. Satiation involves giving a person reinforcers in such quantities and frequencies that he becomes sated. This provides another way to decrease behavior. It is usually not employed, because of practical limitations of providing large quantities of a reinforcer; . the temporary nature of satiation effects with some reinforcers such as food; the deleterious effects of providing large quantities of some reinforcers, such as food; and the gradualness of the change induced. There is some indication that satiation can be an effective procedure if the reinforcer is inappropriate for the person, so that it may expose one to ridicule (use of a pacifier by a five-year-old) or because it is inconvenient or irritating to others—for example, hoarding magazines or towels on a hospital ward (Gelfand and Hartmann, 1975).

Respondent Behavior

Respondent behaviors include those that involve the autonomic nervous system, such as heart rate and blood pressure, whereas operants (behavior that "operates" on or affects the environment) involve the skeletal muscles. We usually associate the former with involuntary reactions and the latter with voluntary behaviors. Until fairly recently, a wide separation was made between these two classes in terms of their controlling variables. Thus, respondent behavior was thought to be influenced mainly by what happened *prior* to the behavior and operant behavior by what happened *after* the behavior. We now know that the separation between these two types of reactions, in terms of whether they can be influenced by their consequences, has been greatly exaggerated (Miller, 1969). Heart rate, blood pressure, and a wide range of other visceral responses can be brought under operant control; that is, they can be influenced by what happens after they occur. Both types of behavior are discussed here, to offer a more complete understanding of the establishment and maintenance of problematic behaviors; however, the separation between respondent and operant behavior is somewhat arbitrary. Examples of respondent reactions include increased heart rate immediately before taking the stage to give a speech; pupil dilation on entering a dark room; sweaty palms before a test; increased heart rate on seeing a mouse; and goose pimples on a chilly day.

Cognitive variables play an important role in the development and elimination of respondent reactions (Bandura, 1969, in press). Within social learning theory, physiological reactions are viewed as having an informational role in indicating what consequences might occur given certain actions or their absence, such as defensive behavior. This is stressed rather than the view of emotional arousal as a drive that activates avoidance behavior. Within the former view, it is the cognitive appraisal of arousal that to a large extent determines the level and direction of motivational inducements to action (Bandura, in press, p. 17). Respondent reactions and operant behavior are considered to be coeffects of mediational factors (self-arousal). Thus, "stimuli influence the likelihood of behavior by virtue of their predictive function, not because they are automatically connected to responses by occurring together" (Bandura, in press, p. 3). Any of the relationships discussed in the following section may be modified by cognitive processes.

Eliciting events can be divided into two general classes: those that elicit a behavior without any previous learning (unconditioned stimuli) and those that affect behavior only after learning (conditioned stimuli). Most respondent behavior of clinical import is learned, such as fear of heights, stage fright, and nervousness at social gatherings. Prior to a conditioning history, a dentist's office will not lead to increased heart rate, nor will a pointed gun. These latter events are initially neutral in relation to heart rate, that is, originally did not influence behavior. Only after an experience of painful drilling at a dentist's office may approach to his office cause discomfort. Thus, respondent conditioning involves the temporal pairing of neutral events with cues that already elicit a given reaction, as in the classic experiment in which Pavlov (1927) paired a bell with food and developed a conditioned response of salivation.

Two variables that affect the amount of conditioning that takes place by pairing a neutral event with a conditioned or unconditioned stimulus include the intensity of the unconditioned event and the number of pairings between it and the neutral stimulus. As the intensity and the number of pairings increase, so does the amount of conditioning that occurs. The greater the intensity of pain in our example of the dentist's office, and the more frequently the dentist has to drill on any one occasion, the greater the probability of a conditioned reaction of "fear" on future occasions when the person either thinks about or approaches the dentist's office.

A third variable is the time relation between the presentation of the neutral and unconditioned event. The closer together they occur in time, the greater the probability that a conditioned response will develop, although, with humans, close contiguity between two events does not seem to be required to achieve successful conditioning, because of the influential role of symbolic representation (for example, anticipation) (Bandura, 1969). Even backward conditioning (presentation of the unconditioned event before the neutral one) is effective with humans, whereas it is usually not with animals.

These variables are of import in the development of respondent reactions, such as anxiety, anger, and pleasurable feelings, as well as in the design of procedures to eliminate problematic respondent behavior. The intensity of the antecedent event is critical in determining the magnitude and latency of unconditioned respondents. The greater its intensity, the shorter will be the time period between its presentation and the occurrence of a response (the shorter the latency) and the greater will be its magnitude. For example, the more intense the drilling near a nerve, the greater may be the resultant pain and the shorter may be the time between the event and the pain. A very weak unconditioned event, such as a warm stove, may not elicit any response. With conditioned responses, the *degree of similarity* of the presented event to the one present during conditioning is important in relation to whether a reaction will occur, and, if it does, to its magnitude and latency. Thus, in the example of the dentist's office, the probability and magnitude of a conditioned reaction taking place on future occasions depends mainly on how similar the events presented on the next visit are to those originally present. For example, Is the office identical? Is the dentist wearing the same white coat? Is the client again there to have a cavity filled? Cognitions concerning the arousal value of events substantially influence the effects of the described relationships. For example, the sense of personal mastery in relation to events that may otherwise evoke defensive reactions may instead occasion approach behavior and successful performance (Bandura, in press).

Respondent Extinction. Respondent extinction is one method that has been employed to eliminate problematic emotional reactions. This involves repeated presentation of an event without pairing this with events it has typically been associated with in the past. For example, a child may be *gradually* exposed to speaking in front of adults, thus avoiding the anxiety reactions usually experienced when his mother tried to force him to speak in certain situations. As extinction progresses, magnitude of the reaction decreases and latency increases. Note that the conditioned event must be presented for a respondent extinction procedure to be in effect. Flooding, a procedure designed to eliminate avoidance reactions, has been conceptualized as involving a respondent extinction procedure in that feared events are presented without being paired with aversive events (Stampfl and Levis, 1967).

Counterconditioning. Counterconditioning has also been employed to alter problematic emotional reactions. This procedure involves the pairing of some event with a response that is incompatible with the reaction typically elicited. Thus, using our example of the dentist's office, we might change the uncomfortable reaction by repeatedly presenting portions of the event, such as the sight of the dentist's chair or drill with a state of deep relaxation. This procedure may be carried out symbolically (in the imagination) or events may actually be presented. Note that a different event (relaxation) is now repeatedly associated with the dentist's office. By employing such a procedure, the function of an event is being altered from one that elicits unpleasant emotional reactions and leads to avoidance behavior (leaving or staying away from some situation) to one that elicits a pleasant or neutral reaction and leads to approach behavior. A counterconditioning procedure may also be used to change an event from one that elicits pleasant reactions and approach behavior (alcohol or drugs) to one that elicits unpleasant reactions and avoidance behavior.

The Interaction Between Respondent and Operant Behavior

Both respondents and operants are involved in almost any reaction or chain of behaviors. Anxiety involves not only respondent components in terms of elicited increases in heart rate or "butterflies" in the stomach but may also occasion operant avoidance or escape responses. Seeing a lover after a long absence may elicit a sexual response as well as be the occasion for operant greeting behaviors. Thus an event may not only elicit respondent reactions, but may also occasion operant behaviors. It is often important in relation to selection of intervention method to distinguish between a presenting problem that represents a deficit or surfeit in respondent conditioning from one that represents an incentive problem, in which appropriate behaviors are available but simply not reinforced. For example, bed wetting may result from a lack of incentive for maintaining a dry bed or from a deficit in respondent conditioning in which fullness of bladder is associated with awakening. A respondent reaction should be observed every time the eliciting stimulus is presented, given that other factors are held constant and fatigue is not a factor. Failure of the reaction to follow the principles of respondent behavior should be a signal that operant factors are involved, such as reinforcement from significant others, or

that components of the eliciting stimulus have not been identified.

The Role of Symbolic Processes

Covert behaviors influence overt behavior in their role as
eliciting, discriminative, and reinforcing events (Bandura, 1969;
Mahoney, 1974a). And, as mentioned previously, awareness of
the relationships between our behaviors and consequences facilitates learning; however, it is not essential. There are probably
many consequences that maintain our behavior that we cannot
identify or have misidentified. What we think a contingency is
may have a greater influence on our behavior than what it actually is. There is considerable evidence for vicarious conditioning processes in which learning is established via observation of
others (see Bandura, 1969, 1971a). A substantial literature has
been accumulated within social learning theory attesting to the
role of symbolic process in influencing behavior (see, for example, Bandura, 1969; Mahoney, 1974a). Anticipated consequences enable separations between performance and later reinforcers. They also unfortunately allow inaccurate anticipations
that are dysfunctional such as expecting to be rejected in social
situations in which, given display of existent skills, such rejection would not occur. Inaccurate anticipations may thus interfere with the display of appropriate skills. Social learning theory
models are essentially mediational models that recognize the
role of symbolic processes such as attention and relational
processes.

The role of attentional factors is evidenced in the literature investigating resistance to temptation and expectancy features within counseling, as well as in self-monitoring. Relational
features include comparative processes in which we compare
some consequences with our own past experiences, with what
we have observed watching other people and with socially acquired performance criteria (Bandura, 1971b). Thus, as Mahoney (1974a) points out, our evaluations of our own behavior
are made relative to past, vicarious, and ideal standards. Standard setting interacts with performance feedback to alter the

effects of this feedback. Retentional deficiencies and errors of inference may also influence the effects of external events. As Mahoney (1974a) points out, "the actual contiguity of events may be far less important in learning than their perceived relationship."

Symbolic processes have traditionally occupied an important role in many behavioral procedures (see, for example, Wolpe, 1958). Many behavioral procedures involve the client in imagining relevant events, such as covert modeling, in which the client imagines himself or some other person interacting with a feared event (see, for example, Cautela, 1971b). Each procedure that involves the presentation of actual events, such as modeling, has generated its covert replica. Thus, in covert positive reinforcement (Cautela, 1970b) the client imagines engaging in a typically avoided behavior, and then imagines a pleasant event. Covert negative reinforcement involves imagining the ending of a covert aversive image contingent on the imagined performance of a desired response (Cautela, 1970a). In covert extinction, the client imagines performing a behavior without its usual consequence (Cautela, 1971a) and in covert sensitization, the client imagines some dysfunctional approach behavior paired with an imagined aversive event (Cautela, 1967). Utilization of covert events, of course, presents a measurement problem.

Thus covert events have been assumed to function as eliciting events for respondent reactions, as discriminative cues for operant behaviors, as responses in their own right, and as consequences that may be negative, positive, or neutral. They have been employed in covert conditioning therapies (see Mahoney, 1974a, for a thoughtful review) both as events to be influenced (such as the frequency of positive self-statements) as well as the antecedents and consequences that may influence them. In addition, they have been presumed to play an important role in the complex processes that affect the attention and relational features assumed to be involved in learning. Cognitions are also considered to play a critical role in the degree to which various intervention procedures are effective in altering behavior. For example, Bandura (in press) has recently argued that it is the extent to which interventions alter the personal sense of self-efficacy that will determine their effectiveness. Processes that influence self-efficacy include what a person has actually accomplished, vicarious experiences through viewing the performance of others, verbal persuasion, and information provided from physiological reactions. Support is offered for the greater effect on self-efficacy of enactive interventions that provide more dependable information concerning what can actually be accomplished, compared to vicarious and emotive modes of intervention (see Chapter Eight for further discussion of these intervention modes).

Generalization

Antecedent events that are similar to those present during either operant or respondent conditioning will also tend to elicit or occasion similar behaviors. If a person slows down when he sees a police car in back of him, he may also tend to have this reaction when he spots cars that are similar to a police car. This is known as *stimulus generalization* and occurs with both operant and respondent behaviors.

The term *response generalization* refers to the fact that behaviors that are similar to a behavior that is reinforced will also tend to be increased in terms of future probability. If a child is reinforced for telling a particular type of joke, he may tend to offer additional jokes that are similar in nature. That is, he may display his "joke repertoire." Generalization is discussed in more detail in Chapter Eight.

Use of Conditioned Reinforcers

Conditioned reinforcers are events that have acquired some reinforcing potential through learning. Conditioned reinforcers that are paired with a variety of reinforcers become generalized reinforcers, in that they are capable of reinforcing behavior related to a wide variety of deprivation states. Examples include money, approval, and tokens or points. Because of this characteristic, in addition to a variety of other advantages described hereafter, token or point programs are often employed to alter behavior.

Token Programs. A token program is a motivational system for systematically arranging the increase in desired behaviors and the decrease in inappropriate behaviors. Points or tokens are awarded for behaviors to be increased and a loss of tokens may also be agreed on for inappropriate behaviors. Tokens are exchanged for agreed-on "backup" reinforcers. A token program is artificial in that it is not a normal part of the environment, and tokens are gradually faded out as natural reinforcers take effect—such as social approval or enjoyment of activities in their own right. Token programs have been employed in a wide range of settings, including the classroom, home, and day-care facilities, as well as in a range of residential settings, including mental hospitals, institutions for the mentally retarded, reformatories, and half-way houses. It has been suggested that one of the reasons for the effectiveness of token programs is the extent to which a person's behavior is made more visible to the token dispenser as well as to the individual receiving the points or tokens (Ferster, 1972). For example, a teacher who can offer tokens "selectively to produce specific increments in a child's behavior is also becoming more observant and hence more sensitive to other aspects of the child's repertoire" (Ferster, 1972, p. 138). That is, her attention to the child will increase and she is likely to prompt desirable behaviors. "On the child's part, the token amplifies the product of his conduct so that he can observe his progress and competence" (Ferster, 1972, p. 138).

There are a number of occasions in which it may be desirable to employ a token program (Ayllon and Azrin, 1968b): (1) when there are few naturally occurring appropriate reinforcers available; (2) when appropriate reinforcers are available, but it is doubtful that they will be applied consistently in an unambiguous form; (3) when it is difficult to arrange immediate presentation of reinforcers; (4) when the goal is to establish some event as a reinforcer; for example, approval; (5) when satiation effects may be a problem; and (6) when there is a need to remind significant others to reinforce appropriate behavior.

Tokens allow reinforcement of behavior at any time. They also permit a sequence of behaviors to be reinforced without interruption (Kazdin and Bootzin, 1972). Because tokens may be exchanged for a variety of backup reinforcers, their effectiveness is relatively independent of specific deprivation states and they will function as a reinforcer for people with different preferences, because different reinforcers may be purchased (Kazdin and Bootzin, 1972). Tokens also provide a visible record of improvement.

There are a number of additional advantages in using tangible reinforcers, such as tokens, rather than praise and approval (Ayllon and Azrin, 1968b, p. 77): "(1) The number of tokens can [have] a . . . quantitative relation to the amount of reinforcement; (2) . . . tokens are portable and can be in the subject's possession even when he is . . . removed from [the situation] . . . in which . . . tokens were earned; (3) no maximum exists in the number of tokens a subject may possess; (4) tokens can be used . . . to operate devices for the automatic delivery of reinforcers; (5) tokens are durable and can be continuously present during the delay; (6) the physical characteristics of tokens can be easily standardized; (7) the tokens can be made fairly indestructible so they will not deteriorate during the delay; and (8) tokens can be made unique and nonduplicable so one can assure that they are received only in an authorized manner."

The behaviors to be reinforced must be in the client's repertoire and provisions made for them to occur or no tokens can be earned. And it is very important to pair the giving of tokens with social approval, since this may be depended on to maintain behavior when tokens are gradually withdrawn. The first behaviors reinforced may be far removed from the final desired goal. The closest possible approximation to the final goal is included in the initial program. As this behavior becomes more frequent, a closer approximation is required for the same number of tokens and so on until tokens are being earned for the final objectives. When a behavior has occurred regularly for a few days, the number of tokens offered is gradually decreased, and, if other behaviors are to be changed, a new behavior can be added to the program and tokens offered for it. Social reinforcers should be continued for appropriate behaviors. Whether simple or complex, there are a number of essential ingredients of token programs (Ayllon and Azrin, 1968b), described in the following sections.

Pinpointing of behaviors to be reinforced. Pinpointing informs the client how tokens can be earned. Behaviors are described so as to require minimum interpretation as to whether they occurred (Ayllon and Azrin, 1968b). Selecting behaviors that can be tracked by virtue of their effect on the environment (such as raking up leaves on a lawn) has the advantage of not requiring supervision to see whether it is accomplished. Behaviors should be selected that will continue to be reinforced after training (Ayllon and Azrin, 1968b). This will keep attention focused on selecting behaviors that will be of value to clients rather than behaviors of value only to staff, parents, or teachers. Be sure to select behaviors that the client performs with some frequency so that reinforcement can occur often. This may require selection of approximations to desired outcomes.

Identification of appropriate reinforcers. Activities or items are selected that can be earned during the first day, as well as some that may take a few days to earn. Reinforcers should be defined with the same precision devoted to definition of behaviors. If, for example, an ice-cream cone is included as a reinforcer, the amount should be specified (for example, one, two, or three scoops). Careful definition prevents arguments and accusations of unfairness. As many dimensions of the reinforcer as possible should be specified in physical terms. If a reinforcer is access to a game, how long is this access to be, where can the game be played and with whom? Use of a variety of backup reinforcers will encourage desired behaviors. It is important, of course, not to allow noncontingent access to backup reinforcers.

Assignment of point values to behaviors and points required for reinforcers. There should be a reasonable compensation for behaviors and a reasonable cost for reinforcers. What is reasonable will become apparent when the token program is put into effect. If the balance is off, the program will simply not produce a change in behavior. If reinforcers can be accumulated too easily, satiation may occur, or a client may be able to earn all reinforcers available in the first two days, and thus no contingencies would encourage further appropriate behaviors. If too little is offered, there may be no incentive for altering behavior. Token programs may be poorly designed in that they offer too much for too little or too little for too much.

To balance a token program, all points that could be earned daily and weekly are added, using some convenient amount, such as a daily total of 10 or 100 points. Next, point values are arranged so that some reinforcers can be obtained very soon and so that others will require a greater accumulation of points. The delay selected is informed by what is thought possible. Some clients will require more frequent, immediate offering of backup reinforcers than others. The design of token programs is always a trial-and-error process, in the sense that it is through feedback as to how the program works that alterations in the original program are then made.

Explaining the value of tokens. A verbal explanation of the value of tokens or points is usually sufficient. However, with clients such as nonverbal children, further efforts may have to be made to establish their value by pairing tokens with backup reinforcers. For example, a child may be given a token, led over to a table with a variety of reinforcers, and shown that he can receive one item if he gives the trainer a token. Repetition of this pairing a few times should succeed in establishing the exchange value of tokens. The trainer should be sure to verbalize the contingency each time.

Arranging for points to be awarded following desired behaviors. Critical to the effectiveness of token programs is that points are awarded following desired behaviors. Making sure that behaviors are clearly defined will make it easier to identify and reinforce them. It must be decided when points are to be awarded and who is to give them. Points or tokens should be given as soon after behavior as is possible.

Arrangement for securing backup reinforcers. Just as it is important to award tokens immediately following desired behavior, it is also important that backup reinforcers be offered as agreed on. A time and place for this must be arranged.

Monitoring the number of tokens earned for each behavior. Arrangements must be made to keep track of the number of tokens or points awarded so that reinforcers can be exchanged in accord with this number. It is also important to keep track of what points are earned for so that behavioral requirements for awarding of points can be altered. For example, if a desired behavior has stabilized at a given level for a couple of weeks, the points offered for this can be reduced, while points for another behavior can be offered. Tracking is usually easily accomplished by use of chart.

Monitoring reinforcer use. By keeping records of what reinforcers are frequently purchased, their value can be adjusted accordingly. Let us say that a goal is to encourage use of a reinforcer that is not selected very often, such as reading the newspaper. The point value could be reduced to encourage use of this reinforcer. Or, if a reinforcer is being used more than is desired (let us say that candy is an item), its cost could be increased, or a limit placed on how often it can be purchased.

Pairing tokens with social approval. Token economies are artificial, in that they are not a natural part of the environment. It is thus necessary to pair tokens or points with a naturally occurring reinforcer, such as social approval, to maintain behavior when the token system is removed.

Token systems may be quite simple and informal or more complex in that they include many behaviors and reinforcers. In some, reinforcement contingencies are the same for all participants while in others different contingencies may apply to different people. The degree of training that is necessary for staff, parents, or teachers to carry out an effective program depends on its complexity and the degree and type of resistances encountered. Various procedures have been introduced to encourage client participation, to deal with lack of client response to the program, and to assure that contingencies are enforced (see, for example, Kazdin and Bootzin, 1972). Client participation can be encouraged by use of reinforcer and response priming and by selection of behaviors that are possible for the client to perform so that tokens can be earned. Client participation in planning the program decreases client resistance. This accentuates the client's responsibility for his behavior (Kazdin and

Bootzin, 1972). Steffy (1968), for example, reports the participation of aggressive psychotic clients in planning reinforcement
programs and arranging contractual agreements. Clients may be
involved in carrying out selected aspects of the program, such as
giving out or banking tokens.

It is, of course, important that tokens can only be gained
via designated behaviors. Stealing of tokens can be prevented by
marking tokens, by giving each client his or her own special
token card, on which tokens are recorded or by staff distribution of tokens to individual containers (Gambrill, 1976). Selection of behaviors that result in a behavior product (some change
in the environment) will help to prevent awarding of tokens for
behaviors that have not been carried out, although this will not
preclude giving tokens to someone other than the person who
completed the behavior.

Token programs employed with a large group typically
report the failure of the program to affect the behavior of some
clients. For example, 18 percent of chronic schizophrenic patients were unaffected by a program geared to alter their job
preferences (Ayllon and Azrin, 1965). This problem may be
remedied by the use of stronger reinforcers and individualized, rather than ward-wide programs. Token hoarding, which
decreases use of available reinforcers, can be discouraged by de-
valuing tokens if they are not spent within a certain time
(Atthowe and Krasner, 1968). Considerations relating to the
training and alteration of staff behavior are discussed in Chapter
Twenty-One.

If a token program is implemented and does not seem to
work, a review of the exact procedures employed should be
made to ascertain what requisites for a viable program are missing. The people who are to offer the tokens may not do so in
the manner in which they are supposed to. Perhaps they cannot
readily discriminate behaviors to be reinforced and need more
practice in picking these out, or perhaps behavioral definitions
must be clarified. These individuals may have too much to do,
or may find it aversive to offer tokens. Perhaps they do not
understand the importance of offering tokens immediately following behavior, of verbalizing the reason for gaining a token,
and of offering tokens consistently. They may forget to pair

tokens with verbal praise or may be sarcastic when offering them. Perhaps the token dispenser is not clear about who is to reinforce what behavior. Responsibilities may have to be clarified as to who should reinforce what behaviors (Ayllon and Azrin, 1968b). The faults in a program are best discerned from observation of the behavior of the token dispenser in relation to those receiving tokens. Required records may not be kept. Perhaps recording procedures developed require too much time and are not designed to offer the most useful feedback to the token dispensers. The reinforcer menu must also be examined to make sure there are indeed items that are reinforcing, and that these are priced reasonably in relation to required number of tokens. This should also be scanned to make sure that some reinforcers can be obtained within the first day. Perhaps reinforcers on the reinforcer menu are available without the use of tokens. The behaviors selected for reinforcement may seldom occur, thus permitting few opportunities for their reinforcement. Perhaps the behaviors have no utility from the point of view of the client. The tokens offered for various behaviors may be too much or too little. As can be seen, there are a number of requisites for the design of a viable token economy.

Summary

Behavioral principles describe relationships between behavior and environmental events. What happens before our behavior affects these relationships as well as what happens afterwards, and a number of parameters influence the relationships that are established, such as the schedule, frequency, and amount of reinforcement. The importance of schedules of reinforcement has been especially emphasized, because of the profound effects such schedules have on behavior. Basic procedures, such as positive reinforcement, are defined not only by a certain procedure, but also by the effect they have on behavior. Some consequences decrease behavior, whereas others make it more likely on future occasions. Artificial reinforcers in the form of tokens or points may be employed when natural reinforcers are not effective.

There are many advantages to employing positive means

of influence rather than punitive means, including the development of specific alternative behaviors, and the pleasantness of positive influence compared to aversive influence. Behavioral principles provide methods to establish new behaviors as well as to alter behaviors already present, such as model presentation and shaping, and point to the influential role that cognitions play in regulating behavior. The principles related to respondent conditioning provide valuable information concerning the development and alteration of emotional reactions.

3

Almost all forms of helping share certain common features. All involve introducing clients to a new way of viewing their problems and potentialities. Other common features include obtaining needed assessment information, securing the client's cooperation, establishing a helping relationship, and providing feedback as to progress. In addition, all must attend to ethical concerns inherent in the helping process. Some of these features are described in detail in other chapters and some of the facilitating conditions for others, such as establishing rapport with clients, are assumed to be known (and hopefully mastered) by the reader. This chapter addresses the need for understanding the client's view of the problem; for forming a common conceptualization of the "problem"; and the need for

70

Important Features
of Behavioral Practice

structuring counselor-client contacts as these relate to behavioral practice, as well as nonspecific therapeutic factors and methods for securing client involvement.

Understanding the Client's View of the Problem

As with all counseling efforts, it is critical to identify problems of concern to the client and to understand his frame of reference for viewing these problems. Clients have their own more or less explicit view of what their problems are related to. They have various assumptions about their lives and possibilities (Frank, 1961). These assumptions are often quite inaccurate, and, in addition, discourage effective action. Often clients accept verbal statements alone as indicating the values they hold (in the absence of behavior in accord with such statements), and they are thus confused in terms of understanding what changes they would like. For example, a client may say he really likes people but make few attempts to approach others. A client's seeking of help indicates that his views have not enabled him to resolve his problems. Skilled listening and supportive statements encourage the client to offer needed information. Most clients approach the counseling situation with a variety of concerns, including difficulties in committing oneself to change and submitting to the influence of a helper, not finding it easy to trust a stranger and be open with him, not seeing problems clearly, and feeling overwhelmed by problems (Brammer, 1973). Recognition of the difficulty in sharing such information may help the client to share needed data and encourage the client to view the counselor as someone who is in touch with the client's experience. Understanding the client's view of his problem can indicate ways a new framework may be helpful to the client in obtaining desired outcomes.

Forming a New Conceptualization of the Problem

If the counselor sees the world as the client does, he will have little to offer (Levy, 1968). Thus an integral aspect of the counseling process is the formation of a new conceptualization of the problem, a conceptualization that is shared by both the counselor and client, that will be helpful in solving this problem, and that may be helpful in preventing or solving other problems that arise. This process is gradually initiated during the first steps of assessment, along with helping the client to describe desired outcomes and related environmental and personal events. The client's view of problems may be in conflict with a behavioral framework, in which there is an active attempt to increase the influence that clients have over their internal and external environments and in which people are considered to affect those with whom they interact. The client may not see his own role in maintenance of his problem. He may believe that he has little control over what he does, thinks, and feels. Commitment to a disease-model interpretation of a problem, in which a client views himself as "sick," may induce him to search for a "pill-like" cure. The client may not be willing to engage in the step-by-step work that may be required within a behavioral model. Only after the rationale for this model is carefully explained may client cooperation be gained. Or the client may view himself as abnormal and his feelings as "crazy." Casting his problem in terms of learning theory helps to "normalize" his reactions, to decrease fears that he may be mentally ill. Davison notes that, "In essence the argument (obviously buttressed by the prestige of the therapist role) presented to the client is that, while his feelings may appear very odd, peculiar, crazy, or 'sick,' such feelings can be produced in 'normal' people as well by subjecting them to certain environmental-developmental situations. Furthermore, his feelings are explicable in terms of the same psychological processes which psychologists invoke to explain such human behavior as rote learning, acquisition of sensory motor skills, and sensory deprivation experiences" (Davison, 1966, p. 266). It is important to reduce unwarranted fears, since these may make the problem considerably worse. Through a new "attribution" of his problem, the client is helped to view it in terms of a process (learning) that affects all behavior. The client may view himself as having no role in maintaining behaviors of others he complains about, and must be guided during assessment to understanding the interaction between his own behavior and the behaviors he complains about. The client comes to "reinterpret" problem behaviors (Kopel and Arkowitz, 1975).

It is important that the client and counselor arrive at a common view of the presenting problem, as well as at a common agreement as to what will be done to change it. This mutual sharing of conceptualizations is a vital aspect of behavioral intervention (Meichenbaum, 1975b; Wolpe, 1958). This common view is a motivating factor in that, if the client accepts it and if it makes sense to him, there will be a greater willingness to try out procedures that flow from this account of the problem.

Within a behavioral framework, the counselor wishes to increase the client's understanding of how his behavior is related to specific thoughts and environmental events and to "give the client a sense of control and a feeling of hope, particularly in terms that will lead to specific behavioral interventions" (Meichenbaum, 1975b, p. 364). Alternative views of problems are offered and the client asked to consider them. The counselor is thus active in altering how the client thinks about his problem. The client's conceptualization is not accepted at face value, but must be molded to fit one that will be helpful in terms of change efforts.

Mutually agreed-on views are fostered in a variety of ways, including the way in which the presenting problem is discussed, the types of questions asked, the assessment procedures used, the rationales that are offered, as well as homework assignments that may be given (Meichenbaum, 1975b). Focused counselor summaries of material can help to pull material together within a new framework. Helpful summaries collect together points that the client himself has brought up that will help the client to see his problem in a more useful (and more accurate) framework. Identifying similar themes among a variety of seemingly disparate events can also help to open the client to alternative frameworks. As in helping efforts within other frameworks, it may be necessary to confront discrepancies, distortions, games the client plays (such as "Yes, but . . . ." tricks), smoke screens, and evasions (Egan, 1975). However, confrontation should be carried out responsibly and nonpunitively. As Egan notes, some counselors use confrontation as a club or, conversely, lose ground because they are afraid to challenge the client at all. (See Egan, 1975, for a helpful discussion of manner of confronting and possible client reactions.)

Interactions between the client and counselor may also be employed to identify relevant behaviors and events. The client can be asked to carry out a task in the natural environment that can then be discussed during the interview, using questions and comments that will encourage a certain conceptualization, such as pointing out relationships between behavior and environmental events, or relationships between types of self-statements and what the client feels and does. Or an assessment procedure serving this purpose could be arranged in the office situation, such as having a mother observe the interaction between her child and another person. Specific conceptualizations of these situations are then encouraged by the type of question asked, making an attempt to have the client reach conclusions that match those held by the counselor. The principles of behavior that relate to desired outcomes are discussed. The client's acceptance of new views of his behavior and related factors will be influenced by the counselor's skill in establishing a relationship (a power base) during initial exploration of the problem. This base should rest on genuineness, respect for the client, accurate empathy, and the client's perception of the counselor as a skilled helper. Skilled use of gentle confrontation as needed and of advanced, accurate empathy, in which new views of behavior are offered, is employed to encourage new frameworks. Intervention procedures can then be linked with information gathered during assessment.

Although the self-influence possibilities over one's life and problems are emphasized and the client thus is given an increased sense of responsibility over his life and the way it affects others, this is done in a way that nullifies self-blame (Wolpe and Lazarus, 1966). Self-blame as well as blame of others for unfortunate events in one's life are actively discouraged. Blame rarely helps in arriving at constructive solutions to problems and it usually makes people feel unhappy. Enhanced client understanding of the effects of the mutual interaction between his behavior and the environment will hopefully discourage such blame and encourage instead the search for functional relationship between behavior, thoughts, feelings, and environmental events. An important aspect of a behavioral conceptualization of problems includes a stress on the learning factors involved in the establishment and maintenance of the problem as well as the use of these principles in designing intervention programs. The framework stresses "action" in relation to resolving problems as well as "understanding" of related factors. Self-exploration in which the events related to problems are identified is considered to be a means to an end—action that leads to more satisfying living. Such exploration may sometimes lead to realization of the need for change and new behavior.

"To the extent that counseling increases the client's knowledge of how he typically behaves and the effects he typically intends, counseling increases his ability to predict and control his behavior" (Strong, 1970, p. 390). However, it will not do so unless appropriate incentives, needed skills, and necessary comfort levels are present. Only if such understanding by itself frees needed resources will this stage be sufficient. The next important stage is planning and carrying out specific actions in real life. Many counselors never get beyond self-exploration and self-understanding; that is, they do not include the important phase of designing action programs based on such self-understanding in which the client puts new information into practice (Egan, 1975).

Each intervention mode offers a different rationale to the client for effects that are achieved. The nature of the rationale provided seems to be related to outcome. It has been found that greater gains occur when the client attributes change to his or her own efforts (Kopel and Arkowitz, 1975). Such attribution is encouraged by having the client learn general principles of behavior and participate as much as possible in the selection of assessment and intervention methods and to gradually assume more responsibility for these. The emphasis should be on the client's active use of the principles in order to avoid perception of these as magical procedures. That is, the client should believe that he is mainly responsible for his improvement (Kopel and Arkowitz, 1975). By being encouraged in self-observation, either in the natural environment or during simulated conditions in the office, the client learns to reevaluate his behavior as it relates to given situations and to start acquiring a pattern of self-reinforcement. The client is more likely to attribute gains to his own doing if the reinforcing events or punishing events employed are weak. That is, he is more likely to infer motivational influence to his own behavior than when strong external aids or consequences are employed. Use of weak consequences is more likely to lead to a changed perception of himself in which he views himself as capable of influencing his behavior (Kopel and Arkowitz, 1975). "In the case of positive reinforcement, the potential problem stems from the client inferring that he merely emitted the desirable behavior in order to secure the reward. This external attribution may decrease the extent to which the individual infers that he is the kind of person who emits the positive behavior" (Kopel and Arkowitz, 1975, p. 200). It is important not to replace self-attributions for behavior with external attributions, since this may result in a decrease of positive behaviors (Lepper, Greene, and Nisbett, 1973). Developing patterns of self-reinforcement will encourage self-attribution. Thus the self-management components of intervention are important to highlight to the client. Many, if not most, behavioral methods can be viewed without strain as enhancing the client's self-mastery over his life. Some authors have suggested that one index of success in counseling is client acquisition of a new conceptual framework for understanding his or her behavior (Kaul and Parker, 1971).

Structuring Counselor-Client Contacts

There is a continuing need throughout assessment and intervention to explain the roles and requirements of the client and the counselor, the sequences of the counseling process, and the rationale for procedures. Introductory explanations include an overview of client and counselor responsibilities and of the framework that will be employed. This "socialization" of the client is an ongoing task, because different client behaviors may be required during different phases of assessment and intervention (Gambrill, Thomas, and Carter, 1971). It is a particularly extensive part of behavioral intervention, in which a goal may be to develop client skills in applying a behavioral framework to problems that arise. If the client is to do this, he should understand the rationale for each step in the process as well as be familiar with its components, such as what type of questions to ask. To the degree to which such information encourages the client to carry out mutually agreed-on assignments, provision of explanations also functions as an intervention. Counselor-client contracts structure the helping process by identifying, among other items, the duration of intervention as well as desired outcomes. Because short-term intervention appears to be as effec-

tive as longer-term change efforts both with delinquents and
their families and with social agencies (Reid and Shyne, 1969;
Stuart and Tripodi, 1973), establishing a duration of change
efforts seems advantageous, in view of the savings in time and
money that short-term intervention offers. Behavioral interviews are structured in other ways as well. Any assignments the
client has agreed to carry out are reviewed during the initial part
of the next interview (or before by telephone) to stress their
importance and to assess their results so further assignments can
be designed. A record of interventions should be made so that it
is readily apparent what type of assignments have been fruitful.
Assignments are reviewed at the end of the session to ensure
that the client understands what he has agreed to and times of
counselor-client contact are established between interviews
when data will be collected—for example, by telephone.

Behavioral interviewers tend to be more directive than
psychoanalytically oriented psychotherapists; they more frequently give advice and instructions, provide information, influence the conversation, and talk more (Sloane and others, 1975).
Counselors may err by being too directive or by being too nondirective. Overly directive counselors may view the client as a
problem rather than a person and not recognize the need to
help the client to explore his behavior and to begin to understand factors related to it. In contrast, the completely nondirective counselor errs by assuming that self-understanding is sufficient to allow the client to alter his behavior. One important
way in which a behavioral interviewer influences content is in
terms of concreteness, that is, in helping the client to identify
specific desired behaviors, thoughts, feelings, and factors that
influence these rather than speaking in terms of vague generalities. Another way involves prompting and reinforcement of
constructive client behaviors in the interview (such as positive
self-statements and concrete behavioral descriptions) and discouraging unconstructive client behaviors such as negative self-
statements, "psychoanalyzing," and vague generalities. Unless
the counselor is cognizant of the principles of reinforcement
and employs them in a helpful way during interviewing, these
principles may actively work against him (Egan, 1975). If spe-

cific examples of a problematic behavior are desired, and if a client's vague statements are followed by nods and "Um-hums" from the counselor rather than prompts for appropriate behavior, such vague statement may continue to be offered. An agenda of items to be addressed within an interview should be prepared beforehand, to the extent possible. If prior information is available about the nature of the client's problem, it may be necessary to consult the literature regarding this problem before the interview to determine typical referents and how it may be rendered observable and countable. Examples are frequently related factors, types of intervention procedures used with such problems, their relative effectiveness and efficiency, and their advantages and disadvantages. A list of possible intervention methods may be generated as the assessment phase nears completion. The counselor is considered to be responsible for directing the flow of conversation and tasks within the interview so contact with the client will be maximally useful. It is the counselor's responsibility to maintain focus within the interview on tasks to be accomplished and to do so in an efficient way and in a way that is comfortable for the client. Obviously, unanticipated events may warrant a diversion from the pursuit of agreed-on objectives, such as a new problem that has arisen that requires immediate attention (Gambrill, Thomas, and Carter, 1971). Perhaps a client has just lost a job, been injured, lost a significant other, or been threatened with eviction. Client discomfort when discussing a given topic may require temporarily halting focus on agreed-on tasks. Perhaps the client will have to be trained in deep muscle relaxation to enable him to more comfortably discuss difficult topics (Bernstein and Borkovec, 1973). Sometimes the client may not answer questions but may instead diverge at length into unrelated content. If so, the counselor attempts to lead the client back to the focus of questions in a polite and informative manner. It may be necessary to restate the purpose of the question as well as the purpose of a given interview. The client may be offered a free time at the end of the interview to discuss anything he might like, with the agreement that time prior to this will be devoted to pursuit of agreed-on tasks. As in other practice models, additional encouragement and support is given to draw out clients who are quiet. This may entail restating questions in alternative ways, restating the rationale for questions, and offering support and encouragement in relation to the individual's role as a client and in relation to problems that may be experienced in the natural environment. It may be necessary to reaffirm the mutual purpose of contact, and, if a written contract has already been formed, to bring it to the client's attention. The client may wish to change the agreements stated in the contract. If frequent changes are requested, attention should be devoted to the possible reasons for the "floating problem." Perhaps the original contract did not include a problem of concern to the client. The client may be unable to identify a source of his distress and the counselor may not have identified it during assessment. If so, the interview dialog should return to the early assessment phase to attempt to determine whether some problem of import has been neglected. Or perhaps the client is looking for an easy answer to his distress, that is, instant relief. Information provided by the counselor concerning the gradual nature of change may not have been sufficient to counter this unrealistic hope, and so the client becomes disappointed and ready to move on to another problem in which fast relief may be experienced. The client may have to be reminded of potential benefits of task completion. This may require pointing out the effect of unnecessary digressions. Precounseling inventories that the client is requested to complete prior to the first interview may be used to help to structure initial sessions. These may involve the client in initial attempts to identify specific desired positive changes; they encourage clients to state their goals positively (Stuart, 1975). These can also be employed to encourage the client to attend to the relationships between his behavior and that of others. Requested completion of precounseling inventories will also help to stress the active role that the client is expected to assume.

The type of interaction the client may anticipate may differ greatly from that offered. Unless explained, this difference may have negative effects on change efforts. For example, Mayer and Timms (1970) found that lower-class clients interviewed at a family service agency disliked the social worker's passivity and reluctance to give advice. Being unaware that the counselor's approach to problem solving differed from their own, they interpreted this as a lack of worker interest, failure to understand, a confusion as to how to proceed, and a lack of power to help. Poorly motivated clients can often profit from counseling if they are informed what to expect (Orne and Wender, 1968).

A recent description of a good helper that is in accord with behavioral practice and that indicates many aspects of structuring as well as establishing a helping relationship is offered by Egan (1975, p. 23):

> A good helper knows that helping is a great deal of *work*. He attends to the other person both physically and psychologically. He knows what his own body is saying and can read the nonverbal messages of his client. He listens intently to the other, knowing that effective counseling is an intense process in which much can be accomplished if two people are willing to collaborate. He responds frequently to the other, for he is working at understanding him. He responds from the frame of reference of his client, for he can see the world through the client's eyes. He respects his client and expresses his respect by being available to him, working with him, not judging him, trusting the constructive forces found in him, and ultimately placing the expectation on him that he live life as effectively as he can. He genuinely cares for the person who has come for help; that is, he is nondefensive, spontaneous, and always willing to say what he thinks and feels, provided that it is in the best interests of his client. A good helper is concrete in his expressions, dealing with actual feelings and actual behavior rather than vague formulations, obscure psychodynamics, or generalities. His speech, while caring and human, is also lean and to the point.

The Therapeutic Context

A number of influences are present in all therapeutic endeavors, including arousal of hope, the expectation of help, demand characteristics, and an initial cathartic interview. Placebo effects alone may create changes. For example, subjects with mild fears respond favorably to suggestion alone (see Borkovec, 1973) and almost two thirds of mild and moderate insomniacs responded as favorably to a placebo as to hypnotic medication (Nicholis and Silvestri, 1967). In both instances, however, the placebo effect was more marked with clients with mild or moderate problems than with clients who presented severe problems. The potency of the effects mentioned earlier is demonstrated in the recent study by Sloane and his colleagues that compared the effectiveness of behavior therapy and psychoanalytically oriented psychotherapy with ninety-four clients, presenting moderately severe neuroses and personality disorders (Sloane and others, 1975). A waiting-list control group was promised therapy in four months' time to assess the role of unspecified factors. All three groups of clients significantly improved in three months. However, the "placebo" group did not improve as much on specified desired outcomes selected for change. The contribution of placebo effects and demand characteristics to effective change highlights the importance of maximizing these effects by encouraging hopeful expectations of change. Lick and Bootzin (1975) point to a number of possible ways through which expectancy manipulations may enhance improvement in the treatment of fear reactions. These include an increased tendency to test reality after undergoing an effective intervention, resulting in increased extinction of fear reactions and self-reinforcement for improvement; increased compliance with intervention procedures; and an alteration of cognitive events related to fear reactions after treatment; that is, the client may, when presented with previously fear-arousing events, say, "I am not afraid of . . ." rather than, "Oh my goodness, there is an. . . ." A fourth effect may result from the demand characteristic operating following treatment to show improvement.

A great deal of effort has been devoted to trying to determine the relationship between certain types of counselor behaviors and positive outcome, particularly within client-centered intervention (see, for example, Truax, 1966). Past research indicated that at least minimal levels of accurate empathic understanding, nonpossessive warmth, and genuineness facilitate positive change and it has been argued that these relationships between counselor behavior and outcome cut across schools of psychotherapy (Truax and Mitchell, 1971). Some recent studies do not support the importance of these factors except in client-centered therapy (Bergin and Suinn, 1975). However, it could be, as these authors point out, that these conditions are related to positive change but are not being measured appropriately. Supporting this interpretation are studies that find significant correlations between client-perceived empathy and outcome, even though there was no relationship between tape-rated empathy and outcome (Sloane and others, 1975). Clients who themselves reported higher levels of warmth, empathy, or genuineness in their counselor showed greater improvement, even though these variables as rated from sessions were unrelated to outcome. Clients rated the personal interaction with the counselor as the single most important part of counseling. Only in psychotherapy (and not in behavior therapy) did clients who were liked by their counselors show greater improvement than those who were less liked (Sloane and others, 1975). A recent study of behavioral intervention with families of delinquents found that both counselor structuring and relationship skills were strong predictors of outcome variance (Alexander, Barton, Shiavo, and Parsons, 1976).

As in all helping efforts, placebo effects and demand characteristics will be enhanced to the extent to which the counselor skillfully builds a base of social influence. For example, these effects will be enhanced if the client perceives the counselor as an expert. This will depend on the level of helping skills the counselor displays, his reputation as an expert, and the role he assumes (for example, his credentials). It has also been suggested that his confidence in his theory and model of helping is a source of behavior expertness (Strong, 1968). That is, if he exerts substantial effort to understand, use, and evaluate his framework of helping, this will be evident in his interaction with clients. Enthusiasm and confidence will characterize his statements and he is more likely to work hard for his client.

Many counselor behaviors serve not only to encourage positive placebo effects but also help to direct interview content in relevant directions. For example, clear counselor questions help to focus the client on important material and serve to indicate to the client that the counselor knows "what she is about." Respect for the client encourages positive effects and increases the possibility that the client will accept new conceptualizations of his problem and carry out agreed-on assignments, because this respect is likely to increase the attraction value of the counselor. Respect includes verbal as well as nonverbal behaviors, including careful attending; suspending critical judgment; regarding the resources of the client and cultivating these; displaying accurate empathy, in which the counselor demonstrates to the client that he is trying to understand the client; reinforcing constructive action of the client and refusing to reinforce unconstructive actions; and being genuine—nondefensive, consistent, sharing appropriate self-disclosures, and being tactfully spontaneous (Egan, 1975; Truax and Carkhuff, 1967).

Counselor trustworthiness is another important characteristic that influences the effects of counseling. Dimensions that influence this characteristic include behaviors of the counselor such as maintaining confidentiality, demonstrating respect, and avoiding behaviors that might indicate the presence of ulterior motives, such as voyeurism, selfishness, or personal gain (Egan, 1975).

A lack of understanding of the client and a failure to establish an influence base on the part of the counselor will limit the possibilities of new understanding by the client and will decrease the likelihood that the client will agree to carry out needed activities in real life. Failure to establish a power base and to indicate to the client at an early stage that counseling can be of help no doubt is partially responsible for the high dropout rates in a variety of helping efforts (Baekeland and Lundwall, 1975).

Securing the Client's Involvement

Typically, within a behavioral model, the client is an active participant in both assessment and intervention in terms of carrying out agreed-on assignments in the natural environment. Reconceptualization of the problem and explanations provided to the client help to engage the client in change efforts through challenging interfering belief systems, highlighting the need for specific changes, clarifying expectations, and offering an alternative way to view events. Within a behavioral approach, commitment is actively pursued and is usually crystallized in the form of written contracts and explicit statements of expectations about the client's and counselor's role in the change process. The setting of time-limited change efforts also facilitates involvement. A client may be willing to try out a change program for a limited time period. If this initial program produces benefits, he may then be willing to pursue further change efforts. Another factor related to client involvement is precision of instructions. Special efforts are made to make these as clear as possible, rehearsal experience is provided whenever possible prior to the client's carrying out a task in the natural environment, and feedback is consistently provided. These factors increase the possibility that mutually agreed-on tasks will be successfully completed. Much of the work of obtaining client involvement may be accomplished before the signing of a client-counselor contract. Many sessions may be necessary in which a trusting relationship is established and the client guided in viewing his problems in new ways that will encourage him to become involved in the change process. Change efforts can be encouraged by counselor praise for client efforts, participation in reviewing results of assignments, and recognition of the difficulty of change. Excessively high or low levels of praise should be avoided, because they will be counterproductive. The prime source of encouragement hopefully arises from the positive effects achieved by the client by acting differently in the natural environment.

Even though the client agrees that counselor suggestions are good ones and agrees to follow them, he or she may not do so. As we all know, good intentions do not necessarily lead to completed deeds. Special contingencies may be required to secure client involvement in carrying out agreed-on assignments. These may be established at an early point. For example, further counselor contact may be made contingent on task completion. Daily collection of needed information by phone, which may only take a couple of minutes, can also help clients to complete assignments. Knowing that someone will call at a certain time to collect information can function as an incentive to do so and provides an opportunity to reinforce clients for their efforts. Patterson and Hops (1972) made provision of further information contingent on clients' giving a brief five-minute overview of material they agreed to read during the week.

Reinforcement from significant others for desirable behaviors is frequently used as an incentive for clients to complete assignments. Sometimes it is also necessary to build in contingent response cost, in which positive events are removed on failure of the client to carry out agreements. For example, the wife of an alcoholic man was advised to discontinue provision of certain positive events contingent on her husband being drunk (Miller, 1972). Response cost involving material items has also been employed. Elliott and Tighe (1968) formed an agreement with their clients that if an assignment was not met—let us say not to use tobacco in any form during a one-week period—they would forfeit some portion of their deposit. Checks may be made out to a client's least favorite charity and are then mailed out if an assignment is not completed (Boudin, 1972). Typically, not more than one check is lost. Commitment plus a refundable deposit has been found to be more effective than commitment alone in reducing dropouts in a weight reduction program (Hagen, Foreyt, and Durham, 1976). There were fewer dropouts when a twenty-dollar deposit was required compared to a five-dollar deposit or no deposit at all. Patterson and his colleagues also employ a refundable deposit in their parent training program.

Failure of the client to become involved in working out specific change programs and in acting on these may result from "rushing" the client; that is, not allowing sufficient time for exploration of the problem, for ferreting out the client's goals, values, and attitudes related to possible problem areas and failing to guide him by successive approximations (at his own pace) to considering and hopefully even suggesting new conceptualizations of her difficulties. It may be necessary to cycle back to initial steps in the helping process.

Involuntary clients present special difficulties. Involvement may be facilitated by locating ways in which counselor-client contact may be of benefit from such clients' point of view. Even though they may not consider the behavior that got them in trouble—say, stealing from stores—to be an undesirable behavior, the consequences that followed this behavior, such as detention in a juvenile hall, with possible incarceration in a longer-term facility, may be considered distinctly undesirable. Obtaining client agreement with change objectives and intervention procedures by the use of signed contracts decreases the involuntary aspect of change efforts.

Prompting facilitates client attendance at agreed-on meetings. For example, Ayllon and Roberts (1975) found that attendance of parents at training sessions where they would learn how to enhance their child's cognitive skills increased from 17 percent to 77 percent when they were telephoned two days in advance of the meeting to remind them of the training session. Promptness at meetings increased to 100 percent when parents received a bonus of one dollar for each session for which they were on time.

Clients sometimes perceive their actual or potential distress with different degrees of concern. Perhaps all has gone well with a client for a few days, and he suggests termination of contact, when in the counselor's opinion, successful intervention will require many more steps. The rationale for the pursuit of these tasks may have to be reviewed and the client reminded of his discomfort on prior occasions. Client involvement can also be facilitated by being sensitive to areas that are difficult to discuss, that perhaps evoke anxiety or anger in the client. Procedures may have to be offered to help the client to influence these emotional reactions, such as self-instruction training for stress management, so that necessary topics can be usefully discussed. Requesting the client to fill out a "motivational balance sheet" on which he lists the advantages and disadvantages of a decision to pursue a specific change facilitates compliance with agreed-on plans (Hoyt and Janis, 1975). There are thus a variety of ways that client involvement can be facilitated.

Increasing Counselor Influence. The use of paradoxical intention (Haley, 1973) offers an alternative to persuasive manuevers to facilitate client involvement (Johnson and Alevizos, 1975). This stems from the view of counseling as a social influence process and as each client possessing a certain susceptibility to influence that may be either enhanced or decreased by actions of the counselor. The following first set of methods attempts to increase the social influence of the counselor, thus facilitating client acceptance of ideas and assignments. As Johnson and Alevizos note, most of these suggestions have not been tested. Thus they are offered here in a spirit of caution. Each must be used with respect to an individual client's characteristics and with due concern for ethical considerations. The reader is referred to Johnson and Alevizos (1975) and Haley (1973) for a detailed description of these procedures.

Establishing a positive compliance set. The counselor can make simple, uncontroversial, and relatively undemanding requests of the client during the first interview—for example, in suggesting what to talk about. A dramatic example of initially establishing such a set is shown by the research concerning the "foot-in-the-door technique," in which subjects who previously answered a few small questions were more likely to comply with larger requests (Freedman and Fraser, 1966). As Johnson and Alevizos emphasize, the client should never be engaged in a power struggle. If difficulty is encountered, he is reassured of his own ultimate control in his life. This is an important point to bear in mind, because of the importance of attribution of change to self-induced efforts.

Starting where the client is. Empathizing with the client's problem can facilitate cooperation. Identification with resistance is often used with children. Let us say that a ten-year-old is referred for bed wetting and he is resistant and yelling. Milton Erickson handled such a child by saying, "You know your parents ordered me to cure you of bed wetting. Who do they think they are to order me around?" (Haley, 1973). Any statements that indicate that the counselor likes the client can facilitate cooperation. Confronted with a young girl who gave him three months to improve her life, Erickson said that he accepted her imminent suicide and advised her that she should have one last fling before dying, buying new clothes, and so forth. Such identification with and expansion of the client's mode of behavior and thinking so that change is facilitated is basic to "strategic therapy" (Johnson and Alevizos, 1975).

Emphasizing the positive aspects of behavior and motivation. Problem behavior may be well-intentioned. For example, the counselor may point out that it is natural for an overprotective mother to be concerned about her child. Interventions should be carefully selected to allow the mother to continue in the role of a "good parent" that is initially emphasized. This view sets the stage for helpful intervention efforts.

Emphasizing the "newness" of procedures. Clients have often tried a number of different approaches for alleviating their problem. If counselor suggestions sound to the client like a method that she tried and was unsuccessful, she is likely to say, "Oh yes, I tried that already and it didn't work." There are two ways to avoid this. One is to find out exactly what the client did try before making any suggestions and to point out the differences between what had been tried before and the new procedure. A second possibility is to suggest an outlandish procedure (Haley, 1973).

Condoning lack of cooperation and disordered behavior. "Acceptance combats resistance before it has a chance to occur" (Johnson and Alevizos, 1975, p. 6). Acceptance of the client's hesitancy in sharing relevant information can help to remove this source of difficulty. The counselor may say, "You might be hesitant to tell me certain details or things about yourself. I think that if I were in your shoes I might do the same. Nonetheless, don't tell me anything you don't want to until you're ready" (Johnson and Alevizos, 1975, p. 6). This approach is often more effective than explaining the rationales for needed information, exhorting clients, or trying to use empathy. Such attempts may cast the interaction into a contest of wills. Note that the suggested strategy changes the issue from whether the client *will*, for example, share information, to *when* it is appropriate or reasonable. It also diffuses the issue of control, because the counselor has joined the client's position. Prescriptions may also be made for a disordered behavior; for example, a child can be asked to display a tantrum. Such prescription of problematic behavior is a frequently employed method in strategic therapy (Raskin and Klein, 1976). It places the client in a double bind—one way or the other, he will satisfy the counselor. These procedures can thus help to remove the use of the problematic behavior as a manipulative ploy.

Offering practice in resistance. This procedure consists of practicing the resistant response. In this manner, "the client learns that he can be resistive, that the counselor knows that he can be, and that these reactions are not very productive and are not much fun" (Johnson and Alevizos, 1975, p. 7). An example is taking turns with a child who is yelling.

Making accurate predictions. As Johnson and Alevizos point out, strategic counselors capitalize on natural occurrences by predicting these and using their accurate prediction for enhancing their influence. The client's response may be predicted. It is wise, for example to forecast possible negative reactions the client may have to a procedure. This indicates to the client that the counselor recognizes possible difficulties with the procedure. These become expected hardships rather than unexpected disadvantages. "Predicting these reactions keep them more under the control of the therapist, disinhibits the client to discuss them, and, if they occur, demonstrates the clinician's ability to predict what his client will do or think" (Johnson and Alevizos, 1975, p. 8). Predictions can be presented so as to challenge the client's abilities to carry out a procedure. Hopefully the client will be stimulated to prove the counselor wrong, that he can indeed do it. Prediction of possible setbacks can be employed for a similar purpose, to harness client motivation to prove otherwise or to avoid undue discouragement.

Using uncertainty and confusion. These methods are usually employed only for highly resistant clients or for those who try to control the intervention process. Client uncertainty can be created by not responding as the client expects. As Johnson and Alevizos (1975, p. 9) point out, "The paranoid who complains that spaceships are after him will have to deal differently with someone who, after hearing his report, draws the shades, turns out the lights, and fearfully asks how they can be avoided." Confusion can also be induced by repeated obscure counseling statements.

Discussing with clients whether they will cooperate is often quite unproductive. *Offering the client a choice* between alternatives may succeed in eliminating the issue of cooperation. Advantages of offering the client a choice are the preference for a choice situation (Felixbrod and O'Leary, 1973) and greater change when this can be attributed to one's own efforts. A good example of the use of alternatives is modifying bathing behavior in a residential center by asking a boy *which* shower, bathroom, or color of towel he would like (Mahoney, 1974a). A summary statement at the end of the interview can be employed to pose alternative intervention procedures and the client asked which he prefers. Note that emphasis is shifted from whether a client will cooperate to how and when he will. Use of imagined approach behavior offers a way for a very anxious client to begin to approach feared objects. Selection of an alternative can be facilitated by first describing an alternative (for example, first describing flooding, which involves the presentation of highly anxiety-arousing situations), and then describing a more comfortable procedure that involves a graduated, self-regulated approach to feared events. A good example for encouraging a recalcitrant client to collect needed data, offered by Johnson and Alevizos (1975), is suggesting that an unpopular relative assist in gathering this information.

Using arousal or frustration. Participation of a recalcitrant client may be provoked by drawing inferences about him that are probably quite untrue and hopefully will provoke him into participating in order to "put the record straight." Examples of the use of such provocation would be telling a silent teen-ager to remain silent while his parents present their views or offering a child who refuses to attend school activities at home that are clearly below the level of his competency (Johnson and Alevizos, 1975). Presenting long verbal digressions prior to offering any suggestions may enhance acceptance by arousing the impatience of the client to hear the latter. A variety of procedures may be employed to prevent talk against a procedure. Such talk may encourage scanning only for material in support of resistance rather than a careful weighing of pros and cons. For example, a topic can be raised at the end of the interview and the client can be asked to think about it. As noted by Johnson and Alevizos (1975, p. 15), "The good clinician may need to be just as adept at stopping client talk when that is called for as he is in disinhibiting such talk when that is necessary."

Hinting at new approaches. A new way to view a problem may be suggested indirectly, and the client allowed to "discover" it for himself at a later time. This is one way in which new conceptualizations may initially be mentioned. In addition to verbally mentioning new ideas, these may also be introduced by special means of structuring assessment or intervention. For example, including a home observation session during assessment in the treatment of depressed housewives suggests involvement of significant others.

The Use of Strategic Interventions. In addition to these methods of enhancing client cooperation and commitment, there are other procedures geared to overcome client resistance. As Johnson and Alevizos (1975) point out, a hallmark of strategic intervention is a central focus on overcoming client resistance. The assumption is made that the client often possesses needed skills, but is not performing them and that intervention will allow him to be free to employ his resources. Johnson and Alevizos focus on performance problems rather than on learning problems. Many counseling methods make use of the procedures described in the following paragraphs, although the rationale given for their use differs.

One method involves continuation of a symptom in some modified form suggested by the counselor (Newton, 1968). One rationale provided for this is that the client's resistance is mobilized against the symptomatic behavior rather than against a change in this behavior. A couple that argues frequently, for example, may be instructed to schedule their arguments at a certain time. Unrealistic fears may be emphasized by asking the person to act out such fears. For example, one client seen by a colleague was afraid that he could "go crazy." When asked what he would do if this occurred, he said that he would run down the street screaming and waving his arms bizarrely. He was then asked what would be so bad about this, and he replied that people would see him and that he would be arrested and locked up. At this point, it was suggested that both he and the counselor go outside and engage in his envisioned activities and see if anybody would pay attention to them. They both went outside and ran down the street yelling and waving their arms about, and in fact no one paid the slightest heed. The client was amazed and stopped worrying that he would "go crazy." Obviously this method (like any other) will not be effective in every instance of such a presenting complaint. It was very effective in this case, where an unrealistic social fear was present and other maintaining consequences such as social attention were not a factor.

Scheduling symptoms brings them under client control. Supposedly "involuntary" actions now occur during certain times or in certain places. By scheduling symptoms, the client learns to delay and to perform the behavior only under certain circumstances (Johnson and Alevizos, 1975). A good example, described in Chapter Fourteen, is of a man who suffered from insomnia and was asked to try to stay awake all night. Symptom scheduling may include arranging an aversive consequence, such as carrying out the sympton in an uncomfortable spot—for example, sulking only while sitting on a special sulking stool kept in an unpleasant spot (Goldiamond, 1965).

The technique of *reframing* (Watzlawick, Weakland, and Fisch, 1974) is a cognitive means of providing an alternative way to view a problem or situation. An example is offered in Chapter Thirteen, in which a direct request for behavior change failed with a woman who was subjected to daily belittling remarks by one of her superiors. Being asked to go up to this man the next time he made such a remark, to take him aside, and to tell him that when he did this it turned her on, altered her own behavior when with him (even though she never actually said this to him) and resulted in a subsequent change in his behavior. The behavioral methods of stress control provide a new way for the client to view emotions—as being able to influence them—as does rationale emotive therapy (Ellis and Harper, 1975). As Johnson and Alevizos (1975) note, the strategic therapists often make unique use of this by behaviorally presenting to the client a totally opposite conceptualization of his problem.

Another form of reframing is helping the client to *view the symptom as an asset*. Erickson (Haley, 1973), for example, encouraged a woman who vomited uncontrollably to schedule this behavior so as to get rid of unwanted relatives in her home. "An emphasis upon the positive aspects of any problem makes it less of a problem. And giving permission for the functional gains which a problem can provide gives the client permission to restrict the problem to those situations in which he really wants such functional gains" (Johnson and Alevizos, 1975, p. 23).

In some cases, it may not be optimally effective to offer the client a rationale for procedures (Haley, 1973). Some of the procedures designed to enhance client cooperation, described in the latter part of this chapter, may be less effective if the rationale for them is explained (Johnson and Alevizos, 1975). It may also be helpful to inform the client that he will discover meanings that will supplement those provided by the counselor. "Holding back a rationale can, indeed, serve a therapeutic purpose, not the least of which is the client's discovery of rationales of which the therapist would not be aware" (Johnson and Alevizos, 1975, p. 28).

Summary

A number of factors important in most forms of interpersonal helping are also of importance within behavioral practice. This includes the need to understand the client's problem and forming a new conceptualization of the problem, one which will make sense to the client and enable positive change. This new conceptualization is gradually formed, for example, through counselor questions and assignments to observe certain events in the natural environment. Counselor-client contacts are structured in such a way as to facilitate formation of a positive counselor-client relationship, as well as to encourage a new view of problem-related behaviors. Contextual therapeutic factors comprise an important component of behavioral intervention, as they do with other methods of interpersonal helping, and should be enhanced to the extent possible. The client's involvement is wooed in a number of ways, including formation of a more helpful conceptualization of problems; careful description of and rationale for tasks to be carried out; practice of required tasks; feedback in terms of accomplishment; and solicitation of the client's overt commitment to participate in the change effort, concretized in a written agreement. Additional procedures may have to be employed to obtain client involvement, including refundable deposits or use of various "strategic methods." Selection of these methods should always be informed by ethical considerations and possible costs and benefits to the client.

4

Carrying out an assessment of a client's problem is like unraveling a puzzle or locating the pieces of the puzzle, as the case may be. It is a puzzle that the client has not been able to solve. Typically, various unsuccessful solutions have been attempted. So many unsolved problems may have accumulated that few coping efforts are made any longer, except the one that brings the client to your office or agency. Perhaps the client has been prodded by some significant other or social agency to encourage him to seek help. The point is that the client, his significant others, or society have not been able to solve a problem. Hopefully, the unsuccessful problem solver confronts a successful problem solver—a counselor who is an expert in helping clients learn how to solve their problems.

A Framework
for Assessment

Depending on the counselor's theoretical orientation, certain pieces of the puzzle are sought rather than others, and a puzzle completion may be declared at any of diverse points. The purpose of this chapter is to identify the components of assessment within a behavioral framework. This assessment framework is directly informed by the principles of behavior described in Chapter Two, recognizing contextual needs in the helping process described in Chapter Three, such as forming a mutual conceptualization of the client's problem.

The purpose of assessment is to describe the presenting problem and to identify related factors that can be influenced, thus enabling solution or resolution of the problem. It is only by obtaining a view of a client's current life that factors related to presenting problems are discovered. Each major life area is examined, including relationships with significant others, work, social life, and recreational activities. What is a typical day like for the client? Does he like his work? Does he have any friends? Is his health satisfactory? Do circumstances in any of these areas relate to achievement of desired outcomes? Assessment is a multifaceted endeavor (see, for example, Kanfer and Saslow, 1969; Wolpe, 1958; Lazarus, 1973a; Bandura, 1969). A behavioral assessment requires a careful description of the problematic behavior and desirable alternatives, as well as identification of related antecedents, consequences, and relevant organismic variables, in addition to collection of further information that will help to inform selection of intervention method. As with psychodynamic theories, little emphasis is given to the use of trait labels for clients. Instead, behavioral therapists are interested in the "function" of behavior (Mischel, 1973). However, rather than employing behavior as only a "sign" of underlying causes, a behavioral assessment involves an exploration of how factors in the current environment relate to the behaviors. Behavioral therapists recognize the great variability of behavior over situations and the lack of success in predicting behavior in one situation from a knowledge of behavior in other situations (Mischel, 1968). Interestingly, people tend to use trait labels more when describing other people than when describing themselves. When describing ourselves, we tend to use situational cues, such as, "I dropped it because it was slippery," rather than "I guess I'm clumsy." Mischel (1973) speculates that this is because we have more information about the relationship of our behavior to situational variables than we have about the behavior of others.

Response Factors

Let us first take a look at what is involved in viewing the behaviors that may be related to a problem. What do we know when we are told that someone is an alcoholic, is depressed, or is anxious? We must be attuned to the role of three possible components of behavior—the verbal, the behavioral, and the affective (Bandura, 1969). There is abundant evidence that these components of a response may *not* be related (Bandura, 1969). There is often a lag, for example, between changes in self-reports of fear and changes in overt behavior such as approach toward feared events (Lang, 1968). Affective components of anxiety (physiological changes) may or may not accompany verbal reports and behavioral changes. In obtaining a description of a presenting problem, a behavioral counselor attempts to determine the relative importance of each component, because this may influence selection of intervention procedure. A behavioral framework thus assumes multiple response systems, which may or may not be related, depending on the learning history of each individual. This view implies a conceptualization of the "unconscious" as referring to behaviors having a behavioral and possibly affective component without an accompanying cognitive component—a verbal description of the behavior (Bandura, 1969). There is no reason why all three components would always be developed at the same time.

It is often important to consider the respondent elements of a problem as well as the operant components. For example, enuresis may be related to a lack of respondent conditioning (waking has not been associated with a full bladder) or a failure of significant others to offer incentives for appropriate use of the bathroom (an operant problem). The response form (in this case, enuresis) may not provide information as to whether there is a deficit of respondent or operant conditioning. Further information must be obtained to determine this. Just as a behavior that appears to be an operant may have important respondent components, the reverse is also true: A behavior that appears to be maintained by antecedent events, such as anxiety, may have important operant consequences, such as attention from others. Respondent reactions must be considered, if they might interfere with change efforts, as when a mother, because of her "anger," may be unable to ignore undesirable behaviors of her child.

Topographic Description Versus Functional Analysis

A topographic description of behavior entails a description of the form of the behavior. For example, we may say that we saw someone running down the street. A topographic description describes only the form of the behavior. It does not inform us about the function of this behavior; that is, it does not identify possible antecedents and consequent conditions that may be related to the behavior (Ferster, Culbertson, and Boren, 1975). A person might run because he is being chased by a lion (which the observer cannot see, because it has not yet rounded the corner); because he enjoys the feeling of running itself; or because he is hungry and anticipates a good lunch at home. The same is the case for any behavior. A person who abuses alcohol may do so to avoid or escape unpleasant thoughts; because he enjoys the relaxed feeling he gets; because it upsets his wife and he does not like her and so enjoys her discomfort; or for all these reasons. A behavioral assessment requires a functional analysis, in which there is an attempt not only to describe the form of the behavior, but also to identify antecedents and consequences related to the behavior. The form of the behavior is not assumed, as it is in some other orientations, to provide any information as to why the behavior is occurring. If we are informed that three men all drink a fifth of bourbon a day, we have no idea as to the variety of factors related to drinking in each instance. These must be identified through assessment. Verbal behavior, as well as overt and covert behaviors, may have a variety of functions, as illustrated by a child's speaking the word *toast* without any information concerning prior stimulus conditions. The child might be reading a word; or there might have been a prior auditory stimulus that strengthened an echoic (imitative) performance. Perhaps the child has been deprived of food, which led to his speaking because it produced food on prior occasions under the control of such deprivation. The child might be telling his parents of the presence of toast or, conversely, be telling them that there is no toast today (Ferster, Culbertson, and Boren, 1975). It is thus useful to separate the topography of a performance from the change in the environment that it produces. The tendency to employ a binary classification system, in which people are labeled as either having something or not having something (for example, as being an alcoholic or not) has obscured the myriad of varying patterns included in these groups. It has clouded perception of the unique characteristics of each person's behavior and the environmental, cognitive, and physical events related to it. Great efforts have gone into such classification attempts with little success (Mischel, 1968, 1973).

Just as the same behavior may have different functions, different behaviors may have identical functions. Calling out the word *toast*, banging on the table with a knife, or throwing Cheerios on the floor are behaviors that may all be maintained by parental attention. All three behaviors may belong to the same response class. We do not know much about which classes of responses are related to each other, although we do have some information that changes in one behavior sometimes entail changes in other behaviors as well. One set of behaviors is sometimes affected by reinforcers applied directly to other behaviors, because of covariations among behaviors. Such covariations are usually unmeasured. For example, Wahler, Sperling, Thomas, Teeter, and Luper (1970) found that a decrease in nonspeech deviant child behavior also resulted in a decrease in stuttering. Negative as well as positive "side effects" of change have been found in other studies. Sajwaj, Twardosz, and Burke (1972) found that when a teacher ignored persistent and annoying speech initiated by a retarded boy in one setting in a preschool, systematic changes occurred in other behaviors in the same setting and in other settings. Desirable effects included increased speech initiated to other children and increased cooperative play. Undesirable effects included a decrease in task-appropriate behavior and an increase in disruptive behavior. Note that such effects cannot be considered as "symptom substitution" in the traditional sense, as it is likely that such behaviors covaried because of the child's learning history. In fact, ignorance of such covariations may result in mistaking such covariations as symptom substitution.

The Consequences of Behavior

The importance of the relationship between behavior and its consequences and the unique patterns that may result from specific types of relationships calls for a careful search for maintaining consequences of undesirable behaviors, as well as for desirable behaviors that could be reinforced. If a desired behavior does not occur, in a given situation, various possibilities may account for this, including infrequent reinforcement, punishment of the behavior, satiation, or a failure to develop the behavior; that is, a behavior deficit may exist and new behaviors may have to be established. Perhaps a child who now seldom raises his hand in class to answer questions did offer answers in the past and was "put down" by the teacher. Or, perhaps even though he raised his hand he was never called on, and so the behavior gradually decreased. As noted by Ferster (1972, p. 140), "It is particularly difficult to observe the functional significance of behavior when the performances are distorted by multiple contingencies, particularly punishment. In these cases, very strong behavior may be observed only indirectly because only indirect forms are emitted."

Consequences may have a number of sources, including social reactions, affect, situational events, physiological factors, and cognitions. The following example of performance anxiety in test situations illustrates the variety of response components that may be involved as well as the multiple sources of maintaining events. The term *anxiety* may refer to the sensory experience of increased muscle tension and a feeling of dread (affect); to cognitive components ("worrying"; images of receiving a test back marked with a *D*); and to a behavioral component (avoidance of test situations if possible). Taking a test may be followed by negative self-evaluative statements (cognitions); heightened anxiety (affect); extreme fatigue (physical factors); parents calling and saying, "I certainly hope you did as well as your brother; or a girl friend saying, "Gee, I hope you didn't blow it" (social factors). An alternative set of consequences might be as follows: positive self-statements for a job well done; anticipations of a high grade (cognitions); feeling good (affect), girl friend saying, "Let's go out on the town tonight and celebrate" (social factors); or a pleasant tiredness from a job well done (physical factors). The sum total of consequences for behavior has been termed the *reinforcing event* (Tharp and Wetzel, 1969). This event is mostly positive, mostly negative, or may be evenly balanced.

It is often helpful to write down the various consequences for a behavior together with their incentive value, as illustrated in the following example concerning school attendance (Kunkel, 1970, p. 147). It can be seen that there are no positive consequences (C^+) for school attendance (B, or behavior), whereas there are negative consequences (C^-) and often a lack of effective consequences (C^0).

From parent's point of view:

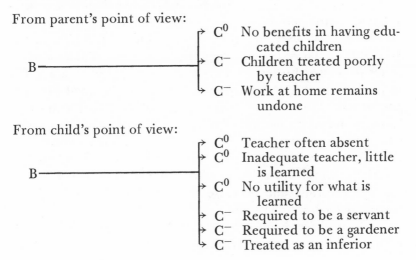

C^0 No benefits in having educated children

C^- Children treated poorly by teacher

C^- Work at home remains undone

From child's point of view:

C^0 Teacher often absent

C^0 Inadequate teacher, little is learned

C^0 No utility for what is learned

C^- Required to be a servant

C^- Required to be a gardener

C^- Treated as an inferior

The Antecedents of Behavior

There is abundant evidence that behavior is situationally determined, that given behaviors tend to occur only in certain situations (Mischel, 1968). For example, we typically do not say "Thank you" when there is no one present. Antecedent events may elicit respondent reactions (that we usually label *emotional reactions,* such as anger, fear, or elation), and may increase or decrease the probability of selected operant behaviors. Such events assume these functions because of the unique reinforcement history of each person. Relevant antecedents may include a variety of sources. A student who complains of anxiety in test situations may anticipate failure, may have received a call from his parents the night before telling him how important it is to pass the medical school examination, may be fatigued from staying up all night studying, and may have seen a sign saying "Examination for Entrance to Medical School," which elicited further anxiety.

The sum total of antecedents for a behavior can be termed the *antecedent event.* This event functions as an occasion for the behavior or else decreases its likelihood. A student who is reasonably relaxed during examinations may have a very different constellation of antecedent events, including cognitive variables (anticipations of doing well on the test); affect (feeling comfortably aroused in anticipation of the test); social factors (verbal reassurance from a friend sitting next to him, looking at other students who feel confident of their abilities to do well); physical factors (getting a good night's sleep the night before); and situational variables (a large room with many students prior to an examination in which he has performed well in the past). One goal of assessment is to identify antecedents that facilitate desirable behaviors and those that are related to undesirable reactions. During intervention, procedures are selected to enhance the former and decrease the presence of cues for problematic behavior.

It is often helpful to list the various sources of antecedent influence over behavior, as illustrated in the following example.

Antecedents

One hour before examination	A^-	⎤
Thoughts of failure	A^-	⎥
A nervous roommate who also has exams	A^-	⎬ Anxiety
Reassurance by a friend	A^+	⎦
Supervisor seems in a good mood	A^+	⎤
All important work has been completed	A^+	⎥ Asking supervisor for
It is near the end of the day	A^+	⎬ the rest of the
Worry that you will be considered undependable	A^-	⎦ afternoon off

Varieties of Problematic Behavior

The important role of what happens before and after behavior points to various ways in which behavior may be problematic (Staats and Staats, 1963). Most problems presented by clients are high-cost behaviors, in that, although they are maintained by positive consequences or by the removal of negative consequences, they usually entail a high cost in other ways.

Inadequate or Inappropriate Reinforcing Functions. Events may assume atypical reinforcing qualities. Avoidance and escape behaviors may be maintained by the removal of events that do not objectively warrant this reaction, such as sight of a tiny spider. Approach behaviors, such as running motorcycles into baby carriages (Raymond, 1956), may be reinforcing to the perpetrator, but not to the victims. Excessive use of drugs and alcohol also fall into this category.

Often, reinforcement for desirable behaviors is applied inconsistently. A parent may only praise her child when she happens to remember to do so, which occurs infrequently. Inconsistent reinforcement may weaken desirable behavior and maintain undesirable behavior. Events that should function as reinforcers may not. Adult attention does not function as a reinforcer for many children labeled *autistic* (see Lovaas and Newsom, 1976). A failure of adult attention to become a positive emotional event may make it difficult for a child to learn necessary repertoires of behavior. Perhaps such events have never been paired with reinforcers. A radical change in one's situation, such as giving up a career to become a housewife, or the death of a significant other, may entail the removal of an important source of reinforcement, and therefore a low frequency of behavior may result.

Inadequate or Inappropriate Stimulus Control. Inappropriate emotional reactions, such as intense anxiety in anticipation of greeting someone, would fall in the category of inadequate or inappropriate stimulus control, as would the broad range of psychosomatic reactions in which stress elicits various changes in physical structures leading to, for example, head-

aches, ulcers, or high blood pressure. Enuresis may represent inadequate stimulus control, in that fullness of bladder does not
lead to waking. Events that should function as cues for appropriate behaviors may not. Recognition of a given state of inebri-
ation may not function as a cue to stop drinking; or events that
should function as cues for appropriate behaviors may cue
inappropriate behaviors. Seeing a lone adult who needs help
may be a cue to rob the person rather than help him. The stimulus control for a behavior may be too wide, that is, spread over
too many situations. A student who has a problem trying to
study may try to work in a wide range of locations, rather than
studying only in one or two places that would thus acquire
stimulus control over study behavior (Fox, 1962). On the
other hand, the stimulus control over a behavior may be too
narrow. A client who complains of few social contacts may restrict attempts to initiate conversations to only a few people.

   Behavior Deficits. A client may lack needed skills; for
example, a woman may not know how to initiate conversations
or arrange future contacts. A student may not know how to organize his study time or know how to take helpful notes, or a
child may lack skills in how to play cooperatively with other
children. Perhaps it has been so long since a client engaged in a
behavior, that even though many of its components exist in his
repertoire, prompts and incentives will be required to generate
the whole chain of behavior. Behavior surfeits are often related
to behavior deficits (Ferster, 1961). If appropriate behaviors are
missing, it may be that the only way reinforcement can be obtained is through inappropriate behavior. Responses may fail to
occur with sufficient frequency or intensity, in an appropriate
form, or under expected conditions (Kanfer and Saslow,
1969).

   Behavioral Excesses That Annoy Others. Many behaviors
that come to the attention of counselors involve behavior excesses, such as assaultive behavior. It is often the frequency of a
behavior that causes problems for a person, rather than its
unique form (Ferster, 1973). For example, we all may tap a
pencil occasionally; however, if we started doing this at a rate of

200 times per minute we might become somewhat bothersome to those around us. A behavior may occur with an excessive frequency, intensity, or duration, or occur under socially inappropriate circumstances (Kanfer and Saslow, 1969).

Motivational Versus Behavior Deficits

Failure of a behavior to occur may indicate that the behavior exists, but is simply not reinforced (or is perhaps punished), or that the person does not have a behavior in his or her repertoire. The distinction between motivational and behavioral deficits is important, because different intervention efforts usually are indicated in the two instances. If lack of a behavior is related to a motivational deficit, intervention must arrange appropriate reinforcement contingencies. There is no need to establish behavior, although there may be a need to prompt the occurrence of the behavior by, for example, verbal instructions. If the absence of a behavior indicates a behavioral deficit, then intervention must arrange the establishment of this behavior, perhaps by model presentation or shaping. Motivational deficits are often mistaken for behavioral deficits. A teacher may say that a student does not know how to do elementary addition problems, or a husband may say that his wife does not know how to talk to him about baseball. These behaviors may not be occurring because they are not reinforced. Bed wetting may present a failure of respondent conditioning, in that fullness of bladder is not associated with awakening, or with a motivational deficit, in that reinforcement is not offered for a dry bed.

Motivational and behavioral deficits can often be distinguished by arranging appropriate conditions for the display of the behavior. The client may be asked to role play various behaviors or asked whether similar or identical behaviors occur in other situations. If behaviors occur, then a motivational deficit is involved. Observation of the client in a range of situations may reveal appropriate behaviors in other situations; or offering a reinforcer for the behavior may result in its occurrence, again indicating a motivational rather than a behavioral deficit.

Inhibitions Versus Behavior Deficits

Behavior deficits are sometimes incorrectly assumed to exist, when in fact requisite behaviors are indeed present, but emotional reactions prevent their display. A woman may not initiate conversations with men with whom she would like to speak because anticipation of doing so makes her anxious. An important aspect of assessment thus is determining whether emotional reactions may be responsible for the failure of appropriate behaviors to occur. Simulated situations and behavioral interviewing can be used to determine if needed behaviors exist. Contexts for role playing should be made as comfortable as possible. If appropriate behaviors are displayed, then possible interfering factors, such as anxiety, are sought.

A disruption in behavior caused by some aversive event (let us say the woman mentioned in the last paragraph decreased a variety of social behaviors following a rejection) indicates that the behaviors involved may be weak to begin with (Ferster, 1972). As Ferster (p. 6) points out, an anxiety reaction, for example, "is not so much a thing of itself as it is a general condition of a larger repertoire. If the baseline behavior operant repertoire were better maintained through positive reinforcement, aversive stimuli of a given magnitude could not disrupt it." This points to the importance of examining possible other factors that may be related to the development of inhibitions. (The assessment of anxiety reactions is discussed further in Chapter Eleven.) If related behaviors are stronger, the person may perform some response that terminates the aversive event, such as using positive self-instructions to remove anticipated anxiety reactions rather than allow an entire repertoire to be disrupted. "A passive person who reacts diffusely and helplessly to the unfavorable aspects of his social world is clinically parallel to the disruption of the ongoing operant repertoire by an aversive stimulus" (Ferster, 1972, p. 136).

Factors to Consider During Assessment

Assessment is a multifaceted endeavor requiring attention to a number of factors, including social and cognitive events, affect and physiological factors, as well as setting events such as states of deprivation. Client assets, both cognitive and behavioral, must be carefully assessed, as well as the possible role of racial and ethnic factors, which may influence desired outcomes and procedures selected to attain them. Problematic behaviors are typically part of a chain of behavior that may involve a mix of cognitive, affective, and behavioral events. Factors related to problem areas may facilitate or hinder attainment of desired outcomes. The client's attempted solutions may have exacerbated problems and these, too, may have to be considered. In addition, client expectations concerning the intervention process must be determined and any misconceptions discussed.

Social Factors. An important part of our environment is presented by other people. Verbal reports of anxiety may be maintained by positive attention from significant others, such as spouse or friends (Lazarus, 1968). Social reinforcement from significant others may become an important maintaining factor, even though it was not involved in the initial occurrence of a problematic reaction. For example, a woman may have experienced severe anxiety when a distance from her home, and may be unable to identify any precipitating cause. Following descriptions of her discomfort to her family, she may receive unusual amounts of sympathy and support, which may encourage such verbal reports. A peer group may provide support for illegal behaviors such as stealing cars and robbing older people. As with any other consequence, social reactions may either increase or decrease behavior (examples where these reactions may increase behavior have been offered). Often, however, they decrease behavior; for example, if one says to a spouse when, for the first time, she or he apologized for being late, "Well, it's about time you recognized how inconsiderate you usually are," the spouse may decrease apology behavior. Other people also influence behavior in their role as models.

With any presenting problem, the possible influence of significant others in the maintenance of a problem must be carefully explored. There will always be the possibility that change efforts will *not* be directly focused on the person presented as the problem, but on others who may be responsible for maintaining the behavior. If a parent complains that her three-year-old will nòt follow instructions and has temper tantrums, the focus of intervention will probably be on changing how she interacts with her child, because it is assumed that the people with whom we interact exert a powerful influence on how we behave. Or change attempts may include a direct focus on all involved parties, as in marital discord.

A way of diagraming interaction sequences that helps to point out who is reinforcing who and whether positive or negative reinforcement is involved entails representing the behavior of each person on one line (see, for example, Kunkel, 1970). The sequence is started at some point in time—for example, when a child asks her mother for a cookie. For the mother, this is a change in her environment. Let us assume it is an aversive event and that, when presented in the past and she gave her daughter a cookie, it was removed. It is likely that the parent's behavior is maintained by negative reinforcement, and her daughter's behavior is maintained by positive reinforcement, as depicted in the following diagram.

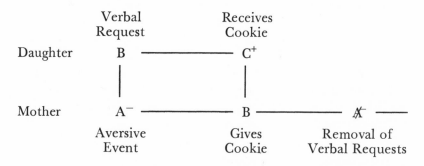

If significant others are involved in a problem, it is important to assess their skills and motivations related to the problem. Let us say that a mother complains that her three-year-old is unmanageable. You must determine whether this mother has reinforcing behaviors in her repertoire and whether she is willing to offer these at appropriate times. It is just as important to identify the assets of significant others as those of the person complained about. These individuals often become "mediators" of change (Tharp and Wetzel, 1969). Behavior deficits may be a problem not only with the individual complained of, but also with potential mediators.

How significant others view the client's problems and what they have to gain or lose from a change in the client's behavior is also important to determine. They may view the problem as the client's own fault, and may not recognize their own role in the maintenance of the behavior. They may anticipate negative effects of improvement in a problem. A husband may worry that if his wife loses fifty pounds she will be attractive to other men and he might lose her. A teen-ager may worry that if he starts to get good grades in school his peers may hassle him.

Appropriate sources of reinforcement have to be provided for changes in the behavior of significant others, as well as cues to help them remember to act in new ways. This triadic model of intervention includes at least three parties, the consultant, mediator, and the target person (Tharp and Wetzel, 1969). This is depicted in Figure 1, together with the various sources of reinforcement for each participant. Potential sources of support for the mediator include other individuals with whom the mediator interacts, the consultant, and the person with the presenting problem. Persons with whom the mediator interacts may or may not support behavior change attempts. In

Figure 1. Potential Sources of Reinforcement in Triadic Model

Foster care worker	Foster parent	Child
Probation Officer	Spouse	Spouse
Psychologist	Attendant	Patient
Social Worker	Teacher	Student

Source: Adapted from Tharp and Wetzel (1969, p. 59).

some instances, they may seriously undermine mediator behavior. Changes that may take place in the target person's
behavior will affect not only the mediator, but also other people with whom this person interacts, as is illustrated in the
arrow going from the target to others who influence the mediator. Perhaps a wife likes to drink with her husband, and anticipates loss of a drinking companion if her husband decreases his
drinking. Requesting her to support such a change will be resisted. The same might be true of a fellow employee who is a
drinking companion. Perhaps a teen-age son may also find a decrease in drinking unpleasant, because he will no longer be able
to castigate his father, which he thoroughly enjoys.

Problematic behavior may be related to a lack of significant others. A woman who is depressed may be socially isolated, with few skills for meeting others. Drug addiction or
drinking may be partially maintained by making the lack of
social contact less painful.

The positive and negative events that we receive from others are related to the range of social skills available. A low frequency of positive consequences from others warrants a careful
examination of the client's social skills to ascertain whether
there are behavior deficits that should be rectified, or perhaps
emotional reactions reduced that interfere with their display.
Does the client have any friends? How often does he see them?
Is he married, or does he have a lover? Has he ever had any
friends or any lovers or been married? The lack of any close
relationships in the past as well as the present may signal extensive deficits both in forming emotional attachments to others
and in offering positive experiences to others. How does he
handle service situations with waiters, bus drivers, sales personnel, and so forth? Do deficits in any of these areas relate to
desired outcomes?

Cognitive Factors. Each of us presents to himself an important part of his own environment in the form of thoughts
and related images, including what he anticipates is going to
happen, how he views past events and how he evaluates his own
behavior and that of others. These symbolic processes influence
our behavior (Bandura, 1969). Fear of elevators may be asso-

ciated with vivid images of the elevator plunging to the ground. Anger may be fueled by the vivid reliving of perceived slights. Self-labeling may be involved in problematic reactions. A client may experience an unusual feeling state and consider it indicative of mental illness. He may become unduly attentive to the possible occurrence of such states, and may label ones that are only similar as also being indicators that he is "going crazy." A depressed client may engage in very few positive self-evaluative statements and a great number of punishing self statements. Cognitive distortions may include arbitrary inference, in which conclusions are drawn in the absence of supporting evidence or in direct contradiction to such evidence; magnification, in which the meaning of an event is exaggerated; overgeneralization, in which a single incident is considered indicative of total incompetence; and dichotomous reasoning, in which polar differences are emphasized (Beck, 1970). An important aspect of intervention is often addressing and altering misconceptions (Wolpe, 1973a).

Irrational expectations of others and irrational anticipation of the possible outcome of one's actions are often related to presenting problems (Ellis, 1962). The expectation of dreadful consequences, coupled with the self-denigration, may interfere with appropriate behaviors as well as encourage inappropriate ones. The client's "internal dialog" and the way in which this relates to his presenting problem must be examined (Meichenbaum, 1975b). Exactly what does the client say to himself or not say to himself in situations related to his problem behavior? It is assumed that there is a close relationship between the nature of self-statements and overt behavior, in that someone who copes well in a given situation has an internal dialog that is different from that of someone who does not cope well. Clients who complain of anxiety and depression often have an internal dialog consisting of anticipated bad consequences. Individuals who have difficulty maintaining attention to tasks, such as hyperactive, impulsive children, evidence omissions of a variety of cognitions that may maintain attention such as setting response standards, noting when attention is drifting, producing motor reactions (such as shaking the head) in order to remain vigilant, and playing cognitive games to make the task more interesting (Meichenbaum, 1971). Assessment should thus include an exploration of whether there are classes of thoughts related to the presenting problem that should be directly focused on. It may be decided that these thoughts will change, given that behavior changes, and that a focus on the latter will be sufficient.

Affect. As with other factors, affect may be an antecedent or consequence of behavior. Affective components include anxiety—"I drink when I feel anxious," anger—"I take a drink when I get mad at my wife," and depression—"After a few drinks, I forget about feeling sad" (Lazarus, 1973a). Perhaps a woman avoids situations where men are present because she is highly anxious when around men. She may have a past history of punishment when attempting to meet men that is related to her anxiety in such situations. This history may interfere with the performance of appropriate behaviors. She may appear nervous, talk too fast, have insufficient eye contact, and give brief, swift smiles. In each presenting problem, the possible presence of inappropriate respondents should be explored.

If the behavior is indeed a respondent one, then it should follow the principles of respondent behavior. The magnitude of the reaction should positively correlate with the intensity of the eliciting event, and the latency should inversely correlate with the intensity. Thus, the greater the intensity of the stimulus, the greater the magnitude of the reaction should be, and the swifter the reaction. Also, the reaction should be consistent. Every time the eliciting stimulus is presented, given that other factors are held constant and fatigue is not a factor, the reaction should be observed. Failure of the reaction to follow the principles of respondent behavior should be a signal that operant factors are involved, such as reinforcement from significant others, or that components of the eliciting stimulus have not been identified. Respondent behavior may be implicated in behavior in the following ways:

First, neutral events may become aversive, and may elicit unpleasant arousal and occasion avoidance or escape behavior. The latter behaviors decrease or remove unpleasant events and may be labeled as problematic either by the person himself or by others. Thus, the resultant avoidance or escape behaviors, as well as the unpleasant arousal, may be problematic. Social situations, for example, may be avoided because of discomfort when in such situations, or going out of the house may be avoided, as in agoraphobia, because leaving the house makes one "anxious." Not only is the anxiety distressing, but the resultant operant behavior may also interfere with obtaining positive reinforcers. A person who is "fearful" of social occasions may avoid them and thus may not experience the pleasure of social interaction or the opportunity of meeting new people.

Situations containing aversive events may not be avoided even though discomfort is experienced; however, other behaviors occurring in the situation may be adversely affected by this anxiety. For example, a female who complained of severe fear of being called on when in law class still attended school, because this was the only way she could obtain a law degree. However, when called on, she could barely speak because she "was so nervous," even though she was well prepared. This behavior had a negative effect on her grades.

Second, neutral events may elicit positive arousal and occasion approach behavior that may be labeled as problematic. For example, the sight of a female in public may elicit sexual arousal and occasion exhibiting behavior.

Third, events that should elicit respondent reactions and cue appropriate operant behavior do not. Adult attention may not be pleasurable. Females may elicit neither positive or negative reactions from a male interested in increasing contacts with women.

Physical Factors. Drugs or alcohol, as well as nutritional deficiencies or hormonal changes, may affect behavior. Such factors may be related to presenting problems. For example, fatigue related to overwork may substantially decrease both the amount and the quality of the interaction between a husband and wife. The influence of many of these factors on behavior is relatively unknown. It is likely that the influence of some physical factors may place boundaries on how much change may be possible in given instances. For example, a physical deficit such as paralysis related to genetic or environmental factors may place limits on the degree of physical activity possible and may lessen exposure to appropriate learning experiences. Whenever a physical basis may be related to a presenting problem, as, for example, with the problem of seizures, intervention should be preceded by a physical examination.

Setting Events. The term *setting events* refers not to specific consequences or antecedents of behavior, but to other factors that may affect behavior, such as maturational levels (Bijou, 1975). In addition, various states of deprivation and satiation influence the effectiveness of various reinforcers as well as the likelihood of behaviors associated with attaining them. In discussing development of children during preschool years, Bijou (1975, p. 831) notes that "Setting factors from social sources, for example the emotional 'tone' of family, sometimes characterized along such dimensions as happy versus sad, and outgoing versus isolated, increase the probabilities of some of a child's social behaviors and decrease the probabilities of others."

Behavioral and Cognitive Assets. Clients may have special skills or areas of knowledge that can be useful in change programs. An adolescent who has moved to a new neighborhood and who is having trouble making friends may be a good baseball player, and this skill can be taken advantage of in arranging situations in which new friendships may be formed. An isolated elderly person may be an accomplished knitter and be able to join a group to teach knitting skills to others. A client who works in administration may possess excellent record-keeping skills, which may be of value in monitoring change efforts. Exploration of behavior assets entails identification of what the client does well, including appropriate social skills (Kanfer and Saslow, 1969) as well as cognitive coping skills such as reappraisal of situations, selective attention, problem-solving skills, and calming self-talk. One important source of possible assets that should be scanned relates to the client's self-control skills (Kanfer and Saslow, 1969). Useful questions to pose, suggested by Kanfer and Saslow (1969), include the following:

(1) Under what conditions can clients control problematic behaviors and to what extent are self-control skills responsible for this, in contrast to influence by other people? (2) Can the client exercise self-control so as to avoid situations in which problematic reactions occur? and (3) To what extent can self-control skills be usefully employed during intervention? Separate assessment should be made of self-reinforcing and self-punishing behaviors, because these have been found to be relatively independent (Kanfer and Duerfeldt, 1968). It has been argued that the use of self-punishment requires a greater amount of external support for the punishing consequences (see, for example, Logan, 1973). In addition, clients will differ in types of self-reinforcement preferred; for example, concrete activities or positive self-statements. Very little is known about such preferences. Some clients will have useful self-observation skills that will facilitate the gathering of assessment information. Such skills are important in noting the relationships between reactions and various events. For example, if a client is aware of his physical signs of anxiety, the environmental factors that increase them may be more easily noted. Often clients are not aware of physiological signs related to a problem area such as frequent anger, associated overt behaviors such as an increased tendency to offer aversive experiences to others, or to related environmental and private (covert) events (Ferster, 1972). Their sense of self-efficacy may be decreased, because of a tendency to attribute achievements to external factors rather than to personal competency (Bandura, in press). A goal of intervention is usually to train the client to be a more accurate observer of his own reactions and to related factors.

Assessment may reveal a lack of problem-solving skills and a need to train the client in these processes. Actually, all presenting problems can be viewed as related to an absence of relevant problem-solving skills, or to a failure to employ skills that are available. Whether it is learning how to resolve a conflict with one's mate, how to handle a temper outburst of a child, or how to alleviate a depressed mood, in each instance the client is confronted with a problem in need of resolution. Offering training in problem solving that can be employed in a range of situations gives a possible benefit of allowing application of new skills in a range of situations.

The Role of Racial and Cultural Factors. The norms present in given racial and cultural subgroups may expand or limit the possibilities for change. For any given problem area, it is important to determine whether group norms will be supportive of or hinder change efforts. If, for example, a woman wishes to become more assertive with her husband, her culture may not be friendly toward such efforts. She may be criticized not only by her husband and children, but also by other family members and neighbors. A teen-ager who starts to become interested in school and in getting better grades may know that this interest will not be supported by his friends who look down on such students and consider them "goody-goodies." Information obtained from the client in the interview as well as data he may collect in the natural environment can be used to identify relevant ethnic and cultural factors.

Behavior Chains. Each of our behaviors is part of a chain of behavior. A client, significant other, or some agent of society, artificially extracts from this chain a behavior that is called problematic. For example, a woman client may inform you that she often gets anxious. She may be unable to identify the sources of her anxiety, which may consist of a long sequence of events. She may become anxious only after she has not asserted herself in a series of interpersonal exchanges both at work and in her social life. A husband may complain that his wife screams at the children. Neither parent may recognize that screaming at the children only occurs after a number of softer verbal requests and ineffective threats have been given and the child continues to engage in behavior that is aversive to the parents. The parents may not recognize their role in the maintenance of such behavior. A student may complain that he cannot study. He may not recognize, until gathering assessment information, that when trying to study he engages in a variety of behaviors that are incompatible with study behavior. During assessment, it is necessary to identify the components of a behavior chain including relevant stimulus events that are related to problematic behaviors. It is also necessary to identify missing components and these often include setting events, as well as behaviors either of the client or of significant others.

Clients usually identify the components of a chain in a way that minimizes their own contribution (Wazlawick, Beavin, and Jackson, 1967). A husband may say, in response to a complaint by his wife that he is rude to her, "If she didn't nag me as soon as I step in the door, then I wouldn't have to tell her to shut up." He conveniently does not mention what he does before his wife starts to nag him. Perhaps she has attempted to initiate a conversation with him and he has ignored these attempts. Thus clients often see their world in relation to "problematic" significant others in terms of a trichotomy of events that starts with a "bad" behavior by the other person. During assessment, additional components of the chain must be identified.

Thus a number of areas are reviewed for possible relation to presenting problems. Behaviors, thoughts, and feelings to be decreased and increased are identified, as well as conditions that facilitate or hinder these. Factors sought include (for behaviors to be increased) antecedents that should be increased; antecedents that interfere with these and should be removed; positive consequences that should be increased; and negative consequences that should be removed; and (for behaviors to be decreased) antecedents that should be removed; negative consequences that should be increased; and positive consequences that should be removed.

Facilitating and Hindering Factors. The various personal and environmental sources to which presenting problems are related may facilitate or hinder achievement of desired outcomes. Assets of the client such as observational skills that will allow him to gather needed information in the natural environment will aid assessment and intervention efforts. Often clients do not take advantage of their resources in pursuing desired changes. Beneficial effects on other behaviors of change in the presenting problem will help intervention efforts, as will the existence of needed tools for achievement of behavioral objectives, such as a quiet place to study when an increase in study behavior is an objective. Items of importance to consider include (1) whether the mediator and client possess needed behaviors; (2) whether change will be a positive event for all involved parties; (3) whether offering positive incentives for appropriate behaviors is a positive event; and (4) whether the presenting problem is linked with other problems either of the mediator or of the client. In the least complex situation, the answers to the first three areas would be yes and the answer to the fourth question, no. Conditions such as uncooperative significant others, an absence of needed tools, or an absence of self-monitoring or observational skills will pose hindering influences on intervention. Clients often are initially unaware of what factors stand in the way of achieving desired goals.

Presenting problems vary greatly in the complexity of related factors. A behavior may be maintained by a variety of consequences, both negative and positive, which may be self-presented and/or provided by significant others. Presenting situations can become more complex by the addition of other involved parties for whom appropriate behaviors may not exist, or for whom change will not be positive. A grandparent may start to visit a family and reinforce inappropriate behaviors of a child. A mother may lack verbal statements that her child finds reinforcing. Significant others may punish a client for change efforts or a problem may be linked with other problem areas that must be addressed, such as a high frequency of negative self-statements or a lack of assertion. Thus intervention may not be directed at the presenting problem in itself, but to alteration of factors related to this. An increase in appropriate behaviors may adversely affect other aspects of a client's existence unless steps are taken to alter this pattern. For example, a woman may avoid thinking about painful memories and imagined social slights by drinking, and thus a decrease in drinking might increase such thoughts. It is helpful to list all the factors that would facilitate goal attainment, as well as those that impede it. Let us say that a client initially states that he is inactive and uncreative in his social relationships. Possible hindering factors may include being afraid to meet others, feeling physically unattractive, obsessively thinking about past interpersonal failures, not having enough interesting things to talk about, not being active enough in social exchanges, and having too great a need for attention (Egan, 1975). Facilitating factors may include caring about others, being an intelligent human being who can usually identify the appropriate behaviors in given social situations, having two people who have shown interest, high motivation to change, and being in a large city that provides a range of resources for meeting other people. Once facilitating and hindering factors are identified, they can be ordered in terms of their importance.

Possible Consequences of Attempted Solutions. Sometimes solutions previously attempted by the client create more problems (Watzlawik, Weakland, and Fisch, 1974). For example, sometimes the direct expression of feelings, even though carried out in an appropriate manner, may exacerbate the situation, as in the example presented by Watzlawick, Weakland, and Fisch (1974), in which a couple's attempts to decrease the overly helpful behaviors of in-laws only led to arguments. Recognition of the relationship between some existing problems and faulty solutions will prevent the possibility of considering these as separate, rather than as related problem areas.

Assessment of the Client's Expectations. Client expectations concerning the possibility of achieving beneficial results from intervention influence outcome, as do expectations concerning the intervention approach employed. Favorable expectations are associated with positive outcomes (Goldstein, 1962). The client's expectations should be discussed early in the intervention process. Client expectations are more fully discussed in Chapter Three.

Examples of Behavioral Assessment

The application of social learning principles is illustrated in the following two examples. The first offers an example of an uncomplicated presenting problem and the second a case that is more complex in relation to associated factors.

Mrs. L. and Charles. Mrs. L. sought help because of her "uncontrollable" six-year-old son, Charles. She and her son lived in a large house with an older woman from whom they rented space. Mrs. L., who had been divorced for some time, retained friendly contacts with her former husband. Charles and his father saw each other about once a week. Mrs. L. stated that her son's behavior had gradually become more unruly; that he would not follow instructions and would not allow her any privacy, for example, breaking into the bathroom when she occupied it whenever he chose. No particular incidents seemed to be related to his behavior becoming more unruly. Mrs. L. had tried a number of strategies to change his behavior, all to no avail. She had first tried to reason with her son, explaining, for example, that everyone had a right to privacy; she then tried threatening her son with punishment; however, she rarely, if ever, followed through with it.

Based on the descriptions of interactions that occurred, it was hypothesized that the boy's behavior was maintained by the attention he received from his mother. She had stated that his unruly behavior necessitated more and more attention being shown to her son. Because unruly behavior was reinforced in her presence, she became a cue for such behavior. As the child's following instructions and allowing his mother privacy were low-frequency behaviors, it was hypothesized that such behaviors were not being reinforced. Baseline data revealed that they did not even occur frequently enough to come into contact with positive consequences. Reinforcement theory thus directed attention to possible maintaining factors in the natural environment that might be related to problematic behaviors. Related antecedent situations were also explored. It was found that these behaviors were particularly prevalent in the early evening. Bedtime had also become a dreaded time for Mrs. L., because of the great hassles that occurred then.

Reinforcement theory also directs attention to finding positive consequences to offer for desirable behaviors. Attention of the mother was one possible reinforcer; however, since attention seemed ineffective, and because a number of behaviors were involved in the initial contract between Mrs. L. and her son, it was decided to temporarily also employ points that could be traded in for various backup reinforcers. (See Chapter

Two for a discussion of point and token programs.) The frequence with which a behavior is reinforced is highly related to the ease with which it can be established, and it is thus important to assess the likelihood that mediators (whether others or the self in a self-management program) will be able to consistently provide positive events following desirable behaviors. Mrs. L. stated that she was very willing to offer positive consequences following desirable behaviors. Behaviors included being in bed and quiet by 8:30 P.M.; speaking nicely to his mother at the dinner table; an absence of name calling; making polite requests for items, such as "Could I please have the bread"; speaking with moderate intensity rather than yelling; allowing his mother privacy when she was in the bathroom (not speaking to her or making any unnecessary noises outside and not opening the door); and following instructions. The mother seemed very interested in improving her relationship with her son, so it did not seem that there were any factors that would hinder achievement of outcomes. Her husband as well as her landlady stated that they would support the program.

Comment. The desired outcomes were not linked to any other problem area. Others in Mrs. L.'s life supported her aims, and she possessed reinforcers to employ and seemed capable of dispensing them consistently. The identified outcomes were positively anticipated by the mother, and their achievement would in no way interfere with other areas. Programs could be designed in accord with the self-management skills she possessed, including careful record keeping, consistently regulating her behavior to meet objectives, and being able to tolerate the inevitable delay before changes in behavior would take place. Achievement of outcomes would benefit all concerned. Charles would be subjected to less nagging and he would actually obtain more positive consequences from his mother. The household would be a more peaceful one to inhabit for all concerned, and Mrs. L. would acquire more effective child management skills. There were really no hindering factors in this case. Reinforcement principles pointed to the rearrangement of the relationships between relevant behaviors and their consequences in the natural environment.

Karen and James. Karen and James sought help with Karen's "drug problem" (use of heroin) and for the increasing discord in their marriage. Before her marriage, Karen, age thirty-two, had had a very active social life in a large city and worked part-time as an editor for a small newspaper. This social life was maintained after she started living with James. Two years prior to initial counselor contact, he persuaded her to move to a sub-urban area that would be closer to his work but further from hers, and assured her that there was no reason their social life could not be continued. However, the move had a number of negative consequences for Karen. She had already given up her job, for reasons unrelated to the move, and had hoped to find a similar or better one in her new locale. She could not locate any job at all in the new area, however, and decided to try her hand at her long-term interest in writing, and shared this goal with both James and her friends. However, she only wrote two arti-cles during a two-year period, one of which she sent off to one magazine, but which was rejected. Transportation was more problematic in the new area, and gradually she saw less and less of her friends. This trend was hastened by James' increased absorption in his work.

A few months after the move, Karen met some new friends, some of whom used heroin, although they assured themselves that they could stop any time they wished to and that it was just a "kick" to get high. Even though she had used heroin for a year in her early twenties, Karen always felt that because she stopped using this long ago, there was no danger that she would become "hung up." Gradually her usage in-creased. In addition to just getting high, she now used it to try to work on her writing and to remove her sense of isolation and boredom. An increasing amount of her time, which had become rather empty since leaving the city, was now filled with the process of obtaining money for drugs and then getting them. Money was not a problem for the first year and a half after their move, because James had agreed to support her while she tried her hand as a free-lance writer. After this time, she had agreed to contribute her financial share (one third of all expenses) from her writing.

Two years passed with little progress made. When James threatened to leave her unless she started to contribute to their financial expenses, she obtained a job in a book store, which she disliked intensely. The marital relationship started to deteriorate in a number of ways. James felt that Karen was not meeting her commitment to contribute financially to their life and she persistently accused him of not spending enough time with her and of not helping to make new friends. As his dissatisfaction increased, his verbal behavior toward her became more harsh, and he shared less and less of his time, thoughts, and feelings with her. She, in turn, became "fearful" of these harsh reactions and either avoided him or tried to placate him. Their sexual interaction dwindled in frequency. It finally became obvious by her inability to account for a large sum of money he had left with her during a trip, that the money was being used for something else. She confessed that she was and had been using heroin for over a year, and that she had started to steal money from the cash register when she worked and was terrified of getting caught. This confession was the first in a series, each of which led to protestations of love, new resolutions, and restitution of possible damaging behaviors. For example, James gave Karen $500 to gradually replace in the register. Karen swore she would stop using drugs and special "withdrawal" arrangements were made to help her get through the uncomfortable physical experiences. The mildness of these experiences was later explained by her failure ever to stop drug use. James, on his part, agreed to spend more time with Karen and sought other ways in which Karen desired him to change; however, Karen would usually tell him, "Love me more; love me like you used to," and he was unable to obtain more specific referents, or found it impossible to offer many requested, such as sexually desiring Karen. Finally, after another "confession" in which Karen revealed that she spent the money that he had given her to replace in the cash register on drugs, they agreed to seek help.

Assessment revealed that the function of drug use gradually changed over the years. Barbiturates and quaaludes had at first mainly been employed to enhance social interactions.

However, with the move away from an urban area, away from many of Karen's reinforcers, drug use was maintained by negative reinforcement (removal of feelings of boredom, worthlessness, and isolation). As other reinforcers disappeared in her life, drug use changed in nature (now heroin was used) and in function (to remove negative events rather than to enhance positive ones).

This series of events entailed less sharing of positive events between Karen and James. They spent less time together and time they did share was often marred by accusations and counteraccusations or silence, because neither was effective in altering the behavior of the other. Their relationship thus increasingly assumed an avoidance component. Karen said that she had no doubts that she wished to remain with James, that she loved him and was happy with him, with the exception that she wanted to spend more time together. James stated that he cared deeply for Karen and wished to continue their relationship, given that she assumed some responsibility for her own support and gave up use of heroin. James would support Karen's efforts toward greater self-management in the work area and in increasing drug-free days. Karen knew that he would insist on a separation if she continued using drugs and this provided another incentive for her involvement in a counseling program. Karen was talented in the writing area. She was not trying to pursue an occupation for which she had little skill. Her writing had often received high praise from a number of critics who were not her friends. She also had excellent social skills in terms of meeting others and maintaining enjoyable contacts.

Each client thus had a number of assets that could be usefully employed in change efforts, including the positive events that Karen and James could share together, their agreement that drug use should stop, and Karen's writing and social skills. Deficits included a lack of self-management skills on Karen's part in relation to her work, as well as an inability to say no in order to avoid unwanted intrusions on her work. General objectives included (1) decrease use of heroin; (2) increase Karen's social contacts; (3) Karen would obtain full-time or part-time employment and contribute to the financial support of their life (one fourth of all expenses); (4) Karen would spend more time "writing"; (5) Karen and James would spend more time together; and (6) James would not become "angry" with Karen as she spent more time away from home. The desired outcomes reflected in Objectives 2 through 6 all related to the first objective. Initial and intermediate steps and programs to obtain each were identified.

   Comment. This problem is considerably more complex than the problem experienced by Mrs. L. and her son. Both presenting problems in the second example were related to a variety of other problems, and behavior deficits were involved, such as lack of self-management skills involving work and Karen's lack of assertive skills, such as the ability to say no. This example illustrates the utility of gathering information concerning the recent past as it relates to a presenting problem. Looking back over the last three years provided valuable information concerning reinforcers that might be increased. Each area of Karen's and James' life was explored, and factors associated with the presenting complaints were found in almost every one.

   It was through a focus on the antecedents and consequences of drug use that relevant sources related to this problem were identified. A focus on past as compared with present satisfactions in the marriage revealed sources related to marital discord in addition to the strain caused by drug use, such as deprivation of social contacts. Many assets were available to build on, and the pursuit of a variety of objectives contracted for was facilitated by these assets.

Sources of Assessment Information

   A number of sources are employed to gather needed assessment information, including self-report measures, observation of the client in either simulated or real-life situations, and physiological measures. Reports of significant others and archival reports such as arrest records or attendance records may also be usefully employed when relevant. Problems of reliability (the consistency with which observations are made) and validity (the extent to which a measure actually measures what it is supposed to—for example, the extent to which its values correlate with values obtained via independent measures) are not limited to self-report but also occur in other modes of measurement. For this reason, it is best to employ multiple sources both for assessment and evaluation. Unfortunately the newness of the field has often precluded collection of critical data concerning validity and possible reactive effects of various measures and intermeasure relationships.

Self-Report Measures. Questionnaires as well as client self-reports for use within the context of interviews are both employed within a behavioral model of practice. Although the reliability and validity of self-reports has been much maligned in the past, self-reports have not been shown to be any more problematic than other types of measurements (Walsh, 1967). For example, social desirability factors may alter behavior during direct observation, just as such factors may influence responses on a questionnaire. With any measure, possible sources of invalidity must be carefully considered.

Questionnaires. Preinterview questionnaires that clients complete prior to the first interview may be employed. The information is reviewed by the counselor and is used in the first interview. Data is offered concerning problem definition, possible maintaining conditions, and environmental and personal resources of the client that may be usefully employed. Two areas for which preinterview questionnaires have been developed include marital discord (Stuart and Stuart, 1972) and depression (McLean, 1976). Some behavioral practitioners ask clients to complete a life history questionnaire (Wolpe and Lazarus, 1966) that provides basic demographic information as well as an overview of major areas of the client's life. In addition, questionnaires related to specific areas may be employed such as the Assertion Inventory (Gambrill and Richey, 1975) to gain an overview of client reactions in this area. Questionnaires may also be employed to gather normative data regarding a client. For example, a couple experiencing marital discord could be requested to complete the Locke-Wallace Inventory (Locke and Wallace, 1959). Initial responses on this inventory can be compared to responses following intervention as one measure of change. In addition, with certain measures there may be a relationship between score and possible results with different treatment procedures. Thus some measure that may be based on self-report may be used to rule out certain treatment procedures and to indicate the use of others. Hopefully in the future we may have more information of this type, which would enable more efficient selection of intervention programs.

Behavioral interviews. The conduct of a behavioral interview is described in Chapter Five. As in all interpersonal helping modes, the client is encouraged to share relevant information related to his or her problem in a way that the counselor views as helpful to the client. Imagined role playing, in which the client is asked to imagine himself in a given situation and to verbally describe it to the counselor, including his feelings and thoughts while in the situation, may be employed within the interview to gain more understanding of problematic behaviors and maintaining conditions.

Self-monitoring and observation of significant others. A third source of information is gathered by the client in the natural environment. A client may, for example, be asked to keep track of how often he says anything nice to himself and to write it down, or he may be asked to note how often a child complies with a request. Self-monitoring is discussed in Chapter Seven.

Observation by Trained Observers. Observation may take place either in simulated, artificial situations, or in real-life situations. If a situation is simulated, an effort is made to make it as lifelike as possible, so that the client behavior observed is more likely to be representative of what actually occurs in real life. Checklists are sometimes employed to assess the client's behavior during situations; for example, Paul (1966) employed a checklist to assess clients' degree of anxiety when giving a speech. The process of observation is described in Chapter Seven. Role playing or behavior rehearsal of a situation and observation of the client's reactions while participating in it is frequently employed as an assessment device. Behavioral avoidance tests in the office have been employed to assess the intensity of fear reactions; that is, how close a client will approach a feared stimulus such as a spider (see, for example, Bandura,

Blanchard, and Ritter, 1969). Role playing is extensively used in assessing social skills. Arkowitz, Lichtenstein, McGovern, and Hines (1975) arranged an interaction between a female and male to assess the behavioral competence of males. Eisler, Hersen and Miller (1973) employed a female assistant in a series of fourteen test situations designed to assess the assertive behavior of male psychiatric patients. Measures included the number of scenes in which compliance occurred and the number in which the client requested a behavior change.

One difficulty with the use of role-playing measures of social skill is identifying the criteria that should be employed to determine how satisfactory a given reaction is (McFall, in press). Judges are usually employed to rate client reactions, using audiotape or videotape transcriptions of the interaction between the client and the role-played others. Ratings of judges are not as satisfactory as empirically determining what reaction works best in what situation via tests in the natural environment; however, very little data of this sort is available.

Physiological Measures. It may be relevant to employ physiological measures; for example, determining drug use by random urinalysis or determining degree of muscle tension by use of electromyographic recordings. Portable galvanic skin recorders, for example, can be employed to assess degree of physiological arousal when in real-life situations.

Reports from Significant Others. Information gathered from significant others may be employed to check on the accuracy of client-gathered reports. A spouse may be asked to keep track of how often their partner is sober, so that this report can be checked against the client's self-report. Reports of significant others are not necessarily more accurate than reports of the client; in fact, in relation to some behaviors, such as drug use, they may be less accurate, because significant others may be unable to discriminate when the client is under the influence of a drug.

Archival and Trace Records. At times it is appropriate to employ an archival record such as school attendance or arrest record. It should not be assumed, however, that these records are necessarily more accurate than client reports. For example, it has been found that clients with drinking problems overestimate their arrest history as compared to official records (Sobell, Sobell, and Samuels, 1974). Some behaviors leave traces (behavior products) that can be observed and recorded, such as the number of cigarette stubs in ashtrays, the number of leaves left on a lawn after raking, and the number of points earned.

Summary

The successful application of behavioral procedures depends on adequate assessment. A variety of factors must be attended to in terms of their possible relationship to presenting problems, including social cues and consequences, cognitions, affective reactions, physiological factors, and situational events. These factors may function as antecedents or consequences for desirable or undesirable behaviors. Behavior is conceptualized as consisting of multiple response systems, including cognitive, behavioral, and emotional components that may or may not be closely related. Assessment procedures are tailored for each client, and include a careful search for useful behavioral and cognitive coping skills, attention to cultural and ethnic factors, identification of faulty reinforcing systems, and the possible role of behavior deficits. Each major area of the client's life is scanned for relevant factors.

5

     The steps involved in conducting a behavioral assessment are described in this chapter. Additional detailed information related to special areas is offered in subsequent chapters. These steps include constructing a problem profile and beginning problem definition; establishing priorities and initial specification of objectives; forming a counselor-client contract; specifying behaviors, related events, and client assets; forming hypotheses about functional relationships; selecting a procedure for collecting data and gathering and evaluating baseline data; and identifying specific objectives to be pursued, as well as subgoals. A critical part of assessment, discovering personal and environmental assets, is described in detail in Chapter Six. There are, of course, situations that may arise that would necessitate

Steps in
Assessment

the abandonment of the usual assessment procedure, such as a
crisis situation, and some steps are often combined with others.
For example, information concerning the controlling conditions
for behavior may be collected at the same time that the frequency of a problematic behavior is determined. Some objectives can be clearly identified at an early point and plans of
action formulated, whereas others must await the completion of
further assessment efforts. A careful attempt is made to explain
the rationale for assessment, as well as intervention procedures,
in language appropriate for the client. Social history and identifying information is gathered as needed, and, as with other
helping endeavors, there is an initial stage of self-exploration in
which the counselor aids the client in sharing relevant informa-

tion concerning problems and related factors (Egan, 1975). A more helpful conceptualization of the problem is then gradually introduced by pointing out alternative views of the client's problem.

Commitment is actively pursued and is crystallized in the form of written contracts that include explicit statements of expectations about the client's and counselor's roles in the change process and clear descriptions of desired outcomes. The helping process is a goal-directed one, in which specific desired outcomes are identified and pursued. The client is usually an active participant in both assessment and intervention in terms of carrying out agreed-on assignments, and often assumes an increasingly active role in formulating intervention plans and analyzing contingency relationships. The client's participation in such efforts will be highly influenced by available assets. Special efforts are made to offer clear instructions for tasks and rehearsal is carried out as necessary to assure that agreed-on assignments are understood. A variety of methods are employed to collect needed information, including behavioral interviewing, observation, simulated situations, client self-monitoring, and self-report questionnaires. Life history information that may inform understanding of the client's problem is also collected during initial interviews. Assessment is a continuing process within a behavioral framework as new, relevant information may also emerge after intervention efforts have been initiated.

Collection of a Problem Profile and
Beginning Problem Definition

Often a variety of problems are presented and a task of the first meeting with the client, given that one area does not take precedence, is to start to identify them (Gambrill, Thomas, and Carter, 1971; Schwartz and Goldiamond, 1975). These areas may be listed in the form of problems, such as "being depressed," or listed in terms of a beginning definition of desired outcomes, such as "to be more relaxed." Because beginning statements of desired outcomes are a step closer to identifying specific objectives, when a choice exists between writing down a problem and writing down a desired outcome, the latter should be selected. A detailed description of desired outcomes is usually completed only after additional assessment information is gathered. Forming a problem or outcome profile helps the client start to determine what he would like to change. Such a list often reveals areas that are interrelated. The client is requested to provide information about *current* problems and desired changes and to offer an example of each, including information describing relevant situational factors. In addition, notation of *who* would like a given outcome is important, because the client, counselor, or significant others may differ in their opinions. Specific observable examples are prompted by the counselor's questions. For example, the client may be asked what the outcome would be if counselor and client were successful. The client is then asked how this differs from his current situation, and what beneficial effects attainment of the desired outcome would have. Possible undesirable effects of attaining desired outcomes are also explored. For example, attention from significant others may decrease if a problem such as anxiety is removed. These questions provide information concerning the by-products of change (Schwartz and Goldiamond, 1975). The client is encouraged to discuss problems in terms that help to solve them, rather than to offer insoluble problems. For example, the client may say, "My life is miserable because of my background." Since the past cannot be changed, this offers no solution to his current dissatisfaction. He could be asked, "What would you do differently if you were not miserable?" and he may reply, "I would go out more, not sit around the house." This statement is "instrumental" (Hurvitz, 1970); it offers a possible way to change. The client may have to be encouraged to view the problem he is presenting as his, rather than blaming it on the failure of others or of vague entities such as the capitalistic system. This is not to say that private problems do not often reflect public concerns (Schwartz, 1969); however, simply blaming difficulties on such larger societal factors without involving oneself in a change effort will not help to alter either individual or societal conditions.

Prompts may have to be employed occasionally, such as "Is there anything else that concerns you right now?" General or invidious labels are discouraged and positive self-statements are encouraged. If a client reports that he is an "alcoholic" or that he is "crazy," he is asked to provide behavioral referents for such terms. If several members of a family request help, each person is asked to offer a profile of desired outcomes. If only one area is presented, the behavioral referents for this can begin to be listed. Problem areas may be noticed by the counselor that are not mentioned by the client; these may be discussed and, with the client's understanding of the basis for their identification, added to the list. For example, a thirty-six-year-old male listed the following problem areas: drinking, arguing with his wife, and being dissatisfied with his job. This client's demeanor during the interview, as well as reports he offered describing interactions at work and with his wife, indicated an extreme lack of assertion. This was discussed with the client and added to the list. Thus, the problem profile consists of problems identified by the client as well as those noticed by the counselor and discussed with the client. After the list is completed, it is reviewed to make sure that nothing was omitted. The question might be asked, "Is there anything else you would like to add?"

The client may be unable to identify what is troubling him except in vague terms such as, "I just feel miserable"; "I feel down all the time"; "I'm so anxious"; "I can't relax"; "I feel depressed"; or "I don't know what to do with my life." It is assumed that behavioral and cognitive omissions or commissions are related to distressing feelings, and help must be offered to the client to identify these as well as related conditions. Helpful questions include: "What kinds of things do you do that seem to increase this feeling?" and "What kinds of things do you do that make you feel better?" It is crucial to obtain descriptions of the client's life in major areas such as work, family, and social life. Information about types of thoughts he presents to himself will indicate the extent to which a part of discomfort is self-presented in terms of how he thinks about himself and the possibilities in his life. Knowledge concerning conditions that are frequently related to various presenting problems can help to generate appropriate questions. For example, depressed housewives often do not schedule any free time for themselves. Another useful question to ask the client is what he would do differently if the desired outcome was attained, if he were not depressed or unhappy. Areas of strength can begin to be identified during this early phase by asking the client what he likes about his current life, what is going well for him and what solutions to problems have been attempted (Schwartz and Goldiamond, 1975). Figure 2 illustrates a problem profile gathered by a child welfare worker when a father stated that he wished his son returned to his custody (Stein and Gambrill, 1976b). As can be seen, a number of problem areas are presented. Information contained on the profile includes who labels an area as a problem, who has the problem, and examples of, as well as the situations in which the problem occurs. Desired outcomes can then begin to be formulated in relation to each problem area.

A problem area may concern the need to make a decision, as in the following case. Judith was an unmarried twenty-eight-year-old woman who said she was unhappy, depressed, and at times suicidal. She was currently working in a job she disliked, having dropped out of law school a year earlier "because of an inability to handle the work." She also reported that she had trouble meeting men, had few friends, and that her life had no direction. When asked whether she had wanted to leave law school, she stated that she had not, but was not 100 percent sure that she wished to be a lawyer, and so did not know what to do. She could not see herself having what she considered to be boring jobs the rest of her life, nor did she wish to settle down immediately into a marriage and not work. Thus, even though she had a long-range goal of getting married, she still wanted to pursue a career. Her dilemma was that she was not sure whether she really wanted to be a lawyer. She was also worried that her extreme anxiety in test situations would arise again if she went back to school. Judith desired changes in a variety of areas. Her depression and unhappiness was related to desired outcomes in these areas, including increasing social contacts and resolving her indecision concerning law school.

Figure 2. Problem Profile

Problem label	Who labels	Who has the problem	Date	Examples	Situation
Discipline	father	father/son	10-1-74	Son will not do chores	Home
				Son will not come home at appointed hour	Home
				Result: father/son argument	Home
				Result: son locks self in room	Home
				Result: son leaves house	
Finances	father	father	10-1-74	Collecting unemployment	
				Unused work skills: printing-press operator and ware-houseman	
Inadequate housing	father	father	10-1-74	Has studio apartment	
				Wants two-bedroom apartment	
Cannot get along with relatives	father	father	10-1-74	Disagree over father's childrearing practices	During visits, in presence of child
Like to visit more often	father	father	10-1-74	Visits only bimonthly	Visits occur in foster home or nearby park
Child care	counselor	father	10-1-74	After-school care arrangements needed during father's working hours	
Child unmanageable	case record	father/son	11-73	None provided in record	
Drug abuse	court	father	5-73	Two arrests for possession of heroin	"Street arrest"
				One admission to hospital detox. unit	Hospital

Source: Stein and Gambrill (1976b, p. 12).

Careful note is made of client assets that are evident. This approach reflects the assumption that the client already possesses resources that may be employed in the change effort. These also should be written down. To encourage the client to scan his positive behaviors, these can be listed on the same sheet as are problem areas or desired outcomes. For example, a column could be added to the outcome profile illustrated in Figure 2 representing client assets pertinent to each area. Egan (1975, p. 142) recommends listing problems (baggage) and resources, as follows.

Baggage

Being depressed

Failure to make a go of first marriage

Looking upon self as failure

Poor relationship with father, extending over years; doing nothing to improve it

Failure to be a good disciplinarian as a high school teacher

Having a part-time menial job with income far less than wife's

Resources

Interest and talent enough to make music a career

Genuineness and sincerity

A caring and supportive wife

A demanding but good relationship with stepson

Ego-strength: has not cracked in face of a number of crises

Genuine care and respect for others

Good motivation: coming to counseling in order to face up to job, emotional, and other real-life issues

Simplicity in life-style: being an uncomplicated, open person

Friends to help him get better part-time job for money for further training in music

Integrity: sticking to values, commitments; honesty (even with hostile exwife and her relatives)

Establishing Priorities and Initial Specification of Objectives

It may not be possible to pursue all desired outcomes at once. The client may have to make a choice as to which one to start with. The rationale for selection of a workable number of outcomes is shared with the client, as is the desirability of a clear mutual agreement on the focus of contacts. The client is requested to review the written outcome or problem profile and to rank the areas in terms of their importance. He can be asked, "Which outcome would you like to pursue first?" or "Which area is of most concern to you right now?" After selecting the most important one, he is then requested to select a second, and so on, until all areas are ranked. In selecting outcomes to address first, it is better to select too few than to select too many. If too many are selected, the client may be overburdened by assignments between sessions, and progress may be hampered in relation to outcomes of greatest concern. Selection of desired outcomes to pursue first is essentially a decision-making step, and a variety of criteria may be employed when evaluating alternatives (Carter, 1973). Such criteria include:

1. Annoyance value of the current situation to the client.
2. Danger value of the current situation.
3. Interference of the current situation in the client's life.
4. Likelihood that the outcome will be attained with intervention.
5. Centrality of the problem in a complex of problems.
6. Accessibility of the problem. (Can you get at it?)
7. Potential for change. (Can you do something about it; do you have the resources and skills?)
8. Probable cost of intervention (time, money, energy, and resources).
9. Relative frequency, duration, or magnitude of the problem.
10. Ethical acceptability of the outcome to the counselor.
11. Likelihood that new behaviors will be maintained in the postintervention environment (on this point, see Ayllon and Azrin, 1968b).

Clients will usually select problem areas that have the highest annoyance or danger value. An area selected may be related to other areas listed on the profile. For example, the client mentioned on page 136 selected drinking as the most pressing problem. Lack of assertion was related to arguing with his wife and not liking his job, which in turn were related to drinking. Thus, all desired changes on his profile were interrelated. With other profiles, there may not be any relationship between areas. Further assessment information may be required to determine the relevance of some of the listed criteria, including centrality of the desired outcome. Only after such information is gathered may it become clear that skills and resources beyond the counselor's capabilities will be required. At other times, it may be quite clear that certain problems will have to be addressed before others. For example, a court may mandate that a father prove himself not to be using drugs before it will consider restoring a child to his care. This requirement may take precedence over a marital problem that the client raises that does not seem to be related to parenting skills or drug abuse.

Desired outcomes that are inaccessible should not be selected, nor should outcomes that have a small potential for change. At times, the counselor may pursue an outcome that has a low potential for change because of other factors, such as involvement of the court. A child may have been removed from a mother's custody on the grounds that she neglected her child and was a heavy drinker. A condition for the child's return may be a decrease in drinking. If the mother indicates that she would like her child returned, and given that a decrease in drinking is a court requirement, this objective may be accepted and an effort made to decrease drinking even though it appears that there is little possibility of change. The "relevance of behavior rule" (Ayllon and Azrin, 1968b) emphasizes selection of only those behaviors that will continue to be reinforced in the postintervention environment. This rule is especially important for programs in institutional settings, in which behaviors selected for change have often been those that benefit only the staff rather than the residents.

Some desired outcomes do not warrant intervention, because it is likely that they will be eliminated in the natural course of events. In one instance, a father was concerned that there was something wrong with his two-year-old son, because the boy had started to pick at and notice all types of threads, including the strands in corn cobs. It seemed likely that this was a temporary interest and intervention was not recommended. This behavior disappeared after a couple of weeks.

The relative frequency, magnitude, or duration of a problematic behavior is often related to its annoyance value. However, not until more specific information is gained about these factors can an informed decision be made according to these criteria. Counting a behavior may indicate that it occurs much less frequently than was thought, as shown in the following example, reported by Thomas and Carter (1971).

Mrs. S. was a twenty-six-year-old woman who listed the following areas as problematic: crying spells, depression, inability to hold a job, arguments with her husband, and stuttering. She selected stuttering as the problem she wished to start with. She was requested to gather information concerning the frequency of this behavior as well as the surrounding conditions (what happened right before and after). The information she collected revealed that she only stuttered six times during a one-week period and she reported that she no longer considered herself a "stutterer" and wished to select another desired outcome.

Mutual agreement on a client-selected behavior may not be possible because of ethical objections a counselor may have. A teen-ager's objective of "getting back" at a teacher whom he feels has wronged him may not be accepted. The counselor may decide not to participate in a change effort that concerns another person without the involvement of this person. Whenever possible, all parties whose behavior is involved in a problem should participate in assessment and intervention, including selection of desired outcomes. If parents wish to increase the frequency with which their thirteen-year-old boy follows instructions, the counselor should explain why the boy should also be involved. Whenever more than one client is involved, each is requested to identify desired outcomes and to rank them in order of importance.

There will be times when a significant other—that is, someone who influences a problem—will refuse to participate.

The counselor must decide whether he or she can ethically carry on without their involvement and also whether there will be enough potential for change with an uncooperative significant other. Efforts should be made to involve the person. As a first try, the client can be requested to talk with the other person. If this fails, permission can be solicited to contact the individual, pointing out how important it is that both parties be involved in a change program and giving a rationale for this. If permission is granted, the significant other can be contacted. The counselor can point out that the client has consulted a helping source and can indicate that he or she recognizes the difficulties that must be posed for this other person because of the client's problem (McLean, 1976). For example, a woman who is depressed may no longer carry out many household tasks. The counselor can stress that he thinks he could help to improve this situation and that it would be easier to do so if the other person involved would participate in the change effort. The counselor should avoid laying blame on either party and, instead, show a recognition of the difficulty that *both* individuals must be experiencing and offer to help in alleviating this. If these efforts fail, the counselor may decide that it would be ethically irresponsible not to offer help to the client, if he judges that help might be effective.

During these first two steps in the assessment process, the client is helped to identify what it is he would like to change. He can be asked, "How would things be different?" Realistic goals must be sorted from unattainable ones. The identification of specific behaviors and related situations is continued in further assessment steps.

Forming a Counselor-Client Contract

All contracts contain the following features: (1) responsibilities of involved parties; (2) the privileges of involved parties —what will be gained if responsibilities will be carried out; (3) costs that may be involved for failure to carry out responsibilities; (4) time limits of the contract; (5) a method of evaluating whether responsibilities are carried out and privileges are awarded; and (6) signatures of involved parties. Time limits may be suggested by the wishes of the client and by the counselor's estimate of the length of time that will be required to achieve desired outcomes and their approximations. In some cases, a court may force the client and counselor to adhere to certain time limits. Separate time limits may be established for achievement of an overall goal (such as return of a child from foster care to his natural parents) and the various desired outcomes that may have to be achieved by attaining this goal (such as decreasing parental drinking and obtaining adequate housing). A written contract forces clients and counselors to concretize the objectives of services as well as mutual responsibilities. Contracts help to prevent unfair or hidden agendas that a counselor or client may have. The responsibility of the counselor is to provide, to the best of his or her ability, whatever help is needed. The counselor is also responsible for clarifying expected compensation; for describing the nature of and rationale for procedures that are employed, as well as prospects for success and any possible disadvantages; and for identifying protections assured to clients, such as confidentiality. Responsibilities of the client include providing needed information, complying with agreed-on assignments, keeping appointments except when emergencies arise, and notifying the counselor when appointments cannot be kept. A time at which both the client and the counselor will evaluate progress should be indicated on the contract, as well as specific criteria and social contexts to be used for measuring the success of treatment (Schwitzgebel, 1975). Time limits facilitate positive effects (Reid and Shyne, 1969). They are of particular import when time is of the essence—for example, when children are in out-of-home care (Gambrill and Wiltse, 1974). Also, a client may be willing to pursue a time-limited goal, although unwilling to participate in a long-range one.

Treatment contracts may be formed at different points during assessment. A contract formed at an early stage may describe expectations relevant to contracts with all clients as shown in Figure 3. This has the advantage of clarifying a number of expectations in the beginning of contact. The renegotiation clause highlights the openness to alteration in contract

Figure 3. Contract

For the agreed-on outcomes to be obtained, cooperation is required. The signatures below indicate that:

On your part, you agree   *On our part, we agree*

1. Appointments

Attend sessions we set up. If you find it impossible to attend, please notify us at least 24 hours in advance.

Keep appointments we set up. If we cannot meet them, we shall try to notify you the preceding week, barring emergencies.

2. Records*

You will be assigned a record book in which you will make regular entries.

We shall explain purpose of entries, analyze them regularly, and provide feedback.

3. Program requirements

You will try to fulfill various other specified assignments, as made.

We shall similarly explain purpose of assignments, analyze them, and provide feedback.

4. Research, training, and confidentiality

Data from your records can be useful for consultation with other staff members, training of staff, and research publications that help other professionals and thereby other clients. You consent to the use of such data for these purposes, with restrictions noted.

We shall preserve the confidentiality of your records and take every precaution to ensure that any data disseminated are not identified with you, in accord with prevailing practice with medical and psychiatric records and research. Any other type of dissemination is specified.

5. Carry-over

Attainment of the desired outcome need not end our relation. Your cooperation in follow-up and its analysis is necessary.

We shall explain the role of follow-up required, your role, and provide feedback.

6. Regular Fees

Regular fees are required.

Conditions and personnel for our sessions and their analysis will be provided.

7. Additional charges

Additional charges for supplies, and so on, may be made.

Supplies and other items will be provided as indicated by additional charges.

*Please note: Item 2, Records, is indispensable for attaining our objectives.

Renegotiation Clause: The requirements and goals are open for renegotiation at any time on the request of either party, at which time any changes that are agreed on will be entered into a new written contract, or written amendment.

Signed _____ Client   Signed _____ Consultant
                                                 _____ Consultant

Source: Schwartz and Goldiamond (1975, pp. 95-96).

components by mutual agreement. This contract is particularly good in highlighting the active role the client will have during assessment and intervention, as well as in identifying counselor responsibilities.

Contracts are also important when counselor-client contact is not completely voluntary. An example of a contract formed between counselors and parents who wished to have their child returned is presented in Figure 4 (Stein, Gambrill, and Wiltse, 1974). The overall goal is identified (to return the child to his parents), as well as general objectives, and consequences if objectives are not attained. A direction of change for each problem area is identified—for example, to decrease drinking and decrease arguments with spouse. Specific plans for each area as well as specified objectives for each are described in writing in subsequent attachments to the main contract. Obligations of both the counselor and the client are included in these attachments. Contracts formed during the early stages of assessment may clarify agreements to start work on certain problems and specify conditions that will permit gathering of needed assessment information regarding additional desired outcomes. Subgoals as well as desired outcomes should be included in a contract as soon as available. For example, a plan to achieve the third goal listed in Figure 4 may include the parents visiting with their child for two hours per week for the first two weeks, four hours the next week, and all day for the following two weeks, if counselor observation and reports by the parent and child indicate the continuing success of the visits. Contracts may be written and signed following completion of assessment, as in the illustration in Figure 5 (Ayllon and Skuban, 1973). The results of assessment can then be included in the contract.

The careful identification of objectives and description of procedures that will be employed enable the client to give informed consent. Informed consent requires that the client understand the results of assessment, the nature of treatment, the risks involved, the prospects of success, and alternative methods of treatment (Schwitzgebel, 1975). The explicit description of objectives, methods, risks, and benefits of intervention provides for a degree of self-determination that contrasts

Figure 4. Sample Contract

This contract is entered into between _____ , Social Worker for the Alameda Project of Children's Home Society, _____ , Child Welfare Worker for the Welfare Department of the Alameda County Human Resources Agency, and _____ , parents of _____ , at present a dependent child of the Alameda County Juvenile Court.

In keeping with the wish of both parents to have their son returned to their home on a permanent basis, both _____and_____ agree to recommend such a return on a trial basis to the Alameda County Juvenile Court contingent on the compliance of the parents to engage in a program to modify the following behaviors that all parties agree are currently problematic and, further, that all parties agree require modification prior to such a return. It is understood by the parents that failure to comply with such a program will result in a statement to the Alameda County Juvenile Court that, in the opinion of both social workers, such a return is not feasible at the present time and that alternate plans for the care of the child, such as guardianship or adoption, should be explored.

The general goals of the modification program are as follows:

1. Elimination of drinking behavior by both parents
2. Participation by both parents in the program sponsored by the Alcohol Abuse Program
3. Visit their child, _____ , in the foster home, according to the prescribed schedule
4. Increase the amount of time _____ engages in employment
5. Obtain suitable housing
6. Demonstration by both parents of adequate parenting skills

The specific plan for each particular problem area as well as the roles of the parents and of the social workers are attached. The first stage of this contract relates to Problem Areas 1, 2, and 3. Development of plan for the remaining problem areas is contingent on the parents' successful completion of the first stage of the contract.

This contract will be in effect for a period of six (6) months. The first stage of the contract will be for a period of two (2) months, August 8, 1974 to October 8, 1974.

Parents: Social Workers:

_____   _____
Mother   Children's Home Society

_____   _____
Father   Alameda County Human Resources
                                                Agency

_____
Date

Note: This contract sample focuses on long-term goals that must be achieved prior to restoration.

Source: Stein, Gambrill, and Wiltse (1974, p. 22).

Figure 5. A Contingency Contract for Therapy

1. *Overview of problem and therapeutic program*

The overall objective of this therapeutic program is to develop and stabilize Mike's behavior patterns so that he may be considered for admission to school this fall. In general, this will involve strengthening some requisite behaviors such as following commands from an adult, and eliminating others such as the screaming and tantrums that accompany most of his refusals to follow instructions.

Mike has a discouraging behavior history for most teachers to consider working with. Because his characteristic reaction to requests is to throw tantrums, he is considered "untestable" by standard psychological means. This does not necessarily mean that he cannot do the items on a test, but rather that he has little or no control over his own behavior. His uncooperativeness quickly discourages most people from making much effort to work with him. What is clearly needed is an intensive rehabilitation program designed to enable Mike to build patterns of self-control that would lead to the elimination or drastic reduction of his disruptive behavior. This, in turn, would open other possibilities for developing Mike's potential, that is, the avenues which are blocked by his unmanageable behavior.

The overall goal of this 8-week program will be the development of self-control with its reciprocal outcome of decreasing or eliminating tantrums and disruptive behaviors. Implementation of this program will require that the child and his trainer engage in such activities as trips to the zoo, museums, parks, movies, swimming pools, shopping centers, supermarkets, and so on as well as having lunch and snacks together. These settings are included to expose Mike to a maximal number of normal situations where expectations of a standard of conduct are imposed by the setting itself.

As much as possible, the techniques used in the day program will be designed with the ultimate objective of utilization in the home. An attempt will be made to see that procedures used in the program are transferred to home management at the termination of treatment. The therapist will give instructions weekly to the parents by phone to ensure that efforts both at home and in rehabilitation do not conflict.

2. *Behavioral objectives of therapy*

a. The objective of the therapeutic program is to teach Mike to comply with between 80 to 100 percent of the verbal commands given to him by an adult(s). Compliance will be defined as Mike's beginning to perform the behavior specified by the command within 15 seconds after it has been stated and then completing the specified task.

b. In addition, we intend to eliminate or drastically reduce Mike's excessive screaming and tantrums. The goal is not to throw a tantrum more frequently than once out of 30 commands and for no longer than 1 minute at a time.

c. Evaluation of treatment outcome: The decision as to the attainment of these specific objectives will rest on Mike's performance during a 30-minute test session to be conducted in a classroom situation. At this session, the therapist, the parents, and an additional person will make 10 verbal requests each of Mike, for a total of 30 verbal requests. Mike must comply with 80 to 100 percent of these requests for the program to be considered a success. In addition, he must have thrown not more than one tantrum, and for not more than 1 minute, during this final evaluation.

Figure 5 *(continued)*

3. *Time and place of therapeutic intervention*

   a. The therapeutic program will start on _____ and terminate on _____ . Evaluation of the effectiveness of treatment will be held on or about the termination date of the therapeutic program.

   b. Location: The meeting place will be at the _____ . Session activities, however, will involve time spent elsewhere, for example, having lunch, trips to shopping centers, amusements, and other special events. If the facility is not available, some other place agreeable can be designated as meeting and base center.

   c. Days of training: Therapy sessions will be scheduled 5 days per week. The specific days may vary from week to week to comply with the objectives of the program. The family will be advised of the therapy schedule 1 week in advance.

   d. Hours per day: Therapeutic sessions will be scheduled for 7 hours a day. Session time may be extended when therapeutically necessary as decided by the therapist.

   e. Absenses: There will be 4 notified absences allowed. The mother is expected to notify the therapist at least 1 hour before the scheduled therapy session. Any additional absences will require an additional fee of $10 per absence.

4. *Fees*

   Achievement of the behavioral objectives is expected to take 7 weeks of training from _____ . This training will cost a total of _____ . The monies will be disbursed in the following manner.

   a. A check for 2/3 of the total amount will be given to the therapist at the beginning of therapy.

   b. The balance of 1/3 will be paid to the therapist on the achievement of the program objectives as specified above on about the date of termination of the program. In the event that the above objectives are not reached by this date, therapy will be discontinued and the balance will be forfeited by the therapist.

   c. All expense incurred during training will be defrayed by the therapist. This will include admission to baseball games, the city zoo, swimming pools, and so on, as well as the cost of field trips, lunch, and snacks.

*   *   *   *

By my signature, I do hereby attest that I have read the above proposal and agree to the conditions stated therein.

_____
Parent

_____
Supervising Therapist

_____
Cotherapist

_____
Date

Source: Ayllon and Skuban (1973, pp. 22-23).

markedly with simply obtaining the client's consent to treatment
without any clear identification of these items. The mutual
signing serves as a model of the type of interaction that will
occur between counselor and client—that both have responsibilities, that there should be clarity as to what these will be, and
that their work together will be reviewed at a predetermined
time. Also, signing of contracts may increase the client's commitment to the change process.

Counselor-client contracts are tools for facilitating change
efforts. They often have to be amended as additional desired
outcomes are identified and additional assessment information
is needed. Objectives may be attained much sooner than expected and a new contract designed, in which time limits are
adjusted accordingly.

Specifying Behaviors, Related Situations, and Client Assets

An important step in the application of a behavioral
model is to identify the behavioral referents for each desired
outcome as well as related events. Some of this information will
be gathered during prior steps. A hallmark of the behavioral
model is the identification of desired outcomes and approximations to them (subgoals) in observable terms. Unless vague
terms are made precise, there may be, unknown to the counselor and client, a lack of agreement concerning what is to be
changed, as well as difficulty in identifying relevant environmental factors. Also, the seriousness of a behavior cannot be
judged accurately if we do not know how often it occurs.
Examples of behaviors and the situations in which they occur
are given in Table 1. These behaviors are countable, and information is provided concerning the situation in which it occurs.
Examples of behaviors that are countable include arithmetic
problems completed, "snacking" (eating between meals), initiations of conversations, temper tantrums, positive self-statements, negative self-statements, hands trembling, crying, and sitting over one hour with the head down and not saying a word.
Terms that need to be specified include *being sad, being in-
secure, not liking someone,* getting angry, being anxious, being

Table 1. Summary of Home Settings for Willie's Behavior, Including Social Consequences[a]

Home Setting	Problem Behavior	Social Consequences	Desirable Competing Behavior
Awakening (school days only)	Complains about stomach or head pains	Mother gives medication and tells him he's OK	Defined by problem behavior
Dressing	Very slow	Mother prompts and sometimes helps	Defined by problem behavior
Breakfast (school days only)	Refuses to eat	Mother prompts	Defined by problem behavior
Leave for school	Refuses to go	Mother and father argue with him and sometimes spank him	Defined by problem behavior
Chores	Refuses to work or does jobs "half-way"	Mother argues or reasons with him	Defined by problem behavior
Outside play	Frequently returns to house to "ask if mother is there"	None obvious	Defined by problem behavior
Inside play	Asks or demands mother's help	Mother helps	Cooperative play with siblings
When mother attends to siblings	Asks or demands mother's help	Mother argues with him or helps	Cooperative play with siblings
When mother plans shopping trip or visit to friends	Asks or demands to go with her	Mother complies	Defined by problem behavior
Bedtime	Complains of fears of dark and "crooks" breaking into house	Mother reasons with him and leaves room light on	Talk with siblings

[a]Data based on mother's report.

Source: Wahler and Cormier (1970, p. 286).

depressed, and being overly dependent. If possible, responses should be defined objectively, clearly, and completely (Hawkins and Dobes, in press). The first criterion requires that the definition refer to observable characteristics of the behavior or of the environment. Clarity is being able to accurately repeat and paraphrase the definition. The third characteristic, completeness, requires identification of the boundary conditions of the definition, so that what responses are to be included and excluded in the response class are clearly discernible.

A helpful question to ask when specifying behaviors is whether two or more people could easily agree as to its occurrence. If the answer is no, further pinpointing is necessary. This is not the case when private events (thoughts or feelings) are recorded, because these are only accessible to the individual experiencing them. However, the thought or feeling still must be clearly defined, so its occurrence can be readily discerned. It is helpful to identify behaviors that have a definite beginning and end, such as following instructions, hitting, making a favorite meal, and washing the car. The duration of a behavior may be important. A wife may complain, for example, that she is unable to maintain a conversation with men in social situations for beyond five minutes and that she lies in bed for many hours before falling asleep.

When the criterion of countability is applied, many statements of problematic behavior turn out to be lacking, such as "inability to act in a mature manner." The specific referents for such global descriptions, as well as the situations in which they occur, must be identified. The same applies to such terms as *aggressiveness, hostility,* and *inhibition.* Clients often employ mental descriptions of behavior and are also prone to using abstractions from behavior (Wahler and Cormier, 1970). The term *inattention* may refer to looking around the room or being out of one's seat. The term *jealousy* may be used to describe one boy hitting another. The client's abstraction may simply be translated into another one based on the counselor's theoretical framework (Wahler and Cormier, 1970). If abstractions are accepted, their use is encouraged. If employed, they should only be used as summary terms for a cluster of specified behaviors (Staats and Staats, 1963). Only in this way will the client and counselor know for sure to what the other is referring.

Some clients concentrate on motives rather than on behaviors (Watson and Tharp, 1972). A client may say, "I guess the problem is that I'm just lazy," or "I just don't want to do it." Such statements are offered as explanations for problems. However, motive analysis can lead one away from the identification of relevant behaviors. Because of their frequent use of traits and motives to explain behaviors, clients are not accustomed to identifying behaviors in situations. Often they do not realize that problematic behaviors occur only in certain situations. A parent may report that her six-year-old daughter is always enuretic, or a client might say that he "feels angry all the time."

A behavioral model focuses on what the client does, in what situations, and how significant others respond, that is, what they do before and after given client behaviors. "What" and "When" questions are used rather than "Why" questions. Asking the clients why they do something presumes that they know the answer and is often frustrating to clients, because they probably do not know and it seems that they should (Kadushin, 1972). "Why" questions encourage the offering of "motivational" reasons that are usually uninformative, such as "I'm just lazy." Instead, the client could be asked, "What happens when. . . ?" One looks closely at what actually happens in the natural environment. Attention is directed toward behavior by questions that focus on it, such as, "Can you give me an example of what he does?" When one example is gained, then another can be requested until it seems that the set of behaviors to which the client refers when he employs a given word have been identified. Information can also be gained by asking what the person complained about would do if he displayed a state *opposite* to that complained of. A wife could be asked, "What would he do if he loved you?" or "What would he do if he were kind to you?" The counselor must exercise care not to impose his or her referents on the client. It is best not to suggest referents. Rather, the client should be guided toward their identification by the questions asked or by offering examples of specific behaviors from other settings. Clients tend to be negative scanners of their own behavior and have a ready repertoire of negative labels to describe it. Very often desired changes are posed in negative terms such as *being less miserable* or *feeling less nervous*. Attention is directed to what would be done differently if a client were less miserable. The client can be asked, "How would you know if you were less miserable?" or "What would you do differently?"

Specification must also be carried out when problematic emotional behavior such as anxiety is concerned. The referents of the term used must be identified, as well as the situations in which such reactions occur. Terms that refer to partially private events, such as emotional responses, create unique problems for the verbal community that attempts to develop their correct use because of the private nature of some of their referents (Skinner, 1953). Thus, each individual may refer to a somewhat different mix of referents when using a term denoting an emotion.

Information concerning surrounding conditions may be obtained from questions such as, "When does this usually take place?" "What is going on when this happens?" "Are there any times when this hardly ever occurs?" "Does this occur at certain times of the day more than others?" and "What happens right afterwards?" It is usually found that the behavior varies in accord with the presence or absence of certain environmental factors. A child may only be enuretic at home and never when he or she visits friends or relatives. Only when a client is turned down after making a request of someone may he "feel angry." These questions are designed to offer information about the consequences of problematic behaviors as well as about relevant antecedent events. Sources of positive reinforcement or avoidance of unpleasant events will usually be revealed.

The question, "When did this start?" or, if a client complains of general unhappiness, asking, "When did you start to feel this way?" may offer useful information as to a change in the client's environment that is related to the present complaint. A child may have started to wet his bed after another child came to live in the home, or a client may report that he has been feeling generally unhappy since he lost a job he really liked.

Selecting Behaviors to Increase. Identifying behaviors to be increased is given particular attention during assessment, because it is usually easier and more comfortable to decrease some behaviors by increasing others. The client may find it hard to offer examples of behaviors that he would like to see more of, because his attention has been focused on those he would like to decrease. This is often found when, from the client's perspective, the problem is some significant other, such as a child or spouse. So much unpleasant interaction may have taken place that the client has become a "negative scanner" of the other's behavior, only attending to behaviors that he does not like. Helpful questions include: "What does he do that you like?" and "What would you like him to do?" Answers to the first question will sometimes be "Nothing," perhaps because of a history of negative interaction, and also because the client may not recognize the importance of reinforcing approximations to desired behavior. Special help in identifying behaviors to be increased may have to be provided, including practice in selecting approximations to desired behaviors. Possible pleasurable behaviors may be suggested by the counselor or pleasurable behaviors shared by others may be noted. Clients could be asked what an ideal marriage, future, or child would be like, depending on what is relevant, and general labels then specified in terms of discrete behaviors (Hunt and Azrin, 1973).

Any person, no matter how deviant his repertoire, evidences approximations to desirable behaviors. Some of these may be incompatible with undesirable behaviors and simply increasing these will decrease the latter. Incompatibility may be of two types. Two behaviors may be physically incompatible in that they cannot be performed at the same time. A child cannot sit in his seat and at the same time run around the room. A child cannot be simultaneously compliant and noncompliant, or isolate himself from other children while at the same time approaching them. Thus, some types of desirable behaviors are obvious once their undesirable counterparts are specified. In other instances, competing behaviors may not be so easily identified. In these situations, behaviors must be located that are *functionally* incompatible with the undesirable behaviors (Wahler and Cormier, 1970). This requires a search for behaviors that are not correlated with the problematic behavior. If a child does not cry while playing with other children, such play could be increased to decrease crying. A woman may not feel depressed when she is working on her job or when cooking meals for her family, and these behaviors could be increased to decrease "depression." When desirable behaviors are identified, the conditions that interfere with or prohibit their display can then be explored, as well as the conditions that would facilitate their performance. Some examples of desirable counterparts of problematic behaviors include following instructions (not following instructions); raising hand before talking (talking out of turn); complimenting someone (saying mean things); being on time (being late); hanging clothes in closet (throwing clothes on floor); and talking with spouse for five minutes when entering house after work (not communicating). (See also Table 1.)

Use of Preinterview Checklists or Questionnaires. One way for the client to contribute information in relation to the identification of behaviors to be increased and decreased and the situations in which these occur is to employ a preinterview questionnaire. Because it is completed prior to the first interview, this contact can proceed on the basis of this additional information. Preinterview questionnaires have been developed for couples and families (Stuart and Stuart, 1972, 1975) and for clients who are depressed (McLean, 1976). The former two require each person to identify specific behaviors to be increased and decreased as well as to answer a range of other items of import to assessment. Each person is encouraged to scan the behavior of significant others for positive behaviors. Wahler and Cormier (1970) have developed checklists, for home, school, and community settings for children, that include a range of situations within each context as well as a variety of behaviors that might be of concern to significant others. Such checklists may help clients to realize that behavior differs in different contexts and encourage them to drop overinclusive terms such as *always* or *never*. Little writing is required, because the client simply checks whether certain behaviors are a problem. A request to note desirable behaviors should be included on these checklists.

Other Assessment Methods. It is usually necessary for the client or counselor to gather information in the natural environment in order to identify relevant thoughts, behaviors and related situations. Clients are often requested to keep daily logs. (Guidelines for observation and recording are described in Chapter Seven.) Simulated situations may be arranged in the office. If a client is having trouble asking an employer for a raise, he can be requested to role play this interaction while his behavior is observed to identify appropriate and inappropriate behaviors. Whenever possible, a sample of problematic behaviors as well as cognitive and behavioral assets should be gathered (Gambrill, Thomas, and Carter, 1971).

Relevant thoughts and feelings may be determined by imagery procedures. The client can be asked to close his eyes and imagine himself in the problematic situation and to describe the thoughts and feelings he has before, during, and after the presenting problem. The client is requested to "run a movie" through his mind of some critical incident (Meichenbaum, 1975b). This will indicate whether there are thought patterns that may interfere with appropriate behaviors. An inquiry can be made as to the range of situations in which similar feelings and thoughts occur, to determine the pervasiveness of negative thought patterns. This imagery assessment procedure will also reveal available cognitive coping skills.

Special Types of Presenting Problems. Some behaviors are very aversive to others or to the client even though they occur infrequently, such as occasional alcoholic binges or sporadic temper outbursts. Appropriate behaviors that are related to the low-frequency behavior must be located. Patterson and Reid (1970) reported a case in which a ten-year-old boy set fires occasionally. They hypothesized that fire setting was related to infrequent reinforcement at home and at school and their intervention program attempted to increase positive reinforcement from peers, teacher, and parents. This reinforcement could be arranged frequently. A twice-yearly alcoholic binge may be related to numerous daily aversive events in a client's life both at work and in the home, coupled with a low frequency of positive reinforcement. The conditions responsible for these events as well as for the low frequency of positive reinforcement must be identified (Hunt and Azrin, 1973). Thus, with low-frequency inappropriate behaviors, related appropriate behaviors and thoughts are located and reinforced and sources of related aversive control removed.

Some desired changes do not appear to be behavioral—for example, losing weight, getting better grades in school, or having more friends (Watson and Tharp, 1972). In such instances, the question is asked: "What must be done differently to alter the situation?" If a client wishes to lose weight, how must he change his behavior to accomplish this? What antecedent conditions should be changed? What chains of behavior are involved and how should these be altered? Behaviors that must be increased if the goal is to be achieved are identified, as well as behaviors that must be decreased. Even though the presenting problem may not sound like a behavioral one, when one examines how this goal will be reached, it is through changes in behavior. If a student wishes to get better grades, the behaviors necessary to achieve this goal must be determined. The student may have to narrow the range of stimulus control over his study behavior, cease engaging in nonstudy behaviors in situations in which he does study, spend more time studying, and learn how to take notes.

It is often more difficult to realize that you are not doing something you should do, than to recognize a behavior surfeit (Watson and Tharp, 1972). It is more difficult because the event does not happen. A focus of assessment efforts is on identifying what should be done differently in related situations, and determining whether the client possesses needed skills. A woman interested in increasing her social contacts with males may not know where to go to meet men nor have appropriate skills for initiating conversations or arranging future contacts. A student may not know how to organize his study time or how to take helpful notes. A child may lack skills in how to play cooperatively with other children.

Identifying Personal and Environmental Assets

A consistent focus during assessment is determining assets that can be usefully employed to facilitate change efforts in relation to each desired outcome. Questioning in relation to locating these assets is carried out as appropriate during assessment, and a list may be made noting them for each desired outcome. Clients often overlook a range of personal assets that can be of value. Perhaps more frequently, however, with a clinical population, there may not only be deficits in self-observation skills but there may also be overly stringent or overly generous standard setting in relation to self-evaluation and often a failure to offer self-reinforcement for appropriate behaviors. This resource identification allows a "constructional" approach to intervention through building on client assets (Schwartz and Goldiamond, 1975). Available recreational and vocational skills are also important to assess. (See Chapter Six for a detailed discussion on locating environmental and personal assets.)

Limiting Personal and Environmental Factors

Either environmental or personal factors may limit a client's choice of objectives (Kanfer and Saslow, 1969). Economic hardship, limited vocational skills, and limited possibilities for forming meaningful social contacts are often real factors that must be contended with. Similarly, personal characteristics, such as deficient speech skills or physical handicaps, may inform the boundaries of change.

Forming Hypotheses About Functional Relationships

The information gathered during behavioral interviews, simulated situations, and in the natural environment is employed to generate hypotheses about the factors related to attainment of desired outcomes. Review of client-gathered recording forms may reveal similar consequences following certain behaviors. For example, they may show that when a child asks his parents for something in a nice way, they ignore him.

Failure to reinforce appropriate asking may be related to "demanding" behavior. Observation of a husband and wife during the interview may indicate that the wife does not talk very much and, when she does, is ignored by her husband. Thus her low frequency of talking may be caused by a failure of her husband to reinforce such behavior. The husband may appear exhausted and inquiry may reveal that he is carrying two jobs. This may be related to a complaint by his wife that she never sees her husband and that he seems to have little interest in making love with her. Observation of a mother and her child in a playroom may indicate that a mother makes very inefficient use of instructions (she asks her child many times to do something and provides no consequences for his behavior whether or not he complies). Hypotheses relate to what appears to be maintaining behavior surfeits, what personal or environmental omissions seem to be responsible for low frequency or the complete absence of desired behaviors and factors that may be related to both, such as setting events (for example, fatigue) or behavior deficits in other areas (lack of assertive behavior related to alcohol abuse). Counselor hypotheses can be checked out as needed by collecting additional assessment information to see if original assumptions are confirmed. Hypotheses are shared as appropriate with the client and form a part of gradually introducing the client to a new conceptualization of his problem. The appropriateness of sharing such hypotheses with the client is influenced by the possibility that the client will be able to understand what is being said and whether he can usefully employ this information. Care must be taken not to overload a client with information he cannot absorb but rather to pace this with what can be understood and used.

Selecting a Monitoring Procedure and Gathering a Baseline

A hallmark of the behavioral model of practice is an empirical orientation in which plans are informed by data collection. Gathering a baseline (a record of repeated measures of the naturally occurring frequency, duration, or intensity of a specified behavior over some time period before trying to alter behavior) allows comparison with the frequency, duration, or intensity of the behavior after intervention efforts have been initiated. (Monitoring methods are described in Chapter Seven.) Useful case management information is provided by continuing to monitor behavior after intervention, in that change (for the better or worse) can be carefully tracked on an ongoing basis and intervention plans rearranged as necessary. Additional advantages of a baseline include gathering an accurate estimate of the actual severity, variability, and range of behavior (perhaps this has been over- or underestimated by the client), determining any systematic changes that occur prior to intervention perhaps from assessment alone, and allowing the observer to become more familiar with the repertoire of the person observed, as well as with possible environmental events associated with behaviors of interest. For example, perhaps a wife is recording how often her husband says something pleasant to her, as well as what she says following such statements, and finds that she seldom supports such statements. Such observation can offer information concerning possible functional relationships between selected behaviors and environmental events, including the actions of significant others.

Specific observable responses to be increased and decreased will have been identified in previous steps. This process may have necessitated observation of the client and significant others either in simulated situations or in the natural environment. In order to permit data collection concerning the frequency of a behavior, decisions must be made as to what response characteristic is most appropriate and how to observe it. Possible response characteristics that could be recorded include frequency of behavior, magnitude, duration, and latency. A decision must be made concerning which of these will allow an accurate representation of behavior and what can be collected in terms of expense and resources available. For example, insomnia may be measured by latency to falling asleep, number of hours slept, or number of times the client awoke in the night. The exact method selected will usually reflect a compromise between expense involved in gathering data and the precision (accuracy) of a given method. Ideally, the data collection method would provide a complete view of the actual frequency of selected behaviors, that is, a quantitative continuous measure. Often one must settle for less precise measures; for example, rather than measuring the amount of time one is late for work, simply noting whether the client was or was not late (a dichotomous measure). Of course, information is lost as one progresses from continuous recording to less complete forms of recording. However, the important point is to select a method that will provide reasonably accurate information in a manageable way. A recording procedure must then be selected—that is, a way to record the response characteristic that has been selected—and a decision made concerning who is to record the information and when it is to be collected. (See Chapter Seven.) For example, if behavior leaves a product, such as a number of answers on a test, these products can be counted. However, most behaviors of concern do not leave observable products, and therefore some other recording procedure must be used, such as time sampling or interval recording. A data recording form must be developed that permits easy, accurate collection of information. Codes may be developed for specific behaviors to simplify monitoring. Only behavior or related events are recorded. Inferences are avoided. It is often helpful to note nonverbal behavior as well as verbal behavior in gathering a complete description of relevant antecedent and consequences events.

After selecting an appropriate response measure, deciding on a recording procedure, and testing it out to make sure that it produces accurate and reliable information (see Chapter Seven), baseline information can be collected. Gelfand and Hartmann (1975) recommended reviewing a data collection checklist prior to collection of data. Items on this list include rechecking behavioral definitions; making sure equipment needed for data collection is at hand (for example, pencils, stopwatches, data sheets); making sure data sheets are labeled and dated; checking whether enough information is being collected; and arranging (if possible) for a reliability check if none has been taken within the past five to six days. Collection of baseline information should be continued until a stable rate of behavior is obvious, or until it seems obvious that behavior is not consistently changing in the desired direction without any change efforts. Data should be collected over an entire week if the behavior can occur on weekends as well as weekdays, because different conditions are often present on weekends, which will cause the behavior to be different in frequency on Saturday and Sunday. If behavior can only occur in certain situations (such as a classroom), it is only collected there. Behavior is usually collected for at least five to seven days and, if a formal analysis of data is to be carried out, a minimum of ten data points is desired within each condition, including baseline (Jones, Vaught, and Reid, 1973). Baseline data may indicate a gradual change in behavior day to day. Number of instructions followed may gradually increase (a positive trend) or ability to approach a feared object may gradually decrease (a negative change). A change program can be initiated if the change is in a direction opposite to that desired, or if the change is in the desired direction but is very gradual. A successful program should increase the rate of change (in the latter case) and reverse the trend in the former case. A sudden shift of behavior in the desired direction may indicate a reactive effect of recording, and thus data collection should be continued. A decreasing frequency of a problematic behavior during baseline will make it difficult to ascertain whether or not a change attempt made any difference, because the rate of behavior was already decreasing. With low-frequency behaviors, or when it is necessary to initiate intervention immediately, a pre-baseline (the client's estimate of the frequency of a behavior) can be accepted. Baseline information may already exist with some behaviors, such as frequency of arrests or attendance at a drug rehabilitation program.

The most problematic type of baseline data indicates large day-to-day fluctuations in behavior. This is a clue that different contexts in which the behavior takes place may not have been taken into account. Let us say that the baseline reveals very different rates of a child's compliance at home in the afternoon and in the evening. The presence of the father in the evening may be critical to these varying rates. It may be necessary to separately record the frequency of behavior under these different situations. Compliance when the father is present could be recorded separately from compliance when only the mother is present. Separate recording of these two behaviors in situations may then result in a stable baseline.

One rule of thumb that has been generated to decide how many baseline sessions to include is: "Three plus one additional day for each 10 percent of variability—that is, number of days of baseline = 3 + 10 ([highest rate − lowest rate]/highest rate). For example, if the number of homework problems solved varied from 6 to 20 during the first three days of baseline, continue to take baseline data for seven additional days—10 [(20 − 6) ÷ 20] = 7" (Gelfand and Hartmann, 1975, p. 232). Of course, what is ideal often diverges considerably from what it is possible to collect, and these practical considerations may make this rule impossible to follow.

Grouping data into larger time segments, such as instructions followed per week, rather than instructions followed per day, may also decrease day-to-day variability; however, this will obscure possible controlling factors. Information is often gathered regarding the situations in which a behavior occurs as well as its duration or magnitude, and examination of weekly records will indicate the frequency of behavior in different contexts. For example, smoking may be more frequent on weekends than during the week, because the client participates in more social events that are cues for this behavior. Examination of baseline data will thus reveal situations in which behavior has a high probability and those in which it has a low probability. A decrease in smoking and an increase in desirable alternatives may be most easily attempted in the latter. Also, different incompatible behaviors may be possible in different situations, and such data allow their careful arrangement. A chart with days along the top and codes for situations along the left is useful for recording the frequency of a behavior in each situation (Watson and Tharp, 1972). This chart can be reviewed after a few days of data have been collected to ascertain the relationship between a behavior and given events. If a goal is to encourage similar behaviors in other situations, baseline data should also be gathered in these situations. This data can then be compared with later generalization probes.

Identifying Objectives

Specific objectives must be identified for each problem area of focus. Specification of desired outcomes allows the client and counselor to fully understand the purpose of their contact, permits the counselor to assess whether she has the skills available to attain outcomes, and guides the selection of change plans. Some objectives can be determined at a very early point; for example, a need for a different housing space may be quite clear during the first interview, as well as the characteristics that such a space must have. (See, for example, the profile in Figure 2.) Steps to alter this problem may be initiated while identification of additional desired outcomes and other assessment steps are pursued. With vague presenting problems such as depression, general unhappiness, an impossible spouse, or an uncontrollable child, specific objectives may not emerge until further assessment information is collected. Specification of objectives entails three components: (1) description of what behaviors are to take place; (2) in what situations; and (3) with what frequency, duration, or intensity. Examples include ten long-division problems completed per hour (in math class); one occurrence of snacking per day (eating of any food outside of mealtimes); zero tantrums per day; and four initiations of conversation with an eligible male per week. Criteria that will be employed in judging performance should be included in the description of objectives. If neatness is a criterion that will be used to assess math problems correctly completed, this must be defined. Snacking may be defined as consumption of any food outside of mealtimes or as eating high-calorie foods outside of mealtimes.

The objective in the first example in the previous paragraph refers to a behavior to be increased whereas the last two examples refer to behaviors to be decreased. In other instances, the goal may be to stabilize a variable behavior or to vary the frequency of a stable behavior. A young woman may only sporadically visit places where she can start conversations with eligible males and the goal may be to have such visits occur on a more regular basis. Or a man may use the same opening line whenever he attempts to initiate a conversation, and a goal might be to vary his opening statements. Another goal may be to maintain a behavior at its current frequency.

Objectives must be clearly specified for each separate problem area. Multiple objectives may be required to address one problem. Let us say the presenting problem is a six-year-old who does not get along at school. Assessment may indicate that he does not get along with his teacher or his peers. Components of the former might include not completing assignments in class and not following instructions. Problems with his peers might include isolating himself from them. The objectives in this example might include increasing assignments completed on time from zero to all assigned, increasing instructions followed from 25 percent to 80 percent, and increasing time with peers during free time from 10 percent to 60 percent. Each of these may require further specification. It may be necessary to identify level of correctness and perhaps neatness in relation to assignments, and to identify how the child is to interact with his peers. A series of intermediate steps may be required for each. The most common error made in attempting to identify objectives is a lack of precision as to exactly what is to be done. Another common error is stating objectives negatively, in terms of "not doing" something; for example, *not* being rude to service people, *not* getting upset. This has been called the "dead man's error"—these objectives could be satisfied by a dead person (Lindsley, 1968b). Objectives should be stated in positive terms whenever possible, identifying what the client should do *more* of and attempting to increase this behavior. In the first example, the identified behavior to increase might be making polite requests; in the second, it might be remaining calm in certain situations. A variety of specified objectives are given in the following list.

1. Spend one half-hour talking about husband's work each weekday.
2. Complete four typed pages of dissertation each weekday.
3. Return greeting in appropriate fashion (say "Hi" or "Hello" and look at the person and smile).

4. Wash the dishes and put them away within one hour after dinner each weekday.
5. Wash hands only when they are actually dirty and never when it is thought that they are "contaminated."
6. Attend school four days a week.
7. Complete all assigned homework on time.
8. Sign up for food stamp program within one week.
9. Telephone an acquaintance and talk for fifteen minutes each day.
10. Wear orthodontic device during all waking hours.
11. Initiate one topic of conversation during each conversation you have that is longer than ten minutes.

One error to guard against is considering the problem to be *time spent* on some activity rather than specifying a behavior. An example is that of studying. The practitioner who accepts as the problem too little time spent studying may set a goal of increasing time spent on studying and find that the client is spending more time "studying," perhaps sitting with a book in hand, but finds to his dismay that there is no improvement in achievement. Simply spending more time at a given task does not necessarily lead to greater production. The problem selected for change should be behavior, such as problems completed, pages written, pages read, and so forth. It is helpful to scan objectives to ensure that they have been fully specified. Are necessary behaviors identified? Are there ways in which the client could act that would conform with the description of an objective, but that would not bring him closer to his goals? If such deficiencies are found, performance criteria are not yet complete. Is it necessary to establish a time period for given behaviors, and has this been done? Is the context in which the behavior is to occur noted? Has a frequency or duration criterion been set? Objectives should also be scanned along ethical dimensions. Will achievement of the objectives be of benefit to the client, or is it really for the benefit of someone else?

Scaling of Objectives. A scale may be designed that identifies a series of increasingly desired outcomes for each problem

area, as in the example in Table 2. This depicts possible outcomes in a program designed to decrease colitis attacks and to
alter perception of stressful interpersonal interactions (Youell
and McCullough, 1975). The most unfavorable outcomes are
represented by the baseline frequency of the behaviors to be
changed. Formation of such a list has been termed *goal attainment scaling* (Kiresuk and Sherman, 1968).

Table 2. Goal Attainment Scale for Client

Date: 10/24/73	Colitis Attack	Cognitive Hypothesis Testing
Most unfavorable outcome thought likely	One per day	Every stress transaction per week seen as attack on self
Less than expected success with treatment	One every other day	One out of 4 times per week considers that a stress transaction might not be attack on self
Expected level of treatment success	One per week	Completes Treatment Steps 4 and 5 *after* every stress transaction[a]
More than expected success with treatment	One every 2 weeks	Completes Treatment Steps 4 and 5 *during* stress transactions some of the time[a]
Best anticipated success with treatment	None per month	Completes Treatment Steps 4 and 5 *during* stress transactions all of the time[a]

[a]Intervention steps over Sessions 5-18 were as follows: (1) review of self-report
material on audiotape; (2) attempt by the counselor to reconstruct a "functional narrative" of interpersonal transactions by questioning the client; (3) review of client's
emotional reactions and thoughts during interactions; (4) requesting the client to
consider whether she had actually been rejected during an encounter or whether
some other possibility might be more likely; and (5) instructing the client to contact
the person involved in the encounter to determine the accuracy of her original hypotheses, that she had been rejected.

Source: Youell and McCullough (1975, p. 743).

Criteria for Selection of Objectives. Criteria that apply to
selection of desired outcomes were discussed previously. These
include annoyance and danger value to the client and to others,
and degree of interference in the client's life. A very important
one is amenability to change. If there is no access to any of the

factors that influence a behavior, change in this behavior should not be selected as an objective. There must be some leverage to alter relevant antecedents or consequences. Selection of goals that are easiest to attain has been suggested as a criterion, on the basis that this will provide an early success experience for the client, so that skills learned in handling easier problems can then be employed with more difficult problems, and so that significant others will expect more positive behaviors. This criterion must be balanced against the criterion of annoyance value. Both criteria can be considered by selecting the behavior with the highest annoyance value, but working on this in small steps, with each step having a high probability of success.

Objectives selected should lead to benefits for the client rather than to losses. This criterion calls for careful identification of the situations in which new behaviors will be displayed and anticipation of the possible consequences that might occur. If an objective requires many small steps, it should only be selected if it is possible to work on it in an incremental way. Importance of a problem area in relation to the overall functioning of a client is another criterion that must be considered. If a college student wishes to go to medical school, but is having a problem studying, cannot get along with his parents, and just had a fight with his roommate, it would be most important in terms of his overall life to address the studying behavior. If a woman is not particularly happy in her job, is very lonely since she has no friends or dates, and worries that she is not a good card player, it would be important to pursue social contacts as well as her job, because both areas are central to her existence.

Specification of objectives is a critical requirement of a behavioral model. Unless you and the client know exactly what changes are to be pursued, it will not be possible to achieve these effectively and efficiently, nor will it be possible to evaluate progress. Many studies of interpersonal helping have found a lack of specification even in situations where major decisions rest on the extent to which changes occur, such as in foster care (Gambrill and Wiltse, 1974).

Identifying Subgoals and Client Assets. To most effectively achieve desired outcomes, it is important to identify and build on client assets. The skills needed to reach a given objective should be carefully matched against those that the client already possesses. Subsequent steps build on client resources in a way that enables gradual and comfortable change, taking advantage of already existing skills. The first steps encouraged are those that represent the closest approximation to the goal that is comfortable and achievable. If a client is interested in increasing the frequency with which he introduces topics of conversation, the first goal may be to introduce a topic, with which he is relatively comfortable, during two conversations he has each day that last five minutes or more. The next step might include initiating more topics per conversation, including ones that are somewhat more difficult for him to introduce. Each step should be described in specific terms that require a minimum of interpretation (Ayllon and Azrin, 1968b).

Progress achieved with initial steps provides information as to what the next subgoals (intermediate steps) should be. Weekly assignment sheets describing the client's current relevant repertoire as well as the subgoals selected for that week can be employed to concretize agreements as to goals, to maintain attention on use of client assets, and to provide a record of weekly progress (Schwartz and Goldiamond, 1975). An example of an assignment sheet is shown in Figure 6. One goal for this client was to become more independent. The client decided that he should learn to drive a car and then buy one, so he could leave his parents home for even a short time. He had already passed the written test for his driver's license, one of the requisites for obtaining a license. The second item concerned career choice; the third, both independence and a feeling of weekend depression. The latter was considered to result from lack of reinforcement on weekends, which could be averted by planning activities for those days. The fourth item addressed the problem of loneliness and his shyness with girls.

Additional examples of program worksheets are given in Figures 7 and 8. The first is an example offered by Schwartz and Goldiamond (1975) and the second is a worksheet employed with a father who wished his son returned from foster care (Stein and Gambrill, 1976b). See Figure 2 for problem profile. Note that subgoals are based on available client assets. Obliga-

Figure 6. Program Worksheet: Robert Jones, June 28

Available Assets	*Subgoals*
1. Passed written test for driver's license.	1. Pay tuition at auto school. Take at least *one* lesson.
2. Received catalogues from art school.	2. Discuss with professors X and Y about next steps.
3. Spent last Sunday in Loop.	3. Plan and carry out activity for Saturday and Sunday in downtown Chicago (or Hyde Park).
4. Had coffee with Jean two times.	4. Ask Jean to lunch.

Program Notes

1. A great step forward toward eventual "independence."
2. Career choice.
3. Break the weekend "depression," also tied to "independence."
4. The next time you have coffee with Jean, you might suggest that you have lunch together.

Source: Schwartz and Goldiamond (1975, p. 120).

Figure 7. Program Worksheet: John Smith, June 17

Available Assets	*Subgoals*
1. Has ability to conceptualize and some organizational skills, many legal skills.	1. Arrange schedule so that work done is done between 9 A.M. and 5 P.M. Leave materials at work, leave briefcase at work.
2. Can enjoy wife and children if not hassled by work, distractions.	2. At home, spend at least thirty minutes with children (if they wish) and at least one hour with wife alone.
3. Go out with wife at least one time this week.	3. Enjoy each other's company on the occasions that they go out or have time alone.
4. Has control over certain contingencies; for example, can set own hours.	4. Analyze work situation and bring in lists of changes that would facilitate Goal Number 1.
5. Is keeping current record exceptionally well.	5. Keep new records.

Program Notes

1. Start out day by *initiating* chat with office mate. Take him into your confidence, tell him you're going to try to complete your work at office. Enlist his cooperation.
2 and 3. Tell kids and wife of resolution; ask for their help.
4. Use legal pads; separate pages for categories.
5. Refer to past records for guides.

Source: Schwartz and Goldiamond (1975, pp. 177-178).

Figure 8. Program Worksheet: Mr. R., February 16

Available Assets	Subgoals
1. He knows where the employment office is and can fill out required forms.	1. Register at the state unemployment office within four working days.
2. He can identify relevant agencies and complete required forms.	2. Register with two employment agencies in the city within four working days.
3. He has access to a newspaper and knows where to look for printing press operator jobs.	3. Review the newspaper want ads daily, specifically looking for job advertisements as a printing press operator.
4. He has adequate telephone skills to set up appropriate appointments.	4. Make appointments for interviews for any open positions as a press operator.
5. He has needed interview skills to make an adequate impression and has had experience as a printing press operator.	5. Follow through on any appointments he is able to make by presenting himself for the interview on time.

Source: Stein and Gambrill (1976b, p. 21).

tions of the counselor should be included on the program worksheet. For the worksheet directly above, counselor tasks included contacting Mr. R. by telephone each day to discuss progress, and meeting with the client to offer him help should any difficulty be encountered in trying to accomplish subgoals.

Some subgoals involve increasing requirements of the same behavior, whereas others involve different behaviors. Let us say that an objective is to increase the number of homework assignments completed from an initial level of one per week to fifteen per week. The intermediate steps might be two, four, six, and so on, up to the accomplishment of the desired level. In other instances, the list of intermediate behaviors will involve different behaviors, rather than simply more or less of the same behavior. If a client wishes to increase social contacts, the following behaviors may be involved:

1. Locating places where he or she can initiate conversations with people with whom he or she would like to increase the frequency of contacts.
2. Visiting one of these places two times a week and initiating a brief conversation (1 minute).
3. Visiting such places two times a week and initiating two longer conversations (5 to 15 minutes).

4. Visiting such places three times a week and initiating one longer conversation (16 minutes to one hour).
5. Arranging for a future brief meeting say over coffee or a beer (for at least one hour).
6. Arranging for an evening meeting (at least two hours).

The particular behaviors contained in the list depends on the unique repertoire of each client. With some clients, it may also be necessary to provide training in how to increase opinion statements, how to disagree in a way that does not put others off, and how to terminate interactions.

Weekly assignment sheets allow the careful monitoring of progress. Each subgoal is discussed·as to whether it was accomplished. If selection of goals has been in accord with client skill and comfort levels, it is likely that they will be achieved. These accomplishments become the available repertoire informing selection of the next set of subgoals. If goals are not reached, then a discussion is held to try to determine what hindered their accomplishment. A first question to raise is whether the program was carried out as agreed on. If not, the reasons for this are pursued. Perhaps instructions were not clear or the client did not fully understand the relationship of subgoals or the procedure selected to achievement of outcomes. If either of the latter reasons were related to failure of the client to carry out agreed-on assignments, procedures and rationales can be reviewed and the assignment pursued in the next week. Such a review will also help to bring out previously unexpressed client objections to subgoals or procedures and will prohibit premature abandonment of effective plans. Notes recorded by the client during the week may point to factors that hindered compliance.

Perhaps the most common reason for failure to meet subgoals is that the steps agreed on were too big for the client and smaller approximations are needed. Subgoals should always be selected that the client is very likely to attain; it is always better to go too slowly than too fast.

The client can be encouraged to gradually assume more responsibility for identifying subgoals and for selecting programs to achieve them by filling out a weekly worksheet in which he first identifies how subgoals relate to final goals (Schwartz and Goldiamond, 1975). This serves as a check that subgoals are clearly related to contracted goals. The client can also be requested to write down agenda items for next session, including items that may not necessarily relate to contracted goals but that he or she would like to discuss. More responsibility is then gradually assumed for stating subgoals and for identifying programs and variables related to attainment of subgoals.

Impediments to Identification of Objectives. The identification of specific outcomes and subgoals may seem a (deceptively) easy matter. This misperception of its simplicity may be one of the impediments to its completion. Such a misperception hinders devotion of attention to this task, which can often be a difficult one, requiring time and the collection of additional information. Another impediment is the view that subgoals seem unworthy of attention. One subgoal by itself may not seem particularly valuable. Thus, another difficulty is the failure to see the many tasks that may be required to achieve a given goal, and the failure to see the relationship of each one to the attainment of that goal. A foster care worker who tells a natural mother that she must relocate in a new apartment if she is to get her child back may fail to identify essential features of the required housing space, and may fail to realize that perhaps the client does not have the skills to carry out the many behaviors required for accomplishment of this objective. Does the client know where to look for vacancies? Does she know what to find out about each apartment? Does she feel comfortable enough to talk to landlords? Can she manage her behavior so as to complete each necessary step? Sometimes a counselor seems to be uninterested in identifying the specific behaviors that are required to obtain a given objective, as if this task would detract from the pleasure involved in interpersonal helping. To some, the task seems mechanical. However, nonrecognition of individual variability is far more "mechanical." With each person, the behaviors that need to be developed may be somewhat different. Determination of this requires the careful identification of what the client can now do, and matching this against what he would like to do.

Another factor that hinders specification of objectives is

a lack of requisite skills for accomplishing this critical task. A counselor must be able to recognize when an objective is specified and when it is not. Questions of use in scanning objectives include the following: (1) Are behaviors identified? (2) Have initial subgoals been identified? (3) Are situations identified? (4) Are performance criteria identified; that is, will it be clear when an objective has been accomplished? (5) Could two or more people agree as to whether a task has been accomplished? and (6) Is there any way the objective could be satisfied in an unsatisfactory way? A vague goal, such as "helping with housecleaning more often," could be met by a wide range of behaviors, including cleaning the windows once a month, vacuuming the living room once a week, vacuuming every day, wiping down the kitchen once a week, and straightening up the house every day. None of these may refer to what a client would like to achieve.

A lack of commitment to a "constructional approach" to change (see Schwartz and Goldiamond, 1975) in which client assets are carefully considered may hinder careful identification of appropriate subgoals and outcomes. A lack of exposure to the value of specific identification of outcomes and subgoals for case management purposes may also impede efforts in this direction. If subgoals are clearly identified and the client runs into difficulty, the troublesome factors can more readily be located.

A lack of interest in forming a clear client-counselor contract may also discourage identification of clear desired outcomes and subgoals, as will a lack of interest in evaluation of change efforts. Only if objectives are clearly stated can careful evaluation take place. Lastly, the process takes time and effort. Unless there is some incentive for doing so, it is unlikely to be accomplished. Perhaps not until the benefits are seen will this process be carried out in each case.

The Reactive Effects of Assessment

Identifying desired outcomes in specific terms and locating environmental and personal factors that are related to their achievement may themselves induce some changes in client behavior. In the following passage, Sobell describes this effect with clients with drinking problems.

> Merely performing a behavioral analysis of a situation may have the effect of a therapeutic intervention. More specifically, a self-awareness of how certain situational factors influence behavior, emotional states included, may be sufficient for some clients to take action to modify or avoid those situations. Likewise, the informational value of recognizing both the immediate and delayed consequences associated with drinking behavior may have some direct immediate implications for the [client]. For instance, a client may have been unaware of the powerful influence of short-term consequences on his behavior. Additionally, when behaviors and situations are specified as precisely as possible and vague terminology such as *dependency needs, self-destructive needs, power needs,* or *alcoholism*, is avoided, the problem may to some extent become less mysterious to the patient. [Sobell, Sobell, and Sheahan, 1973, p. 3]

Whether or not assessment will actually result in a change of behavior depends on whether the client possesses skills needed to alter his behavior. For example, a client may now realize that the reason he drinks when things go well is because he worries that he cannot handle the new requirements on him at such times. This realization will not be helpful unless he possesses needed skills, such as social or vocational ones, that allow him to do well in these contexts.

Summary

During initial contact between client and counselor, an overview of desired outcomes is gathered, and one or more areas are selected on which to focus. The behavioral referents for each area are determined, as well as relevant antecedents and consequences. Behaviors and thoughts to be increased, as well as behaviors to be decreased, are identified. Location of specific behaviors in situations is facilitated by careful selection of questions, role playing, and information collected by the client or counselor in the natural environment. Special attention is devoted to selecting client assets that can be usefully employed in change efforts. A count of how often a behavior, thought, or feeling occurs prior to intervention is gathered, so that change programs can be accurately evaluated and the severity of problems determined.

The obligations of the counselor and client are concretized in a written, signed contract that describes the obligations of both the counselor and the client, the objectives of intervention, the nature of intervention, the duration of treatment, as well as the criteria to be employed for measuring success. Contracts are amended as appropriate over the course of assessment and intervention. Completion of assessment may be required to identify some of these factors. The objectives of intervention are precisely described, including intermediate ones. Initial subgoals are selected in accord with client assets, and subsequent subgoals build on increasing client skill.

6

The identification of resources that can be employed in change efforts is an important aspect of assessment. They include available reinforcers, available mediators, available contexts for change, available use of response cost or punishing events, and personal assets.

Reinforcers

Behavioral intervention entails rearrangement of the relationships between behavior and its antecedents and consequences. There is a particular emphasis on increasing desirable behaviors. This focus requires a search for positive reinforcers that can be employed in change programs. Whenever possible, natural reinforcers (those already present in the natural environ-

Locating Environmental and Personal Resources

ment) are employed. There is a variety of types of positive reinforcers, including social reinforcers such as attention, high-probability behaviors such as reading and walking, consumables, material items, informative feedback, and self-reinforcers.

The ideal reinforcer is nonsatiating, can be delivered consistently, and is nondistracting. If reinforcers are too distracting, their sampling may interfere with the performance of behaviors. Satiation occurs when so much of a reinforcer is provided that it no longer increases behavior that it follows. For example, food may serve as a reinforcer for someone who is hungry, but not for someone who has just consumed a large meal. Satiation can be avoided by using a range of reinforcers and by making special training sessions brief, if this is possible. For example, Gelfand and Hartmann (1975) recommend training sessions fifteen minutes in length with preschool children, and no longer than thirty minutes for older children. Brief and frequent sessions are usually more effective than infrequent longer sessions with children. A third way to avoid satiation effects is to use a conditioned reinforcer (such as tokens, money, or points) that are unrelated to specific states of deprivation. Satiation can also be avoided by offering reinforcers in small amounts (one raisin rather than a box of raisins). Thus, it is also important that reinforcers be offered in small amounts.

The time interval between the occurrence of a behavior and a consequence is often critical; therefore, the reinforcer should be deliverable immediately. If there is a time lapse between a behavior to be increased and the delivery of a reinforcer, an alternative behavior that is not desirable may occur during the time lapse, and the delayed reinforcer will increase the undesirable behavior. If a reinforcer cannot be delivered immediately, tokens or points may be employed to bridge the gap between performance of desired behaviors and reinforcers. With older children and adults, if contingencies between behavior and consequences have been described, delay in delivery of reinforcers can be bridged by cognitive means—for example, by self-statements that remind one of these contingencies (Bandura, 1969).

If reinforcers are to be dispensed by a mediator, they must be under the control of this person; otherwise, the client will have access to the reinforcer without carrying out desired behaviors. Selecting reinforcers that are not usually available will help to prevent unauthorized access and will offer something extra, rather than placing something freely available on a contingency, which may be experienced negatively. An obvious requirement of a reinforcer is that it be practical. It must be within the means of available resources, be easily transportable, and readily available.

It is as important to specify reinforcers as it is to specify behaviors. If the dimensions of a reinforcer are not identified, it will not be possible to offer the reinforcer consistently, or to gradually increase the amount of reinforcement. Lack of specification of reinforcers can cause disagreement between clients or between counselors and clients. If time with a parent is to serve as a reinforcer, it is important to identify its duration, when it is to take place, and what will be done during this time. If a candy bar is to be employed as a reinforcer, the agreement should identify the size of the candy bar. Each person has a unique reinforcer profile—that list of items that can function as reinforcers. Each person might rank given reinforcers differently in importance. An attempt is made to locate reinforcers that can be employed, that can be employed ethically, and that are strong, rather than weak.

How to Locate Reinforcers. There is a variety of ways to locate possible reinforcers. These include verbal or written reports of the client or of significant others, observation of the client, and trying out different items in the natural environment. The advantage of verbal or written reports is that one does not have to enter the natural environment to gather needed information. The disadvantage is that verbal reports may not be as accurate as information gained from direct observation of the client. Ayllon and Azrin (1968b), for example, found that, although some hospital residents indicated that they did not want anything, observation by staff led to the discovery of several reinforcing events. They also found that residents would reject items that they had requested.

Three factors must be balanced in the selection of procedures employed to attempt to determine reinforcers: (1) predictive accuracy expected of a given procedure; (2) constraints about entering certain situations; and (3) the costs involved in employing any one procedure. The information provided by self-reports indicates *possible* reinforcers. Not until items are made contingent on selected behaviors, and a future increase in the behavior is found, can we be sure that a reinforcer has been identified and is being appropriately employed. The various means for attempting to identify reinforcers are listed as follows:

1. *Observe the client's behavior* and see what events follow his behavior and what his high-probability behaviors are. Some behaviors are more probable than others. If we counted the number of times during the day that we engage in given behaviors, we would find

that some occur very frequently, such as getting up from a chair, drinking coffee, reading a magazine; some occur fairly often; and others occur very seldom. High-probability behaviors can be used to reinforce low-probability behaviors (Premack, 1959, 1965). That is, if Behavior A (drinking a cup of coffee) is more probable than Behavior B (completing case reports), and you wish to accelerate the rate of B, you can do so by making A contingent on B, so that to drink a cup of coffee you must complete some portion of the case report. It should be noted that a distinction must be made between response probability and response frequency. The term *probability*, as originally employed by Premack (1965), refers to a situation in which a person has free access to a variety of behaviors and the probability of each is determined by the relative amount of time spent in each. The term *response frequency* indicates the rate of occurrence of a behavior whether or not its availability is contingent or noncontingent (Mahoney, 1974a; Danaher, 1974). The high frequency of some behaviors, such as chore completion, may result more from the contingencies placed on them than from their status as Premackian reinforcers, as Mahoney (1974a) points out. The failure of many programs attempting to employ relatively trivial "high-probability behaviors" such as getting up from a chair or opening a window may be due to a confusion of response frequency with probability. In Mahoney's view, the success of some of these programs is probably caused by the "cueing" function of "high-probability activities"; that is, they serve as reminders to perform low-frequency behaviors to be increased.

2. *Ask the client.* The client may be asked what he likes, what he likes to do and with whom, and what he likes to receive and from whom. Information may also be gained as to what he does in certain situations, to identify high-probability behaviors. Clients may also be asked what they would like to do that they do not do, or whether there were things they used to do that they

liked. If general statements are employed, like "love" or "kindness," the referents for these terms must be identified as well as the mediators of these events. Tone of voice and the frequency with which some event or item is mentioned may provide cues as to reinforcing potential. The items that are mentioned should be written down and the client requested to rank them in terms of desirability. Addison and Homme (1966) developed a pictorial display of reinforcers for children. The child is asked to look through a series of pictures and point to the one he or she would like. These include such items as being wheeled around by the counselor in a chair.

3. *Ask significant others.* Parents could be asked what items their child likes, what he likes to do, with whom he spends time, and what he does during different times of the day. Significant others may be surprisingly ignorant concerning reinforcers for those with whom they interact. Tharp and Wetzel (1969) note how surprising it is that the primary mediators of a problem child often know little about his favorite activities and events. The same may be found with spouses. Often, significant others have relied so heavily on aversive control that they have not devoted attention to the discovery of positive reinforcers. The importance of items identified by significant others must be checked out, either by asking the person involved, or by making them contingent on some behavior and seeing whether the behavior increases.

4. *Employ variations of identified reinforcers.* See which reinforcer the client selects (Ayllon and Azrin, 1968b). For example, different types of magazines could be made available to see which ones the client prefers.

5. *Employ a written schedule.* The Pleasant Events Schedule (MacPhillamy and Lewinsohn, 1972, 1975), for example, contains a variety of items. The client is requested to rate how pleasurable each item is on a three-point scale and to indicate how often each event happened in the past month. This schedule can be use-

ful in identifying events that are not being employed as reinforcers. A list can be made, from the Pleasant Events Schedule, of highly enjoyable items, which can then be ranked in terms of importance. Keat (1974) has developed a survey schedule of rewards for children aged five to twelve years.

6. *Be aware of specific states of deprivation.* Deprivation may point to reinforcing events. For a client who lives alone and has little contact with others, social attention may be a powerful reinforcer.

Types of Reinforcers. There are many different types of reinforcers, social events being one of the most important sources. Other types of reinforcers include behaviors that have a high probability of occurring, consumables, material items, informative feedback, and self-reinforcers.

Social reinforcers. Social reinforcers include events mediated by others (approving words or statements, written statements of approval, nonverbal approval), as well as certain activities. Social reinforcers have a number of advantages. They do not take much time to give. No prior preparation is required, as may be needed for an activity. Satiation is not as much of a problem as it is with food. Social reinforcers typically do not distract from desirable behaviors. A very important advantage of social reinforcers is that they are part of the natural environment. Social approval is an important conditioned reinforcer used to establish and maintain behavior. The use of social reinforcers will thus decrease problems of maintaining behaviors. Examples of each type of social reinforcer are presented in the following list. Many were drawn from the lists presented by Madsen and Madsen (1970, pp. 116-120) and MacPhillamy and Lewinsohn (1972).

APPROVING WORDS AND STATEMENTS

Yes.	Thank you.
Good!	I'm glad you're here.
Great!	You're tops on my list.
Fine answer.	I like the way you explained that.
Uh-huh.	That's a nice expression.
Keep going.	That's interesting.

Great job!	I like that.
Terrific!	I really enjoyed being with you.
Beautiful work.	That's very imaginative.
Indeed!	That was very nice of you.
Right.	You look great!
How beautiful.	That's a good point to bring up.
Yeah!	I agree.

Approving words or statements may refer to what a person is saying, something he is doing, or to some physical attribute.

NONVERBAL EXPRESSIONS OF APPROVAL

Facial

Looking
Smiling
Winking
Nodding
Grinning
Laughing (happy)
Chuckling
Cheering
Pressing lips affirmatively
Rolling eyes enthusiastically

Bodily

Clapping hands
Signaling O.K.
Thumbs up
Nodding head
Jumping up and down

Touching

Touching hands
Ruffling hair
Touching head
Arm around shoulder
Dancing
Caressing back of neck
Kissing
Hugging
Squeezing hand
Nudging
Leaning over
Placing face close to person's face.
Tickling
Cupping face in hands
Guiding with hand

WRITTEN WORDS AND SYMBOLS

Bravo!	Excellent
Congratulations	Outstanding
Very good	Yes!
Well written	+
Gold star	√

Written words and symbols are often used in educational settings.

High-probability behaviors. High-probability behaviors share many of the advantages of social reinforcers. Many are a part of the natural environment. They are readily available and can be employed to maintain as well as to establish behavior. If a variety of activities are available, satiation should not be a problem. They are more distracting than are social reinforcers, in that participation in an activity often precludes continuation of other behaviors. Also, some activities require prior preparation and so may not be able to be sampled immediately following behavior. Many high-probability behaviors involve social interaction; others consist of events that can be sampled alone. The following are selected from the Pleasant Events Schedule (MacPhillamy and Lewinsohn, 1972), and from Madsen and Madsen (1970).

BEHAVIORS INVOLVING SOCIAL INTERACTION

Walking with someone
Talking about old times
Preparing for holidays together
Visiting friends
Meeting someone new
Flirting
Going to the movies with someone
Going bowling with someone
Playing cards
Doing something nice for someone
Attending a club meeting
Being asked for help
Selling something
Being at the beach
Teaching someone
Talking about politics

Introducing people who like
    each other
Visiting relatives
Giving someone a gift
Playing basketball
Playing pool
Listening to jokes
Making people laugh
Going on a picnic
Helping someone
Singing in a choir
Playing Frisbee
Answering questions
Attending church
Giving a massage
Being with a spouse

OTHER BEHAVIORS

Listening to music
Walking
Sewing
Playing with a cat
Watching television
Reading the newspaper
Looking at beautiful scenery
Playing the guitar
Shopping
Gardening
Taking a bath
Working on a crossword
    puzzle
Writing letters
Cooking

Going fishing
Taking a trip
Skiing
Going to the library
Swimming
Taking a bus ride
Visiting a museum
Taking a nap
Wearing nice clothes
Painting
Refinishing furniture
Gathering natural objects
    (rocks, driftwood, and so on)
Doing odd jobs around the
    house

Writing in a diary
Being relaxed
Watching people
Looking at flowers

Running
Caring for house plants
Visiting garage sales
Reading a book

Preferences

For vacation days
Choice of dinner
Choice of where to sit
Choice of clothing to wear
Choice of furnishings
For a night's entertainment
Staying out later
Staying up later

Freedom From Tasks

Child care
A night out
Sleeping late
Having peace and quiet
Somebody doing the dishes
Longer lunch hour

Consumables. A variety of consumables have been employed in changing behavior. Disadvantages to their use include satiation effects and availability. Carrying them around may be awkward. Consumption of the item may distract the client from performance of desired behaviors. Some of these problems can be dealt with by employing consumables in small amounts, such as raisins, which are easy to carry around and do not take long to consume. Eatables are particularly valuable when social events do not function as reinforcers. Some examples of consumables are:

Ice cream
Popcorn
Raisins
Lemonade
Peanuts

Potato chips
Carrots
Celery
Coffee
Beer

Material items. Using material items as reinforcers usually involves engaging in an activity. If clothes are reinforcers, some activity in relation to these will occur, such as looking at clothes, wearing them, or showing them to others. If foreign stamps are a reinforcer, the collector may enjoy looking at stamps, showing them to fellow stamp collectors, and buying stamps. In beginning to search for reinforcers, the behaviors associated with various items may not be immediately evident. It may be helpful to scan for items first and then to think of the activities that are related. The advantages and disadvantages of material items as reinforcers are similar to those discussed under high-probability behaviors.

Some reinforcers can also function as generalized reinforcers (Holland and Skinner, 1961), in that they allow access
to a wide range of reinforcing events. Examples are money, approval, and tokens. Money can be used to purchase a variety of
items or to obtain access to a variety of activities. Tokens may
be traded for a range of items on a reinforcer menu. If we have
someone's approval, a variety of reinforcers may be available
from that person. Some examples of material items are:

Toys	Flowers
Tokens	Bean bag
Points	Silly putty
Gold stars	Perfume
Badges	Cassette tape
Photographs	Marbles
Beads	A tool
Records	Books
Clothes	Magazines
Birthday card	

Informative feedback. The term *feedback* as it is typically
employed has two separable components: an evaluative or approval one, and an informative one as to progress. Leitenberg,
Agras, Thompson, and Wright (1968) investigated the separate
effects of performance feedback and praise in changing phobic
behavior. Informative feedback consisted of showing the client
how long he or she remained in a feared situation. Informative
feedback can be employed separately from other reinforcers.
Such feedback can be used whenever performance criteria can
be established; for example, in terms of achievement on tests or
output on a job. Often, such criteria are already available, as in
sheltered workshops, schools, and job settings. On other occasions, they may be set; for example, number of positive statements said to children per day or number of times snacking
occurred. Feedback as to performance has been found to affect
behavior positively (Leitenberg and others, 1968); however, this
effect has often been temporary (Pommer and Streedbeck,
1974). Examples of informative feedback include time spent in
a given situation, problems completed correctly, grades, and
number of cigarettes smoked, tasks completed, calories consumed, or pounds lost.

Self-reinforcers. Self-reinforcers are consequences presented by the individual himself following behavior, and include thoughts and covert statements as well as self-presented social, material, or activity reinforcers. The following self-reinforcers are examples:

Thoughts

Thinking about a pleasant past event
Thinking about a pleasant anticipated event
Fantasizing some pleasant event
Just sitting and thinking
Thinking about people one likes
Meditating
Thinking about a hobby
Thinking about an interesting question

Positive Self-Statements

I really look nice today.
That was a good job.
That was a nice thing to do.
It worked; I was able to do it.
I did it.
That was really clever of me.
It gets easier every time.

Significant Others

Significant others (mediators) are those who interact or who could interact with clients and influence problem-related behaviors. The focus on the relationship between behavior and the environment points to their involvement whenever possible.

Finding Significant Others. Whenever the problem is an interactional one—for example, between spouses or between a parent and a child—each person is a significant other for those with whom he interacts, and thus the determination of significant others is easy. Gaining the cooperation of these individuals may not be easy. The advantage of working with mediators (significant others) is their continuing role in relation to the target person.

In many contexts, such as classrooms, work situations, and recreational groups, peers provide an important source of social support (Patterson, Littman, and Bricker, 1967; Solomon and Whaler, 1973). If they dispense more reinforcement than do authority figures such as teachers, a change in how this is distributed should be a more effective alteration than cultivating a change in weaker sources of support. In the classroom, peer influence has been helpful in modifying both management problems (Surratt, Ulrich, and Hawkins, 1969) as well as academic achievement (Willis, Crowder, and Morris, 1972). Preschool children have been enlisted to help parents train handicapped siblings (see, for example, Cash and Evans, 1975).

If significant others are not cooperative or do not seem to be available, a careful search of the client's social environment may reveal others who could be trained to provide support for behavior change. People differ greatly in terms of the social network in which they move. Many have a very limited network. The long-term resident of a mental hospital may have no contacts left in the community who would support desirable behaviors. This situation led Fairweather and his colleagues to establish a network of social contacts among people in the hospital and to move an entire group of clients into a home in the community (Fairweather, Sanders, Cressler, and Maynard, 1969).

The environment should be carefully examined to ascertain whether there are sources of social reinforcement that could be more effectively utilized to maintain or establish desirable behaviors. Each area of the client's existence should be viewed from this perspective. Friends, relatives, or acquaintances might be discovered who could, with training, fulfill this role; or "community caretakers," who are essentially invisible, because they are usually ignored in relation to their potential helping role, may be discovered, such as bartenders, hairdressers, and waitresses (Moed and Muhich, 1972). Some who occupy these roles may already be active in supporting desirable behaviors. Others may not only provide no support, but they may even punish these behaviors.

In addition to attending to possible increases of social supports from those with whom a client already interacts, new contacts may have to be cultivated. Social agencies may provide potential mediators, such as "big brothers" and "big sisters."

Contacts can be formed within recreational settings. There is currently a great waste of potential mediators, including the elderly. Elderly people can achieve the same criterion levels in child management as college students (Gelfand, Elton, and Harman, 1972). Cultivation of potential mediators has a number of advantages. This provides a way to support adaptive behavior of many more people than would be possible through continued dependence on professionals. It avoids deficiencies peculiar to traditional modes of intervention, such as difficulty in bridging from artificial to natural environments, as well as avoiding the "deviant-smithy" activities of social control agents, such as labeling and concentration on pathology (Lofland, 1969). Training mediators provides a source of trainers for others, which further avoids reliance on professionals and also has the advantage of offering intervention via peers. Also, functioning as a mediator may be highly rewarding for an individual.

Characteristics of a Good Mediator. Mediators must have access to reinforcers as well as the ability to dispense these on contingency in a consistent way. Even if significant others possess important reinforcers for a client, if these are not offered following appropriate behaviors and withheld following inappropriate ones in a consistent fashion, it is unlikely that positive changes will occur. In deciding on what significant other(s) to employ, the capabilities of each to support desirable behaviors must be assessed. An ideal situation exists when training a person how to manage behavior more positively and effectively functions as a pleasant or beneficial event for him. Foster grandparent programs not only reduce poverty among the aged poor and makes them feel more useful in their daily lives, but also children who received such care improve in their behavior (Greenleigh Associates, 1966).

Mediator Problems that May Occur. Significant others are not always cooperative. Teachers may say they do not have time to be involved; parents may be reluctant to give up reliance on aversive control, even though it has not been effective. Time may have to be devoted to discovering incentives that can be offered to mediators to change their behavior as well as to providing information describing the rationale for change efforts and benefits to be expected. Given that a client will continue to be in contact with a given person, the time taken to modify the behavior of a recalcitrant mediator is well worth it. Cues may have to be arranged to remind the mediator to provide reinforcement for appropriate behaviors, as well as training given in how to identify behaviors. Some of the mediator problems that may be found are given in the following list, together with suggestions for solving them.

First, *significant others may not possess reinforcers.* Parental attention, for example, may not be a reinforcer; and parents may not control access to desired items such as cars, money, or recreational possibilities. Unless parental access to reinforcers can be arranged, parents cannot be employed as mediators of change. A goal of intervention might be to increase the reinforcing potential of given individuals, such as establishing parental attention as a reinforcer or increasing the reinforcing qualities of a spouse.

Second, *significant others may find it aversive to offer positive reinforcers.* They may consider this bribery. Additional efforts may have to be made to differentiate bribery from the use of positive reinforcement, to point out the advantages of positive incentives, and the benefits of the change program to the mediator. The objection raised to the use of positive incentives is often of the form, "I don't want to offer her a reward for doing something she should be doing anyway." A teacher may say this about a student, a parent about a child, or a supervisor about a social worker who is not carrying out expected tasks. We also confront a situation in which there is a desire to attribute the cause of behavior to internal rather than environmental factors, and therefore not to recognize that many behaviors are maintained through what happens in the environment, rather than because of internal feelings and attitudes. Teachers who object to the use of positive incentives as bribery often deny that the money they earn for teaching is one of the important incentives for this activity. There may be a concern that the person will become dependent on positive reinforcers and will continue to demand them in the future. To date, there is no evidence to support this belief.

It should be noted that the term *bribery* is usually employed to refer to giving someone something for carrying out an unethical action. Thus the use of positive reinforcers to increase desirable behaviors could not accurately be considered bribery. It should be pointed out that any artificial reinforcers that are introduced, such as points or tokens, are only a temporary measure and that, as behavior stabilizes, these will be faded out and the natural reinforcers of praise, approval, and self-reinforcement will maintain the behavior. Mediators may be concerned that clients will become dependent on reinforcers introduced and will continue to demand these. Discussion may be required to indicate that there is no evidence that this occurs and that artificial reinforcers will be removed.

Interaction between two people may have become so aversive that it is unpleasant for one to offer positive events to another. There may even be a desire to hurt the other. A husband may be unwilling to offer his wife positive reinforcers. A more gradual approximation to offering positive events must be identified, perhaps first having him remove his attention contingent on certain behaviors of his wife. At times, this interpersonal distaste may prohibit successful change, as in the following example. "A very seriously predelinquent adolescent boy had repeatedly engaged in fist fights with his stepfather. The stepfather had hated the child for years. After four weeks of a closely proctored intervention plan, the boy's misbehavior was rapidly decreasing. The father, fearful that the boy might stay in the home if he reformed, disobeyed every instruction that our staff gave him. The case disintegrated; the boy ran away. It was very clear that the boy's continued presence in the home was so punishing to the father that the rewards our staff offered him—praise, encouragement, attention—were swamped" (Tharp and Wetzel, 1969, pp. 131-132).

One significant other may be punished by another if positive reinforcers are offered. A husband may be jealous of his wife's spending more time with a child and criticize his wife for this. An attendant may fear that he will be ridiculed by fellow employees. Or some external constraint may be present, as is illustrated in the following example. "Our staff strongly urged a widowed mother to call the juvenile authorities when next her daughter, Annie, sneaked out of the house at night. The mother was unable to do so, because this might have resulted in the daughter's being adjudicated delinquent. If the daughter were confined to a detention or correction home, the mother would have lost the pension that she administered for the daughter, and that was the family's major support. It was economically unfeasible for the mother to behave in her daughter's best interest" (Tharp and Wetzel, 1969, pp. 130-131). As Tharp and Wetzel (1969) have noted, the mediator should only be requested to engage in behaviors that are compatible with his role position and that will not be punished.

Third, *significant others may be unable to terminate reinforcement for inappropriate behavior.* Parents may be unable to control outbursts when their child engages in annoying behaviors and may sporadically reinforce such behavior. Teachers may be unable to ignore disruptive behavior on the part of their students. Special procedures, such as desensitization, may be required to enable them to tolerate such behavior so that they can withhold reinforcement for undesirable behaviors while reinforcing appropriate behaviors.

Fourth, *significant others may continue to use punishment or response cost ineffectively.* Positive reinforcement for appropriate behaviors may be diluted by being combined with punishment (Patterson, 1971a). Mediators may continue to employ high frequencies of punishment and response cost, even though these are ineffective and even though the limitations of punishment have been carefully described. Offering incentives for use of positive reinforcement may be necessary; however, this may not overcome a preference for aversive control.

Fifth, *significant others may forget to reinforce appropriate behaviors.* Cues, such as carrying tokens in a pocket, may have to be provided so that mediators will remember to reinforce behavior. The mediator may be so preoccupied with other matters, such as discord in some other interpersonal relationship, that he or she fails to reinforce behavior even though a cue is provided. The mediator may be overburdened, time-wise. He or she may have too many behaviors to reinforce and so forget some. Such problems will have to be addressed before the mediator can be effective as a change agent.

Sixth, and last, *significant others may not be able to iden-*

tify appropriate and inappropriate behaviors. Additional training may be required so the mediator can readily identify behaviors to reinforce and behaviors to ignore.

When Direct Work with Significant Others Is Not Possible

There are other possibilities for achieving change if mediators are uncooperative. The client can be trained to change the behavior of the mediator. Graubard and his colleagues (Graubard, Rosenberg, and Miller, 1971) trained children to alter the behavior of their teacher. An adolescent may be trained how to alter parental behavior if parents refuse to cooperate in a program (see, for example, Fedoravicius, 1973). Clients can be trained in self-management skills, that is, how to pinpoint and bring about changes they would like to make and how to maintain desirable behaviors (Watson and Tharp, 1972). They can be trained to scan their environment to locate reinforcers. Many people do not take advantage of possible sources, and may not even be aware of their existence.

Working directly with a client as his or her own change agent is called for when contact by the counselor with a mediator would have negative effects for the client. If the problem is lack of assertive behavior in relation to undue harrassment from a superior at work, or lack of assertive skills in asking for a raise, appropriate behaviors can be established and rehearsed in an artificial environment until the client feels comfortable with the idea of displaying these in the natural environment and is very likely to be successful (Wolpe and Lazarus, 1966).

Direct work with the client is also necessary when the behaviors to be increased will be displayed to unknown individuals. If lack of social contacts is a problem and the goal is to establish a repertoire in how to initiate contacts, these new behaviors will often be tried out with unknown persons. Here again, behaviors can be established and practiced in a simulated environment, the client can be trained to identify promising situations in which to perform these, and the behaviors can then be tried out in real-life settings.

Available Contexts for Change

Existing environments that may facilitate favorable change or maintain adaptive behaviors should be taken advantage of, because their use requires only that they be found and the person located within them (Baer and Wolf, 1970). Feldman and his colleagues integrated each of fourteen children with behavioral problems into one of fourteen recreational groups, each composed of children displaying acceptable behavior. Prosocial skills increased significantly and there were no negative consequences for the other group members (Feldman, Wodarski, Flax, and Goodman, 1972). Location of a client with a deviant repertoire in a group of people displaying adaptive behaviors permits appropriate modeling and reinforcement, and is more supportive of positive change than some of the traditional alternatives, such as institutionalization, or placing the client in a group setting where other members also exhibit deviant behavior. Selection of context must be carefully matched with objectives. Examples of possible settings include the YWCA, garden clubs, Girl Scouts, senior center recreational activities, bridge clubs, and youth centers.

Response Cost or Punishing Events

If possible, use of response cost and punishing events should be avoided in favor of positive reinforcement of desirable behaviors and withholding of reinforcement for undesirable behaviors. However, there are instances in which stronger sanctions may have to be placed on undesirable behaviors, while at the same time positive incentives are used for desirable behaviors. Response cost is preferable to the presentation of aversive events, because it entails less negative reactions. Examples of the use of response cost include losing toys for several days when these are left out, not being permitted to play pool for fifteen minutes, and paying a fine of ten points. Examples of the use of punishment includes saying no and frowning following a behavior, or helping with the dishes after supper contingent on abusive talk during dinner. (The latter may also involve a response cost component if this activity will interfere with some other desired event). Self-presented aversive events have included snapping the wrist with a rubber band (Mahoney, 1971) and losing points. If time out is to be employed, an appropriate location must be selected.

Discovering Personal Assets

Discovering the client's assets so these can be supported and made use of in problematic situations is an important part of assessment. Perhaps a client has some excellent thought patterns that allow him to focus attention while in work-related situations, but does not employ these skills in social situations when he is anxious. Perhaps he is very skilled in searching the social sphere for reinforcers, but not very good at this in relation to vocational concerns. A client may have a repertoire of reinforcing behaviors that he employs with friends but does not share with his spouse. Self-reinforcement skills may be available but not be employed in problem-related areas. Determination of the client's resources in terms of appropriate thoughts and behaviors enables the therapist to use these in problem-related situations and to point out to the client how these are already usefully employed in other situations. Clients are usually rich in the many assets they do have that could be usefully employed in a wider range of situations. Some of these skills may be located by finding out what is going well for the client (Schwartz and Goldiamond, 1975), and what problems he has successfully solved. Imagery procedures may be employed to discover useful thought patterns (see Chapter Five).

Summary

The stress on the relationship between behavior and the environment implies a focus on finding reinforcers in the natural environment that can support desirable behaviors, as well as significant others to offer these. The capabilities of significant others as change agents should be carefully assessed, as well as various reinforcers, in terms of their potential value, and community resources that may offer valuable contexts for change. Locating resources is an important part of assessment and includes determination of personal assets in terms of existing desirable behaviors and thought patterns that can be employed in change endeavors.

7

Within a behavioral framework, a variety of sources are employed for the collection of information, the verbal reports of clients within the interview being just one. Others include arranged interactions in the office and observation in the natural environment by the counselor, trained aide, or client. Since the client is in direct contact with relevant behaviors in the natural environment, and since an aim of intervention is often to offer him skills in how to identify relevant behaviors and related events, the client is often requested to gather needed assessment information or data that will allow evaluation of progress. In choosing who is to observe and record behavior, two important criteria should be kept in mind: whether the person will be able to provide accurate information, and how easy it will be for him or her to gather this. When a client complains about someone else's

Observation
and Recording

behavior, say a child's or a spouse's, since he or she is in contact with this person, access is given. Access is also given if the client is requested to observe his or her own behavior. Decisions must be made as to how behavior is to be recorded. Factors affecting this include the behaviors being observed, how frequently the response occurs, and practical considerations, such as resources available. Private events such as thoughts and feelings must by necessity be recorded by the person who experiences them. If a behavior occurs frequently throughout the entire day, one can select one period within the day in which to sample behavior. If it is suspected that behavior varies in different situations, information should be gathered in each to check this out. Behaviors differ in how easy they are to detect, and this variability may also influence the selection of a monitoring procedure. For example, it may be difficult for a person with poor posture to note when his shoulders are slumped, because he is so used to having his shoulders in this position. A decision must also be made concerning the daily length of the sampling period; for example, all day, two hours, one hour, or ten minutes. The time interval that offers representative information may be determined by trying out different intervals.

Clarity of instructions and the possession of needed skills affect how easy it will be to collect information. Vague instructions or failure to assure that the client knows how to carry out an assignment will make completion more difficult than necessary or may prohibit the collection of adequate material. Instructions should clearly identify:

- What is to be observed and recorded.
- Who is to do it.
- When it is to be done.
- How it is to be done.
- Where the recording form is to be kept.
- Who has access to the form.
- How incentives should be arranged to ensure that observation and recording occur.
- Over how many days it is to be observed and recorded.
- What to do if difficulty is encountered.

Observational Procedures for Identifying Behaviors and Relevant Antecedents and Consequences

The following section describes observational methods than can be employed to identify relevant behaviors and their antecedents and consequences; since different methods are sometimes employed, depending on who gathers data, the methods are separately described for client- and counselor-gathered information.

Client-Gathered Information. Initially, clients are often unable to accurately describe what happens in the natural environment or how their own reactions vary in diverse situations. A mother may not recognize that she reinforces her child for unmanageable behavior; or an anxious client may say that he is always anxious, not realizing that his "anxiety" varies in relation to certain events, such as feeling "put down" at work or being placed in a submissive role by his wife. A mother may not be able to identify what she means by the term *unmanageable* in relation to her child or *cold* in relation to a spouse.

The client may be requested to observe his own behavior or the behavior of some significant other and to record relevant behaviors and situations. A mother may be having difficulty identifying behaviors of her child that she would like to see more of or less of. She could be requested to note these in a log as they come to her attention, as well as to note what happens right before and afterwards. A client who states that she often gets depressed could be requested to keep a diary and to record what happens before and after she feels depressed, and what she does in this state. Preinterview questionnaires may also be used to identify relevant behaviors and situations. If problematic behaviors only occur in certain situations, the client may note relevant behaviors and related events at that time.

A form allowing room to note the date, what happened right before, the behavior, and what happened right afterwards (the ABC form) can be used to record discrete behaviors and criteria for their occurrence, as well as relevant environmental events (Bijou, Peterson, and Ault, 1968). Careful instructions should be given as to what is to be written down in the "before" and "after" columns, that it is what happens *immediately* before and after that is to be recorded, and that comments should be brief so that recording will not become arduous. Clients are instructed to continue acting normally during collection of such assessment information. The client may be asked to read some written material prior to gathering information, describing criteria for pinpointing behavior, the reasons for being specific, and the importance of environmental events (Patterson and Gullion, 1968; Patterson, 1971a). Recording the antecedents and consequences of behavior helps point out to clients the relation between their own behavior and the behavior complained about. It is often the client himself who maintains objectionable behaviors by reinforcing them, and who hinders the development and increase of desired behaviors by failing to follow them with positive events.

The client may prefer to jot down interactions related to problem areas in a daily log. A more standardized form may be preferred that includes date, time, situation, who is involved, what the client said or did, what happened, what the client then did, and what the client would have preferred to do.

Gathering information on an hourly basis can sometimes help the client to identify factors related to general complaints such as depression. Schwarz and Goldiamond (1975) suggest that every hour during the day the client record the activity being engaged in (work), the setting (sitting at desk), who was there (self), what was wanted (to get work done), what happened (little accomplished), and comments (just sat and daydreamed at desk). For example, Schwartz and Goldiamond (1975) present a case in which hourly records revealed the variety of events that contributed to the inability of a client to complete work, such as taking work to a secretarial pool rather than having a private secretary and going to other people's offices rather than having clients come to him. Whenever an agreement is made to carry out some task outside the interview, it is helpful to give the client a form to take home that describes what is to be done and what to do if difficulty occurs (Figure 9). Recording problems can be caught early by collecting information frequently, perhaps every other day, by telephone or through the mail.

Recording assignments should be as easy as possible to complete successfully. Forms should be easy to fill out and portable, so that the client has access to them as needed. Some forms provide code categories for frequently related events. The recorder notes by insertion of the relevant code what he was doing at the time he engaged in the behavior. The categories of (R) reading, (E) eating, and (W) working are some that have been employed when monitoring smoking. The client should be encouraged to record observations as soon as possible, as memory is fallible. Clients may request the counselor to accept their recollections in lieu of recorded information. Temptation to do so should be resisted, because such data may be misleading.

It is helpful to check the following points before the client starts to gather information: (1) Is a form readily available that permits easy recording? (2) Does the client know what

Figure 9. Recording Agreement for ABC Form

Observer:_____ Date:_____ Who is to be observed:_____

To be observed and recorded:
    What happens right before and after the following behavior(s):

When to observe: Situation(s):_____
                        Over how many days:_____
                        Times:_____
When to record:_____
How to record:_____

Where recording form is to be kept:_____
Who may have access to record:_____

When record is to be shared with counselor:_____
Are data to be graphed?   Yes_____   No_____
If questions arise, telephone worker at:_____
                        during times and days of:_____

and how to record? (3) Have cues been established, if needed, to remind the client to record? (4) Has who is to have access to the record been made clear? (5) Does the client know whether a significant other he is observing should be aware of his observations? (6) Has the client been cautioned to continue acting as he normally would? (7) Will the recording assignment interfere unduly with the client's activities? (8) Does the client know when information is to be reviewed by the counselor? (9) Does the client have access to the behavior he is to observe?

If the client has repeated difficulty gathering needed information, clearer instructions may be needed, or incentives may have to be offered. Practice may help to shape up needed recording skills. The client could be requested to tape-record relevant interactions at home. If it is not feasible for the client to gather information, or, if this is tried and is unsuccessful, the counselor may gather this information.

Counselor-Gathered Information. Information may be gathered in simulated role plays at the counselor's office. A couple with communication problems could be requested to discuss a selected topic and reach a conclusion and this discussion could be taped for later study; or a client could be asked to interact with the counselor as he normally would with some other person in a given situation. An effort should be made to replicate real-life conditions as closely as possible, so that the behavior observed will accurately represent what usually occurs. If it is decided that information can be gathered most rapidly and accurately in the natural environment, the client's permission must be obtained for this. If the behavior of concern occurs in the classroom, the teacher's permission, as well as the principal's, is required, in addition to the parents' permission. A time convenient for all involved parties must be selected that will provide a representative sample of behavior. A way to introduce the observer must be arranged, such as informing children that the observer is interested in learning to work with children. It is important to discuss this matter of how the observer will be introduced, to make sure a parent or teacher, for example, does not frighten a child by saying that "He is coming to watch you." Arrangements should be made to remain as unobtrusive as possible. A chair can be located at the back of a classroom, for example, or to the side of a livingroom, and if more than one observational vantage point is desired, chairs can be placed at other points as well. The observer should vary the apparent object of his interest to avoid the actual person of greatest interest from becoming too self-conscious. Time should be allowed before recording begins to allow those observed to become somewhat accustomed to the observer's presence. This period of time can be used to refine behavioral definitions and to practice recording (Gelfand and Hartmann, 1975). It may take a few minutes, a few hours, or observation over a couple of days for behavior to occur at its usual rate in the observer's presence. Arrangements must also be made to ensure accessibility to relevant behaviors. If observation takes place at home, rules may be established that everyone in the family must be present, that no guests be present during periods of observation, that the television be turned off, that interaction be limited to two rooms where the observer can see family members, that no calls are to be made out and incoming calls are to be answered briefly, and that no conversations with the observers occur during observational periods (Patterson, Reid, Jones, and Conger, 1975). Approaches of children can be discouraged by making items that they might like to play with, such as handbags, unavailable; by not attending when they approach; or simply informing them "I cannot talk to you while I'm working." Observations should be taken at the same time each day unless there is an interest in sampling behavior during different situations, such as after school and during mealtimes.

It is important to be clear about the aims of observation. One purpose might be to identify specific behaviors to be increased and decreased that seem to be related to a problem, as well as related antecedents and consequences. The ABC form could be used for this purpose. Observation may be facilitated by developing a form using code categories. Such forms also permit the gathering of information as to the frequency of behavior, and are described in the next section.

Recording the Frequency, Duration, or Magnitude of Behavior

Information concerning the duration, frequency, or magnitude of behavior is collected during assessment as well as after intervention is initiated. Such data, collected prior to intervention, enable determination of the actual seriousness of a behavior, and monitoring following intervention enables evaluation of change programs. This information may be gathered either by the client or counselor depending on the capabilities of the client and the resources available to the counselor. Behavior may be monitored in a number of different ways, which are described below.

Client-Gathered Information. A variety of ways to monitor behavior have been generated, many to make recording less burdensome. These include continuous recording, in which the number of times a behavior occurs is counted; time samples, interval recording, and duration measures that are based on units of time rather than discrete behaviors; and measurement of behavior products, magnitude, and distance. Choice of method should be determined by ease of data collection and the probability of offering representative information. These factors will influence the selection of response characteristic to measure, situations in which behavior is observed, the number of days over which information is collected, and the length of daily observational time. Data collection forms that permit easy accurate recording must be designed and duplicated, unless some mechanical device is used, such as a wrist counter (Lindsley, 1968a).

Data is collected during baseline and intervention as well as at various follow-up periods, in order to assess the durability of behavior changes. The specific observable behaviors identified as related to desired outcomes will often indicate when during these periods data should be gathered. If a client experiences anxiety only when in social situations, an appropriate response measure may be gathered only when he is in such social situations. If a mother says that she has trouble at bedtime with her child, data may be collected only during this time. Convenience to the client and counselor will also affect selection of time and situations to sample behavior. Let us say that a counselor wishes to have some measure of a client's ability to say no to an unfair request during training sessions, but is too busy with carrying out the training procedure to monitor all instances of this behavior. Probes could be made in the beginning and end of the training session in which behavior is observed in response to an unfair request. Such data probes can also be employed to assess generalization effects with other people in other situations or in response to other training events (as in concept formation).

Continuous recording. All instances of a behavior, thought, or feeling may be counted each day or for some selected period within each day. A wife may count the number of times that she receives a compliment from her husband. A mother may be asked to count how often her child follows an instruction. Table 3 contains a variety of examples of continuous recording of behaviors by clients. Clients have also recorded thoughts and feelings. For example, frequency of auditory and visual hallucinations have been recorded daily (Moser, 1974). Clients on a weight reduction program were requested to record "fat" thoughts (discouraging self-verbalizations) and "thin" thoughts (encouraging self-verbalizations) each day, in a behav-

Table 3. Examples of Continuous Recording by Clients

Behavior	How Defined	How Monitored	How Measured
1. Pages read of school work	Each page read	Self-monitored on study recording form	Number of pages per day
2. Head banging of a retarded nine-year-old girl	Striking nose, chin, or ear with fist or hitting her nose or chin against a wall, chair, or other object (Prochaska, Smith, and Marzilli, 1974)	Parent recorded frequency for 10 minutes of every hour. Time started and stopped recording was noted and frequency of head bangings. The particular 10 minutes of each hour varied	Daily number per minute
3. Assertive behavior of females	Elaborated opinion statements—a sentence that begins with a personal pronoun such as "I," and contains a compound sentence (Richey, 1974)	Self-monitored, using waist counter	Number per session
	Number of conversations initiated that are more than just a greeting (Gambrill, 1973)	Self-monitored, using recording form	Weekly rate
4. Zaps	A statement that hurts or offends a person (Patterson, 1971a)	Wrist counter, wrist recorder, behavior check sheet	Number per day
5. Homosexual contacts	Extended conversations, dates, physical contacts with men (Rehm and Rosensky, 1974)	Self-monitored by client	Number of contacts per week
6. Use of bronchometer for asthmatic attacks	Times used (Sirota and Mahoney, 1974)	Self-monitored by client	Weekly frequency
7. Enuresis	Bed wet in the morning	Monitored by mediator	Weekly frequency
8. Instructions followed	Compliance with request within five seconds	Monitored by parent using wrist counter	Rate per day
9. Whines and shouts of a four-year-old boy	Verbalizations that were of such a pitch and loudness that the observer considered them whines or shouts (Hall, Axlerod, Tyler, Grief, Jones, and Robertson, 1972)	On weekdays, the mother kept a daily record from 9:00 A.M. to 6:00 P.M. and the father noted the frequency from 6 to 9 P.M. The father also recorded data from 9:00 A.M. to 9:00 P.M. on weekends. Recording sheets were posted in the kitchen and parent's bedroom.	Whines and shouts per day

ioral diary (Mahoney, Moura, and Wade, 1973). Gottman and McFall (1972) requested clients to note when they failed to talk when they wished to.

Frequency measures can reflect changes in rate over both short and long periods of observation; specify the amount of behavior displayed; and are applicable with behaviors across individuals (Bijou, Peterson, and Ault, 1968). Such measures are particularly valuable for behaviors that have a definite beginning and end and that occupy a relatively constant time period. Behaviors can be listed along the top of a sheet and days down the left and a mark made in the appropriate square on the behavior check sheet each time a behavior occurs. This form could either be small, so that it could be placed in a pocket, or larger, if it is to be posted so that involved parties can easily see it. During collection of a baseline, the person being observed is usually not informed of this, because such knowledge might affect his or her behavior. During intervention, feedback is often provided to involved parties by posting the form in a visible spot.

The monitoring form should be readily accessible. If only one behavior is counted, a wrist counter can be used. One parent counted how often he said something positive to his son by keeping beans in his right pocket and moving a bean to his left pocket each time he said something positive. He then counted up the number of beans in his left pocket at the end of the day. Wrist recorders have been created that permit the monitoring of many behaviors (Epstein and Hersen, 1974).

Total frequency counts are often too troublesome to obtain. An alternative is to select some time during which the behavior occurs and to record all instances only during this period (see Table 3, Item 2). A child's rate of compliance could be monitored only during the dinner hour. Recording responsibilities could be divided among two or more people. A convenient recording form for continuous recording during selected periods includes room for the date, time (start and stop), total time, number of behaviors, and daily rate (Research Rehabilitation Foundation, 1972). Noting the daily rate of behavior permits easy graphing, because rates of behavior are already determined. A disadvantage of recording only during selected periods is that frequencies of behavior in somewhat different environments may not be accurately reflected. Behaviors should be carefully specified before attempting to observe and record in the natural environment. The more often and more regular the occurrence of the behavior, the shorter the sampling period can be in terms of offering a representative estimate of the frequency of a behavior. Sampling periods must be selected more carefully if the behavior occurs only under certain situations or is much more likely under certain situations. In these instances, a decision should be made to sample behavior during the period in which it is likely to occur.

Determining the rate of behavior. Finding the rate of behavior in terms of some common index, such as number per day or per hour, allows comparison of a variety of different behaviors, either of the same person or of different people. If all instances of a behavior, thought, or feeling are counted, then the rate is the number per day. Or, if behavior is monitored for the *same* amount of time each day, number per time period over days could be accurately compared, because the time periods are the same. If observation periods differ from day to day, then it is necessary to convert the count of behavior to rate by dividing the number of hours or minutes of observation into the number of behaviors observed. Let us say that Mr. Reed counted how often he praised his son, and on Monday he was home for five hours, but on Tuesday he was only home for three hours. Use of a simple daily count may give a very inaccurate picture of what is happening. If saying pleasant things was monitored over a sixteen-hour day, and it was found that the frequency during this time was 5, the rate per hour would be 5 divided by 16, or about .31 per hour. Let us say that the frequency of negative comments was also monitored during this time, and it was found that 30 occurred. The rate per hour of negative comments could be found by dividing 16 into 30.

One-shot recording. Some behaviors can take place only once in a selected time period. The behavior (termed *one-shot* behavior by the Research Rehabilitation Foundation, 1972) either does or does not occur during this period, which can be a month, week, day, or hour. Examples of one-shot behaviors include making breakfast for one's children before they go off to school, drinking during lunch, and being on time for work. The behavior check sheet, or a recording form allowing room to note the date and whether the behavior occurred, can be used to record such behavior. The percentage of days on which the behavior occurred can be found by dividing the number of days in which behavior was checked into the number in which it occurred.

Time samples. A client may not have time to continuously record a behavior even during a selected period. Or, such a count may be difficult, because a behavior may not have a definite beginning and ending, such as a good mood, or may last for varying periods of time, such as wearing an orthodontic device. Time sampling, in which behavior is sampled at fixed or random times selected to offer representative information about behavior, provides an alternative to continuous recording. The times selected ideally are random, so that a person will not be able to predict when his behavior will be checked. Preselected times can be written down on a monitoring form and for each the client records a yes or no, depending on whether the behavior was taking place. Time samples may also be gathered without specifying particular times. The observer simply notes behavior when he or she happens to remember to do so—for example, by marking a plus or a minus in a square. An eighth-grade student monitored her study behavior using such a self-recording sheet (Broden, Hall, and Mitts, 1971).

A cueing device such as a portable timer or kitchen timer may be required to remind the client to check on behavior (Foxx and Martin, 1971). This signal should not be audible to the person whose behavior is being monitored, since it might cue him to alter behavior. Random times to observe can be preselected and the timer set for each of these in turn. For example, a parent may check on whether a teenager is studying at 3:10, 3:40, and 4:45 P.M. during his afternoon study period. Table 4 contains examples of client-gathered time samples. The daily percentage of times in which the behavior occurred is determined by dividing the number of occasions on which the behavior was checked into the number of times the person was performing the behavior. If a parent checked five times on Wednesday to see whether her son was doing chores and found him doing chores only once, the daily percentage for Wednesday would be 20.

Table 4. Examples of Client-Gathered Time Samples

Behavior	How Defined	How Monitored	How Measured
1. Wearing orthodontic device (a school-age boy)	Head band and plastic neck band both in place (Hall and others, 1972).	Five times a day the mother observed Jerry to determine whether he was wearing his orthodontic device. On weekends, checks were made before breakfast, between breakfast and lunch, between lunch and supper, shortly after supper, and within 30 minutes of bedtime.	Percent time orthodontic device was used
2. Mood	+ = a good mood − = a bad mood	On 3- × 5-inch index card, five times daily (on arising, breakfast, lunch, dinner, and prior to retiring)	Number of minus ratings per day (Epstein and Hersen, 1974)
3. Intensity of abdominal pain	Rated on a scale where 1 = no pain and 10 = the most severe pain ever experienced (Sank and Biglan, 1974)	Rated every half hour	Average daily abdominal pain rating
4. Obsessions of a 22-year-old male	Uncontrollable thoughts about being brain damaged, persecuted, and "odd" (Mahoney, 1971)	Each day was divided into two-hour periods, and the client marked an X in all time blocks during which the behavior occurred	Weekly number of two-hour time blocks in which obsessions occurred
5. Positive self-thoughts (same 22-year-old male)	Statements about himself that were positive (Mahoney, 1971)	Each day was divided into two-hour periods, and the client marked an X in all time blocks during which behavior occurred	Weekly number of two-hour time blocks in which obsessions occurred

Duration. Measures of duration are useful for behaviors that are continuous rather than discrete and when the objective is to increase or decrease the length of time of a behavior. Latency to sleep onset is one measure employed in the treatment of insomnia (Tokarz and Lawrence, 1974). Time spent in conversations with strangers and acquaintances has been employed as a measure (Gambrill, 1973). If a person is often late for appointments, an objective might be to decrease the length of time of lateness. This could also be measured by the one-shot method, in which case it would be worded "being on time for work or appointments." Use of duration as a measure allows the setting of approximations to behaviors, rather than using an either/or criterion, as in the one-shot method.

The behavior must be carefully specified, so that its onset and termination can be clearly identified. Duration is not necessarily the measure of choice for behaviors that vary greatly in length of time, such as tantrums or biting one's nails. If recording the duration of behaviors is too time-consuming, a time sample could be used instead, in which the client checks whether the behavior is occurring at random times and determines the percentage of instances in which it did occur. Another possibility is to employ continuous recording by arbitrarily imposing a required time lapse between behaviors before recording another instance. For example, a client could monitor lip biting by using a criterion of five seconds' duration of the response followed by the absence of the behavior for five seconds (Epstein and Hersen, 1974). A stopwatch can be a valuable aid in measuring duration. If observation periods of different lengths are employed, the proportion of time in which the behavior occurred can be determined. The duration of individual units of behavior can also be determined; for example, finding the duration of social contacts of various types, such as strangers and acquaintances (Gambrill, 1973).

Measurement of a behavior product. Rather than measuring behavior itself, effects of behavior could be recorded. This method is useful when other forms of observation may interfere with the behavior being observed, or when it is too time-consuming to observe behavior directly (Ayllon and Azrin, 1968b). For example, it may take too much time to monitor all behaviors involved in a weight reduction program. A record of one or two self-management behaviors may suffice. Other examples include wood that is stacked, a floor that is swept, or a bed that is made.

Magnitude. At times the most reasonable measure to employ is the magnitude of behavior. For example, intensity of abdominal pain was rated on a scale from one to ten by a client every half hour (Sank and Biglan, 1974).

Distance. It may be appropriate to employ distance as the response characteristic assessed; for example, maybe a client wishes to be able to travel farther from home without fear.

Counselor-Gathered Information. The client may not have time to gather needed information, or it may be decided that information can be more readily gathered by using trained observers. Decisions must be made as to when to observe, over how many days to observe, and the length of each observational period. Behavior is usually sampled for ten minutes to one hour per day in the same situation(s). If it is suspected that the frequency of a behavior differs greatly in different situations, samples may be gathered in a variety of contexts. A child, for example, may display different behaviors during free play activities than while working on assignments.

The guidelines for making recording easy for clients apply to trained observers as well. There is nothing more frustrating than trying to count behaviors when you are not prepared to do so. Lack of preparation becomes obvious as behaviors start to occur more swiftly than they can be recorded, or as you realize that you have not clearly identified behaviors, and so are having to spend time deciding whether that was an instance of X behavior. Be sure to specify behaviors before trying to count them. The use of specially designed recording forms may make recording easier.

Continuous recording. Frequency counts can be gathered when the behavior occurs only during a limited period of time. Phillips (1968) employed frequency counts in a home-style rehabilitation setting for predelinquent youth. For example, aggressive phrases were counted for three boys for three hours per day while they were engaged in woodworking activities (Phillips, 1968). Frequency counts may also be gathered during simulated interactions in the office. Parent-child interaction can be observed in a playroom or a social situation arranged between the client and another adult to assess the client's social competence in selected situations. Observations may only be made at the beginning and end of training sessions. Counselor-gathered frequency counts are illustrated in Table 5.

Interval measures. Interval samples are a form of time sampling in which some period is selected and broken into smaller units of time, such as fifteen-second intervals. The recorder simply notes by a check mark whether the behavior occurred during each interval. Not every instance of the behavior is recorded—only whether it occurred within the selected time period. Once the occurrence of a behavior has been noted during an interval, attention can be devoted to other behaviors until the next time interval starts. Interval measures provide close approximations to frequency and duration measures and have been employed with a range of behaviors, including attending, studying, playing, and disruptive behavior (see Table 6). This procedure is appropriate if a behavior occurs often during a period of time. It allows the recording of many behaviors and/ or consequences. An interval-recording form is shown in Chapter Seventeen. The rows may stand for behaviors or their consequences, and the columns (which may be ten, fifteen, or thirty seconds long) represent time intervals. Usually the intervals add up to some convenient period, such as five minutes. Interval sampling was used to record verbalizations of a preschool child using ten-second intervals timed with stopwatches (Reynolds and Risley, 1968). Each time a verbalization occurred within a ten-second interval, a *T* was written in the square. Only one *T* was marked no matter how many seconds talking occupied. If talking extended into the next interval or occurred at all during that interval, a *T* would also be recorded there. Frequency of talking was calculated as the percent of ten-second intervals in which a *T* was recorded. One row was used to record teacher attention. It was therefore possible to examine the relationship between teacher attention and talk of the child. Three 5-minute samples were taken each day during free play periods. Additional symbols may be employed, such as circling a code mark to indicate a certain type of interaction—for example, aggressive

Table 5. Examples of Continuous Recording by Counselors or Trained Observers

Behavior	How Defined	How Monitored	How Measured
1. Attendance of welfare recipients at self-help group meetings	Who appeared at group meetings (Miller and Miller, 1970)	Weekly attendance noted	Number per meeting
2. Aggressive statements of 3 teen-age boys in home-style rehabilitation setting	Stated or threatened inappropriate destruction or damage to any object, person, or animal (Phillips, 1968)	By house parent—recorded for 3 boys for 3 hours each day during woodworking	Number per day
3. "Ain't," spoken by 3 teen-age boys in home-style rehabilitation setting	By its occurrence	By house parent—recorded for 1 boy for 3 hours each day on a counter	Number per day
4. Verbal reinforcement during conversation between a male and female	A single word or utterance that the male interjected into the conversation in reaction to a statement by the female; defined as indicating interest or encouragement from the listener for the speaker to continue, or agreement with something the speaker said (Arkowitz and others, 1975)	Counted from audiotape	Number during 10 minutes' conversation
5. Greeting responses of four retarded children	Hand wave; the hand had to be empty, raised above the elbow level; there were at least two back-and-forth motions either of an arm from the shoulder or elbow or a single hand from the wrist, which did not contact any part of the subject's body or any other person. These were further classified as spontaneous, prompted, or incorrect (Stokes, Baer, and Jackson, 1974).	Responses were counted during training and probe sessions	Percentage of greeting responses

Table 6. Examples of Interval Measures Gathered by Trained Observers

Behavior	How Defined	How Monitored	How Measured
1. Verbalizations of 4-year-old preschool girl	Any speech of the child heard by the observers except random noises such as shrieking, humming, or laughing (Reynolds and Risley, 1968)	Interval recording form using 10-second intervals; a behavior was noted in the interval if it occurred during that interval	Percentage of 10-second intervals in which talking occurred
2. Teacher attention	Any time a teacher spoke to, gave equipment to, or touched a child	Interval recording form using 10-second intervals; a behavior was noted in the interval if it occurred during that interval	Percentage of 10-second intervals in which teacher attention occurred
3. Objectionable behavior of 4-year-old boy; verbalizations of boy and verbalizations of mother to boy	Biting shirt or arm, sticking out tongue, kicking or hitting, calling people derogatory names, saying no loudly (Hawkins, Peterson, Schweid, and Bijou, 1966)	Recorded in the home for each successive 10-second interval whether each behavior occurred	Percentage of 10-second intervals in which objectionable behavior and verbalizations occurred
4. Deviant, cooperative, and isolated behavior of a 6-year-old boy and his brother	*Deviant behavior:* kicking, hitting, pushing, name calling, throwing objects at someone; *cooperative behavior:* asking for a toy, requesting the other's help, conversation, and playing within three feet of each other; *isolated behavior:* the absence of verbal, physical, or visual interaction between the boys (O'Leary, O'Leary, and Becker, 1967)	20-second rate, 10-second rest for 30 minutes each day in the home	Percent cooperative behavior; percent isolated play; percent deviant behavior

versus nonaggressive behavior (Bijou, Peterson, and Ault, 1968). Consistent guidelines must be followed in recording behavior, as with any recording method. For example, a decision must be made whether a behavior is counted as occurring if it took place at any time during the interval or only if it occupied a certain proportion or more of the interval. Failure to establish consistent rules may result in low agreement between observers, because of fluctuating standards when recording.

The maximum frequency of a behavior using this recording method is determined by the size of the time unit selected, which should be related to the frequency with which the behavior occurs. If a ten-second interval is employed, the maximum rate of behavior is six per minute, whereas a five-second time interval yields a rate of twelve per minute. With a frequent behavior, the unit should be smaller, to more accurately reflect its rate. If behaviors occur at a high rate, the interval selected should be small enough so that two complete responses could not occur in one interval, but the interval should be at least as long as the average duration of one response (Gelfand and Hartman, 1975). Use of intervals that are too long will result in an underestimate of the frequency of the behavior and so may lead, for example, to an underestimation of the decrease in undesirable behavior in a program designed to decrease behavior. Intervals that are too small would have the opposite effect. Whenever small time intervals are used, it is helpful to use an audible timing device (Weight, 1969). Intervals can be programed on a cassette tape by recording verbally Interval One, Two, Three, and so forth, at every ten-second interval (Quilitch, 1972). This avoids the necessity of shifting attention from behavior to a stopwatch and helps to coordinate observation and tabulating time during observer agreement checks. The interval number should be recorded, rather than just a tone, because the former procedure produces superior observer agreement (Whelan, 1974).

To assess the effects of intervention, the percentage of intervals in which a behavior occurred during baseline is compared with the percentage after intervention. Let us say that behavior was observed for a fifteen-minute period, using fifteen-second intervals, and that talking to a peer was noted in twenty intervals. Sixty (the total number of intervals) would be divided into twenty and the result multiplied by 100 to obtain the percentage of intervals in which this behavior occurred.

Behaviors and consequences may be recorded at the interval rather than within an interval. For example, Goodwin and Coates (1976) developed a procedure for the simultaneous recording of behavior and consequences. Classes of student behavior, including on-task behavior, scanning, social contact, and disruptive behavior, were arranged along a dimension of appropriateness. Teacher consequences included instructing, rewarding, neutral behavior, and disapproval. The observer notes at each five-second interval what the student is doing, as well as the teacher's response, and inserts a check in the appropriate space. This procedure may not be as accurate as continuous interval sampling with brief or low-rate behaviors. A variant of interval recording alternates between recording and observation periods. Behavior is observed for a given period of time, say fifteen seconds, and then recorded for a preset period, for example, five seconds (O'Leary, O'Leary, and Becker, 1967). This procedure may help to improve the accuracy of data collection because it is less demanding on observers. Intervals can be precorded on a tape-recorder by saying "Interval 1, observe" (fifteen seconds of silence, for example); "Interval 1, record" (five seconds of silence), and so on. Numbering the intervals helps to clearly identify the recording interval and to match this with the interval noted on the data collection form. The accuracy of interval recording is affected by the rate and pattern of responding. Such recording accurately represents low and medium rates, but underestimates high-rate behaviors (Repp, Roberts, Slack, Repp, and Berkler, 1976). This same study found that time samples were even more inaccurate when compared with continuous recording.

Time sampling. Both time sampling and interval recording depend on units of time rather than on discrete behaviors. Neither results in frequency measures; rather, both attempt to offer a representative estimate of the frequency of a behavior. The term *time sampling,* as used here and in the description of client-gathered information, refers to recording procedures that involve a much longer span of time between intervals than does interval recording, where ten-, fifteen-, and twenty-second intervals may be employed and where behavior is sampled over a brief period of time, such as ten or thirty minutes each day. Time sampling is useful when a behavior may occur over a long time span and when it does not have a definite beginning or end. For example, ward staff monitored the talking of four female hospitalized residents by making twenty observations on each patient per day (Bennett and Maley, 1973). The observer approached the area where the resident was located and watched her unobtrusively for one minute. A talking response was noted if the patient was audibly verbalizing while facing another person. Behavior may or may not be prompted when collecting a time sample. Prompting is most often employed with behaviors that are under strict stimulus control, such as responding to someone initiating a conversation (see, for example, Liberman, Teigen, Patterson, and Baker, 1973), or to assess or evaluate changes in many discrete behaviors that make up a complex skill, such as social skills of severely handicapped children (see, for example, Sailor and Mix, 1975). In either case, it would waste time to wait around until the behavior occurred. As noted by Doke (1976), it is important to assess the effects of such prompted probes themselves prior to initiating intervention, so that changes caused by the probes alone are not confounded with changes caused by intervention.

Time sampling can also be employed if one is interested in finding out the range of behaviors engaged in by a person in a selected context. Data can be summarized by counting the total number of times the client was observed and the total number in which each behavior occurred, and by dividing the former into the total for each behavior. If behavior was observed at seventeen intervals during one shift, and a person was found to be sleeping during ten, talking during two, and reading during one, we would determine what percent of seventeen each of these behavior occupies.

Duration. It may be decided that a duration measure can be most accurately gathered by someone other than the client. Duration of thumb sucking may be monitored by observers (Skiba, Pettigrew, and Alden, 1971) or latency of verbal response (Gambrill, 1973). Examples, together with descriptions of how behaviors are defined, are presented in Table 7. With this measure, as with others, behavior may be sampled only at certain times during the day. For example, nurses recorded the daily duration of rational talk by interviewing each patient four times a day for ten minutes (Liberman and others, 1973). Note that in this case the behavior of interest was prompted by the nurses.

Measurement of a behavior product. An advantage of measuring a behavior product is that it does not interfere with the rate of the behavior, because the observer is not present when the behaviors are performed (Ayllon and Azrin, 1968b). Staff in a residential setting could record the daily number of tokens spent by each resident. Phillips (1968) divided bathroom-cleaning behavior into a series of sixteen tasks, each of which was behaviorally specified. Number of tasks completed per day was recorded. Clark, Boyd, and Macrae (1975) measured number of correct responses on tests of students' abilities to write correct biographic information. Measures of the amount of litter in randomly selected yards in an urban low-income housing project were gathered to evaluate the effectiveness of antilitter procedures (Chapman and Risley, 1974). Measurement of a behavior product can be used to check the validity of other measures. Assessment of some products, such as a child's writing, require relatively complex judgments. However, such judgment can be reliably made, given careful definition of behaviors or patterns of behavior (Hopkins, Schutte, and Garton, 1971).

Magnitude. Special equipment is usually employed with counselor-gathered measures of magnitude. For example, intensity of anxiety when in various situations could be monitored by recording changes in skin resistance. Noise level could be recorded via a decibel counter.

Distance. It may be appropriate to measure proximity of a child to his peers in a program designed to increase peer interaction or the degree of approach of a client to a feared stimulus.

Gathering Data Describing a Group

At times, it may be most relevant to collect a group measure. The number of positive and negative interactions between

Table 7. Duration Measured Gathered by Trained Observers

Behavior	How Defined	How Monitored	How Measured
1. Working	Looking at the blackboard, counting on fingers, pencils, crayons, and so on; writing on paper (Surratt, Ulrich, and Hawkins, 1969)	Timer switched on	Percent time working
2. Responding to instructions	Time between instruction and compliance	Stopwatch (Fjellstedt and Sulzer-Azaroff, 1973)	Latency
3. Claustrophobia: 51-year-old woman	Time spent in a small, dark room (Leitenberg and others, 1968)	Elapsed time meter; stopwatch (used by client)	Mean time in seconds per session
4. Punctuality of 3 teen-age boys in home-style rehabilitation setting	Minutes late or early (Phillips, 1968)	Recorded by houseparents	Returning from school, completing errands and going to bed
5. Latency of verbal response	Time between end of recorded verbal statement and start of reply (Gambrill, 1973)	Stopwatch	Average latency over all presented situations
6. Male talk time	Number of minutes during which the male spoke during a 10-minute interaction (Arkowtiz and others, 1975)	Stopwatch	Number of minutes of speaking
7. Rational talk	Speech without inclusion of delusional content. Each nurse was given a list of delusional statements and topics for each patient (Liberman and others, 1973)	Four times a day, each patient was interviewed by a member of the nursing staff for ten minutes. Rational talk was timed with a stopwatch	Minutes of rational talk per day
8. Thumb sucking of a third-grader, in the classroom	Any response resulting in the thumb either touching the lips or going into the child's mouth (Skiba, Pettigrew, and Alden, 1971)	Two observers in the classroom started a stopwatch whenever the thumb was placed on the lips or in the mouth	Duration in seconds

clients during weekly group meetings may be important to determine (Flowers, Booraem, Brown, and Harris, 1974). Finding the rate per session allows comparison of different groups or a behavior of one group over many sessions. If the group size differs on different occasions, the rate of a behavior can be determined by dividing the number of behaviors by the number of people, and then dividing this figure by some time measure. Miller and Miller (1970) determined the weekly number of welfare clients who attended self-help meetings. Percent of children observed eating was employed as a measure in a program designed to increase consumption of balanced meals (Madsen, Madsen, and Thompson, 1974). A time sample using fixed or random intervals may be employed to describe the behaviors of a group. A form allowing notation of location, position, whether the person is awake or asleep, facial expression, social orientation, and activities was reliably employed by mentally retarded residents of a state school and hospital (Craighead, Mercatoris, and Bellack, 1974). Data can be summarized by gathering all recording forms for a day and counting the number of residents engaged in each behavior over all intervals. Let us say that ten residents were observed during seventeen intervals and that a total of thirty-five were watching television. The number of intervals, multiplied by the number of residents, yields the total number of opportunities for any one behavior over all intervals. To find the percentage contribution of any one behavior, the number found performing this would be divided by the total number possible. The frequency of given behaviors before and after intervention can be compared.

Measures have been devised to determine the number of individuals participating in planned activities (see, for example, Doke and Risley, 1972). The number of residents taking part in such activities is determined at fixed or random times. This measurement procedure approximates an interval-recording procedure to the extent to which behavior is observed at frequent intervals—for example, every minute. It should be noted that such group measures may mask important individual differences. Such an observation instrument has been developed by Liberman, DeRisi, King, Eckman, and Wood (1974) to assess the percentage of time that a group of individuals engage in a variety of behaviors. One person is observed for a five-second period and his behavior is coded, using predetermined code categories. Following a thirty-second interval, the second person is observed, and so on until each person in the group has been observed. Four such observation periods, separated by at least one hour, are conducted each day. These observations have been employed to assess behavior in different day-care treatment centers.

Effects of Monitoring Behavior

Being observed or self-monitoring (keeping a record of some discriminable behavior, thought, or feeling) may alter the frequency of behavior. This is revealed by comparing early baseline information with data collected at the end of the baseline phase. The more obtrusive the monitoring procedure, the greater the likelihood of reactive effects. Positive or negative surveillance effects may be found. The former includes the increase in desirable behaviors or decrease in problematic behaviors. Parents tend to decrease their rate of negative behaviors and increase their rate of positive behaviors when observed (Patterson, Cobb, and Ray, 1973). Students who monitored their study time had significantly higher grades than those who did not (Johnson and White, 1971). Maletsky (1974) found that self-monitored scratching behavior decreased. The daily frequency of positive statements made by a mother to her child increased when these were self-monitored (Herbert and Baer, 1972). Negative surveillance effects are more rare and include an increase in problematic behavior or a decrease in a desired behavior. McFall (1970) found that smoking decreased when clients monitored how often they successfully resisted urges to smoke. These findings highlight the role of motivational variables on the reactivity of self-recording. That is, behavior seems to change in a direction desired by the person who is observing and recording behavior. However, the effects of self-monitoring usually dissipate over time (Kazdin, 1974b). A feedback model has been proposed to account for the reactivity of self-recording (Kanfer, 1970). This includes self-observation, self-evaluation, and self-regulation.

Determining the Quality of Data

The quality of data is determined by its reliability (the consistency with which it is recorded) as well as its validity (the extent to which it measures what it is supposed to). The degree of consistency—that is, the extent to which two or more observers can agree on the occurrence of whatever is being observed—relates directly to the degree of validity possible. If behavior is very inconsistently recorded (perhaps because of response definitions constantly shifting), it will not be possible to demonstrate high validity. There are a number of sources of inaccuracy.

Systematic observer inaccuracies may be related to expectancy effects—that is, inaccurate coding of behavior caused by assumptions of how a person (or the self) should behave—or incorrect use of behavioral definitions or the recording procedure. Two observers may have differences in the direction in which their data are biased, as revealed from comparing their data. One, for example, may consistently underestimate the frequency of an inappropriate behavior and another may consistently overestimate the frequency. Baseline data may have to be collected over additional days to allow time to become accustomed to observation so that behavior returns to its usual rate. Systematic changes may occur in observer behavior (unrelated to the actual behavior of the person being observed) over time, perhaps because of fatigue. This observer drift can be determined through occasional recalibration of the observer by comparing his results with those of a criterion observer. Observers are more accurate in their collection of data when they are aware that their results will be checked (see, for example, Taplin and Reid, 1973). Awareness of being observed may also affect behavior. This has been called the "guinea pig" effect (Campbell and Stanley, 1966).

Assessing the Consistency of Recording. The data gathered during baseline and intervention provide case management information. Inaccurate data may give false impressions concerning changes in behavior and this can substantially interfere with informed selection of plans. Such data could lead to the continuation of a program that in actuality is creating little change, or, on the other hand, abandoning a program that is actually very effective. Lack of consistent data will make it impossible to detect change, whereas if data are consistent, small as well as larger changes can be noted. A measurement of the consistency of recording should be gathered during the baseline period (before intervention), as well as after change efforts have been initiated, to assure that behaviors are well enough defined so that two or more observers can agree and that behavior definitions remain the same over time. Information is consistent (or reliable) to the extent that measurements from independent observers are in agreement. At least two observers who gather information independently are required to obtain information concerning consistency. For example, a teacher as well as a student may monitor the number of weekly assignments completed. Both parents may be requested to monitor behavior during weekends. Azrin and Powell (1969) used fellow employees to obtain independent records of pill-taking behavior. Each day a participant observer was given a written schedule that indicated when they should seek out the subject, observe him or her, and note whether or not a pill was swallowed. Observations were also made of the subject at other times, to prevent the observer's presence from becoming a cue for pill taking. Fifth-grade students in elementary school have been employed as peer observers. In these instances, agreement between observers was 95 percent or greater.

Behavior should be observed and recorded independently, for the same duration of time, if possible, and observers should be unaware of the nature of change efforts. Prior to data collection, both observers should make sure that they are familiar with behavioral definitions being used and with the data sheet, as well as use of any special timing devices. Observers should be placed so that the actions of one do not influence the other by virtue of audible sounds (for example, of a wrist counter) or actions (recording a behavior on the data sheet). Data recorded by the observers should be checked right after the observation period and any disagreements discussed and rules developed to resolve these. Each observer should be questioned concerning what he was observing and noting on the record sheet. Often disagreements are caused by failure of the coding categories to exhaust all possibilities (Gelfand and Hartmann, 1975). Inconsistency may be caused by a number of other factors, including "observer drift," in which observers gradually alter the way in which they record behavior, perhaps because of boredom, using shortcuts that result in inaccurate data, or forgetting or changing response definitions. The greater the tendency for observers to show low consistency, the more frequently consistency should be checked.

The precise manner in which consistency is determined depends on the response measure employed (for example, continuous recording, interval recording, or a duration measure) as well as the data collection procedure employed. Three basic decisions must be made in order to assess the consistency of data collected (Johnson and Bolstad, 1973). First, a score unit on which consistency will be assessed must be selected. This may be a single response, such as instructions followed, or a composite score, such as total deviant score, which is based on the sum of many behaviors. If data has been collected on a *response class*—for example, dependent behavior—consistency estimates could be determined either for each component behavior (working with the component sum in each interval) or for the total score, depending on whether it is important to consider each component behavior separately. Secondly, the time span over which scores are to be summed must be selected. Let us say that two observers gather a series of consistency checks within one observational period, each of which contains eight or more recording intervals. Consistency can be assessed for each one or over all intervals during the observational period. When checking interval behavioral definitions, it is best to check the consistency of each set of intervals in order to provide the observers with immediate feedback concerning any disagreements. Trial consistency (assessing consistency within one set of intervals rather than all sets) offers a more conservative estimate of consistency than session consistency. A third decision that must be made is to select a statistical method to summarize data. The easiest methods of determining consistency estimates are not necessarily the most accurate. For example, percentage agreement methods are often employed to assess the consistency of continuous or duration measures. In the former case, the number of target behaviors each observer counted is tallied and the larger number divided into the smaller number and the result multiplied by 100 to obtain a percentage. If, for example, both observers reported that a child followed instructions five times, their agreement would be 100 percent. If one observer counted five and the other three, their agreement would only be 60 percent (3 divided by 5). This procedure for calculating agreement does not necessarily indicate that the two observers counted the same behaviors, because agreement is based on total number observed (Johnson and Bolstad, 1973). Thus, this estimate of agreement must be interpreted conservatively. Consistency of duration measures and time samples can be determined by dividing the larger estimate into the smaller one. If interval sampling is employed, the number of intervals in which both observers record the same behavior (agreements) is divided by the number during which at least one person recorded a behavior (agreements plus disagreements). If intervals were included in which neither observer indicated a behavior, this would inflate the estimate of agreement, because there may be many intervals in which no behavior occurs (Bijou, Peterson, Harris, Allen, and Johnston, 1969). Consistency checks gathered during one week can be averaged to yield a weekly index.

More accurate methods for determining consistency are more complex. Their use with continuous or duration measures requires breaking up the observational period (for example, thirty minutes) into eight to twelve intervals during data collection (Gelfand and Hartmann, 1975). If a continuous or duration measure is used, each recording interval will be scored zero or some positive number. If interval data is recorded, each interval will be scored either zero, indicating that no behavior occurred, or one, indicating that it did occur in that interval. With continuous and duration measures, the number of intervals in which both observers agreed, plus the number in which they disagreed, can be divided into the number of agreements in order to arrive at a consistency estimate. Correlation coefficients provide more accurate estimates of reliability for response measures than do percentages of agreement (Whelan, 1974). The reader is referred to other sources for detailed description of calculation methods (Gelfand and Hartmann, 1975). Large changes can be detected even with relatively unreliable measures. However, in order to describe small changes, consistency must be high. Percentage agreement for interval data should be greater than 80 percent and if a correlation method is used for any type of response measure, it should be greater than .6 (Gelfand and Hartmann, 1975).

Adults gather more accurate data than do younger children (see Kazdin, 1974b). Self-monitored reports by adolescents of room cleaning were highly divergent from data gathered by an independent observer (Fixen, Phillips, and Wolf, 1972). Clients tend to underestimate their performance of undesirable behaviors and overestimate their performance of desirable ones. Frequent consistency checks (reliability probes) are particularly important when observer drift (that is, gradual changes in how behaviors are scored) occurs. This can be detected by recording three criterion tapes representing behavior being coded and by requesting both observers plus a third observer to code at the beginning, middle, and ending phase. If the responses of the two observers differ from the third, this may indicate "observer drift" (Gelfand and Hartmann, 1975). Consistency can be enhanced by thorough initial training of observers, by periodic retraining (or calibration) sessions, by not allowing observers to become fatigued, and by reinforcing collection of accurate data.

Two of the most common reasons for inaccurate data are a failure to specify behaviors and a failure to provide an easy recording procedure. Both possibilities should be checked if a lack of consistency is found or if there is a failure to gather needed information. Perhaps a client cannot discriminate when the behavior occurs; perhaps recording is too intrusive. Noting certain behaviors may be aversive, and so avoided, such as amount smoked, degree of tension, daily weight. In some cases, a positive alternative can be monitored instead, such as resisted urges to smoke (McFall, 1970), or times caught self being relaxed. Self-reports are behaviors that themselves may be controlled by contingencies, and these contingencies may differ from those that influence the actual behavior (Kazdin, 1974b).

Systematically observing behavior is a novel requirement, and a cue may be needed to remind the client to observe and record at appropriate times. Any item can be employed that serves as a reminder. Keeping the recording sheet in an observable spot may function as a cue to observe and record. Watson and Tharp (1972) suggest the use of negative practice for "unconsciously performed" behaviors to heighten awareness of them, so that they can be accurately monitored. A man who habitually engaged in knuckle cracking was requested to spend five minutes each morning and night cracking his knuckles while paying close attention to the behavior. Such practice will also hopefully have beneficial effects during intervention, in that the client will be more aware of beginning to engage in the undesirable behavior. This can then be employed as a cue to perform an incompatible desirable behavior. A second method suggested by these authors is using significant others to remind the client that he is performing a behavior. This method should not be selected if reminders are offered in a critical or punishing manner.

There are many events that do not permit assessment of consistency, such as thoughts. Only the client has access to the frequency of his thoughts and only he has access to the frequency of feelings, unless these are also monitored by special recording devices. When independent assessment is not possible, special attention should be devoted to assuring that response definitions remain the same by periodically gathering examples of the thoughts or feelings and examining these to make sure they fall within agreed-on definitions. Reliability of reporting can be increased by offering training in behavior definitions and by making reinforcers contingent on agreement with reports of independent observers (Fixsen, Phillips, and Wolf, 1972).

Observer Accuracy. Observers may have high reliability but low observer accuracy. Observer accuracy (the extent to which ratings by observers match behavioral coding of a criterion) may be determined by having observers occasionally code a criterion tape (perhaps an audio- or videotape of the behaviors of concern) to make sure their coding matches the behavioral definitions originally agreed on (Johnson and Bolstad, 1973).

Questions of Practicality and Validity. The use of observational methods will of necessity be limited by practical considerations of time and resources available. Even though it is deemed very desirable to supplement client self-report with observational measures in the natural environment, this may not be possible. Observation in the clinic may be used instead. Selection of procedure must also be informed by validity concerns; that is, Does the procedure employed provide an accurate reflection of the behavior of concern? If the client is interested in developing better public speaking skills, who will measure these and where will they be assessed? It is often not possible to select the source having maximal social validity, say members of the audience; however, some approximation to this may be possible—for example, by gaining the report of a significant other who views the behavior of the speaker. The tendency to select a measure that is not really relevant simply because of practical issues should be resisted. Behavior does not have to be observed continuously, but only for selected periods of time; or probes may be employed. The more suspect a source of information is, the greater attempt should be made to gather additional sources of information. It should be noted that a confusion is sometimes made concerning questions of validity and the extent to which measures from different sources are actually related to each other (Lick and Katkin, 1976). A behavioral framework assumes multiple responses that may or may not all be related to a particular event. A person, for example, may report anxiety but fail to indicate anxiety as measured by physiological indicators. This does not necessarily call into question the validity of self-report as much as raise the possibility that, for this person, the experience of anxiety may be mainly a cognitive one rather than a physiological one.

The Use of Incentives

It may be necessary to establish special contingencies to encourage clients to gather data. Further contact can be made contingent upon receiving an agreed-on amount of client-gathered data (Patterson and Hops, 1972). Daily collection of needed information by phone, which may only take a couple of minutes, can also encourage clients to complete assignments.

Summary

Useful information may be obtained from observational data collected in the natural environment or in the office. Either the client or counselor may gather this information. Clients should be carefully prepared to gather information and supplied with a recording agreement form describing what to record and what to do if questions arise. The rationale for recording should be explained so that the client understands why efforts are being made to gather information. It is important that the time selected for recording offer a representative account of relevant behaviors and the situations in which they occur. There are a variety of ways to monitor behavior, including continuous recording, time samples, interval recording, duration measures, measures of a behavior product, and magnitude. The means selected should faithfully reflect the behavior observed and be practical to carry out. Information should be collected in the least reactive way possible. Special cueing and incentive arrangements may be required to assure data collection. Ideally, reliability estimates are determined; however, this will not always be feasible.

8

There is a close relationship between assessment and intervention within a behavioral framework. The information collected during assessment should directly point to possible change methods in a given case. Steps involved in selection of intervention plans include the survey of plausible intervention alternatives, evaluation of each one concerning its applicability to the case at hand, selection of the most appropriate methods and finally, the description of how the procedures will be implemented (Carter, 1973). The selection of change plans is essentially a decision-making procedure and sufficient time should be devoted to this to select a plan that is most likely to succeed and that will be comfortable for the client.

Selection and
Evaluation of
Intervention Plans

Surveying Alternative Plans

A list of possible methods that might be appropriate can be made after assessment information is reviewed and relevant literature examined as necessary. The client is a participant in this process, and he may be asked to help to identify possible plans of action in relation to each desired outcome and hindering factors that influence attainment of outcomes. This will enable him to obtain practice in problem solution, one step of which is identifying possible plans of action. The following factors should be considered (see Carter, 1973).

The Response Systems Involved. Covert as well as overt

behaviors may be of import. For example, the client may display a high frequency of negative self-statements that are related to problem areas, and a procedure that directly addresses these, such as thought stopping, may be selected. Or emotional reactions, such as unadaptive anxiety reactions, may be involved. If these are very intense, it may be necessary to reduce them through use of a procedure carried out in the office or home, such as training the client in progressive muscle relaxation before encouraging him to carry out new behaviors in real life.

Nature of Probable Controlling Conditions. Both covert as well as external events may be antecedents for problematic behaviors. Significant others may be involved in the maintenance of such behavior. Or behavior deficits may exist, such as a lack of desirable alternative behaviors, which will have to be developed through verbal instructions, model presentation, or shaping. Cues for inappropriate behavior may be readily removable, such as not having cigarettes available when trying to decrease smoking. This is often impossible, because these events may be parts of the environment, such as other people with whom contacts are desired. Rather than arrange that certain events not be presented, their eliciting, discriminating, and reinforcing functions may have to be altered.

Nature of Behavioral Objectives. The goal may be to increase or decrease behavior, or perhaps to vary its frequency. If behaviors are to occur in new situations, cues for their performance may have to be arranged. The points mentioned in relation to response systems involved are also relevant here.

Evaluation of Alternative Plans

A variety of criteria should be considered when evaluating possible plans, including acceptability to counselor; acceptability to client; competence of the counselor in relation to method (Can he or she do or learn it in a reasonable amount of time?); relative effectiveness with this particular type of client based on literature; relative estimated efficiency in terms of cost-time estimate; and feasibility in given case (Carter, 1973).

A method may be effective, efficient, and plausible to employ, but be rejected by the client because of the discomfort it might cause. For example, flooding, which is an anxiety induction procedure, may reduce anxiety more rapidly than graduated symbolic desensitization but may be rejected because of its discomfort (see Chapter Eleven).

A counselor cannot ethically agree to employ weak change procedures if strong ones are feasible, given that client discomfort is not a consideration. A client might prefer a verbal means of change, such as talking about his problems, to a procedural mix that includes homework assignments and direct intervention in the natural environment that requires effort on his part. If it is likely that verbal procedures alone will only have a small chance of effectiveness, this should be explained and additional efforts made to point out the advantages of employing other procedures.

We do not have very much precise information concerning the efficiency of various procedures in terms of cost-time data. Patterson and his colleagues are among the few investigators who have reported such data (see Chapter Nine). There are, however, many indications concerning relative time involved in carrying out different procedures. For example, some studies indicate that positive reinforcement of desirable behaviors, combined with time out for undesirable behaviors, is more efficient than is differential reinforcement (positive reinforcement combined with ignoring of undesirable behaviors) (see, for example, Wahler, 1969a). Change methods may require competencies that would require a great deal of time to learn, and this may necessitate referral to another practitioner. Also, the procedure selected must be feasible to employ.

A number of separate steps are involved in evaluating each alternative, including a review of available environmental resources and limitations (Carter, 1973). Can significant others be consistent mediators? Do they possess positive reinforcers? Can significant others be created for this client? What are the economic and material resources of the client, of significant others and of the community? For example, is money available to use as a reinforcer? What reinforcing contexts are available in the community? Can these be employed for this client? Does he meet eligibility requirements to participate in these? Will there be any disadvantages of such participation?

Assessment of the client's resources and limitations is also necessary. What are his assets? Will he be able to be his own manager of change? What social and self-control skills can be used to advantage? Is he a good observer of his behavior? Are there any physical conditions or firmly held attitudes that limit use of certain procedures? What does he do well that can be of value? Assessment of the client's reinforcer profile will indicate items and events that can be employed as reinforcers, as well as their ranking in terms of importance. Information concerning a client's profile of punishing events may also be required. Possible intervention contexts are also reviewed. These might include home, school, job, or community settings. Perhaps a group context would be best. Each procedure has somewhat different requisites which must be satisfied if the procedure is to be effective.

Operant extinction, for example, has many requirements including being able to identify and control the reinforcer; a behavior of concern that is maintained on a rich schedule of reinforcement; and tolerance by significant others of an increase or continuation of the behavior (Gelfand and Hartmann, 1975). If the reinforcer maintaining the behavior is appropriate for the client, differential reinforcement of other behavior can be employed. If the reinforcer maintaining the behavior cannot be identified or influenced, some other procedure must be employed, such as punishment. Operant extinction will not be effective if the behavior is not maintained on a high level of reinforcement. In this case, punishment, restraint, or stimulus change could be employed. The same is true if the continuation of a behavior would be very irksome to significant others or to the client. Punishment should only be employed when there are no ethical objections to its use, when unauthorized escape is not possible, or when the punishing event (or response cost) can be delivered immediately and consistently. If unauthorized escape is possible, restraint or stimulus change may be selected. There are thus many considerations in selecting a procedure to decrease behavior. Whenever punishment, response cost, stimulus change, or restraint is employed, appropriate behaviors should be reinforced as well.

The more extensive the behavior deficits that a client exhibits, the more likely model presentation, feedback, and intructions will be necessary. If deficits are less pronounced, arranged practice opportunities or instructions may result in an increase in behavior. Possibilities for employing stimulus control (the rearrangement of antecedents) should always be carefully considered, as well as possibilities for rearranging consequences of behavior. The former possibility is often overlooked. Often there will be a need for shaping, that is, the gradual increase of behavior in accord with initial levels of discomfort and skill.

Selection of the Best Alternative

Based on the evaluation, plans are selected. Alternative plans may be selected in case the first one does not work out. A plan should be selected that is the easiest one to carry out given the satisfaction of other considerations such as effectiveness, comfort to the client, and desires of the client. The "best" alternative therefore is not necessarily the one that the literature suggests would be the most effective, because the latter may pose operational difficulties or may be rejected by the client in favor of another procedure. A procedure should be selected that matches as well as possible the unique characteristics of the client, the problem, and factors related to this problem. Reading facility of the client may permit the use of written or verbal instructions rather than the use of actual model presentation. Efforts are being made to try to predict the effects of given interventions with given clients in terms of their responses on inventories. For example, Rotter's (1966) locus of control scale supposedly indicates the degree to which a person is affected by internal versus external factors. It would be presumed that someone showing high external control may not do well in a program requiring support of behavior through self-reinforcement. As Bandura (in press) notes, Rotter's scheme is concerned with beliefs about action-outcome contingencies and not with personal efficacy. "Perceived self-efficacy and beliefs about the locus of causality must be distinguished, because convictions that outcomes are determined by one's own actions can have any number of effects on self-efficacy and behavior. People who regard outcomes as personally determined but who lack the requisite skills would experience low self-efficacy and view activities with a sense of futility" (Bandura, in press, p. 27). From this point of view, a scale assessing self-efficacy would offer more valuable information. Careful effort to match client characteristics with particular intervention procedures avoids failures caused by assumption of the client uniformity myth (Kiesler, 1966).

Intervention procedures may involve an enactive, vicarious, or emotive mode of intervention (Bandura, in press). That is, they may involve the client in direct performance of behavior or in observation of a model performing the behavior, or may concentrate on altering emotional reactions related to target behaviors. There is considerable evidence for the superiority of enactive modes of intervention in altering behavior (see Bandura, in press). Enactive modes of intervention provide more realistic information to the client concerning what can be accomplished (be mastered) and greater changes in self-efficacy, which, Bandura contends, is a critical determinant of what the client will attempt and how long he will persist in trying to cope. Thus he would argue that "reducing physiological arousal improves performance by raising efficacy expectations rather than by eliminating a drive that instigates defensive behavior" (Bandura, in press, p. 137).

Successful performance however does not automatically lead to an increased sense of self-efficacy. There are a number of factors that may attenuate its effects, including making a discrimination that the achieved performance relates only to selected situations, that success was caused by external factors rather than to personal competency, that performance is caused by effort rather than ability (Bandura, in press). Such "cognitive misappraisals that attenuate the impact of disconfirming experiences can be minimized without sacrificing the substantial benefits of powerful induction procedures . . . providing opportunities for self-directed accomplishments after the desired behavior has been established" (Bandura, in press, pp. 21-22). If it is necessary first to use symbolic procedures—for example, if anxiety is very high and gradual exposure to anxiety-eliciting events cannot be arranged in real life–in vivo procedures (those that involve exposure to actual events) should be blended with symbolic ones as soon as this is feasible.

Whenever possible, positive procedures rather than punitive ones should be selected. There should be an emphasis on increasing desirable behaviors rather than decreasing undesirable ones. This is more comfortable for the client, as well as more effective. In addition, the development of self-management skills should be arranged whenever possible, because this will offer the client more influence over his environment. Plans that will have undesirable secondary effects should be avoided. Determination of this will require thinking through with the client possible effects of a plan, including their possible impact on significant others. A check should be made of the plan to make sure it will not overburden the client or significant others with too many things to do. Whatever role and mode of intervention is selected a way to prompt appropriate behaviors may have to be selected. This may consist of verbal instructions, physical guidance, model presentation or response priming (requiring the client to perform the initial components of a chain of behaviors). Artificial prompts (those that are not part of the natural environment) should only be introduced when necessary, and minimal prompts should be employed—only those necessary to encourage the behaviors. These are then faded out as the client himself assumes the prompting function or some aspect of the environment does so.

Formulation of Specific Steps in the Change Plan

Formulating specific steps in the change plans entails the precise description of how the plan is to be carried out with this particular client. Who will be involved? What context will be employed? What reinforcers will be used? What contingencies will be arranged? What will the order of application be? Will there be alterations in procedures as intervention progresses and what criteria will be employed for introducing these changes (see Egan, 1975)? Reading may be necessary to research the use of certain procedures with given problems as well as to find out exactly how these have been employed in similar cases. The formulated plan must be evaluated in relation to the change objectives. Is this plan designed to reach these goals? Do objectives have to be modified in light of evaluation of possible plans and ways they can be implemented?

Selection of Intervention Role. An intervention role will also have to be selected. This may include verbal, instigation, replication, or direct intervention. Many traditional models of intervention rely heavily on verbal interchange between counselor and client. Within a behavioral model, this interchange is complimented by other interventive roles.

Instigation. The most frequently used role within a behavioral model is instigational intervention, in which change efforts are carried out in the natural environment by the client through agreed-on assignments. The focus is on behaviors that occur outside of the relationship between the counselor and client (Kanfer and Phillips, 1969). One advantage of an instigational approach is that it does not require direct observation by the counselor or direct intervention. This approach does require the cooperation of the client or significant others who may be involved. Disadvantages include the necessity of some client self-management skills and reliance on client-gathered data. Considerable persuasive skills may initially be required to encourage clients to carry out agreed-on tasks, or special contingencies, such as refundable deposits, may be agreed on. Reinforcement in real life hopefully will encourage clients to continue new behaviors. In order for an instigation to be carried out, the following conditions must hold:

1. The client or mediator must correctly discriminate the behavior he is to carry out and the appropriate stimulus context for its emission.
2. The behavior to be carried out must be present in the person's repertoire.
3. Stimulus conditions under which this behavior is to be carried out must be available in the environment. An important component of these stimulus conditions is a cue that controls the emission of the appropriate behavior; otherwise, the person may "forget" to engage in the behavior.

4. The worker must have sufficient ability to influence the client so that the assigned behavior is
likely to be carried on. [Gambrill, Thomas, and
Carter, 1971, p. 57]

Arrangements should be made as to when feedback on the results
of the instigation will be offered to the counselor, as well as what
to do if questions arise. Any instigation can be viewed as to
whether these requirements have been satisfied. This list can
serve as a checklist prior to presentation of the instigation and
when compliance is assessed. If compliance was not complete,
the requirements can be reviewed to ascertain which requisites
were not satisfied.

Instigations are employed with mediators as well as clients. Client-counselor agreements entail performance of novel
responses in familiar or new stimulus situations or the display of
existent behaviors in novel stimulus contexts. As suggested in
Chapter Six, there is little reason to suppose that changing the
behavior of mediators is any easier than changing the behavior
of anyone else. Attending to someone when they are behaving
appropriately may be a novel response. For example, often
parents attend to their children only when their behavior
reaches a certain level of aversiveness. They often do not attend
to children when they behave well. Attempts to increase the
probability of reinforcement of appropriate behavior by pointing out the great importance of this may be insufficient to
induce a change in behavior. Special contingencies may be required that offer a payoff to the mediators for each instance in
which they offer praise for appropriate behaviors and some way
of helping to "cue" them as to when praise should be offered,
or direct intervention in the natural environment may be required. In spite of the common use of instigations in behavioral
practice, there are few reports of the number and type of instigations employed in a given case and compliance with these. A
variety of instigations may be involved (see, for example,
Thomas and Carter, 1971).

Replication. Replication involves attempts to simulate
aspects of the natural environment for the purpose of observation or change efforts. Symbolic desensitization, in which the

client engages in imagined rehearsal, is a replication method. The client replicates part of the natural environment in his imagination. This intervention role is particularly useful when behaviors must be developed prior to carrying out homework assignments. For example, certain social behaviors may be developed first by behavior rehearsal in the office, and, when the client has acquired skill and comfort with them, he can try them in real life. In replicational methods, reinforcement can be provided immediately. This method is also helpful when the verbal skills of a client are limited. Rather than describing what he does, the client can be requested to role play his behavior so that the counselor can directly observe this. Simulated conditions should represent those in real life as closely as possible, in order to enhance generalization effects.

Direct intervention. In a direct intervention role, the counselor enters the natural environment and directly observes or influences behavior. Valuable assessment information can often be obtained by observing the client in contexts related to problematic behavior. This role does not necessarily require rapport with the targets of change unless social reinforcers are employed. It may be used in institutional settings, but has been employed in other contexts as well. For example, the counselor may demonstrate to a parent how to occasion appropriate behaviors. This role is particularly useful when clients cannot verbalize their problems or engineer their environment for change. Reinforcement can be applied immediately, as in replication. It is also useful with clients who need help in making initial responses, because the counselor can prompt their behavior.

Implementation of Change Plan

The procedures selected are carefully described to the client, including their relationship to objectives. Information collected during assessment can be reviewed, pointing out the relationship between what was discovered during this period and the specific plan now proposed. The client is informed as to what will be expected of him, as are significant others. Agreements are made describing what records are to be kept, how progress is to be evaluated and when it will be reviewed, and questions concerning procedures and rationales for their selection should be solicited from the client.

Any necessary instigations are described and the client's agreement with them solicited. Instigations indicate what is to be done in the natural environment. For example, a mother may agree that she will ignore her child's tantrums and positively reinforce desirable behaviors such as following instructions and helping siblings. It must be determined whether the client has the necessary skills for implementing programs. This is often done through role playing. Does a mother, for example, have verbal statements in her repertoire that will be reinforcing to her child? If not, these will have to be established. If direct intervention is to be employed, arrangements for this must be made with the client and significant others. Many examples are offered in later chapters illustrating the variety of procedures that may be employed in given cases.

The duration of the intervention phase is informed mainly by the social relevance criterion; that is, are clients and significant others satisfied with the degree of change? The scientific criterion may also influence this; that is, has the behavior, in comparison with the baseline information, stabilized at a new and obviously different rate (see Gelfand and Hartmann, 1975)? A sufficient number of data points will be necessary in each phase in order to satisfy the latter criterion.

Arranging a Facilitating Environment for Training Sessions. Behavioral programs may be carried out either at home or in the clinic. In either case, the learning that will take place will be maximized by arranging a distraction-free environment that discourages competing responses. Any setting events that may interfere with learning, such as fatigue of the client (or counselor) or hunger, should be avoided. Training sessions should not be arranged at a time when they may prohibit other desired activities. Perhaps a person likes to watch a particular television show in the evening and would resent a training session being planned at this time. All needed materials should be at hand and organized as needed. These may include recording forms, timers, and special stimulus events. Reinforcers used must be at hand. If reliability data is to be gathered, a second observer must be present. Another observer is helpful if carrying out the program will occupy most of the time of one person. A second person can then record information to evaluate progress. The intervention program should be carefully described to all involved parties, so that they understand the rationale for this event and so that appropriate behaviors are more likely to occur. Often a prior period will be necessary in which the counselor and client get acquainted.

An Example of Multiple Problem Intervention. Assessment often reveals the presence of a number of problem areas. For example, in a case presented by Humphreys and Beiman (1975), it was found that a twenty-eight-year-old male, in addition to a public-speaking anxiety for which he sought counseling and that caused him to faint during oral presentations, had problems in a number of other areas. He was unsure of his vocational plans; was uncomfortable in social situations and had started to avoid them; was unassertive, especially with his father-in-law, who subjected him to frequent harangues; had a fear of crowded places; and avoided eating in restaurants or attending movies. This discomfort seemed to be related to his lack of social skills as well as to self-arousal through cognitive ruminations about the negative effects of his previous public fainting episodes. In addition, Tom and his wife had frequent fights (about four to six per month), during which the wife belittled him and at times physically attacked him. Table 8 illustrates the various procedures employed over a series of eighteen sessions. As the authors note, assessment was carried out as needed during all sessions and client progress praised. Tom assumed increasing responsibility for selecting homework assignments (behavioral programing). The client's interviewing skills in relation to seeking employment were assessed through role playing, and feedback was offered concerning how his verbal and nonverbal behavior could be improved. The steps in problem solving were explained to him and were employed to help him narrow his range of vocational choices. In addition, weekly homework assignments were agreed on that engaged him in the process of seeking a job. He obtained a job during the week of the ninth session and said that he was pleased with this. Progressive relaxation was employed to offer him relaxation skills that he could employ when in anxiety-provoking situations, and these skills were also used during desensitization sessions. His social skills were assessed through behavior rehearsal, and model presentation and feedback were employed to develop additional skills. Homework assignments were designed to gradually increase his participation in conversations, and to gradually introduce him to situations where crowds were present. He himself developed a series of homework assignments related to his fear of public speaking, the last of which involved him in making a presentation to 250 people. Both in vivo (using actual situations) and symbolic desensitization (imagining events) were employed to decrease anxiety in public-speaking situations. For example, the client made oral presentations to the counselor in his office and additional people gradually joined the audience during the later practice sessions. Videotape feedback was offered during these sessions. All procedures were first carefully discussed with Tom so that he would understand their rationale. By the eighth session, Tom reported asserting himself with his father-in-law who in the past had determined the family's activities and who had insisted on paying the bills. Tom now assumed more responsibility for these areas. By the ninth session, he reported that he had attended a luncheon, a party, and a banquet without the usual discomfort he experienced in such situations. An arrangement was made to have Tom's wife see a counselor separately; however, she refused to continue and the counselor discussed with Tom alone what he could do to decrease fighting. He reported that the frequency of fights decreased to about one or two a month.

Sometimes there is a temptation, when multiple problems are presented, to work on too many at once. This tendency may be encouraged by the client who would like to see rapid progress in all areas. Addressing all problems at once may overburden the client and the rationale for selecting a manageable number must be carefully explained. It is explained that other problems will be addressed as progress is shown with initial ones.

Selection of a Monitoring Procedure

A final step prior to initiation of change efforts is selection of a way to monitor behavior so that progress can be care-

Table 8. Assessment and Treatment Procedures for Each Session

Procedure	1	2	3	4	5	6	7	8	9	10	11	12	13	14	15	16	17	18
I. *Assessment*																		
A. Information gathering	X	X	X	X														
B. Diagnostic summary: Problem conceptualization and treatment proposals					X													
II. *Treatment*																		
A. Uncertain vocational goals																		
1. Behavioral programing						X	X	X	X									
2. Examination of alternatives						X												
3. Behavioral rehearsal with feedback						X												
B. Relaxation training						X	X	X	X	X	X							
C. Inadequate social skills																		
1. Information giving[a]							X											
2. Behavioral rehearsal with feedback							X											
3. Behavioral programing							X	X	X									
D. Unassertiveness																		
1. Information giving[a]									X	X								
2. Behavioral rehearsal with videotape feedback										X	X							

	1	2	3	4	5	6	7	8	9	10	11	12	13	14	15	16	17	18
E. Fear of crowded places																		
1. Hierarchy construction																		
2. Systematic desensitization proper							X		X	X	X							
3. Programed self-relaxation and refocusing of attention												X	X	X				
F. Marital difficulty																		
1. Information giving[a]										X	X							
2. Behavioral programing											X	X	X	X	X	X		
G. Public speaking phobia																		
1. In session in vivo desensitization, modeling, videotaped feedback																X	X	
2. Extrasession in vivo desensitization																X	X	
III. *Review of progress and principles*																		X

[a]Involved discussion of general principles and specific application of principles to client's life.

Source: Humphreys and Beiman (1975, p. 313).

fully evaluated. Monitoring is very important when a series of intermediate objectives will be pursued, because feedback enables the client and counselor to know when to increase requirements. As behavior stabilizes at each criterion, the next one can be introduced. For example, if a parent now reinforces her child two times a day, the criterion can be increased to four, and so forth. A plan to obtain this information is arranged prior to initiation of the intervention plan. The same criteria that inform the selection of a baseline procedure apply to selection of a monitoring plan, and often the same method is employed (see Chapter Seven). If the client is to gather this information, a time is arranged when this will be shared with the counselor. Progress is reviewed regularly, employing a clear display form for the data.

Guidelines for Record Keeping

Records of what has been done and what has been accomplished as a result are important. The type of record that is maximally useful depends on who is going to make use of the record. The prime consumers of records are those who work directly with clients and administrators who wish to track the effectiveness of their staff. Continued funding may be contingent on such tracking. The different requirements for these two purposes are discussed separately in the following section, although in actuality all information described is important to counselors, clients, and administrators.

Recorded information of importance to counselors. A record should be kept of interventions employed, describing the problem they relate to, their rationale, exactly how they were implemented, the results, reliability checks, and the location of information describing the results. Such records are very valuable if a case is transferred to another counselor or consultation is sought, because a precise record of what has already been tried will be available. A careful description of the specific procedure employed enables one to assess the quality of the procedure employed; that is, whether it was carried out in a way that the literature would indicate is most effective and that satisfies ethical requirements. Only if the procedure employed is carefully described can its quality be determined. This is especially important if intervention is not effective. It enables one to determine whether progress has been negligible because an intervention was not applied appropriately. Conversely, it enables the determination that a certain procedure, even though applied appropriately, simply was not effective. Such information is also important if the counselor wishes to document the relationship between an intervention and outcome. The latter point pertains to the counselor as a generator of useful clinical research information, a subject that is discussed further in Chapter Twenty-Three. An occasional spot check or probe may be sufficient to gather needed information. Unfortunately, there is often no time to gather and record the information necessary to determine whether a procedure was appropriately employed or employed at all. This is especially problematic when the procedure is carried out by some significant other in the natural environment. Let us say a mother has been instructed to employ differential reinforcement to increase appropriate behaviors of her child and to decrease inappropriate ones. In order to determine whether she actually did redistribute positive reinforcement for these two classes of behavior, one would have to know their distribution during baseline (prior to intervention) and compare it with the distribution following intervention. It would be expected that an increase in positive child behavior would be accompanied by an increase in her positive consequences for such behaviors and that a decrease in inappropriate behaviors would be accompanying by a decrease in positive consequences such as attention for these behaviors. Only if we have such information can we know whether differential reinforcement was employed.

Creation of special forms makes it easier to record procedures employed. An example of a form to keep track of desensitization procedures employed is described in Chapter Eleven. A checklist to assess the quality of shaping procedure employed was described in Chapter Two.

Recorded Information of Importance to Administrators. The "Behavioral Goal Record" is employed by one community mental health center. On it the counselor specifies one to four goals each week, in addition to the method that will be used to accomplish these (Liberman, King, and DeRisi, 1976; Austin, Liberman, King, and DeRisi, 1976). For example, one desired outcome may be for a client to attain a job and a subgoal, filling out three job applications during the first week. This subgoal would be listed under the first week and under it, the intervention that will be employed to facilitate its accomplishment; for example, prompt and reinforce. Monthly goals are indicated at the top of each column, and four weeks of data can be placed on one sheet. If records are kept in this manner, the progress of the agency, of different counselors, or clients of the agency can be graphed in terms of the percentage of monthly goals accomplished. A difficulty with this form of record keeping is failure to weight goals in terms of their difficulty. The important point concerning record keeping is to make records truly meaningful to the counselor, client, and administrator who would like to be able to evaluate agency services. Appropriate record keeping is encouraged in some agencies by basing salary increments on such skills (Rinn and Vernon, 1975). "The Therapist Evaluation Data Sheet" (Rinn and Vernon, 1975, p. 9), employed by a community mental health center, monitors whether the counselor has formed a counselor-client contract; has established behavioral goals and selected intervention procedures based on behavioral principles; has gathered a multiple baseline graph; has dictated clinical impressions of the client after the initial interview and made a diagnosis (which is a state regulation); has presented a description of each session with the client, including noting whether client data is available; has shared with the referring source the goals and plans selected prior to completing them and informed this source of progress after intervention is initiated; and, lastly, records a note at termination concerning any innovations employed and problems encountered. Each counselor at the clinic is evaluated monthly on five client files that are drawn at random from her caseload. The spirit in which this evaluation effort is carried out is reflected in the title of the evaluation program, "Catch a Fellow Worker Doing Something Good Today" (Bolin and Kivens, 1974). Other incentives employed to encourage effective counselor behaviors include college credit arranged through local universities and praise and recognition for setting realistic, meaningful, and specific goals and for attaining them. All too often supervisors and administrators offer no differential incentives for performance of their clinical staff. Graphs of client progress provide another important source of records.

Graphing Data

The careful evaluation of change efforts is one of the hallmarks of a behavioral approach. Repeated measures gathered during baseline are compared with such measures collected after intervention. Graphing data is a useful means to visually display what is occurring and thus serves as a source of feedback for both clients and counselors as to whether progress is being made. Feedback concerning degree of progress may increase the client's motivation to pursue further change efforts (Leitenberg, Agras, Allen, Butz, and Edwards, 1975) and there is considerable evidence that knowledge of prior success contributes to further success (for example, Feather and Saville, 1967). Also, feedback as to progress serves as a reminder of the objectives of intervention.

The use of graphs for feedback during intervention highlights the importance of making the graph visible both in terms of where it is placed and its size. It should be placed in a visible spot such as a refrigerator door so that concerned parties can see it often, and should be large enough to readily show what is happening, at least eight by eleven inches, with values spread out over almost the entire length and width of the paper.

The graphing method selected should clearly represent the data and allow easy plotting of information. Decisions must be made as to how data should be averaged (over what period of time), how many graphs are needed to describe what is happening, and what form of data should be employed (absolute number, such as frequency of discrete responses, intervals, or time; relative number, such as proportion of intervals or time; or rate per unit of time, such as instructions followed per minute or per hour). Use of observational periods of different durations requires selection of relative number or rate rather than absolute number. If the behavior being graphed has few opportunities for occurring each day, such as making one's bed in the morning, data should be grouped, rather than being plotted each day, in order to see trends more clearly. With such behaviors, data could be plotted each day and transferred to number per week on another graph at the end of each week. If data are grouped, more information will have to be collected during each phase of a change program (baseline, intervention, and follow-up, for example). It is helpful to select the number of days or sessions in terms of the multiple of the number of days grouped (Gelfand and Hartmann, 1975). For example, if data are grouped in terms of four days, baseline might be collected over twelve days (four times three) in order to provide three data points. The number of data points available is especially important if reliability is to be checked or any statistical analysis is to be performed to evaluate progress. If by chance the data collected show a cyclic trend, it is helpful to group the data over the length of the cycle in order to more clearly discern intervention effects (Gelfand and Hartmann, 1975). More than one graph is desirable if a multiple-baseline design is employed or if generalization probes are made although this can also be noted right on the same graph if such probes have only been made occasionally, using a different symbol for the probes from that for the regular data points. A third situation where two graphs may more clearly represent data is when the intervention program involves a combined acceleration-deceleration method (one behavior is being positively reinforced and another either ignored or followed by time out, for example) and the rate of both behaviors has been determined. Clients often collect and graph their own data after receiving instructions.

How to Construct Graphs. Some time measure (days or weeks) is represented along the horizontal axis and some response measure (number, rate, duration, or percentage) on the vertical axis. Figure 10 shows the number of conversations initiated per day by a thirty-four-year-old woman during baseline and intervention. Days are represented along the horizontal axis and number of conversations along the vertical axis. This graph shows a marked increase in the number initiated following intervention as noted by the increased steepness of the slope of the line. It is easier to discriminate the data line from the graph's

Figure 10. Number of Conversations Initiated During Baseline
and Intervention

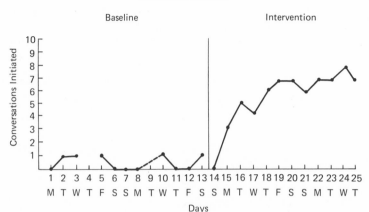

horizontal line if the zero point on the vertical axis appears slightly above the horizontal line (compare Figures 10 and 16).

Days when the behavior could not occur can be noted on the chart by not connecting the data points on either side of this time, as illustrated in Figure 10 between Wednesday and Friday of the first week during baseline. The client was ill on Thursday and stayed in bed all day. Days when a behavior cannot occur are not included on a graph. If a student is monitoring a classroom behavior that can only occur on weekdays, only weekdays are plotted. Or if a father only has his children on weekends, only weekend days can be noted on the graph.

If the behavior could have occurred but was not monitored, a dotted rather than a solid line can be drawn between the days on either side, as shown in Figure 10 during the second week of baseline. The behavior could have occurred on Tuesday, but was not monitored.

Frequency distributions. Simply plotting the number of times a behavior, thought, or feeling occurs per day, as in Figure 10, is the most typical form of graph employed. The monitoring forms described in Chapter Seven permit easy transference of data to graphs. Daily totals for one week, starting on Sunday the 14th, were 0, 3, 5, 4, 6, 7, and 7. The number of conversations initiated for Sunday is indicated on the graph by placing a point at the intersection of Monday and zero, and so on, until points have been placed on the graph for each day. A line is then drawn connecting these points.

Data gathered after a change plan has been initiated should be included on the same graph that presents baseline information, so that changes can be readily seen. Each procedural stage can be noted on the graph and emphasized by a vertical line between different phases and by not connecting the data points between phases. Labeling of graphs is well worth the effort, because different phases can easily be seen and what is plotted is clear.

Graphing the rate of behavior. Rather than plotting the daily frequency of a behavior, thought, or feeling, the counselor may wish to plot the daily rate of a behavior. Perhaps a client monitored a behavior for a different time period each day, and, to consider these different periods, the counselor must convert the data to a rate measure by dividing time into the number of behaviors. The only difference in the graph is what is indicated to the left; instead of frequency, a rate measure will appear. As with frequency measures, this data is readily transferable from recording forms.

Graphing percentages. A third response measure that may be used is percentage. Perhaps the counselor is using a monitoring procedure in which the client checks a behavior, thought, or feeling at various times throughout the day; for example, whether or not he is relaxed. Here too, the recording form employed allows easy determination of the daily percentage and the ready plotting of these data on a graph (see Figure 11).

Graphing other types of information. Measures of duration or magnitude or of a behavior product, such as number of points earned, may also be graphed. Figure 12, presented later in this chapter, represents the amount of time spent in clarinet practice, a Campfire honors project work, and reading for book reports by a ten-year-old girl.

Cumulative records. In a cumulative graph, the number of behaviors found on any one day is added to the number found on the previous days. Let us take the example of the number of positive self-statements a client recorded during baseline (3, 2, 0, 1, 3, 4, and 0). The first point on this graph will appear in the same place as it would in a frequency distribution. Thus, one

Figure 11. Percent of Instructions Followed

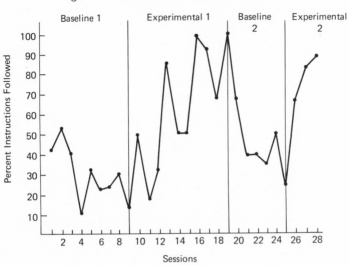

Source: Zeilberger, Sampen, and Sloane (1968, p. 49).

would place a point at the intersection of Monday and 3. However, from that point on, the method of plotting is different, in that it is cumulative; additional amounts are added to what already exists. To determine the placing of the appropriate point for the second day, 2 would be added to 3 for a total of 5, and a point placed at the intersection of Tuesday and 5, and so on. If a behavior did not occur on one day, the total for the preceding day and the day on which zero behaviors occurred is the same.

An advantage of cumulative graphs is that the rate of change can be determined from the slope of the line between the data points. The higher the slope the higher the rate of behavior. Note that a cumulative graph can only go up; it cannot go down, because values are added to each other. Thus, if one is trying to construct such a graph and the line between data points goes up and down, one has not succeeded. (For a more detailed description of graphing, see Katzenberg, 1975).

Bar graphs. Bar graphs, or *histograms* as they are sometimes called, are useful for summarizing data that cannot be otherwise grouped meaningfully. One response measure is plotted to the left, and one of a variety of measures may be indicated along the bottom of the graph (such as different individuals or groups of individuals). A teacher, for example, may wish to keep track of the number of problems each child in her class completes each week. The children's names would be recorded along the bottom line and a bar drawn up to the number each child completed. Bar graphs also permit notation of the range of values for each person by the insertion of a line related to each bar, namely a line that ranges from the lowest value for that person up to the highest value.

Evaluating the Effectiveness of Intervention

A behavioral approach is ideally suited for the evaluation of change efforts, because the targets of change are well specified and arrangements are made for their repeated measurement during assessment and intervention. This section describes a variety of designs that can be employed to assess effectiveness. Each entails the comparison of some measure of behavior during a period when a special procedure is not in effect (a baseline) with one in which it is in effect. A series of observations of the behavior to be changed is collected in each phase. The baseline allows estimation of what the level of behavior would have been in the future, if the intervention had not been introduced (Sidman, 1960; Risley, 1969). The degree of confidence that can be assumed in relation to a change occurring depends greatly on the length of time over which a baseline is gathered as well as on its stability (Risley, 1969) and on whether multiple data sources indicate similar changes. The longer and more stable the baseline, the greater confidence one can have; the greater the variety of divergent measures indicating similar changes, the more confidence is warranted. Usually, behavior of single individuals is involved, although groups of people can be treated as a single individual within such designs. Progress can also be evaluated in terms of the degree to which specific goals were reached, as in goal-attainment scaling or in terms of the percentage of problems in which improvement occurred (see Chapter Five).

The AB Design. This design requires measurement of behavior during baseline as well as during intervention. A comparison is made between the level of behavior predicted on the basis of the baseline measurement with the level obtained during intervention (see Figure 10). The AB design will inform one as to whether a change occurred and describe its magnitude but will not provide any information as to whether the change was caused by the intervention. Changes may have been caused by other variables, such as history (for example, illness or a change of job), maturation, the effects of being observed, and so forth (Campbell and Stanley, 1966). This design incorporates the minimum essential ingredients for assessing degree of change. The following designs described also offer an indication as to whether the intervention is responsible for the change. At times, this can be an important clinical question.

The Reversal Design. The reversal design involves two AB phases in which the second A period consists of the reintroduction of baseline conditions and the second B period, the reintroduction of the intervention procedure. The duration of the intervention periods depends on the success of the intervention, the stability of the behavior being assessed, and the method employed for graphing data (Gelfand and Hartmann, 1975). For example, if graphing is being done by weeks, more days would be needed. The reversal phase is often brief, because of the inconvenience associated with increasing a problematic behavior. Figure 11 presents an example of this design. During intervention, the mother reinforced desirable behaviors and used a brief time out following aggressive or disobedient behaviors. The percentage of instructions followed increased in both intervention phases. The successful reversal of the behavior provides support for the hypothesis that parental behavior is closely related to the child's behavior. The use of an AB design would not have given this assurance.

This design has a number of disadvantages, including possible irreversibility of behavioral effects. For example, one would not wish to reinstate behaviors that are dangerous. Clients may refuse to reinstate conditions that will increase a behavior that is aversive to them. Behaviors may not return to baseline levels for a variety of reasons. Perhaps behaviors developed are maintained by other reinforcers. If, for example, a child is initially reinforced by parental attention for playing cooperatively with other children, such play may itself acquire reinforcing properties, and so the removal of parental attention will no longer affect the behavior. Some skills are not easily lost, such as knowing how to swim. Thus, this design should only be selected if the behavior of concern is relatively harmless; if approval of significant others exists for reinstating the problem behavior; if baseline conditions are under the counselor's control; and if it is unlikely that factors outside of the intervention context will affect the behavior of concern (Gelfand and Hartmann, 1975).

Multiple Baseline Designs. This discussion of the AB and ABAB designs has pointed out the weaknesses of the former and the difficulties in arranging the latter. Multiple baseline designs provide a way to secure more confidence as to whether a given intervention is responsible for change than does the AB design; they do so in a manner that does not require reversal of positive changes. Such designs involve application of the intervention program to a selected subsample of individuals, groups, behaviors, or situations, and involves measurement of several behaviors over a period of time, either of one person or a group of individuals, thus creating several baselines (Risley, 1969). These may be different behaviors of the same person in the same situation, the same behavior of one person in different situations, or the same behavior of many people in the same situation. In each case, the intervention is applied to one behavior at a time. If a change occurs in its frequency and no change takes place in the frequency of the other behaviors, then the intervention is applied to the next behavior. As the number of behaviors increase that have changed in frequency only after the intervention is introduced, confidence grows that change is related to intervention. Thus in each type of multiple baseline design, many behaviors are baselined, the intervention applied to one at a time, and all behaviors are monitored. In this design, because behaviors are selected that are likely to be similarly affected by a single intervention procedure, the range of behaviors to which this design is applicable is more restricted than with the ABAB design (Gelfand and Hartmann, 1975).

Multiple baselines across situations. In yet another design, involving multiple baselines across situations, one behavior of one person or of a group of individuals is measured in different

situations. In a classroom, time, type of activity, teacher, location, and composition of the student group are some possible
dimensions. Hall, Cristler, Cranston, and Tucker (1970) reported a study in which a teacher measured the time of student
return to the classroom following recess at three different periods: noon, morning, and afternoon. The reinforcer employed
was the listing of the name of those coming back within the
allowed time on a "Today's Patriots" list (see Figure 12).

Figure 12. A Record of the Number of Pupils Late in Returning to Their
Fifth-Grade Classroom After Noon, Morning, and Afternoon Recess.
No Charts—Baseline, Before Experimental Procedures.
Patriots' Chart—Posting of Pupils' Names on "Today's Patriots"
Chart, Contingent on Entering Class on Time After Recess.
No Chart—Posting of Names Discontinued. *Patriots' Chart*—Return to
Patriots' Chart Conditions. *Unpatriots' Chart*—Posting of Names on
"Unpatriots' " Chart Contingent on Being Late After Recess (FR 2)
Every Two Days, (FR 3) Every Three Days, and (FR 5) Every Five Days.

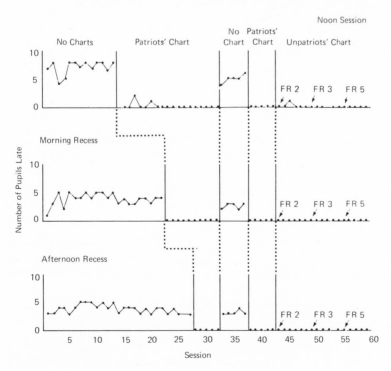

Source: Hall and others (1970, p. 249).

Steps in the use of this type of multiple baseline design include the following: (1) identification of a behavior of an individual or a group of individuals that occurs in different situations; (2) baselining of the frequency, duration, or intensity of this behavior in the different situations; (3) selection of an intervention strategy and the application of this to the selected behavior in *one* of these situations, while at the same time monitoring the frequency of behavior in all situations; and (4) examination of the data following a suitable period of intervention. If but one individual is included, the frequency of the behavior during intervention is compared with that in the other situations. If a group of individuals is employed, the behavior of the group members in each situation is averaged and these averages compared. If the comparison indicates that the procedure resulted in a positive change not seen in the other situations, this same procedure is then applied to the next situation, and so on until the intervention is applied in all situations. Behavior is continuously monitored in all situations.

Multiple baseline across individuals. In the design of multiple baseline across individuals, one behavior of several people in the same situation is measured. Steps in the employment of this design include the following: (1) specification of a behavior of an individual or a group of individuals in one situation; (2) collection of a baseline in this one situation for each person; (3) selection of an intervention strategy and application of this to the behavior of one person or one group of individuals, while monitoring the behavior of all individuals or groups of individuals; and (4) comparison of the behavior of the one person or one group with that of the other individuals or groups. If this comparison shows that the intervention produced a positive change not shown by the others, it is applied to another individual or group, and so on until all individuals or groups are involved (see Figure 13).

Multiple baseline across behaviors. In the design of multiple baseline across behaviors, baselines are obtained on two or more behaviors of the same person. The same individual is involved, and the same situation, but different behaviors within this situation. (See Figure 14 for an example. Data collection and the program were carried out by a parent.)

Figure 13. A Record of Quiz Score Grades for Three High School French-Class Students. *Baseline*—Before Experimental Procedures. *After-School Tutoring Contingent on D and F Grades*—Pupils Required to Stay After School for Tutoring if They Score D or F on Daily Quizzes.

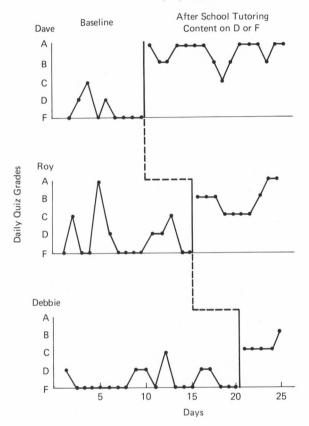

Source: Hall and others (1970, p. 251).

Use of a multiple baseline design requires extra time and effort—for example, in taking three different baselines and waiting until stability appears in each. Also, reliability should be checked in each situation or with each behavior or time. A major difficulty may be finding behaviors that are independent —each behavior can be modified separately without changing the rate of the other behaviors (Kazdin, 1973b; Kazdin and Kopel, 1975). Although generalization of positive effects is

Figure 14. A Record of Time Spent in Clarinet Practice, Campfire Honors
Project Work, and Reading for Book Reports by a Ten-Year-Old Girl.
Baseline—Before Experimental Procedures. *Early Bedtime Contingent on
Less than Thirty Minutes of Behavior*—One Minute Earlier Bedtime for
Each Minute Less than Thirty Engaged in an Activity.

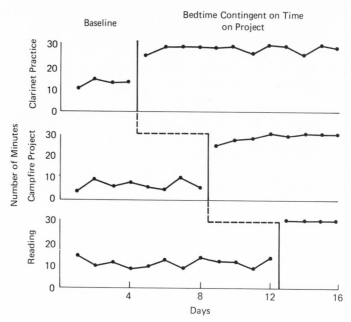

Source: Hall and others (1970, p. 252).

desirable in terms of the client's interest, it is not possible to
have the same degree of assurance that the intervention was
responsible for the change. Behaviors also cannot be developmental requisites for each other (such as standing, walking, and
running of a child), because these would have to be treated in a
certain sequence (Gelfand and Hartmann, 1975). It should be
noted that the examples of multiple baseline studies given were
carried out by parents and teachers.

The Changing Criterion Design. The changing criterion
design is especially suitable where a goal is pursued in a series of
steps and when changes in behavior can be expected fairly soon
after a new criterion is required (Hartmann and Hall, 1976). A
baseline is first taken of some behavior such as cigarettes

smoked or reading rate and then a criterion established for reinforcement. During the first step of intervention, the reinforcer is offered for a given level of performance (or behavior product, such as weight loss). If behavior changes, a new criterion for reinforcement is selected and used. If behavior change coincides closely with changes in criteria level for reinforcement, assurance develops that the program is responsible for the changes. Influence on the behavior is demonstrated by replicating an intervention program across a series of specified criteria. As with all time-series designs, phases should be long enough to ensure that a change is not naturally taking place due to factors such as maturation or history (Campbell and Stanley, 1966). If possible, "treatment phases should differ in length, or, if of a constant length, should be preceded by a baseline phase longer than each of the separate treatment phases. This is to ensure that stepwise changes in the rate of the target behavior are not occurring naturally in synchrony with criterion changes. The baseline should also be stable (having a zero slope) or should be changing in a counter-therapeutic direction" (Hartmann and Hall, 1976, p. 530). Each intervention phase must be long enough to permit the behavior to stabilize at a new rate before introducing a new criterion. This design does not require a reversal of effects and is suitable for the many programs in which the criterion for reinforcement is changed in a stepwise fashion.

   Simultaneous Treatment Design. It is often necessary to decide which particular program will be most effective with a client. The simultaneous treatment design permits collection of such information in an efficient manner (Browning and Stover, 1971). This design is diagramed below. A represents the baseline

$$
\begin{array}{c}
\text{B} \\
| \\
\text{A} - \text{C} - \text{B} - \text{C or D} \\
| \\
\text{D}
\end{array}
$$

condition, and the vertical entries of B, C, and D represent three different intervention conditions. This design was employed to

discover the most effective treatment strategies to alter uncooperative and disruptive behavior of a six-year-old boy in
a class of thirty-six first-grade students (McCullough, Cornell,
McDaniel, and Mueller, 1974). These behaviors included roaming around the classroom, sleeping, daydreaming, arguing with
other children, and playing at his desk with pencils and other
school materials. These behaviors were labeled *uncooperative*,
and *cooperative* behavior was defined as doing class assignments
and not engaging in any uncooperative behavior. Baseline data
were collected over five days by a teacher and her aide during
two-hour periods in the morning and afternoon. Each period
was divided into fifteen-minute intervals. A minus was recorded
for one interval if during that time Cedric exhibited any uncooperative behavior, and a plus was recorded if he worked on assignments and showed no uncooperative behavior. Two treatment
strategies were then compared: A, where social reinforcement
(verbal praise and physical contact) followed cooperative behavior while uncooperative behavior was ignored; and B, which
paired social reinforcement with cooperative behavior and time
out with uncooperative behavior. During time out, Cedric was
removed from the classroom and placed in an empty room for
two minutes. During the last two days, the teacher conducted
treatment B and the aide, treatment A, while also alternating
treatments between morning and afternoon sessions. Treatment
A was offered by the teacher during the first two days. This
allowed partial control for sequence and experimenter effects.

The most effective strategy was selected on the basis of
the information collected during Phase Two and this was then
implemented in Stage Three. Figure 15 illustrates that Condition B was more effective than was Condition A. These results
supported the author's hypothesis that Cedric's behavior varied
as a function of the teacher's reinforcement and suggested the
most effective procedure for altering his behavior. This information was collected rapidly, in four days, and allowed the teacher
and her aide to pursue their regular class activities.

Sequential Treatment Designs. A sequential design allows
determination of the effects of a series of treatment strategies.

A-BC-B-BC design. One type of sequential design presents
a composite treatment variable (BC), removes one component

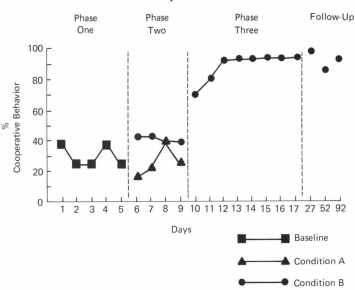

Figure 15. Percentage of Observation Periods in Which Cedric
Showed Cooperative Behavior

Source: McCullough and others (1974, p. 291).

of this (Phase B) and then reintroduces the combination (BC). This permits determination of the effects of one of the treatment components on behavior. This design was employed to assess the effects of the noxious scene in covert sensitization (a form of imaginal aversive conditioning) in relation to the client's responses on a card sort containing a hierarchy of sexually arousing scenes and the number of daily urges toward "immature girls" (Barlow, Leitenberg, and Agras, 1969). Operant rates of these behaviors were recorded during a baseline period (A). This was followed by the use of covert sensitization (BC) in which deviant sexually arousing scenes were paired in the imagination with verbal descriptions of nausea. The specific effect of the noxious scene was examined in Phase B (which consisted only of the presentation of the noxious scene), followed in turn by the reintroduction of Phase BC. Figure 16 shows that total score on the card sort decreased dramatically during both BC phases but increased during Phase B, thus suggesting the effectiveness of the pairing procedure. This example illustrates the

Figure 16. Total Score on Card Sort Per Experimental Day and Total
Frequency of Pedophilic Urges in Blocks of Four Days Surrounding Each
Experimental Day. Lower Scores Indicate Less Sexual Arousal.

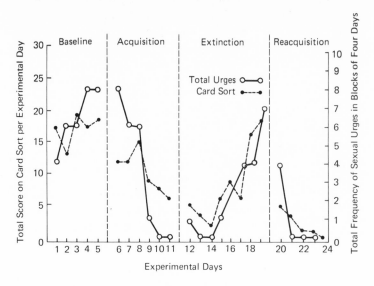

Source: Barlow, Leitenberg, and Agras (1967, p. 599).

potential contribution to practice knowledge that counselors
can make during their everyday practice in a way that is also
directly relevant to case management.

Combined designs. A variety of combined designs have
been employed in the attempt to assess the additive effects of
various procedures. For example, Leitenberg and others (1968)
investigated the additive effects of feedback and praise in relation to the amount of time a knife-phobic client remained in
the presence of the phobic object while behind a closed door.
This design could be diagramed B-BC-B-A-B-BC-B. The procedures in effect during these various phases can be seen in Figure
17. Feedback consisted of informing the client how much time
she had spent in the presence of the phobic object and praise
consisted of verbal reinforcement whenever she exceeded a progressively increasing time criterion. The results showed that
feedback alone was the critical variable in change. This conclusion was strengthened by the reversal obtained in Phase A.

Figure 17. Time in Which a Knife Was Kept Exposed by a Phobic Patient
as a Function of Feedback, Feedback Plus Praise, and
No Feedback or Praise Conditions

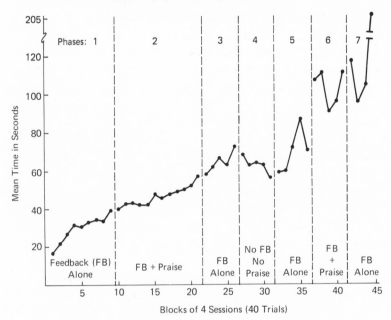

Source: Leitenberg and others (1968, p. 136).

Carryover and order effects are possible, contaminating factors
in the latter types of single-organism designs (Hersen and Barlow, 1976).

Evaluating Expectancy Effects. Single-organism designs
also allow determination of the role of client expectations (Barlow, 1974). A positive expectancy phase entails telling the
client that he will get better but not offering what is thought to
be the effective intervention. A negative expectancy phase entails telling the client that he will get worse, but offering the
intervention. For example, a study by Barlow (1974) showed
that expectancy effects were not responsible for changes in sexual arousal by covert sensitization, because no changes occurred
under a positive expectancy condition, but such changes did
occur during the negative expectancy condition, even though
client self-report did not match these changes.

Factors to Consider when Evaluating Effects of Proce-dures. In addition to the questions that may be raised because of the specific type of single organism design carried out, there are a number of additional factors that may limit confidence in whether a specific procedure did indeed lead to a given effect (Kazdin, 1973b). Questions that arise may concern both internal validity (the extent to which effects are caused by the intervention employed) and external validity (the degree to which the results can be generalized to other populations of behaviors, people, or situations). (See Campbell and Stanley, 1966, for a further discussion of these points.) As Kazdin (1973b) notes, factors may covary with the intervention, which thus makes it impossible to know the actual role of the intervention alone. For example, different instructions often accompany different reinforcement procedures (see, for example, Ayllon and Azrin, 1965). Another example is the informational function that reinforcement may have (indicating the contingencies in effect) separate from the reinforcement function per se (Bandura, 1971b). Thus token programs carry an informational function as well as incentive functions (Kazdin, 1973b). External validity is threatened by a number of factors, for a discussion of which the reader is referred to Campbell and Stanley (1966). Some examples that may limit external validity include using a special sequence of treatments (generalization may be limited to situations where this same sequence is employed) and the effects that observers may have on outcome.

When Intervention Fails

The most appropriate rule to follow when intervention fails is "Grandma's Rule" (Lindsley, 1968b, p. 12), which says to try and try again. An examination of data describing the effects of intervention will indicate whether behavior has changed, and, as Lindsley (1968b) emphasizes, "the child always knows best" (p. 13); that is, whether in fact a change occurs is the final arbiter of the effectiveness of an intervention procedure no matter how convinced one might have been that it will be effective. There are a number of question that should be raised, however, before making a decision that the intervention plan selected was not viable. The initial change procedure selected should be the one most likely to work at the most comfort to the client in the most efficient manner with the least side effects. Hopefully much thought has gone into this selection and the intervention plan should not be lightly discarded. First, was behavior actually monitored? Is the report of little progress based only on the client's or counselor's "feeling" that nothing is changing? Clients may request the counselor to accept their feelings concerning degree of progress, by saying, for example, "Yes, I know you said I should monitor the behavior, but I know what is happening without it. It didn't seem necessary." Such a statement may be made even though the counselor has made careful efforts to share with the client the rationale for monitoring. Actually, no one really knows what is happening, because no one cared enough to keep track of how often the behavior, thought, or feeling occurred, and this can be pointed out. The main point is not to accept a "feeling" that there has not been any change (the same holds for a report of positive change based on a "feeling"). Possible objections to the monitoring or intervention plan that have not previously been shared by the client can be explored. He could be asked, "Is there any way the monitoring process could be made easier for you? Let's take a look at the program we agreed on. Is there any way we could change it that would appeal to you?" If no legitimate issues emerge here, such as a monitoring procedure that was too difficult or client selection of an alternative intervention plan that would probably be as effective, the same instruction can be reinstated.

If the behavior was monitored and no change occurred, the question that should be raised is whether the intervention program was carried out as agreed on in a consistent fashion. This can only be determined by careful questioning as to the details of the program. For example, if the client agreed to practice relaxation and was asked to keep track of the times, duration, and outcome of practice sessions, these records should be carefully reviewed. How many times did he practice? For how long each time? Answers to these questions will reveal the extent of practice. If little practice took place, it is not surprising if little progress has occurred. If a mother agrees to increase the frequency with which she reinforces a child, and is to monitor this for a period of each day, records are reviewed to see how often she offered such reinforcement. The frequency of reinforcement or practice of a behavior is critical to behavior change, and this is why careful review of exactly what was done by the client is important to assess the effectiveness of a procedure. A procedure that is not applied will not work. Frequent client counselor contact by telephone or postcard between sessions can help to identify, at an early point, when procedures are not being employed. These contacts can be used as an opportunity to determine difficulties with a plan at an early point. Such questioning will often reveal that the client did not employ the procedure at all or as agreed on, and possible reasons for the failure must be determined. Perhaps an incentive will be required, such as making further contact dependent on completion of agreed-on prior steps. Failure to carry out a plan should also be used as an opportunity to determine unexpressed client objections to the plan. However, a viable plan should only be abandoned if legitimate objections are raised. Careful review will help to determine whether failures were caused by skill or motivational deficits.

Continued failure to carry out plans in a consistent fashion in spite of careful discussion of their rationale and despite careful arrangement for facilitating incentives and prompts calls for a discussion of this between counselor and client. This discussion should only occur after everything feasible has been done to enhance the possibility of assignment completion. Other intervention modes may be necessary, such as replication or direct intervention. An instigational approach will not be effective with all clients.

Careful monitoring and questions may reveal that the plan was implemented as agreed on and it was not effective over a reasonable amount of time. The counselor should keep in mind that some intervention procedures may take a few days to create a behavior change, even to attain an approximation to a desired outcome. The need for response prompting should always be checked, as should the need for procedures that will maximize the effectiveness of reinforcers. The intervention plan must either be improved or a new plan selected, perhaps drawing from alternatives previously generated. Requisites for the plan should be carefully checked to make sure that none were overlooked. If no other plan seems to be a likely possibility or other attempts have also failed, it is time to obtain consultation or to offer the client the option of being referred elsewhere.

The Generalization and Maintenance of Change

It does little good to develop appropriate behavior in the office for example, without the display of this behavior in relevant situations. And little has been accomplished if changes are not durable. New behaviors created in one context may occur in others, but their fate will depend on whether they are reinforced in these other contexts (a maintenance problem). Let us say that a child does not follow instructions either in school or at home, and that a program has successfully increased the frequency of instructions followed at home. Perhaps he will also start to follow instructions at school; however, if the teacher does not reinforce this behavior it will not persist. And if the teacher has persistently failed to reinforce instruction following, it is unlikely that an initial increase will occur. This example illustrates the two different kinds of deficits in extratherapy responding (Koegel and Rincover, in press). Lack of correct responding in extracounseling sessions has been labeled a *problem of generalization*, whereas initial correct responding followed by a subsequent decrease in behavior has been labeled a *deficit in maintenance*. This distinction is important if these two problems have different intervention implications, and there are indications that this is the case. For example, in a study in which autistic children were trained in behaviors such as nonverbal imitation, the thinness of the reinforcement schedule used during training influenced durability of change in other settings (the thinner the better) and periodic use of noncontingent reinforcers in extratherapy settings further increased durability (Koegel and Rincover, in press). Without these special programs, change was not durable in other settings. In another study with autistic children, the problem of generalization was found to be a problem of antecedent stimulus control (Rincover and Koegel, 1975). When the cue that was functional during training was identified and used in the extratherapy setting, generalization took place. Thus maintenance was a matter of reinforcement control and, when the discriminability of training and extratherapy settings was decreased, greater changes were seen in other settings.

Generalization. Generalization may occur across behaviors (response generalization) or across situations (stimulus generalization). There are a number of studies indicating that changing one behavior influences another that has not been the direct subject of focus (Kazdin, 1973b). Behaviors that tend to be similar in form to the behavior focused on tend to be most likely candidates for change, although in some instances behaviors very different in form have changed (see, for example, Wahler and others, 1970; Wahler, 1975). Unfortunately, there have been few systematic attempts to investigate the variables that influence both the durability of change efforts as well as the generalization of change efforts to new situations. What few studies exist indicate a lack of generalization of change from one setting to another (Kazdin and Bootzin, 1972). For example, Wahler (1969a) found little generalization of positive effects between the home and school setting in the elimination of a child's disruptive behavior. Some studies have found negative contrast effects (see Johnson, Bolstad, and Lobitz, 1976). Careful attention is required during intervention programs to make sure that the variety of significant others, reinforcers, reinforcement schedules and types of reinforcement employed during training match those in the environment where the behavior is expected to occur after intervention. Thus conditions provided in the training setting should match those in the natural environment as closely as possible. If, for example, the desired goal is for a child to follow more parental instructions, practice in this should be provided during training in relation to both the father and mother.

Whenever possible, intervention programs should be carried out in the natural environment, involving those individuals integrally involved in influencing problematic behaviors and desirable alternatives. This is often not possible initially, and training is thus carried out in some artificial setting such as the office. Whenever the natural environment is not the locus for change efforts, a program must be designed to arrange the display of appropriate behaviors in settings related to desired outcomes. One cannot simply count on generalization of effects. Instead, careful planning is called for, including the use of multiple training agents, so that behavior will not just be under the influence of one person; multiple settings, so that it will not be limited to one setting; multiple types and sources of reinforcement; and multiple models. It has been found that skills mastered by autistic children when instruction was offered in a one-to-one training session did not generalize to a group setting, even when groups as small as two children were used with one teacher (Koegel and Rincover, 1974). A procedure employing a gradual increase in group size together with increased intermittency of reinforcement did enable the children to continue to improve their performance in a classroom of eight children with one teacher. This was important, because the aim was to see if severely disturbed children could be gradually integrated into a regular classroom situation. In each setting in which the behavior is to occur, the question must be asked, "What are the environmental sources of control?" The term *generalization* has often been used to refer to any behavior change occurring in the nontraining session. As noted by Johnston (1975), this use is misleading, because it suggests that only one process is at work when a number of different phenomenon need to be described, explained, and controlled.

Probes for generalization can offer useful information concerning the extent to which change in one situation affects behavior in other situations, or the extent to which a change in one behavior affects a change in another. If this is done, data must be gathered concerning the baseline frequency of the behavior in these other settings.

Maintaining Change. Little is gained by inducing temporary positive changes. In order to assure continuation of such changes, a maintenance plan is usually required. Questions concerning the durability of behavior change have been asked from two different perspectives. One is from a "magical" perspective, in which intervention is expected to create permanent changes, durable under all conditions. This view is quite unrealistic, because behavior is influenced by the environment, and if the environment changes, so will behavior. Only if changes in behavior are supported by the social environment will effects persist. Although there are procedures to enhance the possibility of maintenance of positive changes, such as developing self-reinforcing behaviors, the environment may offer little support for new behaviors and they may gradually drift back to original levels. A concern for the persistence of change is an integral aspect of selection of initial intervention strategies. The rationale for the involvement of significant others during change efforts is their continuing role in relation to the client. The focus within behavioral practice on altering contingencies within the client's social network thus helps to assure maintenance of positive changes. Change has not been achieved within an artificial environment, but occurs directly in the natural environment. This is not to say that drift may not occur. That is, significant others may start to return to earlier patterns of reinforcement. There are probably certain characteristics of ongoing relationships such as parent-child and marital interactions that facilitate a drift toward less frequent use of positive events to alter behavior. Positive behaviors are easy to ignore and punishment, although ineffective in the long run, can be quite effective immediately. Occasional tracking of pleasing and displeasing events may serve as a cue to guard against the reestablishment of old coercive interaction patterns as well as to "catch" the beginning stages of a downward trend in positives (Weiss, 1975). Periodic monitoring can be encouraged by postcards sent to involved parties at six-month intervals, requesting counts of pleasing and displeasing behavior for one week (Weiss, 1975). Changes in the mediator's behavior that alter a client's behavior may lead to a so-called chain reaction, in which, because of these positive changes, the mediator begins reacting to the client in a more positive way, which occasions even further appropriate behaviors on the part of the client (Patterson, McNeal, Hawkins, and Phelps, 1967). In such cases, maintenance of behavior is very likely.

Careful arrangement must be made for assuring that the mediator's new behavior will be reinforced. Positive changes in the client's behavior (such as a child or spouse) may be sufficient to maintain such changes; however, often additional incentives, such as counselor attention and praise or tokens, may initially be required. Any artificial contingencies must be gradually removed. Counselor attention should become less important as environmental reinforcers become more important. If any artificial reinforcers have been utilized to obtain desired changes, such as points, credits, or tokens, these must gradually be faded out, that is, given less and less frequently until none are used at all and the behavior still takes place at a satisfactory rate. Fading of artificial reinforcers can be accomplished either by requiring more behaviors for a given number of points or by providing fewer and fewer credits for a given behavior. This is usually accomplished by a transfer from a continuous schedule of reinforcement (offering reinforcement every time the behavior occurs), to an intermittent schedule in which reinforcement is only offered after a certain number of responses are performed or following the passage of a certain time interval. Thus maintenance of behavior requires movement to a schedule of reinforcement that is typically provided in real life. Although behaviors will usually be established by continuous reinforcement, in which all behaviors are followed by positive consequences, successful maintenance requires movement to an intermittent reinforcement schedule because most behavior is only followed by intermittent positive consequences. Following continuous reinforcement, consequences may be provided only after every second behavior, then every fourth behavior, and so forth. The rapidity with which the schedule is thinned should be informed by what happens to the behavior. Behavior maintained at the same level indicates an effective thinning schedule. If the behavior decreases substantially, this indicates that the schedule is being thinned too rapidly, and a return should be made to an earlier schedule temporarily. Learning to anticipate positive outcomes by self-presented statements may facilitate persistence of behavior when backup reinforcers are delayed.

Persistence of behavior change may also be enhanced by introducing increasingly longer delays between behavior and reinforcement as well as by increasing the client's self-reinforcement skills. Self-reinforcement involves three steps: the observation of one's behavior, an evaluation of behavior according to some criteria, and the offer of self-reinforcement dependent on whether one's behavior meets these criteria (Kanfer, 1970). To increase self-reinforcement the client is trained in all three steps. For example, adolescents in a classroom in a psychiatric hospital program were trained to monitor and regulate their own behavior in order to increase the durability of a behavioral intervention program (Santogrossi, O'Leary, Romanczyk, and Kaufman, 1973). This resulted in a beneficial impact on problem behavior. Reinforcement for cooperative behavior was first offered by the counselor, and, when the rate of problematic behavior had decreased substantially, the self-evaluation program was introduced. Each student rated his own performance, decided how many tokens he deserved, and announced his decision to the teacher and his classmates. Failure of similar attempts stresses the importance of reinforcement for accuracy of self-evaluation when self-evaluation is first introduced. A shaping procedure can be employed to gradually increase accuracy of evaluation (Santogrossi and others, 1973). In order for self-reinforcement to persist, it will probably have to be reinforced occasionally. This question has not received much attention to date.

Occasional meetings with the counselor or, better yet, meetings as needed with a "buddy" sympathetic to self-reinforcement efforts can be used to maintain self-reinforcement. Making sure to blend self-reinforcement with pleasing changes in the environment such as cues concerning the adequacy of one's performance may also help to maintain self-reinforcement (Bandura, 1969). The importance of providing self-directed mastery experiences, after capabilities have been developed, in which expectations of personal efficacy are strengthened and generalized is suggested by recent studies (see, for example, Bandura, Jeffery, and Gajdos, 1975).

In addition to arranging for significant others to reinforce new behaviors and for an increase in self-reinforcement, new activities themselves may assume reinforcing qualities. For example, if learning new skills is consistently reinforced, learning itself may become reinforcing. This was the hope of the program for juveniles at the National Boys Training School. It was hoped that by pairing learning with items and activities that were already reinforcing, learning would become a reinforcer (Cohen and Filipczak, 1971). "Many forms of behavior, such as communicative facility and manipulatory skills, which permit an individual to regulate his environment more effectively, persist with little external support because they are functional in producing rewarding outcomes. New performances are also partially sustained by the sensory feedback that they naturally produce" (Bandura, 1969, p. 238).

Occasional self-monitoring may also help to maintain positive changes. Perhaps a woman client feels that her rate of positive self-statements is decreasing. The first useful action for her to take would be to keep count for a few days of their frequency to see if her "feelings" are accurate. Self-monitoring may, of course, be reactive and thus result in an increase in such thoughts. If a decrease in thoughts is found, then intervention procedures can be temporarily reintroduced to increase them. The durability of behavior changes may thus be enhanced by a change in the frequency or magnitude of reinforcement, the locus of reinforcement, or the form of reinforcement (Bandura, 1969).

Special maintenance programs will be required whenever the natural environment does not offer reinforcement for new behaviors or when this reinforcement will tend to decrease over time. The sheer persistence of given behaviors for many years, such as a high frequency of negative self-statements, may necessitate occasional self-monitoring and periodic reintroduction of change procedures for a long time in order to maintain positive changes. The relevance-of-behavior rule, which emphasizes teaching only behaviors that will continue to be reinforced after training, provides the greatest assurance of maintenance of positive changes (Ayllon and Azrin, 1968b). The rehabilitative process may never end for some individuals. There may be a continuing need for supportive services. This is especially true for multiple-problem families with limited material resources as well as personal resources and with individuals who have severe physical, affective, or cognitive limitations, unless a prosthetic environment can be found for such individuals (see Chapter Twenty-One). In referring to some of the clients seen in community mental health centers, Liberman, King, and DeRisi

(1976, p. 579) have said, "There is no neat compartmentaliza-
tion of terminated versus open cases. Yesterday's successfully
terminated case becomes tomorrow's open case in crisis."

Summary

Selection of an intervention plan is directly informed by
assessment efforts. Such efforts provide information concerning
personal and environmental resources, the objectives of change,
the initial repertoire of the client, characteristics of the various
response systems involved, and the relationship of presenting
problems to other areas in the client's life. Thus both facilitating factors and those that may hinder change efforts if not
addressed are carefully considered in the development of change
plans. The usual intervention role is instigational: mutually
agreed-on assignments are carried out by the client in the natural environment. Client logs enable careful monitoring of
changes so that informed decisions can be made as to next
steps. Client acquisition of skills in behavioral analysis and in
programing of change is encouraged by gradually requesting the
client to assume more responsibility for selecting next steps and
procedures.

Graphs as well as logs provide useful case management
information. Progress is regularly reviewed by both clients and
counselors, and may be evaluated within a variety of designs,
some of which also enable determination of the effects of procedural components. These designs permit counselors not only
to obtain information critical for informed case management,
but also to add to knowledge concerning effective procedures.
Maintenance of positive changes is considered in the initial
selection of intervention plans in terms of including significant
others in change programs and establishing self-reinforcement
skills. Arranging for the persistence of positive changes is an
integral aspect of behavioral intervention and, when it is unlikely that the natural environment will maintain such changes,
special maintenance programs must be arranged. The effects of
generalization cannot be counted on to assure behavior in different contexts. Rather, the entire host of intervention methods
employed in inducing change in one situation may be needed to
arrange for the behavior in other situations.

9

There is an extensive literature describing the use of behavior methods with children and their significant others, including parents, siblings, peers, and teachers. In keeping with a social learning framework, the child's behavior is assumed to be influenced by those with whom he interacts, and there is a focus on significant others as well as on the child during assessment and intervention (Patterson and Reid, 1970). An impressive amount of support now exists for the idea that social reinforcement from parents is sufficient to maintain deviant behavior (see Patterson, 1971b).

Many family members do not possess effective reinforcement skills that encourage desired behaviors, and thus resort to aversive methods such as demands for immediate change, nagging, yelling, and so forth, until the target of these unpleasant

Behavioral Intervention with Children, Adolescents, and Their Families

events finally complies simply to end them (Patterson and Reid, 1970). Compliance encourages these annoying behaviors, because they have "paid off." Demands for immediate change generate counteraggression and bad feelings that may lead to further unpleasant interaction, spiraling into a series of unpleasant exchanges. This coercive interaction sequence is contrasted with one in which each party employs positive means to influence the others, as in a reciprocal relationship. The thrust of intervention that flows from this conceptualization of family conflict is to offer children and their significant others positive means of bringing about changes they would like, to replace the aversive or ineffective procedures previously relied on.

Coercive behaviors, such as yelling, demanding, and hitting, may be strengthened by either positive or negative reinforcement. A parent may offer praise for undesirable behaviors that are at other times complained about, or such behavior could be encouraged by the removal of negative events, such as when a child finally cleans up his room after his mother has nagged him. Observational studies of parent-child interaction have shown that parents of problem children offer richer schedules of positive consequences for coercive behaviors than do parents of nonproblem children (Sallows, 1972). However, data such as the modest correlation between deviant behavior and positive consequence for such behaviors indicate that other factors, such as the kinds of reinforcement and punishment employed and antecedent events, may be even more crucial (Patterson, 1976). An examination of parents who generate aggressive children will highlight variables of importance in understanding the development of deviant child behavior.

Distinct differences have been found between parents who generate aggressive children and those who do not. The former type of parent is less likely to track the minor incidents that typically lead to high-amplitude responses such as a fistfight between two children (Patterson, Cobb, and Ray, 1973). These parents are less likely to disrupt chains of aversive behavior and more likely to use ineffective reactions such as yelling or nagging when they finally do react, which may be reinforcing and so increase problem behavior if not followed by punishment. They tend to ignore desirable behaviors. Attending to negative behaviors that are of a specially unpleasant magnitude will encourage such responses in the future. This is how tantrum behavior can be rapidly shaped by parents and teachers. Because of ineffective child management skills, coercive behaviors may increase and the parent is increasingly trained to yell, hit, and nag at higher rates. As he becomes more aversive to his children, they are likely to offer him less positive events, which will influence him to decrease the positive events he offers to his children even more. Effective mothers "track" their children's behavior more closely and intervene in the beginning of a chain of disruptive behavior. They may do so by introducing items or situations that will encourage prosocial behavior. Effective mothers anticipate situations that might lead to coercive child behaviors and reinforce desirable behaviors.

In many families, the presence of an aggressive child is complemented by high levels of aversive behaviors among all family members. Noxious behaviors may include shouting, yelling, or talking loudly; attacking or attempting to attack another person; making fun of, shaming, or embarrassing another person intentionally; high-rate behaviors that, if carried on long enough, would be aversive, such as jumping up and down; and negative commands in which immediate compliance is demanded and aversive consequences implicitly or actually threatened if compliance is not immediate (Patterson, Ray, Shaw, and Cobb, 1969). It is within this social system that the identified child learns his coercive skills (Patterson, 1976). A key factor within such systems is the relationship between an aversive action by one person and its effect in initiating similar reactions in another family member. For example, with both aggressive and nonaggressive boys, 22 percent of the coercive initiations were preceded by aversive behavior of another family member. Children have ample opportunity to learn coercive behaviors (Patterson, 1976). Observations in the homes of normal children revealed that coercive behaviors that attempt to influence others through providing pain (such as hitting) occurred between .02 and .5 times per minute. Such high rates of aversive behaviors have been found in other settings such as nursery schools. The opportunities for vicarious learning of aggressive reactions are augmented by high rates of aggressive episodes in children's cartoons and adult television shows. Children observe the consequences of coercive actions and note that they are often quite successful in influencing the environment. Some of their experience accrues from being victims of siblings; they first learn to effectively counter the coercive behaviors of their sisters or brothers and then learn to imitate them (Patterson, Littman, and Bricker, 1967). If their aggressive attempts are effective in controlling the reactions of peers and siblings, this will increase the probability of such behaviors.

Children vary considerably in the frequency with which they display coercive behaviors, and there is a consistent downward trend from a high point in infancy to lower levels at the time of entry into school (Patterson, 1976). The average rate of deviant responses for a sample of normal three-year-olds is higher (.820 coercive responses per minute) than the average rate (.750) for boys aged five to fifteen referred for treatment because of aggressiveness (see Patterson, 1974, 1976). Thus boys who have been identified as aggressive perform coercive behaviors at a rate almost equal to that of a normal three- to four-year-old. It can only be hypothesized at this point that the decrease in frequency of some types of coercive behaviors is related to decreased parental tolerance for these behaviors (Patterson, 1976).

In addition to the mother who does not track her child's behavior—the "diffusion parent" (Patterson, Cobb, and Ray, 1973)—there is also the "selective diffusion parent," who may track prosocial behaviors but tolerate high rates of coercive child behaviors. Such a mother may feel she must tolerate higher rates of coercive behavior because a child is ill or has a disability, or perhaps she feels guilty because she is working full-time and feels she cannot be a good parent. Because of her ineffective reinforcement procedures, the child's behavior will become worse, which will support the mother's guilt feelings that she is a bad parent (Patterson, Cobb, and Ray, 1973).

It should be noted that children labeled as deviant by their parents do not necessarily have higher rates of deviant behavior than their siblings or peers who are not labeled as deviant (Lobitz and Johnson, 1974; Arnold, Levine, and Patterson, 1975). There is thus an overlap between referred and nonreferred children in their rates of deviant behavior. However, parents of referred children have a more negative attitude toward the labeled child and offer him more commands and negative feedback. They also punish prosocial behavior more than parents of nondeviant boys. Parental attitude is thus a better predictor of referral for these children than child misbehavior. "Dichotomously speaking, it seems clinicians are working with two types of families: (1) those families in which the child's behavior is deviant and the parents label it appropriately and (2) those families in which the child's behavior is not deviant in comparison to his peers but the parents label it so. . . . It was interesting to note that even in families where the child's behavior was clearly deviant, significant differences were not found between the target child and his siblings in terms of observed deviant behavior. Thus, even in those clearly deviant cases, there seems to be more to the labeling of deviance than an objective assessment by parents of child deviance. . . . What appears to be required at this point are assessment procedures which establish the determinants of variance in the perception of child deviance" (Lobitz and Johnson, 1974, pp. 28-29). This point highlights the need to alter the parental attitudes during intervention and to locate possible reasons why particular children are labeled as deviant.

Deviant families, compared to normal families, are more silent, talk less equally, have fewer positive interactions and are in general less active (Alexander, 1973; Winter and Ferreira, 1969; Mischler and Waxler, 1968). These findings highlight the lack of reciprocity in such families. A number of studies have found a direct association between degree of marital discord between parents and the degree of deviancy in their child (for example, see Johnson and Lobitz, 1974). And it has often been noted that the presence of severe marital discord interferes with teaching parents more effective parenting skills (Patterson, 1974). Parents who have higher levels of marital discord are more negative toward their children and have more deviant children (Johnson and Lobitz, 1974). To date, there is no information as to what comes first, marital discord or problematic parent-child interaction, or whether an increased coerciveness between family members leads to both.

This discussion has indicated some of the ways in which family members influence each other. As one member increases his or her use of aversive events, other members are also likely to increase theirs. Assessment procedures are described in the following section, after which basic procedures in which parents are trained are described. A program employed with parents of "aggressive" children is then presented. A final section describes procedures related to other areas, such as excessive dependency.

Assessment

Behavioral interviewing as well as observation by either the client or trained observer are usually employed to gather assessment information. Simulated situations in which the mother is asked to interact with her child in the office while observed by the counselor may be used in lieu of observation in the home. For example, Wahler, Winkel, Peterson, and Morrison (1965) observed parent-child interaction in a playroom at a clinic. For each child, two classes of behaviors were selected: a deviant one and an incompatible one. For one child, the undesirable behavior was commanding behavior, defined as any verbal or nonverbal instruction to his mother (for example, pushes her into a chair, saying "Now we'll play with this!"). The incompatible behavior was labeled cooperative behavior and was defined as nonimperative statements, actions, or questions. For another child, the two classes of behavior identified for change were dependent behavior, defined as asking questions, nonverbal requests for help, and independent behavior, which included any behavior in which the child played alone with no verbal comment from his mother.

Self-Report Measures. Preinterview questionnaires can be employed as described in Chapter Five. Initial interviews are sometimes held separately with the parents and child. The intake interview with parents of aggressive children held by the Oregon Research Group (Patterson and others, 1975) includes obtaining information describing previous agency contacts and their duration. Parents complete an adjective checklist describing their child and are verbally administered the symptom checklist, which asks them to indicate whether a variety of behaviors such as bed wetting, irritableness, and aggressiveness are problematic and whether they are problematic at home, school, community, or other situations. They are asked to check a given problem only if they feel that it is a *current* problem and if they wish to change it. For areas indicated, examples are obtained concerning how they usually handle the problem, who usually does the disciplining and how consistent they are. Their ideas of the causes related to problems are also solicited. Here there is an attempt to ascertain parental beliefs about various determinants of behavior. Inquiry is made as to whether there are problems with other siblings and what they expect to be the outcome of their work with the clinic. Their expectations will indicate the changes that must occur for the parents to consider the program a success. An interview is held with the child while the parents are being interviewed. One aim of this interview is to rule out gross brain damage, extreme retardation (IQ less than 50), or obvious psychosis (Patterson and others, 1975). Another aim is to determine what the child would like altered in the family and how well (from his viewpoint) he is doing at school.

The quality of interpersonal relationships can be assessed by subjective scales such as the Subjective Units of Irritation Scale patterned after Wolpe's Subjective Anxiety Scale (Sherman and Cormier, 1972). The importance of assessment of self-reported quality of relationships is highlighted by the tendency of some parents to mislabel a child as deviant even though he does not have an unusually high rate of deviant behavior. The general level of discord in a family can be assessed by a Subjective Units of Anger Scale ranging from zero (never gives me any trouble; he is a joy to be around) to 100 (can make me the most angry I have ever been). Viewing ratings of family members can help to identify sources of perceived trouble. For example, one child may receive high scale values from all other family members. This also offers a way to assess the effects of intervention programs. In addition, self-report measures may also be employed to identify desired outcomes and related situations. The Behavior Problem Checklist developed by Quay (1972) has been employed to obtain parental report of the general level of deviant behavior of a child. This inventory contains fifty-five items, each of which is rated on a three-point scale.

Observation by Trained Observers at Home or in the Clinic. The amount of observational data collected and the way this is gathered (for example, trained observers or tape-recorded interactions collected at home by the parents) depends on available resources. If possible, observational data describing parent-child interaction should be gathered in addition to self-report data, because parents are not necessarily accurate observers of their child's behavior. They have a bias toward reporting improvement when there is none. In one study, when parents' reports were compared with observational data, nontreated children actually became worse during a five-week period, but 67 percent of the parents said their children had improved (Walter and Gilmore, 1973). Also, parents may label a child as deviant when he has no higher rates of deviant behavior than nonlabeled children (Lobitz and Johnson, 1974). The importance of carefully defining and counting behaviors is emphasized by studies indicating judgments were based on stereotypes of the child in the absence of careful observation long after the child's behavior had changed (see, for example, Wahler and Leske, 1972).

If observation is to be carried out in the home, the rationale for this should be explained and the parents provided with a set of rules to follow during these sessions as well as the rationale for the rules (see Chapter Seven). In the Oregon program, trained observers are employed and data is collected during six sessions at baseline, for two consecutive days during intervention, and at three-week, six-week, and twelve-month follow-up periods. Each session lasts about one hour. Behavior is coded at thirty-second intervals, and a total of five minutes of observational data is collected on each family member during a one-hour session. Behaviors as well as their consequences are noted. Assessment may take place in the clinic by requesting parent and child to interact with each other and observing this interaction (Wahler and others, 1965). These sessions may be especially structured in order to view relevant behaviors. For example, a parent may be asked to give instructions to her child or family members may be requested to discuss a problem. It should be noted that behavior in the office does not necessarily reflect behavior at home (Martin, Johnson, Johansson, and Wahl, 1976). Observation may be employed to identify behaviors to increase and decrease and their related antecedents, and to gather a baseline count of behavior to be altered. Code categories may be very complex or very simple, depending on what is needed and the resources available. For example, a target behavior may be instructions followed and the child's behavior examined to determine their frequency. The parents' reactions to instructions followed can be observed to note the frequency with which positive events are offered after such behaviors and the frequency with which following instructions is ignored or followed by a punishing consequence. Additional examples of counselor observation of children are offered in Chapter Seven, Tables 5 and 6.

Client-Gathered Information. Examples of monitoring by parents are offered in Chapter Seven, in Tables 3 and 4. As can be seen in Table 3, recording responsibilities can be divided between parents. As with all recording assignments, there is a careful attempt to make the assignment easy for the parent as well as useful in terms of information generated. This often involves the use of continuous recording during a selected time period or the use of time samples. Observation is often employed by parents to identify behaviors to be increased and decreased, as well as to monitor behavior. Parents are usually asked to record the frequency of selected positive behaviors as well as behaviors to be decreased, to encourage them to attend to positives in their child.

In the Oregon program for aggressive children, parents are requested to note the daily occurrence or nonoccurrence of each problem noted on a symptoms checklist called the PDR (Parents Daily Report) (Patterson and others, 1975). A high correlation (+.69) has been found between the total number of deviant behaviors counted by trained observers during observational periods and the mean frequency for symptoms indicated by parental report (Patterson and others, 1975). Data are collected each weekday by telephone at a time convenient for both the clients and counselor. Phone contacts last about five minutes and discussion is confined to data collection. There is often a need for "call backs" (if the parent is not present) and clients may fail to offer appropriate information. Efforts by the parents to engage in discussion of intervention should be resisted and the importance of initial steps, such as reading *Families* (Patterson, 1971a), emphasized. Parents are encouraged to handle problems as they usually do and are assured that intervention will be initiated as soon as the baseline period is completed.

Information collected may reveal that identified problems do not seem to occur or that ones not mentioned are now complained about. In the Oregon program, objections to assessment procedures are followed by "admissions of inadequacies" and a focus is maintained on "seeing what happens" after intervention. Debate is avoided, because it is usually ineffective and impedes getting to the main business of altering family problems. It takes about six or more interviews for data collection to progress smoothly, as parents learn what is expected. Most parents need coaching in the use of specific referents concerning their child's behavior. Positive feedback is offered as they acquire skill. For example, the counselor may say, "Thank you, Mrs. X. You are really learning how to specify behavior and the data we are collecting will be very useful in your program" (Patterson and others, 1975, p. 40). Regular tabulation, scoring, and graphing of data is important so this can be used to inform intervention efforts. One easy way to summarize data is to add the number of checks for deviant behavior each day over the total of all behavior categories and situations. This provides a social aggression score. Help should be offered to clarify any definitional ambiguities that may cause problems in monitoring behaviors. If parents are recording instances of noncompliance, guidelines can be shared: for example, noncompliance may include talking back or dawdling (more than thirty seconds) when asked to do something. Parents are coached to make the request or command very clear, to ask only once, not to nag if noncompliance occurs, and to count noncompliance only if a request has specifically been made; that is, standing orders do not count (Patterson and others, 1975).

Parents may be requested to tape record interactions at home at a preselected time that is especially problematic, such as right before dinner or at bedtime, in addition to other periods which they select (Johnson, Christensen, and Bellamy, 1976). This information is reviewed to determine rates of problematic behavior and to view interactions between family members. The child may also be requested to keep track of behaviors or to note what happens right before and after selected behavior.

Training Significant Others in Effective Reinforcement Practices

Perhaps the most important aspect of offering significant others more effective child management skills is training them how to employ positive reinforcement and prompting to increase desirable behaviors already present and to shape new ones. In addition, parents learn the importance of withholding attention from undesirable behaviors and learn how to employ time out or response cost to decrease undesirable behaviors. They may also be introduced to the use of satiation, stimulus change, overcorrection, and the use of rules. Contingency contracts and negotiation training are used, especially with older children. Token programs may be employed when many behaviors are of concern or when parental attention does not function as a reinforcing event. Training may be carried out in the home itself or in the office. The selection of training site will depend on a number of factors including possibility of the trainer entering the home, wishes of the parent, and success achieved from offering training first in the office situation. A number of devices may be employed during training to offer parents feedback. These include hand gestures, light signals, or use of a "bug-in-the-ear" system, in which instructions are transmitted to the parent through a transmitter earplug, a system that provides immediate feedback (see, for example, Krapfl, Bry, and Nawas, 1969).

Increasing Desirable Behaviors. Both positive reinforcement and prompting can be employed to increase desirable behaviors that already exist in the child's repertoire. Considerable attention is devoted to training parents in both of these skills and the rationale for the use of positive means of influence is carefully explained to parents.

Positive reinforcement. The key ingredient in training parents in effective reinforcement practices is to show them how to use positive reinforcement to strengthen behaviors and how to establish new ones. This entails teaching them how to pinpoint desirable and undesirable behaviors, to use or develop effective reinforcers, and to apply these contingently so that appropriate behaviors are increased and inappropriate ones decreased. Incorrect ways of employing positive reinforcement are identified, including offering rewards to a child for terminating an aversive behavior such as crying. This will increase the possibility of crying on similar occasions. Parents sometimes inadvertently arrange for the increase of an undesirable behavior, for example, reinforcing a child for taking his thumb out of his mouth.

Rules for the effective use of positive reinforcement to strengthen behaviors include the following (Homme, Czanyi, Gonzales, and Rechs, 1969; Ayllon and Azrin, 1968b):

Reinforce often.
Reinforce accomplishments rather than obedience.
Reinforce immediately.
Reinforce consistently.
Do not mix criticism with praise.
Identify specifically what is being praised (approve behavior rather than the entire person).
Use a variety of reinforcers.
Use multiple sources of reinforcement (for example, father, mother, and teachers).
Construct situations so that praise will be possible by arranging desired alternatives to current activities.
Reinforce *after* desired behaviors occur.

Parents are trained to specifically describe approved behavior and to praise this rather than the whole person. Thus a mother might say, "Thank you for helping me put the dishes away," instead of "You're a good boy for helping mother." Being specific helps the child to learn what it is that he does that is approved of, and his "whole person" is not on the line. Let us say a child fixes breakfast for her younger sister and brother without being asked. One mother may say: "How nice. What a grown-up girl. You are an angel" (Becker, 1971, p. 107). A second may say: "Ruby, you are such a good helper to me. You set out their glasses and cereal bowls and filled them without spilling. Your brother and sister must appreciate having a sister like you" (Becker, 1971, p. 107). The first mother praises the child and not the behavior. As Becker notes, as a *person* Ruby may be worried about being grown-up, and she knows she is not an angel. The second mother showed appreciation by describing the nice things Ruby had done. Parents are encouraged to ask the child to verbalize why he is receiving praise or a reward and, after he correctly expresses the relationship, to say, for example, "Yes, you earned a treat because you did a good job of cleaning up the yard." This will help the child to identify appropriate behaviors. Giving and withholding love contingent on certain behaviors such as in the statement "Mother will love you if. . . " are discouraged (Krumboltz and Krumboltz, 1972).

It cannot be assumed that significant others possess effective praise statements. Such a repertoire may have to be established, perhaps with the help of the involved child. He could be asked what he would like his parents to say when he does something that pleases them. Parents are encouraged to develop a variety of ways to reinforce behavior. For example, in a toilet training program developed by Azrin and Foxx (1974), parents are asked to develop a "Friends-who-care-list," which is a list of people admired by a child including fictional as well as real characters such as Captain Kangaroo. Approval from such sources can then be offered such as "Your pants are dry. Just like Captain Kangaroo's." In addition, hugs and kisses can be offered. Important components of using praise effectively include establishing eye contact and speaking with enthusiasm (Patterson and others, 1975). The latter may be especially difficult for some parents. Using a variety of reinforcers prevents satiation effects, in which a given event no longer functions as a reinforcer, as in the following example: "Kirk was learning to be responsible for putting away his toys. His mother always said 'Good job' in response to Kirk's gradually improving behavior. But one day he said, 'Good job, good job, that's all I ever hear. I get so tired of hearing you say good job.' Chagrined at her own rigidity, Kirk's mother devised alternative ways of letting him know how much she appreciated his increasing responsibility for maintaining and caring for his own toys and equipment. Instead of merely resorting to synonyms such as 'fine' or 'much better,' Kirk's mother reduced her direct verbal remarks to him and began to describe the child's improved performance to his father. 'Dad, you know what Kirk did today? He picked up all his toys in his room without my having to remind him. And he did it all by himself' " (Krumboltz and Krumboltz, 1972, pp. 17-18). Praising the child's behavior in front of others is another way to offer reinforcement. For example, a mother may say to her husband at dinner, "Sara cleaned her room today and put all her toys away."

Parents and teachers often mix criticism with praise (Patterson, 1971a; Becker, 1971). For example, a father may say, "Joe, it was good that you washed your hands before coming to the table but you did a poor job on washing your face." To many parents, it seems that criticism works since the problem behavior temporarily stops. The temporary nature of this "criticism trap" (Becker, 1971) is highlighted. Parents are trained to distinguish between praising and critical statements and given help in how to avoid the latter. Cues may be provided to help them remember to praise rather than to criticize. For example, if tokens are given to a child for appropriate behavior, simply having these available may remind the parent to praise rather than criticize. Practice in offering praise will also help to increase the likelihood of this reaction. Parents may be encouraged to put up signs reminding them to praise, not to criticize. Asking them to keep track of the number of times they praise and criticize their child may also help to cue them to increase praise (Becker, 1971).

Use of criticism is discouraged by learning more effective ways of dealing with inappropriate behaviors—for example, by praising appropriate behaviors—and learning how to handle situations when a parent must remind a child of some inappropriate behavior. Here, the parent is trained to select some behavior to praise first and then to mention the other behavior, as in the following example from Becker (1971, pp. 103-104).

> When called in the morning, Mary dressed quickly and came downstairs for breakfast, but she forgot to wash her hands.
> *Mother:* "My, you were quick this morning. Breakfast is almost ready. Your dress looks pretty, Mary. I like that yellow."
> *Mary:* "So do I, Mommy."
> *Mother:* "Did you wash your hands and face?"
> *Mary:* "Oh, I forgot. Be right back."
> This is very different from the criticism in the following example:
> *Mother:* "Mary, let me see your hands. You forgot to wash, didn't you?"
> *Mary:* "But they're not dirty."
> *Mother:* "Go wash them and your face, too."

Praising first assures the child that he is still liked, and thus he will be more ready to attend to the parent. Children tend to turn off with parents or teachers who criticize.

Parents are encouraged to ignore minor deficiencies in their concentration on reinforcing positive behaviors. Many parents initially seek out and criticize failings of their children. The following example shows how to ignore a minor deficiency (from Becker, 1971, p. 108).

> Kathy packed her own lunch and is ready for school on time.
> A. *Mother:* "Kathy, you forgot to put away the mayonnaise, but I love you for being such a good helper this morning."
> B. *Mother:* "Kathy, you sure got your day off to a good start. You got dressed and ready for school ahead of time and even packed your own lunch. That's pretty good for a ten-year-old girl. As a special treat, why don't you buy some cupcakes for your lunch on the way to school."
> Mother gives Kathy twelve cents.

The situation often arises that a child is doing something that must end because of bedtime or mealtime. Transfer of attention from one activity to another can be encouraged if a parent does not demand an immediate change but rather allows some time to become involved in the idea of doing something else by giving some advance notice. This may be smoothed by briefly entering into the child's play activity, as in the following example from Becker (1971, p. 104).

> It is almost bedtime and Billy has his cars and roads (wooden blocks) spread all over the living room. Billy is intent in his play.
> *Mother:* (*Getting on the floor and entering into Billy's play*) "My car can stay right on this road and go over this bridge."
> *Billy:* "I have to stop for gas here." (*Billy goes through all the steps of putting gas into the car.*) "Zoom, zoom, I'm on the way to the circus to see the lions."

> *Mother:* "Billy, it's nearly bedtime. In the next few minutes I want you to put your cars and blocks away and get your pajamas on. When you're all ready, I have a special treat for you."
>
> Billy asks what it is, but Mother says it's a surprise. Billy returns ready for bed in less than five minutes. He finds two chocolate-covered graham crackers and a glass of milk waiting for him. He smiles.

Offering a desirable event or surprise contingent on appropriate behavior increases the likelihood of such behavior as does providing a child with a choice of two acceptable alternatives, as in the following example from Becker (1971, p. 105).

> It's time for bed and Kenny wants to watch television some more. He's just started watching a new show.
>
> A. *Mother:* "I should have caught you before this one started. I'll tell you what. You hurry and get on your pajamas and then you can decide whether you want to finish watching this show or have a story, but you have to be in bed ready for sleep by eight o'clock."
>
> Kenny races for the bedroom as the first commercial comes on.
>
> B. *Mother:* "Kenny, get ready for bed now or no story tonight."
>
> *Kenny:* "Oh, Mom. I want to see the Hill-billies."
>
> *Father:* "You heard what your mother said. Now get going."
>
> Kenny trudges off, stamping his feet.

In the first example, the parent recognizes her child's interest and makes use of it to encourage the child to get ready for bed. He is offered a choice between two reinforcers. Children as well as adults enjoy exercising choices. In the second example, the parent demands immediate change, offers no positive consequences or choice, and implies a threat if compliance does not occur.

Parents are encouraged to praise appropriate behavior

consistently at first (that is, every time it occurs) and, to maintain behavior, to reinforce it on an intermittent schedule. They are also trained to reinforce behavior immediately, that is, right after it occurs. The effects of reinforcers can be enhanced by using a variety of reinforcers, as well as by using multiple sources of reinforcement. Reinforcer sampling, in which a small amount of the item or event is sampled, may also encourage behavior by increasing the potency of reinforcers (Ayllon and Azrin, 1968a). Training parents to make effective use of positive reinforcement includes teaching them to focus on improvements. They are encouraged not only to find their children doing something good, but also to "catch them doing something better" (Becker, 1971). A focus on rewarding accomplishments rather than obedience (Homme and others, 1969) encourages the development of accomplishment or "mastery" as a reinforcer. The importance of frequently reinforcing behavior is stressed. Reinforcing approximations to final objectives enables frequent reinforcement. Modeling, rehearsal, and feedback are often used to establish effective reinforcement practices as described later in this chapter. For some parents, extensive training is required. It should be noted that differential parental attention to positive behaviors does not always have positive effects (Herbert, Pinkston, Hayden, Sajwaj, Pinkston, Cordua, and Jackson, 1973). A possible explanation of the occasional adverse effect of differential reinforcement of other behavior is that the overall density of reinforcement is decreased. Enriching the frequency of reinforcement for appropriate behavior in addition to the use of time out may preclude this adverse effect.

Training parents in how to prompt desired behaviors. Parents may arrange for their child to observe a model who is reinforced for a behavior. If a child grabs some item during dinner, rather than say something about this, one parent could demonstrate polite asking behavior shortly thereafter and the other parent could praise the specific behavior involved (so that it is clear exactly what is being reinforced). Another example is as follows:

> Paul, a cystic fibrosis child, had to do upside-down
> tilting exercises as part of his treatment. The tilted

block of wood and the upside-down position were
frightening to him, and he resisted doing these
exercises. To help him overcome his fear Paul's father did exercises with him, attempting to make
the exercises seem like a game. His dad would say,
"Time for my exercises," and then do sit-ups,
which were similar to Paul's. Paul simple watched
at first. For a while he was reluctant, but gradually
his dad's interest and enthusiasm took hold. He decided to attempt one exercise with his father
helping him. After that point Paul performed his
exercises, which they called his "upside-downies,"
more frequently, until they became a regular routine, with his father's assistance. From seeing the
example set by his father, Paul soon began to act as
if his "upside-downies" were a game as well as an
exercise. [Krumboltz and Krumboltz, 1972, p. 50]

Desired behaviors can be prompted by verbally reminding
the child of the contingency in effect, or posted rules that describe the relationship between a behavior and its consequences
may prompt behavior. Physical guidance may also be employed.
Reminders may be offered by a posted chart on which earnings
are recorded and/or required behaviors described. An example
of reminders for task requirements is shown in the following list
(from Becker, 1971, p. 152):

1. Fill sink with water.
2. Add two capfuls of detergent.
3. Wash dishes, then cups and glasses, then silverware,
   then pots and pans.
4. Dry them and put them away.
5. Wash counter.
6. Clean sink.
7. Put away detergent, towels, and dishpan.

After behaviors occur regularly, these cues can be abbreviated.
For example, this list was replaced with a sign saying "Do
dishes." This can later be removed, but behavior still tracked
and recorded.

Developing new behaviors. Parents often withdraw all

help and attention when they decide it is time for a child to do something different, such as help himself more. Rather than reinforce approximations to desired behaviors, they expect the behavior to take place right away. This is illustrated in the following example with two mothers who had helped their children dress and decided it was time for them to learn to dress themselves in the morning (Becker, 1971). The first mother, Mrs. Rushmore, simply told her little girl one morning that it was now her job to get ready and returned to the kitchen. Karen put on her socks and underpants and sat on the bed. When her mother returned and found her sitting on the bed, she scolded her and told her to hurry up or she would be late for school. The mother checked five minutes later and Karen now had her slip on and was reading a picture book. Again the mother scolded her and nagged her to get ready. This mother withdrew all attention and help from Karen immediately and made the additional mistake of only attending to Karen when she dawdled. No praise was offered for any approximations achieved. "Not getting dressed" received all the attention. The mother trained her daughter to dawdle in the morning and Karen trained her mother to yell and nag from the time she got out of bed until she left for school in the morning.

The other mother told her daughter that it was time for her to do more things for herself. She started preparing the night before by reminding her daughter what she would wear the next day and together they set out these clothes where Linda could easily find them. The morning started with the mother hugging her daughter and saying, "Let's see how far you can get dressed yourself while I put the coffee on. I'll be right back to check" (Becker, 1971, p. 36). She returned within a minute, praised Linda for putting on her socks, underpants, and slip, and praised her for being a good girl. This mother rewarded accomplishment, praised approximations, made arrangements the night before that would make these approximations more likely, and checked soon, so she could offer praise as soon as any approximation had occurred.

The number of approximations that will have to be reinforced in order to attain a particular objective will depend on the complexity of the skill and the capabilities of the child. It is important not to offer too many reinforcements for any given approximation, because that behavior may then interfere with the display of other variations which may be closer to the final goal, as well as not to offer too few reinforcements for a given approximation, so that behavior does not drift back to less desired behaviors. An important part of shaping is the immediacy with which approximations are reinforced. Prior to shaping, an agenda should be arranged that consists of identification of the desired goal, the intermediate steps that may be required to reach this goal, and skills available. This agenda serves as a guide so that closer approximations can readily be reinforced. In addition, an appropriate reinforcer should be determined. Examples of the use of shaping are offered in Chapter Nineteen. Prompts should be employed as needed to occasion behaviors. Model presentation may also be employed to prompt and develop new behaviors.

Decreasing Undesirable Behaviors. Parents are trained how to withhold attention following undesirable behaviors and to reinforce alternative desirable behaviors. The disadvantages of physical punishment are carefully discussed and response cost and time out offered as alternatives. Time out is used with younger children, whereas response cost is more appropriate for older children. Additional procedures that can be employed to decrease undesirable behaviors include satiation, stimulus change, and overcorrection. Parents are encouraged to employ operant extinction and positive reinforcement of alternative behaviors as a first endeavor to decrease undesirable behaviors. If this is not effective, procedures that combine positive reinforcement with a mild form of punishment, such as time out or overcorrection, can be employed. The importance of combining time out, response cost, or overcorrection with positive reinforcement of appropriate behaviors is strongly emphasized.

Withholding reinforcement (operant extinction). Let us say that a child cries at bedtime, and that his mother typically goes upstairs and reads a story to him until he falls asleep. In order to decrease crying, the mother could be instructed to no longer attend to the child when he cries at bedtime. Williams (1959) successfully employed such a procedure (extinction) to eliminate crying at bedtime; however, the amount of crying at first increased to about forty-five minutes. This temporary increase in undesirable behavior is characteristic of the behavioral effects obtained when reinforcers are no longer provided for a behavior. However, it can be avoided by reinforcing alternative behaviors. Withholding of reinforcement is especially likely to work when all sources of support can be controlled and when the behavior is relatively harmless (Krumboltz and Krumboltz, 1972). If reinforcers cannot be withheld, an extinction procedure is not in effect. Even occasional reinforcement may maintain behavior at a high rate. It is thus important that parents learn to withhold attention consistently after undesirable behaviors, while reinforcing appropriate behaviors. Special help, in addition to practice, is sometimes required to help parents not to attend to undesirable behaviors. Parents can be trained to use self-instructions that help them in this process, such as "Take it easy"; "Don't attend to that. It will only make it worse"; "It's hard but I can do it"; and "Remember to attend to good behavior." It should be recognized that it is difficult not to attend to inappropriate behaviors, and, of course, some behaviors must be attended to, as described in the next section.

Reinforcing alternative behaviors. This method of decreasing undesirable behaviors is preferred, because it does not entail the use of aversive events and it can be highly successful in decreasing undesirable behavior. Parents are coached to withhold attention following undesirable behaviors and to reinforce positive alternatives. For example, if fighting with a brother is a problem, parents may ignore fighting and reinforce cooperative behaviors, for example, by providing attention when the brothers have been playing well together for a short period of time, offering praise when one offers to share a toy with the other, and so forth. Other examples of the differential reinforcement of other behaviors follow.

> Four-year-old Bruce was unafraid of the water; in fact, so unafraid that he would wander out toward the deep end of the pool even though he was unable to swim well enough to protect himself. I knew I could frighten him into staying on the shallow side of the rope, but I did not want to make him afraid of the deep water. I simply

wanted him to stay in the shallow water until he was a better swimmer. Whenever we went swimming, I would arrange for one of his brothers or sisters to play one of his favorite water games, "Dunk the Doughnut" or "Ring Around," in the shallow end of the pool. The games improved his swimming ability and kept him diverted from the deep end of the pool. We were able to teach him to swim without instilling a fear of deep water. . . .

Every time I tried to wash my Volkswagen, little Becky would hang around, be in the way, and get splashed. I tried to reason with her and then, exasperated, I tried force—that was a mistake. She began to wail. I didn't want her parents to think I was mistreating her, but I didn't want her under the hose either. Finally, I said, "Becky, how would you like to pretend you're driving my car in the rain?" She loved playing inside the car. [Krumboltz and Krumboltz, 1972, pp. 172-173]

Differential reinforcement of other behavior (DRO) is the most widely employed procedure in which parents are trained to increase desirable behaviors and to decrease undesirable ones. In DRO, parents learn to redistribute their attention. Adverse effects of differential reinforcement have sometimes been found (Herbert and others, 1973). Making sure there is an increase in the amount of positive reinforcement offered may preclude such effects.

Training parents in how to use punishment effectively. Parents often make ineffective use of punishment. They may use severe physical punishment, which encourages their child to fear, hate, and avoid them. Or they may use weak punishment, such as a small slap coupled with yelling. If the only time a child receives attention is when he is criticized, these parental actions may assume reinforcing qualities and actually encourage inappropriate behaviors. Parents are also often inconsistent in their use of punishment, or fail to prevent escape from the contingency. If a child is placed in his room after kicking his father and can escape out the window, this consequence would not be very effective.

Because of the negative emotional reactions created when physical punishment is used, the failure of this method to increase any particular other behaviors on the part of the child, as well as the fact that it may decrease other desired behaviors (the child may become afraid to do anything), physical punishment is discouraged. Only if other methods have failed to alter behavior or if the behavior presents a clear danger to a child may physical punishment be selected to accompany the use of positive reinforcement. For example, running into the street has so much potential danger that a parent may employ physical punishment. Physical punishment has been successful after other methods have failed to alter self-mutilating behaviors (see Lovaas and Newsom, 1976). Typically, milder forms of punishment, such as response cost or time out, can be used in place of physical punishment and should be tried before resorting to such consequences. Effective use of punishment requires that it be used consistently and immediately following undesirable behaviors, and that alternative positive behaviors are reinforced. Parents are trained to warn the child before invoking the punishment, so that the warning signal itself will come to influence behavior. They are coached to make such statements in a calm nonblaming manner, and to specifically identify the behavior of concern.

Response cost. Response cost involves loss of some positive event contingent on behavior. For example, in the contract described on page 342, Maude loses points if she swears, steals, or does not comply with parental requests. Arrangements between behaviors and response cost should be discussed with the child before contingencies are imposed.

Time out. This procedure entails the removal of a child from a reinforcing environment to one that is not reinforcing, contingent on a specific behavior. It is an especially useful procedure for high-rate behaviors of children two to twelve years old. Ideally, the time out is terminated contingent on an improvement in a specific behavior. If two children are playing together and one grabs a toy from the other, his mother could inform him that he will have to leave the play area and go to his room until he is able to share his toys with his friend. There is no need to make the time out of long duration; in fact, there is a distinct disadvantage to this, in that prosocial behavior cannot be reinforced during time out. As Patterson has noted (1971a), some parents like long time-out periods, because they get the child out of their way. Such periods should be as brief as possible (three to five minutes) and can be measured with a kitchen timer. As with the use of positive reinforcement, extinction and punishment, the success of the procedure is intimately related to the way in which it is carried out. The behavior to be followed by a time out must be specifically defined, and a time out area that has little or no reinforcing value must be selected. The bathroom is sometimes used, after items that might be fun to play with or to break are removed when possible. It is important that time out be consistently employed, that is, every time the behavior occurs. The entire procedure is first explained to the child, including a description of the behavior that will result in time out and the length of the time-out period, for example, five minutes. When an undesirable behavior occurs, the parent is trained first to label the behavior: "[Jenny], that was a hit, and means a time out and you are to go to the bathroom for five minutes" (Patterson and others, 1975). There should be no screaming, nagging, scolding, debating, dragging, or shouting, and the statement should be expressed in a matter-of-fact, calm way. The behavior is simply described and the consequence arranged in a perfunctory manner. Ideally, the child walks there by himself without trying to argue, debate, scream, or yell. In actuality, this seldom happens at first. Rather, children attempt to debate with their parents over whether the behavior was as labeled, to say that they did not mean it, to ask them for another chance, and to tell them that they are unfair, do not love them, and so forth.

Parents are trained to respond to noncompliance with their request by adding time to the time-out period. They could, for example, add five minutes for each minute of failure to follow instructions. The child is informed of this addition by the parent examining his watch and saying after one minute, "That's five minutes more." This can be continued until thirty minutes are accumulated, at which point the parent can be instructed to walk away after equating noncompliance with a removal of some privilege, such as the opportunity to view television that evening. It is important that this consequence be enforced. Consequences for noncompliance should be arranged beforehand and practice offered in voicing these. Time-out periods should shorten rapidly if the procedure is used consistently and correctly and if prosocial behaviors are reinforced. Each attempt to leave time out, talk to people, yell, kick the door, or open it should result in one more minute of time out. And if the child leaves before the time out is over, a backup consequence is expressed, such as "Unless you go to TO [time out area] immediately, your bike will be locked up for five days," and then he is to be ignored. If a child was originally sent into time out for refusal to follow an instruction, this request is repeated as soon as the time out is over. He is returned to time out for each further noncompliance. Threats by the child, such as "I don't care. Do whatever you want," or "I like it in there," should be ignored. The information collected by the parents in relation to behaviors of concern will indicate whether or not time out is working. Usually, if time out has not decreased to two or three times a day during the second week, there is something wrong with the procedure being employed.

Model presentation, rehearsal, and feedback are employed when teaching parents how to use time out, to ensure that they understand the procedure and receive practice in handling problems that may arise, such as attempts by the child to debate (Patterson and others, 1975). The counselor role plays the part of the parent and asks a parent to role play the child. Specific labeling of the behavior is modeled: "Jenny, that was a hit [and so on]." The parent is coached to try to argue back, which offers the counselor an opportunity to show the parents how to handle this situation. They are also shown how to accompany the child to the time-out area, close the door, and leave, as well as what to say when screaming continues during time out. A rule is established that five minutes of quiet must occur before the time out is ended. In this way, the parents ensure that they will not reinforce screaming by terminating time out when this is taking place. Items broken or damaged during time out should be paid for in part from the child's allowance and he is so informed. To arrange this, a child who gets no allowance may be offered a small one (Patterson and others, 1975). Messes made during time out should be cleaned up by the child.

Parental complaints of failure of time out to work may require a home visit in which their use of this procedure is observed. Such visits often reveal that parents are being overly lenient in defining the inappropriate behavior that is to result in time out or that they have selected an inappropriate place. One couple placed their child for her time-out period in the hallway where she could interact with her brothers and sisters (Patterson and others, 1975). In another instance, the parents selected an attic above the kitchen for the time-out area. This had a trapdoor opening into the kitchen and the child took this opportunity to throw down various objects at her parents as they were eating their meal. Parents may also provide reinforcement during the time out. Patterson and his colleagues reported an example where a home visit revealed that after the child was placed in time out, the parent would hold the door and debate with the child through the door and open the door frequently to make sure that the child was all right. Debates were continued after the child was removed from time out. Failure to go into time out may be dealt with by a loss of points if the child is on a point program or by accumulation of chore time.

Time out is not the procedure of choice for extreme behaviors such as stealing or assault committed by older children (rather, response cost can be employed, such as requiring a certain amount of chore completion). Time out should be introduced at an early point in a chain of disruptive behavior. A very important point to keep in mind is to combine time out with positive reinforcement for appropriate behaviors, and it is best to initiate such reinforcement prior to using time out (Patterson, 1971a). The more reinforcing the "time-in" environment, that is, the greater the range of pleasurable activities possible, the more effective the "time out" environment will be. In fact, enriching the time-in environment through the increase of appropriate reinforcers, may preclude the necessity for use of time out.

Time out for undesirable behaviors, combined with positive reinforcement for desirable behaviors, has been found to be effective when positive reinforcement combined with ignoring undesirable behaviors (extinction) has failed (see, for example, Wahler, 1969a). Time out offers a mild punishment that does not have the adverse effects of physical punishment for influencing the rate of problematic behaviors.

Satiation. If a behavior is harmless and a parent can tolerate it, a child may be permitted or even encouraged to repeat it until satiation occurs, that is, until he no longer shows an interest in performing the behavior, as in the following example. "When his mother gave him mashed potatoes for dinner, two-and-a-half-year-old Randy would eat nothing else. When she put other food in his mouth, he would just hold it for a while and then spit it out. His mother, applying the satiation principle, began giving him only mashed potatoes at every meal. After three days of eating nothing else Randy asked for some of the other food that was on the table. Although he would not eat a large variety of other things, Randy did broaden his taste. Two years later his parents learned that Randy suffered from a severe overbite, making it difficult for him to chew food. His preference for mashed potatoes and other soft foods probably resulted from the difficulty he had in chewing" (Krumboltz and Krumboltz, 1972, p. 146). Satiation will not work, of course, if the activity continues to be reinforcing, as in the following example. "The babysitter found seven-year-old Jimmy underneath his house playing with matches. She decided to try to satiate him on burning matches by insisting that he continue to light matches, anticipating that he would tire of the activity. A number of Jimmy's friends gathered around the house while he lit the matches. Jimmy would clown and throw the matches about as his friends laughed and joked with him. He would label some of his matches 'torpedoes,' light them, and slide them toward his audience. He would call others 'bombs,' tossing them high in the air to watch them fall. The crowd loved the show. After fifteen minutes the babysitter gave in, took all the matches away from Jimmy, and made him go into the house. Later Jimmy bragged to a friend how he had vexed his babysitter. A week later his mother caught him playing with matches under the house again" (Krumboltz and Krumboltz, 1972, p. 152). Notice that the requirement of repeating the behavior was terminated before the activity became aversive.

Stimulus change. The cues for inappropriate behaviors may be removed. Distraction methods are often employed by parents to interest a child in another activity. Setting events associated with problematic behavior can also be altered. For example, a child may become difficult to manage because he gets too little sleep; obtaining more sleep may help to decrease this tendency.

Overcorrection. The procedure of overcorrection (Foxx and Azrin, 1973b), in which inappropriate behavior is stopped and a positive alternative practiced, provides another way to decrease behavior (see examples in Chapter Nineteen). Overcorrection is similar to time out in that it temporarily interrupts offensive behavior; unlike time out, however, it uses the period of time to train alternative appropriate behaviors. Use of overcorrection places many more demands on the trainer. If a maintaining consequence of inappropriate behavior is to prevent demands, then overcorrection is indicated, because time out under such conditions would serve as a positive event (Birnbrauer, 1976).

Rules. Rules rather than written contracts are often used with young children. A rule identifies an "if-then" relationship. Families differ in terms of the number of rules, whether they are negative or positive, as well as who establishes and enforces them. Helpful rules have a number of characteristics, one of which is clarity (Homme and others, 1969). Clear rules help parents understand when to reinforce, ignore, or punish and enable the child to understand the consequences of given behaviors. Rules help children to predict their environment in a consistent fashion. The more clear the rule, the easier it will be to enforce.

Clarity of consequences will make a rule easier to enforce, as will selecting consequences that are positive and easily offered. Some parents make the mistake of selecting events that are not reinforcing. For example, a parent might say, "Eat your breakfast on time or you will miss the school bus." This will not be effective if the child does not care if he misses the bus or not. A vague statement of behaviors and consequences would be, "If you finish your homework, I'll take you to a movie as soon as I get a chance."

Rules should be stated positively and be short and easy to remember. Instead of saying, "If you're not in bed in one half hour, then I will not read you a story," one should say, "If you are in bed in a half hour, I'll read you a story." Parents may need practice in changing negative statements of rules into positive ones. This process is encouraged during the pinpointing stage of assessment and intervention, in which parents learn to focus on positives. Parents may have to be reminded that rules describe relationships between behavior and consequences. Thus, instead of saying, "I want you to clean your room on Saturday," one would say "Clean your room on Saturday before going out to play." There are two problems with the first statement. No consequence was arranged and it was expressed in terms of encouraging obedience by the "I want . . . " rather than accomplishment (Homme and others, 1969). Another example of a statement that encourages rewarding of obedience rather than accomplishment is "Clean up your room for mother," rather than "You can earn two points if you clean up your room by four this afternoon."

In addition to absence of a reinforcer if the rule is not followed, response cost may be arranged. For example, a mother might inform her child that if he spills his milk, he will have to clean it up. This may be a general rule in the home: Whoever makes a mess must clean it up. Parents must be cautioned that they should only establish rules that are possible for the child to follow, given his or her developmental achievements. Often parents have unrealistic expectations of what their child can accomplish, which causes frustration for them as well as for their children. Parents often make the mistake of having too many rules, so many that even they may forget their intricacies. They are coached to use only as many rules as are really necessary and to start out with one new rule rather than many.

The task of stating the rules can be gradually transferred to children by asking them to express the rule when the behavior occurs or fails to occur. Identification by the child of the many situations to which a rule may be applied can be encouraged by adding statements of the general rule, such as "You and Mary had a nice time together today. When you are nice to her, she is nice to you" (Becker, 1971, p. 146). A final step in this process would be to then have the child try to employ these rules to reason out what to do in new situations. The following example is from Becker (1971, p. 146).

Jimmy is angry at Mickey and threatens to beat him up. Mother shows him that there is a rule he has learned which goes against this.

Mother: "I can see you are angry. But what's the Golden Rule?"

Jimmy: "Don't do to someone else what you wouldn't want him to do to you?"

Mother: "That's right. Maybe we can find a better way to settle the issue. Hey, suppose he is really just trying to get you all upset. Have you thought of that? If you just ignored what he did, you would fool him if he's expecting you to be all upset."

Jimmy: "Maybe. I'll give it a try. And besides, if I hurt him, he would just want to hurt me back."

When a rule is broken, the child should be asked to correct his behavior. Let us say he forgets to close the front door when coming home from school. He can be reminded of the rule and requested to go outside and reenter, because this will recreate the chain of behavior related to door-closing behavior (Guthrie, 1935).

Contingency Contracts

Contingency contracts are written agreements between two or more people that specify relationships between behaviors and consequences (Patterson, 1971; Homme and others, 1969). Contracts offer a tool for training clients how to negotiate positive changes, and show them how to employ positive reinforcement and response cost effectively. Communication training, which is described later in this chapter, often accompanies use of contracts. Contracts have been used when communication has broken down, especially with teen-agers and their parents (for example, see Stuart, 1971b; Tharp and Wetzel, 1969; Weathers and Liberman, 1975b). Contracts describe who is to do what for whom under what circumstances. The exchanges that are to occur between parents and their children are described and expectations of all participants are made explicit. Participants are encouraged to start noticing what they would like to see more of (in addition to less of) and what they feel willing to offer in exchange for this. Contracts thus facilitate positive scanning of each other's behavior and the view that something must be offered for change, rather than simply the expectation of change, as in the past. Contracts discourage blaming others and encourage assumption of responsibility for helping to bring changes about. They encourage use of positive contingencies, in which a reward is offered for task completion, in contrast to negative ones, in which parents impose a negative contract such as, "In order to avoid punishment, you must perform . . . ."

Identifying explicit responsibilities ensures that they will be completed. "Contracts make explicit the everyday expectations that family members have of each other and provide positive reinforcement or incentives for the carrying out of responsibilities. Family roles and behaviors become clearly defined through negotiation rather than vaguely expected through demands. In developing a contract, family members learn to establish specific goals for each other, respond to each other's desirable behavior with positive feelings, and to negotiate, bargain and compromise with each other" (Weathers and Liberman, 1975b, p. 209). It is important that an atmosphere of compromise be established when developing contracts, so that no participant feels that he or she will lose face (Stuart and Lott, 1972). The importance of variables associated with the counselor's behavior in establishing contracts is emphasized by a study by Stuart and Lott (1972), in which the contracts formed depended more on the counselor and his interventions than on the client.

A number of guidelines have been generated for designing effective contracts (Homme and others, 1969):

1. The contract reinforcement should be immediate.
2. Initial contracts should call for and reinforce small approximations if the task is difficult. (Additional contracts are based on previous performance levels.)
3. Reinforcement should be given frequently in small amounts.
4. The contract should call for and reward accomplish-

ment rather than obedience to the manager. Obedience leads to dependence on the manager.

> *Improper Contract:* Do as I say, and I will give you a reward.
>
> *Proper Contract:* If you do X, you will get Y.

5. Reinforcement should come after the performance, not in anticipation of a performance.

> *Improper Contract:* You can watch television if you clean your room later.
>
> *Proper Contract:* Pick up your clothes in your room, and then you can watch television for an hour.

6. The strength of reinforcement must be fairly weighted to the amount of performance.

7. The contractual terms must be clear in amount of performance expected for amount of reinforcement. Both responsibilities and rewards must be described in specific terms. For example, the statement "Make your bed before you leave for school in the morning," is more specific than "Help more around the house." Family members are at first inclined to use vague terms, perhaps because they initially do not know how to be specific, or because such vagueness seems to facilitate negotiation. However, each person can then interpret these vague terms in his own way. Conflicts are simply postponed until a disagreement arises as to whether a contract has or has not been fulfilled.

8. The contract must be honest, carried out immediately, and according to the terms of the contract. No coercion should be employed in deciding on terms.

9. The contract must involve positive reinforcement rather than negative reinforcement.

10. Contracts must be used systematically.

11. Basic requisites of employing positive reinforcement must be satisfied. Examples of such requisites include possession of needed behavior included in the contract and lack of unauthorized access to reinforcers. Contracts should offer advantages for *each* partici-

pant over current available conditions in terms of reinforcers gained and costs avoided. It is important that the terms of the contract be promptly fulfilled as agreed on. Regular review of contracts helps to assure this or to locate difficulties, such as contracted behaviors that are too difficult for a participant and that prevent completion of contract terms. Examples of contracts appear later on in this chapter.

One of the assumptions that informs the use of contingency contracts is that receiving positive reinforcement in social exchanges is a privilege rather than a right (Stuart, 1971b). That is, one does not have the right simply to demand change. Rather, successful interpersonal relationships are viewed as involving exchanges in which there is a reciprocal exchange of positive events and the value of any relationship between two people is considered to be a function of the range, rate, and amount of positive events mediated by that exchange (Stuart, 1971b).

Making expectations explicit increases freedom in interpersonal exchanges. "When contracts specify the nature and condition for the exchange of things of value, they thereby stipulate the rules of the interaction. For example, when an adolescent agrees that she will visit friends after school (privilege) but that she will return home by 6:00 P.M. (responsibility), she has agreed to a rule governing the exchange of reinforcers. While the rule delimits the scope of her privilege, it also creates the freedom with which she may take advantage of her privilege. Without this rule, any action taken by the girl might have an equal probability of meeting with reinforcement, extinction or punishment. If the girl did not have a clear-cut responsibility to return home at 6:00 P.M., she might return one day at 7:00 and be greeted warmly, return at 6:00 the next day and be ignored, and return at 5:30 the following day and be reprimanded. Only by prior agreement as to what hour would be acceptable can the girl ensure her freedom, as freedom depends upon the opportunity to make behavioral choices with knowledge of the probable outcome of each alternative. Just as contracts produce freedom through detailing reciprocal rule-governed exchanges, so must contracts be born of freedom, since coerced agreements are likely to be violated as soon as the coercive force is removed" (Stuart, 1971b, pp. 4-5).

Contracts include not only identification of the privileges that each participant expects to gain, but also the responsibilities required to earn the privilege. For example, responsibilities of a teen-ager may include completing certain chores. Parents usually have a tendency to select too many responsibilities for their children. Because the reinforcers they may have to offer are sometimes limited, especially for teen-agers, they are encouraged to keep tasks to a minimum (Stuart, 1971b). It must be possible to monitor responsibilities completed and privileges received so that privileges can be exchanged in accord with earnings. A monitoring form for a contract between a father and his teen-age son is illustrated later in this chapter. Whereas the absence of earned privileges may be sufficient to increase appropriate behaviors, or decrease inappropriate ones, it may also be necessary to impose a cost for failure to carry out responsibilities. Costs offer the aggrieved party an appropriate means of indicating disapproval. "In families without explicit or understood behavioral contracts, the failure of a child to meet curfew is often met with threats of long-term 'grounding.' Faced with the threat of not being permitted to go out for weeks on end, the teen-ager is often persuaded to violate his contract even further and remain out later because the magnitude of the penalty is fixed and not commensurate with the magnitude of his violation. When sanctions are built into the contract, they may be of two types. One is a simple, linear penalty such as the requirement that the adolescent return home as many minutes early the following day as he has come in late on the preceding day. The second type of sanction is a geometric penalty which doubles or triples the amount of makeup time due following contract violations" (Stuart, 1971b, p. 6). If costs are added, positive incentives should be arranged to clearly outweigh these. Inclusion of a bonus adds another positive incentive for appropriate behaviors and helps to encourage positive scanning of behavior. This may include extra money, extra time with friends, or unusual privileges, such as freedom to have a party.

All parties should take part in negotiating contract terms when possible. This process of negotiation may be the most important element in contingency contracting (Weathers and Liberman, 1975b). With young children, the parents may assume more responsibility at first for deciding on task requirements and reinforcing events. This responsibility should gradually be assumed by the child so that he receives experience in setting appropriate tasks and selecting reasonable rewards (Homme and others, 1969). The steps involved in contingency contracting include the following (Weathers and Liberman, 1975b): (1) identifying rewards for others (What does he want that we can offer? What do they want that I can offer?); (2) identifying rewards for self (What do we want that he hasn't offered? What do I want that they haven't offered?); (3) setting priorities and rewards (What is most important for us? What do I want most?); (4) empathizing (How does he feel about doing this for us? How do they feel about doing this for me?); (5) setting costs on providing rewards (How hard would it be for us to do this for him? How hard would it be for me to do this for them?); (6) bargaining (What are we willing to give for what we want? What am I willing to give for what I want?). Identifying rewards can be facilitated by the use of preprinted cards listing commonly valued reinforcers (Weathers and Liberman, 1975b). Reinforcers for a teen-ager may include letting him stay out longer on weekends and weekdays; giving him a certain amount of allowance per week; letting him watch television more often; no longer going through his things; no longer listening to his phone calls; not being critical of his clothes, hair, friends, and so on; no longer nagging him about a certain topic. Reinforcers for the parents might include the teen-ager's doing a certain amount of homework each evening; making his bed and hanging up his clothes before he goes to school; not talking back as much when arguing; bring his friends in to meet his parents; improving his grades in selected courses to specific grades; getting up in the morning without a hassle; and playing his stereo more quietly. The parents are considered one team and the teen-ager the other team; each team is asked to select one item that they think would please the other team so that they can test out their judgment as to what the other persons value. Finding out what significant others like and dislike can also be facilitated by the use of lights or tokens, by giving a green light or token the meaning of "like" and a red token or light the meaning of "dis-please" (see, for example, Thomas, Carter, and Gambrill, 1971). Family members can be asked to exchange light signals or tokens in accord with these meanings during discussions; that is, to give a green token to a family member when he or she says or does something that is liked and a red one when the family member does or says something that is disliked (see Stuart, 1971a). Cards are exchanged between teams, and the recipients indicate why the reward offered would be pleasing. During this process, appropriate responses are prompted and reinforced by the counselor and rephrasings are offered. This process is continued until three cards have been offered to each team. Each team is then asked to identify and specify two additional reinforcers they would like and to explain why they would like them. Each team then ranks their five items in terms of their importance.

Family members also receive training in the exchange of empathic statements; that is, in placing themselves in someone else's position. One team is asked to read one of the cards listing a desired reinforcer to the other team and to empathize with how hard it would be for the other team to perform the behavior described (Weathers and Liberman, 1975b). The counselor is active during this process by prompting, restating, and reinforcing empathetic statements. Weathers and Liberman note that some adolescents will be very resistant to empathizing with their parents and that glib comments such as "It would be difficult for him to do it" should not be accepted. Cards listing reinforcers that have been discussed are given to the other team. This process is repeated until all reinforcers have been discussed. The last phase allows for assignment of cost values to reinforcers. Each team is asked to rank their reinforcers in terms of how difficult or costly each will be to perform.

These steps set the stage for negotiation training, which is described later in this chapter. Families are reminded of the rules to be followed: that agreements should be honest and fair, and that coercive nonverbal or verbal behavior should be avoided. Family members are instructed to "(1) suggest possible deals; for example, parent to adolescent—'If you will take out the trash daily you can use the telephone after dinner'; (2)

make counterproposals; for example, 'I would rather vacuum the living room to get to use the phone after dinner'; (3) make compromises: 'If you either take out the trash or vacuum the living room, you may use the telephone after dinner'; and (4) specify exactly what is being traded for—specify when, where, how often, and who is the judge and arbiter for deciding compliance to the various terms of the contracts" (Weathers and Liberman, 1975b, p. 212). Privileges and responsibilities exchanged are written down in contract form.

Contingency contracts have been employed with delinquents and their families with somewhat uneven results (Weathers and Liberman, 1975a; Tharp and Wetzel, 1969). In one program, contracts, together with other behavioral methods, were employed with seventy-seven predelinquent children by eight specially trained paraprofessionals who provided consultation to parents and teachers (Tharp and Wetzel, 1969). A wide range of problem behaviors were addressed both in the home and at school. This program was successful in reducing 89 percent of the problem behaviors addressed by 50 percent or more. Unfortunately only an AB design (see Chapter Eight) was employed, which makes it impossible to attribute positive effects to the intervention employed. The following case example of a teen-ager involved in this program illustrates the procedure.

> Salvador had been seen by the police after an incident in which he chased his stepfather with a butcher knife. He was a severe management problem in a home composed of his crippled stepfather, a passive mother, and an infant stepbrother. He was sullen and defiant in most parental contacts.
>
> Sal's stepfather had provided him with an old car which Sal drove at will and for which he was repaying the stepfather with money earned on a part-time job. The basis of the intervention plan was that Sal would repay the money in the form of improved home behaviors.
>
> From home chores, baby sitting, coming home on time, and relinquishing the car keys, Sal earned points which were converted into car payments. Car payments had to be up to date on a weekly basis. If they were not, he was restricted in car usage to the degree that he was in arrears.

The details of the expected behaviors, their
value in car payments, and the details of payment
were formally negotiated and written out in contract form [see Figure 18] by the behavior analyst.
Both Sal and his father signed the contract. [Tharp
and Wetzel, 1969, p. 113]

If the Contract Fails. Even after careful planning, some
contracts will not work. A number of points should be checked,
including the following: Are behaviors possible? That is, do occasions arise when they can be performed and can the person do
them? Are reinforcers given for behaviors carried out? Are these
events reinforcing? Is it possible for the client to gain so many
points that no further behaviors are necessary to obtain reinforcers? After a contract is put into effect, daily contact should be
held with the involved parties to check whether the contract is
working and, if it is not, a discussion should be held as to how it
could be improved.

Token or Point Programs

Token or point programs are frequently employed with
children and their parents (see, for example, Christopherson,
Arnold, Hill, and Quilitch, 1972). One aim of a token program
may be to increase the reinforcing potential of parental approval by pairing this with backup reinforcers offered in the
token program. Or, perhaps approval is an important reinforcer
but is not applied in a consistent fashion. Tokens have the advantage of having a standardized exchange value (Ayllon and
Azrin, 1968b). A program can be developed to encourage consistency of quality of praise while employing a token program.
All arrangements should be written down so that behaviors and
resultant benefits or costs are clearly understood by the participants. Initially, very simple programs may be employed that
include few behaviors and few reinforcers. Tokens or points are
often used in contingency contracts. (See Chapter Two for additional details concerning the design of token programs.)

Negotiation Training

Negotiation training is designed to offer parents and their
children positive skills in resolving conflicts. Training in the use

Figure 18. Sample Contract, Negotiated by the Behavior Analyst,
Between Target and Mediator

CONTRACT
English Ford Automobile

Section I

Sal R. is buying a $400.00 English Ford from his stepfather at the rate of $5.00 per week. This money is to be earned in the following way:

Item	*Value*
1. Remaining home or bringing in the car keys on Sunday through Thursday nights by 9:30 and giving them to his stepfather or placing them in an agreed upon place.	40¢ per night
2. Remaining home or bringing in the car keys on Friday and Saturday nights by 12:00 and giving them to his stepfather or placing them in an agreed upon place.	60¢ per night
3. Mowing front and/or back lawn once a week on day and at time of Sal's choosing. This task must be completed within one day.	60¢ per week
4. Feed dog daily prior to evening meal (Monday through Friday).	10¢ per feeding
5. Arrive for evening meal at 6:30 or at time specified by mother in the morning. Mother shall indicate any changes prior to the 6:30 meal.	5¢ per meal
6. Straighten room each morning before leaving house or by noon. Mother and Sal are to decide what straightening up room means.	5¢ per day

Total possible—$5.00

Section II

A. Penalty for failure to make car payments
   1. The penalty for payment failure shall be computed at the rate of 15 minutes of restricted car use the following week for each $.05 under the required $5.00 per week payment.
   2. These restrictions will be imposed by the current car owner, Mr. G.
   3. Failure to make any car payment at all will result in restriction of car privilege for the following week.
B. Payments are to be computed on Sunday evenings.
C. Additional car payments may be made if purchaser acquires a job and has access to additional money.

This contract can be rewritten or in other ways changed by either Sal or Mr. G. at their request and at any time. All changes must be made in consultation with Mr. Douglass.

Signed:

_____   _____
Mr. R., Purchaser   Date

_____   _____
Mr. Paul G., Owner   Date

Source: Tharp and Wetzel (1969, p. 114).

of contingency contracts is one form of negotiation training. Alteration of clients' communication patterns is typically involved in this process. Clients learn to increase verbal and nonverbal behaviors that encourage resolution of conflicts and to decrease behaviors that exacerbate conflict. One form of negotiation training that has been usefully employed with parents and their teen-age children concentrates on development of effective verbal behavior (Kifer, Lewis, Green, and Phillips, 1974). The negotiation process was divided into three component behaviors. The three behaviors included complete communications, identification of issues, and suggestion of options. A complete communication was defined as "statements that indicate one's position (what one thinks or wants) regarding the situation being discussed and that are followed in the same verbalization by a request for the other person to state his position or respond to the position just expressed. Examples: (1) 'I want to spend my summer job money on a bike. Is that OK with you?' (2) 'I want you to run for Student Council. What do you think about it?' " (Kifer and others, 1974, p. 359). Identification of issues was defined as "statements that explicitly identify the point of conflict in the situation. This statement may contrast the two opposing positions, or try to clarify what the other's position is if this is unclear, or identify what one thinks the conflict is really about. Examples: (1) 'You want me to buy clothes, but I want to buy a bike'; (2) 'The real issue is that I want you to learn responsibility.' Subjects were encouraged but not required to use the word *issue* when performing this behavior to make its occurrence more explicit. Suggestion of options was defined as statements that suggest a course of action to resolve the conflict, but not merely restatements of that person's original position. Examples: (1) 'How about if I spend some on clothes and use the rest to buy a bike if you'll help pay for it?' (2) 'I could get a part-time job and learn responsibility that way.' Subjects were encouraged but not required to pose options in the form of questions to increase the likelihood of receiving an answer to the option" (Kifer and others, 1974, pp. 359-360).

Clients were first asked to identify the three most troublesome problem situations between them at the time. (One parent and a child was involved in each pair, because two single-parent families took part in the program, and in one instance the father declined to participate.) Each pair discussed each situation for five minutes and were asked to try to reach a solution acceptable to both. Weekly training sessions seventy-five minutes long were held with individual pairs of clients, using a three-step format for each session: presession role play, discussion and practice, and postsession role play. A total of nine to ten hours were devoted to each pair of clients. The trainers first described a hypothetical parent-child conflict situation and asked the pair to role play the situation for five minutes. Then the clients were given a sheet describing the same situation they had discussed, as well as a list of response options and consequences. The trainer and subjects took turns matching each option with its likely consequence. A sample situation together with possible options and consequences is given in Figure 19.

Figure 19. Sample Sheet Used in Classroom Sessions

Situation

You have worked all summer for money and your mother insists that you spend it on clothes, but you want to spend it on something else.

Options

1. Tell her it is your money and it is none of her business what you spend it on.
2. Spend it on ugly clothes you know she hates.
3. Since she will not let you spend it the way you want, give it to charity.
4. Do not spend it on anything; put it in savings and let it collect interest.
5. Spend some on clothes she wants you to get and some on what you want.
6. You buy clothes if she will buy what else you want.
7. Sell them to a friend after you buy them.
8. It is easier to buy the clothes than hassle with mother.

Consequences

1. Get her mad at you and maybe have money taken away.
2. You have to wear the clothes you bought.
3. Feel good in helping a worthy cause.
4. End up with more money than you originally had.
5. Find out the clothes were a good thing.
6. Be miserable about the whole thing.
7. Never learn how to negotiate.

Source: Kifer and others (1974, p. 359; Roosa, 1973, p. 4).

Each client then selected the consequences that were most desirable to him, and practiced arriving at his selected options, with the child playing his own part the first few times and the parent and child switching roles later on. Clients were coached to use all three behaviors in their proper order, that is, to use complete communications, then to identify issues, and then to suggest options. One client first practiced all behaviors until she performed all three during a role play and the other client then did the same. Feedback in the form of social reinforcement was provided including smiles, praise, and head nods. Following discussion and practice a postsession simulation was conducted during which the parent and teen-ager again discussed a hypothetical conflict situation without instructions. Although encouraged to discuss current problems, only one pair did so.

The results of negotiation were divided into two types of agreements, complaint and negotiated. Complaint agreements were defined as "agreements by one person to the original position of the other such as 'All right, I'll spend all my money on clothes' " (Kifer and others, 1974, p. 360). Negotiated agreements were defined as "agreements to a suggested option that is not merely the original position of either person. Such agreements can take the form of a compromise, a deal (A gets his way but must in turn do something for B), or a new alternative (a different course of action). Example: 'OK, I guess a job would be fine.' Agreements need not restate the course of action agreed upon. This was done in the examples to preserve the identity of situations" (Kifer and others, 1974, p. 360). This training procedure was effective in increasing negotiation behaviors. However, reminders often had to be given after a week's lapse to cue the use of all three behaviors involved in negotiation. Agreements were reached in conflict situations in each pair that were more real than before training. The authors note that this procedure is designed for clients who have their emotional behavior under reasonably good control. That is, it is unlikely that such negotiation behaviors would be employed during "the heat of battle." If clients attempt to solve problems at the wrong times, when emotions are running high, instructions should be given that enable them to select a more appropriate time to solve problems.

Helpful communication also contains the following elements (Alexander, 1974): (1) brevity—statements should be reasonably short to avoid aversive monologs, the possibility of "acting out," and the confusion that they induce; (2) directing statements to their target—that is, encouraging clients to speak to the person they are expressing feelings about rather than through third parties; (3) source responsibility—in which the person speaking recognizes that he or she wishes something by using "I" statements, such as "I would like" or "I will be responsible for"; (4) congruence between verbal and nonverbal messages—verbal messages may be altered by nonmatching nonverbal expressions; and (5) interruptions and feedback—it may be helpful to train clients to interrupt someone who is speaking to them in order to clarify points. They are also trained to provide feedback on the messages they receive. If being interrupted is highly aversive to a client, some other method may be suggested for requesting clarification, such as raising the hand slightly to indicate that the client does not understand.

The Use of Games. Just as behavioral contracting can be carried out in a "gamelike" atmosphere (Weathers and Liberman, 1975b), negotiation training can also be conducted in such a framework. This often helps to discourage aversive patterns of family interaction (Blechman, Olson, and Turner, 1976; Blechman, Olson, and Hellman, 1976). Training is given in how to play the game, and the family is asked to use this format to discuss one problem each week at home. During an exploratory study of the use of such games, families received six training sessions followed by two later sessions (Blechman and Olson, 1976). A part of training is teaching family members to identify appropriate and inappropriate problem-solving behaviors. Appropriate behaviors include pinpointing specific behaviors that would please family members, proposals for compromises, supportive or approving statements that facilitate problem solving, and requests for information necessary for problem resolution, including asking others how they feel about given options. Speculation about why a problem behavior occurs is discouraged. The game board consists of fourteen squares divided into four components of the problem-solving process: (1) selection of problem; (2) description of more pleasing behavior; (3) consequence choice, where family members decide how the new behavior will be rewarded; and (4) contract settlement, in which a contract is agreed on, written, and signed by all involved parties. Movement to a more advanced component is contingent on successful completion of earlier ones. Players are rewarded for appropriate behaviors by opportunities to select bonus cards from a pack of such cards and by movement through the game board. At home, family members write down on cards problems that arise and place them in the pack of problem cards. Rewards that may be employed to increase desired behaviors can be placed in another pack and possible costs may be ascertained and placed in the "Risk" pack.

The one who raises the problem (red) identifies family members who contribute to the problem (blue). For example, a mother might complain that everyone in the family leaves their clothes on the floor. A rule is established that only one problem will be dealt with during a session. This is selected either because of its obvious importance or by a role of the dice. The aggrieved party may use the time until discussion of the problem to collect information about it, including ideas as to how it could be improved and relevant antecedents and consequences that may be shared when the problem is discussed. The rule of discussing only one problem per week allows time for the contract from the previous problem to have effect. Previous contracts are reviewed in terms of progress, which is assessed by one family member tracking the behavior during the week. If no change has occurred, the problem is reentered in the problem deck for later discussion, and if the problem has been successfully altered, this contract is terminated.

A case example of the use of contracting and negotiation training is offered in the following section.

Example of Contingency Contracting and Negotiation Training

Behavioral procedures were extensively employed in the Alameda Project (Stein and Gambrill, 1976a, 1976b) in working with natural parents and their children who were in foster care. The example described here concerns Mike, age fourteen, who ran away from home and refused to return, stating that he no longer wished to live with his father because they continually fought. He said his father was "unfair," never giving him credit for anything that he did, and that it was impossible to "please" him, so "Why bother trying?" The father agreed that they could not discuss issues without "getting into a hassle" and added that Mike "never did anything he was asked to do." While noting that he did want his son at home, he thought that a foster home was the best current solution. It was suggested that the problems they identified could best be addressed if the boy remained at home while the counselor would help them with their problems. Although a dependency petition had been filed, Mike was placed under his father's supervision after three weeks in temporary placement.

Assessment took place over a two-week period and included one office and three home visits. During home visits, parent-child interaction was observed and recorded, because verbal communication was cited by both clients as the most important problem. Examples of this were that (1) all discussions resulted in arguments; (2) the father said that Mike did not listen to him when he was talking, and did not comply with any of his requests, such as doing chores or being home at specified times; and (3) the son stated that his father "always yells and shouts" and will not listen to his "half of the story." During the initial office interview, it was noted that both the father and son frequently interrupted each other, and that the interrupter would increase his voice tone to be heard above the speaker. The father's statement that his son "never did anything" did not appear to be entirely accurate, because both agreed that the boy did do some things. The issue was that he did not do them as his father thought they should be done. When asked to clarify this issue, it seemed clear that the father did not fully describe task requirements.

The initial program designed to address the issue of household responsibility is described as follows, including the contract that was formulated between the father and son regarding this area. This case provides a good example of starting an intervention in one problem area while continuing to gather needed assessment information in relation to other areas. Thus, a program to address the problem of chore completion was initiated while arrangements were made for the worker to gather assessment information regarding the verbal interaction between Mike and his father.

Intervention Program 1: Household Responsibilities. The father was asked to identify two household responsibilities that he thought his son should fulfill, and the frequency with which they should be done. He cited cleaning up the kitchen each evening within one hour after dinner, and washing the car once each week. The son agreed that these were fair requests. Next, to clarify the father's expectations for each chore, he was asked to describe, in writing, what the kitchen and the car would look like after they were "cleaned up." The father wrote that the dishes would be washed and stacked, the counter top and table wiped clean, the trash emptied and the floor swept. The car would be washed on the outside, vacuumed and dusted on the interior, and the ash trays and trash bag emptied. After being shown the list, Mike said that he understood what his father wanted and thought it was fair. A chart for the daily recording of these chores was designed (see Figure 20).

The worker suggested that Mike's allowance of $5.00 each week be earned by the son for completing chores, with a set sum of money for each chore. The father agreed willingly; the son, somewhat reluctantly. Sums awarded for given chores are described in Figure 21.

It was suggested that, based on what the father and son had said about their problems with verbal communication, as well as on observations of interrupting and shouting behavior in the office, it would be best if no verbal communication occurred between them relative to the chore program. Any problem that arose was to be written down. To encourage the father's participation in the program, he was asked to cite two things that he enjoyed doing in the evenings. He said he liked to watch television. The counselor suggested that his first half hour of television watching be contingent on his not discussing chore completion with Mike. A second list (see Figure 20) was designed to note conversation relative to chores. One half hour following chore completion the son would place a checkmark in the chart if the father did not discuss chore completion. If the father did discuss chores, there would be no check mark, and

Figure 20. Checklist for Daily Chores, Weekly Car Cleaning, and No Dialog

Clean kitchen	Mon.	Tues.	Wed.	Thurs.	Fri.	Sat.	Sun.
Wash and stack dishes							
Clean off counter and table top							
Sweep floor							
Empty trash							
Clean car							
Wash exterior							
Vacuum and dust interior, empty ash trays							

Cleaning kitchen: To be completed within 1 hour following dinner. A check mark is to be placed next to each chore each evening after it is done by Mike. Between 1 and 1½ hours after dinner, Mr. Jones will check the chores that have been completed and make the appropriate check marks.

Clean car: To be done once each week. Mike will check off task completion by each item on the list. Mr. Jones will verify task completion as well as the check marks.

No-Dialog Checklist

Mon.		Fri.	
Tues.		Sat.	
Wed.		Sun.	
Thurs.			

Mike will place a check mark each day of the week, if no dialog has occurred relative to task completion.

Source: Stein and Gambrill (1976b, p. 104).

the father would forfeit the first half-hour of television. The purpose of written agreements was explained and a contract was drawn up and signed (see Figure 21). Telephone contact was arranged over the next three days, and the clients were invited to telephone the counselor if any difficulties arose. Agreements of all parties were written down and a copy was given to the clients (see Figure 21).

Intervention Program 2: Verbal Communication. Arrangements were made for three home visits over the next week: once during dinner, once in the early evening immediately fol-

Figure 21. Contract Between Clients Regarding Household Chores

This contract is entered into between Mike Jones and his father Frank Jones.

Mike agrees to:

Each evening, within one hour following dinner, Mike will clean up the kitchen. This includes washing and stacking the dinner dishes, cleaning off the counter and table top, emptying the trash, and sweeping the kitchen floor.

Each time Mikes completes one of these tasks, he will place a check mark next to the task completed under the appropriate day.

Mike further agrees to wash the car once each week; this includes washing the exterior, vacuuming and dusting the interior, and emptying the ash trays. Mike agrees to place a check mark next to each of these tasks when they are completed. Mike further agrees to place a check mark on the "no-dialog" list each evening and following car washing if no verbal exchange takes place between father and son regarding chores.

Mr. Jones agrees to:

Refrain from all discussion of task completion. Should any task not be completed to Mr. Jones' satisfaction, he will write down which aspect of the task wasn't completed and how it should have been done.

To pay Mike a weekly allowance, not to exceed $5.00. This amount of allowance earned is contingent on task completion and is payable on the schedule listed below.

Mr. Jones agrees to forego his first nightly half-hour of television watching should he engage in any dialog with Mike regarding task completion.

Allowance Schedule: Maximum $5.00

Each of the four tasks involved in cleaning the kitchen has a value of $0.10 or a maximum daily value of $0.40 and a maximum weekly value of $2.80.

Washing the exterior of the car is valued at $0.75, vacuuming and dusting the interior and emptying the ash tray at an additional $0.75. Maximum value for cleaning the car is $1.50.

Bonus: If all kitchen cleaning tasks are completed each night, there will be a weekly bonus of $0.35. If car-washing tasks are completed once each week, there will be an additional $0.35 bonus. This bonus for each chore category is payable only if all of the tasks within that category are completed.

Cost: For each task not completed Mike will forego the value of that task. For example, if on any given evening Mike fails to sweep the floor, he can earn only $0.30 for that evening.

Signed: _____ J. Jones

_____ M. Jones

Source: Stein and Gambrill (1976b, p. 105).

lowing dinner, and on Saturday morning between 10:00 and 11:00 A.M. in order to observe Mr. Jones and Mike, and to try to clarify the problems cited as "verbal communication." It was explained that the counselor's main role during these visits would be to observe and record rather than to discuss problems, but that a brief part of each session would be devoted to going over the chore completion program and dealing with any difficulties either party had. A promise was made to share the results of observation and to plan programs to modify any problems that were identified.

The data presented in Table 9 was collected during three hours and fifteen minutes of home observation. A coding form

Table 9. Baseline Data Describing Verbal Interaction
Between Mike and His Father

Total Recording Time: 3 hours, 15 minutes.
Length of Recoding Intervals: 5 minutes.[a]
Total Number of Intervals: 39.
Total Number of Responses Recorded: 77.

Type of Verbalization	Frequency			
	Father		Son	
No communication (10 intervals)	Frequency	Percent[b]	Frequency	Percent
1. Disapproval	10	20	—	—
2. Yelling or Shouting	9	18	8	29
3. Command Negative	11	23	—	—
4. Ignoring	—	—	12	43
5. Incomplete Instructions	9	18	—	—
6. Approval	2	04	3	11
7. Command Positive	3	06	—	—
8. Attending	2	04	3	11
9. Positive Verbal Exchanges	3	06	2	07
	49		28	

[a]More than one response can be recorded in any single interval. Also one statement, such as a disapproving comment or negative command may be made in a "yelling" tone of voice, and would be coded twice.

[b]Percentages are to the total number of verbalizations made by each person.

Source: Stein and Gambrill (1976b, p. 107).

was employed utilizing the following verbal categories: (1) *Command Positive (Present):* Request begins with a positive, such as "Would you please," or "I would appreciate it if you would. . . " and is for something in the present, for example, "Please pass the salt" (2) *Command Positive (Future):* Immediate compliance is not demanded, and listener is permitted to state a position; for example, in response to a request to go to the store, the listener may state, "It will be difficult for me to do that because. . . ," and a compromise way of obtaining what is needed at the store is made. (3) *Attending:* Listener looks at the speaker and responds almost immediately after the speaker has finished talking. (4) *Positive Verbal Exchange:* An exchange of information about any topic, such as the son's school or the father's work, where each party attends and responds to the other and no negative methods of communication are employed. (5) *Yelling or Shouting:* Statements are made in a loud tone of voice. (6) *Disapproval:* Sentences begin with a negative comment, such as "Why don't you ever. . ." or "You never . . . ." (7) *Incomplete Instructions:* A request is made; however, the expectations are not clearly described. For example, a parent may say, "I'd like you to take out the trash," but does not say when this is to occur. (8) *Command Negative:* Immediate compliance is demanded. No opportunity is given to the listener to state a position. A threat of negative consequences for noncompliance may be included (for example, "You do this, or else. . . ") (9) *Ignoring:* Statements or questions are not answered. Repeated requests culminating in yelling or shouting may result. (10) *Approval:* Sentences beginning with a positive comment, such as "I like it when. . . ." The counselor noted at each five-minute interval which, if either, of the clients was speaking and the category into which a verbal statement fell. A statement was defined as any complete utterance beginning as soon as one person started to speak and ending when that person finished. Complete sentences and utterances such as "uh-huh" were included.

The clients were shown what was recorded and examples of statements defining each category were offered. The effects of their pattern of interaction were explained, including how this contributed to the presenting problem. For example, the high frequency of disapproving relative to approving statements was noted as well as the frequency with which the father demanded compliance with his requests and the high number of incomplete instructions. Incomplete instructions, negative commands, disapprovals, and a low frequency of positive verbal responses contributed to Mike's feeling that he "never did anything right," and facilitated his ignoring and noncompliant behavior, which, in turn, encouraged the father's yelling and shouting. The son had probably learned to model his father's behaviors. It was explained that such patterns gradually become established over time, so that each person becomes a cue to the other for such communication. Issues or problems are rarely dealt with, because each party responds to the "attack rather than the problem" (Patterson and others, 1975).

In addition, the counselor noted that the father had a repertoire of approval statements, although he used it infrequently, and that the son did attend to him when his remarks were positive. Hence, one objective was to increase the frequency of the father's approval responses and the son's attending behavior. An additional objective was to teach the father and son how to discuss problems in a positive manner that would lead to resolutions; that is, how to negotiate areas of disagreement. A new counselor-client contract was recommended, the objective of which would be to dismiss the court dependency, contingent on successful completion of the programs. The clients were congratulated for their progress with the chore completion program.

The father was asked to make one of the following verbal responses to his son each evening after checking the chore completion list given that some chores had been completed: (1) "The kitchen looks really nice, Mike—thank you for cleaning up," or (2) "I appreciate the way you cleaned up after dinner." Mike was to listen to his father's statement, and after he had finished, to simply say, "Thank you, Dad." There were to be no negative comments made by either party. Both the father and son agreed to maintain a record of approval and attending responses by placing check marks on a chart indicating their presence following an exchange. The reinforcer for Michael was having his Saturday night curfew extended by one hour, earned at the rate of ten minutes each evening, five minutes each for approvals and attending behaviors. If the entire hour was not earned, Mike could have whatever extra time he did earn. The father had expressed a wish to save $10 each week to be used in any way he wished. This was to be accumulated at the rate of $1.50 for each check mark that appeared for him. Michael agreed to save this money for his father. The father gave his son the money each evening it was earned. All details of the plan were written down and a copy given to the clients. A recording chart was also prepared and given to the father and son. The social worker agreed to telephone Mr. Jones and Mike twice each week for the first three weeks and once each week following that for the duration of the contract, to monitor the program and to discuss any difficulties. Plans were also made to meet with Mr. Jones and Mike once each week on Thursday evenings between the hours of 7 and 8:30 P.M. Negotiation training was initiated during these sessions. In addition, the worker monitored the chore completion and verbal response records, as well as any written disapproval notes by either father or son. The agreed-on plan for negotiation training is described in Figure 22.

Figure 22. Plan for Negotiation Training

The objective of this program is to teach both parties methods of discussing issues in which there are differences of opinion, such that these differences can be resolved in a manner that is satisfactory to both clients. To accomplish this the worker agrees to meet with the father and son each Thursday evening between the hours of 7 and 8:30 P.M. The focus of these meetings will be as follows:

1. To teach each party how to state an issue of concern in a specific manner so that the other person understands the focus of the concern.
2. To facilitate Step 1, the worker will teach father and son how to "paraphrase" what the other has said. Paraphrasing involves having the listener repeat, in his words, what he has heard the speaker say. The speaker responds by stating either agreement or disagreement with what has been said.
3. Finally, the worker will assist father and son in learning how to "trade" to resolve differences of opinion. Trading involves identifying what each party is willing to give or contribute to problem resolution.

The father and son agree to

1. Be present at their home during these regularly scheduled meetings.
2. To practice the tasks learned in negotiation sessions. These practice sessions will occur on [date] in [place] and at no other time.
3. In any practice area in which there is disagreement or difficulty, both parties agree to write down their view of the difficulty. This should include a statement of the aspect of negotiation training (for example, being specific, paraphrasing, trading) that is difficult. Within the identified area of difficulty, each party should write down who was speaking, what was said, their perception of the difficulty, and how it could have been resolved.
4. The worker agrees to go over any issues that are listed and to assist father and son in methods of resolving them.

Source: Stein and Gambrill (1976b, p. 114).

The•chore completion chart was maintained over four-teen weeks of intervention and the data recorded were graphed to show the percentage of chores completed each week. Chore completion ranged between 90 and 100 percent for the entire program compared to the prebaseline period (client estimate) of zero. The father complied with the suggestion that no dialog regarding chores occur during the first two weeks of the chore program. After completion of negotiation training, verbal inter-action was again observed, over three and a half hours, using the same observational form employed during baseline. A descrip-tion of their interaction following training is presented in Table 10. There were dramatic decreases in negative communication

Table 10. Postnegotiation Training Observational Data

Type of Verbalization	Frequency			
	Total Recording Time: 3 hours, 30 minutes. *Length of Intervals:* 5 minutes. *Total Number of Intervals:* 42. *Total Number of Responses Recorded:* 99.			
No Communication (3 intervals)	*Father*		*Son*	
	Frequency	Percent	Frequency	Percent
1. Disapproval	3	05	—	—
2. Yelling or Shouting	2	04	—	—
3. Command Negative	0	—	—	—
4. Ignoring	1	02	2	05
5. Incomplete Instructions	2	04	0	—
6. Approval	12	22	9	23
7. Command Positive	10	18	—	—
8. Attending	11	20	12	30
9. Positive Verbal Exchanges	14	25	17	43
	55		40	

Source: Stein and Gambrill (1976b, p. 117).

categories and increases in positive categories following training. The court dependency was therefore dismissed as per the con-tract agreement.

A Training Program for Parents of Aggressive Children

An example of the steps involved in utilizing a social learning framework with aggressive children is discussed in the following section. It draws on the program developed at the Oregon Research Institute (ORI) (Patterson and others, 1975). In the ORI program, parents learn to specify, track, and record a series of child behaviors as well as to arrange contingencies for problem behaviors. Learning to observe and collect data is a central aspect of this parent training program as it is with others (for example, see Lindsley, 1966). Parents learn to attend more carefully to their own behavior and to their child's behavior. The emphasis throughout is on change within the family, with all involved family members taking an active part in the process. This framework is conveyed in the description of the program given to the child: "This is a place where families learn how to change what is going on in their own home. Parents and kids learn how to change some of the things that really hurt them. Today we will be asking you (the child) about some of the things that you think would make things better for you" (Patterson and others, 1975, p. 25).

Assessment. After a brief discussion with both the parents and the child, separate interviews are held with the parents and the child. The program is described to the family, stressing the hard work that will be involved over three to four months. Parents are informed that contact with the staff will be frequent at first, including daily brief telephone calls to gather data collected by the parents. The need for involvement of *both* the mother *and* the father is emphasized and the rationale for collection of a "breakage fee" is explained. This covers the cost of books and equipment that might be lost and serves as a source of "response cost" for failure to honor agreed-on assignments or to keep agreed-on appointments. Most parents receive the entire $10 back at the end of the program.

Parents learn that they will be requested to read *Families* (Patterson, 1971a) and that intervention will not begin until they have completed this and taken a test on its contents. This book describes reinforcement principles. Parents who receive training in the general concepts of behavior management are more able to deal with a range of problematic child behaviors compared to parents who receive training only in how to alter specific target behaviors (Glogower and Sloop, 1976). Improvements were also maintained better by the former group. Understanding such principles seems to encourage their use. If the parents wish to discuss their child's problems at school, it is explained that these problems will be addressed following intervention in the home. Progress through the sequence of program components is contingent on completion of earlier steps. For example, parents do not receive their first appointment for a "pinpointing interview" until they have read the book. And not until baseline data is collected on pinpointed behavior is intervention initiated. Subtraction of one dollar from their deposit for continued noncompliance helps to ensure cooperation. Admission to a parent training group may be contingent on reading *Living With Children* (Patterson and Gullian, 1968) as well as on collecting consistently good data for several days.

Data is collected before, during, and after intervention, so allowing ongoing feedback concerning progress. At the end of the home-observation period, parents are given a copy of *Families* to read. They are requested not to try to apply concepts explained in the book at this point. Telephone contact is made within two days to check on whether any problems have arisen. *Living With Children* may be used if reading skills are limited. Most parents are not accustomed to reading such material, and problems in completing this assignment arise with some families. Some parents, for example, express disagreement with the approach. Parents are encouraged to continue reading even though they do not agree with the ideas and are informed that the principles will make better sense when they are applied. They can also be requested to write down their disagreements so that these can be discussed at a later time. A second problem that may arise is attempting to apply principles and failing. Parents are warned that, although the principles sound simple, application is a complex matter and that they should wait until their comprehension of the principles is checked. A third problem that may arise is reading difficulty. Often one parent reads the book quickly and the other lags behind. The "slow" parent is telephoned and asked how the reading is coming along. If further delay ensues, the referring agent can be asked to telephone the parent and ask how things are going, and, if the answer is fine, to ask for specifics. Interpretive comments as to why the delay is happening are avoided. For some parents, nothing seems to work. Need for extensive assistance in getting the parents to read the manual or listen to a tape recording of the manual is a poor omen for them carrying out new child management skills (Patterson and others, 1975). Usually, however, initial steps progress smoothly. Following the completion of the book, which usually takes two weeks, a brief test is given to assess comprehension.

After satisfactory completion of the test on *Families*, attention is directed toward identifying behaviors to be observed by the parents. The child is informed that he will also have an opportunity to identify things that he would like changed in the family and is asked to write down items that occur to him. The father is then asked what problem he would like to focus on. Continual efforts are made to involve fathers and to overcome their idea that the program can be left up to the mother. Practice is provided in pinpointing, tracking, and recording behavior by giving each parent a wrist counter and asking them to count some agreed-on behavior during a five-minute discussion with the counselor about what child behaviors concern them most. The number counted by the father and mother is compared and problems of definitions discussed. Calculation of a rate score is demonstrated and the couple given practice in arriving at this figure. It is recognized that tracking behavior while doing other things is difficult, but, as they practice, this will become easier. They are asked to select two behaviors to increase and two to decrease. Both parents record the four behaviors over the next three weekdays during one specially selected hour each day. One behavior can be counted with a wrist counter and others can be tabulated on a piece of masking tape attached to the wrist. Telephone calls to collect data are arranged and data are collected each weekday. During phone contact, the parents are asked if there are any problems in defining or counting behaviors. Calls are made to the father one day and the mother the next to keep both parents involved. Requests for assistance in solving problems are answered by suggesting that the parents do whatever they usually do until intervention. The following example of the presenting picture of a child seen in this program is from Patterson and others (1975, p. 31). This case is discussed in more detail later.

Maude, The Malevolent

Maude was only ten when referred to ORI at the behest of the school. In addition to frequent stealing episodes, and even more frequent lies, she was almost totally without friends. Her "entrance" into a game being played on the playground could be marked by her shouted commands and freely dispensed kicks and blows to those who non-complied. What was most infuriating to peers and teachers alike was her ability to look an accusing adult in the eye and say, "No, I didn't take the money," even though faced by three eye witnesses (including the teacher). If defeated in such an encounter, she generally planned revenge such as writing notes to the teacher in the most florid prose imaginable. The notes were directed to those teachers most likely to be upset by the language. While only four feet tall, she could reduce most adults half again her size to smoldering impotence.

Her parents fared no better. Her presence in the home consisted of running battles with both of her older sisters. What she did not accomplish by verbal invectives could be won by stealthy attacks upon their belongings, for example, a favorite picture smashed, an article of jewelry "lost," or money "mislaid." Attempts to control her behavior were met with denials, lies, debates, giggles, and sobs. Occasionally one or both parents would severely spank her but both were convinced that it did little good. She was so difficult to manage that the parents had long ago given up any pretense of asking her to do chores.

The mother seemed very angry with Maude and reported later that she spent long hours ruminating about her daughter's myriad misbehaviors. She was convinced she could not be changed and had often considered institutionalization. She reported that Maude knew just what to say or how to act in order to get under her skin.

The parents listed the following as problems of greatest concern to them:

1. Steals.
2. Lies.
3. Swears at home and school.
4. Fights with peers.

5. Not liked by other children.
6. Teases siblings.
7. Does not mind.

Intervention. After data are collected for three days, the next session is held, during which the first contract is established. The contracts employed by the Oregon Research Center are usually in the form of simple token economies in which points are accumulated for behaviors completed. Reinforcers that can be purchased with the points are identified. Frequent daily reinforcement may be necessary initially. Token programs are often employed with aggressive children, because such children are not as responsive to adult social reinforcers and tend to increase coercive behaviors when parents try to punish them. It is assumed that through pairing parental praise with points and their backup reinforcers, approval will gradually acquire a reinforcing function, allowing the gradual removal or fading of the token program in which artificial reinforcers are employed. Initial contracts focus only on two or three behaviors that are easy to monitor. Later contracts can include more behaviors as well as longer delays in offering backup reinforcers.

The definitions of the four behaviors selected by the parents are recorded on the back of the contract sheet. A convenient amount (ten) of daily earnable points is selected. When asked what they would like to earn, children as well as parents at first usually select items that are either too far removed (going to a football game in the fall when it is now spring) or too large (going on a weekend fishing trip). Items should be selected that can be offered on a daily basis, are ethical to offer, will function as reinforcers, and that the parents are willing to offer. The child and parents are also asked what the consequences should be if the child forgets or has a really lousy day (Patterson and others, 1975). Both the parents and the child usually have to be toned down from vengeful possibilities to focusing on a consequence that will help the child practice a different behavior. This might include a half hour earlier bedtime or letting siblings choose what is to be viewed on television for the night. It is important to avoid behaviors that will require an effort for parents to monitor or supervise. The first contract employed with "Malevolent Maude" is shown in the following list (Patterson and others, 1975).

10 points	Stay up until 9:00 P.M. and watch television.
8 points	Go to bed 8:30, get special dessert.
6 points	Go to bed 8:30.
4 points	Go to bed 7:30.
2 points	Go to bed 7:00.
Minus or 0	Wash dishes and go to bed 7:00.

The family is given a copy of the written contract to post in a conspicuous spot, such as the refrigerator door. Daily telephone contact is continued over the next few days.

Effective use of positive reinforcement should be modeled for the parents and practice offered in its use. The parent may be requested to observe the counselor interacting with her child from behind a one-way mirror. Extensive training may be required to develop skills in positive reinforcement as well as to encourage parents to only reinforce appropriate behaviors. Skills are established in a step-by-step manner, in a context of constructive feedback in which parents are praised for approximations to effective behavior. If these discussions take place in parent groups, other members are involved in offering feedback. The need for consistent use of positive reinforcement or punishment without nagging or debating with the child is emphasized. Role playing includes how to handle various reactions of the child to enforcement of contracted rules, such as arguing back. Parents learn how to track noncompliance; that is, attend to it, label it, and be consistent in their use of consequences. They are coached to use only a single prompt for the desired behavior and then to use a time out immediately.

As noted by Patterson and his colleagues, it is at this point that parents of unsuccessful cases will begin to reinterpret what has been said or modeled. Their version of a procedure may not work at all or they may not even try to carry out agreed-on procedures. These are signals that further steps must be taken to attempt to change parental behavior. If difficulties occur, new problems should not be added to the contract. Points of concern may be mentioned by the child when he is asked how the contract is going. Failure of a point program to affect behavior (few points are being earned) usually relates to inconsistent tracking of behaviors by the parents, forgetting to award points, or failure to provide backup reinforcers (Patterson and others, 1975).

If the first contract is successful, additional behaviors can be added to the contract and negotiation training initiated. Positive behaviors are emphasized by asking one parent at the beginning of the session to review the good things that happened since the last session, using the contract as a reminder. (Parents are required to bring the contract to the session.) Effective parental behaviors are identified and praised, such as smiles, touches, clear labels, enthusiasm, absence of zapping (punishing statements such as put-downs), and eye contact. Negotiation training is initiated in which family members learn to describe problems in concrete terms, in a way that indicates that it is a problem for them, and with an absence of blame of other family members. The counselor first models an appropriate way of stating a problem, as in the following example. "Try to talk about a problem in terms of how it makes *you* feel. Do it without putting the other person down. For example, let me pretend I'm you: 'The problem I'd like to work on is the television going so loud all the time. It makes me nervous to have it so loud. I'd like to include that in this week's program.' If all of you agree that it really is a problem, then discuss how to set up a program for it" (Patterson and others, 1975, p. 70). The father is then asked to try to pinpoint a problem. The family is reminded not to zap one another and that the zapee (the victim) is always right as to whether a comment is a zap. A scorecard on which number of zaps are recorded for each family member can help to identify and to decrease zaps when these are frequent. Each person is asked to make a mark by the person's name and label the behavior every time he yells, interrupts, or zaps. It is emphasized that this should not be done in a spirit of punishment but in terms of trying to help each family member to track and influence his or her own behavior. The child is encouraged to try to help the parents define the behaviors they mention. It is helpful to tape this discussion. Replaying the tape can be used to identify parental behaviors consistent with good

reinforcement practices. After the other parent is asked to identify a behavior to add to the list, the child is then requested to
do so. The counselor should be sure to coach him to explain
how it makes him feel, and to try to be specific.

When new behaviors are added to the contract, points are
readjusted so that the total represents the same number. Backup
consequences should be strengthened. For example, a cost can
be placed on failure to earn any points for a week. Payoffs
should still occur frequently, either daily and/or biweekly. A response cost for some low-frequency behavior such as stealing,
truancy, or assault can also be added at this point. The rationale
offered for this is to provide practice in not doing the behavior
and the child is asked to participate in selecting a response cost.
A certain number of hours of chore completion is often arranged and it is emphasized that the parents must supervise this or
at least check on its completion if a behavior product results,
such as wood being stacked. An hour or two may be enforced
for minor deeds and five or six for serious misdeeds such as
assault. Parents often fail to enforce contingencies. This may be
discovered by asking the child. As always, it is vital to specifically describe the behavior; for example, stealing can be defined
as the child's possessing anything that does not belong to him,
and he is told that it is his responsibility to avoid situations in
which it seems he is guilty (Patterson and others, 1975).

Telephone contact is decreased to three times a week,
still alternating between speaking to the mother and to father.
Specific questions will help to reveal if the program is being employed and with what effects. For example, the father can be
asked how many points his son earned for specific behaviors, as
well as how many the father gave out, or when time out was
used. These calls are crucial for determining inadequacies in
contracts at an early point as well as problematic situations that
may interfere with the program. Other children over five years
of age may be involved in later sessions, to fill them in on what
is happening and to provide an opportunity for the counselor to
observe parents' skills as they describe examples of good behaviors of their child.

The contract formed with Maude and her family during
the third family conference is shown in Figure 23. The minus

Figure 23. Contract Between Maude and Her Parents

Name _Maude_   Dates _April 10_ through _17_

Behaviors (points)	Monday	Tuesday	Wednesday	Thursday	Friday	Saturday	Sunday
−5 steal (1)							
−1 swear (3)							
−1 noncomply (2)							
clean room (2)							
dishes (1)							
lie (1)							
TOTAL							

TO for: noncomply _____   Backup Reinforcers

Stealing   _____
gets: 2 hours of work _____   10 points   mother reads to her 30 minutes
            _____   8 points   get special dessert
                                               6 points   stay up until 8:30 P.M.
                                               4 points   no TV
                                               0 points   go to bed at 7:30
                                              −5 points   go to bed at 6:30

Source: Patterson and others (1975, p. 77).

figures indicate the number of points lost for given behaviors. An absence of reinforcement occurs for behaviors of less concern to parents. Numbers in parentheses indicate the number of points earned per day for each behavior. Thus, if Maude did not swear all day, she received three points. Time out was used only for noncompliance.

Patterson and his associates speculate that this procedure will be effective with one out of three children and that additional programs are required for the other families. These programs may entail intervention in the classroom, a focus on marital conflict, offering training in the home, or perhaps training the parents to help their child learn academic skills.

Supplementary Home Observation and Training Sessions. It has been estimated that there are about 20 percent of families where training must be offered in the home itself. If little progress occurs during the first two or three weeks, this is a cue that such training may be required. Home visits may only be necessary to secure information relative to a given problem, such as time out failing to work. During these sessions, the first half hour is devoted solely to observation, usually during the dinner hour. This period should reveal ineffective use of punishment and/or reinforcement procedures. After observation, a conference with the family is held, during which positive procedures are first noted and then one observed problem in child management is described, effective procedures modeled for the parents and the parents asked to role play them. The counselor then returns to his observer role and asks the parents to try to use what he has just demonstrated. One area in which a problem often occurs is ineffective use of time out. Parents are often too lenient in the definition of problem behaviors. With many families, two evening meetings are sufficient to establish a working program (Patterson and others, 1975).

Patterson and his colleagues have been among the few who have gathered careful data concerning the efficiency and effectiveness of their program, although the absence of a control group to which clients were randomly assigned limits their assessment of effectiveness. Twenty-seven children participated in one program, fourteen of whom had problems in school as well as at home. Treatment time per family averaged 31.5 hours in the home and 28.6 hours in the classroom (Patterson, 1974). In addition, about 1.9 hours of consultation were provided during a twelve-month follow-up period. A strength of this study was evaluation through independently gathered observational data. This indicated that deviant behavior decreased by 43 percent, a level that was maintained at a six-month follow-up. The rate of appropriate behavior in the classroom increased 29 percent and was maintained at a four- to six-month follow-up. It has been found that when parents are trained in behavioral methods of influencing a child, there is also a decrease in the rate of aggressive behavior of siblings (Arnold, Levine, and Patterson, 1975). As Arnold and his colleagues note, this is important, because the siblings of aggressive boys also evidence aggressive behavior at a high rate. In fact, there were no initial differences between the rates of deviant behavior for referred and nonreferred children in the same family.

Training Parents in the Home

Training may initially take place in the home. Patterson and his colleagues sometimes conduct "marathon intervention" in the home, during which counselors work in pairs in three-hour sessions (Patterson and others, 1975). The counselors first review data on the contract from the prior day and the parents are asked to describe what happened each time points were awarded or removed and when they used time out. During observation, the counselors indicate to the parents when they respond to behavior appropriately and also note when they do not. Their lack is carefully pinpointed and the parent is asked to rehearse appropriate behavior the next time a contract-related behavior occurs. Both father and mother are present during these sessions. If a verbal request does not prompt appropriate parental behavior, this is modeled by the counselor. While one counselor tracks and models effective reinforcement procedures, the other observes. They reverse roles every thirty minutes. Prompts are faded as appropriate behaviors increase in frequency and sessions arranged less frequently. Efforts are usually terminated if change is not noted after three to four sessions.

Cues may be employed to signal the mother to employ various consequences. For example, Hawkins and others (1966) used a cueing procedure to signal a mother when to reinforce her four-year-old boy (respond with attention and approval), when to tell him to stop some objectionable behavior, and when to place him in his room and lock the door (a time out). "Peter had been brought to a university clime because he was extremely difficult to manage and control. His mother stated she was helpless in dealing with his frequent tantrums and disobedience. Peter often kicked objects or people, removed or tore his clothing, called people rude names, annoyed his younger sister, made a variety of threats, hit himself, and became very angry at the slightest frustration. He demanded attention almost constantly, and seldom cooperated with Mrs. S. [his mother]. In addition, Peter was not toilet trained and did not always speak clearly. Neither of these latter problems was dealt with in the study. Peter had been evaluated at a clinic for retarded children when he was three years old and again when he was four and a half. His scores on the Stanford Binet, Form L-M, were 72 and 80, respectively. He was described as having borderline intelligence, as being hyperactive, and possibly brain-damaged" (Hawkins and others, 1966, p. 100). The child and mother were first observed at home and it was noted that many of his behaviors appeared to be maintained by his mother's attention. When he behaved inappropriately, the mother would try to explain to him why he should not act that way or would try to interest him in some other activity by offering toys or food. Such inappropriate use of a distraction procedure may increase problematic behavior. Even though the mother occasionally removed a toy or other object, Peter was often able to talk her into giving it back to him. Disciplinary measures invoked by the mother, such as placing him in a highchair, occasioned tantrum behavior that was quite effective in maintaining parental attention in the form of verbal persuasion and arguments. Objectionable behaviors identified during observation included "(1) biting his shirt or arm, (2) sticking out his tongue, (3) kicking or hitting himself, others or objects, (4) calling someone or something a derogatory name, (5) removing or threatening to remove his clothing, (6) saying "No!" loudly and vigorously, (7) threatening to damage objects or persons, (8) throwing objects, and (9) pushing his sister" (Hawkins and others, 1966, p. 101).

Intervention consisted of six one-hour sessions (twice per week), held in the home while Peter, his mother and his three-year-old sister were present. Each time an objectionable behavior occurred, the mother was signaled first to tell Peter to stop and, if the behavior recurred during the session, she was instructed to place him in his room. When the counselor noted him playing in a desirable manner, the mother was signaled to offer him praise and attention.

The training program was effective in decreasing objectionable behavior and increasing desirable alternatives. Objectionable behaviors decreased from between 18 to 113 per session during baseline to between 1 to 8 per session during intervention. Positive effects were maintained over a twenty-four-day follow-up period. The mother reported that her son was well behaved and much less demanding and that she found it necessary to use time out only about once a week.

Training in the home was also employed by Zeilberger, Sampen, and Sloane (1968). The mother learned to use time out for inappropriate behavior, to ignore minor disruptive behaviors, and to praise appropriate behaviors of her four-year-old boy. Training sessions were held for one hour each day, with the objective of teaching the mother how to decrease physical aggression (hitting, pushing, kicking, biting, and scratching), yelling, and bossing (directing another child or adult to do or not to do something), and to increase following of instructions. Percentage of instructions followed during the first baseline period averaged 30 percent (see Figure 11). The average during the last seven sessions of the first intervention period was 78 percent. The aggressive behavior decreased substantially. Yelling also decreased even though no direct plan was devised for this, which raises the important question of what behaviors are functionally linked to what other behaviors. That is, when will a change in one behavior lead to a change in other behaviors? The decrease in instruction-following when baseline conditions were reinstated lends support for considering parental attention a reinforcer of the boy's behavior.

Some home intervention programs have addressed sibling interaction. For example, O'Leary, O'Leary, and Becker (1967) employed prompting, shaping, and instructions to increase cooperative behaviors of a six-year-old boy and his brother, both of whom frequently engaged in assaultive and destructive behaviors at home. Unlike the intervention procedure in the Hawkins (1966) study, the child's behavior was first brought under the influence of counselor-offered instructions and consequences, and this influence was then transferred to the mother. If the mother can assume such responsibilities initially, it saves time to teach her directly to employ the procedures as in the Hawkins study. Appropriate behavior was first reinforced by M&M candies and later by points that were exchanged for small toys. It was necessary later to introduce time out for some deviant behaviors that were not controlled by reinforcement of alternative behaviors. A description of the children is presented as follows.

Psychiatric History

Barry had been under psychiatric treatment for two years and was described by his psychiatrist as "seriously disturbed." He was reported to be extremely hyperactive, aggressive, and destructive. His EEG was symmetric and within normal limits. Although it was not possible to give him an intelligence test, the psychiatrist felt that his intelligence was within normal limits. He was diagnosed as an "immature, braindamaged child with a superimposed neurosis," although the nature and cause of his brain damage could not be specified.

Parental Report

According to Mr. and Mrs. A. [parents], Barry fought with his brother whenever they were alone. He damaged toys and furniture. He had temper tantrums and failed to follow parental instructions. . . . He roamed away from home, and he would occasionally enter strangers' houses.

Mrs. A. reported that the boys angered her by screaming, yelling, and hurting each other when they were alone in the basement playroom. [O'Leary, O'Leary, and Becker, 1967, p. 114]

Observation revealed a great deal of commanding behavior by six-year-old Barry in relation to Jeff, age three. If his brother did not do what he asked, Barry would coerce him physically. They would break each other's toys, which occasioned further fighting. The mother usually remained upstairs while the boys played in the basement playroom. She only responded to the screaming, yelling, and fighting that could be heard. Three classes of behavior were focused on. Deviant behavior included kicking, hitting, pushing, name calling, and throwing objects at each other. Cooperative behavior included asking for a toy, requesting the other's help, conversation, saying "Please" and "Thank you," and playing within three feet of one another. An absence of verbal, physical, or visual interaction between the boys was defined as isolate behavior.

A baseline was taken over a five-day period for about thirty minutes each day using a twenty-second rate, ten-second rest interval recording procedure. During the first two days of intervention, cooperative behaviors were reinforced by placing an M&M in the child's mouth, and at the same time saying "Good." Only every second or fourth such response was reinforced on the next two days and on the fifth day the brothers were informed that they would be given an M&M if they asked each other for things, said "Please" or "Thank you," answered each other's questions or played nicely together (building things together, pulling each other in the wagon, taking turns, or carrying out a request). These prompts were repeated each day. A token system was also introduced on the fifth day by telling the boys that in addition to receiving M&M's, they would also receive checks on a blackboard for cooperative behavior and that these would be removed for deviant behaviors (which were described). Checks were separately recorded for Barry and Jeff and when a check was awarded, the boys were told specifically why the check had been awarded and who received it. Backup reinforcers included candy, bubble gum, kites, comic books, puzzles, and other small toys. Total cost of the program was $10.67. The number of checks required to earn a backup reinforcer was gradually increased. On the twelfth day, M&M's were discontinued. Cries and screams that resulted on days on which insufficient checks had been earned to receive a backup reinforcer were ignored.

Cooperative play increased from 46 percent of recorded intervals during baseline to 85 percent of all intervals during intervention. A reversal procedure was employed, which would probably not be employed in practice (see Chapter Eight). During the second intervention period, the mother was instructed on how to run the token program, a time out was introduced for kicking, hitting, pushing, name calling, and throwing objects at each other, and a requirement was made that points must be earned over several days before a backup reinforcer could be purchased. Hand signals were employed to help the mother administer reinforcement and consequences appropriately, they were gradually eliminated as the mother acquired skill. When time out was invoked, the boys had to remain in the bathroom for five minutes and to be quiet for a period of three minutes before they could come out. Only after the mother demonstrated ability to employ consequences appropriately in the counselor's presence was she then encouraged to use these procedures at other times.

Use of Videotape Feedback

Parent training has also been carried out by videotaping parents interacting with their children and by replaying the tapes to help parents identify appropriate and inappropriate child management techniques (Bernal, Duryee, Pruett, and Burns, 1968). This method was employed to help a mother manage the behavior of her eight-and-a-half-year-old son who was a severe disciplinary problem. She was instructed to decrease her very high output of indiscriminate reactions to her child and to respond to him in a soft tone even when correcting him. If ignoring his behavior did not reduce it, she was then to order him to stop, and if he did not, to spank him. It was hoped that cues antecedent to the spanking, such as the verbal warning and the frown, would become established as conditioned negative reinforcers, which then would influence behavior on their own. It was also hoped that offering her more effective procedures would decrease severe spanking of her son, which often occurred. In addition, she was trained to reinforce appropriate behaviors. Portions of videotapes of the mother and her son interacting were replayed to demonstrate to the parent points where she should ignore or reinforce behavior. Cues were presented to her as she interacted with her son during later practice sessions. One of the advantages of videotape feedback was allowing the parent to view her progress.

Encouraging Completion of Parent Training Programs

Follow-up data on the effect parent training programs have on the behaviors focused on during intervention are encouraging, although there is a trend for father-absent families and families of lower social class to be associated with poor outcome (Patterson, 1974). There is a need for additional follow-up data (see O'Dell, 1974). It is important to note that there is often a high dropout rate in terms of program completion, although not necessarily higher than that of other parent training programs (Bernal, 1975). Many programs assume that learning general principles of behavior will help parents apply these to other problems (for example, see Patterson and others, 1975), and there is some evidence that this actually occurs (Arnold, Levine, and Patterson, 1975). The dropout rate indicates the importance of identifying incentives that encourage parents to remain in programs. Some of these have already been mentioned, such as the use of a deposit that is refundable if the program is completed. A recent study showed that parents who initially paid a contract deposit equal to the twelve-week program fee, which was refundable contingent on attendance at sessions and completion of assignments, completed more assignments, intervened in more problems, and had a lower dropout rate than did parents without this arrangement (Eyberg and Johnson, 1974). The precise agreements were as follows. "(1) the entire session deposit (that is, $7 or $3 according to income) was returned if both parents in intact families attended and brought at least four sevenths of the assigned data; (2) one half of the session deposit was returned if only one parent attended with the requisite data; (3) no money was returned for a missed session unless there was a prior cancellation due to illness or other unavoidable circumstance; (4) if parents did not collect the requisite data for a given week, the therapists canceled the treatment session in the telephone contact and applied Contingency 1. In the single-parent families, of course, these rules applied solely to the mother. Special fee arrangements were made for the few families who could not forward an advance payment. In all cases, however, a sufficient advance payment was required to apply the contingencies as outlined, and fees were collected on a weekly or monthly basis. Therapy time was also used as a reinforcer to be applied either contingently or noncontingently to families. Parents in the noncontingent group were seen for their twelve scheduled treatment sessions irrespective of their completing weekly assignments. No parent in the contingent group was allowed to come to or remain at a scheduled treatment session unless he had completed assigned daily tasks and brought to the session four sevenths of the assigned data" (Eyberg and Johnson, 1974, p. 597).

Special incentives may be arranged for parents. For example, in an early study, the mother received points that were saved for a driving lesson for offering reinforcement to her children (Patterson and Reid, 1970). She had always wanted to learn to drive and eagerly anticipated her first lesson, which she earned by the end of one week. In addition, her children were given training in how to reinforce her by saying pleasant things to her. Each took turns going up to the mother and saying something nice to her. Points were given to the children that were exchanged for events such as ice-cream orgies. These procedures were included, because observation showed that the mother obtained little reinforcement in the family. Only if parents are reinforced for changes in their behavior will these new behaviors be maintained. And it is quite obvious that positive changes in a child's behavior are not necessarily sufficient to maintain new behaviors of some parents. Currently, the Oregon project employs a "parenting salary," in which the parent receives five to fifteen dollars per week contingent on performance as a parent. No information is as yet available concerning the effectiveness of this payment.

Promise to work on a problem of concern to parents in another setting such as the school may be made contingent on progress in altering parent-child interaction in the home (Patterson and others, 1975), or an agreement could be made to devote attention to a problem a parent has, contingent on such progress. For example, in one case in the Alameda project (Stein and Gambrill, 1976a) where intensive services were offered to natural parents who wished their children returned to them from foster care, a mother asked the counselor to help her decrease daily long telephone calls from her mother. The counselor promised to help her with this after problems of direct concern to the issue of restoration of the child were addressed (Stein and Gambrill, 1976b).

It is important to focus on problems of concern to parents, and care must be exercised in interviews not to impose problems. However, even though substantial changes may occur in behaviors addressed, parents may say, "I still feel the same way about him." Perhaps these are parents who "mislabel" their child as deviant because of their own negative attitude toward him. It will be necessary to determine the basis for this attitude and to modify it rather than, or in addition to, the child's behavior. The method selected for trying to achieve this aim would depend on the source of the attitude. Perhaps a parent feels burdened with too many responsibilities and blames this on her child rather than arranging her life so as to decrease these responsibilities. Perhaps a mother or father really do not want to keep a child, but feel they must, and therefore counseling is needed in terms of alternative arrangements.

Some parents may be more inclined to complete a program if training is provided in a group. A group setting provides varied models for appropriate behavior, normalizes child management difficulties (in that parents discover that others have similar problems), and provides multiple sources of reinforcement (see, for example, Rose, 1977).

Siblings as Mediators

Siblings have been involved in helping parents manage disruptive children (Lavigueur, 1976) and preschool children have been employed to help alter their retarded siblings' behavior. In one pair, the older child was four years and three months old, and the infant was two years and seven months. The older children observed a training film that demonstrated the use of prompting, modeling, offering verbal information, and the appropriate use of reinforcement.

Dependent Children

Dependent behaviors may include not making decisions and not accomplishing certain tasks that the child is physically capable of doing, such as dressing himself, going to school by himself, or cutting his own food. Often these behaviors are not required by parents; that is, the parents help the child with these tasks. A program to increase independence arranges reinforcement for independent behaviors and the removal of support for dependent behaviors. The extent to which some parents have reinforced dependent behaviors is at times startling.

An eight-year-old boy, for example, may be helped by his mother to butter his toast, cut his meat, and dress. Parents can introduce an independence training program by informing the child that they wish him to take more responsibility for a task. Expectation of sudden changes is discouraged, and help should be given to the child to gradually assume more responsibility. Shifting responsibility for certain tasks to the child, such as getting up and off to school on time, removes these as problems for parents. They are now the child's problems. Parents are forewarned that the problematic behavior may temporarily become worse and are coached to refrain from reintroducing old patterns of helping until the new system has a chance for success. For example, Becker (1971) reports an example where a six-year-old girl refused to get up in the morning, dress, and eat breakfast on time without help. Her mother nagged her from the time she awoke until she was out the door. The mother offered this help in part because she was afraid that her daughter would be late for school. (Note how she assumed responsibility for her daughter's behavior). The mother purchased an alarm clock for Karen, informed her that getting out on time was now her responsibility, refrained from nagging, and praised any successes that occurred. It was judged that the requisite behaviors—getting dressed and getting out of bed when the alarm went off—were in Karen's repertoire. During the first two weeks, Karen was late six times. Over the following six weeks, she left the house a bit late, but hurried to school and was on time.

Parents often keep children dependent by not taking the time to teach the child skills that would enable him or her to take over certain tasks. A parent may have not taken the time to show a child how to tie his shoes or cut his meat without dropping it on the floor. Bed-making behavior may have never been modeled for a child. Failure to reinforce approximations is often related to lack of "independent behaviors" such as self-help skills.

Whining and Complaining

Excessive attention to minor complaints and hurts can encourage a child to become a "whiner" or "complainer." Here, too, it is necessary to reverse the reinforcement contingencies that are currently in effect and to encourage the parent to praise the child for not complaining. For example, if a child falls and hurts himself slightly, the mother might say, "I bet that hurt, you are brave for not crying," rather than, "Oh my goodness, did you hurt yourself?" The intent is not to encourage never expressing reactions to pain, but encouraging a frequency and intensity of behavior that will benefit the child. Few people, including peers, would find a ten-year-old who cries and whines frequently very pleasing to be around. The parent is trained to encourage lack of complaining by failing to attend to minor complaints. In response to a complaint about another child, she might say "I'm sorry, you have to solve it yourself" (Becker, 1971).

Noncompliance

Noncompliance is perhaps the most frequently complained of behavior. High frequencies of saying no to parental requests usually take place because of a failure to use positive means of influence. If saying no is effective in influencing parental behavior, it will become even more frequent. As Becker (1971) points out, parents and teachers often provoke such reactions by being too abrupt in their demands for change or too bossy, or by modeling negative behavior themselves. Thus, they may respond to requests from their children by saying, "No, not now." Parents are coached to avoid demands for immediate change. Rather than saying "I want you to go to bed now," they could first become involved briefly in the task that the child is engaged in if this is possible, then make the new activity as desirable as possible. Some parents make too many requests. They are always asking their children to do things. If this is found, they are encouraged to make requests of their child only when they really want him to do something. An important point to keep in mind when coaching parents to increase compliance is to select behaviors that are easy for the child to perform and ask him to do them. He may even be asked to do things he likes to do (Becker, 1971). The important point is to increase the frequency with which he is reinforced for following instructions—it does not matter, initially, what the instructions are. To hasten the training process, the parent may be coached to give many instructions to a child within a short time, being sure to praise each one, and perhaps also to award tokens or points. As easy instructions are complied with, more difficult ones can be given. This will also give the parents practice in refraining from use of threats and nagging. Rather than say, "Get the paper for me," the parent could say, "Will you do me a favor and get the paper?" (Becker, 1971). Offering alternatives also helps to avoid negative reactions, such as saying, "You can take turns playing with the truck, and do not shout, or you will have to play by yourselves." And parents are encouraged not to make the mistake of acting insulted by a disrespectful child (Becker, 1971). This is also important to remember when dealing with verbally abusive children; parents are coached to praise polite behavior and ignore abusive behavior or invoke a response cost.

Decreasing Children's Fears

An example of decreasing a child's fear related to school is discussed in Chapter Seventeen, and an example of a child's fear of dogs is described in detail in Chapter Eleven. Most reported programs for decreasing the fears of children have employed differential reinforcement of other behavior and stimulus fading in which initial cues for comfort are gradually removed. Training the child in new self-instructions has also been employed. For example, Kanfer, Karoly, and Newman (1975) compared the effectiveness of sentences that emphasized the child's competence, such as "I am a brave boy (or girl). I can take care of myself in the dark" with sentences that concentrated on decreasing the unpleasant qualities of the aversive situation (a dark room), such as "The dark is a fun place to be. There are many good things in the dark" (p. 253). The former type of self-statement was more effective than one that attempted to decrease the aversive qualities, or a neutral sentence, such as "Mary had a little lamb, its fleece was white as snow." Emotive imagery, in which the child imagines a positive event in the context of a graduated portion of a feared stimulus, has also been employed to decrease childrens' fears (Lazarus and Abram-owitz, 1962).

Summary

Behavioral intervention in child-related problems focuses not only on the child but also on his significant others (parents, peers, and siblings). These individuals form an important part of the child's environment in terms of providing cues for appropriate as well as for inappropriate behavior and consequences that may encourage or discourage these behaviors. A wide variety of presenting problems have been successfully addressed, including dependency, fear reactions, stealing, aggression, hyperactivity, negativism, and fire setting. Multiple sources of assessment information are employed, including verbal reports of the parents and the child, observation in the clinic or home, and self-monitoring. Assessment often reveals a coercive family interaction pattern in which members use aversive control to influence each other and fail to prompt and reinforce appropriate behaviors. A major focus has been on training parents in more effective child management skills, including how to observe and record behavior as a first reaction to a problem; how to use prompts and positive reinforcement effectively; how to employ contingency contracts, time out, and response cost; and how to make effective use of rules. Parents are also encouraged to offer models of appropriate behavior to their children. With some children, it is necessary to use time out contingent on inappropriate behavior in combination with positive reinforcement of desired behavior. Negotiation-training procedures have been developed to help family members communicate more positively with each other, and these procedures, as well as contingency contracting, have often been employed with children labeled as delinquent and with their parents. With some families, it is necessary to hold training sessions in the home.

10

Although over 90 percent of adults marry, there has been a continual upward trend in the rate of divorce with an increase of 80 percent in the past ten years alone (National Center for Health Statistics, 1973). It is estimated that 25 percent of women now age thirty-five will have dissolved their first marriage by the age of fifty (U.S. Bureau of the Census, 1972), which is probably a conservative projection in view of the increasing number of divorces among older adults. Almost one half of first admissions to state mental hospitals are related to marital stress as the main precipitating cause (Beisser and Glasser, 1968). There has been a steady increase in the number of women who abandon their husbands and children and disappear to start another life. Factors related to the increase in divorce include the increasing acceptance of divorce as "normal"; the increase in alternatives available to women, especially

358

Enhancing Marital
Interaction

economic ones; and the rising standard of expectations for happiness in marriage, which makes it more difficult to remain in an unsatisfactory marriage (Weitzman, 1974). Also, it is now recognized that growing up in a troubled marriage may present more problems for a child than does parental divorce. Moreover, at no other time in history has marriage been expected to last for so many years. The dissatisfaction with marriage is also reflected by the numbers who report unhappy marriages and who seek help for their troubled marriages each year.

What Is a Good Marriage?

How people define a good marriage may be directly related to problems they may have in their marriage. The criterion employed in defining such a state varies among marriage researchers and marriage counselors, as well as among the general population (Laws, 1975). Is a happy marriage one that lasts? This criterion has been accepted by many, although soundly rejected by others, who point to the one couple in five who remain in a state of matrimony even though they describe themselves as unhappy (Renne, 1970). Inappropriate expectations may be directly related to marital stress. For example, the expectation of a sustained high level of very positive events without some effort to maintain this level is an inappropriate expectation. The level of satisfaction expected from a marriage and how realistic this expectation is, and the possibility of attaining desired outcomes outside of marriage, affect marital happiness.

A good marriage can be defined as one in which satisfaction is expressed by both participants, in which each person mediates important positive events for the other, and in which pleasant events exchanged clearly outweigh the unpleasant. In distressed marriages, the exchange of positive events relative to aversive ones dwindles, creating dissatisfaction, further stressful interactions, and mutual avoidance. It has been suggested that the strength of a marital relationship is "a direct function of the attractions within and barriers around the marriage and an inverse function of such attractions and barriers from other relationships" (Levinger, 1965, p. 19).

The factors required to facilitate a good marriage at one point in the career of a long-term relationship may differ from those required at other points. After a couple marries, a variety of types of interactions and potential reinforcements and annoyances from these interactions are likely to occur, including sexual interaction, possibly children, living in the same household, arrangement of earning and allocation of money, and an interest in social activities and communication with other people (Azrin, Naster, and Jones, 1973). The demands placed on the couple by some of these events, such as children, limit opportunities for personal independence. Thus, marriage leads to new sources of reinforcing as well as annoying events. Over time, and as events (such as vocational aspirations, children, and so forth) change, these sources will also change, requiring a constant rematching between interest in certain reinforcers and the degree to which they are offered. Many couples cannot manage this matching process. Distressed couples, as compared with nondistressed couples, engage in more conflict and fewer recreational activities together and offer each other fewer pleasing behaviors and more displeasing behaviors (Birchler, Weiss, and Vincent, 1975). During casual conversation and problem-solving attempts, the former group also engages in fewer positives and more negatives than do nondistressed couples.

A Behavioral View of Marriage

Within a behavioral framework, marriage is viewed as entailing an exchange of behaviors that may be predominantly pleasant or unpleasant. This formulation rests on social exchange theory, which assumes that whenever two people interact, each strives to maximize pleasure and satisfaction while also trying to minimize costs, and that continued social interaction is maintained by a high level of pleasurable events relative to painful ones, as well as by each participant's view of alternative relationships (possibilities) and the comparative rewards and costs of those alternatives (Thibaut and Kelley, 1959; Homans, 1950). Satisfaction in a marriage may alter if new possibilities arise that potentially could provide more positive events. Social exchange theory further assumes that feeling for another person is related to the level of pleasurable events received from that person, which in turn is influenced by what may be available from other relationships (Thibaut and Kelley, 1959).

As interaction between two people continues, sooner or later one person will become displeased with some aspect of the partner's behavior. Perhaps a wife may be displeased with her husband's failure to help with household chores, or a husband may dislike his wife's negative comments about his parents. Ideally, such changes are dealt with in a positive manner, in which desired behaviors are encouraged by offering positive consequences for them. However, many people do not possess the skills required to bring about change in a positive way, or a partner may not respond to these skills. Talking about the desired change is often the first strategy attempted. Although this may result in change in some cases, in most it probably does not. Agreements are forgotten and the aggrieved party may then *demand* a change in the partner's behavior (Patterson and Hops, 1972). If compliance does not follow, the aggrieved party may present punishing consequences, such as nagging or threats, in order to coerce the partner into compliance. Let us say that Mrs. L. is sitting in the living room reading the paper, while her husband is cooking the evening meal. She has agreed to set the table prior to dinner, but has shown no inclination to do so, even after being asked politely by her husband. He may seek her out again, repeating his request. Repeated failure to comply may lead to an escalation of negative verbal statements on his part such as, "Look, it's your job to set the table and you're just sitting reading. How about helping out?" The repeated requests disrupt her peaceful reading and the increased negativism in her husband's demands may be very unpleasant. In order to end these requests, she may rise and set the table. Her husband has succeeded in altering her behavior, but he has employed coercive means to do so.

This process often escalates, in that higher levels of punishment are required to attain compliance. Demands for change tend to produce counterattacks, rather than any change in the problem behavior. As the exchange of aversive events increases, the potential of either party to alter the behavior of the other decreases. Since problems between the couple are rarely resolved, each new situation calling for problem solving becomes a cue for "pain control" and coercive attempts (Weiss, 1975). This situation is complicated by the increase in the number of behaviors to be changed (that displease one party), which in turn will increase the number of "automatic" fights (Patterson and Hops, 1972). In a coercive interaction pattern, two people train each other to become increasingly destructive (Patterson and Hops, 1972). The aversive behavior of one person is gradually shaped to higher and higher levels by ignoring lower-level unpleasant behavior and by finally "giving in" to the coercive behavior. Confrontations may, of course, be avoided through immediate compliance. At least such compliance avoids more unpleasant negative escalations. However, when one partner employs punishing consequences, the other is also likely to increase his or her use of such consequences. For example, a woman may train her husband to realize that only after a severe physical attack by him will she stop nagging him. These coercive behaviors may also be brought to the fore by a change in expected levels of positive exchanges over time, caused by the attempt of one party to regain original levels. As the exchange of negative events increases, it is assumed that attempts to negotiate certain changes in each other's behavior are more likely to be accompanied by aversive events to which the other person responds, rather than to the problem supposedly being discussed. It is also assumed that this aversive quality will tend to characterize other communication, so that even attempts to offer support are accompanied by qualifications and criticisms. As the unpleasantness of interaction increases, the partners learn to avoid each other and exchange less positive interactions (Birchler, Weiss, and Wampler, 1972). Distressed couples, in fact, share fewer recreational activities (Weiss, Hops, and Patterson, 1973) and report three times as many conflicts as do nondistressed couples (Birchler, Weiss, and Wampler, 1972). Although members of a distressed marriage do possess problem-solving skills, as shown by their ability to employ these when interacting with opposite-sex strangers, they do not employ them with their mates (Vincent, 1972). This view suggests several sources of marital discord: (1) reinforcers gained from the marriage may be very few in number; (2) reinforcers may be provided for only one or two states of need (for example, sex and financial); (3) reinforcers offered by one person may be taken for granted; (4) previous reinforcers are no longer of interest; (5) one (or both) partners do not recognize new interests of their partner; (6) more reinforcers are offered than are received (operant extinction); (7) the couple cannot talk about sources of dissatisfaction due perhaps to anxiety or lack of communication skills; (8) marital demands interfere significantly with sources of reinforcement outside of the marriage; and (9) aversive influence, rather than positive influence, may be employed to coerce satisfaction (Azrin, Naster, and Jones, 1973).

The Reciprocity Hypothesis. Some investigators have assumed that positive events are reciprocated on an equitable basis in nondistressed families, whereas they assume that in distressed families there is an inequitable exchange in which one partner coerces positive events from the other by presenting punishing consequences, such as nagging or demanding behavior. These behaviors coerce the other to offer a positive event, in order to terminate such consequences. When couples have been requested to count pleasing and displeasing events offered to them by their partner, high correlations have been found for average levels of pleasing behavior (Wills, Weiss, and Patterson, 1974). Lower correlations were found for displeasing behaviors. Comparison of the interactions of distressed and nondistressed couples showed that the former are significantly more negative toward each other and less positive than are nondistressed couples (Birchler, Weiss, and Vincent, 1975). The difference was especially evident in nonverbal behaviors, including smiles, head nods, frowns, and eye contact. The exchange of positives was greater for nondistressed couples, particularly in the context of resolving differences. Distressed couples also reported more daily conflicts with each other.

These findings support a definition of *reciprocity* as referring to a relationship between the rate of positive events exchanged between two people, but do not provide support for a definition of reciprocity that assumes there is a temporal relationship between the behavior of one person and the immediate consequence provided for this behavior by the spouse (Gottman, Notarius, Gonso, and Markman, 1976). A high rate of positive events could be distributed in a noncontingent fashion (bearing no functional relationship) to the immediately preceding spouse behavior. In order to provide support for the latter definition of reciprocity, it would have to be demonstrated that a positive event from a husband (or wife) was more likely to be offered following a positive event from the mate than was another type of event, and there is no evidence that temporal positive reciprocity discriminates between distressed and nondistressed couples. Rather than temporal reciprocity being critical, a "bank account" model seems more descriptive of satisfying and stable marriages in which positive deposits exceed negative withdrawals. There is some support for this assumption, because couples in happy marriages who are married longer show less reciprocity than nondistressed couples who have been married only for a short time; supposedly the longer-married couples have more positives "deposited" (Gottman and others, 1976).

Marital satisfaction seems to be influenced more by unpleasant than by pleasant events, in that a modest change in the former may lead to a large change in satisfaction (Wills, Weiss, and Patterson, 1974). Moreover, pleasurable and unpleasurable events are independent—a change in one may not result in a change in the other. It cannot be assumed, therefore, that increasing the positive events exchanged in a marriage will necessarily alter the exchange of negative events; rather, attention should be devoted to each.

There is a greater imbalance in aversive control in nondistressed couples than in distressed couples (Wills, Weiss, and Patterson, 1974). In such marriages, distress may be denied by the coerced spouse (Jacobson and Martin, 1976), or the coerced partner may view the marriage as better than currently available alternatives (Thibaut and Kelley, 1959). Interestingly, the low rate of positive behaviors offered to the spouse in distressed marriages is not found when members of such dyads interact with a stranger (Birchler, Weiss, and Vincent, 1975). Members of nondistressed as well as members of distressed couples offer more positive social reinforcement to strangers when conversing with them than to their mates. The implication of this finding is important, because it means we cannot tell from a person's rate of positive events with one person whether she or he will also offer a mate a high rate of pleasant events, and it may also mean that there is an inevitable decline in positive events exchanged in long-term intimate relationships.

Distress often stems from the methods the couple employs to try to bring about change in each other's behavior and to reach decisions. As these methods become more aversive, the range of reinforcers mediated by the spouse declines, as does the satisfaction provided by the marriage. This view of marriage is concerned with the strategies used by the couple to attempt to alter each other's behavior and to make decisions, and with offering the couple more positive skills to resolve current as well as future problems. The objective is to help couples learn how to negotiate and contract for changes in their relationship (Weiss, 1975). To accomplish this, clients must learn how to identify specific changes they would like in each other's behavior, how to communicate, and how to identify the exchange value of behaviors. The focus of assessment and intervention is clearly on the dyad. The partners are helped to realize that they currently exchange pleasant events, despite problems; to discover and initiate other interactions with each other that could be of positive value; to set up a reciprocal relationship in which each person feels assured that when an effort is made to reinforce the spouse, this effort will be reciprocated by the partner, that the spouse in turn will offer support for positive events received from his partner, and that reinforcers will not occur if they are not offered; to establish this reciprocal exchange as characteristic of their interaction pattern; to employ a wide range of reinforcers so that the marriage will help to satisfy many needs; and to discover reinforcers for each other (Azrin, Naster, and Jones, 1973). Assessment will reveal the procedural components required for each couple, and the progression of the components may differ from couple to couple depending on the unique assessment picture. The assessment and intervention procedures involved in this type of training program, described hereafter, draws mainly on the Marital Studies program developed at the University of Oregon. Further on, programs are described that deal with more circumscribed areas of interaction, such as decision making.

Couples approach marital counseling with many agendas, which may or may not be mutually shared. They both may wish to maintain the relationship and be very motivated to engage in change efforts. On the other hand, they both may feel that divorce is imminent and be searching for someone else to make a final decision for them. Or one person may be very committed to trying to improve the relationship, whereas the other has given up. Another possibility is that neither is sure what he wants. When commitment is unclear, a trial period can be suggested, in which an attempt is made to improve the interaction, in order to obtain further information that would facilitate making a decision on whether to continue living together. Information concerning possible outcomes may be gathered by asking the couple to act "as if" their marriage were a success for a period of three to five weeks. This approach may be coupled with more specific intervention procedures (Stuart, 1975). The results attained within this time period can then be reviewed and a decision made as to whether to proceed with the change program. Whatever decision is made should be made by the couple; however, the counselor may help by offering guidelines for problem solving. The opinion of the counselor as to what should be done can be considered another source of information, which may be of value to the couple.

Assessment

This stage begins a process of "shaping a new interpersonal vocabulary" (Stuart, 1975), in which partners learn to communicate with each other in a more constructive fashion. One aspect of this process is to decrease the use of "terminal hypotheses," which attempt to offer an explanation of a behavior (or of its absence) in a manner that provides no information as to how to alter the situation. An example of such a statement would be, "You leave the dirty dishes in the sink because this is just what your mother did." Even if this statement were quite accurate, no way to change the behavior has been added. As Stuart points out, such statements are negative cues for change efforts and thus decrease the likelihood of their occurrence. Instead, the couple learns to employ "instrumental hypotheses," which account for behavior and feelings in such a way that something can be done to change the situation (Hurvitz, 1970). For example, an instrumental statement in the above situation might be, "I'll put the dishes away by seven at night every other day if you'll put them away by this time on the alternate days."

Couples also learn to particularize general statements. A husband may say that it is his "wife's work" that bothers him. This statement does not identify what his wife should do differently. Only after additional interviews may he identify the behavioral referents of "her work" such as "coming home after 4:30 from work," "working on weekends," and "spending all of the money she earns on herself" (see, for example, Patterson and Hops, 1972). This aspect of training teaches the partners to be *specific* concerning their dissatisfaction with each other. Clients typically have greater ease identifying items they do not like than selecting behaviors to increase. Therefore, examples of what other couples find pleasing and displeasing in their marriage may be offered by the counselor. Or the partners could be requested to describe what an ideal marriage would be like or asked to describe what they liked about each other when they first met (Azrin, Naster, and Jones, 1973).

One procedure that may be useful when partners express vague expectations is to have each one list his or her expectations and to ask the partner to describe how each expectation would be satisfied in behavior. For example, a husband may say that his wife should be a good cook. His wife can be requested to operationalize this statement—to say, for example, "He would like me to cook spaghetti three nights a week." The husband can then be asked if this definition satisfies his expectation. This procedure will help to uncover expectations that are held only because they are impossible to fulfill and discourages the assumption that each already knows what the other thinks (Weiss, Hops, and Patterson, 1973). It also encourages reticent partners to share what they think.

A variety of assessment measures have been employed, including self-report concerning the self and the partner, observation by partners of aspects of each other's behavior, and observation by trained observers. Useful data may also be gathered by requesting clients to tape-record selected interactions at home. If possible, multiple sources should be used for purposes of assessment and evaluation.

Self-Report Measures of Self and Partner. A number of self-report measures are available, in addition to a Marital Precounseling Inventory (Stuart and Stuart, 1972). The aim of each is to provide information concerning areas of change and related factors.

Marital precounseling inventory. Stuart and Stuart (1972) have developed a Marital Precounseling Inventory that assesses nine categories: goals for behavior change, resources for change, degree of marital understanding, power distribution, congruence of priorities, communication effectiveness, sexual satisfaction, congruence in child management, and general marital satisfaction. Respondents are continually encouraged to be specific in their desires for change. Completion of this inventory offers clients an early socialization experience into a behavioral model by directing client attention to positives and to specific behaviors, and the counselor is offered a rich source of information that can be employed during the initial interview.

Living with someone requires making decisions concerning matters of mutual concern such as where to live, how to allocate resources such as time and money, what type of people to socialize with, how to raise children, and so forth. The ability to select mutually acceptable alternatives, and to achieve this in a positive way, is an important aspect of a pleasing marriage. Distressed couples often lack such skills. This may result in repeated unsuccessful and aversive attempts to reach decisions, in the avoidance of issues, in choice through sheer passage of time, or in the selection of alternatives that are punishing to one party. Decision-making responsibilities for various areas are allocated differently by each couple. In traditional marriages, the husband is awarded power to decide where the couple lives, selection of major material items such as choice of house and car, whether his wife will work, and so on. Today this situation has changed considerably, as women are requesting or demanding an equal say in the selection of alternatives. An important part of assessment is to determine whether the decision-making pattern of the couple is a constructive one. Is each person satisfied with the allocation of decision-making responsibility? What is the pattern? In what areas would each like to exercise more power? Does the husband or wife assume most of the responsibilities? Are they spending considerable time debating as to who is to make what decision rather than having established a satisfactory allocation of responsibility for different areas? Successful couples either share responsibilities equally, or decide to share them unequally, by agreement, whereas unsuccessful couples are characterized by one party usurping decision-making power in certain areas, and the other party contesting it, with little mutual decision making (Stuart, 1975; Stuart and Lederer, in press). Assessment will reveal whether decision making is a problem for a couple and the way in which each person would like to reallocate responsibilities.

Marital adjustment scales. The Locke-Wallace Marital Adjustment Scale provides an overview of marital satisfaction that can be employed as one source of evaluation (Burgess, Locke, and Thomas, 1971; Kimmel and Van der Veen, 1974). The client is requested to indicate overall satisfaction with his marriage on a seven-point scale and how much he agrees with his spouse in various areas of his marriage such as handling family finances and sexual interaction. Information is also gained concerning mutual participation in outside activities and on how disagreements end. Client scores on this measure have not been found to correlate with a daily measure of satisfaction (Robinson and Price, 1976). The Marital Happiness Scale (Azrin, Naster, and Jones, 1973), in which each spouse ranks ten different areas on a scale of one (completely happy) to ten (completely unhappy), offers a continuous measure of daily satisfaction. Respondents are requested to ask themselves the following question as they rate each item: "If my partner continues to act in the future as he (she) is acting today with respect to this marriage area, how happy will I be with this area of my marriage?" Respondents are coached, via written instructions, to exclude feelings based on past experience and to try not to allow the rating of one category to influence another. Areas include items such as those mentioned above (for example, household responsibilities, personal independence, spouse independence, communication, and sex). They are also asked to rate their general happiness each day on a scale from one to ten. The Marital Status Inventory (Weiss and Cerreto, 1975) provides another index of marital satisfaction. This latter instrument describes fourteen possible cognitive and overt steps taken toward the goal of divorce, such as "I occasionally have thoughts about divorce," and "I have consulted a lawyer and/or filed for divorce."

Areas of change questionnaire. Indications of areas in which each spouse desires change can be obtained by asking each person to complete the Area of Change Scale (Weiss, Hops, and Patterson, 1973), which is a thirty-four-item inventory describing specific spouse behaviors. The respondent indicates, on a seven-point scale (very much less, −3, to very much more, +3) whether he would like his spouse to change ("I want my partner to help with the shopping") and whether it would please his partner if the respondent were to change in this way ("It would please my partner if I helped with the shopping"). This inventory provides information concerning desired areas of change as well as the possibility of deriving conflict agreement and disagreement scores. An agreement is scored if both agree on an area of change and a disagreement is scored if a directional difference is found. An example of a disagreement would be if the husband said that he wanted his wife to help with the children much more and the wife said that her husband wanted her to help with the children much less. As would be expected, distressed couples have much higher mean conflict values—28.0—than do nondistressed couples—6.9 (Birchler, Weiss, and Vincent, 1975).

Potential problem area checklist. Areas in which conflict occurs can be identified by sharing with the couple a list of twenty-six potential problem areas within marriages (Weiss, Hops, and Patterson, 1973; Weiss and Margolin, in press). This checklist conveys an expectation that all couples may have something to offer in relation to each area and thus may facilitate contributions. Areas listed include running the household; family economics and family living (for example, finances and money management, meals, shopping, household chores, transportation, husband's and wife's work, child care, family recreation and leisure time, adult recreation and leisure time, friendships); value and philosophy, including areas like education, religion, traditional versus contemporary outlook, politics; personal factors, including such items as affection and closeness, sexual adjustment (including contraception), jealously and extramarital affairs, personal habits, health, personal improvement, temperament and personality differences, and kinship responsibilities that concern husband's and wife's parents and other relatives or dependents. (Examples of specific behaviors are cited later in this chapter.)

Each spouse is asked to identify the three most problematic areas and the three most satisfying areas and to indicate what the partner does that is pleasing and displeasing in each of the six areas. Partners are encouraged to be as specific as possible and to try to offer as much information as possible to their mate. Each problem area is then ranked in terms of importance, and the three areas selected as being most satisfying are also ranked on a scale of one to three in terms of importance. Involvement of the couple in this task helps identify areas of satisfaction and dissatisfaction in their relationship. Areas so identified may be used later when the couple is requested to discuss conflictual areas in their marriage to assess their skills in conflict resolution.

The Marital Activities Inventory. A focus on the importance of positive events highlights the need to determine pleasurable activities the couple now shares and to locate ways to in-crease such experiences. The Marital Activities Inventory (Weiss, Hops, and Patterson, 1973) lists eighty-five recreational activities that couples may find enjoyable. Each person is asked to indicate how often they have engaged in each activity during the last month and how often they have done it alone, with the spouse, or with others. Each also indicates whether they desire any change in the frequency of each activity as undertaken *together with their partner*. Many couples, particularly after children are born, forget to devote attention to themselves *as a couple* in terms of doing things together (without the children). They stop reacting to each other as two adults, an experience that no doubt was very important in their original attraction to each other.

Partner Observation of Self and Other. In addition to self-report measures, partners have also been asked to gather obser-vational information as a means of assessment. In addition, they may be requested to observe a tape-recorded or videotaped interaction between themselves and to identify positive and negative behaviors.

Observation of pleasant thoughts. Patterson and Hops (1972) attempted to assess cognitive aspects of marital relation-ships by asking each partner to observe and record pleasant thoughts about the other partner. If desirable, the partner could also be asked to note in a log the spouse behavior that may have been associated with the positive thought. Frequency of posi-tive thoughts has been found to be associated with frequency of affectional interactions (see Weiss and Margolin, in press).

Spouse-observation checklist. Partners can be asked to keep track on a daily basis of the number of pleasing and dis-pleasing partner behaviors. These are defined as responses asso-ciated with one spouse that the other finds pleasing or displeas-ing, independent of the intent of the acting or speaking partner. Clients are carefully instructed to remember that what is pleas-ing is always in the eye of the beholder. A list has been com-piled of 400 discrete behaviors that may be performed either by one spouse or both and that have pleasing or displeasing conse-quences (Weiss, Hops, and Patterson, 1973). Twelve major areas of marital interaction are included: companionship, affection, consideration, sex, communication process, shared activities, child care and parenting, household management, financial decision making, employment and education, personal habits, and appearance, and self and spouse independence. Within each of these areas, examples of pleasing and displeasing behaviors are listed. Both affectional as well as instrumental pleases and displeases are usually selected. Examples of pleases and displeases for two problem areas are given in the following quote from Weiss (unpublished material available from R. L. Weiss, Psychology Department, University of Oregon, Eugene, OR 97403).

MEALS AND SHOPPING

Pleases	*Displeases*
Spouse prepared an interesting or good meal.	Spouse prepared a tasteless meal.
Spouse helped with shopping.	Spouse served leftovers from the night before.
Spouse packed a lunch for me.	
Spouse got up and made breakfast for me.	Spouse forgot to buy food we needed.
Spouse prepared a favorite food or dessert.	Spouse did not come to a meal when asked.
Spouse helped with cooking.	Spouse was late in coming home for a meal.
Spouse did errands with me or for me.	Spouse fixed a food I dislike.
Spouse had dinner ready on time.	Spouse offered unsolicited advice while I was preparing a meal.
Spouse carried groceries into the house.	Spouse left something out of the refrigerator.
Spouse bought some food item especially for me.	Spouse violated his/her diet.

PERSONAL HABITS AND APPEARANCE

Pleases	*Displeases*
Spouse dressed nicely.	Spouse bothered me when I was concentrating.
Spouse got a haircut or hairdo.	Spouse mumbled.
Spouse cut my hair.	Spouse came home late and didn't call.
Spouse left me hot water for a shower.	Spouse hogged the covers.
Spouse paid attention to his/her appearance (shaved, took a bath, and so on).	Spouse belched.
	Spouse wore sloppy clothes.
Spouse made an attractive shirt or dress.	Spouse wore curlers when I was at home.

Pleases	*Displeases*
Spouse met me on time.	Spouse smoked during meal-time.
Spouse let me sleep in.	
Spouse ran bathwater for me.	Spouse missed the ashtray with cigarette ashes.
Spouse took care of his/her correspondence.	Spouse monopolized the bathroom.
	Spouse used my toilet articles (razor, hairbrush, toothbrush, and so on).
	Spouse left his/her toilet articles lying out in the bathroom.
	Spouse used all of the toilet paper without getting a new roll.

The term *affectional pleases* refers to actions or statements by a spouse that convey acceptance, approval, or worthiness as a person; affectional displeases include actions or statements that convey rejection and disapproval as a person (Weiss, Hops, and Patterson, 1973). Affectional events differ from instrumental behaviors in three ways. First, affectional events are things that a spouse directs toward his or her partner, such as kissing him or her when she or he comes home or smiling at him or her in a warm way. Second, affectional events are very brief. A positive or nasty comment takes only seconds to make, unlike instrumental behaviors, which may take time to perform —such as getting tickets to a concert and arranging for dinner reservations. Third, such events convey acceptance and approval, or rejection and disapproval. Examples of affectional events follow (unpublished material available from R. L. Weiss, Psychology Department, University of Oregon, Eugene, OR 97403).

Pleases	*Displeases*
Spouse hugged or kissed me.	Spouse turned away when I asked for a kiss or hug.
Spouse asked about my feelings.	Spouse refused to listen to my feelings.
Spouse said he/she likes me.	
Spouse touched me affectionately.	Spouse hit or pushed me.
Spouse brought me a present.	Spouse swore at me or called me names.

Pleases	*Displeases*
Spouse called me just to say hello.	Spouse forgot my birthday or our anniversary.
Spouse expressed feelings and thoughts to me.	Spouse called me just to complain about something I did.
Spouse tried to cheer me up.	Spouse said he/she didn't want to talk about his/her problem with me.
Spouse asked me how my day was.	
Spouse smiled at me or laughed with me.	Spouse tickled me.
	Spouse teased me.
Spouse said he/she was glad to see me	Spouse read the paper during mealtime.
Spouse teased me.	Spouse got angry and wouldn't tell me why.
Spouse cuddled close to me in bed.	
Spouse warmed my cold feet.	Spouse fell asleep while I was talking to him/her.
Spouse went to bed when I did.	Spouse pinched or poked me.
Spouse brought me home something to read.	Spouse threatened me.
	Spouse yelled at me for smoking.
Spouse brought me a cup of coffee, tea, etc.	Spouse told me how to do something I already know how to do.
Spouse greeted me affectionately when I came home.	
Spouse gave me a massage, rubbed lotion on my back, and so on.	Spouse read a book (or watched television) and wouldn't talk to me.
Spouse confided in me.	Spouse criticized me in front of others.
Spouse asked for my opinion.	
Spouse complimented something I made.	Spouse dominated the conversation.
Spouse answered my questions with respect.	Spouse interrupted me.
	Spouse did something for me instead of showing me how.
Spouse forgave me for something.	
Spouse apologized to me.	Spouse nagged or became angry about chores I hadn't completed.
Spouse called to tell me where he/she was.	
Spouse thanked me for doing something.	Spouse criticized my parents or relatives.
Spouse skillfully calmed me down when I was being unreasonable.	Spouse brought up bad times from the past.
	Spouse commanded me to do something.
Spouse listened sympathetically to my problems.	Spouse spoke sarcastically to me.
Spouse was patient when I acted crossly.	Spouse refused to talk about a problem we share.

Efforts are now being made to group all events into major categories thought to be important for marital exchange including communication, companionship, and services (Weiss, 1975). This will allow the creation of individual profiles for specific areas of marital interaction, which hopefully will offer more precise identification of area deficiencies.

Partners may be asked to record the frequency of pleases and displeases, employing the entire list, or only to note those extracted from or added to the list that are uniquely relevant to their own relationship. They may be asked to select behaviors that they consider of special importance for gaining an enjoyable marital interaction. (Prearranged exchanges or an "act of God" should not be included.) Each may be requested to note the frequency of each event two times during the day for a one-week period. An example of a recording form appears in Figure 24.

Distressed and nondistressed couples can be differentiated in terms of the ratio of pleases to displeases. For distressed couples, this ratio is 4:3 whereas the ratio for nondistressed couples is 29:7 (Birchler, Weiss, and Vincent, 1975). These ratios are related both to scores on the Locke-Wallace inventory and to daily ratings of marital satisfaction (using a seven-point scale) that partners have also been asked to complete on a daily basis. The advantage of having each spouse complete the latter is that this procedure will help to indicate to both partners the relationship between rates of pleases and displeases and their marital satisfaction.

It should be noted that some authors (for example, Stuart, 1975) recommend only the selection of pleases. This emphasis is made since there is evidence that negative information carries more weight than positive information (Kanhouse, Hanson, and Reid, 1972) and thus gathering both involves a risk that the negative information will have a greater impact on partners than will positive information (Stuart, 1975). In addition, couples often tend to engage already in a great deal of negative scanning, and a total concentration on positives will discourage this. Negatives that bother a spouse can still be addressed within this emphasis by simply learning to identify desired changes in positive terms, that is, to identify behaviors to be increased.

Figure 24. Example of Weekly Please and Displease Recording Chart

PLEASES DATE:	AM	PM	AM	PM	AM	PM	AM	PM	AM	PM
kissed me										
answered the phone when I was busy										
asked for my advice										
turned up the heat										
called me on the phone from work										
took her blouse off first when undressing										
PLEASES GRAND TOTAL										

DISPLEASES DATE:	AM	PM	AM	PM	AM	PM	AM	PM	AM	PM
yelled at me for smoking										
turned away from me when asked for a kiss										
dropped clothes on the floor										
missed toilet bowl when urinating										
punished child										
broke promise to repair something										
DISPLEASES GRAND TOTAL										

Source: Hops (1976, p. 438)

Partner observation of recorded interactions. Partners have been requested to observe a videotape of their interaction and to identify desirable self and spouse behaviors (Weiss and Margolin, in press). This task can indicate the degree to which partners agree on what behaviors are helpful and these tapes can also be employed to develop client discrimination of helpful and dysfunctional behavior.

Counselor Observation of Partner Interaction. Interaction between the partners can be observed either in the office situation or at home. Usually it is more convenient for counselors to gather this information in the office. The situation is structured in some way in order to observe relevant aspects of interaction. For example, the couple may be asked to discuss one major problem and one minor problem and to arrive at a solution (Weiss, Hops, and Patterson, 1973) or to discuss some preselected topic such as expectations of each other as husband and wife (Carter and Thomas, 1973). Usually such discussions are brief, lasting about ten minutes. The interaction can be recorded in order to identify appropriate and inappropriate behaviors. The following sample instructions to a couple are from Patterson and others (1975, p. 88). "I'd like to have you spend the next ten minutes trying to solve your disagreements about ＿＿＿＿＿＿ . I wish to get a general picture of how you go about this so proceed as naturally as you can. I will be making a tape of it so that I can study it before our next meeting, at which time we will go over it together."

There is often a lack of honest and direct communication between distressed couples. Honest communication includes questions raised by one spouse to which the partner could respond candidly without any penalty, and direct statements where one spouse expresses his or her wishes rather than concealing intents (Knox, 1971). Appropriate communication skills are necessary in order to identify desired changes in each other's behavior as well as to arrive at mutually satisfactory decisions in relation to the many problems that arise in day-to-day living together. Each must know how to share positively with his or her partner changes that he would like to see, as well as know how to listen when the partner speaks. This includes knowing what types of questions to ask (when general statements are made, a spouse might say, "Could you give me an example?"), as well as learning what behaviors to avoid because they are dysfunctional (such as blaming the partner). Observation of distressed and nondistressed couples in a problem-solving situation has shown that the former display significantly fewer positive reinforcers and effective problem-solving behaviors, and significantly higher rates of aversive behaviors such as blaming and criticism (Birchler, Weiss, and Vincent, 1975; Vincent, Weiss, and Birchler, 1975).

Distressed couples are more likely than nondistressed couples to enter into "negative problem-solving loops," in which a series of negative statements are made that interfere with effective problem solving. Distressed couples evidence inappropriate communication patterns whether discussing low- or high-conflict areas—for example, whether arriving at a consensual ranking of dog breeds in terms of preference, or discussing an actual unresolved marital conflict (Gottman, 1975). Although more statements by each person were coded by their spouse as positive in nondistressed than in distressed marriages (57 percent, as compared to 36 percent), there was no difference in the *intent* of the communication (what the spouse meant to convey—that is, a positive or a negative), a finding that highlights the importance of communication problems in distressed marriages (Gottman, 1975). That is, in distressed marriages, spouses are less successful in offering communications that match their intent—many statements that are offered with a positive intent are coded as negative by the spouse. Such data have been obtained in an inexpensive and unobtrusive manner by offering each spouse signaling buttons on which each can register the intent of the statement (positive or negative). With couples who have not been married very long, distressed couples could readily be discriminated from nondistressed couples, regardless of the conflict level of the task. With couples married six and one half years or longer, distressed and nondistressed couples could only be discriminated on the high-conflict tasks (Gottman, 1975). Perhaps, as Gottman notes, distressed couples who have been married for some time learn to avoid disagreement and exchange more positive messages in low-conflict areas. This is consistent with the picture of the "stable but unsatisfactory" marriage in which couples present a happy front in social situations.

We also have more information now on what happens during the beginning, middle, and end of a problem-solving process in distressed and nondistressed couples. Distressed couples propose plans and talk about their communications in the first third of their discussion, whereas couples who are not distressed usually engage in summarizing and agreeing in the first third. Most disagreement in nondistressed couples occurs in the first third of the discussion, whereas most disagreement for distressed couples occurs in the last third (Gottman, 1975).

It should be noted that an observer's description of a behavior may not reflect its function in a particular context

(Gottman, 1975; Gottman and others, 1976). Let us say that in the following exchange a counselor codes the wife's statement as a criticism:

Husband: Let's spend Christmas at your mother's.
Wife: You always get tense at my mother's.

Within one coding method, this would be categorized as a mind-reading statement: she is attributing feelings—or thoughts, motives or actions—to the husband (Gottman, 1975; Gottman and others, 1976). It seems that although this type of statement occurs in the dialog of all couples, it is the *non*verbal components of a mind-reading statement that determine whether it functions as a sensitive feeling probe or as a criticism. Rather than asking about feelings in a Rogerian manner ("How do you feel about that?"), many partners tend to mind-read with positive nonverbal cues. Such statements are followed by agreement and by the elaboration of feelings, that is, by a positive reaction. The nonverbal components of statements are extremely important (Mehrabian, 1972). Allowing partners themselves to code statements as positive or negative will help to avoid imposition of faulty counselor assumptions concerning the function of statements.

The Marital Interaction Coding System (Weiss, Hops, and Patterson, 1973) allows sequential coding of couple interaction. Code categories employed in this system identify problem-solving statements, positive and negative interaction responses, such as agree or criticize, as well as nonverbal behaviors that either facilitate or interfere with effective problem solving. Problem-solving sessions during which the partners interact typically last around ten minutes. They are requested to discuss a problem identified during one of the previously mentioned assessment procedures. Some of the code categories that have been employed to assess interaction between couples are illustrated as follows (Weiss, Hops, and Patterson, 1973, p. 319).

Verbal Code Name	*Nonverbal Code Name*
AG Agree	AS Assent
AP Approval	AT Attention

Verbal Code Name	*Nonverbal Code Name*
AR Accept Responsibility	CO Compliance
CM Command	LA Laugh
CP Complaint	NC Noncompliance
CR Criticize	NO Normative
CS Compromise	NR No Response
DG Diagree	NT Not Tracking
DR Deny Responsibility	PP Positive Physical Contact
EX Excuse	SM Smile
HM Humor	TO Turn Off
IN Interrupt	
NS Negative Solution	
PD Problem Description	
PS Problem Solving	
PU Put Down	
QU Question	
SP Solution (Past)	
TA Talk	

The term *problem description* (PD) refers to statements about the problem without suggestions for change; *problem solution* (PS) refers to statements that suggest or produce a change that could lead to a problem solution; and *compromise* (CS) involves a mutual exchange of behaviors that lead toward the resolution of a problem. These behaviors occurred infrequently when distressed couples were requested to discuss a problem and to arrive at a solution (Weiss, Hops, and Patterson, 1973). They tended rather to discuss their problem in a very general way, failing to make specific suggestions for change and failing to maintain focus on the problem. They brought in irrelevant material and interrupted each other so that the discussion soon revolved around issues that had nothing to do with the problem they were there to discuss. Attempted digressions, or sidetracking of the discussion was frequent. Other nonconstructive behaviors noted included *excuses* (EX), which concerned denial of responsibility by invoking implausible explanations or spurious reasons, and *complaints* (CO), which included statements expressing a person's suffering, usually offered in a whining tone of voice. Gottman and his colleagues (Gottman and others, 1976) employ a variation of this coding system in which one group of coders code the content from verbatim transcripts of interaction, employing the following eight summary areas: agreement, disagreement, mind reading, problem solving, problem talk and/or feeling, communication talk, summarizing self, and summarizing other. Other coders code nonverbal behavior using a hiearchical decision rule based on the importance of certain nonverbal behaviors, with facial expressions given primary importance, followed by positive and negative voice cues, followed by positive and negative body positions.

A second method of assessment, one that is more readily accessible for immediate use in that it does not require training in a number of code categories, consists of listening to an audiotape of the partners' interaction (or viewing a videotape, if one is available) and identifying possible problem areas (Carter and Thomas, 1973; Thomas, Walter, and O'Flaherty, 1974). Possible problem areas include surfeits (too much of a behavior) and deficits (too little of a behavior). The following examples (from Thomas, Walter, and O'Flaherty, 1974, pp. 238-238) should be considered only as illustrative; problems unique to each couple should be identified.

Temporal remoteness. An interactant dwells excessively on referents pertaining to the past or the hypothetical future.

Detached utterance. An interactant talks on a subject that does not show a clear semantic connection to the immediate focus of the discussion (for example, irrelevant examples, ideas, or hypothetical situations).

Positive talk deficit. An interactant fails to compliment or say nice things about the other as a person or about what the other says or does.

Positive talk surfeit. An interactant excessively compliments or says nice things about the other person or about what the other says or does.

Overtalk. An interactant speaks considerably more than his partner (or the others with whom he is interacting), considering the interaction session as a whole.

Undertalk. An interactant speaks considerably less than his partner (or others with whom he is interacting), considering the interaction as a whole.

Rapid latency. An interactant speaks very quickly after the speech of another.

Slow latency. An interactant responds very slowly after another interactant stops speaking.

Obtrusions. An interactant too frequently makes utterances while another is speaking. Such intrusions become interruptions if they produce an immediate and apparently premature termination of the speech by the other.

Quibbling. An interactant endeavors to explicate, clarify, or dispute a minor, tangential, and irrelevant detail.

Overresponsiveness. An interactant speaks too long and what he says goes beyond what is called for in responding to the partner's talk. (Overresponsiveness applies to the speeches of the interactant in response to what is requested or suggested by others whereas overtalk applies to speaking more than one's partner, or others, in the interaction, considering the entire interaction session.)

Underresponsiveness. An interactant says too little in relation to what a previous question or comment appears to call for. (This too applies to speeches of the speaker and is to be distinguished from undertalk.)

Pedantry. An interactant uses too many big words where simpler, better known words would be adequate (for example, saying *trepidation* for *fear* or *viscissitude* for *change*).

Dogmatic statement. An interactant makes a statement in a categorical, unqualified, all or none, "black or white" manner.

Overgeneralization. An interactant misrepresents real-world referents (behaviors or other events) by understating such characteristics as their amount, importance, or quality. For example, overgeneralization of amount may involve the use of the word *always* when an event occurs sometimes.

Topic content avoidance. An interactant clearly and openly averts the opportunity to talk about an assigned or agreed-on topic.

Topic content shifting. An interactant introduces new or different content from an assigned or agreed-on topic.

Topic content persistence. An interactant speaks excessively on an assigned or agreed-on topic.

Excessive cueing. An interactant employs more verbal cues than are necessary, as indicated by asking too many questions or making too many requests, directives, commands, or suggestions.

Poor referent specification. An interactant fails to speak concretely and specifically in regard to the referent and, instead, his speech tends to be general and abstract.

Opinion deficit. An interactant fails to express a preference or an opinion regarding referents when the discussion seems to call for some evaluation by him.

Opinion surfeit. An interactant expresses preferences or opinions excessively regarding the referents when the interaction does not seem to call for this much expression of opinion by him.

Excessive agreement. An interactant agrees excessively with the statements of others.

Excessive disagreement. An interactant disagrees excessively with the statements of others.

Too little information given. An interactant provides too little information considering what should or might be provided at that point in the discussion.

Redundant information given. An interactant excessively repeats information already given or known.

Too much information given. An interactant provides an excessive amount of information concerning a subject compared with what is necessary.

Negative talk surfeit. An interactant expresses too frequent or too lengthy negative evaluations of others, events, or other aspects of his surroundings. When these negative evaluations are applied to the behavior of others with whom he is interacting, the interactant is faulting.

Negative talk deficit. An interactant fails to express negative evaluations, especially in situations in which they would be warranted.

Illogical talk. An interactant makes an illogical statement, considering what others have said.

Type of content is involved in most categories—for example, pedantry, dogmatic statement, negative talk, and positive talk. The first three offer examples of unconstructive behaviors, whereas the last one offers an example of constructive behavior. Obtrusions and excessive cueing involve the control and direction of conversations. An example of the results of reviewing the recorded verbal interaction of a couple is presented in the section on developing communication skills in this chapter.

The function of specific partner behaviors can be determined by having each spouse indicate whether he likes or dislikes given behaviors during an exchange. For example, signal systems have been developed allowing people to indicate like (a green light) and dislike (a red light) of another person's behaviors while talking (see Thomas, Carter, and Gambrill, 1971; Stuart, 1971a). A client may be given different colored chips and instructed to give a green chip to a family member when he likes what the other person said or did and a red chip when he dislikes what the other person said or did. The advantage of this procedure is that the clients themselves indicate the function of events. It is likely that their perceptions will be more accurate than those of trained observers, who may unknowingly impose their preference system on the clients.

Intervention

As with all presenting problems, the assessment stage of practice also has intervention implications in terms of starting to offer clients a more helpful vocabulary in talking about problem areas and developing a more helpful framework that may be employed to alter problems; for example, by using observation as a first reaction to a problem. Thus pinpointing desired changes is an aspect of intervention as well as of assessment. Initial interviews function as training sessions, in that couples are coached on how to pinpoint desired changes. The behaviors identified must be observable and countable, so that either spouse will readily be able to see if they occur. Completion of the self-report inventories described earlier will help to prepare the couple for initial sessions. This process of pinpointing behaviors to be increased or decreased helps each spouse learn what behaviors are valued by the other (Weiss, Hops, and Patterson, 1973). It also discourages "crystal ball" phenomena, in which partners expect their mates to know what they want and discourages thoughts that they know what their partners are thinking. Typically, each spouse has been quite nonspecific about his or her complaints, which makes it impossible for the partner to know what to do differently even if she or he were favorably disposed to altering his or her behavior. Pinpointing desired changes, in which the behavioral referents for such general phrases as "She just doesn't love me" or "He is so inconsiderate" are identified, may occupy three or four interviews.

Learning to be a Positive Scanner. A history of unpleasant interaction and avoidance often results in an inability to notice positive aspects of a partner's behavior (Hops, 1976). Attention to such behaviors can be cultivated in a variety of ways. Either audiotape or videotape can be employed to record a brief portion of the couple's interaction, and each person in turn asked to identify behaviors of the spouse that she or he likes. When recording behaviors that are pleasing at home, each can be requested to inform the other when he or she records a please and to tell the spouse what he or she did to warrant this. For example, if a husband comes home and asks his wife what she did during the day, she may record a please and tell him that she liked his asking about her day. This immediate feedback helps the couple to identify pleasing events as well as displeasing events or when intent goes awry—that is, when the effect of a behavior differs from that intended. Requesting each to acknowledge a pleasing behavior of the spouse and to thank him or her or offer some other positive recognition helps to emphasize the mutual dependency of the couple (Weiss, Hops, and Patterson, 1973). A spouse may be asked to offer the partner a "love day" during which they increase the number of positive behaviors typically offered. Awareness by the partner of the spouse's attempt to increase positive behaviors hopefully will heighten attention to such positives. Data collected by each spouse can be reviewed daily or weekly, noting especially positive behaviors (Azrin, Naster, and Jones, 1973). Learning to view positive behaviors of the spouse as gifts, rather than as expected, will also increase appreciation of positive behaviors. Offered levels of reinforcement often become expected levels of reinforcement, no longer to be praised and perceived as gifts, but to be expected as one's right and therefore simply to be complained about when absent. Evidence for this pattern is supported by the finding that even happy couples offer a higher rate of reinforcement to strangers than to their own mates.

Positive scanning can be encouraged by audiotaping or videotaping short segments of the couple interacting together, and then replaying this tape, asking each spouse to count the positive events in his or her own behavior (Hops, 1976). Another short segment of interaction can then be recorded and each spouse requested to listen to or view the tape and to select positive behaviors of his partner. This procedure can be repeated until there is an increase in the number of positive events that are noted. The focus on positive behaviors encourages each person to act more positively, so there are usually more positives to count. This procedure will heighten the discrimination of positive behaviors of the mate. Inability of one or both partners to identify strengths of the mate may mean that they are so angry at the partner they cannot think of his or her positive aspects, that they lack patience for entering into a change program, or that they believe that nothing will change. They can be encouraged to do more thinking *on their own* before talking further with the mate or with the counselor.

One problem that may arise is rejection of identified behavioral referents as being meaningful to the original complaint. Thus a husband may complain that his wife does not love him. When asked what she would do if she did love him, he may say, "She would kiss me when I come home in the evening," "She would not bother me when I read the paper before supper," and "She would have supper ready at six every night." When asked if there were additional things she would do differently, he may be unable to identify anything further. The examples offered may be rejected as not really capturing what he means when he says, "She does not love me." It may be necessary to repeat the rationale for identifying specific behaviors, including the need to monitor behavior in order to evaluate progress, to clarify expectation so that the mate will know what to do differently, and to remind the couple that it is only through our behavior that we affect others. Assurance can also be provided that as other referents are identified these will be considered. The couple can be encouraged to "table" their objections temporarily and see what happens after a change program is initiated.

Developing Communication Skills. The next phase continues the development of a new interpersonal vocabulary, stressing the ideas that one cannot *not* communicate (Watzlawick, Beavin, and Jackson, 1967), that *measured* honesty is needed for satisfactory relationships, that there should be an emphasis upon positive information, and that problematic behavior always involves an interaction between two people, that is, both partners are involved (Stuart, 1975). The importance of nonverbal as well as verbal behavior is emphasized. Another guideline stresses the differential information value of negative and positive information. Clients in fact often request their mates to selectively disclose their feelings (Levinger and Senn, 1967). Spouses are encouraged to include the first speaker's behavior when describing an interactional sequence so that they recognize their initial role in the interaction. Observation of the couple's interaction patterns during assessment will reveal communication problems that exist. The couple can be coached in more appropriate skills, which include effective listening and sharing behaviors as well as a decrease in aversive and sidetracking behaviors (Patterson and Hops, 1972). Often neither spouse listens to the other when she or he is talking; rather, they intrude with interruptions, denials of responsibility, counter-complaints, and so forth. In addition to these surfeits, there is often a deficit of behaviors that would encourage pinpointing, such as the request for specific examples, acceptance of responsibility, agreement, offering concrete suggestions, and paraphrasing the partner's comments to make sure they are understood. One partner may dominate the other in terms of talk time and often neither partner knows how to express his or her preferences positively by offering concrete examples. Rather, requests for change are often accompanied by criticism or blame or even ridicule or sarcasm. Appropriate sharing behavior includes being specific about what one would like the other to do, focusing on behaviors to be increased, suggesting alternatives, and avoiding blame. Silent spouses may be encouraged to offer more opinions by setting norms that equalize talk time. Any behaviors that deflect the couple from the topic at hand or that are aversive, such as "put-downs," sarcasm, or ridicule (that is, "zaps"), are identified and discouraged. "Zaps" are defined as putting the other person down by means other than a simple description of the problem (Patterson and others, 1975). For example, a spouse may say to his mate, "You're sloppy." (A zap is always in the eyes of the "zapee.") Such comments sidetrack effective problem-solving efforts, because the partner will tend to react to the attack rather than to the problem.

Good communication is defined as having the impact one intends to have (Gottman and others, 1976). As noted in the discussion of assessment, distressed partners often do not have the impact they intend to have; that is, their messages are misinterpreted by their partners. Helpful and dysfunctional communication behaviors are given in the following list (see also list given in discussion of assessment).

Helpful Behaviors	*Behaviors and Thoughts to be Avoided*
Asking the partner for feedback as to what she heard.	Mind reading (assuming that one knows what the other person is thinking or feeling).
Disregarding gloomy expectations about what reactions a partner will have if one does level with him.	
Asking what can be done to make things better.	Continued restatements of one's own position (the "summarizing self syndrome," Gottman and others, 1976).
Recognize the reasonableness of one's partner's position.	
Giving feedback about what one thought one's partner said.	Gunnysacking (complaining about stored-up displeasures).
Editing statements before they are expressed and deleting dysfunctional behaviors such as attacking one's partner's character.	"Yes, butting" (Gottman and others, 1976, p. 12), in which the partner refuses to accept any of the other person's suggestions.
	Following a complaint with another complaint.
	Insults.
	Sarcasm.

Partners are encouraged to "level" with each other in a positive way, which means use of helpful behaviors as mentioned as well as avoidance of dysfunctional behaviors. It is also important that they learn to recognize hidden agendas, especially negative ones (Gottman and others, 1976). A hidden agenda exists when one issue seems to be being discussed—but actually another is at stake. Hidden agendas can create very problematic interactions, as shown in the following exchange (based on an example from Gottman and others, 1976, p. 90).

Message	*Probable Hidden Agenda*
Husband: "I wish you would see a doctor. You look positively frazzled."	*Wife:* "He thinks I'm unattractive."
Wife: "I don't think we should have another child until I finish school."	*Husband:* "She doesn't want to stay with me. She's not committed to me."

Message	*Probable Hidden Agenda*
Husband: "I'm not going to do the dishes."	*Wife:* "What he needs is more important than what I need."

The coverants (thoughts) indicated in the right column represent hidden agendas in that they are unexpressed assumptions that may influence the behavior of the person who has them, in a way that is bewildering to the partner, who is not privy to them. Being polite is also stressed (Gottman and others, 1976). This includes the following: saying what one can do and what one wants to do rather than what one will not or will not want to do; showing appreciation to one's partner for things done that one likes; being courteous and considerate; expressing interest in one's partner's activities; allowing one's partner to finish speaking before starting to speak; saying things that one's partner will like; criticizing one's ideas, not oneself (otherwise one's partner may feel compelled to come to the rescue); and focusing on the present situation, not on old resentments. It should be explained that offering and receiving new behaviors may seem unnatural at first, because it is different from what has been happening, and that what is important is whether it becomes natural over time. Many people equate naturalness with a lack of planning and consider that their marriage can only be successful if it is positive in an unplanned manner. It is unlikely whether this can indeed occur; it obviously did not work for the couples who seek counseling. Clients can be asked what is so bad about wishing to please a partner in a planned way. Planning is sometimes confused with insincerity. Stipulating that affectional behaviors are only offered when the person actually feels them is an important boundary condition. Insisting that a partner change—for example, offer more positive events—while at the same time insisting that this happen naturally, places both the partner and the counselor in an impossible condition if this charge is accepted.

A couple may have to learn to distinguish between problem solving, information gathering, and catharsis. Difficulties may arise if one partner is just "sounding off" and the other thinks he or she is trying to problem-solve. The specific behaviors in need of change will vary from couple to couple. Focusing on communication patterns not only helps clients to learn more effective strategies for resolving areas of conflict in their relationship, but also, as more effective skills are developed, helps them increase the rate of rewarding interactions and helps them decrease the frequency of aversive interactions (Jacobson and Martin, 1976).

Training is typically carried out in the office with the help of audio- or videotape feedback in addition to counselor coaching, rehearsal, and model presentation of effective communication skills. Tape recordings of discussions at home should be gathered to check on skill acquisition. For example, if the couple mentions only vague complaints, the same topic can be discussed by the counselor, who models the careful identification of specific behaviors. Or the counselors may model gathering needed information before any change attempt is made. Positive listening and sharing behaviors can be illustrated and the couple then requested to rehearse them in subsequent discussions. Feedback has been provided in a number of forms, including verbal instructions, role playing by the counselor, written instructions, videotape, and audiotape. During this feedback, the destructive results of ineffective communication patterns are emphasized and more effective behaviors modeled. Written instructions based on an analysis of a tape recording of a couple's interaction during a ten-minute period have been found to improve communication skills. An example of this follows (from Carter and Thomas, 1973, p. 102).

> One of the primary areas of difficulty we observed in your communication has to do with your style of addressing specific problems. We can refer to this as your problem-solving style. We wish to point out certain key features of your problem-solving style that we feel are in need of improvement:
>
> 1. *Not maintaining specificity.* As a general rule, you did reveal an ability to discuss details surrounding a specific, concrete problem. For example, both of you contributed specific information that helped in clarifying the topic of

whether or not one of your sets of parents
should have been invited for Thanksgiving. However, the specifics of that situation were soon
abandoned when the abstract issue of what holidays mean to one or the other of you was introduced. Although that particular incident is now
in the past, we would suggest that when you discuss similar situations in the future you make it
a rule to maintain a focus on the specifics of *the
situation itself* and not allow the situation to be
submerged in a discussion of abstract issues or
principles. It would help if you would cue each
other when you find yourselves slipping away
from specifics. A statement like "Let's get back
to the specifics" might help in this connection.

2. *Diverting the focus of discussion.* This defect is
related to the one just mentioned, that of not
maintaining specificity, but it differs in that the
problem here involves a more blatant *shift* of
topics rather than the topic simply becoming
more abstract. For example, in one exchange,
Mrs. T. said, "I think when I'm trying to do
something to make something for our children
that you should be right there with me. They're
not just my children, it's not just my responsibility. It's for us to do together for our children.
. . ." Mr. T.'s reply was, "Well when I'm cutting
the grass out in the backyard or working on my
truck or something like that, do you come and
say 'Do you want me to help you cut the
grass?' " Mrs. T. then fell into the discussion of
whether or not she works in the yard and how
much, and the whole discussion seemed to take
one giant step aside from the original topic of
sharing responsibility for the children. We feel it
would have been better if Mr. T. had maintained
a focus on the original topic, but when he did
deviate from it, Mrs. T. could have suggested that
they return to the original focus of discussion instead of allowing herself to go along with a topic
shift. Mutual problems generally require the *exclusive* attention of both parties for a concentrated period of time. Too many side issues serve
to dilute and weaken your problem-solving efforts.

The recommendation was made that the couple should avoid talking about things in vague and general ways and should instead keep their discussions specific and to the point, centered on actual, rather than hypothetical, events. The amount of content that was specific increased substantially over baseline levels (from a high of 40 percent during baseline to one of 65 percent). Measurement of discrete behaviors is easily done simply by reviewing the tape-recorded material and counting well-defined target categories—in this case, specific statements.

One way to help the couple learn to identify zaps is to replay a tape of their interaction and ask them to write down zaps on a piece of paper. Alternative ways to express feelings can then be modeled and the tape replayed, and the "zapper" can be given the opportunity to express himself or herself in a more concrete, constructive way. Thus, rather than saying, "You're sloppy" (which, incidentally, does not inform the partner what to do differently), the spouse may say, "You leave your clothes on the bedroom floor rather than hanging them up in the closet." Thus the "zapper" receives practice in describing problems in a more positive way with an absence of blame, sarcasm, ridicule, or negative labels. Replaying of taped interaction may also be employed to identify other sidetracking behaviors, such as attempts to change the topic, attempts to offer tangential explanations for actions, bringing up hypothetical possibilities, and so forth. Some couples may have become so accustomed to the mutual exchange of unpleasantries that much practice is required to identify negative comments. An advantage of videotape over audiotape is that feedback can be offered for nonverbal as well as verbal behaviors. Because the nonverbal component of behavior is such a critical part of communication, it is important that both areas be addressed. In the absence of videotape, the person could be requested to watch himself or herself in a mirror as the couple talks, or a partner could be requested to identify nonverbal behaviors that both partners would like to see more of or less of that occur when they talk to each other. Couples may be asked to select positive and negative behaviors in their taped interactions, so that their ability to discriminate them can be checked.

The sequence of feedback and instructions with modeling and rehearsal is carried out with other behaviors that are problematic for the couple. Rehearsal provides practice in using the new behaviors and further opportunities for the counselor to encourage appropriate responses and discourage continued use of ineffective ones. The couple is requested to practice during specially scheduled problem-solving sessions. These usually last about thirty minutes. The scheduling of these sessions is important, because couples often attempt to solve problems many times during the day. Confining such attempts to a selected period prevents possible aversive interactions from intruding on other activities and highlights the importance of attention to problem solving. The partners are usually coached to select one problem they would like to discuss during this session. If a couple has a high "zap" rate, a condition should be established that if either partner counts more than a certain number of zaps, the session is to be ended. Or they could be trained how to "stop action" (Gottman and others, 1976), in which one partner calls a halt to the discussion, a check is made concerning how both partners are feeling, and intents and impacts of statements are clarified. If one partner has trouble refraining from interrupting the other, a small card placed in front of the speaker could be employed to indicate who has the floor. Some of these sessions are tape-recorded by the couple and reviewed by the counselor to monitor progress. These tapes provide a basis for further feedback to the couple. Communication skills can also be enhanced by daily half-hour sessions in which the couple reviews their day. Rules unique to each couple may be added, such as a requirement that each spouse must ask two questions of the other to show his or her interest. Poker chips may be exchanged to signal positive evaluations. Stressful exchanges can be recorded for later review. The couple may also be asked to read material describing behaviors and methods that will facilitate their interaction; for example, *Families* (Patterson, 1971a) or sections of *The Mirages of Marriage* (Lederer and Jackson, 1968).

Developing Problem-Solving and Negotiation Skills. After couples have been trained to identify specific behaviors and to focus on positives, and have acquired skills to effectively listen to and share their preferences with each other in a positive way, these skills can then be employed in problem solving and in negotiating changes; that is, in learning more positive ways to influence each other (Stuart, 1975). In negotiation training, partners are taught how to identify specific changes that each would like to see in the other's behavior and to identify what items or behaviors each is willing to offer in exchange. Important concepts that the couple learns include the notion that changes are indeed negotiable—that is, if a given change is desired, they *can* identify a way to encourage the behavior. In addition, they learn to compromise with each other. They also learn to focus on the future rather than on old complaints of problems (Hops, 1976).

A refusal to compromise characterizes the arguments of many couples. Learning to place specific values on given behaviors and consequences makes the process of compromising easier, in that it is clear what is being offered for what. Thus, a wife may agree to come home from work at six o'clock every evening if her husband cooks the meals on three nights of each week. An important aspect of this training is attempting to alter a person's perception of having a right to certain behaviors on the part of the spouse and cultivating the attitude that a person earns positive events from a spouse by offering such events to him or her (Stuart, 1969). Contracts are employed as a tool to explicitly describe agreements and provide an orderly way to ensure change based on the assumption that each person can gain only by honoring contractual obligations (Weiss, Hops, and Patterson, 1973). Contracts arrange the immediate reinforcement of desired spouse behaviors. This is important, because such behaviors typically have not been attended to and reinforced in the past. In fact, they currently may even be followed by punishment. Contracts clarify expectations; identify benefits and costs; act as a continuing reference point in case of disagreement as to terms; and also function as cues that remind spouses of their agreements with one another (Rappaport and Harrell, 1972). Contracts can be modified easily and signing them serves as a sign of commitment of spouses to the counseling effort. Contracts should also identify the duration of the negotiated agreement as well as rules for renegotiating and should be signed

by all involved parties. Contracts can be used as a valuable tool
to help spouses to learn the steps involved in negotiating change
in a positive way.

After desired changes are identified, a next step is to
identify consequences to offer for support of these changes.
Positive and negative consequences may have three different
sources. They may originate from the spouse—receiving a back
rub or having dinner out; from the environment—having a beer
or signing up for an art class; or from the counselor—a reduced
fee or fine of an agreed-on amount of money (Weiss, Hops,
and Patterson, 1973). Potential negative and positive events that
may be employed as consequences may be identified during pinpointing which behaviors please and displease each spouse. The
Marital Activities Inventory, which lists recreational events a
couple may enjoy sharing with each other, provides an additional source of consequences. Examples of positive and negative consequences from each source are offered in Table 11.
This table clarifies the valence of a consequence (positive or
negative) and the recipient.

Table 11. Illustrative Contingency Matrix

From:	Positive Consequences:		Negative Consequences:	
	To Husband	To Wife	To Husband	To Wife
Spouse	Backrub	Dinner out	Lose spending money to spouse	
	Sexual variety	Shopping trip	Specified spouse chore	
Environment	Free time	Hairdresser	Clean garage	Lose free-time units
	Beer	Art class	Clean oven	Wash windows
Therapist	Reduce Rx fee	Movie tick-ets	Fine or loss of deposit money	

Source: Weiss, Hops, and Patterson (1973, p. 328).

Behaviors and consequences can be placed on a negotiation training form as shown in Table 12.

There are a variety of characteristics that all contracts
should share. They should include a focus on increasing behaviors rather than an emphasis on decreasing behaviors (Homme

Table 12. Negotiation Training Form

Husband	Wife
Problem Behavior:	Problem Behavior:
Accelerate: _____	Accelerate: _____
Decelerate: _____	Decelerate: _____
Reward:	Reward:
1. From Wife: _____	1. From Husband: _____
(H+)	(W+)
2. From Environment: _____	2. From Environment: _____
(Nonspouse +)	(Nonspouse +)
3. Therapist: _____	3. Therapist: _____
(T+)	(T+)
Penalty:	Penalty:
1. From Environment: _____	1. From Environment: _____
(Nonspouse −)	(Nonspouse −)
2. From Wife: _____	2. From Husband: _____
(H−)	(W−)
3. From Therapist: _____	3. From Therapist: _____
(T−)	(T−)

Source: Weiss, Hops, and Patterson (1973, p. 330).

and others, 1969). It is better to identify a behavior that will compete successfully with a cherished behavior rather than ask a spouse to relinquish or to punish such behavior (Weiss, 1975), because the couple's interaction is already probably suffering from an overabundance of aversive events. Also, it is usually easier to present positive events following the occurrence of a behavior than to acknowledge the nonoccurrence of something (Birchler, Weiss, and Vincent, 1975). For example, one could focus on increasing interaction with the wife rather than on decreasing newspaper reading of the husband. This does not mean to say that undesirable behaviors should not be considered, but that their change should be attempted by increasing incompatible alternative behaviors that can compete successfully with them. Need for a separate focus on such behavior is emphasized by the fact that positive and negative behaviors are independent and that negative behaviors seem to have more impact than positive ones on marital satisfaction. An example of a negative contract would be, "If I don't throw my shoes and socks on the livingroom floor, you won't forget to pack my lunch," in contrast to a positive contract, which might be, "I will put my shoes and socks in the closet when I take them off, if you will pack my lunch." (This is not to say that the latter is a "good" contract, as a later discussion on types of contracts will explain.) The contract should be entered into in good faith, that is, without fraudulent intent. Positive consequences originating from a spouse must be *intended* to be offered, contingent on agreed-on behavior, and both parties must be honest concerning their willingness to engage in behaviors described in the contract.

Furthermore, the contract must be fair—the positive and negative consequences offered for given behaviors must be reasonably balanced with the behaviors in question and should arrange for reinforcers to closely follow behavior. What is fair is in the eye of the beholder. The counselor may not always agree with the partners' judgment of fairness, but if it is not way out of line, their estimate of its fairness should be accepted. An example of an unfair contract would be as follows: "If Kate has dinner ready on time for a whole week, makes the bed by the time I get home every day, scrubs and washes the bathroom every other day, and washes the car on the weekend, I will take her out for a beer at the local pub on the weekend." In a contract where the wife will sleep in the nude one night if the husband takes her out for dinner once a week for the next three months, the positive consequence is too far removed, perhaps too little too late.) In addition to avoiding the mistake of offering too little too late, one must also take care not to offer too much too soon. In neither case would the contract be a balanced one in terms of offering a fair exchange. The need for making all terms in the contract explicit has already been emphasized. Both expected behaviors as well as positive and negative consequences must be clearly defined. It would not be satisfactory to simply say, "I will give you some money, if you wash the dishes every night," or "For every night you don't wash the dishes, you will have a nasty surprise before bedtime."

All involved parties must agree with all items on the contract. No one should be allowed to agree to a contract that involves a behavior that is aversive to offer. Let us say that a wife does not like to have intercourse with her husband. She should not be permitted to enter into a contract where intercourse is offered as a positive consequence (as a W+—see Table 12). This would place her in a situation where her husband controls the rate of a behavior that is a problem for her. However, some approximation to this behavior that she is willing to offer might be included instead, such as "cuddling" in bed for fifteen minutes. "Cuddling," of course, would have to be defined. In addition, one must take care that negative events arranged (H— or W—) do not involve increasing undesirable behaviors. For example, a contract where the wife does not sleep in the nude (W—) if her husband does not engage in future planning conversations with her should not be formed if sleeping in the nude is an avoidance behavior that should not be strengthened, because the husband's response failure would increase an undesired spouse behavior. The contract should also provide for fairly immediate reinforcement and access to positive consequences should be available only *after* the behavior occurs. If such consequences are available before the behavior, there is no contingency between completion of the behavior and its reinforcement, and thus no reason to expect it to change in frequency.

Types of contracts. The first type of contract employed in marital counseling was a quid pro quo agreement in which a change in one person's behavior was contingent on a change in the spouse's behavior (Stuart, 1969; Lederer and Jackson, 1968). For example, it might be arranged that if a husband speaks to his wife for twenty minutes each day after work, she will have dinner ready on time (6 P.M.) the next night. Nonoccurrence of one behavior insures nonoccurrence of the other. This is a difficulty with quid pro quo contracts: problem behaviors are "linked," so that if one does not change, neither will the other. This type of contract also necessitates one partner having to change his behavior first. Contacts in which independent consequences are arranged for desired spouse behaviors are preferred—a change in one problem behavior may occur independently of the other, because separate consequences are arranged (Weiss, Birchler, and Vincent, 1974). For example, the husband may receive a night out with his friends if he talks to his wife for twenty minutes each day and the wife may receive breakfast in bed Saturday and Sunday morning if she has meals on time during the week. Such agreements have been called "good faith" contracts. The following example also illustrates a contract in which independent consequences are arranged.

> H agrees to wash dishes three nights, *and* W agrees to cook gourmet meals. If dishes, then backrub (H+). If meals, then twenty minutes' conversation (W+).
>
> No dishes, no backrub (not —H+)
> No meals, no twenty minutes conversation (not —W+)

This type of contract eliminates the problem of who must go first. A "parallel" exchange is possible, in which both partners can initiate change but even if one does not, the other aspect of the contract can be carried out. For example, if the husband does not do the dishes and so does not receive a backrub, the agreement in relation to the exchange between meals and conversation can still be carried out. Rewards consist of nonproblematic behavior (backrubs [H+] and conversation [W+]). If either changes his or her behavior (if the husband washes the dishes three nights or the wife cooks gourmet meals), positive consequences occur *other* than in problem behaviors. Although such contracts offer benefits for displaying desired behaviors if one partner does not carry out his or her part of the agreement, "bad faith" may generalize to the other element of the contract (Weiss, Birchler, and Vincent, 1974).

Penalties as well as benefits may be required to encourage new behaviors. For example the following could be added to the contract above:

> No dishes, H must pick up clothes (H—). No meals, W washes car (W—).

Penalties may consist of an absence of nonproblematic spouse behavior or "outside" events such as washing the car (W—) or picking up clothes (H—). Failure to engage in a behavior should be followed by only one type of penalty. Either the partner does not get a reward (not H+ or not W+) or he or she is punished by a penalty unrelated to the spouse (Table 12). Including both would weight consequences on the negative side. The more problematic the interaction pattern between a couple, the more outside sources of consequences should be employed at first. Although an aim of negotiation training is to directly involve spouse consequences more frequently, to do so immediately, when there is resentment and unwillingness to offer things to the partner, would be strategically premature (Birchler, Weiss, and Vincent, 1975). Counselor sanctions selected from the contingency matrix developed for each couple may be added to the contract (see Tables 11 and 12).

There is no evidence at this point that the good faith contract is more effective than the quid pro quo contract, or that any contract at all is required, in contrast to each spouse simply agreeing to a series of changes without any specification of explicit contingencies (Jacobson and Martin, 1976). The "happiness contract" (employed by Azrin, Naster, and Jones (1973), along with a variety of other procedures, approaches the latter description. In the program developed by Azrin and his colleagues, each person listed activities typically done for the partner, activities received from the partner as well as several requests for improving the marriage. Reinforcement contingencies were not stated in specific response-reinforcement relationships, but rather as a global cluster of responses that produces a global package of reinforcers. That is, each spouse agreed that if one partner failed, either by intent or oversight to comply with any of his spouse's new requests on schedule, the offended partner would notify the offending partner of the omission and would make clear his intention to begin a sustained omission of *all* current activities done for the partner as well as new requests on the following morning if the initially omitted request had not been fulfilled by then (Azrin, Naster, and Jones, 1973, p. 374). Details in offering a given satisfaction were specified in the agreement only as much as each person felt was necessary. Specification was initially urged by the counselor in order to avoid later misunderstandings. However, the main criterion was whether the recipient of the activity was satisfied. For example, if a person complained while doing the dishes, her partner might not consider this as a satisfactory completion of the activity. An emphasis on the centrality of satisfactions, rather than on behavioral detail, allowed partners to vary and substitute activities as long as prior agreement was obtained from the partner. As with other contracts, each person was requested to sign the contract (Azrin, Naster, and Jones, 1973). It seems, however, that the more aversive the interaction between the couple (the more resentment and lack of good faith and trust), the more likely it will be that a step-by-step setting of new contingencies will be required. If more formal contracts, such as the good faith contract, are employed, less formal contracts can be used as the couple develops negotiation skills. Suggestions for change can be deposited in a "suggestion box" and review by the couple during weekly discussion meetings (Gottman and others, 1976).

A range of events, such as fatigue and little time because of a heavy work schedule, lack of energy caused by poor eating habits, or loss of a cherished job, may be related to a decrease in marital satisfaction on the part of one or both partners. Responsibilities in relation to such events may be incorporated into contingency contracts.

Establishing Decision-Making Skills. Many of the same inappropriate behaviors that hinder conflict resolution also hinder effective decision making, including inability to focus on one problem and failure to be precise as to suggestions. A five-step process may be employed to develop decision-making skills, including (1) agreement to work together on a problem; (2) choosing one part of the problem to work on; (3) listing possible solutions; (4) selecting solutions to try out; and (5) deciding how this solution will be carried out (Thomas, O'Flaherty, and Borkin, 1976; Thomas, 1976). Training in more appropriate decision-making skills is typically carried out in the office. The couple is asked to select a problem to discuss, and verbal instructions and cues are employed to shape appropriate behavior. Cues are used to coach the couple to move from one step to another. For example, a husband and wife wanted their nine-year-old son to make more of his own decisions (Thomas, O'Flaherty, and Borkin, 1976). The partners were next requested to select one special aspect of this problem they felt was small enough to make a decision about. The couple was coached to be more specific when the partners employed vague terms. At an early point with this couple, the counselor intervened and asked for clarification of the term *Carl's decisions*. Tendencies to move on to other steps, such as offering solutions, were discouraged, the counselor prompting the couple to return to clarification of key terms in the problem, such as exactly what decisions the parents would like their son to make. They indicated that they wanted their son to make his own decisions concerning what books to read, what books to get from the library, what to watch on television, and what to wear.

The importance of agreeing on this phase of the process before moving on to subsequent decision-making steps is highlighted by asking whether the couple agrees that this is the part of the topic they wish to work on, and one member is requested to paraphrase the agreement. This procedure will hopefully encourage the couple to do likewise during subsequent decision-making sessions. The couple is then asked to list as many solutions as they can think of that might alleviate the problem. It is emphasized that their only task at this point is to suggest solutions; that is, they are not to evaluate solutions yet. Some of the solutions the couple mentioned earlier developed are listed as follows (from Thomas, O'Flaherty, and Borkin, 1976, p. 372). "[Some solutions were] to offer Carl choices like 'Would you like egg or cereal this morning?' 'Which book would you like to read—A, B, or C?' (suggested by W, the wife); to give Carl a choice and then have the father leave the room, in order to decrease the likelihood of his making the choice for the boy (suggested by H, the husband); to send Carl to the library by himself to obtain books (suggested by H); to take Carl to the library and let him decide which books to take (suggested by H); to have Carl take out the food he wants when food is being prepared (suggested by H); to have Carl select his own clothes (suggested by H); to let Carl decide what television programs he wants to watch (suggested by W); when Carl asks a question involving a decision that he can make himself, to turn the question back and to ask him to decide for himself (suggested by H); and when Carl asks his father a question, the father is to stop and think before answering, in order to avoid making the decision for Carl (suggested by H)." If the couple drifts off the topic, the counselor prompts the partners to return to the topic of discussion. A red light is illuminated as a cue that the couple has drifted off task and if this fails to refocus them appropriately, the counselor then intervenes with verbal instructions. The use of a light as a prompting device has the advantage of enabling conversation to continue between the couple without interruption. Suggestions are written down and the couple is asked to review the list so that each partner is familiar with the suggestions. Then the couple is requested to select the suggestion that they think offers the best solution. The couple decided that Carl would decide himself what books he wanted to read and that he should select his own books from the library. After solutions were offered, the couple was prompted to review their suggestions, to make sure both agreed, and were then asked to plan exactly how they would carry out their solution, including what was to be done, by whom, when, and how. This led to a discussion of what to do if the parents did not agree with a decision that Carl made. It was decided that the boy should be permitted to make his own decisions—that neither the father nor the mother would have veto power over them. Because it seemed that the father might need a cue to remind him not to interfere in Carl's decision, the wife said that she would remind him, if he did intrude, by saying they had "made an agreement." The parents were then requested to give a summary of their plans.

This training took place over four ninety-minute sessions. Feedback was provided both via counselor statements as well as by light signals (red for "off topic" and green for "on topic"). Data collected for eleven couples indicated that this coaching procedure was successful in increasing appropriate verbal units for each step in the decision-making process. Training is typically provided for about three problem areas and information should be collected as to whether plans are implemented (Thomas, O'Flaherty, and Borkin, 1976). Without this, the program may simply succeed in "talk with no action." Periodic reviews of a sample of the couple's decision making can be reviewed and additional coaching provided as needed during follow-up sessions. Intrusions by the counselor should be kept to a minimum; otherwise, clients may become frustrated by being interrupted frequently. During the problem-solving session concerning Carl (about one hour), only eleven coaching comments were made, six of which dealt with initiation or ending of steps in the decision-making sequences, and five related to redirecting the conversation by requesting clarification. It is not necessary to have feedback via colored light devices. Such feedback could be offered by the counselor simply having two different color cards, and by placing a card in one of two spots to indicate "on-task" or "off-task" behavior.

Learning to Cue and Offer Positive Consequences
for Desired Behaviors

A behavioral model of social interaction stresses the extent to which each person influences the behavior of the other. Thus any behavior that is a source of complaint by either party must be viewed in relation to the behavior of the complainant. Let us say that Mrs. Z. complains that her husband does not notify her when he is going to be late for supper. Assessment may reveal that when he has telephoned her in the past, she has berated him for his lack of consideration and demanded that he come home as planned. She has discouraged his telephoning by presenting him with an unpleasant interaction when he did call. Or let us say that a husband complains about his wife's cooking. We may find that various things are wrong with meals, such as their being late or not heated properly, when he has come home in a grumpy mood and ignored his wife's greetings. It is thus important to determine the "chain" of behavior that is involved in a complaint, in order to identify the extent to which the behavior of each person serves as an occasion or as a consequence for the behavior of the other. Often, the aggrieved party overlooks his or her own role in the complained about behavior. There is a tendency to report situations in a trichotomy, in which one party says, "He did _____ so I did _____ and then he did _____" (Watzlawick, Beavin, and Jackson, 1967). For example, "He yelled at me so I got my coat and said I was leaving and he said 'Good riddance.'" Reporting interactions in such a way makes the complaining party appear guiltless. The complainer may not mention that before he yelled at her she had been nagging her husband about myriad items.

In cases where a low frequency of an event is complained

about, such as a failure to come home from work on time or not spending much time talking, there should be a search for the consequences usually provided for such behaviors. This will often reveal that there is a lack of positive consequences for desired behaviors and may even reveal the presence of punishing consequences. For example, a husband may prefer to work late, because he finds his house in a total uproar when he arrives home and is immediately faced with a barrage of requests from his wife to take care of many small tasks, such as pick up some milk at the store, get the children in for dinner, set the table, mow the grass after dinner, and so forth. It may be much more peaceful simply to work late at the office. Or a wife may not enjoy talking with her husband because he rarely offers her an opportunity to talk about topics of interest to her.

Assessment may reveal that a couple possesses appropriate communication skills as well as skills to select specific desired changes, negotiate behavior changes, and to make joint decisions, but fails to provide positive consequences for desired behaviors. Each may know specifically what the other would like to be different but may simply not provide cues that facilitate this change nor consequences that will maintain it. Identification of reinforcers such as praise and approval and the conditions under which to provide these (following desired behavior) may be sufficient to increase desired behaviors, as the following example illustrates.

Tom and Betty described themselves as basically happy, but troubled by Betty's habit of leaving items such as clothes, newspapers, and magazines all over the house. Tom did not like to be in an untidy house and Betty disliked it too, because guests might come over and the house would be disorderly. She said she simply forgot to pick up the items. A program was initiated in which cues were arranged to remind her to pick up items and place them in appropriate spots; for example, to return magazines to the magazine holder. These cues were designed by Tom in accord with the principle that they be pleasing to all involved parties as well as serve as a cue for appropriate behavior. For example, he made a collage of nudes, which he posted in the bathroom with a reminder to hang up towels. On top of the television set in the livingroom was placed a sign that contained a picture of a hand with a finger pointing out into the livingroom, with the phrase, "Have you picked up stray items?" Cues were also placed in the kitchen and bedroom. A two-week baseline revealed a daily average of forty misplaced items. Betty received points dependent on how many items below her baseline were misplaced daily. She received five points each day on which only 30 items were misplaced, ten if only 20 were found and fifteen if only 10 were found and so on. Betty requested that points be tradeable for purchase of a birthday cake, since in her country she had only received a birthday cake on her birthday and she had a great liking for such cakes. Since her weight was not a problem, the cake was selected as the backup reinforcer. She had to earn fifty points to obtain a cake. Tom was requested to praise his wife for putting away items and for neater-looking rooms. The criterion for awarding points was raised weekly in accord with the decreasing number of items left around the house. During the first week of intervention, the daily average number of misplaced items decreased to twenty, then to ten the second week and to seven the third week, where it remained for the following three weeks. Both Betty and Tom said that they were satisfied with this daily average and the cues were removed one at a time and the point program gradually faded out. Tom was encouraged to continue to praise his wife for her new behaviors.

Both Tom and Betty were so pleased with the results of the program that they decided to use cueing to try to increase the regularity with which Betty took her birth control pills. Tom made a sign to post in the bathroom, which pictured a very pregnant woman and contained the words, "Do you want to look like this?" Betty's taking of birth control pills increased from 80 percent to 100 percent. With most couples, a more complex intervention will be required to increase positive transactions.

Stimulus Control Procedures. The introduction of novel stimuli facilitates the development of new behaviors. Goldiamond (1965) reported two examples of the use of stimulus control procedures to encourage appropriate behaviors of couples. The first example concerned a twenty-nine-year-old graduate student, Mr. A., who said that his wife had committed "the ultimate betrayal" a couple of years ago with his best friend. The husband had suggested that his friend keep his wife company while he (the husband) studied in the library at night and this association led to a sexual encounter between the friend and his wife. "Since that time, whenever he saw his wife, he screamed at her for hours on end, or else was ashamed at himself for having done so and spent hours sulking and brooding" (Goldiamond, 1965, p. 118). A program was designed to reduce yelling, but there was a concern that sulking might increase, because this behavior seemed to belong to the same response class as yelling. A stimulus control procedure was selected. Mr. A. was assigned a special sulking stool located in the garage. He was free to sulk to his heart's content (p. 119), but had to do so on this sulking stool. When he was finished, he could then leave the garage and join his wife. The stool was deliberately placed in an undesirable location. This procedure was successful in decreasing sulking time, as revealed by his daily records. Stimulus control was also employed to decrease bickering in the bedroom and to increase more pleasant interactions. Since it is easier to develop new behaviors in novel stimulus situations, a stimulus was sought that would alter the room entirely and would be easy to apply and withdraw (Goldiamond, 1965, p. 120). A yellow night light was put in, which was turned on when both felt amorous and was otherwise kept turned off.

Example of a Behavioral Approach to Marital Counseling

The following case was presented by Weiss (1975) and concerns Ellen and Tom, aged twenty-seven and thirty years old, respectively, who had been married for four years and had a two-year-old son and a three-year-old daughter. Ellen was attending college and Tom worked as an accountant. Two meetings were held between the cotherapists and the couple to arrange the collection of self-report inventories, samples of problem-solving interactions (four ten-minute interactions) and spouse observation at home over a two-week period. The values obtained for these measures are presented in Table 13. The Locke-Wallace inventory supported a picture of high marital dissatisfaction, as did the Marital Status Inventory. For example,

Table 13. Pre- and Postintervention Data Comparison

	Husband		Wife	
	Pre	Post	Pre	Post
Self-Report Data				
Locke-Wallace Marital Adjustment	72	77	43	78
Marital Status Inventory (steps to divorce)	4		9	
Areas of change (conflict scores)	23	3	18	2
MAITAI (% activities with spouse of total				
activities)	58%	52%	48%	45%
Laboratory Data (rate/minute)				
Positive responses	1.30	4.25	1.39	4.50
Problem-Solving Statements	.30	1.60	.40	1.00
Positive Social Reinforcement Responses	1.00	2.65	.99	3.50
Negative Responses	.10	.50	.85	.35
Nonspecific Problem Description	2.50	1.60	1.89	1.40
Home Data (mean frequency/day)				
Instrumental Behaviors:				
Pleasing	7.28	10.60	7.42	13.14
Displeasing	3.57	1.00	6.00	.57
Affectional Behaviors:				
Pleasing	4.00	10.10	3.71	11.14
Displeasing	4.14	1.85	3.14	2.14
Shared Recreational Events Perceived as Pleasing	5.80	5.10	2.42	5.43

Source: Weiss (1975, p. 19).

Ellen answered *true* to nine of the fourteen items on the Marital Status Inventory. The scores for areas of change conflict was higher than the mean score previously found for distressed couples (a total of 41). As can be seen from Table 13, the baseline problem-solving sessions, during which they discussed child rearing and sex, revealed a high rate of nonspecific problem description and a low rate of problem-solving statements. Neither was very supportive of the other's behavior during these interactions. Most of their activity together related to the areas of household management and child care, with few affectional or sexual exchanges. They had not had intercourse for the prior two months.

The impression of the counselors was that both were socially skilled individuals, who had, during the course of their marriage, shaped each other to behave in a manner unpleasant to both. The husband described himself as in the powerless position of having to wait for Ellen to initiate sexual activity. His wife viewed him as unspontaneous and unenthusiastic. Tom's labeling of Ellen as "flighty" and "less intelligent" was encouraged by his reinforcement of behaviors that fit such labels. For example, whenever she displayed "little-girl" behaviors, he offered her aid immediately. Cycles seemed to take place in which Tom would take Ellen for granted (for example, he would not help around the house and would not be playful with her). Ellen would then try to woo his attention, and, when this was not successful, would finally express her pessimism about their relationship. This would scare him as to the possible consequences of separation, and he would then become very reinforcing to her. Each struggled to maintain certain strongholds in their relationship. Tom controlled the finances and Ellen's control was maintained through her infrequent interest in sex. Both withheld rather than shared affection. Whenever one partner became very pessimistic about the relationship and started to consider separation, the other became more encouraging. Both were reluctant to end the relationship and said they cared about one another, even when angry. Sexual contact was reported to be very enjoyable when it did take place. Both were reluctant to recognize the association between their own behavior and the downward trend in their marriage. In their view, their marital happiness was subject to unexplainable cycles. Their marital difficulties, as would be expected, caused massive disruptions in their daily lives.

Intervention took place during ten weekly sessions spread over three months, with about three phone calls between each session. Phone contacts lasted about five minutes and sessions between one and two hours. A total of twenty-three hours of time was involved.

Communications training was not carried out with this couple at first, since assessment revealed that both the husband and wife were verbal and socially skilled and it was thought critical to provide immediate therapy benefits. Intervention focused first on increasing positive time together. A list of shared pleasant events was constructed and the first assignment was to increase these and to provide each other with a "love day," defined as a day when one spouse increased his or her rate of pleases, using the other's please list as a guide. This assignment turned out to be premature. Tom and Ellen had difficulty carrying it out and were not excited about it. Each was worried about losing face. Coercive behaviors were far too prevalent and each resented the other for withholding gratifications. Discussion was devoted to try to change attributions of one's distress to the partner as a bad person into consideration of a bad relationship as the culprit. It was pointed out that they had developed unconstructive ways of interacting with each other during the course of their relationship, which led to a lack of gratification for both of them. This pattern, in turn, resulted in feelings of desperation and anger, and they then attacked what seemed to them to be the source of the problem, the other person, rather than their unfortunate habits of interaction. It was stressed that each had to realize that it was *not* the spouse that was the villain, but the habits that prevented marital satisfaction. The cause of their distress was the negative effect of relationship non-payoff.

Following this discussion, the original assignments were reinstated and there was an increase in shared recreational events (from 4.4 to 7.5 per day) over nine days. However the "love days" were again a failure, because of overly high expectations of each other, and this assignment was dropped. A vacation during which Ellen and the children visited her mother offered an opportunity to create more satisfying phone conversation skills. Typically, their phone conversations when apart had been quite aversive. This time, prior to Ellen's departure they developed a menu of telephone pleases and displeases, role played phone calls, and scheduled the calls that occurred. These stimulus control methods were successful in making these calls positive rather than negative events. Following her return, Tom and Ellen were trained in conflict resolution skills, which included teaching them to label communication modes (to discriminate whether a problem-solving or expression mode was appropriate), as well as appropriate reactions within each mode, and teaching ways to offer a "time out" from arguments. This training was initiated to replace their pattern of arguments, in which Ellen would propose an idea that Tom would ignore. Ellen then typically withdrew, which resulted in attempts by

Tom to draw out suggestions, which were then met with Ellen's silence. Tom would then get angry and an argument would ensue. Thus communication training for this couple was brought in at a later point. (Possibly it would have been more effective to introduce this training earlier.) This training resulted in a decrease in the number of arguments and displeases and an increase in their rate of pleases.

The following session was spent discussing the positive happenings of the past week and in forming a contingency matrix (see Table 11 for an example) as a prelude to establishing the first contingency contract. Now that the number of conflicts between the couple had decreased and they could spend more positive time together, the counselor felt it was time to deal with the so far avoided areas of sex, control of finances, and attention. The counselor speculated that the expectations of dealing with these difficult issues led to the decrease in positive events that occurred during the next week. Both expressed increasing dissatisfaction at the next session. The counselor pointed out that he felt this was caused by the inability of the couple to exchange the important reinforcers of sex, money, and affection and that they should begin to contract for such an exchange. As with many couples, a long discussion was required to encourage each person to disclose their own investment in their power situations. This discussion occupied so much of the interview that there was not time to establish a contract.

Prior to the next scheduled meeting, conflicts increased and Ellen announced that she wished to separate. A meeting time was arranged and the possible costs and benefits of separation were discussed. The counselors advised against separation at this time, but assured the couple that they would, of course, respect whatever decision the couple made. They felt that Ellen and Tom had not yet tried to share some of the important gratifications of married life. Ellen was not willing to make a decision and the couple agreed to think about the matter. At home, Tom, who did not wish a separation, increased his attentiveness toward his wife and opened separate checking accounts so his wife could have some influence over the money. This resulted in Ellen wishing to try to work out their problems and they had intercourse for the first time in months. As Weiss (1975) points out, they thus carried out an informal contract. This "high" period was attributed by the couple to the mysterious cycles to which their relationship seemed prone. The counselors, however, pointed out the relationship between their behaviors and these ups and downs, and the need to structure positive events, in order to ensure the regular exchange of important reinforcers. Again, this discussion occupied so much of the interview that there was not time to form a contract and an appointment was scheduled within two days to accomplish this. The first contract formed is shown in Figure 25. This is a good-faith contract making use of external rewards such as reduction in

Figure 25. A Contract for Two Low Base-Rate Behaviors That Symbolized Each Spouse's "Hold Out" in the Relationship. (A $25 Performance Deposit Had Been Required Early in Intervention. Therapists Had Fined Clients the Previous Week for Not Keeping Data for Several Days.)

Consideration and Sex

Wife	Husband
Accelerate	*Accelerate*
1. Initiate one sexual intercourse with Tom	1. Initiate and engage in one 20-minute conversation with six positive statements; for example, "I never thought of that," "That was interesting," "That is a good idea," "That is a new way of looking at it."
2. Engage in one sexual intercourse with husband	2. Initiate and engage in one 20-minute affectional period that will include behaviors like foot rubs and touching and patting
Reward:	*Reward:*
1. One album of Ellen's choice	1. $6 worth of clothing
2. Reduction by $2 of therapist penalty	2. Reduction by $2 of therapist penalty
Penalty:	*Penalty:*
Do dishes for 3 days	Make lunches for 3 days

We the undersigned agree to the conditions of the above contract. We further agree to accept the partner's initiation of the above activities or suggest a more convenient alternate time.

Wife _____   Husband _____

Therapists:

_____   _____

Date _____

Source: Weiss (1975, p. 22).

fees. In such parallel contracts, neither partner has to risk the cost of losing face by going first. The agreements described in the contract were met during the following week, and both partners expressed satisfaction with the program as well as with their relationship.

Two additional contracts were formed during the remaining two sessions, one with the help of the counselor (Figure 26)

Figure 26. Contract for Specific Communication Behaviors
(Attention and Interest)

Conversation Alone and With Others

Wife	Husband
Accelerate:	*Accelerate:*
1. Initiates 3 ten-minute conversations with husband about husband's feelings, thoughts, and so on. Conversation begins with an open-ended question by wife.	1. During one occasion when company is present, husband will bring wife into conversation, make positive statements about her (for example, "That was interesting," "That was a good idea") and do affectional things with her (for example, touch her hair, hold her hand, put his arm around her).
2. During the conversation wife keeps eye contact and makes comments on topic.	2. Husband will do each of the above behaviors at least once for a total of five.
3. If child interrupts the conversation, wife acknowledges the interruption (for example, "I want to finish hearing this but . . ."), attends to child, then returns to the conversation. If the interruption is long, wife brings up the conversation later (for example, "I want to finish hearing about _____")	
Reward:	*Reward:*
Two games of cards of wife's choosing.	During three consecutive mornings wife makes coffee or tea for husband.
Penalty:	*Penalty:*
Wife picks up children's room and living room for 3 consecutive days.	Husband does laundry once.

We the undersigned agree to the conditions of the above contract. We further agree to accept the partner's initiation of the above activities or suggest a more convenient alternate time.

Wife _____   Husband _____

Therapists:

_____   _____

Date _____

Source: Weiss (1975, p. 23).

and one by the couple (Figure 27). Both felt that the contracts so far were very useful in ensuring positive exchanges.

Figure 27. Client-Generated Contract

Companionship and Support for Wife's School Work

Wife	Husband
Accelerate:	*Accelerate:*
Get up with Tom and cook breakfast (3 mornings during the week)	Pick kids up at day care Monday night. Watch kids while wife in class Monday night. Watch kids 5 hours on Sunday
Spouse reward:	*Spouse reward:*
One present costing $3 or less from husband	One present costing $3 or less from wife
Penalty:	*Penalty:*
Sweep, vacuum, dust	Wash and wax floor

We the undersigned agree to the conditions of the above contract. We further agree to accept the partner's initiation of the above activities or suggest a more convenient alternate time.

Wife _____   Husband _____

Therapists:

_____   _____

Date _____

Source: Weiss (1975, p. 23).

Self-report information collected after the last session (see Table 13) revealed positive gains in the Areas of Change Inventory (a postintervention score of 5) and improvements in the Locke-Wallace and Marital Status Inventory. Percentage of activities with spouse compared to total activities decreased after intervention, partly because of Ellen's full-time return to school. Notice that there was disagreement on the way in which shared activities were counted. Postintervention analysis of the couple's problem-solving skills from recorded data were also encouraging, as can be seen in Table 13. The increase of negative responses on the part of Tom, viewed in conjunction with the increase in positive responses, may be due to an overall increase in expressiveness. This finding is in accord with other data, which indicates a decrease in negative reaction from the wife, but either no change, or an increase in negative responses, from the husband. Spouse-recorded measures also reflected an improvement in the relationship.

The influential role of stimulus control in this relationship was highlighted by the fact that discussions leading to "revelations" of the cause of difficulties failed to have an impact on interaction at home (Weiss, 1975). Thus, in spite of their new perceptions of the causes of their distress, when they returned home, the cues occasioned old, inappropriate behaviors. The contracts provided a useful stimulus control function for such behaviors. The relationship between their marital satisfaction and the behavior of the partner was emphasized through tracking pleases and displeases. For this couple, increasing the exchange of affectional events seemed especially important. With other couples, the exchange of instrumental events may be more of an issue.

Brief Reciprocity Counseling

Reciprocity counseling has been successfully carried out over a four-week period with two one-hour meetings each week (Azrin, Naster, and Jones, 1973). One interesting feature of the program designed by Azrin, Naster, and Jones (1973) is use of a contract that does not specify unique relationships between behaviors and reinforcers. A "Current Satisfaction Procedure," in which each person was requested to list ten satisfactions currently received and ten satisfactions currently given to the partner, was employed to increase the awareness of reinforcers already exchanged. This homework assignment was given after some practice in the office with instructions as to how to be specific. The lists developed by each person were read aloud at the next meeting and agreement reached concerning the specific nature and extent of reciprocity that already existed in the marriage. A "Perfect Marriage Procedure" was employed to aid the clients to identify interactions that could be reinforcing to them. Each was asked to list interactions that would represent his or her idea of an ideal marriage for each of nine problem areas (household responsibilities, rearing of children, social activities, money, communication, sex, academic or occupational progress, personal independence, and spouse independence). Instructions were given to be as selfish as possible. This also was given as a homework assignment. The counselor introduced a "Feedback Exchange Procedure" at the next session, in which clients exchanged their Marital Happiness Scale forms for the previous day as a way of informing each person how the mate felt about him or her in relation to each of the nine problem areas. They were requested to exchange these each evening, discuss the ratings, and initial the partner's scale. This enabled each person to assess each day how well he or she had succeeded in pleasing the spouse in each area and to discuss needed points. An "Appreciation Reminder Procedure" was used to encourage each partner to mention to the spouse "any novel, unusual, unanticipated, unscheduled satisfactions given to the spouse such as an unscheduled vacuuming of the house" (Azrin, Naster, and Jones, 1973, p. 372). During the counseling session, each client was asked to offer recent examples of such items and to routinely follow this procedure at home. The clients' success with using this procedure was checked at every session by asking how they were carrying out the procedure and whether they had experienced any problems. The "Fantasy Fulfillment Procedure" was employed during the first session to identify, agree on, and list new satisfactions. First, each person was asked to decide (independently) what his partner could do to increase his own happiness in relation to three problem areas. As in the "Perfect Marriage Procedure," clients were asked to be as selfish as possible. They were asked to do this with the next three problem areas during the second session. When a suggestion was made by one client, the partner was asked by the counselor whether she or he would comply with this. If there was no agreement, compromises were found with the help of the "Frequency Fulfillment Procedure," which helped couples learn that every desire should be fulfilled, at least in part. In this compromise method, the desire was translated into a continuum of possible activities rather than in an all-or-none manner. This might involve different frequencies of a behavior, different durations, or behavior in different situations. The couple was coached to employ this compromise procedure whenever one person refused to comply with a request. Items identified through this procedure as well as by the "Reciprocity Aware-ness Procedure" were attached to a Happiness Contract (see sec-tion on contracts). This contract was reviewed at the second session in order to permit each client to reevaluate satisfactions agreed on in view of the past few days. Each new satisfaction that had been listed was read by the counselor and the person asked whether it was being followed; if not, why not; and whether any changes were desired. At the third session, the "Positive Statement Procedure" was introduced, which required each spouse to add a positive note to any negative statement that he made and if possible, to state this positively in the first place. Each was told to stop the partner whenever a negative statement was made without a positive note and was told that he or she should not respond until a positive note was added or the statement rephrased in a positive way. For example, rather than saying, "That was a dumb thing to say," a positive version would be "That may be true, but did you ever view it from this perspective—?" At the same session, a "Sex Feedback Proce-dure" was introduced, which consisted of giving each client a copy of a marriage manual (Ellis, 1966) in which certain phrases, sentences, and passages were underlined, and asking each client to rate the degree of desirability of the activity on a scale from one to five. Copies were exchanged during the next session and the couple was asked to discuss the ratings. During the fourth session, the "Fantasy Fulfillment Procedure" was continued by asking each person to decide new satisfactions for the last three problem areas. Counselor promptings and instruc-tions were deliberately faded out during this session to enable the couple to learn to carry out this process without counselor help.

Ninety-six percent of the clients reported higher levels of marital happiness as a result of the program. It was not neces-sary to offer reciprocity counseling in all problem areas, because some areas, such as child rearing, were not relevant. Marital hap-piness ratings continued to increase at a one-month follow-up period. This approach minimizes the need for clients to keep records of their behavior and is very short-term in nature. No attempt was made to teach the clients the principles of behav-ior. This program also differs from other behavioral marital counseling procedures in arranging global reinforcers for global responses, use of a subjective outcome measure (self-reported happiness), and requirement of less behavior specification (Azrin, Naster, and Jones, 1973). These characteristics make this program ideal for counseling.

Working with Only One Partner

Ideally, marital counseling involves both partners. However, if one partner refuses to cooperate, even though many attempts have been made to involve him (it usually is a "him"), and if the person who has sought help is considered to be a relatively accurate observer of the marital interaction and can carry out agreed-on assignments fairly well, unilateral intervention may be attempted. For example, Scheiderer and Bernstein (1976) offer a case of a fifty-two-year-old woman, Mrs. X., who originally sought help because of chronic low back pain that had occurred daily since she was fifteen and for which no physical basis could be found. This pain interfered with her freedom of movement in her job as well as with falling asleep at night. She described her marriage as most unsatisfactory, saying that her husband spent his time at work or involved in his hobbies and that they spoke to each other only rarely. Mrs. X. was very sensitive to criticism and did not view herself as competent, in spite of having several good friends and a good relationship with her two college-age daughters.

It was hypothesized that Mrs. X.'s back pain was associated with tension caused by her negative self-evaluation in her marriage and social interactions, and a number of intervention programs were initiated. First, she was trained in progressive relaxation to alleviate her back pain, with emphasis on the lower back, which was tensed through arching. It was assumed that her husband's indifference to her was related to her own low opinion of herself. These thoughts were shared with the client, and she was informed that she could learn to acquire control over her self-evaluative thoughts. A first assignment was to note, in summary form, the antecedents, her overt verbal behavior and thoughts, and the consequences of all social interactions that lasted more than five minutes. "This procedure made Mrs. X. more aware of how she was allowing her own internal evaluative thoughts to supercede the actual feedback she was getting from other people" (Scheiderer and Bernstein, 1976, p. 48). She was also asked to list ten positive self-evaluative statements and to say these covertly (to herself) as appropriate during her interactions. One statement included was, "I'm just as important a person as my husband." She was also asked to make a list of positive things "she could do for and say to other people as well as to herself" (Scheiderer and Bernstein, 1976, p. 48), and to write down examples of positive actions and comments other people offered to her.

Mrs. X. was asked to spend more time with her husband, even if she had to follow him around the house or turn off the television set. Discussion topics included the day's activities, current events, or information offered by friends. Increasing communication would hopefully set the stage to bring up more serious concerns at a later time. Mrs. X., with the help of the counselor, attempted to define problem areas in the marriage and to create programs to increase desirable behaviors. The principles of reinforcement and extinction were shared with her. One objective was to increase the frequency with which her Mr. X. spoke to her in a positive and complimentary way either about things she did well or about routine jobs such as errands and housecleaning. The importance of modeling appropriate behaviors herself was emphasized as well as the need to reinforce his desirable behaviors. She was instructed to ignore unjustified criticism and to tell herself covertly that "she hadn't done anything to justify it," and, if a conversation developed a negative tone, to alter this tone even if she had to change the topic. A menu of reinforcers for her husband was constructed by Mrs. X., including offering him a sandwich or dish of ice cream, doing an errand for him, buying him a small item like a record, and, when she offered one of these reinforcers to him, she was to verbalize the contingency—for example, she might say, "I just wanted to make a pot of coffee for you to show you that I really appreciated your starting the car for me this morning" (Scheiderer and Bernstein, 1976, p. 49).

Assertive training was indicated by Mrs. X.'s reluctance to freely disclose positive thoughts and feelings to her husband as well as by her difficulty in making even small requests of him. Twelve assertive responses were defined and were ranked in order of their difficulty of performance for her. An item of low difficulty was asking her husband to stop at the store on the way home. Telling him that she would accompany him on a vacation only if he agreed to visit her out-of-town relatives was an item with considerably more difficulty. An agreement was made to carry out one response each week, provided she had successfully completed the one for the prior week. Later on, other assertive behaviors were identified related to interactions with her employer.

Mrs. X. also expressed a dissatisfaction with her low frequency of social activities, especially with Mr. X. She had not been successful in trying to involve him in these activities and experienced not only anger and rejection when turned down, but also intensified back pain. The counselor thought that this self-imposed social deprivation contributed to her feelings of being unworthy and undeserving. A program was arranged to provide continued opportunities for Mr. X. to spend more time with his wife, as well as to have Mrs. X. learn that she could go out by herself. She was asked to identify twenty enjoyable activities, such as shopping or going to a movie, and each week to choose one to enjoy alone or with a friend, and one to which she could invite her husband to enjoy with her. Mr. X. "was free to refuse an invitation, but these occasions provided Mrs. X. with experience in accepting a refusal without self-criticism and in selecting an alternative activity" (Scheiderer and Bernstein, 1976, p. 49). This series of programs was carried out over twenty sessions spread over seven months. In addition to the programs mentioned above, a weight reduction program was initiated at the client's request. The frequency and duration of back pain had gradually decreased and written contact six months after termination indicated that she had no further back problems. Beneficial changes also occurred in the marriage. These as well as other changes are described in the following quotation from Scheiderer and Bernstein (1976, pp. 49-50):

> Mr. and Mrs. X. spent every evening meal together as well as a period of at least 30 minutes dis-

cussing the day's events, problem solving, or listening to music. Once a week, they went to a social function, for example, a dog show, the movies, a restaurant, or an office party. Mrs. X. described the changes as a return to "courting days" and the changes were best illustrated by their decision to resume sexual intercourse (usually once a week) after several years' abstinence. Her weight had decreased from 220 pounds to 175 pounds.

Mrs. X. also became more at ease in social activities whether alone or with a friend. She joined a history club and the U.S.O., and was able to develop two new close friendships. She reported feeling more comfortable with other people in public and could state her opinion without fear of criticism. She engaged in one social activity per week alone, with a friend, or in conjunction with a social organization.

As a result of her experience as a behavioral engineer, Mrs. X. was much more aware of how other people's behavior interacted in a complex way with her own. Thus she no longer labeled herself the sole cause of her problems. It was suggested that because she had learned many specific skills which could be helpful to other people, she might consider joining some type of volunteer organization (for example, a "hotline" for distressed people or "mental hospital companion") and thus utilize her listening skills. She was aware of her limitations as a "therapist," but felt very self-confident in her interactions with other people, and proud that the therapist had made this suggestion.

Many behavioral programs for improving marital interaction refuse to accept a case if one spouse will not participate. This places the partner that is seeking help in a most unfortunate situation. However, only if it is decided that the requisites for working successfully with only one partner are present should an agreement be made to pursue changes in this unilateral fashion. Prerequisites include accurate observation of the marital interaction and ability to identify problems and to implement programs. Although only one spouse is involved in the program, the focus is on the marital *interaction*.

Marital Therapy in Groups

Liberman (1975) has designed a workshop for couples in which three to four couples meet for ten weekly sessions with two counselors. The aims of this Married Couples Workshop are "to help make bad marriages good and good marriages better." It is explained to the couple that marital conflict and dissatisfaction take place under the following conditions: if too few pleasing behaviors are offered; if pleasing exchanges are limited to only one area; if pleasing behaviors and events that do occur are taken for granted or ignored and as a result, fewer and fewer occur; if one partner offers many more pleases than he or she receives; or if aversive control (such as criticism, tantrums, nagging, threats, or violence) is used to obtain desired outcomes. The objectives to be achieved during the course of the workshop are clearly identified, and include getting clients to understand the concept of reciprocity; to increase the range of social, emotional, and instrumental behaviors that please their partner; to acknowledge and reinforce the pleasing behaviors of the partner; and to achieve competency in a variety of verbal and nonverbal communication skills. The following skills are taught (see Liberman, 1975, pp. 3-4):

Giving pleases to spouse; acknowledging pleases from spouse; requesting pleases (including physical affection) from spouse in direct, assertive manner; expressing empathy by giving accurate feedback to spouse on what spouse said and felt; expressing negative feelings and thoughts to spouse in a direct, assertive, spontaneous, and nonaccusative manner; requesting pleasing alternatives or the termination of negatives in a direct, assertive manner; coping with unexpected or persistent hostility or negatives by:

1. Turning interaction into mutually pleasing subjects or activities
2. Giving repeated and persistent pleases even in the face of hostility
3. Taking a time-out
4. Giving empathy

In addition, couples learn what the components of contingency contracts are, how to write one, and how to monitor adherence to contract terms.

Screening of prospective group members is recommended. Requirements for group participation include participation of both spouses; their verbal acknowledgment of interest in joining the workshop; their willingness to commit themselves to remaining together for the duration of the workshop; agreement to refrain from discussing the past following the first session and to focus instead on the present and future; to pay a fifteen-dollar "good-faith" contingency deposit, one dollar of which is returned for each session attended and the full amount if all sessions are attended; and agreement to attend sessions, participate in group exercises, and complete homework assignments.

First Session. The rationale of the procedures employed during the workshop is explained in the first session: that "love consists of a reasonably mutual and equal giving and getting of pleasing behaviors between partners and that each person's needs and desires can be met only to the extent that the other person's needs and desires are met also" (Liberman, 1975, p. 11). Each person is asked to take home and fill out the Areas of Change Inventory and Marital Adjustment Scale. Written instructional materials are used throughout to complement verbal information given during group discussions.

Ground rules established for sessions include offering each couple fifteen minutes to report on their progress, assignments, or problems, provided they have completed their homework assignment. If assignments have not been completed, they are allowed only five minutes. Participants are informed that the group leader will interrupt any person who uses gunnysacking or starts talking about the past. (The term *gunnysacking* refers to unloading negatives on a partner.) The rationale for using a group setting is described. Each participant then receives an opportunity to specify behaviorally a goal or problem. Prompting and models are employed to encourage selection of positive alternative goals. Information from the scales completed prior to this session can be employed by the leader in helping each couple in their problem defining and goal setting.

The concept of reciprocity is explained and participants are given a handout describing "Recording of pleases" and a list of pleases. Each member is asked to review this handout and to identify ones that are important to him or her. The first homework assignment is given, in which each spouse is to list ten pleases that he or she thinks that he or she is giving and ten pleases that she or he thinks she or he is receiving. Partners are encouraged to catch their partner doing something nice and to share this with their partner. As a second homework assignment each is to note and record each day at least one please received from the spouse. Participants are encouraged to be sure to acknowledge pleases received. A third assignment requests each person to indicate, for each of eight potential problem areas such as money and leisure time, the type of interaction that would make their marriage seem perfect. During the first session, couples also receive instructions on how to initiate and acknowledge pleases. Also, the importance of *how* things are said rather than why things are said is stressed. Models are presented and nonverbal behaviors are emphasized, including eye contact or looking, postural orientation, appropriate facial expression, and gestures. In this session each participant receives at least one practice turn in giving and acknowledging a please. In a fourth assignment, each spouse is to practice, at home, giving and acknowledging pleases three times daily.

Second Session. At the beginning of the second session, each spouse is asked to read out loud the ten pleases she or he currently gives to and receives from his or her spouse. This provides an opportunity to further prompt and model behavioral precision in definitions. The pleases each spouse received during the week are then reviewed, which provides further opportunity to check on specificity. The feelings that these received pleases engender are also explored. Appropriate questions and comments by group members are encouraged in all sessions. The first homework assignment for the second session is given—to chart at least one daily please and to exchange and discuss each night the pleases exchanged. Next, attempts of each person to offer to acknowledge pleases from his partner is reviewed. Particular attention is devoted to those couples in the group who complete assignments.

Another task during the second session engages each spouse in listing one new please he would like from his or her partner. This "Fantasy Fulfillment Procedure" is used as a prelude to developing a contingency contract, and tries to point out that "any desire or fantasy sought from the marriage is capable of fulfillment at least in part" (Liberman, 1975, pp. 25-26). Each stated interest is translated into possible activities, in contrast with the usual "all-or-none" character of marital conflict. For example, if one person desires more independence and time to work on hobbies, the leader might help him translate this general goal into explicit requirements, including definition of how often, duration of aloneness, and place where this will occur. A couple may agree that the husband will spend thirty minutes three times a week in the garage working on his hobbies. Couples are then assisted to compromise and agree on giving the spouse an aspect of the fantasy. Assignment two commits each to carry out at least one of the agreed-on desires.

Throughout the program the relation between behavior change and how one feels about someone is emphasized—that behavior change is a route to emotional change. During the second session, Liberman also shows a film that depicts various ways to ask for affection and how to terminate undesired physical contact without hurting the partner's feelings, as well as how to acknowledge positive contact. Couples then engage in a hand massage exercise for the purpose of learning how to ask for physical pleasures and how to offer verbal feedback during physical contact. Prompting and modeling are liberally employed during the practice session. Group leaders then model appropriate and inappropriate ways to ask for sexual contact and couples take turns role playing these ways while group members supply feedback. The third assignment is to practice asking for and giving physical affection and providing verbal feedback at least five minutes a day.

Third Session. At the beginning of the third session each spouse is asked to read the pleases received during the week and to share how he or she felt and how he or she acknowledged the pleases. An assignment is given to continue charting daily pleases and to acknowledge them as well as to exchange charts nightly for discussion. Each couple then describes to the group how they exchanged behaviors, activities, or tangible reinforcers in the "Fantasy Fulfillment Procedure." If the couple had trouble, the leader tries to help, for example, by encouraging the spouse to select a more modest approximation to fantasy. For example, "Instead of wife agreeing to initiate sex once a week, she might agree to initiate a hug or kiss" (Liberman, 1975, p. 32). The physical contact assignment is reviewed, stressing that positive feedback in relation to hugs and kisses have as much impact as such feedback during sexual intercourse. The leader may ask a successful couple to model the physical pleasuring they practiced during the week. If a couple had trouble, the leader attempts to identify the specific problems and deficits and employs behavior rehearsal to develop more appropriate behaviors. Leaders are coached to accept "small improvements; . . . to avoid intellectualizing, rationalizing, and other forms of verbal game playing, and to get to the behavioral level: practice, prompt, model, give positive feedback, and give assignments" (Liberman, 1975, p. 33).

The importance of the daily exchange of positive statements and actions is further highlighted by discussing progress in giving and acknowledging pleases. Couples are asked to role play some of their interactions. Training in appropriate communication skills is continued during this session, with an emphasis on teaching participants how to express negative feelings without hurting their partner and how to acknowledge such feelings. Appropriate and inappropriate behaviors are first identified and modeled by the group leaders. Appropriate behaviors include being direct, owning up to feelings, being spontaneous, and being assertive. Inappropriate behaviors include being indirect, being accusatory, gunnysacking (storing up grievances), withdrawing, sulking, and being aggressive (Liberman, 1975).

Each couple is then given an opportunity to rehearse a situation (one that has occurred recently) related to the expression of negative feelings. The recipient of the information is asked to share with the group how he or she felt, in order to highlight the fact that negative feelings can be shared in such a way that they do not hurt and anger. As always, prompting, further modeling, and feedback are offered as needed during and following each role play. The same sequence is followed for acknowledging negative feelings. Reading may be assigned from the Minnesota Couples Communication Program (MCCP).

Guidelines are offered for discussion of negative feelings. These include the following points: (1) What to talk about (discussing only one, specific issue); (2) how to talk (owning one's feelings; expressing feelings directly; giving positive feedback; and practicing empathy, which helps to slow down conversations); (3) when to talk (a time should be set that is mutually convenient and when interruptions are unlikely); (4) where to talk (distracting places such as at a party should be avoided); (5) duration (the couple should decide in advance on the duration of the discussion, as well as on rules for the conversation); and (6) termination (agreeing that stopping the discussion need not be an end to the discussion of issues) (Liberman, 1975). An assignment is given for each couple to practice having such a session for five to ten minutes each day. One spouse is to first share a negative feeling, while the other tries to respond with reflection, shared meaning, empathy, and checking out. When the partner sharing the negative feeling is satisfied that his partner understands how he feels, the partner then shares a negative feeling.

Fourth Session. At the beginning of the fourth session, each client reads the pleases received during the past week. As usual, these are reviewed to make sure they are specific, that they were acknowledged, and to see how the recipient felt. The same homework assignment is repeated: to continue to record pleases, to acknowledge them, to exchange record sheets each night, and to discuss pleases exchanged. Homework assignments regarding expression of negatives is reviewed and each couple is given an opportunity to role play an example. Each participant is also given an opportunity to rehearse appropriate forms of negative expression, using a real situation from their relationship. Emphasis is placed on the importance of empathic reactions, reflection, and requests for clarification in slowing down exchanges so they do not escalate. A second assignment is given: to continue daily practice sessions in sharing negatives.

Contingency contracting is introduced at the fourth session, the rationale for this explained, and the steps involved identified. The counselor points out that this procedure will provide a way to gain agreement concerning issues that once produced discord and that each couple will learn to compromise where each partner feels that he or she gets something by giving up something (Liberman, 1975). The steps involved in this training process include selecting items (behaviors or events) that each person thinks will please his or her partner; requesting feedback from the partner on pleases selected; and selecting items pleasing to oneself and explaining why they would be pleasing. Items are then ordered in terms of desirability as well as cost (responsibilities). The last step is to negotiate and identify for each privilege and responsibility how frequently, how much, when, where, and with whom.

In selecting responsibilities for oneself, each person looks through a list of cards describing various behaviors and events and selects one that he or she thinks will please his or her partner. This is read out loud to the group and the person explains why he or she thinks it will be pleasing to the partner. Items written on the cards should be specified. The partner then indicates whether this behavior or event would in fact be pleasing. Feedback may indicate that the behavior is unacceptable, in which case another card is selected. Feedback from the group is useful in making sure that behaviors or events selected are realistic. If the partner does accept the selected behavior or item, this card is then placed under the category of responsibilities. A blackboard can be used to note items selected. The next step entails selecting a responsibility for the partner. Each participant selects a card that indicates some behavior or event that would be pleasing to him- or herself and reads this card aloud. If agreed to, the card is given to the partner, who places it under his responsibilities list. (Leaders should make sure that items selected are possible, that is, have a good likelihood of happening.) The first two steps are then repeated. At the end of this exercise each spouse has two well-defined behaviors listed as responsibilities.

The next task, called "Building Empathy," entails spouses sharing with each other how each would feel if the behaviors were actually carried out. Each person is requested to indicate how much value each listed behavior has and how hard it would be to carry out. Responsibilities are ranked in terms of how difficult they would be to actually carry out. Each couple goes through this process in front of the rest of the group. A last assignment is given in which each spouse is to select one day during the week as a "love day" during which she or he increases the number of pleases offered the partner. Examples might include extra hugs and kisses, cooking a special meal, or washing the dishes.

Fifth Session. At the beginning of the fifth session, daily charting of pleases is reviewed by each spouse and pleases received are read aloud. As always, members are encouraged to use great detail and asked to share how they acknowledged the pleases. Sessions in which sharing of negative feelings was practiced are reviewed to make sure these are going well. Couples who have done well are asked to role play an interaction in front of the group. Training in asking for pleases is then initiated. The leader models appropriate ways of asking, and couples are given strategies for responding both negatively and positively to such requests. It is important "to demonstrate and instruct each spouse in how to say no without sounding angry, inciting rejection, or cycling into recriminations" (Liberman, 1975, p. 54). Each couple is given an opportunity to role play asking for a please and saying no in response. Types of pleases that are difficult to request for each person are discussed. Responsibilities selected during the fourth session are reviewed for their appropriateness. Couples that may not have had an opportunity to complete this step are provided with one. Assignments include the following: (1) daily charting of pleases; (2) daily sessions in which each couple practices asking for pleases and if necessary responding assertively with no; (3) a weekly love day for each person; (4) sharing of negative feelings on an "as-needed" basis. It is emphasized that the spouse with the negative feeling has the obligation of indicating to the partner that he or she wishes to share a negative. Discussion will be required to identify negatives that should be ignored and those that should not. If something really bothers a person, or if small annoyances such as leaving clothes on the floor are likely to pile up into a larger annoyance, they should be mentioned. However, some people may have a tendency to make too much of small things that should be ignored. Couples are instructed that when one has to say no, offering some alternative to the denied request can help to sustain reciprocity. For example, a husband could constructively say no to his wife's request for sexual intercourse and maintain reciprocity by adding, "I feel too tired today because of a tough time at work, but I would like to sit next to you on the sofa with my arms around you and listen to some music" (Liberman, 1975, p. 57).

Sixth Session. Review of daily charting of pleases is carried out at the beginning of the sixth session and couples are asked whether their feelings are beginning to match noticing of partner pleases. When one spouse complains that the partner is not doing his assignments, the aggrieved party is encouraged to express his hurt and negative feelings in a direct way. The counselor emphasizes that each person progresses at a different rate. Group members can also be used to provide appropriate feedback to both the recalcitrant and the compliant spouse. Contingency contracting is continued by first choosing a privilege for the self. This may consist of some behavior of the self, some behavior of the spouse, or some solitary or mutual activity that would be pleasing. Each is encouraged to ask, "What would I be willing to work for?" Some activity may be chosen that is already being sampled, but that the person would like at an increased frequency or duration. A wife, for example, may currently give her husband one five-minute back massage per week and he may select two fifteen-minute back massages per week. Again, specification is very important, including "where, when, how often, and with whom." These specifics are noted down on cards. The group, as well as the spouse, participates in assessing how realistic each selected privilege is, and the spouse must agree with the selection. Each spouse then selects a privilege for the other. The partner is free to accept, reject, or modify the selected item. If the item is accepted, the partner indicates how this would be pleasing to him or her. The item selected is given to the partner and he places this in his privilege stack and ranks it in terms of its importance.

Negotiation training is initiated during this session and each couple is helped to establish a contingency contract entailing the exchange of at least one responsibility and privilege. Couples are reminded to employ the communication skills they have been learning in this process. One format for carrying this out is for each couple to go through the process in front of the group, with the leaders prompting them as needed. Group members are reminded that both responsibilities and privileges must be specific, so that each person understands to what he is committing himself, and they must be realistic and accepted by the partner. The rules for contingency contracting are also spelled out; that is, partners must understand that the privilege is contingent on the agreed responsibility being carried out. Different privileges or responsibilities may be selected if desired at this point. The contract agreed on is to be in effect for one week. It is thus important that responsibilities and privileges could indeed occur during a one-week period. Parallel contracts are used rather than quid pro quo contracts; thus, the responsibilities of one partner cannot be the other person's privileges, because the other may not have carried out his or her responsibility and so may not have earned the privilege. Each person has the option of fulfilling the terms of his or her contract or of not doing so. One spouse may fulfill his or her contract while the other spouse does not (Liberman, 1975, p. 77). The contracts formed for each couple are typed, and signed by both parties.

Remaining time in this session is employed to rehearse any communication skills couples are having trouble with. As always, leaders intervene quickly to discourage complaints about failures and do not spend too much time on resistant clients. Assignments for the next week include charting of pleases and exchanging forms at the end of the day and discussing these, setting weekly love days, discussing compliance with the contingency contract, and monitoring degree of compliance and daily practice of communication skills.

Seventh Session. Daily pleases are reviewed in the usual manner in the seventh session. Daily recording of pleases can be faded out for successful couples, although couples may wish to continue this process as prompting for reciprocity needs. Each member of the couple then reports on the extent of his or her partner's compliance with the contract, whether she or he completed responsibilities and sampled privileges. Reported dissatisfactions are employed as a cue to ask the couples to practice their communication skills in trying to refine their contracts in a more satisfying direction. If any couple finds contracting very aversive, the matter is not pushed. Communication skills discussed during the sessions are reviewed and each couple is given an opportunity to rehearse a situation in which one of these skills should be employed, using real-life situations. Couples who report success can be asked to role play an example. This will provide a model for other group members and will help the group to identify problem areas that may not have been noticed. During this review of skills, leaders reinforce closer approximations to desired behaviors. Assignments include continuation of recording of pleases or their gradual fading out. Couples could, for example, record these only every other day. Weekly love days are to be continued and the same or revised contingency contract is agreed to and is to be monitored. Couples are also urged to use their communication skills daily.

Eighth Session. In the eighth session, homework assignments are reviewed with each couple being allowed about ten to fifteen minutes. Communications skill training is continued, this time emphasizing skills to employ in dealing with hostility, anger, and bad moods. Situations that may induce these feelings are discussed, including aversive experiences outside of the family or failure of a partner to carry out a promise. The leader identifies appropriate and inappropriate ways of dealing with such situations and models these. Examples of incorrect reactions include escalating the discussion with negative comments or angry remarks, saving up recriminations and unloading them all at once, withdrawing, or sulking, reassurance, or reasoning. Correct reactions include offering of pleases, diversion to some mutually enjoyable activity, brief time-out periods, and the use of empathic reactions. Appropriate reactions may be linked together. For example, a brief time out may be employed, followed by suggestions of a diverting activity. If time out is used, members of couples are coached to inform their partners where they are going, when they will return, to share feelings as to why they are going out, and to show willingness to talk about the issue at a later time. Couples are discouraged from using generalizations (such as, "You're always angry"), invoking recriminations, or sulking in response to anger. Each person is then asked to select some situation where he or she was confronted with hostility, displaced anger, or a bad mood; to demonstrate how the situation is usually handled; and then to practice a more appropriate way. Assignments for the ninth session include noticing and verbally acknowledging pleases from partners. Continuation of a contract is optional. However, couples are encouraged to negotiate agreements as differences and conflicts arise. The various steps involved in contingency contracting—pinpointing of behavior, empathizing, negotiating, and compromising—should be used as a tool for conflict resolution (Liberman, 1975). Couples are also encouraged to continue using communication skills.

Ninth Session. In the ninth session, assignments are reviewed, including use of reciprocity awareness, communication skills, and contingency contracts. A new area introduced during this session concerns distribution of time for family, social, and recreational activities. This area is broken into four parts: (1) time for being alone and for doing activities, singly or with other friends outside of any other family member; (2) time for doing things together with spouse—just the couple alone; (3) time for doing things together with spouse and children—family alone or with other families and children; and (4) time for doing things with spouse and other couples without children. The importance of distributing time among areas is emphasized, and each person is asked to make an impromptu inventory of how he currently distributes his time and to offer suggestions for improvements. The remaining part of the session is devoted to problem solving or reciprocity enhancing. Assignments are optional at this point, with the one exception that each group member selects something that he or she will do between now and the final meeting two weeks away.

Tenth Session. In the tenth session, assignments are reviewed. Major areas covered during the group meetings are reviewed to identify areas that need further discussion, rehearsal, prompting, or model presentation. For example, each couple is asked how it is doing in the area of communication skills. Group members are encouraged to employ the group leaders as consultants "in behaviorally specific ways." For example, a wife may specify, "I'd like some help in learning how to ask my husband to do some favors for me," rather than saying, "I want to be able to make my husband nicer to me" (Liberman, 1975, p. 95).

Guidelines for Maintaining Positive Changes

Positive changes will only be maintained if they continue to be reinforced. Thus, in behavioral counseling programs, spouses are encouraged to continue to offer positive statements in relation to behaviors of their spouses that please them—without, of course, offering these so frequently they become unpleasant rather than pleasant. Partners are encouraged to try to discover new ways to show their mates that they appreciate various behaviors. Periodic discussions between mates in which they share positives exchanged during the day or week may also help to remind each person to reinforce pleasant events from the other. It is all too easy to start to take pleasurable events for granted, rather than as events to be earned and appreciated for their being offered. Learning to establish norms for decision making hopefully will decrease arguments about areas that have been identified as too unimportant to argue about. An emphasis on ending arguments in a positive way—that is, to arrive at a mutually satisfactory plan of action, rather than concentrating on winning—will also help to maintain positive communication modes. Gottman and his colleagues (1976) recommend selecting items from a "fun deck" of cards, each of which contains some activity that might be fun to do together, such as baking bread or going on a picnic. As one participant said, this is a positive version of Russian roulette. Recognizing that one will actually never know all facets of another person will hopefully encourage an ongoing curiosity about what the other person thinks, feels, does, and fantasizes about. Maintaining the ability to discriminate negative and positive hidden agendas may also help to maintain positive interactions. This skill may be maintained by occasionally monitoring the frequency of positive and negative thoughts about the spouse or the frequency of positive and negative spouse behaviors. If the negative behaviors or thoughts are found to be high, this should cue self-exploration for possible negative hidden agendas, perhaps caused by a failure to "level" with the partner or to a failure to reinforce the partner for positive changes. The data that indicate a greater number of positives offered to strangers than to the partner even in happy marriages (Birchler, Weiss, and Vincent, 1975) signal the need to occasionally monitor the frequency of positives and to ensure that this remains high. Scanning of a checklist of helpful and dysfunctional communication behaviors may help to cue a partner to desist from negative behaviors and to increase positive behaviors. A number of additional helpful guidelines for maintaining positive changes are offered by Stuart and Lederer (in press). Randomly scheduled "love days" may also serve to highlight the positives one partner offers to another.

When Separation is Decided On

Counseling may result in a decision to separate. Given that each person will be able to construct a happier existence via such separation, this decision should certainly not be considered a failure either by the counselor or by the partners. What is needed at this point may be a discussion of factors that may make separation easier for the couple. Information concerning economic matters, means of forming new social contacts, child care, and so forth, has been found to be an important aspect of separation counseling (Weiss, 1975). Training partners in stress management and problem-solving skills may be indicated if anxiety increases during this period (see Chapter Twelve).

Summary

The application of behavioral principles to the field of marital interaction is fairly new. However, in the short history of such efforts, some promising procedures have emerged. There is an emphasis on the pleasurable behaviors exchanged by mates, in offering clients skills that will permit them to recognize satisfactions already exchanged and to identify and offer new satisfactions. Integral ingredients of behavioral programs include helping couples to be specific in relation to the changes they would like to see and offering them more positive ways to communicate with each other. Both skills are considered to be essential to offer new satisfactions that may be required during the career of a marriage that is considered to be an emergent rather than a fixed one. Contracts are often employed as a tool to help couples learn to exchange more positive events, and clients are coached to gradually assume more responsibility for identifying important contract components. As with other behavioral procedures, there is an emphasis on increasing positive events rather than on decreasing negative events, although, because exchanges of negative and positive events do not seem necessarily to be related, if negative events are predominant, intervention should also consider this fact.

11

Anxiety is a cause of discomfort to clients seen in a wide variety of settings. Because a typical consequence of anxiety is avoiding situations that contain anxiety-eliciting events, these reactions are not only discomforting, but also usually entail curtailment of activities that may be limiting in terms of lost opportunities for enjoyment and achievement. Unadaptive anxiety is defined as reactions that are evoked in situations in which there is no objective reason for anxiety, or anxiety that is out of proportion to the presenting situation (Wolpe and Lazarus, 1966). There is usually no objective reason to feel extreme discomfort when in the presence of authority figures, when a few blocks from home, or when seeing a tiny spider. Reasonable discomfort may sometimes be advantageous, such as when parking your car in a dark city lot in the evening; however, refusal to leave home because of high fear in such situations is limiting indeed.

Anxiety Reduction Procedures for Specific Stressors

Anxiety has been found to be a contributing factor in a wide range of presenting problems including depressive reactions (Wolpe and Lazarus, 1966), obsessive-compulsive behavior (Walton and Mather, 1963), and excessive alcohol consumption (Kraft and Al-Issa, 1967). Such reports emphasize the prevalence of anxiety reactions and their role in maintaining other problematic behavior, and point to the need to ensure that these reactions are not overlooked in assessment.

Behavioral Components of Anxiety Responses

Anxiety is viewed as a learned behavior that is composed of different types of reactions (cognitive, affective, and behavioral) that may or may not be closely related. For example, someone may report high fear, but may not display it when

439

confronted with an actual situation. The complex nature of fear is highlighted by the frequent finding that verbal reports of improvement lag behind decreases in avoidance behavior (Lang, 1968). The organization of fear reactions and the order in which they change are unique for each person. The particular pattern displayed by the client must be identified. This may include verbal reports of fear, motor components, and somatic changes (Lang, 1968). The person may say "I am afraid of . . ." (verbal component). The verbal aspect of anxiety may also be shown in disturbances in speech patterns. Certain situations, objects, or people may be avoided (motor component). Muscular and autonomic concomitants of anxiety, the somatic component, may be displayed by changes in respiration, cardiac rate, and blood pressure, and by a decrease in skin resistance. Cognitions often play an important role in the development and maintenance of anxiety reactions, and attending to them may be critically important to alter anxiety. Some writers, such as Bandura (in press), assume that potential threats are activated mostly through cognitive self-arousal. "Perceived threats activate defensive behavior because of their predictive value rather than their aversive quality" (Bandura, in press, p. 36).

It is not uncommon to find a verbal and somatic component, but not a motor component; that is, anxiety-eliciting events are not avoided. This may occur in situations in which positive reinforcers are present. Social gatherings may provoke anxiety; however, the presence of attractive females may result in approaching these situations in spite of discomfort. Or, avoidance behavior may not occur because behavior is maintained by negative reinforcement unrelated to the anxiety-arousing events. A teacher may feel great anxiety on speaking before his class, yet do so to avoid being fired.

The Development and Maintenance of Anxiety

Either external or internal events, such as physiological reactions or thoughts, may become associated with anxiety reactions (Schachter, 1966). These events assume three functions. They elicit anxiety, cue avoidance behavior, and reinforce negativity. The anxiety reaction, as well as the avoidance behavior, may be labeled *fear*. This self-label may be applied in other instances and itself become an eliciting event for anxiety. It is thus usually through a conditioning history that events acquire the capacity to elicit anxiety. An important part of this history concerns self-statements that are learned in relation to various situations, perhaps through modeling. The manner in which a person thinks about given events is often related to anxiety (Meichenbaum, 1975b; Ellis, 1962). Events in one system—the behavioral, the autonomic, or the verbal—may be cues for reactions in other systems. If a person has a fear of spiders, he may not take vacations in the country. If social events are feared, such as parties, he may not attend such functions. Avoidance behavior allows the person either to escape from unpleasant situations or to avoid exposure to them. Avoidance also precludes non-anxiety-provoking exposure to these events, which might decrease anxiety. Such behavior conserves the potential for given events to elicit anxiety.

Anxiety may be related to behavior deficits and to attention from significant others, as illustrated by the following case. Maria was a twenty-nine-year-old woman who had dropped out of law school because of extreme anxiety in test situations. She intensely disliked her current job and was debating about whether to reenter law school. She was most apprehensive about pursuing this alternative, because of her previous panic reactions in test situations. Initial interviews revealed that Maria lacked study skills. She organized her time poorly and she did not arrange her environment so as to limit distractions. She received a great deal of attention from her boy friend concerning her fears and her decision as to whether to return to school. This topic occupied much of their conversational time. She was concerned that unless he felt sorry for her and viewed her in a "helpless role" she would not be able to maintain his interest.

In this situation, poor study skills prevented Maria from efficiently and enjoyably preparing for examinations. Knowing that she was not well prepared contributed to her test anxiety. Verbal reports of anxiety were heavily reinforced by an important significant other. If behavior deficits or reactions of significant others are related to anxiety, special procedures are required, as illustrated in the case example on pp. 485-488.

Verbal reports of fear may relieve the person from carrying out distasteful tasks. A woman who complains that she is fearful of going far from home may no longer have to do the shopping or pick up the children. Such reports may preclude behaviors that, although to some degree pleasurable, may also be followed by unpleasant responses from significant others. A woman may develop anxieties at the time she is thinking about taking on a career outside of the home if she anticipates negative reactions from family members (Fodor, 1974). Thus conflictual decisions may be avoided through anxieties.

Bandura (in press) has recently proposed a theory of self-efficacy that relates to the development, maintenance, and alteration of anxiety reactions. He says, "It is hypothesized that expectations of personal efficacy determine whether coping behavior will be initiated, how much effort will be expended, and how long it will be sustained in the face of obstacles and aversive experiences" (Bandura, in press). Four sources of information are presumed to relate to one's expectations of self—efficacy, including performance accomplishments, vicarious experiences, verbal persuasion, and physiological states. An efficacy expectation is defined as the conviction that one can successfully execute a behavior to produce a desired outcome. In concert with this proposal, intervention procedures, including those developed to decrease defensive behavior, are conceived of as ways of creating and strengthening expectations of personal efficacy.

Establishing a New Conceptualization of Anxiety

If anxiety is of concern, and if its central role is not evident to the client, its contribution to the problematic behavior should be described. Unadaptive anxiety is presented as a learned reaction, which is elicited in situations in which it is not objectively called for, in that no real danger exists (Wolpe, 1958). The dangers are often literally in the client's mind, in the form of anticipated unpleasant consequences and negative evaluations. Such thoughts can be demonstrated by asking the client to share what goes through his mind in anticipation of, in the presence of, and following anxiety-eliciting events (Meichenbaum, 1975b). What does he tell himself? The self-defeating and self-fulfilling nature of these thoughts, including the helpless stance that they imply, are emphasized. It is obvious that thoughts such as "I am really dumb," and "Nobody likes me," or "I really blew that one," are not geared to inspire confidence and bravery. Focus on thoughts that are related to anxiety reactions highlights the client's role in the maintenance of such reactions and leads naturally to an emphasis on the development of anxiety management skills. Anxiety is presented as an opportunity to employ coping skills, as a reminder that such skills should be used (Suinn and Richardson, 1971; D'Zurilla, 1969; Meichenbaum, 1975b).

Assessment

The conditions in which anxiety is *currently* experienced must be ascertained, as well as variables that may aggravate or attenuate it. Essentially, a process of discrimination training is involved in isolating anxiety sources (Lang, 1968). The client is gradually trained to discriminate the crucial events related to anxiety. It is by no means always easy to determine these events. Many sessions may be required to ferret out relevant sources.

Either external or internal events may elicit anxiety (Wolpe and Lazarus, 1966). The first class refers to those in the external environment, such as heights and people, and the second class to thoughts or physiological reactions, such as feelings of dizziness or rapid heart beats. Thoughts are a crucial mediating component of anxiety in relation to external events, as illustrated in the following example.

Ralph was a thirty-seven-year-old chemical engineer who was unable to accept many jobs because of his fear of riding elevators. When approaching an elevator, he would have a series of thoughts such as, "I wonder when this elevator was last inspected? What if the cable breaks? The elevator will smash against the floor. What if it gets stuck between floors and the doors won't open?" The range of situations in which negative thoughts occur is determined and the client learns to identify the contributions of his own thinking style to his anxiety.

What originally may appear as a number of separate

anxiety sources may all be related to one theme. Situations such as a friend passing by without saying hello, not receiving an invitation to a party, and being interrupted during a conversation may all be interpreted as rejection and as indicating that the person is "no good." If a theme is multidimensional in relation to anxiety, the dimensions may be aspects of the event itself; for example, if fear of authority figures is the problem, the aspects may be their position, sex, age, or factors other than possible dimensions of the class. For example, no fear of authority figures may be felt when a man feels that he look particularly good on a given day. These other factors, like characteristics of the event itself, may either increase or decrease anxiety.

Experimental studies and clinical reports indicate that it is not necessary to determine the origin of the anxiety reaction, or to explore its possible "unconscious meaning," in order to alter the reaction. The origin may be lost in the learning history of the person, or the factors responsible for its current maintenance may be different from those at work when it was established.

Appropriate thought patterns and behaviors should be noted during assessment so that they can be encouraged. That is, the clinical potential of the client's imagery and self-instructional capabilities is assessed (Meichenbaum, 1975a). Can the client cope well in some stressful situations, and if so, how does he do this? It is also important to determine the client's self-reinforcement pattern. Does he use reasonable standards to give himself pats on the back or are his standards overly demanding and therefore prohibitive of a high frequency of positive statements? Does he dilute his coping skills by inappropriately attributing them to external factors rather than to his own capabilities?

Information pertinent to locating anxiety-eliciting events and coping patterns can be obtained from a variety of sources, including counselor questions, self-report inventories, information gathered by the client in the natural environment, or arranged situations in the office, including imagery assessment, in which the client is asked to imagine himself in the situation together with accompanying feelings, thoughts, and behaviors.

The lack of correlation between various measures of anxiety calls for the use of multiple sources of information.

Self-Report and Self-Monitoring. An overview of the client's life-style, in terms of work, family, recreation, and social life may provide clues concerning factors related to anxiety. Useful questions include the following: "When did you first notice this reaction?" "What seems to make it worse?" "Are there any things that make it less intense?" "What have you tried that seems to help?" "Would you feel more or less anxious if . . . ?" "If you found yourself in _____ situation, would you be anxious?" "What goes through your mind in this situation?" "In what other situations do you feel anxiety?" "Can you give me an example of when you last experienced this?" The more specific the question in terms of the situation involved, the more likely the client will be able to provide accurate information in terms of his response in that situation. Initially, clients often incorrectly discriminate sources related to anxiety reactions. An imagery procedure, in which the client closes his eyes and tries to vividly imagine a situation, is often helpful in identifying sources of anxiety. The client is asked to imagine himself in the anxiety-provoking situation together with relevant feelings and thoughts that occur to him, as well as information about the imagined events that relate to his discomfort. He is asked to describe (out loud) what he is experiencing (Kazdin, 1976), and this description can be tape-recorded for review by the counselor and client to determine anxiety sources and the behavioral referents of anxiety.

Structured self-report inventories such as the Fear Survey Schedule (Wolpe and Lang, 1964) and the Assertion Inventory (Gambrill and Richey, 1975), on which clients rate their degree of anxiety to a variety of situations, may help to identify general sources. Many of these structured inventories incorporate a Likert scale, in which the client is asked to respond to items in terms of degree of reaction (such as on a scale of from 1 to 5). Structured inventories offer the advantage of economy of time, in that they usually do not take long for the client to complete, and they can be scored objectively in the sense of arriving at a specific score for each client, such as degree of anxiety in social situations. This enables comparison between individuals as well as one way to evaluate progress of intraindividual change over time. Such inventories are valuable as a screening device, that is, to point to possible problematic areas that can be further specified via some other means such as behavioral interviews, self-monitoring, or observation of the client in actual situations. Additional assessment methods, such as self-monitoring and observation of the client, are useful when the client is unable to verbally describe the antecedents and consequences related to his anxiety reactions. In self-monitoring, the client is asked to gather information in the natural environment; that is, to note when anxiety is experienced as well as related antecedents and consequences, including self-statements. This may be facilitated by use of a portable tape recorder, on which the client notes information as relevant situations occur. Ratings of the degree of anxiety elicited by various situations can be indicated by using the Fear Thermometer (Walk, 1956), which is a ten-point scale ranging from 1 (completely calm) to 10 (extremely anxious). In addition, the client may be requested to note how he knows he is anxious by writing or recording the cognitive, physiological, and behavioral indications of his anxiety. Review of this information will hopefully help to isolate specific sources of anxiety as well as the behavioral referents for the client's anxiety.

Simulated Situations. Conditions that approximate those in the natural environment and that relate to a client's anxiety may be employed to gather needed assessment information. Let us say a woman has a fear of elevators in a certain building where she works. If there is an elevator in the building where the interview is being held, she can be accompanied to the elevator to see how closely she can approach with differing degrees of anxiety. The client should be encouraged to verbalize her thoughts and feelings during such experiences. Behavioral approach tests in which clients are instructed to progressively approach a feared stimulus (Lang and Lazovick, 1963) have been employed extensively as a behavioral measure of fear. Potential problems with this include possible demand characteristics in the testing situation that are not present in the natural environment. These characteristics may overemphasize the degree of avoidance behavior by the demand to present oneself as a fearful individual during initial testing, or may overestimate possible approach behavior, because of the client's perception that he is in a protected environment—with the counselor in a clinic (Orne, 1962). Such simulated tests of avoidance behavior will only offer accurate information to the extent that conditions in the natural environment are replicated. The unpredictability that is often one aspect of a feared event in real life may not be matched in the test situation; for example, asking a snake-phobic client to approach a securely caged snake, in contrast with a freely moving snake.

Simulated situations are often used to assess anxiety in interpersonal situations. For example, Paul (1966) requested students with public speaking anxiety to give a speech in front of a small audience. During the speech, various characteristics of the subjects, such as speech blocks, throat clearings, and trembling hands, were rated by trained observers. Role-played situations, in which clients are asked to role play their reactions to videotaped or audiotaped presenting situations, are also frequently employed. These assessment devices are discussed in Chapter Thirteen.

Observation of the Client in the Natural Environment. Helpful information can often be gained by observing the behavior of the client in the natural environment. For example, the author accompanied a client who had a verbally expressed fear of driving. The client was asked to indicate when she started to feel uncomfortable, to verbalize her thoughts, and to try to identify events associated with her anxiety. It was found that curves and roads with narrow shoulders were related to her anxiety. The client drove slightly on the wrong side of the median strip and so passed oncoming cars very closely, which made her nervous (not to mention the counselor's reaction). She gripped the wheel very tightly and sat forward in an uncomfortable position, which probably aggravated her anxiety, as muscle tension often does. This journey into the client's natural environment revealed important factors that had not been previously mentioned, and indicated that, contrary to her statement, her thoughts were an important component of her anxiety reaction. For example, when approaching a curve she would imagine a stalled car on her side of the road and imagine crashing into it. The presence of an observer may alter the client's behavior. Possible reactive effects of observation can be checked by employing multiple sources of information and comparing them. Helpful information can sometimes be offered by significant others who are a part of the natural environment, if the client agrees to their participation.

Physiological Indicators. Physiological measures that may be associated with anxiety, such as skin conductance (electrodermal measurement), cardiac changes, or changes in muscle tension (measured by electromyograph recordings) may be employed to assess the extent of involvement of physiological reactions for particular clients. Portable apparatus is available for gathering conductance and electromyograph recordings, some of which provides audible feedback—for example, as a tone that increases in loudness as anxiety increases. Such feedback may be employed during presentations of stimuli in the office situation—for example, slides of relevant events, during self-monitoring or when the counselor accompanies the client into the natural environment. A number of studies have shown that there is a relationship between stress and an increase in the spontaneous fluctuations in electrodermal reactions (see Katkin, 1975). In contrast, the cardiac reaction to stress may show either an accelerative or decelerative change (Lacey, 1967). It should be noted that there are wide individual differences in how different people react physiologically to stressful stimulation (Lacey, 1967). (See Lick and Katkin, 1976, for further information describing the use of electrodermal and cardiac measures). The mode of presentation of stimuli seems to be related to changes in physiological reactions. For example, Grossberg and Wilson (1968) found that instructions to imagine relevant events produced greater physiological arousal than did instructions to listen to tape-recorded scenes. Other studies have found a linear relationship between measures such as heart rate and skin conductance and the vividness with which clients visualize events (see Lang, Melamed, and Hart, 1970). Physiological measurement can be employed to rank scenes in terms of the degree to which they elicit anxiety (see, for example, Barabasz, 1974).

Pictures of Related Events. Pictures related to a client's anxiety may be displayed and the client asked to describe what is happening, including the thoughts of the actors represented (Meichenbaum, 1976). This method may be especially useful with clients who have difficulty describing their reactions and related events using other means.

Overview of Anxiety Reduction Procedures

A wide variety of behavioral procedures has been developed to decrease anxiety. These methods entail guided reexposure to anxiety-eliciting events (Wilson and Davison, 1971). The use of incompatible responses to eliminate fear reactions was proposed by Guthrie in 1935 and they were employed to eliminate a child's fear reaction by Jones in 1924. Wolpe's unique contribution was the development of systematic desensitization based on relaxation, in which events are imagined in the presence of a relaxed state. The effects of this procedure were originally attributed to the principle of reciprocal inhibition, which states that "If a response antagonistic to anxiety can be made to occur in the presence of anxiety-evoking stimuli so that it is accompanied by a complete or partial suppression of the anxiety response, the bond between these stimuli and the anxiety response will be weakened" (Wolpe, 1958, p. 71). However, incompatible states seem to be facilitating rather than necessary conditions (Wilson and Davison, 1971). This model stresses the role of respondent conditioning in the establishment and maintenance of anxiety reactions.

A second model of anxiety has emphasized the relationship between anxiety reactions and consequences and the alteration of such reactions by reinforcing gradual approach to actual objects (Leitenberg and Callahan, 1973). Here there is a focus on changing what happens after approach behavior occurs. This has been variously called *in vivo* or *performance desensitization, shaping,* or *reinforced practice,* and is contrasted with symbolic desensitization, in which anxiety-producing events are imagined. Comparative studies indicate the greater effectiveness of performance-based interventions that involve display of approach behavior. For example, whereas performance desensitization eliminated physiological reactions to both actual and imagined threats, symbolic desensitization, which involves imagined events, decreased autonomic reactions only to imagined threats (Barlow, Leitenberg, Agras, and Wincze, 1969). Performance desensitization permits more information concerning coping skills and therefore, Bandura (in press) would argue, achieves greater changes in perceived self-efficacy. A variety of response induction aids may be employed to help the client perform adequately, including modeling of threatening activities, graduated tasks, performance requirements, enactment over graduated temporal intervals (involving short intervals at first), joint performance with the therapist, protective aids to reduce the likelihood of feared consequences and reduction in the severity of the threat itself (Bandura, Jeffery, and Wright, 1974). These aids are gradually withdrawn as the client develops coping skills. Self-directed mastery experiences are then offered (Bandura, Jeffery, and Gajdos, 1975). Performance desensitization is typically employed along with symbolic methods (see, for example, Wolpe, 1973a).

A third model has stressed the importance of arranging exposure of the client to anxiety-producing events within a respondent extinction method. Anxiety induction procedures such as flooding and implosion, in which the worst that could happen is imagined or experienced, have also been found to be effective. Covert modeling, in which the client rehearses approach behavior to feared situations, has also been successfully employed (see, for example, Kazdin, 1973c).

There has been increasing emphasis on a cognitive mediational model of anxiety, in which the person contributes to his own anxiety via arousing self-statements, and the development of procedures that establish self-management skills for anxiety control (Goldfried, 1971; Goldfried, Decenteceo, and Weinberg, 1974; Meichenbaum, 1975b). Anxiety is conceptualized as an opportunity to employ coping skills, rather than as an occasion for further discomfort. Anxiety management procedures, in which new self-instructions and coping skills are developed and in which the client learns to view his anxiety in a new way, have been found to be more effective than symbolic desensitization (Meichenbaum, Gilmore, and Fedoravicius, 1971). Desensitization itself has been viewed as training in self-control (Goldfried, 1971). Procedures in which coping reactions are developed include stress inoculation (Meichenbaum, 1975b) and differential relaxation, in which the client is trained how to relax and instructed to use this skill whenever he starts to feel anxious (Wolpe and Lazarus, 1966).

The behavioral procedures that have been developed to decrease anxiety differ along a number of dimensions: (1) the stimulus level employed (gradual exposure, use of the target situation, or exposure to an extremely negative event); (2) mode of representation (actual or imagined); (3) whether the identification of specific anxiety-eliciting events is required; and (4) whether training is explicitly provided in coping skills that can be employed in the natural environment. Anxiety reduction procedures for dealing with specific stressors are described in the following sections. These include symbolic desensitization based on relaxation, including the development of self-management skills; covert modeling; reinforced practice; modeling and reinforced practice; guided participation; and anxiety induction procedures.

The wider the range of situations in which anxiety is elicited, the more probable it is that a procedure other than systematic desensitization would be more effective (that is, one that focuses on the development of coping responses that can be employed in a range of situations). These methods do not necessarily require identification of specific anxiety sources. The possible role of behavior deficits must be explored, as well as the consequences of anxiety, in terms of reinforcement from significant others or avoidance of unpleasant situations. The client may hold misconceptions that are related to his anxiety reaction. Anxiety in social situations may be related to a belief that he must always please others, that everyone must like him. Irrational beliefs should be identified and steps taken to correct such misconceptions (see Chapter Twelve). Performance desensitization should be used together with symbolic desensitization as soon as this is possible, given the client's anxiety levels and the situations that can be arranged.

Symbolic Desensitization Incorporating Self-Management Skills

Systematic desensitization based on relaxation has been successfully applied to a wide range of problems, including alcoholism (Kraft and Al-Issa, 1967), anger reduction (Rimm, deGroot, Boord, Heiman, and Dillow, 1971), bronchial asthma (Moore, 1965), and auditory hallucinations (Slade, 1972), to name but a few. This procedure is designed to remove anxiety reactions to specific events or situations, particularly when direct action is not possible (Lazarus and Serber, 1968). Most interpersonal anxieties permit graduated direct action, and other procedures, such as role playing and reinforced practice in the natural environment, should be used rather than symbolic desensitization. The latter procedure may be used to lower anxiety so that these other procedures can then be employed. Desensitization based on relaxation is uniquely designed to address reactions in which there is a large affective component to the anxiety reaction. If there is a large cognitive component, procedures addressed to this content would be selected instead (see Chapter Twelve). Symbolic desensitization is not as effective if a client has anxiety reactions in a large number of situations (Marks, 1969); however, the incorporation of anxiety management training into the traditional procedure may overcome this limitation.

The procedure involves construction of a hierarchy of items for each area in which anxiety occurs. This consists of a series of items ranked in accord with the amount of anxiety each produces, ranging from items that induce hardly any to those that elicit high anxiety. Desensitization is begun with items that elicit a small amount of discomfort. In addition, the client is trained how to present incompatible self-instructions. Thus the main components include: (1) isolation of the events that elicit anxiety and formation of stimulus hierarchies, each related to a discrete theme and consisting of graded steps in relation to how much anxiety each elicits; (2) training in relaxation; (3) training in self-instructional and coping skills; and (4) the systematic pairing of visualized scenes with relaxation or with anxiety, followed by successful coping reactions. The counselor should determine at an early point whether the client can imagine scenes with clarity and whether he can learn how to relax; however, both relaxation and clarity of imagery seem to be facilitating, rather than necessary, conditions for success.

The effective process in desensitization has been variously conceptualized as a counterconditioning process (Wolpe, 1958), in which anxiety-provoking events are paired with incompatible reactions; as an operant-shaping procedure (Lang, 1969), in which the client learns to say, "I am not afraid in the presence of fear-arousing events," or to present competing responses such as "I am angry"; as a means of arranging response exposure to feared events and thus the respondent extinction of anxiety reactions (Wilson and Davison, 1971); and as a process that permits the covert rehearsal of approach behavior (Lang, 1969). Although there is considerable debate as to the theoretical rationale for the effects of desensitization and the relative importance of respondent versus operant processes, there is no doubt that the procedure can be effective in decreasing verbal, emotional, and behavioral components of anxiety in relation to a variety of sources.

There are a number of advantages of symbolic desensitization, including the ability to present any type of scene. This is not possible in in vivo desensitization, in which actual events are employed. It is uniquely suited for desensitization to anxiety-arousing imagery (Bandura, 1969). Minimal discomfort is induced, because the approach to anxiety-eliciting events is gradual, although this is also true of graduated in vivo desensitization and graduated modeling. It is useful when client discomfort is too high to initiate approach behavior in the natural environment. Such approach may be made possible if preceded by desensitization. The procedure readily lends itself to a group context (Paul and Shannon, 1966).

Disadvantages of the method include the following: (1) it is necessary to identify anxiety-eliciting events; (2) clients may be unable to clearly visualize events, thus precluding their imagined presentation; (3) the counselor has only indirect control over critical events (however, this is true with all procedures involving imagined events); (4) additional procedures are required to assess progress in the natural environment; and (5) as traditionally employed, clients do not receive as much practice in *coping* with anxiety as they do in anxiety management procedures. This disadvantage can be eliminated by the inclusion of coping responses in which anxiety occurs and is successfully reduced (Goldfried, 1971; D'Zurilla, 1969; Meichenbaum, 1974).

In presenting the procedure of symbolic desensitization, the counselor describes the procedure to the client and explains the underlying rationale, including the reasons for the construction of hierarchies, the role of relaxation, and the use of coping as well as mastery responses. Desensitization is presented as a procedure that will develop skills in managing anxiety. The process of forming a common conceptualization of anxiety is important, and may require several sessions (Meichenbaum, 1975b).

The necessity for the formation of hierarchies is explained in terms of employing events that elicit just small amounts of anxiety to ensure that a response of relaxation or a coping response will occur in the presence of anxiety-eliciting events, rather than, as in the past, a response of anxiety. It is pointed out that relaxation training will also facilitate the occurrence of such reactions. The need for regular home practice sessions to become skilled in relaxing is strongly emphasized. An analogy can be made to the learning of any skill in which practice is an essential component.

Identification of Anxiety Sources. The various assessment sources described earlier are employed to locate anxiety-eliciting events. A wide variety of events may be found to elicit anxiety, which are then organized in terms of thematic groupings, as described in the case history of Mr. M. Mr. M. was a twenty-two-year-old medical student who reported becoming increasingly anxious when blushing, and, since he had become more anxious, said that the blushing occurred with greater frequency. He had become alarmed, because he was beginning to avoid certain situations because of anxiety that he might blush. He tended to blush under five different conditions:

1. Conversation related to sex: He became anxious if sexual topics were mentioned either in lectures or during casual conversation. Specific topics included illegiti-

macy, extramarital relations, developmental changes of puberty and adolescence, and jokes that made reference to sex, masturbation, homosexuality, and female or male genitals.

2. Conversations or lectures dealing with physical diseases in which flushing might be manifested, such as hypertension and polycythemia.

3. Conversations or lecture material dealing with mental disorders.

4. Being singled out, which included such situations as introducing his wife, attempting to tell a lie, meeting a friend unexpectedly, and entering a room after the start of a lecture.

5. Physically examining a female patient.

A broad list of fears, such as follows, may originally be presented (from one of the author's cases). Note that many are internal in source (losing control, becoming mentally ill, fainting, and becoming nauseous). Neither the list of fears or their thematic groupings are sufficiently specific to be usable in a hierarchy.

Original List of Fears

Being alone	Feeling disapproved of
Being in a strange place	Being ignored
Falling	Darkness
High places on land	Psychiatrists
Looking down from high build- ings	Looking foolish
	Losing control
Feeling angry	Fainting
Sudden noises	Becoming nauseous
Sight of deep water	Becoming mentally ill
Mentally sick people	Taking written tests
Prospect of surgical operation	Feeling different from
Feeling rejected by others	others

Once the anxiety sources have been isolated, events that are related by a common factor are categorized together. The following represents the thematic groupings of the fears originally presented.

Thematic Groupings

Agoraphobia

Being alone

Acrophobia

Falling
High places on land
Looking down from high build-
     ings

Mental illness

Becoming mentally ill
Mentally sick people
Psychiatrists
Losing control
Feeling angry
Fainting
Feeling different from others

Rejection

Feeling disapproved of
Feeling rejected by others
Being ignored
Looking foolish

The unknown

Being in a strange place
Sudden noises
Darkness

Illness

Prospect of surgical operation
Becoming nauseous

Some themes are easy to discern, because they are related to an externally observable referent, such as heights. Fears that do not refer to an observable external referent, such as fear of rejection or fear of failure, may be more difficult to discern and to arrange in a hierarchy.

Construction of Stimulus Hierarchies. When the sources of anxiety have been identified and common themes determined, together with any other factors that affect such reactions, then hierarchies can be constructed. A stimulus hierarchy consists of a graded series of events, all related to one particular theme, that evoke gradually increasing degrees of anxiety, starting with a situation that elicits just a small amount of discomfort and ranging to those that provoke high discomfort. Hierarchies may involve a spatial-temporal dimension in which a specific situation or event induces anxiety and in which scenes can be graded in accord with how close the client approaches them (such as time until an examination), or they may involve events related to a theme (such as criticism, being ignored, or being watched) that does not involve a closeness dimension (Paul, 1969b). What is aimed for is a scale with the intervals representing equal increments of anxiety starting with situations that elicit just a small amount of discomfort and ranging to those that provoke great discomfort.

Prior to the construction of hierarchies in which items will be imagined, it should be determined whether relevant anxiety-eliciting events can be visualized in the imagination with some degree of emotional clarity, by selecting an item related to the client's anxiety and asking him to imagine this. The client should close his eyes when doing so, to shut out distracting events, and sufficient detail about the situation must be at hand so that it can be realistically described. A signal can be arranged beforehand, such as raising the right index finger when anxiety is experienced. Some investigators have found that self-reported clarity of imagery is unrelated to outcome (Kazdin, 1974a); however, this finding may be caused by the failure to locate appropriate assessment devices for imagery (Danaher and Thoresen, 1972). It is possible to enhance the imagery skills of clients so that they learn to imagine events with greater emotional impact, by asking them to carefully describe details, for example, but this may be more time consuming than employing a procedure that does not require imagery, such as in vivo desensitization. The hierarchies that are employed when in vivo desensitization is used involve a gradual exposure to actual events, and so may be quite different in content than when imagined scenes are employed.

The subjective anxiety scale can be used to rate the degree of anxiety elicited by each scene (Wolpe and Lazarus, 1966). This scale ranges from 0 to 100, 0 representing complete calmness and 100 representing extreme discomfort. The client is requested to rate each hierarchy item on this scale. This rating provides a subjective indication of the increments of anxiety between scenes and the degree of anxiety of the weakest scene. It is helpful to place each item on a separate small index card and have the client rank these in terms of subjective anxiety. If it is necessary to add scenes, this can readily be done by making up additional cards and inserting them between the items already formulated. Traditionally, hierarchies are constructed with small subjective levels of anxiety between items (for example, about 10 units), and start with an item that has a rating of about 10. It should be noted that the necessity of hierarchy construction is questioned by reports of successful desensitization using only the highest hierarchy items (Suinn, Edie, and Spinelli, 1970) or abbreviated hierarchies. An advantage of graduated desensitization is that it does not induce much discomfort at any time. A disadvantage is that it may be less efficient in terms of time.

The number of scenes in a hierarchy varies from just a few, say five, to many more, perhaps thirty, depending on how many dimensions influence the degree of anxiety and on the intensity of the anxiety. The greater the number of dimensions and the more intense the anxiety, the more items may be required. In designing a hierarchy in which many factors affect anxiety, some must be held constant, while others are varied. It is important to carefully specify scene content, because if this is not done, the client may vary the setting from scene to scene during desensitization, and thus unwanted and worse yet, inexplicable, variations in anxiety may ensue. Marquis and Morgan (1969) recommend asking the client to review hierarchies after their completion to make sure all dimensions have been identified.

Clients differ widely in the ease with which they can, after some instructions and beginning help, set up hierarchies on their own, at home. As a help toward this, anchor points can be established (Rimm and Masters, 1974). The client can be requested to describe a scene at the lowest end of his hierarchy and one at the highest end, being careful to make the scenes very specific. The process of identification of specific scenes can be modeled for the client and the client requested to complete the rest of the items, trying for graded steps in subjective anxiety. These items should be reviewed to ensure that they are sufficiently specific.

Examples of hierarchies. The following lists show hierarchies related to a variety of themes. Items are arranged from the least to the most anxiety producing.

1. Alone in house with parents 5 minutes' travel time away.
2. Alone in house with parents 10 minutes' travel time away.
3. Alone in house with parents 15 minutes' travel time away.
4. Alone in house with parents 20 minutes' travel time away.

5. Alone in house with parents 25 minutes' travel time away.
6. Alone in house with parents one half hour travel time away.

1. One hour before examining a female patient aged 40.
2. One half hour before examining a female patient aged 40.
3. Fifteen minutes before examining a female patient aged 40.
4. Walking down hall toward patient's room.
5. Entering room and greeting patient.
6. Explaining purpose of visit.
7. Examining heart with stethescope.
8. Examining breasts.
9. Abdominal examination.

The final list is from MacDonald (1975a, p. 319).

1. Standing on the front porch in the late afternoon with your Dad, about ready to go inside, looking down the block and seeing a Beagle three houses away minding his own business and trotting toward you.
2. Sitting in the _____ family's kitchen with the rest of your family, hearing Mr. _____ say, "He surely was a hard egg, wasn't he?" and watching Dumplin' who's lying down at the kitchen entrance, look at you, get up, and trot around the table to a spot three feet from you.
3. Standing in your Gramma and Grampa's front yard playing ball with your Dad and Sister and watching a Schnauzer exploring about fifty feet away.
4. Sitting in your back yard, alone, playing with your G.I. Joe and looking up to see an unfamiliar collie running down your driveway and past the garage.

In this last hierarchy, item prompts were more extensive, because the client, an eleven-year-old boy, had a record of "breaking treatment rules." Additional prompts enable more influence over imagined content. Many investigators have successfully employed standardized hierarchies. These have been employed during group desensitization as well as during individual sessions.

Relaxation Training. The identification of anxiety sources and the formation of hierarchies are usually combined with training the client in deep muscle relaxation (see Chapter Twelve). When it is not possible to use relaxation, other positive events that may facilitate exposure to feared situations may be employed, such as positive imagery (Lazarus and Abramovitz, 1962), game playing (Marshall, Boutilier, and Minnes, 1974), music (Lowe, 1973), or laughter (Ventis, 1973).

Desensitization Incorporating Self-Management Skills. After hierarchies have been constructed, appropriate self-instructions and coping skills developed, and relaxation training completed, desensitization can be initiated. The procedure consists of the systematic pairing of imagined hierarchy items with relaxation (a mastery reaction) or with a coping response (successful reduction of anxiety), starting with scenes that provoke a small degree of discomfort.

The use of signals. Instructions are given that if discomfort is felt, either during relaxation instructions or scene presentations, this should be signaled, for example, by raising the right index finger. If a signal is given on scene presentation, the client can be requested to continue imagining the scene while visualizing the use of coping reactions to decrease the anxiety. Signals of anxiety between scenes may be followed by instructions to keep out all other thoughts and to attend to feeling calm and relaxed. A signal may also be employed to indicate when scenes are clearly imagined. The duration of scene presentation can be timed from this signal.

Relaxation instructions. The first activity that is carried out is relaxing the client. Either you or the client may present relaxation instructions. It is helpful to determine the subjective anxiety level prior to relaxation. This will provide some indication of how much time should be spent in presenting instructions. Scene presentation is usually not initiated if the subjective anxiety level is twenty or higher, because absence of a state of relaxation may prevent the client from tolerating exposure to and coping with anxiety-eliciting events. However, the level of subjective anxiety required for positive effects varies from person to person, and, as noted previously, alternative procedures such as flooding, in which high anxiety exists during exposure to anxiety-eliciting events, are also effective. It is advisable not to allow the client to speak during relaxation and scene presentation, in order to maintain relaxation.

Relaxation instructions prior to scene presentation usually do not include instructions to tense the muscles. The relaxation proceeds from the point where the client happens to be. Such instructions may consist of a countdown from one to ten, employing the procedure described in Chapter Twelve or an earlier phase may be employed, as also described in Chapter Twelve. The instructions and suggestions of relaxation should be presented slowly, allowing time for the relaxation of each muscle group. The pace with which the muscle groups are covered depends on the time required to relax particular muscles. The following example illustrates instructions that are presented.

> Close your eyes. Get in a comfortable position. (Pause.) Try to put all worrisome thoughts out of your mind and let your only concern be to let yourself go and become relaxed and comfortable. (Pause.) As I mention each muscle group, give your attention to relaxing this group, remembering what it felt like when this muscle group was relaxed. Notice the feeling in each muscle as it becomes more relaxed. (Pause.) Relax the muscles of your arms and hands. (Pause.) Focus on any tension that you may feel in these muscles and try to relax this tension. (Pause.) Let the relaxation spread from your hands and forearms up into your upper arms. (Pause.) Just think about being calm and tranquil. (Pause.) Picture yourself saying "Just relax and be comfortable." (Pause.) Signal me if these muscles feel completely relaxed. (Signal.) Focus now on the facial and scalp muscles. Try to smooth out your forehead muscles. (Pause.) Let these muscles and the muscles of your scalp become very relaxed. (Pause.) Let this relaxation spread down to your eyes. (Pause.) Focus on the difference between varying degrees of relaxation. Let your eyelids become more relaxed. (Pause.) Let this sensation of

relaxation spread to the muscles of your cheeks and mouth. (Pause.) Each time you exhale, let your body become more relaxed. (Pause.) Try to let your whole face become more relaxed, including your jaw muscles and the muscles around your mouth. (Pause.) Try to let go further and further, becoming calmer and calmer. (Pause.) Signal me if your scalp and facial muscles feel completely relaxed. (Signal.) Let the relaxation spread down into your neck and chest. (Pause.) Let these muscles become more relaxed. (Pause.) Try to let this spread to the muscles in your back (pause), shoulders (pause), and stomach. (Pause.) Just think about relaxing and becoming more calm and comfortable. (Pause.) Each time you exhale, try to carry the relaxation further. Focus on the feeling of relaxation. (Pause.) There is nothing else you have to concern yourself with now. (Pause.) Let the muscles in your back and shoulders become more relaxed; let the tension drain from them. (Pause.) Each time you exhale, try to take the relaxation even further. (Pause.) Signal me if the muscles in your neck (pause), back (pause), chest (pause), shoulders (pause), and stomach (pause) are completely relaxed. (Signal.) Continue to relax the muscles in your arms (pause), face (pause), neck (pause), chest, and shoulders as you attend to relaxing the muscles of your legs and feet. (Pause.) Let the relaxation spread down into your right (left) leg and foot. (Pause.) Focus on the changes in sensation that occur. (Pause.) Let this relaxation spread to the muscles of your left leg and foot. (Pause.) Signal me if the muscles in your legs and feet feel completely relaxed. (Signal. Pause.) Let the relaxation spread over your whole body and let yourself become more calm (pause), more relaxed (pause), more tranquil. (Pause.) Each time you exhale, try to carry the relaxation further. (Pause.) Please signal me if your whole body feels completely relaxed and if you feel calm and tranquil. (No signal.)

If a signal is presented, scene presentation can begin. If a signal is not presented, the subjective anxiety level can be determined by requesting the client to signal if the level is over ten, and if a signal is presented, if the level is above twenty, and so on, until a point is reached where no signal occurs. A high level of discomfort would warrant further relaxation instructions. The location of tension can be determined by mentioning each group and asking the client to signal if tension is felt. Additional instruction can then be given to relax this tension. Relaxation may be deepened by asking the client to imagine a calming scene or by employing a countdown procedure coordinated with the client's breathing. The client is informed that a countdown from five to one will be made and that as this occurs, he is to try to take the relaxation deeper with each count. If further attempts to increase relaxation are unsuccessful, desensitization could be initiated anyway, using hierarchy items that elicit small amounts of anxiety. Reports of subjective anxiety together with careful observation of the client will usually provide an accurate estimate of degree of relaxation. Such reports could be complemented by the use of physiological indicators if desired.

If a client is skilled in relaxing deeply or happens to be very relaxed before relaxation instructions are initiated, these may occupy only two or three minutes. The muscle groups can then be covered in a more general fashion with more limited suggestions of relaxation between the mentioning of particular groups.

Use of neutral scenes. When relaxation instructions have been completed, prior to the first desensitization session, it is advisable to first present a neutral scene, a scene to which no anxiety is anticipated, to determine the possible presence of anxiety-eliciting components in the treatment situation itself (Wolpe, 1958). An example of a neutral scene might be standing on a street corner waiting to cross the street, or sitting at home reading the paper.

If neutral scenes provoke no anxiety and can be clearly imagined, then scene presentations from the hierarchy can be initiated. If anxiety is signaled on the imagination of a supposedly neutral scene or clear visualization cannot occur, determination should be made as to whether that particular scene happened not to be neutral or whether some other factor is involved, without disrupting the state of relaxation. Other scenes that are thought to be neutral can be presented and, if no anxiety is elicited by these and clear visualization can take place, desensitization can be initiated. If repeated signaling of anxiety to neutral scenes occurs, this could be employed as an opportunity to use coping imagery. The factors responsible for this anxiety can be explored after the end of the session.

Scene presentation. At the initial session, the least anxiety-provoking item is presented first. This item typically has a subjective anxiety rating of about five or ten units. Three types of scenes are employed, unlike traditional symbolic desensitization (Meichenbaum, 1975b). One is the traditional mastery response, in which a scene is presented to which no anxiety reaction occurs. In the remaining two, the client is encouraged to employ self-instructions and coping skills such as deep breathing to decrease anxiety, which is signaled on imagining a scene or is suggested by the counselor in response to scene content. The client's attention is focused on the use of anxiety as a reminder to employ coping skills to decrease the anxiety.

In this form of imagined rehearsal, the client receives more practice in coping with anxiety. Also, because anxiety will be experienced in the natural environment, it is more realistic to include coping scenes. The duration of coping scenes that have been used range from thirty seconds to two minutes (Meichenbaum, 1974). The reactions of the client are employed as a cue as to what instructions to employ.

The manner in which items are introduced is as follows. (The hierarchy for the scenes used was presented earlier in this chapter.)

> I am going to ask you to imagine some scenes now, and I would like you to try and imagine them as clearly as you can. Only imagine what is described. You will remain, in general, relaxed and comfortable. Imagine that it is fifteen minutes before you are to examine a forty-year-old female patient. You are sitting at your desk completing reports. Signal me when you clearly imagine the scene. (Pause of ten seconds after signal.) Stop imagining that scene and keep on relaxing. (Pause.) Just let yourself go further. See yourself taking a slow, deep breath and slowly exhaling. Focus on the feel-

ing of relaxation that this induces. There is nothing to be concerned about now. Just enjoy feeling calm and relaxed. (Pause.) Imagine the same scene. (Repeat scene and request the client to signal when the scene is clearly visualized. Pause for ten seconds after signal.) Signal me if you feel the slightest discomfort. (Signal.) Continue to imagine this scene. You can feel yourself starting to feel tense and you use this as a reminder to say "Just relax." "Stay calm." See yourself taking a deep breath, slowly exhaling it, beginning to feel calmer. (Pause.) Stop imagining that scene and just relax now. Signal me if you feel any discomfort. (No signal.) Let yourself become more comfortable and tranquil. Each time you exhale, take the relaxation further. (Pause for a few seconds.) Now, imagine that you are walking down the hall toward the patient's room. Signal me when you clearly imagine the scene. (Pause for ten seconds after signal.) Stop imagining the scene and just keep on relaxing. (Pause.) Imagine the same scene again; you are now walking down the hall toward the patient's room. Signal me when you clearly imagine this scene. (Signal.) See yourself this time starting to feel uncomfortable. You feel some tenseness in the pit of your stomach. You start to think about how you can escape the situation. (Examples from the client's own experience should be employed.) Notice what you have been feeling. These are signals to use coping reactions. (Pause.) Visualize yourself taking a slow deep breath and holding it. (Pause.) (The particular self-instructions and coping devices employed are tailor-made for each client.) Stop imagining that scene and just focus upon being relaxed. You can deepen relaxation by thinking silently to yourself the words *relax, tranquil,* and *calm.* Picture these words to yourself. Give your attention to relaxing and letting go further and further. (Pause for a few seconds.) Signal if you feel relaxed. (Signal.) Imagine that you are now entering the room and greeting the patient. She smiles at you and says hello. Signal me when you clearly imagine the scene. (Pause ten seconds after the signal.) Signal me if you feel any discomfort. (Signal presented.) Continue to imagine this scene and imagine yourself coping with this anxiety by use of the breathing method that you practiced. (Pause.) Imagine yourself saying, "Just relax; take it easy." Picture these words to yourself. Imagine that you are able to feel more relaxed and comfortable. (Pause for a few seconds.) Stop imagining that scene and relax. (Pause.) Imagine the same scene; you are entering the patient's room and greeting her. Signal when the scene is clearly imagined. (Pause five seconds after signal.) Stop imagining that scene and signal if you felt any discomfort. (No signal.)

Each scene is presented at least twice. When anxiety is experienced on imagining a scene, it can be employed as an opportunity for the client to employ coping responses. This scene is then repeated until no anxiety is felt on imagining it, or until the client can readily reduce the anxiety. At this point, the next scene is introduced.

The subjective anxiety level experienced should be checked periodically. It is common practice to terminate sessions with an item that arouses no discomfort. If, when nearing the end of a session, a scene is presented that arouses anxiety, a weaker one is introduced prior to termination. A brief amount of time is allowed in which the client is requested to focus on sensations of relaxation and calmness.

The sequence of mastery and coping imagery. Mastery responses are encouraged at the beginning of sessions during the first two or three scenes, to enable the client to become accustomed to the procedure and to facilitate a relaxed state (Meichenbaum, 1974). Following this, coping imagery can be presented following signaled anxiety. If the client is able to recapture a state of relaxation, then coping imagery can occasionally be presented by the counselor. In these scenes, the client is requested to imagine himself in a situation in which he is becoming upset and anxious, and this is used as a cue for coping imagery. If the client is unable to cope with the anxiety, the scene should be terminated and relaxation instructions presented. The scene can be presented again, but this time with the inclusion of specific suggested coping activities (Meichenbaum, 1974). If the client fails a second time to reduce the anxiety generated by the scene, a weaker one should be employed. If coping imagery is successful in decreasing anxiety, counselor suggestions of specific positive self-instructions and behavioral skills to employ can be gradually faded out over sessions. Rather than suggesting specific skills, the counselor asks the client what he could say to himself to feel more relaxed. He is asked to identify some self-instructions that would be useful. The main guideline to employ in relation to selection of instructions is to enable the client to mentally rehearse the use of behavioral and cognitive coping skills that can be employed in stressful situations (Meichenbaum, 1974).

Duration of scenes. A single prolonged exposure to a fear-eliciting item has been found to be more effective than several shorter ones of an equivalent duration in reducing both subjective reports of anxiety and behavioral avoidance (Ross and Proctor, 1973). This would suggest use of fewer but longer scene presentations during desensitization. Observation of the client will provide feedback as to how long anxiety-provoking material should be presented. If it is thought that an item might provoke a large reaction, it can be presented for a brief time. The duration can then be gradually lengthened and coping imagery introduced. Scenes in which there is a mastery response, that is, no anxiety is experienced on imagining the scene, are typically shorter than those followed by coping imagery. Coping reactions require time for the client to rehearse the use of cognitive and behavioral skills.

The duration of scenes is also affected by the nature of the scene itself. Some scenes describe activities that require time to be carried out, such as walking up four flights of stairs or going for a ten-mile drive in the country.

Time interval between scenes. Relaxation instructions are presented between scenes. The time allotted for these depends on the degree of relaxation of the client. A brief interval between scenes, about five to ten seconds, can be used when relaxation is satisfactory. If it is not very deep or a scene has been disturbing, more time is allotted to relaxation instructions. Subsequent items are introduced when the client is again relaxed. The usual time between scenes is about thirty seconds. The client is encouraged to be an active participant in maintaining relaxation, by using self-instructions.

Extraneous disturbing thoughts may intrude during the intervals between scenes. This might be obvious by observable changes in the client or by anxiety signals, or such thoughts may be discovered on inquiry following termination of the session. Another indication is an unanticipated anxiety signal following a scene presentation. If such intrusion is recurrent, between-scene intervals should include suggestions to keep out all disturbing thoughts and the presentation of a calming scene. Signaled anxiety to such thoughts could be followed by coping suggestions.

Progression to stronger hierarchy items. Progress to a higher item is usually not made until anxiety to lower items can be successfully handled. The number of times a scene is presented prior to a request for a signal as to whether discomfort was felt and/or successfully reduced may vary, depending on the size of the increment in subjective anxiety between items. With small increments, an inquiry could be made after every second repetition. Requests for feedback after every second presentation can also indicate whether discomfort is decreasing over repetitions. If zero discomfort is indicated on two presentations, this scene can be increased in duration, a coping scene can be introduced, or the next item can be presented, after a pause during which suggestions of relaxation are given. It should be noted that abbreviated hierarchies have been successfully employed, thus calling into question the necessity of a highly standardized progression.

Number of scenes required. The number of scenes presented during any one session of a given length of time depends on a number of factors, including the amount of time initially required to relax the client; the amount of anxiety provoked by scenes, which affects the amount of between-scene time devoted to relaxation instructions; the time required for the construction of clear images; and the duration of scenes. As skill in relaxation is acquired, and the client becomes familiar with the procedure, less time is spent on preliminaries, allowing more for scene presentations. If multiple hierarchies exist, scenes from each may be included during a session. This has the advantage of preventing a decreasing vividness of items, which sometimes occurs when scenes from only one hierarchy are employed.

Geer and Katkin (1966) reported the successful treatment of insomnia by a variant of systematic desensitization, in which only one scene per session was presented for a total of nine sessions. The number of presentations required before successful coping reacions follow a scene varies, depending on the effectiveness of coping reactions, the subjective anxiety rating of the item, and the duration of exposure.

Questions following each session. If signals of anxiety were presented during the session, either spontaneously or on inquiry, the degree of discomfort evoked by various scenes can be determined at the end of the session. If no anxiety signals were presented, even though a great deal was experienced, the client should be requested to be sure to signal when discomfort is felt. Repeated lack of anxiety when scenes can be clearly imagined may indicate that the scenes presented are too weak, or that scene content is irrelevant to anxiety, or that the client is avoiding anxiety-provoking material.

Imagery should also be checked on termination of a session. It may be found that the client is changing the scene content from time to time. This may result in seemingly random signals of anxiety. If so, instructions can be repeated to imagine the scene only as described. Shifting of content can usually be precluded by making scene descriptions very specific.

Subsequent sessions. It is common practice first to present the last scene from the previous session on a subsequent session (Marquis and Morgan, 1969). If there is any doubt about the subjective anxiety rating of items in subsequent sessions, the client may be requested to examine them and to correct ratings if they have changed. Practice between sessions may result in a decrease in subjective anxiety.

Duration, spacing, and number of sessions. The duration of sessions usually varies from twenty to thirty minutes, depending on the availability of time and the durability of the client. Some clients (and counselors) become fatigued more swiftly than others and so sessions will be shorter. The duration usually increases as treatment proceeds, because less time is spent on preliminaries. More lengthy sessions may also be effective; for example, Suinn (1970) successfully employed a two-hour time span on one day, followed by one hour on the following day.

The number of sessions per week varies, depending on the availability of time. Usually one or two a week are held. Whether there are many sessions per day or a session only once a week, the important factor determining reduction of anxiety seems to be the amount of imagined anxiety and rehearsal of mastery and coping responses. A variety of factors influence the total number of sessions required to successfully decrease anxiety, including the number of anxiety themes presented; the degree of involvement of related events in the themes; the intensity of the anxiety reactions; and the amount of practice, both imagined and actual, in performing mastery and coping responses. Assignments between sessions provide additional practice in the use of skills. When only one theme is present and the anxiety is of a moderate degree, only a few sessions may be required. For example, the medical student who complained of blushing, eliminated the anxiety after six desensitization sessions. Meichenbaum (1972) successfully employed eight one-hour group sessions with students anxious about tests. Suinn (1970) employed one two-hour session.

As anxiety decreases in relation to one or two themes, a decrease may also occur in relation to others that have not been dealt with directly. The degree to which this occurs is partially dependent on the extent to which separate themes are interrelated. Andrews (1966) would explain the reduction of "non-treated fears" by the assumption that successful treatment rids the client of a general avoidance pattern that he has developed, thus reduction of other anxieties would be expected. The development of coping skills should enhance generalization of effects and so reduce the number of sessions required.

Notation System. It is helpful to keep a record of what has been done during sessions. Such records permit continuity of scene presentation from session to session. If someone else takes over treatment, records are vital, and together with formulated hierarchies, enable the carrying on of treatment without any break in continuity. One system that can be used simply requires indication of the theme, the item number, and the number of times each type of imagery response occurred for each item.

Difficulties that May be Encountered. If treatment is progressing smoothly, a decrease of anxiety to scenes presented during sessions will occur, as well as a transfer of this effect to the natural environment. If these effects are not found, the procedure should be halted and the reason for this located. Lack of change may be caused by overlooking behavior deficits or reinforcing consequences of anxiety. It may also relate to insufficient imagined and actual practice in using coping skills.

Perhaps insufficient time has been devoted to obtaining a common conceptualization of anxiety and the possibilities of achieving self-control over anxiety by cognitive and behavioral coping reactions. If the style of the client's thinking is related to anxiety, then it is very important that this be pointed out and an alternative offered, that is, a change made from learned helplessness to learned resourcefulness (Meichenbaum, 1974). Lack of effects may also be related to inadequacies in level of relaxation, difficulties related to imagery, or inadequate hierarchies.

Inadequacies in relaxation level. One of the conditions that facilitates the effects of desensitization is attainment of a state of relaxation. A number of factors may be related to difficulty in achieving and maintaining such a state. Insufficient relaxation instructions may be given when inducing a relaxed state or between scene presentations. Insufficient practice of relaxation could be the cause of difficulty. Inquiry should be made as to whether the client is practicing as directed and, if not, the rationale is repeated concerning the importance of regular practice. The client may fail to signal when discomfort is experienced, and the rationale for doing so can be reviewed.

Inaccurate reporting of degree of relaxation may stem from an incorrect use of the subjective anxiety scale and if this is suspected, inquiry can be made as to how this scale is being employed. The careful establishment of items at the high and low ends of hierarchies will usually prevent this.

It may be necessary to spend more time teaching the client to discriminate the presence of different degrees of anxiety. This may be done by going back to the training phase of relaxation, perhaps using graduated release of tension rather than immediate release, thus emphasizing various stages of tension. Lack of awareness of states of tension can be a major obstacle to the delineation of anxiety sources, because the client will not be able to determine the circumstances in which he feels more or less anxious (see Chapter Twelve for additional discussion of difficulties in relaxation and how to remove them).

Difficulties related to imagery. The client may say, "I can see the scene clearly in my mind, but feel no anxiety. If I were actually in the situation, I would feel very anxious." Sometimes this can be overcome by increasing the vividness of scenes or by requesting the client to describe what he is imagining. Scene content should be specific and scene description vivid. Lack of clear visualization is sometimes caused by scene descriptions that are not sufficiently detailed. Persistent difficulty of this type may be caused by a lack of engagement in the scene, an attempt to avoid anxiety-eliciting material even in the imagination. If neutral scenes can be clearly imagined, then it is likely that an avoidance component is responsible. Additional training in cognitive and behavioral coping skills may be required, or in vivo methods may have to be employed.

The office situation may be so different from real life that although no avoidance component prevents the formation of clear images, no anxiety is provoked on imagining scenes. The first maneuver that may be attempted is to increase the vividness of scenes by embellishing them with further descriptive details. If this fails, recourse may be made to in vivo methods. People vary in the ease with which clear images can be constructed and in the extent to which emotional reactions are evoked on imagining situations. The client may be trained to present clearer images.

Fluctuations in anxiety and erratic progress may take place because of unprogramed shifting of unspecified scene content. Repeated signaling to the same scene or unexpected anxiety to a scene whose previous presentation evoked little or no anxiety may be a consequence of such shifting. If this occurs, instructions can frequently be repeated to imagine only what is presented and not to vary the scene. Increasing the concreteness and vividness of the scene may also help. Decreasing vividness as one type of scene is repeated many times can be circumvented by presenting scenes from more than one hierarchy during a session, or by employing more unique descriptions of each scene.

During the interval between the presentation of a scene and the occurrence of a signal indicating that it can be clearly visualized, its repeated clear construction, punctuated by fading, may take place. Not until the scene remains in the imagination for a while may a signal be presented. Thus, clear visualization is taking place but is not reported. The repeated presentations may result in reports of anxiety on scene termination. This can be avoided by presenting scenes for only a set period of time, without requiring a signal indicating clear visualization. If discomfort then decreases over presentations, it is probable that the repeated signaling was caused by this type of exposure. Or coping responses can be requested.

Inadequate hierarchies. Scene content may be irrelevant to anxiety or the correct general source could be contained in the hierarchy, but there may be an inadequate delineation of the dimensions that affect the reaction. The client may vary content related to unidentified sources from scene to scene or even within the same scene. This may be evidenced in erratic progress during sessions, in that anxiety signals will appear unexpectedly. If this is found, time should be devoted to trying to identify other dimensions that influence anxiety. Any that are discovered can then be included in the hierarchy. The formation of hierarchies is often an evolving process, in that additional refinements in terms of anxiety sources are discovered. The importance given to the inclusion of accurate anxiety-eliciting content depends on whether exposure to the specific anxiety-eliciting events is considered most important (Wilson and Davison, 1971) or whether emphasis is placed on practice in the use of coping skills. Practice could be obtained with *any* anxiety eliciting source, as in the procedures described in the next chapter. If desensitization is conceptualized as imagined rehearsal, then the more similar this rehearsal to the actual situation, the more carryover of effects to the natural environment one would expect. Hierarchies may also be inadequate in relation to errors such as inclusion of too strong a scene at the weak end of the hierarchy, or sequential scenes that are too divergent in terms of anxiety elicited.

Developing Self-Instructions and Coping Behaviors

Self-instructions such as "Just relax," "Take it easy," and "Think about the word *calm*," are helpful in decreasing anxiety. Instructions that focus attention on other factors in the situation are also valuable. For example, if anxiety occurs during a social encounter, this can be a cue to attend to what the other person is saying, what he is wearing, or what he looks like. Each client is encouraged to develop a list of positive self-instructions that are especially effective for him and these are employed to influence anxiety reactions both during desensitization sessions as well as in the natural environment.

Deep breathing is another skill that can be used to control anxiety. The chest is slowly filled with air by taking four or five short deep breaths, holding each one for about five seconds (Meichenbaum, 1974). The air is then slowly released, while attending to changes in sensation, particularly to increases in relaxation, and while thinking about words such as *calm* and *relax*. The procedure is repeated a few times, providing an opportunity to experience the sensations of relaxation and increased calmness that deep breathing induces. This procedure can first be modeled for the client, and practice in using it then provided.

Deep breathing and self-instructions can both be used to influence anxiety in stressful situations. It has been found that desensitization is more effective when coping reactions—that is, experience in successfully reducing anxiety—are included. Development of coping skills emphasizes the achievement of self-management of anxiety.

Self-Directed Desensitization

Self-directed desensitization, in which the client listens to tape-recorded relaxation instructions and scene presentations, has been found to be effective in decreasing anxiety (see, for example, Baker, Cohen, and Saunders, 1973). An initial session is held between the client and counselor to form relevant hierarchies, and progress should be regularly reviewed and procedures checked. A study comparing self-directed desensitization with counselor-administered desensitization found greater self-reported gains in behavioral improvement during a follow-up assessment with those clients who employed self-directed desensitization (Baker, Cohen, and Saunders, 1973). Self-administered desensitization has been employed in institutional settings (see Dawley and Guidry, 1973). The problem with self-administered programs is how to maintain involvement in programs, which, if completed, are successful. The problem of involvement is highlighted by the study by Rosen, Glasgow, and Barrera (1976), which reported that 50 percent of the subjects did not progress beyond the relaxation-training portion of the program.

Arranging Practice in the Natural Environment

Homework assignments arranging for graduated approach to feared situations are arranged as soon as the client can engage in them with a moderate amount of comfort. These experiences provide further practice in the use of cognitive and behavioral coping skills and further opportunities to view anxiety not as distressing, but as an opportunity to exercise self-management over tension. A record should be kept of such encounters, which is shared with the counselor on a regular basis. Successes should receive abundant praise and the client encouraged to gradually assume more responsibility for designing assignments. Typically, there is a lag between what can be imagined successfully and what occurs in actual encounters (Bandura, 1969).

Assignments to practice coping skills may not necessarily relate only to hierarchy items. Selection of other situations in which stress occurs allows for practice even when the client is not yet ready to try out these skills in situations related to hierarchy items.

Responses Incompatible with Anxiety

Systematic desensitization as traditionally designed employs relaxation as a response incompatible with anxiety. As Wolpe (1958) pointed out, other reactions, including assertive behavior, anger, and sexual reactions, are also incompatible with anxiety, and these reactions can be usefully employed to decrease anxiety when appropriate. In addition, a number of other reactions have been employed, including Asian defense exercises, running, and directed physical activity such as hitting a pillow. Imagining positive events while in the presence of feared events has been employed with children (Lazarus and Abramowitz, 1962). This procedure ("emotive imagery") requires identification of a highly positive event that can be thought about or experienced while gradually approaching a feared situation. For example, a child with a fear of dogs and a love of sports cars may be asked to imagine that he goes outside his house and sees a magnificent, bright red (his favorite color) sports car. This is described in great detail and, toward the end of the scene, the presence of a small dog down the street is noted. Thus the positive imagery is used in place of a response of relaxation. Arranging positive responses may also be done in actuality, such as having a child who has a fear of the dark enter a somewhat dark room to receive a telephone call from a favorite relative. As comfort increases, the scenes or situations are altered to gradually expose the child more to the feared event.

Covert Modeling

Requesting the client to imagine himself (or another person) performing adequately in a fear-arousing situation has also been found to be effective in decreasing anxiety (Cautela, 1971b, Kazdin, 1973c). Imagining a coping reaction in which fear is experienced and successfully reduced is more effective than imagining a mastery model in which fear is not experienced (Kazdin, 1973c). An example of a coping model is: "Imagining that the person (model) puts on the gloves and tries to pick up the snake out of the cage. As the person is doing this he sort of hesitates and avoids grasping the snake at first. He stops and relaxes himself, feels calm, and picks up the snake" (Kazdin, 1973c, p. 89). As Mahoney (1974a) points out, part of the effectiveness of covert modeling may result from information that is offered concerning appropriate stress-reducing responses. This may explain the greater effectiveness of covert modeling compared to just imagining the situation (exposure only). For example, athletes often use covert modeling to refine their performance (Suinn, 1972). Covert modeling can be employed within special training sessions as well as in the natural environment. Imagining a variety of models and model reinforcement is more effective than imagining only one model or an absence of model reinforcement (Kazdin, 1975). Covert modeling, in which clients imagine themselves or others coping successfully with threats, is not as effective as performance facilitated by modeling (Thase and Moss, 1976).

Reinforced Practice

The use of actual rather than symbolic events has a number of advantages. First, there is no need to worry about generalization from the imagined state to real situations, because actual events are employed. Also, for the same reason, all relevant cues should be present. Although there are only a few studies comparing the effectiveness of reinforced practice with symbolic desensitization, they favor the superiority of in vivo methods in terms of efficiency (Crowe, Marks, Agras, and Leitenberg, 1972). "Independent performance can enhance efficacy expectations in several ways: (1) it creates additional exposure to former threats, which provides participants with further evidence that they are no longer aversively aroused by what they previously feared—reduced emotional arousal confirms increased coping capabilities; (2) self-directed mastery provides opportunities to perfect coping skills which lessen personal vulnerability to stress; and (3) if well executed, independent performance produces success experiences, which further reinforces expectations of self-competency" (Bandura, in press, p. 22).

Considerable ingenuity has been shown in gaining access to relevant events, such as arranging with a planetarium to provide showings of thunder and lightning to a woman with a severe fear of such events, and gaining cooperation of airport officials to allow access to hangared planes to use with clients who have flying phobias. Pictures of feared events may be employed as approximations to the actual event. Ingenuity has also been shown in response induction procedures that facilitate performance of feared behavior, such as the use of game playing with children during in vivo exposure (Croghan and Musante, 1975).

Covert positive reinforcement, in which the client imagines a pleasant experience following approach behavior, or covert modeling, in which the client imagines himself performing well, may be employed to encourage such responses in addition to self-reinforcing statements. Self- or social reinforcers could be made contingent on approach behavior. A sixty-three-year-old man who had developed an extensive checking ritual performed each evening prior to bedtime received such reinforcers as a hug and kiss from his wife and opportunity to work on a crossword puzzle for decreasing the time he spent in this ritual. On the first night on which he succeeded in reducing this to sixty minutes, he and his wife resumed sexual relations, which had ceased ten years before (Melamed and Siegel, 1975b).

Approach to feared events is *self-regulated* in accord with degree of client apprehension. A series of graded steps is employed and the client is instructed to go as far as he can, starting at the least anxiety-provoking step and then stopping when anxiety becomes too high. As comfort increases with one degree of approach, the next is selected for practice. Abundant praise should be given for progress, as well as feedback as to the amount of progress achieved in each attempt. It has been found that feedback is more important than praise in getting progress started (Leitenberg, Agras, Allen, Butz, and Edwards, 1975). This highlights the need for careful arrangement for such feedback. Initially, practice is usually carried out in the presence of the counselor, but additional sessions may be conducted alone. During self-observation, the client provides his own feedback as to progress (Emmelkamp, 1974); for example, how long he can remain in the feared situation without feeling unduly tense. Clients who are anxious when out of doors have recorded the amount of time they are able to remain outside. Here, too, approach is graduated in accord with client comfort and clients are instructed to leave anxiety-provoking situations when they start to become uncomfortable. Repeated exposures to the feared situation may be made during one session. The advantage of this procedure is that the client carries it out on his own; however, arrangements should be made for regular contact with the counselor to share information as to progress and to allow opportunities for counselor praise.

Practice may be preceded by training the client in anxiety management skills which he is instructed to employ during practice sessions. This may be particularly helpful when anxiety is high, since it will offer an additional source of incompatible cues, and thus it may lower anxiety sufficiently so that exposure to feared events will occur. The client is instructed to provide self-reinforcing statements following approach behavior.

There are several factors involved in reinforced practice that are designed to enhance the reduction of avoidance behavior and anxiety. As in symbolic desensitization, a series of graded steps is employed, each of which is initially accomplished under circumstances that afford protection against feared consequences (Bandura, 1971a). The difference in reinforced practice is that exposure occurs to real events. Praise from the counselor serves as a further incentive for approach behavior, as does feedback. Competent verbal behavior is encouraged and anxiety-provoking statements are discouraged. Examples of tasks employed in reinforced practice for public speaking anxiety include "(1) reading a list of unrelated words, numbers, and sentences; (2) reading a speech which someone else had written; (3) reading an original speech; (4) delivering an original speech from extensive notes; and (5) delivering an original speech from a single note card and without use of a podium" (Kirsch, Wolpin, and Knutson, 1975, p. 167). Tasks employed with a seven-year-old boy with a school phobia included "(1) getting out of the car and approaching the curb; (2) going to the sidewalk; (3) going to the bottom of the steps of the school; (4) going to the top of the steps; (5) going to the school door; (6) entering the school; (7) approaching the classroom a certain distance each day down the hall; (8) entering the classroom; (9) being present in the classroom with the teacher; (10) being present in the classroom with the teacher and one or two classmates; and (11) being in the classroom with a full class" (Garvey and Hegrenes, 1966, p. 148). This last procedure was carried out during twenty consecutive days, with about twenty to forty minutes of counselor time involved each day as he accompanied the child in carrying out these approximations.

Reinforced practice has been employed with infants. Graduated approach and events eliciting positive reactions were employed to decrease the anxiety of a one-year-old infant to baths (Bentler, 1962). Margaret reacted with violent emotion, not only to the bathtub, but also to the faucet, water in the tub, being placed in the basin, as well as to faucets or water in any part of the house. Distraction, toys, and body contact were used to elicit positive reactions. Intervention took place over a month. Toys were first placed in the empty bathtub and the infant was given free access to the bathroom and to the toys. She was then placed on the kitchen table around the sink while the sink was filled with water and had toys floating in it. The toys on the table were gradually moved closer to the water and then were moved to the other side of the basin, so that Margaret would have to step into the basin to reach them. She was then washed in the bathroom sink. The mirror situated over the basin provided another source of distraction. She finally progressed to being washed in the tub while receiving affection and hugs from her mother.

Modeling and Reinforced Practice

An effective and efficient way to reduce defensive behavior is to have the client observe a model perform the desired approach behavior, and then to arrange optimal conditions for him to engage in similar activities until performance is skillful and comfortable (Bandura, 1971a). The client is given an opportunity to practice approach to the feared event in a self-regulated way, as in reinforced practice, but this time also observes someone else performing the desired behavior without unfavorable consequences—that is, he observes effective ways of handling threatening situations. This procedure thus provides an opportunity for vicarious as well as actual extinction of anxiety reactions. Approach to the feared situation is carried out in a protected environment, as in reinforced practice. A coping model is more effective than a mastery model (Meichenbaum, 1971). It is more effective if the model shows signs of anxiety and then demonstrates to the observer how anxiety can be reduced through the use of self-instructions and behavioral coping reactions (see examples in the next chapter). There are a number of components involved in successful use of this procedure, including: (1) observation of a model performing approach behavior; (2) self-regulated approach in graded steps; (3) use of a protected environment; and (4) encouragement and feedback from the counselor. Both live and symbolic models have been found to produce effects, and the procedure has been employed with both children and adults across a broad array of fears. Children's fears of hospitalization and surgery were successfully reduced by having them observe a filmed model going through various steps in this experience such as talking with nurses and doctors (Melamed and Siegel, 1975a).

Anxiety should decrease over repeated modeling trials. Such trials are continued until fear is sufficiently reduced to permit approach behavior. As with reinforced practice, clients may or may not be trained in anxiety-neutralizing procedures and requested to use these self-control skills during exposure to feared events. Whether this is necessary depends on the intensity of the anxiety reactions. The more intense the anxiety, the more probable that training the client in skills for coping with anxiety will facilitate the lowering of anxiety and so increase the probability of exposure to feared objects. Such training should also result in more generalized effects. Covert modeling may also be employed, in which the client imagines a model coping with the feared situation. This permits rehearsal of approach behavior and has been found to be effective (Mahoney, 1974a). Greater changes in avoidance behavior and self-report have been found when same sex and same age models are used (Kazdin, 1974a).

Guided Participation

Guided participation is a variant of modeling with reinforced practice that includes all features of this procedure and, in addition, offers physical assistance in enacting feared activities. The counselor physically assists the client to approach feared events. For example, in a study with people who had a fear of heights, the counselor physically assisted clients in climbing responses, in addition to modeling progressively more threatening behaviors. In another study, the client placed his hand on the counselor's arm as the counselor modeled approach behavior. Physical assistance is gradually faded as clients become less fearful. As in reinforced practice, approach is self-regulated and a protected environment is offered in relation to degree of exposure. This procedure has been shown to be more effective than modeling with verbally guided enactment, more effective than systematic desensitization (Ritter, 1969), and more effective than covert modeling (Thase and Moss, 1976). The physical contact involved in guided participation provides another source of cues that are incompatible with anxiety-producing cues, and thus should facilitate exposure to feared events. Modeling plus participation has been found to be more effective than either procedure alone (Lewis, 1974). Self-directed performance, during which the client is asked to perform alone the activities previously executed with the counselor's assistance, facilitates the effects of participant modeling (Bandura, Jeffery, and Gajdos, 1975). Self-directed performance permits independent mastery responses.

Anxiety Induction Procedures

Wolpe speculated that in order to decrease anxiety, it was necessary to inhibit the anxiety reaction reciprocally in the presence of feared events. Another view espoused by the developer of implosive therapy is that what is required is non-punished exposure to feared events (Stampfl and Levis, 1967). The use of anxiety induction procedures assumes that anxiety is maintained, because it is reinforced by the removal of unpleasant events, and that exposure will allow extinction of the anxiety reaction; that is, the feared event is presented, but no longer paired with an aversive event. Or, put another way, this allows a discrimination to develop between rational and irrational hypothesized outcomes (Franks and Wilson, 1974). The person is in the presence of the feared object and in fact nothing horrendous occurs.

There are two variants of anxiety induction procedure,

implosion and flooding (Morganstern, 1973). In anxiety induction methods, no attempt is made to fortify the client with anxiety management skills prior to exposure to feared situations or to graduate the discomfort involved.

Implosive Therapy. There is an attempt in implosive therapy to present the most extreme version of feared stimuli imaginable to the client, the idea being that nothing horrendous will actually happen and the client will be able to "reality test" and see that he has been jousting with ghosts in the dark. These ghosts are made very colorful indeed in implosion and a requisite for use of this procedure is an excellent imagination for horrifying events on the part of the counselor. No doubt those who write scripts for horror movies would have considerable skill in creating scenes for implosive therapy. For example, "A person afraid of a snake would be requested to view himself picking up and handling the snake. Attempts would be made to have him become aware of his reactions to the animal. He would be instructed to feel how slimy the snake was. Next, he would be asked to experience the snake crawling over his body and biting and ripping his flesh. Scenes of snakes crushing or swallowing him or perhaps his falling into a pit of snakes would be appropriate implosions" (Hogan, 1966, p. 26). Psychoanalytic as well as behavior theory were originally used to inform the design of implosive therapy, and it was assumed that whenever a client has a difficulty either aggressive or sexual content may be related to it, even though the client does not mention such content (Stampfl and Levis, 1967). Thus, if a client is compulsive, it is assumed that this is in some way related to the anal stage of development, and therefore scatological content is included in scenes, such as having him imagine a visit to the outhouse during a trip to the country and falling in. The inclusion of content related to sexual and aggressive themes is not necessary for effects to be achieved.

Flooding. Flooding is analogous to presenting the top hierarchy item over and over again. The client is repeatedly exposed to the target stimulus, not to an extreme version of it, as in implosion. Let us use the example of public speaking anxiety. A hierarchy for successive approximation is illustrated earlier in this chapter. This procedure was compared with flooding as well as with implosion (Kirsch, Wolpin, and Knutson, 1975). In the flooding condition, students practiced only the top hierarchy item on five occasions. In implosion, students practiced the top item during two sessions, and during the other three delivered a speech without notes, delivered one to an audience that had been instructed to react hostilely with boos and catcalls, and delivered a speech under pressure of being videotaped. Flooding was found to be most effective in decreasing anxiety, as measured by a behavior checklist during performance. Some studies suggest that this procedure is more effective than systematic desensitization in the treatment of agoraphobia and obsessive-compulsive behavior (Crowe and others, 1972).

Flooding may be carried out symbolically or in actuality, although there is evidence that in vivo exposure is much more effective (see, for example, Stern and Marks, 1973). When scenes are presented in the imagination, they should be made as vivid as possible and situations that arouse the greatest anxiety are presented. Both imagined and actual flooding may be employed. Emmelkamp (1974) employed a series of flooding sessions with agoraphobic clients. Each session consisted of forty-five minutes of imagined flooding followed by in vivo flooding during which the client spent forty-five minutes walking through the streets along a route jointly determined by the client and counselor. Flooding plus self-observation (described earlier in this chapter) has been found to be more effective than either procedure alone (Emmelkamp, 1974). Because prolonged exposure is more effective than short periods of exposure, it does not seem that it is the duration of exposure per se that is the effective ingredient in flooding (Franks and Wilson, 1974).

Restructuring the Social Environment

Significant others may support "phobic behavior" and fail to reinforce competent behavior. Lazarus (1966) was one of the first to point to the possible role of social reinforcement for phobic behavior and the importance of changing inappropriate reinforcement patterns. Emmelkamp (1974), for example, found that with some clients phobic responses appeared to play an important part in marital relationships. In one instance in which both the client and counselor reported progress, the husband informed an independent observer that there had been no improvement in his wife and that only he himself could help her. Thus phobic behavior on the part of one family member may offer a source of reinforcement for other family members. Or, significant others might have adapted to "phobic behavior," as in the following example. Intervention should include a reprograming of inappropriate reinforcement patterns.

Illustration of the Use of
Multiple Anxiety Reduction Methods

Very often, many different anxiety reduction methods may be employed with a client. This is well illustrated in the following example of an eleven-year-old boy with a dog phobia (MacDonald, 1975a). Significant others had made a number of accommodations to the boy's fears. His mother made round trips to his school four times a day so he would not be exposed to dogs, and the father had ceased to participate in a number of outdoor sports, because his son would not go beyond the yard around the house. The boy did not participate in any school activity programs, because of possible exposure to dogs, and was described as withdrawn. Most of his time at home was spent in his room.

The phobia had developed over a series of three incidents. During one, a dog had charged into the yard and knocked over the boy. This was six years earlier. Now he refused to go outside unless accompanied by a friend or family member. The following intervention procedures were employed: relaxation training hierarchy construction, systematic desensitization, desensitization adjuncts, skill training in appropriate ways to interact with dogs, modeling procedures and reinforced practice, programed outdoor activities, and social-environmental restructuring. A brief description of each component is provided as follows.

1. *Relaxation training.* Seven training sessions were given. Home practice became regular when the child was given a record card and asked to note down the time of each of his sessions.

2. *Formation of hierarchies.* This was conducted over eleven sessions. Examples of items can be seen on page 459.

3. *Systematic desensitization.* This was started on the eighth session and extended over ten sessions.

4. *Desensitization adjuncts.* The boy was given a set of fourteen dog photographs during the fifth session and was to choose two each day and post these in his room. He was also requested to write a happy story about himself and a dog. At the tenth session, he was given a five-minute tape recording of a barking dog and cassette recorder and was instructed to play the tape following a relaxation session when he was relaxed, and to increase the volume over practice sessions. When reactions to this tape were mastered, another tape was introduced, which consisted of simultaneous barks and howls from a number of different dogs.

5. *Dog interaction skill training.* This boy had an absence of skills for interacting with dogs. At the fourth session, he was taught to interpret dog body language such as tail wagging and bristled neck fur. A model-prompt-reinforce sequence was employed to encourage head rubbing, back patting, and ear scratching skills, using a stuffed animal. This procedure was also employed to shape command giving, with special attention devoted to voice firmness. Textual material was also employed. The boy was requested to read sections of a dog trainer's manual.

6. *Modeling procedures and reinforced practice.* A series of sessions was conducted to provide safe exposure to the feared stimulus in progressively less controlled situations. A second goal was to train the child in dog handling and outdoor play skills. First the boy watched two models engage in ear scratching, dog feeding, patting, and simple command giving. The models engaged in an instructional dialog between each other, in order to direct the boy's attention to relevant events. During the second session, a replication of important components of the last session was first carried

out. The boy then watched two models engaging in ball throwing and playing tag behind a chain-link fence. They encouraged him to interact indirectly by giving the dog commands, throwing the ball over the fence, and running alongside the dog near the fence. In the third session, direct contact with a dog was arranged. A sequence was followed in which a male model described and modeled an interaction such as ear scratching. The counselor imitated this through the fence while verbalizing nonanxious reactions, and then the boy was asked to imitate the behavior. Appropriate imitation was reinforced and hesitation or avoidance was ignored. This sequence, modeling-imitation-prompting-reinforcement, was repeated several times for several interactions, including back patting and dog biscuit feeding. In the fourth session, there was direct contact without separation, following a warmup phase (repeat of elements from the third session). Prompting and mild verbal punishment were employed to encourage approach behavior. A variety of novel events were introduced during subsequent sessions to encourage generalization of fear reduction. Content of the first three sessions was included with a new dog during the fifth session, and during remaining sessions more active interactions were encouraged.

7. *Programed outdoor activity.* Starting with the tenth session, a series of assignments was given that required progressively longer outdoor time periods. The purpose of this was to arrange for the acquisition of play and social skills that would be incompatible with those of a "dog phobic." These assignments included approximations to walking home from school starting with just 10 percent of the route; tennis and bike riding lessons; trips to the comic book store; and walks to watch Little League baseball, starting with staying for just one inning.

8. *Social environmental restructuring.* The counselor held five meetings with the parents. They were instructed to stop cuing their child to be afraid and to offer praise

for appropriate reactions to animals as well as for other instances of "competent" behavior.

The results of this program were very positive. The boy stayed outdoors without worrying about dogs by the sixth session. An eighteen-month follow-up revealed maintenance of positive changes. He was no longer designated by teachers as socially isolated and withdrawn, regularly played outdoors both alone and with friends, and did not avoid situations that might involve a meeting with a dog.

Selection of Anxiety Reduction Procedures

Assessment will reveal the extent to which different response systems are involved in defensive behavior. These may or may not be highly correlated. In terms of a parallel effects view, physiological-attitude-behavior consistencies represent correlated coeffects rather than outcomes of a process, and therefore one cannot assume that these will be highly correlated (Bandura, 1969). Assessment will also indicate the extent to which significant others reinforce appropriate behaviors and fail to reinforce desired behavior. The wider the range of situations in which defensive behavior occurs, the more relevant is a procedure in which the client is trained in general coping skills. In cases where physiological arousal is high, a procedure especially directed toward altering such responses should be seriously considered, in conjunction with other methods. Thus, progressive relaxation training may be employed that heightens client awareness of states of tension and offers skills in decreasing them. The importance of recognition of physiological cues in relation to outcome is emphasized by the finding that subjects who respond with increased physiological arousal during initial hierarchy items and who can verbally discriminate their physical reactions associated with arousal are more likely to respond favorably to intervention (Lang, Melamed, and Hart, 1970).

If cognitions are important antecedents for anxiety, cognitive restructuring may be employed, which focuses on changing negative thought patterns (see Chapter Twelve). The development of coping skills can be complemented by reinforced practice and modeling procedures, which are indicated when overt behavioral components are outstanding. There is strong suggestion that using a graduated series of actual events is more effective than imagined events (Bandura, Blanchard, and Ritter, 1969). More accurate feedback will be provided, and there will be less need to be concerned about generalization. Symbolic procedures are particularly useful when direct action is not possible, such as with anxiety-arousing cognitions, when graduated approach is not possible, or when imagery is an important antecedent for anxiety. Such procedures should be blended with gradual approach as soon as possible. Symbolic desensitization requires the identification of the specific antecedents of anxiety, whereas other methods, such as differential relaxation, require only that the client be able to identify the occasion for employment of his new coping skill, such as increased muscle tension. More general coping skills may be developed when anxiety sources cannot be identified.

Most procedures entail provision of feedback and praise for client progress, the formation of a conceptualization of anxiety as something the client will learn to develop control over and as a cue to employ coping reactions, and training in coping skills. In each case, the relationship between significant others and the client should be examined to determine whether these others are reinforcing defensive behavior and failing to reinforce competent actions.

Some information exists describing the interaction between the type of anxiety and the most effective treatment procedure—for example, flooding or reinforced practice is more effective than imagined desensitization in decreasing agoraphobic reactions (Emmelkamp and Wessels, 1975) and animal phobias (Bandura, Blanchard, and Ritter, 1969). Minimal information exists concerning the relationship between various personality inventories and outcome, although what information is available appears promising in terms of facilitating selection of intervention procedures. For example, Farmer and Wright (1971) found that both muscle relaxation as well as directed muscle activity such as pounding a cushion with the fist (Lazarus, 1965a) was effective in decreasing snake phobias of subjects who scored high and low on Fisher and Cleveland's (1958) barrier score, whereas directed muscle activity was effective only for low-barrier subjects.

Evaluating Progress

The uniqueness of the particular response systems involved in an anxiety reaction, the relative contribution of each, and the fact that often changes in one response system, such as the ability to approach feared events, are not matched by similar changes in other response systems, such as verbal report or physiological measures, make it especially important to evaluate progress across multiple response systems (Lick and Katkin, 1976). The client may even be forewarned that there is some lag between changes in attitude (verbal reports of fear) and actual approach behavior but that over time these will tend to converge. Gathering information on overt approach behavior as well as physiological measures (or self-report concerning arousal) will enable the counselor to make sure that there is not too much lag between what the client will do and the arousal reported. That is, one would not necessarily wish to encourage repeated approaches to a feared object with continuing high arousal, although this may occur in the initial stages of implosion or flooding programs. However, if arousal fails to decrease over sessions, some other procedure should be considered, perhaps one that will offer the client more direct control over his arousal through stress management training.

It must also be remembered that different contingencies may control verbal reports that may influence actual arousal or approach behavior. If social reinforcement is maintaining verbal reports of anxiety, these may persist even though physiological arousal in the presence of feared events decreases.

Summary

A variety of procedures have been developed for the removal of behavioral inhibitions. An integral aspect of all behavioral methods for anxiety reduction is cultivation of a new conceptualization of anxiety in terms of its development and control. Systematic desensitization is uniquely suited for situations in which gradual exposure to anxiety-eliciting events cannot be arranged (perhaps because of the intensity of the anxiety or the source of this reaction), and in situations in which new behaviors do not have to be established. Desensitization sessions permit imagined rehearsal of approach toward feared events. Training in progressive relaxation and the use of hierarchies enable gradual exposure to anxiety-eliciting events and assure successful coping and mastery reactions. The effects of desensitization can be enhanced by the development of behavioral and self-instructional coping skills. Homework assignments are combined with imagined rehearsal as soon as possible to permit additional exposure to feared events and feedback on progress. A variety of adjuncts to relaxation may be employed during such assignments including positive imagery and self-reinforcement for progress. Social consequences from significant others are restructured as necessary. Comparative studies show that performance-based interventions are more effective than vicarious procedures, in which the client watches a model, and than symbolic procedures, in which feared events are imagined. A number of response induction aids can be employed to encourage coping behaviors, including observation of a successful model. Anxiety induction procedures have also been effectively employed to decrease anxiety, and here, too, there is evidence that actual exposure is more effective than imagined exposure. An emphasis on the development of coping skills that can be employed in a variety of situations will hopefully help to maintain appropriate behaviors.

12

There has been a recent emphasis on developing coping skills that can be employed whenever stressful situations arise (see Suinn and Richardson, 1971; Meichenbaum, 1975b; Goldfried, 1971; Novaco, 1975). A characteristic of all these procedures is training the client to discriminate the antecedents of stress in terms of cognitions or feelings, and to employ these as cues to utilize coping reactions. These procedures do not require construction of a hierarchy. Possibilities of generalization are enhanced because of the focus on general skills and the use of negative thoughts and emotions as cues for positive coping behavior. The client has a built-in reminder to use these new resources. This approach to anxiety reduction stresses a cognitive-mediational model of anxiety.

The conception of training clients in general stress man-

492

Developing
Self-Management Skills
for Regulating Stress

agement skills that can be employed in a range of situations is by no means new. Jacobson, for example, developed relaxation training in 1938 and suggested that clients use it in their daily activities to relax unnecessary tension. What is new is the development, refinement, and testing of such procedures and their comparison with other anxiety reduction methods such as traditional systematic desensitization. The emphasis on developing a new conceptualization of stress that is apparent in some of these procedures is also not new, as can be seen from reading Wolpe's (1958) early book on the subject. There is, however, a renewed emphasis on the importance of self-management skills, and a growing literature in relation to learned helplessness (Seligman, 1975) and on procedures that alleviate it, which has informed the development of stress management methods.

These procedures are particularly useful when it is not possible to locate anxiety- or anger-arousing environmental sources, and when more general skills are needed, because of the range of situations in which stress occurs. Some procedures focus more on thoughts, whereas others emphasize sensory awareness training in relation to physiological concomitants of and cues for anxiety or anger. Assessment should reveal which response systems are particularly involved—the affective, cognitive, or behavioral. Intervention procedures can then be selected in accord with such information. Procedures that emphasize the role of thoughts in relation to anxiety will be discussed first, followed by a description of methods that focus on affective components of anxiety. Methods developed for management of inappropriate anger will be described.

The Use of Stress Inoculation Training with Multiphobic Clients: Self-Instruction Training

Many clients experience discomfort in a range of situations; that is, they are multiphobic. A program that trains clients how to manage anxiety in a variety of situations has been found to be more effective than traditional systematic desensitization (Meichenbaum, Gilmore, and Fedoravicius, 1971). This training program focuses on altering the cognitions that mediate anxiety. People who experience anxiety in situations tell themselves things that are different from the self-statements of people who do not experience stress. It has been found, for example, that, in evaluative situations, people who have high test anxiety spend more time worrying about their performance and about how others are doing, and ruminate over alternatives and are preoccupied with feelings of inadequacy, anticipation of punishment, loss of status, and increased physiological reactions (Mandler and Watson, 1966). Negative thoughts may also hamper competent interpersonal behavior.

The stress inoculation program is designed to achieve three goals: to educate the client about the nature of stress reactions; to have the client rehearse coping skills; and to offer the client opportunities to practice coping behaviors in which anxiety is experienced and successfully reduced (Meichenbaum, 1975b). Coping reactions are more effective in decreasing anxiety than are mastery reactions, in which no anxiety is imagined (Meichenbaum, 1971). The training program is offered over a four-week period using six one-hour sessions. The educational phase is analogous to the formation of a mutual conceptualization of anxiety described in the previous chapter. This includes finding out how the client has felt and what he has thought about when confronting feared situations in the past, and finding out how he currently copes with stressors in general and his target fears in particular. A conceptualization of anxiety is offered in terms of two elements—heightened arousal, and a set of anxiety-producing thoughts and self-statements (desires to flee, a sense of helplessness, thoughts of being overwhelmed [Schachter, 1966]). The goals of treatment are explained in terms of the two major elements of anxiety reactions. Treatment is viewed as helping the client learn to control physiological arousal as well as to substitute positive self-statements for anxiety-producing thoughts. Training in progressive relaxation is employed to offer skills in controlling arousal levels and practice is provided in using coping self-statements when confronting stress. Clients also learn to relabel their reactions in more appropriate ways—for example, rather than labeling physiological arousal a sign that they are crazy, it may be labeled as tension and thus may now be considered a cue to cope.

The client is encouraged to view anxiety as a series of phases rather than as one large panic reaction (Meichenbaum, 1975b). This reaction is divided into four phases: preparing for a stressor; confronting or handling a stressor; possibly being overwhelmed by a stressor; and, lastly, reinforcing oneself for having coped. Examples from the client are solicited that could be employed in each of these four stages. These statements are then practiced during Sessions Two, Three, and Four, first out loud and then covertly. Training in relaxation and the use of breathing exercises are also provided during these sessions. Examples of coping self-statements are shown in the following list from Meichenbaum (1975b, p. 371).

1. *Preparing for a Stressor*

What is it you have to do?
You can develop a plan to deal with it.

Just think about what you can do about it.
That's better than getting anxious.

No negative self-statements; just think rationally.

Don't worry; worry won't help anything.

Maybe what you think is anxiety is eagerness to confront it.

2. *Confronting and Handling a Stressor*

Just "psych" yourself up—you can meet this challenge.

One step at a time; you can handle the situation.

Don't think about fear; just think about what you have to do. Stay relevant.

This anxiety is what the doctor said you would feel. It's a reminder to use your coping exercises.

This tenseness can be an ally, a cue to cope.

Relax; you're in control. Take a slow, deep breath. Ah, good.

3. *Coping with the Feeling of Being Overwhelmed*

When fear comes, just pause.

Keep the focus on the present; what is it you have to do?

Label your fear from 0 to 10 and watch it change.

You should expect your fear to rise.

Don't try to eliminate fear totally; just keep it manageable.

You can convince yourself to do it. You can reason your fear away.

It will be over shortly.

It's not the worst thing that can happen.

Just think about something else.

Do something that will prevent you from thinking about fear.

Describe what is around you. That way you won't think about worrying.

4. *Reinforcing Self-Statements*

It worked; you did it.

Wait until you tell your therapist about this.

It wasn't as bad as you expected.

You made more out of the fear than it was worth.

Your damn ideas—that's the problem. When you control them, you control your fear.

> It's getting better each time you use the proce-
> dures.
> You can be pleased with the progress you're
> making.

Many of these statements serve to redirect attention to the task at hand—taking a test, speaking to a new person or trying to write a report. This is an important goal in increasing such thoughts. As noted by Meichenbaum (1975b) the self-statements developed encourage the client: (1) to assess the reality of the situation; (2) to control negative, anxiety-producing thoughts; (3) to recognize and use the anxiety as a cue to employ coping skills and possibly to relabel the anxiety; (4) to cope with fear experienced; and, lastly, (5) to provide self-reinforcement for coping reactions. Coping skills that the client already possesses are determined during assessment and their use in problematic situations is encouraged.

The last step in stress inoculation provides opportunities to practice coping reactions under actual stressful conditions. This is initiated after the fourth session. Prior to the first exposure, the counselor models the use of coping reactions in dealing with a stressful event and the client is requested to imitate the counselor's behavior, first using verbalized self-instructions and then covert ones. The intensity of the stressful event should be such that the client is able to cope successfully with it. As skill is acquired with one level, higher-level stressors can then be arranged.

Having an effective coping response at one's disposal and perceiving the relationship between one's own thoughts and actions and the removal of unpleasant events interfere with a pattern of learned helplessness (Seligman, 1975). As Meichenbaum (1975b) points out, stress inoculation alters the client's perception of himself as being helpless, to an attitude of "learned resourcefulness." This helps to alter a self-concept of not being able to handle stress, to a self-concept of being able to do so. Stress inoculation training provides clients with a graded set of exposures to stress, thus hopefully inoculating them to high stress levels in a variety of situations. The anxiety itself or negative thoughts serve as built-in reminders to employ coping skills (Suinn and Richardson, 1971). "People's sense of self-competency affects their susceptibility to self-arousal. They fear and avoid threatening situations that they believe exceed their coping skills but behave affirmatively when they judge themselves capable of managing circumstances that would otherwise be intimidating. Perceived self-competence not only reduces anticipatory fears, but also, through expectation of eventual success, sustains coping efforts in the face of difficulties" (Bandura, Jeffery, and Gajdos, 1975, p. 142).

Rational Emotive Therapy (Rational Restructuring)

The ability of our thoughts to negatively affect our lives has been stressed for many years by Ellis (1962). He has particularly emphasized training the client to identify irrational cognitions and to reevaluate them in more realistic terms. "Rational-emotive therapy," as Ellis has labeled his system, has recently been placed in a behavioral framework by Goldfried, Decenteceo, and Weinberg (1974). Here, too, the client is trained to perform a situational analysis of his reaction, including identification of the external events that provoke his reactions, the specific thoughts these events induce, and the beliefs related to the thoughts. Frequently occurring irrational beliefs include the following (from scattered places in Ellis, 1962):

1. "The idea that it is a dire necessity for an adult human being to be loved or approved by virtually every significant other person in his community" (p. 61).
2. "The idea that one should be thoroughly competent, adequate, and achieving in all possible respects, if one is to consider oneself worthwhile" (p. 63).
3. "The idea that certain people are bad, wicked, or villainous and that they should be severely blamed and punished for their villainy" (p. 65).
4. "The idea that it is awful and catastrophic when things are not the way one would very much like them to be" (p. 69).
5. "The idea that human unhappiness is externally caused and that people have little or no ability to control their sorrows and disturbances" (p. 72).
6. "The idea that if something is or may be dangerous or

fearsome, one should be terribly concerned about it and should keep dwelling on the possibility of its occurring" (p. 75).

7. "The idea that it is easier to avoid than to face certain life difficulties and self-responsibilities" (p. 78).

8. "The idea that one should be dependent on others and needs someone stronger than oneself on whom to rely" (p. 80).

9. "The idea that one's past history is an all-important determinant of one's present behavior and that because something once strongly affected one's life, it should indefinitely have a similar effect" (p. 82).

10. "The idea that one should become quite upset over other people's problems and disturbances" (p. 85).

11. "The idea that there is invariably a right, precise, and perfect solution to human problems and that it is catastrophic if this correct solution is not found" (p. 87).

Bandura (in press) has noted the various ways in which cognitive appraisals may attenuate the effects of successful coping reactions. The person may perceive that only in certain situations will his behavior be effective. Or he may credit his achievements to external factors and not to his own ability. "Here the problem is one of inaccurate ascription of personal competency to situational factors" (Bandura, in press, p. 21). The effect of successful performance on one's sense of self-efficacy will also vary, depending on whether accomplishments are attributed to ability or to effort expended.

Rational restructuring involves a reappraisal of the rationality of the client's thoughts and guides the client toward the selection of positive alternatives, thus again providing the client with an active coping skill that can be used in everyday life. Let us say that someone had the following thought: "I must look awful today." One would first examine the rationality of the thought. The irrational aspect of this thought may rest on the assumption that "I must look good every day or people won't like me." Secondly, the implications of the statement, if it were true, are examined. One could address the implications of actually looking awful by saying to oneself, "If I don't look as good as possible, so what? What dire events will befall me?" There would then be a focus on more positive beliefs, such as saying covertly, "I still have something to offer and people with genuine interest in what I have to say won't be affected by superficialities."

Use of this method involves the following steps:

1. Identification of anxiety.
2. Examination of thoughts about the situation that may be related to the discomfort. The client learns to ask, "What am I saying to myself that is making me upset?"
3. Reevaluation of these thoughts in terms of their rationality and implications—the client is encouraged to examine the rationality of his thoughts. Have hasty negative judgments been made? Do irrational expectations exist, such as "I want this person to really fall for me immediately?" What are the implications of these thoughts even if true?
4. Evaluation and thinking of more realistic and positive statements.
5. Noting any resulting decrease in anxiety.
6. Reinvolvement in the interaction or task at hand.

The fifth step is important, because the client is thus encouraged to become aware of the relationship between altering his thought patterns and resultant increases in comfort. The sixth step focuses the person back on the task or interpersonal encounter in which he was involved. It is best to have the client rehearse this skill before trying it out in actual situations. Rehearsal can be carried out in the office by selecting a situation and asking the client to close his eyes and imagine himself in this situation and to describe out loud both the situation and what he says to himself. He may then be asked to rationally reevaluate these thoughts, to offer positive alternatives, and to refocus on the task or interaction at hand. These steps would first be verbalized and then practice provided in carrying them out covertly. After practicing with an easy situation, progress can be made to a harder one. An example of what someone might say in practicing follows. The situation involves feeling discomfort when telling a woman that one would like to see her again.

> *Negative statement.* "If I tell her that, she will think I am over-eager, hard up, and then I will really mess up my chances. Also, if she doesn't tell me that she would like to see me, then I'll feel awful, because this means she doesn't want to see me again, ever."

> *Reevaluation.* "Telling someone that you would like to see her again is not such a big deal. It very well might please her very much and also I am honestly expressing my feelings. And, if I don't, I may be missing out on seeing her again. If she does not reciprocate by saying she'd like to see me, that doesn't necessarily mean she never wants to see me again. Even if she doesn't want to see me again, at least I have tried and have honestly and courageously stated my feelings."

Practice in using this procedure may also be provided by behavior rehearsal. Situations are recreated in the office and the client requested to rehearse his new coping skills while involved in tasks or encounters. If the anxiety arises in interpersonal settings, use of a group provides a ready source of participants who can help to recreate various situations.

The main difference between rational restructuring and stress management is the greater emphasis in the former on examining the sources of irrationality related to a client's self-statements. If irrational beliefs are firmly held, it may be necessary to engage the client in a careful examination of them.

Sometimes the use of rational restructuring is initially distracting to clients when employed in actual situations and an alternative procedure, such as stress management or "thought stopping," that does not have this effect can be offered. These can be employed when the client is involved in anxiety-arousing situations, while rational restructuring can be used during covert or overt practice sessions, allowing for the appraisal of client statements. As skill is developed with rational restructuring, the client may become able to reevaluate during actual situations. Helpful sources that the client may be asked to read include *Talk Sense to Yourself* (McMullin and Casey, 1975), *A New Guide to Rational Living* (Ellis and Harper, 1975), and *"I Can If I Want To"* (Lazarus and Fay, 1975).

There is less empirical support for the effectiveness of rational emotive therapy than for the self-instructional training. These procedures are similar in their focus on the role of dysfunctional thoughts (private monologs) in distress, and on offering training in and reinforcement for client observation and change of dysfunctional thought patterns (see Mahoney, 1974a). Both also employ graduated performance tasks, as well as modeling. Greater emphasis is given within rational emotive therapy to acceptance of a value system stressing self-acceptance and to a formal logical analysis of premises. Both emphasize covert verbalizations, unlike covert modeling, which emphasizes covert imagery. As Mahoney (1974a) notes, both methods are very different from "positive thinking" or the use of "autosuggestions" popularized by best-sellers in their use of specific, task-relevant self-statements and graduated performance tasks.

The cognitive-restructuring method developed by D'Zurilla, Wilson, and Nelson (1973) encourages clients to verbalize past experiences involving feared situations. Here, too, clients are provided with an understanding of their fears in terms of learning theory. Irrational ideas underlying their fears are exposed and challenged, as in rational restructuring. Clients thus engage in prolonged verbal exposure to threatening situations and are encouraged to relabel threatening stimuli, thus providing a rational explanation for the development of their fear and to attribute fear to internal cognitions rather than to external events (Wein, Nelson, and Odom, 1975). As with other behavioral methods for stress reduction, there is a reattribution of the fear behavior from the feared event to the client's incorrect interpretation of his anxiety. Cognitive restructuring has been found to be as effective as systematic desensitization in decreasing avoidance behavior and more effective in reducing subjective anxiety (Wein, Nelson, Odom, 1975).

Thought Stopping

Recurrent unconstructive ruminations are sometimes problematic. One twenty-eight-year-old male, for example, had the recurrent thought that he was going to become mentally ill and lose control. This thought was related to a wide variety of external and internal events. Thought stopping was employed, in conjunction with other procedures, to decrease these thoughts. This procedure was originally discussed by Wolpe (1958). The client is trained to identify negative thoughts, to covertly tell himself to stop them, and to focus on the task at hand. The potential of achieving control over one's thoughts can be dramatically demonstrated to clients by requesting them to verbalize their negative thoughts and by shouting at them, "Stop!" Typically, their speech will be interrupted. (The one time I found this demonstration a total failure was with a compulsive talker. Shouting "Stop!" had literally no effect on her speech or her physical appearance. This is unusual.) This procedure is repeated with an inquiry each time as to whether the client's thought pattern was interrupted. If it was blocked, the client gradually assumes blocking control and learns to covertly say, "Stop," when negative thoughts start to occur. Rimm and Masters (1974) have presented the most detailed description of thought stopping, breaking the procedure down into four phases. During the first, the client describes the situation in which his negative thoughts take place, as well as the thoughts themselves. The thoughts are thus placed in the context in which they usually occur, including the presence of positive thoughts and constructive attention focusing. The client is interrupted in his verbal description when negative thoughts first occur by loudly saying, "Stop!" This step is repeated until the client reports that the thoughts were blocked. In the second phase, the client imagines the same sequence of events and is requested to raise a finger when a negative thought just starts, at which point the counselor loudly says, "Stop!" This stage is also repeated until the client reports successful blocking of thoughts. Phase Three provides for the client's overt blocking of thoughts just as they begin. Notice the focus on "catching" the negative thought-chain when it first begins. This is important, because it is easier to disrupt a chain of behavior or thoughts at the beginning than at the end. My own experience is very similar to that of Rimm and Master's (1974) in viewing the client's success as often feeble at this point. As these authors point out, repeated modeling by the counselor as well as encouragement are usually necessary. During the fourth stage, the client practices the covert blocking of his thoughts. An important part of thought stopping is teaching the client to redirect attention and thoughts to constructive events, because a blank mind refuses to stay blank. The situation in which the client finds himself provides cues for attention. The ruminations concerning mental illness with the twenty-eight-year-old male client mentioned earlier were particularly frequent during interpersonal encounters. He was trained to identify a number of dimensions in such encounters on which he could focus, such as attending to what the person was saying, what the person looked like, and so forth.

Rimm and Masters (1974) have noted the similarity of covert and overt assertion. Overt assertion is thought to be incompatible with anxiety and is widely employed as a method to decrease interpersonal anxiety. Provision of self-instructions such as "Stop" asserts control over one's thought processes and may share some of the same inhibitory features as overt assertion, and may also redirect attention to more positive events. Given this assumption, Rimm and Masters (1974) suggest that thought stopping be complemented by requesting the client to covertly say positive self-assertive statements appropriate to problem-related situations, following blocking of a thought by saying, "Stop." These self-assertions are similar in nature to the coping self-statements described by Meichenbaum (1975b). An examination of the possible sources of irrationality of thoughts should be carried out before training the client in thought-stopping procedures. The combination of thought stopping and self-reinforcement has been found to be more effective than thought stopping alone (Hays and Waddell, 1976).

Thought stopping has been employed with children as well as with adults. For example, Campbell (1973) reports the case of a twelve-year-old boy who frequently experienced negative thoughts concerning the violent death of his sister, which he had witnessed nine months earlier. The boy spent increasing amounts of time ruminating about the incident, had stopped eating and sleeping, and was doing very poorly in school. Many events now seemed to occasion the ruminative thought chain. Baseline information was collected with the help of his mother. This revealed that he experienced an average of fifteen ruminations each day, each sequence lasting about twenty minutes. A variation of the usual thought-stopping procedure was employed, in which the boy was asked to evoke the negative thought and then to loudly count backwards from ten to zero as fast as possible. On reaching zero, he was to turn his thoughts to one of a number of pleasant scenes, which had been identified earlier. When he could successfully stop the thoughts by counting out loud, he then received practice in achieving this with subvocal counting. The counselor instructed him to employ this procedure whenever the negative thoughts occurred and to practice it once each evening. He also agreed to keep records of the frequency of the negative thoughts and the relative duration of each thought chain. He was seen once a week for four weeks. The frequency of ruminations decreased from fifteen to three after the first interview and decreased further thereafter. Weekly telephone calls to check on progress were made following treatment. At a three-year follow-up, his mother reported that he no longer suffered from obsessional thoughts nor from problems with sleeping and eating, and that he was now an honor student.

Coping Skills That Emphasize the Role of Affective Reactions

Clients differ as to which response system is most heavily involved in their anxiety reaction. Within social learning theory, emotional reactions are considered to be a "source of information that can affect perceived self-efficacy in coping with threatening situations. People rely partly upon their state of physiological arousal in judging their anxiety and vulnerability to stress. Because high arousal usually debilitates performance, individuals are more likely to expect success when they are not beset by aversive arousal than if they are tense and viscerally agitated. Fear reactions generate further fear of impending stressful situations through anticipatory self-arousal" (Bandura, in press, p. 15). If the client learns to decrease arousal, this should increase expectations of mastery. If there is an important affective component in a client's anxiety reaction, one of the following procedures may be employed to help clients discriminate finer dimensions of arousal and to employ them as cues to attain a positive affective state.

Progressive Relaxation Training. The aim of providing training in relaxation is to increase the discrimination of muscle tension and to train the client to relax even small degrees of tension (Wolpe, 1958). Relaxation is presented as a skill to be learned. To avoid the perception of relaxation as something that is imposed, the counselor should stress that it requires practice and that voluntary control of muscle tension must be learned. Relaxation training has been effectively employed in the treatment of a variety of problems, including anxieties (Wolpe, 1973a); insomnia (Borkovec and Fowles, 1973); high excitement and tension of psychotic children in response to minor irritations (Graziano and Kean, 1968); tension headaches (Lutker, 1971); and the symptoms of Huntington's chorea (MacPherson, 1967).

Time involvement. In the Paul (1966) method of tension-release relaxation training, all major muscle groups are demonstrated during the first training session. This may require about forty-five minutes. As the client acquires skill in relaxing, less time will be necessary to attain a state of relaxation. Individuals vary in the speed with which they learn to relax. It is important to take the time required to demonstrate tension and release of each muscle group.

The client is requested to practice relaxation at home twice a day for about fifteen minutes. This practice consists of tensing and relaxing those muscle groups that have been demonstrated, attending to changes in sensation, in addition to allowing time at the end of the practice session to relax all muscles as much as possible. Either audiotaped or self-presented suggestions can be employed. It is important to provide a rationale for such practice, so that the client will be motivated to carry it out. Only if relaxation is practiced will skill be acquired, and this rationale must be shared with the client. Selection of suitable times and situations should be discussed. The requisite conditions for home practice are the same as those for practice in the office: a comfortable spot, an absence of distracting noises, and an absence of time pressure. If the client feels pressed for time, it is unlikely that he will focus attention on relaxation. Some clients find it helpful to relax right before going to sleep. This may also facilitate falling asleep. The probability of practice can be increased if the counselor regularly checks with the client—for example, every other day—to determine when and how long practice was carried out, whether correct procedures are being employed, and how the client is progressing.

Method of training: general procedures. The method presented here is a variant of Wolpe's (1958) form of the relaxation training procedure developed by Jacobson (1938). Training consists of systematically going through the major muscle groups of the body and arranging for the tensing and relaxation of each one, with instructions to note the differences between relaxation and tension. Repetitive pairing of the word *relax* with a change from a tensed to a relaxed state lends control to this word as a cue for relaxation.

The same procedure is followed for each muscle group. First, the client is requested to tense the group, and to hold this tension for about five seconds, while noting the changes in sensation that take place. Second, he is instructed to release tension in this muscle group immediately on hearing a cue word such as *relax* (Paul, 1966). Then he is again requested to attend to changes in sensation, noting the difference between tension and relaxation of this muscle group. Third, the client is requested to continue focusing on this muscle group for about forty seconds, during which additional requests are made by the counselor to experience the sensations of relaxation; and to try to allow the muscles to relax further (additional relaxation instructions are offered later in this chapter). The suggestions and instructions of relaxation offer a model to the client of the type of instructions that can be self-presented at home during practice sessions. This same process of tension release is repeated one or two more times or until the client reports that this muscle group is very relaxed. If the development of cognitive and behavioral coping skills are more heavily emphasized, fewer tension and release cycles may be used (Meichenbaum, 1972).

Instruction should be given in a calm, confident, slow, evenly paced manner, although each counselor will develop his or her own unique style. Counselor statements focus the client's attention on changes in sensation and encourage the perception of relaxation as a skill. Two types of statements should be avoided (Bernstein and Borkovec, 1973): (1) ones that assume a given state exists, such as "You are deeply relaxed," because such a state may not exist, and also because such statements cast relaxation under external control of the counselor, which may interfere with the conceptualization of relaxation as a self-controlled skill; and (2) direct suggestions, such as "relax more deeply," because these again encourage the external control of relaxation.

The client is informed that, over practice trials, relaxation will be carried deeper and will be acquired sooner. It should also be mentioned that partial muscle tension may be felt initially, and that it is the discrimination of this residual tension that will be learned, in addition to learning how to relax it. Also, when the client is tensing muscles in the arms, legs, and neck, it may be necessary to ask the client to try not to involve other muscles, because discrimination of tension in one muscle may be precluded by the simultaneous tensing of others.

Preparation of the setting and client. The client assumes a comfortable position, preferably in an overstuffed chair, with his or her arms resting on the arms of the chair. Paul recommends that the legs be extended, with the head resting on the back of the chair, and that the eyes be closed. If, when instructed to assume a comfortable position, a posture is taken that requires unwanted muscle tension, the client should be requested to assume a more relaxed position. The head should be resting on some support. All possible sources of distraction should be removed, such as ringing telephones.

The use of signals. After tension and release of a muscle group, and after additional time has been allowed for its relaxation, the client is requested to signal by raising his right index finger if the muscles in this group feel completely relaxed. If no signal is presented, then the tension and release of this group is repeated. If a signal is presented, instructions are given to continue to relax these muscles as the tension and release process is performed with other muscle groups.

Enhancement of relaxation by self-presented coping reactions. Learning to become relaxed is a skill and the aim of relaxation training is to train the client in this skill. An important aspect of such training is specific self-instructions and coping skills that can be employed not only in the training procedure but in the natural environment as well (Meichenbaum, 1974). These skills will enable the client to decrease anxiety. The importance of learning and using these skills and instructions should be emphasized. Anxiety thus becomes a cue to employ skills to decrease it, rather than, as in the past, a cue for further anxiety. The client is guided in thinking about his anxiety in a new, more positive way.

Taking a deep breath may be employed as one coping device. The counselor might say, "See yourself taking a slow deep breath, slowly filling your chest cavity. Good. Now exhale slowly. As you see yourself exhaling note the feeling of relaxation and control you have been able to bring forth. Fine. Now stop the image and just relax" (Meichenbaum, 1975, p. 374). Self-instructions, such as "just relax" and "take it easy," are also important in managing anxiety.

Sequence of muscle groups. The first muscle group dealt with is dominant hand and forearm. Counselor statements may be as follows.

> We will start with your right [left] hand and lower forearm. I will soon be asking you to make a tight fist with your right [left] hand and to note the feelings in these muscles when you tense them. Focus on the changes in sensation when you make a tight fist. [Pause.] Make as tight a fist as you can and tense the muscles of your lower forearm. [Pause.] Hold this tension. [Allow about five to seven seconds.] Note the sensation of tension in these muscles. [Pause.] When you hear the word *relax*, release all tension immediately. [Pause.] Relax. Focus on the difference between tension and relaxation. [Pause.] Notice that relaxing is an

active movement. [Pause.] Notice how these muscles feel as they become relaxed. [Pause.] Just try
to let these muscles relax further and further.
[Pause.] There is nothing else you have to be concerned about at this time except relaxing. [Pause.]

It is important to include suggestions of mental as well as physical relaxation in a way that focuses on the client's active use of
these suggestions to alter his state of relaxation. It seems that
the major contribution of relaxation is more a mental than a
physical process (Rachman, 1968). The counselor might say,
"You can deepen the relaxation and relax away feelings of tension by thinking silently to yourself the words *relax* and *calm* as
you relax. Think or picture these words to yourself as you
slowly exhale. This is especially helpful between sessions when
you practice relaxing or whenever you feel tension or anxiety"
(Meichenbaum, 1975b, p. 373). Loudness of voice can be
matched with instructions by giving tension instructions in a
louder voice compared to relaxation instructions. About forty
seconds are allowed for such counselor statements.

The client is then requested to signal by raising his right
index finger if the muscles in the right (or left) hand and forearm feel completely relaxed. He should be cautioned not to signal unless these muscles feel completely relaxed. If a client
raises his right index finger, then the counselor would say,
"Continue to relax the muscles in your hand and forearm as
you now devote attention to the muscles in your upper right
[left] arm." If no signal is presented, then the tension and release process is repeated. "We will go through the same process
again with the muscles of your right [left] hand and lower forearm, and will try this time to carry the relaxation even further.
You will first tense these muscles and hold this tension for a
while and then, when you hear the word *relax*, will release this
tension. Again, try to attend to the differences in sensation in
these muscles when they are tensed and when they are relaxed.
Make a fist with your right [left] hand and tense the muscles in
your lower forearm." If tension and release is repeated two or
three times with a muscle group and complete relaxation is still
not signaled, suggestions can be offered that may help to re-

move interfering conditions as described later in this chapter. Sufficient time should be allowed for each phase of the tension and release process, including a time after the release of tension during which the client is requested to try to relax the muscle group further, focusing on the sensations that are experienced.

The second muscle group involves the biceps of the dominant arm. Counselor statements involved in tension and release of the biceps muscle are as follows: "This time you will be paying close attention to the biceps muscles of your right [left] arm. [Pause.] Please keep your arm resting on the arm of the chair. Tense the biceps muscles of your right [left] arm as tight as you can. Note the sensations when this muscle group is tense. Hold this tension. [Allow about five to seven seconds.] Relax the muscles in your arm. [Pause.] Try to let go of tension in these muscles while you attend to the differences in sensation as these muscles become relaxed. Just enjoy the feeling of relaxation. Note that relaxation is a letting go of tension [pause]; something that is under your voluntary control, just as tensing your muscles is under your voluntary control. [Pause.]" Such instructions are continued for about thirty seconds. The tension and release process may then be repeated.

For the third group, hand and lower forearm of nondominant arm, repeat procedure used for dominant arm. For the fourth group, biceps of nondominant arm, repeat procedure used for biceps of dominant arm.

The fifth group involves muscles in the forehead. Counselor statements may be as follows: "We will now turn to the muscles in the head region, starting first with the muscles in the forehead. There are two major muscle groups in this region, one involved in frowning and the other involved when the forehead muscles are raised. We will start with the muscles involved when raising your forehead. Raise your forehead muscles up toward the ceiling. [Pause.] Hold this. Feel the tension in your forehead as you continue to tense these muscles. [Pause.] Relax the tension in your forehead. [Pause.] Let these muscles smooth out. Notice the difference in these muscles as they become more relaxed." Such statements are continued for about forty seconds and then the process is repeated.

Counselor statements for the other group of forehead

muscles may be, "Let's turn now to the second group of muscles in the forehead, those involved when you frown. Frown as hard as you can, attending to the sensation in your forehead as you do so. Hold this." From this point, the procedure is the same as that presented for the previous group.

The sixth group involves eye and nose muscles. Counselor statements may be, "We will now turn to the muscles of the eyes and nose, starting with those around the eyes. Squint your eyes together. Hold this tension. Notice the sensations around your eyes when these are tense. [Repeat procedure used with other muscles.] The muscles in the cheeks and upper lip can be tensed by wrinkling your nose. Wrinkle your nose. Notice the changes in sensation in the muscles of your upper lip and across your cheeks as you hold this tension. [Continue procedure as with other muscles.]"

The seventh group involves muscles in the lower part of the face. Counselor statements may be, "Let's turn at this point to the muscles in the lower part of the face. These include the jaw muscles and the muscles around the mouth. Clench your teeth together and pull back the corners of your mouth. [Pause.] Note the changes in sensation as you do this. [Pause.] Feel the tension in the mouth muscles and in the muscles in front of your neck. Hold this tension. [Pause.] Relax. Try to let the tension drain away. [Pause.] Notice the difference in sensation between tension and relaxation. Let your teeth part and try to take this relaxation further. [Pause.] There is nothing else to be concerned about now. [Continue procedure as before.]"

Some clients feel self-conscious when tensing their facial muscles. If the client is not really tensing them and holding the tension for a sufficient time, it may help to request that he open his eyes and observe the counselor demonstrate what he is to do.

The eighth group, neck muscles, can be demonstrated by requesting the client to pull the chin downwards toward the chest while at the same time trying to prevent it from touching the chest (Bernstein and Borkovec, 1973). These muscles can also be demonstrated by pressing the head against a wall while in a seated position or by holding some flat object, such as a book, in back of the client's head and requesting him to exert pressure against this.

The ninth group, chest, shoulders and upper back, can be demonstrated by asking the client to take a deep breath and hold it, and, at the same time pull back the shoulder blades as if trying to make them touch (Bernstein and Borkovec, 1973). Special attention is devoted to the thoracic muscles, which control respiration, because the respiratory rhythm can be used as an adjunct to relaxation (Wolpe and Lazarus, 1966). These muscles can be demonstrated by taking a very deep breath and then exhaling it completely, attending to the fact that no effort is required to push the air out during exhalation. This is repeated a few times, until exhalation is perceived as a letting go of muscle tension, as a relaxation of the respiratory muscles. Special emphasis may be placed on learning deep breathing and less on repetition of tension and release cycles (Meichenbaum, 1974).

The remaining (tenth through sixteenth) muscle groups can be dealt with in the following sequence, using the procedures developed for the previous groups. The *abdominal* muscles can be demonstrated by asking the client to tighten up his stomach muscles, as if in anticipation of a hard punch in the stomach. The stomach muscles can also be tensed by pulling them in tightly. The muscles of the *upper dominant leg* can be demonstrated by asking the client to tense his upper leg, noticing the tension in the muscles as he does so. For *dominant calf and lower leg,* the client is requested to pull his toes up toward the head. This tensing exercise creates tension in the calf muscle. Periodically, the caution to refrain, as much as possible, from tensing muscles in other parts of the body should be repeated. For the *dominant foot,* the client is requested to push down with the toe and to arch the foot (with the caution not to tense the muscles very hard, because a cramp may result). For the *nondominant upper leg* and *nondominant calf and lower leg,* repeat procedures used for dominant leg. For the *nondominant foot,* repeat procedures used for dominant foot. Time is allowed at the end of each practice and training session to relax all muscles as far as possible, starting from whatever point of relaxation exists.

Relaxation training may be carried out at home by the

use of taped instructions (for example, see Bernstein and Borkovec, 1973). If this is done, it is advisable to initiate training in the office and to contact the client regularly to ensure that appropriate procedures are being followed, to determine whether progress is occurring, and to offer verbal reinforcement to the client for his efforts. Relaxation skills should be checked by observation of the client.

Assessment of degree of relaxation. The degree of relaxation is assessed after tension and release of all sixteen muscle groups. The counselor slowly goes over the major muscle groups that have been demonstrated and provides instructions to continue relaxing these muscles. Then the client is requested to signal if he feels tension anywhere in his body. If no signal is presented, the session can be terminated after allowing a couple of minutes for the client to enjoy the relaxed state. Sessions are terminated by employing a countdown from one to five, within which suggestions for increasing movement are presented, such as stretching the legs, moving the hands and fingers, and moving the head around (Paul, 1966). This countdown occurs with increasing degrees of voice loudness. Thus, a session could be terminated by employing the following instructions: "I am now going to count to five and when I reach five, you will open your eyes and feel calm and refreshed. One (pause); two, stretch your legs (pause); three, move your head around (pause); four, move your hands and fingers around (pause); five, open your eyes."

On close observation, the counselor may not concur with the client that a relaxed state exists. Such observation will present many indications as to the degree of relaxation. Clues include the smoothness of the facial muscles; the regularity of breathing; the position of the hands, which should appear loose and relaxed; and the degree of movement. Typically, in the deeply relaxed individual no movement occurs. If there is frequent swallowing, eye blinking, hand movement, or other general movement, it is highly likely that a state of deep relaxation does not exist. Posture is another indicator of degree of relaxation. If this is rigid or of such a nature that a great deal of muscular tension is required to maintain it, then deep relaxation is not possible.

If observation of the client reveals a lack of relaxation

even though he has signaled that he is completely relaxed, additional relaxation instructions should be given, focusing on the areas of tension noted by the counselor. Following this, the state of relaxation can again be assessed by requesting a signal if complete relaxation is felt.

A lack of relaxation could be caused by going too fast over each muscle group. It is very important to allow sufficient time to enable the client to experience the sensations of tension and relaxation in each muscle group so that he can learn to discriminate finer degrees of both states. Moving too fast will prohibit learning this skill. Or, perhaps the client has signaled complete relaxation when he did not experience this. The level of relaxation may be reported to be deeper than it is, to please the counselor. This problem can usually be avoided by stressing how important it is to be honest in accurately communicating degree of relaxation, and by providing a rationale for this. Inaccurately judging the degree of relaxation may occur because such a persistent state of tension exists that any drop in it appears to be a very relaxed state. Additional training may be required for such clients. In such instances, the use of a *graduated* release, rather than an immediate release of tension, may be helpful in increasing discrimination of different stages of relaxation (Wolpe, 1958). If further relaxation instructions are not successful, the session should be terminated and appropriate questions asked to try to determine the difficulty.

If the client indicates by his failure to present a signal that he is not completely relaxed, the counselor can mention each muscle group, one at a time, and request the client to signal whether tension is still experienced in this group. Further relaxation instructions can be given when tension is found or the tension and release process can be repeated. The state of relaxation can then be reassessed.

Questions asked after the session ends. Feedback should be obtained as to how the client feels. Did he enjoy the relaxation session? The client should be requested to describe how he feels, so the counselor can determine the extent to which sensations are focused on and to discover unique words employed by the client that can be used by the counselor on subsequent sessions (Bernstein and Borkovec, 1973). Was there anything that could have been added to enhance the state of relaxation? Is there anything that could be avoided, to enhance this state?

Specific questions should be asked concerning any problems that arose during the session. Perhaps there was difficulty in relaxing a particular muscle group. If the client persistently tenses a muscle group, additional practice may be required to develop discrimination of tension in this group and to learn how to relax it. Perhaps relaxation was difficult because of the presence of interfering thoughts. The client may be more comfortable sitting up than in a semireclining position. Any problems that arise are addressed and praise is offered for client progress.

Attaining relaxation more rapidly. Fewer steps are necessary as skill in relaxation is acquired. Contraction of muscles is usually carried out only during the training phase. After tension can be perceived in a muscle group, and the client can release it, there is no further need to tense this group prior to relaxing it. This applies to training sessions in the office as well as to practice sessions at home. The client would start from whatever point of relaxation already exists and then carry it as far as possible. When relaxation is employed differentially—that is, when the client learns to release whatever tension exists when engaged in everyday activities (Wolpe and Lazarus, 1966)—and when relaxation is employed in symbolic desensitization, the relaxation starts from whatever state of relaxation already exists. There is no tension phase.

Bernstein and Borkovec (1973) have described a step-by-step process to move from the procedure described earlier, in which a tension and release cycle is carried out with sixteen muscle groups, to relaxation without tension. The basis for this change is the increased discrimination of various states of tension and relaxation. The client learns to recognize more subtle variations and acquires skill in attaining deeper states of mental and physical relaxation. At this more advanced stage, relaxation can be increased over the entire body rather than within specific muscle groups. Advanced steps should not be employed until the client has mastered earlier phases.

Procedures for seven muscle groups

1. The muscles of the dominant arm are tensed and relaxed as a single group.

2. The same procedure is carried out for the muscles of the other arm.
3. All facial muscles are tensed at once.
4. The neck muscles are tensed, as described in the sixteen-group procedure.
5. The chest, shoulder, upper back, and abdominal muscles are tensed at once, while taking and holding a deep breath.
6. The muscles of the dominant leg and foot are tensed by raising the leg slightly and tensing the upper leg, calf, and foot.
7. The same procedure is followed for the nondominant leg and foot.

It is important to ascertain the level of relaxation that is attained. Practice periods at home will now incorporate this seven-group procedure, if the client reported satisfactory relaxation. Additional attention may have to be devoted to particular muscle groups.

When the client can acquire a state of relaxation using seven muscle groups, those covered may be reduced to four. It will be helpful to include the breathing response as an adjunct to relaxation.

Procedures for four muscle groups

1. Both arms are tensed and released.
2. The face and neck muscles are tensed and released.
3. The chest, shoulders, back, and abdomen are tensed and released.
4. Both legs are tensed and released.

A time for questions should be allowed following each procedure to determine whether the client attained a relaxed state. It is better to move too slow than to move too fast.

In *relaxation without prior tensing,* the same four muscle groups are employed; however, the tension and release process is no longer followed. Instead, the client focuses on any tension that already exists in each group, starting with the arms. He is asked to identify any tension in this group and is requested to relax these muscles, recalling what it was like when they were relaxed on other occasions (Bernstein and Borkovec, 1973). These authors have called this phase "relaxation through recall." After instructions to relax each group, about thirty seconds are allowed for additional relaxation instructions, and the client is requested to signal at the end of that time whether the muscles in his arms and hands feel completely relaxed. If a signal occurs, progress is made to the next muscle group. The tension and release process can be reintroduced if the client has trouble relaxing a particular muscle group. Practice at home should also employ the recall method.

A countdown procedure can be added to the recall process after the client is relaxed. The client is informed that a procedure will be added that will help to increase the degree of relaxation. This involves counting from one to ten while instructions are given to carry the relaxation further. Suggestions for relaxation of each major muscle group are given between numbers.

The final phase of relaxation training can then be counting slowly from one to ten, with instructions to relax occurring between each number. The client's state of relaxation should be assessed after each procedure, and attention should be devoted to relaxing any residual tension that is felt. At this point, a deeply relaxed state should be achievable within one minute.

Practice at home should continue twice a day during each phase but the last, in which practice once a day may be sufficient to maintain relaxation skills. Progress to a more advanced stage of relaxation skill should usually not be made unless the client has faithfully practiced earlier stages twice a day as recommended. These practice sessions are very important in the opportunities they provide for discrimination of different states of tension and relaxation and for acquiring skill in learning to relax.

Bernstein and Borkovec (1973, p. 37) suggested the following timetable for each phase of relaxation. As these authors note, this timetable is conservative, for many clients progress more rapidly. It is suggested that each step but the last be repeated twice before moving on to a more abbreviated one.

Procedure	*Session*
16 muscle groups, tension and release	1, 2, 3
7 muscle groups, tension and release	4, 5

Procedure	Session
4 muscle groups, tension and release	6, 7
4 muscle groups, recall	8
4 muscle groups, recall and counting	9
Counting	10

Difficulties and suggested solutions. The client may have intrusive, worrisome thoughts. Such thoughts can be reduced by frequent instructions to put all worrisome thoughts completely out of mind, stressing that the only concern at the present time is to relax. These instructions can be coupled with the presentation of a calming scene that can be employed when inducing relaxation. Ideally, such scenes are determined prior to the initiation of relaxation instructions to make sure that one is selected that is calming. The client can be requested to describe a time when he felt very relaxed and happy. The scene should be described in detail, because the more concrete and vivid the description, the easier it is to imagine the situation. If a beach scene produced a calming effect, the sounds, sights, and feelings that would be present in such a situation are slowly, concretely presented. The wording might go as follows: "Imagine yourself lying on a beach on a warm summer day. Notice the sensations you feel as you lie in the sun. [Pause.] Imagine the gentle sounds of waves breaking on the shore and an occasional gull in the distance. [Pause.] Notice a breeze as it blows over you and how it feels in contrast to the heat of the sun. [Pause.] The sky is very blue, with just a few white clouds, which are moving slowly. Notice the warmth of the sun on your right hand and forearm. [Pause.] There is nothing else to be concerned about except to relax and be calm and tranquil. [Pause.] Let this calmness spread over you and just enjoy feeling tranquil and relaxed as you feel the warmth of the sun. [Pause.] " Suggestions that are seductive or hypnotic in manner should be avoided during the description of such scenes as well as during other aspects of relaxation instructions. Intrusive thoughts may also be decreased by a more continual stream of suggestions, including requests to focus on particular sensations and mental states.

Occasionally, difficulty in relaxing occurs because of a fear of "letting go," particularly in relation to instructions from another person. This difficulty can usually be avoided by stressing that relaxation training is a skill that the client will learn and control. If such a difficulty persists, other interventions could be employed, such as in vivo desensitization or self-instructional training.

Relaxation may induce new feelings that are of concern to the client, such as feelings of warmth or lack of orientation (Bernstein and Borkovec, 1973). Labeling these feelings as a common aspect of relaxation and as something to be enjoyed may remove this concern. Reorientation can be arranged by requesting the client to remain still but to open his eyes during relaxation.

Discrimination of different stages of relaxation may be enhanced by requesting the client to keep a record of any changes he notices in anxiety and to write down what he feels, very specifically, in terms of autonomic reactions or muscle tension, including the location of such tension. Training the client to employ a specific word, such as *relax*, for decreasing tension a few times each day, may also sharpen perception of the differences between tension and relaxation.

Some clients report that their muscles are relaxed but that they still feel anxious. Careful questioning during relaxation training will usually catch this problem. The client should be asked whether he feels relaxed all over, whether his mind is more calm, whether he feels more calm "inside." Additional training can be carried out, focusing particularly on mental relaxation. Suggestions of both types of relaxation should routinely be included in relaxation training as well as during home practice sessions.

A failure to focus attention on sensations and on mental calmness can often be rectified by repeated instructions to attend to these factors. The statements that the counselor uses to focus attention can also be employed by the client in other situations to enhance mental calmness and this possibility should be shared with the client. A variety of events may interfere with such focusing, including noises and intrusive thoughts.

A failure to follow instructions, such as talking during the session, moving about frequently, or failing to practice at home may require repetition of the rationale for such procedures. If clients do not carry out required practice sessions, the counselor should try to find out why practice sessions are not a pleasant experience (Bernstein and Borkovec, 1973). Perhaps an unsuitable place or time is selected, thus prohibiting attainment of a state of calmness and relaxation. Perhaps the importance of practice is not accepted. The client may be more willing to practice if he effectively employs self-instructions to cope with anxiety while going about his everyday activities. If these attempts are successful, he may be more willing to engage in further practice that will enhance these coping skills. The consequences of repeated failure to practice are pointed out not in a critical, but in an informative manner. The more relaxation is practiced, the more skill will be acquired. If the counselor makes sure that a state of relaxation has been attained in the office situation, the client will have a reference point for what a relaxed state feels like.

Occasionally, clients fall asleep during relaxation instructions. A state of relaxation can be differentiated from sleep by asking the client a question that requires a signal. A tendency to fall asleep can be decreased by presenting instructions in a somewhat louder voice, by including shorter instructions following release of tension, by requesting the client to focus on your voice, and by arranging sessions at a time when the client is not tired (Bernstein and Borkovec, 1973). A sleeping client can be awakened by gradually increasing voice loudness until it is obvious that the client is no longer sleeping.

Differential Relaxation. Differential relaxation consists of releasing unnecessary tension during daily activities (Jacobson, 1938). Such tension is often experienced by clients who complain of anxiety, and, through training in progressive relaxation, they can learn to discriminate the initial signs of negative arousal and learn to relax this tension. Training in progressive relaxation should be combined with instructions to employ relaxation in the natural environment. Relaxation may be enhanced by employing a word that has been paired with relaxation during training, such as *calm* or *relax*. Client discrimination of muscle tension may be enhanced by homework assignments in which clients observe their degree of relaxation three times a day, in addition to those times when they feel anxious, and record the degree of subjective anxiety (using the subjective anxiety scale, which ranges from one to 100). They may also be asked to write down in a log specific physiological cues such as tension in particular muscles, upset stomach, and so forth (Deffenbacher, 1976). Each client can thus form a personal set of cues related to increasing tension. Through self-observation, these cues can be identified in real-life situations and can function as a signal for self-initiated relaxation instructions. Practice in decreasing anxiety by relaxation instructions can be offered through induced-anxiety training, in which the client assumes a relaxed position and the counselor then presents suggestions of anxiety until a predetermined level is reached, at which point the client is instructed to employ relaxation instructions.

Conditioned Relaxation. The term *conditioned relaxation* has been employed to refer to the procedure of pairing a word such as *calm* with a relaxed state so that the word becomes a cue for relaxation (Paul, 1966). Such pairing is a typical aspect of relaxation training, and differential relaxation may be increased in effectiveness by use of such a cue word. Arrangements may be made for a certain number of pairings. The client may be requested to repeat the cue word each time he exhales for a specific number of times, and to employ this procedure when he feels relaxed. This pairing can be supplemented by the counselor's repeating the cue word in synchrony with the client's exhalations (Russel and Sipich, 1974). A cue word related to a pleasant scene may also be employed to induce a relaxed state. In this procedure, the client is requested to relax and to vividly describe out loud a pleasant, relaxing scene (Gurman, 1973). He is then asked to select a cue word for this scene, to practice twice daily thinking about this catchword and achieving a relaxed state, and also to use this word during the day when he starts to feel anxious (Gurman, 1973). Anxiety-relief conditioning may also be employed to lend relaxing potential to a given word (Wolpe, 1958). Removal of some unpleasant event is made contingent on saying a word such as *calm*.

Use of Biofeedback Devices. Feedback may be provided to heighten awareness of differing levels of tension (Coursey,

1975). Biofeedback depends on the availability of appropriate instruments such as a monitor of electrodermal activity. Feedback can be heightened by employing a device that generates an audible sound in accord with arousal level. Such devices can be usefully employed during assessment as an indicator of arousal.

The Role of Problem-Solving Skills

A lack of effective problem-solving skills may be related to anxiety. Such a lack may place the client in circumstances that are realistically tension-producing, such as not knowing what to do if a landlord refuses to make repairs, dealing with an unwanted houseguest, locating a job. It may be necessary to train the client in general problem-solving skills, including how to define problems, how to generate alternatives, defining criteria to employ in selecting an alternative to pursue, and then finding out whether this alternative is effective (D'Zurilla and Goldfried, 1971). The perception of problems as normally occurring in everyone's life helps to place problems in perspective—rather than being awful and uncommon, they become everyday challenges to be dealt with. One aspect of problem solving involves identification of when a problem exists. Some clients create problems for themselves by mislabeling their feelings, thoughts, or behaviors as signs that they are crazy or are possessed by some other unhappy state. These labels are anxiety provoking, as well as dysfunctional in other ways because they offer no information as to how to alter behavior that may be associated with them. The client can be trained to more appropriately label his behavior, for example, rather than considering himself crazy because of unusual feelings, he may consider himself unique. Problems may also be created by failing to distinguish between thoughts and overt behavior. That is, a client may think that because he has had a thought of injuring someone, this is the same as committing the act. It is important that clients learn to discriminate between thoughts and actions and to distinguish between a thought that may be a cue for a latent behavioral tendency and a thought that is simply silly and should be ignored (Lazarus and Fay, 1975).

Learning How to Handle Anger

Responding aggressively in social exchanges can cause as many problems as responding in an unduly submissive manner. Counterattacks are occasioned and people may begin to avoid those who are aggressive in their exchanges. Social skill training, as well as self-instruction training, have been employed to develop appropriate reactions to possible provocations. Gittleman (1965) employed behavior rehearsal and positive rewards to train children how to deal in a better way with minor provocations, such as being bumped when going down the hallway. A series of possible reactions was established to such situations, ranging from a positive response (saying, "Excuse me," even though the other boy bumped into the first boy) to negative reactions, such as turning and hitting the boy. Points were awarded in accord with degree of positiveness of the reaction. Behavior rehearsal was carried out in a group setting in which two boys would role play a situation and points were awarded by the boys who were watching.

Model presentation and instructions have also been employed to increase alternative reactions of adults to provoking situations (Foy, Eisler, and Pinkston, 1975). Target behaviors included hostile comments, irrelevant comments, compliance, and requests for change. Intervention focused on decreasing the frequency of the first three and increasing the frequency of reasonable requests for behavior change. Social skill training is indicated when the client does not know how to express anger appropriately—for example, by using "I" statements rather than than accusatory "you" statements—and does not know when to express anger, that is, if appropriate, to express it as soon as possible rather than storing it up and having an outburst (see Chapter Thirteen for further details). A program that emphasizes the role of cognitions is called for when a client seems to be too easily provoked and when part of this provocation is provided by his own self-statements.

Novaco (1975, 1976) developed a stress management training program to offer people skills in managing provocations and in regulating their anger arousal based on a similar program developed for anxiety reduction (Meichenbaum, 1974). Several individuals involved in the study had assaulted others. The training program was conducted in a group setting. The initial stages consisted in conducting a situational analysis including identification of situations that provoked anger; exploration of thoughts and feelings in anger-inducing encounters; working toward a common conceptualization of stress reactions in terms of emotional arousal and cognitive activity; and encouraging clients to understand the role of their own thoughts in relation to feelings experienced. Participants were encouraged to recognize the anger-producing self-statements that occurred when they were provoked (Novaco, 1976). Assessment methods were employed, such as asking the client to close his eyes and to relive a recent anger-producing event while reporting his feelings and thoughts. A basic assumption was that anger is encouraged and maintained by one's thoughts. The negative self-statements provoked included a variety of beliefs, such as the necessity of success, intolerance for mistakes, unreasonable expectations of others, and the necessity of retaliation (Meichenbaum and Turk, 1976).

Clients were trained to employ a situational analysis of anger—that is, to note the thoughts that occurred when they started to feel angry—and were trained how to use relaxation skills to reduce arousal and self-instructions to control attentional processes, thoughts, images, and feelings. Here, too, as with anxiety, the client learns to view his emotional reaction as a series of events, rather than as an all-or-nothing reaction over which he has no control. The client comes to realize that it is not the event itself that automatically triggers a reaction, but rather what he believes and says to himself about these events (Ellis, 1962). The following examples (from Novaco as cited in Meichenbaum and Turk, 1976, pp. 6-9) illustrate the types of statements encouraged in different stages of an anger reaction.

Preparing for a Provocation

What is it that you have to do?
You can work out a plan to handle this.
You can manage this situation. You know how to
regulate your anger.
There won't be any need for an argument.

Time for a few deep breaths of relaxation. Feel
comfortable, relaxed and at ease.

Confronting the Provocation

Stay calm. Just continue to relax.
As long as you keep your cool, you're in control
here.
Don't take it personally.
Don't get all bent out of shape; just think of what
to do here.
You don't need to prove yourself.
There is no point in getting mad.
You're not going to let him get to you.
Don't assume the worst or jump to conclusions.
Look for the positives.
It's really a shame that this person is acting the
way she is.
For a person to be that irritable, he must be aw-
fully unhappy.
There is no need to doubt yourself. What he says
doesn't matter.

Coping with Arousal and Agitation

Your muscles are starting to feel tight. Time to re-
lax and slow things down.
Getting upset won't help.
It's just not worth it to get so angry.
You'll let him make a fool of himself.
It's reasonable to get annoyed, but let's keep the
lid on.
Time to take a deep breath.
Your anger is a signal of what you need to do.
Time to talk to yourself.
You're not going to get pushed around, but you're
not going haywire either.
Try a cooperative approach. Maybe you are both
right.
He'd probably like you to get really angry. Well,
you're going to disappoint him.
You can't expect people to act the way you want
them to.

Self-Reward

It worked!
That wasn't as hard as you thought.
You could have gotten more upset than it was
worth.

You're doing better at this all the time.
You actually got through that without getting
   angry.
Guess you've been getting upset for too long when
   it wasn't even necessary.

Humor was employed as a response incompatible with
the extreme anger reactions of a twenty-two-year-old woman
who referred herself for counseling (Smith, 1973). These outbursts occurred with her husband and her three-year-old child.
She reacted to her child's misbehavior "with extreme rage responses which consisted of screaming at the top of her voice,
jumping up and down, smashing things, and physically attacking
her child" (p. 577). She would also throw things at her husband
and physically attack him when becoming angry. Systematic
desensitization produced negligible progress after seven sessions.
It was impossible for her to imagine even slightly provoking
scenes without becoming extremely angry. At this point, the
hierarchy items were embellished with humor that had a slap-
stick quality. For example, one item, concerning misbehavior
by her child when driving, began, "As you are driving to the
supermarket, little Pascal the Rascal begins to get restless. Suddenly he drops from his position on the ceiling and trampolines
off the rear seat onto the rear view mirror. From this precarious
position, he amuses himself by flashing obscene hand gestures at
shocked pedestrians" (Smith, 1973, p. 577), and so on. This
introduction of humor was very effective, and during the very
first session all scenes on the hierarchy of anger-inducing situations were presented. Eight sessions followed, during which the
client reacted with laughter and seldom reported feeling angry.
As her anger decreased, she became able to use more appropriate child management methods with her son, such as differential reinforcement. Significant others reported a marked
change in her outbursts and the depression she had originally
complained of improved considerably.

Summary

Some behavioral procedures for stress reduction train the
client in coping skills that can be employed in a range of stress-

ful situations. A few procedures focus particularly on the cognitive mediators of anxiety in terms of negative thoughts and irrational expectations, whereas others focus on the affective cues for arousal. Selection of procedure is informed by assessment, during which components of the client's anxiety reaction are determined and antecedents identified. The wider the range of situations in which anxiety occurs, the more appropriate are these self-initiated general coping skills. The self-management aspects of control over stress are emphasized. Self-instruction training methods have been developed for anxiety, anger, and pain management. Social skill training will also be required with clients who have difficulty controlling their anger if their reactions are related to a lack of appropriate assertive skills.

13

A lack of effective social skills has been implicated in a wide range of presenting problems, including marital discord (Eisler, Miller, Hersen, and Alford, 1974), depression (Lazarus, 1971), sexual dysfunction (Edwards, 1972), dependency (Patterson, 1972), and antisocial aggressive behavior (Wallace, Teigen, Liberman, and Baker, 1973). The role of anxiety and skill deficits in interpersonal situations has long been recognized in the behavioral literature. Salter (1949) was the first to note the range of situations in which interpersonal anxiety may occur and to point to the inhibitory role of effective social behavior on anxiety reactions. Wolpe (1958) considered effective social behavior to be highly related to well-being. When the consequences of a lack of effective social skills are examined, as well as the broad array of situations in which it may take place,

Development of Effective Social Skills

this is not surprising. Opportunities are lost and unpleasant events tolerated, because of ineffective social skills. A coveted promotion may be forgone, because of an inability to ask an employer for this position. The opportunity to meet someone interesting may be lost, because of discomfort with the thought of approaching the person and starting a conversation. These consequences affect the client's internal dialog so that he may then engage in a range of negative self-statements and ruminations. Resentment and anger may accumulate, until, finally, one more event sets off an inappropriately strong reaction, which results in criticism or being avoided. Stressful physiological responses may also take place. Behavior that reduces unpleasant thoughts and feelings may occur, such as drinking, social isolation, or attention to physical symptoms.

Difficulties in social situations arise in clinical as well as nonclinical populations. Zimbardo, Pilkonis, and Norwood (1975) reported that over 40 percent of college students experienced uncomfortable shyness in interpersonal situations. Effective social behavior includes the expression of positive as well as negative feelings; however, the emphasis in the clinical and experimental literature has been on the latter. Social skills training has been employed with a range of populations, including psychiatric patients, both inpatient and outpatient (see Hersen and Bellack, in press), college students who complain of few social contacts (see, for example, Glass, Gottman, and Shmurak, 1976), adolescents (see Sarason and Ganzer, 1973), and depressed clients (see Lewinsohn, 1974). Social skills training is involved in behavioral marital counseling in terms of developing more appropriate communication skills, and in enhancing parent-child interaction via developing more effective negotiation behaviors and increasing positive statements exchanged. Recent applications of social skills training have been made with the elderly (Berger and Rose, 1976), with professional women (Brockway, 1976), and with homosexual men (Duehn and Mayadas, 1976).

A Definition of Effective Social Behavior

Social skill has been defined as "the complex ability both to emit behaviors which are positively or negatively reinforced and not to emit behaviors that are punished or extinguished by others" (Libet and Lewinsohn, 1973). Thus social skill relates to receiving positive events from others, in removing annoying or unpleasant ones, and avoiding behaviors that are punished or ignored by others. The advantage of this definition is that it has an efficiency concept built in. Not only does the competent person secure high levels of reinforcement from others, but he also does so efficiently; that is, without performing many behaviors that are ignored or punished. Assertive behaviors tend to be more effective than aggressive or submissive behaviors, and one goal of intervention is to help the client to differentiate these three types of behavior.

Appropriate social skills (assertive behaviors) are differentiated from both aggressive and submissive behaviors. Aggression is defined as the "hostile expression of preferences by words or actions in a manner which coerces others to give in to these preferences; any act which suppresses or takes away the rights of another person" (MacDonald, 1974, p. 32). The aggressive person "puts down," hurts, or humiliates people. Goals are achieved at the expense of causing bad feelings in others (Alberti and Emmons, 1974). Anger is expressed at the other person rather than at the situation and reactions express intention of hostile action. Submission is defined as "the act of allowing one's rights to be ignored, as any act which yields humbly to the preferences of another person" (MacDonald, 1974, p. 32). The submissive person allows others to choose for him. He does not achieve desired goals. His reactions indicate that he is in the wrong and that the other person is right. Assertion is defined as "the open, calm, confident expression of preferences by words or actions in a manner which causes others to take them into account" (MacDonald, 1974, p. 32). It is assumed that it is best to express oneself in as positive a way as possible. This implies the use of the "minimal effective response": one that requires a minimum of effort and negative emotion and has a high probability of positive consequences (Rimm and Masters, 1974).

Let us say that someone has been waiting in line to get into a movie and, as he gets near the ticket office, the person in front of him lets in six other people. An aggressive reaction might be, "Hey, get back there. What the hell is going on?" This conveys antagonism through swear words, or offensive or sarcastic statements. Strong, sharp opposition to the other's behavior is indicated. An assertive reaction entails the statement of a request or demand for a behavior change using minimal negative emotion such as, "Listen, we've been waiting for awhile. Why don't you move to the end of the line?" A submissive reaction includes the expression of annoyance in a manner that is not readily noticeable, such as coughing or sighing; a complete absence of overt reaction, that is, simply allowing the people to move into line; or leaving the situation. Personal attacks are avoided in assertion. Rather the client is encouraged to "own his feelings": through the use of "I" statements such as "I feel hurt when. . ." or "It bothers me when. . . ." Only one systematic attempt has been made to gather normative data as to how a selected population (college women) defines various behaviors in a given situation using all three response possibilities (MacDonald, 1974). There is a need for additional information of this type.

Let us look at the following possible reactions to a statement from a waiter in a restaurant:

Waiter: "Please sit over here."

Patron 1: "Well, OK." (Agrees even though he does not want to.)

Patron 2: "No, it's my right to sit anywhere I want. I'm sitting over here."

Patron 3: "I would prefer to sit over here. Could we?"

Patron 1 readily submits to another person without even voicing his preferences. Unless the waiter is unusually perceptive and has a high desire to please his patrons, he will not notice or respond to the hesitation reflected in the first response. Patron 2 is overly confrontationist and may be inaccurate in assuming that he can sit anywhere, because some tables may be reserved. Rather than state his preference, he gives an ultimatum, which is likely to "put off" others. Patron 3 states his preference and asks if this can be granted. He could also have indicated a reason why. This is an example of an assertive response. A preference is stated in a polite but firm manner. The individual is neither overly confrontive nor overly submissive.

The role of ineffective social behaviors is illustrated in the following example. Mr. K. stated that he was generally miserable, that he disliked his job and was unhappy in his marriage of ten years. He was thirty-five years of age and had been employed as a hairdresser for many years. No children had resulted from the marriage. Mr. K.'s lack of assertive behavior was striking both at work as well as at home. It was first noticed when he dejectedly reported that his wife disliked the apartment he had found. His wife assured him that she would like any apartment he selected and refused to participate in locating one. When she saw it, she found all sorts of faults with the apartment and berated Mr. K. for his poor selection. When moving the furniture into the new apartment, he would ask her where she wanted a particular chair placed and she would tell him that she would make up her mind later. If he then put the chair down temporarily, she would criticize him for his poor choice. She repeatedly arranged situations so that it was impossible for him to win, given his lack of assertion. During a joint interview, it was also noted that she made frequent belittling remarks about him. Most of these revolved around the theme of his inadequacy as a man. He simply hung his head and looked hopeless following such comments. She broke down in tears saying that she wanted him to be a man. Mr. K. did not assert himself with his wife and he felt very resentful toward her.

His lack of effective social behavior at work led to many unfair impositions being placed on him. Extra work was foisted on him, which resulted in his being hectically busy when the other men lounged around reading magazines. He felt very resentful about this unjust situation, but never spoke up and told the scheduling clerk that he was receiving an unfair load of work, nor did he ever say anything to the other employees. In addition, he was subjected to frequent teasing and heckling from fellow workers, because he offered them so much reinforcement for their reactions, turning red and getting upset. These events would eventually "get under his skin" and he would finally explode in an extreme outburst. Explosive inappropriate verbal outbursts often occur when a person is unassertive.

The Situational Nature of Ineffective Social Behavior

Ineffective social behavior is typically situational; that is, clients usually experience difficulty only in certain situations. For example, positive feelings may be appropriately expressed, but difficulty may be encountered when trying to express negative feelings. A variety of dimensions may affect social competence, including (1) the degree of intimacy involved; (2) whether the feeling is positive or negative; (3) various characteristics of relevant people including status, age, and sex; (4) perceived status of self in the situation; and (5) number of people present (MacDonald, 1974). Some people experience anxiety when trying to express themselves in intimate relationships, but experience no discomfort in service situations with store clerks and waitresses. Clients may have difficulty asserting themselves dependent on the social power base of the person they are interacting with, such as attraction or coercive power (French and Raven, 1960). Ineffective behavior may occur only in interactions with people holding positions of authority over the individual, such as a supervisor at work.

The situational nature of assertive behavior is illustrated in a recent study in which thirty-two assertive situations were presented to sixty hospitalized male psychiatric patients (Eisler, Hersen, Miller, and Blanchard, 1975). Half required the expression of negative assertiveness and the other half required positive reactions. The partners in the situations were either male or female and either familiar or unfamiliar. The following examples illustrate certain categories used (p. 332).

Male-Positive-Familiar

Narrator: You have been working on a difficult job all week; your boss comes over with a smile on his face. Your boss says: "That's a very good job you have done; I'm going to give you a raise next week."

Male-Positive-Unfamiliar

Narrator: You are the leader of the company bowling team. Your team is slightly behind when one of the men on your team makes three strikes in a row to even up the score. You are really proud of him. He says: "How did you like that one?"

Female-Positive-Familiar

Narrator: Your wife has just bought a new outfit and is trying it on. You really like it and think that she looks very nice in it. Your wife says: "Well, how do I look in this outfit?"

Female-Positive-Unfamiliar

Narrator: You are in a restaurant and the waitress had just served you an excellent meal cooked just the way you like it. You are pleased with her prompt, efficient service. She comes by and says: "I hope you enjoyed your dinner, sir."

Male-Negative Familiar

Narrator: You have had a very busy day at work and are tired. Your boss comes in and asks you to stay late for the third time this week. You really feel you would like to go home on time tonight. Your boss says: "I'm leaving now; would you mind staying late again tonight and finishing this work for me?"

Male-Negative-Unfamiliar

Narrator: You go to a ballgame with reserved seat tickets. When you arrive you find that someone has put his coat in the seat for which you have reserved tickets. You ask him to remove his coat and he tells you that he is saving that seat for a friend. He says: "I'm sorry, this seat is saved."

Female-Negative-Familiar

Narrator: You are in the middle of watching an exciting football game on television. Your wife walks in and changes the channel as she does every time you are watching a good game. Your wife says: "Let's watch the movie instead; it's really supposed to be good."

Female-Negative-Unfamiliar

Narrator: You are in a crowded grocery store and are in a hurry because you are already late for an appointment. You pick up one small item and get in line to pay for it. Then a woman with a shopping cart full of groceries cuts in line right in front of you. She says: "You don't mind if I cut in here, do you?"

Behavior varied as a function of the social context presented. Responses to negative scenes were characterized by longer replies, increased eye contact, greater affect, more speech volume, and increased latency of response. Subjects tended to talk longer to other men than to women. The men were significantly more assertive with women than with men. Situational differences dependent on sex were also found in a role-playing situation in which women responded to a series of twelve taped situations, half of which involved a male and half of which involved a female (Gambrill, 1973). There were twice as many "no responses" to situations involving a male. Examples of some of the situations used are as follows (Gambrill, 1973).

> You are attending a lecture for the general public and during intermission a pleasant-looking man your age comes up to you and says, "Are you enjoying the lecture?" You say. . . .

> You have been engaged in a short conversation with a woman you have just met in a bookstore and now want to end the conversation. You say. . . .

> You are sitting in the bus terminal waiting for a bus from San Francisco to Berkeley. A woman sits down next to you and you decide to start a conversation. You say. . . .

> You have been conversing with a man about your own age in the first meeting of a class you are taking. You have been talking about the content of the class but now want to change the topic to talk about the Berkeley political scene. You say. . . .

The situational nature of assertive behavior is also revealed by the lack of generalization effects for all social behaviors when assertive training is employed with selected behaviors (see, for example, McFall and Lillesand, 1971).

The Components of Effective Social Behavior

Patients rated high in overall assertiveness speak louder, respond more rapidly, give longer replies, evidence more profound affect, show less compliance, and request more changes in the other person's behavior than patients rated low in assertiveness (Eisler, Miller, and Hersen, 1973). Characteristics of an open body expression are encouraged and those of a closed body expression discouraged (Laws and Serber, 1974). An open body expression is characterized by a generally relaxed posture, a lack of obvious muscular tension, and movement tends to be easy and graceful. It includes facial expression of smiling and laughing, the head is usually up, and eye contact is direct. Body movements and head orientation tend to be toward the other person. In contrast, a closed body expression is characterized by a generally rigid posture, presence of obvious muscular tension, and fidgety activity; and movement tends to be stiff, strained, or jerky. This includes a tightly drawn facial expression and frowning; head position is often down, and there is a lack of eye contact. Body movements and head position tend to be away from others.

The specific components of effective social skills depend on the particular interpersonal situation involved. Some social behaviors are in response to an instigation by another person, whereas others require more initiative—for example, responding to someone initiating a conversation, in contrast to initiating a conversation. A second variable is the valence of the affect involved, whether it is negative or positive. Situations involving negative assertion are discussed first. These include a variety of behaviors such as refusing requests, responding to criticism, discouraging unwanted interactions, requesting a change in someone else's behavior, disagreeing with another person, and resisting interruptions. In each case, difficulty may only be in relation to specific individuals (strangers, acquaintances, intimates) or contexts (service-related—as in stores and restaurants—authority, family).

Unfortunately, there is very little information available as to what mix of behaviors actually works best in given social situations. From the data so far available, it is certain that there will be situational differences both in optimal verbal and nonverbal components. Various approaches have been taken so far to attempt to determine the effective social responses (see McFall, in press). Some employ judges and base decisions on majority opinion. Others identify differences between groups, such as between highly assertive and very nonasssertive individuals. Very few studies have attempted to define situational competence by determination of what behaviors are most effective. One of the few reports describing such an attempt investigated different ways for a person to initiate a conversation with a stranger (Twentyman, cited in McFall, in press). Twelve male and female undergraduate students tried out three different initiating remarks when approaching same- and opposite-sex undergraduates in real-life situations. One requested permission to talk to the person ("Hello. Do you mind if I talk to you?"). A second employed an indirect approach ("Hi. Haven't I seen you somewhere before?"). A third employed a direct approach and admission of awkwardness in terms of meeting others ("Hi. I'm trying to meet people. Do you know of any good ways of doing this?") (Twentyman, cited in McFall, in press, p. 25). Immediately following this initiation attempt, the person approached was asked to complete a questionnaire on which she or he rated the effectiveness of each statement. The first approach was liked more than the second in all sexual combinations and was rated more favorable than the last approach when men approached men or women, but not when women approached either men or women. In view of the lack of such social validity information in terms of actual behavior, the suggestions made in the following section are offered tentatively.

Negative Assertion in Response to Someone Else Taking the Initiative. The ability to say no to unwanted requests is perhaps the one behavior most often mentioned as problematic for a wide variety of clients. Some requests entice one to engage in a tempting behavior such as having a drink when a decision has been made to try to stop drinking. Others relate to behaviors having no such tempting components—for example, refusing a request to borrow money. Both involve someone else taking the initiative in making the request. Responding to criticism also involves initiation from another person and is discussed under negative assertion, because of the negative content implied in the word *criticism.*

Refusing requests. The inability to clearly and politely refuse requests makes life difficult for many people. The client's response can be examined to see whether the word *no* is mentioned, and whether a clear refusal is made in a polite way, without excuses. The statement may describe the reason for the refusal, but not in the form of an excuse, because no excuse is necessary. One could say in response to a request to borrow money, "No; I need all the money I have for this week." Offering excuses opens the door for others to try to counter them and, if pressured, it is more effective to simply repeat the same statement of refusal. The following statements of refusal illustrate different approaches (from McFall and Bridges, 1970, pp.

12, 17; see also McFall and Lillesand, 1970). In each case, the word *no* is mentioned first, the answers are direct and concise, and no excuses are given; however, a reason is offered.

> Your roommate is constantly borrowing dimes from you in order to buy cokes, candy, and so on but never seems to pay you back. You are getting rather annoyed at this and have decided to stop lending money. Now your roommate comes up to you and says, "Hey, can I borrow a dime for a coke?" What would you say?
>
> 1. "No, you've never paid me back in the past, and I'm tired of losing money."
> 2. "No, sorry, you owe me too many dimes already."
>
> Suppose you want to sell a book for five dollars. A mere acquaintance of yours comes up to you and says, "Gee, I really need the book and I can't find it anywhere, but the trouble is I can only pay you three dollars for it. What do you say?" What would you say?
>
> 1. "No, I can't sell the book for any less than five dollars. I need the money."
> 2. "No, I can't. I paid five dollars for it and I think it's only fair if you pay that, too."

The statement of refusal may contain an empathic element, in which it is recognized that someone else has a problem and would like the favor performed, such as, "I know you are late for your appointment but I don't have time now to drive you over." An alternative may even be suggested, such as, "Why not take the bus? They run every fifteen minutes." A variety of manipulative attempts may be employed in response to a refusal and the client must learn how to respond to these so he does not allow himself to be manipulated into doing something he would rather not do. These include (1) flattery—"Gee, I always thought you were a generous person"; (2) criticism—"You really have a problem"; (3) the "poor-soul" routine—"You know I wouldn't ask you unless I was down to my last penny"; (4) the "once-in-a-lifetime" request—"You know I've never asked you before and I promise I'll never ask again"; (5) the promise of "never-more"—"I promise this is the last time I'll ever ask"; (6) guilt-induction attempt—"I really feel bad that you turned me down." These may all be combined in a last-ditch effort that may go something like: "Gee, I always thought you were a generous person. You really have a problem not being able to lend your own friends some money. You know I wouldn't ask you unless I was down to my last penny. You know I've never asked you before and I promise I'll never ask you again. I promise this is the last time I'll ever ask. I really feel bad that you turned me down." These may be countered (1) by repeating refusal; (2) by saying, "That may be true, but I won't lend you the money" (the first part of this answer has been called *fogging* [Smith, 1975]; this method permits the deflection of manipulative criticism while keeping decision making in one's own hands); (3) by saying, "I'm sure that's true, but. . . "; (4) by saying, "Yes, that's true, but. . . "; (5) by saying, "I'm sure you need the money, but. . . "; (6) by saying, "I know you are disappointed but. . . ." It is more appropriate to react to guilt-induction attempts with anger rather than guilt, because it is really not very considerate of others to deliberately try and induce a negative feeling, and, if such attempts persist, this can be verbalized. "Negative inquiry" may also be useful when confronted with criticism after refusing a request. Here, criticism is solicited either to make use of it, if it is helpful in some way, or to draw it out, if it is being used in a manipulative manner. This also forces others to be more forthright in their statements (Smith, 1975). The person requesting the favor may say, "You are really being immature." An example of negative inquiry would be, "What's immature about not wanting to lend you money?"

Nonverbal components of refusal behavior are important, including direct eye contact and body posture oriented toward the person. Speech should be loud enough to be heard and slow enough to be understood with a relative absence of stammers and hesitations.

Refusing desirable requests (resisting temptations). Another type of request that may prove problematic is when we are asked to do something that for certain reasons we might like to do, but for other reasons would prefer not to do. If a client is trying to lose weight and someone offers her a delicious piece of cake, the exchange might go as follows:

> *Mrs. T. (for Temptress):* "I know you are on a diet but I just made this delicious cake. How 'bout just a tiny piece?" (Mrs. T.'s "tiny pieces" are in fact quite large.)
>
> *Mrs. R. (for Resister):* "No, thank you. I'm really trying to stick with my diet." (Mrs. R. should certainly avoid thanking Mrs. T. more than is socially necessary, because it really was not very nice of Mrs. T. to tempt Mrs. R.)
>
> *Mrs. T.:* "You know how delicious my cake is. Just a small piece couldn't hurt. Let me cut you one."
>
> *Mrs. R.:* "None for me. I really like the way my clothes look now that I've lost weight."

Probation may be violated because of lack of skill in how to say no to peers who tempt a teen-ager to engage in activities that may violate his probation. A training program designed to offer such skills was designed by Sarason and Ganzer (1973). One aspect of training is offering deflecting techniques. For example, when asked to "hit" a gas station that they happen to be passing, the boy might suggest getting a beer first to talk it over. The response elements described earlier are also of import here, including directness, empathy, self-disclosure (for example, "I just got off probation"); repeating the statement; and negative inquiry. The main point is that the client does not allow himself to be manipulated into doing or accepting something that he does not wish to. Anticipation of future undesirable consequence, such as returning to jail or tipping the scale at a higher weight, as well as the positive consequences of successful refusal can be verbalized or imagined to increase the probability of successful refusal behavior.

Common misconceptions related to a reluctance to refuse unwanted requests include the belief that one has to please everyone; that it is awful to hurt or disappoint other people and that this should be avoided at all cost; that others have more of a right than the client to determine what he will do and not do; and that saying no cannot be done in a nice way.

Frequent fears related to saying no include the concern that the exchange will escalate; that is, the other person will become abusive or will not like you anymore if you do not do what he wants. Training provides a repertoire of reactions to escalation.

Responding to criticism. Clients often report an undue sensitivity to criticism from others and demonstrate poor skills in responding to it. As with any other situation, sensitivity usually occurs only in certain situations; for example, a client may be able to handle criticism from his wife very effectively but have trouble responding in authority relationships at work when criticized. Clients are encouraged to avoid reactions that are hostile or defensive, or that hedge or counterattack, and are encouraged to agree with any truthful aspects of the criticism. Let us say that an employee is late for work and his boss says, "This is the second time you've been late in a month, Gary. This is going to have to stop." Gary could say, "Yes, I have been late twice in the last month but I assure you that this is the last time." It is appropriate to request specific information from your detractor if this is needed for clarity. Thus if an employer says, "You could have done a better job on these reports," one could ask, "I would like to write good reports and it would help if you could be more specific about how they could be better. Could you give me some examples?" It may be necessary to prepare the client for various reactions to his remarks. Let us imagine a continuation as follows:

> *Employer:* "Look, you've been here long enough to know how to do these reports."
>
> *Employee:* "Well, it seems there are still some ways you would like them to be different and it would help if you shared these with me."
>
> *Employer:* "Well, they certainly could be longer."
>
> *Employee:* "What particular sections would you like more detail on?"

Note that there is no criticism in return.

Fogging may be employed to defuse a detractor; one can admit the possibility that the criticism may have some foundation even though one does not think so. For example, a client might say, "That may be true, but...." An empathic reaction could be included, such as, "I can see how you might feel that way, but...." A variety of misconceptions may be related to an undue sensitivity to criticism and a lack of appropriate verbal reactions to such situations, including the belief that one must never make a mistake, or that it is a terrible thing to be criticized, or that if one does make a mistake, it reflects on the total person.

Negative Assertion Involving Taking the Initiative. Successful social interchanges require the ability to take the initiative in altering one's social environment. This may include requesting a change in an annoying behavior, disagreeing with someone, resisting interruption, or terminating an unwanted interaction. Negative assertion requiring initiative also includes recognition of personal limitations, such as apologizing when one is at fault, or admitting ignorance.

Requesting a change in an annoying behavior or negative event. Just as it is important in social interaction to be able to refuse requests, it is also important to be able to make requests of others. There are two types of relevant situations—when an annoying event is or has been present, and when a positive motivator is present, such as initiating a conversation with an interesting person. An example of the former is as follows: Iris was watching her favorite television show, *Wide World of Sports*, when her husband came in, greeted her pleasantly and sat down beside her. He then said, "There's a really good program on now —the Russian Ballet. Hope you don't mind if I switch the channel." At this point he gets up and switches the channel. A group of female runners disappear, replaced by two delicately balanced dancers. Possible reactions are as follows:

> *Wife 1:* "You know I was watching that show. I really like it."
> *Wife 2:* "You have a nerve to just switch off what I was watching. What's the matter with you?"
> *Wife 3:* "Bill, I'm watching that show and want to see the end of it. Please turn it back on."

Neither Wife 1 nor Wife 2 ask for a change of behavior. Wife 2 attacks Bill, and Wife 1 meekly states her preference. Stating a preference is often not enough. One must also ask for a change of behavior; that is, inform the other person what one would like.

The client's responses are examined for the following qualities: Was there a clear request for a behavior change? Was there an avoidance of attack on the other person? Was a reason stated? Often the reason is stated first. Let's say a person is in a movie and someone behind is kicking his seat. He might turn around, look at the person, and say, "It's difficult to concentrate on the movie when my seat is being kicked. Please try not to kick my seat." Another example of making a request for a behavior change when an annoying event has occurred is shown as follows (from Galassi and Galassi, 1974, p. 9).

> You have gone to dinner at a nice restaurant. You decided to splurge this evening and ordered a steak dinner. You ordered a rare steak. However, when you cut into the steak, you find it is well done.
>
> *You:* Waiter, I'd like to see you a moment.
>
> *Waiter:* Is everything OK?
>
> *You:* No, I ordered a rare steak and this is well done.
>
> *Waiter:* OK. (Begins to walk off.)
>
> *You:* One moment; I would like you to return this steak and bring me a rare one.
>
> *Waiter:* I distinctly remember you ordering a well-done steak, sir.
>
> *You:* That's impossible. I always order my steak rare.
>
> *Waiter:* I have it written down right here on my slip.
>
> *You:* You must have misunderstood me, then. Would you please return this steak and get me a rare one?
>
> *Waiter:* All right, I'll be back in a few minutes.
>
> *You:* Thank you.

If one is confronted with an unpleasant event that one would like to remove, such as a colleague playing "Oldies but

Goodies" while one is trying to work, one should examine one's response to determine if a direct request for a behavior change was made and whether one's response indicated that the noise bothered one, rather than being voiced as an attack on the other person. The same nonverbal behaviors of importance in refusing requests are also important here.

Misconceptions related to a reluctance to express preferences include the belief that one does not have a right to request changes of others or that it is better to simply "let things go" and not say anything. And, with things that are not that annoying, learning to live with them may be fairly easy. However, if the behavior or event is quite bothersome, not saying anything will usually have negative effects over the long run. Teaching the client pleasant ways to request changes removes the belief that such requests must be made in a nasty way. Fear of negative reactions may prevent a client from requesting changes and offering skills in how to deal with a variety of responses will help to remove this.

Disagreeing with others. A client may have difficulty expressing opinions that differ from those of others. He may not express these at all or do so in an offensive manner, such as by saying, "You don't know what you're talking about," or "No, I'm afraid you're not right." Or, he may disagree without elaborating on his reason for his disagreement, which does not add much to conversations nor support his assertion.

Appropriate disagreement statements contain the recognition that it is the person himself who disagrees, rather than blaming or putting down his partner (Gambrill and Richey, 1976). The use of the personal pronoun *I* is encouraged, as well as the use of elaborated opinion statements such as, "I think there is another way to look at the issue, because. . . ." Interest in the other person can be shown by following this by a question directed to him, such as "Have you ever looked at it from that angle?"

Clients may experience difficulty in disagreeing because they wait too long, meanwhile building up anger and annoyance. They are encouraged to express their disagreement at an early point without interrupting others unless they are forced to do this. Differing opinions may not be expressed because the client feels that his opinions are not as valuable as those of others, that people will not like him if he disagrees with what they say, or that one has to be abusive to differ with others.

Resisting interruption. Perhaps a wife constantly interrupts her partner whenever he starts to talk, or mistakes the natural pause pattern between sentences for a signal that he has finished speaking (Gambrill and Richey, 1976). Skills relevant to resisting interruption include verbal gestures, such as raising the hand to indicate "Wait a minute," as well as direct verbal statements, such as "I'd like to finish my thought." Clients who allow themselves to be interrupted do not act as if they have a right to be treated with the same consideration as others.

Apologizing when one is at fault. Everyone at times does things that he is sorry for, in that he might have hurt another person unnecessarily or entailed some other cost. Apologizing often requires taking the initiative, although at times the person may confront one with the misdeed and ask for an apology. Let us say that a client borrows someone else's sweater and loses it on a camping trip. The person can be informed that the item is lost and that he is sorry. A statement of apology may include an empathic statement, such as "I know this was your favorite sweater. . . ." Undue criticism should not be tolerated. Difficulty in offering apologies is sometimes related to the belief that one must never make mistakes.

Admitting ignorance. Clients are sometimes placed in difficult situations when they allow people to assume that they know more than they actually do. For example, an English teacher reported an encounter in which someone assumed she knew a great deal about Medieval English, although this was not her specialty. She became increasingly uncomfortable, because she allowed this assumption to stand but was in the position of really not knowing much about the field. She was afraid that if she said, "My specialty is the Renaissance and I really am not very familiar with Medieval English," she might receive a reaction such as "I'm surprised that someone who is an English teacher doesn't know more about that period"—that is, that she would be considered poorly informed. However, no one can know everything, and she could have simply responded, "English is such a large field, it's impossible to keep up with everything." Admitting ignorance also allows clients to acquire information, because they are not pretending that they know it.

Terminating unwanted interactions. Enjoying family, work, and social life requires knowing how to end unwanted conversations as well as how to initiate and maintain desirable ones. Many clients make complaints that they get "caught" in conversations that they do not wish to have. They experience this because they do not take the initiative and express their desire in a firm but polite manner, being sure to look at the other person. One tactic that others employ to keep us in interactions is to continue a steady stream of speech, which forces us to interrupt this in order to leave. Often clients say, "I can't interrupt him." However, others should be sensitive to cues that are offered, such as a decrease in eye contact, a shift of body posture away from the person, and attempts to speak. The client has a perfect right to break into the other's conversation if no natural pause is provided in the exchange. He might say, "Excuse me, I'm sorry to interrupt you, but I have to leave now." It is not necessary to offer an excuse, although he may share the reason for departure. Statements of interest in leaving may have to be repeated if the other person is persistent. Often, when a client reports he would like to discourage a conversation, observation of his behavior shows that he offers a high frequency of gaze behavior, of smiles, of head nods, and in some cases, even asks questions, rather than avoiding these behaviors.

Positive Assertion: Someone Else Takes the Initiative. Social interactions occur in which positive assertion is called for, some of which involve another person taking the initiative— for example, when someone offers a compliment, attempts to initiate a conversation or arrange for a future meeting.

Accepting compliments. Many people feel they have to be modest when receiving a compliment. When someone says, "You really look nice today," their response might be, "It's probably because it's such a nice day," rather than accepting the compliment by saying "Thank you," without rushing to offer a compliment in return. If a compliment is offered on some item that has been purchased, this can be recognized by saying "Thank you" and information related to the item may be offered, such as disclosing where it was purchased.

Responding to another initiating an exchange. Some clients who would like to have more social contacts discourage the initiation attempts of others by inappropriate nonverbal behavior, such as a low frequency of gaze behavior and frowns rather than smiles, as well as by offering minimal or negative verbal behavior. A young woman who was interested in meeting more men offered the following report of an exchange she had on the tennis court when a man came up to her and said "Hi, do you come here often?" She barely looked at him, becoming very nervous because he was very attractive, and simply said no (which was not true) and walked away. Behaviors to be increased to facilitate encounters include smiles, eye contact, and body posture oriented toward the person; answering questions with more than yes or no—that is, using elaborated statements such as "Yes, I come here often because it's usually free and really has a nice surface"; and by using the answer-question rule (Gambrill and Richey, 1976)—that is, by then turning the exchange back to the other person; for example, by saying, "And how about you? This is the first time I've seen you here." This type of statement also shows an interest in the other person, in that the client notes that she has not seen him before.

Responding to requests for a future meeting. Opportunities for further contacts may be lost because of inappropriately reacting to a request from someone else for a future meeting. Such reactions may include saying no when one wished to say yes, putting a decision off and perhaps not knowing how to get in touch with the person again, saying no because alternative arrangements were not suggested that would be more appealing —for example, arranging some neutral place to meet, such as in front of a movie rather than meeting at someone's house (see Gambrill and Richey, 1976).

Positive Antecedent: You Take the Initiative. Positive assertion includes taking the initiative in initiating conversations with others, maintaining conversations, arranging future contacts, asking favors, complimenting others, and showing affection.

Initiating conversations. Valuable opportunities to meet

others are often lost because of shyness in starting conversations. As with any other social skill, the relative contribution of behavior deficits, inaccurate discriminations, and negative thought patterns, as well as cognitive and behavioral assets, must be determined. A client may have appropriate skills for initiating conversations, but display these at the wrong time. Even though a client may already know a variety of ways to initiate conversations, he may benefit from learning and practicing additional ones.

There are many ways to initiate conversations, illustrated as follows (from Gambrill and Richey, 1976, p. 57).

> Ask a question or make a comment on the situation or mutual activity that you are *both* involved in.
>
> Compliment the other person on some aspect of his or her behavior, appearance, or some other attribute.
>
> Make an observation or ask a casual question about what the other person is doing.
>
> Ask if you may join another person or ask him to join you.
>
> Ask another person for help, advice, an opinion, information.
>
> Offer something to someone.
>
> Share your personal opinion, or experience.
>
> Greet the person and introduce yourself.

A client may make a number of mistakes in the way he initiates conversations. Comments could be too personal; they could be delivered in a negative or sarcastic way; they could imply a personal criticism, such as "Boy, you look awful"; they could imply an assumption about the other person that is offensive; or they could be judgmental, dogmatic, or egotistical, all of which may put off others (Gambrill and Richey, 1976). Nonverbal behaviors are important in initiating conversations, including eye contact, facial expression, and orientation of the body toward the person. Such voice qualities as loudness, as well as an absence of hesitations and stammers, are also important.

Negative thoughts related to a reluctance to initiate conversations include an undue sensitivity to rejection or to the possibility of rude or hostile replies. There is often a striking absence of positive thoughts concerning the immediate and ultimate positive consequences of taking the initiative in this situation.

Maintaining conversations. Listening as well as speaking skills are important in maintaining enjoyable conversations, and both areas should be assessed if the client is interested in increasing social contacts. When listening, does the client look at the other person, and offer occasional verbal and nonverbal feedback in the form of "Hm-hms" and head nods? Does he wait until others have finished speaking before starting to talk? Do his questions match what the other person has been saying? Does he offer information about himself as well as pick up on information offered by others and use this as the basis for questions and comments? Is he able to reciprocate talking with listening or does he speak too much or too little? Does he initiate some topics of conversation and attempt to change the topic of conversation when he is bored with the current one? Does he ask questions about the person? Are elaborated opinion statements offered as well as yes and no replies? Is he prepared with a variety of topics to speak about? Failure to share opinions and to introduce topics of conversation may be caused by the client's feeling that his opinions are not very valuable or interesting.

Arranging future contacts and terminating exchanges. An important aspect of having enjoyable social contacts is arranging for future meetings. This may entail use of the telephone as well as in-person arrangements. Some important elements include degree of enthusiasm, having an interesting place to go to, suggesting another time if the first one is not satisfactory, not being apologetic, and telling the other person that one enjoyed being with him and would like to see him again. Thus one would avoid statements such as "I'm sorry if I'm bothering you, but someone told me about a movie. I don't know if it is any good, but if you happen to be free anytime could you go with me?" This statement is full of apologies, is not enthusiastic, and does not suggest a specific time.

It is also important to know how to end conversations in a polite way. The client's repertoire can be examined to determine whether he has the skills to do this. Does he wait for a natural pause in the conversation? If a pause does not occur, can he politely interrupt the other person? A failure to interrupt a talkative person when a natural pause does not occur is usually related to the misconception that it is always impolite to interrupt someone, whereas it could be considered insensitive of others not to notice attempts to "gain the floor" to speak.

Asking favors. Sometimes clients have no trouble refusing unwanted requests, but find it difficult to ask favors of others. Or, the client may incorrectly assume that others should know what it is he would like and become resentful when this is not forthcoming. It is important to be able to identify situations when it is appropriate to ask given favors. And, as with any social behavior that requires an initiation, the attention of the other person must be gained through effective verbal and nonverbal behavior, including loudness of voice, eye contact, and body positioning. Words should match nonverbal behavior. Being clear as to exactly what is desired as well as stating the reason for asking the favor may increase the chance of compliance. An example of asking a favor is presented as follows (from Galassi and Galassi, 1974, p. 13).

> You have a class to attend from 7 to 8:30 P.M. and you are expecting a very important call somewhere between 7 and 11 P.M. Your roommate is planning to stay around the dorm tonight. You want to ask her to listen for the phone and take a message if the call comes in before you get back.
>
> *You:* "[Claire], I have an important call I'm expecting tonight. Will you please listen for the phone and take the message if it comes before I get back from class?"
>
> *Other:* "You know I hate to be confined to the room all night."
>
> *You:* "I'll be back no later than 9."
>
> *Other:* "That's still two hours."
>
> *You:* "The call is quite important to me."

Other: "It can't be that important. They'll probably call back."

You: "I need to get the message tonight."

Other: "Then why don't you stay home from class?"

You: "I would rather not have to miss class if possible."

Other: "OK—I guess I'll stay in and listen for the call."

Some clients report that they do not ask favors because they feel crushed when turned down. That is, they have the misconception that to be turned down is "awful." Or they may have the misconception that they will be obligated to this person or feel they have no right to ask favors. However, just as others have a perfect right to say no, the client has a perfect right to ask.

Complimenting others. Most people enjoy receiving compliments that are sincerely expressed and this provides one way to increase their enjoyment during social exchanges. A client may be able to identify appropriate times and ways to give compliments, but may have misconceptions about offering them that interfere with their expression. For example, a man may feel that it is "unmanly" to express compliments. Possible misconceptions should be addressed. As with other assertive behaviors, nonverbal behavior should match verbal behavior and the client's "compliment-giving repertoire" should be checked to make sure that he is not diluting compliments by incongruent nonverbal behavior such as looking away or frowning. An example of giving a compliment appears as follows (from Galassi and Galassi, 1974, p. 10).

One of your friends whom you haven't seen since last semester drops by your room to say hi. You notice that this friend who was quite heavy has lost about twenty pounds.

You: My, [Claire], you really look great. You've lost a lot of weight.

Other: Thank you.

You: How did you do it? Dieting takes real will power. I really wish I had your determination.
Other: Oh, it wasn't that hard.
You: Whatever you did, you really look great.
Other: It's good to see you again.
You: It's good to see you again.

Showing affection. The client's impact in personal encounters may be decreased by a failure to show appropriate signs of affection. He may be hesitant to ever touch someone when offering a positive comment or to hug someone when saying goodbye. This may be combined with inappropriate reactions in response to affection shown by others, such as becoming tense when touched. One source of irrational fear that is raised by clients who wish to increase their social contacts with both men and women is that members of the same sex may interpret such displays of affection as indicative of homosexual interests. A decision will have to be made as to whether or not one will limit one's spontaneous displays of affection because of this risk. The degree of comfort with one's own sexuality will influence which alternative is selected. If the client has concerns in this area, these should be addressed. If the risk is taken, two things are important to bear in mind. One relates to the possible misperception of the other person's concern. That is, the concern may only be in the client's mind and not exist at all in the thoughts of others. The other relates to whether the source of a "problem" is located in oneself or in the other person, and to how much responsibility the client should accept for other people's reactions. Let us say that a person the client is interacting with is "homophobic," that is, has an irrational concern in relation to any hint of homosexuality, imagined or actual, especially as it impinges directly on himself or herself, and that after an appropriate display of affection, this person avoids the client. The client should be encouraged to see this reaction as an inappropriate one to his own behavior, if his own behavior would be considered appropriate in most other contexts, and to perceive the other person's reaction as his or her own limitation. If interaction continues, then perhaps the topic can be discussed. This oversensitivity to the display of affection seems especially keen among men in Western society, compared with men in other countries such as Greece, where physical affection displayed between men is socially condoned.

Assessment

Indications of a skill deficit and its relationship to the presenting problem may be gained from information gathered in the natural environment as well as from information gathered during interviews. The client may display an undue deference to the counselor, offer examples of interactions that indicate a lack of effective expression, or interact with a significant other in an unassertive manner in the office. Examples that point to a lack of appropriate behaviors may be offered when the client is questioned about what happens right before and after incidences of his presenting problem. He may report that it is only after his supervisor unjustly criticizes him or his wife arranges social events for the evening that he does not like, that he starts to feel depressed. Often the client with an assertive problem makes no mention of this during initial contact. However, with the growing popularity of assertion training and the availability of training manuals for the public, client recognition may occur more frequently in the future (Fensterheim and Baer, 1975; Smith, 1975; Alberti and Emmons, 1974; Gambrill and Richey, 1976).

The question of concern during assessment is whether the client displays ineffective social behavior in relation to given situations. The effect of this on his life is carefully determined, both in relation to client-presented problems as well as to others noted by the counselor. An important part of assessment is to determine whether appropriate skills are available. If they are present, intervention will address factors that interfere with their display, such as oversensitivity to negative reactions or certain misconceptions that one does not have a right to express feelings in an appropriate way. If the client does not possess needed skills, intervention procedures that will establish them, such as model presentation and behavior rehearsal, would be selected. The interview can be employed to determine the range of situations in which interpersonal difficulties are experienced, the models the client has been exposed to in the past, and the types of consequences, positive or negative, that follow both adaptive and inappropriate social behaviors. Descriptions of exactly what he does and says, thinks and feels in relevant situations should be obtained. It is often useful to check the client's report against information gained during interviews with significant others such as a spouse, or with data from other sources, because often the client will not be able to identify important deficits or surfeits in his social behavior and may misinterpret the reactions of others—for example, he may think that they reacted negatively, when in fact their reaction was favorable.

Self-Report Inventories. Self-report paper-and-pencil inventories, such as the Assertion Inventory (Gambrill and Richey, 1975), may be employed to gain an overview of degree of comfort in various interpersonal situations as well as information as to how the situation is usually handled. The client is requested to indicate degree of discomfort (on a scale from one to five), as well as how likely she is to carry out the behavior if the opportunity arose (on a scale from one to five), in relation to 40 situations. A total anxiety score as well as total response probability score can be derived from this inventory. Structured paper-and-pencil inventories such as the assertion inventory are screening devices that may point to the relevance of certain areas. More specific information must be gained via other assessment methods, such as behavioral interviews, self-monitoring, role playing, or observation in the natural environment. A fifty-five-item Interpersonal Situation Inventory has been developed for psychiatric patients (Goldsmith and McFall, 1975). Patients respond to each situation with one of five alternatives, ranging from being able to handle a situation and feeling comfortable in it to not being able to handle it and feeling uncomfortable in it. Another alternative allows the client to indicate that the situation is not personally relevant. Such inventories offer information as to the range of interpersonal situations in which difficulty exists related to the expression of both positive and negative feelings.

Other self-report inventories, such as the Conflict Resolution Inventory, concentrate on more discrete situations, such as refusing requests (McFall and Bridges, 1970, p. 5). Examples from this inventory include the following:

> You have volunteered to help someone, whom you barely know, to do some charity work. He/she really needs your help but when he/she calls to arrange a time, it turns out that you are in the middle of exams.

> You and two close friends are looking for a fourth person with whom to share an apartment. Now your two roommates come to you and say that they have found someone they would like to ask. However, you know this person and secretly dislike him/her.

> On your way back to the dorm, you meet a slight acquaintance who asks you to carry a heavy package home for him/her since he/she is not going home for a while, but it would be quite cumbersome, since you are carrying packages of your own.

> You are studying for an exam but your best friend asks you to go to a concert with him/her. He/she makes you feel that if you were a true friend you would go.

Response alternatives included (1) "I would refuse and would not feel uncomfortable about doing so"; (2) "I would refuse but would feel uncomfortable doing so"; (3) "I would not refuse but would feel uncomfortable because I didn't"; (4) "I would not refuse even though I might prefer to, but would not feel particularly uncomfortable because I didn't"; and (5) "I would not refuse because it seems a reasonable request."

Rehm and Marston (1968) created a Situation Questionnaire consisting of thirty items such as calling a girl up just to talk and dancing with a girl on a date. A briefer inventory pertaining to ability to interact effectively in heterosexual situations was developed by Twentyman and McFall (1975). This consists of twenty items with each item scored on a seven-point scale. Self-report information can inform the counselor as to whether the client can identify appropriate behaviors, but will not inform him as to whether the client can appropriately display these. This can only be determined by further questioning and observation. A Discrimination Test on Assertive, Aggressive and Nonassertive Behavior has been developed by Jakubowski to assess the extent to which a person can select the appropriate alternative for a series of sixty items (see Lange and Jakubowski, 1976).

Self-Monitoring. The client may be requested to keep a log of relevant situations in the natural environment, noting the situation, what was said and done, satisfaction with the response, subjective rating of discomfort, what he would have liked to say or do, and what he thought about and felt. An example of a client-gathered log is shown in Figure 28. It is also helpful to ask clients to write down what an effective response would be, if they can. We can see from the righthand column that this client was only able to come up with an effective reaction for some of the situations. She clearly had difficulty saying no, as well as in initiating conversations. Data gathered over the rest of the week supported the hypothesis that these were two areas of difficulty for her. She also had difficulty in making reasonable requests of her secretary, which had the consequence of often making her seem unreliable to others, because letters would not be answered on time. Separate columns indicate those situations in which she had an initiatory role. This is particularly important in ongoing relationships such as marital interactions, in which people tend to "forget" their role in marital difficulties.

Praise should be offered for effective behaviors that are noted. Reactions that will have a positive effect on interactions are encouraged, even when someone's reaction toward the client is negative. A good example of this is the empathic assertion advocated by Lazarus (1973b) in which one tries to empathize with the other's situation; for example, by saying to a clerk who has snapped at you, "It looks like you are really very busy today." Information may be collected by recording relevant incidents on a tape recorder. This has the advantage of allowing review of this material during sessions and encourages the client to offer more details concerning his experiences.

Role-Playing Methods. Role playing offers a valuable tool to assess the client's behavior. He can be requested to role play

Figure 28. Example of a Client-Gathered Log

Date	Time	Situation	Who Is Involved	What You Said or Did	What Happened	What You Did	What You Would Have Liked to Do
9/13	9:00 A.M.	Work	Secretary	Request that urgent letter be typed	She said she did not have time	Said "OK"	Repeat request and try to convey urgency: "This is a really important letter. Do you think there is some other way we could get it typed?"
9/13	11:30 P.M.	Work	Colleague		Asked if I could talk	Said "OK"	Say no, because I was really into work and it was not urgent that we talk: "Gee, I have to finish this now. Could we talk later this afternoon?"
9/13	12:00 P.M.	Work	Colleague		Asked to have lunch with me	Said yes	Say no, because I really find this person a bore.
9/13	7:00 P.M.	Home	Friend		Telephoned and asked if he could come over	Said yes	Say no—really felt like being alone.
9/14	3:00 P.M.	Faculty meeting	New man	Nothing	Nothing		Would have liked to go over and start a conversation with him.

behavior in the office situation, with reciprocal roles assumed by the counselor after determining how significant others may act. This information may be gained by first requesting the client to role play the part of the significant other. Reciprocal roles may be played by other people, such as secretaries, who may be available. Behavior in a number of different situations should be sampled to determine the range of contexts in which behavior may have to be modified to reach desired outcomes. For example, if a male indicates that he has trouble meeting women, situations might include initiating a conversation with a woman, introducing a new topic of conversation, and trying to arrange a future meeting (Gambrill, 1973). Video- or audiotape can be used to record role-played interactions. It is best to make the role play as lifelike as possible, carefully describing the environmental context, so that both nonverbal and verbal behaviors can be accurately assessed. If a client is having difficulty expressing a complaint to his employer, the role play should be initiated with the client leaving the room and then reentering it so that his posture, eye contact, and gait can be assessed when he first presents himself. Perhaps he avoids looking at the counselor, enters the room with drooped shoulders, and shuffles his feet in an uncertain way. It is important to change nonverbal behaviors as well as verbal behaviors, which might be: "I know you are busy and might not have time now, but. . . ." Situations may be presented by film, audiotape, or videotape and the client's responses observed and recorded for assessment purposes. Films for assessment of assertive behavior of high school girls and women have been developed (Jakubowski-Spector, Pearlman, and Coburn, 1973; Steel and Hochmann, in press). Role-playing situations have been developed for a number of different populations and situations, including psychiatric patients (Eisler and others, 1975), institutionalized delinquents (Freedman, 1974), women college students (MacDonald, 1974), initiating social interactions (Rehm and Marston, 1968; Gambrill, 1973), the elderly (Berger and Rose, 1976), refusal situations (McFall and Marston, 1970). Audiotape has often been employed to present situations (see, for example, Rehm and Marston, 1968). One scene is presented at a time and the client's response to the scene recorded for later review. Videotape scene presentation has also been employed (see, for example, Galassi, Galassi, and Litz, 1974) as well as live confederates who interact with the client. For example, Arkowitz and his colleagues (1975) requested their subjects to interact with a female confederate and to get to know her. They assessed the client's talk time, number of silences, number of verbal reinforcements, number of head nods, number of smiles, gaze time, and appropriate speech content. Few differences emerged between frequently and rarely dating subjects. The only differences found were in the number of silences and the higher rating in social skill received by the frequent daters. (Examples of scenes used to assess social behavior in various contexts are given earlier in this chapter.)

Asking the client to verbally describe his thoughts and feelings during the role-played interactions, as well as his perception of what the other person was thinking and feeling, will help to identify useful and dysfunctional feelings and thoughts. Attention is directed to nonverbal as well as verbal behavior. Nonverbal components of verbal messages account for a great percentage of the impact of communications (Mehrabian, 1972). Important nonverbal behaviors include eye contact, smiles, body positioning, and facial expression. These should be defined so they are easily discernible, so that the counselor and client will be able to determine what he should do more or less of and so that they can be reliably identified when assessing the effects of intervention. Looking has been defined as the client turning his head 45 degrees toward his partner with his eyes focused between the top of the head and the chin; smiling defined as a 45-degree crease in the client's cheek with his teeth showing (Eisler, Hersen, and Agras, 1973). Some measures do not permit this type of precise specification—for example, reinforcing comments—although one can identify types of statements that fall into this class—for example, affection, approval, agreement, showing interest, and so forth.

It is important that nonverbal behaviors match verbal behavior; for example, smiling while telling someone one cannot see him would not be appropriate. *How* the client says things is as important as *what* he says, including latency of response and loudness and fluency of speech. The client's reactions are examined to see whether eye contact was adequate, whether words were stated loudly and clearly enough to be understood, whether there was a relative absence of hesitations and stammers, and whether he faced the other person rather than speaking to him from the side or in back of him. In each situation, the particular components that make up an effective reaction may be somewhat different. Exactly what these differences consist of is still unknown. Video- or audiotape recordings of simulated interactions are useful for reviewing client behaviors.

Observation of the Client in Real Interactions. Role-playing methods are artificial and may not reflect the client's actual behavior in real-life situations. For this reason, role playing may be supplemented by observation of the client interacting with a significant other either in the office or at home, or by observation of the client in other social situations. Lewinsohn (1974), for example, employs home observation in which depressed clients are observed interacting with significant others. He also has employed observation of depressed clients during group therapy (see Chapter Fourteen). Observation of the social interaction between clients and significant others is used extensively in behavioral marital counseling, where the main aim may be to improve the interaction of the couple. Such observation is especially valuable when desired outcomes concern modification of the interaction between two people. Valuable information can also be gained by observing the client in other real-life situations. It is often easy to arrange this. Let us say a client has difficulty in service situations. He could be accompanied to a store and his behavior observed to identify effective and ineffective components. As with simulated situations, asking him to share his cognitions will enable identification of helpful and dysfunctional thoughts. Attention should be devoted to the intrusiveness of measures during simulated situations or during collection of observational information.

Physiological Measures. Little attention has been devoted to the measurement of physiological changes that may accompany social interaction. Heart rate and pulse measures have been employed to assess the possible role of anxiety during interpersonal exchanges (Borkovec, Stone, O'Brian, and Kaloupek, 1974; Twentyman and McFall, 1975). Means used to gather such measures are quite intrusive, and the relationship between physiological arousal and social skills displayed is complex, in that arousal may or may not be associated with degree of social skill (Borkovec and others, 1974). Such a measure would be important to the extent that the subject reported high arousal in social exchanges. A self-report index of discomfort could be employed, instead of a more intrusive direct physiological measure; for example, requesting the client to rate his degree of anxiety during social encounters and determining whether the average rating improved.

The Relationship Between Thoughts and Effective Social Skills. What one says to oneself affects what one does. Many people have suggested this relationship through the centuries, and now there is a growing body of data to support it. What one thinks affects what one gets, or what one avoids, as the case may be. It has been found that a major contributor to ineffective behavior in dating situations is the nature of the internal dialog (Schwartz and Gottman, 1976). Less assertive men have more negative self-statements and fewer positive self-statements than do more assertive men, but do not differ from more assertive men in their knowledge of appropriate behaviors. Training in self-instructional procedures directed toward altering cognitions has been found to be more effective than a skill-acquisition program (coaching and rehearsal) with socially anxious male college students (Glass, Gottman, and Schmurak, 1976). Subjects were trained to become aware of the negative self-statements they made and to produce incompatible positive self-statements. Many studies have failed to find skill differences between high-frequency and low-frequency daters (see, for example, Arkowitz and others, 1975), and between less and more socially anxious men (see, for example, Valentine and Arkowitz, 1975). However, skill deficits are more outstanding in other populations, such as psychiatric patients (see Hersen and Bellack, in press). People with high or moderate social anxiety interpret the same feedback as more negative than do people with low social anxiety and have a greater expectancy that others will evaluate them negatively (Smith and Sarason, 1975).

The importance of self-evaluations is highlighted by the finding that socially anxious men underestimate positive aspects of their performance and overestimate negative aspects compared to less socially anxious men (Valentine and Arkowitz, 1975), and have a more accurate memory for negative information and a less accurate one for positive information (O'Banion and Arkowitz, 1974), which is likely to be associated with negative self-evaluations as well as with infrequent self-reinforcement for social behaviors (Valentine and Arkowitz, 1975). These findings point to the importance of cognitive factors in relation to effective social skills and the need to assess the nature of the client's internal dialog in such situations. If negative thought patterns are found, intervention should include a focus on altering them. Just as with anxiety in noninterpersonal situations, negative self-instructions may take place in anticipation of, during, or following encounters. Let us say that a woman is thinking about going over to a person and starting a conversation. Her sequence of thoughts might be as follows: "I would really like to meet him. I haven't seen him here before. But what would I say? I would probably stammer and stutter and make a fool of myself. He might think I'm a pushy woman." Negative thoughts during encounters may decrease her ability to be an enjoyable person to talk to, because she may be only half attending to the conversation. And, even though she might make a good impression, she may say afterwards, "See, I never should have done that. It was just a waste of time." It has been found that high-anxiety speakers in a public-speaking situation are likely to make statements to themselves such as "I must be boring," when they see two or three people leave while they are talking. The person low in speech anxiety is more likely to attribute such leaving to external circumstances (Meichenbaum, 1975b). People who have trouble handling angry feelings may also present provocative thoughts to themselves before, during, and after exchanges. The same assessment procedures that are of value in determining thought patterns in relation to other stressful events can be employed here.

Many clients anticipate negative consequences from being more assertive. They may anticipate that others will scream at them, perhaps even assault them, and certainly put them in their place. Others may anticipate negative consequences that are indeed likely. An employer may not be at all pleased when a

client starts to request what he feels are needed changes in relation to his work. Usually, however, the results of assertion are
positive both for the client and for significant others, in that
assertion encourages mutual respect and removes feelings of
resentment, and so facilitates positive encounters. The irrational
and rational anticipated consequences are separated through discussion (MacDonald, 1974) and the client prepared for possible
negative ones through establishing positive self-instructions and
self-reinforcement patterns. Convincing the client of the irrationality of some of his concerns can be encouraged by asking
him to observe appropriate models in the natural environment
and to note what happens after effective social behavior, as well
as what happens after his own successful behaviors (MacDonald,
1974). If negative consequences are likely to follow new behavior, the short- and long-term benefits and costs of engaging in
more effective social behavior should be discussed, and the
client must make a decision as to his preferred alternative
(MacDonald, 1974).

Social Skill Training

Social skill training usually consists of a variety of components, including behavior rehearsal, feedback, prompting,
model presentation, programing of change, and homework assignments. Textual material may be employed to offer instructional information. For example, written material was employed in a study designed to increase initiation of social
contacts by women (Gambrill, 1973). The client could be requested to read portions of *Your Perfect Right* (Alberti and
Emmons, 1974) to clarify differences between aggressive, assertive, and submissive behavior. With undergraduates, instructional control coupled with guided practice (coaching and behavior rehearsal) has been sufficient to increase assertive
behavior (McFall and Twentyman, 1973); however, with other
populations, such as psychiatric patients, modeling has been
required to achieve effects with complicated components of
assertion such as resisting pressure (see Hersen and Bellack, in
press). Mere practice without coaching has been ineffective with
psychiatric patients. Both outpatient and inpatient psychiatric

populations have responded well to skill training procedures (see Chapter Nineteen).

The Value Stance Involved in Social Skill Training. Social skill training is designed to increase the influence that a person exerts over his or her social environment by increasing the expression of both positive and negative feelings as well as to increase comfort in interpersonal situations. A value stance as well as an intervention strategy is associated with such training. It is assumed that people have a right to express their feelings in a manner that neither subjugates others nor oneself, and that well-being includes this expression (Wolpe and Lazarus, 1966). It is thus for the overly reticent as well as for those who are overly aggressive in their encounters. The former group fail to assert their rights, whereas the latter group achieve their rights at someone else's expense. Such training implies that it is adaptive to express oneself in appropriate ways, to be able to distinguish situations in which restraint is called for from those in which assertion would be most adaptive, and to act in such a manner. It is considered nonadjustive and unfair to be taken advantage of, to allow oneself to be unduly imposed on, and to be intimidated. There is nothing wrong in refusing invitations or requests if one does not wish to act in accord with them, and, on the other hand, it is not sickly sentimental to compliment people when one feels like it, or to express pleasure. There is also the assumption that life will be more enjoyable and more interesting if one is active in the construction of his or her own social environment. The risk entailed in being more active is assumed, and steps taken to deal with undue anxiety concerning possible negative reaction, by the development of positive self-instructions.

Motivating the Client to be More Assertive. A critical aspect of social skill training is forming a conceptualization of effective behavior as important. Attention is devoted to enhancing the discrimination between submissive, assertive, and aggressive behavior; to encouraging the belief that one has a perfect right to express feelings, both negative and positive; to pointing out the losses involved in a lack of assertion; and to highlighting the relationship of unassertive behavior to the presenting problem if this is not evident to the client. Discussion centers around the disadvantages of ineffective social behavior, if the client is not already aware of these. Specific situations are selected in which nonassertive behavior has occurred, and these are carefully examined, pointing out what befell the person both in terms of negative consequences such as doing things he did not wish to do, aggravating others unnecessarily, losing opportunities, and having unpleasant feelings such as anxiety and resentment.

It is often helpful to illustrate to the client how his behavior appears to others. This can be done by assuming the role of the client and duplicating his usual nonassertive behavior, perhaps even exaggerating it, to highlight how this behavior strikes others. This enactment is often a shock to clients and frequently leads to statements such as, "My goodness, no wonder no one ever listens to me," or "Do I look like that?" Also, statements are frequently made indicating new awareness of specific actions. A client may realize, for example, that he infrequently looks at others during exchanges.

The negative effects of a lack of assertive behavior is often made quite apparent to clients through assessment efforts. For example, a client may realize, by keeping a log, that he rarely states his preferences and that instead he expects others to know what he wants. The client comes to recognize the losses entailed through ineffective behavior and the possible relationship of this behavior to his presenting problem, which may be marital discord, depression, or drinking. Possible detrimental effects on others are also revealed through assessment.

Sometimes a client has conceptions that interfere with his willingness to become more assertive, and discussion may be necessary to alter them. Various beliefs may have to be challenged, such as the belief that one should never hurt people's feelings and that therefore one should never criticize others or complain; that it is childish or inappropriate to express positive emotions; that one is indebted to another person and must silently suffer whatever impositions the other wishes to inflict; or that one must always please others.

The client may initially feel that to be assertive is to be aggressive; that he will hurt other people's feelings; that they will not like him; and that he has no right to impose his preferences on others. The role of assertive responses in inhibiting anxiety is pointed out, drawing on examples from the client's history as well as on other illustrative examples (Wolpe and Lazarus, 1966); and the natural motivating role of the client's emotional reaction, whether positive or negative, is pointed out (Wolpe, 1973b). For example, if the client is angry about poor service in a restaurant, the anger can serve as a motivator for assertive behavior. The positive benefits of effective social behavior may be emphasized by requesting the client to observe models of effective behavior in his own social environment, noting carefully what happens after such behavior.

One maneuver that is often effective in altering interfering conceptions is to ask the client whether he thinks it fair for a person to be treated in such a manner and whether he would treat someone else this way; that is, he is encouraged to accept his personal rights. Often the answer is a very definite no, the reason being that it would be unfair to do so. Thus, the client states that he would not inflict on others what he readily bears himself. If the client already recognizes the inequalities in his relationships, highlighting them further offers additional incentives for participation in the work necessary to alter behavior. The counselor stresses the manner in which unexpressed feelings such as anger and resentment build up and create anxiety and hinder positive relationships.

If the problem lies in the other direction—that is, antisocial aggression—the negative consequences of this, as well as the beneficial effects of appropriate assertion, are emphasized. Here, too, the client learns to influence his social environment in a more effective way. The effort that may have to be devoted to encouraging assertive behavior is illustrated in the following example.

Mrs. M., a sixty-seven-year-old widowed retired school teacher, complained of an intense phobia of water. It became apparent in gathering information about her current living situation that she was extremely unassertive in her personal relationships, including her living companion, Mrs. R., a woman a few years younger than herself.

Mrs. M. spent most of her time at home except for daily walks around the neighborhood, weekly visits to a church in town, and weekly visits to an old-age home, where she pushed a book cart around the floors of the home. She said she would like to go out more frequently, especially in the company of some of the other woman she knew, but if she did this it would have to be done without the knowledge of Mrs. R., because the latter objected strongly to Mrs. M.'s going out, especially when Mrs. M. wished to go out with other people. Mrs. M. did not like to lie to Mrs. R. Mrs. R. herself did not like to go out and therefore would not accompany Mrs. M. on any outings. Mrs. M. curtailed her activities, because Mrs. R. did not approve of them.

Mrs. R. was also very controlling in the home and Mrs. M. did not assert herself in relation to these controlling maneuvers. For example, Mrs. R. insisted that Mrs. M. watch television with her every evening, including the requirement of Mrs. M.'s attention during commercials when Mrs. M. would have preferred to doze. If Mrs. M. looked away from the set, Mrs. R. would berate her severely. Mrs. M. especially felt bored and reluctant to watch television commercials, but acquiesced to Mrs. R.'s verbal pressure. Mrs. M. would have preferred to go to bed early, because early in the evening she took a sleeping pill that made her very sleepy, and she thus had to struggle to stay awake during the evenings. Mrs. R. would also frequently criticize Mrs. M. if she did not like something that Mrs. M. was doing. Mrs. M. reported that she never asserted herself with Mrs. R., because she felt that she was a difficult person to live with because of her water phobia and should give in to Mrs. R. to make up for this. In actuality, one could not imagine how Mrs. M. would be difficult to live with, because she was such an amiable person, and on inquiry it was apparent that the water phobia did not affect Mrs. R. in any significant way.

Much discussion was necessary before Mrs. M. agreed to be more assertive with Mrs. R., even in a small way. This discussion centered around two subjects. The first concerned her misconception that she was a difficult person to live with and therefore must acquiesce to Mrs. R. The second centered around the injustices she was enduring. She was asked whether she would treat another person in such a manner and whether she thought it was fair to do so, and stated that she would never dream of treating another person that way, because it would be unfair.

Additional myths related to a failure to assert oneself relate to mistaking a lack of assertion for politeness or trying to be helpful (Lange and Jakubowski, 1976). Exploring the actual consequences of a lack of assertion in such instances often helps to point out the actual disadvantages—often to the other person involved—of nonassertive behavior.

Selection of Procedure. Once the client perceives the need to change his behavior and agrees to try out more effective reactions, he must be carefully instructed concerning what types of responses to employ, as well as when to use them. Selection of procedural mix depends on the nature of the client's cognitive and behavioral deficits and surfeits in relation to relevant situations, as well as to his comfort levels. If appropriate behaviors exist, but are not performed because of anxiety, intervention focuses on training the client in behavioral and cognitive anxiety management skills. If skills are absent, a procedure geared to develop them, such as model presentation and behavior rehearsal, is selected. Discrimination training is required when skills are available but not performed at appropriate times. A careful scanning during assessment interviews of skills in varied interpersonal situations often reveals many appropriate social behaviors that simply have to be placed under new stimulus control, that is, prompted in other situations. For example, available appropriate ways of saying no to a spouse may be of utility in work situations but not be employed there. Thus the selection of procedures flows directly from assessment, which will reveal relevant cognitive, affective, and overt behaviors, as well as important contexts.

Components of Social Skill Training. Typically, there are a variety of components involved in social skill training. These include behavior rehearsal, feedback, prompting, model presentation, programing of change, and homework assignments. Training is often carried out in a group context.

Behavior rehearsal. Role playing during assessment may reveal that the client has many effective components of needed behaviors and it may be decided that these can be "shaped" by offering further instructions and prompts during rehearsal. Not only does behavior rehearsal provide for learning new behaviors, but it also allows their practice in a safe environment and so serves to reduce discomfort. Covert modeling or rehearsal in which the client imagines himself or someone else dealing effectively in social situations has been found to be as effective as actual rehearsal (Kazdin, 1975). Home sessions during which the client engages in covert rehearsal can be used to supplement office sessions. The value of actual rehearsal is emphasized by a study that found significant effects after only twelve minutes of rehearsal (Lawrence, 1970). The situations employed during role playing should be explicitly described, so that actual conditions are closely replicated. Coaching or prompting may be employed during rehearsal to encourage appropriate behaviors.

Feedback. Positive feedback is offered following each rehearsal. That is, positive aspects of the client's performance are carefully noted and praised. The focus is on what the client did in a better way, with the counselor noting even small improvements. Thus approximations to final behaviors are reinforced. Critical comments, such as "You can do better" or "That wasn't too good," are avoided. Such feedback helps the client to discriminate behavior he should do more of and less of. A structured format for feedback in a group setting has been developed at the Oxnard Mental Health Center to promote systematic feedback and to assure involvement of all group members (Liberman, King, DeRisi, and McCann, 1975). Some of the group members are asked to rate a series of behaviors in each scene on a scale from one (very poor) to five (excellent, and little or no room for improvement, respectively). These behaviors include facial expression, use of hands, voice loudness, posture, eye contact, voice fluency, and content. The rating is offered in comparison with the client's last role play. The "average" rating of the group members is placed on a blackboard beside each behavior. Group members who gave high ratings or whose ratings deviated from those of the others can then be asked to give reasons for their ratings. They have found that even withdrawn clients tend to carefully monitor the rehearsals of the other group members with this system of group feedback. Modeling effects are enhanced, because attention to rehearsals is heightened.

As noted previously, the client is coached in learning responses that are as positive as possible. Such behaviors are more likely to be effective, because they are less likely to lead to negative escalation of exchanges that may induce client discomfort.

Prompting. Instructions or signals can be used to prompt (bring about) a response. They can be employed prior to rehearsal or model presentation as well as during rehearsal. Instructions are given before the client rehearses a behavior, thus "prompting" him to engage in certain behaviors rather than others. Perhaps he did not look at his partner during the role play and is coached to look at the other person while he (the client) is speaking. Care must be taken to identify *specific* behaviors. Liberman and his colleagues (1975) have developed a series of hand signals that can be employed during rehearsal. Their advantage is that the scene can be continued while coaching is provided in relation to specific behaviors. More direct communication may be arranged by use of the "bug-in-the-ear," which is a remote control device that allows the counselor to speak to the client unheard by others (Weathers and Liberman, 1973). If the reciprocal role is being played by the counselor, such prompts may be more difficult to give unless their precise meaning is arranged beforehand. Prompts should gradually be faded out as client skills increase.

Model presentation. Model presentation and rehearsal are usually employed when assessment reveals that the client lacks requisite behaviors in certain situations. This is most accurately determined by observing the client enact situations, as mentioned in the section on assessment. If this is not possible, because of the client's reticence, he may be more willing to do so after watching a model presented by the counselor, or, if in a group situation, by one of the other group members. The advantage of model presentation is that an entire chain of behavior can be demonstrated to the client and the client then requested to imitate it. Nonverbal behaviors, which are very important in social interaction, can be demonstrated as well as verbal behaviors, and the client's attention drawn to those that are especially important. The effectiveness of model presentation in establishing new behaviors, in decreasing avoidance behaviors, and in facilitating behaviors is well documented (Bandura, 1969). Models are more effective if they are similar to the client in sex and age, if they are perceived to have a high status, if their reactions are followed by positive consequences, and if the client's attention is directed toward desired response elements (Bandura, 1969). For example, the client may be requested to notice the model's eye contact, his hand motions, and the orientation of his posture toward the other person. The model may verbalize appropriate positive thoughts during the role play if effective social skills are hampered by negative thoughts. At first, appropriate self-statements can be verbalized out loud by the client when imitating the model's behavior, and then, by instruction, gradually moved to a cognitive level. The effects of modeling are enhanced if the observer has an opportunity to practice the observed behavior and if he is requested to identify important components of and general rules associated with the modeled behavior. For example, it has been found that observers who summarize the model's behavior are more able to learn and retain information (see, for example, Bandura, Grusec, and Menlove, 1966). Following model presentation the client is requested to practice (rehearse) the modeled behavior. Praise is offered for effective behaviors or approximations to them, and coaching given in relation to needed alterations. Models are represented as needed, and rehearsal, prompts, and feedback continued until desired responses and comfort levels are demonstrated.

Effective behaviors may be modeled by the counselor, or written scripts, audiotape, videotape, or film may be employed. The advantage of written material is that it can be referred to on an as-needed basis. Essential elements of various responses can be highlighted and written models offered. A checklist can be provided for each situation, so that the client can check his behavior, thoughts, and feelings against it to assess his own responses. The client may be instructed to watch people with effective behavior who are in similar roles prior to model presentation and rehearsal in the office (MacDonald, 1974), and to write down in a log the situation, what was done, and what happened. This increases exposure to a variety of effective models, offers examples to use during rehearsal, increases discrimination as to when to employ certain behaviors, and permits vicarious extinction of anxiety reactions through observation of positive reactions following effective behavior. The opportunity to see how negative reactions can be handled may be provided as well. Client observations are carefully discussed, noting effective elements as well as other situations in which such behaviors may be usefully employed. These situations provide valuable material for rehearsal during office sessions in addition to the client's observations of his own behavior in the natural environment.

McFall and Lillesand (1971) employed model presentation coaching and rehearsal to increase refusal of unreasonable requests. Assessment included recording of the student's responses to nine prerecorded stimulus situations. During training, a tape-recorded narrator first described a scene. The student then responded covertly or overtly to the scene, then listened to one male and one female assertive model, and was coached regarding the components of a good assertive reaction. Further feedback concerning the student's response was offered, and the entire sequence then repeated. Covert rehearsal produced greater improvement than did overt rehearsal. The imagery of the client can be checked during covert modeling by asking the client to verbalize what he is imagining (Kazdin, 1976). These descriptions can be recorded for later review. Imagining multiple models and favorable consequences is more effective than imagining only one model or a lack of positive effects.

Programing of change. Specific goals should be established for each session. Perhaps only one or two nonverbal behaviors will be focused on in any one session. Or, the client's initial repertoire might be such that he will be able to practice all needed verbal and nonverbal behaviors. Assessment of the client's behavior in relation to given situations will reveal the behaviors he already possesses, and training will build on these. Thus goals are individually established for each client during each session. Reinforcement for improvement is always in relation to the client's past performance rather than in terms of comparisons with other people. Any improvements are noted and praised, even small ones. This process offers the client a model of how to alter his own behavior (to identify small changes to be made, practice them, and offer praise for improvements).

Hierarchies ranked in terms of the degree of anxiety or anger that situations induce can be employed to gradually establish new social skills. Rehearsal starts with situations inducing a small degree of anger or anxiety and, as these are mastered, higher-level scenes are introduced. Escalation of scenes is carefully programed in accord with the skill and comfort level of the client. Rehearsal may be required for each item in the hierarchy. If a client is too uncomfortable to engage in role playing, a script may be offered and responses read from it rather than asking the client to ad lib an imitation of a model. As comfort increases, role playing can be introduced. A hierarchy employed with a twenty-two-year-old male who engaged in destructive acts concerned making requests of the nursing staff (Wallace and others, 1973). Eight scenes were included that varied staff responses (yes or no) and the latency of the reply (five seconds to no response at all).

The use of homework assignments. Only after needed skill and comfort levels are attained are assignments mutually agreed-on that the client will carry out in the natural environment. Prior preparation may also be required if negative reactions are anticipated. Only those are chosen that offer a high probability of success at a low cost in terms of discomfort. In order to avoid the possibility of negative outcomes, the counselor needs to have an adequate understanding of various relationships in which assertive behavior is proposed (Wolpe, 1958). New assertive behaviors will not always immediately change the behavior of others in a positive way. The behavior of significant others may change only slowly and more effective behavior may initially create even more negative feelings and actions. In these instances, coping skills should be developed to handle such reactions before asking the client to carry out new behaviors. Ideally, significant others are also involved in the counseling process, so that they may facilitate change efforts. However, this will not always be possible.

With some behaviors, such as assertive behaviors in service situations, unknown individuals may be involved. Here the client is trained to identify situations in which a positive reaction to new behaviors is likely. For example, if an assertive problem exists in situations, he can first select clerks who appear friendly and who smile at him rather than ones who scowl and look as if they have had a bad night. Homework assignment cards may help to prompt completion of objectives (Liberman and others, 1975). These indicate the date the assignment was given, description of assignment, when it is to be completed, and date completed. Or, one assignment sheet containing the same information can be offered to the client, on which he records all assignments (Gambrill and Richey, 1976). When effective social behavior occurs without difficulty in easy situations, more difficult ones are then attempted. The positive outcomes from success in easy situations and the consequent weakening of anxiety encourage effective behavior in other situations. Clients are instructed to reinforce themselves for effective behavior.

The first instance of effective behavior may not be an exact replica of one that has been rehearsed. Practice, coaching, and model presentation provide instruction concerning the essential elements of effective behavior, and clients are encouraged to vary their reactions in appropriate ways. Mrs. M., for example, first asserted herself with her living companion in an unrehearsed situation. She was out sweeping her small yard and Mrs. R. yelled out the window and told her to stop. Mrs. M. responded, "I want to sweep and I am going to do so," at which point Mrs. R. retreated and made no further mention of the matter. Other effective behaviors followed, and Mrs. M. was amazed to find that Mrs. R. did not flare back at her when she stated her preferences but rather seemed surprised, treated her with greater deference, and did not make as many controlling attempts.

As with any other assignment, a careful check is made at the next meeting to find out what happened. Client records aid in the discussion of assignments. Information reviewed includes what was said and done; when it was said and done; how the client felt before, during, and after the interaction; whether self-reinforcement was provided for trying to influence one's social environment even though the attempt might have failed; and what response occurred following the client's behavior. Feedback and reinforcement is offered for appropriate behaviors, additional instructions given as necessary, and further assignments agreed on.

The Use of Logs During Intervention. Careful notes

should be kept by the client, recording instances of effective behavior, noting what was said, in what specific context, what happened consequently, and how he felt. If an ineffective response was given in a situation, the client can be asked to write down one that he thinks would have been more effective. This will provide added practice in selecting appropriate behaviors. For example, a thirty-six-year-old female physicist, who long ago had been trained as a nurse and who now taught at a prestigious university, was greeted after summer holidays by her chairman with the statement, "Hello, nursie." Ms. B.'s statement (which she felt was ineffective) was, "That was a long time ago." Her proposed, more effective statement was, "Why did you call me that?" Focusing attention on identifying more effective responses decreases attention to hurt feelings, helplessness, and anger.

Client logs provide a daily record of progress and thus enable the selection of new assignments. Behaviors are checked to see whether they were appropriate for the occasion. Of particular interest here is catching responses that are aggressive rather than assertive. It is not desired that responses that would be perceived by most others to be aggressive increase in frequency, and there is sometimes a tendency to go overboard in asserting oneself in the initial stages. This can be settled down to an appropriate level by coaching. The client must be able to discriminate between situations that require some restraint or more subtle forms of assertion because of special circumstances, such as danger of losing one's job, and situations in which direct assertion is appropriate. Thus in some situations more covert forms of assertion may be required.

Social Skill Training with Psychiatric Patients

Social competence has been found to be more important than psychiatric diagnosis in discriminating people who were hospitalized from those who were not (Zigler and Phillips, 1961). Of a sample of psychiatric patients, 80 percent reported some difficulty in interpersonal situations in a recent study by Goldsmith and McFall (1975). As discussed in Chapter Nineteen, psychiatric patients often have ineffective problem-solving skills in interpersonal situations. Social skill training has been employed both with inpatient populations as well as with outpatients. It has been found that model presentation is more effective than practice (rehearsal) alone with this population (Eisler, Hersen, and Miller, 1973), and modeling and instructions together are more effective than either alone (Hersen, Eisler, Miller, Johnson, and Pinkston, 1973).

In the most systematic attempt made to develop and evaluate an interpersonal skill training program for male psychiatric patients (Goldsmith and McFall, 1975), the first step was to obtain a sample of problematic situations that were difficult for this population. A group of seventy-four outpatients was asked to give specific examples of interpersonal situations that were difficult for them. They were asked to describe the context, to identify the participants and purpose of each interaction, and to describe the flow of interaction, that is, who said what to whom. Situational contexts reported included dating, making friends, having job interviews, interacting with authorities, interacting with service personnel, and interacting with people viewed as more intelligent or attractive or who appeared in some way different. Those interpersonal contexts most frequently mentioned included initiating and terminating interactions, making personal disclosures, handling conversational silence, responding to rejection, and being assertive. The fifty-five problem situations generated from this step were then presented on audiotape to twenty male inpatients, who indicated which of five alternatives best described the way they would respond in the situation. Alternatives ranged from feeling comfortable and being able to handle the situation satisfactorily to feeling uncomfortable and being unable to handle the situation. A fifth possibility they could check meant that the situation would probably never occur for them. An item was retained only when more than 80 percent reported some difficulty, more than 20 percent reported both discomfort and inability to handle it, and less than 25 percent indicated that the item was not relevant. This step-by-step process follows the recommendations by Goldfried and D'Zurilla (1969) for systematically and empirically developing a skill training program for specific behavioral problems and specific populations. The next step was to obtain information concerning appropriate and inappropriate reactions to these five situations. Eight staff members at the psychiatric hospital listened to the fifty-five taped situations and role played each situation. The competence of these responses were then evaluated by other staff members. At least four of the five judges had to rate a response as competent for it to be classified as such, with no judge having rated it as incompetent. The judges were asked to identify what it was about the response that influenced their evaluation. If a "principle" was mentioned by more than one judge, it was retained for use in coaching clients. Two examples of problem situations and rated alternatives are as follows (C is the number of judges who rated the response as competent, and I is the number who rated it as incompetent). These examples are from Goldsmith and McFall (1975, pp. 131, and 143-144, respectively).

> You are seated next to two strangers at a large dinner party. As you sit down to eat, the person on your right looks at you and smiles, but doesn't say anything. You say, "Hello." The person nods, smiles again, and keeps looking at you. You say:
>
> 1. "Is there something wrong?" ($C = 1; I = 1$)
> 2. "Haven't I seen you someplace before?" ($C = 0; I = 0$)
> 3. "How did you come to be invited to this party? Do you know the host?" ($C = 3; I = 0$)
> 4. "Do you have the strange feeling you've seen me before?" ($C = 1; I = 0$)
> 5. "I notice you're smiling." ($C = 0; I = 0$)
> 6. (Look around to see if there is somebody else more receptive.) ($C = 0; I = 0$)
> 7. "I'm Bill Williams. Who are you?" ($C = 5; I = 0$)
> 8. "What is your name? My name is Bill Williams." ($C = 4; I = 0$)
>
> You are standing in a long checkout line at a department store. A woman standing in front of you has turned around and smiled at you several times. You'd like to chat to pass the time. You say:
>
> 1. "You know, frankly I hate shopping. It's these lines that always discourage me." ($C = 2; I = 0$)
> 2. "Could I help you with the bags?" ($C = 1; I = 0$)

3. "This is a real interesting store. Just picked up some snake meat and brass toilet seats." ($C = 3$; $I = 0$)
4. "I think this line would go a lot quicker if we could talk." ($C = 0; I = 3$)
5. "I hate standing in line!" ($C = 1; I = 1$)
6. "How are you?" ($C = 3; I = 0$)
7. "Looks like you have yourself a bundle of groceries." ($C = 2; I = 0$)

Training consisted of three one-hour sessions spread over five days. The patient first listened to an audiotaped description of a problem situation, and by audiotape was coached in the components of effective behavior in that situation. He then listened to a competent response and then heard a review and summary of the training material as well as a description of the likely consequences of various response alternatives. At this point, the audiotape was stopped and a brief discussion held with the client to make sure that he understood the material and was willing to try out the attempted proposed behavioral solution. The recorded situation was then replayed and the client rehearsed responding. His responses were taped and played back and evaluated, first by the client and then by the counselor, who offered corrective feedback. This rehearsal and feedback was repeated until both the client and the counselor agreed that the criteria for effective behavior had been satisfied on two consecutive role plays. The training then advanced either to a new situation or to another component behavior of the same situation. A total of fifteen minutes was devoted to each of eleven problem situations over the training sessions. This skill training procedure was found to be more effective on a number of behavioral and self-report measures both in the training context and in more real-life situations than was a psychotherapy control or an assessment-only group. Readmission rate also provided suggestive evidence of positive transfer of effects to the natural environment.

Social skill training is often carried out in a group context with psychiatric patients. For example, Field and Test (1975) used a series of twelve group meetings to develop the assertive behaviors of severely disturbed patients. Relevant situations were identified by holding individual interviews with each client as well as by talking with significant others in the hospital. The meaning of assertive behavior was discussed during the first two sessions, drawing from material presented by Alberti and Emmons (1974). Over the next ten sessions, the counselor would first introduce a problem situation and then solicit discussion from the group concerning their own experiences with this situation. Possible responses to this situation were modeled by the counselors, and a discussion then held. At that point, the larger group broke up into smaller groups consisting of no more than three patients per one staff person, and the patients rehearsed reactions to this situation and received feedback and further model presentation as needed. The larger group then reconvened and each client role played his behavior and was videotaped. These tapes were played back and the group participated in offering feedback to each client. In order to sustain attention of clients to what was occurring in the group, clients were reinforced with tokens for making appropriate comments to the person who was role playing. Liberman and others (1975) also found it necessary to devise special means to maintain attention of patients to the task. One means they employed was to ask each client to rate selected aspects of each role play, such as eye contact, facial expression, use of hands, voice loudness, on a scale from one (very poor desirable behavior is lacking) to five (excellent, little or no room for improvement). Those ratings were shared with the group following the role play.

The skills of the patients were tested in three situations. One involved saying something to a neighbor who is playing his music loudly, a second involved a sales clerk who tries to pressure the client into buying a torn blouse, and a third involved an apartment house manager who is reluctant to rent an apartment because he knows the client was a patient at a mental hospital. Prompts were offered by the counselor, such as "I understand you want to rent this apartment," or "I've been told that you have been a patient at Mendota, and I don't rent to any patients" (Field and Test, 1975, p. 132). The clients who had experienced the skill training group evidenced less compliance when under pressure and responded with a shorter latency period following such training.

Videotape models have also been employed to increase appropriate social interaction among psychiatric patients. For example, Gutride, Goldstein, and Hunter (1973) developed four videotapes; one showed how a person may react to another person who approaches him, a second modeled initiating exchanges, a third showed how to initiate interaction with groups of people, and a fourth showed how a person could resume relationships with people outside of the hospital, such as relatives, friends, or business associates. Multiple models were employed to attempt to enhance generalization and specific effective behaviors were identified. Groups of five to eight patients met with two group leaders three times a week over four weeks. The groups were led by undergraduates who had received twelve hours of training in the use of model presentation, role playing, and social reinforcement. The procedure employed at each session involved first showing one of the tapes, during which the rationale for display of the behavior was presented and attention was drawn to specific effective behaviors of the models. The importance of nonverbal behavior was highlighted during intervals when the tape would be temporarily stopped. After this presentation, a discussion was held, during which the relevance of the situation for each of the group members was explored. The rest of the session was devoted to behavior rehearsal of the scene modeled, or of some variant of this related to the client's special situation. These role plays were videotaped and played back to the group, where corrective feedback was offered. Behavior of patients was assessed during mealtime for two weeks following training as well as during training sessions. Such assessment in the natural environment is unfortunately more the exception than the rule, and thus the extent to which positive effects generalize to real-life situations with psychiatric patients is still unknown.

Another study by the same authors focused on such areas as eating behavior. Models were employed to demonstrate appropriate behaviors such as eating skills, and the rationale for the development and display of appropriate behavior was emphasized (Gutride, Goldstein, and others, 1974). Greater improvement was found for acute patients than for chronic patients, and for simple than for complex skills. Arranging incentives for appropriate behaviors is of major importance in maintaining new skills and is often a considerable problem, whether these incentives are offered by relatives or attendants in a hospital. Some additional studies designed to increase appropriate social behavior of psychiatric patients are described in Chapter Nineteen.

Most studies test degree of generalization by inserting "probe scenes" (which are different from scenes used during training), and by observing the client's reactions to these scenes. For example, Hersen and Bellack (1976) employed social skill training with two male chronic schizophrenics. One subject was nineteen years old, with a diagnosis of schizophrenia, catatonic type, with paranoid ideation. When admitted, he was delusional, evidenced flat affect, and appeared especially anxious in interpersonal situations. His psychiatric symptoms and his gradual withdrawal had progressed over a four-year period. The other patient, a twenty-seven-year-old male with a diagnosis of schizophrenia, undifferentiated type, also was withdrawn, very anxious, avoided eye contact, and stuttered often. Behaviors identified for these men included the following:

1. *Ratio of eye contact to speech duration.* Defined as the total length of time (in seconds) that the client looked at his partner while responding to a prompt. (Total duration of eye contact was divided by the total duration of speech.)
2. *Speech duration.* The length of time (in seconds) that the client spoke to his partner. Timing was ended after pauses of three seconds or longer, until the client started to speak again.
3. *Number of requests.* Verbal requests for new behavior from the partner were scored on an occurrence or nonoccurrence basis for each scene. The client had to show more than mere noncompliance. He had to show content that he wished his partner to alter his behavior, for example, to ask his boss to ask him (the client) to stay late some other time.
4. *Number of compliances.* This also was rated on an occurrence or nonoccurrence basis. If the client did not resist the partner's position, a compliance was scored.

5. *Ratio of speech disruptions to words spoken.* Events included as speech disruptions included pauses, repetitions, stutters, and expletives such as "Ah," "Oh," "Um," and so forth. A ratio was calculated by dividing the number of disruptions by the total number of words spoken.

6. *Number of appropriate smiles.* This was recorded on an occurrence or nonoccurrence basis for each positive scene from the time a prompt was given to the end of a response. This reaction was defined as a forty-five-degree crease in the cheek with the teeth showing.

7. *Appropriate affect.* This "was scored on a five-point scale (one, a very flat unemotional tone of voice and absence of appropriate facial and physical gestures; five, full and lively intonation (emotional expressiveness) with corresponding facial and physical gestures appropriate to each situation)" (Hersen and Bellack, 1976, p. 241).

8. *Overall assertiveness.* This was rated on a five-point scale ranging from one (very unassertive) to five (very assertive).

During training, the purpose of social skill training and its nature were explained to the client. Videotaped baseline probes were conducted during baseline and three probe sessions were held during each week of training. In addition, follow-up probes were held at two, four, six, and eight weeks after training. Training sessions were held in a videotape lab. The subject sat on a sofa together with two role models. The counselor communicated with the client over an intercom. A series of eight training scenes was employed, half of which involved the expression of positive feelings (such as initiating a conversation) and half of which involved the expression of negative feelings (such as refusing an unacceptable request). One scene at a time was introduced. The scene was first described, and the appropriate role model then delivered the prompt for the client's response. Immediate feedback was provided concerning the client's reaction. Constructive feedback was employed, in which positive aspects of the client's behavior were supported whenever they occurred, and specific behaviors to increase or decrease were noted as appropriate. For example, the counselor might say, "That was better, but you still looked away at the end. This time try to look at Jim for the whole time" (Hersen and Bellack, 1976, p. 242). If needed, appropriate behavior was modeled by one of the role models. This sequence was repeated as often as necessary, until some improvement was noted. The next scene was then introduced. All eight scenes were introduced at each of the sessions that were held over a four-week period. There were five twenty- to forty-minute sessions per week for one client, and five to six thirty- to ninety-minute sessions per week for the other client. Training concentrated on one of the four target behaviors each week. For example, during the first week of training, an attempt was made to increase the ratio of eye contact to speech duration, whereas in the second week attention was devoted to speech duration. Figure 29 presents the results of the training for one client based on ratings by judges of the client's videotaped interactions.

As noted by Hersen and Bellack (1976) the focus on discrete behaviors in a sequential fashion may be especially valuable with a population in which there may be difficulty in focusing on complex stimulus inputs. And, although social reinforcement was effective for these patients, this certainly will not be true of all patients. Additional reinforcement may be added by offering tokens for appropriate social behaviors, if this can be linked with a token program in the setting itself. A third point mentioned was the interest of these clients in increased interpersonal effectiveness. Not all patients have such an interest. Thus there will probably be limitations in terms of the type of client for whom social skill training is appropriate.

Instructions and rapid performance feedback were successful in increasing the assertive behaviors of two patients who were residents of a veterans administration hospital (Eisler, Hersen, and Miller, 1974). One patient, a twenty-eight-year-old house painter, had been admitted after he had fired a shotgun into the ceiling of his home. His history revealed periodic rages following a consistent failure to express anger in social situations. His behavior was assessed by asking him to role play interpersonal situations related to the current life experiences in which he was unable to express anger. These included being

Figure 29. Probe Sessions During Baseline, Treatment and Follow-Ups for Subject V. Data Are Presented in Blocks of Eight Scenes.

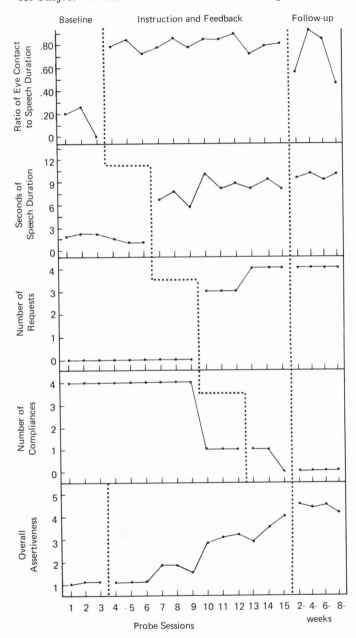

Source: Hersen and Bellack (1976, p. 243).

criticized by a fellow employee at work, disagreeing with his wife about her inviting company over to their home without checking this with him first, and his lack of ability to refuse requests by his eight-year-old son. An assistant played the complementary role in each situation, that of his wife, son, or fellow employee. The client's reactions were videotaped, as well as observed through a one-way mirror. Assessment of his reactions revealed expressive deficits in four components of assertiveness including eye contact (he did not look at his partner when speaking to him), loudness of his voice (one could barely hear what he said), speech duration (his responses were very short consisting of one- or two-word replies), and behavioral requests of his partner (he was unable to ask his partner to change his behavior). He was informed that during training sessions, he would learn how to respond more effectively in these interpersonal situations. Twelve situations that were unrelated to the client's problem areas but that required assertive behavior were employed during training sessions. Each was role played five times in different orders over training sessions. Instructions were offered to the client by the counselor through a miniature radio receiver (Bug-in-the-Ear—Farrell Instrument Company, P.O. Box 1037, Grand Island, NE 68801). Instructions related to only one of the four response areas at any one time. Thus during the initial scenes he was coached to look at his partner when speaking to him, and during the second series he was coached to increase the loudness of his voice but received no instructions concerning any other response. During the fourth series, he was coached to speak longer, and during the last, instructed to ask his partner for a behavior change. He received feedback concerning his performance after each role play. This procedure permitted a multiple-baseline analysis of the four behaviors, in which intervention was applied only to one behavior at a time, meanwhile gathering information concerning the frequency or duration of all behaviors. Each response increased after specific instructions were given regarding this, and effects generalized to the specific situations that were problematic for this client. Ratings of his behavior were made by reviewing videotapes of his performance. A similar training procedure was successful in increasing the assertive behavior of a thirty-four-year-old male with a history of alcoholism. His current admission had been related to an inability to handle increased responsibility at work after he was promoted to a managerial position at a small motel. It was difficult for him to confront those who worked for him when they performed poorly; he complied with unreasonable demands made on him by his employer as well as by his motel guests; and was unable to resist pressure from salespersons. More rapid gains for both patients might have occurred if training had been directly concerned with their specific problematic situations.

As with other client populations, anxiety as well as skill deficits may interfere with appropriate actions in various interpersonal situations, and reassurance and encouragement are often necessary to involve the client in role playing. For many clients, however, appropriate interpersonal behavior must be taught; that is, a lack of appropriate behavior is not just caused by anxiety. Reading from a script offers an approximation to role playing that is often less anxiety provoking. A hierarchy of scenes can be employed for role playing, graduated in accord with the client's anxiety. Role playing is initiated with scenes that induce low levels of discomfort. If the client is too anxious to read from a script, relaxation training may offer him useful coping skills as a prelude to initiating graduated role playing. When there are many deficits, most investigators recommend concentrating on one behavior at a time, as was illustrated in the previous example, where eye contact was first focused on, then voice loudness, and so on (Eisler, Hersen, and Miller, 1974). Most skill training programs employ scenes related to real-life problems and repeat each role play a number of times. For example, in a case reported by Eisler (1976), six real-life scenes were enacted ten times in various random orders, focusing on one behavior at a time, such as eye contact, and offering feedback after each performance. Sixty rehearsals were provided over five separate sessions. After obtaining a stable increase in the first behavior, instructions were then given concerning the next behavior. Often modeling must be used to supplement instructions. In fact, there are a number of studies showing that instructions alone (without modeling) are not sufficient to develop appropriate social behaviors with psychiatric patients (see

Hersen and Bellack, in press). The client should be free to select components of the modeled response he feels most comfortable with, as long as the mix selected will offer effective behaviors. Assignments in which the client tries out his new behaviors are an important aspect of social skill training, and these are graduated in accord with client skill and comfort levels.

The degree of possible generalization in terms of the stability of positive change and the range of situations in which new behavior will occur are still unknown. Many of the training programs described earlier were very brief. Longer programs involving more varied situations and time for more rehearsal should enhance positive effects, as should appropriate homework assignments. Attention to other important factors, such as encouraging significant others to reinforce appropriate social skills and development of self-monitoring and self-reinforcement skills, should also enhance positive changes.

Social Skill Training to Increase Social Contacts

Another area where social skill training has been employed is related to minimal dating and social contacts in general (see, for example, McGovern and Burkhard, 1976; Gambrill, 1973). With a college population, it has been found that simply arranging a series of practice dates results in a significant increase in dating behavior (Christensen, Arkowitz, and Anderson, 1975). The success of such interventions indicates the difference in the intervention needed with this population compared to a psychiatric population, as does the greater effectiveness of cognitive self-instructional programs compared to skill training programs. It seems that with students, the appropriate skills are often available, but are not displayed because of interfering cognitions and feelings. There are some data, however, showing that shy males may not be as able to interpret interpersonal cues as well as socially comfortable males (Twentyman, cited in McFall, in press). They are also uncertain as to how to find out if the women they take out are enjoying themselves (Boland, 1973). This is in contrast with confident men, who are more likely to say to themselves, "If I'm having a good time, she's having a good time" (McFall, in press, p. 25).

Undergraduate males who describe themselves as confident "reported feeling less anxious than shy subjects when preparing to phone an unknown coed for a date and when interacting face-to-face with a 'live' coed. They also tended to show less autonomic arousal when interacting with the coed. In simulated heterosexual situations, they were less likely than shy subjects to avoid initiating interactions. Independent raters perceived confident subjects as being less anxious, more skillful, and more sustained in their interactions than shy subjects. Behavioral diary data indicated that confident subjects, in contrast to shy subjects, spent more time relating to more women in more situations" (Twentyman and McFall, 1975, p. 393). A brief instructional program in which women engaged in a series of homework assignments and were offered textual instructions concerning, for example, how to initiate conversations, where to meet others, and how to have enjoyable conversations was effective in increasing the frequency of social contacts and the proportion that the women initiated (Gambrill, 1973; Gambrill and Richey, 1976). Each woman was provided with self-monitoring forms and requested to keep track for two weeks of all interactions that were more than just a greeting with individuals with whom she wished to increase contact. Information requested included first name, age, and sex of the person; date, place, and duration of the interaction; who initiated the conversation and, if the subject did, what she said; the response of the other person; and her degree of enjoyment of the interaction. Each person was also requested to select two interactions during the week (if two occurred) that were particularly pleasant or unpleasant and to record additional information concerning them, such as whether she contributed her share of talk to the conversation, disagreed when she felt like it, or initiated some topics of conversation. The purpose of requesting this information was to help women identify behaviors that they might like to change by utilizing material in the manual. Each also completed the Assertion Inventory (Gambrill and Richey, 1975). Further assessment information was gained by requesting each woman to respond to a series of twelve tape-recorded scene presentations related to the following areas: (1) responding to an initiation; (2) expressing disagreement; (3) initiating a con-

versation with a stranger; (4) arranging for an immediate continuation of an interaction with a stranger; (5) arranging for
future contact; (6) terminating a conversation; (7) changing the
topic of conversation. The subject was to listen to each taped
description and to respond as if she were actually in the situation. Responses were tape-recorded.

At the first group meeting, each subject received a wrist
counter, monitoring forms, an Activity Inventory to aid in the
selection of places to go to meet people, a copy of the first
three sections of a social interaction manual, a form concerning
use of self-reinforcement, and an individualized behavior assignment based on preintervention social contacts. Each woman was
requested to double her number of initiations with strangers
and/or acquaintances, depending on individual goals, and to
continue monitoring social interactions. An overview of the
manual sections distributed at each session was provided. Textual material presented various ways to initiate conversations
and criteria to employ in selecting places to meet people. The
women were also asked to covertly compliment themselves and
to award themselves points on their wrist counters after engaging
in a behavior that pleased them (one point) or that pleased
them very much (two points).

During the second session, each woman filled in a summary form that enabled the concise recording of weekly social
interactions and each shared with the group whether she had
completed her assignment for the week and, if so, what she had
done. Instructions were given to maintain or increase the frequency of initiating conversations and to arrange one brief
meeting with a stranger during the next week and one longer
one with a stranger or acquaintance, depending on individual
goals. Forms were provided to record relevant information such
as who arranged the contact, what was said, when and where it
took place, and the first name of the person. The textual material distributed concerned arranging future meetings, disagreeing
with others, and maintaining conversations.

At the third session, the women were again requested to
share details with the group concerning their assignments and
were instructed to continue to covertly compliment themselves
following performance of target behaviors, and to continue to

initiate conversations and to arrange meetings. Textual material distributed discussed specific behaviors, thoughts, or feelings that may interfere with enjoyable social exchanges and described a variety of ways to terminate conversations.

Women who participated in this program increased the frequency with which they initiated social contacts, as compared to women who participated in a self-help control group, and initiated a higher proportion of their contacts.

Social Skill Training for Adolescents

Social skill training programs have been developed to offer adolescents additional effective social behaviors. For example, Sarason (1976) and Sarason and Ganzer (1973, 1971) used modeling, rehearsal, and feedback to offer juvenile delinquents additional skills to resist pressure from peers. The following example illustrates a modeled interaction involving a newly paroled youth pressured to go out drinking (from Sarason and Ganzer, 1971, p. 139).

(George knocks on the door and Tom answers)

Tom: Hi, George, how're you doing?

George: Hey, man, we're glad to see you back. Gotta celebrate your return. We got a couple cases of beer out in the car. Come on, we're gonna have a party.

Tom: Oh, you know I got to stay clean.

George: What do you mean, you gotta stay clean? Come on, this party was planned just for you. We even got a date with Debbie lined up for you. It won't hurt just this once.

Tom: Well, you know I'm on parole. I can't go drinking . . . I might get caught and if I get caught now, I'll really get screwed.

George: Oh, man, we won't get caught. We never get caught doing anything like that.

Tom: Well, maybe you guys have never gotten caught, but the night I got in trouble I was out drinking and ended up stealing a car. (Pause) You know, I just got back.

George: Look, man, you don't have to drink. Just come to the party and have a little fun. What are we gonna tell Debbie anyway?

Tom: You know being there is the same as drinking to the fuzz. And Debbie won't have any trouble finding someone else.

George: You mean you don't want to go out with Debbie?

Tom: Not to this party. Maybe to a show sometime or something like that.

George: Boy, I sure don't understand you. You have sure changed since you got back from that place. You trying to kiss us off?

Tom: No, that's not it, man. If you want to do something else where we wouldn't get into trouble, (pause) like go to a show, the dance or something, that would be okay but . . . well . . . I know some guys who were in there for a second or third time and they don't get the breaks anymore. You know what it is to be on parole.

George: Okay, look, let's just have one quick beer now out in the car, okay? For old times' sake.

Tom: No, man, I know where that leads. Then it would be just one more and then pretty soon we'll be drunk. I can't do it, man.

George: Jeez! What is the matter with you, man? Just one beer?

Tom: Maybe another night. My old man expects me to help him work on the boat tonight anyway. I'll be in trouble with him if I take off. Look, I'm sorry, maybe some other time, okay?

George: Okay. Can't be helped, I guess. Look, we'll be at John's place. Come on over later if you can.

Tom: Sure. See you tomorrow, anyway.

The scenes employed in this program were identified by interviewing youths and finding out their perceptions of problems that might exist for them when they left the institution. They were asked to role play these difficulties and these role plays were tape-recorded and edited for use as scripts.

Freedman (1974) attempted to identify skill deficits of

institutionalized male adolescent youths. He first identified potential problem areas by consulting a number of sources, including youths. A second group of boys was then asked to rate the commonness and difficulty of each situation. Forty-two situations were identified and ninety narrative descriptions of situations developed pertaining to these. A sample each of institutionalized boys, nondelinquent boys, and five adult authorities then role played responses to each of the ninety items. Raters judged the effectiveness of the various reactions and identified the components of the reactions that made them effective or ineffective. Based on this step, a forty-four-item Adolescent Problem Inventory was developed. An example of a situation describes one boy who is walking down the street and another boy who deliberately bumps the first boy as he passes. Possible reactions include ignoring him and saying nothing and simply walking on (this receives the highest rating) to the lowest rating, in which the first boy would push or fight with the other boy. When the scale was administered to both institutionalized adolescents and a group of nondelinquent boys, the former group showed a significantly lower overall competence score.

Developing Job Interview Skills

Social skill training has also been employed to develop appropriate job interview skills. Prazak (1969), for example, developed a program to teach participants to talk about available skills, to answer questions, to develop an appropriate presentation of self in terms of appearance and mannerisms, to appear enthusiastic and to end interviews. Clients first viewed a videotape of an effective model in an interview situation. The participants then role played interviews that were videotaped for review. Constructive feedback was employed in which clients were praised for behaviors that matched those of the model. These tapes were also useful in assessing the clients' deficiencies and strengths in terms of existing interview behaviors. In order to help identify assets each client was requested to record their assets in a notebook and to memorize them. Clients learned how to handle difficult questions in terms of an erratic work history, jail sentences, hospitalizations, and so forth. They were encouraged to keep their answers short, to bring up obvious problems themselves before the interviewer brought them up, and never to use psychiatric or medical labels. Polaroid pictures were taken of each client before and after training in appropriate grooming and postural skills. Clients were taught to maintain eye contact during interviews, to shake hands firmly, and to end the interview by asking whether they could telephone the interviewer later to find out if they obtained the position. Training in interviewing skills is also a part of the job-finding club developed by Jones and Azrin (1973).

The Role of Physical Characteristics
in Interpersonal Exchanges

Responses from others are partially determined by the variable of attractiveness. For example, Glasgow and Arkowitz (1975) found that physical attractiveness discriminated significantly between a high-frequency dating group and a low-frequency dating group. This dimension must be considered when a client is desirous of increasing positive social interactions in terms of helping the client to remove characteristics that may interfere with achievement of this goal, such as dressing in a sloppy fashion and enhancing characteristics that might enhance his impact, such as improving his posture. Failure to attend to this dimension may dilute the positive impact the client has on others.

When Direct Assertion Fails or
May Have Negative Consequences

In some situations, direct assertion may have serious negative consequences. Subtle tactics were recommended by Wolpe and Lazarus (1966) in the case of a law clerk who was subjected to harrassment during daily prolonged lectures by his superior. He did not wish to give up his clerkship. The client was asked to discover any areas of vulnerability that his superior, Mr. J., might have, through casual conversation with the office secretaries. It was discovered that Mr. J. was hypochondriacal. The client was instructed to feign a worried expression and to interject some statement relating to Mr. J.'s health during the next lecture. Thus, in the next interview, the client stared at the left cheek of his superior. Almost immediately, Mr. J. stopped short and irritably asked what was wrong—whereupon the client asked him if he felt well. The interview was abruptly terminated less than two minutes later. After one other such occasion, Mr. J. avoided the client and the unpleasant interviews were at an end. It is not recommended that a lifestyle of "one-upmanship" be developed, but that the client be able to employ such manuevers in situations where more direct assertion is prohibited, in that it would entail very negative consequences (Wolpe, 1958).

Perhaps direct assertion will hurt some significant other as well as be ineffective; nevertheless, it may be possible to find a way to change behaviors without negative consequence. Watzlawick, Weakland, and Fisch (1974) present some ingenious resolutions in such situations. They offer an example in which in-laws persisted in offering unwanted help to a young couple. The in-laws visited four times a year, staying each visit for about three weeks, and taking over all household responsibilities during their stays. The husband was concerned that they would be hurt (because they were only trying to be "good parents") if their efforts were rejected. The authors also use this example to illustrate how attempted solutions to a problem often exacerbate it. Here, the couple's attempt to assert their independence was interpreted as ingratitude and frequent scenes in public occurred as to who was going to pay the check.

The husband said that tangible proof of achieving his goal of greater independence from his parents would consist of his father telling him of his own accord, "You are now grown up; the two of you have to take care of yourselves and must not expect that mother and I are going to pamper you indefinitely" (Watzlawick, Weakland, and Fisch, 1974, p. 118). A way was sought to provide the experience to the in-laws of being "good parents" in a way that would also bring about a decrease in their "helping behaviors" for this couple. The couple was instructed to allow the house to become dirty and the laundry to pile up prior to their next visit and to allow the in-laws to carry out all household chores, repairs, and responsibilities without any suggestion that they not engage in these tasks. The in-laws cut the visit short and the father told his son "that he [the son] and his wife were much too pampered, that they had gotten much too accustomed to being waited on and supported by the parents, and that it was now high time to behave in a more adult fashion and to become less dependent on them" (p. 119). The in-laws could now be good parents by "weaning" their son.

When Not to be Assertive

It is important to teach clients when not to be assertive. One such situation occurs when unwanted negative consequences may occur, as in the example with the law clerk discussed above. If it is obvious that someone is very upset, such as a waiter in a restaurant, or if the slight or annoyance is a minor one, it may be best for all concerned to remain quiet or to select another time to express oneself (Alberti and Emmons, 1974). Expressing negative feelings to a person who is already very upset may result in a rapid negative escalation and thus entail more cost in terms of emotion than one wishes to endure. It is also unlikely that assertion will be effective at that time. Minor things that bother one in a significant other, such as a mate, are best left unmentioned. Asking someone to change his behavior is an implied criticism, and a more positive way to try to alter behavior is to support desirable behaviors through verbal approval. A rule that would seem to facilitate pleasure would be to praise positive behaviors, ignore minor annoying ones, and assert oneself calmly at an appropriate time when it really matters.

If treatment is successful, anxiety is lessened in interpersonal situations and assertive responses are only employed when the client happens to feel like doing so. The client will now be indifferent to many situations that previously caused discomfort, such as imagined digs and slights, and the misconception of many situations as rejecting, which occurred previously due to oversensitivity, should be removed.

Reframing of problems may also be useful in situations in which clients become angry, according to Watzlawick, Weakland, and Fisch (1974). These authors offer the example of a young executive assistant who became very angry when one of her superiors belittled her, which often occurred in front of others. This situation had become so unpleasant that her superior was about to recommend her dismissal and she was thinking of resigning. She was instructed to wait for the next incident and then at the first opportunity, to take him aside, tell him with obvious embarrassment something to the effect that when he talks to her in that way, it "turns her on," and then leave quickly before he could say anything. The client found the idea enormously funny. She stated that the very next day her superior's behavior had changed and that he had been polite and easy to get along with since that time. She had not made the "confession" to him. The authors speculate that the effective ingredients in such a change procedure is that now the client saw that she could deal differently with a threatening situation and that this knowledge altered her behavior, which in turn affected the other person's behavior (see Chapter Twelve for additional discussion of procedures for helping clients influence inappropriate anger reactions).

Learning How to Deal with Rejection

Many clients who are anxious in interpersonal situations and some who are aggressive are oversensitive to the reactions of others. They are so worried about the possibility of being slighted or receiving a critical remark from others that they avoid engaging in a variety of appropriate behaviors, such as voicing opinions, requesting behavior changes, and initiating conversations, or become unduly defensive. A number of points have been mentioned in this chapter that relate directly to helping clients become less sensitive to negative comments or actions from others. One is the inhibitory effect of assertion on anxiety (Wolpe, 1958). As a client becomes more assertive and reaps the benefits of more effective behavior, these consequences will encourage further assertive behavior. Knowing what to say to oneself after receiving a critical comment is very important. Rather than saying negative things, the client is encouraged to develop an alternative repertoire of thoughts, including praise for being assertive; he learns a repertoire of thoughts and actions that will enable him to deal effectively with his own emotions in the face of rejection. This training will enable him to more accurately discriminate and label other people as being rude, rather than blaming himself as in the past. Training will also provide verbal statements that can be made in situations where a rude or hostile remark is voiced. As with any other behavior, the degree to which new reactions to critical comments are practiced will influence how readily these new behaviors become a comfortable and skilled part of one's social repertoire.

The Self-Management Aspects of Effective Social Behavior

Self-reinforcement can be employed to facilitate the development of new social behaviors (Richey, 1974; Rehm and Marston, 1968). Such reinforcement is also important in maintaining new behaviors, particularly when these will sometimes be followed by punishing consequences. Clients should be instructed to reinforce themselves for trying to exert more effective influence over their social environment, even though their attempts are not always successful. If a woman tries to speak up more during a meeting and fails to gain the floor, she still should praise herself for trying. Some overt form of reinforcement may temporarily be needed to encourage new behaviors, such as awarding herself points on a wrist counter, or on an unobtrusive waist counter, such as a belt with beads (Richey, 1974). Different degrees of success could be awarded a different number of points and these points could then be traded for various items on a reinforcer menu, such as buying a copy of a favorite magazine or telephoning a friend. Rehm and Marston (1968) instructed their subjects to award themselves between one to three points, depending on the degree of assertiveness. (See Chapter Eight for further discussion of the maintenance of behavior.)

The Assertive Person

If treatment is successful, stress should be lessened in interpersonal situations, so much so that often, assertive responses may not even be employed, because the client is now indifferent to situations that previously caused discomfort, and thus may only employ his assertive behavior when he happens to feel like doing so. Furthermore, the misconception of many situations as slighting or rejecting, which occurred previously because of oversensitivity, should not occur. Assertion should result in a change in self-concept, caused in part by the more positive responses from others because of the client's more effective behavior and in part by the fact that he can now influence many situations that previously controlled him. This changed self-concept may facilitate further new behaviors.

Summary

Social skill training is designed to increase competence in social interactions and may be carried out in either individual or group meetings. It is assumed that well-being is related to effective social behavior. Social skill deficits have been related to a wide variety of presenting problems. Careful assessment is required to determine whether skills are absent; to identify relevant situations; to determine whether there are discrimination problems in relation to when behaviors can most profitably be displayed; and to determine whether negative thoughts and irrational anticipations interfere with the display of effective behaviors. A variety of routes may be employed to gather assessment information, including self-report, role playing, and observation in the natural environment.

A number of procedures are usually involved in skill training, including behavior rehearsal, feedback, prompting, model presention, programing of change, and homework assignments. The more outstanding the deficits, the more likely that model presentation will be required. Intervention also includes attempts to replace interfering negative thought patterns with positive self-instructions. Homework assignments graded in accord with client comfort and skill levels are an important aspect of social skill training, and client-recorded logs describing relevant behaviors and the situations in which they occur are regularly reviewed, to offer further feedback and to encourage use of similar skills in other situations. Learning to provide self-reinforcement for effective social behavior is an important aspect of social skill training and aids in the maintenance and generalization of more effective behaviors.

14

Depression is ranked as the second most frequent mental disorder today and has consistently been referred to throughout the ages as one of the plights of men and women. It has been estimated that from 4 to 24 percent of the population may experience periods of depression sufficiently severe to warrant clinical aid (Schwab, Brown, Holzer, and Sokolof, 1968). The three demographic factors associated most highly with risk of depression include being female, married, widowed, separated or divorced, and a mother (McLean, 1976). Marital maladjustment is related to depression, especially for men (Coleman and Miller, 1975). Its mention as a problem throughout the ages has not been accompanied by a concomitant development of commonly accepted definitions of and conceptualizations of this state nor of ways to alter it. The term *depression* itself is poorly

Behavioral Intervention with Depression

defined. As Lewinsohn (1974, p. 63) notes, "It is sometimes used to refer to a normal mood state, an abnormal mood state, a symptom, a symptom syndrome, as well as a disease process and possibly to a series of disease processes." Most people are familiar with one or more of the symptoms associated with depression. These may include affective symptoms such as dejected mood; self-dislike; loss of gratification; loss of attachments; crying spells and loss of mirth reaction; motivational symptoms, including the loss of motivation to perform a variety of activities, a lower activity level, and suicidal wishes; and cognitive symptoms such as low self-evaluation, negative expectations, self-blame and criticism, indecisiveness and a distorted self-image, as well as physical symptoms including loss of appetite, sleep disturbance, fatigue, and fatigability (Beck, 1967).

Each client may have a different cluster of symptoms. There thus does not seem to be any particular defining feature of "depression."

Two major distinctions have been made among different types of depression: psychotic and neurotic depression and endogenous and reactive depression (American Psychiatric Association, 1968). There has been difficulty in obtaining agreement in classifying clients in relation to the first distinction. The second is defined on etiological grounds. Endogenous depressions are assumed to be related to internal biochemical or genetic factors and reactive depressions to external factors such as stress. Although these two types can be differentiated in relation to different clusters of symptoms related to each, there is no evidence, to date, that placement in one category or the other bears any relation to treatment outcome.

Theories of Depression

The oldest theory of depression generated by the Greeks invoked the presence of black bile in the body fluids. This search within the genetic history or physical makeup of the person for the cause of depression has continued into the present and some depressive behavior may have a physiological basis (Akiskal and McKinney, 1973). Psychodynamic formulations of depression emphasize internal psychological mechanisms. Freud ([1917] 1955) compared melancholia with grief reactions and assumed that depression was related to a real or fantasized object loss in which a narcissistic identification with the object resulted in an inability to differentiate external loss from a loss within the ego, which in turn led to a loss of self-esteem. Repressed hostility turned against the self was also posited to play a role in depression (Abraham, 1927). Bibring (1953) widened the range of sources that may be related to depression and pointed to the role of helplessness in relation to aspirations. Critical factors related to depression were assumed to occur in early childhood. Psychoanalytic theory of depression, dealing as it does with unobservables, renders the generation of testable hypotheses difficult, if not impossible, and thus there is no body of data providing information concerning the validity of this theory of depression.

Reinforcement Theory of Depression. Ferster (1965) was one of the first to link the state of depression with the reinforcement history of the person and to call for a functional analysis of depression in which antecedents and consequences related to this state would be investigated rather than simply describing the topography (form) of the state. It was emphasized that the repertoires of a depressed person and a normal person are often essentially indistinguishable in terms of the types of behavior that take place (Ferster, 1973). For example, everyone may sit looking out of a window occasionally. However, the frequency, as well as the maintaining conditions, with which the behaviors might occur may be very different. It was assumed that only through a functional analysis of behavior could the depressed person's repertoire be understood. Within this view, cognitions as well as affect were assumed to be secondary to the functional relationships between behavior and the environment, which were considered to be directly related to depression. Depression was defined as a decreased frequency of positively reinforced behavior: "To observe the actual behaviors alluded to in the clinical definition of depression, we need look to the frequency of various classes of the depressed person's activity as compared with those of a person who is not depressed. The most obvious characteristic of a depressed person is a loss of certain kinds of activity coupled with an increase in avoidance and escape activity such as complaints, crying and irritability. A depressed person may sit silently for long periods, or perhaps even stay in bed all day. The latency of a reply to a question may be longer than usual, and speaking, walking or carrying out routine tasks will also occur at a slower pace. While he may at a particular time answer questions, ask for something, or even speak freely, the overall frequency is low. Certain kinds of verbal behavior such as telling an amusing story, writing a report or a letter, or speaking freely without solicitation may seldom occur" (Ferster, 1973, p. 857). There is a failure to handle or avoid unpleasant social consequences and a tendency instead to blame and criticize either others or oneself. To the extent to which social behaviors decrease, there may also be an effect on reinforcers associated with physiological processes such as eating and sex, in that social behaviors are associated with them. The collateral (related) social repertoire associated with such reinforcers may no longer occur. For example, a man may no longer telephone his girl friend to arrange dates or arrange to have supper with friends. Ferster (1973) also emphasized the increased frequency of avoidance and escape behaviors such as complaints and requests for help.

As with other labeled categories such as alcoholism, the category termed *depression* is considered to be a phenotype that may be related to a number of different environmental conditions, or genotypes (Ferster, 1973). The reduced frequency of positively reinforced behavior that is considered to be the hallmark of depression may be related to a variety of maintaining factors. As Ferster notes, "no matter what the physiological substrate of the depressed individual's behavior, it is still necessary to identify the functional relation between the behavior and the environment that prompts, shapes and maintains it" (Ferster, 1973). A number of conditions have been assumed to relate to depression.

Factors that interfere with the cumulative development of behavior. Failure of the child's repertoire to interact successfully with that of the mother in such important situations as feeding not only may result in a loss of behaviors that would normally result from successful reinforcement of these interactions, but may also result in a corresponding lack of perceptual development. Developmental problems are most outstanding in infancy and early childhood, because the child's repertoire is usually rapidly expanding at these times. One by-product of a lack of reinforcement is large-scale emotional reactions such as rage, and, if these reactions succeed in influencing the behavior of the mother, the enlargement of the child's perception of the environment is blocked because the emotional reactions take precedence over the smaller magnitude component activities involved in a normal interaction (Ferster, 1973). Such a developmental history blocks the establishment of adequate ways of interacting with other people, and entire areas of interpersonal reactivity may not be available as a means of interacting with the others (Ferster, 1973). This view of the possible development of repertoires labeled as *depressed* would turn attention to increasing behaviors that are reliably followed by reinforcement, on the assumption that the increase in appropriate behaviors will decrease reliance on inappropriate ones.

Moreover, talking about factors related to the client's behavior serves to increase the client's verbal activity, which is one step in the direction of increasing other activities.

Schedules of reinforcement. Reinforcement schedules in which a large amount of behavior is required to produce a change in the environment are particularly susceptible to disruption (Ferster and Skinner, 1957). "Call[ing] on a large number of persons before . . . consummat[ing] a sale, studying all semester for a final examination, working on a term paper, writing a novel, persuading someone, carrying out an experiment which requires long and arduous procedures without indication of success before completion, [dealing with a] difficult therapeutic encounter where much thought and stress go into small indicators of progress, and . . . routine housework, which may require a fixed and large amount of repetitive work, all exemplify a schedule of reinforcement which can potentially weaken the behavior severely. The result is frequently seen as an abulia in which the novelist, for example, is unable to work for considerable periods of time after completing the previous work. The effect of such schedules of reinforcement are hard to observe at times even though the predominant result is long periods of inactivity" (Ferster, 1973, p. 864).

Changes in the environment. Behavior may be weakened by a sudden change in the environment as when a close companion dies (Ferster, 1966). To the extent to which a person's repertoire is related to someone who dies, there will be a total dampening of their behavior. The extent to which behavior is maintained by negative rather than positive consequences is another factor that determines whether a change in the environment will weaken behavior. For example, compare work-related behavior maintained by escape and avoidance to work maintained mainly by positive consequences. In the former case, if a person is placed in a "free work environment," little behavior may result, since there is an impoverished repertoire in relation to positive reinforcement. Behavior can also be weakened through punishment including criticism, fines, being jailed or withdrawal of privileges (Skinner, 1953). Extinction may result in a decrease in behavior to the extent to which punishment is carried out in relation to a range of behaviors.

In a number of cases, depression has begun after some

environmental event that entailed a loss of positive reinforcement such as death of a spouse or injury, which deprives a person of an important set of skills (Paykel, Meyers, Dienelt, Klerman, Lindenthal, and Pepper, 1969). Changes in the environment that seem to represent successes, for example, a promotion, may in fact entail a loss of reinforcement, or a shift from a variable schedule of reinforcement that maintains high rates of behavior, to a schedule that requires a high steady output prior to reinforcement.

Anger as a factor in depression. The prominence of "anger" in the depressed person's repertoire, perhaps related to the low frequency of positive reinforcement, will further decrease this frequency, since angry acts are usually punished, or their monitoring in order to avoid their expression requires attention that is then not available to act in more positive ways on the environment. "The repression of punished behavior appears to be a serious contributor to depressions because it commits such a large part of the person's repertoire to activities which do not produce positive reinforcement" (Ferster, 1973, p. 867). One cannot expect people one is angry at to offer one positive reinforcement. Because of its relation to the loss of positive reinforcement, anger may come to serve as a preaversive event, which may further decrease one's repertoire.

Other important factors. All of the above situations represent conditions in which many behaviors are no longer reinforced. Many of the conditions may be operative in any one instance. For example, excessive punishment, as well as the effects of intermittent reinforcement or of extinction, may be present. It is one or more of these conditions that are assumed to lead to the development of a limited repertoire of observation of depressed people, which further reduces positive reinforcement. That is, depressed persons usually have distorted, incomplete, or misleading views of the environment. First of all, they have a *limited* view of the world (Ferster, 1973). Their behavior is inappropriate to the changing circumstances of the external environment. Depressed persons are more likely to use magical avoidance to influence their environment—for example, pouting or complaining—rather than actively trying to alter it. A negative view of the world may relate to the large number of aversive events that befall depressed persons, perhaps because of their limited view of the world. Thirdly, the depressed person seems to have an *unchanging* view of the world, which hinders the cumulation of relevant skills and experiences.

Ferster views the depressed person as being reactive to the environment, as based on prompts, commands or aversive events initiated by others. Thus, reinforcers in his interactions are usually appropriate to the repertoire of other people rather than to the depressed person. The depressed person's repertoire is characterized by indirect actions such as complaints, rather than by direct actions that influence the environment. The proper focus of intervention is assumed to be the achievement of an increase in positively reinforced behaviors (Ferster, 1966, 1973). Bizarre or irrational behaviors are considered to confuse the objective description of a depressed person's repertoire, since they divert attention from the need to develop positively reinforced behaviors. High frequency of such behaviors does not mean that they are strongly maintained but rather that such behaviors occur by default because they are simpler and more likely to be reinforced than other behaviors (Ferster, 1973). It was assumed that, for some people, not being able to behave at all is worse than engaging in inappropriate behavior. Insufficient positive reinforcement and aversive control have also been highlighted by other behavioral writers, including Moss and Boren (1972); Lazarus (1968); Lewinsohn, Weinstein, and Shaw (1968); and Liberman and Raskin (1971).

A low rate of response contingent-positive reinforcement is assumed by Lewinsohn and his colleagues to elicit depressive behaviors such as dysphoria, fatigue, and other somatic symptoms and to offer an explanation for other aspects of the depressive syndrome, such as the low rate of behavior (Lewinsohn, 1974). The depressed person is viewed as being on a prolonged extinction schedule. Depressive behaviors are often maintained and strengthened by sympathy, interest, and concern from family members; however, because others view such behavior as unpleasant, they will avoid the depressed person, which in turn will decrease the rate of positive reinforcement further. The total amount of response - contingent positive reinforcement attained by a person is viewed as a function of three variables. One is the number of events assumed to be potentially reinforcing for a person. This will be influenced by individual differences, by biological variables, and by sex and age. A second variable is the number of potentially reinforcing events that can be provided by the environment, and the third variable concerns the instrumental behavior of the person, that is, the extent to which skills are available and are displayed, that result in reinforcement from the environment (Lewinsohn, 1974).

A critical aspect of this conceptualization is that reinforcement be response-contingent, that is, a result of the person's behavior. As Lewinsohn (1974) points out, it is well known that "giving" (that is, noncontingently) to depressed individuals does not alter their depression. Some evidence has been gathered to support this view. For example, Lewinsohn and Libet (1972) investigated the relationship between daily ratings of mood and number of pleasant events. A relationship between these factors was found for two thirds of their subjects. Many of the activities associated with mood changes involved social interactions. A second group involved affect and states assumed to be incompatible with feeling depressed, such as being relaxed, and a third group involved activities that are assumed to lead to feelings of adequacy, competence, or independence. It has also been found that depressed persons engage in fewer activities and rate fewer items as pleasant. This finding supports Costello's argument that the loss of interest in the environment so characteristic of depression is related to loss of reinforcer effectiveness rather than decrease in the sheer number of reinforcers. Data gathered from a group of depressed and nondepressed persons revealed that the mean number of daily activities sampled for the former group was 23.4 and for the latter 33.4 (Lewinsohn and Graf, 1973). Use of self-report regarding pleasant events sampled, although it may suggest the overall amount of positive reinforcement, does not necessarily indicate the amount of *response-contingent* reinforcement, which is considered so crucial. Thus, it is not clear whether use of the pleasant-event schedule can throw much light on this view of depression.

The role of social skills. Lewinsohn and his colleagues

focused especially on possible deficits in social skills among depressed persons and hypothesized that depressed persons would have less skill compared to nondepressed persons. A person was considered to be skillful to the degree that he receives positive (and avoids negative) social consequences. Extensive analysis of social interactional data obtained in five therapy groups and eighteen homes indicated that people who are active, are quick to respond, are relatively insensitive to an aversive person, do not miss a chance to react, distribute their behaviors fairly evenly across members in group situations, and display positively reinforced behaviors, maximize their rate of positive reinforcement—that is, they are socially skillful (Lewinsohn, 1974). Observation of the social exchanges of depressed and nondepressed people has shown that the former emit interpersonal behaviors at about half the rate of nondepressed persons, have a more restricted range of people with whom they interact and evidence a longer latency of responding to others (Lewinsohn, 1974). In addition, their interactions display less reciprocity in terms of the number of actions devoted to other people. That is, depressed people tend to do either more or less than others. They also emit fewer positive reactions toward others, which is probably related to their receiving less (Libet and Lewinsohn, 1973).

Depressed people occasion fewer behaviors from others compared to nondepressed persons (Shaffer and Lewinsohn, 1971), which suggests that the former group of people receive less social reinforcement. Depressed individuals are more sensitive to the quality of social reinforcement compared to nondepressed people (Stewart, 1968). The largest difference found between depressed and nondepressed people occurred following a negative social reaction in which they were ignored, criticized, or disagreed with. This may mean that they have a greater tendency to avoid or withdraw from painful situations. Finally, the total amount of positive reinforcement obtained is less in depressed compared to nondepressed persons (see Lewinsohn, 1974). It is still uncertain whether a net loss of reinforcers can induce depression or whether depression may occur when there is only loss of control without loss of reinforcers. "Would a Casanova who slept with seven new girls every week become depressed if he found out that it was not his amatory prowess, but rather his wealth or his fairy godmother that made him popular? This is a theoretically crucial case, but we can only speculate about what would happen" (Seligman, Klein, and Miller, 1976, pp. 197-198).

Cognitive Theories. Beck (1967) emphasized internal psychological processes, particularly cognitive aspects of depression. He rejected the view of depression as an affective disorder in which cognitions related to low self-esteem were secondary to the affective disorder. He considered the cognitions the primary cause of the depression, including a negative view of the self, of the outside world, and of the future and a tendency to set high performance standards. An examination of thought content of depressives revealed distortions and unrealistic perceptions, in which clients exaggerated their faults and the obstacles in their path. The role of helplessness has been emphasized within cognitive theories of depression. For example, Lichtenberg (1957) assumed that depression increased in severity as belief in hopelessness progressed from a specific situation (least severe) to a whole behavior style of total dissatisfaction with the environment (most severe). Cognitive theorists have made an important contribution to the understanding of depression in terms of the description of the type of thinking that occurs in depression.

Bandura (1969) pointed to the excessively high standards held by some individuals and the potential effects of such standards in that such a person would offer infrequent self-reinforcement. Because of excessively high performance standards, success experiences will be few and failure experiences many, which will reduce positive reinforcement and, in turn, lead to cognitive and emotional effects of such a loss. Self-reinforcement requires two other components—self-monitoring and self-evaluation (Kanfer, 1970). Fuchs and Rehm (1975) point out that, in contrast with nondepressed individuals who monitor behavior-consequence sequences and accurately observe outcomes in each sequence, depressed persons selectively attend to external negative events that immediately follow their behavior, regardless of actual contingencies. Distortions in self-monitoring include selectively attending to immediate external events rather than delayed or external consequences of behavior and selectively attending to negative events. In contrast with non-depressed persons, who set realistic explicit criteria for their behavior and who objectively evaluate their behavior by comparing behavior to preset criteria, depressed persons set unrealistic, perfectionistic, global standards for themselves, making attainment impossible. Because of these tendencies, depressed persons often do not reach their goals and therefore evaluate themselves negatively.

Nondepressed persons offer themselves both overt and covert rewards contingent on attaining self-established criteria and so maintain their behavior even in the relative absence of external control and in spite of delayed consequences, and may administer punishment if they fail to meet these criteria. These processes aid nondepressed persons to suppress unproductive behavior and to resist temptation in their pursuit of long-term goals. In contrast, depressed persons offer themselves low rates of self-reward and high rates of self-punishment (Roth, Rehm, and Rozensky, 1975). The passivity of depressed persons implies a failure to employ self-control to bridge loss or delay of external reinforcement (Fuchs and Rehm, 1975). That is, the passivity and dependency characteristic of depressed individuals may result from impairments in self-monitoring, self-evaluation, and self-reinforcement (Kanfer, 1971). These characteristics help to account for the lower frequency of behaviors among depressed persons especially in the absence of external reinforcements. Potentially productive behaviors are reduced by the excessive self-punishment. This self-management view of depression also complements the stress on the development of increased influence over positive and negative environmental events.

The Concept of "Learned Helplessness." The role of response-contingent reinforcement in depression complements the "learned helplessness" view of depression, as well as cognitive theories of depression. "Learned helplessness concentrates on those depressions which begin with a reaction to loss of control over gratification and relief of suffering and in which the individual is slow to initiate responses, believes himself to be powerless and hopeless and has a negative outlook on the future"

(Seligman, Klein and Miller, 1976, p. 187). This view would argue that it is not trauma by itself that has bad effects but the inability to control trauma (see Seligman, 1975). The belief that trauma is uncontrollable appears to have three effects. A motivational effect is seen in the lowered probability that escape behavior will be initiated. Motivation to react is undermined by previous experience with reinforcers over which one has exercised no control. There is also an affective or emotional component, in which failure to control aversive events leads to depression as well as a cognitive effect, in that learning that responding and consequences are independent makes it more difficult to learn on future occasions that responding does make a difference. This view of depression complements a life stress model in which depression is related to stressful conditions, such as a change in work conditions. The low percentage of individuals for whom such stressful events are followed by depression—the estimates range from 10 to 20 percent (Klerman, 1974) to 33 percent (Brown, Harris, and Petro, 1973)—would point to many individuals possessing and exercising coping skills in such situations. Only those who feel powerless in the face of such events may become depressed. The role of powerlessness over interpersonal events due to ineffective coping skills has been stressed by many behavioral writers (McLean, 1976; Stuart, 1967b). Depressed individuals indeed perceive reinforcement as more response-independent than do nondepressed individuals on skill tasks (Miller and Seligman, 1973). The learned helpless view of depression emphasizes attainment of client influence over consequences through exposure to successful experiences.

Bandura (in press) has emphasized the distinction between efficacy and outcome expectations. "People can give up trying because they lack a sense of efficacy in achieving the required behavior, or they may be assured of their capabilities but give up trying because they expect their behavior to have no effect on an unresponsive environment or to be consistently punished. These two separable expectancy sources of futility have quite different antecedents and remedial implications. To alter efficacy-based futility requires development of competencies and expectations of personal effectiveness. By contrast, to change outcome-based futility necessitates changes in prevailing environmental contingencies that restore the instrumental value of the competencies that people already possess" (Bandura, in press, p. 28).

Summary. A behavioral view of depression emphasizes the multiple factors that may be related to this state and the carrying out of a functional analysis to determine related antecedents and consequences rather than a topographic analysis. Special attention is devoted to sources of positive reinforcement and to developing coping skills that will offer the client more influence over his or her environment so that their frequency is increased. There is an emphasis on increasing appropriate sources of positive reinforcement, rather than an emphasis on decreasing inappropriate behaviors that are considered to be secondary concomitants of a low frequency of response-contingent reinforcement. It is assumed "that the only thing that separates depressed people from nondepressed people is the use of interactional and coping skills" (McLean, 1976, p. 74).

Assessment

As with other presenting problems, a variety of methods are available to gather relevant assessment information and often multiple sources are employed. The goals of assessment include: evaluation of the intensity of the depression, including suicidal risk; identification of specific behavioral excesses and deficits; formulation of hypotheses concerning maintenance of the client's depression; and description of an intervention plan that includes specific behavioral goals and appropriate procedures for reaching these (Lewinsohn, 1975). Lewinsohn stresses the important role of "structuring" the intervention process with depressed clients, in order to arrive at a clear mutual understanding of expectations, goals, and time commitments involved. An overview of the program is presented, including the length of the assessment phase, which usually lasts two weeks; the review sessions that will be held following this phase; the need for home observation and the rationale for this; and the necessity for gathering self-monitored data. The client is introduced to the use of behavioral terms during assessment, and these are employed in review sessions when working toward an identification of objectives. A three-month time limit is agreed on, although this is extended in case of need. Special contingencies may be required to encourage clients to gather needed information such as making further sessions contingent upon collecting this data. Problem areas that are often related to depression are indicated in Figure 30.

Self-Report Measures. Preinterview questionnaires have been developed that provide a range of relevant information to peruse prior to the first interview (McLean, 1976). Responses to this questionnaire offer indications of degree of impairment in relation to three response modalities. The cognitive-affective modality includes items such as rate of suicidal ideation, decision-making ability, concentration, rate of laughter per day, rate of crying per day, and rate and duration of depressive thoughts. Areas included under the behavioral modality encompass work performance (interest in work, feelings of competence, time lost, and percentage accomplished in one day), and social interaction (for example, frequency of self-initiated social activity; average daily time spent with friends over the last two weeks; frequency of social events attended per week and satisfaction experienced when attending these events; frequency of sexual intercourse; and interest in sexual intercourse). If married, social interaction includes time spent talking to spouse, time spent in shared activities with spouse each day, and marital satisfaction over the past week. Amount and type of physical exercise are also noted under the behavioral modality. The somatic response modality includes average number of hours of sleep, agitation (pacing, hand wringing), weight loss, fatigue, and appetite. Information on social resources is gained as well as employment status. Clients are also requested to list specific goals they would like to attain and to specify how they would like to see their personal and social worlds altered. The first session may be made contingent on completion of the questionnaire, in order to increase the possibilities that it will be attended to.

One useful measure of depression that can be employed to monitor daily changes in mood is the Depression Adjective Checklist (Lubin, 1965), which consists of seven parallel lists of adjectives. The client checks the word that best describes how he feels. This scale discriminates well between depressed and nondepressed clients. The Beck Depression Inventory (Beck, 1972) samples a broader range of behavior that may be associated with depression compared to the Lubin Depression Adjective Checklist. The former inventory includes 21 different characteristics of depression, which the client ranks in terms of severity of the symptom. It taps self-report of cognitive, physiological, and overt behaviors.

"Mood monitoring" is initiated right after the first interview. Daily ratings of mood along a scale ranging from normal mood to extreme depression (Aitken, 1969) help the client and counselor to identify environmental events that may be associated with mood ratings (Lewinsohn, 1974). This is illustrated in the following example. "In the case of Mr. B., it was discovered that he tended to feel most depressed on Sundays. This was taken up with him, as it was very clear that he had little to do on Sundays. He then took up coaching a basketball team on which his son was one of the players and this was accompanied by a reduction in his DACL [Depression Adjective Checklist] ratings. In the case of Mrs. G., after an initial period of treatment during which her DACL ratings had come down, they then shot up rather dramatically at a point where her relationship with her husband had again deteriorated. The obvious correlation helped to reinforce for her the association between her relationship with her husband and her depression" (Lewinsohn, 1974, p. 102).

Information concerning the rate of sampling of pleasant activities during the preceding thirty days and the degree of enjoyment gained from these activities can be determined by asking the client to complete the Pleasant Events Schedule (MacPhillamy and Lewinsohn, 1972, 1975). This schedule lists 320 items—for each the client notes whether or not he engaged in the activity over the last month and indicates the enjoyment experienced. Three scores can be derived from this inventory: an activity level, defined as the sum of the frequency ratings; reinforcement potential, defined as the sum of the pleasantness ratings; and obtained reinforcement, defined as the sum of the product of the frequency and pleasantness ratings for each item.

Figure 30. Flowchart to Facilitate Therapeutic Decision Making in the Behavioral Treatment of Depression

Skill Areas	Problem Areas	Intervention	Pre-Post Scaled Improvement Criteria
Communication	average marital interaction?	Communication feedback training (± control) with regularly scheduled practice	(1) spouse report (2) analysis of home conversation audiotape
	quantity and range of interaction sources constricted?	Regularly scheduled communication practice, content prompting and cueing with established sources, and initiation of verbal interactions with appropriate new sources	(1) frequency and duration of verbal interactions with both familiar and new sources (2) client-satisfaction rating and communication interchanges with both familiar and new sources
Behavioral Productivity	quantity of and appropriateness?	Establish goal behavior that is acceptable to social environment as well as patient, construct graduated performance assignments using contingency management and successive approximations	(1) goal attainment scaling of objective and observable treatment goals (2) feedback from significant other, when available (3) record of objective events (for example, work record, places visited, tasks accomplished, physical exercise)
	recognition of by significant others?	Conference with client and significant other to establish what are desirable behavior goals, teach both significant other and client contingency management	(1) feedback from significant other, when available (2) client report of feedback received from significant other re client behavioral productivity
Social Interaction	unfamiliar with potential social environment in community?	Provide information and examples, outline advantages/disadvantages	(1) quiz client in discussion format (2) ask for additional information which client discovered on own initiative
	interacting with social environment unrewarding?	Provide information re alternative sources of interaction, role play alternative interaction styles and provide feedback and graduated performance assignments	(1) client self-report (2) rate of self-initiated social encounters/events participated in
	avoidance behavior due to anxiety?	Assertive training role play interaction styles in individual and/or group sessions, graduated performance assignments, relaxation training, where appropriate	(1) performance on graduated performance assignments (2) subjective report of social anxiety—satisfaction (3) frequency and nature of spontaneous social events initiated by client

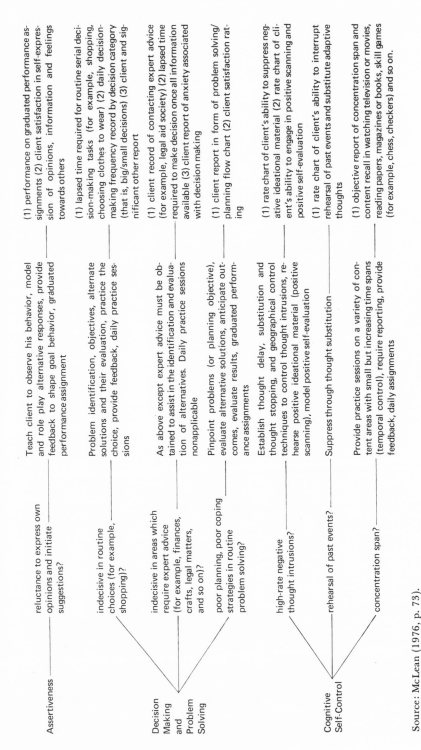

Area	Question	Intervention	Evaluation
Assertiveness	reluctance to express own opinions and initiate suggestions?	Teach client to observe his behavior, model and role play alternative responses, provide feedback to shape goal behavior, graduated performance assignment	(1) performance on graduated performance assignments (2) client satisfaction in self-expression of opinions, information and feelings towards others
	indecisive in routine choices (for example, shopping)?	Problem identification, objectives, alternate solutions and their evaluation, practice the choice, provide feedback, daily practice sessions	(1) lapsed time required for routine serial decision-making tasks (for example, shopping, choosing clothes to wear) (2) daily decision-making frequency record by decision category (that is, big/small decisions) (3) client and significant other report
Decision Making and Problem Solving	indecisive in areas which require expert advice (for example, finances, crafts, legal matters, and so on)?	As above except expert advice must be obtained to assist in the identification and evaluation of alternatives. Daily practice sessions nonapplicable	(1) client record of contacting expert advice (for example, legal aid society) (2) lapsed time required to make decision once all information available (3) client report of anxiety associated with decision making
	poor planning, poor coping strategies in routine problem solving?	Pinpoint problems (or planning objective), evaluate alternative solutions, anticipate outcomes, evaluate results, graduated performance assignments	(1) client report in form of problem solving/planning flow chart (2) client satisfaction rating
	high-rate negative thought intrusions?	Establish thought delay, substitution and thought stopping, and geographical control techniques to control thought intrusions, rehearse positive ideational material (positive scanning), model positive self-evaluation	(1) rate chart of client's ability to suppress negative ideational material (2) rate chart of client's ability to engage in positive scanning and positive self-evaluation
Cognitive Self-Control	rehearsal of past events?	Suppress through thought substitution	(1) rate chart of client's ability to interrupt rehearsal of past events and substitute adaptive thoughts
	concentration span?	Provide practice sessions on a variety of content areas with small but increasing time spans (temporal control), require reporting, provide feedback, daily assignments	(1) objective report of concentration span and content recall in watching television or movies, reading papers, magazines or books, skill games (for example, chess, checkers) and so on.

Source: McLean (1976, p. 73).

Self-reports of pleasant events possess good validity when compared with ratings of peers and independent observers. Test-retest reliabilities range from .66 to .85 (see, for example, MacPhillamy and Lewinsohn, 1972). The relationship between enjoyment and frequency of reinforcers sampled offers helpful assessment information. If, for example, sampling of events is high but average enjoyment rating is low, perhaps social skill training to increase social contacts is needed, or negative thoughts may interfere with enjoyment (Lewinsohn, Biglan, and Zeiss, 1976). Items marked as enjoyable by the client are extracted from the overall list, and the client is requested to monitor them daily. Lewinsohn and his colleagues extract 160 such items. Ratings of daily mood and monitoring of all 160 events are usually gathered over at least a two-week period.

Given that the client is also rating his daily mood, the relationship of mood to overall activity level as well as particular activities can be determined. Activities that seem to be associated with mood are brought to the client's attention. Events that are highly correlated with a more positive mood can be selected and made the focus of special intervention efforts to increase their occurrence (Lewinsohn, 1974). An example of a list of such events appears in Figure 31. Graphs depicting daily mood ratings and number of pleasurable events sampled are employed when assessment information is reviewed. Graphing the information often shows striking relationships between activity levels and mood changes. Activities associated with improved mood are selected as events to increase. The spirit in which this is carried out is described by Lewinsohn (1975, p. 48): "Several sessions, individual and joint, are sometimes necessary to present the information and to agree upon treatment goals. This process requires a great deal of skill and sensitivity on the part of the therapist and cannot be rushed. It involves considerable interaction between patient and therapist. The end product is a mutually acceptable "contract" (understanding) as to the nature of the client's difficulties and the desirable treatment goals and procedures."

Only through self-report can information be obtained concerning negative thoughts that may be related to depression. The client may be requested to keep a diary in which these thoughts are noted for later review or the client may be asked

Figure 31. Activity Schedule

Name_____ Date_____ Raw Score_____ Weighted Score _____

Instructions: Place check marks in the frequency column to correspond to the number of times an activity takes place during the day. For example, if you go for a walk two times during the day, place two check marks in the frequency column. Only activities that were at least a little pleasant during the day being considered should be checked. If an activity differs in pleasantness from your initial ratings, write in how pleasant the activity was for that particular day, using the following rating system: 2 means a little, 3 means a fair amount, 4 means much, and 5 means very much.

| Activity | How Pleasant | | |
	Initially	Today	Frequency
Talking with other teachers	3		
Developing own teaching materials	4		
Talking with students			
Teaching students	4		
Cleaning house	3		
Carrying on conversation with daughter	4		
Taking a trip (to)	5		
Going on a date			
Hearing a lecture	3		
Attending class	3		
Going to a play	4		
Going to a concert	2		
Attending a church discussion group	4		
Playing a game	2		
Eating at home	2		
Dining out	3		
Having a drink with a friend			
Solving mathematical problems	4		
Solving crossword puzzles	2		
Listening to music	3		
Watching animals	3		
Watching sports	1		
Reading for teaching purposes	3		
Reading for entertainment	4		
Looking at interesting buildings	2		
Looking at beautiful scenery	4		
Watching TV	2		
Singing alone			
Singing with others	3		
Dancing	2		
Performing on a musical instrument	1		

Source: Lewinsohn (1974, p. 103).

to telephone when having such thoughts and the "internal monolog" can be taped for later review (K. Mahoney and M. J. Mahoney, 1976). Particular attention is devoted to the possible presence of excessively high performance standards, an absence of positive self-evaluation, and sources of irrationality. Frequency of positive and negative thoughts can be estimated via self-monitoring. For example, Mahoney (1971) requested a client to note whether a negative or positive occurred each two-hour interval. A log such as the one in Figure 32 can be helpful in revealing situations that are associated with depression.

Observation. Information gained concerning the inter-action of the depressed person with significant others has yielded a valuable source of information. In fact, Lewinsohn considers home observation his most powerful assessment pro-cedure and points out that it has other beneficial effects as well, such as focusing attention on behavioral and interpersonal prob-lems rather than on the client alone, and helping to set the stage to involve significant others. "The necessity of arranging for the home observation gives us a natural opening to relate to the spouse, children, and others close to the client in ways that are potentially more constructive than the usual information-gath-ering oriented kind of social history interview with the relative" (Lewinsohn, 1974, p. 94). The necessity for planning the home observation offers information in and of itself in that resistance to seeing problems in terms of disturbed interpersonal relation-ships are revealed as well as communication problems with sig-nificant others (Lewinsohn, 1974).

Home observations take place around dinner time for about an hour each visit over three visits. Behaviors of the client and the social consequence of these are coded every thirty sec-onds using ten action categories (psychological complaint, somatic complaint, criticism, praise, information request, infor-mation giving, personal problem, instrument problem, other people's problems, talking about abstract impersonal, general topics, and so on); seven positive reaction categories (affection, approval, agree, laughter, interest, continues talking about topic, and physical affection); seven negative reaction categories (criticism, disapproval, disagrees, ignores, changes topic, inter-rupts, and physical punishment) (Lewinsohn and Schaffer, 1971). The content of conversation is also coded. This may in-clude, for example, school, the self, others, and the counselor. The purpose of this home observation is to identify behaviors that may be related to "depression" and to obtain a baseline count of their frequency. Related conditions have included an absence of interaction between the depressed client and his or

Figure 32. Client-Recorded Log for June 4th

	1 TIME	2 ACTIVITY	3 (setting) WHERE	4 WHO WAS THERE	5 WHAT YOU WANTED	6 (what happened) WHAT YOU GOT	7 COMMENTS
T1	7:00 A.M.	Eating breakfast	At home	Wife, two-year-old son	A good day. Peace at home. Things back to normal.	Good breakfast. Was patient with son, conversed with wife	A good start. I'm optimistic—feel good today.
T2	8:00 A.M.	Driving	Highway	Self	To get to work	Slow, jams, got there	Damn traffic, but there's nothing I can do about it.
T3	9:00 A.M.	Mail	At desk	Mr. X. (next desk)	To get mail out of way	Chatter and demands for advice from this young ambitious man	Complied with his request, but seething inside.
T4	10:00 A.M.	Work	Desk, on telephone	Constant interruption	Get work done. Get important papers typed.	Delay as no one free in secretarial pool	Frustrated—depressed —work fell off
T5	11:00 A.M.	Same	Same	Same	Same	Same	Just sat at desk shuffling paper.
T6	12:00– 1:00 P.M.	Lunch	Cafe	Was alone	Relax—have drink	Nothing	Didn't help. Still depressed.
T7	1:00-5:00 P.M.	Work	Desk, other offices	Coworkers	Get work done.	Some of work done	Will have to take work home to catch up.
T8	6:30 P.M.	Finally got home	Highway	Self	Get home, relax, catch up on work	Angry at traffic	Finally got home, worn out—had sandwich, spoke with wife, went into office
T9	10:00 P.M.	At desk	Home office	Alone	Get some work done— catch up and possibly be ahead for tomorrow.	Nothing. Sat, shuffled papers—had several drinks	Really discouraged, depressed
T10	10:00 P.M.	Desk	Home office	Wife	To be on good terms with wife	Argument. She wanted to know when I was coming out.	Upset
T11	11:30 P.M.	Tried to sleep	Bed	Alone; wife in spare bedroom	Wife—good relations, good feeling	Tossed and turned— slept poorly, restlessly.	A typical night after my wife and I have had a fight.

Source: Schwartz and Goldiamond (1975, pp. 164-165).

her spouse; a failure of the client to reinforce behaviors directed toward her by significant others; a high frequency of talk about depression; and devotion of only a small portion of talk time to topics of interest to the client. The following case examples illustrate the value of home observations (Lewinsohn, 1974, pp. 95-96):

> The client, Mary K., was an attractive, twenty-four-year-old female. She was referred to the Psychology Clinic following a fainting spell. Prior to this she had been depressed for several months. In addition to feelings of dysphoria, she also complained of a stiff neck, a urinary infection, a constant preoccupation with having a brain tumor. Except for the urinary infection, medical examinations had not revealed any physical basis for the other symptoms or complaints. Mary K. had been married to Bill, who is about her age, for three years and both were employed as teachers since their graduation from college. During the preceding spring, however, Mary resigned her job "because the pressure was too much." She had obtained employment as a retail clerk. During the summer of 1967, Bill was taking graduate courses and was preparing for a new position to begin in the fall.
>
> The K.'s were seen for a total of 10 sessions, including the intake interview, extending over a period of less than six weeks. The results of the home observations, or rather what appeared to us as the salient features, are presented in Table [14]. The table shows the proportion of time spent on

Table 14. Percentage of Total Time Spent on Each Conversation Topic during Initial (July 14 and 15, 1967) and Final (July 28 and 29; August 7, 1967) Home Observations

Topic	Initial (%)	Final (%)
"His" (for example, music, school)	36	14
"Hers" (for example, work, somatic complaints, cat, and so on)	12	23
"Mutual" (new home, going out, and so on)	36	45
Not talking	16	12

Source: Lewinsohn (1974, p. 95).

topics of interest to her, to him, and to both of them. It is clear that more topics of interest to him than to her were being discussed, and that more time was devoted to the former than to the latter. Table [15] shows the number of positive and nega-

Table 15. Incidences Expressed as Rate per Minute of Behavioral Categories During Initial and Final Home Observations

Category	Mr. K.		Mrs. K.	
	Initial	Final	Initial	Final
Laughs	.07	.06	.33	.13
Listens attentively to other conversations	.45	.33	.63	.20
Shows affection	.03	.02	.00	.02
Complies with other request	.01	.02	.05	.01
Shows sympathy	.10	.03	.05	.02
Continues topic	.30	.52	.41	.23
Total	.96	.98	1.47	.61
Interrupts	.11	.04	.06	.05
Nonsympathetic	.06	.03	.02	.00
Shows boredom	.06	.09	.00	.02
Misses chance to reinforce other	.02	.01	.03	.00
Changes topic	.28	.32	.31	.48
Ignores	.10	.10	.15	.01
Total	.63	.59	.57	.56
Initiates conversation	.24	.12	.23	.33

Source: Lewinsohn (1974, p. 96).

tive reactions for the case. As can be seen, she "dispenses" a greater number of positive reactions than he does. The immediate effect of the home observations was to shift the focus of the interviews away from somatic concerns to everyday, concrete happenings at work and home. The home observations and other data that had been collected in this case also stimulated a great deal of interaction between the K.'s, both in and out of subsequent joint interviews. She expressed dissatisfaction with the small number of affectionate interactions between them. The therapy sessions subsequently evolved primarily around very concrete, down-to-earth kinds of interaction between the two, the general goal of the therapist being to increase the number of positive interactions between them. At the end of treatment, the K.'s reported that things were definitely better between them, and they both seemed wholeheartedly committed to the idea that most of their problems lay in the interactions between them.

Mrs. G. was born in 1930. In the intake interview, she reported herself to be on the brink of total despair, finding it increasingly difficult to keep going, spending large amounts of time in bed; generally she appeared to be confused and very upset. She complained of having difficulty sleeping because of obsessive ruminations about incidents in which she believed she had been rejected by other people. She also mentioned recurring fantasies in which she saw her children killed by wild animals or in an automobile accident or by drowning. She also complained about the absence of close friends, blaming the situation on her husband, who professed no need for people. She said that she no longer had any feeling for her husband that she had neither the capacity nor the desire to love him. She indicated an interest in discussing past experiences about which she felt a great deal of guilt.

Two home observations were conducted during the diagnostic phase. During the first visit, the family was moderately defensive, whispering to each other, at least initially, and generally giving the appearance of not wanting the two observers to see or hear very much. The family's defensiveness diminished during the second observation period. The main finding which emerged from the data was that Mrs. G. initiated many interchanges with others, but that they initiated very few with her. . . . Others in the family would continue talking about a topic introduced by her, but the data showed that Mr. G. rarely took an active role in his interactions with Mrs. G. The lack of any positive interaction categories was also very striking, as was the absence of topics of conversation that might have been of interest to the adults. Most of the conversation centered around the food, the children, school, and other topics such as the dog, the Christmas tree, the children's clothing, which appeared to be of very little intrinsic interest to Mr. and Mrs. G.

The coding procedure described has also been employed in a therapy situation and a number of measures of social skill have been derived, including the following (Libet and Lewinsohn, 1973; see also Lewinsohn, 1975).

1. *Activity level.* Total number of actions displayed by a person per hour.
2. *Interpersonal efficiency.* Ratio of the number of behaviors directed toward the client divided by the number of behaviors he displays toward others. A low ratio indicates that the person is on a low schedule of reinforcement. One can also assess efficiency from the other person's vantage point; that is, the relation between what one offers and what is received from a person (the interpersonal efficiency-other ratio).
3. *Interpersonal range.* The number of people with whom the person interacts. The Interpersonal Range Measure is employed to measure this, which can vary from 0—directs all actions to one person—to 1—distributes actions equally among all people (Libet and Lewinsohn, 1973).
4. *Use of positive reactions.* The extent to which a person reinforces actions directed toward him by others.
5. *Action latency.* Length of time between a reaction to a person's statement and the next action of the person. This can be assessed both for positive and negative reactions.
6. *Silence.* The number of time intervals per hour during which the person neither acts or reacts to others.
7. *Initiation level.* The number of actions per hour, given that the person has engaged neither in an action nor a reaction in the preceding interval.
8. *Sensitivity to an aversive reaction.* The extent to which a person is turned off by a reaction from the most aversive person in the group.

Differences have been found in the behavior of depressed persons in home and therapy settings (Libet, Lewinsohn, and

Javorek, 1973). Depressed men tended to initiate fewer
questions, offered fewer comments and had a longer latency in
responding to reactions, were more affected by adverse reactions, and occasioned fewer positive reactions. Findings were
essentially similar for women in the group; however, the differences were not significant. In the home situation, depressed
men displayed fewer actions, but initiated more actions, which
was attributed to their lower participation in conversations initiated by others. Depressed men as well as women were also
more silent, more slow to respond to other people's reactions,
and occasioned a lower frequency of positive reinforcement.
The activity level measure (the total number of verbal actions
displayed per hour) best differentiated depressed people from
nondepressed people.

Coding systems that are considerably easier have been developed to assess the interaction of depressed individuals. For
example, McLean, Ogston, and Grauer (1973) asked clients to
discuss a problem at home for one half hour and to tape-record
this discussion. These tapes were reviewed, noting positive and
negative initiations and reactions at thirty-second intervals.
Scores were determined based on the proportions of interaction
for each participant. Simply recording the activity level of each
client during a discussion also offers a simplified index.

Observation by significant others such as a spouse can be
employed to check client self-report. Such checks are very important with depressed clients, because they often distort their
experiences—for example, attending only to what they consider
to be their failures and ignoring their successes. Rush, Khatani,
and Beck (1975) requested wives as well as their depressed husbands to keep a log of activities engaged in by their clients (the
men). Comparison of these two sources of information helped
to reveal failure of clients to attend to positive experiences.

A rating scale has been developed to assess the behavior
of hospitalized depressed psychiatric patients (Williams, Barlow,
and Agras, 1972). Observers check the behavior of the patient
at random intervals during each half hour from 8 A.M. until 4
P.M., note whether the patient is talking, smiling, or engaged in
a variety of types of motor activity, and note time spent out of
his room.

The Risk of Suicide

There is no doubt that there is an increased risk of suicide among depressed people (Mendels, 1970) and thus an appraisal of the probability of this risk should be made. Suicide attempts may or may not be manipulative, that is, maintained by their social consequences, and, as McLean (1976) has noted, it is very difficult to differentiate cases where it is and those where it is not with any degree of certainty. Lewinsohn employs the suicide risk scales created by Lettieri (1974), which are based on information routinely collected during intake interviews. Weights are assigned to answers and a total risk-taking score is derived, which ranges from 1 to 9. Scores above 6 indicate a high risk. A high risk estimate warrants close monitoring of the client and daily contact. An example of a client with a high risk would be "an older male, divorced within the past six months; shows evidence of somatic symptoms (loss of weight, appetite poor, sleep poor, excessive fatigue); absence of feelings of irritation or anger; refusal of help; one or more previous suicidal attempts; few or no family members in area; pattern of divorce or repeatedly being discarded by a lover or spouse; presence of confusion, hallucinations and/or delusions" (Lewinsohn, Biglan, and Zeiss, 1976, pp. 102-103).

Intervention

Selection of intervention procedures is directly informed by the results of assessment. Information collected during this phase will indicate the various factors that seem to be responsible for "depressive" behaviors. The range of situations that may be involved, together with related interventions and criteria for each to evaluate progress, are indicated in Figure 30. The assumption that guides the selection of intervention procedures is the assumed relationship between depression and a low frequency of positive reinforcement. There is a stress on increasing this frequency by enhancing the client's coping skills, especially those that influence his interpersonal environment. It is considered essential to provide an adequate schedule of positive reinforcement in order to decrease depression, and it is felt that

altering the person's schedule of activities and social interactions is the most reasonable source for altering the schedule
of reinforcement. It is also considered essential to conduct a
careful assessment to determine those events that will function
as reinforcers for each person. The assessment picture is often
complicated by the presence of a variety of other problems such
as insomnia, physical difficulties, and obsessive thinking. This
varied assessment picture calls for individual tailoring of intervention programs. The variety of intervention methods that
may be employed are described in the next section.

Increasing Pleasant Activities. A procedure for identifying
pleasant events has already been described. It is important to
locate items or activities that are particularly reinforcing for
each client. Trying to increase the total number of pleasant
events seems to be as effective as increasing a few target activities (Lewinsohn, Biglan, and Zeiss, 1976). Increased sampling of
such events can be encouraged by making assignments well
within the client's capabilities and by trying to increase encouragement from significant others. In addition, reinforcement
from the counselor provides an important source of support
that can be provided on a daily basis at first through phone contact. Lewinsohn and Graf (1973) employed therapy time as an
incentive to encourage sampling of pleasant events.

Behavioral Productivity. One assumption, that successful
performance is the most powerful antidepressant, focuses attention on behavioral productivity (Burgess, 1969; McLean, 1976).
These performances may or may not involve items indicated as
pleasant events. A graded series of task assignments is arranged.

> If the history indicated the loss of a specific
> reinforcer which was available, or partially avail-
> able, efforts to reinstate it were endeavored. If
> reinforcement losses were more generalized or non-
> specific, the client was required from the first to
> emit a few performing behaviors which required
> minimal effort for successful completion. Typi-
> cally, depressed individuals undertake tasks which
> they fail to complete. The result is not only the
> loss of reinforcement for task completion, but also
> the occasion for anxiety arousal with respect to
> that failure. In addition, the interruption of a chain

of responses is often reinforced by social attention. In order to achieve reinforcement for task completion it was important initally to select simple, easily executed performing behaviors for which the completion probability was high. The client's attention was drawn to the importance of successful completion, rather than to the nature or value of the task. Gradually task requirements were increased so that behaviors accelerated in frequency, duration, quality, and successively approximated former behaviors from the client's repertoire. [Burgess, 1969, pp. 194-195]

Daily contact was held with clients during the first week. This approach was employed with a twenty-six-year-old, married, college graduate who described the onset of his depression as coinciding with his first postgraduate employment, nine months before the initial interview. He said he needed considerable assistance in doing his work and had become less and less able to perform without assistance and viewed himself as a failure. He was very anxious regarding his failure to perform in any situation. Task planning was initiated with easily accomplished behaviors such as making a telephone call, mowing the lawn, or drying dishes. These behaviors were praised by the counselor and became self-reinforcing when he felt satisfaction from having done something. He reported on the execution of tasks during interviews and planned successfully more complicated activities including job interviews, employment test taking, and vita writing. His wife was encouraged to reinforce completed behaviors with attention and praise, and to ignore depressive behaviors. After two weeks the client reported feeling much better. He had initiated contact with some friends and had written letters for the first time since his recent marriage (Burgess, 1969). Initial steps taken must often be very small, to ensure their completion. The varied behavioral components involved in a task may not become evident until the task is attempted as in the example below.

A severely depressed, hospitalized client of the writer had stated that she wanted to become "a better mother." One of the sub-tasks this involved was providing meals. To overcome her indecision over what to provide for a menu, we suggested she poll her family for ideas. This done, she prepared her shopping list in advance. Being thrift-conscious she prepared herself by itemizing anticipated costs of the purchases from a food-chain ad in the local paper and using the ward calculator. She left, with the list and money (including an extra $10 floater) to purchase the groceries for her weekend visit home. Two hours later she returned disheveled with no groceries. The second item on the list was peas, but in the store there were fresh peas, canned, frozen and dehydrated peas, and peas in sauce, to say nothing of the choices available considering brands. The task had not been graduated carefully enough and when it was, the shopping and meal preparation were completed with no further difficulty. [McLean, 1976, p. 80]

Guidelines for increasing behavioral productivity include the following (McLean, 1976, p. 80):

1. The performance task be graduated into as small units as are necessary in order to reduce the task demands to the point that successful performance is guaranteed;
2. graduations of the task must be explicit so that performance data can be monitored by the client;
3. in order for the client to become oriented towards competence and performance success, attention must be focused on the task and on what has been accomplished already, instead of worrying about how much there is yet to do;
4. reinforcement must be contingent upon performance, preferably social reinforcement by "significant others."

Opportunities for social interactions between the client and significant others may be used as reinforcers to encourage behaviors, as may other high-probability behaviors.

Increasing Social Skills and Social Interaction. Social skills are given special importance in terms of viewing the depressed person's repertoire, and during assessment actual and potential sources of social reinforcement are examined in detail, as well as the client's skills in the social arena either through home observation or observation in group sessions. Complaints concerning social interaction are often made by depressed people, and there is increasing evidence that social interaction is especially important in relation to maintaining depressive behavior. Differences between depressed and nondepressed persons in terms of social skills have already been described. Each client differs in terms of the exact skills that he or she already possess and those that must be prompted and/or developed. Individual differences accentuate the need for careful identification of required skills for each client.

A first step is to identify problematic social relationships. These may occur in a variety of settings, such as in home, work, school, or recreational contexts. Social relationships may be problematic because of their absence, because of discomfort experienced, or because of a lack of certain social skills (Lewinsohn, Biglan, and Zeiss, 1976). Determining what areas create anxiety will provide information in terms of possible contribution of inhibitory factors in relation to nonuse of available skills or to their distortion because of unadaptive emotional reactions. For any relationship area identified by the client as problematic, it is then necessary to gather more precise information in terms of what behaviors should be increased and decreased. Self-monitoring in relation to specific areas in terms of anxiety, degree of contact, and mood may offer more discrete information (Lewinsohn, Biglan, and Zeiss, 1976) or home observation may be made of the client and his or her significant others or the client's behavior observed during group sessions.

Increasing pleasant events may result in more social interactions as may a special program designed for this goal (Gambrill, 1973). Anxiety in interpersonal situations may call for offering the client self-management skills for influencing his anxiety and/or graded approximations to anxiety-producing social situations.

Group Intervention. A group context was employed by Lewinsohn, Weinstein, and Alper (1970) for depressed persons. Specific desired changes were identified for each client, such as increasing the rate of positive behaviors toward others or responding more quickly after occasioning a negative reaction from someone else. Feedback was offered to each client based on the findings from observation and specific goals established for each client. The group members and the counselor reinforced approximations to the achievement of goals while the client tried out new behaviors in the group context. The social skill training program of Liberman and others (1975) is very similar, and components of it are described in Chapter Thirteen. Homework assignments graduated in accord with each client's comfort and skill levels provide additional opportunities to try out new skills and to gradually build up a series of successful experiences in real-life situations.

Developing Cognitive Self-Management Skills. Most depressed clients have a high rate of intrusive negative thoughts, including ruminations about past negative events and thoughts about the hopelessness of the future and their meager possibilities of improving their perceived plight. Many also have excessively high performance standards. Concentration on establishing more appropriate standards and on increasing successful performances may be sufficient to shift these perceptions to a more positive stance, or it may be decided that progress will be attained more rapidly if a special program is designed to decrease negative thoughts and increase positive ones in their place. There are many ways through which covert and overt verbal behavior could be related. Covert negative self-statements could be partially maintained by the attention gained by their expression or function as a cue to terminate unpleasant behaviors, such as working, and take a nap instead. The relationship between self-statements and mood is well illustrated by those studies in which mood is altered by the type of self-statements (Velten, 1968; Coleman, 1975).

There are a few reports of the use of the Premack Principle to increase positive thoughts (using high-probability behaviors to increase low-probability behaviors). Todd (1972) employed this method with a forty-nine-year-old married woman suffering from chronic depression. Six positive self-statements about herself were generated and written on a card, which was placed inside her cigarette pack. The Premack Principle was explained to the client and she was requested to read one or two of the positive items prior to smoking a cigarette and to add additional positive thoughts to her list as these occurred to her. She complied with these instructions and added seven positive items the first week and seven the second and reported that she felt much better about herself than she had for a long time. A number of other procedures were employed with this client, as is usual in remedying depression, including marital counseling, systematic desensitization for anxiety reactions, conditioned relaxation for psychosomatic complaints, behavior rehearsal, assertive training and assignment of increasingly more demanding tasks in order to reinstate social behaviors. Time with the counselor was contingent on compliance with task completion.

The high-probability behaviors employed to alter the frequency of various coverants (thoughts) may, as Danaher (1974) suggests, serve a cueing function rather than a reinforcing function. That is, they remind the client to offer positive self-statements. Vasta (1976) employed temporal cueing to increase the positive self-statements of a twenty-one-year-old college student who had been in counseling for almost a year and a half following a suicide attempt. The client and counselor first discussed the definition of *positive self-evaluation* and arrived at a mutual understanding of this term. The client was asked to record on an index card any positive self-evaluations that had occurred in the preceding hour, each hour, starting at 11 A.M. and ending at 8 P.M. A list was constructed of the client's assets, divided into the categories of physical, intellectual, and personality. The thirty-three items that were generated were written down on index cards and the client was asked to read these over each morning before he left for school. Neither procedure resulted in any appreciable change in the rate of positive self-statements, which remained at about .5 per hour. During the third phase, the client was asked to carry the cards with him and to record any spontaneous positive self-statements, as in the prior procedure. In addition, he was now to read one positive self-statement from each of the three categories of assets if no positive self-statement had spontaneously occurred during the prior hour. This procedure resulted in an immediate increase in the rate of positive self-statements to about thirteen per hour.

Following three weeks of this procedure, the client was then asked to only record the time of occurrence of positive self-evaluations. Although there was a slight decrease in the rate of positive statements (to about 1.1), they remained well above the baseline level for five weeks. The client's interpersonal functioning improved markedly during the last two phases of the procedure. He held several job interviews during this time, made some new friends, and started to date a woman for the first time in two years. He reported feeling much better. This study demonstrates the use of cueing to increase positive self-statements. Notice that the frequency of cueing was high, in that the client offered a great many positive responses each day.

Thought stopping (see Chapter Twelve) may also be helpful in decreasing negative thoughts, especially if combined with positive self-instructions that focus the client's attention on a task involving a chain of behavior, such as engaging in a pleasant activity. Logs that the client keeps of his daily activities may help him to more realistically view his accomplishments. These may reveal cognitive distortions that can be discussed by the client and counselor in terms of the disjunction between what the client thinks he has accomplished (perhaps nothing) and what he actually did during a week (Rush, Khatani, and Beck, 1975).

Learning to establish reasonable criteria for self-reinforcement should be employed when the client selects unreasonably high standards, as illustrated in the following case example. Jackson (1972) described the case of a twenty-two-year-old housewife who had seen a number of counselors over the past two years for feelings of depression, worthlessness, inactivity, and frequent negative self-statements. Prior counseling efforts had attempted to offer her insight into why she was depressed and to increase her activity. These attempts were only temporarily effective. Mrs. M. was extremely harsh with herself, even restricting herself from pleasurable activities. Her sensitivity was only to her own unacceptable performances and she tended to act in a mechanical manner. She stated that offering herself pleasurable experiences was against her upbringing, and so consequences she presented to herself were mainly unpleasant ones. Even compliments had become a cue for self-criticism. The client was asked to identify tasks she performed frequently and considered important, and she selected housekeeping. She was asked to record the total amount of time each day that she spent dusting and washing and drying dishes and to record the number of rewards she gave to herself each day for these activities (defined as "praising yourself, doing something you like, or feeling contented as a consequence of doing housework"). In addition, she rated her daily depression on a ten-point scale. These recordings were to be made about the same time each evening. The baseline revealed a zero frequency of self-reinforcement.

Mrs. M. was first helped to lower her goals for self-reinforcement to more reasonable ones, so that self-reinforcement could occur more frequently. Each goal was written down, identifying the performance clearly before the task was attempted. After finishing a task, she was asked to assess her performance in view of what she had set out to do. If she decided that she had met or surpassed her goals, she was to do something pleasant immediately. This could consist of a positive self-statement or some event such as telephoning a friend or having a cigarette. To facilitate carrying out this procedure, she was given a box of poker chips and told to award herself as many as she felt she deserved, and to record the number she took for each task. This process was modeled for the client during the interview and Mrs. M. practiced the entire procedure until she had mastered it. Positive self-reinforcements increased to about four per day following intervention and there was a decrease in self-rated depression. Interestingly, she spent less time on housework, which she attributed to being more efficient and having a more easy-going attitude toward this activity. She began to apply the procedures she was learning to other areas, such as social interaction. On the fifteenth and twenty-first days, interviews were held with the client and new tasks were assigned. On the twenty-first day, which was the fourth interview, she reported that she felt better and stopped observing and recording, but continued the self-reinforcement program. Two months later she was requested to resume monitoring the frequency of positive self-reinforcement, depression, and time spent on housework. Rather than saying something such as "It's not good enough" following completion of a task, she now had a feeling of satisfaction and offered herself verbal approval.

Cognitive factors were emphasized by Fuchs and Rehm (1975) in a group program for depressed clients. Participants were informed that their moods were a function of their own behavior and that they would learn skills that they could use to gain greater control in achieving desired outcomes. The aim of the program was to establish self-monitoring, self-evaluative, and self-reinforcement skills. During Session One, self-control principles relevant to depressed behavior were discussed, as was the tendency of depressed persons to note negative events and short-term results of behavior. Homework assignments were given, requesting members to monitor each day's positive activities, to keep track of their moods on an eleven-point scale from 0 (worst or most miserable feelings ever experienced) to 10 (best or most elated feelings ever experienced) following each positive event noted, and to graph their data (daily average mood and total number of activities). An emphasis on self-monitoring was continued during the second session, in which logs were reviewed, noting relationships between mood and activities. Self-evaluation was discussed during the next two sessions. The importance of setting realistic and obtainable goals was stressed as a means of accurate self-evaluation. Each participant was requested to select goals, based on their logs, that they said they would enjoy but that did not occur very often and to develop specific subgoals under each. Participants were encouraged to select goals that were discrete, obtainable, overt, and immediately discernible in terms of behavior. Illustrative subgoals might include "phoning a friend to chat" and "going to the library for a book about cats." Participants were requested to try to refine subgoals, based on continued monitoring. During the fourth session, a weighting system was introduced, in which clients were asked to award points for accomplished subgoals according to the difficulty or subjective importance of the goal (ranging from 1 to 5).

The concept of self-reinforcement was introduced at the fifth session. Participants were asked to construct "reward menus" for themselves, to assign "prices" to each item, and, during the next week, to offer themselves rewards as points were earned, to covertly reinforce themselves. Compared to a nonspecific therapy group and a waiting-list control group, individuals in the self-control group reported higher gains in self-reward as well as in beliefs in personal self-control.

Tharp, Watson, and Kaya (1974) reported use of self-management by four female college students who reported depressive feelings. They were instructed to pay special attention to the antecedents of such feelings and to employ the skills they had learned in one prior self-change effort. Their self-management methods are described as follows.

> Case 1 simply rated and recorded her natural units of activity as to "good" and "bad" feelings. This redistributed her attention in favor of her happy states. Such recording appears to interrupt the self-escalating process typical of depression. It is not always enough.
>
> Through recording, Case 2 discovered that her depressed periods were preceded by unfortunate interactions with others, leading to feelings of unworthiness, and so on. She set as her goal an increase in self-reliance, paying less attention to others' evaluations of her. She reinforced stopping ruminating about others with access to a favorite hobby. After sixty-four days she reported that her depression had stopped. This program had *altered the function of the antecedent,* so that rejection led to thoughts of self-reliance, which were then reinforced.
>
> Case 3 had suicidal thoughts. She first tried to break into her morbid ruminations with neutral or happy thoughts, but the results were insufficient. On Day 60, she began the plan of substituting "my good dream" (a pleasant fantasy) at the *onset* of thoughts that she knew would lead to depression. For example, a bus driver shouted at her "Get to the back!" which greatly embarrassed her. After ten minutes, she felt she was sinking into a deep depression, so before going on to work, she spent fifteen minutes with her "dream." After seven days of her plan there was a sharp reduction in depression, and she was still using the plan effectively at a three-month follow-up.
>
> Case 4 hypothesized that she was grossly

alienated from the expression of her honest
thoughts and feelings and took as her target behavior an increase in such expression. Her initial frequency was low, but on Day 45 she began a systematic reinforcement schedule for "honest"
statements, either to herself or aloud. This greatly
increased their frequency. [Tharp, Watson, and
Kaya, 1974, p. 624]

Lazarus employed imagined anticipation of positive
events to decrease depressed feelings. The basis for the use of
"time projection" is that because depression can be viewed as
related to inadequate or insufficient reinforcers, if the client can
imagine himself freed from his inertia so that he imagines engaging in a pleasurable activity, a reduction of the depressed mood
may occur (Lazarus, 1968). Imagining pleasant thoughts breaks
the chain of depression-inducing coverants. The use of this procedure is illustrated as follows.

A middle-aged woman was deeply depressed
following the death of a good friend. She consulted
a psychiatrist who prescribed drugs and explored
her guilt feelings and overdependency, all to no
avail. The patient spent most of her time in bed.
An operant conditioner was of the opinion that her
withdrawn behavior was being maintained and supported by positive reinforcement in the form of
concern and sympathy from friends and relatives.
There was no evidence to support this contention.
It seemed to me that following the shock and grief
which accompanied her good friend's demise, she
had entered a self-perpetuating state of mourning,
resulting in a weakened behavioral repertoire and a
chronic nonreinforcing state of affairs, which rendered her refractory to most positive stimuli. . . .
she was asked to concentrate on each of her positive reinforcers in turn. "Imagine yourself eating a
dish of delicious ice cream. Enjoy it to the full. See
the creamy texture; dig your spoon in; bring it
toward your mouth; smell and taste the delicious
flavor; feel the smooth texture with your tongue.
Relax and really enjoy it." Next, to enhance her
ongoing positive feelings, she was asked to imagine
herself enjoying a hot shower. Thereafter, the cru-

cial *anticipation* of positive reinforcement was introduced in the following way: "Think about the enjoyable things you can do tomorrow. How about a bit of gardening, followed by a hot shower, after which you can play one of your favorite Mozart recordings, while indulging in another dish of ice cream." (At this point the patient interrupted the sequence and joked that I would replace her depression with a problem of obesity. She then remarked, "My God! That's the first time I've laughed since Myrna's death.")

We continued the time projection sequence by advancing, in imagination, day by day, and filling each day with a variety of "nonfattening reinforcers." She was required to immerse herself as realistically as possible in each activity until she could feel all the accompanying pleasures and the full enjoyment of each pursuit. Toward the end of the session we had advanced seven days into the future. The important *retrospective contemplation phase* was then carried out. "Now look back over the past week that you have just lived through. In retrospect it's been a pretty busy and rewarding time. Try to capture a good feeling about it all. It's been an enjoyable week. Now we can let that week become two weeks and two weeks soon becomes one month as we advance further into the future. . . ." . . . We then extended the time projection sequence several years into the future. This patient was followed up two years later and indicated that apart from "normal downs," she had experienced no undue misery or depression. [Lazarus, 1971, pp. 228-229]

Unfortunately, there are no data supporting the effectiveness of time projection.

Anticipation of positive events may be combined with assignments to sample such events (to attempt to develop self-control of negative expectations) (Anton, Dunbar, and Friedman, 1976). Clients were first requested to keep a daily activity log, in which they listed the eight most important activities of the day without regard as to why these were important to them. They were also asked to rate each item on a seven-point scale ranging from 1 (extremely unpleasant) to 7 (extremely pleasant).

During the second session, they were informed that they would be selecting six pleasant events to be performed over the next two weeks, three of which would be carried out by the client alone and three of which were to involve at least one other person. Selected activities were to be potentially enjoyable to the client, were to take at least fifteen minutes to carry out but not more than one day. Three positive anticipation statements were then constructed for the first two activities. These statements were to begin with, "I will enjoy...," and specifically described some aspect of the activity (see Figure 33). Time was then allowed each client to close her eyes and

Figure 33. Two Examples of Anticipation Statements

Activity planned   lunch in the park with Edna.
Date planned for   Wed.
I will enjoy   getting sandwich and salads from deli to take out.
I will enjoy   sitting on the grass in the park and seeing the sun come through the
trees.
I will enjoy   talking with Edna, and the peace of the park.

Activity planned   going to plant nursery.
Date planned for   Sat.
I will enjoy   looking at all the annuals.
I will enjoy   looking at things and imagining/designing what I will do for my garden.
I will enjoy   looking at the house plant section and selecting a plant to hang in the
kitchen.

Source: Anton, Dunbar, and Friedman (1976, p. 70).

imagine each activity as if it were actually happening. Examples of activities selected included going to a lecture, browsing in an antique shop, working in the garden, and spending time reading. "She was instructed to rehearse covertly each of the three statements about the activity and to create a vivid image for each statement. For example, one subject imagined herself in the park sitting on the grass and seeing the sunlight filter through the trees (see Figure [33]). She was asked to continue repeating the statements and imagining the activity until she could identify a positive feeling while doing so. If the subject had difficulty creating vivid imagery, the therapist assisted by describing the activity with vivid adjectives" (Anton, Dunbar, and Friedman, 1976, p. 69). An assignment was given to practice this "positive anticipation" three times a day at home. This mix of selecting an activity to carry out, engaging in positive anticipation, and performing the activity was carried out over four more sessions. Additional uses for positive anticipation were pointed out, such as using this to help to carry out some task by imagining the task completed and how good it would feel.

Anticipation of activities resulted in disappointment if the client expected someone to react in a particular way for an activity to be pleasant and this did not happen, or if the client did not have enough information about the activity to predict its enjoyability. This calls for an emphasis on anticipated positive events that are independent of particular reactions of others and for obtaining sufficient information to be able to tell if some activity will be enjoyable. As a result of this program, there was a substantial lowering of scores on the Depression Adjective Checklist (Lubin, 1965) for seven of the nine participants. The authors noted that the two clients showing little or no change had very few social skills, lacked interpersonal relationships, and had almost no available reinforcers. It would seem obvious that positive anticipation will not be maintained if there is nothing positive to anticipate.

Many depressed clients complain of a limited concentration span and a program may have to be instituted to gradually increase this, perhaps by offering a reinforcer following gradually longer periods of concentrated activity.

Marital Interaction. Distress in marriage has been found to be present in up to 70 percent of cases where depression is a presenting problem (McLean, 1976). Many investigators have focused on the role of family members in the maintenance of "depressive" behaviors (for example, Liberman and Raskin, 1971). Significant others are trained to shift their attention from depressive behaviors to constructive behaviors. The interplay between data gathered in home observations, objectives identified, and interventions carried out is illustrated in the examples previously presented. A combination of training in social learning principles, spouse-offered feedback concerning the verbal behavior of his or her mate, and training in use of contingency contracts was employed successfully during an eight-session training program to alter depressive behaviors (McLean, Ogston, and Grauer, 1973). Depression and problematic marital interaction were described within a behavioral framework and couples were instructed to avoid blame and discussion of past events, to employ positive reinforcement to increase specific behaviors, and not to offer "constructive criticism" unless solicited. Homework assignments provided an opportunity to try out this new knowledge at home. Cue boxes that had button-operated red and green lights and an electric counter on line with each light were given to the couple to be used over four weeks during daily twenty-minute discussion sessions at home. The lights permitted immediate feedback to each spouse concerning their partner's perception of verbal statements. Instructions were given to offer the green light whenever they felt their partner was supportive, constructive, complimentary or otherwise positive and to signal the red light each time they considered their spouse to be sarcastic, contemptuous, indifferent, or negative to them. Topics were to center on conflict-filled issues, such as differences in child-rearing practices, refusal of one person to alter his or her behavior, financial priorities, and so forth. Appropriate use of the lights was modeled by the counselor. Taping of these discussions would have allowed more discrete feedback from the counselor in terms of each couple's progress (Thomas, Carter, and Gambrill, 1971; Thomas and Carter, 1971). Instead of using a cue light, couples can be instructed to hold a daily twenty-minute "talk time" in which they review how each other's day went or discuss other content of interest to one or both. This time is ended by offering positive feedback or some positive commitment of benefit to the spouse (McLean, 1976).

For the first three weeks, each spouse was asked to comply with requested changes in their behavior independent of whether their own requests were met. Contingency contracts were employed over the remaining five weeks; receipt of a behavior was contingent on displaying a behavior desired by the spouse. This intervention package resulted in a significant change in frequency of problematic behaviors, in Depression Adjective Checklist scores, and in verbal communication style.

Often significant others unintentionally reinforce depressive behavior. For example, McLean (1976) offered an example of dependent behavior of a depressed housewife that was partially maintained by support from her husband and her children. If she verbalized any hesitancy to carry out one of her agreed-on responsibilities, they would "help" her. For example, if she said, "I don't know if I feel like cooking supper tonight," they would say, "That's OK, Mom, we'll cook it tonight." There is, thus, a need for periodic checks to make sure that significant others reinforce behaviors incompatible with depression and ignore depressive behaviors.

Problem Solving and Decision Making. One of the characteristics of depressed persons is an inability to make decisions, even in small matters such as what to prepare for supper. This can be viewed as a failure to employ effective problem-solving or decision-making skills. Problem solving has been defined as a process that offers a variety of potentially effective response alternatives for handling a problematic situation and increases the likelihood of choosing the most effective option from among various alternatives (D'Zurilla and Goldfried, 1971). Thus the aim of training clients in problem-solving skills is to offer them a general coping strategy for a variety of situations. Such training is one of the procedures employed to aid clients with drinking problems as described in Chapter Fifteen. Another format developed by Goldfried and Goldfried (1975) for the development of such skills is described as follows.

General orientation. General orientation refers to the spirit in which one approaches a problematic situation and encourages the recognition of problems as a normal part of everyone's life, the assumption that there is something that can be done about problems, a willingness to recognize problems when they arise, and discouragement of a tendency to act impulsively. The client may have a variety of irrational expectations related to the first two points that must be addressed, perhaps employing cognitive restructuring, in which the client learns to reevaluate negative statements. As Goldfried and Goldfried point out, recognizing when a problem occurs may be difficult for clients. They are trained to identify feelings or cognitions that accompany a problem so that these can be used as cues to initiate problem solving. Feelings and cognitions are put to constructive use in this way rather than being themselves the focus of attention.

Problem definition and formulation. In order to solve a problem, it is necessary to specifically identify the problem in concrete terms, including details or conflicts that make a situation problematic. Irrelevant details must be excluded and objectives clearly identified. For example, if a depressed client says, "I just can't get my work done," a first step would be to identify what it is he or she would like to accomplish, what would he or she like to be different. A twenty-eight-year-old teacher who made such a complaint said she would like to mark papers in the evening at home and to prepare her next day's classes in the afternoon periods while at school. Conditions that interfered with accomplishing work in the afternoon included feeling very sleepy after consuming a large lunch. Accomplishing work in the evening was difficult, because her roommate played opera loudly all evening and she could not concentrate. In this stage of the training process, clients are given practice in trying to identify what hinders and what would facilitate achievement of objectives. This prepares them for the next step.

Generation of alternatives. In this stage, the client is encouraged to generate alternatives.

Decision making. In the decision-making stage, the possible negative and positive consequences related to each alternative are examined and the alternative that offers the most positive outcome is selected. Clients are encouraged to consider the following points (Goldfried and Goldfried, 1975, p. 140) in evaluating alternatives:

1. The personal consequences, particularly as they relate to the major issues or conflicts of the situation
2. The social consequences that the course of action would have, particularly on the significant others in the person's life
3. The short-term consequences as they relate to both his own problem and the effects on others
4. The long-term consequences that the solution will have on future personal-social functioning, and the possible prevention of a similar problematic situation in the future.

The alternative selected must then be described in detail in terms of how it will be carried out. This will also involve consideration of various alternatives; however, all will be related to one course of action.

Verification. Consequences resulting from the course of action are observed and if results are positive, the problem-solving process is ended. A negative result would call for recycling through former steps.

Deficits may occur at any of the above points. The client may fail to gather needed information prior to making a list of alternatives. Some clients do not consider their own past as sources of information, that is, they do not look back on their own behavior in similar situations and try to identify the relationships between outcomes, situational factors, and their own behavior. Model presentation is therefore helpful in enhancing problem-solving skills. The client can be requested to observe an effective problem solver who verbalizes his thoughts, so that the client can also observe the internal dialogue related to effective problem solving, including what questions to ask, what information to seek, how to maintain attention in the task. He then can attempt to problem-solve—first expressing his thoughts aloud.

Decision making can be gradually increased by starting with small decisions, such as what type of meat to have for dinner and progressing on to more difficult ones. Significant others should be coached to reinforce decisions made.

Case Examples

The following three case examples illustrate the application of behavioral methods with depressed clients. The first concerns a young woman who lived alone, the second a married woman who sought help at a community mental health center, and the third a married male.

Case 1: Miss A. Z. The following case example indicates the relationship of a lack of reinforcing activities to depression as well as the possible maintaining consequences for suicidal attempts. It is a good example of intervention that combines immediate intervention to decrease the possibility of another suicide attempt, while at the same time working on other areas related to depression. This case concerned an unmarried twenty-five-year-old secretary referred to a family service agency by a psychiatric hospital.

Presenting Problem(s): Miss A. Z. was referred following hospitalization for a second suicidal attempt. After repair of severely cut arteries, she was discharged from the hospital with a diagnosis of "severe depression." As she viewed her problems, she had cut her wrists because she was very unhappy. Each time that she cut them, she was alone and had been alone for several days, was feeling very depressed, and had no plans in the foreseeable future for any activity that might relieve her depression. Being alone and having no plans can be considered to be the eliciting stimuli for the response of depression. Depression, in turn, can be considered to be the discriminative stimulus for the operant behavior of attempting suicide. The expected reinforcement for cutting her wrists was attention from the friend whom she called to help her and from the hospital attendants who treated her; such attention would remove the aversive stimulus of loneliness and also reinforce the suicidal acts.

Goals: The referring hospital sought the prevention of future suicidal attempts. Miss A. Z. stated that her suicidal attempts were the result of dissatisfaction with her "work, social life . . . everything." She wished to reach a point at which she would be free of depressive and suicidal ruminations, or at least be able to conquer them when they arose. She wished that she could be content with her job, could have friends other than the two middle-aged couples who were her only social contacts, and could be hopeful about her future.

Miss A. Z.'s three problems, while assuredly interrelated, received somewhat differing treatments. Each problem will, therefore, be discussed separately.

Depression and Suicide: (1) Tentative projection of behavioral and environmental changes: Miss A. Z. first had to become able to control her ruminations when they occurred, and then had to learn to achieve satisfactions in her life sufficient to obviate depression. (2) Relevant conditions and treatment plan: Miss A. Z. expressed keen interest in religion, reading, and knitting. As she described these prepotent behaviors, religion and reading were clearly dominant. Accordingly, she was given two tasks to perform when she anticipated depression while alone at home; these were to think about the glories of God and how she could help God's will to be done on earth, and to translate selected sections of the *Bible* and the *Apocrypha* into modern English. (3) Rationale: Miss A. Z. was trained to emit two kinds of operant behavior that would compete with depression. As she could not both glory in the works of God and be depressed, or concentrate upon the meaning of biblical passages and dwell upon her own loneliness, the treatment was systematically geared to forestall depression. Reinforcement for the new responses stemmed from relief of the aversive experience of loneliness, positive reinforcement by the therapist for depression-free periods and energy to engage in other problem-solving activities.

Dull Work Situation: (1) Tentative projection of behavioral and environmental changes: Miss A. Z. had either to find new satisfactions in her current job or find new work. (2) Relevant conditions and treatment plan: Miss A. Z. was a trained stenographer but was employed as a posting bookkeeper. She found the work uninteresting and was frustrated by its lack of stimulation. Her goal was to find new secretarial employment involving creativity and social responsibility. She was hindered in attaining her goal because she "feared change" and because she feared that several job changes in the past would label her as a "poor employment risk." Her statement about fearing change was explored objectively (rather than receiving an "understanding" response from the therapist), and she was able to give up such statements immediately. She was then told that the local job market was such that persons of her skill were much in demand and that her work history would not deter employers. The criteria of jobs that would be interesting to her were reviewed and she was aided in determining what she would ask for. Finally, she was asked to contact an employment agency within

five days and to have at least two interviews within
the next ten days. (3) Rationale: Miss A. Z. fortunately possessed skills much in demand. Had she
not been skilled, treatment might have begun with
aiding her to locate and undertake appropriate
training. It was necessary to help her to overcome
her inactivity that was maintained by negative expectations for herself (fear of change) and for prospective employers (who would reject her because
of her work history). She was encouraged to assert
herself, a counterconditioning procedure, and was
reinforced in this effort with training in specific
relevant behaviors (asking for exactly the kind of
work that she wanted) and with relevant information about job availability. A schedule was set for
her, to enable her to overcome her tendency for inaction. Reinforcement for abiding by the timetable
was furnished by the therapist in the form of abundant encouragement and praise, by her own sense
that she was taking charge of her problems, and by
the promise of new rewards inherent in a new job.

Social Isolation: (1) Tentative projection of
behavioral and environmental changes: Miss A. Z.
complained of having no friends her own age and
was so fearful of peer contacts that she constantly
withdrew from young adults despite her intense desire to be with them. The steps to be taken to
accomplish her goal were first becoming as attractive as possible, then locating peers, developing
approach behaviors, and developing behaviors appropriate to the maintenance of new friendships.
(2) Relevant conditions and treatment plan: Miss
A. Z. expressed herself well and was appropriately
responsive to the therapist. She was somewhat unkempt, and specific suggestions were made to improve her appearance. Short-term suggestions
included changing her hair style and making her
clothing more youthful and attractive. Long-term
suggestions centered on engaging her in a weight-
reduction program. It was determined that she possessed basic social skills in ample supply, but that
she lacked assertiveness necessary to put her in
contact with peers. She was therefore given assertive training which consisted of having her approach one stranger in church and begin a two-
sentence conversation, note exactly what aspect of

the encounter was anxiety-arousing, and undergo counterconditioning to overcome this barrier. She was interested in religion, reading, knitting, and swimming and could use these interests to join groups in which she might encounter peers. Furthermore, she expressed an interest in attending college and was encouraged in this direction. As friendships arose, she was guided in means of developing them. During this experience, it was brought to light that since high school, she had never maintained a close contact with a young person within ten years of her age. (3) Rationale: Miss A. Z. was encouraged to alter her appearance, which was an important stimulus for the responses of others to her. For changes made in her appearance, she was reinforced first by the therapist, but more importantly by coworkers and, eventually, by friends. She was given counterconditioning (assertive) treatment to overcome a respondent condition (anxiety) and then became able to emit a wide range of operant (social approach) behaviors. [Stuart, 1967b, pp. 28-31]

Within one week the client found a new job that not only offered more money, but also more satisfying work. She joined a church group and later on social groups and enrolled in college courses that provided another opportunity for social contacts as well as educational reinforcers. According to her verbal report, she learned to view her depressed periods as "choices" rather than "inevitabilities" and to anticipate success rather than failure. She learned to exercise more influence over potential reinforcers in her environment.

This case demonstrates a careful scanning of the client's repertoire to identify not only needed changes in relation to the presenting problem, but also client assets. As Stuart (1967b) points out in his discussion of the case, multiple sources of reinforcement were employed to enhance the possibility that Miss A. Z. would carry out agreed-on assignments. In addition to his support and encouragement, reinforcing effects accrued from her new behaviors in the natural environment. Assignments were carefully graded in accord with skill and comfort levels thus helping to ensure their successful completion. This is especially important with depressed clients, since they are especially prone to ready acceptance of failure. A reduction in fee was also employed to provide an additional incentive for weight loss. Each week that a predetermined amount of weight was lost, the counseling fee was decreased by one third. Verbal behaviors related to depression were consistently discouraged during interactions with the counselor. Instead, "they were critically examined and their frequency quickly decreased" (Stuart, 1967b). Given that the counselor has carefully arranged for greater reinforcement from the natural environment by virtue of increasing client skills, the need for counselor support should naturally decrease over time.

Case 2: Sarah Jane. The following example highlights the variety of behavioral and environmental factors that must be considered for a thorough understanding of a presenting problem (Liberman and Roberts, 1976). Sarah Jane, a thirty-six-year-old, married ex-nurse with two children, contacted the mental health center three days after moving to a new town. She looked at least ten years older than her years because of white hair, obesity, pallid complexion, and an immobile facial expression. When asked to describe her presenting problem she reported that she had been depressed for year and had been hospitalized twice, once for five weeks and again for two weeks. She said that she felt little interest in living and could not function properly at home.

Sarah Jane was referred to the Day Treatment Center, where she signed an agreement to participate in the Center's Incentive System (see Liberman, King, and DeRisi, 1976). Sarah Jane was assigned to the supervising mental health nurse, on the assumption that having a nurse for a counselor would provide a good model and source of support. Two weeks were spent gathering assessment information from Sarah Jane and her husband. Deficits as well as behavior excesses were identified. Behavior deficits included a failure to perform housework and child-care activities, poor grooming, and infrequent conversations with her husband and children. Behaviors identified to increase in each of these three areas respectively included cleaning, clothes washing, making beds, shopping, cooking, and making snacks for the children; fixing her hair more stylishly, wearing more colorful clothes and ironing her clothes; and spending at least fifteen minutes each day talking with her husband and reading to her children. Behavior excesses included complaining about how worthless and helpless she was and spending a great deal of time in bed. Sarah Jane was spending an excessive amount of time in bed. She was taking "naps" several times a day, and regularly, from 4 to 6:30 P.M. and went to bed at 8 P.M. Several possible explanations for the precipitation and maintenance of Sarah Jane's depression emerged. Her marriage had been unsatisfactory from the beginning. Jack, her husband, had taken a new job in a distant city and returned home only on weekends. Sarah Jane felt deserted and burdened with all of the family responsibilities. Her husband offered her more attention and spent more time with her when she became depressed. She had terminated her job as a public health nurse when she began to feel unhappy and to lose her self-confidence.

The treatment plan developed included ignoring Sarah Jane's negative self-references while she was at the Center, offering social approval for improved grooming, a contingency management program that she would carry out at home, and marital therapy once her depression started to lift. Since the literature reveals no clear benefit of medication in neurotic depression, she was removed from her drug regimen. With the help of the nurse, she prepared a small notebook to be used as a behavioral diary. Each page was divided into two columns: (1) "Constructive Activities " and (2) "Nap Time." Sarah Jane was instructed how to use a high-frequency behavior (time in bed) to reinforce desirable but lower-frequency behaviors (constructive activities at home). She was urged to use time in bed only *after* she first completed a designated amount of housework, shopping, or interactions with her children. A list of household activities that were classed as "constructive" was compiled. She kept track of the time spent in constructive activities as well as the time spent in bed. At her counselor's suggestion, she visited a beauty parlor and had her hair styled in a more becoming manner. She seemed pleased when people would make positive comments about her new hair style and enjoyed the idea of keeping a diary of her activities. Daily meetings were held between Sarah Jane and her counselor to review her diary entries, as well as the graph, which indicated the cumulative number of hours spent constructively. She often attempted to provoke a reaction from the counselor by telling her how difficult it was for her to complete her household chores and how worthless she felt as a mother and as a wife. The counselor ignored these statements and instead made additional inquiries concerning Sarah Jane's accomplishments. There was a gradual increase in constructive activities during intervention as revealed by a cumulative record of such activities. Nap time used and nap time earned was displayed on a bar graph. A number of changes were visible in Sarah Jane after one month in the Day Treatment Center. Her appearance had improved, she initiated more conversations with other patients as well as with staff members and assumed the job as menu planner and food supervisor for the luncheons served at the center. She herself said that she felt better and was observed to smile occasionally. Marital counseling was initiated at this point, because difficulties in her marriage seemed intimately related to Sarah Jane's depression.

The marital therapy was conducted jointly by the nurse-counselor and a psychiatrist for sixty minutes once weekly. A first task was to teach Sarah Jane and Jack to look at each other, to express their positive and negative feelings directly to each other, and to offer positive feedback when something pleasant was said. Additional practice in these skills was held at home, using the programed manual *Improving Communication in Marriage* (Human Development Institute, 1969). Behavioral rehearsal with coaching was employed to give Sarah Jane and Jack experience in talking directly and emotionally with each other. Appropriate conversational skills were modeled, with an emphasis on eye contact, use of hands, posture, facial expressions, vocal tone and fluency. At the first session, it was suggested that a verbal agreement be made to exchange a desired behavior with each other. It was decided that each night that Sarah Jane talked with Jack for fifteen minutes or more on a topic of interest to him he would come to bed with her instead of staying up later. At the second session, the couple expressed satisfaction with their exchange and it was decided to negotiate a contingency contract. Sarah Jane wanted Jack to spend more time with the family and Jack wanted Sarah Jane to dress more modishly and to show more affection toward him. Sarah Jane had opportunities to practice, under supervision, the kinds of behaviors that Jack considered to be affectionate. The first contract was in effect for four weeks, and a second contract was then established for two weeks. In the first contract Sarah Jane's responsibilities included sitting and talking with her husband during breakfast Monday through Friday, and cleaning the living room for two hours each week. Jack's responsibilities included arising from bed at 10 A.M. on Saturday and Sunday and engaging in some mutual activity with his wife between 10 and 11 A.M. on Tuesday, Thursday, Saturday, and Sunday. The second contract included these responsibilities as well as—for Sarah Jane—dressing in clothes that appealed to her husband and initiating affection (kisses, hugs, hand holding, caresses) toward her husband. Jack, in turn, agreed to arrive home by 5:30 P.M. each day and to avoid expressing hostility or "uptightness" (coldness, rejection, annoyance, silence, or withdrawal) when Sarah Jane asked him not to pursue sexual relations. Compliance with the terms of each contract was regularly reviewed. A receipt system was employed to monitor contract compliance. Each time a term of a contract was fulfilled, the partner wrote out and handed a receipt to the other. For example, Jack gave Sarah Jane a receipt for initiating affection and she gave him a receipt for coming home on time. It was explained that although the exchange of receipts might seem artificial at first, it would help to keep them both aware of the new contingencies in their relationship and to remind them to offer compliments, praise, or recognition to their spouse for more pleasing behaviors. It was stressed that use of receipts would be gradually eliminated as more positive interactions developed.

Both spouses issued and received about five receipts per week over a nine-week period, for a total of about 90 for both Sarah Jane and Jack. Considering that Sarah Jane had an opportunity to engage in about 157 contracted behaviors during this nine-week period and Jack had an opportunity to engage in 114, this represented only about 33 percent of possible opportunities. After ten sessions, Jack and Sarah Jane expressed a renewed willingness to continue their marriage and seek further improvements. They had resumed sexual intercourse and reported satisfaction with their sexual experiences for the first time in years. Both, however, reported skepticism about the outcome of their marriage but felt that therapy had encouraged their efforts to do as much as possible to strengthen the union.

One month after the initiation of marital therapy, the self-control contingency concerning nap time was discontinued, because Sarah Jane had shown steady improvement in house-keeping and childcare functions. A new goal was selected— exploring opportunities for volunteer work outside the home. It was hoped that part-time work would be a step toward gainful employment, with the natural reinforcers of a job supporting Sarah Jane's resistance to depression. Marital therapy sessions were now made contingent on Sarah Jane checking out five volunteer opportunities each week. In the third week, Sarah Jane began a volunteer job at a hospital, for three days per week. About four months after her admission to the Day Treatment Center, Sarah Jane informed her counselor that she was too busy and involved with her home and volunteer job to continue coming to the Center and it was mutually agreed to terminate treatment. The marital therapy sessions were also terminated, and instructions were given to gradually fade out their contract and use of receipts.

A three-year follow-up by telephone indicated that a mutual decision was made to terminate the marriage about one year after counseling had ended, and that both Sarah Jane and Jack were happily involved in jobs and social relationships. Sarah Jane had continued working as a volunteer for over a year and after her divorce returned to college for a refresher course in pharmacology and obtained a job in a doctor's office. Three months later, she was let go with one day's notice. Although she was angry and hurt, she turned her attention toward locating another job and found one as a night nurse in a hospital. She had joined a weekly adult discussion group at her church that she said was very helpful to her in making decisions. When asked whether she was going out with men, she replied that she was not ready for that yet. She said she had many friends from church and that she went to parties and dinners. She felt that for the first time in her life she could let her hair down and have fun, and could joke and be playful with friends. She mentioned that keeping her daily activities in the diary while attending the Center and repeating them each day to the psychiatric nurse had helped, by giving her a goal to reach that was not far away. Jack reported a "sense of release" from the pressure of being married and said that he had an active social life.

In accord with the information that emerged from assessment, various intervention procedures were employed in this case, including counselor instructions and regular counselor feedback. During the initial stages of intervention, when review of Sarah Jane's diary and feedback was offered only twice a week rather than every day, progress slowed considerably. This emphasizes the importance of daily feedback and daily monitoring of agreed-on assignments. Counselor instructions required considerable self-management skill on the part of the client in terms of daily recording, daily attendance at the Center, and contingent use of nap time. An important source of feedback was provided by graphs, which clearly showed progress in daily number of constructive activities. The Center offered opportunities to reinforce a range of constructive behaviors, as well as an environment that would not support "depressive" talk.

Community-based reinforcers were creatively employed, such as volunteer work, and there was also a careful programing of assignments and contingencies in accord with Sarah Jane's skills; for example, starting with just three hours per week of volunteer work. Such work also increased social contacts with others and helped to support adaptive behaviors. Those with whom Sarah Jane interacted in the volunteer group became the natural reinforcers for appropriate behavior, and Johnie gradually decreased her own, more artificial reinforcement in the center. And last, but far from least, was addressing the marital interaction. Marital therapy provided an opportunity for Sarah Jane and Jack to determine if their coercive and distant relationship could become more satisfying. However, the improvements that occurred were insufficient to maintain the marriage. The main effort of marital therapy seemed to be to encourage a change away from the stagnation of their old marital relationship. Further attempts to increase the exchange of positives between the couple may have led to additional improvements in their relationships. As noted above, only about five contracted behaviors were exchanged each week. Considering that some of these were items like displaying affection, this seems very low.

Case 3: Mr. S. Although financially successful, Mr. S. reported little personal, marital, or job satisfaction. His visit to the counseling center was precipitated by his wife throwing him out. His main presenting complaint was of severe and prolonged depression, which interfered with his marriage and his work. His daily work routine indicated many conditions that were dysfunctional. He did not have his own secretary, even though he occupied a high position in the firm, and had to spend time going to the typing pool to find someone who could do his work. In addition, he usually went to see clients who were consulting him, rather than having them come to him. Because he did not get work accomplished at the office, he would bring work home with him and retreat to his study to work. His family saw little of him, although when he did spend time with his wife and children, this was enjoyable for all of them. Client-recorded logs helped to identify situations associated with depression.

Objectives included making work more pleasurable and spending more time with his family. This was to be accomplished by obtaining his own secretary, to spend at least one hour an evening with his wife and an hour each evening with his children and to go out with his wife alone two times a week. The shift from initially stated vague goals and the building on available behaviors are emphasized in the following quote: "The client stated goals initially either in such negative terms as 'not being a mass of tensions' and 'not being scared of people,' or in such vague positive terms as being able to handle 'aspects of things,' 'enjoy family,' and 'improve marital relations.' The contract is not concerned with eliminating depression, eliminating work problems, or eliminating marital tensions, and so on. Rather, the contract is stated in terms of constructing or putting together repertoires which already exist and which are to be maintained by the natural reinforcers in the environment. The absence of such reinforcers produces the presenting problems" (Schwartz and Goldiamond, 1975, p. 71).

Available resources included enjoyment by his wife and his children of time spent with him as well as his own pleasure from such contacts; available work skills; and his good record-keeping abilities, which facilitated the collection of needed assessment information. The first subgoals established at the end of the second interview are described in Chapter Five. As noted in Chapter Five, use of the program worksheet format for agreed-on assignments encourages recognition of available client skills. Subgoals for the following week are shown in Figure 34.

Figure 34. Program Worksheet, Mr. S., June 24

Current Relevant Repertoire (Session 3)	Subgoal: Subterminal Repertoire (for Session 4)
1. Was successful on three days. Worked at home on weekend.	1. (a) Try procedure on all workdays. (b) No work on Sundays.
2. Successful in time with children and wife on four days; on days home without work, exceeded expectations.	2. Try to meet criterion (thirty minutes with children and one hour with wife) on all weekdays. Spend all day Sunday with children and wife.
3. Went out Saturday night to movies.	3. Repeat on Saturday P.M. and do one thing together on weekdays.
4. Made a list of changes at work.	4. Ask for larger office.
5. Keeping excellent records.	5. Continue, and soon we will have graphs as a visible reinforcer.

Program Notes

1. Tell office mate you made it last week on three days and want to shoot for more this week. Also ask him how he'd feel if he had present office all to himself, and explain.
2 and 3. Discuss notion of chart with family.
4. Try to approach head of firm; good list; we'll try them one by one.
5. Try to figure out what to graph on yourself.

Source: Schwartz and Goldiamond (1975, p. 180).

Other subgoals were added as prior ones were accomplished. For example, the client agreed to ask his employer if he could change his working hours to 8 A.M. to 4 P.M. in order to eliminate rush-hour traffic. As frequency of interaction with his family increased, subgoals concerned a focus on the quality of the interaction. Interaction logs kept by the client indicated problematic interactions as well as positive interactions. This log requested the client to note the time and place of the interaction, with whom the interaction occurred, what he said, what the other person said, and what the client then said, together with comments regarding each interaction. Counselor comments can be added to the far right of the log when these logs are reviewed. An example of an interaction that needed attention was saying yes to colleagues, rather than no, when he was very busy and did not wish to be interrupted. An example of a positive interaction occurred with his wife at home when he suggested that they go out and get some ice cream and she said that she had to do the dishes. He suggested that she do them later and they went out for ice cream. The counselor supported this type of interaction, because it was positive and spontaneous.

Another goal of the client concerned getting along better with others at work. He said he was awkward when interacting with personnel. He was asked "to observe and record how others in the office interacted with one another around the water cooler" (Schwartz and Goldiamond, 1975, p. 190). It was discovered from this observation that Mr. S. lacked skills to initiate conversations. He was asked to observe how others initiate, maintain, and end interactions, and to begin using these methods, starting with short, work-related conversations with fellow workers at their desks. After this was accomplished, he initiated short (two to three minutes) conversations not related to work, then began to invite people to take coffee breaks with him to discuss business, and so on.

A six-month follow-up indicated that Mr. S. had left his job and became a senior partner in a company of his own. Relations with his children and wife continued to be positive. He said he no longer felt so depressed and that when he did, was able to relate his feelings to specific events at home or work. He would then try to arrange events that would alter these contingencies and try to set up others that would prevent their occurrence. (Schwartz and Goldiamond [1975] provide an annotated verbatum description of the first interview with Mr. S.)

Sleeping Problems

Sleeping difficulties are often complained of by persons describing themselves as depressed. Such difficulties may take a variety of forms including difficulty in falling asleep, frequent awakening at night, or early-morning wakening (Karacan and

Williams, 1971). Pharmacological treatment has been, and still is, most frequently prescribed for sleep difficulties; however, there are indications that this has a number of disadvantages including increased tolerance for medications as well as possible exacerbation of sleeping difficulties (see, for example, Kales, Preston, Tan, and Allen, 1970). A behavioral approach emphasizes self-management of sleeping difficulties.

Assessment. As with any other problem, it is important to identify the exact nature of the complaint. A baseline will provide a check on the client's verbal report of difficulty and information concerning related antecedents and consequences can be gathered at the same time. In addition, the client can be requested to complete a "General Sleep Questionnaire" (Borkovec and Boudewyns, 1976). If the client has been on medication, it may take up five weeks for the sleep cycle to return to normal (Oswald and Priest, 1965). Also, it should be borne in mind that sleep habits vary with age and sex (McGhie and Russell, 1962). Self-monitoring is usually employed to gather needed assessment information although reports of others, such as nurses, roommates, or spouses, have also been employed. For example, the client can be requested to monitor how long it took him or her to get to sleep the previous evening and the number of hours slept. Assessment may reveal that anxiety is associated with sleep difficulties perhaps related to self-presented negative thoughts. This may also reveal a faulty use of stimulus-control arrangements of antecedents that would encourage sleep.

Intervention. Some clients have exaggerated beliefs concerning the ill effects of sleep loss or mistaken assumptions about their sleep needs. Education as to patterns of sleep may help to alleviate anxiety associated with failure to attain a certain amount of sleep. As with other interventions, the effects of suggestion, as well as client and therapist expectations, make up an important component of the overall treatment effectiveness (Nicholis and Silvestri, 1967). Procedures most frequently employed to alleviate sleeping difficulties include progressive relaxation training, and stimulus and temporal control. Training the client in progressive relaxation has been found to be successful in reducing number of nightly wakenings and improving ratings of how rested clients feel on awakening (Borkovec and Fowles, 1973), as well as reducing difficulty in getting to sleep (Gershman and Clouser, 1974). After learning deep muscle relaxation, the client is instructed to relax when he goes to bed. Tape-recorded relaxation instructions were successfully employed with an eleven-year-old child who had slept poorly for many months (Weil and Goldfried, 1973). She was instructed to play the tape at bedtime and within a few days fell asleep before the tape ended. The thirty-minute tape was gradually decreased in length to five minutes. Continued improvement in her sleep was noted at a six-month follow-up.

Combining relaxation with stimulus control appears to enhance effects. Many clients contribute to their sleeping difficulties by thinking about the problems of the day or of the morrow after they lie down to go to sleep. Or they use bedtime as a cue for worrying about whether they will get to sleep and visualize the dreadful day they will have tomorrow, feeling tired, and how hard it will be to get up in the morning, and how miserable they will feel. Such thoughts are not usually conducive to quickly falling to sleep. As Bootzin (1973) pointed out, for such individuals, the bedtime situation has become a cue for behaviors that are incompatible with falling asleep. Stimulus-control procedures are designed to rearrange this influence. Clients are instructed to rearrange their bedrooms, since it is easier to develop new patterns of behavior in novel stimulus situations; not to take naps during the day, since this decreases the need for sleep and sleep becomes associated with inappropriate temporal and physical events; and to reduce distracting stimuli at bedtime, such as loud noises or bright lights (Borkovec and Boudewyns, 1976). In addition, clients are instructed to remain in bed for no longer than ten minutes if they do not fall asleep. If they do not fall asleep within this time they are to get up and do something else—anything else that has not been associated with difficulty in falling asleep in the past, such as going to a different room or reading a book (Bootzin, 1973). This procedure is designed to separate the cues for falling asleep from cues for other activities and to produce rapid onset of sleep. They are not to get back into bed unless they feel sleepy and the same process is repeated as often as necessary until the client falls asleep. Inclusion of temporal control in which the client goes to bed and arises at specified times has been found to enhance effects (Tokarz and Lawrence, 1974). Learning to replace worrisome thoughts with positive fantasies and positive self-instructions should also facilitate falling asleep. Intense anxiety associated with difficulty in sleeping related to an identifiable theme may indicate a need for desensitization in addition to the procedures described. Lewinsohn and his colleagues currently employ a combination of progressive relaxation training and stimulus control procedures with depressed clients who have sleep latencies of thirty-five minutes or more (Lewinsohn, Biglan, and Zeiss, 1976).

"Paradoxical" instructions have been reported to be effective where other measures were judged to be inappropriate for individual clients; however, to date only case studies exist to support this claim. For example, Mr. M., a forty-three-year-old male, complained of severe sleep disturbance of ten years' duration and had made a superficial suicide attempt occasioned by financial difficulties (Borkovec and Boudewyns, 1976). He was referred by his psychiatrist, who felt that continued use of sleeping medication was neither effective or advisable. Mr. M. was very skeptical about the effectiveness of psychological counseling. He was obsessed with the idea that he had to have some sleep. He was informed that the reason he could not sleep was that he was trying too hard. As expected, he countered this by pointing out that it was reasonable that he should be concerned, since his lack of sleep interfered with his life. The counselor suggested that he might overcome his concern by doing just the opposite of what he wanted, that is, to try and stay awake all night. The next morning the client informed the counselor that he had tried this and, in an "I told you so" attitude, informed the counselor that he had not slept all night. He was congratulated for following instructions and was asked to do the same the following night. As Borkovec and Boudewyns (1976) point out, one of the significant factors of paradoxical intention is that the counselor never loses credibility. If the client stays awake, he is reinforced for cooperating, and if he goes to sleep, progress occurs. The next morning the client informed the counselor that he had again tried to stay awake but had fallen asleep for a couple of hours. According to the hospital records he had slept for seven hours! He continued the procedure and reported six and a half to seven hours of sleep per night.

Summary

Depression is considered a general category that may encompass a variety of behavioral, affective, and cognitive surfeits and deficits. A behavioral approach emphasizes the importance of a functional analysis of depression in terms of the behavioral referents involved as well as related antecedent and consequent factors. Inappropriate behaviors are considered to be secondary effects of a low frequency of response contingent positive reinforcement and there is a focus on increasing the client's influence over appropriate sources of positive reinforcement by enhancing needed skills and thus altering the sense of "learned helplessness" that has developed. As with other presenting problems the client, to the extent possible, is an active participant in gathering needed assessment information and carrying out agreed-on assignments in real life. Skill areas that may be of concern in depression include cognitive self-control skills, decision-making and problem-solving skills, and social skills.

15

There is little debate that drinking is one of the major public health problems in the United States in terms of involvement in highway fatalities, job absences, aggressive behavior, and a range of medical disorders. Problem drinking is involved in over 50 percent of first admissions to mental hospitals. However, there is disagreement as to what is an alcohol problem. When is someone a problem drinker? Is alcoholism a disease requiring medical intervention or is it caused by learning inappropriate reactions to the stresses and strains of everyday life? In this chapter, the terms *alcoholic* and *alcoholism* are avoided and the terms *problem drinker* and *problem drinking* used instead, to avoid many assumptions that are no longer supported concerning the factors related to drinking (Knupfer, 1972).

Behavioral Intervention with Problem Drinkers

Some Mistaken Beliefs About Problem Drinking

It seems that the suffix *-ism* encourages the belief that one knows something about the person who is said to have the *-ism*. If a case report states that Mr. L. has been repeatedly hospitalized for alcoholism, there is a tendency to infer characteristics of Mr. L. that may have no basis in fact. In actuality, all we know from this report is that someone thinks that Mr. L. consumes too much alcohol. The basis for this statement will become clear as some of the myths about problem drinking are explored.

"There Is an Alcoholic Personality." Repeated efforts to locate personality variables related to problematic alcohol con-

667

sumption have failed (W. R. Miller, 1976). We do not seem to
be able to make any predictions, based on any personality measures, as to who will become an alcoholic. And only broad predictions are possible in terms of demographic and cultural variables. For example, males aged thirty-five to forty-five are more
likely to be problem drinkers than men who are either younger
or older. Men are more prone to be problem drinkers than are
women. People who have had an opportunity to observe and
learn patterns of appropriate drinking are less likely to become
problem drinkers than are those who have not had this opportunity. The former individual has had an opportunity to learn
when it is appropriate to drink, how much can be safely consumed without social censure, and the purposes drinking is to
serve, for example, as a facilitator of a pleasant time at cele-
brations.

The factors related to the development of problem drinking in women seems to differ from those with men. More
women appear to be solitary drinkers (Wanberg and Knapp,
1970), perhaps because more women are in a situation where
they can maintain other roles and still drink (such as housewives
compared with women who work). They drink to the point of
insensibility more often (Wood and Duffy, 1966) and the
course of alcoholism is reported to be more severe (Sclare,
1970). Antecedents for drinking often relate to acceptance of
the female role (Curlee, 1969). A recent study of four women
with a mean age of forty-five, all of whom were unemployed,
revealed that frequent antecedents included feelings of depression and anxiety (Tracey and Nathan, 1976). Their report that
they felt better after starting to drink supports the idea that
they used alcohol as self-medication.

"Alcoholism Is a Disease." The traditional view assumed that a person either was or was not an alcoholic, and the
aim was to identify whether the disease was present or not. In
line with this assumption, a *cure* was defined as the absence of
drinking, and resumption of drinking was considered a *relapse.*
The consideration of problem drinking as a disease opened the
hospital wards to problem drinkers, who in the past had been
dealt with as criminals. The hospitals had always been open to
the more affluent, who could be admitted, under some other

diagnosis, to detoxify (go through the initial physical discomfort of being without alcohol). Although this saved many people from the county jail, it encouraged a treatment model based on the disease concept, with a resultant failure to focus on relevant environmental factors.

Although problems with alcohol consumption may certainly entail an absence of ease (*dis-ease*) for the person who drinks as well as for significant others, there is no evidence to support the notion that problem drinking is a disease. Studies of the natural history of problem drinking have failed to reveal a consistent progression of symptoms (see, for example, Park and Whitehead, 1973). Contrary to this notion are data that indicate that alcoholism is self-limiting, that there is spontaneous recovery in many cases and that this may account for up to three fourths of all recoveries (see, for example, Knupfer, 1972). The supposed irreversible loss of control over drinking that is held to be a major criterion of the disease of alcoholism has been seriously questioned by studies in which problem drinkers consumed alcohol but did *not* evidence craving or a loss of control (see, for example, Marlatt, Demming, and Reid, 1973), by studies illustrating that problem drinkers can become controlled drinkers (Sobell and Sobell, 1972), and by reports showing that problem drinkers will modulate their drinking to be permitted to remain in an enriched environment (Cohen, Liebson, and Faillace, 1973). Also, a diagnosis of alcoholism does not provide information as to what treatment methods will be most effective.

Within a behavioral framework it is assumed that a given drinking pattern has been learned and that alteration of this pattern requires a situational analysis of drinking behavior. There is a considerable amount of data that support the conceptualization of drinking as a behavior maintained by its consequences (Marlatt, 1976a; Lloyd and Salzberg, 1975).

"First Drink, Then Drunk." The goal of intervention in the past was total abstinence, and this goal is still embraced by some self-help treatment centers such as Alcoholics Anonymous. However, research has shown that total abstinence is not always necessary and that many problem drinkers can become controlled social drinkers (Sobell and Sobell, 1973, 1976; Lloyd

and Salzberg, 1975), and that problem drinkers do *not* manifest craving for alcohol after consuming alcohol (Marlatt, Demming, and Reid, 1973). A *controlled* drinker is defined as a drinker who must select carefully the time, place, and circumstances of drinking and who must limit the amount he drinks (Sobell and Sobell, 1973). He is a drinker who has had a problem with alcohol and who successful employs self-management skills in regulating alcohol intake (Miller and Muñoz, 1976). This goal allows the person a greater feeling of control over his drinking behavior than does the belief that "first drink, then drunk." This is not to say that there may not be some clients who would prefer or need to select the goal of abstinence. This goal may be warranted for medical reasons, for example, cirrhosis, or for some individuals who are likely to lose control of their social behavior and/or their drinking whenever they drink.

"There is Agreement as to What a Problem Drinker Is." There is little agreement among investigators concerning the criteria to be employed for a diagnosis of problem drinking (W. R. Miller, 1976). This lack is mirrored by laymen when they consider someone with whom they interact to be a problem drinker. A level of drinking in a subculture in which drinking is common might not be considered to be a drinking problem, whereas this same level might be considered a severe problem in a subculture in which there is little tolerance for drinking. Also, people who relate to a person who is starting to escalate his or her drinking will apply the label *alcoholic* at different points in the career of the drinker, depending on their degree of contact with the person either while he or she is drinking or during the aftermath of drinking, which may be characterized by hangovers and failure to fulfill commitments. A significant other such as a spouse may be the next to the last to apply the label. The last is usually the drinker himself. Knupfer (1972, p. 258) has accepted the position that "if either he thinks it [drinking] is a problem or his wife does, or his boss does, or he gets arrested for drunkenness, then it is a problem." She also "reserves the right to decide that it is a problem even without these conditions if he drinks, say, a fifth of whiskey a day." As she employs the term *problem*, it includes behaviors related to drinking that put the person "at substantial risk of social or medical damage" (Knupfer, 1972, p. 258).

The Effects of Alcohol

The amount of alcohol consumed is closely related to the effects that are induced. Weight is associated with these effects. If a client weighs 120 pounds and consumes three drinks (a drink is defined as any amount of beverage that contains about one half ounce of pure ethyl alcohol), the blood alcohol concentration (the amount of alcohol in the blood—BAC) that will be reached within one hour will be .80 mg percent (milligrams of alcohol per 100 milliliters of blood), a level at which there is definite impairment of muscle coordination and driving skills and which is considered legally drunk in some states. Light and moderate drinkers begin to feel some effects at .20 mg percent. This is the approximate BAC reached after one drink (Miller and Muñoz, 1976). Other factors that affect the blood alcohol level include *how fast* drinks are ingested and if food is consumed while drinking or a full stomach exists before starting to drink. When alcoholic beverages are consumed along with a meal, the blood alcohol concentrations may be decreased by 50 percent.

A variety of undesirable physical effects have been related to alcohol although some, such as the higher incidence of cirrhosis of the liver, have also been related to nutritional deficiencies that occur together with drinking. Physical changes that occur with mild quantities of alcohol include an increase in heart rate; slight dilation of blood vessels in arms, legs, and skin; a slight lowering of blood pressure; a stimulation of the appetite (well known by the owners of restaurants); and a marked increase in urine output.

Ingestion of alcohol has both immediate and long-term effects on memory and includes the blackout, which involves either a partial or total loss of recall for some time after the onset of drinking. Blackouts usually occur in the advanced stages of a drinking problem. Alcohol intake also affects the quality of sleep. Sleep may occur in smaller segments of time being broken by wakefulness, and there is a suppression of dreaming (REM) sleep (Williams and Salamy, 1972). Problem drinkers have a lowered resistance to pneumonia and other infectious diseases. Although this has usually been attributed to nutritional deficiencies concomitant with drinking, recent evidence indicates that this may occur in well-nourished drinkers as well. One criterion for assuming dependence on alcohol is occurrence of the "withdrawal syndrome" following abstinence. This may include tremulousness, nausea, perspiration, and insomnia.

Learning to Abuse Alcohol

Of the 68 percent of adults who consume alcoholic drinks, only about 9 percent report problems related to drinking, which indicates that there are 12 to 15 million problem drinkers in this country (Cahalan, 1970). A strong argument can be made in favor of a reinforcement interpretation of drinking (Hunt and Azrin, 1973; Bandura, 1969). This argument is supported not only by the success of treatment approaches based on this assumption, but also by studies that indicate that drinking can be influenced by its consequences. For example, when access to social reinforcers is made contingent on sobriety, drinking decreases (Nathan and O'Brian, 1971). Data that indicate a major relationship between cultural factors and drinking support this behavior. Some subcultures such as the Scandinavians, Jews, and Moslems discourage drinking, whereas others, such as the French and Italian, reinforce drinking. The rates of problematic drinking in these cultures reflect such reinforcement patterns, in that less problematic drinking takes place in the former. The lower rate of problem drinking among married as compared to single people suggests that aversive events will be encountered more often following drinking, in the form of time out from positive family events (Hunt and Azrin, 1973). The lower rate of problem drinking among the regularly employed also suggests that drinking would interfere with an important source of reinforcement. The higher rate of problem drinking among the self-employed can be explained by the lack of negative consequences from employers resulting from drinking.

A behavioral analysis of drinking emphasizes identification of the antecedents and consequences of drinking. These include both positive as well as negative events. Pleasant consequences include the relaxing state that alcohol induces, as well as, for some, the taste of alcohol and the social support from friends and family for drinking in social situations such as at parties (Hunt and Azrin, 1973). Another positive consequence includes tolerance for activities that would typically be punished in a sober state, such as talking about certain topics or making sexual advances. Consumption of alcohol may lead to an increased perception of personal "power" or control (McClelland, Davis, Kalin, and Wanner, 1972). The rate of social interaction among alcoholics is higher when they consume alcohol, which suggests increased social interaction as a positive reinforcer for drinking (Griffiths, Bigelow, and Liebson, 1973). In addition to the presentation of positive events following drinking behavior, drinking may also be maintained by the removal of painful or annoying events. Anxiety, anger, or depression may be dulled after drinking, as may withdrawal symptoms resulting from temporary abstinence. These sources of reinforcement, which include subjective as well as physical, social, and addictive factors, combine to produce and maintain drinking behavior in the absence of factors that would lead in the opposite direction, that is, toward abstinence or toward a nonproblematic drinking pattern.

On the other hand, a variety of factors interfere with the development of problematic drinking (Hunt and Azrin, 1973). These also include social and subjective factors, as well as physical ones, such as initial nausea, dizziness, lack of coordination, inability to focus clearly, and sexual impotence. Part of this pattern of reinforcement will be influenced by individual reactions to alcohol (Jellinek, 1960). Unpleasant social reactions may result from significant others, such as family members, as well as from authorities, if drunkenness occurs in public settings. The deterrent impact of various factors depends on whether reinforcers such as a family or job exist, as well as how important these possessions are, and how immediately the aversive events follow drinking. The aversive consequences of drinking usually do not occur immediately. Some, such as cirrhosis of the liver, may not occur for years, and others, such as family members finally getting fed up with behaviors that occur in a drunk, may not occur for months. Not until many absences from work may an employer become concerned. A spouse may "cover up" for her mate for many weeks and months, as may fellow employees. It is not until such significant others label their friend or mate a *drunk* that they no longer will protect him or her from the aversive consequences of drinking. The negative aftereffects of drinking (the hangovers) are also temporally removed from the drinking. Thus, the ultimate aversive consequences of drinking are removed in time, while positive effects and removal of negative effects are more immediate. This reinforcement pattern perpetuates alcohol consumption. This conceptualization differs from the traditional stress reduction theory related to alcohol use, in that it is far more inclusive in terms of the factors considered to be related to alcohol use, and includes economic, social, and cultural factors.

Direct observation of drinking behavior in the laboratory and on special wards has revealed that social stress augments drinking (Miller, Hersen, Eisler, and Hillsman, 1974), as does the presence of cues for drinking such as bottles or pictures of liquor (Miller, Hersen, Eisler, Epstein, and Wooten, 1974), and the presence of models who consume alcohol (Caudill and Marlatt, 1975). For example, subjects who observed a heavy drinking model consumed twice as much in a wine-tasting test compared to subjects in the no-model group. The role of three potential sources of tension or arousal as determinants of drinking was examined by means of a "tasting task" in which the subject perceived his role to be a taster of wines. These included fear of pain (fear of a painful electric shock), threat of interpersonal evaluation (male drinkers being rated by females along selected dimensions of physical attractiveness), and anger (subjects were deliberately criticized and angered by a confederate prior to the tasting task). Threat of a painful shock sometime during the tasting task had no differential effect on alcoholics and nonalcoholics (Higgins and Marlatt, 1973). However, male subjects who expected to be evaluated by females in another task right after the tasting experiment drank almost twice as much wine as men in the low-threat conditions (Higgins and Marlatt, 1975). Lack of opportunity to express anger by retaliating against a person who provoked them increased consumption of wine in the tasting task, whereas expression of anger decreased consumption. Consumption by nonangered subjects fell between these levels (Marlatt, Kosturn, and Lang, 1975). These findings lend support to fear of social evaluation and lack of assertion as determinants of excessive drinking of alcohol. The role of stress alone as the antecedent of drinking has been seriously questioned (Cappell and Herman, 1972).

The following example illustrates some of the reinforcing qualities of alcohol. Joe worked in a large law firm in a Midwestern city. It was his habit after work to have a drink with some of his fellow workers before driving home. Over the years, as his responsibilities increased and he felt more pressured at work, he started to drink during lunch and, instead of one drink after work, managed to get down two or three. As his job pressures increased, he became more irritable at home, which negatively affected his interaction with his wife and children and encouraged longer evening visits to a bar. He no longer accompanied his fellow workers in the evening, since he had received signals from them as well as direct verbal admonishment concerning his drinking. He now went off by himself to another bar farther away from the office.

Joe, who originally could be described as a social drinker, changed his drinking pattern markedly over the years. Rather than refusing to assume unwanted responsibilities at work, he accepted tasks that he disliked. Work was no longer pleasurable to think about or do and, as he drank more, it became more difficult to manage, because of hangovers the next morning. What had seemed pleasurable at home, such as playing with his children when he arrived home, now gave him a splitting headache and he would instead yell at them and tell them to go outside. Over the years, drinking assumed different functions for Joe. Originally it facilitated positive interaction. Now it helped him escape the unwanted pressure at work and gave him time away from his wife, who had fallen into the unfortunate habit of nagging him about his drinking. This example illustrates that drinking alcohol may be maintained both by positive consequences (increased relaxation and conviviality), as well as by the removal of negative events (such as worry about work and family), and that factors initially associated with drinking may differ considerably from those currently relevant.

Drinking Patterns of Problem Drinkers
Compared to Nonproblem Drinkers

Only fairly recently has information been gathered as to how people with drinking problems differ in "how they drink" compared to people who do not have such a problem. Problem drinkers will almost always drink more than twelve drinks within a four-hour period; generally order straight drinks; take larger-size sips no matter what type of drink; and drink faster than normal drinkers. In contrast, normal drinkers rarely drink more than 12 drinks within a four-hour period; usually order mixed drinks; take many rapid and small sips; and drink considerably slower than problem drinkers (Sobell, Schaefer, and Mills, 1972). This is important information if we wish to individually tailor treatment goals, which might include, rather than abstinence, the goal of becoming a controlled social drinker. Here, it is important to teach the person a different drinking pattern.

Assessment

Being informed that Mr. L. is a problem drinker provides no information relevant to intervention. We must identify his pattern of drinking, including what and when he drinks; the situations in which drinks are consumed; and relevant consequences. Within a behavioral approach, what is an alcohol problem must be individually defined for each client. There is no attempt to classify people on an either/or basis—"he is or is not an alcoholic"—but rather to identify for each person his or her pattern of drinking and the factors related to this pattern. Antecedents may include social situations in which drinking enhances conviviality and relaxation and/or negative events, such as anxiety or anger, that are dulled by the effects of alcohol. The nature and frequency of various surrounding conditions are usually determined through self-report and self-monitoring, although this information can be augmented by the report of significant others. The history of drinking may help to reveal important related factors, although it must be kept in mind that the original conditions related to the establishment and maintenance of drinking behavior may differ considerably from those that are currently related to drinking. There is an attempt to identify those situational factors that facilitate drinking, as well as those that decrease its probability and, during intervention, an attempt to decrease the presence of the former and increase factors that will encourage alternative behaviors and controlled drinking. A variety of sources are employed in gathering needed assessment information.

Self-Report Measures. The social history of drinking is usually provided by the client, although additional material may be obtained from significant others or from public records, such as arrests for drunken driving. The context in which self-report data is gathered should be carefully considered in judging its accuracy (Marlatt, 1976b). Thus, a client who is under duress to accept treatment may not be as cooperative in providing detailed information nor go as far out of his way to offer accurate reports as a client who is very interested in altering his drinking pattern. A recent study investigating the accuracy of self-report revealed that alcoholics tend to overestimate their arrest history as compared to official records (Sobell, Sobell, and Samuels, 1974). In 37 percent of the cases, subjects' reports correctly matched their arrest records, 37 percent overestimated arrests, and 24 percent underestimated them. Some have questioned the accuracy of arrest records, which may partially explain the overestimation (see, for example, Ball, 1967). As with trying to assess other presenting problems, it is best to employ multiple measures in order to guard against possible inaccurate reporting from one source.

Self-report questionnaires have been developed for gathering information concerning alcohol abuse and related problems. For example, Marlatt (1976b) has developed a Drinking Profile, which consists of a structured, behaviorally oriented interview. This offers demographic information, data concerning drinking patterns, beverage preferences, antecedents and consequences of drinking, periods of abstinence, and information about the initial development of the drinking problem. The client is also asked about his motivation to stop drinking and his expectations of treatment outcome. A scoring manual is available for coding open-ended items (those items to which a variety of responses are possible).

Another self-report questionnaire, the Alcohol Use Questionnaire, consists of sixty-five items (Horn, Wanberg, Adams, Wright, and Foster, 1973). Scores can be derived for a number of factors, including physical severity, familial involvement with drinking, psychosocial benefit from drinking, marital difficulties associated with drinking, weekend controlled drinking, anxiety related to drinking, and alcoholic deterioration. Such questionnaires provide valuable assessment information regarding not only the extent and pattern of drinking, but also about problems related to drinking. They thus aid in deciding what particular intervention procedure to employ. Horn and his colleagues have also developed a Follow-Up Assessment Questionnaire.

Self-Monitoring Measures. Clients are often asked to keep records of their drinking behavior during both assessment and intervention. Such information in the former phase provides a baseline for drinking (how often drinking occurs before intervention) as well as description of related antecedents and consequences. This information is usually collected over a two-week period. Sobell and Sobell (1973) developed an Alcohol Intake Sheet, which provides space for recording the date, type of drink, percent of alcohol content in the liquor, time the drink was ordered, number of sips per drink, amount of total drink consumed, and the environment where the drink was ingested. A separate entry is made for each drink. Entries are made daily, and recording forms are filed in a loose-leaf binder and brought to group sessions, where they are reviewed by the client and counselor. The Center for Behavioral Medicine, associated with the Hospital of the University of Pennsylvania, employs a somewhat different form, which allows recording of time (when started and when finished), place, situation (with whom), mood, kind of drink, quantity (in ounces), percentage of alcohol, and ounces of alcohol (Pomerleau and Brady, 1975). A more simple form calls for the notation of the date, time, type of drink, amount and situation on three-by-five-inch, lined index cards (Miller and Muñoz, 1976). A *drink* is defined as any amount of beverage that contains about one half ounce of pure ethyl alcohol, which is the amount of alcohol in one bottle of beer (12 ounces); in one ounce of distilled spirits (30 ml); in one small glass of fortified wine (2½ ounces); or in one glass (4 ounces) of table wine (12 percent). These drinks all contain the same amount of alcohol. The client would count one drink for each bottle of beer, four-ounce glass of wine, or ounce of hard liquor consumed.

All of these forms provide needed information about the situations in which drinking occurs, the amount consumed daily, and the type of drinks ingested. Continued monitoring during intervention provides valuable information that enables the evaluation of progress. As with all self-monitoring, provision of careful instructions to the client helps to ensure accurate data collection, as does routine review of records. Additional incentives may be required, such as collection of a monetary deposit in advance, which can be earned back in weekly amounts contingent on the return of carefully recorded reports (Marlatt, 1976a). Self-monitoring also has beneficial effects for clients in terms of awareness of drinking patterns. The client is encouraged to analyze a specific behavioral pattern—his drinking. The records provide realistic feedback and serve as a safeguard against subjective distortion of drinking patterns (Sobell and Sobell, 1973). Self-recording encourages clients to recognize and discuss the significance of situations where drinking, moderate or abusive, occurs, and facilitates early intervention by identifying the onset of abusive drinking.

Collateral Sources. Information collected by the client may be checked through collateral sources, such as significant others, or official records (arrest records, hospital admissions) —with the client's permission, of course. Such sources should not be involved if this would have negative repercussions for the client. One measure employed to measure the effects of a behavioral program with alcoholics is the Daily Drinking Disposition (Sobell and Sobell, 1973). This is based on self-report as well as collateral sources. Daily consumption of alcohol was assigned to one of five categories: (1) drunk days (consumption of more than six ounces of 86-proof liquor); (2) controlled drinking days (consumption of six ounces or less of 86-proof liquor or its equivalent); (3) abstinent days (no drinking); (4) incarcerated days (client was in jail or in the hospital). This method of monitoring allows the generation of a drinking profile over time, showing the number of abstinent, controlled drinking, and drunk days for each client.

Measures of Blood-Alcohol Concentration. Blood alcohol concentrations as measured by breath-analysis tests have been employed as a measure of outcome (Miller, 1975; Sobell and Sobell, 1975). Probes are usually made on a random basis, with the client's prior permission. These probes may also provide the basis for dispensement of various rewards contingent on the results of the test. Assessment of breath samples is quite precise, with an average maximum deviation from actual blood samples of .003 percent (Huntington, 1972).

Physical Examinations. Physical examinations should be arranged in cases where it seems likely that prolonged drinking may have resulted in problematic medical conditions such as malnutrition or cirrhosis. Prescribed medication may be desirable to cushion the effects of withdrawal from alcohol.

Direct Observation. Direct observation of drinking behavior either in the laboratory or in the natural environment is usually not possible purely for practical reasons. Such observation has yielded useful information, some of which has been described above. "Working" for alcohol (operant responding) in an inpatient treatment program has been related to treatment outcome (Miller, Hersen, Eisler, and Elkin, 1974). Clients rated as more successful during a follow-up period showed fewer pretreatment responses for alcohol than did clients rated as treatment failures. Differential pretreatment rates of *ad libitum* consumption (alcohol is freely available) have also been found to be related to outcome. Clients who showed the greatest improvement at a six-month follow-up did not drink during sessions at a bar that was set up in a hospital (Skolada, Alterman, Cornelison, and Gottheil, 1975). Thus direct observation in artificial environments seems to yield predictive information in terms of treatment outcome. To date, the rate of drinking in artificial situations has not been compared with the rate of drinking in the natural environment as assessed via observation (Marlatt, 1976a), although there have been efforts to measure drinking in natural settings (for example, see Kessler and Gomberg, 1974).

Intervention

A behavioral approach to the reduction of excessive alcohol consumption has proceeded along three avenues. The earliest was the use of aversive conditioning; that is, the attempt to pair unpleasant events such as nausea and shock with the consumption of alcoholic beverages. A second avenue emphasizes acquisition of self-management skills to monitor, understand, and alter behavior by means of situational analyses and the use of alternative responses. A third avenue stresses the establishment of environmental contingencies for appropriate alcohol consumption. There is a lack of comparative data about which intervention methods work best with various clients. The important thought to bear in mind when selecting procedures is that intervention should be tailored for *each* particular client. The client's drinking pattern and related problems must be known, so that the intervention mix selected will be well matched to this pattern. The self-management of drinking will first be discussed, followed by a discussion of the regulation of environmental contingencies related to alcohol use. Finally, the use of aversive conditioning will be described.

The Self-Management of Drinking

A characteristic shared by problem drinking, drug abuse, obesity, and smoking is their self-inflicted nature. It is the individual who raises the drink, food, or cigarette to the lips or inserts the needle in the vein. Behavioral programs for the self-management of drinking have focused on all three aspects of the components involved in a situational analysis of drinking: the behavior itself, the antecedents of drinking and the consequences of drinking. The reader is referred to the excellent guidelines described by Miller and Muñoz (1976) for further examples and details.

Self-Control Through Rate Reduction. The amount of alcohol consumed is the critical variable in determining blood alcohol levels. We have also seen that the drinking pattern of people with a drinking problem differs from that of social drinkers. The object of intervention emphasizing self-control through rate reduction is to teach the person how to establish reasonable limits for drinking, how to monitor drinking behavior in the natural environment, and how to slow down drinking. A systematic plan of rate reduction has been described in a self-help manual by Miller and Muñoz (1976). This program consists of the following steps.

Setting limits. The first step is to determine reasonable blood alcohol concentrations. Tables describing the blood alcohol concentrations reached after one, two, three, and four hours of drinking according to body weight and number of drinks consumed help the client to determine for his own body weight the number of drinks that can be consumed within a certain period of time in relation to given effects (Miller and Muñoz, 1976). The effects of various blood alcohol concentrations are used as a guideline to establish a maximum blood alcohol concentration (BAC). The client is encouraged to select two different limits: (1) an upper limit on any single occasion, and (2) an amount he thinks he should set as a regular daily limit. For example, Mike drank about 30 beers, 15 mixed drinks, and 5 glasses of wine each week. He consumed 5 to 6 drinks a day, except on weekends, when he drank more heavily. He decided that his BAC should not go higher than .07. Limits selected were 4 drinks in one hour, or 6 drinks in two hours, or 6½ drinks in three hours, or 7 drinks in four hours. He then selected a regular limit by comparing his own drinking with the national average, which is about 18 to 21 drinks per week. He decided that his daily drinking should not exceed this national figure and set 3 drinks per day (not more than 21 per week) as his regular limit. Hourly BAC levels were determined by referring to tables. For example, if he limited himself to 1 drink per hour, his BAC would be almost zero.

Miller and Muñoz recommend completing a personal agreement form in which limits are identified (Figure 35). Agreements as to limits may be included in a counselor-client agreement as shown in Figure 36, later in this chapter.

A partner or buddy may be involved to help clients adhere to personal agreements. Such a person can be useful by discussing progress with the client, using positive feedback, and avoiding criticism or admonishments. The buddy can aid in devising methods for achieving greater self-control over drinking and also can share in earned rewards. As Miller and Muñoz (1976) stress, this person should not be employed as a policeman who provides penalties, since this will cause dislike of the person. Rather, self-responsibility is stressed.

Self-monitoring of drinking. An important component of

Figure 35. Personal Agreement Form

I have decided that on an *average day* I should not have more than _____drinks. (Regular Limit)

This means that in the *average week* I should not consume more than _____ drinks.

I have decided that on *any* occasion I should not have more than the following: (Absolute Limit)

        _____drinks in 1 hour, or
        _____drinks in 2 hours, or
        _____drinks in 3 hours, or
        _____drinks in 4 hours.

Signed: _____
Date: _____

Source: Miller and Muñoz (1976, p. 28).

rate reduction is keeping track of what is consumed. This can readily be done by using an index card with columns to note the date, time, type of drink, amount, and situation (Miller and Muñoz, 1976). Difficulties may occur for the client with self-monitoring, such as other people wondering what he is doing. Miller and Muñoz (1976) offer recommendations for handling such situations and illustrations of what can be said to others if recording is observed. One could, for example, seek out a private spot to record information, such as in the bathroom. One could say "I'm trying to cut down and I want to keep track of my drinks," or "It's something I'm doing for myself." As these authors point out, most people will not even notice record keeping or will readily accept such explanations.

    The client is encouraged to transfer his daily records to a weekly summary chart each Sunday so trends can be observed. This chart includes total number of drinks consumed for the week, whether he stayed within his regular limit, the highest number of drinks on any one day, the number of hours spent drinking on highest day, and whether he stayed within his occasional limit.

    Learning to drink more slowly. An emphasis on slowing down the drinking rate stems from the lower blood alcohol levels that result when the same amount of alcohol is consumed over a longer time period and from the finding that people who have trouble regulating their alcohol intake tend to drink faster. They also tend to order and consume stronger drinks such as ale, martinis, liquor (straight or on the rocks), rather than mixed drinks or beer. One way to slow down is to consume less concentrated beverages and thus to ingest less alcohol per sip. The client is encouraged to become aware of the type of drinks he consumes and which ones he tends to gulp, and to try to switch to less concentrated drinks that he tends to sip.

Taking smaller sips and spacing sips will result in a slower alcohol intake. Clients are encouraged to increase the number of sips per drink. The following guidelines (Miller and Muñoz, 1976) are offered for the number of sips in relation to type of drink.

Beverage and Amount	Sips
Small mixed drinks	6-8
Tall mixed drink	10-12
4 oz. of 12% wine	6-8
2½ oz. of 20% wine	6-8
12 oz. of beer or ale	12-14
1 oz. of liquor on rocks	6-8

Allowing at least sixty seconds between sips as well as putting the glass down and removing the hand from the glass between sips are methods recommended to break the chain of behavior of raising the glass to the lips. Clients are also encouraged to space their drinks. The guidelines they establish for their limits inform them as to how many drinks they can have in one hour, two hours, and so forth. Spacing of drinks may be facilitated by ordering nonalcoholic beverages between alcoholic drinks. Clients are encouraged to assume an experimental approach to their drinking behavior by identifying new types of drinks and noting how they react to new drinking patterns.

Learning to refuse drinks. Another important skill is learning how to refuse drinks. Examples of what to say are given to the client. One might say, "No, thank you," or "No thanks, I have just finished one." In the face of persistent efforts by others, one might repeat the original statement, "No, thanks," and elaborate on the refusal: "No, I just don't want another drink right now," or solicit the other person's help, "I'm really trying to cut down; how about helping me?" The particular situation in which the drink is offered, for example, whether the person is a stranger or a significant other such as a drinking companion or spouse, will determine the exact words that would be appropriate. The client is encouraged to practice refusing drinks if he anticipates trouble in this area. He can practice with the counselor, with a friend or alone using a tape recorder.

Self-reinforcement. As with all self-management programs, self-reinforcement is an important component of the program. Careful monitoring of drinking provides a basis for self-reinforcement. Any progress toward attainment of goals should be reinforced not only by positive self-statements, but also by offering oneself concrete rewards such as buying a favorite magazine, going to a movie, or visiting a museum. The particular reward selected must be individually tailored. The following suggestions for self-rewards are offered by Miller and Muñoz (1976, p. 55). Some material rewards that require money are *objects* (magazines, record albums, books, cosmetics, clothing, games, furniture, and so on); *food* (pastry, ice cream, fancy meals, and so on); *stepping out* (movie, restaurant, dance, play, museum, park, shopping, and so on). Rewards that require mainly time include: social time (with people to talk, play games, go somewhere, converse on the phone, kiss, make love, and so on); sit-back-and-appreciate time (for concentrating on something that is interesting, reading a book, watching television or people, reading letters, and so on); do-my-own-thing time (for things that one "never has time to do," like painting, drawing, potting, puttering, writing, building something, playing an instrument, and so on); and do-nothing time (resting, daydreaming).

Self-Control Through Environmental Planning (the Control of Antecedents). The steps described above concern the exercise of self-management skills *during* drinking. The term *environmental planning* refers to regulating the antecedents of behavior so that cues for appropriate patterns of drinking will be increased and those for inappropriate drinking will be decreased (Thoresen and Mahoney, 1974; Miller and Muñoz,

1976). The client learns to identify the cues for appropriate and inappropriate drinking and to regulate these through preplanning; that is, by arranging for the presence of cues for appropriate drinking and for the decrease or elimination of cues for inappropriate drinking. Rearranging antecedents, also known as *stimulus control*, is also an essential ingredient of self-management programs for smoking, overeating, and drug abuse. Antecedents for drinking may include special places, certain people, times, or activities, as well as emotional factors. The information collected during self-monitoring provides descriptions of relevant antecedents.

Places where drinking occurs. Drinking is more likely to occur in some places than in others. Some drink mainly in bars, while others drink at home. The self-monitoring forms will indicate the situations in which drinking tends to occur. It is helpful to use a summary sheet to note times and situations in which drinking occurred during a certain time period (such as a week) and drinks consumed in each.

Self-monitoring will also help to identify places in which drinking is usually controlled. Ideally, the client would then try to avoid (stay away from) those places where he tends to overdrink and to increase the frequency of visits to places where drinking is controlled. Miller and Muñoz (1976) encourage their clients to think of staying away from such places for awhile as a "vacation," until the client develops self-control skills that will enable the control of drinking in these situations.

Miller and Muñoz (1976) recognize that clients may not be willing to forgo visits to favorite drinking spots and, in lieu of this, recommend altering the environment within such places, since it is easier to establish new behavior patterns in novel stimulus environments. Such rearrangement of the environment removes some of the cues for overdrinking and new cues will hopefully become associated with moderate drinking. For example, if the client has a favorite table or stool in a bar, he could move to a new one or take somebody along who will make it less likely that he will overdrink. He could go at a different time of day, or different day of the week and order different types of drinks. He could also change the environment around at home by moving furniture, changing the lighting, sitting in a different chair and changing what he drinks.

People with whom the client drinks. Self-monitoring will also indicate *who* accompanies the drinking client. Most problem drinkers ingest alcohol in the presence of other drinkers (Cahalan, Cisin, and Crossley, 1969). Clients are encouraged to identify and seek out those with whom they tend to regulate drinking and to identify and take "a vacation" from those with whom they tend to overdrink. If the client is unwilling to avoid those who encourage problematic drinking, he is asked to try to find out *why* he tends to drink more with certain people. Perhaps certain people "push" drinks on him and he has difficulty saying no; perhaps certain people make him anxious and drinking dulls this anxiety (Miller and Muñoz, 1976).

Times when drinking occurs. Self-monitoring will indicate the times of the day and the days of the week when drinking tends to take place and will enable alternative planning for these times. Some drinkers only start drinking at home, after work. Others may drink throughout the day. Some people only drink on the weekends, whereas others drink on a daily basis. And there is the well-known binge drinker, who disappears every six months for a week or so, during which heavy drinking occurs. Paydays may be especially problematic in that they often occur on Friday when one does not have to worry about getting up the next day.

A client may decide not to cash his paycheck right after work (Miller and Muñoz, 1976), or he could only take so much money to the bar and arrange a ride home at a certain hour. He may make an agreement with himself to honor the maximum limit he has set for himself during certain time periods, and to switch to soft drinks when this is reached. Time spent at the bar could be reduced or drinks carefully spaced. All of these efforts involve preplanning. Some involve not having resources to purchase drinks (only having a certain amount of money). Others arrange the interruption of the chain of behavior involved in drinking—for example, making an appointment at a certain hour. The latter heightens the possibility of controlled drinking if the appointment requires a certain degree of sobriety. Other methods involve decisions concerning limits on drinking and selection of alternative behaviors that discourage drinking.

Activities related to drinking. Many games available in drinking establishments such as bars involve "waiting time" when it is easy to take sips of drinks to "pass the time." Waiting for a turn to play pool, for example, may be a high-probability time for sipping drinks (Miller and Muñoz, 1976). The client is encouraged to try to identify activities that are incompatible with drinking, such as talking to someone or dancing, as well as those that facilitate drinking, such as watching television and playing cards.

Emotional factors. The relationship of drinking to stress reduction has already been noted. The client is encouraged to identify feeling states that seem to be associated with overdrinking. These might include fear of social evaluation; anger, perhaps experienced when the client is thwarted and does not express negative feelings; depression and disappointment resulting from sone imagined or actual loss; conflict with some significant other; indecision in relation to an important matter, such as whether to leave a spouse; or boredom from not having anything to do. Alcohol may remove the discomfort of such feelings. Again, self-monitoring will reveal feeling states that have often preceded drinking. Alternative behaviors must be developed that will either eliminate such emotional antecedents or will allow them to be handled in ways other than drinking.

Self-Control Through the Development of Alternative Behaviors. After antecedent emotions are identified, careful planning is necessary to identify alternative behaviors related to each source of emotion.

Learning how to feel relaxed. Some clients state that drinking is the only way they can feel relaxed; that, after a couple of drinks, they unwind and can start to enjoy themselves. The client can be trained in one or more alternative means for achieving this state such as progressive muscle relaxation, deep breathing, or other types of positive self-instructions.

Learning how to influence anxiety related to specific stressors. Anxiety, either rational or irrational, may be associated with drinking. A client may be worried and anxious because he has lost his job, is having trouble finding another one, and sees his family facing increasing privation. Drinking may decrease his concerns. Another client may unrealistically worry about losing what is in fact a very secure position. Realistic and unrealistic worries must be separated and self-management skills offered to the client that will allow him to exert more influence over his anxiety. If anxiety is severe and specific stressors are involved, a formal program of desensitization may be employed. A high frequency of negative self-statements may be associated with stress, and the client can be trained to offer positive self-statements.

Perhaps the client has realistic worries, but makes the mistake of thinking about these much of the time, even when he is in no state to make a decision, or worries in lieu of taking actions that would help him make decisions. He may need self-management skills that allow him to exert stimulus control over his thoughts; that is, to think about certain topics only at certain times and places.

Learning to solve problems. Drinking may be associated with trying to arrive at some solution or resolution of a problem. It may serve to remove thoughts regarding the necessity for making a decision as well as the frustration induced by faulty problem-solving skills. It may be necessary to offer the client problem-solving skills.

Learning how to deal with situations requiring negative assertion. Frustration and anger may result from not maintaining one's rights; for example, taking on an unfair amount of work, or tolerating undue harrassment from a significant other. Perhaps only when the client has assumed some unfair responsibility, caused by failure to say no, does drinking occur. The development of assertive behaviors for these situations will remove this antecedent of drinking.

Learning how to deal with situations requiring positive assertion. Drinking may be related to social isolation, which, in turn, is related to a lack of appropriate social skills for meeting and maintaining contacts with others. Perhaps the client does not have ready topics at hand to discuss; perhaps he or she is not sure how to ask to see someone again and loses contact with potential friends; perhaps he or she offers little in the way of reinforcement to others when they are speaking. Appropriate social skills may have to be developed to enhance rewarding social encounters.

Learning how to deal with family conflicts. Lack of negotiation skills for resolving differences among family members may cause recurrent marital or parent-child conflicts that lead to drinking. Repeated failures to solve family problems may result in avoidance of the spouse, with increased amounts of time spent away from home as the reinforcing value of the spouse dwindles compared to the aversive experience now offered. It may be necessary to train the client in positive negotiation skills.

Learning how to deal with depression. As with other labels for vague emotional states, the specific behavioral referents for *depression* must be identified, as well as related factors. Events related to a feeling of depression could include conflict over a decision; recurrent fighting with a spouse; failure to initiate desired contacts; or failure to arrange future contacts with a person. Thoughts may also be related to depression. A lack of positive self-instructions and a high frequency of negative self-statements could induce a "down" feeling, as could a low frequency of pleasurable events.

Learning how to handle boredom. The same factors related to dealing with depression apply to boredom, the uncomfortable feeling of having nothing interesting to do. Judicious scheduling of enjoyable activities for times associated with being bored may be required.

Learning to identify alternative behaviors. Instructions should be provided to help the client identify the setting events for heavy drinking and to select socially acceptable alternative responses in these situations (Sobell and Sobell, 1972). The client can be asked to generate a list of possible alternative behaviors in each situation and to evaluate the likely outcomes of each in terms of probable long-term consequences and appropriateness for the given situation. Efforts should also be made to construct situations where he can experiment with and practice various alternative responses so that discrimination between effective and ineffective reactions would be enhanced. The following example of the generation and evaluation of alternatives is offered by Sobell and Sobell (1972, pp. 19-20).

Subject R. R. was divorced for eighteen months prior to this hospitalization and his wife admitted that she had assumed that the divorce action would stop his drinking so that they could remarry. However, R. R., who was fifty years old, spent the next eighteen months living with a young common-law wife. During this time R. R. incurred thousands of dollars worth of debts and his drinking also increased. About the time R. R. entered Patton [hospital], his exwife contacted him and suggested reconciliation. As had been the case prior to his divorce, his exwife then began to dictate his life—handling the debts, when they would remarry, where he would work, and so on. For R. R., an ineffectiveness at asserting himself was elucidated as one of the setting events that led to his heavy drinking and eventual divorce. In addition, R. R. now had at least two other matters to handle: a common-law wife and the considerable debts incurred. An example of the interfering behaviors of R. R.'s exwife is that while he was still in the hospital she took it upon herself, without consulting R. R., to contact his finance and insurance companies about the debts, incidentally mentioning that he was now a patient in a "state mental hospital."

In one of the early treatment sessions, R. R. discussed a desire to return to his exwife but realized that changes would be necessary in both of their behavior patterns in order to prevent the marriage from deteriorating once again. With the therapist, he discussed four of the various alternative ways in which he could respond to his present situation:

1. He could return to his common-law wife and attempt to pay off his incurred debts.
2. He could declare bankruptcy and try to live alone.
3. He could return to his exwife, remarry her, and continue his passive life.
4. He could return to his exwife and assume some of the responsibility within the family structure.

R. R. then analyzed the four delineated alternative responses for their probable long-term consequences:

1. He realized that his original association with his young common-law wife was meant to spite his first wife, and that he had let his common-law

wife spend exorbitant amounts of money in order that he could impress and keep her.

2. R. R. did not believe that declaring bankruptcy would be a feasible alternative, because, as a fifty-year-old aerospace technician who had not worked for two years as a result of government cutbacks, it would be extremely difficult for him to find work and live alone.

3. It was obvious to R. R. that returning to his ex-wife under the same conditions that existed prior to his divorce would probably precipitate his returning to his heavy drinking shortly after discharge.

4. In order to return to his exwife and avoid a resumption of heavy drinking, R. R. knew that it would be necessary to confront her concerning her assertiveness and impulsiveness, both of which had functioned as setting events for his previous drinking. He also realized that he could not depend on his wife to decrease these behaviors, and that he would have to learn effective ways of interacting with her and handling problem situations.

R. R. selected the last alternative as being the most beneficial in terms of long-term consequences, and portions of succeeding treatment sessions were devoted to training him in the desired behaviors. Some of the sessions were conducted with R. R.'s exwife present, at which time they both were able to discuss their marriage and the difficulty he had in handling her assertiveness. They also discussed specific ways in which he could effectively respond to situations that might occur and, in fact, he practiced many of these suggested responses during the sessions.

Clients who did well in a behavioral program using the above training as one component seemed to learn how to carry out a situational analysis in other situations, including identification of specific antecedents, generating alternative reactions, evaluating each, and selecting for practice the one that had the most beneficial consequences. One example of this application of skills to new situations follows (Sobell and Sobell, 1972): "J. A. was able to analyze an experienced desire to drink as resulting from the fact that his brother was living in his house, free-loading off of him and attempting to seduce his wife. J. A. then generated a number of possible responses to this situation, including migrating to Chicago. After analyzing the various alternatives in terms of long-range consequences, he decided upon confronting his brother and demanding that he move out of the house. To J. A.'s amazement, his brother did move out, and J. A.'s marital relationship improved considerably thereafter" (Sobell and Sobell, 1972, p. 60).

Arranging Contingencies in the Natural Environment That Support Sobriety

Some clients may be able to establish and maintain sobriety by learning additional self-management skills; others may also require increased community-based reinforcement for sobriety. Sources of reinforcement for drinking and available self-management skills will influence which mix of procedures is selected.

A Community Reinforcement Approach. One of the most innovative and effective intervention procedures for decreasing alcohol abuse entails maximizing the natural deterrents of alcoholism, which include interference with other sources of satisfaction such as loss of a job, friends or family, and the inability to engage in a variety of recreational activities (Hunt and Azrin, 1973). Since a result of alcohol intake is postponement or omission of positive events, the deterrents to alcohol use can be maximized to the extent that the positive events postponed are of high quality and frequency and are varied in their nature.

The purpose of the community reinforcement approach is to rearrange vocational, family, and social reinforcers of the alcoholic such that "time out" from these reinforcers will occur if drinking takes place. This is accomplished by enriching these sources of reinforcement and then making continued access to them contingent on sobriety. Referrals are made for any special problems such as legal difficulties the client may have. A broad focus is employed in identifying possible reinforcers postponed, including vocational, recreational, social, and family events. The results obtained using this approach with a group of hospital-

ized alcoholics, a group that has a very poor prognosis, indicated that these men drank less, worked more, and spent more
time with their families and out of institutions than did men in
a matched control group. For example, the mean percentage of
time spent drinking was 14 percent for the men (there were
only men) in the program and 79 percent for a control group
that experienced the usual hospital treatment procedure. Unemployment was 5 percent for those in the program, 62 percent
for the control. Gains were maintained at a six-month follow-
up. Each of the components of this program are described in
the following sections.

Vocational counseling. Clients who did not have a job received intensive job counseling. The process of job finding was
viewed as requiring a number of complex skills best learned in a
structured situation emphasizing client motivation, maintenance
of behavior, feedback, imitation, and practice (Azrin, Flores,
and Kaplan, 1975; Azrin, 1976). The client's family was viewed
as a strong source of support and assistance, and a letter was
sent, to each family member or person who lived with the
client, that explained how that person could help the job
seeker. Suggestions included limiting use of the phone by other
family members, helping with transportation, offering emotional support, and making suggestions for job search. Job seeking was considered to be a full-time activity and help was
offered to the client to aid him to schedule his time. In addition
to seeking family support as an aid to alleviating discouragement, commentaries from former job seekers who were successful in obtaining employment were played on audiotape for the
clients. Counselor support and support from other group members were also provided. Job seeking was considered a group
effort, and group sessions permitted use of a buddy procedure,
cooperation in arranging transportation, role playing, supervision of manner of telephone inquiry, review of resources, and
sharing job leads. Clients were encouraged to consider many
types of jobs. Self-help was emphasized, so that if a job was subsequently lost the client would know how to go about obtaining
another one. Written instructions concerning dress and grooming were given to the client and discussed. A variety of procedures were used to identify job leads, including talking to

friends and relatives, placing a situation-wanted advertisement, and *carefully* perusing help-wanted ads. Clients were trained how to keep helpful records. Role playing was used to rehearse appropriate interview behavior. Release from the hospital took place as soon as the client obtained a job. This program has been found to be highly successful in helping clients to obtain employment. Comparison of a group of clients who sought jobs using this program with a control group indicated that, within two months, 90 percent of the counseled job seekers obtained employment, as compared to 55 percent of noncounseled job seekers (Azrin, Flores, and Kaplan, 1975).

Marital and family counseling. This aspect of the procedure "attempted to (1) provide reinforcement for the alcoholic to be a functioning marital partner, (2) provide reinforcement for the spouse for maintaining the marital relation and (3) to make the drinking of alcohol incompatible with the improved marital relation" (Hunt and Azrin, 1973, p. 94; see also Azrin, Naster, and Jones, 1973). The Marriage Adjustment Inventory (Manson and Lerner, 1962) was employed to identify problem areas. The husband and wife met together with the counselor in order to identify specific activities in each problem area that the spouse agreed to perform to make the partner happy, such as preparing meals, listening to the spouse with undivided attention, picking up the children from school, redistributing finances, engaging in sexual activities of a particular type or at a minimal frequency, visiting relatives together, and spending a night out together. Clients were requested to read a marriage manual, which offered specific instructions about sex (Ellis, 1966), to encourage communication about sexual interaction. Complete sobriety was a requirement by all wives as one of the agreements.

Problems encountered included a disinterest in identifying what would make the marriage more pleasant; doubt on the part of wives that they could withhold pleasant events following drinking; a refusal of a spouse to initiate some unaccustomed activity; the identification of new problems; and the decision that agreements already made were not desirable. Attempts to identify potential positive changes included suggesting satisfactions that other couples enjoyed; the articulation of possible satisfactions in specific terms; asking each client what an ideal marriage would be like; and inquiring as to what satisfactions they shared in the past or expected to share when they were first married. Difficulty in withholding pleasant events was aided by requesting the spouse to discontinue physical and social contact with the client. In the extreme case, this involved moving out of the house. Refusal to offer new activities, such as a different type of sexual behavior, was overcome by applying reinforcer sampling (Ayllon and Azrin, 1968a), in which clients were encouraged to try it only for a limited period of time, such as a week. Training clients how to create agreements of their own helped when new problems arose or when clients were disinterested in continuing existing contracts. In some cases, both the client and his wife stated that they had no desire to return to the marriage. Informing them that no attempt would be made to have them live together until distressing situations were removed helped to alleviate this source of resistance to counseling efforts.

One of the most innovative aspects of this community reinforcement program was the arrangement of "synthetic" or foster families for clients who were unmarried and who did not live with their parents. "Families" were composed of people who might have some natural reason for maintaining contact with the client, such as relatives, an employer, or minister. These people were encouraged to invite the client over to dinner on a regular basis and to expect the client to help with chores or offer other reasonable services. Here too, sobriety was a requisite for these pleasant events. If a client lived with his parents, similar arrangements were made as described between spouses.

Social counseling. Friends of the client often consist of other heavy drinkers. The aim of the social counseling program was to increase social interaction with friends, relatives, and community groups who did not tolerate drinking and to reduce interaction with those who encouraged drinking. In order to provide an alternative setting for enjoyable social interaction without drinking, a tavern was converted into a self-supporting social club for the clients. A variety of activities was provided there, including dancing, card playing, talking with female companions, attending picnics and fish fries, watching movies, and playing bingo. Saturday night was the club's main meeting night. Wives were invited to attend and clients were encouraged to invite friends as guests. The client paid his own membership dues after a period of one month. Sobriety was a requisite for entrance into the club and no drinking was allowed in the club itself.

Reinforcer-access counseling. Enhanced adjustment and pleasure in work, family, and social life are often hindered by a lack of access to facilities such as newspapers and telephones as well as by deficits in basic social skills, such as introducing interesting topics to talk about. Access to such facilities was arranged. Telephones were installed in the homes of clients, often at project expense, during the first month, and daily newspapers were delivered free of charge for the first month. Access to a telephone made it much easier to call others to arrange social contacts or just chat, and reading the daily newspaper offered topics of conversation. It was hoped that payment for these facilities would be eventually assumed by the men themselves. Clients were helped to obtain driver's licenses to give them easier access to a variety of events. Increased access to such facilities would, it was hoped, increase the attractiveness of activities other than drinking and encourage clients to maintain jobs so they could continue paying for these services.

A counselor visited the client once or twice a week for the first month following discharge from the hospital, to remind the client of alternative reinforcers, help with any problems that may have arisen, and check on the progress of the client's sobriety, work, and social life. Counselors visited twice a month after the first month and then once a month. Interestingly enough, time out from positive events as a result of drinking rarely took place since clients rarely drank. However, clients stated that they believed that such time out would occur if they did drink and that anticipation of such consequences helped them to stay sober.

A modified form of this community reinforcement approach for decreasing alcohol intake was found to be even more successful than the one described (Azrin, 1976). A two-year follow-up indicated that initial benefits were maintained. Additional components included a buddy system, in which each client had a peer advisor who met with him regularly; an early warning system, entailing daily reports to identify stressful situations that might lead to drinking; group counseling; written contracts; and a positive motivation program to assure self-administration of Disulfiram (Antabuse).

Contingent Use of Social Services. A creative use of community reinforcers to maintain sobriety was also demonstrated with alcoholics convicted of repeated public drunkenness charges (Miller, 1975). Here too, positive incentives were made available contingent on sobriety. Twenty men were studied. Each had a minimum of eight arrests for public drunkenness in the last twelve months; had a sporadic work history; resided in a rooming house, hotel, or mission; and was unmarried, the majority being divorced. Social services usually available whether or not clients drank were made contingent on sobriety. Sobriety was assessed by agency workers and clients' employers by observations of gross intoxication, including odor of alcohol on the breath, staggered gait, and slurred speech. In addition, random breath-analysis tests were given once every five days. If blood alcohol concentration was over 10 mg/100 ml of blood volume or there were signs of drinking, goods and services from the agencies were withheld for five days.

Goods and services desired by these men included housing, employment, medical care, clothing, meals, cigarettes, and counseling. Special arrangements were made to permit men to live and eat at the Salvation Army housing facility for the duration of the program, dependent on maintaining sobriety. Both services were removed for a period of five days if sobriety was not maintained. Employment for clients was sought through a local agency that provided unskilled jobs on a day-to-day basis and through the state employment agency. Employment was also terminated for five days if the client drank. Necessary medical care was continued independent of sobriety; nonessential care such as dental treatment was not. If clients were eligible for veterans' assistance, they received canteen booklets that could be traded for cigarettes, meals, or clothing at the Veterans Administration Hospital, contingent on sobriety.

Results obtained with this group were compared with those of a group who received the traditional services of the skid row community agencies, that is, who received services whether intoxicated or sober. Men in the behavioral program had a lower arrest rate for public drunkenness (.30 for a two-month period, compared to 1.30) as well as a higher number of hours worked per week (12 hours compared to 3.2). Eight out of ten subjects in the behavioral program were arrested at least once for public drunkenness prior to the program, whereas only three were arrested afterwards. The number of subjects in the control group who were arrested at least once increased from eight to nine.

The populations employed in both studies described (those who have been hospitalized repeatedly for alcoholism and those who have a recurrent arrest record for public drunkenness) are notoriously resistant to efforts to alter their drinking. These successful programs were multifaceted, identifying and dealing with a range of relevant antecedents and consequences for drinking and sobriety. The usual procedure of providing a wide variety of services and goods whether or not a person is drunk and often providing more services to clients when they are drunk than when they are sober is often countertherapeutic and may actually help to maintain the chronic inebriate's drinking patterns (Miller, 1975). It seems only reasonable to utilize available reinforcers contingent on appropriate behavior. When appropriate contexts are not available, they can often be created, as illustrated by the conversion of a tavern into a social club and by the creation of "families" for those who have none (Hunt and Azrin, 1973).

Behavioral Contracting. Written contracts between the client and the counselor or between the client and a family member have been employed to reduce problematic drinking. Contracts provide a systematic way to schedule the mutual exchange of reinforcers so that positive consequences are provided for appropriate drinking patterns or for complete abstinence, and costs are imposed for inappropriate drinking. A recent report in which contracting was employed involved a forty-four-year-old married male (Miller, 1972). A major source of marital conflict related to his drinking, which had increased substantially over the past two years. Self-monitoring for a two-week baseline period revealed his preferred drink to be bourbon and that he consumed seven to eight drinks per day (defined as one and a half ounces of alcohol either straight or mixed). These data were corroborated by reports from his wife. The couple decided that between one and three drinks per day was acceptable, and the husband agreed to this limit and to consume these drinks in the presence of his wife prior to the evening meal, unless they went out for the evening or entertained at home. A fine of twenty dollars, payable to his wife, to be spent by her as frivolously as possible, as well as withdrawal of her attention (she would leave his presence immediately) was to follow drinking in any other situation, as determined by observation, liquor on his breath, or "drunken comportment."

The contract also stipulated that the wife would pay a fine of the same amount to the husband if she engaged in any negative verbal or nonverbal reactions to her husband's drinking. In addition, contingent on such behavior, he would immediately withdraw his attention. The husband agreed to increase attentive behaviors toward his wife when she engaged in noncritical, nonalcoholic-related conversation. She, in turn, agreed to provide attention and affection to her husband whenever he voluntarily limited his drinking (stopped after one or two drinks or did not drink at all). Although both found anticipation of giving twenty dollars to the other a highly unpleasant event, the couple could afford it, since they both worked.

Only after the husband incurred a few fines did drinking decrease to below acceptable limits. This stabilized at about two drinks per day by the thirtieth day and as drinking decreased, both the husband and wife reported a more enjoyable relationship. A six-month follow-up, during which the client monitored the number of drinks for ten days, revealed a maintenance of positive effects. In this case, the undesirable effects of drinking were confined to the marital interaction and intervention was directed to this one area. If additional areas are involved, interventions that relate to these should be employed.

The following case offers an example of a contract between a client and his wife and a counselor (reported in Stein and Gambrill, 1976b). The family came to the attention of the court because of allegations of child abuse against the father regarding Steven, his nine-year-old son (Stein, Gambrill, and Wiltse,

1974). Mrs. W. was not involved in the incident. The child was removed from the parent's home after the abuse incident and was made a court dependent, leaving four other children at home. Both the parents and Steven stated that they would like to be reunited. Assessment focused on identification of factors that were related to the child abuse. Abusive behavior was facilitated by frustration with the children's failure to complete chores and that this was aggravated by the father's drinking. One goal of the program was to decrease the father's drinking from 7 drinks per day to two drinks per day. It was observed by both the counselor and Mrs. W. that the father did not show the effects of alcohol until after a third drink. Mr. W. said that drinking after he came home from work helped him relax and quenched his thirst. (A separate program was established to increase chore completion.)

Alternative ways to achieve both goals were selected and included in a contract (Figure 36). Positive consequences for controlled drinking included discussing his job with his wife and earning time alone. Mrs. W. agreed to have nonalcoholic beverages available, to refrain from speaking with her husband about his job if he drank more than two drinks in the evening, and to keep a record of "time alone" that he earned. In exchange for this, she earned free time (Figure 37). Separate programs were designed to increase the children's chore completion and to set up a visiting schedule between Steven and his parents, including arrangement for counselor observation of parent-child interaction during a portion of these visits for assessment purposes.

Over an eleven-week period, the father's drinking decreased to an average of two and a half drinks a day and then declined to zero, and Mrs. W.'s free time increased from zero to eight hours per week. Following three and a half months of intervention, Steven was returned to his family. Follow-up contact maintained for six months indicated that parent-child interaction was satisfactory and drinking remained at a zero level.

Contingency contracting has been successfully employed among outpatient alcoholics to maintain Disulfiram injection (Bigelow, Strickler, Liebson, and Griffiths, 1976). A security deposit was made by the client, portions of which were forfeited for each failure to visit the clinic. Pointing out the bene-

Figure 36. Plan to Reduce Alcohol Consumption

The goal of this modification program is to reduce the number of drinks that the father consumes each day from seven drinks per day to two drinks per day. The father states that his drinking serves two functions: (1) to quench his thirst, and (2) to assist him in relaxing. This program is designed to make the father's drinking of alcoholic beverages contingent on his drinking of nonalcoholic beverages to quench his thirst and on his engaging in other relaxing behaviors while he is at home. (Note: The father's drinking occurs primarily at home.)

Before the father can drink an alcoholic beverage, he will first

Step 1. Quench his thirst by drinking a nonalcoholic beverage such as orange juice, Pepsi Cola, or lemonade, and

Step 2. Attempt to relax by either watching television, reading, or taking a bath.

If he meets those two conditions, he can then drink an alcoholic beverage. The total number of drinks per day may not exceed two. For complying with this program, the father will receive the following reinforcers.

1. If he complies with Steps 1 and 2 above, his wife will allow him to discuss his job with her; and

2. For each day he has two drinks or less, he will earn one hour of time alone.

The mother agrees:

1. To have nonalcoholic beverages readily available in the refrigerator;

2. Not to engage in discussion about her husband's job unless he has complied with Steps 1 and 2 of his modification program; and

3. To keep records of "time alone" that he has earned and to negotiate with him as to when that time will be used.

The social worker agrees:

1. To monitor the program during weekly interviews with the parents;

2. To discuss any problematic areas in the implementation of the program, and, if necessary, make alterations in the program; and

3. Not to allow the father to discuss his job unless he has complied with Steps 1 and 2 of his program on the day of the interview.

Source: Stein and Gambrill (1976b, pp. 181-182).

fits of such ingestion decreases resistance to such intervention. In the community-based program developed by Azrin (1976), significant others were placed in the position of helping to remind the client to take this medication rather than in a "watchdog" position. Also, Antabuse was presented "as a chemical time-delay device which gave the client time to think over a

Figure 37. Plan to Increase Mother's Free Time

The desired outcome of this plan is to provide the mother with time alone, as a respite from child-care responsibilities and as an opportunity for her to pursue activities of her own choosing. Time alone will be contingent on the mother's monitoring the father's drinking program.

The mother agrees to:

1. Have nonalcoholic beverages readily available in the refrigerator;
2. Keep records of "time alone" that he has earned; and
3. Reinforce him by allowing him to discuss his job if he has complied with Steps 1 and 2 [see Figure 36] of his drinking program.

If the mother complies with this program, she will earn two (2) hours per week of time alone.

The father agrees:

1. To negotiate with _____ as to when she will use her two hours of time alone each week; and
2. During her "time alone," to be responsible for managing the home, including caring for the children and other household chores.

The social worker will review this program at his weekly interviews with the parents and attempt to facilitate its implementation and maintenance.

Source: Stein and Gambrill (1976b, p. 183).

decision rather than to act impulsively" (Azrin, 1976, p. 343) and resort to drinking. Routine taking of Antabuse was aided by linking this with a well-established habit or event, such as mealtime, and the client was to take the Antabuse only in the presence of a spouse or friend.

Aversive Conditioning

A presentation of the use of behavioral methods with alcohol abuse would not be complete without discussing the use of aversive conditioning, in which there is an attempt to pair drinking with aversive consequences such as shock or nausea in order to suppress drinking (Davidson, 1974). Both avoidance conditioning, in which the client can avoid the aversive event, as well as escape conditioning, in which alcohol is paired with an aversive event, have been used. Recent efforts are more sophisticated in their application of behavioral principles than

earlier efforts, and are often included as but one aspect of a
total intervention program, which may include procedures described above, such as developing alternative behaviors (Sobell
and Sobell, 1972). Both actual as well as imagined aversive
events have been employed. The use of aversive conditioning
alone has not been especially promising. For example in a
recent study, 31 percent of the subjects who experienced an
aversive conditioning program were abstinent after one year,
compared to only 7 percent of a hospital control group (Vogler,
Ferstl, Kraemer, and Brengelmann, 1975). This percentage fell
to 20 percent after one year. As the authors of this study note,
"Electrical aversion conditioning techniques in and of themselves are not likely to generate profound changes for more than
a moderate percentage of drinkers. Those who do succeed probably receive adventitious reinforcement for their sobriety"
(Vogler and others, 1975, p. 173).

   The Use of Actual Aversive Events. Pairing nausea with
alcohol appears to be more effective than pairing shock with
alcohol, although there have been no carefully controlled
studies to date. It has been argued that nausea is a more "bio-
logically appropriate" stimulus for successfully developing a
conditioned aversion to the taste and smell of alcohol than
shock (Wilson and Davison, 1969). The client is administered a
substance such as emetine, and instructed to concentrate on the
sight, smell, and thought of alcohol, and then to taste and swal-
low it (Lemere and Voegtlin, 1950). A variety of alcoholic
beverages are included in this procedure. Over a one- to ten-year
follow-up period, 51 percent of 4,096 clients remained abstinent. Inclusion of clients who became controlled drinkers
would enhance this rate. The lack of a control group makes it
impossible to determine whether these results were attributable
to the aversive conditioning procedure or to some other treatment component, such as hospitalization or even spontaneous
remission. Middle- and upper-class clients who were older and
who had a stable employment history had the most favorable
prognosis. Booster sessions during the first year increased the
likelihood of abstinence (Voegtlin, Lemere, Broz, and O'Hallaren, 1942).

   Shock has been employed in a number of studies with

less impressive results (Nathan, 1976). Studies combining aversive conditioning with other behavioral procedures indicate that aversive conditioning was not critical (Sobell and Sobell, 1972). Conditioning has been carried out in specially created "bars" and "home situations" in hospitals, to simulate the context in which drinking takes place, on the rationale that the more similar the conditioning context to real life settings, the greater the generalization of effects (for example, see Sobell and Sobell, 1972). These efforts are preceded by a careful analysis of each client's drinking pattern, including identification of his favorite drinks. Avoidance conditioning, rather than escape conditioning, was employed, since it was thought that this paradigm would facilitate establishment of self-control skills. Seventeen sessions were held, during which the client sat at the "bar" or in the "home environment," depending on where each subject did most of his drinking. Drinking responses were punished on a variable-ratio schedule, in which a variable (unpredictable) number of drinks resulted in a shock. This schedule of punishment generates behavior that is resistant to extinction. Nondrinker subjects (those who selected abstinence as a goal) were shocked on a variable-ratio schedule for ordering any type of drink and a shock might also occur from any time the glass was touched until it was released. (The drink could be consumed.) At later sessions, if a nondrinker had not ordered any drinks in prior sessions, he was offered a free one (no shock would be paired with this) at the beginning of the session. If he refused this and poured it down the sink, shocks were withheld, and a free drink was offered every fifteen minutes under the same conditions. If the drink was accepted, shock contingencies were reinstated.

Clients who had selected the goal of becoming a controlled drinker received a shock on a variable-ratio schedule for ordering a straight drink; for taking a sip larger than one sixth of the total volume of the mixed drink, one twelfth of a 12-ounce beer, or either 2½ ounces (20 percent alcohol content) or 4 ounces (12 percent alcohol) of wine (glasses were marked by strips of tape that divided them into equal sip portions); ordering a drink within twenty minutes of having previously ordered a drink; or ordering more than three drinks. Selection of behaviors to pair with shock was in accord with the differences in drinking patterns that have been identified between social drinkers and problem drinkers. If more than three drinks were consumed during a session, the procedures in effect for the non-drinker subjects were instated.

During sessions practice was also offered in resisting pressure to drink, and subjects who had selected the goal of becoming controlled drinkers were educated concerning different types of drinks. This program also placed heavy emphasis on the identification of the setting events for heavy drinking for each client and training the client in alternative socially acceptable responses in these situations. Setting events were defined as those that immediately preceded or accompanied heavy drinking in the recent past as well as those identified to have such a role through self-monitoring. Another component of this program consisted of showing the client videotapes of his behavior both while drunk and sober. This was appropriately entitled videotape "contrast." Also, each client was given a card to keep in his wallet with a list of "do's" (such as examples of appropriate reactions in a certain situation) and "don'ts" (such as, "Don't drink after a quarrel with your wife").

It is not possible to identify the special role of each particular component of this multifaceted endeavor in the successful results achieved; however, the role of the aversive conditioning aspect is questionable, because of the failure to find generalized suppression of drinking during probe sessions when shock contingencies were removed. As mentioned previously, the authors felt that training in situational analysis was especially important.

The results with aversive conditioning in relation to suppressing alcohol intake are equivocal. Other procedures that do not employ aversive conditioning are available that have yielded more promising results. In consideration of the unpleasant nature of undergoing aversive conditioning, these can be selected as procedures of choice.

The Use of Aversive Imagery. Symbolic procedures have included all the various paradigms that have been included in aversive conditioning using actual events. Thus, the thought of drinking can be paired with an imagined aversive event (classical conditioning), relief from an imagined aversive event can be paired with refraining from drinking (aversion relief), or avoidance of an imagined aversive event can follow refraining. The overall results of these procedures has not been impressive (O'Leary and Wilson, 1975), although individual case reports have seemed promising (see, for example, Cautela, 1970c). As with aversive-conditioning procedures employing actual events, more promising alternatives are available. A symbolic procedure could be combined with other procedures, such as training the client in appropriate self-control skills or arranging contingencies in the natural environment which will support sobriety. Although rendering the "ultimate aversive consequences" of drinking more current provides a possible intervention mode, this has not been reported in the published literature.

Covert sensitization. In covert sensitization, a behavior to be decreased (such as drinking) is paired in the imagination with an aversive event (Cautela, 1966). It is hoped that through this pairing the behavior will become aversive and the client will avoid (refrain from) the undesirable behavior. Thus the aim of this procedure is opposite that of desensitization, in which one wishes to decrease anxiety in the presence of a particular stressor and increase approach behavior to this. The advantages of covert sensitization are that any type of relevant event can be presented, since the imagination is employed for its representation and the client can carry out sessions at home after careful instructions have been provided.

In order to employ this procedure, it is first necessary to gather an explicit description of the problematic behavior and the events that surround this. It is best to write down or record the description of these events, so that they can be presented in rich detail to the client during covert sensitization sessions. It is also necessary to identify an aversive event that can be imagined. This must be individually tailored for each client since each person is terrified or nauseated by different events.

As originally designed (Cautela, 1966, 1967), imagined nausea was employed, increasing the symptoms of nausea as the person approached the maladaptive behavior; the client was trained in relaxation; and a relaxed state arranged prior to presentation of the first scene. Requisites for the use of this procedure include the ability of the client to imagine situations related to the maladaptive behavior, as well as the aversive event, with some degree of emotional clarity. Some clients are unable to experience nausea when this is described. Other aversive events, such as snakes or maggots, may be employed.

The aversive event may be paired with various components of the chain of thoughts, feelings, and behavior that may be involved in drinking. For example, Anant (1968) first paired suggestions of feeling sick and vomiting with imagined drinking, and then with the desire to take a drink, and, finally, made the relief from nausea contingent on the client imagining successful determination to control his drinking urges. The following case gives an example of a scene used in covert sensitization. The client was a twenty-nine-year-old nurse who said that drinking "helped her get through a date or a party or being home in her apartment" (Cautela, 1966, p. 36). She experienced hangovers the next day and would then take a few drinks to calm herself down. Desensitization was employed to decrease anxiety in social situations, but even though she could imagine scenes without discomfort there was no transfer of effects to actual situations. Cautela (1966) reasoned that drinking was still associated with other events in social situations, and that when these events cued the urge to have a drink, this led to anxiety, since she thought she "had" to have a drink. Covert sensitization was employed to render the drinking in social situations aversive and thus change the function of these environmental events.

> She was asked to relax and indicate by raising her index finger when she felt completely relaxed. She was asked to signal when she could do this vividly. After she gave the signal the patient was told: "Now I want you to imagine that you ask the waitress to give you your favorite drink. She brings the drink. Just as you reach for the drink you start to feel sick to your stomach. As you hold the glass in your hand you feel yourself about to vomit. As you are just about to put the glass to your lips you vomit. It comes out of your mouth all over the table and the floor. It is a real mess. When you can visualize the whole scene clearly and feel a little sick to your stomach, raise your finger. The pa-

tient raised her finger about ten seconds after the instructions. She was then given similar instructions about being at a party, but this time she vomited all over the hostess' dress. When she signaled this time she was asked to relax and try to erase the scene from her mind. She was then asked to imagine she was about to take a drink at a dance; when she did she started to feel ill, but this time she would not try to drink it and then she would immediately feel calm. She was given 10 more trials in this manner in the first session. On every other trial she was told that she refused to take the drink and she immediately felt calm.

After the trials were over she was told to do the same thing at home. She was cautioned to visualize the scene very clearly and visualize herself starting to feel ill as soon as she saw the glass. She would then vomit as soon as the glass touched her lips. [Cautela, 1966, p. 37]

Covert sensitization was also carried out, using beer and wine, in imagined scenes. The client was instructed to practice the same procedure at home, being sure to visualize the scenes very clearly and to imagine herself starting to feel ill as soon as she saw the glass. She did not carry out home practice sessions since she reported that visualization of these scenes made her ill. (Instructing the client to maintain records of home practice sessions according to the time and number of trials encourages accurate reporting of such practice.) Seven more sessions were held in the office, once each week, and the client later started home practice sessions once a day. She reported that she had completely stopped drinking and that she felt fine when she went out unless she thought about having a drink. "She expressed great satisfaction in stating that she didn't have to drink to have a good time" (Cautela, 1966, p. 38). She was asked to continue home practice sessions if she felt tempted, and did so on three occasions over an eight-month period. A follow-up interview at this time indicated that she had not had a drink since intervention ended. Instructions to employ covert sensitization when tempted indicate the emphasis placed on the self-management features of this method.

Cautela (1970c) stresses the importance of conducting a

sufficient number of conditioning trials in achieving positive
effects. He recommends continuing treatment for at least six
sessions after the client has stopped drinking or has lost the
desire to drink. Overgeneralization, in which an aversive reaction is experienced in inappropriate situations, such as when
drinking is discussed on the television, does not seem to be a
problem. As with other aversive-conditioning procedures,
effects seem to be very specific to the exact stimulus that is employed, which should caution the counselor to be sure to
include all relevant cues for drinking in covert sensitization
trials. Unfortunately, to date, the only evidence for the effectiveness of covert sensitization rests on case studies. These, however, do suggest that the method has some promise. Covert
sensitization has also been employed with other problematic
reactions such as obesity (Cautela, 1966), drug abuse, and
sexual responses (Barlow, Leitenberg, and Agras, 1969).

Covert modeling. Covert modeling, in which the client
imagines himself successfully coping with a situation, has been
effective in decreasing drinking (Hay, Hay, and Nelson,
1977). One case presented concerns a forty-eight-year-old man
with a thirty-year history of alcohol abuse. He had been committed to a state institution for detoxification and rehabilitation. This was one of many hospitalizations. According to his
report, there had been no prior period of abstinence in the natural environment. Assessment revealed five situations that
seemed to be related to drinking. Covert rehearsal was presented
as a self-control skill that he could use in the natural environment. Each scene was carefully described, including successful
coping reactions, and when the client signaled that he clearly
imagined the scene, its description was continued for another
thirty seconds. An example of a scene is given as follows.
"Imagine yourself walking in town and running into a group of
your old drinking buddies. They have already been drinking
heavily and ask you to join them. They are drinking white lightning. They look happy and you are alone. In the past you
would have taken a drink and probably have become drunk.
Now cope with the situation. Imagine yourself feeling the
'urge' to drink but refusing and slowly turning and walking
down the street" (Hay, Hay, and Nelson, 1977, p. 71).

Two sessions per week were held, over a period of three

weeks. The client was requested to rehearse the scenes each day with the help of a tape recording prepared by the counselor, on which scenes were described, and was instructed to employ covert modeling any time that he anticipated or was in a high-probability drinking situation. As with covert sensitization, the self-control aspect of this procedure is emphasized. The client was also trained in progressive relaxation. Progress after discharge was monitored by daily self-report postcards, pre-addressed to the hospital, on which the client recorded the quantity and type of any alcohol beverage ingested. The counselor phoned the client once a month. Weekly postcards were requested after two months and phone calls were then made monthly. Covert modeling was continued during three one-hour sessions during the first six months following discharge. During the eleven months of posthospitalization, the client maintained his full-time job, and reported drinking on only three days. These reports were corroborated by his sister.

Blood Alcohol Concentration Discrimination Training

In this procedure, clients are trained to estimate blood alcohol levels from proprioceptive cues and to employ these cues to regulate their alcohol intake (Caddy and Lovibond, 1976). Periodic external feedback is necessary to maintain discrimination of different blood alcohol levels. As this procedure has usually been combined with a variety of other procedures, such as education concerning the effects of alcohol, self-control training in the principles of stimulus control and self-reinforcement, and aversive counterconditioning (see, for example, Vogler, Compton, and Weissbach, 1975), it is not possible to assess the effects of this procedure alone.

Case Example

The following example illustrates the variety of methods that may be used to decrease alcohol consumption (Lazarus, 1965b, pp. 739-740).

Mr. K. A., aged forty-two years, a chemical engineer by training, had been the managing direc-

tor of a large industrial concern from the ages of
thirty-one to thirty-eight years. He was then forced
to resign since his addiction to alcohol seriously
interfered with his work. In an endeavor to support
his wife and two children, he drifted unsuccessfully
from job to job. He twice sought treatment in an
institution, but each time the beneficial effects
were extremely shortlived. His wife then obtained
a judicial separation and the patient went to live
alone in a boarding house. He was then consuming
more alcohol than ever before.

He had grown accustomed to "drinking with
the boys" from the age of seventeen years, but
within ten years he was almost entirely a solitary
drinker. . . . He met and married his wife when he
was twenty-four years old and attained a satisfactory heterosexual adjustment.

At work he was inclined to be overconscien-
tious and found that "a good many stiff drinks
were needed before I could keep the office out of
the home and stop worrying about work."

He was referred for behaviour therapy by his
cousin, a physician. . . . The patient was rather
emaciated and had pronounced tremors in both
hands. He also complained of frontal headaches,
gastric spasms and was prone to "blackouts" after
spells of heavy drinking. He was admitted to a
nursing home for two weeks, medically investigated and treated for anemia. Stelazine (2 mg.
t.d.s.) was also prescribed for a month. The therapist visited the patient at the nursing home and
obtained further details of his life history. Mr.
K. A. was then given a nontechnical explanation of
the behaviour therapeutic rationale with special
emphasis on the need to eliminate the CAD [condi-
tioned autonomic drive—anxiety] as well as the
drinking habit. He agreed to cooperate with the
therapeutic proposals.

On his discharge from the nursing home, a
programme of aversion therapy was initiated. The
sight, taste and smell of alcohol were paired with
strong . . . shocks to his left palm and forearm. He
was also provided with a portable faradic unit and
instructed to switch on the current whenever the
need for a drink arose. In order to offset the effects of discrimination learning, aversion therapy

sessions were conducted at the patient's boarding-house as well as in the consulting room. Within two weeks he had become extremely sensitive to and anxious about the . . . shocks. The following technique of conditioning "anxiety-relief" was then employed: A glass of brandy was placed before the patient. He was instructed to lift the glass and to try and drink its contents. As soon as his fingers touched the glass, a mildly unpleasant current was passed into his hand. As the glass approached his lips, the current was made distinctly noxious. The shock would cease about half a second after replacing the glass on the table and withdrawing his hand. After one session he seldom raised the glass more than six to eight inches off the table and would then immediately replace it, showing obvious signs of relief at the fact that he had thus avoided the noxious stimulus.

Progressive-relaxation procedures were also administered together with additional diagnostic interviews in which attempts were made to elucidate the basic dimensions of his anxieties. . . . It was clear that Mr. K. A. reacted with anxiety to numerous innocuous stimuli. These were finally divided into three separate but related categories: (1) hypersensitivity to statements of personal devaluation; (2) difficulties at work; and (3) dwelling on past and present regrets. The specific items making up each of these themes were ranked in order of the amount of anxiety evoked.

Devaluation series. He reacted to being called *thin; unkempt; stupid; selfish; callous; weak; sick;* a *drunk;* an *animal; gutless* and *spineless;* and *a failure.* These remarks were generally less upsetting when directed at him by an acquaintance, but when said by his mother or his wife, he was inclined to feel "desperately unhappy."

Work series. Situations connected with his work, which made the patient unhappy, included: being reprimanded for arriving late; forgetting to telephone a client; misquoting a price; not knowing the answer to a client's questions; failing to obtain promotion; the boss expressing dissatisfaction with his work; being shown up by a fellow employee; and being dismissed.

Past and present regrets. Circumstances that

he regretted included: having disappointed his late
father by failing one year at school; the vast
amount of money he spent on drink; having cursed
his mother; recalling [past] homosexual encounters; remembering his adolescent drinking sprees
that set him on the road to chronic alcoholism; the
occasions when he was unkind to his wife and children; the day he lost the position of managing director; and the fact that his family left him.

Systematic desensitization . . . was administered by instructing Mr. K. A. to imagine or reflect
upon these items while in a state of deep . . . relaxation. During some of the more exacting items he
was inclined to weep and ask for a drink. His reactions of anxiety, guilt and remorse were counter-
posed by deep relaxation again and again. Finally,
after twenty sessions (held three times a week), the
patient reported as follows:

"None of these things bother me any more. I
sort of feel 'Who cares!' or 'So what!' or 'That's
just too bad!' or 'That's forgiven and forgotten!' —
I'm just human and that means no one can expect
me to be perfect."

It was also apparent that Mr. K. A. had high
levels of unexpressed resentment. His previous
training had taught him always to "bottle up his
feelings." The therapist encouraged the outward
expression of his resentments, but stressed that
these should be "acted out" in a reasonable and
assertive (as opposed to an aggressive) manner. The
patient was assisted in this regard by means of "behavior rehearsal"— . . . in which the patient's . . .
expression of resentment was . . . rehearsed by enacting imagined interpersonal encounters.

At this stage, approximately nine weeks had
elapsed since his initial interview. . . . Apart from
the small quantities of alcohol he had imbibed during the aversion therapy sessions, he had been totally abstinent. He had gained nearly twenty
pounds in weight and there was no sign of his former tremors. He stated: "I've never felt so fit in
my life." A wealthy relative then offered him a
free holiday at the coast for a month. The therapist
had strong misgivings about the wisdom of this
venture, but Mr. K. A. was adamant that he would
be "all right." Before leaving for his holiday the

patient had indicated that he very much desired to effect a reconciliation with his wife and children. He had approached his wife on two occasions and had been rebuffed each time.

The therapist telephoned the patient's wife and arranged for an interview. She stated that although she felt a good deal of compassion for her husband, she had nevertheless become sensitized to the entire aura of drunkenness, "especially to the way he looks and the things he says while drunk." She agreed to undergo a course of desensitization . . . designed to render her relatively impervious to her husband's past misdemeanors. After nine sessions she stated that she could contemplate living with him, but that she was still "terribly afraid that he'll go back to the drink again."

Mr. K. A. returned from his holiday and stated in a matter-of-fact tone of voice that he had imbibed no alcohol whatsoever. He went on to say that he had met the personnel officer of a chemical plant who had offered him a senior post with excellent prospects. "Much against my own better judgment I took your advice and told him that I am an exalcoholic—but he didn't change his mind."

He was delighted to learn that his wife had undergone therapy during his absence. "It might be different from now on," he said, "I've never really felt before that she was on my side."

He was instructed to return for booster treatments of aversion conditioning every month. After four weeks he telephoned to inform the therapist that he felt "happy at home, happy at work and happy within myself." He therefore insisted that he required no further treatment. Approximately two months later he telephoned again to report that he had "done a terrible thing." He explained how, impelled by sheer curiosity, he had entered a bar and had a tot of brandy and then another. "I didn't feel any compulsive need to devour the whole bottle and get picked up in a gutter . . . After two drinks I quit." The therapist advised the patient to make another appointment. He then explained that although the consensus of opinion was that teetotalism was essential, conclusive evidence on this point was sorely lacking. An experiment in controlled drinking was therefore inaugurated on the understanding that its failure would necessitate retraining along lines of complete and total abstinence. The patient was hypnotized and exposed to repeated suggestions that should he ever engage in solitary drinking, or have more than two tots of any harsh liquor, or more than two glasses of wine or beer, he would immediately develop violent abdominal cramps with nausea and vomiting for periods of up to ten minutes.

A systematic follow-up investigation showed that the patient remained a successful social drinker for over fourteen months.

Selecting Goals: Abstinence or Controlled Drinking

Selection of controlled drinking as a goal has a number of advantages. Clients may be more willing to seek help with this goal than with a goal of abstinence, and pursuit of and failure with a controlled drinking program may render a client more willing to enter a program where the goal is abstinence (Miller, 1975). It provides the client with alternative behaviors that do not preclude the sources of social reinforcement available to the social drinker (O'Leary and Wilson, 1975). Also, self-esteem is enhanced by possession of skills to regulate drinking, in contrast with the fear that after one drink all may be lost.

Generalization and Maintenance

If programs are carried out in artificial environments, such as hospitals, arrangements must be made for new drinking patterns to occur in real life situations. Some programs have attempted to facilitate generalization by carrying out conditioning in artificially created situations, such as bars or home environments that are designed to simulate the natural environment (Sobell and Sobell, 1972). Successful transfer to real life situations may require more planning than simple dependence on generalization effects, such as training the client in self-management skills and how to select friends who will support sobriety as well as training significant others to support desirable behaviors. Booster sessions, during which additional conditioning sessions are provided, enhance the maintenance of effects achieved with aversive conditioning (Voegtlin, Lemere, and Broz, 1940). These sessions should concentrate on the client's preferred beverages, because drinking a favorite beverage is involved in 75 percent of relapses. If the client has been hospitalized, a careful examination of the natural environment should be made prior to release, in order to develop necessary arrangements to maintain positive changes, or to select an appropriate "bridging" environment, such as a halfway house. Procedures that focus on altering reinforcement patterns for drinking in the natural environment and developing self-management skills have the advantage of already dealing with real-life contexts, and thus enhance the possibility of maintenance of appropriate behaviors. Any artificial procedural components must be gradually eliminated.

Periodic contacts following intervention may aid in maintaining change. Additional follow-up contact simply to obtain information about program effectiveness seems to offer a continued source of support. For example, Sobell and Sobell (1976) contacted their clients every three to four weeks over a two-year postdischarge period. Almost all the clients reported that they liked these contacts. Comments concerning these meetings centered around knowing that they could talk with someone who knew them and was familiar with their problems, knowing that someone cared about them, keeping them aware of their problems, keeping them on guard. These men, who had been hospitalized and who had experienced a disruption of their social contacts and family lives, experienced follow-up contacts as therapeutic. Follow-up contacts help to catch trouble spots. Relapse is often associated with posttreatment association with old drinking companions (Lemere and Voegtlin, 1950) and a check can be made concerning such contacts, support offered for sobriety, and training provided in any additional skills needed.

Summary

Within a behavioral view, problem drinking is viewed as a behavior maintained by a variety of consequences, which may differ in each case. A situational analysis is required, to identify relevant antecedents and consequences as well as the particular pattern of use for each client. Behavioral intervention with problem drinkers has progressed from a primitive use of aversive conditioning—in which drinking was paired with aversive events, while relevant cognitions, environmental contingencies and alternative behaviors were ignored—to a sophisticated multi-faceted approach that carefully considers consequences in the natural environment and the development of self-management skills and alternative behaviors that will enable the client to successfully manage his drinking behavior. Attention is focused on all factors that may be related to drinking, and alternative behaviors and contexts are offered that will support abstinence or controlled drinking. Preliminary data indicate that this broad-spectrum approach to assessment and intervention within a behavioral framework is successful with a range of clients who have drinking problems.

16

As with alcohol abuse, it is impossible to obtain accurate rates of the extent to which various drugs are consumed in excessive amounts without medical prescription. Substances of concern include opiates (mainly heroin), amphetamines, barbiturates, cocaine, psychedelics, and toxic inhalants. Although there have been a number of articles that discuss drug abuse from a behavioral perspective, the development and evaluation of intervention programs is still in the early stages (see Callner, 1975).

Myths About Drug Abuse

The myths about drug abuse are similar to those surrounding alcohol abuse. These include the assumption that drug use is related to certain personality types; that once an addict-

Drug Abuse

ing drug is sampled, use will steadily increase; and that agreement exists concerning the definition of drug abuse. Actually, as with alcohol abuse, there are a variety of patterns of drug abuse, ranging from the "junkie" who has a habit costing hundreds of dollars a day and who leads a life entirely centered around drugs, to the person who holds a job and uses opiates only on weekends, to the person who samples drugs a couple of times a year on special occasions.

As with problem drinking, the effectiveness of procedures should be viewed in terms of the natural history of drug use and nonuse. What do we know about how many people stop taking drugs without any special intervention? Long-range follow-up studies of people who abuse drugs clearly show the incorrectness of the stereotype "Once an addict, always an addict" (O'Donnell, 1972). Relapse has been found to be very probable after abstinence in an institution or for any short period of voluntary abstinence; however, over time, some studies have shown that abstinence increases at a fairly steady rate. For example, a study of 453 subjects five years after discharge from Lexington, a residential treatment center (Duvall, Locke, and Brill, 1963), indicated that only 9 percent of subjects were voluntarily abstinent six months after discharge; 17 percent two years after discharge; and 25 percent five years after discharge.

The less the involvement in the drug subculture, the more probable was eventual abstinence. Self-concept as a patient using medicine or as an addict seeking kicks was indirectly related to abstinence. For those with self-concept as patients, the determining factor was their physicians; if the physicians continued to prescribe, the subjects continued to be addicted, whereas if they refused to prescribe, the subjects became abstinent and did not use other drugs or substitutes. For those whose self-concept was of addicts seeking kicks, addiction tended to continue if narcotics were available, and if they were not available, subjects tended to shift to substitute drugs.

Criminal record was mildly predictive of posthospital drug patterns. The greater the number of sentences after the onset of addiction, the greater was the probability that men would show a pattern of continued addiction to narcotics or of addiction to substitutes. Abstinence was found mainly among men with no sentences, or with only one or two sentences.

Several variables connected with employment were associated with abstinence. Those in the health professions showed the largest proportion in the abstinence patterns, and those in illegitimate occupations showed the smallest. Those whose work patterns had been steady before addiction began were somewhat more likely to be abstinent from narcotics, but were about equally likely to be addicted to narcotics. The real difference was that they were less likely to spend much time in prisons or other institutions, and to have shifted to other drugs.

Men with no history of alcoholism before addiction showed posthospital patterns either of addiction to narcotics or of complete abstinence. Those with early histories of alcoholism were no more or less likely to show a pattern of complete abstinence, but were more likely to show patterns of addiction to substitutes than to narcotics.

Variables recorded at the time of first hospitalization—such as prognosis; status as voluntary, probationer, or prisoner; length of hospital stay; and psychiatric diagnosis—were not found to be predictive of posthospital drug patterns. [O'Donnell, 1972, pp. 247-248]

Abstinence rarely appears to be voluntary among narcotic users who have been addicted for some time (O'Donnell, 1972). A recent study (Boudin, Valentine, Ingrham, Brantly, Ruiz, Smith, Catlin, and Regan, in press) found that degree of success of a behavioral treatment program was related to how many years the client had been addicted to heroin, previous cost of the habit, and the number of times the client had been previously enrolled in methadone programs.

There is little agreement as to what constitutes drug abuse and how it should be handled by professionals or laymen. This is clearly reflected in the history of legislation regarding opiate use. Before opiate use was considered a criminal act, a large proportion of opiate users were members of the middle class, including large numbers of housewives, who would purchase laudanum on a nonprescription basis (Duster, 1970). (Perhaps this is why there was not a greater interest in a woman's movement at this time—because a large portion of housewives were "stoned" at home.) This pattern changed radically when legislators decided that the use of morphine was bad and passed the Harrison Act, in 1914. Overnight, people who had thought of themselves as respectable citizens were "criminalized." The description of the panic that occurred and the lines that formed at the local pharmacies is vividly described in *The Legislation of Morality* (Duster, 1970). With this change in the legal status of opiates, their use decreased among the middle class and, over time, increased among the poor in large urban areas.

Learning to Abuse Drugs

Drug use, like alcohol use, is considered to be a behavior maintained by its consequences, although respondent conditioning is also heavily involved (Wikler, 1965). Factors related to opiate use often differ from those related to alcohol abuse because of the differential availability associated with these substances. Whereas alcohol is readily available and the consumer is enticed daily to purchase this substance through billboards, magazine advertisements, and friends, opiates are legally obtainable only through medical channels.

Learning to be a drug user shares one characteristic with learning to become a prostitute. People are usually initiated through someone who is already an initiate. Initial unpleasant physical effects of a drug may be reinterpreted by peers who initiate the novice into drug use (see, for example, Becker, 1963). The initiate may be informed that feelings of dizziness and nausea are not really that bad, that they disappear quickly and are only initially experienced. For example, one old-time user of opiates, a client of mine, said to an initiate, "The nausea you might feel is nothing like being sick. You just go to the bathroom and throw up and that's it. There's no retching and it only happens one time. It's nothing like really being sick." Attention is drawn by the initiator to the potential positive effects in addition to minimizing and relabeling negative effects.

Assuring a steady source of drugs and resources with which to purchase these requires what sociologists have called an *apprenticeship,* because there are so many skills to be learned (Becker, 1963). If the user holds a job, it is unlikely that the money thus earned can support a habit, and therefore it often does not pay him to work. Attention must be devoted to other ways to achieve funds, which accounts for the high number of offenses related to drug use. Thus, becoming an opiate user often leads to the development of an entire life-style centered around obtaining the money to buy drugs, getting the drugs, and then using them.

Inclination to "try out" a drug may be related to a variety of reinforcing contingencies. The possibility of winning a respected reputation in a subculture seems to be related to the rush toward drug use when heroin was first introduced into a neighborhood. After it was clear that drug use resulted in some untoward effects, it became even more of a challenge to "triumph in a situation where previous heroes have failed" (Feldman, 1968, p. 135). The sense of control over one's environment that drug use is thought to provide has been stressed by some investigators (Coghlan, Gold, Dohrenwend, and Zimmerman, 1973). The effects of drugs may be far more reliable than the effects of other people's reactions. Delinquent drug users, for example, viewed themselves as having greater control over their drug-taking behavior than over their behavior in other situations. Use of drugs enhances feelings of power, maturity, and independence (Retka and Fenker, 1975). The consequences associated with using other drugs may be somewhat different. The "up" feeling created by amphetamine use, or the visionary experiences resulting from psychedelics, may be uniquely pleasurable to different people. Factors associated with use of psychedelics among male college students include responding to a dare as proof of one's flexibility or of one's maturity and intellectual depth, curiosity, feeling of missing something if one does not try it, and seeking answers to philosophical or personal problems (Lipinski and Lipinski, 1967). Kraft (1970) considered social anxiety to be the major factor associated with repeated drug use.

Maintenance of drug abuse may be related to somewhat different reinforcement contingencies, because the physiological effects of drugs change as use continues. For example, as a tolerance is established for opiates, a greater dosage is required to feel the effects, and the "flash" may disappear altogether. Over time, the definitive criterion for an addiction may take place: withdrawal symptoms consequent on abstinence, followed by drug use to relieve these symptoms. Thus negative reinforcement, the removal of the aversive effects of withdrawal symptoms, may acquire a larger role. The opinion that addiction is maintained by the quest for euphoria and the fear of abstinence distress has been questioned for some time, because tolerance for the euphoric effect develops rapidly; and the opportunity of gradual withdrawal is typically available but not taken advantage of. Lack of success of a "drying-out period" reduces the significance of avoidance of withdrawal symptoms in maintaining drug use. It is no wonder that such periods do little to alter usage, considering that the client returns to the natural environment, where all the old cues and consequences for drug use are present.

Respondent conditioning has been emphasized by some writers (see, for example, Wikler, 1965), who consider conditioned responses to be mainly responsible for long-term drug use and posttreatment relapse. Wikler, for example, considered that initial use was associated with various emotional states such as anxiety, anger, guilt, or depression. Drug use is followed by tension reduction, and physical dependence gradually develops. Thus Wikler emphasized the negatively reinforcing effects of drug use. Following the development of physical dependence, continued drug use may be maintained to reduce the unpleasant symptoms associated with withdrawal. Wikler emphasized the extent to which situations, such as friends and neighbors, became associated with physical withdrawal symptoms, and assumed that, because of the repeated pairing of these situations with withdrawal effects, these events themselves acquired the capacity to elicit such effects. Behaviors associated with withdrawal can be elicited months after complete abstinence by reexposure to eliciting events (Wikler, 1965). A possible chain of behavior involved in heroin use is depicted in Figure 38.

Perhaps even more important than drug use itself is involvement in an addict subculture and the learning of a new set of behaviors and reinforcers that are incompatible with socially accepted behavior (O'Donnell, 1972). One factor that influences movement away from a peer group that finds use unacceptable (as well as the behaviors that accompany it) toward a group that supports drug use is assured availability of drugs. A new environment is provided by the new peer group, in which new skills, attitudes, and values are developed, and in which the addict becomes increasingly alienated from society (O'Donnell, 1972, p. 242). Furthermore, many individuals already exist in a subculture that will support drug use.

Figure 38. Highly Simplified Conjectural Chain for Heroin Addiction

0 — Withdrawal symptoms, conditioned anxiety and autonomic states in a heroin addict

R_1 — Thoughts about fixing, anticipation of high (craving) or relief from withdrawal symptoms; drug talk

S_1 — Sight of connection or usual purchase place

R_2 — Purchase of heroin

S_2 — Sight, feeling of balloon of heroin, sight of addict friends

R_3 — Walk to setting safe for fixing

S_3 — Sight of heroin, kit; sight and sounds of others fixing in safe setting

R_4 — Shooting heroin

S_4 — Hit and conditioned reactions to it; private cognitive states, autonomic states

R_5 — Relaxed behavior, nodding, pleasant private cognitions

C+ — Mood changes, reduction of tension, cessation of abstinence phenomena, cessation of pain in presence of anxiety, approval of others, relief from guilt

Source: Droppa (1973, p. 150).

Assessment

A behavioral framework entails the same concern for identifying the pattern of drug use and related antecedents and consequences as described under assessment of alcohol abuse. A variety of assessment procedures may be employed, including self-report, official records, urinalysis, and collateral sources such as significant others. Special precautions should be taken to ensure the confidentiality of records relating to drug use, because of the illegality of such use. Only through assessment will the client's unique patterns of drug use be identified and related factors be determined. Perhaps in no other population are there so many individual differences of potential import, including the drugs employed; their differential physical and psychological effects; how these drugs are acquired (legal or illegal channels); how drugs are used (main-line, orally); the intensity and variety of events that cue drug taking; whether the person considers himself an addict and whether this is considered to be a good or bad thing; and degree of involvement in an addict subculture.

Self-Report. The history of drug use is typically provided by the client, although this should be supplemented by other sources of information such as official records. Overreporting number of arrests by clients has led some investigators to question the accuracy of arrest records. For example, Ball (1967) interviewed fifty-nine exconvict narcotic addicts concerning their current use of drugs and their arrest records, and checked their reports against hospital and arrest records as well as urine samples obtained at the time of the interview. Arrests were overreported by 38 percent of the sample, accurately reported by 32 percent, and underreported by 29 percent. Certainly the conditions under which self-report information is collected will greatly influence its accuracy, for example, whether treatment is voluntarily sought. As with other presenting problems, it is wise to employ multiple sources to obtain needed assessment information.

Callner and Ross (1976) have developed an assertion scale for use with drug abusers. Items included relate to the areas of authority ("I never feel shaky and overly nervous when I think of asking a boss for a raise"); positive feedback ("I often don't say some of the nice things I am thinking about some people"); drugs ("I have no trouble telling friends not to bring drugs over to my house"); negative feedback ("I have a hard time criticizing others even when I know that they are wrong and I am right"); and heterosexual ("I never have a hard time getting up enough nerve to call up girls to ask them out for dates") (p. 662).

Self-Monitoring. Either monitoring forms or a diary may be employed to collect relevant assessment information. The monitoring form might include information such as date, time, drug taken, dosage, and situation. Thoughts and feelings that may be antecedent to actual drug use may also be monitored, such as urges to take a drug or thoughts about drugs (Boudin and Valentine, 1973). It is helpful to record relevant situations associated with such thoughts and urges, so that the situational events or other coverants that may be related to these can be identified. Wrist counters may be employed to help clients to monitor their behavior (Boudin and Valentine, 1973).

If a client is willing to record a number of items, Boudin and Valentine (1973) present some evidence that show that it may be possible to predict onset of a drug crisis (ingestion of the drug) by paying close attention to behaviors that precede drug taking. They offer as an example a case of a woman in her twenties who previously had used heroin. She monitored, on a daily basis, marijuana use, mental contentment, thoughts about drugs, and urges to use drugs. Right before an incident of drug use, thoughts and urges increased dramatically, as did frustration ratings. Mental contentment and marijuana use decreased. The need to consider multiple antecedents is indicated by a failure to take drugs on other occasions in which thoughts and urges about drugs increased, yet frustration did not. Obtaining a baseline has often proven a problem with clients (Droppa, 1976). Special measures may have to be taken to encourage data collection, such as frequent contact between the client and counselor to gather information recorded.

Card sorts, in which the client is requested to sort cards naming various drugs according to their arousal value, provide another source of self-report information (Barlow, Leitenberg, and Agras, 1969).

Physiological Measures. Urine can be checked for a variety of drugs, including opiates and amphetamines, and random urinalysis tests have been employed in some programs to monitor drug use. It has been found, however, that laboratories are often highly inaccurate in their analysis procedures. When artificially prepared samples were sent to government-approved laboratories, it was found that one laboratory unaware of the test accurately identified only 49.4 percent of the samples (Gottheil, Caddy, and Austin, 1975). The laboratory that was unaware of the test reported 66.3 percent false positives, whereas the other laboratory, which was aware of the test, found only 3.8 percent false positives. The suggestion is made by those who carried out this study that periodic "blind" proficiency tests be conducted and that satisfactory performance on these tests be mandatory for continued federal licensing. Another problem with urinalysis is encountered when clients are simply asked to bring a sample of their urine to a laboratory for analysis, because there it is unknown whether this is indeed their own urine. The client's physiological reactions to drug-related stimuli, such as the names of drugs, may be useful in measuring drug-related reactions. Assessment of the client's physical condition is important in that different drugs seem to have somewhat different physical side effects. Continued drug use may be obvious by track marks.

Collateral Sources and Official Records. Significant others may be asked to provide assessment information with the permission of the client. Often their reports will not be as accurate as the client's, because significant others may not be privy to the client's drug habits. Arrest records, days gainfully employed, days attended school, or hospital records may be employed; however, as noted under the discussion of client self-report, arrest records may not be as accurate as client self-report. Records of some behavior product, such as money spent on drugs, may be employed.

Observation. Direct observation of *behaviors* related to drug use is feasible and offers a potentially valuable way to monitor potential drug use. For example, the client could be observed in role plays during which he responds to pressure to take drugs or participates in other social exchanges related to drug use, such as initiating conversations (Callner, 1975).

Intervention

There are only about thirty reports of behavioral intervention in relation to drug abuse, many of which were undertaken in hospital settings. Most describe case reports involving opiate addiction, and many do not include clients with characteristics most common to the street addict, such as lower socioeconomic status, high school education or less, and criminal record (Callner, 1975). There is a lack of information concerning which intervention method works best with which client. The goal is typically abstinence, unlike alcohol abuse, where it may be to become a controlled drinker.

All too often, there has been a failure to conduct a careful assessment of the antecedent and consequent events that are related to drug use and a failure to select a procedural mix that is especially designed to address assessment profiles. That is, seldom has a multiform intervention approach been employed. Aversive conditioning using electrical, chemical, or verbal events has been used in many studies in efforts to reduce drug use. Such studies have involved actual or imagined punishment of drug taking or respondent conditioning, in which antecedents of drug taking are paired with aversive events in the attempt to alter the stimulus function of these events. A respondent-extinction paradigm has been employed in other studies, in which there is an attempt to block (for example, through methadone) the usual effects of heroin. None of these paradigms arranges for alternative behaviors in situations triggering drug use other than avoidance of drug use (in successful cases). In all fairness, it should be noted that many of the mentioned studies were carried out in a spirit of inquiry, that is, to determine whether a given method would be effective. If aversive conditioning could effectively reduce drug use, this would be far less costly and time-consuming than multiform intervention, in which, perhaps in addition to aversive conditioning, conditions are arranged in the natural environment to support nondrug use and desirable alternative behaviors are encouraged along the lines of Hunt and Azrin's (1973) community reinforcement approach, and alternative skills offered to the client relating to situations occasioning drug use. As with alcohol abuse, the client may have to learn how to select and meet new friends who do not use drugs, and, as with clients who abuse alcohol, important skill areas may be absent that must be developed, such as recreational and vocational skills. Reinforcer sampling may be needed to develop new sources of appropriate reinforcement and to enhance self-reinforcement skills. Problem-solving skills may be needed to handle new situations (Sobell and Sobell, 1972). Only when there is strong support for nonaddictive behavior might aversive conditioning alone be effective. So long as drug use has a functional value for a person—for example, by providing a prime source of enjoyment; providing prevention from boredom; as a main source of social contacts; and as a main coping skill for dealing with stress and frustration—aversive conditioning could not be expected to maintain abstinence. Intervention should be individually tailored in relation to the unique set of antecedents and reinforcing consequences associated with drug use.

Developing Alternative Behaviors. Behaviors incompatible with drug use can be developed such as self-control skills for handling social anxiety (see, for example, Kraft, 1969). Encouraging results were produced by a multifaceted program, in which a goal was to establish an effective repertoire for handling problems of daily living and to create a sense of individual responsibility (Copeman, 1973). This residential program included initial detoxification as well as aversive conditioning, in which a range of cues for drug use were paired with shock. A group context was employed to develop appropriate social behaviors. Rational-emotive therapy (Ellis, 1962) was used to address irrational thoughts, and training in problem solving, including how to obtain a job, was offered. Of fifty young black men and women, all of whom had records of drug-related crimes, and who were pressured to enter the program, fourteen completed the program. Seven remained free of drugs for almost two years, and the other seven for one year. Two clients who relapsed received "booster sessions" and subsequently remained free of drugs.

Training clients to analyze stimulus conditions related to drug use may also be helpful. Self-monitoring of drug use and associated behavior and cognitions may aid such efforts (Boudin and Valentine, 1973). Assertion training and systematic desensitization have also been employed to develop behaviors that provide alternatives to drug use. For example, Flannery (1972) employed assertion training to decrease use of LSD and marijuana in a twenty-year-old female. Marijuana was used by the client for tension control. The scenes used during desensitization were related to work, school, relationships with parents, and her boyfriend, who used drugs. Thought stopping was used to reduce negative self-statements, which were felt to occasion drug use. She was also trained how to increase positive self-statements. A total of twelve sessions were held, during which drug use was eliminated. Follow-up six months later indicated a use of marijuana and LSD less than once a month.

Relaxation training and desensitization were employed

over fifty-two and twenty-six sessions, respectively, to decrease use of Dexamyl by two clients, eighteen and twenty years old (Kraft, 1969, 1970). Hierarchy themes concerned social fears such as talking to other people, dating, and enjoying parties without drugs. Following desensitization clients were instructed to expose themselves to offers to buy drugs. An eleven- and ten-month follow-up indicated that both clients remained drug-free and were working full-time. The reader is referred to the discussion of problem drinking for a description of the range of alternative behaviors that may be relevant to successful reduction in drug use and for the community sources of reinforcement that may be developed.

The Use of Contingency Contracts. Counselor-client contracts, in which expected behaviors and responsibilities are carefully identified, have been employed to decrease drug use. Here, the counselor does not attempt to deal directly with drug use (as in aversive conditioning), but to establish new contingencies that will increase incompatible behaviors. Boudin (1972) combined contingency contracting with self-administered aversive conditioning via a portable shock apparatus with a female graduate student who consumed around 60 to 70 mg of amphetamine daily, which she obtained from the university health center. She was concerned that she had become addicted to the barbiturates she took as a secondary effect of taking the amphetamines, expressed feelings of panic, and was suicidal. A three-month contract was drawn up between the counselor and Miss X. The conditions of the contract are shown in the following list (from Boudin, 1972, pp. 605-606).

1. Miss X. had to submit a weekly schedule to the therapist and keep him continuously informed of her whereabouts.
2. Three check-in times were established every day. Each morning, noon, and night, Miss X. would call and describe her projected activities up to the succeeding check-in period. Any "potentially dangerous situations" (those situations where drugs or drug users were in close range, which increased probability of using drugs) were communicated to the therapist in order to be discussed at the next check-in time.

3. During any clearly "potentially dangerous situation," Miss X. called the therapist so that immediate counsel could be given, resulting in one of the following three outcomes: (a) Miss X. could remain in this situation under certain conditions; (b) Miss X. had to extricate herself from the situation; or (c) Miss X. had to be removed from the situation by the therapist.

4. Miss X. had to give up all drugs which were accessible to her. Since she was living in a house with other drug users, and knew where various drug supplies were kept, these people had to be informed of our arrangement. Miss X. had to make a formal announcement individually to her suppliers to remove any drugs from accessibility to her, and to refrain from giving or selling her any drugs, even if she requested them. The therapist was present at all of these interactions, to further confirm that Miss X. was in earnest.

5. The therapist had to arrange his schedule so that Miss X. knew where he was at all times.

6. The therapist had to agree that he was to be accessible and available in all crises, twenty-four hours a day.

7. A subsection of the contract dealt with the self-application of shock, as described by Wolpe [1965]. Miss X. was instructed in the use of a small portable shock dispenser which she carried with her at all times. Any awareness of what was termed *volitional behavior,* behavior leading to the acquisition of drugs, or any drug-searching behaviors (for example, searching the medicine chest), was a discriminative stimulus for the self-application of shock.

8. A joint bank account between Miss X. and the therapist was established in the amount of $500 (all of Miss X.'s money). Ten signed checks in the amount of $50 each were held by the therapist, who had only to sign any of these checks to make it valid.

9. It was agreed to by the therapist and Miss X. that any drug use or suspected drug use by Miss X. would result in the loss of a $50 check. Originally, this check was to be sent to the National Welfare Rights Organization, but since

Miss X. was active in supporting their work, it was decided that this would not really be an effective decelerating consequence. It was finally mutually agreed upon that a $50 check would be sent to the Ku Klux Klan for any infringement of the rules as determined in the contract.

10. Miss X. would receive rent, food, and spending money from the therapist whenever necessary as long as she could account for her expenses.

The first notable aspect of this contract is the frequent client-counselor contact provided: three times a day and during crisis periods. Arrangements were made for crisis times, when Miss X. agreed to telephone the counselor. This provided for extra help on an as needed basis, which is often lacking in traditional once-a-week counseling. The use of a portable shock apparatus would hopefully help her decrease the urge to take drugs by pairing this with an aversive event. Items 8 through 10 in the list describe the contingencies in effect.

Only three days after signing the contract, Miss X. announced that she felt much better and wished to terminate the contract. However, the counselor refused to do so and reminded her of her presenting complaints. Over the subsequent three months, two crisis periods arose. One involved the visit of her boyfriend, who was an amphetamine user, at a time when the counselor was away for the weekend. This resulted in a $50 check being forwarded to the Ku Klux Klan. A second situation arose over the need to complete a term paper and her feeling unable to do so without amphetamines. In this instance, she agreed to stay at the home of the counselor for a three-week period, during which time the paper was completed. A variety of reinforcers, including food, liquor, cigarettes, sleeping locations, and rest periods, were made contingent on the number of pages she completed and typed each day. Miss X. left the country for a preplanned year abroad three months later, and reported no drug use during that time, even though drugs were available.

The use of volunteers to maintain contact with clients would decrease the burden on the counselor in a program requiring close contact between the client and counseling source. They could be instructed to contact the counselor only when they could not handle a situation. Behavioral contracts can only be effective if meaningful reinforcers and costs can be imposed. This may require a prior period in which appropriate reinforcers are enriched along the lines of the community reinforcement program for alcoholics (Hunt and Azrin, 1973).

Contingency contracting and behavior rehearsal were employed with a twenty-one-year-old man and his twenty-three-year-old wife, both of whom were on three-year probation for possession of marijuana (Polakow and Doctor, 1973). The wife's drug use was reported to be related to her husband's use. The husband had a long history of arrests for drug possession and sales. The husband employed barbiturates and marijuana daily and could not find and maintain a job. The marriage was threatened by his total involvement with drugs and drug-related activities. Intervention was conducted over a nine-month period, with weekly sessions. "The initial six contacts were used to ascertain the contingencies involved in their drug usage, behavior potential for prosocial activities, and sources of possible reinforcement for incompatible nondrug activities" (Polakow and Doctor, 1973, pp. 375-376). This revealed that efforts by the wife to reduce the husband's drug use were actually functioning as reinforcers for such use.

A contract was made between the counselor and the clients which specified one activity not related to drugs per week, which would result in one week less of probation. The activity had to be verifiable. The wife agreed not to mention drug use to her husband and to offer positive reactions for statements on his part to stop using drugs and his efforts to locate a job. The husband said that he would start looking for a job on a four-week contractual sequence, which allowed for development of job-finding behaviors. "In the first phase the contract made reinforcement contingent on simple approximations in the form of looking through the want ads to identify potential jobs. In the second phase of contracting, reinforcement was contingent on looking through the wants ads, selecting potential jobs and actually making contract with the employers (via telephone) to gain additional information regarding salary and types of skills required. During the third phase, the client was required to look through the want ads, select appropriate jobs, call for information and, if suitable, actually make an arrangement for a job interview. In this phase, reinforcement was contingent on performance of all specified behaviors. Once appointments were made, the reinforcements became available for attendance at employment interviews" (Polakow and Doctor, 1973, p. 376). This program arranged for small increments in job-finding behaviors. The husband obtained a job during the second cycle of the contract, at which time a new contract was formed to reinforce job retention. For each week of job attendance, one week was removed from the probationary period.

Requirements for activities not related to drugs were increased to two per week at the fourteenth session; and to three per week at the twentieth session; four per week at the twenty-fourth session; five at the twenty-sixth session; and seven at the twenty-eighth session. Rehearsal was regularly employed to anticipate novel activities. During the twentieth session, both clients started to participate in group training to develop social skills and to provide further social reinforcement for activity not related to drugs. Discussion of drug use was not permitted during these group sessions. Also at the twentieth week, the counselor started to help the clients form their own contracts. They were asked to negotiate and form a contract for any behaviors they desired in the other. Probation was dismissed, no violations or arrests having occurred for the nine-month contract period. The husband had maintained regular employment for seven months. Follow-ups at three, six, and twelve months indicated a continued abstinence from drugs, continued employment and an improved marriage.

Counselor-client contingency contracts were also used successfully with a twenty-four-year-old female barbiturate addict who was on probation for possession of dangerous drugs (Polakow, 1975). The initial six sessions were devoted to identifying the contingencies that were related to drug use, as well as resources for activities not related to drugs. In addition, possible alternatives to decrease barbiturate use were explored, as well as various routes to increase social behaviors not related to drugs. The contract required client participation in covert sensitization sessions in exchange for time taken off her total probation period (one week off for each session). In addition, she agreed to participate in one activity not related to drugs each week. The number of such activities she agreed to engage in was gradually increased as in the case described earlier. Behavior rehearsal was employed to help her to deal with activities that might be anxiety producing. At the end of a year, she had been drug-free for three months and had obtained a job. "During the next three months she was 'paid' for maintaining employment and for continuing in the therapy sessions, now devoted to positive reinforcement of non-drug activity" (Polakow, 1975, p. 54). Follow-up contacts were made at six, twelve, and eighteen months. She had maintained her employment and reported that she had not resumed drug use. A review of police and court records indicated that there had been no subsequent arrests.

The Use of Aversive Events. Some aversive events have been employed in a punishment paradigm, in which drug taking is followed by an aversive event, whereas others employ a respondent conditioning paradigm, in which the event is paired with stimuli that elicit or occasion drug use. Because both respondent and operant conditioning are involved in both these procedures and because it is difficult to time actual or imagined events precisely, it is a moot point in many of these studies as to whether punishment or respondent conditioning is the most outstanding ingredient. Both alcohol and drug abuse require a "chain" of behaviors. This is especially true with drug use, where legal sanctions necessitate finding sources and raising money to purchase substances. The variety of behaviors included in such a chain is illustrated in Figure 38. The use of covert aversive events is particularly convenient, and portable shock devices, which are used by the client in the natural environment, may provide an additional way to regulate drug use (Wolpe, 1965). Although there is a range of design limitations in these studies (Callner, 1975), some show promise in decreasing drug use, and can be combined with additional procedures in a multiform intervention design.

Covert sensitization. The results of covert sensitization alone, in which imagined drug use or events associated with drug use are paired with imagined aversive events such as nausea or social rejection, have been mixed (see, for example, Droppa, 1976), probably because of the lack of individually tailored intervention methods. Other studies report its successful combination with other methods. Group covert sensitization was employed with teen-age LSD users who had a history of multiple drug use and who volunteered for treatment. Drug use was paired with imagined nausea and escape scenes were also provided, in which avoidance of drug use was followed by relief from nausea (Duehn and Shannon, 1973). At an eighteen-month follow-up, six of the seven subjects reported that LSD had not been used since intervention and that there was no desire to use that substance.

A variety of imagined aversive events have been employed during covert sensitization, in accord with the subject's unique profile of aversive events. Three examples of scenes employed during covert sensitization follow. Scenes 1 and 3 include imagined relief from aversive events contingent on refraining from drug use.

[Scene 1]

I want you to imagine now, as clearly as you can, that you are with John and he suggests that you go to a friend's apartment in Squirrel Hill and see what's happening. You get there and there are a few people sitting around and you don't know anybody but John. You notice a fit and a bag of stuff lying on the table and everybody else is stoned. Somebody reaches for the works and starts to cook up and you really feel like getting down. You wait your turn and finally pick up the fit. You're looking around for the spoon and you find it. You pick up the bag of stuff and you start to feel shaky. You notice that your muscles are real tight and your head is starting to ache; it feels like a tight band around your head, tightening and tightening, and your head is pounding. You look around for some water and notice a sharp and painful pounding sensation traveling up your arm from your fingers. It is traveling up to your shoulder and it is burning and really hurts like hell. You start to pour some stuff into the spoon but your head is aching worse and you start to feel sick to your stomach. Your throat feels heavy and warm and your stomach feels queasy. The aching band around your head gets tighter and tighter and your arm is throbbing so bad that your hand is shaking and you can hardly hold the spoon.

You decide not to shoot up right now. You put the spoon and the stuff back on the table and say to yourself, "I don't need to do up now; I can control myself." Right away you start to feel better; your arm is hurting less and less and you can feel the headache fading; it is nearly gone. Your hand has stopped shaking and your nerves are steadier. Your stomach feels better. You decide to split from there and tell John you're going. You are feeling better and better as you walk down the stairs into the clear air outside.

[Scene 2]

Imagine very clearly that you are on your way home from work and you have with you a homemade script [prescription] for Percodan. You decide to get it filled. While driving you are worrying about getting caught. You imagine yourself arriving in the vicinity of the drugstore. You park the car. You are getting out of the car, walking over to the door and going into the drugstore. You walk back past the counters to the pharmacy counter. You give the script to the pharmacist and he takes it and looks at it, then looks at you, then looks closely at the script. You start to get more and more nervous and you feel a churning knot in your stomach. The druggist goes into the back of the store and you see him pick up the phone and start to dial. You begin to panic, but control the feeling of wanting to run, trying to think what to do. The druggist does not come back to the counter and you slowly, deliberately, turn and walk toward the door. You notice two men in plain clothes walk in the front door. You are shaking as they come up to you and one of them says, "We want to ask you a few questions about your prescription." He flashes a badge and you know it's all over.

[Scene 3]

You imagine, very clearly, as if it were happening right now, that you are at work, sitting at your desk, and you are feeling a vague nervousness, a feeling that you want to take some Percodan. You reach in your pocket and get out two Percs. You start to get up to get some water and notice that your hand is starting to shake uncontrollably. As you get up, you shiver, feel chills all over; chills are going up and down your spine. You start to feel tense and jumpy as you stand there and you get cold and clammy all over. You feel your stomach starting to turn over and you are shivering. Your head starts to tighten up and you feel pressure at the back of your head. It feels like your head is being tightened in a steel band against your forehead. You are shivering and shaking and at the same time you start to feel sick to your stomach. You taste bile coming up into your throat, your head is pounding and you are shaking all over.

You decide to put the Percs away. As you put them back into your pocket, you start to feel relieved. Your headache is fading, your muscles are beginning to relax and your stomach feels better. You say to yourself, "I can control my drug use, I don't need to use this." You feel better and better. You imagine that you are walking in the park on a pleasant, breezy spring day. You see the patterns of sunlight on the leaves and everything is very relaxed and beautiful. [Droppa, 1976, pp. 141-142]

Electric shock. Portable shock devices may be used to enhance the client's ability to resist drug use (Boudin, 1972; Wolpe, 1965). This requires a motivated client. Some successful case studies have been reported in which shock has been combined with other procedures such as assertion training, development of self-control techniques and relaxation training (see, for example, Lesser, 1967).

Extinction Procedures. Imagined as well as actual events have been employed in extinction procedures designed to decrease drug use. As with the use of aversive conditioning, it is likely that success can be facilitated by careful consideration of the antecedents and consequences related to drug use, including identification of behavior deficits involved and the development of appropriate alternative behaviors.

Covert extinction. In covert extinction, a behavior is imagined without its usual reinforcing consequence (Cautela,

1971a), the theory being that, without reinforcement, the behavior will decrease. This procedure was employed with four female amphetamine addicts ranging in age from sixteen to forty-seven who mainlined 100 to 200 mg three to five times a day (Götestam and Melin, 1974). A specific description of the chain of behaviors involved for each client in drug use, including relevant situations, is required when this procedure is used. Thus, the first step was to obtain such a description from each client. One client, a thirty-year-old woman, typically injected drugs in public toilets. During covert extinction trials, she was asked to imagine herself having a craving, going to the public toilet, preparing the syringe, and shooting up *without feeling anything*. After 100 trials, she went AWOL (all four patients went AWOL) and shot up, but felt nothing. She reentered the hospital and completed another series of 100 trials and then went home, where she remained drug-free at a nine-month follow-up. She continued using covert extinction when she felt a craving to take the drug, and reported that it helped such feelings to dissipate. One of the other clients also returned for completion of treatment. Three of the four women were abstinent nine months after discharge.

Chemical procedures. Use of narcotic antagonists such as cyclazocine or methadone also depend on a blocking of the usual effects of drugs. Recent reports describing results of methadone programs have been discouraging (see, for example, Anderson and Nutter, 1975). Use of this procedure requires a high degree of client self-determination.

Combining Aversive Conditioning and the Development of Alternative Behaviors. Many programs have employed a variety of intervention procedures, some of which have taken place in the hospital. For example, following detoxification, a combination of aversive conditioning, using both shock and aversive imagery, relaxation training, and systematic desensitization was employed in the hospital with a thirty-year-old female with an eight-year history of barbiturate and heroin use and a twenty-four-year-old male addicted to heroin for six years (O'Brien, Raynes, and Patch, 1972). This permitted a direct focus on the problematic behavior itself (pairing drug use with an aversive event), as well as a focus on related factors, such as anxiety. Both clients were first detoxified on methadone, over about eighteen days. Assessment included identification of the events, both external and internal (thoughts and cravings), that were associated with drug use. Sessions 4 through 6 were devoted to training the woman in relaxation, including pairing of a cue word (*alpha*) with a relaxed state. Aversive conditioning and relaxation were employed during the next sixteen sessions. Scenes associated with heroin use were described to the clients, using their own jargon, and items related to drug use were displayed to them. Scenes were included involving all sites of injection on their bodies, in the hope that each would assume an aversive quality by being paired with shock. Progressively smaller parts of the entire behavioral chain involved in injecting heroin in various situations were presented. About seven scenes were paired with shock on each session, for a total of about 112 pairings over the sixteen sessions. Neither subject reported any desire to use heroin at the time of discharge, and the woman, at a follow-up one and a half years later, reported continued abstinence.

Behavioral contracting has also been combined with the use of aversive procedures (Boudin, 1972; Boudin and Valentine, 1973). Wisocki (1973) used a variety of procedures with a highly motivated twenty-six-year-old heroin addict over twelve weekly sessions. Thought stopping was used to eliminate positive thinking about drug use as well as negative self-statements that interfered with prosocial behaviors and job seeking. The client was also taught to use covert reinforcement (Cautela, 1970b) for nonuse of drugs. This procedure entails imagining a positive event following a behavior to be increased. Covert sensitization was employed to develop an aversive reaction to use of heroin, using flying insects, spiders, sewage, and contracting leprosy as aversive events. Such events were paired with thinking about buying heroin, seeing a pusher, and preparing to inject heroin. Ten scene presentations were made during each session, and the client was instructed to practice three times a day at home. Covert reinforcer sampling was used to enhance the client's self-image. This involved the client imagining engaging in a variety of behaviors he identified as positive. At an eighteen-month follow-up, the client reported continued abstinence from drugs. In addition, he had married and was experiencing an active and enjoyable social life.

Summary

Drug abuse is viewed as a behavior that is maintained by a variety of consequences and that may be related to diverse antecedent events. Here, too, there is a need for an individual assessment of the unique antecedent and consequent factors related to substance abuse. The application of behavioral methods to the area of drug abuse is fairly recent. A variety of methods have been employed, including contingency contracting, covert sensitization, and covert extinction, in addition to the use of actual aversive events. There is an increasing recognition of the need to develop appropriate alternative behaviors that will successfully compete with drug abuse. Often, the drug abuser, like the problem drinker, learns only one reaction to unpleasant events—to resort to substance abuse. Intervention must include the development of appropriate alternative behaviors in stress-provoking situations as well as the establishment of more functional behavior related to other motivational sources for drug abuse.

17

Children who have problems at home often have difficulties at school as well. If problems occur in both settings,
intervention may be initiated in both at once, depending on
whether two programs can be managed successfully and on
whether intervention in the school is employed as an incentive
to encourage parental participation in a home program, in
which case gains would have to be made in the latter setting
before a program was initiated in the school (see, for example,
Patterson and others, 1975). As in other settings, there is a
focus on the relationship of the child's behavior to that of significant others such as peers and teachers. Although the child's
behavior is the source of complaint, attention is directed toward
identification of antecedent and consequent environmental
events that relate to his behavior, which usually include behav-

746

Behavioral Intervention in Educational Settings

iors of others. Problematic reactions are considered to be related to deficient environments. "In many respects the classroom is a barren wasteland when one compares it to other, normally reinforcing interactions. Most of the reinforcers in the system are highly formalized, such as grades and test scores. The control of social behavior is achieved more as a function of threatened or applied aversive consequences than by positive social reinforcers" (Patterson, Shaw, and Ebner, 1969, p. 15).

There is an extensive literature describing the application of behavioral methods within a variety of classrooms, including special education classes, classes of retarded children, and classes of normal children in elementary school, junior high school, and high school. Some programs have been directed toward altering the behavior of one child, whereas others are concerned with the behavior of an entire class. Individual contingencies (consequences given to one child) as well as group contingencies (consequences awarded to a number of people such as all class members) have been employed. Children have been trained to alter inappropriate behavior of the teacher, to help their peers to develop more effective behaviors, and to manage their own behavior. However, the main focus of intervention has been to enhance teacher skills in relation to influencing classroom behavior and academic achievement. The teacher is trained in how to provide attention for desired behavior, and is coached in how to reinforce approximations to desired behaviors and to gradually increase the criterion for reinforcement as behavior improves. He or she is encouraged to ignore behaviors that interfere with learning but that are not dangerous or destructive, and to employ time out or response cost for inappropriate behaviors that cannot be ignored, such as destruction of property or rough fighting. Increasing teacher praise for appropriate behaviors of one pupil has beneficial effects on the behavior of other children in class (Broden, Bruce, Mitchell, Carter, and Hall, 1970).

Teachers often provide more attention for disruptive behaviors than for appropriate classroom behavior. One large survey of public school teachers indicated that 77 percent of their interactions with children were negative, while only 23 percent were positive (Madsen, Madsen, Saudargas, Hammond, and Egar, 1970). Teacher commands given in relation to inappropriate behavior often increase this behavior. One study found that the teacher's saying "Sit down" when children are out of their seats actually increased the frequency of standing behavior (Madsen, Becker, Thomas, Koser, and Plager, 1970). Soft teacher reprimands that can only be heard by the child being spoken to are more effective in decreasing disruptive behavior than are loud reprimands. A substantial number of studies indicate that student behavior is a direct result of contingent teacher attention. For example, calling a child "bad" may actually increase inappropriate behavior (O'Leary and Becker, 1967). Redistributing this attention has been found to alter a wide variety of behaviors, including crying (Hart, Allen, Buell, Harris, and Wolf, 1964), and speech (Brison, 1966). In the latter study, the teacher was trained to praise approximations to speech; within four weeks the child was speaking, whereas he had not spoken for the year before. On-task behavior and social behaviors of older children have also been increased by redistributing teacher attention. The effects of such a change will in part be determined by the extent to which undesirable behaviors are maintained by peer attention. If this is an important maintaining condition, arrangements should be made to "co-opt" this reinforcement in support of the program by using group contingencies.

Assessment

Limitation of students and the teacher to one physical location (the classroom) for a set period of time facilitates collection of observational data by a trained observer. In addition to direct observation, other assessment methods have been usefully employed, including self-report and self-monitoring by the teacher and/or students.

Observation in the Classroom. Observation of teacher-student interaction offers valuable information as to the nature of problematic behaviors and reinforcement contingencies operating in the classroom. Either the teacher or trained observers may be employed to gather needed information in the classroom. The teacher may continuously record a specific behavior by using a wrist counter. Teachers have also employed a variable time-sampling procedure in which a student's behavior is noted at preselected intervals marked by a timer (Kubany and Sloggett, 1973). For example, a student's behavior may be observed eight or nine times during a fifty-minute class period. A timer is present and when it rings, the teacher observes and records the student's behavior. A baseline gathered by a teacher in this manner indicated that one seventh-grade social studies student was on task only 53 percent of the time. Additional behaviors can also be coded if desired. For example, with this student, passive (P) behavior (not on task but not disrupting others) and disruptive (D) behavior (out of seat, talking without permission or making other noise) were fairly equally distributed over the remaining intervals sampled. On-task behavior increased to 83 percent of intervals after a program was initiated in which the entire class was awarded one minute of free time for card playing at the end of the class period each time the student was on task. The teacher indicated that the monitoring procedure was not inconvenient and that, after the first few bell rings, the class did not seem distracted by the bell. The percentages gathered by this recording method reflected the actual frequency of the behavior very closely. For example, making only four or five observations per session generated a record that was very similar to one based on eighty observations per session.

The teacher may not have time to monitor behavior, or his or her data may be supplemented by data collected by the counselor or some other trained observer. Parents, for example, may be employed as observers after receiving training. A number of coding procedures have been developed. Some arrange for notation of teacher reactions as well as student behavior. One system allows notation of four categories of increasingly off-task student behavior—attending to task, scanning (off task alone), social (off task with others) and disruptive (fighting, throwing objects, and so on)—as well as four categories of teacher behavior (instructions, praise, ignore, and elsewhere). Behavior is coded at the end of every five-second interval (Goodwin and Coates, 1976). This monitoring system indicates the frequency with which a teacher offers effective consequences for student behaviors. Changes in the percentage of intervals in which on-task behavior is praised and disruptive behavior ignored could be employed as one measure of change. High levels of reliability can be achieved with this monitoring system after a few hours of training.

Interval recording is often used for classroom observation, usually by observers other than the teacher. In Table 16, we see that a child in nursery school changed activities with great frequency, as indicated by the brackets. Vocalizations were noted (V) as well as proximity of the child (P) or physical contact with another person (T). In the bottom row, contact with physical objects (E) or with children were noted. The child changed her activity twelve times in the 6-minute observational period (fifteen-second intervals were employed). The teacher offered approval five times, contingent on the child's verbal or

Table 16. Sample Line from a Data Sheet of Nursery School Girl
Who Changed Activities with High Frequency

1 2 3 4	5 6 7 8	9 10 11 12	13 14 15 16	17 18 19 20	21 22 23 24
/ / / /	/ / / /	/x /x / /	/ / /x/	x /x/ / /	/ / / /
			V	V V	V
P P P	P	P P P	P	T T P	P P
	E E	E E E	E	C C	

Source: Bijou, Peterson, and Ault (1968, p. 181).

proximity behavior (see *X*'s above top line) and we see that the child spent most of the 6-minute period alone or in close proximity to another child. Even though rate of activity change and not peer interaction was the subject of the study, the other data on social behavior provided interesting information: decline in rate of activity change was related to an increase in rate of appropriate peer behavior. Interval recording has been used to determine the rate of hyperactivity. Recorders noted the presence (a slash) or the absence (an *O*) in the interval at the end of each twenty-five seconds during 45-minute math and reading classes (Ayllon, Layman, and Kandel, 1975). The percent of intervals in which hyperactivity occurred was assessed before and after intervention. The average rate of appropriate and inappropriate behavior in a given classroom or during certain activities in one classroom (such as reading and play) can be determined by observing a child who is not considered deviant by the teacher along with the labeled child. This allows a calibration of children who are labeled *deviant* and may reveal a negative attitude toward this child, in that rate of appropriate and inappropriate behaviors of these children may be very similar. Existence of a negative teacher attitude may call for different intervention methods, ones more focused on altering his or her attitude.

If trained observers are employed, permission must first be gained from the teacher, the school principal, and the child's parents. A way must also be arranged to introduce the observer to the class. The teacher might introduce the observer by saying, "This is _____ . She'd like to see how we do things at our school." It is important to discuss with the teacher what he is planning to tell the children about the observer. Methods of remaining unobtrusive include sitting in the back of the room and entering and leaving the classroom during a natural change in classroom activity. The observer should thank the teacher when leaving and make arrangements for further observation periods as necessary.

Self-Report and Self-Monitoring Measures. Self-report measures have only infrequently been employed in relation to educational settings. Since it is likely that people can be mislabeled in this setting as well as in others, such as the family (in that being labeled as *deviant* may not accurately reflect a high rate of inappropriate behavior), determination of attitudes is important. A subjective units of irritation (SUI) scale modeled after Wolpe's subjective anxiety scale (1958) can be employed to assess interpersonal relationships (Sherman and Cormier, 1972). The teacher is given a number of three-by-five-inch index cards, each of which has a student's name written on it, and asked to rate each student in the class from zero (a model student who never irritates her) to 100 (the worst student she could imagine). This measure can also be employed to assess changes in the quality of a relationship with a decrease in SUI score representing an improvement in the relationship. Decreases in subject units of irritation correlate well with decreases assessed by other measures, such as a decrease in overall rate of disruptive behavior. Such measures can provide a concurrent measure to evaluate progress. Self-monitoring by students has also been employed. For example, in one study (Broden, Hall, and Mitts, 1971), an eight-year-old girl recorded her study behavior by noting at different times during history class whether she was studying. She was given a recording form containing three rows of ten squares and when she happened to remember, she recorded a "+" in a square if she was studying or had been studying for the past few minutes and a "−" if she was not studying. This self-recording procedure increased study time from a baseline of 30 percent to 78 percent.

Archival Records and Behavior Products. Attendance records and class grades or grades on tests may be pertinent to a behavior change program. Such information can be obtained from examining records kept by the school.

Reinforcers in the Classroom. The classroom provides a wide variety of reinforcers, many of which are often not employed contingently to increase desirable behaviors. Some examples of these follow (see Madsen and Madsen, 1974, pp. 122-123).

Touching

Patting shoulder	Leaning over
Touching arm	Touching hurt
Straightening clothes	Kissing a hurt
Hugging	Putting face next to child
Touching hand	Tweaking nose
Shaking hands	Tickling
Squeezing hand	Cupping face in hands
Patting cheek	Gentle pull at hair

Activities and Privileges: Approval

Individual

Leading student groups
Representing group in school activities
Displaying student's work (any subject matter)
Straightening up for teacher
Putting away materials
Running errands
Caring for class pets, flowers, and so on
Collecting materials (papers, workbooks, assignments, and so on)
Choosing activities
Show and tell (any level)
Constructing school materials
Dusting, erasing, cleaning, arranging chairs, and so on
Helping other children (drinking, lavatory, cleaning, and so on)
Reading a story
Exempting a test
Working problems on the board
Answering questions
Outside supervising (patrols, directing parking, ushering, and so on)
Classroom supervision
Omitting specific assignments

First in line
Assisting teacher teach
Leading discussions
Making gifts
Recognizing birthdays
Grading papers
Special seating arrangements
Responsibility for ongoing activities during school
    holidays (pets, plants, assignments)
Decorating room
Presenting hobby to class
"Citizen of the Week" or "Best Kid of the Day"

Social

Movies
Decorating classroom
Presenting skits
Playing records
Puppet shows
Preparing for holidays (Christmas, Thanksgiving,
    Easter)
Making a game of subject matter
Outdoor lessons
Visiting another class
Field trips (subject matter)
Planning daily schedules
Musical chairs
Competing with other classes
Performing for PTA
Dancing
Going to museums, fire stations, courthouses, pic-
    nics, and so on
"Senior Sluff Day"
Participating in group organizations (music, speech,
    athletics, social clubs)
Talking periods
Recess or play periods
Early dismissal
Parties
Talent shows (jokes, readings, music, and so on)

Performance feedback, whether self-scored or provided
by others, can facilitate appropriate behavior. For example,
feedback and graphing of number of arithmetic errors by first-
grade pupils decreased the number of such errors (Fink and

Carnine, 1975). The classroom situation provides many reinforcers that can be employed in response cost, such as loss of
recess.

Reinforcers can be maximized in a number of ways, including arranging for children to observe others being reinforced. Reinforcer sampling may be employed: the child is
allowed access to a reinforcer for a brief period of time prior to
making it contingent on some behavior. A teacher might read a
chapter of an adventure story early in the day and then use subsequent chapters for task completion later in the day. Teachers
are encouraged to use naturally occurring reinforcers, curriculum being one of the most important in classroom settings. For
example, receiving desired textual material can be made contingent on completion of a certain amount of work on material
that is not so highly desired. Teachers are also encouraged to
employ a range of reinforcers, and to ensure that reinforcers do
not compete with each other by scheduling two or more at the
same time. Cues may be arranged, such as lights, to signal that
reinforcers can be gained for on-task behavior. The vast differences that exist between teachers in their use of classroom activities is nicely illustrated in the following example.

> As a reward for her second-grade class, Miss Robb
> granted a special privilege. "Whoever finishes both
> pages in his workbook without any mistakes today
> may come in after school and help me wash the
> blackboard." Each day Miss Robb would have a
> different activity which would qualify children to
> be chosen for the special privilege of helping her
> wash the blackboards. The second graders vied
> with each other to qualify for the reward. Miss
> Robb managed to arrange things so that over the
> course of the year every child in the class received
> this reward several times.
>
> The next fall a new teacher arrived to teach
> the third-grade class. Miss Gibson made it clear that
> she would tolerate no nonsense. "If any of you
> causes any trouble, you will have to come in after
> school to help me wash the blackboards."
>
> The same children who valued the honor of
> washing blackboards after school for Miss Robb
> now felt shamed when they were required to per-

form the same activity for Miss Gibson. [Krum-
boltz and Krumboltz, 1972, p. 110]

And, finally, high-probability behaviors, such as running around
the room, have been successfully employed to increase appropriate behaviors, such as sitting at one's desk (Homme, deBaca,
Devine, Steinhorst, and Rickert, 1963).

Intervention

The usual concern of a counselor relates to the behavior
of one child in school. Parents may, for example, indicate that
their child has problems in school as well as in the home. Or
teachers may request aid with particular children, or with the
disruptive behavior or academic underachievement of an entire
class. Behavioral methods employed when the focus is upon the
behavior of one child will be described in the following section,
as well as examples of programs for entire classes of students.
An entire class may be involved, even though one child is the
topic of concern, in order to arrange for peer support of desirable behaviors. Ideally, natural reinforcers should be employed
or established, such as teacher attention; however, this may not
be possible and therefore home-based incentive programs may
be employed. One guideline that is very important is not to require too much of the teacher. If he feels overburdened, he will
probably "turn off." He will also turn off if he feels he is being
criticized. If a high rate of deviant behavior occurs, it may be
necessary to employ a behavior modifier to gain control over
the behavior, who eventually turns the program over to the
teacher, who can then continue it at little cost to himself (Patterson, 1971a).

A wide variety of intervention procedures have been employed to alter student behavior in the classroom. Stimulus control (rearranging antecedent conditions), as well as contingency
management (rearranging consequences), have been employed.
There has been a special focus on altering the distribution of
teacher attention, on the use of token programs, and on methods of training teachers. Students have been trained to alter the
teacher's behavior as well as to alter the behavior of their peers.

Contingency contracts, in which explicit arrangements are made between selected behaviors and consequences, offer one way to gradually have the student assume more responsibility for self-monitoring and self-evaluation of his own behavior. A lack of cooperation by teachers need not prohibit changing classroom behavior as indicated by the successful use of home-based reinforcement programs; that is, reinforcers are offered by the parents for appropriate class-related behaviors. Behavioral procedures have also been employed to decrease anxiety associated with school attendance and to increase appropriate social interaction. Recently there has been special emphasis on developing self-management skills of children in relation to impulse control and task performance, and procedures have also been developed to enhance study skills.

Altering Stimulus Conditions. Desired behaviors can be prompted through use of instructions or posted rules. Rules that offer positive consequences for appropriate behaviors are emphasized, and teachers are encouraged to illustrate desired behaviors by praising children who offer good examples of following rules, noting specifically the basis for the praise (Becker, Thomas, and Carnine, 1971). Posting of rules and their enforcement increase desired behaviors; however, posting of rules alone has little effect (Madsen, Becker, and Thomas, 1968). Teachers are coached not to have too many rules, to select ones that are easy to enforce, and to be prepared for rule testing where children "misbehave" to see whether the rule will be enforced. Repeating rules less frequently over time as desirable behaviors increase in frequency helps to teach children to prompt their own desirable behaviors; however, reinforcement for such behaviors should still be offered. The failure to reinforce desirable behaviors was strikingly demonstrated in a study of the natural rates of teacher praise and disapproval over Grades One through Twelve. Verbal approval rates of teachers decreased over grade with a large decrease after Grade Two. Almost never did teachers praise expected behaviors by saying, for example, "Good, you came in on time" (White, 1975).

Teachers can also be trained to increase facilitating events for desired behaviors. These include skills, tools, or physical conditions that are essential or important if a behavior is to occur. Completing math problems, for example, may require a quiet place to work and certain arithmetic skills. It is important that teachers possess adequate curriculum design skills and apply these to each child to assure that tasks given match existent skills. Inappropriate curriculum design is often the cause of disruptive classroom behavior. Such incorrect design results in a lack of reinforcement for task completion—either the task is too hard and so the student cannot successfully complete it, or it is too easy and the student becomes bored. The introduction of highly structured methods of distributing and collecting academic assignments and materials under precise temporal requirements has been found to successfully decrease disruptive behavior (Ayllon, Layman, and Burke, 1972). This is one illustration of the importance of structuring classroom activities.

Public posting of the names of those individuals who achieved a certain criterion may increase appropriate behaviors. For example, posting the names of children who returned to class promptly after recess decreased the number of students late for class (Hall and others, 1970). Public posting of the highest scores increased story-writing performance (Van Houten, Hill, and Parsons, 1975). Such posting has also been found to increase appropriate staff behavior. For example, publicly posting the percentage of training sessions conducted by staff working in a school for the retarded dramatically improved their performance (Panyan, Boozer, and Morris, 1970).

Altering Teacher Attention. Most behavioral programs have attempted to rearrange the consequences provided by the teacher so that appropriate behaviors are reinforced and inappropriate ones either ignored or followed by response cost or time out. Guidelines shared with teachers include the following:

> 1. Specify in a positive way the rules that are the basis for your reinforcement. Demonstrate the behaviors you desire by praising the children who are good examples of following the rules. Rules are made important to children by providing reinforcement for following the rules. Rules may be different for different work, study, or play periods. Keep the rules to five or less. As the children learn to follow the rules, repeat them less frequently, but continue to praise good classroom behaviors.

2. Relate the children's performance to the rules. Be specific about the behaviors children show that mean "paying attention" or "working hard." "That's right, you're a hard worker." "You watched the board all the time I was presenting the example. That's paying attention." "That's a good answer. You listened very closely to my question." "Jimmy is really working hard. He'll get the answer. You'll see." "Gee, you got it. I didn't think you would. That's good working." Relax the rules between work periods. Do not be afraid to have fun with your children when the work period is over.

3. Catch the children being good. Reinforce behavior incompatible with that you wish to eliminate. Select incompatible behaviors to reinforce that will be most beneficial to the child's development. Focus on reinforcing tasks important for social and cognitive skills in the process of eliminating disruptive behaviors.

4. Ignore disruptive behaviors unless someone is getting hurt. Focus your attention on the children who are working well to prompt the correct behaviors in the children who are misbehaving. Reinforce improvement when it does occur.

5. When you see a persistent problem behavior, look for the reinforcing events. It may be your own behavior.

6. You can use as a reinforcer any activity the child likes to participate in, as well as social attention, praise, or more tangible reinforcers.

7. In looking for reinforcers to use to strengthen behaviors, remember these:

reinforcers controlled by parents

the social worker's attention

games and puzzles

honors and privileges

helping teacher

playing teacher's role

recess

praise and attention

being right

being first

toys and edibles

trinkets

a class party

art activities

music

extra gym periods

8. Reinforcing events must immediately follow the behavior to be strengthened.

9. Social reinforcers do not work for all children. When necessary to get appropriate behavior going, strengthen the reinforcers being used.

10. If a point system backed up by tangibles or special activities is introduced, always accompany the points given with praise and words telling the children what they did well. These steps will help make praise alone effective as a reinforcer, as well as completing the tasks that are the basis for reinforcement. "You finished all of your arithmetic problems. That [is] really [good. You earned] nine points for that." Relate the payoff to what he did to earn it. "You earned this model airplane by working really hard on arithmetic and reading. I'm proud of your improvement." Slowly require the child to work for longer periods with less tangible payoffs, but give lots of praise and other forms of social reinforcement.

11. Seek special training or consultation if elaborate token systems seem to be the answer for you.

12. Punishment is most likely to be required when the unwanted behavior is very intense (so that there is potential danger to self or others) or very frequent (so that there is little positive behavior to work with).

13. If punishment is necessary, first try isolating the child in a room by himself with only a chair and a light. The child should remain in the time-out room until he is quiet for several minutes. Give one warning prior to the use of time out, so that the warning signal can be used most of the time as a punishment without the need for time out.

14. Any use of punishment should be accompanied by the use of reinforcement of behaviors incompatible with the punished behaviors.

15. Hold consistently to your rules for reinforcement, extinction, or punishment. This means do not sometimes reinforce and sometimes punish the same behavior. Do not give in after deciding a behavior should not be reinforced. Only if you show consistent reactions to the children's behaviors can they learn what is reinforced and what is not. [Becker, Thomas, and Carnine, 1971, pp. 161-163]

Ignoring behavior alone is ineffective (Madsen, Becker, and Thomas, 1968). When use of praise for desired behavior and ignoring undesirable behaviors are not effective, other procedures must be added. However, systematic use of teacher attention should be continued. Time out, for example, has been successfully employed, in special classrooms, to decrease disruptive behaviors (Drabman and Spitalnik, 1973). Use of time out poses some difficulties in terms of getting the child to the time out area and selecting an appropriate spot. Response cost has been found to be as effective as a reward system in decreasing disruptive behavior (see Bucher and Hawkins, 1973). However, a potentially bad side effect of a cost program may be found in encouraging teachers to look for bad rather than good behaviors. Both rewards and costs can be effectively combined as illustrated in the token system described later.

Many studies have focused on decreasing disruptive behavior in the hopes that academic performance will therefore increase. For example, reinforcement has been offered for refraining from disruptive behavior. The purpose of such programs is thereby to increase appropriate classroom performance, the most important of which is academic performance. However, such approaches do not always result in an increase in academic achievements (Ferritor, Buckholdt, Hamblin, and Smith, 1972). A number of recent studies show that inappropriate classroom behavior can be decreased by reinforcing incompatible behaviors. For example, one study found that when children were reinforced for sitting, making eye contact with the teacher, and performing academically related activities, their disruptive behavior decreased (O'Leary and Becker, 1967). Reinforcement for academic achievement has been employed to alter hyperactive behavior of children previously maintained on Ritalin (Ayllon, Layman, and Kandel, 1975). A check-point system similar to that described later in this chapter (O'Leary and Becker, 1967) was used, in which checks were awarded by the teacher for correct academic performance. This included addition of whole numbers under 10 and workbook responses to stories read each day. Hyperactivity was assessed using some of the code categories developed by Becker, Madsen, Arnold, and Thomas (1967), such as gross motor (getting out of seat, standing up, running, hopping, skipping, jumping, walking around, moving chair, and so forth); object noise (tapping pencil or other objects, clapping, tapping feet, rattling or tearing paper, throwing book on desk, slamming desk); disturbance of others' property (grabbing objects or work, knocking neighbor's books off desk, destroying another's property, throwing objects at another person without hitting him); contact (hitting, kicking, shoving, pinching, slapping, striking with object that hits someone, poking with object, biting, pulling hair, touching, patting, and so forth); verbalization (carrying on conversation with children when it is not permitted, answering teacher without raising hand or without being called on, making comments or calling out remarks when no questions have been asked, calling teacher's name, crying, screaming, singing, whistling, laughing, coughing, or blowing loudly); and turning around (turning head or body to look at another person, showing objects to another child). Medication was first removed, resulting in a marked increase in hyperactivity. The percentage of hyperactivity and of academic performance while on medication and during the final six-day period (without drug therapy, but with a reinforcement program) can be seen in Figure 39.

This study clearly showed that, for these three children, reinforcement for academic performance decreased hyperactivity. The academic gains made under the reinforcement program were in sharp contrast with the lack of academic progress shown by these children while under medication (Ayllon, Layman, and Kandel, 1975). A multiple-baseline design across math and reading performance, in which the reinforcement program was first introduced only for math responses, supported the efficacy of the reinforcement program. Only in math did behaviors change. Reading responses remained at their baseline level until the program was also employed there. The authors report that the influence over hyperactivity by improvement in academic performance was rapid, stable, and independent of the duration or dosage of medication received by each child prior to the program. Parents were relieved that their children could get along in a normal fashion in school without drugs and the teacher was pleased that she could now increase social and academic skills of the children more easily, as they were more responsive to her.

This study supports the reciprocal relationship between

Figure 39. The Percentage of Intervals (for One Student) in Which
Hyperactivity Took Place and the Percentage of Correct Math and
Reading Performance

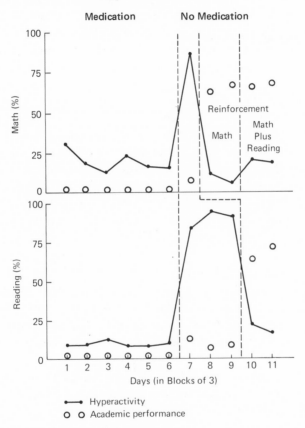

Source: Ayllon, Layman, and Kandel (1975, p. 142).

academic performance and disruptive behavior. The disruptive-
ness to work of such behaviors as talking or walking around the
room was supported by the students themselves, who made
comments such as, "Shut up. I'm trying to do my work" and
"Quit bugging me, can't you see I'm reading?" during times
when they could earn points. The authors conclude that "This
study offers a behavioral and educationally justifiable alternative to the use of medication for hyperactive children" (p. 145).
They note, however, that these results may be attainable only

with students who have well-developed academic repertoires. When disruptive behavior is stronger, there may have to be an initial phase during which there is a direct focus on such behaviors. It should also be noted that no generalization of effects to other academic periods occurred even though the teacher and students were the same. This again highlights the need for special programs to arrange display of appropriate behaviors in other settings.

Token Programs in the Classroom. Token programs can be introduced when naturally available reinforcers such as teacher approval or grades do not support desirable behaviors, which was the case with a classroom (of 17 nine-year-old children described as emotionally disturbed) in which a token program was introduced (O'Leary and Becker, 1967). Instructions were first placed on the blackboard: "In seat, face front, raise hand, working, pay attention, and desk clean." Tokens consisted of ratings placed in small booklets on each child's desk. These could vary from 1 to 10 and were awarded in accord with how well the children followed instructions. Ratings were tradeable for a variety of backup reinforcers, including candy, pennants, comics, and kites. Instructions were repeated to the class each day of the token program. Each child was first rated five times a day and this was decreased later to three times a day. The length of time between earning tokens and exchanging them was gradually extended after three days by requiring two days prior to trading them (over the next four days), three days for the next fifteen days, and four days for the next twenty-four days. This gradual fading of the token program served to gradually increase the reinforcing potential of teacher praise and attention.

The ratings took about three minutes for the teacher to complete. The rating procedure encouraged the teacher to reinforce approximations to appropriate desired behavior. The teacher was coached to offer verbal praise while giving out the ratings, such as, "Good, Gerald, I like the way you raised your hand to ask a question" (O'Leary and Becker, 1967). The teacher also ignored inappropriate behavior of students while reinforcing appropriate behavior of other students. As the authors note, this permitted her to almost totally dispense with the use of social censure. This program was very successful in decreasing deviant behavior. The daily mean of deviant behavior during baseline ranged from 66 to 91 percent, and decreased to 3 to 4 percent during intervention. The program was totally carried out by the teacher, although observers were employed to collect data in the classroom. Time out was not employed at all.

Token programs have been used to increase academic performance in such areas as penmanship (Hopkins, Schutte, and Garton, 1971) and the creativeness of compositions (Maloney and Hopkins, 1973). An extensive literature exists describing the use of token programs to decrease disruptive behavior in classrooms as well as to increase academic performance with pupils varying widely in functioning level (see O'Leary and O'Leary, 1976; Birnbrauer, 1976). There is no doubt that these programs are very effective in achieving the former goal. There is less support for their efficacy in maintaining academic performance, but this seems related to a failure to focus directly on academic performance; a failure to arrange appropriate maintenance programs, including the need to train new teachers as the child progresses from class to class; and lack of appropriate curriculum design. Use of naturally existing backup reinforcers is emphasized.

Token programs have been found to be more effective in increasing appropriate teacher attention to on-task behavior than instructions to praise on-task behavior and ignore off-task behavior (see Breyer and Allen, 1975). For example, one teacher used no praise at all (on five of the ten baseline days) and was ten times more likely to use reprimands for inappropriate behavior than positive statements for on-task behavior. All children in her class displayed academic and social deficiencies that had prevented their promotion to the second grade. She was first given a list of positive teacher comments and was asked to select two or three new comments each day and to use these to reinforce students. She agreed to a goal of fifteen positive comments per hour and also agreed to decrease her use of negative comments to 60 percent below baseline. Praise increased threefold; however, she did not reduce her rate of negative statements.

A token program was then introduced in which the

teacher observed and scored each of her fifteen students on a variable-interval, eight-minute schedule for on-task behaviors. After every second interval she circulated among her students and tallied the number of points each student had earned on a tally sheet at their desk. Three points were earned for each on-task behavior such as listening, seat work, voluntarily reading out loud, and completion of daily assignments. Points were tradable at the "Good-Study Store" for a variety of prizes at the end of each day. The token program resulted in an immediate and strong reversal of the frequency of praise and reprimands. Reprimands decreased 50 percent and positive comments doubled in frequency. The teacher reported that she was much more comfortable with the token program than with the praise-and-ignore condition since she viewed the focus of the program as being the students rather than herself. The greater changes in the student's behavior during the token program may also have caused the teacher to like the token program more than the praise-and-ignore condition.

As the authors point out, it is very likely that the prior praise-and-ignore phase, in which the teacher learned to identify particular approval statements, may have facilitated the effects of the token economy. It is also likely that the greater attention to reinforcement for on-task behavior in the token program by virtue of frequent dispersement of tokens helped the teacher to self-monitor her behavior more closely. A token program may thus be less threatening to teachers in encouraging them to alter their rate of positive and negative comments than simply training them to praise more frequently and to ignore off-task behavior.

An example of a token program in an elementary school class of twenty-five to twenty-nine students designed to increase academic performance (McLaughlin and Malaby, 1972) was carried out by the teacher of a combined fifth- and sixth-grade class. The main target behavior was assignment completion in spelling, language, handwriting, and math. Behaviors that earned and cost points are described in Table 17. Variation in points awarded for items correct was related to the number of items on a test. In the case of food for animals, the amount of food brought determined the reward received. Penalties were made

Table 17. Behaviors and the Number of Points
That They Earned or Lost

Behaviors That Earned Points	Points
1. Items correct	6 to 12
2. Study behavior 8:50-9:15	5 per day
3. Bring food for animals	1 to 10
4. Bring sawdust for animals	1 to 10
5. Art	1 to 4
6. Listening points	1 to 2 per lesson
7. Extra credit	Assigned value
8. Neatness	1 to 2
9. Taking home assignments	5
10. Taking notes	1 to 3
11. Quiet in lunch line	2
12. Quiet in cafeteria	2
13. Appropriate noon hour behavior	3

Behaviors That Lost Points	Points
1. Assignments incomplete	Amount squared
2. Gum and candy	100
3. Inappropriate verbal behavior	15
4. Inappropriate motor behavior	15
5. Fighting	100
6. Cheating	100

Source: McLaughlin and Malaby (1972, p. 264).

quite severe to prevent a student from gaining reinforcers if he or she engaged in a cost behavior during the week.

The students helped to select the privileges, choosing from those naturally available in the class. A ranking by the students of the desirability of various items was employed to assign point values (see Table 18). Students could select special jobs or projects each week.

There were at least eighteen assignments per week, although this figure varied from week to week. Students recorded points awarded on a form by their desks and the teacher recorded points won or lost in her grade book. Monday morning was selected as point exchange time. This process was supervised by student bankers, each of whom took responsibility for one of the privileges, subtracting the necessary number of

Table 18. Weekly Privileges

| | Price in Points | |
Privilege	Sixth	Fifth
1. Sharpening pencils	20	13
2. Seeing animals	30	25
3. Taking out balls	5	3
4. Sports	60	40
5. Special writing on board	20	16
6. Being on a committee	30	25
7. Special jobs	25	15
8. Playing games	5	3
9. Listening to records	5	2
10. Coming in early	10	6
11. Seeing the grade book	5	2
12. Special projects	25	20

Source: McLaughlin and Malaby (1972, p. 264).

points from a student's point total. Each banker gave the teacher a list of those students who purchased privileges. Because of the involvement of students in carrying out this program, the teacher time required was modest, about twenty to twenty-five minutes each week. This is a critical point, given the many other tasks which teachers must carry out.

As a result of the token economy, assignments completed increased from 69 to 94 percent during baseline, to 100 percent when exchange days were varied rather than always held on Mondays. The decrease in assignment completion when points and fines were no longer contingent on such behavior supported the influence of these incentives. The program was rated as favorable by twenty of the students, who made comments such as, "I completed my work on time easier, I liked to earn privileges" and "It made school fun." Five students did not like the program and their negative comments included, "Privileges cost too much" and "The fines were too high." There were individual differences in relation to percent increase in assignment completion. This program provides a good illustration of the effective combination of a reward and cost program.

Contrary to what might be expected, token cost programs in which tokens are removed following inappropriate behaviors have been found to be as effective as token reward systems (for example, see Kaufman and O'Leary, 1972). The teacher either added tokens to each child's token container in the front of the room or removed them. Different results might ensue if the tokens had to be physically removed from the children.

Training teachers how to use a token program may be aided by initial use of a model (Ringer, 1973). For example, a token system was first introduced into a fourth-grade class of thirty-seven students by a token helper, who moved in a random fashion around the class initialing squares on a card by each student's desk if the student was behaving appropriately. The child was verbally praised as well. The program was originally discussed and mutually agreed on by the teacher and the "token helper." The teacher was encouraged to praise students for on-task behavior and the token helper immediately initialed the card of any child commended by the teacher. Pupils who earned initials in twenty squares were permitted to visit the principal's office, where the principal praised each child individually and placed a rubber stamp with the school emblem on the card. The teacher gradually assumed more responsibility for dispensing tokens.

As with any behavior change program, special procedures are typically required to achieve maintenance of positive changes after tokens are removed. The development of peer praise for appropriate behaviors and gradually increasing the delay of reinforcement are two procedures that have been found to enhance maintenance (Jones and Kazdin, 1975). Training children to accurately evaluate their own behavior has also been attempted to increase the longevity of effects (Drabman, Spitalnik, and O'Leary, 1973).

Teacher Training. A variety of formats have been employed, including formal instruction in the principles of behavior modification, formal practicum training in observational and experimental techniques, feedback from the counselor while in the classroom, instructions coupled with counselor praise of teacher behavior, modeling by a "token helper" (Ringer, 1973), and role playing. For example, Hall, Lund, and Jackson (1968) held up a colored square to indicate that they wanted the teacher to praise. Brief signals presented over the PA system have also been employed for this purpose (Van Houten and Sullivan, 1975). More formal programs train teachers how to observe, record, and graph behaviors, as well as how to reinforce on-task behaviors and ignore off-task behaviors. The teacher may be willing to read a book describing classroom management procedures (for example, Madsen and Madsen, 1970; Buckley and Walker, 1970). As with other training efforts, it has been found that practice using behavioral principles in the classroom, rather than just reading or talking about these concepts, is important (McKeown, Adams, and Forehand, 1975). Instructions alone in terms of identifying behaviors and systematic use of attention are not effective in increasing appropriate teacher praise (Cossairt, Hall, and Hopkins, 1973). Frequent feedback— for example, every ten minutes—is helpful in increasing appropriate use of praise (Cooper, Thomson, and Baer, 1970). Teachers, like parents, are trained to identify specific responses and to collect information (a baseline) as their first reaction to a problem.

Teachers often have more difficulty using praise contingently to increase desirable behaviors than learning the complexities of token programs. Teachers as well as parents often display a reluctance to use positive reinforcers. Essential to success of a teacher training program is assuring reinforcement for changes in his or her behavior, especially during the one- or two-week period it may take to create changes in the students' behavior. Reinforcement props are needed during this time, including the counselor's presence in the classroom and praise for efforts for carrying out the program (Patterson, 1971a). As with some parents, positive changes in the child's behavior are often insufficient to maintain appropriate child management skills. One incentive employed has been grades in behavioral training courses; however, these also are only offered over a brief time span. Jones and Eimers (1975) developed a skill-training package using role playing and focusing on training teachers to set limits and to prompt and reinforce on-task behavior during seat work and group discussions. Training sessions were held after school once or twice a week and lasted ninety minutes. One teacher received six sessions and the other seven sessions. Role playing centered around the use of mock classroom lessons in which the roles of "teacher," "good student," and "bad student" were alternated between participants. One person played "teacher" and tried to conduct a lesson; one played the "good student"; and the other participant was instructed to engage in misbehavior, such as making "wise" or "smart" remarks, throwing objects, hassling others, and so forth. During role playing, the counselor modeled correct behavior, the teacher rehearsed behaviors, and corrective feedback was offered. "Teachers" were asked first to critique their own behavior. "Students" were asked to share how they experienced the "teacher's" behavior. Rehearsals of specific strategies were repeated until all agreed that mastery had been achieved. The first training sessions included a discussion of the types of problems typically found in an elementary school and an identification of basic skills in offering mild disapproval. These included "(1) early identification of potentially disruptive behavior; (2) a repertoire of brief, low-intensity, nonpejorative verbalizations and gestures signifying that the student was out of order, such as "just a second," "wait," "that's enough," or simply the child's name; (3) physical proximity to and orientation toward the offending student; (4) quickness of responding following the onset of disruption so that the disruptive behavior was interrupted if possible; and (5) facial expression and tone of voice consistent with disapproval" (Jones and Eimers, 1975, p. 426). Teachers were trained to "cruise"—to continually move within the semicircle of students in the context of a group discussion, so that approval and disapproval could be offered in close proximity. Limit setting was also discussed in Session 1. During Session 2, time out was discussed and a time-out area was selected in each teacher's classroom. Use of this procedure was practiced, including giving brief warnings, brief dismissals of "wheedling" by students, composure in the face of provocation, and how and when to summon backup help if physically resisted or threatened (Jones and Eimers, 1975). Disapproval for disruption and approval for on-task behavior of the disruptive student were also modeled and practiced. Teachers were instructed never to use disapproval by itself but to always pair this with immediate approval of a "good student" and to approve the offending students as soon as appropriate class participation occurred.

During Session 3, skills were offered as to how to make a transition to a discussion period, including teacher statement of behaviors expected during the transition and rules to be followed during the next activity. Methods of prompting appropriate student behavior were then discussed and rehearsed. Positive attention to on-task behavior during seat work was practiced during the fourth session. Teachers were instructed to praise at least four students each time they walked around the class. Various forms of verbal and nonverbal approval were practiced. Additional sessions provided an opportunity for offering skills in how to deal with "helpless students" who seemed to occupy more than their share of teacher attention. The trainers visited each teacher's classroom at least once a week to assess the teacher's skills. This training program was successful in decreasing disruptive behavior and increasing student productivity during arithmetic periods in a class of twenty-eight students. It is fairly economical in terms of teacher and trainer time and requires no extra time of the teacher in the classroom, as does implementation of a token economy.

Evaluation of teacher training programs requires assessment of their effectiveness in creating positive changes in both teacher and student behavior. The extent to which new skills are maintained over time and generalized to other classes is also important. As with other behaviors, generalization must be programed. In addition, efficiency is an important concern. Even though teachers may possess appropriate classroom management skills and curriculum design skills, they may not use them. Merit and bonus payments for specific teacher behaviors may be required to encourage such performance (for example, see Harris, Bushell, Sherman, and Kane, 1975).

Group Contingencies. Positive consequences for deviant classroom behavior often arise from the peer group rather than from the teacher (Minuchin, Chamberlain, and Graubard, 1967). One advantage of a group contingency is the arrangement for peer support of appropriate behavior. Consequences may be gained by an entire group, such as a class of students, depending on the behavior of this group or some subgroup or individual within it. Group consequences for individual performance are useful when one student has a problem not common to the other group members. Patterson, for example, employed a "work box" that recorded the number of points gained by a student for on-task behavior in class. These points were tradable for a party for the entire class. Group contingencies offer a means of influence in relation to the entire class, which is very important when a teacher has many students to consider. Such contingencies in the classroom have been successfully employed to alter hyperactive behavior, off-task behavior, to increase academic performance, and to maintain appropriate social behavior (Hayes, 1976). One beneficial effect of group contingencies for academic performance is an increase in spontaneous tutoring efforts (Hamblin, Hathaway, and Wodarski, 1971). Some studies report an increase in popularity of students when group consequences relate to a student's performance (Alden, Pettigrew, and Skiba, 1970). Thus the sociometric status of individual students may be affected by group consequences. A potential disadvantage of such contingencies is that peer influence may become peer pressure (O'Leary and Drabman, 1971). Group contingencies are used extensively in China, where the achievements of a group of children are emphasized and students are expected to help each other (Bronfenbrenner, 1970).

A group contingency may be applied to a level of performance. An example would be offering free-time activities to the entire class contingent on each student completing twenty-five of thirty-five arithmetic problems. Here, each student's privileges depend on a level of group performance. Contingencies based on low performance (for example, the average of the lowest four scores) accelerate learning of the slower student more than do individual performance contingencies, and appear to do so because they increase the amount of spontaneous peer tutoring (Hamblin, Hathaway, and Wodarski, 1971). This is defined as informal helping patterns displayed between students that might increase the academic performance of the pupil receiving help. In a study with fifth-grade students, about 10 percent of available time was spent by students in tutoring when individual contingencies were in effect, compared to about 80 percent under the group contingency. A prompt in relation to such tutoring was offered every other class day. Students were informed that if they wanted to, they could tutor another student in their group after they finished their own assignment. Play money was employed as a reinforcer, and could be traded once a week for edibles, toys, or sundries.

High-performance group contingencies maximize differential performance; that is, the slower students perform the worst and the gifted students the best (Hamblin, Hathaway, and Wodarski, 1971). A mixture of contingencies would avoid fostering "excellence among the elite" at a cost to slower students as well as maximizing gains of the slower student at a cost to the faster students. Slower students benefit more when low-performance group contingencies are employed, compared to more gifted students.

A group contingency can be cast into a game framework by involving competition for privileges that are already available in most classrooms (Barrish, Saunders, and Wolf, 1969). This framework was used in a fourth-grade class in which students were divided into teams and disruptive behavior (for example, talking, whispering without permission, or leaving one's seat and/or seated position during a lesson without permission) by any student resulted in a check against his team that might result in a loss of privileges for his entire group. Checks were placed on a chalkboard in the classroom. Either one or both teams could win. The game and its rules were carefully explained to the class. Students were informed that they were going to play a game each day during math period and that the class would be divided into teams, and that, if neither team received more than five marks, the team (or teams) would receive the privilege of wearing victory tags and a star would be placed by each member's name on the winner's chart. If both teams won, all students could line up early for lunch. If only one team won, they could line up first for lunch and they could have thirty minutes at the end of the day for special projects. The losing team would not have access to these privileges and would have to work on their assignments during the last thirty minutes of the day, and students would have to remain after school as usual if they did not do their work during this thirty-minute period.

Out-of-seat behavior and talking out decreased from

about 82 and 96 percent respectively during baseline to 9 and 19 percent during the "good behavior game." The game was usually won by both teams and wins occupied about 82 percent of class periods. This game did require extra time by the teacher to think up special projects. The problem of one or two students consistently earning check marks against the team was handled by placing them on individual contingency programs, because it was not thought fair to penalize their teammates for their high rate of disruptive behavior. These students acquired points against themselves alone. The authors point out the possibility that the many comments made by teammates to these students in relation to the check marks they were accumulating for the team may have functioned as reinforcement for their behavior. Fourteen of the twenty-one students said they liked the game and seven said they did not. Those who liked it mentioned being able to read better when it was quiet and said that it was fun. Those who did not offered comments such as, "No, I hate being quiet" and "It's not fair, because we have the guys who talk a lot." The teacher felt it was an easy program to use, because it did not require a change in any class activities or rules. The problem of students who acquire many marks was also addressed, by allowing the team to decide whether to exclude a person that day from the group if an individual member precluded winning by obtaining four or more marks in a day. If excluded, this student would not be able to participate in any activities won by his team that week and was placed behind a screen in the back corner of the room on the following day to study alone (Medland and Stachnik, 1972).

A timer that records duration of appropriate behavior can be used to visually indicate to the class proximity to group reinforcement (Kubany, Weiss, and Sloggett, 1971). Such a timer was employed to decrease the disruptive behavior of a first-grade boy. For each two minutes of accumulated time, the boy earned a treat for the entire class. The timer ran only when the boy was quiet and in his seat. It was turned off by the teacher when he misbehaved.

Teaching Students to Change the Teacher's Behavior. Graubard and his colleagues have taken the refreshing approach of training "deviants" how to change the behavior of "normals"

(Graubard, Rosenberg, and Miller, 1971). That is, rather than focusing on the behavior of the teacher, he taught students how to occasion more positive behaviors from the teacher. Graubard notes that, "We feel that it is necessary to teach deviants to change other people, not only for self-protection, but also because the positive use of power leads to self-enhancement and positive feelings about the self. If children are to be more than recipients of someone's benevolence, they must learn how to operate on society, as well as to accept being operated upon. Moreover, our clinical data indicated that in the process of learning to change others, the 'deviant' changes his own behavior and receives feedback and reinforcement for this change" (Graubard, Rosenberg, and Miller, 1971, p. 83).

One study took place in a school in which teachers were hostile to the special education program and in particular toward adolescent minority members of the program. Previous directives to treat all children equally had no effect on teacher behavior. Seven of these children aged twelve to fifteen were trained as behavior engineers, including two Caucasian, two black, and three Chicano children. Each student was assigned two clients (teachers) and had the responsibility of increasing the rate of teacher praise and decreasing the rate of negative teacher comments. The children were instructed in behavior modification theory and methods, and were told that they were going to take part in an experiment. Scientific accuracy was stressed as being very important. They recorded all remarks directed toward themselves during a two-week period and these remarks were then sorted into two piles, negative and positive. Student training included making eye contact with teachers, asking for extra help, and making reinforcing comments such as, "Gee, it makes me feel good and work so much better when you praise me" and "I like the way you teach that lesson." They were also taught to use the "Ah hah" reaction—that is, when a student understood an assignment, he was to ask the teacher to explain it again, and, halfway through the second explanation, to exclaim, "Ah hah! Now I understand. I could never get that point before." In addition, they learned to ask for extra assignments and to extinguish undesirable teacher behaviors through breaking eye contact and ignoring provocations. Behaviors were practiced with the help of videotape feedback.

The results indicated a significant increase in positive contacts and a significant drop in negative ones. This study and others like it illustrate the potential for training individuals in low-power positions to change the behavior of others when the latter are not open to more direct change efforts.

Peers as Mediators. Peers provide an important source of social support (Solomon and Wahler, 1973). In the classroom, peer influence has been helpful in modifying both management problems (Surratt, Ulrich, and Hawkins, 1969) as well as academic achievement. The most successful peer programs have given careful attention to maintenance of appropriate behavior on the part of the behavior engineers. For example, in a study in which 23 eighth-grade students tutored forty-three children in Grades Two through Eight, the tutors were divided into five teams (Willis, Crowder, and Morris, 1972). Each tutor was regularly observed by the school counselor who employed a checklist of twenty items on which each tutor was rated. Items included "Praises often when correct," "Gives red chip for error," "Keeps accurate records," "Shows enthusiasm," and so on. The team with the highest efficiency rating was awarded a trophy. In addition, praise for good work was regularly offered. The behavioral program was compared, in terms of gains made, to a regular reading program staffed by a certified, degree-holding teacher. Results showed that the children in the behavioral program made thirteen months' progress whereas those in the traditional reading program were slightly further behind at the end of training. Tutoring programs not only help those tutored, but also the students who carry out the training (Davis, 1972).

In one study, a fifth-grade student modified the on-task behavior of four first-grade students (Surratt, Ulrich, and Hawkins, 1969). The rate of "nasty comments" made by a student was decreased by training a preferred peer to ignore and move away from the child contingent on such behavior (Lovitt, Lovitt, Eaton, and Kirkwood, 1973). Peers have been employed to enhance speech skills (Bailey, Timbers, Phillips, and Wolf, 1971). Peer behavior managers have been trained to supervise small groups of children working on programed instruction material (Greenwood, Sloane, and Baskin, 1974). Patterson and Reid (1970) used a peer who was skilled in football playing to coach a student who was less skilled. A group contingency was employed in which all students were allowed out five minutes early for recess, contingent on improvement in football-catching behavior during daily sessions. This procedure resulted in a marked increase in positive social interaction between the student and his peers.

Teaching Deviant Children to Change Normal Peer Behavior. It is well known that children who are in special classes are often stigmatized by their classmates when they return to a regular classroom. Being teased, ignored, and ridiculed are part of the social roles forced on special education children (Graubard, Rosenberg, and Miller, 1971). A training program was designed to help children to decrease such stigmatizing reactions and to increase more positive reactions from their "normal" peers. The program was carried out in weekly thirty-minute sessions over a nine-week period. Operant theory was explained and illustrated to the children and they were asked to make a list of those children who made school unpleasant for them, and to specifically describe and record behaviors of these children that they wished to change. They counted, for example, the number of hostile physical contacts on the playground with their "arch enemy" or the number of snubs directed toward them. They were also asked to identify children with whom they wanted to increase contact and to count the positive contacts with such children. Data collected were given to the counselors each day. Each of the three students selected three student peer clients. The students were trained in the following procedures:

1. *Extinction,* or walking away from the chase-the-cap game, breaking eye contact with the provocative children, and ignoring negative remarks. (The children received primary reinforcers such as candy from their counselor for each instance in which they succeeded.)
2. *Reinforcement,* or explicitly sharing toys or candy or giving compliments to those children who made positive contact with the behavior engineers.
3. *Reinforcing* incompatible responses, by first initiating and reinforcing the children participating in active ball games, and so on.

4. *Setting contingencies* such as helping the children with homework, crafts, and school activities was also used. [Graubard, Rosenberg, and Miller, 1971, p. 92]

The average number of positive contacts increased from an average of about four to about eighteen, and the average number of negative contacts decreased from twenty-six to six. Hostile physical contacts and teasing decreased, and positive behaviors, including invitations to parties and to play ball, increased. The authors note that

At least with reference to positive contacts, the students, as behavior engineers, are able to manage a fairly subtle posture, gradually bringing in a new client in successive weeks of treatment. They are doing about as well in exercising control over human behavior as many a graduate does in a Ph.D. thesis, or professionals who charge $50 an hour, for that matter. . . . Behavior modification appears to be a powerful tool that can give "deviant" children the social skills and power to change the behavior of others towards them. While the "deviant" children undoubtedly changed their own behavior, the important thing remains that they did dramatically change the behavior of others towards them. [Graubard, Rosenberg, and Miller, 1971, p. 96]

Graubard and his colleagues also showed that the perceptions of normal children toward special education children can be improved by offering various kinds of reinforcing activities in special education classrooms, sponsored by the special education students. Activities included wrestling, boxing, fishing derbies, craft classes, and listening to music. These were available only if other children participated in the activities with the special education children, and, in many cases, other children could participate only at the invitation of a special education student. Special education children increased in sociometric status and there was a substantial increase of visits to special education classrooms.

The Use of Contingency Contracting. Written or verbal contracts that identify the exchange value between behaviors and reinforcers have frequently been employed to modify class-room-related behaviors. These may be drawn up between the teacher and the student or between parents and their children as described in the next section. Ideally, the student assumes responsibility for identification of more and more components of the contract, so that he learns to self-contract (Homme, Csanyi, Gonzales, and Rechs, 1969). (The use of contingency contracts is described in detail in Chapter Nine.)

Home-Based Incentive Systems. Home-based incentive systems may be employed when it is not possible to use school-based systems. Perhaps school programs are tried and fail, or perhaps cooperation cannot be gained from a teacher to implement a program in the classroom. A home-based system was employed with 23 third-grade children in an urban public school (Ayllon, Garber, and Pisor, 1975). The teacher of this class had experienced increasingly difficult management problems. Each day three or four students were sent to the principal's office, and on two occasions about a third of the students left the classroom through the windows. A token system was introduced in the classroom allowing students to earn a point for each page of work completed with at least 70 percent accuracy. This reinforcement for academic achievement was effective only for the first day (disruption decreased from 85 to 20 percent). Students were then also offered a point for each fifteen-minute period in which they did not engage in disruptive behavior such as being out of their seat or any motor behavior that interfered with the activities of another student. Various reinforcers were employed, such as comic books (3 points), rental of a doll for thirty minutes (5 points), admittance to the game room (40 points), and recess time (20 points). Two incidences of disruption during a fifteen-minute period resulted in loss of all points for the day. The teacher used a kitchen timer to keep track of time intervals and records of disruptive behavior were kept with the help of a list of student names and columns to indicate fifteen-minute periods, which was attached to a clipboard. Addition of this procedure was also only temporarily effective in decreasing disruptive behavior. After seven days, there was a rapid increase in inappropriate behaviors.

At this point, it was decided to increase potential incentives by using a combined school- and home-based incentive system. A two-hour meeting was arranged with the parents where the problem with the children was explained and their help was sought. Parents who did not attend were contacted by phone or at their place of work. Most children lived in single-parent homes. Parents were informed that, starting with the following Monday, the teacher would give the child a good behavior letter (see Cohen, Keyworth, Kleiner, and Libert, 1971) if their child had been good that day in school. "Good" was defined as not exceeding two disruptions in any one 15-minute period during the school day. The signature of the teacher appeared on the letter, as well as the date and the child's name. The letter included a reminder to praise and reward the child and expressed the teacher's pleasure with the child's behavior. Parents were to use their own judgment in supplying rewards and punishment and were encouraged to ask their child for the letter each weekday and to show their displeasure when a letter was not brought home. Telephone calls were made by the teacher to the parents when letters were not sent home. These calls were made regularly at first, and then only occasionally, as reminders. Consistency of praise for letters and sanctions for their absence was strongly emphasized.

During the first twelve days in which the combined program was employed, disruption fell from 90 percent to a mean of 10 percent. Thus, the combined program was successful in maintaining change whereas the school-based program was effective only in creating an initial change. "Children who received letters generally appeared elated and often consoled those without letters since the consequences were well known among friends" (Ayllon, Garber, and Pisor, 1975, p. 624). A notable aspect is the success of the program in spite of the very limited training provided to parents. The authors speculate that this success might have been caused by the parents' freedom to select rewards and sanctions themselves, because parents are usually most familiar with items and activities that would function as meaningful consequences for their children. A variety of rewards were used, including praise, movies, extended television privileges, and money. Sanctions included removal of television privileges and an earlier bedtime hour. Advantages of providing backup reinforcers at home include use of natural reinforcers and involvement of parents in what is happening with their children at school. The "Good Behavior Letter" provided feedback on a daily basis. In addition, home-based reinforcement may be successful in influencing behavior, whereas school-based programs may not.

Parents as Tutors of Their Children. Parents have been successfully trained to enhance the academic skills of their children. For example, Ayllon and Roberts (1975) trained women who averaged a third-grade educational background to develop the cognitive skills of preschool children in four areas:

> 1. *Receptive language.* The child is required to respond to an instruction in a nonvocal manner. In this case, his task was to identify a verbally named object by pointing to a picture of it.
> 2. *Expressive language.* The child is required to respond to instructions in a vocal-verbal manner. In this case, his task was to identify vocally a pictured object, representing not only an understanding of the instruction and a knowledge of his environment but also the ability to verbalize and communicate this knowledge.
> 3. *Prepositional language.* The child is required to position an object according to a specified spacial arrangement. In this case, his task was to place a figure relative to a box according to verbally presented instructions. This task represents a high-order receptive response form, requiring not only knowledge of the environment but also knowledge of the interrelations of parts of the environment.
> 4. *Body awareness.* The child is required to identify parts of his own body. In this case, his task was to respond to combined vocal and nonvocal instructions by identifying vocally a portion of his own anatomy. [Ayllon and Roberts, 1975, pp. 110-111]

The parents were trained how to use reinforcement in the form of praise and consumable items. The effectiveness of reinforcement to increase learning skills has been shown in a number of studies (for example, Staats and Butterfield, 1965). Often children labeled as *having learning disabilities* have simply reflected the cuing and reinforcement deficits in their environment.

Skindrud (undated) trained parents of eight- to twelve-year-old boys to conduct home tutoring sessions. Programed reader texts were employed and sessions required forty-five minutes of the mother's time. Procedures were demonstrated to the mother and telephone contact was maintained weekly to collect data on oral reading and work rates that were to be gathered daily. In addition, periodic evaluations of progress were made. The professional time involved in training mothers ranged from three to twenty hours. The highly disruptive behavior of one boy required greater supervision time. The results of this program exceeded the normal rates of reading growth for the average child as well as the pretutoring rates for the children involved. In two cases, there was an average gain of one year in reading grade level for every nine weeks of tutoring. Observation in the classroom indicated a decrease in disruptive behavior. This effect of improvement in academic skills on disruptive classroom behavior has been often noted. Mothers have been extensively employed as behavior change technicians in programs for disadvantaged preschool children (see, for example, Risley, Reynolds, and Hart, 1970). The mothers worked with the children on specific programs involving training in math, language, and reading skills.

Decreasing Dysfunctional Emotional Reactions
Related to School

Fears related to school have been addressed within an operant framework in which gradual approximations to feared events are arranged and reinforced (see, for example, Lazarus, Davison, and Polefka, 1965). Events incompatible with fear have included being accompanied to school by the counselor or parent; the use of distraction and humor during these occasions; as well as encouragement and "emotive imagery" (Lazarus and Abramovitz, 1962), in which the child imagines pleasant images while in fearful situations such as a visit to Disneyland; and making the first excursions unrelated to staying at school. The term *school phobia* generally refers to a child's refusal to attend school; however, such refusal may or may not be associated with anxiety, which is implied by the term *phobia*. Refusal could simply be related to truancy because school is not a rewarding experience. The term is only applicable when anxiety is a factor. A distinction is sometimes made between two types of school phobias: Type I, which can be treated rapidly and which is characterized by a rapid onset and good communication between family members, and Type II, characterized by a longer history of school avoidance and the presence of other family difficulties (Kennedy, 1965). The child in the following example represents Type II.

The role of both anxiety and the secondary reinforcers of attention from significant others resulting from avoidance behavior is illustrated in the following case example of a nine-year-old boy with a school phobia (Lazarus, Davison, and Polefka, 1965). It was important during intervention to address both factors. Because of the high level of anxiety present initially, gradual approach to the feared situation was arranged in the company of the counselor, and the boy was encouraged to pair pleasant imagery with the school situation, described as follows in Step 2. As anxiety decreased, various rewards were then established to encourage further approach behavior. The history of the problem and family history is first presented, followed by a description of intervention procedures.

History of the Problem

When he was referred for therapy Paul, age 9, had been absent from school for 3 weeks. The summer vacation had ended six weeks previously, and, on entering the fourth grade, Paul avoided the classroom situation. He was often found hiding in the cloakroom, and subsequently began spending less time at school each day. Thereafter, neither threats, bribes, nor punishments could induce him to reenter school.

Paul's history revealed a series of similar episodes. During his first day of kindergarten he succeeded in climbing over an extremely high wall and fled home. His first-grade teacher considered him to be "disturbed." Serious difficulties regarding school attendance were first exhibited when Paul entered the second grade of a parochial school. It was alleged that the second-grade teacher who, according to Paul, "looked like a witch," generally intimidated the children and was very free with physical punishment. Paul retrospectively informed his parents that he felt as though "the devil was in the classroom." At this stage he became progressively more reluctant to enter the school and finally refused entirely. A psychiatrist was consulted and is reported to have advised the parents to use coercion, whereupon Paul was literally dragged screaming to school by a truant officer. Paul was especially bitter about his experience with the psychiatrist. "All we did was talk and then the truant officer came." In the third grade, Paul was transferred to the neighborhood public school where he spent a trouble-free year at the hands of an exceedingly kind teacher.

Family History

Paul was the fourth of eight children, the first boy in a devout, orthodox Roman Catholic family.

The father was a moody, anxiously ambitious electronics engineer. A harsh disciplinarian —"I run a tight ship"—he impulsively meted out punishment for any act that deviated even slightly from his perfectionistic standards.

The mother, although openly affectionate and less rigid and demanding than her husband, took pains to respond towards her eight children in an unbiased fashion. She stressed, however, that "Paul touches my nerve center," and stated that they frequently quarreled in the father's absence.

Although reticent, essentially aloof and somewhat withdrawn, he was capable of unexpected vigor and self-assertion when he chose to participate in sporting activities. From the outset, the therapist noted his labile and expressive reactions to all stressful stimuli. The extent of his subjective discomfort was easily gauged by clearly discernible responses. As the magnitude of anxiety increased, there was a concomitant progression of overt signs—increased reticence, a postural stoop, a general constriction of movement, tearfilled eyes, mild trembling, pronounced blanching, culminating in sobbing and immobility.

Procedure

After the initial interview, it was evident that Paul's school phobia was the most disruptive response pattern of a generally bewildered and intimidated child. Although subsequent interviews revealed the plethora of familial tensions, situational crises, and specific traumatic events . . . the initial therapeutic objective was to reinstate normal school attendance. Nevertheless it was clearly apparent that the home situation in general and, more particularly, specific examples of parental mishandling would ultimately require therapeutic intervention.

The application of numerous techniques in the consulting room (for example, systematic desensitization) was abandoned because of the child's inarticulateness and acquiescent response tendency. It was obvious that his verbal reports were aimed at eliciting approval rather than describing his true feelings. Desensitization in vivo was therefore employed as the principal therapeutic strategy.

The school was situated two and one half blocks away from the home. The routine was for Paul to leave for school at 8:30 A.M. in order to arrive by 8:40. The first recess was from 10:00-10:30; lunch break from 12:00-1:00; and classes ended at 3:30 P.M. At the time when therapy was initiated, the boy was extremely surly and dejected in the mornings (as reported by the parents), refused breakfast, rarely dressed himself, and became noticeably more fearful toward 8:30. Parental attempts at reassurance, coaxing, or coercion elicited only sobbing and further withdrawal.

Accordingly, the boy was exposed to the following increasingly difficult steps along the main dimensions of his school phobia:

1. On a Sunday afternoon, accompanied by the therapists, he walked from his house to the school. The therapists were able to allay Paul's anxiety by means of distraction and humor, so that his initial exposure was relatively pleasant.
2. On the next two days at 8:30 A.M., accompanied by one of the therapists, he walked from his house into the schoolyard. Again,

Paul's feelings of anxiety were reduced by means of coaxing, encouragement, relaxation, and the use of "emotive imagery" (that is, the deliberate picturing of subjectively pleasant images such as Christmas and a visit to Disneyland, while relating them to the school situation; see Lazarus and Abramovitz, 1962). Approximately fifteen minutes were spent roaming around the school grounds, after which Paul returned home.

3. After school was over for the day, the therapist was able to persuade the boy to enter the classroom and sit down at his desk. Part of the normal school routine was then playfully enacted.

4. On the following three mornings, the therapist accompanied the boy into the classroom with the other children. They chatted with the teacher, and left immediately after the opening exercises.

5. A week after beginning this program, Paul spent the entire morning in class. The therapist sat in the classroom and smiled approvingly at Paul whenever he interacted with his classmates or the teacher. After eating his lunch he participated in an active ball game, and returned to his house with the therapist at 12:30. (Since parent-teacher conferences were held during that entire week, afternoon classes were discontinued.)

6. Two days later when Paul and the therapist arrived at school, the boy lined up with the other children and allowed the therapist to wait for him inside the classroom. This was the first time that Paul had not insisted on having the therapist in constant view.

7. Thereafter, the therapist sat in the school library adjoining the classroom.

8. It was then agreed that the therapist would leave at 2:30 P.M. while Paul remained for the last hour of school.

9. On the following day, Paul remained alone at school from 1:45 P.M. until 2:45 P.M. (Earlier that day, the therapist had unsuccessfully attempted to leave the boy alone from 10 until noon.)

10. Instead of fetching the boy at his home, the

therapist arranged to meet him at the school gate at 8:30 A.M. Paul also agreed to remain alone at school from 10:45 A.M. until noon provided that the therapist return to eat lunch with him. At 1:45 P.M. the therapist left again with the promise that if the boy remained until school ended (3:30 P.M.) he would visit Paul that evening and play the guitar for him.

11. Occasional setbacks made it necessary to instruct the lad's mother not to allow the boy into the house during school hours. In addition, the teacher was asked to provide special jobs for the boy so as to increase his active participation and make school more attractive.

12. The family doctor was asked to prescribe a mild tranquilizer for the boy to take on awakening so as to reduce his anticipatory anxieties.

13. After meeting the boy in the mornings, the therapist gradually left him alone at school for progressively longer periods of time. After 6 days of this procedure, the therapist was able to leave at 10 A.M.

14. The boy was assured that the therapist would be in the faculty room until 10 A.M., if needed. Thus, he came to school knowing the therapist was present, but not actually seeing him.

15. With Paul's consent the therapist arrived at school shortly *after* the boy entered the classroom at 8:40 A.M.

16. School attendance independent of the therapist's presence was achieved by means of specific rewards (a comic book, and variously colored tokens that would eventually procure a baseball glove) contingent on his entering school and remaining there alone. He was at liberty to telephone the therapist in the morning if he wanted him at school, in which event he would forfeit his rewards for that day.

17. Since the therapist's presence seemed to have at least as much reward value as the comic books and tokens, it was necessary to enlist the mother's cooperation to effect the therapist's final withdrawal. The overall diminution of the boy's anxieties, together with general gains which had accrued to his home situation, made

it therapeutically feasible for the mother to emphasize the fact that school attendance was compulsory, and that social agencies beyond the control of both therapists and parents would enforce this requirement eventually.

18. Approximately three weeks later, Paul had accumulated enough tokens to procure his baseball glove. He then agreed with his parents that rewards of this kind were no longer necessary. [Lazarus, Davison, and Polefka, 1965, pp. 225-227]

The authors note that numerous setbacks occurred during intervention, which lasted four months. The counselors' reactions to these setbacks were influenced by the intensity of Paul's anxiety. If it was judged that social consequences were mostly responsible for displays of avoidance behavior, rewards were offered for increased approach behavior. Premature exposure to anxiety-producing situations may have made Paul more, rather than less, reluctant to approach the classroom. Also, high anxiety would interfere with appropriate classroom behaviors, such as attending to the teacher and interacting with his classmates. On the other hand, inappropriate use of emotive imagery or relaxation might have reinforced avoidance behavior.

Three different counselors were involved in the intervention program, two being graduate students. Thus it is not necessary that such programs be carried out only by the counselor. The authors note that there was little disturbance when counselors were exchanged, and felt that it often had an advantage, in that, following a setback, a change of counselors offset the negative effects of being associated with sensitizing experiences (Lazarus, Davison, and Polefka, 1965). After normal school attendance was established, a conference was held with the family in which the implications of the father's harsh tendencies were discussed as well as the mother's inconsistent behavior and the parents agreed to try out some recommended actions. A ten-month follow-up indicated that Paul had maintained the progress made and, according to the parental and school report, had made additional gains.

Very often problems occur at school as well as at home.

The following case example describes behavioral intervention with a five-year-old boy with multiple problems, one of which concerned "separation anxiety" (Patterson and Brodsky, 1966). His parents had been asked to remove him from kindergarten and said that when he was separated from them at school, he started to bite, kick, throw toys, scream, and cry. The teacher had multiple black-and-blue marks on her legs. The child revealed a general negativism in his interactions with adults and his play skills with other children were limited. Much of the time he ignored other children. Being at school was assumed to entail deprivation (a lack of reinforcement from peers and teacher), which in turn elicited a negative emotional state ("separation anxiety"). This, in turn, occasioned high-amplitude behavior (such as kicking and screaming), which was reinforced by removal from the aversive situation as well as by positive social reinforcement for such behavior. The authors speculate that children who are "selective responders" (conditioned to respond only to social reinforcers dispensed by a limited number of people) are prone to develop this reaction to deprivation and consequent "separation anxiety" (Patterson and Brodsky, 1966). Karl was not responsive to social reinforcers offered by peers or his teacher. Thus being placed in a classroom constituted an environment with few social reinforcers. He also had no control over the length of the deprivation period. He had learned that he could avoid the anxiety associated with deprivation altogether by throwing temper tantrums.

Intervention was directed toward decreasing the anxiety and also establishing appropriate behaviors that would compete with inappropriate tantrums. It was also necessary to train his peers, parents, and teacher to respond appropriately to desirable behaviors. The mother was requested to bring in notes describing occasions on which she praised Karl for not being afraid when left at school, for following instructions and for being "grown up." A "Karl Box" was used in the kindergarten during recess period. Karl was informed that the buzzer would sound each time he played with another child without hurting him (Patterson and Brodsky, 1966). He earned praise from the counselor, as well as candy, which he could distribute during snack time among the other children. The buzzer from the box was also used as a reinforcer for not crying when his mother walked away from him during sessions in the office. The mother was trained how to break tasks up into small steps so that Karl could be encouraged to do more on his own at home—for example, tie his shoes and butter his bread. She awarded points for such behaviors and when he accumulated ten, he could trade them in for a plastic toy from the counselor. During sessions held in the home the counselor observed parent-child interaction; coached the mother to provide immediate reinforcement for appropriate behaviors; and, when new tasks were attempted, such as combing his hair, taught her to reinforce the attempt at first and then to withhold praise until some improvement occurred. During the course of the program, duration of tantrums decreased, negativism (saying no), and isolated behaviors decreased, and initiations of interactions between Karl and his peers increased. These changes were at first dramatic, but then declined; however, they remained well above original levels.

A "work box" that signals reinforcement has been successfully employed in a number of studies to develop appropriate behavior. For example, in one study, signals were presented on a variable-interval schedule contingent on sitting still and attending for a brief time period (Patterson, 1965). An announcement is usually made to the class concerning the work box and group contingencies are usually employed in which reinforcers are earned for the entire class (Patterson, Shaw, and Ebner, 1969).

Decreasing Test Anxiety. Performance in school is often hampered by anxiety in evaluation situations. As Allen (1972) has noted, fear of evaluation is related to a variety of factors such as procrastination, somatic complaints, and excuses. Highly test-anxious individuals are self-centered in that they are preoccupied with present and future evaluations of their work (Sarason, 1975). They seek external cues as a means of coping with tasks and high anxiety may interfere with discriminations between appropriate and inappropriate cues. There are a number of programs that have been developed to offer people skills for dealing with anxiety in test situations. Progressive relaxation training and self-instructional training have been usefully employed (Donner and Gurney, 1969; Meichenbaum, 1972). The client may also benefit from frequent rehearsal of the test-taking situation. For example, one client has failed to pass his qualifying examinations and had one last opportunity to take this test when he sought consultation. He reported that he panicked in this examination situation, even though he knew the material. It is critical to determine whether the client has appropriate study skills and is well prepared when an anxiety response in examination situations is presented, because anxiety is realistic if the student is poorly prepared. In this situation, appropriate study skills were available and a rich fund of information was at hand. Training in progressive relaxation was employed to offer him greater influence over his anxiety and rehearsal periods were agreed on, during which he would go to a room similar to the room in which the examination would be held and would practice answering one question. At first, he could have up to two hours to answer the question and this was gradually decreased to the length of time that would be available for each question during the examination. A series of questions were generated for these sessions. At the time that he sought consultation, there was a six-month period prior to his examination. A total of thirty "rehearsal examinations" were held. He took his examinations on schedule and received a high pass.

Decreasing Public Speaking Anxiety. Many students complain of undue anxiety in public speaking situations. Desensitization and social skill training have been used to decrease anxiety and develop appropriate behaviors (see, for example, Paul, 1966; Paul and Shannon, 1966; Fawcett and Miller, 1975). Social skill training to increase participation in discussions focused on simple and complex question asking, summarizing another person's point of view prior to making a statement, or asking a question and initiating a statement without being prompted (Wright, 1976).

Increasing Interaction with Peers

Children who are socially isolated have less opportunities for social learning. Such children are more likely to drop out of school (Ullman, 1957) and more likely to develop mental health problems (Cowen, Pederson, Babijian, Izzo, and Trost, 1973). Social isolation may reflect a deficit in social skill, anxiety in social situations, or a lack of reinforcement for peer interaction. When adult attention maintains isolate behavior, redistributing attention, so that social reinforcement is offered for increased interaction with peers and is withheld for proximity to adults, can increase peer interaction. For example, in a study with a preschool child, attention was initially given when the child stood near, then played beside, and finally interacted with another child (Allen, Hart, Buell, Harris, and Wolf, 1964). Special efforts were made to increase interaction with peers, including instructing the teacher to direct her social reinforcement (looks and comments) to the child as a participant in a group activity—for example, "You three girls have a cozy house." Reinforcing "on feet" behavior and ignoring regressed crawling increased social interaction of a preschool child with her peers (Harris and others, 1964).

Another approach to increasing interaction with peers has focused directly on enhancing reinforcing skills of children. The more reinforcers a child gives, the more he receives (Charlesworth and Hartup, 1967). Thus reciprocity seems to characterize peer interaction as well as family interaction. This approach takes advantage of available natural reinforcers. Social reinforcement may include imitation of another child, smiling and/or laughing, giving (of tangible objects), affection (physical contact signifying friendliness) and verbalization (Charlesworth and Hartup, 1967). In one study with preschool children aged three to five who interacted infrequently with their peers, four 5-minute videotapes, accompanied by a narrative soundtrack in which the actions of the children were described, were shown to the children. Each depicted a social reinforcing behavior, such as imitation (Keller and Carlson, 1974). The models were six-year-old children. Observation of these videotapes increased participation in social interaction and the frequency with which children engaged in giving and receiving social reinforcement. Only those behaviors that were seen most frequently in the child's repertoire, such as laughing, verbalizing, and imitating, increased, whereas affection and token giving, which were initially at low levels, did not. Model presentation thus appeared to have a facilitating effect, in which the videotapes served to increase the children's expectancy that certain behaviors would be reinforced, rather than training novel reactions. Viewing a film showing children approaching other children to join in play activities has resulted in increased social interaction with peers (O'Connor, 1969), as has the use of group contingencies (Patterson and Reid, 1970). Verbal coaching has also been used to increase social skills of children. One program included instructions from an adult on the social skills relevant to friendship making, a series of twelve-minute play sessions with other children to practice social skills and a review of play sessions together with the coach (Oden and Asher, 1975). Instructions stressed participating in the activity, cooperating, communicating with the other person, having friendly fun and being nice. For example, the children were asked to get involved and to attend to the game or activity. They were coached to take turns, to share materials, to offer suggestions if problems arose, and to offer solutions if a disagreement arose about the rules. They were encouraged to talk to the other person, to say things about the game itself, to ask questions about the other person, to share information about themselves, to say something nice when the other person did well, to offer the other person encouragement, and to smile. Training was given to a group of nine-year-old children over a four-week period. Children who received this training increased on play sociometric ratings significantly more than a control group, and this result was maintained at a one-year follow-up period.

Videotape models have been employed to enhance the social skills of older children (see, for example, Goodwin and Mahoney, 1975; Thelan, Fry, Dollinger, and Paul, 1976). Six male residents of a group home (ages twelve to sixteen) observed fourteen 5-minute tapes in which an actor portrayed a young male in various problematic interpersonal situations. Unsuccessful coping was shown, as well as gradual mastery of the situation. Behaviors modeled included expressing positive (for example, empathic) feelings, consulting a staff member about a problem, and dealing with an accusation. Following observation of the model, each boy role played the behavior modeled, then viewed the tape a second time and repeated the role play. As suggested by the failure of positive changes to be maintained in the home situation, it is unlikely that such procedures alone will induce enduring change. Staff may have to be coached how to respond positively to new appropriate behaviors and cueing procedures may be needed to remind the youth to display their new behaviors. Additional examples of social skill training are offered in Chapter Thirteen.

Creating a Positive Self-Image

Self-image can be defined as the sum total of the statements that a person makes about himself: what he says *to* himself *about* himself (Homme, deBaca, Cottingham, and Homme, 1968). Because behavior is influenced by anticipated consequences, what a person says to himself can affect what he does. Thus a child who thinks poorly of his abilities is less likely to exercise available skills and to take risks. This suggests the reinforcement of statements made by the child such as "That was a fine job." The child can be reinforced, for example, for going over to the teacher and whispering, "I am a fast learner." In addition "earshotting" can be employed—the teacher comments on a specific behavior of a child within earshot of the child, by saying, for example, "George completed all five of his assignments today" (Homme and Tosti, 1971). Simmons and Camp (1975) have developed the *Great Expectations Program Manual* for increasing children's self-esteem.

Self-Instructional Methods

Children as well as adults have been trained in self-instructional skills that permit a wider range of alternative behaviors in relation to given situations. Areas in which such methods have been employed include learning to influence impulsive behavior, improving problem-solving skills, and encouraging creative responses.

Decreasing Impulsive Behavior. The "Turtle Technique" is a self-control procedure that helps young children control impulsive and aggressive reactions to provocations (Schneider and Robin, 1976). Training is initiated by telling a story to the child about a boy named Little Turtle who disliked school and who, in spite of his vows to stay out of trouble, always managed to find it. For example, he would get mad and rip up all his papers in class. One day when he was feeling especially bad, he met an old tortoise who talked. " 'Hey there,' he said in his big bellowing voice, 'I'll tell you a secret. Don't you realize you are carrying the answer to your problem around with you?' Little Turtle didn't know what he was talking about. 'Your shell—your shell!' he shouted. 'That's why you have a shell. You can hide in your shell whenever you get that feeling inside you that tells you you are angry. When you are in your shell, you can have a moment to rest and figure out what to do about it. So next time you get angry, just go into your shell' " (Schneider and Robin, 1976, p. 159). The story continues, describing how, the next day when he started to get upset, Little Turtle remembered what the tortoise had said, and pulled in his arms close to his body, put his head down so his chin rested against the chest, and rested for awhile, until he knew what to do. The story ends with the teacher coming over and praising him for this reaction and Little Turtle receiving a very good report card that term.

Following this story, practice is held in which the teacher demonstrates the turtle reaction, and the children practice it to various imagined frustrating experiences. Thus the child learns a new reaction to the cue of anger or frustration. This is combined with teaching the child relaxation skills, again employing the story of Little Turtle, who returns to the Tortoise, telling him that he still has some angry feelings, even though he has used the turtle response. Starting with the stomach muscles, the children are given practice in tensing and relaxing major muscle groups of their body. Tensing and relaxation are then incorporated into the turtle response by tensing the body when assuming the turtle position, as a count is made from 1 to 10, followed by relaxation of the muscles, which is maintained for a few moments. The children are encouraged to use frustrating experiences as a cue to employ the turtle reaction. This reaction is presented as one that is harder to do than "acting out."

Learning the turtle reaction is combined with teaching the child problem-solving methods. As with adults, this consists of selecting problematic situations, giving examples of various reactions to these and identifying their consequences (D'Zurilla and Goldfried, 1971). For example: " 'If I hit Johnny, the teacher will get angry. She will punish me, and it will ruin my day. On the other hand, if I choose to control myself and ask the teacher to help me get my toy back, the day will continue to be good, and I can show myself how big I am. If I rip my paper up because I made a mistake on it, I will only have to start again. Another choice is to cross out my mistake neatly and continue so I do not waste time. That way I will have more time to play' " (Schneider and Robin, 1976, p. 160). Problem-solving instruction sessions are held daily in class, during which recent problem situations are discussed. Cues are provided for the children, such as the teacher asking, "What are your choices?" The children are instructed to incorporate problem-solving efforts during use of the turtle technique; that is, to use this time to imagine behavioral alternatives to their frustrating situation and the consequences of each. In this way, the child learns to expand his range of alternatives.

Peers are rewarded for supporting other children's efforts to employ the turtle method. They are encouraged to praise and applaud the child who is using the technique, and to cue fellow students to use the turtle method in situations that might lead to a fight. Peers, in turn, are reinforced by the teacher for their support. Training sessions are held for about fifteen minutes each day for about three weeks and are then reduced to twice a week. Within a few weeks after introduction of the turtle technique, children start "doing turtle in my head" without prompting and without going through the physical withdrawal reactions. It is important that children learn to discriminate when they should employ the turtle technique and when they should fight back. As noted by the authors, "A turtle has to stick its neck out to get ahead" (Krumboltz and Thoresen, 1976, p. 162). Children must learn when it is appropriate to consider self-defense an appropriate alternative. This technique is now being used with adults in cases of marital abuse. The husband is trained to use the cue word *stop*, is given relaxation instructions, is taught a modified version of the turtle position, and is trained to use this time to solve problems. Another manual developed for aggressive children is called the "Think Aloud" Program (Camp, Blom, Herbert, and Van Doorninck, 1976).

The Use of Self-Instructions to Enhance Task Performance. A number of procedures have been developed to enhance the problem-solving skills of young children (see, for example, Meichenbaum and Goodman, 1971; Spivak and Shure, 1974). The goal of such programs is to develop self-instructions that can be employed to size up and successfully address task demands. The training procedure includes model presentation of the use of self-instructions during task performance and practice in using self-instructions. Children are trained to use covert statements for orienting, organizing, regulating, and self-rewarding functions, in order to enhance their self-control. Children are first encouraged to overtly express self-instructions during task performance and then to "covertly" express these. A cognitive training method employed with second-graders who had been placed in "opportunity remedial class" because of behavior problems such as hyperactivity and poor self-control and/or had low IQs included the following steps.

> First E performed a task talking aloud while S observed (E acted as a model); then S performed the same task while E instructed S aloud; then S was asked to perform the task again while instructing himself aloud; then S performed the task while whispering to himself (lip movements); and finally S performed the task covertly (without lip movements). The verbalizations that E modeled and S subsequently used included: (1) questions about the nature and demands of the task so as to compensate for a possible comprehension deficiency; (2) answers to these questions in the form of cognitive rehearsal and planning in order to overcome any possible production deficiency; (3) self-instructions in the form of self-guidance while performing the task in order to overcome any possible mediation deficiency; and (4) self-reinforcement. The following is an example of E's modeled verbalizations that S subsequently used (initially overtly, then covertly): "Okay, what is it I have to do? You want me to copy the picture with the different

> lines. I have to go slow and be careful. Okay, draw
> the line down, down, good; then to the right, that's
> it; now down some more and to the left. Good, I'm
> doing fine so far. Remember, go slow. Now back up
> again. No, I was supposed to go down. That's okay.
> Just erase the line carefully—good. Even if I make
> an error I can go on slowly and carefully. Okay, I
> have to go down now. Finished. I did it." [Meich-
> enbaum and Goodman, 1971, pp. 116-117]

An error was deliberately included because prior research indicated a marked deterioration in performance following errors.
Children were also exposed to a model demonstrating a strategy
of searching for differences that would allow successful elimination of incorrect alternatives: "I have to remember to go slowly
to get it right. Look carefully at this one (the standard), now
look at these carefully (the variants). Is this one different? Yes,
it has an extra leaf. Good, I can eliminate this one. Now, let's
look at this one (another variant). I think it's this one, but let
me first check the others. Good, I'm going slow and carefully.
Okay, I think it's this one" (Meichenbaum and Goodman, 1971,
p. 121). This training program was carried out during four half-
hour sessions spread over a two-week period. It was effective in
improving performance on a variety of psychometric tests that
measure cognitive impulsivity, performance IQ, and motor
ability.

Another program designed to enhance problem-solving
skills presented pictures to children enrolled in the third,
fourth, and fifth grades that depicted problems the children encountered (Stone, Hinds, and Schmidt, 1975). Each picture was
accompanied by three sheets: the first labeled *facts,* the second
choices, and the third *solutions.* The children worked in groups
of four. They were offered cues for appropriate behavior that
were gradually faded out. Each group recorded relevant facts,
choices, and solutions. Feedback and reinforcement were then
offered concerning their work. A recent program focused on the
type of questions children ask and found that a modeling procedure was effective in increasing helpful questions in relation to
problem resolution (Denney and Connors, 1974).

Resisting temptation. Self-instruction training has been

successfully employed to help children to resist temptations to wander off task (Patterson and Mischel, 1976). Task-facilitating instructions that refocus attention on the task were found to be more effective than temptation-inhibiting plans. For an example of the first, the trainer may say, "When 'Mr. Clown Box' says to look at him and play with him, then you can just look at the pegboard and say, 'I'm going to look at my work' " (p. 212). For an example of the second type, the trainer may say, "When 'Mr. Clown Box' says to look at him and play with him, then you can just not look at him and say, 'I am not going to look at Mr. Clown Box' " (p. 212). Interestingly, although the former type of instructions were more effective in decreasing the duration of time devoted to the Clown Box, there was no difference in the frequency of these looks. This study, as well as others, indicate that even very young children (mean age of four) can learn self-instructions that help them to regulate their attention to tasks.

What the child thinks about, not what is physically in his view, determines his ability to delay (Mischel, 1973). It is possible to cognitively transform a desired stimulus so as to increase the time before it is sampled (Mischel and Baker, 1973). For example, if the child has been instructed to think of a desired object, such as pretzel sticks, as little brown logs—or marshmallows as round white clouds or cotton balls—he can delay longer than if he focuses on the consummatory properties of the rewarding events such as the pretzels' crunchy, salty taste. And if the children imagine abstract representations of the objects, such as pictures, they can wait longer than if they imagine the real objects.

Enhancing Creativity. Self-instruction training has been employed to increase "creative responses" of undergraduate students (Meichenbaum, 1975a). The procedure employed is similar to the stress inoculation procedure described in Chapter Twelve. The first step is to inquire as to what kinds of thoughts occur during situations of relevance. Attention is often directed to inadequacies, such as "I am not original," and there is a tendency to devalue the importance of the task at hand. Even when creative responses are offered, they are attributed to an easy test or labeled as *unimportant* or *unoriginal*. Here, too, as in developing self-instructional control over stress, there is an attempt to develop self-recognition of the effects of such statements. Thus, after some of these statements are offered by group members, the counselor then wonders out loud about the possible effects of such statements on creativity. The purpose of this stage of the procedure is to have clients become aware of their negative self-statements. During intervention, students learn to use these statements as cues for offering positive self-statements and behaviors.

Creativity is presented as a process or style of thinking, rather than as only a product, and as a skill requiring practice. Various conceptualizations of creativity are discussed and possible self-statements associated with each identified. Some of these are offered in Table 19.

At the end of the first group meeting, each subject was asked to try to identify what he said to himself in relation to relevant situations and to interview both his creative and uncreative friends to try to determine their thinking style.

Session 2 was employed to develop incompatible self-statements along the lines of those mentioned. During Sessions 3 and 4, models were presented of effective self-statements while working on tasks. The counselor talked out loud to himself during these tasks. Subjects were then asked to work on tasks while talking quietly to themselves and to offer themselves self-instructions covertly. Each type of self-statement (see Table 19) was covered separately, first discussing the self-statements, then presenting a model, followed by practice. As Meichenbaum (1975a) notes, it is important that the self-statements generated be meaningful to each person. They should not merely be automatically repeated. Rather, a set is generated for each person and each person is encouraged to accompany self-statements with appropriate affect, such as expressions of joy and feelings of surprise. During the final two sessions, discussions were held concerning how the self-instructions could be applied to "real-life" problems. Subjects were requested to bring to these meetings materials on which they could work while employing self-instructions. Each subject seemed to gravitate to a unique set of instructions.

This training program was successful in increasing origi-

Table 19. Examples of Self-Statements Used in Creativity Training

---

Self-statements arising from an attitudinal conceptualization of creativity

Self-inducing self-statements
What to do:

> Be creative, be unique.
> Break away from the obvious, the common place.
> Think of something no one else will think of.
> Just be free-wheeling.
> If you push yourself you can be creative.
> Quantity helps breed quality.

What not to do:

> Get rid of internal blocks.
> Defer judgments.
> Don't worry what others think.
> Not a matter of right and wrong.
> Don't give the first answer you think of.
> No negative self-statements.

Self-statements arising from a mental abilities conceptualization

Problem analysis—what you say to yourself before you start a problem

> Size up the problem; what is it you have to do?
> You have to put the elements together differently.
> Use different analogies.
> Do the task as if you were brainstorming or doing Synectics training.
> Elaborate on ideas.
> Make the strange familiar and the familiar strange.

Task execution—what you say to yourself while doing a task

> You're in a rut—okay, try something new.
> How can you use this frustration to be more creative?
> Take a rest now; who knows when the ideas will visit again.
> Go slow—no hurry—no need to press.
> Good, you're getting it.
> This is fun.
> That was a pretty neat answer; wait till you tell the others!

Self-statements arising from a psychoanalytic conceptualization

> Release controls; let your mind wander.
> Free-associate, let ideas flow.
> Relax—just let it happen.
> Let your ideas play.
> Refer to your experience; just view it differently.
> Let your ego regress.
> Feel like a bystander through whom ideas are just flowing.
> Let one answer lead to another.
> Almost dreamlike, the ideas have a life of their own.

Source: Meichenbaum (1975a, p. 132).

nality and flexibility on tests of divergent thinking. Meichenbaum (1975a) notes that it is likely that maximum effectiveness
of such a program would have to tailor particular sets of instructions to individual differences. For example, when a disinclina-
tion rather than an inability to use one's imagination is present,
awareness of negative self-statements and an increase of positive
self-statements may be focused on. For clients who are low on
both intelligence and creativity, a greater emphasis on problem
analysis and task execution may be required.

Developing Effective Study Habits

Many students have ineffective study habits. Inadequate
stimulus control, in which study behavior is not effectively controlled either by time or place is usually involved (Fox, 1962),
as well as strained ratios (too much work for too little reinforcement) and inadequate information about progress. Not having
special places and times to study renders the student subject to
a host of competing behaviors that are associated with these
times and places. Many studying behaviors are only indirectly
relevant to or may even compete with effective learning, such
as underlining and copying (Fox, 1962). Behaviors that must be
established include placing the initiation of study under stimulus control (if this first step does not occur, no others are possible), and making the study occasion an effective stimulus for
good study habits.

Behavioral programs have emphasized the development of
self-management skills that will allow the student to effectively
influence his own study behavior. These programs usually include self-monitoring, stimulus control procedures, self-instructional procedures (such as thought stopping), and self-reinforcement (Groveman, Richards, and Caple, 1975). It is hoped that
increased study behavior will result in improved grades. Intervention is preceded by a baseline period during which number
of pages read and hours studied for each course are self-monitored.

A study schedule may be established for all courses (Walter and Siebert, 1976) or for only one course at a time, starting
with the course that gives the student the most trouble (for

example, physics). A procedure employing successive approximations for increasing efficient study behavior has been described by Fox (1962). This had two main components: gradually increasing time in study situations and then increasing other appropriate study behaviors. The student was first asked to go to the library each day after his physics class and to leave all his books except his physics book back on the first floor. He was to select a special place to study in the library and to study only there. This was an attempt to purify the stimulus control over study behavior so that study places would become an occasion only for study behavior rather than for a host of other behaviors, such as letter writing, talking, or daydreaming. In order to decrease the probability of daydreaming being associated with special study places, the student was told that if he experienced discomfort or began to daydream, and was unable to terminate this (for example, by use of thought stopping), he was to make a decision to read one more page and then to leave the library immediately to see his friends for coffee or do anything he pleased, even though his interest might have been renewed. This would hopefully serve to decrease the aversiveness of studying the subject. Only a short study time was required and he was free to terminate this time. The decision to abandon study was now "an approved procedure rather than a display of student irresponsibility" (Fox, 1962, p. 88). Completion of an assignment prior to departure provided positive reinforcement. Breaking up the work into small pieces would also hopefully decrease the aversiveness of studying. The amount of work to be completed prior to leaving the library is increased by one page or one problem each day. This program was continued until the student was working one hour a day on physics. He was then informed that, if he wished, after studying one hour, he could study another hour. It was stressed, however, that he should make an independent decision each time. This was to increase his ability to exert self-control; that is, to make a decision and to carry it out. Once this program was established for a week, work on the next course was begun in the same step-by-step fashion until all courses were addressed.

The student was also instructed in how to survey (read over the boldface and italicized headings in a chapter to get an overview of the material and to serve as a warmup); questioning (reviewing the material again and forming questions suggested by the headings); reading (without underlining or note taking) and recitation (outlining or reciting material while the book is closed). "It is during recitation that the student is emitting the essential behavior to be learned; reading is like watching someone else perform" (Fox, 1962, p. 88). A final behavior was review, in which the student checked his outline against the book or reread the chapter looking for errors of omission or commission. Surveying was encouraged first and was to occupy no more than one minute. When this procedure became routine, the next step, the questioning phase, was added, in which the student was instructed to ask one question for each boldface heading. Later he was asked to generate multiple questions for each one. The reading phase was next tackled; he first was asked to read only to answer questions he had posed or that had occurred to him as he read. A time limit for different types of material, based on his current reading speeds, was established. Recitation was then initiated; he was asked to stop at the end of each section, to close his book and to sit on it (which discourages looking at the book as well as slumping in the chair), and to spend three minutes outlining what he had read. Recitation time was gradually increased, and review training introduced, in which he sought errors of omission and commission. This review then was gradually increased. The student remained "on a schedule in which he made an independent decision after each section to stay and study or leave and play" (Fox, 1962, p. 89). This program was successful in increasing the grades of students who completed it. Some more specific instructions in relation to reading are offered in the following quote (from Groveman, Richards, and Caple (1975, pp. 28-29).

1. *Survey*. Skim over chapter headings and topic headings within each chapter. Read summary paragraph at the end of each chapter, if there is one. Notice core ideas of each chapter. Goal is to help organize ideas when chapter is completed.
2. *Question*. Create a question from the first heading. This is done to increase curiosity about the

chapter and to orient the student towards finding critical information in the chapter. Key
words to ask when reading the chapter are *why,*
when, and *how.* What ideas does the author
really wish to make us aware of?
3. *Read.* Read each chapter to answer the questions that you have developed. Do not plod—
actively seek the answers. Notice words or
phrases italicized. Were all your questions answered?

The student may need special coaching concerning how
to remove distractions, including assertion training to fend off
friends desirous of interrupting his schedule. Self-monitoring of
study behavior has been found to have a positive reactive effect
(Johnson and White, 1971). Feedback concerning progress, such
as hourly rate of words read in a foreign language, also seems to
have a positive effect (Fox, 1962).

Students are trained to establish clear goals, including
identification of tasks to be accomplished, and when each one is
to be completed. They are encouraged to record these tasks and
also to note the date the task was achieved and whether they
rewarded themselves for accomplishing each task. Training may
also be provided concerning how to take lecture notes. Guidelines include the following (from Groveman, Richards, and
Caple, 1975, pp. 37-38).

1. *Good listening.* Sit near the front of the classroom, especially in a large lecture hall. Do not
let your mind wander; stay alert.
2. *Orderliness.* Attend all the lectures—excuses are
easy to find—poor grades are difficult to make
up. Keep class notes for each course in either a
separate notebook or different sections of the
same notebook. Write legibly. Develop a simple
abbreviation system, for example: *i.e.* (*that is*),
& (*and*), ∴ (*therefore*).
4. *Note-Taking Format.* Rule your notebook into
three sections:
a. Section One is two inches wide.
b. Section Two is five inches wide.
c. Section Three is one inch wide.

5. *Five R's of Note Taking:*
   a. Record—during a lecture, record pertinent facts and ideas the instructor has presented.
   b. Reduce—as soon as possible after class summarize notes in two-inch column.
   c. Recite—cover the five-inch column and use the two-inch column as cues to see if you have ideas and facts clear.
   d. Reflect—use one-inch space for your own ideas.
   e. Review—repeat step c every other week.

Guidelines for test taking may also be required. Students are coached to make a schedule for review (not to cram the night before), to use all notes to prepare a summary of main topics and to organize all facts under these topics (Groveman, Richards, and Caple, 1975).

The student may also need help in completing papers. The possible role of perfectionistic standards in both writing or in taking examinations should not be overlooked, because this may be a contributing factor to a failure to perform or a failure to do well. A student may try to produce a final draft on the first try at writing a paper, and, when one does not emerge, may castigate himself unmercifully for what he considers to be dreadful work. Training in setting successive approximations to a final draft may be necessary. Let us say a client has been getting *C*'s on written papers. He or she can be asked to write a *D* paper and, when this emerges more easily, to try to write a *C* paper in a smaller amount of time, and so forth (Goldiamond, 1965). Some clients may be uncomfortable with deliberately trying to write a poor paper and may be trained how to set successive approximations by establishing clear, reasonable goals for each work period. For example, a goal may be to write five rough-draft pages within two hours. Many times a student is unclear as to what is to be accomplished when sitting down to work. If a final draft is attempted when a student is not ready to produce one, the experience will be stressful and unproductive. The client should also be trained how to program reinforcement for completion of agreed-on tasks (see, for example, Passman, 1976). Training students in more effective study skills has been carried out in groups as well as with individual clients (see, for example, Mitchell, Hall, and Piatkowska, 1975).

Summary

No other one setting has received more attention within a behavioral model than the classroom, perhaps because the classroom provides a natural, observational unit that is convenient in that participants remain within a well-defined area, and because of the potential importance of behaviors in educational settings to later achievements. The student's behavior is considered to be a reflection not only of his own skills and reinforcer hierarchy, but also of the way in which these interact with the conditions provided within the classroom by the teacher and by his peers. Numerous studies have shown that appropriate behaviors are often ignored in the classroom and inappropriate ones reinforced by the teacher and the peer group, and that most teacher-student interactions are negative. Teacher training programs have concentrated on increasing the teacher's use of positive reinforcement for appropriate behavior and extinction for inappropriate behavior. Some programs have also concentrated on enhancing the teacher's curriculum planning skills, because their lack is often integrally related to discipline problems and because they offer a natural source of reinforcement in the classroom. Token programs have been used extensively, and backup reinforcers are often offered by parents. Group contingencies provide a way to involve all students and to secure the support of peer reinforcement for desirable behavior. Many behavioral programs focus on increasing student competencies by offering the student additional social, academic, and recreational skills, and skills for influencing his or her emotions. These seem particularly appropriate, as does the goal to make learning itself a reinforcer, within an educational setting, where the basic aim is to increase competencies.

18

    The relationship between mind and body is well illus-trated in the many ways health problems relate to behavior. Both in Canada and the United States, major governmental statements have appeared that emphasize the relationship be-tween health problems such as cardiovascular illnesses, cancer, accidents, drinking excessive amounts of alcohol, smoking, over-eating, and underexercising, all of which are self-inflicted. Health problems are exaggerated by the pollution of the envi-ronment and by the advertising industry "hooking" people on things that are not beneficial to their health, such as food with multiple additives and great amounts of sugar. Health problems have psychological and social repercussions which are often in the foreground when a client presents a health-related problem. The overweight person, for example, may be far more concerned

Behavioral Procedures for Health-Related Problems

with the effects of his girth on his social life than on his longevity. Perhaps a man with asthma has just met a woman he has really fallen for who thinks it especially ridiculous that he continues to smoke in view of his recurrent difficulty in breathing, and he therefore wishes to decrease his smoking. The purpose of this chapter is to introduce the reader to some of the behavioral assessment and intervention procedures that have been employed to remedy health-related problems. Reference will often be made to additional sources where greater detail can be found in terms of carrying out special procedures.

Depending on what behavioral procedures are being considered, it could be argued that behavioral methods have long been available to reduce some medical problems. Anxiety management training can be employed to reduce stress resulting from recurrent muscle tension. Cognitive coping skills can be developed to decrease stress-inducing thoughts. Thus a variety of self-management behavioral procedures offer clients skills to control their degrees of stress. It is well established that stress is related to a variety of medical problems, including heart trouble and high blood pressure. In addition to the use of behavioral procedures to modulate stress, a review of the history of the use of behavioral methods reveals some intriguing applications to medical problems. For example, England and Mahoney (1965) successfully employed behavioral methods to eliminate recurrent bronchial nodules that had previously necessitated surgical removal on two occasions. It was hypothesized that the nodules were related to stress, which in turn was related to a lack of assertive skills on the part of this client. Intervention consisted in training the client in assertive behaviors. A follow-up one year later indicated that the nodules had failed to reappear. In some cases, behavioral methods have been employed not to remove an incurable condition, but to alleviate the severity of the symptoms (MacPherson, 1967). For example, a woman with Huntington's chorea suffered from frequent complete body tremors, over which she had no control. Questioning revealed that these tremors started in her lower left leg. Typically, when she would feel the initial signs of a tremor, her anxiety would increase in anticipation of the discomfort involved in a complete body tremor, which always followed. During intervention, she was trained to discriminate the initial stages of the tremor, shown how to relax and trained to associate the onset of the tremor in her leg with relaxation rather than with an increase in muscle tension. This new reaction succeeded in stopping the spread of the tremor, which in the past had been facilitated by added stress and muscle tension. Thus, although these methods could not cure this disease, it did alleviate one of the uncomfortable concomitants. Additional areas in which behavioral methods have been employed with medically related problems are discussed in the following sections. There is an emphasis on the development of alternative behaviors that will alleviate current or potential problems. Many programs, such as those designed to regulate smoking, focus on preventative measures.

Assessment

As with other presenting problems, a variety of sources are employed to gather needed assessment information and to evaluate progress. Physiological measures are often of import with medical problems and are often employed to supplement self-report and observation. Making sure that physical examinations have been carried out as needed is important in order to indicate when a medical procedure is required for intervention as well as to suggest the degree of organic impairment present and the extent to which this may limit possible change. However, the existence of organic impairment does not mean that change cannot be brought about through nonphysical means —for example, by rearranging contingencies or developing additional self-management skills. Such examinations may in some cases show that a physical basis does not exist, and attention can then be devoted to determining the maintaining conditions for verbal complaints (Epstein, 1976). Self-monitoring will be necessary with some reactions possibly related to medical disorders, such as degree of pain and its onset and offset. In some cases, other measures that are more readily observable may be selected, such as amount of medication requested and consumed, use of special respirators, and so forth. As with other presenting problems, it is important to remember that the contingencies influencing verbal reports may differ from those that influence the occurrence of physical indicators such as pain. If verbal reports of pain persist despite the fact that physiological measures indicate an absence of any physical source of pain, a search should be made for such possible external supports for symptoms (Epstein, 1976).

Respiratory Disorders

Behavioral procedures have been employed with a number of different respiratory disorders, including asthma and chronic cough. There is also an extensive literature describing the use of behavioral methods to attempt to decrease smoking, which is associated with respiratory disorders as well as with a number of other physical difficulties.

Asthma. Relaxation training and desensitization have been employed in the alleviation of asthmatic attacks (for example, Moore, 1965). In one study, although relaxation training alone, suggestion, and desensitization all resulted in subjective improvement, only clients who received systematic desensitization showed objective improvement. Clients were initially moderately to severely handicapped by attacks, with a range of from one to seven attacks per week. Here, too, a lack of concordance between response measures was noted; both at pre- and posttest there was a lack of correlation between subjective measures, measures of the number of asthmatic attacks, and objective measure of breathing function. During relaxation training, two training sessions were offered and clients were requested to practice at home for five minutes each day. In the desensitization condition, three hierarchies were employed: one based on an asthmatic attack, one on any situation that produced a reaction, and a third on a stress formulated to induce an attack based on psychoanalytic theory. Samples of hierarchies used are given in the following lists (from Moore, 1965, p. 271).

Hierarchy 1
    This is based on an asthmatic attack and is given to all patients in the same form.
    1. Very slight wheeze
    2. Just a bit more wheezy
    3. Wheezy, uncomfortable lying down
    4. Very wheezy and have to sit up
    5. Quite wheezy even sitting up in bed
    6. Very wheezy even sitting up
    7. Difficult to get the breath
    8. Feel you cannot breathe
    9. Fighting for breath
    10. Cannot go on fighting, feel as if you are going to die

Hierarchy 2
    This is based on infective or allergic factors, and is prepared individually to suit each patient.
    Example 1. The patient was a girl of nineteen who always had an attack whenever she breathed cigarette smoke, especially in a hot closed room.

1. Hot day at caravan [bus] at Canvey Island [holiday resort]
2. Hot day in London
3. Very hot day in closed room
4. Very hot day in closed room with stale cigarette smoke
5. Very hot day in closed room but one person smoking
7. Sitting in crowded cinema
8. Sitting in crowded cinema with a lot of cigarette smoke
9. Traveling in lift with one person smoking
10. In crowded lift with a lot of cigarette smoke

Each situation was repeated three times, four or five new situations being presented at each session.

Other studies have found relaxation training alone to be effective both with adults (Rathus, 1973) and with children (Alexander, Miklich, and Hershkoff, 1972). Self-monitoring and self-management skills have also been effectively employed (Sirota and Mahoney, 1974). A forty-one-year-old woman who had suffered from asthmatic attacks for seven years had found various treatments over many years all to be unsuccessful in helping her. Her attacks were exacerbated by stress and anxiety, and she was trained in relaxation as a coping response in such situations. She practiced relaxation twice a day for one week, with the help of a cassette tape. In order to encourage self-monitoring of her relaxation and to help to interrupt anxiety chains, she was given a portable timer to be set at random intervals and was asked, when the cue occurred, to evaluate her degree of relaxation, note her anxiety level, and relax away any tension that was present. In addition, a brief postponement of bronchometer use was introduced. Any time she had difficulty breathing and wished to use her inhalant, she set the timer for three to four minutes and practiced an abbreviated (four-muscle group) relaxation procedure. Only if absolutely necessary was she to use her inhalant.

Bronchometer use decreased sharply from a baseline of nine times a day to zero on the tenth day of intervention. A two-month follow-up indicated that positive changes were maintained. The client reported that identifying and altering early

tension reactions (through naturalistic cueing) was very successful in decreasing asthmatic episodes. She reported that the tick-
ing of the timer became a cue for maintained calmness. A new,
self-management, optimistic, response set was reported to be
usefully employed in other areas, including her marriage.

The operant nature of some asthmatic attacks is illustrated by examples where attacks decreased in duration when
significant others, such as parents, were trained to rearrange
consequences following attacks suffered by their children. For
example, Neisworth and Moore (1972) reported a case example
of a seven-year-old boy who was diagnosed as asthmatic at the
age of six months, and who was often hospitalized for this condition. Frequent visits to the emergency room were required by
the age of two due to repeated attacks (coughing, wheezing, and
abrupt inspiration). From that time until the age of seven, he
was seen monthly by a physician. "By the time it was suggested
that the child might be helped by behavior therapy, a pattern of
parental concern and continued attention to the problem had
been well established. Typically, the mother would caution the
child not to overexert himself, not to eat certain foods, and to
be sure to take his medicine. She described the child as 'nervous' and reported that emotional upsets or excitement precipitated the child's attacks. Of particular concern were the child's
prolonged wheezing and coughing at bedtime. Further investigation revealed that both medicine and sympathetic attention
were given especially during the bedtime asthmatic episodes"
(Neisworth and Moore, 1972, p. 96). Attacks at nighttime in
bed were concentrated on, because attacks were most extreme
in this situation. A ten-day baseline revealed an average duration
of about seventy minutes for these attacks. A differential reinforcement procedure was employed, in which the parents were
instructed to no longer provide attention to the boy during bedtime attacks or to offer medication. Decreases in duration of
coughing at bedtime were reinforced by giving him lunch money
to buy his own lunch at school (rather than taking lunch) if he
coughed for less time than the night before. As often happens
when an extinction procedure is first put into effect, there was
an initial increase in the duration of attacks. This was followed
by an abrupt decrease on the seventh day of intervention and

by the thirteenth day of intervention, attacks lasted only about nine minutes. In order to provide assurance concerning the role of social attention on attacks, which is of special concern when presenting problems have a possible physical base, a reversal design was employed, in which parents were requested to reinstate the original contingencies for the behavior. Attacks again increased in duration. A return to intervention procedures again decreased attacks to about seven minutes. The parents were requested to occasionally monitor duration of bedtime coughing as a reminder to continue new contingencies. A follow-up of eleven months indicated that attacks had remained at about two to seven minutes in duration (see Figure 40).

Figure 40. Duration of Bedtime Asthmatic Responding as a Function of Contingency Changes

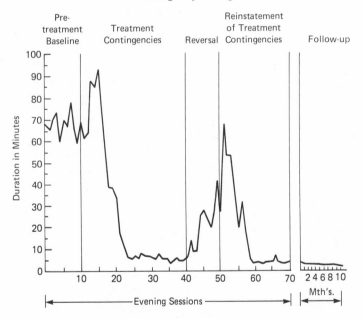

Source: Neisworth and Moore (1972, p. 97).

The operant nature of some asthmatic attacks is also illustrated by the success of operant shaping in decreasing attacks in which reinforcement is offered for increasing periods without attacks (Miklich, 1973).

Time out from positive reinforcement has been successful in decreasing the frequency and duration of children's hospitalizations for asthmatic attacks (Creer, 1970). Because frequent hospitalizations interfere with schooling and normal socialization experiences, it seems desirable to reduce unnecessary stays in the hospital. The clients in this study were two ten-year-old boys who lived in a residential treatment center for children with intractable asthma. When free of attacks, they participated in public school and a variety of other social and recreational activities. Both boys were frequently hospitalized when other children would be seen by a physician and released. Don and Jack seemed especially skilled at exaggerating their asthma attacks by hyperventilating, ignoring early warning signals of an impending attack, and seeking attention while the attacks were relatively mild (Creer, 1970). They also remained in the hospital longer than other children. "This occurred because each S [subject] had a series of physical complaints they would present to the medical staff. Jack, for example, frequently reported that he was experiencing stomach pains. This invariably would initiate a series of examinations and tests, all of which would delay Jack's release from the hospital. Don, on the other hand, sometimes complained of chest pains. Such comments always elicited a complete mobilization of the medical staff because Don had a history of at least two cardiac arrests" (Creer, 1970, p. 117). Time-out conditions in the hospital were as follows:

> Each boy will be placed in a room by himself whenever he is hospitalized. The Ss can receive no visitors other than medical or nursing personnel. Both boys are not allowed to visit with other patients while in the hospital. Only books related to school work are allowed to be in the Ss' possession. Comic books and television sets are forbidden. The Ss can leave their room only to go to the restroom. The nursing staff will prevent the Ss from visiting with other patients on their way to and from restroom. The boys will eat all of their meals in their room by themselves rather than joining the other children in the hospital dining room. These instructions were strictly adhered to all times during this phase of the study. [Creer, 1970, p. 118]

A reversal of contingencies was employed to gather further evidence of the importance of social consequences in maintaining the frequency and duration of hospitalization. During time out, both mean number of hospitalizations and duration of stay fell sharply. For example, during baseline Don was admitted on sixteen occasions, for a total of twenty-eight days. He was admitted only six times during the first time-out period, for a total of eight days. The reversal procedure supplied further evidence for the role of attention.

Behavioral methods have also been employed to alleviate other disorders associated with the respiratory system, such as tracheostomy dependency (Wright, Nunnery, Eichel, and Scott, 1969) and chronic cough (Alexander, Chai, Creer, Miklich, Renne, and Cardoso, 1973).

Smoking. In spite of increasing support for the relationship between smoking and a wide range of illnesses, including lung cancer and cardiovascular disease, more than one third of the adult population smokes (American Cancer Society, 1974). Some smokers have no intention of quitting and so would not appear in a smoking reduction program. These people may believe that smoking is not harmful or may accept the risks involved. Possible deleterious effects may be accepted, but the smokers may believe they are unable to stop. As Straits (1965) has pointed out, smokers may have a range of attitudes, including the uninformed, the unbelieving, the unmotivated, and the unable. Some smokers would like to stop smoking and seek help. A third group of smokers represents individuals who stop smoking without professional help and, as Premack (1970) notes, more attention should be paid to how they achieve this feat.

A major problem with all smoking reduction programs is the temporary nature of effects achieved. Reasons for the disappointing maintenance of progress include a failure to sufficiently consider individual differences in terms of attitudes and of antecedents and consequences related to smoking, and to provide individually tailored maintenance programs. Many behavioral intervention programs designed to reduce smoking have expected gains to be magically maintained. The following discussion introduces assessment and intervention issues. The reader is referred to other sources for additional details (for example, Flaxman, 1976).

Assessment. The purpose of assessment is to determine the rate of smoking, as well as situational and motivational factors related to it. One advantage of smoking is that it is very easy to monitor. A form can be divided into days and times, folded, and inserted inside the cellophane wrapper of the cigarette pack. Smoking is self-monitored on the form. The client is usually asked to note (using abbreviations) what he was doing at the time—for example, working, socializing, watching television, or reading. It has been found that monitoring of cigarettes desired but not smoked (abstinence) decreased smoking, whereas self-monitoring of those smoked increased smoking (McFall, 1970). Self-monitoring will indicate the rate of smoking as well as related antecedents and consequences.

Smoking may be associated with a very wide range of situations, because it can occur anywhere. And, when frequency of inhalation is considered, it is obvious that one is dealing with a behavior that is reinforced hundreds of times per day. A person who smokes twenty cigarettes a day puffs about 150 times a day or 60,000 times a year (Jarvik, 1970). The strength of the behavior is highlighted in studies where tobacco has been unavailable to smokers. Some smokers made lettuce cigarettes (they did not enjoy them) (Jarvik, 1970). And we all know of cases (perhaps ourselves) of smokers rooting through the trash for a stub when there are no cigarettes in the house. Some people report that they tend to smoke when they are nervous, although others report that they smoke when they are excited. Eysenck (1973) accounts for this seeming contradiction by speculating that smoking is employed to regulate the state of arousal. Medical assessment may reveal physical problems, such as emphysema, which may increase the urgency of achieving a decrease in smoking behavior.

Intervention procedures. A smorgasbord of behavioral procedures has been investigated in the attempt to decrease smoking, often with little regard for individual differences. One can take one's pick between a conditioning procedure, which entails rapid breathing of hot, smoky air and which is fairly effective if people do it (Lichtenstein, Harris, Birchler, Wahl, and Schmahl, 1973), or stimulus-control procedures, in which clients agree gradually to decrease smoking, starting with situations in which they do not smoke much anyway (Sachs, Bean, and Morrow, 1970). A cigarette container could be used that opens only at gradually increasing intervals (Azrin and Powell, 1968), or a response-cost procedure in which a certain sum of money is lost if agreed-on goals are not met (Elliot and Tighe, 1968). This variety of behavioral programs is more than matched by sometimes bizarre and sometimes sheerly profit-making schemes devised by others, including a week at sea without any cigarettes. (This did not work well, as anyone with even a rudimentary understanding of stimulus control could have predicted.) Out of all this investigation, some information has emerged. The first major point is that we still do not have an effective way to help people stop smoking, although we do know a lot about what will not work. A planned, abrupt, total quitting seems more effective than gradual withdrawal or immediate termination of smoking (Flaxman, 1974). Incidentally, this is how most people who succeed in quitting through their own efforts do so—all at once. Multiple procedures were employed in this self-control package including substituting new habits for smoking (for example, developing a new hobby or using worry beads for tactile stimulation); offering the smoker self-control skills to help him resist the impulse to smoke (such as thought stopping and altering cues associated with smoking); enhancing motivation by rehearsing reasons for stopping to smoke; making a public commitment; and learning to use self-reinforcement.

Neurological and Muscular Disorders

Behavioral procedures have been employed to decrease seizures and eliminate nervous habits and tics as well as to decrease headaches. As with any other presenting problem, attention is devoted during assessment to the possible role of maintaining factors, such as social attention, as well as to the role of specific precipitating events.

Seizures. A number of behavioral procedures have been employed to decrease the frequency of seizures. Arranging for increased tolerance to seizure-inducing events by gradually introducing such events has been successfully employed to decrease reflex seizures, in which the seizure is evoked by a particular stimulus or class of stimuli (Adams, 1976). A variety of competing responses have been employed—for example, teaching a client to smell strong odors during the epileptic aura in order to arrest the attack (Efron, 1956).

As with many other disorders that appear to have a physical origin, the role of environmental factors can be illustrated by influencing the frequency or duration of the behavioral disturbance by rearranging what happens before or after the behavior. Seizures have been modified by stimulus control (rearranging what happens before) as well as by contingency management (rearranging what happens after). Biofeedback has been employed to decrease seizures related to epilepsy (Sterman, 1973). Selection of procedure is informed by the results of assessment. For example, desensitization was employed to reduce the seizures of a thirty-six-year-old male diagnosed as having Jakob Creutzfeldt Syndrome, a progressive neurological disorder characterized by dementia and violent episodes of bizarre muscular movements (Parrino, 1971, p. 215). These ranged from twenty-two to ninety-five a day during baseline. Surrounding environmental stresses included being relieved of certain responsibilities at work, which Mr. S. perceived as a demotion and mounting difficulties with his wife, whom he suspected of having an affair with one of his best friends. A subsequent divorce and ending of his employment relieved these stresses; however, seizures continued.

During the client's most recent stay in the hospital, the staff had noticed that various emotional triggers appeared to be related to episodes of bizarre muscular movements, and he was referred to a behavior therapy unit. A thirteen-day baseline revealed that seizures occurred from twenty-two to ninety-five per day for an average rate of fifty-eight per day. Seizures were less frequent at work and on weekends when he visited friends and relatives. Level of anxiety seemed to be a predicator of seizure rate. Some of the situations that seem to elicit anxiety included: "Socializing with fellow patients in the unit, particularly when Mr. S. was the focus of attention; meeting someone in authority, friend or stranger (for example, the director of the unit); initiating conversation with an acquaintance during visiting hours; dealing with a particularly difficult female patient in the unit who constantly harassed Mr. S.; and the mention of family-related material (for example, wife's name, children's names)" (Parrino, 1971, p. 217).

The client was trained in deep muscle relaxation and a stimulus hierarchy was formed for each of the situations described. Desensitization sessions were held twice a week over three months, and the client was also taught how to carry out self-desensitization sessions. The following items, directed to the client, represent the hierarchy concerning initiating a conversation with a visitor (from Parrino, 1971, p. 213).

1. A person you recognize appears in the unit.
2. The acquaintance is having a conversation with a staff member.
3. The acquaintance looks in your direction.
4. The acquaintance and you make eye contact.
5. The acquaintance smiles at you from across the room.
6. The acquaintance starts walking towards you.
7. The acquaintance is getting very close to you.
8. The acquaintance extends his hand to you.
9. You shake hands with the acquaintance.
10. You engage in conversation with the acquaintance.

The rate of seizures decreased sharply, from a high point of forty-three per day during the fourth week of intervention to ten per day in the fourteenth week. There was a slight increase in seizures when the client returned to work, and he was encouraged to continue self-desensitization sessions related to anxiety at work. Seizures decreased to zero by the nineteenth week of intervention. Over the course of intervention, the seizures altered in form from gross motor movement to ticlike mannerisms restricted to the facial area. He maintained fulltime employment, became engaged to be married, and all medication was withdrawn. This case illustrates the role of stress on the exacerbation of a physical disorder as well as possible "leftover" conditioning effects, even though the original precipitating causes (marital and vocational stress) were no longer present.

In another case, seizure antecedents were focused on in

an attempt to identify the initial components in the chain of behavior leading to a seizure and to interfere with these components (Zlutnik, Mayville, and Moffat, 1975). A seizure was considered to be the final link in a chain of behaviors, which suggested that this could be decreased by interfering with preseizure behaviors. This method requires that preseizure behaviors be identifiable. With four clients, a punishment procedure was employed in which the change agent would shout no, grasp the client by the shoulders, and shake him once, vigorously. With another client, a differential reinforcement was employed contingent on arm raising, which was a preseizure behavior. The client's hands were placed down at her side, and after five seconds a combination of primary and social reinforcement was offered, contingent on her arms remaining down.

The following case example illustrates the application of this interruption procedure with a seven-year-old boy who had received varying diagnoses of autistic, brain-damaged, and as having a learning disability (Zlutnick, Mayville, and Moffat, 1975). A formal diagnosis of epilepsy had never been made; however, the possible role of functional factors had not been suggested. Frequency of seizures was twelve per day in spite of medication (Dilantin). His seizure behavior comprised distinct components: (1) fixed gaze at a flat surface; (2) followed by his body becoming rigid; (3) followed by violent shaking, and (4) ending with a fall to the floor. Intervention was carried out in a classroom, with twelve other children present, by a staff member of a behavior modification unit. Baseline revealed that the usual reaction of the teacher was inattention. There did not seem to be any relationship between seizures and particular cues. During intervention, the interruption procedure was applied as soon as fixed-stare behavior occurred. Seizures fell from twelve per day to about one to two per day and completely disappeared after seven weeks of intervention. Only when staff members failed to "interrupt" the chain of behavior within ten to fifteen seconds following the beginning of visual fixation did a seizure occur. Medication was faded out completely and although a plan had been made to offer the parents training to influence seizures at home, this did not prove necessary, because they reported a reduction of staring and seizures there also. A sixth-month follow-up revealed that one seizure had taken place during this time.

Family members were directly involved in helping to decrease seizure behavior of a fourteen-year-old girl who had had a history of seizures since the age of eighteen months (Zlutnick, Mayville, and Moffat, 1975). A diagnosis of epilepsy had been made and, in spite of medication, seizure frequency was two a day. Preseizure action consisted of raising the arm to a position parallel to her head followed by a sixty-second seizure consisting of violent shaking and vacant staring. There was 100 percent predictability of seizure behavior from arm-raising behavior. The mother was employed as the trainer, under the direction of a home-visiting teacher who visited the house twice a week. Other children in the family participated by helping to collect data. As with the case described earlier, observation did not reveal any particular people, locations, time, or activity that seemed to be cues for seizures. Seizures decreased to about one every three days with use of the interruption procedure. The father did not become involved in the program. A six-month follow-up indicated that, although seizures had increased by one or two per week, they still were far below their original level.

An interruption in the chain of behavior leading to a seizure may also be arranged through training in the use of positive self-instructions. Ince (1976) reports the case of a twelve-year-old boy who was trained in deep muscle relaxation during which the word *relax* was paired with a relaxed state and then was instructed to employ this when he felt the onset of a seizure approaching. Intervention took place over three months during weekly hour-long meetings. He usually had between nine and ten grand mal seizures and about twenty-five to twenty-six petit mal seizures per week. During intervention there was an attempt to change the function of the initial component in this chain from one that increased anxiety to one that would have the opposite function. Symbolic desensitization was employed to decrease anxiety to a variety of themes associated with seizures, such as having a seizure in the classroom or on the baseball field, being ridiculed by other children, or receiving new, experimental medication. The hierarchy for being ridiculed included scenes concerning "Children laughing at him when he enters school; children staring at him, pointing at him and laughing in his classroom; children calling him names; children telling him that he is 'crazy' or 'retarded,' or that he belongs in an institution; children refusing to play with him or come to his house when he asks them to because he has epilepsy" (Ince, 1976, p. 40).

Tape-recorded relaxation instructions were employed, and the boy was given a copy of these which he took home and was asked to practice twice a day. It was possible that seizures were partially supported by the parents. When seizures would occur at school, for example, the father would be notified and would leave work and take the boy home. However, the parents refused to discuss their possible role. After five sessions over four and a half weeks, the boy reported that he no longer felt nervous about items on the hierarchies. Additional sessions were provided in which a relaxed state was paired with the word *relax* and the boy was instructed to employ this cue word to try to reduce seizures. Five weeks of symbolic desensitization were not very effective in decreasing seizures; however, self-instructional training resulted in an immediate decrease to between one and two grand mal, and three and four petit mal, seizures per week. This decreased further to a complete absence of seizures, which was maintained at a six-month follow-up.

Rearrangement of parental attention was employed to reduce the frequency of seizures of a ten-year-old girl. These consisted of rhythmical head rolling accompanied by hair pulling (Gardner, 1967). Extensive physical examinations had failed to reveal any physical causes for this behavior. Examination of the family interaction revealed a competition with her younger sister for parental attention, as well as some events that could have functioned as a model of seizurelike behavior. One occurred a few months prior to the development of seizures, when the mother experienced a headache of such intensity that she "rocked and banged" in pain and was taken to the hospital. A few weeks before the development of the seizures, the child evidenced increasing somatic complaints.

The parents were seen together in three weekly one-hour sessions, the first of which took place while the child was in the hospital. The intervention plan developed during this session was put into effect when the child returned home. This consisted of the parents ignoring the child when she evidenced seizures or other highly deviant behavior such as tantrums, and offering her attention when she engaged in appropriate behavior. The parents estimated that somatic complaints occurred about six to eight times per week during the two weeks prior to hospitalization and tantrums occurred about five to six times per week. In two weeks of intervention, seizures decreased to zero, somatic complaints were about three per week, and tantrums three per week. Within a month, tantrums decreased to zero. A reversal design was employed in order to provide further confirmation that parental attention maintained seizure behavior. The parents were asked to reinstate original conditions on the twenty-sixth week of follow-up. Within twenty-four hours of reinstatement of attention for the child's somatic complaints, these increased to about one per hour, at which point the child displayed a seizure. The parents then reinstated the intervention plan. Seizure behavior disappeared. Somatic complaints remained at about seven per week and gradually decreased to three per week. Somatic complaints, tantrums, and seizures all seemed to be functionally related to parental attention. Reinforcement of somatic complaints appeared to be a cue that other deviant behaviors, such as seizures, would also be followed by parental attention. The influence over seizure behavior by parental attention supported the learned nature of "seizures" in this case. A follow-up one year later indicated that no further seizures had occurred.

Eliminating Nervous Habits and Tics. Rather than considering nervous habits as "erotic and aggressive instinctual impulses. . . which are continually escaping through pathological discharge" (Mahler and Luke, 1946, p. 441), as in the psychoanalytic view, behavioral theorists view such behaviors as learned habits that may start as reactions to extreme events such as a physical injury and that persist after the original event has passed (Azrin and Nunn, 1973). Such habits may have developed gradually, so that they blend with other behaviors and escape notice by the person. Frequent practice of the habit, as Azrin and Nunn point out, may even strengthen the muscles involved in the habits, while the opposing muscles remain relatively unused. Attention from others may help to maintain the movements. This view suggests a variety of intervention procedures, including increasing client awareness of the movement, interruption of the movement so that it is no longer part of a chain of normal movements, reinforcement of a competing movement, and programing of social reinforcement. A behavioral program including awareness training, competing response practice, and habit-control motivation was employed to reduce the frequency of a variety of nervous habits of twelve clients ranging in age from five to sixty-four. Types of nervous habits or tics included shoulder jerking, head shaking, eyelash plucking, fingernail biting, and thumb sucking. Some of these habits had persisted for over seven years. Clients monitored the number of incidents per minute or day or the percentage of time each day they experienced the habits. These records were collected each day during the initial part of intervention, and validating reports were obtained from significant others who were in a position to frequently observe the client, such as spouses, teachers, roommates, boyfriends, or coworkers.

A variety of procedures were employed to increase client awareness of habits. The response description procedure required the client to describe the details of the movement to the counselor while enacting several incidences of the movement. In this procedure, the counselor informed the client whenever the habit was occurring. In the early warning procedure, the client practiced detecting the earliest sign of the movement such as when the hand approached the face (in a nail biter). Heightened awareness of the habit was further encouraged by competing response practice, in which muscles that were incompatible with the movement were tensed for a few minutes. Situation awareness training required the client to recall all situations, places, and persons where the habit was likely to occur and to describe how he performed the habit in each situation.

In competing response practice, each client was taught a specific response pattern that was incompatible with the old habit. Desirable characteristics of such a response included being opposed to the nervous movement, being capable of being maintained for a few minutes, producing increased awareness of the muscles involved in the movement, being socially inconspicuous and compatible with ongoing activities, and strengthening muscles antagonistic to the habit. For example, for the habits of eyelash pulling, thumb sucking, and fingernail biting, clients were asked to place their hands down at their sides and to clench their fists whenever they detected the movement, until they could experience tension in their arms and hands. If this activity would interfere with an ongoing activity, they were instructed to grasp some object that would be appropriate to the situation, until they could feel tension. The client who suffered from head shaking was asked to slowly and isometrically contract her neck muscles until the head was perfectly still (Azrin and Nunn, 1973). Each client practiced his exercise in the counseling session until he performed it correctly, which usually required less than five minutes.

Client motivation was enhanced by habit-inconvenience review, in which the inconveniences, embarrassment, and suffering resulting from the habit were discussed by the counselor and client. In addition, social support procedures were employed, in which family and friends commented favorably on the client's efforts and reminded him of the need to practice his exercise. The counselor telephoned the client at regular intervals to gather self-monitored data and to praise the client for his efforts. Manual guidance was necessary with some of the children who failed to initiate the exercise by themselves. A public display procedure was employed to demonstrate to dubious significant others that in fact the client could attain self-control over habits these others thought to be neurologically determined and therefore not subject to voluntary influence attempts. Family members were required to observe the demonstration of self-control during sessions and significant others were informed of such control right after counseling sessions.

A symbolic rehearsal procedure was employed to teach the client to be aware of the habit in many situations. He imagined situations in which the habit occurred and imagined that he could detect the movement and that he performed the required exercise. This stage lasted about fifteen minutes. Actual practice in detecting the movement and exercising for three minutes afterward was provided by engaging the client in conversation on a variety of habit-irrelevant topics for a half hour, during which the client could practice detection and practice of the competing response. If he did not detect the habit, attention would be drawn to this by the counselor offering some minimal prompt such as staring at the limb, or saying "Hmmm," at which time the client would carry out the competing exercise for three minutes while the conversation continued. Only one or two counseling sessions were required for the program, in addition to telephone contacts. This program was very successful in decreasing undesirable movements, not only during counseling sessions but also in the natural environment. Massed practice and self-monitoring combined with desensitization have also been employed to decrease tics (Rafi, 1962; Thomas, Abrams, and Johnson, 1971). Electromyograph (EMG) feedback has been successful in decreasing injury-induced muscle tension (Jacobs and Felton, 1969) and chronic teeth clenching (Rugh and Solberg, 1974).

Other Neurological Disorders. Relaxation training has been employed to decrease migraine headaches (Lutker, 1971). This has also been combined with other procedures such as assertiveness training and systematic desensitization (Mitchell, 1969; Mitchell and Mitchell, 1971). Relaxation training combined with feedback of muscle potential seems to be most effective in training clients to decrease the frequency of tension headaches (Blanchard and Young, 1973; Chesney and Shelton, 1976). Whenever headaches are complained of, a thorough medical examination should be arranged, because this symptom is associated with a variety of physical disorders. This is also true of other complaints, such as seizures. Relaxation training has been employed to decrease involuntary muscle movements (MacPherson, 1967; Butler and Salamy, 1975). Provision of EMG feedback from muscles is useful in helping to regain the use of given muscle groups in clients who suffer from neuromuscular disorders (Blanchard and Young, 1974). Shaping was used to develop walking in a five-year-old girl with cerebral palsy (O'Neil, 1972). Behaviors reinforced included pulling herself up to a kneeling position, moving to a standing position, and walking with the support of a cabinet. She was then trained to release her hold on the cabinet and to walk with a crutch, by using a harness that permitted someone standing behind her to support her as she walked. Steps in this program included walking with harness support only, hand support using a stick and spring, support with a weighted crutch, and finally, walking with one weighted crutch. Both social and edible reinforcers were employed in this program. Nancy's doctor had previously informed Nancy's mother that the child would never walk. Systematic desensitization has been employed to reduce the anxiety of clients with cerebral palsy (Silber and Howard, 1972) and observational modeling has been employed to increase the social skills of cerebral palsied children (Cochrane, 1974). A classical conditioning paradigm was employed to decrease attacks of a woman with temporal lobe epilepsy (Efron, 1956). It was found that an unpleasant odor presented during the aura prior to the seizure would arrest the seizure. This odor was paired with a bracelet, which also assumed this function. An eight-month follow-up showed an absence of seizure behavior. Metronome-conditioned speech retraining shows promise in the treatment of severe stuttering (Brady, 1971b). Delayed auditory feedback and a time-out procedure have also been employed (Perkins, 1973). A recent study suggests that self-observation and recording of stuttering are more effective in increasing fluency than contingent monetary gain or loss (Lanyon and Barocas, 1975).

Obesity

It is estimated that forty to eighty million people in the United States are overweight (Stuart and Davis, 1972). The relationship of extra weight to a variety of many major disorders such as cardiovascular disease and diabetes is well known. Adverse psychological consequences are also associated with obesity by virtue of its possible interfering role in relation to work and one's social and sexual life. The interest in reducing girth is attested to by the popularity of the wide variety of weight reduction programs offered to the public and the wide sales of weight reduction "how-to-do-it" books. As with any strategy of change, each program reports some successes with some people. However, the statement that Stunkard made in 1958 seems almost equally true today: "Most obese patients will not remain in treatment. Of those who do remain in treatment, most will not lose significant poundage, and of those who do lose weight, most will regain it promptly" (Stunkard, 1958, p. 87). The methods described in the following discussion, which emphasize behavioral management and environmental control, have shown more promise in decreasing dropout rates in weight reduction programs and in helping a greater percentage of clients lose weight (Leon, 1976). For example, a behavioral weight reduction program was significantly more effective than the Take Off Pounds Sensibly (TOPS) self-help program (Levitz and Stunkard, 1974). The typical self-help program failed to facilitate weight loss. The long-term effectiveness of behavioral programs still remains unknown. Maintenance remains a problem. It seems that there are individual differences in the specific type of program that is most effective and of greatest interest to a person. This calls for individual assessment and tailoring of programs.

Factors Related to Obesity. Obesity seems to be related to a variety of factors, including both overeating and a lack of activity. These two factors are related, in that as activity goes down eating goes up, and as sedentary persons become more active, their food consumption may decrease (Stunkard and Mahoney, 1976).

Obesity that starts in childhood tends to be more difficult to alleviate (Stunkard and Burt, 1967). This persistence of obesity is partially explained by the increase in the total number of adipocytes in the subcutaneous tissue (Hirsch and Knittle, 1971). Although the individual cells shrink during weight reduction, the total number of fat cells does not change. There is also an indication that genetics, as well as metabolism, plays a role here. For example, there is evidence that some obese persons can gain weight on fewer calories than are required by persons of normal weight (Passmore, Strong, Swindells, and El Din, 1963). Some have argued that overweight people are below the physiological "set point" and respond to this with the enhanced sensitivity to palatability noted in fasting, normal weight individuals (Jacobs and Sharma, 1969). The eating experience is more positive for the overweight individual than for the normal weight person. For example, obese college students were found to be more likely to cancel their dormitory food contracts in order to eat in better restaurants (Goldman, Jaffa, and Schachter, 1968). There is increasing evidence that overweight individuals are more sensitive to palatability variables (Polivy, 1975). Also, obesity tends to run in families.

The greater importance of external compared to internal cues for eating has received only modest support (see, for example, Milich, 1975). And the supposition that there is a characteristic obese eating style characterized by a few large bites, rapid eating pace, and short meal duration has not been supported (Mahoney, 1975). It is clear that there are many reasons why some people overeat. The state of being overweight reveals no information about the particular behaviors involved or the antecedents and consequences related to them.

A Behavioral Approach to Obesity. A behavioral approach to weight reduction emphasizes the self-management of eating behavior. Behavior change is emphasized rather than weight loss. One's weight is considered to be a result of behavior in terms of what is consumed and the amount of exercise engaged in. There is a focus on identifying and strengthening antecedents and consequences that facilitate appropriate eating behaviors and identifying and weakening antecedents and consequences associated with inappropriate eating behaviors (Stuart and Davis, 1972). An overview of assessment and intervention procedures is presented in the following discussion. For greater detail, the reader is referred to Stuart and Davis (1972), Ferguson (1975), and M. J. Mahoney and K. Mahoney (1976a). As with other self-management programs, clients are encouraged to become better observers of their own behavior and the factors that influence it, including their thoughts as well as environmental factors, so that they will be able to exert more influence over their behavior and achieve more success in attaining goals they select. Information collected through self-monitoring is reviewed to identify patterns and this information then employed to generate possible alternatives that might help the client reach selected goals. For example, as one of the first steps in their self-management program for weight reduction, M. J. Mahoney and K. Mahoney (1976a) introduce the reader to the components of successful self-control, including specifying the general problem area (such as food consumption), collecting data, identifying patterns and possible related factors, generating possible solutions, selecting one to try out, comparing current data with previous data, and, based on this comparison, extending, revising, or replacing solutions. This procedural guideline is highlighted by employing this series of steps in relation to selected problem areas described later. Hopefully, the client thus will learn a problem-solving strategy to influence behavior that can be used in relation to many problem areas.

Assessment. The emphasis during assessment is on the client's behavior related to eating, such as eating habits, exercise, and food-related thoughts (M. J. Mahoney and K. Mahoney, 1976a, 1976b). Separate assignments may be employed to gather needed assessment information. For example, M. J. Mahoney and K. Mahoney (1976a) include a series of six assignments in their self-management program for weight control, the first of which relates to the problem area of food-related thoughts. Food-related thoughts and the time they occur are noted on a small card, for about a week. Cues can be arranged to remind the client to note food-related thoughts, such as placing small, colored index cards around the house; or the client can be asked to review such thoughts at each hour and to note any that occurred. These are then examined to determine helpful and dysfunctional patterns. Later examination of data collected may reveal that food-related thoughts are inappropriate and self-defeating, for example, "It's just not fair that I cannot eat just what I want to" or "What's the use?" Identification of patterns can then help to inform possible options for altering thought patterns in specific ways. Figure 41 gives examples of negative and appropriate monologs. The second assignment recommended by M. J. Mahoney and K. Mahoney (1976a) involves the client in gathering information about his or her social support system related to eating. He or she is asked to list the following headings on a "Social Support Log" (M. J. Mahoney and K. Mahoney, 1976a, p. 87): *Person, His Actions* (and two columns under this, *Helping Me Avoid Food* and *Feedback on My Efforts*), and *My Reactions*. Clients are requested to rate others' actions and their own reactions as to whether they were poor, neutral, or good. This log is to be reviewed at the end of

Figure 41. Examples of Negative and Appropriate Monologs
Regarding Eating

Problem Category	Negative Monologs	Appropriate Monologs
Pounds lost	"I'm not losing fast enough." "I've starved myself and haven't lost a thing." "I've been more consistent than Mary and she is losing faster than I am—it's not fair.	"Pounds don't count; if I continue my eating habits, the pounds will be lost." "Have patience—those pounds took a long time to get there. As long as they stay off permanently, I'll settle for any progress." "It takes a while to break down fat and absorb the extra water produced. I'm not going to worry about it."
Capabilities	"I just don't have the will power." "I'm just naturally fat." "Why should this work—nothing else has." "I'll probably just regain it." "What the heck—I'd rather be fat than miserable; besides I'm not *that* heavy."	"There's no such thing as 'will power'—just poor planning. If I make a few improvements here and there and take things one day at a time, I can be very successful." "It's going to be nice to be permanently rid of all this extra baggage—I'm starting to feel better already."
Excuses	"If it weren't for my job and the kids, I could lose weight." "It's just impossible to eat right with a schedule like mine." "I'm just so nervous all the time—I have to eat to satisfy my psychological needs." "Maybe next time. . . ."	"My schedule isn't any worse than anyone else's. What I need to do is be a bit more creative in how to improve my eating." "Eating doesn't satisfy psychological problems—it creates them." "Job, kids, or whatever, I'm the one in control."

Source: M. J. Mahoney and K. Mahoney (1976a, pp. 62-63).

the week, noting who provides feedback concerning the client's eating and whether this is positive or negative. These data are important in helping the client determine options for enhancing social support.

Noting what is eaten and when this is eaten is part of a third assignment that involves the client over a four- to six-week period in attempting to gradually alter eating habits. The problem area here is considered to be food consumption and as with all self-management problems, a first step involves collection of relevant data. Information is gathered for a week, including food eaten (type, quantity, and calories), location, time, and social situation (alone or with others). The client may also be asked to note his or her mood (anxious, bored, tired, depressed, or angry (Stuart and Davis, 1972)). After this information is collected for one week, it is examined to identify patterns. The total number of calories consumed each day and the average weekly calorie intake are determined. The client is requested to judge how much activity he gets each week and to find out for this activity rating and, for his desired weight, his daily calorie allowance. This will indicate the daily calorie intake that should be consumed and the client can then examine options for achieving it, including substituting less caloric food or reducing certain food items. In order to make monitoring less cumbersome, only those food items selected for change may be tracked when the client attempts to alter his eating habits.

A fourth assignment involves the client in collecting information concerning eating style. The client is encouraged to employ a form with the main headings of *Before, During,* and *After.* In the *Before* column, headings include *Time* and *Location:* "Were you thinking about food beforehand?" "Did you see any food before you decided to eat?" "Did you respond to a food offer?" In the *During* column, headings listed include "Did you consume a relatively large amount?" "Did you chew it very little or not at all?" "Was the food mostly carbohydrate?" "Did you eat fairly rapidly?" Headings listed in the *After* column include "Did you feel stuffed?" and "Did you leave a clean plate or empty carton?" This information is gathered for a week and then examined for patterns related to eating style. This may reveal that eating is often preceded by food thoughts and that a procedure must be developed to alter these thoughts. Or perhaps records show that the client typically eats very fast and he will decide to set down his fork or spoon between bites of food in order to slow down his pace of eating. Seeing food may be a problem and arrangements must therefore be made to decrease the frequency with which this occurs, perhaps by rearranging food items in the refrigerator or by taking another street home from work, so as not to pass a bakery with delectable items in the window.

A fifth assignment involves the client in taking a look at his energy expenditure after he has been introduced to the principles of energy expenditure and some guidelines for increasing energy output. The first assignment in this four-week assignment asks the client to purchase a pedometer, attach this at the hip or ankle, and to record the reading at noon, at dinner time, and at bedtime.

In a sixth assignment, the client gathers data to determine if he is an emotional eater (M. J. Mahoney and K. Mahoney, 1976a, p. 150). Information can be recorded for one week on a form with three columns: *Emotion Before, Eating Incident,* and *After.* These records are reviewed after a week to determine if eating is related to certain emotions. (Notice that in self-management programs the client is encouraged to always gather data as a response to a perceived problem area.)

Although self-monitoring may have some beneficial effect in relation to weight loss, this effect is usually temporary (Mahoney, 1974b). Clients are urged to continue their typical eating pattern during this time. Information gained via self-monitoring is employed to identify behaviors, thoughts, and situations that should be increased and decreased. Assessment may reveal that the client has poor temporal control over eating behavior; that is, he may tend to eat at many different times during the day. Or perhaps it will reveal that there is poor stimulus control, in that eating behavior occurs in a variety of different situations and is paired with a wide variety of reinforcers, such as watching television and reading magazines and newspapers (Ferster, Nurnberger, and Levitt, 1962). Problems may be found with the client's eating style—he may eat very fast or take large quantities of food onto his plate. One must be careful not to assume that such characteristics are typical of all overweight people, because they are not (Mahoney, 1975). The role of significant others is explored in terms of the extent to which they will support desirable eating behavior. Clients are discouraged from weighing themselves daily, because of fluctuations in weight, poor accuracy of home scales, and the goal of focusing the client on alteration of eating habits rather than on weight loss. Two-week weighing intervals are recommended (M. J. Mahoney and K. Mahoney, 1976a).

It is important for the client and counselor to assess motivation to lose weight. Does the client have good long-term reasons for losing weight? A weight reduction program requires a great deal of effort on the part of the client and if high motivation is not present, it is wasteful to initiate a program. The client should have a physical examination to make sure it is medically safe for him to decrease his food intake and increase his physical activity. Initial interviews provide information concerning weight goals and history of obesity. The importance of realistic goals and establishing approximations to desired outcomes is emphasized.

Assessment may occupy three interviews, during which weight history is taken, client motivation explored, client-gathered data reviewed, and the program described to the client, stressing the need for his active participation. Activity records will reveal the type, frequency, and character of physical exercise. The client may be asked to keep track of the time of the exercise, location, whether he was alone or with someone, the physical activity (type, how long, far or number of times, and calories expended), and feelings after the activity (Jeffrey, 1976).

Counselor-client contracts describing desired outcomes and contingencies may be drawn up. These may entail depositing money or valuables with the counselor and describing conditions for earning them back. In one behavioral weight reduction program, in which deposits are employed, the client received one fourth of his deposit when he reached his desired weight, and one fourth when it was maintained for one year (Jeffrey, 1976). The remaining half of the deposit is paid by the client to himself during intervention for improvement in eating and exercise habits, *not* for weight loss. The entire deposit is lost if the client drops out of treatment. In this program, the client is encouraged to think carefully about his commitment before the contract is signed a week later.

Intervention. A variety of intervention procedures have been employed in behavioral programs related to obesity. Most are based on a reinforcement framework in which eating is viewed as an operant maintained by its consequences and occasioned by situations in which it has occurred in the past. Some procedures, such as covert sensitization (Cautela, 1966), focus on the respondent aspects of eating and are introduced to create an aversion toward certain foods in order to establish an avoidance of these foods (Stuart, 1967a). These are especially useful with foods a person finds very difficult to resist; however, aversive conditioning by itself is relatively ineffective in altering eating patterns. The emphasis during intervention should be on developing and monitoring of new eating habits rather than on loss of weight per se. Such an emphasis on habit control has been found to be more effective for both weight reduction and maintenance (Mahoney, 1974b). In addition to self-monitoring, behavioral programs have included one or more of the following components: "implicit or explicit goalsetting; nutritional, exercise, and health counseling; tangible operant consequences (reward and punishment); aversion therapy; social reinforcement in the form of either therapist, group, or family support; covert conditioning and cognitive restructuring strategies; self-presented consequences (self-reward, self-punishment); and stimulus control procedures" (Stunkard and Mahoney, 1976, p. 54).

   In one weight reduction program, assessment is conducted over three interviews spread over three weeks. Intervention is divided into three phases (Jeffrey, 1976). In Phase 1, twelve weekly one-hour classes are held, in food and exercise management. Topics include nutrition and food exchanges, food buying, food storage, preparation and serving, food eating, food cleanup and review, snacking, enlisting help from family and friends, learning to handle feelings, and physical activity and review. Phase 2 consists of twelve weekly half-hour meetings that address the food and activity management problems of each person. Formal self-rewards in the form of portions of deposits made are stopped, and the client is encouraged to develop his own covert and overt self-reward systems for appropriate eating habits. In Phase 3, five to twenty biweekly or monthly fifteen- to thirty-minute sessions are held to stabilize new eating and activity habits. When desired weight is reached, the maintenance phase is initiated, which also provides for fifteen- to thirty-minute biweekly meetings. Meetings are gradually decreased in frequency, depending on each client's ability to maintain appropriate eating habits. However, some contact is maintained for one year. Jeffrey (1976) stresses the importance of client motivation to lose weight as well as the stability of the client's life situation in achieving successful results.

Goal setting. Identifying specific achievable performance criteria is important, because it permits positive self-evaluation (Stunkard and Mahoney, 1976). This is especially important for clients who select unrealistically high performance standards and then castigate themselves when they cannot meet these. Imagining oneself in a situation related to a selected goal or imagining that one is a counselor helping a friend can offer helpful feedback concerning the reasonableness of goals (M. J. Mahoney and K. Mahoney, 1976a). Clients are encouraged to be flexible about goals they establish, because goals selected may be unrealistic. They are encouraged to set reasonable goals *based on what they are doing at the present time*. As M. J. Mahoney and K. Mahoney (1976a, p. 54) stress, "a reasonable goal is a relative goal," relative to the client's past and current behavior. For example, if a client wishes to increase how much exercise he obtains, he is encouraged to first find out how much he gets right now. Only current behavior of the client should be used as a guide for goal setting.

Nutritional counseling. It is essential that clients ingest a well-balanced diet, and information is therefore provided in terms of daily requirements of various nutrients. Some programs employ an exchange program, in which the client establishes a total caloric intake that would produce a weight loss of about a pound and a half per week, and then selects a plan based on this goal, in which a given number of exchanges from various food categories are permitted (Stuart and Davis, 1972). An exchange plan allows for 20 percent calories in protein, 30 percent in fats, and the remainder in carbohydrates. For example, the daily food plan for a 1,200-calorie daily food plan contains six meat exchanges, four cereal exchanges, two milk exchanges, three vegetable exchanges, three fruit exchanges, and three exchanges from a miscellaneous list (Stuart and Davis, 1972). This plan allows the client to save food allotments from meals for snacks. The client receives a list of possible alternatives under each exchange list.

Baseline information will provide information on the number of calories typically consumed by a client. Considering that it takes a caloric deficit of 3,500 calories to lose one pound, a decrease of 500 calories should result in a weekly loss of one pound. This will vary somewhat from person to person, depending on other factors such as the amount of exercise and fluid retention. Stunkard and Mahoney (1976) note the uncertain relationship between caloric intake and weight loss indicating the role of metabolic differences among people. There is evidence, for example, that some obese individuals can gain weight on fewer calories than nonobese persons (Passmore and others, 1963).

Nutritional counseling that emphasizes the importance of inclusion of all needed nutrients (but in small amounts) assures a balanced diet and also avoids one of the pitfalls of many dieting methods that place the person on a very unusual diet, such as eating only protein, which is very unlike the environment in which eating will typically occur.

Exercise counseling. The fact that Americans lead increasingly sendentary lives has been cited as one of the main reasons for the great numbers in our population who are overweight. Establishing and maintaining an appropriate exercise program is not only relevant to expending calories but also to health in general. Clients are encouraged to identify appropriate methods for increasing their energy expenditure, preferably by expanding their daily activity patterns, such as by walking up the stairs rather than taking the elevator, perhaps by walking part of the way to work rather than driving, and so forth. Emphasis is placed on activities that are fun for each client, which may include hiking, swimming, or biking. Some weight reduction plans encourage the client not only to establish an exercise plan but also to monitor it (Stuart and Davis, 1972). First, baseline information is gathered describing the present level of the client's activities. He may be encouraged to increase this amount by 250 calories each day, using a table describing the average energy expenditure during various recreational activities as a guide (Stuart and Davis, 1972). Stuart and Davis (1972) also recommend trying to identify antecedents that would facilitate an increase in physical activity, such as making plans with other people so that the activity provides social reinforcers as well as physical activity.

Stimulus control. The important role of cues associated with eating was first emphasized by Ferster, Nurnberger, and Levitt (1962). These authors listed a variety of stimulus control procedures for altering these cues. Many of these procedures have been incorporated into current behavioral weight reduction programs, such as those of Stuart and Davis (1972) and M. J. Mahoney and K. Mahoney (1976a). They emphasize the importance of "purifying" the stimulus control of eating behavior so that eating is cued only in certain situations. For example, they recommend the separation of eating from all other activities, so that these activities no longer function as a cue for eating. Clients are encouraged to eat only in a specified room at certain times and are not to engage in other activities such as reading or watching television during this time. They are also encouraged to make high-calorie foods unavailable by not purchasing them. High-calorie foods can also be made more unavailable by freezing them so that the client would have to go through the process of thawing the item. In addition, clients are encouraged not to shop when they are hungry, to shop from a carefully prepared list and to only take enough money to make purchases from the list. They are also coached not to attend dinner parties or other situations where high-calorie foods will be available, when they are in a deprived state. They are encouraged, instead, to eat some small amount of food beforehand so their deprivation will be more moderate. They were also instructed to dispose of food previously eaten to "avoid waste," and to alter the size and appearance of food by using smaller plates and reducing portions. If a client tends to eat fast, he is encouraged to slow down his pace of eating by laying down his utensils occasionally and by following a rule not to pick up more food until he has finished chewing and swallowing food already in the mouth. These procedures serve to interrupt the chain of behavior involved in eating (Ferster, Nurnberger, and Levitt, 1962). Another way to regulate the cues for eating is to identify other activities that could be engaged in at times when there is a great temptation to nibble. A housewife, for example, might tend to eat after her children leave for school. She might call a friend or write a letter instead of eating. Various stimulus control activities may be given out in separate homework assignments (M. J. Mahoney and K. Mahoney, 1976a, 1976b).

A behavioral program emphasizing stimulus control procedures was recently compared with a TOPS (Take Off Pounds Sensibly) self-help program (Levitz and Stunkard, 1974) involving 240 clients in sixteen different TOPS chapters. Fewer people dropped out of the behavioral program and greater weight losses were achieved in this group. This study also compared professional versus nonprofessional leaders in behavioral programs and it was found that clients led by a professional lost a mean of 4.2 pounds compared to 1.9 in the TOPS chapters. Only weight lost in the behavioral program led by professionals was maintained at a one-year follow-up. The increased effectiveness of professionally led groups should encourage careful training of paraprofessionals (Franks and Wilson, 1975).

Stimulus control methods by themselves have not been found to be effective in the absence of other intervention methods (Mahoney, Moura, and Wade, 1973). Although simply giving clients manuals describing stimulus control methods has resulted in weight loss, follow-up was only over a four-month period (Hagen, 1974). Stimulus control methods seem to be most effective when combined with other intervention procedures, such as self-reinforcement (M. J. Mahoney and K. Mahoney, 1976b). Periodic follow-up visits seem to be extremely important in maintaining change (Leon, 1976).

Social reinforcement. There are three possible sources of social reinforcers for developing new eating patterns: from family members, from group members (if intervention is carried out in a group setting), and from the counselor. Although support from the counselor and from group members may be helpful in encouraging appropriate behaviors during intervention, because these sources of support are not a part of the natural environment, it becomes especially important to obtain the support of family members. In the program designed by M. J. Mahoney and K. Mahoney (1976a, 1976b) family members were invited to all sessions and one session was devoted to their role in the program. "They were asked to (1) restrict their feedback to praise (no teasing or criticism); (2) avoid offering the client food (either at or between meals); and (3) cooperate by compromising their own meal and snack patterns in a way which was beneficial to the client" (p. 32). Clients were trained to prompt appropriate behavior from significant others and to reinforce the spouse for appropriate efforts. The nature of the verbal interchange concerning food between the client and one important significant other can be ascertained by having the client record the type of social feedback he received (Stuart and Davis, 1972; M. J. Mahoney and K. Mahoney, 1976a).

Self-reinforcement. In addition to increasing social reinforcement, it is also important to increase positive self-evaluation for developing and maintaining appropriate eating habits. This may be done on a very formal basis: clients draw up written contracts specifying performance goals, explicit time intervals, and incentives to be provided for meeting these goals (M. J. Mahoney and K. Mahoney, 1976a). Contracts are signed and witnessed, and family members or friends help to monitor the contracts to ensure compliance. Reinforcement for habit change is more effective than reinforcement for weight loss (Mahoney, 1974b). Subjects who received modest monetary rewards for weight loss and for a greater frequency of "thin thoughts" (encouraging self-verbalizations) and restraint (refusing a fattening food or excessive quantity) than for fat thoughts (discouraging self-verbalizations) or instances of indulgence (eating a fattening food or excessive quantity) showed greater improvement compared to subjects who lost money contingent on unadaptive behaviors.

Failure to establish reasonable performance standards may lead to severe negative self-evaluations that are very dysfunctional (K. Mahoney and M. J. Mahoney, 1976). Figure 42 shows an example of a token program designed by a client to reinforce appropriate behaviors related to eating.

Self-control over incentives for appropriate behavior is more effective than external control in maintaining weight loss. Clients who rewarded themselves for achieving their goals maintained their weight losses to a greater extent compared to clients who received money payments from the counselor

Figure 42. Token Reinforcement Menu

Responses Earning Tokens		
Response	Amount	No. Tokens
Follow diet	1 meal	3.0
Follow diet	3 consecutive meals	12.0
Follow diet	7 consecutive days	100.0
Walk	1 block	0.5
Walk	6 blocks	6.0
Walk	20 blocks	25.0
Item		
Extra 15 minutes' conversation		3.0
Extra evening out		25.0
Extra babysitter for 3 hours during day		25.0
$2 surprise		300.0
New dress		500.0
Special weekend trip		1500.0

Source: Stuart and Davis (1972, p. 94).

(Jeffrey, 1974). If assessment reveals that a client tends to eat when he is tense, relaxation training may be indicated. "Nonfattening" responses are encouraged when anxious, bored, or depressed.

Cognitive self-management. M. J. Mahoney and K. Mahoney (1976a) have stressed the importance of weight-related thoughts, in recognition of the important role of cognitive processes in self-management (see, for example, Mahoney and Thoresen, 1974). Clients are trained how to record, evaluate, and alter weight-related private monologs with an emphasis on setting reasonable performance standards and on positive self-evaluation. They are trained to "clean up" what they say to themselves. Weight-related thoughts are classified into five categories and examples of appropriate and inappropriate responses in each given. These include: "(1) thoughts about pounds lost (for example, 'I've starved myself and haven't lost a thing'); (2) thoughts about capabilities ('I just don't have the willpower'); (3) excuses ('If it weren't for my busy schedule, I could lose weight'); (4) standard setting ('Well I blew it with that doughnut. My day is shot'); and (5) thoughts about actual food items. Subjects reported that their cognitive restructuring was an in-

valuable component in their weight reduction success" (Stunkard and Mahoney, 1976, p. 59). The nature of these private
monologs can be determined by means of a pocket diary or
phone-answering device that allows clients to call and report
their private monolog at any hour of the day or night (K. Mahoney and M. J. Mahoney, 1976). Or clients can learn to become aware of food-related thoughts by periodically reviewing
their thoughts and noting them down. These records illustrate
the role of cognitions in distress and behavior dysfunction.
Examination of the recorded monologs of a thirty-six-year-old
housewife revealed statements such as, "I can't do anything
right" and "This will never work" (K. Mahoney and M. J. Mahoney, 1976, p. 104). There were many global statements
reflecting on one's total personality, such as "I am a fat slob"
and "I am a failure," which implies a deep-seated inadequacy.
Her inappropriate standard setting contributed directly to such
internal monologs. She expected herself to be perfect and set
very high standards, and a fall from these standards resulted in a
flood of negative self-evaluations. Her prohibitions against certain foods simply increased their attractiveness, as prohibitions
usually do. This high frequency of negative self-evaluations was
accompanied by a very low frequency of positive self-statements. "Ironically, when her unreasonable standards were met,
she felt relieved but never satisfied. Each week had to be better
than the preceding one. She never congratulated herself or
praised her own progress. Her perseverance appeared to be
dominated by anxiety over failure, rather than by anticipation
of success. With her previously rigid standards, of course, failure
increased as her standards rose, and a self-perpetuating vicious
cycle was maintained" (K. Mahoney and M. J. Mahoney, 1976,
p. 104). Mrs. H. was trained to monitor, evaluate, and alter maladaptive self-statements by employing cognitive restructuring
and problem-solving methods. The recorded client monologs
provided practice material for this training. "She was trained to
detect distress (depression, anxiety) to perform quick 'instant
replay' of her preceding self-statements, to evaluate their adap-
tiveness, and to generate alternative statements. She was addi-
tionally taught to cue positive self-thoughts and to practice
positive self-evaluation by calling a phone-answering device and

verbalizing self-praise for what she had accomplished. Tape recordings of these self-praise assignments were reviewed by both the therapist and the client, in order to stabilize, strengthen, and expand positive self-evaluation skills" (K. Mahoney and M. J. Mahoney, 1976, p. 104).

Mrs. H. was contacted sixteen months later and reported that her weight reduction had continued at a slow and comfortable pace, and that she had shared her new skills with her teenage son, who had lost fifteen pounds. She viewed her eating habits and her cognitive behaviors as imperfect, a view that was considered a positive event by the counselor. She now set reasonable standards for her behavior and offered herself more positive self-evaluative statements. In programs for weight reduction that stressed "cognitive ecology," clients reported that this aspect of the program was perhaps the most important (M. J. Mahoney and K. Mahoney, 1976b).

Another cognitive component related to weight reduction is trying to increase the prominence of the "ultimate aversive consequences" of inappropriate eating (Ferster, Nurnberger, and Levitt, 1962). Many inappropriate behaviors offer immediate positive consequences or immediate removal of negative consequences but have long-term deleterious effects. This applies not only to inappropriate eating behaviors but also to smoking and excessive drinking. In an attempt to make these consequences more current, each client is asked to generate a list of such consequences, including only those that are very aversive. It was found that specific situations, such as described by the statement, "I tried on my new dress and showed it to my husband and he said I looked fat," were more effective than global statements such as "I am a fat slob." Some weight reduction programs have included a focus on increasing thoughts related to the aversive consequences of eating, usually by means of the Premack Principle, in which a high-probability behavior is made contingent on covertly expressing one or two negative thoughts related to eating. There is no evidence that this is effective.

Aversive conditioning. Pairing an actual or imagined unpleasant event with an actual or imagined inappropriate eating behavior has been attempted. For example, Stuart (1967a) reported the example of a woman who did very well in increasing appropriate eating behaviors except with chocolate chip cookies, which seemed impossible to resist. Covert sensitization (Cautela, 1966) was employed: a problematic behavior was paired with unpleasant thoughts or images in the imagination. She was asked what event was very unpleasant for her to think about and reported that imagining her husband in bed with another woman was highly unpleasant. She was instructed to imagine being about to consume a chocolate chip cookie and then to vividly imagine the situation she had just described. After engaging in this practice a few times, her desire for chocolate chip cookies decreased substantially. Attempts to assess the efficiency of covert sensitization in changing eating patterns has not always yielded successful results (Elliot and Denney, 1975).

Aversive conditioning may be especially helpful if there is one particular food that is difficult to resist. The unimpressive results, in terms of maintenance of weight loss, from the use of actual aversive events may be caused by the selection of an inappropriate aversive event. Rather than shock, the use of olfactory stimuli may be more effective, such as pairing the smell of certain foods with aversive odors (Stunkard and Mahoney, 1976).

Only recently has attention been devoted within a behavioral framework to helping overweight children decrease their weight (Aragona, Cassady, and Drabman, 1975; Wheeler and Hess, 1976). This is especially important, because overweight children tend to become overweight adults (Stunkard and Burt, 1967).

Anorexia Nervosa

The term *anorexia nervosa* refers to a voluntary decrease in food intake with accompanied weight loss and amenorrhea (Stunkard, 1975). It is most common among females with puberty being the usual time of onset. Although a rare disorder, it can lead to severe consequences, including death. The important role of learning variables in the development of anorexia is suggested by many studies (for example, Crisp, 1970). The client is often not identified until substantial weight loss has occurred, rendering hospitalization necessary. There are two important phases of intervention: in the hospital and after the client returns home. To date, behavioral procedures have shown considerable promise in the first stage, but have not been applied in any systematic way to maintaining weight gains in the natural environment (Stunkard and Mahoney, 1976). Here, too, as with obesity, eating is considered an operant maintained by its consequences, and most behavioral procedures have employed an operant approach in which the client is reinforced for consuming greater amounts of food or for weight gains. Possible respondent components have also been noted, such as the phobic reaction to the thought of being "fat" displayed by some anorexic clients.

The first report of the use of behavior procedures with anorexic clients concerned a twenty-six-year-old female whose weight had decreased from 118 to 47 pounds at the time of hospitalization (Bachrach, Erwin, and Mohr, 1965). Reinforcers in the hospital previously available on a noncontingent basis such as radio, visits from friends, television, and walking with other patients were made contingent on consuming progressively larger meals. Between February 1, 1961, and March 10, 1961, the client gained fourteen pounds. It was then suspected that she was secretly vomiting food, because there were no further increases in her weight. Reinforcers were then made contingent on weight gain; however, her weight did not increase. Her discharge from the hospital was accompanied by instructions to her parents, with whom she lived, as to how to maintain her weight gain. Her parents were encouraged to employ stimulus control procedures such as eating at a certain time of day and only when a purple tablecloth was used, and were coached to only speak about pleasant topics during mealtime. At a one-year follow-up, her weight had increased to 88 pounds. This example illustrates the design of a program to encourage initial weight gain as well as to arrange a maintenance of weight gain in the natural environment.

Access to activity has been found to be an important reinforcer for anorexic patients, and weight gains have been achieved when the sole contingency has such access (Blinder, Freeman, and Stunkard, 1970). Weight gain was accompanied by improvements in interpersonal relationships and increased feelings of well-being. In a hospital program that has been effective in helping anorexic clients gain weight, the first four or five days are used to gather a baseline concerning the client's weight and to observe behavior in order to identify appropriate reinforcers (Brady and Rieger, 1972). Access to physical activity (a six-hour pass to leave the ward on days when a weight gain of at least one half pound occurred) and permission to socialize were employed as reinforcers. Clients gained an average of four pounds a week over a six-week period, and then returned home, usually to distant locations where no follow-up was provided. Feedback concerning weight and caloric intake has been found to be more important than positive reinforcement, namely praise (Agras, Barlow, Chapin, Abel, and Leitenberg, 1974). This study also showed that clients ate more when larger meals were served.

Other Disorders Associated with the Gastrointestinal System

Contingent use of edible reinforcers has been effective in decreasing constipation of children (Tomlinson, 1970; Perzan, Boulanger, and Fischer, 1972). Functional diarrhea (where no underlying physical disorder can be found) has been decreased by the use of systematic desensitization (Hedberg, 1973). A combined cognitive and behavioral program was successful in decreasing colitis attacks of a twenty-two-year-old female (Youell and McCullough, 1975). An attack included tensing and relaxing of the abdomen, abdominal cramps, spasticity of the rectum, and diarrhea. Four weeks of baseline revealed that these attacks occurred seven times a week and were associated with interpersonal encounters in which she perceived herself to be rejected or in some other way harmed. She would ruminate over these events. At the fourth session, a tape-recorded log was introduced, in which the client was asked to continue to record each incidence of an attack as well as antecedent events, but now to use a cassette tape recorder for this purpose. Information to be recorded in the log was to be very specific, including what the client said and what involved others said and did, as well as feelings and thoughts she had. This recorded material became the prime focus of intervention, each situation being reviewed in detail. Possible antecedents for the attacks were identified. In each instance, the client was asked whether she had really been rejected or whether other events might account for the other person's reaction. In each instance, she was requested to contact the person and check out her hypotheses regarding their behavior. Gradually, over the course of intervention, the client learned to prevent colitis attacks by reevaluating whether she had indeed been rejected in interactions where this thought occurred to her and checking out her hypothesis by asking the person. For example, one colitis attack occurred after ruminating that a professor who had questioned her during an oral presentation in class really did not like her. When she talked with him she found that, quite to the contrary, he had been most impressed with the way she had stood her ground and argued back. Colitis attacks decreased to zero by the eleventh week of intervention and remained at zero over a forty-three-week follow-up period. She had attained greater success than had been anticipated by the goals that were established (see Chapter Five). Youell and McCullough (1975) suggest that recording and reviewing the tape-recorded logs may have functioned as a self-desensitizing experience to stress involved in her encounters. In addition, the identification of cues that precipitated colitis attacks and learning a coping strategy (reevaluation of her thoughts together with checking out her hypothesis with the person) probably contributed to positive effects achieved.

Behavioral methods have been employed to decrease repetitive vomiting. For example, the vomiting of a nine-year-old retarded girl decreased rapidly when she was no longer permitted to leave the classroom and when attention was no longer provided for this behavior (Wolf, Birnbrauer, Williams, and Lawler, 1965). Self-correction and positive practice resulted in a sudden substantial decrease in the habitual vomiting of a severely retarded woman (Azrin and Wesolowski, 1975). On vomiting, she was required to clean up the vomit and change her clothes and bedsheets if these had been soiled, and also to practice fifteen times an appropriate way to handle an urge to vomit. "On each trial she was taken to the toilet where she bent over the bowl for several seconds with her mouth open and was required to flush the toilet. She was then returned again to the location of the vomiting to initiate the next trial" (Azrin and Wesolowski, 1975, p. 146). She was also reminded every hour during the day that she should only vomit in the toilet and that she would have to clean up the vomit and practice if she vomited anywhere else. Vomiting decreased from about twice a week to zero. There was no relapse after one year.

Encopresis. Elimination of fecal matter at the wrong time and place seems especially bothersome to significant others and there have been a number of reports describing application of behavioral principles to increase appropriate toileting behavior. Selection of method depends on whether or not appropriate skills are available. If these are present, but simply occur sporadically, then contingency management may be sufficient to increase appropriate toileting behavior. If toileting skills are not present, as is usual with very young children, such behavior must be shaped, as described later in this chapter.

Increasing available toileting skills. Programs are often carried out by parents at home as illustrated in the following case example. This particular case was selected for inclusion since the program was carried out by parents who had many problems of their own (Bach and Moylan, 1975). The father was an alcoholic and the child's mother was diagnosed as schizophrenic and had experienced many hospitalizations. The parents met while both were residents of a state mental hospital. Marital counseling was ongoing at the initiation of assessment for the soiling problem. The client was a six-year-old boy who urinated at inappropriate times and places and, although previously toilet trained, was now incontinent of feces and suffered from constipation. For the last two and a half years, he had been almost totally incontinent, despite consultation with pediatricians and psychiatrists. Prescribed regimens of laxatives, suppositories, and enemas were inconsistently applied by the parents, probably because the procedures were a great source of unpleasantness for all involved parties. The psychiatrist gave the child a diagnosis of "depressed child with encopresis and defective object relationships" (Bach and Moylan, 1975, p. 239), and recommended long-term psychotherapy for the parents as a prerequisite for dealing with the encopresis.

A baseline was taken of daily bed wetting, pants wetting, soiling of pants, and appropriate use of the toilet. Principles of operant conditioning were discussed with the parents and money was selected as a reinforcer for the boy. An unplanned use of this reinforcer was carried out by the father when, during the latter part of the baseline phase, "the child so badgered his father for money in order to accompany his friends to the store, the father violated our instructions and said, 'If you go to the toilet right now and do a *kaka* I'll give you a quarter.' The boy trotted off to the bathroom and expelled his feces into the toilet for the first time in two and a half years" (Bach and Moylan, 1975, p. 240). The boy received twenty-five cents for every bowel movement in the toilet, ten cents for every time he urinated appropriately in the commode, and ten cents for every morning his bed was not wet. The reinforcers were to be given immediately and accompanied by praise. All inappropriate bladder and bowel movements were to be ignored and clothes changed as perfunctorily as possible.

The reward for having a dry bed was immediately effective in increasing this behavior. Appropriate use of the toilet for urination increased from zero per week to forty-five in Week 3 and thirty-five in Week 4. Pants wetting decreased to a rate of two per week. The authors speculate that the variation in appropriate urination from week to week was a function of the boy's diet, time spent at home, and his interest in money.

The program for encopresis did not fare as well. "The first week produced seven occurrences of appropriate bowel movements, and a small but noticeable decrease in soiling. This rate of improvement did not maintain itself, however, and during Weeks 4 to 11 the boy soiled forty times and used the toilet on twenty-two occasions. Marked improvement began with the institution of friendly prompt social praise, and a nickel reward for 'trying to go kaka.' Between Weeks 12 and 20 there were seventy-six appropriate bowel movements and only three incidents. An interesting feature of the nickel reward for 'trying to go kaka' was that the frequency of such rewards dropped to almost zero within five weeks. The child began to respond to his parents' prompting in one of two ways: (1) he told them he had no need to evacuate and refused to go into the bathroom; or (2) he went into the bathroom and successfully evacuated, thereby receiving the higher reinforcement for that behavior instead of the nickel for trying" (Bach and Moylan, 1975, p. 240). The uneven progress was affected by the difficulty the parents had in refraining from punishing the child for soiling and their forgetting to reinforce appropriate behavior immediately. There was a need for very frequent reminders from the counselor. In addition, it was found that the boy had been helping himself to money the parents left around the house which no doubt decreased the value of this incentive. A two-year follow-up indicated that the boy had developed regular bowel and bladder movements before bedtime and that monetary incentives now occurred on a weekly basis. There had been no instances of soiling. The parents reported a great feeling of accomplishment after experiencing three years of frustration.

Time out has been employed in some programs to decrease soiling behavior. For example, a thirty-minute time-out period in her room was enforced in the evening contingent on the soiling by a twelve-year-old girl. During this procedure, soiling decreased from a baseline of 6.3 per week to 3.7. At the eleventh week, avoidance of dishwashing contingent on nonsoiling was introduced. Addition of this procedure decreased the rate of soiling to .93 per week. In cases where soiling is maintained by parental attention, a removal of this, including a refusal to change soiled clothing, has been found to result in a rapid decrease of this behavior (Conger, 1970). Mineral oil, suppositories or mild candy laxatives have been used as prompts for appropriate elimination, which can then be reinforced (Ashkenazi, 1975). Feedback concerning sphincter pressure has resulted in increased continence (Engel, Nikoomanesh, and Shuster, 1974).

Genitourinary Problems

Behavioral methods have been employed with both urinary retention as well as excessive micturation. One program was carried out with a twenty-two-year-old college student with partial paralysis. He could not fully empty his bladder. Self-observation of the cues associated with complete emptying of

the bladder—for example, a tugging sensation in the bladder—
was employed (Fazio, 1974). Prolonged exposure to situations
in which urination typically did not occur has also been employed to decrease urinary retention (Lamontagne and Marks,
1973). Again, it should be noted that a thorough physical examination should precede use of behavioral procedures for problems that may be physically based. However, as mentioned previously, such procedures may be usefully employed whether or
not a physical base is found. Excessive urination has been decreased by systematic desensitization (Taylor, 1972) as well as
by provision of false feedback regarding bladder pressure
(Jones, 1956). The results associated with frequent urination
are dramatically revealed by the steps clients had taken because
of such frequency, including abandoning careers and severely
restricting social contacts. (Sexual dysfunction is discussed in
Chapter Twenty).

   Enuresis. The term *enuresis* refers to the involuntary discharge of urine without any underlying organic pathology after
a child has attained the age of three or four years. The category
includes both diurnal enuresis (wetting during waking hours)
and nocturnal enuresis (wetting while asleep). An appropriate
toilet-training procedure will hopefully prevent both.

   Nocturnal enuresis. Both direct bladder training and the
bell-and-pad conditioning method have been employed to increase continence. The former consists of the following steps
(Starfield, 1972): (1) once a day the child practices holding his
urine as long as he can before going to the bathroom; (2) the
child consumes large amounts of water while holding his urine,
because this will help to stretch the bladder; (3) the child uri-
nates into a cup that has ounces marked on it after he has held
his urine as long as he is able; (4) the child keeps a record of the
number of ounces of urine he passes in each daily session and
checks on the calendar whether he was wet or dry that day; (5)
the family helps to occupy his attention while he is trying to
hold his urine; (6) the parents help him practice starting and
stopping his flow of urine; and (7) the child practices this himself several times a day. This program was used with 198 children over a six-month period. On a follow-up evaluation, one
third were free of enuresis. A more effective program of direct

bladder training included a shaping procedure, in which children were reinforced with tokens and praise for holding their urine two to three minutes longer than on the previous day on each session (Paschalis, Kimmel, and Kimmel, 1972). This program required two hours of parent training and an intervention period of twenty days.

The bell-and-pad device was originally developed and tested by Mowrer and Mowrer in 1938. This consists of a urine-sensitive pad connected to a bell. When the child starts to urinate at night, the bell rings in an alarm box beside the child's bed. This alarm must be turned off manually. The child then goes to the bathroom, often supervised by the parent to make sure that he actually gets up. He then returns to the bedroom, changes the sheet, resets the alarm and goes to bed. In the original procedure, the child received a gold star placed on a chart for each day his bed was dry. Four to eight weeks were required to complete this program. A careful search for the symptom substitution that would be expected from a psychoanalytic point of view indicated an absence of negative change and the presence of positive changes (Baker, 1969). Marked improvement in parental attitude toward the child is often noted as a consequence of no longer having to remove and launder urine-soaked sheets every day. Relapse with this method can be decreased by the use of "overlearning" in which the child is asked to drink two pints of liquid in the hour before going to bed (Young and Morgan, 1972).

A rapid method of toilet-training children. A rapid method of toilet training children that involves an intensive learning procedure has been developed and tested over the past few years. Procedures have been developed for retarded children as well as normal children (Foxx and Azrin, 1973a; Azrin and Foxx, 1974). The procedure for normal children requires that the child be responsive to verbal instructions and this is tested by asking the child to respond to a series of verbal instructions, such as to point to his nose, his eyes, and so on. The first report of this method included thirty-four children with a mean age of twenty-five months. The parents of these children reported difficulties in toileting that led them to seek outside help. Some of the children only spoke a few words and did not dress themselves. Within the intensive learning experience, factors known to be important to learning were maximized, and then were faded out as learning took place. These included a distraction-free environment, a large number of trials, consideration of component responses, reinforcement for correct responses, use of a variety of reinforcers, use of high-quality reinforcers, frequent reinforcement, manual guidance when necessary, use of verbal instructions, immediate reinforcement, immediate detection of incorrect responses, and punishment for incorrect responses. In the procedure for nonretarded children, an imitation procedure was added, as well as a procedure for the verbal and symbolic rehearsal of the benefits of the procedure. Detailed instruction manuals are available for both programs (Foxx and Azrin, 1973b; Azrin and Foxx, 1974).

Training was conducted by a trainer, either in the home of the child or trainer. Family members were asked to leave for the day. This helped to provide a distraction-free environment. The child was given fluids to drink about every five minutes in order to provide frequent opportunities to reinforce correct toileting. Reinforcement was offered for urinating in the potty chair and for each of the component skills preceding and following urination, such as approaching the potty chair, pulling down the pants, sitting on the potty chair, and so forth. Abundant verbal praise was offered, as well as hugs, kisses, and applause, and items of special value to the child, such as specific types of sweets, were used as well. Symbolic reinforcers such as informing the child how pleased various significant others would be (friends, relatives, or heroes) were also offered. Reinforcers were varied often so that they would not lose their effectiveness. Visual observation was used to immediately detect appropriate responses, such as lowering the pants and sitting on the chair. A special signaling potty chair (Star Tinkle, Nursery Training Devices, Inc., Concord, California, approximate cost $10.00) was used with some of the children in this program, although this is not necessary. This chair sounds a musical signal when fluid activates a device in the bowl of the chair. Initially, every appropriate behavior was reinforced to permit a high frequency of reinforcement.

Graduated guidance in which instructions were given and

manual guidance offered only to the extent necessary was employed to develop the component skills involved in appropriate toileting. Verbal instructions were very explicit as to the exact behaviors involved. Imitation was employed to help the child to learn the steps in toileting and the benefits of proper toileting. The child was given a hollow doll that could be filled with water through the mouth and would release water through a hole between its legs. The child was taught to perform all the toileting skills and procedures with the doll, including praising and feeding the doll, and lowering and raising its pants. Practice in imitation was conducted continuously between the child's own practice trials until the child learned component toileting skills.

"The objective of training was not to educate the child to urinate frequently and correctly, but to do so at whatever frequency was necessary to ensure dry pants" (Foxx and Azrin, 1973a). The child's pants were checked every five minutes, and the child was encouraged to check his pants. Reinforcement was given for dry pants. Accidents were discouraged by reprimanding the child when his pants were wet, omitting reinforcers at the next dry pants check, and not interacting with him for about five minutes. The child was required to change into dry pants at the end of the time-out period. Wet pants were thus associated with loss of social interaction. The child was also required to engage in a period of positive practice in which the complete act of toileting was rehearsed. During this period, the child was required to practice going to the potty chair from various locations in the house for ten rapidly conducted trials. Prompted practice trials were held every ten minutes to provide practice in toileting and to associate urination in the potty chair with reinforcement. Close observation by the trainer and frequent "dry pants checks" permitted early detection of wet pants.

Detailed instructions and continuous reinforcement were gradually faded out as the child learned component toileting skills. When a component behavior was completed once without prompting, instructions in relation to this behavior were omitted on the next occasion. When the child initiated and carried out an entire practice trial without instructions, instructions for such trials were then omitted. After unprompted toileting, reinforcers for appropriate toileting were offered on an intermittent schedule, and then discontinued entirely, as were dry pants checks. The important point in the training procedure was the first time toileting occurred without a need for instructions. The trainer functioned primarily as an observer after this first unprompted toileting. Children who were over twenty-six months required an average of two hours of training time. The thirty-four children in the study required an average of four hours of training time.

The parents were required to check the child's pants before each meal or snack, at naptimes, and at bedtime, and to praise the child for having dry pants. When an accident occurred, the child was reprimanded and required to change his pants and practice going to the toilet (positive practice). The parents were instructed not to offer reminders to the child. This procedure was followed only for a few days after training and was discontinued when the child no longer had any accidents.

Following this training procedure, accidents decreased from an average of six per day to a near-zero level for all children and remained near zero during a four-month follow-up period. As Foxx and Azrin note, the motivation desired for maintaining toileting habits was the pleasure of the child's parents and family. This pleasure is quite obvious for anyone who has guided parents in the use of this program. Most of the children experienced the program as very positive, hugging and kissing the trainer (Foxx and Azrin, 1973a). Some children initially reacted negatively to attempts to toilet train them; however, their initial reluctance was decreased by offering them immediate, graduated guidance whenever they failed to respond to a request. Many of the parents described their children as more cooperative and pleasant in their general conduct after the training program. Although no special training was given for bed wetting (enuresis) the mothers of ten children reported that their child stopped wetting the bed at night after completing the daytime training program. It should be noted that bowel training and bladder training were accomplished at the same time, with no need for different training procedures. The success of this program indicates that toilet training is not a futile exercise for children who have the required locomotive skills, manual dexterity, and maturation of the bladder and bowel muscles, which usually occurs at about twenty months of age.

The Azrin and Foxx (1974) manual was employed in a program in which parents toilet trained their own normal children (Butler, 1976). Three weekly classes were held with the parents. Parent-gathered records of soiling and wetting indicated that 77 percent of the parents successfully toilet trained their children. As in the study by Foxx and Azrin (1973a), a substantial proportion (20 percent) of children also stopped wetting the bed at night. Required relaxation (Webster and Azrin, 1973), in which the child receives overcorrection practice in being calm and relaxed by resting in his bed for a set period of time, was found to be helpful with children who reacted negatively to positive practice trials after accidents.

Decreasing Pain Associated with Menstruation. Desensitization has been employed to decrease pain during menstruation (for example, Chesney and Tasto, 1975), and as a method of preparation for childbirth (Kondas and Scetnicka, 1972). A menstrual symptom questionnaire was first given to each woman in the Chesney and Tasto (1975) study. This included items such as depression, weakness, irritability, dizziness, cramps, and nausea. The women were trained in relaxation during two sessions, were asked to practice twice a day and to keep a record of their practice periods. During the third session, the women practiced using their relaxation skills while they imagined neutral scenes unrelated to menstrual pain. Specific scenes associated with the onset of menstruation were imagined, while in a relaxed state, during the fourth and fifth sessions. Instructions were given to practice imagining the scenes while relaxed at home twice each day. Two months following the completion of the program, the women again completed the symptom severity questionnaire. The results indicated that this program was much more effective than a self-directed discussion group and a waiting-list control group in decreasing symptomology, but only for women who suffered from spasmodic dysmenorrhea. The approach was not effective for women with congestive dysmenorrhea. The term *spasmodic dysmenorrhea* refers to pain that begins on the first day of menstruation and is experienced as spasms of pain sometimes severe enough to cause vomiting or fainting. In congestive dysmenorrhea, there is advance warning for several days, during which increasing heaviness is experienced, as well as a dull, aching pain in the lower abdomen and other body parts, such as the breasts and ankles.

Cardiovascular Disorders

The prime objective in programs related to cardiac control is to offer clients increased control over cardiac functions. Biofeedback procedures that offer clients immediate information concerning changes in internal processes and contingency management procedures in which patients are offered a reward for appropriate alterations in cardiac function are two methods that have been frequently employed to alter heart rate and hypertension (see Katz and Zlutnik, 1975). There is no doubt that clients can be trained to alter these functions; however, few studies have demonstrated generalization of self-control skills to the natural environment. One exception is a study by Weiss and Engel (1971) in which patients were trained to alter premature ventricular contractions. It has been suggested that training clients in deep muscle relaxation will help to control hypertension by decreasing anxiety and that assertion training will offer skills to combat aggressive responses associated with hypertension (Blanchard and Young, 1973). Behavioral procedures can be employed to alter the behavioral patterns characterizing the Type A individual, who has a greater risk of cardiovascular disease (Suinn, 1974). A truly preventative thrust entails teaching children behaviors that are incompatible with coronary heart disease (Boyer, 1974). The reader is referred to other sources for a detailed discussion of the use of behavioral procedures with disorders related to the cardiovascular system (Shapiro and Surwit, 1976). It is likely that behavioral methods will increasingly be employed to develop behaviors that are incompatible with cardiovascular disease, in addition to focusing directly on alteration of cardiac functions.

Dermatological Disorders

Skin inflammations may be exacerbated by self-scratching. A variety of behavioral procedures have been employed to de-

crease such scratching, including instructing significant others
not to provide attention to the inflamed areas, and not to discuss the problem (Walton, 1960). The severe scratching of a
five-year-old child was decreased by instructing the parents to
ignore scratching and to offer approval and affection for not
scratching and for appropriate behaviors (Allen and Harris,
1966). Fay had been scratching herself until she bled, which resulted in large sores and scabs on her forehead, nose, cheeks,
chin, and one arm and leg. The mother reported that she had
come to dislike the child intensely, was repelled by her appearance, and wondered if it might not be better to place her outside of the home. She said the marriage itself was in jeopardy,
largely because of constant quarrels with her husband over disciplinary procedures. Assessment in a clinic playroom indicated
that the mother spoke to Fay only to criticize, direct, or explain why she should behave differently. Data gathered by the
mother at home indicated that Fay rarely scratched herself at
certain times, such as during constructive play, and that the
mother berated the child for a wide range of so-called misdeeds.
Tokens were used to reinforce appropriate behavior and not
scratching, because the mother found it difficult to attend to
Fay in a positive fashion. Every twenty or thirty minutes that
Fay had not scratched, the mother was instructed to go up to
Fay and approve her play and give her a gold star to paste in a
booklet. Every second or third gold star was accompanied by an
edible such as a cookie. Tokens were exchanged at midday and
supper time for inexpensive trinkets if no scratching had occurred. Although scratching decreased during the day with this
procedure, it still occurred at night, and so another incentive (a
new Barbie doll item) was added. Each afternoon of a scratch-
free day, such an item was purchased and was given to Fay, contingent on a scratch-free appearance, the next morning. By the
end of six weeks, Fay's sores had healed and a four-month follow-up indicated a maintenance of positive changes.

Substitution of an appropriate behavior has also been
effective in decreasing scratching. For example, a woman substi-
tuted a stroking response for the scratching, then a patting response, and placed herself on a token system (Watson, Tharp,
and Krisberg, 1972). This self-management program was effec-

tive within twenty days in eliminating scratching, stroking, and patting. Desensitization has been effectively employed to decrease arousal related to facial swelling and itching over the entire body of a twenty-three-year-old female (Daniels, 1973). Assessment revealed that this reaction was associated with anxiety resulting from interactions with her husband and his relatives. After two weeks of desensitization, the hives disappeared during the day and were completely eliminated within twelve weeks. A twenty-three-month follow-up revealed a maintenance of positive gains. Behavioral methods have also been employed to decrease the aversiveness of the painful treatment associated with severe burns (Shorkey and Taylor, 1973).

Decreasing Aversiveness of Health Care

Some people avoid needed medical treatment because of the actual or anticipated pain it may entail. Behavioral methods have been employed in relation to a number of treatment procedures to make these procedures less troublesome. For example, systematic desensitization was employed with a hemodialysis patient who had developed a severe anxiety reaction following his first treatment, which had been administered by a student technician. One session, ninety minutes in length, involving desensitization was held and, in addition, only trained personnel were permitted to administer the treatments when these were again initiated (Katz, 1974). Less experienced technicians were gradually "faded" into the procedure (they accompanied the trained technician and gradually took over more of the procedure). Praise and attention were offered for calm behavior. As noted by Katz and Zlutnik (1975), this case should cue hospital personnel to use only trained personnel during the first occasions of treatment procedures. A variety of other medical phobias have been successfully alleviated, including those relating to physical examinations (Freeman, Roy, and Hemmick, 1974), injections (for example, see Nimmer and Kapp, 1974), and dental treatment (Klepac, 1975).

In one study, observation of filmed models encountering various situations in the hospital that the children would experience helped to decrease children's anxiety prior to surgery

(Melamed and Siegel, 1975a). Training clients to reappraise anxiety-provoking events, to use calming self-talk, and to selectively influence their attention can help to control pre- and postoperative stress in adults, as reported by Langer, Janis, and Wolfer (1975). Patients were instructed to direct their attention to the more favorable aspects of their situation whenever they anticipated or experienced discomfort. These self-management methods offer clients greater control over stress and pain and thus help to enhance pain tolerance.

Discrimination training was employed to decrease the aversiveness of painful treatment of burns on a seventeen-month-old girl who suffered from second- and third-degree burns over her body (Shorkey and Taylor, 1973). When the nurses sprayed silver nitrate medication over the bandages, she would cry and move about. Her agitation increased over the weeks, until by the fourth week she refused food, screamed, and became agitated whenever a staff member approached her. A number of procedures, such as interrupting the treatment procedure to sing, talk, or play with her, were unsuccessful. The hospital social worker, who was trained in behavioral methods, was consulted and a discrimination training program was devised so that Lynn would learn to discriminate between the aversive condition of treatment and nonaversive social visits. Nurses were instructed to wear green isolation gowns and not to talk to, handle, or play with Lynn, and to spend as little time in her room as possible during treatment procedures. During social visits, to contrast with this condition, staff and others wore large, red, sterilized bags with armholes and would talk to, play with, and massage her neck and shoulders to reduce tension. To further distinguish these two occasions, green lights were turned on during treatment and red lights during social visits. Lynn's mother initially resisted wearing the red gown, because she felt that her daughter would recognize her with or without the gown. However, without the gown Lynn was quite agitated in her presence, whereas with it, she was calm. Lynn's rate of crying started to decrease on the second day of this program. Crying and agitation continued during the treatment, but she became calm and started smiling at other times. Her physical condition improved considerably.

Rehabilitation

An important aspect of medical care involves regaining skills. This often entails helping clients and their significant others to learn how to handle pain-related behaviors and to participate in needed treatment. Another aspect of rehabilitation involves prevention of secondary effects from illness such as bedsores. For example, paralytic persons have been helped to intermittently relieve pressure from their ischium when sitting in a wheelchair (Malament, Dunn, and Davis, 1975). An alarm sounds if the patient remains continuously seated for ten minutes. This sound can be ended if the client relieves pressure from the seat cushion by pushing up from his chair. The client is instructed to try to prevent the alarm from sounding. Each pushup resets the alarm for ten minutes. This procedure has resulted in a decrease in the formation of bedsores. Further study is necessary to identify how long changes persist without "booster" sessions. Programs initiated in the hospital setting may help to establish self-management skills that can be successfully applied at home in terms of adhering to appropriate regimes. For example, a patient with renal failure who was undergoing hemodialysis agreed to participate in a program in which tokens were gained for observing diet restrictions (Barnes, 1976). These tokens were exchanged for water, up to a limit of 800 cubic centimeters per day. This program helped him to learn to influence his fluid intake, which had previously been excessive. Behavioral methods have been employed in rehabilitation settings for many years (see, for example, Meyerson, Kerr, and Michael, 1967). Self-monitoring and positive reinforcement has been employed to increased fluid intake of burn victims and spinal cord injury patients, so helping to maintain electrolyte balance of the body (Sand, Fordyce, and Fowler, 1973; Fowler, Fordyce, and Berni, 1969).

Chronic Pain and Illness

Only recently has a behavioral framework been applied to the areas of chronic pain and illness (Fordyce, 1976a; 1976b). It is recognized that many of the referents of the word *pain* consist of behaviors such as verbalizing pain, going to a doctor, or resting and that pain may thus involve learning as well as a response to tissue changes. Chronic pain or illness especially provides an opportunity for learning new behaviors, both by the patients and significant others who may have to interact with them in new ways. A functional analysis of behaviors involved in chronic pain and illness entails an examination of the contingencies available at home and at work, as well as of the relationship between clients and members of the health care delivery system (Fordyce, 1976a).

There appears to be three conditions under which respondent pain may acquire operant functions (Fordyce, 1976a). One way is by direct reinforcement of pain behavior from health care professionals as well as from family members who may support such behavior by their attentive concern. This attention may also help to remove discomfort by direct actions such as massages or bringing medication. Pain behavior also results in prescriptions of medication, and a large number of chronic pain patients become addicted or habituated to such drugs. Medical management may also serve to maintain pain behaviors beyond the role of precipitating body damage by prescribing rest. It is assumed that these multiple sources of direct reinforcement for pain behaviors aid in establishing, maintaining, and expanding the rate of operant pain behaviors—those pain-related behaviors that are maintained by their consequences rather than those that result from bodily changes (Fordyce, 1976a).

There are also indirect sources of reinforcement for pain behaviors, in that such consequences permit the avoidance of unpleasant consequences. Avoidance behaviors, such as a limp, may be developed that serve to reduce pain. Such "guarding actions" are automatically reinforced by pain reduction, and also evoke attention from others. Pain behaviors may also permit the avoidance of unpleasant social or work-related situations, as Fordyce notes in the following passage.

> An impotent husband who finds that back pain renders intercourse physically painful also effectively avoids the "pain" of the impotence. The perennially anxious and submissive worker, elevated by

the relentless force of the Peter Principle to a level of job demands for which he or she is ill prepared, finds that pain yields a legitimated time out from the stress of the job.

Recently developed problems are often found. One of the more common illustrations concerns elderly people coming with newly emerged chronic pain problems who are sometimes found to have performance deficits (for example, memory deficit) relating to arteriosclerosis or minor strokes. Pain behaviors provide, for them, a form of time out. It is often less noxious to stay home with pain or a headache than to admit one cannot remember cards well enough to participate with long-time bridge partners. Another form of time out benefits from pain behaviors concerns behavior of the patient's spouse. Pain behaviors may lead to more spouse attention or time spent at home, which may be directly reinforcing. Pain behaviors may also be indirectly reinforcing if they keep an errant mate home more often. [Fordyce, 1976a, p. 160]

A third condition that contributes to the maintenance of pain behaviors is failure to reinforce well behavior. Patients are often chastized for trying to do more. A worker may not be allowed to return to his job because of his medical record. For many patients with histories of illness, there may be no acceptable alternative to the sick role (Fordyce, 1976a). This nonreinforcement of well behavior implies that the elimination of pain behavior will not automatically lead to effective well behavior, and, of course, some well behavior may no longer be available to the patient, because of the illness or its treatment.

Fordyce points out that sometimes depression and pain are mistaken for one another and that cues for the one are often cues for the other. The persistence of symptoms, as reflected in the persistence of distress behaviors that are actually caused by the loss of reinforcement involved in prolonged inactivity, may be misperceived as a failure to resolve the pain problems, when in fact this has been solved. If mislabeling occurs, intervention will be directed toward the wrong goal.

This analysis indicates that a pain problem viewed solely from a medical disease model may be mistreated. The potential goals for an operant approach to chronic pain, according to Fordyce (1976a, p. 165) include:

1. Reduction of pain behavior:
   a. Signals to others that tend to elicit reinforcement
   b. Medication taking
2. Reduction of excessive health care utilization behaviors:
   a. Continued pursuit of unattainable "cure"
   b. Continued pursuit of authentication of the problem
   c. Continued pursuit of attention, additional palliative medication, or more prescribed rest
3. Increased activity level: Restoration of optimal activity level to make posttreatment target behaviors accessible
4. Rearrangement of contingencies for pain and well behavior by family and significant others:
   a. Reduction in direct and nondirect reinforcement of pain behavior
   b. Increase in reinforcement of effective well behavior
5. Establishing and maintaining effective well behavior:
   a. Correcting skill deficits
   b. Remedying problem behaviors from which time out was sought through pain behaviors
   c. Promoting access to sustaining well behaviors
   d. Where indicated, legitimating retirement and helping patient and family to carry it out effectively

Assessment. A first step is to distinguish respondent pain elicited by body damage from operant pain, which is under reinforcement control. And, of course, chronic pain should first be carefully evaluated by a physician. The role of operant consequences in maintaining pain is indicated if medical evaluation fails to reveal a physical basis in proportion to the pain evidenced, or if a physical basis is uncertain. As Fordyce (1976a) emphasizes, an operant analysis cannot establish that a pain problem is operant and not respondent. Additional criteria for patient selection include the chronicity of pain, the potential accessibility of target behaviors in the client's repertoire, cooperation by the spouse, and some capability to influence effective reinforcers such as medication, rest, and attention.

Clients are requested to keep a diary for two weeks, and to record medications taken and the length of time in each twenty-four hours spent sitting, standing, walking, or reclining. A behavioral analysis also attends to the factors that increase and decrease pain behavior. If activities that result in pain are aversive to the client, it is more likely that the pain is operant in nature. The behavior of significant others in response to pain is also ascertained. A list of activities previously engaged in and their value is determined, to identify possible avoidance components present. A decision must be made as to whether inpatient or outpatient treatment is indicated. Addiction or habituation to any medication is an indicator for inpatient treatment, so that this medication can be controlled. Likelihood of compliance with required exercise regimes is another factor. If significant others are strongly reinforcing pain behavior, intervention with the client is not initiated until they are trained to rearrange their consequences. The spouse is considered a very important part of intervention and is included in each step of assessment and intervention.

Overview of Intervention Methods. One aspect of an operant program concerns medication management. The goal of this program is to reduce medication to what seems necessary for maintenance in relation to respondent pain. A baseline is first taken, during which medication is available as needed (within medical limits). Medications are then shifted from a pain-contingent to a time-contingent basis. The client receives a "cocktail" containing his medication at fixed intervals around the clock. The active agent in this cocktail is gradually faded. The patient is given options of increasing the length of time between intervals or of doing away with medication during the night.

Another aspect of the program is increasing exercise. A baseline reveals the tolerance level of the patient in terms of how many of what type of exercise can be done prior to stopping. There is no attempt to push the client. A schedule for exercise is arranged based on the client's current tolerance level.

Exercise periods are usually scheduled two or three times a day every day. Increments in behavioral requirements are preset and never set according to how the patient feels. If exercise quotas are not reached, there is no attempt to give the patient a pep talk. Prior quotas are returned to or the patient could be given the option of leaving the program. Notice that here, too, there is an attempt to reinforce well behaviors rather than pain behaviors. Medications are no longer contingent on expressions of pain behavior, unless, of course, there is some increase of respondent pain. And exercise requirements do not depend on expressions of pain but on previous achievements.

Graphing is initiated after baselines have been gathered and initial quotas established. These show, for example, daily amounts of sitting, standing, walking, or reclining. Graphs serve a variety of functions: they remind the staff to respond to activity of the patient rather than pain behavior, and they provide a topic of conversation related to activity. In addition, progress shown on the graph can be the basis for reinforcement of efforts by the patient and his significant others (Fordyce, 1976a).

A third aspect of the program is expansion of the range of activities engaged in by the client. A baseline is first ascertained and quotas established in terms of distances walked. Duration of time spent in volunteer jobs can be increased as exercise levels reach their ceilings. Participation in recreational programs is planned as appropriate. Videotapes of walking behavior of patients suffering from chronic back pain before and after participating in Fordyce's program are indeed impressive in terms of the gains observable.

Family training provides another essential aspect of this program. A separate interview is held with the spouse. One task of this meeting is to make a list of pain behaviors that consists of ways in which the spouse is made aware that the client is having pain. These may include talking about pain, moving in a guarded fashion or sitting in a special position, asking for medication, and/or expressing a lack of desire to engage in an activity because it would induce pain. The first task the spouse is asked to carry out is to make a covert count of the patient's pain behavior during the first twenty minutes of each visit (the total number of times one or any combination of pain behaviors is displayed). A similar count is to be made during telephone conversations with the patient. Daily figures are collected by the counselor. It is up to each spouse as to whether he or she wishes to inform his or her mate of the monitoring activities. The client has already been informed that the spouse will learn how to be effectively and selectively responsive to pain and well behavior (Fordyce, 1976). The spouse next is asked to observe his or her own reactions when pain behavior of the client occurs. After some of these responses have been identified, alternative ways of responding to pain behavior are developed. This usually requires learning how to be neutral or unresponsive rather than protective or solicitous. For example, a significant other may learn how to break eye contact and to say and do nothing for a couple of seconds after the client has experienced pain behavior. He or she is then encouraged to ask a specific questions about the client's activities, such as "How far did you walk today?" These new reactions are rehearsed and the spouse then counts the number of times he or she reinforces well behavior or activities. Learning alternative behaviors helps the partner to become an effective reinforcer of well behavior and activity. Another important topic to discuss is how to structure activities at home. The client and his or her spouse are aided in developing agreements concerning posttreatment activities. Family members are coached to decrease the extent to which they have taken over tasks the patient can perform. And family members are urged not to take any special protective action when flareups occur, but to maintain quotas and current activity levels.

Following return home, the client is requested to come in daily to the hospital during the first week. This is gradually faded out. It is important to ensure that the client will not be suddenly required to do much more when he returns home. During the hospital stay, passes are given in accord with possible activity levels of patients and degree of training offered to the family members. If there is a strong possibility that significant others will reinforce pain behaviors, passes may be restricted until gains are made in their appropriate use of attention. This program is usually carried out in the hospital; however, if significant others are cooperative and the client reliably compliant in terms of adherence with medication and exercise regimes, there is no reason why it could not be carried out on an out-patient basis.

Follow-Up. Appropriate contacts are made with continuing health care personnel in terms of informing them about medication regimes, and exercise quotas are determined. Both diaries and record sheets for recording exercises are given to the client, as well as a schedule for fading out their use. A fading schedule might consist of recording for two weeks, skipping a week, recording for one week, skipping two weeks, recording a week, skipping four weeks, recording a week and so forth. At regular intervals, these records are mailed to the counselor, who graphs the data. A supportive letter is sent to the client, together with the graph. A critical aspect of the follow-up period is continuing to develop other well behaviors in terms of work, family, and social life, to the extent possible. What is possible will differ from person to person. Community agencies and resources are natural sources for ideas.

The Development of Coping Responses. Patients have been trained how to manage their thoughts to allow increased tolerance for pain. For example, Levendusky and Pankratz (1975) used relaxation training, covert imagery, and cognitive relabeling to gradually withdraw a patient from pain-relieving medication. The covert imagery included imagining his pain as "tightening steel bands, which he could loosen, and as electrical impulses traveling over circuits, which he could manipulate" (Levendusky and Pankratz, 1975, p. 166). This procedure also involved teaching him to relabel physiological cues for pain. These now became cues for the use of coping reactions rather than cues for anxiety and increased pain. The provision of a rationale for the use of self-instructions for pain control is an important ingredient. Turk has applied stress management training to pain control (see Meichenbaum and Turk, 1976). The client learns to employ self-instructions that allow him to have more influence over his pain reactions. Relaxation training has been employed to decrease chronic back pain (Scheiderer and Bernstein, 1976).

Summary

The application of behavioral procedures with medically related problems is a recent endeavor, with certain notable exceptions such as the bell-and-pad method developed in 1938 to decrease bed wetting. However, major strides have already been made in some areas. Some problems addressed represent areas that are notoriously resistant to change efforts, such as obesity and smoking. Although behavioral methods show promise, especially with developing new patterns of eating and self-management skills, additional data are needed regarding maintenance of these new skills. Highly effective methods have been developed to encourage appropriate toileting behavior. Behavioral methods have been employed to reduce the frequency and intensity of symptoms associated with some incurable illnesses, such as Huntington's chorea; to decrease the aversiveness associated with needed medical or dental treatment; to decrease pain-related behaviors that interfere with successful rehabilitation; and to eliminate the aftereffects of illness, such as nervous mannerisms that no longer have a physical basis. Symptoms such as pain, seizures, and difficulty in breathing are often influenced by the reactions of significant others. Rearranging what these others attend to, as well as training the client how to redirect his attention, have both helped to decrease frequency and intensity of these symptoms. A complete physical examination should always precede psychological intervention when the presenting complaint could have a physiological base.

19

Behavioral methods have been employed with a range of severe behavior disturbances, including childhood autism, developmental retardation, psychosis, and severe obsessive-compulsive behavior. This chapter presents an overview of the use of behavioral methods with such disorders, focusing especially on programs that have been carried out in the natural environment (although with some disorders, such as childhood autism, intervention in the hospital is often a prior step to intervention in the home). References to sources offering more detailed descriptions are included in this discussion.

Childhood Autism

Some children fail to an extreme extent in their social, emotional, and intellectual development. Such children have

Severe Behavior
Disturbances

variously been labeled *autistic, psychotic,* and *schizophrenic.* To date, it has not been possible to demonstrate physiological or behavioral specificity between children receiving these three labels and in fact, as noted by Lovaas and Newsom (1976), the boundaries between these children and retarded children are often blurred. The lack of diagnostic information provided by labels, has directed attention to the particular behavioral deviations of each child. This overview draws partially from the excellent review of behavioral intervention with such children by Lovaas and Newsom (1976). The reader is referred to other sources for in-depth description of assessment and intervention methods, such as Lovaas (1976) and Kozloff (1973).

Children characterized by one of these labels have gross deficiencies in behaviors that, if present, would help them to function in the natural environment. Differences characteristic of autism usually appear in the first year of life and certainly by the second year. Such children usually do not react to sensory stimuli in the normal fashion. Social reinforcers, including physical affection, are unimportant and may even be aversive. Smiling and laughing may be totally absent, as may expressions of sadness. Few self-help or play skills are present and these children seem immune to perceiving danger. Speech is usually absent, and if it does occur, it is often echolalic (repetitious of what is said to the child). In addition to these deficits, there are behavioral surfeits in relation to self-stimulation (repetitive stereotypic acts such as rocking, repetitive humming, hand flapping, or prolonged looking at an object). In addition, tantrums and self-mutilation behaviors are often present, sometimes of a very extreme nature, including pulling the nails off the fingers or actually tearing skin from the body. Perhaps in no other instance is more of a challenge presented to the professional, because of the multiple deficits and surfeits involved in childhood autism. The following discussion introduces the reader to some of the procedures employed to increase appropriate behaviors and to decrease inappropriate behaviors. Intervention in hospital settings is first described, followed by examples of intervention programs in the natural environment. A comparison of the relative effectiveness of operant conditioning and play therapy indicated that the former was far more effective (Ney, Palvesky, and Markely, 1971).

Altering Self-Destructive Behavior. There was an effort in early studies to identify the maintaining conditions of self-destructive and self-stimulatory behavior. The results of these studies provided strong support for the operant nature of self-destructive behavior and its maintenance by social consequences. That is, such behavior seemed to be maintained by attention from adults. The frequency of self-destructive behavior was found to vary as a function of consequent attention. When attention was withdrawn or a time out imposed, self-destructive behavior decreased. This formulation of self-destructive behavior indicates that recommendations to offer attention, concern, and understanding to the child when he injures himself are actually dangerous, in that they are very likely to exacerbate such behavior. In one case study, the relationship between a lack of reinforcement for appropriate behavior and an increase in self-destructive behaviors was strongly suggested (Lovaas and Newsom, 1976). Lack of reinforcement for appropriate behaviors seemed to function as a cue for self-destructive behaviors. This suggests that self-destructive behaviors may emerge in the family setting only after appropriate behaviors are not reinforced. Lack of reinforcement for appropriate behaviors becomes a cue that self-destructive behavior will be reinforced. Such behaviors also seem to occur when demands are placed on the child. The tantrum or self-destructive behavior terminates the demand. These early studies emphasized the situational control of self-destructive behavior, a recurrent finding for a wide variety of severely disordered behavior as well as normal behavior. In situations in which self-destructive behavior was not reinforced, it did not tend to occur.

In early studies, the use of aversive events (shock) has been explored, because of the extreme danger of some self-destructive behaviors and because of the fact that use of an extinction procedure may actually result in the child's death. Shock is presented contingent on self-destructive behavior, usually to the arm or leg by means of a hand-held inductorium. Typically only a few shocks are required to completely suppress such behavior. Beneficial side effects of punishment have been found, including an increase of eye contact and desirable imitative responses (see, for example, Risley, 1968). The use of aversive stimuli must be viewed in relation to the long-term pain that may be involved without effective intervention, which may include twenty-four-hour restraints over many years and/or heavy medication. Most important for achieving beneficial effects is combining this use of punishment with the reinforcement of appropriate behaviors. This means that it is critical for those interacting with the child to learn to reinforce appropriate behaviors. As Lovaas and Newsom (1976) point out, if a child must employ self-destruction to gain adult attention, it is likely that these adults would repeat themselves and shape similar alarming behavior, such as feces smearing, unless they were taught to respond to appropriate behavior. Unless there is a commitment to the systematic use of positive reinforcement of alternative behavior, there is no ethical justification for use of punishment. The success of an educative procedure in decreasing self-injurious behavior of profoundly retarded adults offers promise that this less aversive procedure can be effective as well in decreasing such behavior of autistic children. This procedure is described later in this chapter.

Altering Self-Stimulatory Behavior. Unlike self-destructive behavior, self-stimulatory behavior does not seem to be under social reinforcement influence. This behavior seems to be maintained by self-reinforcement in the same way as are playing, thinking, or listening to music (Lovaas and Newsom, 1976). A number of procedures have been employed to reduce such behaviors, including punishment, shaping of incompatible responses, and overcorrection (the latter procedure is described later in this chapter).

Developing Language. The development of language is very important, because it offers a route to the establishment of other repertoires. "In working with nonlinguistic children, we soon realize how handicapped they are without language. Instead of our being able to tell them what to do, we have to move them physically through the desired behaviors. When we have to delay meeting their needs, there is no effective way to tell them to delay gratifications. When they become emotionally attached to us, there is no way to tell them, when we leave for the day, that we will return tomorrow. If they want something, they have no easy way to tell us what they want" (Lovaas and Newsom, 1976, p. 325).

A central aspect of training programs is initial establishment of control over the child's attending responses. Complex behaviors are gradually established by modeling in small steps. Physical guidance is employed if the child fails to respond. "The physical prompts are gradually withdrawn and reinforcement for prompted behavior is later withheld to counteract passive responding. After imitative behavior is strongly developed, stimulus control is shifted from modeling cues to verbal stimuli and appropriate environmental events" (Bandura, 1971a, p. 664). After an imitative response has been established, the meanings of words and the use of words in sentences are taught. The steps in this process have been described in detail by Lovaas (1976). Prompting and differential reinforcement are employed to encourage rearranging words into sentences; this training enables children to combine new words into grammatically correct sentences. The concepts of response classes and stimulus generalization help to account for these effects. That is, when a particular response is reinforced, others that are a member of that response class are also increased in probability. And, in relation to stimulus generalization, when a response is reinforced in one situation, it will also tend to occur in similar situations. Discrimination training is at the heart of this program for establishing verbal behavior; that is, the child is reinforced for a given behavior in the presence of one stimulus and not in the presence of others.

Increasing Self-Care Skills. In addition to developing language skills, a range of self-care skills are required for increased independence, such as dressing, washing, brushing the teeth, and so forth. Shaping, prompting, model presentation, rehearsal, and feedback have been employed to develop such skills. Verbal instructions provide an efficient shortcut to shaping whenever a child is responsive to such instructions. An example of a program for learning to put pants on is described in the following quote from Morris (1976). Notice the step-by-step process, and the way in which help is gradually faded. This program assumes no initial skill in putting pants on. If some skills are present, the program should take these into consideration by starting with the closest approximation.

> Use loose-fitting pants with an elasticized waist. Throughout the program, praise the child for any progress. Also, reward the child at each step with small amounts of his favorite food or drink. You will also need a chart to record the child's progress. The vertical line should state "Number of Steps" and the horizontal line, "Sessions."
>
> 1. Place pants completely on the child.
> 2. Pull pants up to *just below* the child's waist. Place your hands gently over the child's hands on either side of his pants and help him pull up his pants as you say, "*(Name)*, pull up your pants." Praise the child for pulling up his pants.
> 3. Repeat Step 2, except gently move your hands to his wrists.

4. Repeat Step 2, except move your hands to his forearms to gently guide him.
5. Repeat Step 2, except remove your hands from the child's forearms (*you may have to gently prompt him at first on this and later steps*).
6. Pull pants up the child's hips. Then have him pull the pants up the rest of the way. Remember to say to him, "Pull up your pants," and to praise him when he is successful.
7. Pull pants up to the child's knees. Then have him pull the pants up the rest of the way.
8. Have the child sit down with the pants up to his knees. Then have him stand up and pull his pants up the rest of the way. Remember to say, "Pull up your pants," and to praise him.
9. Have the child sit down. Place the pants *just over* his feet up to his ankles. Have him pull the pants up to his knees. Then have him stand up and pull the pants up the rest of the way.
10. Have the child sit down. Place the pants *just over* his toes. Have him pull the pants up to his knees. Then have him stand up and pull them up the rest of the way.
11. Have the child sit down. Place one of the child's feet into one of the pant legs until his toes show. Then have him place his other foot through the other pant leg and pull the pants up to his knees, then stand up and pull the pants up the rest of the way.
12. Have the child sit down. Place the pants in front of the child with the opening of one pant leg just touching the toes of one foot. Then have him first pull the pant leg up until his toes show, then place his second foot in the other pant leg, then pull them up to his knees, and stand up and pull them up the rest of the way.
13. Have the child sit down. Place the pants in front of the child. Have him grab the pants with his hands on both sides of the pants, place one foot through one pant leg, then the other foot through the other pant leg, pull them up to his knees, and stand up and pull them up the rest of the way.
14. Repeat Step 13.

Remember to praise the child each time he successfully completes a step and to say to him,

"(*Name*), pull up your pants" right before he begins to pull his pants up. You may have to prompt
the child a few times at various points to help him
completely learn a particular step. Chart on your
graph the last step that the child successfully completed at the end of each session. [Morris, 1976,
pp. 125-126]

Increasing Social Interaction. For many autistic children,
social attention does not function as a reinforcer. Because this is
so important in developing a wide range of other behaviors,
there was an early emphasis on establishing social events as reinforcers. Some studies arranged this by pairing approach to
adults with the removal of an aversive event (see, for example,
Lovaas, Schaeffer, and Simmons, 1965). (The ethical implications of procedures involving aversive events are discussed in
Chapter Twenty-Two.) In instances when social attention is
effective, it can be employed to encourage approach behavior
(see, for example, Wetzel, Baker, Roney, and Martin, 1966).
Cooperative responses have been developed by reinforcing one
child for interacting with another child. Parents have been
trained, by prompts over wireless microphone systems, to apply
systematic consequences to social and academic tasks. For
example, a mother of a three-year-old autistic child learned to
increase her child's responses to the social requests of "Say,
"Hi," "Smile at me," "Come to me," "Hold my hand," and
"Look at me" (Moore and Bailey, 1973, p. 499). Language development allows the child to interact through this medium
with others.

Training Parents of Autistic Children. Parents are confronted with a wide variety of tasks to accomplish in training
autistic children. The following overview introduces the reader
to the components employed in one training program, part of
which took place in the laboratory and part of which took place
in the home (Kozloff, 1973). Parents were first introduced to
the principles of learning through reading manuals such as *Families* (Patterson, 1971b). This material was discussed, as well as
information contained on parent-recorded logs describing the
child's behavior at home and parental reactions to this behavior.
These logs provided valuable information concerning parental

attitudes about the child's problem, some of which may be critical to address, such as self-blame for problematic behavior, or
attribution of the behavior to a disease process that requires
medical attention. Parents observed training sessions between a
teacher and their child from behind a one-way mirror and their
attention was drawn to specific behaviors and to their consequences, as well as to how the teacher initiated exchanges with
the child. They learned how to record their observations on a dic-
taphone during these sessions, in order to enhance their observational skills. Prompts were given to encourage appropriate use
of labels for given behaviors, such as "he imitates correctly and
she rewards him with approval and food" (Kozloff, 1973, p.
38). Parents learned how to reward appropriate behavior, including praising and/or cuddling and presenting social reinforcement right before offering a small amount of food; how to
ignore irrelevant behavior; and how to use time out for disruptive behaviors. They also learned to gradually shift from a continuous schedule of reinforcement to intermittent reinforcement, and to initiate or structure exchanges with directives or
contract statements, rather than with questions. Parents were
encouraged to alternate the reinforcers and the tasks periodically, to avoid the child's becoming either satiated or bored.

At first they worked with a child on a task the child already knew how to perform; that is, their first task was simply
to maintain an exchange. The parent observed the teacher and
then imitated the teacher's behavior. Coaching was provided by
a counselor behind a one-way mirror, by means of a wireless
intercom system. Opportunities were provided to extend new
skills to other family members. For example, the mother
coached other family members to develop the skills she had
been taught under the guidance of coaching from the counselor.
That is, she was coached in how to coach. She was reminded
through the intercom to praise often and to prompt (give suggestions) when necessary. The second part of the training program took place in the home. A list of problems for each family
was drawn up, including unconstructive exchanges that occurred as well as behavior deficits of the child that were to be
addressed. Home observation, parent-recorded logs, and interviews provided a view of the pattern of exchanges between parent and child, as illustrated in the following example of Michael

and his parents. It was found that there were far more inappropriate responses than appropriate ones, and that Michael engaged in a high rate of bizarre and disruptive behavior. Tormenting his mother seemed to provide some of the fun for these behaviors, whereas other behaviors just seemed to be ways of filling time. He performed very few chores and his mother provided few structured opportunities for constructive activities. Rarely did he respond to attempts by his mother to engage him in an interaction. The mother reinforced inappropriate behaviors and failed to reinforce appropriate behavior in a consistent fashion. Much of her attention and offering of other reinforcers was noncontingent; that is, unrelated to whether inappropriate or appropriate behavior had just taken place. Written instructions were prepared that included directions for decreasing inappropriate behavior as well as how to teach constructive behaviors. Instructions for Michael's parents are shown in Table 20.

Table 20. Instructions for Michael's Parents

To Ignore: Do not look at or talk to Michael while he is engaged in inappropriate behavior. Do not tell him to stop, or try to verbally divert his attention, or scold him, or threaten him with punishment.

To Reward: For the present, give Michael approval (verbal, strokes, and so on). For certain things, food may be given (an afternoon snack for working puzzles for awhile, a drink of juice for a household task, and so on). Make sure, of course, that the reward follows the behavior immediately—within a few seconds.

To Time Out: Without speaking, but with some vigor, take Michael to time-out room. Leave him in two minutes for first offense, four minutes for second offense, and so on. Do not let him out if he is whining or throwing a tantrum.

Child's Behavior	Your Response
Pulling and/or pushing For records	Set aside several periods of the day during which Michael can work for a record (for example, by picking up toys, clothes, working puzzles). Tell him, "As soon as you _____, you can have a record." At any other time, ignore him until he asks at an opportune time of the day. (Eventually, working for records was established ten minutes after lunch. It was initiated with Mrs. Hare [the mother] saying, "It's time to work for a record." She would

Table 20 *(continued)*

Child's Behavior	Your Response
	lead Michael to the table and prompt him to work puzzles.)
For bath	Ignore. Then, when it is proper time, tell him he may take bath or whatever you usually say.
Crying and/or whining	Ignore. This will probably occur after he is ignored for pulling.
Playing with stove, getting into food in refrigerator or pantry, climbing on cupboard, getting into food being prepared (assuming that any of these are disturbing to you)	Time out from the kitchen by removing Michael from kitchen and locking door from inside. Open in approximately three or four minutes and repeat each time he repeats inappropriate behavior. Don't let it escalate; don't wait and let him do it for awhile. Remove him immediately. This will work if he likes being in the kitchen. If he does any of these when you are not in the kitchen with him, remove him and lock the door.
Climbing on refrigerator	Ignore.
Playing with own food (spilling it, slapping it, and so on) or getting up from the table to mess around	Take food away. No food until next meal. Ignore all appeals for food in between.
Spinning objects	Do not chase him or have a tug of war. Take object away quickly and without speaking. Then, say, "As soon as you ————, you can spin this." (Have him perform a simple task.)
Water play	Temporarily, remove him from room and lock door. If he does this during a meal, remove him from the kitchen, and lock him out, and take his plate away. Use this until we attack problem outright.
All bizarre behavior	Ignore.
Self-initiated working at puzzles, looking in magazines, picking up clothing, helping in kitchen, speech (any approximation)	Reward verbally and with strokes; if convenient, with a bite of food. If he is engaged in such activity for more than few minutes, reward him several times. Don't just wait until he stops. Reward him during activity if it is longer than 10 seconds or so. Be on the lookout for appropriate behavior and consistently reward it.

Source: Kozloff (1973, pp. 87-89).

With each family, one or more problems were selected to start with and training sessions were then held in the home, where the parents were coached in use of their new skills. They were encouraged to select a special setting for training their child in new behaviors, a place with a minimum of distractions. Sessions were scheduled at times when the child was likely to be motivated—for example, right before mealtime, because food was employed as a reinforcer during sessions. Eye contact was the first target of focus. This was reinforced whenever it occurred and was prompted by holding up a bite of the child's meal near the parent's eye and waiting for him to make eye contact. Eye contact was followed immediately by praise and a hug and the bite of food. The objective of the next step was to offer the child a repertoire of play and chore behaviors. Parents were instructed to specify the behavior they desired, and to then break this into small steps and to select the closest approximation to reinforce, making sure that this behavior is available and is not too difficult. Options available in terms of encouraging the behavior were noted, including simply waiting until the behavior occurs, asking him to do it, or waiting until a child says he wants something, at which point the parents could state the rule—"as soon as you put in the puzzle piece you can hear a record" (Kozloff, 1973, p. 47). A fourth possibility is setting aside training periods during which the child had a chance to work for the reinforcer.

Very simple tasks were first selected, such as completing a puzzle or fitting shapes into a box. Prompting was employed to encourage approximations to task completion, rewarding the child at first for every correct response with hugs, praise, and a bite of his lunch. As skill was acquired, prompts were gradually faded out and reinforcement given less frequently, until reinforcers were offered only after completion of three or four puzzles. It was important that the child learn to enjoy these interactions with his parents as well as the tasks involved. To assure this, parents were encouraged to allow the child to progress at his own rate; to prevent satiation by offering him small bites of food; to alternate tasks to prevent boredom; and to gradually increase task requirements to promote new skills. They were coached to talk to the child about the task and to praise him for completing it, but to refrain from offering a steady stream of utterances, or the parents' voices might become meaningless. Eye contact was encouraged by making this a prerequisite for receiving puzzle pieces or blocks to be stacked. The parent would hold up a puzzle piece and give it to the child only after eye contact was established.

When appropriate, chore training was also initiated at this stage of training. Certain times of the day were put aside when the child could earn reinforcers for performing tasks such as helping with the dishes or cleaning the kitchen table. Michael, a ten-year-old, learned to do a number of chores, including putting laundry away; setting the table; clearing the table and returning plates, utensils, and food to the kitchen; loading the washer with clothes and detergent, and starting it; and packing his lunch box with food and utensils. Chaining was employed to develop behaviors in which the last behavior in the chain was established first. For example, in developing the behavior of setting the table, Michael started with bringing food to the table, the last behavior required to set the table. Component behaviors were reinforced, working back from bringing food until Michael could complete the entire chain of behaviors, including putting on the table cloth, the plates, utensils, and so forth. Michael's mother also learned to make use of available reinforcers to increase constructive activity. For example, Michael loved to play in the water, and his mother allowed him to wash the dishes as a reward for cleaning the table.

Another major stage in the child's education was speech training. The methods developed by Lovaas (1976) were employed, consisting of presenting some verbal stimulus (for example, a sound to imitate or picture to name), prompting the child to make the correct response, rewarding successive approximations, and then gradually fading prompts. Initial training sessions were held in the laboratory and were very brief, only twenty minutes long. The stages in this training process included encouraging spontaneous speech, developing imitative speech, teaching children to label, and then developing conversational speech. Parents were trained to encourage the attractiveness of exchanges by returning to easier sounds or words for a few days; by offering more prompts; by employing more enthusiasm when reinforcing the child and offering this for closer approximations to the vocal model; or by using other reinforcers or other tasks for a few days (Kozloff, 1973). Words were established by first developing the individual components, and then by reinforcing the child for imitating the entire word composed of the previously established components. During conversational training, the most advanced stage, the child was trained how to ask and answer questions, and how to ask for things. The reader is referred to Kozloff (1973) and Lovaas (1976) for a step-by-step description of the training methods employed.

Another component of the training program was to show parents how to decrease inappropriate behavior by the use of methods such as negative practice, which involves having the child repeat the behavior so many times that it becomes unpleasant to perform.

Some of the changes that occurred in one child's behavior are indicated in Table 21. As the reader may have gleaned, a great deal of counselor time was devoted to this training program with parents, an average of about 120 hours per family over a year. This time, however, must be viewed in relation to the training tasks that the parents are assuming and hopefully will maintain. That is, to the extent to which they develop effective skills, further professional help can be held to a minimum. Most of this time was spent coaching and observing parent-child interactions in the home. The continual need to encourage parents to be consistent in their application of contingencies was identified as the biggest reason for so much time being spent in the home. Home sessions usually lasted for two hours. As Kozloff notes, this may be too small an amount of time initially to spend with families. Many parents, for example, gave their children a great deal of noncontingent reinforcement and so wasted reinforcers that could be employed to strengthen appropriate behaviors. And, with parents who had come to rely heavily on punishment, it was difficult to encourage them to ignore inappropriate behavior. Marathon sessions may more readily break up such typical patterns of behavior. Problems that were identified as interfering with consistent contingency management included parental ambivalence about encouraging a

Table 21. Mike's Behavior Before and After Training Program

Behavior of Child	Program Prior to Training Program	Behavior During Follow-Up
Bizarre-Disruptive	Average of forty-five disruptions per two-hour session, including crying and/or whining, playing in water, getting into food, pulling and/or pushing, playing with stove, climbing, disrupting meals, and spinning objects.	Average of one disruption per session. All but getting into food, crying and/or whining, playing in water, and climbing eliminated.
Constructive Activity	Average duration five minutes per session. Play repertoire limited to simple puzzles and stacking blocks, No chores. Manual dexterity poor.	Average duration fifty-five minutes per session, or an increase by a factor of 11. Play repertoire included complex puzzles, Play-doh, Tinker toys, swing and climber sets, pegboard landscape, coloring with crayons, sewing cards, riding tricycle, "Lite-Brite" toy, musical toys, and so on. Chore repertoire included setting and clearing table, loading and starting washer and dryer, scouring toilet, taking out trash, packing lunch box, washing dishes, dressing. Development of generalized motor imitation. Plays and works with mother several hours per day.
Speech	Mute. No words.	Rate of acquisition of imitative speech positively accelerating. Repertoire included at least thirty-seven words. Beginning to develop labeling vocabulary, including words mama, daddy, food. Object discrimination (pointing to or picking up objects named) quite developed (89 percent unprompted correct responses).
Autistic Aloneness	Values presence and attention of others, but cooperates with parental exchange signals an average of only 49 percent of the time and does not engage in cooperative play.	Cooperates with parental exchange signals an average of 95 percent of the time and engages in games requiring attentiveness to others, such as hide and seek, imitation.

Source: Kozloff (1973, p. 205).

normal life for their child and having a normal life of their own, and marital friction was sometimes observed to interfere with constructive exchanges. "Instead of comforting Mrs. White or helping her to handle Kristen when Kristen engages in her extremely aversive screaming, Mr. White was observed to blame Mrs. White for the fact that Kristen was screaming" (Kozloff, 1973, p. 210). Siblings sometimes interfered with effective application of new skills; for example, Kristen's younger brother "invariably threw a tantrum whenever Mr. White was engaged in a play exchange with Kristen." Additional problems included the following: "The parents themselves may have strong behavior patterns or deficiencies which interfere with their learning or applying the techniques. One parent was very literal-minded, and this prevented her from generalizing the techniques to other situations or behavior problems of the child. Another parent was disorganized in her scheduling of family activities, and her disorganization may have prevented her from running structured orthogenic exchanges with the child on a continuous basis. There may be negative sentiments, or at least a lack of positive sentiments, between the parents and the child. The implications of this are twofold—not only may the parents be less willing to work with their child, but the parents' praise and approval will not be rewarding to the child. Thus, an important source of reinforcement for appropriate behavior will be absent" (Kozloff, 1973, p. 210).

It must be remembered that far more was required of these parents than is required in the usual parent training program. Not only were parents trained to decrease inappropriate behaviors and increase appropriate behaviors throughout the day, but they also took part in daily training sessions with their child, which required them to learn a variety of additional skills. They are thus exposed to more "ups and downs" in terms of progress. "The parents go through many extinction trials for precious little reinforcement from the child. . . . when they are working on harder skills, the amount of reinforcement decreases" (Kozloff, 1973, p. 211). This indicates that reinforcers for parents in such programs must be strengthened. The time involved in the training process could be decreased by a greater use of prepared training materials in the forms of films and manuals. Parents who are already trained could be employed to train other parents.

One of the most well-known cases in the behavioral literature concerns a three-and-a-half-year-old boy admitted when
three years of age to a children's mental hospital with a diagnosis of childhood schizophrenia (Wolf, Risley and Mees, 1964).
He had developed cataracts on both eyes at the age of nine
months, at which time severe temper tantrums and sleeping
problems had developed. Removal of his occluded lenses made
wearing glasses a necessity. However, all attempts to encourage
this behavior had failed and, at the time of hospitalization, his
opthalmologist had predicted that he would lose his sight completely if he did not start wearing corrective glasses within six
months. He lacked normal social and verbal behavior, did not
eat normally, and engaged in self-destructive behavior during his
tantrums, including head banging, face slapping, hair pulling,
and face scratching. After observing the interaction between
Dickey and his mother, it was decided to initiate intervention in
the hospital. Extinction and time out were employed to decrease temper tantrums. As his behavior improved, the criteria
defining "a tantrum" were lowered. The parents often visited
Dickey in the hospital and learned the use of extinction and
time out. Shaping was employed to get Dickey to wear glasses.
About three twenty-minute sessions were spent each day on this
task by attendants. First, a conditioned reinforcer was established by pairing clicks from a noisemaker with small bites of
fruit. Initially, only frames (without lenses) were employed,
because the lenses altered Dickey's perception in such a way
that might make wearing glasses especially unpleasant. A number of glass frames were placed at different locations around the
room and Dickey was reinforced for picking them up, holding
them, and carrying them. He was then reinforced for successive
approximations to bringing them closer to his eyes. Progress was
slow, because of the inexperience of the attendant who was
trying to shape the behavior and because of the use of weak
reinforcers. After two weeks of such efforts, bites of breakfast
were employed and larger ear pieces and a roll bar (which was
attached to the glasses, went over the head, and guided the ear
pieces up and over the ears) were added. Further progress required the experimenters taking over the shaping process and
also using bites of lunch as a reinforcer. These additions were

successful in increasing glasses-wearing behavior, with the prescription lenses. About two weeks after glasses-wearing behavior was established, glasses-throwing behavior became a problem and occurred about twice a day. A time-out procedure, in which Dickey was confined to his room contingent on throwing glasses, was successful in decreasing this behavior. Appropriate verbal behavior was increased by reinforcing imitative behavior with bites of food. Gradually, verbal prompts were dropped and Dickey would name the object upon seeing the picture. He was then trained to respond to questions such as "What did you do outside?" That is, he learned to answer questions about his activities. The parents were trained to employ this method at home to continue to expand his verbal repertoire. Correct mealtime behavior was increased by enforcing a brief removal of his plate, and, if inappropriate behavior continued, a removal from the eating situation contingent on eating with his hands. As words paired with such removal, such as *no,* developed influence over his behavior, these procedures were no longer necessary.

A later study (Wolf, Risley, Johnston, Harris, and Allen, 1967) indicated that Dickey continued to improve after the intervention program ended. He even enrolled in a public school education program. (Another example of a program carried out by parents is offered in Figure 5 in Chapter Five.)

There are a number of studies showing that parents as well as teachers can be trained in the use of effective intervention procedures to encourage appropriate behaviors of autistic children if training teaches them fundamental skills. As with other training programs, opportunity to observe a model interacting effectively with the child is an important component of training; however, this may not be enough to establish skills. For example, in a program for parents of autistic children, only after parents learned to identify correct and incorrect use of each of the following techniques were they able to teach their children a range of new and different behaviors: (1) presenting instructions consistently and clearly, (2) using prompts effectively, (3) selecting successive approximations, (4) applying consequences immediately and appropriately, and (5) using distinctive intertrial intervals (Glahn, 1975).

The Use of Behavioral Methods with the Mentally Retarded

There is an extensive literature describing the use of behavioral methods with mentally retarded children and adults (see, for example, Gardner, 1971; Birnbrauer, 1976). A wide range of target behaviors have been addressed, including self-care skills, disruptive and aggressive behavior, vocational and social skills, and academic behavior. The specificity of these methods renders it easier for nonprofessionals such as parents to learn to usefully employ them. The term *retardation* encompasses an array of severity of behavioral deficits ranging from the broad range of deficits in the profoundly retarded to the much milder deficits in the mildly retarded. The term *"mental retardation* should not be applied on the basis of an intelligence test but rather only if the person also lags significantly behind the norms in the development of motor and self-help skills, academic learning and social behavior" (Birnbrauer, 1976, p. 361). About 90 percent of the mentally retarded are mildly retarded.

One problem that may be present is a limited reinforcer profile. For example, social attention may not be very powerful as a reinforcer. Inadequate stimulus control is a major deficit in the retarded. That is, appropriate behaviors are often present, but do not occur reliably enough to produce consistent reinforcement (Gardner, 1971). With the more severely retarded, behavior can tend to be erratic, unless the individual is under optimal reinforcement conditions in which reinforcement is frequent and of a highly preferred nature. Visual cues such as lights and counters, which signal the accumulation of reinforcement, have been successfully employed to help maintain behavior (Stamm, 1970). A low frustration tolerance may also be present, in which there is a disposition to engage in various disruptive emotional and operant behaviors when behavioral requirements are made or when the reinforcement schedule is lean. This may be caused by a limited history of intermittent reinforcement; positive consequences for unadaptive behaviors by others who may comply with the client's demands to avoid management difficulties; and negative reinforcement of the nonadaptive behaviors, because this allows the person to avoid undesirable situations (Gardner, 1971). Assessment systems have been developed to identify specific areas of deficit (see Sailor and Mix, 1975).

Mentally retarded children and adults have been trained to function as mediators of change for others (see, for example, Klein, Paluck, and Beresford, 1976) and have been trained to gather valuable monitoring information (see Craighead, Mercatoris, and Ballak, 1974).

Decreasing Aggressive and Disruptive Behavior. The same variety of procedures used with normal children has been employed with retarded individuals. In addition to the use of differential reinforcement, time out, response cost, and the presentation of aversive events, "bedrest" and "restitution" have been employed. For example, profoundly retarded adults were required to lie in their beds for two hours contingent on aggressive or self-injurious behaviors (Webster and Azrin, 1973). The rate of such behaviors fell from a baseline of 7.0 a day to 0.2 per day. An alarm sounded if the resident got off the bed, which made monitoring of bedrest easy for staff. Positive effects included an increase in visits from family members. As Birnbrauer (1976) notes, this method will not work for clients who will not follow instructions. In this case, a mix of procedures can be used, including differential reinforcement plus overcorrection. The latter procedure consists either of positive practice in which appropriate behavior is practiced, or of restitution overcorrection, which involves a period of close contact with a trainer during which a client is encouraged to assume responsibility for the disruption caused by his misbehavior by returning the disturbed situation to a greatly improved state (Foxx and Azrin, 1972). The client is prevented from engaging in inappropriate behavior during this time. This procedure, like time out, entails an interruption.

Restitution should be required immediately following an inappropriate behavior, so that there is little or no time to enjoy the consequences of the offensive behavior, and because immediate consequences are more effective than delayed ones. The restitution required should be directly related to the misbehavior; should be extended in duration (for example, thirty minutes), so that the offender cannot engage in other reinforcing activities; and should entail active performance requiring effort.

Praise and approval are minimized during restitution, so that the restitution period does not become positively reinforcing. Either verbal instruction or physical guidance is employed to encourage performance. Hopefully, the annoyance of having one's limbs moved during physical guidance will serve as an incentive to encourage voluntary movement. Examples of the use of restitution training include household orderliness training for the disturbance of objects, social reassurance training for annoying or frightening others, medical assistance for physical aggression, and quiet training for agitation, in which the client is required to be in bed for a set period of time.

In household orderliness training, the client is encouraged not only to correct the specific disturbance he caused, but also to improve the overall appearance of the household. A client who throws a chair, for example, would be required to return the chair to its original position and to straighten all other chairs on the ward, as well as related objects. If a client frightens others, he is required to apologize to all persons present. If verbal behavior does not exist, gestures may be employed to apologize. An example of the use of medical assistance is provided later in this chapter.

Restitution training was employed with a fifty-year-old, profoundly retarded female with an IQ of 16 who had been hospitalized for forty-six years (Foxx and Azrin, 1972). She also had a variety of physical disabilities including impaired hearing, chronic asthma, and lack of muscular control of her left hand. Verbalization consisted only of the statement, "I want to eat." Object throwing had been a problem recorded in her chart since the age of thirteen, and this made it impossible to include her in off-ward or educational activities. Time out, physical restraint, and requiring her to replace furniture to its regular position had all proven to be ineffective. A baseline revealed that she threw about thirteen objects per day. Household orderliness training consisted of returning overturned beds to their original position and remaking the beds completely and neatly. She was then required to smooth out and straighten the bed clothes, push the bed against the wall, and fluff out the pillows of all other beds on the ward. "When Ann turned over a chair or table, she was immediately required to straighten all tables and chairs on the ward, wipe off all furniture with a damp cloth, and empty all trash cans. When she turned over a table containing food, she was required to clean the entire dining room after sweeping and mopping up the debris. Since she failed to follow the trainer's requests initially, Graduated Guidance of her limbs was given. Also, she did not appear to know how to make beds and arrange furniture. Consequently, the Graduated Guidance procedure was instructional as well as motivating. Social Reassurance Training required Ann to apologize to the individuals whose beds or chairs she had turned over and to all other individuals present on the ward, all of whom were usually apprehensive because of her episodes. Although she was essentially nonverbal, she was able to move her head in the appropriate direction (up and down or sideways) when asked if she was sorry for what she had done and whether she intended to create another such disturbance" (Foxx and Azrin, 1972, p. 19). Objects thrown per day decreased to one per day and, after eleven weeks of restitution training, decreased to zero.

Restitution has advantages over other methods to eliminate offensive behavior—it actively teaches appropriate behaviors. For example, the clients in the program described learned how to make beds and to respond sociably to others. Rather than the staff having to spend considerable time and effort to correct the results of the offensive behavior, the client assumed responsibility for this, although this assumption may require initial physical guidance. The importance of a minimal duration of restitution is emphasized by the ineffectiveness of periods shorter than thirty minutes. Overcorrection has also been used to decrease stealing by retarded persons (Azrin and Wesolowski, 1974).

Decreasing Self-Stimulating Behavior. Overcorrection is a generally effective procedure for eliminating self-stimulatory behavior. With some self-stimulatory behaviors, no environmental disruption is created and thus the restitutional phase is not appropriate; however, positive practice of appropriate behaviors may be offered. This procedure was employed with a seven-year-old boy, Mike, diagnosed as autistic, who displayed many classic autistic behaviors such as hand clapping (Foxx and Azrin, 1973c). He was so socially unresponsive that he appeared deaf. He was enrolled in a day-care, intensive learning program. Baseline observations at school and at home indicated that he almost continually clapped his hands. Functional movement training was employed to teach and motivate him to hold his hands stationary, and only to move them for functional reasons, such as when instructed to do so. When he began clapping, functional movement training was initiated for five minutes. He was instructed to move his hand to one of five positions: above his head, straight out in front, into his pockets, held together, or held behind his back. If he failed to respond to a request, he was physically guided. He was required to hold his hands in each requested position for fifteen seconds. Sequence of positions was varied to assure that he was responding to individual instructions. A verbal warning procedure was introduced after the self-stimulatory behavior was absent for a few days. If he was observed to engage in the self-stimulatory behavior, he was asked to stop and only if he failed to stop or engaged in another self-stimulatory behavior during the morning was overcorrection training instituted. Hand clapping decreased from a baseline of 90 percent during the school day to zero on the third day of intervention. The verbal warning procedure was initiated on the thirty-first day and hand clapping remained at a low level during the remaining 100 days of observation. Overcorrection was also employed at home to eliminate hand clapping there. His parents were instructed how to use overcorrection and within two days this behavior decreased to zero, at which time the verbal warning procedure was implemented.

Overcorrection has been successfully employed to decrease several kinds of self-stimulatory behavior of both retarded and autistic children including head weaving, object mouthing, and hand mouthing. Effects can be maintained by verbal reprimands and parents can readily learn to carry out the procedure. Overcorrection has been found to be more effective than noncontingent reinforcement, differential reinforcement of other behaviors, or punishment by physical slaps (Foxx and Azrin, 1973b).

Self-stimulatory behaviors may originally be established because of a lack of functional (reinforced) outward-directed behaviors. As such behaviors increase, the probability of functional behaviors decreases still further. Overcorrection both removes reinforcement from the self-stimulatory behaviors (by interrupting these) and at the same time, provides reinforcement for functional behaviors (Foxx and Azrin, 1973b).

Decreasing Self-Injurious Behavior. A combination of required relaxation, positive reinforcement for outward-directed activities, and hand-awareness training procedure has been successful in decreasing self-injurious behavior of clients ranging in age from ten to forty-six, all of whom had visible swelling from injuries and who struck themselves on the face, head, ears, or eyes, usually with their fist or open hand. Protective clothing or physical restraints had been used with five of the eleven patients. All but one, who was diagnosed as schizophrenic, were classified as profoundly retarded (Azrin, Gottlieb, Hughart, Wesolowski, and Rahn, 1975). The first procedure required the person to relax in his bed for two hours and to keep his arms down along his side. Verbal instructions and gentle physical guidance were used only as necessary. The second procedure involved reinforcing the person for behaviors such as looking at the trainer, following a variety of instructions, catching and throwing a ball, or playing with a musical instrument. The third procedure involved practice in clasping the hands together behind the back for ten-second periods. Verbal and physical guidance was faded out as client skill in these procedures increased. The average number of self-injurious incidents decreased 90 percent on the first day and 99 percent at the end of three months.

Increasing Self-Care Skills. Many mentally retarded children and adolescents do not possess self-care skills such as dressing themselves, brushing their teeth, washing, and feeding themselves. A step-by-step program in which tasks are carefully sequenced is effective in developing such skills, as illustrated by a program designed to teach mentally retarded adolescents to brush their teeth. A careful task analysis is first required to design an effective program that entails identification of the tasks involved in a self-care skill. Teaching techniques must then be selected. The failure to carefully identify the many tasks required for behaviors such as brushing one's teeth, tying shoe laces, putting on a shirt, as well as the failure to arrange a schedule of reinforcement to support the acquisition of such behaviors, are the reasons why many severely retarded or disturbed children never learn to do these tasks. This failure is incorrectly attributed to their mental retardation or to their emotional disturbance. Task analysis was facilitated by studying a videotape of three skilled performers (of tooth brushing) and three retarded persons brushing their teeth, one of whom was described as very good, another poor, and the third average (in relation to the tasks at hand). The following steps were identified by Horner and Keilitz (1975, p. 303).

1. *Pick up and hold the toothbrush.* The student should turn on the water and pick up the toothbrush by the handle.
2. *Wet the toothbrush.* The student should continue to hold the toothbrush, placing the bristles under the running water for at least five seconds. Then, the student should turn off the running water and lay the toothbrush down.
3. *Remove the cap from the toothpaste.* The student should place the tube of toothpaste in his least-preferred hand, unscrew the cap with the thumb and index finger of his preferred hand, and set the cap on the sink.
4. *Apply the toothpaste to the brush.* The student should pick up the toothbrush by the handle, hold the back part of the bristles against the opening of the toothpaste tube, squeeze the tube, move the tube toward the front bristles as toothpaste flows out on top of the bristles, and lay the toothbrush on the sink with the bristles up.
5. *Replace the cap on the toothpaste.* The student should pick up the toothpaste cap with the thumb and index finger of the preferred hand, screw the cap on the toothpaste tube, which is held in the least-preferred hand, lay the tube of toothpaste down, and with the preferred hand pick up the toothbrush by the handle.
6. *Brush the outside surfaces of the teeth.* The student should brush the outside surfaces of the upper and lower teeth on both sides and in the center of the mouth, using either an up and down or back and forth motion, for at least thirty seconds.

7. *Brush the biting surfaces of the teeth.* The student should brush the biting surfaces of the upper and lower teeth on both sides and in the center of the mouth, using a back and forth motion, for at least thirty seconds.

8. *Brush the inside surfaces of the teeth.* The student should brush the inside surfaces of the upper and lower teeth on both sides and in the center of the mouth, using a back and forth motion, for at least thirty seconds.

9. *Fill the cup with water.* The student should lay the toothbrush down, pick up the cup, place it under the faucet, turn on the water, fill the cup, and turn off the water.

10. *Rinse the mouth.* The student should spit out any excess toothpaste foam, take a sip of water, hold it in the mouth, swish it around in the mouth. and spit it out. If any toothpaste foam [remains, this] should be repeated.

11. *Wipe the mouth.* The student should pull a tissue from the container (or pick up a hand towel) and dry his mouth.

12. *Rinse the toothbrush.* The student should pick up the toothbrush by the handle, turn on the water, and place the bristles under the running water until the bristles are free of toothpaste (any toothpaste not removed by the water may be dislodged by drawing the fingers across the bristles), turn off the water, and lay the toothbrush down.

13. *Rinse the sink.* The student should turn on the water, rub around the inside of the sink with the hand to wash any residue of toothpaste or toothpaste foam down the drain, then turn off the water.

14. *Put the equipment away.* The student should put the toothpaste and toothbrush in the proper storage place. (If a glass and hand towel are used, these should be placed in the proper place.)

15. *Discard the disposables.* Any used paper cups and tissues should be placed in a waste receptacle.

Training was carried out by four people who had no previous experience with either mentally retarded individuals or with the training procedure. One, for example, was a junior college student. The eight subjects ranged in age from nine to seventeen years, had a mean IQ of 43.1 as measured by standardized tests and had been institutionalized for about two and a half years. A baseline was taken by placing a toothbrush, tube of toothpaste, disposable cup, and box of tissues near the sink and saying, "[Name], here is everything you need to brush your teeth. I want you to brush your teeth by yourself. Do the very best you can." Sessions ended when behavior using the mentioned items ceased and the subjects responded affirmatively to the question, "Are you finished brushing your teeth?" Four types of procedures were employed during training: (1) no help —the subject was simply given the opportunity to perform a step without assistance; (2) verbal instruction—a statement was made describing the desired behavior; (3) demonstration of the desired behavior in addition to verbal instruction; and (4) physical guidance plus instructions in which the subject would be guided or otherwise physically assisted in initiating the desired behavior but was allowed to complete the step on his own. These procedures were employed successively for each toothbrushing step and all steps were covered in each session. As skill was acquired by each subject, the number of training procedures used in each step of the program was decreased. Training was gradually faded out in this way. The trainers were coached to praise any correctly completed step and then to introduce the "no help" condition for the next step in the sequences; that is, to wait five seconds and see whether this was performed by the subject and to offer a nonspecific verbal prompt if it was not, such as "What's next?" Verbal instruction for the next step was immediately given if inappropriate behaviors occurred (for example, licking the toothpaste tube) or if some other toothbrushing step was displayed. If the correct task was not initiated or inappropriate behavior occurred after verbal instruction, the next training procedure was introduced. Failure of a correct response within five minutes, or inappropriate behavior, resulted in use of the final training procedure: physical guidance plus instruction. This was repeated once if the first attempt failed, and if it again was unsuccessful, then the next step in the sequence started with the no help condition.

Prior to the training program, the first four subjects completed about four to five steps correctly. Three of the children were completing all steps correctly after eighteen to thirty training sessions. Three additional subjects who started with a higher number of tasks completed at baseline (six to ten) were completing all steps correctly after only twenty to twenty-one training sessions. The remaining two subjects completed twelve and thirteen tasks. Tokens accompanied by praise and pats on the back tradable for sugarless gum were employed with the first four subjects; however, only social reinforcement was employed for the other four subjects.

As the authors point out, a disadvantage of using a set of sequences is that a subject's performance measured by tasks completed correctly in sequence may be below the baseline level in terms of knowledge of component responses. That is, someone may remove the cap from the toothpaste before wetting their brush and so not get credit for this during training. Other sequences are necessary in the order in which they are described, such as squeezing out toothpaste after taking off the cap. A separate program could be arranged for each child, allowing for acceptable variations in the sequence, if this did not complicate the training program greatly for staff. Ease of training instructions for staff is a very important consideration in view of the scarcity of staff time. The advantage of programs such as this is that they can be precisely described in writing so that new trainers can readily learn them. The extent to which the high performance levels achieved with this program are maintained is not known, because no follow-up data are provided. It is likely that a special program would be needed to maintain and generalize these new skills.

Spot checks are useful when monitoring self-care behaviors. For example, a child can be observed at various times during the day to determine whether his shirt is tucked in, his shoelaces are tied, his hair combed, and so forth. Examples of ways to gather data on a group of children or adults are described in Chapter Seven.

Increasing Other Skills. An extensive literature is available that describes use of behavioral procedures to increase other skills. Gold (1973) presents a review of the use of behavioral methods in increasing vocational skills. Retarded children have been trained in problem-solving methods in order to increase their cognitive abilities (see, for example, Ross and Ross, 1973). Doll play, live models, film slides, and puppets were employed to teach social responses to a group of children aged four to ten (Ross, 1969). Both logical thinking and social responses increased, compared to a control group of children who had no such training. Parents are often trained how to manage the behavior of retarded children and adults in the home situation (see, for example, Frazier and Schneider, 1975; King and Turner, 1975). A great number of studies have been devoted to increasing academic behaviors and decreasing disruptive behaviors in the classroom (see Birnbrauer, 1976).

Clients Labeled Psychotic

There is an extensive literature describing the use of behavioral methods with clients labeled psychotic both in residential settings (Kazdin and Bootzin, 1972) and in open settings such as community mental health centers (see Liberman, King, and DeRisi, 1976). A variety of areas have been focused on, including increasing appropriate speech, decreasing hallucinations, developing problem-solving skills, and increasing appropriate social behaviors.

Increasing Appropriate Speech. The speech of those labeled psychotic is often inappropriate either because of omissions or behavior surfeits. Two approaches that have been employed to alter this have been reinforcement of appropriate speech and self-instructional training. The latter approach assumes that overt behavior is mediated by covert statements and that changing these can be employed to alter overt behavior. Self-instructional training programs that have been found to be successful with impulsive children and test-anxious college students have been effectively employed to increase appropriate behavior of those labeled schizophrenic (see, for example, Meichenbaum and Cameron, 1973). This procedure was employed with a forty-seven-year-old male hospitalized seven times in the past eleven years, for an average stay of about seven months (Meyers, Mercatorius, and Sirota, 1976). He was diagnosed a chronic undifferentiated schizophrenic with agitated depression and alcohol abuse and was currently on medication (2 mg of prolixin decanote weekly and 300 mg of Melaril and 50 mg of Aventyl daily). His verbal behavior was very inappropriate. He often responded to questions with irrelevant answers, was highly anxious, and failed to attend to the environment. He was seen twice a week over seven weeks for about forty-five minutes each session. A baseline of appropriate reactions was first established over seven weeks by asking him a series of eleven questions. If an answer was simply repeated, if no answer was given, or if an irrelevant answer was offered, it was scored as inappropriate. Over sessions a series of self-instructions were presented, two per session. These included statements such as "Don't repeat an answer"; "I must pay attention to what others say"; "What did they ask me?"; "I must speak slowly"; "People think it's crazy to ramble on. I won't ramble on"; "Remember to pause after I say a sentence"; "I must stay on the topic"; and "Relax, take a few deep breaths."

Appropriate answers and covert self-instructions were modeled for the client by a staff member asking the counselor a question in front of the client. He demonstrated this three times and then the client was asked to imitate his behavior. This procedure was continued until the client displayed three consecutive appropriate verbalizations. Then the counselor presented the self-instructions only covertly, emphasizing, however, that he was still using them, and the same process was repeated. The client was praised for all correct performances. Of the client's verbalizations during baseline, 65 percent were inappropriate. This decreased to 16.7 percent during intervention. At Session 11, a staff screening of the client was held, because it was felt that the client was not showing enough progress. The client reviewed his instructions prior to the meeting and answered seventeen of eighteen questions correctly. The staff were so impressed that plans were initiated to place the client in a half-way house and arrange for day treatment. And, after Session 15, he was placed in the community. A six-month follow-up showed that positive changes were maintained.

Decreasing Hallucinations and Delusions. A range of procedures has been employed to decrease the frequency of hallucinations, including time out (Davis, Wallace, Liberman, and

Finch, 1976), assertive training (Nydegger, 1972), differential reinforcement of other behaviors (Liberman and others, 1973), covert sensitization (Moser, 1974), self-monitoring (Rutner and Bugle, 1969), and desensitization (Slade, 1972). Some of these procedures have been carried out in hospital settings. Desensitization was employed to decrease the frequency of auditory hallucinations of an eighteen-year-old man who was first admitted to the hospital at age sixteen. Auditory hallucinations were defined as "the experience of hearing voices which don't exist, which are unwilled and that occur spontaneously" (Slade, 1972, p. 85). This client was initially seen one year after discharge, when he again complained of hallucinations and feelings of derealization. Two or three different voices were involved, which either abused him or laughed at him. He was working at the time and living with his parents. His father was an invalid who two years before had made an unsuccessful suicide attempt and his mother was a domineering woman who made life difficult for the client.

The client was asked to keep a baseline record to determine the frequency of hallucinations and to identify situations that seemed to provoke them. This data revealed that hallucinations were more likely when he experienced high internal arousal in an environment characterized by low external stimulation. A hierarchy of tension-producing situations was constructed (see Table 22). The client was seen four times over a

Table 22. Hierarchy of Anxiety-Provoking Situations

Item	Description
Low	
1	Sitting alone in bedroom at home
2	Alone in bedroom, thinking about father
3	Talking to mother alone at home
4	Alone in a room with father
5	At work, thinking about father and the family
6	At home, in a room with father, brother and sister
7	At home, talking to mother; father, brother and sister present
8	At home, alone with father; having a verbal argument
9	At home with father, brother and sister; getting annoyed with father and hitting him
High	

Source: Slade (1972, p. 88).

period of nine weeks, and was trained in relaxation, which he practiced one half hour each day. Five weeks of desensitization was then initiated. The mean percentage of auditory hallucinations decreased from a baseline level of 15 percent to 1.9 percent, at a five-week follow-up period. Favorable changes were also found in the client's ratings of mood changes.

Thought stopping with an emphasis on the self-control aspects of this procedure was employed to decrease the frequency of recurrent, frightening, and uncontrollable visual sensations of an eighteen-year-old woman (Fisher and Winkler, 1975). The client reported feelings of depersonalization and unreality and was afraid that she was going insane. She had flashes of dark colors when she closed her eyes after she went to bed at night, and had intrusive sensations of heads of screaming dogs and cats, and of a geometric pattern with a spot of light in the center. She said she could not control these intrusions. The main thrust of intervention was to enable the client to gain control over these intrusions, based on the literature that shows that if an aversive event can be controlled, it does not arouse as much anxiety (Averill, 1973). She was seen for a total of twelve sessions, some of which were devoted to gathering needed assessment information and establishing a relationship. The major aspect of intervention consisted of practice sessions, during which the client would be asked to imagine one of the intrusive thoughts and to put it out of her mind as soon as she could. Through the use of signals (raising her index finger), the counselor was able to tell when she started to visualize the sensation as well as when she had put it out of her mind (lowering her index finger). This allowed the measurement of both onset latency and offset latency. She was unable to imagine the screaming dog and cat, so desensitization using an approach hierarchy was employed to enable her to imagine these in practice sessions. An eighty-five-day follow-up indicated that although some of the sensations still occurred, she could make them go away much more easily. She reported that the increased control she now had over the intrusive thoughts had totally eliminated others.

As Fisher and Winkler (1975) point out, the rationale provided to the client in relation to the intrusive thoughts was probably a very important aspect of the effectiveness of intervention. This rationale presented a view of the intrusive thoughts as troublesome but not bizarre, inexplicable, or uncontrollable experiences. A very good example of altering the conceptualization of the client from one where behaviors or sensations are experienced as signs of mental illness to a more helpful one is offered in a case study by Davison (1966), in which a paranoid delusional system was presented. An alternative view of persistent headaches was offered as related to tension rather than to a spirit who was helping the client make decisions. This reattribution, in which normal, private events are attributed to oneself and to natural causes rather than to bizarre and mysterious causes, paves the way for the introduction of helpful self-management procedures.

Counselor-client contracts have been employed to decrease self-injurious behavior of a fifty-four-year-old hospitalized woman and the rage reactions of a forty-six-year-old male who had been hospitalized for twelve years with a diagnosis of paranoid schizophrenia (Bergman, 1975). In the latter case, the patient experienced rage when staff would not listen to his delusional material. Mr. R. agreed that these rage reactions must cease immediately and the counselor agreed that Mr. R. could discuss the delusional material with him and that the counselor would be nonjudgmental. (This is an example of "symptom scheduling" described in Chapter Three.) After six months, the rage reactions decreased from a daily rate of 4.1 to only one every few weeks. This case example illustrates the potential use of contingency contracts with psychiatric patients.

Developing Problem-Solving Skills. The problem-solving behavior of psychiatric patients differs from that of a nonpsychiatric population. Psychiatric patients are less able to solve problems involving interpersonal situations (Platt and Spivack, 1972) and differ in the type of solutions offered when compared to a normal population (Platt and Spivack, 1974). It has also been found that they are deficient in their ability to generate solutions and are less able to offer a rationale for a particular course of action (Platt, Siegel, and Spivack, 1975). Problem-solving training has been offered in a group setting to hospitalized patients in order to improve their social functioning (Coché and Flick, 1975). At each group meeting, the members were asked to offer an interpersonal problem. The leader assisted in clarification of the problem. Possible solutions were then sought from the group and each discussed in terms of its possible consequences. This four-step procedure was repeated over eight one-hour sessions spread over two weeks. It was repeatedly stressed that there is usually more than one solution to a problem. About three to four problems were discussed at each group session. Feedback was solicited from the patients as to whether they had tried out any solution on a current problem; however, no homework assignments were given. Although hospitalization itself resulted in an increase in problem-solving ability, even greater gains were evidenced by the patients who experienced this series of group meetings.

Self-instructional training has been employed to improve the performance of patients on attentional and cognitive tasks (Meichenbaum and Cameron, 1973). Here, an approach was used that was similar to that described in Chapter Seventeen with impulsive children. Patients were trained to employ statements such as "Pay attention, listen and repeat the instructions, disregard distractions," while working on a variety of activities such as digit-symbol tasks (Meichenbaum and Cameron, 1973). Patients in one group were also trained to monitor their behavior and thinking in addition to interpersonal cues so that they would become more sensitive to the facial expressions and behavioral reactions of other people that might indicate that they were engaged in bizarre, incoherent, or irrelevant behaviors and verbalizations. It was hoped that self-monitoring and attending to interpersonal observations would function as cues for self-instructions such as "Be relevant and make myself understood." The use of structured sensory motor tasks for this training provided a way to gradually approach more anxiety-provoking social situations. These tasks required little self-disclosure or social interaction. As skill in offering appropriate self-instructions increased, more demanding tasks were introduced, such as proverb interpretation and interviewing. Self-reinforcement training was also provided, which encouraged the patients to reinforce themselves for appropriate thoughts and behaviors. As in the training program for impulsive children, a variety of training procedures were employed, including model presentation, rehearsal of self-instructions, gradually moving from saying self-instructions out loud to their covert use, feedback, and successive approximation, in which skills were gradually shaped. The group that received self-instructional training evidenced greater improvement on a number of measures such as the amount of "healthy talk" during an interview, compared with a control group. It should be noted, however, that to date, the generalization of the new skills to the natural environment has yet to be demonstrated and that some studies have been unable to replicate the positive effects found by Meichenbaum and Cameron (see, for example, Margolis and Shemberg, 1976).

One procedure used to help psychiatric patients to discriminate self-instructional behavior offers a detailed explanation of the influence of thoughts on behavior and of the importance of being aware of thoughts (Meyers, Mercatorius, and Artz, 1976). The importance of providing a rationale for procedures was discussed in Chapter Three. An interpersonal situation is then described by the counselor and both productive and dysfunctional thoughts are modeled. The client is then asked to monitor his thoughts while taking part in a series of intentionally vague tasks—for example, walking over to the door and back again. The client is then asked to rehearse a series of positive thoughts and to comment on what he feels, and then a series of negative thoughts, in order to point out the relationship between thoughts and physiological reactions. As a final step, the client monitors his thoughts at intervals in the natural environment. These intervals are cued by a timer set for random times or by initiating an interaction. The effectiveness of this procedure in actually altering behavior is not known as yet.

More appropriate problem-solving skills have also been developed by presenting clients with simulated situations and a range of possible solutions and consequences and increasing their skill in selecting options that will be maximally effective (Roosa, 1973). An example of a situation, along with possible options and consequences, is presented in Figure 43.

Increasing Appropriate Social Skills. With hospitalized patients, token economies have typically included a focus on increasing appropriate social behaviors by prompting and reinforcing these behaviors. Social skills training has been employed with both inpatients and outpatients. In this procedure, specific

Figure 43. Interpersonal Politics and Action:
Association (Neighborhood) Stress Training

Situation: You have been discharged from the hospital, are living with your
family, and are back at work. The neighborhood kids taunt you as
you come to and from work or are in your yard, calling you crazy
man, old nuts and bolts, dummy, and so on. You are becoming
increasingly uptight.

Options: 1. Decide to quit your job and stay in the house all the time.
2. Pick up a stick and go after the brats.
3. Yell and cuss out the kids.
4. Call the police.
5. Talk to your neighbors about the situation and how you feel
   and ask them to control their kids' behavior.
6. Accuse your neighbors of teaching their kids to call you names.
7. Call neighbors and threaten to beat up their kids.
8. Call neighbors and threaten to call police.
9. Tell the kids that this makes you feel bad and explain how you
   are *not* crazy.
10. Ask kids what they think a "crazy" person is and use this as a
    basis for open communication.
11. Continue to try and ignore the kids.
12. Move to another neighborhood.
13. Decide you have too many strikes against you to make any
    more effort of any kind.

Consequences: 1. Neighbors call police.
2. Neighbors are convinced you are crazy.
3. Kids picture of you as "crazy" is reinforced and their taunts
   increase.
4. Get in a fight with the kids.
5. Get in a fight with the parents.
6. Neighbors do nothing about kids'behavior.
7. Neighbors prevent kids from continuing to taunt you.
8. Continue to become more uptight.
9. Return to hospital.
10. Open up complete communication with kids and practice nego-
    tiating behaviors (I want—you want) through getting their feed-
    back.
11. Give kids a better understanding of how it hurts when one is
    made to feel different.
12. Go on welfare.
13. Wife divorces you.
14. Experience loss of money and inconvenience of moving.
15. Practice not dealing with a situation.
16. Experience a terminal case of PLOMITIS. [a joke]
17. Your family is convinced you are still crazy.
18. Alienate neighbors.
19. Gain neighbors respect.

Source: Roosa (1973, p. 5).

behaviors are identified to increase and decrease, and procedures such as model presentation, instructions, rehearsal, and feedback used to increase skills. Additional procedures for increasing appropriate social behaviors are described in Chapter Thirteen.

Obsessive-Compulsive Behavior

Although the presenting problems of obsessive thoughts and compulsive rituals make up only about 1 percent of the psychiatric inpatient and outpatient population, they are noteworthy for two reasons. First, they have been especially recalcitrant to traditional treatment efforts, and, second, they are quite disabling in terms of client distress. Obsessional thoughts include repetitive, intrusive, and frightening ideas, impulses, images, or beliefs. For example, one client seen by the author complained of persistent thoughts that he would "go crazy" and kill someone, and in order to avoid this possibility, he rarely went out of the house. Compulsive rituals involve repetitive motor acts such as checking or a high frequency of hand washing. Such behaviors are often so frequent that they interfere with appropriate behaviors. Those ritualistic behaviors are accompanied by severe psychological distress that is enhanced by the realization that the obsessions or compulsions "don't make sense." Most rituals reduce the client's distress (Hodgson and Rachman, 1972), although others may increase distress (Rosen, 1975). A wide variety of procedures have been employed to reduce obsessive-compulsive behavior, including thought stopping, modeling procedures, desensitization, implosion, symptom scheduling, reprograming significant others, and response prevention.

Response Prevention. Arranging exposure to the anxiety-provoking source followed by a prevention of compulsive rituals has been successful in decreasing such behavior. Such rituals are usually maintained by the removal or avoidance of aversive events, although one must always examine the possibility that they are partially maintained by attention from significant others. The first example illustrates the use of response prevention at home. The client, a forty-five-year-old policewoman engaged in washing and cleaning rituals whenever she came into contact with objects associated with death (Meyer, Robertson, and Tatlow, 1975). She was to be married in two weeks and wished to be rid of her symptoms prior to her wedding. She had not informed her husband-to-be of her symptoms. Assessment did not reveal any other problems or other factors that might be associated with the washing rituals. A tendency to be preoccupied by death-related events was first noticeable at the age of fifteen when her mother died. She developed ruminations that her mother had been buried alive and these thoughts had persisted for many months. When she was twenty-two, her father gave her a book that belonged to a deceased friend. She experienced an impulse to wash her hands after handling the book, because of its association with death. There were no further incidences of this theme until her father died eighteen years later. An unfortunate event occurred two weeks after his death in which she discovered the decomposing body of a neighbor who had died in the next apartment, and her concern with contamination spread to the communal areas of the building in which she lived. "Less than a year later, the wife of her fiancé-to-be died, and thereby he unwittingly became the carrier of contamination from all the things associated with her. Anxiety attacks and palpitations became an almost daily occurrence. Yet she stayed at work, managing to change all her clothes and handbag whenever she got in to work or went home at night. Time went by, and more and more things became potentially contaminated: newspaper articles of death or disaster, pictures of dead people; anything remotely concerned with death. She felt she could not marry in such a state, particularly with her fiancé involved in the symptoms, so she sought help urgently" (Meyer, Robertson, and Tatlow, 1975, p. 37).

Intervention consisted of thoroughly contaminating her by taking her to the hospital mortuary, where both she and the counselor handled a dead body, which was the top item on her hierarchy of contaminating events. She was encouraged not to wash following contamination. Additional items on her hierarchy were handled in a similar fashion and she resisted the urge to ritualize both during these hour-long sessions as well as after the counselor left, although she "temporarily became depressed and fearful." Generous praise was offered for her achievements. The remainder of the course of intervention is described in the following quote:

> At this stage her fiance unknowingly brought in a pile of highly "contaminated" groceries from his own house and left them in the kitchen. The patient could not touch them but called the therapist instead. Directed over the phone, she found she was able to unpack the groceries and distribute them around her kitchen, but relief only came when she had recontaminated the entire flat. Later she wrote, "That was much worse than the dead body."
>
> By the end of a week in treatment, her fiancé was brought into the picture (although his own contaminating presence was never fully explained to him). There were only five more days to the wedding and she was feeling very well—until she remembered the cupboard containing the suitcase of her father's personal things.
>
> Panic-stricken, she thought of concealing till after the wedding the "totally abhorrent" suitcase; but after some delay she plucked up the courage to phone the therapist. That evening the suitcase was opened and unpacked. Again, everything in the flat was contaminated by it, but it was three quarters of an hour before the patient ceased to tremble and settled down. On the evening of the twelfth day in treatment, she wrote "At last I'm beginning to feel pleased with myself." Next day she was married. [Meyer, Robertson, and Tatlow, 1975, p. 38]

Although she experienced tension from time to time, which was alleviated by offering her anxiety management skills, an eight-month follow-up revealed that the desire to ritualize was gone, although it was months before she stopped having "twinges" when touching certain things.

Symptom scheduling has also been employed to decrease ritualistic behavior in the home. For example, Gertz (1966) arranged set times for the rituals to be performed in the attempt to break the association between the "urge" to engage in the ritual and doing it. This was combined with graded task assignments in the home, which arranged exposure to the antecedents for the ritual. A checking ritual was successfully reduced by imposing increasing durations of relaxation immediately prior to ritual performance (Alban and Nay, 1976).

Intervention with compulsive clients is often carried out during a short stay (for example, one week) in the hospital, because response prevention can more easily be arranged in that setting. As Leitenberg (1976) notes, a cautious optimism can now be expressed in relation to altering obsessive-compulsive behavior. Components of successful intervention appear to be prevention of compulsive behavior, together with encouragement of approach to anxiety-arousing situations, objects, or thoughts that typically occasioned such rituals. Anticipation of a response prevention procedure appears to be more anxiety-provoking than the actual experience (Mills, Agras, Barlow, and Mills, 1973).

Less information exists concerning intervention with clients who have obsessive thoughts, although there are some case studies reporting use of thought stopping. A reasonable direction for such intervention to take would be training the client how to use positive self-instructions.

The Role of Significant Others. As with any presenting problem, the possible role of social reinforcement should be explored. If sources of social support are present and not attended to, there is no reason to expect response prevention to be effective. The latter procedure should be effective when the compulsive behavior is "magical" in nature, in that it is performed to remove some threatening event that is not actually a threat. The following example illustrates a situation involving social support from significant others that had to be attended to.

Mrs. A. was a forty-five-year-old woman who was married to a psychologist. They had a ten-year-old son. She presented a variety of unusual behaviors, including the following: completion of chores at home in time with covertly sung nursery rhymes, which was distracting, because she could only take action in relation to a chore on a certain beat of the song; standing all cigarette butts up in ashtrays; and being frozen between the kitchen and the living room if either her son or her husband was speaking. Also, any outside viewer would label Mrs. A. a compulsive talker. She would start talking to someone she knew by literally screaming at them from a distance as soon as she saw them, and would keep up a nonstop speech, forcing one to interrupt her in order to speak themselves. This nonstop speaking was also evidenced when she was interacting with her husband. Needless to say, the receptionist at the clinic did not look forward to Mrs. A.'s visits to the center.

Assessment information was gathered during interviews and at home. Initially her talking occurred at such a rate that in order to accomplish anything an agreement had to be made that she only had two minutes to speak and then the counselor would speak. A timer was employed to signal time periods. One significant item that emerged was that Mrs. A. did not appear to possess appropriate skills for gaining attention from her husband. He tended to go off by himself when at home. She said she had given up trying to engage him in conversation, because she was unsuccessful. He, in turn, said that, as she had come to talk more and more, he had avoided talking with her more and more. Thus one objective of intervention was to develop a repertoire of appropriate conversational skills, so that Mrs. A. could have conversations with her husband (and others) that they would mutually enjoy. This nonstop talking did not occur with her son. Mr. A. agreed that he would spend more time talking with his wife; however, conversations were to be ended if three minutes went by without Mr. A. saying something. Mrs. A. also felt stifled in the role of a housewife. She had no friends and rarely left the house. She said that she would like to have more friends and a program was initiated to increase her social contacts. Of course, the new conversational skills that she was developing were very important for achievement of this goal. Conversational skills were established through model presentation and role playing, as well as through assignments to observe how others converse as she started to increase her social contacts.

Negative practice was employed for the problem of walking from the kitchen to the living room. She was instructed that she was to imagine three times each day that her son and husband were talking loudly while she was in the doorway, and she was to walk back and forth through the doorway ten times on each occasion. No specific intervention was directed toward altering the nursery rhymes or standing up of cigarette butts. As her social contacts increased and mutually enjoyable conversational time with her husband increased, all rituals decreased. Intervention took place over a period of four months, with weekly visits and phone contact every other day to gather data concerning progress. Mrs. A.'s conversational behavior gradually changed during interviews from compulsive talking to conversational reciprocity. A one-year follow-up indicated that positive changes were maintained.

Melamed and Siegel (1975b) used a combination of operant reinforcement, disruption of the chain of compulsive behavior, systematic desensitization of related fears, and response prevention in a self-directed, in vivo exposure program. The intervention program was carried out at home by Mr. R., the sixty-three-year-old client, and his wife. Mr. R. had developed an extensive checking ritual, which was performed each evening prior to going to bed. This checking was time consuming and frustrating to Mr. R. and, in addition, it created conflict with his wife. It was his wife who sought help about this problem. The development of this checking behavior is described as follows.

> The compulsive checking began approximately nine months before the initial assessment interview. This behavior first occurred in reaction to a minor malfunction in the gas line. Despite reassurance from a repairman that the automatic shut-off valve would prevent any accidents, Mr. R.'s concern about a possible fire or explosion led him to engage in a ritualistic trip to the basement to check that the pilot light in the furnace was still on before he could go to sleep. In the course of the next few weeks, the checking behavior generalized to the entire house. He was spending more than three hours each evening checking such things as electrical appliances to make sure that they were turned off, wall sockets and wires to see if they were touching anything, windows and doors to make sure that they were locked, and ash trays to clean them of any cigarette ashes. He was also inspecting all cupboards in the house to make sure

that the pots and pans were so placed that they would not fall and make a loud noise that might frighten him. This generalized to any object which might fall òff a shelf or table.

Each evening, at approximately the same time, Mrs. R. would go to her bedroom and get ready for bed. Mr. R. would then begin his checking in a very systematic manner, examining each room in the house in the same order every night. Mrs. R. had to be in her bedroom before the checking could begin, because Mr. R. was afraid that she might use something after he had checked it or that she might leave her cigarettes burning in an ashtray that he had already cleaned. This behavior was extremely annoying to Mrs. R., and she refused his repeated requests to assist him in his checking.

Mr. R. was afraid to be home by himself, and was, therefore, very reluctant to let his wife go away and leave him home alone. Furthermore, he constantly checked on her while she worked in the basement on her hobbies to assure himself that nothing had happened to her. This behavior caused Mrs. R. to feel very restricted in her own activities. Mr. R. was also severely limited in his social activities. For example, each Sunday he would drive by himself to visit his sister who lived in another state. It took him more than three hours to drive there, but he would return home as soon as possible, often after only ten minutes visit, because he was concerned that something might happen to his wife while she was alone in the house. These fears and concerns resulted in Mr. R. becoming extremely withdrawn from social contacts. In addition, he became quite nervous, which necessitated his taking tranquillizers for about five months prior to therapy. The tranquillizers were prescribed by a psychiatrist with whom Mr. R. had had one therapy contact. In addition, the psychiatrist recommended hospitalization and insulin shock treatment, which Mr. R. rejected. [Melamed and Siegel, 1975b, p. 33]

Mr. R.'s occupation involved checking air brakes at railroad yards. It was thus important, as the authors note, to design

a program that would eliminate the problematic checking behavior, but that would not eliminate behavior necessary for his
job. During the first week, Mr. R. collected a baseline of duration of checking behavior with the help of a stop watch. He
recorded the time he spent checking each room in the house
and the time he started to check and ended checking. He was
also requested to note items that might function as a reinforcer
for him. Pleasant events had drastically decreased since he developed his ritual, including avoidance of reading newspapers or
watching television, "for fear of seeing something that might
upset him." Whereas the prebaseline estimate of duration of
checking behavior was three hours, self-monitoring revealed a
duration of about sixty-seven minutes. Mr. R. reported that he
had been trying to "beat his time" each evening.

Intervention was carried out over a period of fourteen
weeks. First a time limit for checking was agreed on that was
very close to his baseline. He agreed that he would complete
checking within sixty minutes and, if he succeeded, he would
receive a hug and kiss from his wife and could also work on a
crossword puzzle. Baseline revealed that he spent the least
amount of time checking the living room and he was asked to
drop this from his checking ritual. "His wife reported that on
the first night he succeeded they resumed sexual relations,
which had been suspended ten years previously" (Melamed and
Siegel, 1975b, p. 33). The first week, average duration of checking fell to forty-seven minutes; however, Mr. R. reported that it
was difficult for him to fall asleep. He was given training in relaxation and asked to practice this fifteen minutes each night
before falling asleep.

During the second week of intervention, Mr. R. was asked
to discontinue checking the bedroom since he had only been
spending five minutes on this, and now was to spend less than
fifty minutes completing checking. Reinforcements included
working on a crossword puzzle as well as a one-dollar reduction
in fee each day he succeeded in his goal. He was encouraged to
continue to practice relaxation after completing his checking
ritual. Average duration of checking fell to forty minutes the
second week of intervention.

The next week he was given a randomly arranged list of

the three rooms he still checked, and was asked to follow a different order each evening during his checking. Checking was conceptualized as a chain of behavior maintained by anxiety reduction, and arranging a new order of links in the chain was an attempt to disrupt the checking ritual further. However, it did not result in a decrease in the duration of checking; in fact, it increased his anxiety. He was asked to eliminate another room during the seventh and eighth weeks of intervention, and was asked to practice relaxation before as well as after checking, in an effort to decrease anticipatory anxiety. Duration of checking now decreased to about twenty minutes. A response prevention program was initiated in the ninth week, in which he would go to his bedroom at night with his wife, close the door, and remain there until the next morning without any checking. He was asked to try to do this at least once a week. Duration of checking now decreased to thirteen minutes.

Another problem addressed was Mr. R.'s fear of getting a needed hernia operation. Desensitization for his fears of hospitalization was initiated during Sessions 8 through 10. He entered the hospital for the operation the tenth week and remained for seven days. His inability to check while in the hospital had not caused him any discomfort. He continued the response prevention procedure at home during the next week, during which he was contacted by phone to obtain reports concerning duration of checking behavior. A final session was held the fourteenth week with Mr. and Mrs. R. Mr. R. indicated that he did not feel an urge to check and, because he no longer was subject to extreme anxiety, which on earlier occasions had been relieved through checking, he no longer took tranquilizers.

One-month and eight-month follow-ups were held, and at four months after intervention ended, Mr. R. contacted the counselor because of a concern about an urge to initiate checking. Response prevention was conducted for one week. The follow-up periods indicated that he no longer felt nervous when his wife left the house, was socializing more (which had started during the seventh week during intervention), still did not feel an urge to check, and had not resumed use of tranquilizers.

Without offering the client skills to decrease his anxiety (relaxation training) and without gradually eliminating components of the chain of checking behavior, it is unlikely that the response prevention procedure would have succeeded. Unlike the hospital situation, such prevention could not be assured. Only through the careful intervention planning reflected in this case example could the groundwork be laid by successful use of response prevention in the home setting. Operant consequences, both from his wife as well as from himself, were employed, to enhance the probability of achieving a decreasing checking time. Gradual elimination of components of the chain of behavior entailed an in vivo, graded exposure to the anxiety-producing situation. The successful use of instigations allowed the client to assume major responsibility for carrying out his program and, in so doing, to develop an increased sense of mastery over his environment, including his own internal environment, in terms of anxiety. "In the present study, the issue of self-control was particularly important since the client perceived the problem as basically a 'loss of his self-confidence' " (Melamed and Siegel, 1975b, p. 35).

Covert Modeling. Covert modeling, in which the client successfully imagines coping without performing the obsessive-compulsive behavior has also been employed to decrease such behaviors (Hay, Hay, and Nelson, 1977). This procedure was employed with a twenty-seven-year-old inpatient diagnosed as having an obsessive-compulsive personality, anxiety neurosis, and depressive neurosis. She had become preoccupied with cleanliness about six years before this hospital admission, changing her children's clothing at the slightest sign of dirt and continually cleaning her house. She began to be obsessed about the way she performed everyday activities such as turning off lights and opening and closing doors. Her current behavior revolved around checking lights and doors and a new obsession with being third and anxiety concerning the number 3. This behavior interfered with her life in that she could not ride a bus or in a car with only two other people, she would throw away the third item in a box, and she refused to carry three things. She firmly believed that if she failed to engage in these activities something terrible would happen to her. She was asked to record the frequency of checking lights, checking whether she had closed her door and behaviors concerned with the number 3. Covert modeling was applied to one behavior at a time, within a multi-ple-baseline design across behaviors. Scenes were presented by the counselor and the client was asked to imagine coping with urges to check that she had switched off the lights. Eight scenes were imagined during each session. All three behaviors de-creased substantially over the six weeks of intervention. The client reported that even when she now experienced an urge, she felt that she had the skills to cope with it. The multiple baseline suggested a relationship between door checking and light checking. For example, both decreased when covert mod-eling was applied to door checking after its application to light checking. One week after the last intervention session, the client was discharged. Three- and six-month follow-up contacts both with the client and her mother revealed a maintenance of posi-tive changes. She said that she did feel depressed at times be-cause of her inability to locate a job. Follow-up care should have included a job-finding program (Azrin, Flores, and Kaplan, 1975).

Hysterical Reactions

In hysterical reactions, there is a loss of sensory or motor function without any observable anatomical or neurological changes that may be related to the loss of function. This state has been viewed as the person's acquisition of a certain role that is supported by the social environment (Ullman and Krasner, 1969). Such behavior has also been viewed as a conditioned re-sponse that is later maintained by avoidance of anxiety (Liver-sedge and Sylvester, 1955). There are a few reports of the use of behavioral methods with such clients (see, for example, Wolpe, 1958; Brady and Lind, 1961; and Goldblatt and Munitz, 1976).

Summary

Some of the earliest applications of behavioral methods to clinical problems concerned clients with severe behavior dis-turbances, such as childhood autism, profound mental retarda-tion, and deficits requiring hospitalization. Shaping, model presentation, and the development of imitative behaviors have been effectively employed to develop new repertoires for autistic and mentally retarded children. Attention has been directed to increasing language skills, expanding self-care skills, and encouraging appropriate social interaction. Procedures have been developed to decrease severe self-destructive behaviors and self-stimulatory behaviors, such as repetitive rocking, which may be of such a high frequency as to interfere with reinforcement of appropriate behaviors. Overcorrection provides a relatively non-aversive procedure to decrease such behaviors and to develop more appropriate alternatives. Parent training programs have been developed both for autistic and retarded children. There is an extensive literature describing the use of behavioral procedures with clients labeled psychotic. Behavioral programs have been designed to increase appropriate social, self-care, and work skills, and to decrease inappropriate behaviors such as hallucinations and delusions. A variety of behavioral procedures has also been used to address obsessive-compulsive behavior, including response prevention, modeling, desensitization, implosion, and rearranging support from significant others. As in other areas, there has been an interest in the development of useful self-management skills such as problem-solving skills. For example, programs have been developed to teach chronic mental patients, as well as retarded children and adults, more effective problem-solving behavior. Behavioral programs employed with institutionalized populations and those developed to maintain positive behaviors when a client moves from the hospital to the community are discussed in Chapter Twenty-One.

20

Until recently, perhaps the majority of articles describing the application of behavioral methods to sexual disorders concerned sexual variations such as homosexuality, fetishism, exhibitionism, and transvestism, although articles could also be found describing the use of behavioral procedures with sexual dysfunctions such as men's failure to attain or maintain an erection and women's failure to attain orgasm (see, for example, Wolpe, 1958). The pioneering work of Masters and Johnson (1970) served as an impetus for increased application of behaviorally based procedures with problems of sexual dysfunction (see, for example, Annon, 1974; Lobitz and LoPiccolo, 1972). The Masters and Johnson framework was compatible with a social learning theory approach to sexual behavior, which emphasizes careful description and evaluation and rejects the

Sexual Behavior

ascription of pathological causes to sexual dysfunction. A social learning theory approach to sexual dysfunction emphasizes the role of incorrect information, skill deficits, and dysfunctional anxieties concerning sexual performance, or concerning what is considered proper sexual behavior. This approach differs substantially from a traditional psychoanalytic view, in which sexual problems are considered to be signs of underlying personality disorders. Differences exist concerning what is labeled a *disorder* and what is considered to be a sexual *variation,* even within the psychoanalytic ranks itself. The new willingness to discuss sexual behavior and the new recognition that women as well as men have sexual reactions have resulted in the development of programs for enhancing sexual responsiveness. This chapter presents an overview of assessment considerations and

923

intervention methods for nonorganically based sexual dysfunction and sexual variations, beginning with a brief discussion of the human sexual response.

The Sexual Response

The past reluctance to speak about and investigate the sexual response is highlighted by the care with which William Masters prepared for his own career in the study of the human sexual response and sexual dysfunction and its treatment. Anticipating the possibility of being discredited if he did not first establish a career in an accepted and regular line of medicine, he first devoted many years to this endeavor. It is amazing that only since 1966, with the publication of *The Human Sexual Response* (Masters and Johnson, 1966), have the public and the medical profession been privy to a scientific description of the human sexual response. A new era has been initiated with the publication of this book, an era in which more people discuss sex, more people are willing to seek counseling for further sexual fulfillment, and brief intervention procedures have been designed and made available, procedures that do not require a delving into pathological processes previously assumed to lie behind all forms of sexual dysfunction. Masters and Johnson (1966) describe the sexual response as a natural physiologic process consisting of two separate systems of influence that may compete for dominance in any sexual exposure, the biophysical system and its psychosocial counterpart. "Freedom to respond to direct biophysical-system demand requires only from its psychosocial counterpart that the female's [or male's] sexual value system not transmit signals that inhibit or defer the manner in which erotic arousal is generated" (Masters and Johnson, 1970, p. 221). In sexual dysfunction, this natural physiologic process is disregarded or interfered with through a lack of information or misinformation concerning sexual physiology and interpersonal communication processes. Failure to understand these processes results in fear of failure, which is considered to be a prime factor in sexual dysfunction. "These crippling tensions in the marital relationship are gross evidence that two people are contending with sexual functioning unwittingly drawn completely out of context as a natural physical function by their fears of performance" (Masters and Johnson, 1970, p. 12). "Fear of inadequacy is the greatest known deterrent to effective sexual functioning, simply because it so completely distracts the fearful individual from his or her natural responsivity by blocking reception of sexual stimuli either created by or reflected from the sexual partner" (Masters and Johnson, 1970, p. 13).

There is considerable evidence for the important role of learning in the development of sexual reactions to particular people, objects, or activities. The existence of wide cultural variations in the physical characteristics and accoutrements that elicit sexual reactions is but one evidence of the role of environmental factors. Investigations into the backgrounds of those who evidence sexual variations often reveal unusual social learning histories, such as Stoller's (1969) findings that transvestites were often initiated into cross-dressing by their mothers, who dressed them in girls' attire or rewarded them when they (the children) themselves put on girls' clothes. It is likely that the extent to which any particular person, object, or activity becomes related to sexual reactions is also influenced by the type of models that are available as one grows up, the extent to which repeated associations occur between certain objects or people and sexual reactions and the strength of these sexual reactions, and the extent to which sexual reactions are reinforced by significant others (Bandura, 1969). The studies illustrating that sexual reactions can be conditioned to previously neutral stimuli (neutral with respect to a sexual reaction) provide further evidence that sexual reactions can be developed through conditioning. For example, Rachman (1966) repeatedly associated a photograph of women's boots with slides of sexually stimulating nude females and found that subjects eventually exhibited sexual reactions to the boots alone. The possibility of altering patterns of sexual arousal through conditioning has been employed in a number of intervention programs described later in this chapter. Some writers have emphasized the role of sexual fantasies during masturbation in directing sexual reactions (see, for example, McGuire, Carlisle, and Young, 1965).

The role of learning is also highlighted by the repeated failure to find physiological differences between groups such as homosexual and heterosexual males. The importance of environmental factors does not imply that physical factors may not have a profound effect on the sexual response. For example, sexual reactivity may be decreased by alcohol or by drugs such as heroin. Diabetes mellitus may decrease potency in males. Ingestion of estrogen in males for treatment of carcinoma of the prostate can markedly decrease sexual interest (Schumacher and Lloyd, 1976). Certain types of oral contraceptives may decrease sexual interest in women. The possible influence of a variety of physical factors calls for a complete medical examination of the client, and a medical history, including diet and a description of any medications currently taken.

What Is a Sexual Problem?

There has been such a controversy concerning the behaviors to be encompassed by the term *sexual problem,* and such divergencies of opinion at different times, that this question needs to be addressed in its own right. For example, forty years ago, if a woman complained that she was unable to become aroused during intercourse with her husband, her complaint itself would probably cause her to be labeled a problem, because women were not supposed to have sexual reactions, let alone complain about their absence. Analytic theory assumed that only a few women could progress from the "infantile clitoral" orgasm to the "mature vaginal" orgasm. Interestingly enough, and consistent with the male view of sexuality espoused within psychoanalytic theory, no difference between two types of male orgasm were suggested; for example, a "tip" climax and a "full shaft" orgasm. Women's insistence on their own sexuality has resulted in many more women seeking counseling to attain greater sexual fulfillment.

Another controversy involves sexual variations—that is, the behaviors of individuals who are attracted to atypical objects or activity such as homosexuals, transvestites, and fetishists. Not too many years ago, there was relatively little disagreement in the professional literature that all individuals manifesting such behaviors were deviant and that these behaviors were signs of pathology. Only recently did the American Psychiatric Association (APA) declare that homosexuality is not necessarily a sign of mental illness, and call for psychiatrists to devote attention to removing some of the conditions that stigmatize homosexual persons. Even within the organization, there was a vocal minority that vehemently disagreed with the APA decision. The behavioral literature, until recently, has sidestepped the question of what is a sexual problem. Varied sexual behaviors, including homosexual behavior, have been targeted for change with little thought given to societal reactions to this behavior and the possible role of these reactions in the presenting problem and in the request for a change in sexual orientation. Recently, an eloquent argument has been made cautioning counselors against accepting a contract to alter homosexual behavior when in fact the client may be selecting this goal because of reactions of society to the behavior (see Davison, 1976). Even if we agree that the change is desired because of social pressure, what alternatives should be offered to the client? Marks (1976) argues that it is unethical to withhold intervention while waiting for society to become more enlightened. Certainly, however, the possible role of societal pressure on the individual's selection of desired outcome should be discussed with the client, and the client should be asked to rethink his desired outcome carefully. Is this something he or she would really like? Is it a change that *he* desires, not his parents or his brothers or sisters? Thus an important issue in the definition of a sexual problem is the question, To *whom* is it a problem? Is the problem only a problem to the client, or is it a problem to some significant other? And why is it a problem to this significant other? For example, is the significant other a parent who feels that the homosexual behavior of her son is sick and that he must receive counseling? Or is a person a significant other in the sense that she or he is forced to participate against his or her will, as in rape and child molestation? Such questions lead readily to the distinction between victimless and victim-present interactions. In the case of rapists, pedophiliacs, and sadists, a victim is clearly present (we are disregarding, for the purposes of this discussion, the occasional complicity of the victim in his or her own victimization). This distinction is highlighted later in this chapter by the separate discussions of sexual variations involving consenting parties and those in which nonconsenting parties are involved. Ethical issues related to selection of desired outcomes are discussed further in Chapter Twenty-Two.

Assessment

A presenting problem of sexual dysfunction must be viewed within the context in which it occurs, namely the client's existence, environmental, physical, and cognitive, at a particular time. Important factors to consider include interpersonal relationships, especially those with a sexual partner (or partners), if there is a partner; feelings and attitudes concerning sexual behaviors; and interpersonal skills that are typically required to develop a relationship with a potential sexual partner. It is assumed that "there is no such thing as an uninvolved partner" (Masters and Johnson, 1970, p. 2). In addition, possible sensitizing factors must be explored, such as poor diet, fatigue from overwork, selection of distracting environments for attempted sexual interactions, poor health, and alcohol problems. The possible role of physical factors, either as direct causes of a sexual problem or as sensitizing factors, should be checked out, by requiring the client to seek a complete physical examination, as well as by gathering relevant information within the behavioral interview.

Information gained from a review of the past history of the client may offer important information concerning the source of interfering sexual attitudes as well as of unusual sexual patterns or the reasons for interfering anxiety reactions. Life history information can be gained from the Life History Questionnaire developed by Wolpe and Lazarus (1966). During assessment, a specific description of the presenting complaint is obtained, including its development and an identification of related factors. As with any presenting problem, information is collected concerning behavior deficits, assets and surfeits, available self-control skills, potential significant others and reinforcers, and health and other factors that may be related to problematic behaviors. Labels are carefully avoided. Careful attention is devoted to the possible role of thoughts and feelings, to misconceptions the client may have, to erroneous expectations concerning sexual behavior. Masters and Johnson (1970) stress the importance of determining the client's sexual value system, because if an attempt is made to increase sexual behaviors that conflict with this value system, the result will be failure (see Masters and Johnson [1966] for a detailed discussion of their assessment procedures). During assessment, the client is asked to share his or her expectations of intervention—Exactly what does he or she hope to gain?

One important decision that must be made as a result of assessment, as with any presenting problem, is the complexity of the intervention procedure that will be required to alter the problem. This is fully described in Annon's (1974) recent book, *The Behavioral Treatment of Sexual Dysfunction*, where Annon points out that there are some sexual problems that can be alleviated by giving permission (essentially, indicating that it is OK for the person to be engaging in certain feelings, thoughts, or behaviors); some that can be solved by giving information; some that will respond to brief intervention; and other problems that require more complex intervention procedures, because of related behavior deficits, surfeits, emotions, or attitudes. This is an important distinction to make, not only to ensure that clients with more complex problems receive intervention programs suited for them, but also to ensure that a problem that can be altered by a rapid procedure is not addressed by an expensive and time-consuming program.

The assessment of deviant sexual patterns may require a complete assessment of four components: the extent of deviant arousal, the amount of heterosexual arousal, the adequacy of heterosexual social skills, and the appropriateness of gender role behavior (Abel, 1976). Assessment in all these areas is not only required when a deviant arousal pattern is initially presented, but may also yield important information when other presenting problems occur, such as failure of a single male to have successful sexual encounters with women. Let us say that a male complains that he has difficulty in his sexual interactions with women. Assessment might reveal that he experiences just moderate arousal to heterosexual stimuli; that he is also aroused by homosexual stimuli; that he is sorely lacking in heterosexual social skills; and that he displays inappropriate feminine gender role behaviors, which result in his being turned down by women when he asks them out for dates.

Sources of information employed in the assessment of sexual problems include self-report questionnaires and inventories, self-monitoring, observation of related behaviors (such as heterosexual skills involved in establishing social contacts), physiological measures, and behavioral interviewing. As with assessment related to other problem areas, multiple measures should be employed, if possible, and the concordance between them examined for possible discrepancies, in order to attain as accurate a picture as possible of the presenting problem and related factors. Specific sources of information related to sexual problems are described in the following sections. It is assumed that additional sources concerned with related problem areas would be included as needed. For example, if further information was needed concerning possible reinforcing events for a client, the client may be requested to complete the Pleasant Events Schedule (MacPhillamy and Lewinsohn, 1972), or, if a client indicated a lack of assertive behavior that might be related to the presenting problem, he might be asked to complete the Assertion Inventory (Gambrill and Richey, 1975) to attain an overview of discomfort and response probability in relation to a variety of social situations. Situations in which discomfort was indicated could then be further specified via other measures such as behavioral interviewing, role playing, or self-monitoring.

Self-Report Questionnaires and Inventories. A variety of self-report questionnaires and inventories have been developed to obtain information related to the assessment of sexual problems. It is helpful to have the client complete some of these prior to the first interview.

Sexual adjustment inventory. The Sexual Adjustment Inventory (Stuart, Stuart, Maurice, and Szasz, 1975) is a precounseling inventory developed to obtain information concerning physical health; personal, marital, and family difficulties; birth control methods employed; frequency of and satisfaction obtained during sexual activities; sexual functioning; masturbation; decision making; communication; and moods and attitudes. This inventory is based on the assumptions that sexual behavior is learned; that it is more effective to concentrate on strengthening desirable sexual activities than to concentrate on eliminating undesirable behavior; and that learning to communicate and to modify rules of sexual behavior is critical to increasing sexual pleasure between two people. As with other precounseling inventories, this provides the advantage of offering relevant information to review prior to the first interview, and helps clients to start attending to relevant areas such as behaviors to increase and to the joint involvement of both parties in the counseling process. Additional information concerning the marital relationship can be gained by also having a couple complete the Marital Precounseling Inventory (Stuart and Stuart, 1972), which is described in Chapter Ten. The Sexual Response Profile (Pion, 1975) described next may also be employed as a preinterview questionnaire.

Sexual response profile. The Sexual Response Profile is an eighty-item questionnaire that requests the client to offer information concerning knowledge and attitudes about past and current sexual behavior (Pion, 1975). Questions are included as to parental attitudes about the client's sexual activity; sexual information obtained from parents; dating history; situations the client thinks influence sexual activity, such as health, lack of privacy, interest in another person, pregnancy, type of contraception employed if any (condom, pill, intrauterine device [IUD], foam, diaphragm, rhythm method, surgical method, or no method); aspects of sexual experience that the client would like to change; and items employed to enhance sexual arousal such as fantasies, movies, books, music, cologne, alcohol, drugs, or physical contact. This inventory is especially suitable for heterosexual couples.

Sexual pleasure inventory. The Sexual Pleasure Inventory consists of 140 items designed to assess degree of arousal a client associates with sexual activities and experiences. Two versions have been designed, one for men and one for women, each of which contains almost identical items (Annon, 1975d, 1975e). The client notes how pleasurable each item is (or would be if he has not experienced it) on a five-point Likert scale ranging from "not at all" to "very much." Illustrative items from the version for females include contact of tongues while kissing a male, experiencing a male's erection while he dances with the respondent, a female asking the respondent to her house, and having a male flirt with the respondent. Items from the male version include biting a female, wife swapping, seeing the genitals of a female, and using sexual words. As illustrated by these examples, inquiry is made concerning possible arousal value of same-sex persons as well as opposite-sex persons. Items are included in four broad areas, including general items, such as nude art or exotic dancers; items that involve the client personally, such as being seen in the nude or talking about sex; items related to social relationships, such as calling a woman on the phone or a male smiling at the respondent; and items related to physical contact, such as engaging in sexual intercourse. An overall score, as well as scores in each of these four areas, can be derived by summing the client's reactions in each. This inventory is valuable for identifying positive sexual activities and experiences, and can also be employed as one index of degree of change of emotional reactions. For example, if one goal of intervention is to increase arousal to members of the opposite sex, one could compare the arousal value of related items before and after intervention.

Sexual fear inventory. Items included in the Sexual Pleasure Inventory are employed to assess relative degree of fear or unpleasant feelings a client may have to activities and experiences related to sex (Annon, 1975b, 1975c). Each item is rated in terms of the degree of fear or anxiety each would elicit. On the front of the questionnaire, the client is cautioned that it is not necessary for him to have experienced each situation and to react to each item in terms of how he would expect to react if he were confronted with the situation. This inventory can be employed to identify sexual stimuli that cause anxiety, and, as with the Sexual Pleasure Inventory, can be employed as one index to evaluate change after intervention. Both of these scales can be referred to during behavioral interviewing to gather more detailed information in relation to items of import. A comparison can also be made of the fear-pleasure ratings for the same items.

Heterosexual behavior inventory (male and female versions). The Heterosexual Behavior inventory consists of seventy-seven items that assess the range of a client's sexual repertoire and the frequency with which he or she engages in specific sexual behaviors either with a heterosexual partner or alone (Robinson and Annon, 1975c, 1975d). The client is asked to indicate for each activity when he or she has engaged in the activity ("not at all," "one to three times," "four to ten times" or "eleven or more times"), and also to indicate whether he or she engages in the activity on a regular basis. If the client does not currently have a partner, he is asked to complete the questionnaire on the basis of his experiences with his last partner, or if there is more than one current partner, to complete items in terms of the partner with whom the greatest frequency of contact occurs. Unfortunately, this inventory does not request information indicating when experiences have occurred. For example, a woman might have used a vibrator on her partner's testicles (one item on the female version of this inventory) five years ago or a week ago. Also, no definition of the phrase "on a regular basis" is given. Therefore, information that is more specific should be gathered during interviews with the client. Seventeen of the items concern the use of vibrators on various body parts, and twenty-seven items concern solitary sexual activities. Changes in summary scores can be employed as an index of change. Annon (1975a) reports that this inventory is helpful in work with heterosexual couples, because comparison of the responses to inventory items often suggests areas for further discussion. The counselor and clients find that this inventory, together with the Heterosexual Attitude Scale, is useful in making decisions concerning the ordering and selection of appropriate intervention procedures.

Heterosexual attitude scale. The Heterosexual Attitude Scale is identical to the Heterosexual Behavior Scale, except that the client responds in terms of his or her attitude concerning each item on a Likert scale ranging from "dislike very much," "much," or "some," to "like some," "much," and "very much" (Robinson and Annon, 1975a, 1975b). This scale can help to identify experiences and activities that may cause positive or negative reactions, and changes in ratings can be employed to assess the extent to which items yield different self-reported arousal values following intervention. As with the Heterosexual Behavior Inventory, a comparison of the answers of each client can help to identify areas for further discussion. Answers to this inventory can also help in the ordering and selection of intervention procedures. For example, if a couple wishes to increase the variety of sexual behaviors engaged in as a couple, items can first be selected that are reported as relatively positive.

Sexual interaction inventory. The Sexual Interaction Inventory (LoPiccolo and Steger, 1974) permits the determination of scores in a number of areas, including frequency of satisfaction of the male, self-acceptance of the male, mean pleasure by the male, perceptual accuracy by the male of the female, and mate acceptance (male of female). Similar scores are obtained for the female, and a total disagreement score can be determined. Scores on these scales can readily be plotted, and can be employed as one measurement of progress by comparing scores before intervention with scores following change efforts.

Card sorts. The arousal value of specific sexual activities can be indexed by requesting the client to sort cards, each of which describes a particular activity or event, into categories, depending on its arousal value. Individually tailored card sorts have been employed as one source of information in the assessment of deviant sexual arousal. Brief phrases, developed from the client's descriptions of erotic and sexually variant experiences he either has had or would like to have, are written down on individual index cards. Examples of phrases developed for an exhibitionist included: "I have an erection; I'm masturbating in front of an attractive twelve-year-old girl; she's fascinated by my penis," and "It's in the afternoon; the two girls on the motor scooter are looking at my penis; they are really excited" (Abel, 1976, p. 440). Each phrase is rated on a seven-point scale: −3 indicating that the phrase was sexually repulsive, 0 neutral, +3 highly sexually arousing, with −2, −1, and +1, +2 falling between. The total arousal value of scenes can be tabulated each day to provide an ongoing indication of arousal value. Graphing of this information provides a clear display of any changes that may occur (see Figure 16 in Chapter Eight).

Self-Monitoring. The client may be requested to monitor relevant behaviors, such as the frequency of certain types of arousal or the frequency of specific behaviors. A person seeking treatment for exhibitionism may be requested to keep track of the number of times each day he has an urge to expose himself. Conditions related to this urge may also be noted, to try to identify related antecedent and consequent factors. This information may be employed in scene descriptions in covert conditioning procedures, in which detailed descriptions of actual events are required. In Abel's (1976) program, clients are asked to record how often fantasies of exposing himself occur and how often the client actually does expose himself. This information is to be recorded three times a day—at lunch, dinner, and at bedtime—to help identify the high-frequency behaviors to be decreased. Requesting the client to note thoughts related to such urges and to actual behavior is very important, as thoughts may play a critical role in occasioning behaviors to be decreased or in interfering with behaviors to be increased. Considerable data support the finding that such internal cues play an important role in deviant arousal patterns (Abel and Blanchard, 1974).

Data gathered by the client in the natural environment can help to identify the referents of problems that he has difficulty describing. Annon (1975a) reports an example of a client who wished to alter his sexual orientation from homosexual to heterosexual, and who was unable to specify what he meant by the term *homosexual* in relation to himself. He was asked to record in a notebook the surrounding circumstances when he applied the label *homosexual* to himself. This procedure helped to identify the specific behaviors and occasions related to self-labeling, including failure to be aroused when meeting an attractive woman, an increase in the pitch of his voice when talking with other men, and acquiescing to the demands of other men. With this information, possible alternative behaviors to be increased in each situation could be more readily identified.

In their program to increase sexual functioning, Lobitz

and LoPiccolo (1972) require clients to complete a daily record form on which they note any sexual activity that occurred, including its duration, a rating of the degree of pleasure and arousal experienced, and any other subjective remarks about the activity. Each client also records the amount of pleasure and arousal that the partner was perceived to feel.

Physiological Measures. Physiological devices have been developed that can accurately record sexual arousal in males (see, for example, Barlow, Becker, Leitenberg, and Agras, 1970) and in females (see Sintchak and Geer, in press). Direct calibration of penile erection can be recorded by a penile transducer, which encircles the penis and gives off a signal when erection occurs. A pen records the presence of this signal on a polygraph. One such transducer is available from the Farrell Instrument Company, P.O. Box 1037, Grand Island, NE 68801. "By comparing partial erection measures to those recordings obtained during full erection, the client's physiologic erection during sexual stimulus presentation can be quantified as percent of a full erection" (Abel, 1976, p. 441). Physiological measures have been most frequently employed during the treatment of sexual deviation. As noted by Abel (1976), a number of decisions must be made when measuring physiological sexual arousal to stimuli, including the mode of stimulus presentation, what content will be displayed, and the instructional set given to the client. A variety of stimulus modes have been employed to present stimuli, including videotape clips, movies, slides, audiotape, written descriptions, and having the client fantasize experiences. Brief (two-minute) video clips are the most effective in generating erections in homosexuals, voyeurs, pedophiliacs, exhibitionists, sadists, and rapists. Content should be carefully selected to correspond as closely as possible to environmental factors, people, and behaviors that, according to the client's report, are most erotic. Video clips are available for some sexual behaviors such as male homosexuality (Farrell Instrument Company); however, descriptions must often be tailor-made and recorded on audiotape, or fantasy employed. A check on events imagined can be made by asking the client to describe his fantasy out loud.

Verbal reports of arousal may not match physiological arousal. For example, Abel, Blanchard, Barlow, and Mavissakalian (1975) reported a case where a client reported a fetish for woman's sandals. "Using audiotape descriptions, the authors isolated sandal cues only. When such stimuli were presented, however, the client developed minimal physiological arousal. Assuming that the client's arousal must be in some way related to sandals, another audio description was developed to isolate cues specific to a woman's foot, devoid of sandal references. Contrary to the client's verbal report, foot stimuli generated marked erections" (Abel, 1976, p. 442). Abel (1976) also reports instances where men with deviant arousal patterns who reported a lack of heterosexual arousal in fact evidenced such arousal when the proper events were located. Thus verbal report alone is often insufficient to identify arousal patterns. A complete assessment of deviant arousal patterns calls for reviewing information from self-report, physiologic, and motor response sources.

The fact that voluntary control can be exerted over sexual reactions (see, for example, Henson and Rubin, 1971) suggests the importance of the client's motivation in participating in treatment efforts. As Abel suggests, greater credibility should be given to positive erection measures, because suppressing sexual reactions is easier than generating false reactions (see Henson and Rubin, 1971). Ideally, in cases where the presenting problem is one of arousal to atypical stimuli, erection measures should be obtained on the client's arousal to deviant cues, as well as to his ability to suppress arousal to such cues. "Erection measures under both instructional sets allows the therapist to judge the client's ability to voluntarily influence the objectivity of such measures, and thus the therapist has a better understanding of the validity of the erection measures he is relying on" (Abel, 1976, p. 443).

Abel (1976) cautions the counselor concerning selection of content that may only appear to be nondeviant. For example, video clips of a seductive single girl, two lesbians, a heterosexual couple, and a male homosexual couple engaged in genital activity were shown to strictly heterosexual and strictly homosexual males (Mavissakalian, Blanchard, Abel, and Barlow, 1975). The latter group reacted to the heterosexual couple scenes by imagining sexual interaction with the male participant. Thus given groups may respond to specific content in unique ways. Abel also stresses the value of assessing a client's arousal to types of women he is most likely to meet rather than to types of women he is unlikely to encounter. Physiological measures may also be employed to assess the client's anxiety during role plays, although counselor observation and self-report of subjective anxiety may offer sufficient information. The client should be requested to identify the specific events associated with his anxiety reaction.

The Behavioral Interview. The behavioral interview is a critically important component in gathering assessment information related to sexual dysfunction and sexual variations, as it is with other presenting problems. Components of such interviews have been described in detail (see, for example, Masters and Johnson, 1966; Annon, 1974). Perhaps in no other area is it so important to maintain a nonjudgmental stance as when discussing sexual matters. Clients are typically not accustomed to discussing their sexual life even with their own partners—which may be one of the prime reasons a sexual problem exists. Any hint of judgment may seriously interfere with the sharing of needed information and will certainly limit the extent to which a model of objectivity and comfort when discussing sex can be presented to the clients, a model that will encourage their own mutual sharing of sexual attitudes, fears, and experiences. Masters and Johnson (1970) consider constructive communication between a couple to be the most important factor to increase, so that the partners learn to share with each other and to understand each other's needs and interests. The concern with the privacy of material and the value of having an advocate of the same sex have led some counselors to stress the importance of having dual-sex counseling teams, in which, after an initial meeting with all four persons, separate interviews are held by the female counselor with the female client and by the male counselor with the male client, to obtain the partners' separate versions of their sexual problem and their sexual histories. An advantage of separate interviews is to obtain from each partner, uninfluenced by the other, their perception and description of the sexual problem and related factors. Discrepancies between the two accounts provide valuable information concerning areas that may have to be addressed during counseling. Dual-sex counseling teams are, however, not necessary for effective treatment nor are client dyads (see, for example, Lazarus, 1974; Kaplan, 1974). Separate interviews can still be held to gather relevant information from each participant.

Within the behavioral interview, appropriate communication skills are modeled for the client: readiness to share information concerning sexual activities and comfort when discussing sexuality. The counselor may offer relevant information concerning his own sexual history, to help normalize the client's feelings and encourage sharing of information (the case example of Mr. and Mrs. T., described later in this chapter, offers some examples of such sharing). Another important aspect of this modeling is sharing feelings as well as descriptions of behavior, because a person's sexual value system is such an important aspect of sexual reactions. The objectivity with which sexual behaviors and attitudes and related factors are discussed offers a model for the clients. "When the partners in the sexually inadequate relationship can see themselves as they have permitted the cotherapists to see them, when they can have their rationales for sexual failure and their prejudices, misconceptions, and misunderstandings of natural sexual functioning exposed with nonjudgmental objectivity and explained in understandable terms with subjective comfort, a firm basis for mutual security in sexual expression is established" (Masters and Johnson, 1966, p. 62). The behavioral interview also provides a recurring opportunity to focus on the relationship between the partners (assuming that two partners are involved) rather than to locate the source of the problem in one partner or the other.

If two partners are involved and if separate interviews are held with each, during which sexual histories are obtained, at the end of the discussion the counselor should ask whether the client wishes *not* to share any particular information with the partner, in such areas as extramarital sexual experiences, abortion, or incest. Any material so identified must of course not be shared with the other partner without the client's permission. Masters and Johnson stress the importance of having a minimum of privileged information in terms of the desired outcomes of their rapid-treatment form of therapy, which "is so dependent upon partner exchange of vulnerabilities that continuation of therapeutic procedures depends largely upon identification of stable elements in the marital relationship sufficient to support professional circumnavigation of the inadmissable evidence" (Masters and Johnson, 1970, p. 63).

The client usually has a conceptualization of his problem that is not helpful, in that it may be unduly pathologizing and has not led to helpful change. The client's concept of the cause of his problem and its maintenance is determined by the counselor during assessment as is a description of past efforts to alter the problem. As with other presenting problems, an important aspect of the interaction between the client and the counselor is forming a more helpful conceptualization of the problem. A social learning perspective of the problem is nurtured. Examples gathered from the client's history are employed to point out the role of learning variables in his or her own history. For example, one woman who sought treatment (from the author of this book) because she could only become aroused when physically hurt by her partner revealed a past history of receiving money from her brother when she was a small girl in exchange for allowing him to whip her with a light willow branch. This had continued into early adolescence and she described these occasions as acquiring a sexual atmosphere. Another client, a forty-year-old male reported great anxiety when he considered the possibility of sexual activity with a woman. He had grown up in a home in which his mother took repeated opportunities to warn him of the possible danger of venereal disease, of how debilitating such diseases could be, and of how to avoid this possibility through abstinence. A focus on the relationship between partners is also emphasized, and the clients are steered away from blaming physical problems or isolating one interactant as the source of the problem.

Information shared with the counselor through verbal report and self-report inventories will indicate the language system the client employs when discussing sexual behaviors, attitudes, and feelings. If this language system is comfortable for the counselor, it can be employed. The main criterion to employ in selection of language is to use terms that will enhance client comfort and that offer explicit information.

Especially difficult problems are posed when gathering self-report information about variant sexual behavior. As Abel notes, obtaining such information "is usually hampered by both client and therapist characteristics." The client may feel both' ashamed and guilty regarding his behavior and may fear ridicule or admonishment from the counselor, even though reassurance has been provided. In instances where rape or pedophilia are involved, strong attitudes against such acts may be held by the counselor. If these attitudes interfere with the counselor's objectivity, the client should be referred "to a therapist whose personal attitudes will allow a more accurate assessment" (Abel, 1976, p. 439).

As with normative sexual behaviors, it is critical to obtain a complete description of exactly what variant behaviors occur, as well as associated environmental and cognitive factors. If an intervention procedure is to be employed, using imagery procedures in which scenes are recreated in the imagination, it is important to have at hand the client's own words and descriptions of his actions, feelings, and thoughts. Abel suggests that comfort and ease of the counselor with the descriptive words of the client may be increased by using the client's own language when obtaining information. As the exhibitionist says, " 'And as I come up to her, I pull my zipper down, pull it out, and flash her,' the therapist responds, 'So then you pull it out and flash her, and then what do you do?' " (Abel, 1976, p. 439). As Abel notes, it is important to identify the entire chain of behaviors, thoughts, and feelings that precede and follow the variant sexual behavior, because usually intervention will address all of these factors. As when describing any problem, the client may have to be slowed down and asked to describe the situation in greater detail, including related thoughts and feelings, as in the following interchange.

> *Therapist:* "Well, what exactly occurred the day you were arrested?"
> *Exhibitionist:* "Not much, I just found a girl and exposed myself."
> *Therapist:* "Tell me how you got to that final point of exposing yourself. What happened each step of the way?"

Exhibitionist: "Well, it started when I blew up at my wife. I got in the car and just planned to drive around a little. Then, I started looking for college girls, you know, short dresses. I really wasn't thinking about exposing myself. Then, I saw this real sharp one and young, so I slowed down to look. Then, I started thinking about exposing myself, and I circled the block and parked the car in front of her, like I usually do, and leaned over towards the sidewalk side of the car — — —." [Abel, 1976, p. 440]

This account indicates antecedent factors related to the exposure incident that will probably have to be addressed, including improving the client's marital relationship, interfering with his avoidance of his wife after fights and his solitary rides in his car, and decreasing his looking at attractive girls. As Abel (1976) notes, even though he perceives no urge to expose himself during these events, they are components of a chain of behavior leading to exposure.

Intervention

One way of conceptualizing sexual problems is in terms of the procedure that would most readily (within the least amount of time) be effective in enhancing sexual functioning. Annon (1974) has proposed a list of procedures that includes permission giving, offering limited information, brief intervention, and intensive intervention.

Giving Permission. Some clients have a concern that thoughts or feelings they have or behaviors they engage in are abnormal, wrong, or bad. They may experience sexual arousal related to what they consider to be an inappropriate stimulus, such as someone of the same sex, and therefore label themselves *homosexual.* Offering permission entails letting them know that having occasional thoughts and feelings of this nature is not unusual, that it happens with many people, and that it in no way indicates that one will become committed to a homosexual life-style. Such reassurance that the client is normal and offering permission to continue what has been happening is in some instances enough to allay a client's concern (Annon, 1974).

Clients may also have anxieties in relation to specific behaviors. They may, for example, consider that oral-genital sexual contacts are unusual, bad, or wrong and feel a conflict between their guilt about engaging in this type of contact and the pleasure derived from this. Here too, offering permission for this behavior as well as offering limited information concerning the statistical frequency of this behavior may allay their concerns. Permission not to engage in certain behaviors may be helpful when there is pressure on a client to perform in a way that she or he does not desire to; for example, a husband may place pressure on his partner to become multiorgasmic when his wife has no interest in being so. Or a couple may read that the average frequency of intercourse is three times a week and feel they are abnormal because their frequency is once a week, even though both are happy with this frequency.

It is obvious that permission giving has its limits. It is limited to private thoughts or feelings of a nondangerous nature and to interaction between consenting adults. One would certainly not employ this approach with a thought, feeling, or behavior that could be potentially dangerous or unpleasant to someone, such as fantasies of raping women, because there does seem to be a relationship between content of sexual fantasies and situations that assume sexually arousing qualities. If, while masturbating, a male consistently fantasizes inflicting injury on a woman, this situation may acquire sexually arousing properties. Offering permission is also bounded by the counselor's theoretical orientation, the range of available information concerning what is usual and unusual, and perhaps his or her own sexual value system.

Offering Limited Information. A second level of intervention entails providing the client with information related to a sexual concern. Sexual dysfunction may be related simply to a lack of knowledge concerning how to arouse one's partner or a lack of knowledge concerning the normality of certain practices that are currently inducing guilt and so interfering with sexual performance. Unrealistic expectations may be present regarding sexual function. It is very important to distinguish between such cases and those cases where more intensive intervention other than permission giving and information giving is necessary. One area of common sexual concerns relates to genital size. A male, for example, may be concerned that his penis is too short or a woman may be concerned that her breasts are unusually small. Information concerning the variability of genital size may be provided in relation to concerns in this area, as well as information concerning the lack of correlation between genital size and sexual performance (Masters and Johnson, 1966). A woman who believes that she is inadequate because she is not experiencing vaginal orgasms can be informed about the actual site of orgasms. Verbal discussion of such information between the client and counselor can be complemented, if appropriate, by textual readings.

Another area of concern relates to sexual behavior. A married male may believe that he is abnormal because he masturbates occasionally, even though he and his partner describe their sexual interaction as very positive. He can be informed that 70 percent of married college graduates masturbate occasionally and that two out of five married men who are in their late twenties and thirties masturbate an average of six times a year (Kinsey, Pomeroy, and Martin, 1948). Three out of ten wives who are between the same ages masturbate an average rate of ten times a year (Kinsey, Pomeroy, and Martin, 1953). Masturbation ranks first as the most effective means of reaching orgasm for women (Masters and Johnson, 1966). Other common areas of client concern include sexual intercourse during menstruation and oral-genital contact.

Annon (1974) wisely cautions the counselor not to offer statistical information until one knows the client's specific frequency of a certain behavior. Telling a man that 75 percent of men reach ejaculation within two minutes after vaginal entry may reassure a male who takes four or five minutes but may be quite discouraging to a male who takes five seconds. He also stresses the importance of offering *limited* information that directly concerns the client's problem. Tendency to share with clients all that one knows must be securely held in check, because this may only confuse the client and dilute the importance of crucial information. As when offering information related to any other presenting problems, the language employed should be suitable for the particular client. Completion of assessment inventories may help to establish acceptable terms.

Brief Intervention. Assessment may reveal that more intervention is necessary than permission giving and the provision of limited information, but that this intervention can be accomplished in a relatively brief period of time. For example, the rapid intervention procedure developed by Masters and Johnson (1970) for sexual dysfunction takes place over a period of two weeks, during which the couple attends daily conferences with the cotherapists and carries out daily homework assignments. This program requires the couple to free two weeks of their time. Because this is difficult for many couples to manage, other formats for this treatment are used that do not require such an intensive commitment from the couple. Masters and Johnson (1970) also recommend the use of a therapy team comprised of a suitably trained man and woman so that each partner will have someone of his or her own sex to support and empathize with his or her position.

Brief intervention is possible when sexual dysfunction is uncomplicated by other factors, such as severe marital discord, a drug or alcohol problem, or depression. In the latter instances, a more lengthy intervention process will be required in which these additional problems are also addressed. In the remainder of this chapter, sexual dysfunction is first discussed, followed by an overview of behavioral procedures employed with sexual variations.

Increasing Sexual Functioning

The term *sexual dysfunction* includes a variety of sexual inadequacies. Masters and Johnson (1970), for example, identify four major types of sexual inadequacy in the male, including premature ejaculation, ejaculatory incompetence, primary impotence, and secondary impotence. Their definition of a premature ejaculator is a man who "cannot control his ejaculatory process for a sufficient length of time during intravaginal containment to satisfy his partner in at least 50 percent of their coital connections. If the female partner is persistently non-orgasmic for reasons other than the rapidity of the male's ejaculatory process, there is no validity to the definition" (Masters and Johnson, 1970, p. 92). Ejaculatory incompetence is defined as the inability to ejaculate during intravaginal containment (p.

116). Third, "the primarily impotent man arbitrarily has been defined as a male never able to achieve and/or maintain an erection quality sufficient to accomplish coital connection. . . . No man is considered primarily impotent if he has been successful in any attempt at intromission in either heterosexual or homosexual opportunity" (Masters and Johnson, 1970, p. 137). For the term *secondary impotence* to be correctly employed, there must have been at least one instance of successful intromission. The usual pattern is scores or thousands of episodes of successful coital connection followed by failure, often due to fatigue, distraction, or too much alcohol consumption, followed by the establishment of a pattern of erective failure.

The term *primary orgasmic dysfunction* refers to a woman who reports "lack of orgasmic attainment during her entire lifespan" (Masters and Johnson, 1970, p. 227), during all attempts, by whatever means. This is contrasted with *situational orgasmic dysfunction,* in which a woman has experienced "at least one instance of orgasmic expression, regardless of whether it was induced by self or by partner manipulation, developed during vaginal or rectal coital connection, or stimulated by oral-genital exchange" (Masters and Johnson, 1970, p. 240). Vaginismus entails a constriction of the vaginal outlet that makes penile penetration impossible. Masters and Johnson (1970) emphasize the importance of a pelvic examination in diagnosing this state of affairs. "Anatomically this clinical entity involves all components of the pelvic musculature investing the perineum and outer third of the vagina. Physiologically, these muscle groups contract spastically as opposed to their rhythmic contractual response to orgasmic experience. This spastic contraction of the vaginal outlet is a completely involuntary reflex stimulated by imagined, anticipated, or real attempts at vaginal penetration. Thus, vaginismus is a classic example a psychosomatic illness" (Masters and Johnson, 1970, p. 250). The term *dyspareunia* refers to difficult or painful intercourse, and Masters and Johnson (1970) again emphasize the importance of a careful pelvic and rectal examination in determining possible causes for this reaction.

Given the absence of related factors such as severe marital problems, problem drinking, or physiologic problems, a rapid treatment procedure has been found effective for many of the problems just described with clients who are committed to pursuing change. Clients are usually screened for these brief programs and rejection rates as high as 50 percent of client referrals have been reported (LoPiccolo and Lobitz, 1973). Some authors recommend the use of traditional psychological tests such as the Minnesota Multiphasic Personality Inventory (MMPI) to help identify major psychological disturbance that may be an indication that more intensive intervention will be required. For example, Schumacher and Lloyd (1976) report that one fourth of their client population seeking treatment for sexual dysfunction has major psychological disturbance. Lobitz, LoPiccolo, Lobitz, and Brockway (1976) reported that MMPI results could have been helpful (if the authors had attended closely to them) in pinpointing the low self-esteem of a male client that later caused difficulty in pursuing an intervention program for the couple.

The limitation of the success attained with these brief intervention programs to a portion of the client population seeking help should not detract from the success that has been achieved with these programs. It should be noted, however, that most reports describing results are not controlled studies, including the work of Masters and Johnson (1970). Treatment of sexual dysfunction emphasizes the education of the clients concerning the sexual response and the factors that can interfere with this natural reaction (see Masters and Johnson, 1970). Considerable time is devoted to the explanation of sexual function and an attempt is made to put sex "back into its natural context" (Masters and Johnson, 1970, p. 10). Communication between partners is emphasized and modeled for the couple, misinformation is corrected, and each learns to explore and share with the other his or her sexual value system. A graduated approach is employed, in which clients progress from easy to more difficult tasks. Many members of couples have never been able to indicate to each other which activities they find sexually desirable and those that are distracting (Masters and Johnson, 1970). An important aspect of intervention is to have both participants fully understand the process of performance fears and its effects. To remove all performance demands, specific performance instructions are carefully avoided, and the couple is instructed not to engage in intercourse. The partners do, however, engage in a series of in vivo graduated exposure assignments designed to allow them to experience (or to recapture) their natural sexual response. Initial assignments involve them in sensate focus experiences in which they learn to appreciate sensory experiences of touch, smell, sound, and sight (see Masters and Johnson, 1970). This can be considered a form of in vivo desensitization, in which clients become accustomed to touching and being touched without anxiety or embarrassment (Marks, 1976). A refundable penalty fee has been employed to increase client motivation (Lobitz and LoPiccolo, 1972). Other procedures employed to increase sexual functioning include reading erotic literature, erotic fantasy, role playing of orgasmic reactions to decrease inhibitions and anxiety, and the counselors modeling of an acceptance of sexuality (Lobitz and LoPiccolo, 1972).

An overview of behavioral programs for problems of sexual dysfunction is presented in the following sections. The reader is referred to other sources for a more complete description of these programs and of intervention programs aimed at other problems of sexual dysfunction (see, for example, Annon, 1974; Masters and Johnson, 1970).

Erectile Failure. The role of performance anxiety and fear of failure is emphasized in the conceptualization of erectile failure (see, for example, Masters and Johnson, 1970; Wolpe, 1958). Anxiety concerning whether an erection will occur can prevent its occurrence. Fear increases after each failure to attain an erection. Thus fear directly interferes with sexual arousal, the two states being incompatible with each other. As Masters and Johnson (1970) point out, performance anxiety leads to a number of other unfortunate effects. The male now closely monitors the degree of penile erection; that is, he assumes a spectator role during sexual interactions (Masters and Johnson, 1970, p. 196). This spectator role interferes with participating as a sexually aroused partner. Failure to attain or maintain erections may lead to the secondary effects of worries about his manliness and to a depressed mood. The reactions of his partner may exacerbate his anxiety; she may become hostile toward him or may appear obviously unsatisfied, thus making him feel guilty. Now we have in bed not two people, but four, because each assumes a spectator role in relation to performance and satisfaction. This leaves little room for the natural response of sexual arousal to occur. A basic aspect of the intervention method for erectile failure involves removing the possibility of failure via instructions that are given to the couple involving the clients in assignments requiring graduated stimulation. Improving communication is also a point of focus, and educative material is offered.

Case example. The following case example illustrates the importance of individually tailoring intervention programs according to the unique picture that each client presents. This is as much a need in the area of sexual dysfunction as it is with any presenting problem. As with other problems, attention may have to be devoted to client resistance, refusal to carry out agreements, and problems in other areas that interfere with progress in relation to the sexual concern.

Two case studies illustrating the adaptation of intervention procedures to unique client needs are offered by Lobitz, LoPiccolo, Lobitz, and Brockway (1976). One of these studies describes Mr. and Mrs. T., a married couple in their late fifties, who sought help with Mr. T.'s erectile failure. Mr. T. reported that he was sexually aroused by his wife, but that when intercourse was attempted he was usually unable to achieve an erection. If he did achieve an erection, he would lose it immediately. Mrs. T. reported herself depressed and frustrated by this state of affairs, and was considering the possibility of discontinuing all sexual activity. Mrs. T. was depressed not only about the couple's sexual problem but also about her husband's impending unemployment because of a reorganization in her husband's company. The couple reported that they had achieved successful intercourse only four or five times during their two-year marriage. They estimated their frequency of sex at about once every six weeks. Although Mr. T. attempted to initiate sex much more frequently, his wife refused to participate. Although Mr. T. used a variety of sexual methods to bring Mrs. T. to orgasm, such as manual and oral stimulation, she was quite unwilling to use manual or oral manipulation for him in turn, because she found these activities distasteful.

Mr. T. had experienced no erectile problems during his

first marriage, which had lasted for some twenty-five years. This marriage had ended when he was informed by his wife that she was having a relationship with another man and she wanted a divorce. Mr. T. had refrained from sexual activity until he met Mrs. T. He experienced an erectile problem during his courtship with Mrs. T., but attributed his difficulty to his feeling that premarital sex was wrong. However, the problem persisted when they were married. Mr. T. reported no erectile difficulties when masturbating, which he engaged in two or three times a week.

Mrs. T. had also had a first marriage that had lasted for twenty-five years and that had ended in divorce. She reported that her first husband "had been an unskilled, violent, and inconsiderate sexual partner who had frequently forced her to have intercourse against her will" (Lobitz and others, 1976, p. 241). "Most relevant to Mr. and Mrs. T.'s current sexual problem was the fact that Mrs. T.'s previous husband usually had an erection before beginning any overt sexual activity and never allowed Mrs. T. to touch or manipulate his penis in any way" (Lobitz and others, 1976, p. 241). She had not remained celibate after her divorce, having had sexual relations with two or three other men. She enjoyed these encounters, although she did not reach orgasm during intercourse.

Intervention was conducted over a period of fifteen hours, one hour daily, by a male-female cotherapy team. The usual intervention program was initiated with the couple, consisting of daily homework assignments to be carried out in their home. They were each requested to keep a record describing what had occurred, how much pleasure they had experienced, and their level of arousal. These forms were returned to the counselor prior to the next session. Sexual histories for Mr. and Mrs. T. were gathered in separate interviews. Assessment occupied the first two interviews.

During the third session, the counselors explained the process of erectile failure and drew the couple's attention to some unrealistic expectations they held concerning sexual functioning. For example, Mrs. T. expected Mr. T. to have an erection before beginning sexual activity and without any direct stimulation of his penis. "The therapists remarked that very few men functioned this way and that it was an undesirable behavior pattern in any case. The female cotherapist emphasized the pleasure she obtained from caressing her husband and arousing him to the point of erection. The male cotherapist revealed that he did not have erections before beginning sexual activity and also very much enjoyed his wife's caressing his genitals. Both therapists emphasized the research findings (Rubin, 1968) that older men become erect more slowly and required more stimulation; thus Mr. T. was unrealistic in expecting himself to perform sexually as he had in the distant past" (Lobitz and others, 1976, pp. 242-243). This description offers a good example of the way in which counselors share their own experiences and feelings to emphasize points and of the way points are supported by sharing research findings. This stage of intervention, in which unrealistic expectations are identified and more functional and realistic ones established, is a critical antecedent to developing a more helpful view of sexual functioning and laying the groundwork for homework assignments that will help the couple learn more pleasurable behaviors.

Although this discussion seemed to reassure Mr. T., his wife disagreed with the counselors. She objected to the idea that she contributed to her husband's problem by making hostile and derogatory remarks about his sexual functioning. The female counselor tried to empathize with her position in terms of her feelings to no avail, and, when the male counselor pursued the point in spite of her denial, Mr. T. refused to repeat the remarks his wife had made. This interaction offers an illustration of the potential value of a male-female counselor team. The female counselor can empathize with and be supportive of the woman's position and the male counselor can be supportive of the male position. The combination of advocacy by the same-sex counselor and confrontation by the opposite-sex counselor is not, however, always effective, as shown by the interaction described. "The counselors found themselves in a seemingly untenable position for treatment to succeed. Mrs. T. must realize and accept her role in Mr. T.'s problem. However, she refused to do so, and Mr. T. was unwilling or unable to confront her" (Lobitz and others, 1976, p. 243).

The couple finally responded to a face-saving attempt in which the female counselor agreed with Mrs. T. that she had not meant to be hostile by remarks such as, "My first husband was much more masculine" and "Even when he [Mr. T.] gets an erection it's not very big" (p. 243), but that these remarks had negative overtones in spite of her helpful intent. The male counselor supported Mr. T. in repeating that such statements were quite harmful to Mr. T.

Toward the end of the third session, the general intervention strategy was described to the couple. The husband was eager to begin, but, as the counselors had anticipated, Mrs. T. brought up interfering factors such as her busy social schedule and her depression. The counselors had already discussed between themselves various strategies for overcoming Mrs. T.'s resistance and at this point they agreed with Mrs. T. that the demands that would be made by the intervention program would probably be beyond her present abilities. This strategy had its intended effect, in that Mrs. T. insisted that she could carry out the intervention program. "The female cotherapist agreed with Mrs. T. and the male therapist then 'reluctantly' allowed himself to be argued into commencing treatment" (p. 244). The couple were asked to refrain from all sexual activity except masturbation and were asked to take a bath together and to give each other a complete body massage while nude, but not to touch the breasts or genitals.

At the fourth session, the clients reported that they had not experienced much arousal. Their next assignment consisted of adding to the first assignment some hugging and kissing as well as a complete visual inspection of the other's nude body while massaging it and talking about what they saw and how they felt about different parts of the body. This exercise was intended to decrease the embarrassment each felt about their bodies. The results of this assignment were more positive. Mr. T. reported that he had attained a partial erection and that Mrs. T. had been quite aroused. She, in turn, suggested that her heavy breathing and nipple erection were caused by the coldness of their bedroom. The female counselor suggested that Mrs. T. had learned to turn herself off to avoid disappointment and that it was now important to learn to label sexual arousal correctly and to let herself become aroused. At this point, the male counselor suggested that intervention include a focus on increasing Mrs.

T.'s ability to have an orgasm during intercourse. She, however, said that she was content with her present method of reaching an orgasm.

The third assignment built on the former two assignments and this time was to include genital caressing for both Mr. and Mrs. T. It was emphasized that Mr. T. should not try to have an erection nor should he expect one and he should not watch for one to occur. "He was simply to enjoy her caressing his flaccid penis" (p. 245). They were again forbidden to engage in any sexual activities together other than their assignment in order to remove performance pressure. This assignment was also a success. Mrs. T. reached an orgasm through oral manipulation and Mr. T. had had two brief erections in reaction to being caressed by his wife. Mrs. T. said she felt resentful that now that Mr. T. was having erections they were forbidden to have intercourse. The male counselor noted that this was a hostile remark in view of the progress that was being made. This time, Mrs. T. admitted her hostility and then expressed some positive feelings about the progress that had occurred.

The assignment given at the sixth session was for the couple to practice the teasing technique, in which the female caresses the penis until some degree of erection occurs, then stops and allows the erection to dissipate, then resumes touching (Masters and Johnson, 1970). Instructions are given to stop touching the penis as soon as an erection occurs. One purpose of this assignment is to teach the couple that if an erection is lost it can be attained again. This exercise was to be practiced for about twenty minutes. The couple reported during the seventh session that the assignment was successful. Mr. T. had achieved seven erections within the twenty minutes, and Mrs. T. reported no repugnance at touching his penis, which was a sign of progress for her. Mrs. T. had not reached orgasm.

The next assignment given to the couple was for Mrs. T. to show her husband how to manipulate her genitals as she did when she masturbated, and for Mr. T. to show his wife how to touch his genitals. An additional assignment was given to Mr. T.—to try to maintain an erection for five to ten minutes. As the authors note, this was a tactical blunder, because a specific performance demand had been placed on Mr. T., "ensuring that he would assume the role of anxious spectator instead of aroused participant" (p. 246). The assignment was not a success. The husband reported being very aware of the ten-minute expectation and only achieved three brief (thirty-second) erections during the couple's session. The counselors assumed all the blame for this failure and took the opportunity to discuss again the role of performance demands in erectile failure. For the first time, Mrs. T. seemed to accept this notion. Other parts of the assignment had gone well, with Mr. T. learning to manipulate Mrs. T. to orgasm.

The purpose of the next assignment was to help the clients learn how to receive pleasure without any obligation to return pleasure to the partner at the same time. They were to caress each other's genitals while in the positions described by Masters and Johnson (1970), wherein the male sits behind the woman and reaches around her to touch her genitals and where the male lies on his back while the woman sits between his legs and touches his genitals. Reports during the ninth session about this assignment were not positive. The authors speculate that the results of their previous tactical error were still being felt. The husband reported difficulty relaxing and attending to his arousal and had only partial erections, which dissipated quickly. "At this point he had suggested switching positions and his caressing her genitals. To his surprise, once he was sitting behind her, where she could not see him, he had a full erection during the entire ten to fifteen minutes he was caressing her genitals" (p. 247). He informed his wife of his erection and she started to touch him. He reported being able to focus on his arousal this time and maintained his erection until ejaculation. The wife had not been able to achieve orgasm during this assignment.

The assignment given for the following session was for the wife to assume the female superior sitting position (the male lies on his back and the woman sits over him) and to place the penis at the entrance to the vagina. At the tenth session, the clients reported that they had violated the ban on intercourse, because they were unable to restrain themselves; however, they had stopped before either reached a climax. The importance of not moving too swiftly was reemphasized and, at the same time, the beneficial results of a lack of performance anxiety were noted by the counselors. They were given a one-day holiday from home exercises because of reported genital soreness and, as a next assignment, Mr. T. was asked to stimulate Mrs. T.'s genitals with an electric vibrator. She had not reached an orgasm during the past few sessions and reported being increasingly depressed, because her husband had been given notice that his job would end in one month. The counselors also requested Mr. T. to lie on his back while Mrs. T. kneeled over him and "stuffed" his penis into her vagina. In this approximation to intercourse, the wife experiences penile containment while the male experiences no performance anxiety, because this activity is to occur whether or not an erection exists.

At the eleventh session, the clients reported that this assignment had gone well. Mr. T. had maintained a strong erection during the session and they both enjoyed the activity; however, Mrs. T. again did not reach an orgasm. The counselors told her not to try to have an orgasm, because such an effort would place a performance demand on her that would interfere with arousal. They were requested as a next assignment to carry out the same activity with the addition of slow pelvic thrusting. This assignment also went well; however, Mrs. T. still did not reach orgasm despite multiple methods of stimulation. Their last assignment was to resume a normal sex life. They were informed that there might be some relapse at this point (in terms of erectile failure), because a performance demand to function normally might now be felt. This prediction of some relapse helps to remove performance demands that clients may place on themselves at this point (Masters and Johnson, 1970). And, if a relapse does not occur, the male "is too elated by his success to be concerned about the therapist's mistaken prediction. Thus the therapist cannot lose by predicting failure" (Lobitz and others, 1976, p. 249).

In the thirteenth session, the clients reported that they had engaged in several minutes of intercourse, which Mrs. T. insisted they terminate because she was "hot and tired." The counselors confronted her with her behavior, the female counselor displaying a supportive role and the male a confrontative one. He told her that he was convinced she was trying to undermine the intervention program and challenged her to accept a refund of a portion of their treatment fee if the couple would spend the last two days of intervention relaxing at a luxury hotel. This challenge was a success. The couple had intercourse on both days, with Mr. T. ejaculating and Mrs. T. being manipulated to orgasm several times. In order to help maintain gains made, each was asked to develop two lists, one that identified things that contributed to their difficulties and another that identified ways they had found to deal with these problems. These lists are given in Tables 23 and 24.

Mr. and Mrs. T. were also asked to develop a plan for their sexual activities for the following three-month period.

Table 23. Mr. T.'s List

Errors	Corrections
1. "Sex" was kind of a dirty word.	1. Realization that sex and sexual activities are natural, essential and a wonderful part of living.
2. That a woman, particularly a "good" woman, either didn't want sexual intercourse or only wanted it in order to have children.	2. Realization that a healthy woman has just as strong a need and (though latent) drive for intercourse as a healthy man.
3. That masturbation is a type of self-abuse and could or would result in physical or mental damage.	3. Realization that masturbation in moderation is a healthy method to achieve a degree of sexual satisfaction, particularly when heterosexual intercourse is [not] available.
4. That normal sexual intercourse is a manifestation of a male physically dominating a female solely for the male's satisfaction.	4. Comprehension (and this was difficult to accept) that a woman intensely wants and needs penetration to feel fulfilled (completely apart from the needs for procreation).
5. That taking visual delight in the nude figure (or partially clothed figure) of my wife was sinful.	5. Acceptance of the fact that a wife wishes her husband to enjoy the sight of her body.
6. That an erection should "just come naturally" when circumstances indicate that intercourse may be consummated or that I can "will" an erection.	6. Except for teen-agers and those in their twenties, some type of overt stimulation is needed to produce an erection; that "willing" an erection is impossible.
7. That personal gratification in and from intercourse was selfishly wrong.	7. Acceptance that the only way for my wife to be completely satisfied sexually was for me to concentrate on my "selfish" desires.

Source: Lobitz and others (1976, p. 250).

Table 24. Mrs. T.'s List

Errors	Corrections
1. Hadn't been stimulating Mr. T. by caressing his genitals manually or orally.	1. Learned to do this and the places that it felt best.
2. Unmeaningly (*sic*) undercutting Mr. T. on occasion by unthinking remarks.	2. Will be more careful of his ego.
3. Trying too hard for climax.	3. Will try to relax and just enjoy feeling.
4. Start thinking of many things when Mr. T. is caressing my genitals to produce climax.	4. Will try to turn mind off and just participate.

Source: Lobitz and others (1976, p. 251).

They established some conditions for their love making; for example, that time pressure be absent, that they both feel well, and that possibility of distractions would be removed by taking the phone off the hook and by not answering the doorbell. Both agreed to attend to sensations being experienced when they found their minds wandering during love making, and that neither would consider him or herself or his or her partner as a performer. A specific plan was made concerning Mrs. T.'s slow build-up to orgasm. "Normally Mr. T. will continue to caress Mrs. T. for up to twenty minutes, alternately using manual, oral, or vibrator methods. At the end of the period, unless Mrs. T. wishes him to continue, Mr. T. will desist. If Mrs. T. becomes tired or tender at any time, she will tell him so and Mr. T. will desist. Mrs. T. will not feign tiredness or soreness" (Lobitz and others, 1976, p. 252). Plans were also made to experiment from time to time with new positions and for signals that would be employed to initiate love making and how these would be responded to. For example, if the partner did not wish to engage in sexual activity, he or she was to offer a clear and honest reason.

A number of self-report measures were employed to evaluate progress, including (1) frequency of intercourse; (2) duration of foreplay; (3) duration of intercourse; (4) percent of occasions on which orgasm in coitus occurred for each participant; (5) percent of occasions on which there was a problem in attaining an erection; (6) rating of sexual satisfaction for each participant on a scale from 1 to 6; and (7) score on the Locke-

Wallace Marital Inventory. Frequency of intercourse increased from once every six weeks prior to intervention, to twice a week at a three-month follow-up period. Percent of occasions on which orgasm was achieved in coitus was 90 for Mr. T. and 75 for Mrs. T. (baseline was 25 percent and zero). Whereas Mr. T. had had trouble attaining an erection on 100 percent of coital occasions, after intervention such trouble was experienced on 10 percent of occasions. Ratings of sexual satisfaction increased from 1 for both, to 6 for the husband and 5 for the wife.

Premature Ejaculation. In their careful review of histories of couples, Masters and Johnson (1970) found no specific background factors related to the creation of a pattern of premature ejaculation. They consider that "the first few ejaculatory experiences predispose a man to the development of premature ejaculation regardless of his prepubertal and postpupertal environmental background" (p. 101). Following homework sessions in which sensate focus is practiced to heighten attention to and awareness of physical sensations, the woman is instructed in the use of the squeeze technique, originally developed by Semans (1956). In this method, the woman places her thumb on the frenulum and her first and second fingers on the dorsal surface of the penis and applies pressure by squeezing the thumb and these first two fingers together for about three to four seconds. With sufficient pressure, the male will lose the urge to ejaculate and may lose part of his erection. Masters and Johnson (1970) recommend use of an artificial model to offer practice in the use of this method. (The importance of making sure the client understands what a particular action consists of cannot be overestimated—it should never be assumed that the client does in fact understand. A good example of this is a case discussed by Annon [1974], in which a male was instructed to manipulate his partner's clitoris. The client reported that when he had tried this his partner became annoyed with him and had forced him to stop this activity. The counselor at this point showed him a life-sized female model and asked him to demonstrate what he had been doing at which point he approached the model, inserted his finger into the navel region, and moved it about.)

Following loss of ejaculatory urge, stimulation of the penis is resumed and when a full erection is again achieved the squeeze technique is resumed again. Pressure is applied first under instructions of the husband, but the wife soon will learn the signs of an impending ejaculation and learn to apply pressure herself. LoPiccolo and Lobitz (1973) recommend that the male "begin the squeeze procedure in masturbation, rather than by manipulation by his wife. This offers the advantage of reducing his anxiety by allowing him to gain self-confidence about ejaculatory control before he begins again to interact sexually with his wife. This modification is also useful in cases where the wife finds this manipulation and squeeze procedure repugnant" (LoPiccolo and Lobitz, 1973, p. 347).

Success with this assignment is followed by an assignment for intromission, in which the woman mounts her male partner and inserts the penis into the vagina, after practicing the squeeze technique a few times. As the male's ability to be contained in the female without ejaculating increases, pelvic movement is introduced. The reader is referred to Masters and Johnson (1970) for further details of this intervention program. The results they report with their program for premature ejaculations are extremely good. Out of 184 men, there were only four failures to learn adequate control during intervention, defined "as sufficient to provide orgasmic opportunity for the sexual partner during approximately 50 percent of the coital opportunities" (p. 113). Kaplan (1974) employs a group setting for the treatment of premature ejaculation.

Ejaculatory Incompetence. Newell (1976) reported the successful treatment of ejaculatory incompetence by using a penile vibrator, which the client employed at home while viewing erotic pictures. Previous attempts to alter the behavior through a graduated sensate-focus program (Masters and Johnson, 1970) had failed because the client's wife, who felt that the program was altering her sexual reactions, did not cooperate. She had no interest in becoming orgasmic, feared becoming pregnant, and was unwilling to employ contraceptives. Following three weeks of use of the vibrator at home, the client reported that he had been able to experience ejaculation. Prior to this he was unable to recall ever having ejaculated while awake, even during adolescence, although he and his wife engaged in intercourse about once or twice a week (without ejaculation). Follow-ups six months and one year later indicated that he continued his frequency of ejaculation during intercourse with his wife one to three times a week, although he would typically confine ejaculation to "safe periods," even though he was using contraceptives. This case provides an example of an alternative to employ when it has not been possible to involve both partners in a program. It also illustrates the role of pregnancy fears.

Increasing Female Sexual Functioning. Masters and Johnson (1970) describe a primary inorgasmic woman as one who has never experienced a climax by any means of stimulation. The recommended intervention for this procedure is very similar in basic intent to the program for treating men with erectile failure. There is an emphasis on anxiety reduction via graduated in vivo exposure and skill training in attaining sexual arousal. "During coition the nonorgasmic woman is immediately more disadvantaged than her sexually inadequate partner in that her fears for performance are dual in character. Her primary fear is, of course, for her own inability to respond as a woman, but she frequently must contend with the secondary fear for inadequacy of male sexual performance" (Masters and Johnson, 1970, p. 228). Masters and Johnson provide a detailed discussion of the various factors that may be related to orgasmic dysfunction, including religious orthodoxy, considering the male partner inadequate in terms of expectations the woman has of a male partner, and being paired with a male who is a premature ejaculator. Here too, as with the problem of erectile failure, intercourse is prohibited while sexual skills are established.

Nonorgasmic women may be ignorant of how to enhance arousal. One method of enhancing the woman's skills in increasing her sexual arousal is through a graduated masturbation program. A graduated approach is employed in order to accustom the woman to the act of masturbating. The following nine steps are included in one version of such a program (from Lobitz and others, 1976, pp. 255-256).

> *Step 1.* The client is given the assignment to increase her self-awareness by examining her nude body and appreciating its beauty. She uses a hand mirror to examine her genitals and identify various parts with the aid of diagrams.

Step 2. The client is instructed to explore her genitals tactually as well as visually. To avoid performance anxiety, she is not given any expectation to become aroused at this point.

Step 3. Tactual and visual exploration are focused on locating sensitive areas that produce feelings of pleasure when stimulated.

Step 4. The client is told to concentrate on manual stimulation of identified pleasurable areas. At this point the female therapist discusses techniques of masturbation, including the use of a lubricant.

Step 5. If orgasm does not occur during Step 4, the client is told to increase the intensity and duration of masturbation. She is told to masturbate until "something happens" or until she becomes tired or sore.

Step 6. If orgasm is not reached during Step 5, the client is instructed to purchase a vibrator of the type sold in pharmacies for facial or body massage. She is to repeat Step 5 using the vibrator.

Step 7. Once the client has achieved orgasm through masturbation, the husband is introduced to the procedure by his observing her. This desensitizes her to displaying arousal and orgasm in his presence and also functions as a learning experience for him.

Step 8. The husband manipulates his wife in the manner she has demonstrated in Step 7.

Step 9. Once orgasm has occurred in Step 8, the couple is instructed to engage in intercourse while the husband stimulates his wife's genitals, either manually or with a vibrator.

Instructions may be given during Step 1 to also initiate a program of vaginal exercises to increase awareness of the pelvic muscles and to increase their tone. These are listed as follows (from Heiman, LoPiccolo, and LoPiccolo, 1976, p. 52):

1. Contract the [pubococcygeus] muscle, hold for a count of three, then relax. Breathe regularly.
2. Contract the muscle while inhaling, pulling the muscle upward with the intake of breath. This may be harder to do, because you may find your stomach muscles contracting as well. With time you will learn to do this one without contracting the stomach muscles.

3. Contract and relax the muscle as quickly as possible, while breathing regularly.
4. Bear down on the muscle as if pushing something out of the vagina, or trying to urinate in a hurry. You may find yourself holding your breath, but try to breathe regularly.

Lobitz and LoPiccolo (1972) report that "in their most difficult case to date, three weeks of daily forty-five-minute vibrator sessions were required to produce orgasm" (p. 268).

As with other intervention programs designed to enhance sexual functioning, this program must be carefully designed to take into account the unique value system of the client in relation to sexual behaviors, and the unique relationship between the woman and her partner, if a specific partner is involved in the program. Lobitz and others (1976) present an informative case example in which one complicating factor was the male's low self-esteem and his low pleasure level during love making. It should be emphasized that it is not necessary for a woman to have a partner to participate in most of the steps involved in the program described. A group setting is often employed for nonorgasmic women, in which misconceptions are discussed, educative material presented, and graduated assignments given. Marshall (1975) has described a program for reducing guilt that may be associated with masturbation, in which statements concerning the positive benefits of masturbation are prepared and repeated by the client immediately following masturbation. The client could then present a reinforcer to herself or himself by thinking about some pleasant thought or using some actual event, such as taking a walk. Kohlenberg (1974a) has described a program using directed masturbation employed with couples who had not responded to a Masters and Johnson (1970) type of program for primary orgasmic dysfunction. Observation of their own bodies and self-stimulation were first carried out privately and then together. Stimulation by the partner was gradually faded into the self-stimulation. Within six weeks, all three of the women indicated that they had experienced orgasms while masturbating, and orgasm during intercourse occurred several weeks later. A sixth-month follow-up indicated that the women were orgasmic 50 percent of the time during intercourse.

Some women with secondary orgasmic dysfunction can only attain orgasm in a very specialized manner. In such instances, an aim of intervention is to break the rigid stimulus control of orgasm, so that orgasm occurs on other occasions, such as during intercourse. Snyder, LoPiccolo, and LoPiccolo (1975) report an example of a young married woman who could only attain orgasm when masturbating while standing. She was instructed to refrain from masturbating in this fashion and asked to engage in the nine-step program described earlier, while lying down. Additional procedures that were employed with this couple included a Masters and Johnson (1970) program of gradual approximations to intercourse starting with sensate focus and discussion of the couple's marital problems. The counselors pointed out the relationship they felt existed between the couple's sexual problems and other problems such as the wife's dissatisfaction with her career prospects and disagreements concerning interactions with the husband's parents. This case example illustrates the interaction that may occur between problems in the sexual area and other marital problems.

Videotape as well as imaginal desensitization has been employed to increase sexual responsiveness in women. Wincze and Caird (1976) compared these two methods in treating a group of twenty-one women, all of whom complained of high anxiety associated with sexual behavior and inability to obtain sexual pleasure. Seventy-five percent of the women also reported that they did not reach orgasm. During desensitization, thirty scenes were arranged individually and each woman participated in two or three weekly sessions, each forty-five minutes long, until all items could be imagined without experiencing anxiety. A second group of women viewed items recorded on videotape. Both procedures resulted in a decrease in heterosexual anxiety compared to a no-treatment control group; however, only 25 percent of the nonorgasmic women were orgasmic at the end of intervention. It is likely that additional procedures, perhaps following the sensate-focus procedure of Masters and Johnson (1970), would have resulted in these women becoming orgasmic. For additional reports of the use of desensitization see Wolpe (1973) and Brady (1971a). Additional desensitizing effects may be achieved when a specific partner is involved by having the partner present hierarchy items (see, for example, Madsen and Ullman, 1967).

Caird and Wincze (1974) used systematic desensitization with a twenty-four-year-old woman referred because of a strong revulsion to sexual intercourse. Although she found foreplay bearable she said that she had never found sex pleasurable. She had been married five months at the time she was first seen by the counselors. She was trained in deep muscle relaxation and asked to order fifty 3×5 inch index cards, each of which contained a description of one specific aspect of heterosexual behavior in terms of the degree of anxiety each occasioned, using a five-point scale ranging from "no anxiety" to "very high anxiety." Each description corresponded to one of a series of four-minute videotapes that were to be employed during systematic desensitization. The client was asked to sort twenty-five of the cards before and after each session. At each session, the client was requested to attend to a series of video clips, while relaxed, and to imagine she and her husband in each situation and to remain relaxed. "Each four-minute scene was presented in segments of 15, 30, 45, and 60 seconds with 30- to 45-second intervals between segments. Mrs. M. was instructed to close her eyes and augment the relaxation during the inter-trials interval. If during the presentation of the film Mrs. M. felt anxious, she could signal by raising her finger to stop the machine" (Caird and Wincze, 1974, p. 176). The client's husband was present at all sessions. Seven sessions were held over a two-week period, until all fifty scenes were completed. The counselor instructed the client "to engage in sexual behaviour only to the extent that she could do so without experiencing anxiety. It was explained to her husband that he was not to attempt to force his wife into intercourse; that she was to determine when and to what extent sexual activity should take place" (Caird and Wincze, 1974, p. 176). Positive changes were found on self-report inventories as well as via client self-report of sexual activity. Satisfactory intercourse had taken place on a number of occasions and Mrs. M. had experienced orgasm on three occasions. A six-month and nine-month follow-up indicated a maintenance of positive gains. "Not only was Mrs. M. enjoying sex, [but also] her attitude toward it had undergone dramatic changes and she remarked that she had, in subtle ways, initiated intercourse" (p. 177).

Graded exposure has been used to alter vaginismus. For example, Wilson (1973) employed directed masturbation coupled with imagining degrees of penetration immediately prior to orgasm, starting with imagining minimal finger insertion. As she tolerated small degrees of imagined insertion, she then imagined additional degrees, in each case not progressing to a further step until a prior step could be imagined without discomfort and was paired with an orgasmic reaction. When the imaginal hierarchy was successfully completed, graduated real exposure was initiated by her partner. Normal intercourse was initiated within one month.

Sexual Variations

Considering the relative newness of the behavioral approach, there is a fairly extensive literature describing the application of behavioral methods in the attempt to alter a range of sexual variations, including exhibitionism, voyerism, transvestism, gender identity, homosexuality, and pedophilia. This intervention has progressed from a naive application of aversive conditioning procedures, in which ethical considerations were forgone as well as the need for individually tailored programs, to a multiform intervention in which a careful behavioral analysis of sexual behaviors and related factors is conducted (Franks, 1967), although there are still many lapses in the design of assessment and intervention procedures. Sexual variations involving consenting adults, such as homosexuality, have become increasingly suspect as an object of change per se, because of the strong societal pressures (to assume heterosexual behavior patterns) exerted on people with such sexual orientations (Davison, 1976; Wilson and Davison, 1974). It has been in the context of trying to alter deviant sexual arousal that physiological measures of sexual arousal have been further refined. Today it is generally agreed that assessment should be carried out in four areas: the extent of deviant sexual arousal, the extent of heterosexual arousal, the adequacy of heterosexual skills, and the appropriateness of gender role behavior. Assessment may reveal various patterns of sexual arousal. For example, such arousal may only occur in the presence of deviant sexual stimuli, with none manifested in the presence of heterosexual events. It has been assumed that decreasing the former through aversive conditioning would automatically result in an increase in heterosexual behavior; however, this is not necessarily the case (see Barlow, 1973). A program that directly focuses on increasing heterosexual arousal to new stimuli is often required to increase heterosexual responsiveness; for example, by classical conditioning, in which neutral events are paired with events that elicit sexual arousal, or by a fading procedure, in which stimuli associated with heterosexual arousal are gradually superimposed on stimuli that elicit deviant sexual arousal. It is possible to increase sexual responsiveness to heterosexual events by completely positive means, such as fading, without the use of any aversive conditioning procedure. Deficits in heterosexual social skills and in appropriate gender role behaviors will require special programs designed to establish new behaviors. The first series of behaviors discussed involve nonvoluntary participants. This series includes exhibitionism, voyeurism, sadistic fantasies, and child molestation.

Exhibitionism. Aversive behavior rehearsal has been employed to decrease sexual exhibitionism. Wickramasekera (1976) indicates that this intervention program is employed for repeated offenders, as defined by police records, who "are introverted, anxious, moralistic, and nonassertive, and [is] probably contraindicated for the extroverted, sociopathic type of patient whose trait anxiety level is low. It elicits the patient's symptom (exhibitionism) under conditions which overlap substantially with the naturally occurring event, but with certain critical alterations: (1) The 'exposure' is deliberately planned by the therapists and patient several weeks in advance; (2) The 'exposure' is enacted under conditions of reduced anonymity; (3) During enactment, the behavior is subjected by the patient and therapist to cognitive-verbal exploration of associated affect, bodily sensations, and fantasy. The goal is to elicit and 'demythologize' any autistic fantasies that may mediate the exhibitionism in the natural habitat" (Wickramasekera, 1976, p. 167). Sexual exhibitionism occurs under fantasy involvement that decreases the client's critical judgment in terms of the risks that are taken. Wickramasekera's procedure attempts to shift attention to factors based more on reality. Vicarious aversive behavior rehearsal has also been employed successfully. In this kind of rehearsal, the client observes a videotape of an exhibitionist going through an aversive behavior rehearsal procedure. The latter procedure has a number of components, including the following: (1) helping the client to identify the external and internal events related to exhibiting; (2) taking a battery of tests to determine personality factors that may contraindicate use of this procedure and that serve to create "the therapeutic expectation that grave and healing events are about to occur" (p. 169); (3) increasing behavioral commitment to change through requiring the client to offer a complete disclosure of his deviation, including its frequency and chronicity, to significant others such as his parents or wife and to his lawyer; (4) two forty-minute sessions of disclosure and self-confrontation in front of five mental health professionals such as social workers and psychiatric nurses. A barrage of questions are thrown at the client and he is then instructed to engage in specific acts of exposure and masturbation while he is questioned by team members. "He is asked to disrobe and robe several times while encouraged to explore the relationship between current feelings, moods, prior exposures, and their relationship to antecedents and consequences and immediate situational factors" (p. 170). Both vicarious behavior rehearsal and aversive behavior rehearsal have been found to be effective within one to four sessions. Follow-up reports indicate that gains are maintained for up to seven years (Wickramasekera, 1976). For other reports of behavioral intervention with exhibitionists, see Serber (1970) and Reitz and Keil (1971).

The importance of identifying the sequence of behaviors and situations prior to the act of exposure has been emphasized by some writers (see, for example, Abel, Levis, and Clancy, 1970). "It is not a single condition which precipitates the deviant act, but rather a chain or sequence of behaviors. . . . The sequence begins with sexually stimulating memories of previous exposures. This ideational material is followed by driving to a place where he has previously exposed himself. The urge for a new experience now appears. After locating a young girl, the patient circles the area rehearsing mentally. He then stops the car and calls the girl. As she approaches, he anticipates with pleasurable excitement her reaction to the sight of his genitals. Finally, he exposes himself and terminates the sequence by masturbating" (Abel, Levis, and Clancy, 1970, p. 60). As the authors note, this sequence of behaviors suggests the desirability of removing as many phases of the sequence as possible by appropriate means. For example, if an antecedent event is the client's having a fight with his wife, intervention procedures offering the couple improved communication skills may be required. The authors also stress the importance of reinforcing nondeviant sexual activity.

One program employed audiotaped descriptions of scenes paired with shock in order to decrease deviant sexual behavior. This procedure was employed with three exhibitionists who also had histories of voyeurism, two transvestites, and one masochist, all of whom were twenty-one to thirty-one years of age. Four were married and four had recent arrest histories as a result of their deviant behavior. Clients were excluded who had a history of psychosis, retardation, organicity, or homosexuality. A number of assessment devices were employed, including the MMPI, and two ratings scales, one of which consisted of ten phrases, five describing sexually arousing deviant phrases and five describing nondeviant sexual activity. Each client rated the items from "least" to "most exciting." A second rating scale, completed weekly, "consisted of twenty-one items in three categories: (1) specific deviant behavior practiced by the patient, (2) deviant behavior not practiced by him, and (3) nondeviant sexual activity" (Abel, Levis, and Clancy, 1970, p. 60). These three categories were further divided into fantasized and overt behaviors. Each client was asked to indicate the frequency of each listed behavior over a one-week period, and was requested to complete one of these scales each week and to mail it in on Sunday to the counselor. "A verbal description of the patient of his activities—deviant sexual, normal sexual, and general (nonsexual) daily routine—was recorded on audiotape while the penile responses were recorded. The subject described in detail the behavior sequences and thoughts involved in three actual deviant sexual experiences. In addition, he discussed normal sexual experiences and other nonsexual activities" (Abel,

Levis, and Clancy, 1970, p. 61). Portions of these tapes were selected and, for each client, six tapes, each lasting 120 seconds, were produced. Passages were selected that were associated with the greatest penile responses. Some clients were assigned to a contingent shock schedule in which descriptions of deviant material were followed by shock, and one was assigned to a noncontingent shock schedule. Clients were also given the opportunity at each session to avoid shock by describing normal sexual behavior in place of the tape segment typically followed by shock. The results indicated a decrease in erectile responses to deviant sexual material and a continued reaction to nondeviant material.

A self-regulation program, in which clients learned to identify stimuli related to exhibiting behavior and to employ alternative competing responses, was successfully used to decrease exhibitionism (Rooth and Marks, 1974). Covert sensitization has also been employed to decrease exhibitionism (Maletzky, 1974).

Voyeurism. There are only a few reports in the literature describing behavioral intervention with voyeurs. One concerned a forty-four-year-old man who had started "peeping" at the age of thirteen and had continued this behavior up until the time of his treatment, never being caught (Stoudenmire, 1973). He had requested hospitalization at about the age of forty-one to decrease this behavior; however, he had been discharged two weeks later, having been told that there was nothing that could be done for him. He sought treatment because he was worried that he might be discovered and that he might act on his fantasies that he engaged in when observing his teen-age daughters. He peeped on his teen-age daughters and on his neighbors, typically masturbating at the same time.

He and his wife were seen less than once a month over a period of fifteen months. This low frequency of contact was required because of limited financial resources of the client and distance from the clinic. He and his wife agreed to keep records of the frequency of their sexual intercourse (this seemed a reasonably incompatible behavior to increase). He also recorded dates and times of peeping behavior and this showed that he peeped about every other day. The couple was encouraged to increase their frequency of intercourse, especially at those times when peeping tended to occur, in the evening and on weekends, and the client was instructed that when he had an urge to peep he should masturbate, keeping voyeurism at the fantasy level. It was noted during assessment that the client was quite passive and unassertive. Even though he had not requested help in this area, instructions were offered to increase appropriate assertive behavior with his family and friends. One problem that arose during intervention was that he began to drink alcohol. However, this behavior decreased after he had a talk with his doctor, on the counselor's advice, concerning the effects of alcohol. In addition, jealous feelings about his wife's former marriage started to bother him, although he had not thought about this matter previously. The counselor suggested that this was caused by the greater affection he now felt for his wife, and he was trained in the use of thought stopping and asked to apply this when such thoughts occurred. After four sessions, voyeuristic episodes decreased to twice a month and after seven sessions decreased to less than once a month. He now only peeped on neighbors, not on his teen-age daughters. Both he and his wife reported greater satisfaction in their marriage. At a six-month follow-up, positive gains were maintained, according to self-reports of the clients, and neither drinking nor jealous thoughts had returned as a problem.

Decreasing Sadistic Fantasies. There are few behavioral reports concerning alteration of sadistic behavior and fantasies. Davison (1968) reported use of a counterconditioning procedure with a twenty-one-year-old, unmarried, male college student who described himself as a sadist. He reported a lack of heterosexual fantasies and activities and masturbated about five times a week while having fantasies about torturing women. Although he did not feel guilty about this, he was very worried that his behavior might make it impossible to get married in the future. Initial efforts were made to place his problem in perspective, because Davison felt that the perceived gravity of the problem and its implications were as disruptive as the problem itself. The student had read a Freudian interpretation of "sado-masochism" and was very upset about the poor prognosis that was offered. A social learning theory interpretation of his behavior was reviewed for the client. "Mr. M. frequently expressed relief at these ideas, and the therapist, indeed took full advantage of his prestigious position to reinforce these notions" of his behavior as resulting from a "normal psychological process rather than an insidious disease process" (Davison, 1968, p. 85). This is an excellent illustration of the formation of a new conceptualization of the client's problem and the extent to which a pathologizing conceptualization can often be a contributing factor to a presenting problem. A task during this phase of intervention was to alter the way in which the client labeled himself and to offer him a more helpful interpretation of the processes related to his fantasies.

As a first assignment, he was asked to gain an erection using whatever means were necessary and was then to shift his attention, while masturbating, to a picture of a sexy nude woman. Only if he began to lose his erection was he to return to imagining the sadistic fantasy, using this only to regain his erection, and then was to attend to the picture of the nude woman. He was to concentrate on this picture as orgasm approached. The importance of associating sexual arousal with the picture was emphasized. This series of self-managed masturbation assignments was continued over the following sessions. It was assumed that pairing masturbatory arousal with an appropriate sexual stimulus (a *Playboy* photo) would create a pleasurable sexual association with this picture. This effective stimulus could then be used to develop sexual arousal to less provocative female pictures. These events were then made purely imaginal. As Davison (1968) points out, this procedure requires substantial client influence over fantasy content.

He reported at the second session that he had been able to masturbate to a picture from *Playboy* on three occasions without using his sadistic fantasy. At the second session, the counselor started to initiate him into the type of conversations about girls that boys often engage in, but that the client had not experienced. It was felt that this would help to change his orientation toward girls, to make him more comfortable with them. He was also given an assignment to ask a girl out for a coffee date during the coming week and to spend time between classes looking at girls and attending to their attributes. During his next masturbation assignment, he was to now use the picture from *Playboy* as a backup stimulus to a picture of a girl in a bathing suit. If he lost his erection while masturbating while attending to the picture of the girl, he was to use the *Playboy* picture to regain his erection. The *Playboy* picture thus replaced the sadistic fantasy. If necessary, the sadistic fantasy could be employed as a further backup. He was also asked to attend to imagined sexual events and "when masturbating in this way he was to use the *Playboy* image, with a sadistic fantasy as backup" (Davison, 1968, p. 86). His report at the next session indicated a "reluctance to give up the sadistic fantasy" (Davison, 1968, p. 86), and a covert sensitization procedure was employed in which imagined sadistic fantasies such as a girl tied to stakes on the ground was paired with the imagination of "a large bowl of 'soup' composed of steaming urine with reeking fecal boli bobbing around on the top. His grimaces, contortions, and groans indicated that an effective image had been found, and the following five minutes were spent portraying his drinking from the bowl, with accompanying nausea, at all times while peering over the floating debris at the struggling girl" (Davison, 1968, p. 86). As a next assignment, he was asked to masturbate using the picture of a girl in a bathing suit.

At the fourth session, he reported that he had arranged a date, was looking forward to it, and had used the picture of a "bathing beauty" (p. 86) to masturbate several times, using the *Playboy* picture as a backup. He used the *Playboy* girl two out of five times in fantasy with no decrease in enjoyment. "He was to continue using the bathing-suit picture while masturbating to real-life stimuli, but to avoid sadistic fantasies altogether" (Davison, 1968, p. 86). The client reported at the fifth session that he had masturbated several times to bathing-suit pictures of girls and was unable to obtain an erection by his sadistic fantasy and even had difficulty imagining it. "He had also spent considerable time with two girls, finding himself at one point having to resist an urge to hug one of them—a totally new experience for him. He enthusiastically spoke of how different he felt about 'normal dating' and a one-month period without interviews was decided upon to let him follow his new inclinations" (Davison, 1968, p. 86).

He reported one month later at the sixth session that his sadistic fantasy had not reappeared and that he could masturbate to both real and imagined appropriate sexual stimuli. He was encouraged to date girls, because he had not been dating. The client requested help with procrastinating on his studies and two sessions were devoted to this topic.

This program focused on altering sexual fantasies as providing one route to altering sexual-social behavior. However, there were additional methods employed such as offering a model for, and practice in, male talk about girls, giving him assignments to date, directing him to attend to desirable characteristics of girls in real life, and offering him a new more helpful orientation to his problem. As Davison points out: "whether Mr. M. would actually begin dating again regularly, or at all, would seem to depend importantly on factors other than those dealt with in this brief therapy; for example, the client's physical attractiveness, his conversational and sexual techniques, the availability of women attractive to him, and so forth" (Davison, 1968, p. 88).

Follow-up contact was made with the client sixteen months later. He reported that he had not experienced the sadistic fantasies for seven months and that for the other nine months had decided to return to the use of sadistic fantasies during masturbation. In accord with the schedule he had established for himself, he dropped these fantasies and returned to masturbation using heterosexual events. He said that he had gotten to know a number of girls and that "by my old standards I have become a regular rake" (Davison, 1968, p. 89). As Davison (1968) points out the immediate excitation caused by the sadistic fantasies when the client decided to return to them makes questionable the role of the aversive counterconditioning in terms of being effective in and of itself.

Behavioral intervention procedures for rapists are in the early stages of design (see Abel, Blanchard, and Becker, in press). Research in this area poses problems of confidentiality as well as unique issues of public concern. Identity of clients is protected by assigning each client an identification number and filing information by this number. Given the high recidivism rate for men who are incarcerated for rape offenses, develop-

ment of effective procedures to decrease such behavior is sorely
needed.

Treatment of Child Molestation. Kohlenberg (1974b) employed aversive conditioning to decrease deviant arousal, and
employed a program modeled on Masters and Johnson (1970)
to increase appropriate arousal with a thirty-four-year-old male
who had been arrested twice for child molestation. During the
first four weeks of counselor-client contact, Mr. M.'s history
was obtained, relevant baseline information was gathered and an
intervention plan developed. The client only became aroused in
relation to young males of about six to twelve years of age. He
reported that he looked for sexual contacts with young boys
about twice a week. Although this behavior did not currently
result in sexual contacts, it did result in discomfort and stress.
He reported that he thought about such children about twice a
day, and that he masturbated several times a week while fantasizing about children. Although he had sexual contacts with
other adult males several times a year, these did not result in
orgasm. Thoughts of encounters with adults made him apprehensive and tense, and he reported that he tended to form relationships with men who were already committed in some way,
so that sexual contacts would be precluded. His sexual history
revealed that his first sexual contact took place at the age of
eight, with his twelve-year-old brother. Such contacts persisted
for several years and also included his younger brother. He did
not recall ever being attracted to adult females.

Mr. M. was requested to keep a daily record of the number of thoughts about young males, the number of prowling
incidents, and the number of encounters with adults who were
sexually arousing. The counselor required these records as a
condition for the continuation of counseling and the client received a rebate of $5 from his $20 fee for each week such records were turned in. Collection of baseline information over
four weeks revealed a zero frequency of sexual contacts with
adults, five instances of prowling, and between twelve to sixteen thoughts about children each week. Because display of his
sexual behavior to children could result in his arrest, it was decided to first employ aversive conditioning to decrease the sexual arousal value of children. Aversive conditioning, using elec-

tric shock paired with imagined approach to young males, was carried out during the fifth to eighth sessions. Instructions were given by the therapist to imagine a scene; when Mr. M. signaled that the image was vivid, a shock was delivered. During the first session, eleven such pairings were made; six occurred during the second session. Little change was noted in any client-reported measure of behavior. (A finger shocker was employed.)

In vivo desensitization was then introduced, the goal of which was to enable sexual arousal and orgasms for the client with adult male partners. This procedure first required that Mr. M. locate a sexual partner, who was to be at least thirty years old, willing to attend ten weeks of counseling sessions, and have two encounters with the client each week in which he agreed to follow a program that included sexual encounters that did not eventuate in orgasm. A suitable partner whom the client had known previously agreed to participate. Joint sessions were initiated with a discussion of learning principles concerning choice of sexual object, and a first assignment was given for Mr. M. and Mr. C. to have two encounters during the week. "These first encounters were to take place with both men in bed without clothes. As described in Masters and Johnson (1970) for heterosexual couples, they were instructed to take turns giving each other sensate pleasures. Touching and caressing of any kind was permissible, but there was to be no touching of the genital or anal area and sexual arousal was not a goal" (Kohlenberg, 1974b, p. 194). Mr. C. reported that he found these sessions enjoyable, but Mr. M. reported that he felt very tense. Mr. M. was concerned with his own sexual performance and was worried about Mr. C.'s reaction to his own lack of sexual arousal. The effects of the observer role on sexual arousal was discussed, and Mr. C. assured the client that his lack of sexual arousal was not viewed negatively. The clients were again asked to engage in the same assignment, with the objective of becoming relaxed and experiencing pleasant feelings. It was stressed that sexual arousal was not a goal. Positive results were reported with this assignment, with Mr. M. being relaxed and even becoming sexually aroused. The step-by-step in vivo approach employed by Masters and Johnson (1970) with heterosexual couples was employed with Mr. M. and his partner. A higher step was introduced only when relaxation and pleasure were reported with an earlier step. These included: "(1) touching for sensate pleasure; (2) touching for sensate pleasure, some exploratory touching of the genital area; (3) simultaneous genital touching, orgasm not permitted; (4) simultaneous genital touching and belly rubbing with genital contact, orgasm not permitted; (5) no restrictions, orgasm permitted" (Kohlenberg, 1974b, p. 195).

Over time, in these in vivo practice sessions, Mr. M. became aroused with Mr. C. He reported that he now found older men attractive and on several occasions had sexual contacts with other males that he found arousing. The number of thoughts about children decreased markedly. Kohlenberg speculated that increasing sexual behavior toward adult males provided "a repertoire of behavior that was incompatible with 'prowling' for children. That is, those periods of time that normally would have been spent seeking contacts with children were now spent making contacts with adult males" (Kohlenberg, 1974b, p. 195). Arousal value of adult males was not complicated by the aversive characteristics associated with children —for example, being arrested. This study provides an example of using a graduated in vivo program to increase sexual arousal to sexual activities that are more appropriate. Because aversive conditioning produced no change, this reorientation of sexual arousal could have been achieved totally through positive means of intervention. This case example illustrates "the use of behavioral principles to assist a client in achieving his own personally preferred, albeit socially unconventional goals" (Franks and Wilson, 1975, p. 524). For various reactions to the ethics involved in this example, the reader is referred to Davison and Wilson (1974), Garfield (1974), and to Chapter Twenty-Two of this book, on ethics.

Heterosexual arousal to mature females was increased by pairing sexual arousal elicited by pictures of young girls with slides of increasingly older women (Beech, Watts, and Poole, 1971). The results indicated that interest in young girls declined, even though no aversion therapy had been employed. Edwards (1972) employed training in thought stopping and assertion training to decrease pedophilic behavior of ten years' duration. Photographic records of the reenactment of child

molestation behaviors with mannequins have been helpful in revealing behaviors engaged in (Forgione, 1976). A sexual retraining program has been employed with incarcerated homosexual
pedophiliacs, using desensitization as well as sexual retraining in
the direction of fostering sexual behavior with adult males.
Other aspects of this program include education of prison staff
and attaining cooperation of local gay groups (Serber and Keith,
1974). One recent case study describes the use of behavioral
procedures to decrease incestuous behavior (Harbert, Barlow,
Hersen, and Austin, 1974).

Fetishistic Behavior. A number of studies of behavioral
intervention have reported a decrease in fetish-related behavior
and an increase in more appropriate sexual arousal patterns.
Raymond (1956), for example, reported a case of a male who
had been arrested on repeated occasions for behaviors such as
smearing mucus on women's handbags and damaging baby carriages. Assessment revealed that sexual arousal with his wife
depended on engaging in a variety of fantasies about handbags
and baby carriages. In an aversion therapy program, handbags
and carriages were paired with nausea. Not only did these behaviors decrease, but more appropriate sexual behavior with his
wife increased.

One twenty-one-year-old male client occasionally had
entered the dressing rooms of young boys during hockey
matches or their cabins at summer camp and took trousers in
order to use them during masturbation. After aversive conditioning failed to create any change in his trouser fetish, Marshall
(1974) employed orgasmic reconditioning—the client was given
material that described heterosexual activities and a series of
photographs, and was asked to attend to this material while
masturbating. The client was also provided with a bottle of
smelling salts—the counselor suggested that he carry this with
him at all times and that he inhale from the bottle whenever a
deviant fantasy started to occur. He reported employing this
procedure on 90 percent of the occasions on which he started
to have a deviant fantasy. A six-month follow-up revealed that
"his only difficulty was in maintaining heterosexual fantasy
during masturbation in the period between initiation and ejaculation. . . . Fantasy at other times was heterosexual, and no

deviant masturbation-independent fantasy occurred. The subject had not engaged in any trouser-procuring behavior despite many opportunities" (Marshall, 1974, pp. 615-616).

Transvestism. The terms *cross-dressing* and *transvestism* refer to sexual arousal that is associated with wearing the clothing of the opposite sex. There are many reports of the influence of social learning history on the development of such reactions. For example, males may be initiated into cross-dressing by their mothers or may be highly rewarded by their mothers when they themselves put on girls' clothes (Stoller, 1969). Aversive conditioning has been employed with uneven results (see, for example, Moss, Rada, and Appell, 1970). An impetus for seeking consultation is often the reactions of a significant other who raises concerns about the cross-dressing and associated activities of a partner. Carr (1974) reported the case of a twenty-four-year-old male who was recently divorced by his wife after a failure of one consultation attempt to alter his habit of taking enemas and dressing in women's underpants. The association of enemas with sexual arousal dated back to the age of thirteen, when the client had masturbated while giving himself an enema and had achieved an orgasm. This pairing had been repeated up until the present time when he administered enemas to himself on evenings during weekdays or late afternoon on weekends. The discovery that his arousal could be heightened by putting on women's underclothing before and after the enema seemed accidental. However, after a year (at the age of fourteen), the cross-dressing became very frequent, and he would wear woman's undergarments whenever possible. When first seen by the counselor, the client would put on the underwear early in the morning under his other clothes "which heightened his sexual anticipation over the day, leading to the enema and orgasm at the end of the day" (Carr, 1974, p. 172). He could not reach orgasm simply through cross-dressing and reported that he sometimes became bored with this procedure. His frequency of enema and cross-dressing behaviors decreased from five per week to about twice a week after his marriage, "apparently because there was less opportunity for enemas and because sexual intercourse with wife (one to four times per week) provided some alternative satisfaction" (Carr, 1974, p. 172). The frequency of his behaviors increased after his wife discovered his enema bag and his supply of feminine underwear. Thereafter, she made it a point not to be around at times when he was likely to engage in this behavior, which offered him more opportunities to engage in this. His increase in the behavior may also have been related to the fact that she was apparently intrigued by the behavior, as evidenced by her frequent inquiries.

The goals of intervention included a decrease in enemas and cross-dressing and an increase in social contacts and heterosexual behavior. Opportunities for the former two behaviors were decreased by selecting and scheduling competing pleasurable activities, such as movies, going to dinner, and meeting friends, at peak risk times. These activities hopefully would compete with one of the occasions on which the behaviors to be decreased occurred—when he felt lonely or bored. The client possessed opportunities to meet women as well as appropriate social skills. He agreed to engage in one "new and unusual social activity every week to extend his social repertoire—[attending the] opera, horse racing, sailing, skin diving, art shows, riding the ferry, mountain climbing, hiking, beachcombing" (Carr, 1974, p. 173). In order to remove reinforcing value of the enema behavior, he was asked to gradually increase the latency between the enema and the orgasm induced by masturbation. As a further attempt to decrease enema behavior, a program was developed to decrease the anticipatory enema response by engaging in "cognitive replay" twice a day at times when no reinforcement was possible—such as when at his office. He was also asked to confine his dating of women to those who evidenced obvious sexual interest in him and to only participate in sexual activity when very motivated "and once the opportunity for sex arose and the drive was high, not to delay intercourse too long. He had reported that occasionally intercourse was not successful, especially if there had been a long (sometimes two hours) foreplay period" (Carr, 1974, p. 173). He was also asked to keep a daily log in which he kept track of the time of all target events, the participants, how he felt (whether it was pleasurable or not), and what happened right before and after each event. Target events to receive special attention were enemas, cross-dressing, dates, and coitus.

Cross-dressing decreased from five times to week to zero within three weeks, and by the thirteenth week enema behavior decreased from four times a week to zero. Frequency of dates increased from zero to five a week at the end of thirteenth week, and intercourse increased from zero to twice a week. The latter activity increased substantially in the self-reported pleasure associated with it. The client also reported greater feelings of self-confidence and welf-worth. Gains were maintained at a five-month follow-up. This intervention program carefully considered the factors related to behaviors to be decreased and arranged for the increase of incompatible behaviors. The self-management aspects of the program make it likely that gains will be maintained.

Lambley (1974) reported the successful use of reinforcement of heterosexual imagery and planned heterosexual encounters, coupled with graduated in vivo exposure for erectile failure and orgasmic reconditioning for orgasmic failure in a successful intervention with a twenty-six-year-old male transvestite who requested treatment. Behavior rehearsal and feedback were employed to increase his social skills. After five weeks, he met a woman he had known previously and became involved in a sexual relationship with her. His cross-dressing decreased from a baseline of four times a week to once a week, although he still engaged in fantasies about cross-dressing. Cross-dressing behavior decreased to zero by the end of the seventh week, and he reported that he preferred to spend his time with his girlfriend. At that time, however, he started to experience trouble in maintaining an erection and both he and his partner were engaged in a graduated in vivo exposure program designed to overcome this problem. During an individual counseling session, the client was introduced to orgasmic reconditioning. He was to employ his cross-dressing fantasy during intercourse, because it invariably aroused him sexually. After a number of successful uses of this fantasy, he was instructed to reintroduce the heterosexual fantasy during intercourse. A six-month follow-up indicated that positive gains had been maintained. He still had some cross-dressing fantasies but considered these "secondary to his interest in heterosexual activities" (Lambley, 1974, p. 102).

Homosexuality. A large number of studies report the results of attempts to alter homosexual behavior and arousal patterns, primarily those of male homosexuals (see Bancroft, 1974; Barlow, 1973). Initial attempts focused on the use of aversive conditioning. For example, Feldman and MacCullouch (1965, 1971) employed an aversion-relief procedure in which slides of men were paired with shock or threat of shock, and slides of women were paired with relief from an aversive event. Recent efforts have been more enlightened: they have shown concern for multiform intervention based on individual behavioral analysis, including the development of needed heterosexual skills; have questioned the ethical appropriateness of pursuing a change in sexual orientation; and have used positive rather than aversive procedures to alter sexual arousal patterns. This enlightenment is not shared by all, however, as suggested by Barlow in 1973: "It is revealing that in the empirical field of behavior modification, the use of a therapeutic technique [aversion relief] has now been reported in the literature on approximately 150 cases and continues to be employed clinically without any evidence that it is effective" (Barlow, 1973, p. 659). In the past, it was thought that use of aversion relief would increase heterosexual responsiveness, but there is no evidence that this occurs (see Barlow, 1973). However, pairing events associated with deviant arousal with aversive events may occasion an increase in heterosexual responsiveness (Barlow, Leitenberg, and Agras, 1969). Further studies question the necessity of employing aversive conditioning at all in order to increase heterosexual arousal. For example, Barlow and Agras (1973) found that a fading procedure, in which female characteristics were gradually superimposed on a slide of a male while the client maintained a 75 percent erection, was effective in increasing heterosexual arousal. Pairing is another procedure that has been employed to increase heterosexual responsiveness. Here, sexual arousal is paired with heterosexual stimuli. As Barlow (1973) notes, this procedure has been referred to by a number of names, including *counterconditioning, classical conditioning,* and, "when masturbation is used to produce sexual arousal, the procedure has been called *masturbation conditioning* or *orgasmic reconditioning*"

(Barlow, 1973, p. 662). (Also see Marquis, 1970). An example of pairing has been described under the topic of decreasing sadistic fantasies.

Neither pairing nor fading provides for development of other needed behaviors, such as an increase in heterosexual skills or other skills, the absence of which may be related to homosexual behavior. Stevenson and Wolpe (1960) for example, employed assertion training to alter deviant sexual behavior. Behavior rehearsal with women has been employed to teach social and assertive behaviors to six male homosexuals, who subsequently reported increases in heterosexual interest (Cautela and Wisocki, 1971). As noted by Barlow (1973), this emphasis on retraining is similar to Salter's (1948) and Ellis's (1959) approach, "in which homosexual activity is largely ignored and the patient is taught in the first instance to be more assertive and, second, is given instructions and encouragement on appropriate heterosocial and heterosexual behavior" (Barlow, 1973, p. 662). Some clinical reports indicate that systematic desensitization can increase heterosexual responsiveness in the absence of aversion therapy (see, for example, Kraft, 1967). Use of this procedure is aimed at decreasing heterosexual anxiety and would only be appropriate if such anxiety existed.

Only through a careful behavioral analysis will the precise intervention methods that are required for a given client be identified. As Barlow (1973) suggests, this analysis will probably frequently consist of a procedure such as fading to increase heterosexual responsiveness, as well as of social skill training to establish heterosocial skills. "There is an immediate need for a precise delineation of the various behavioral components constituting heterosexual responsiveness and for the development of reliable and valid measurement devices to assess the extent of deficiencies in each component, so that the appropriate technique or combination of techniques can be administered" (Barlow, 1973, p. 667).

Should the desired outcome always be to increase heterosexual responsiveness? Clearly not. The goal should depend on the wishes of the client, which may be enlightened by the counselor's discussion of possible reasons for a requested change in sexual orientation, including external pressures that perhaps should not be permitted to influence the selection of desired outcome. The case examples discussed under the topic of child molestation provide illustrations of instances where the goal is to increase homosexual responsiveness to adult males. The distinction has been made between *homosexual problem behaviors,* which implies that the behavior is a problem because it is not heterosexual, and *problem behaviors of homosexuals,* which recognizes that persons with a homosexual orientation may have problems in living, as may any other group of individuals, but that these problems are not necessarily related to having homosexual orientation (Begelman, 1975). There is a need for descriptive information concerning what may be the problems of homosexual persons. For example, what unique problems, if any, are related to the deviant status of the homosexual in the eyes of many laymen? Recent reports describe the use of assertion training for problems that may be entailed with "coming out" (see Duehn and Mayadas, 1976). The management problems that may be involved for homosexual persons are well described by Plummer (1975).

Transsexualism. The term *transsexualism* refers to the adoption of opposite-sex role behavior as well as thinking, feeling, and behaving in the opposite-sex role (Green and Money, 1969). Clients who display this behavioral, cognitive, and emotional pattern often request sex reassignment surgery. The developmental history of transsexuals is very different from that of homosexuals (see Green and Money, 1969) and clear distinctions should be drawn between transsexualism and both transvestism and homosexual behavior. For example, transsexuals display behaviors such as spontaneous cross-dressing in early childhood. This does not necessarily occur among homosexuals or transvestites (Stoller, 1969). Barlow, Reynolds, and Agras (1973) report a successful program for altering adult transsexualism. Because the only approach to date to alter such behavior has consisted of surgical methods, identification of a psychological approach would have the advantage of precluding the necessity for this radical form of intervention. The client was a seventeen-year-old male transsexual who had thought of himself as a girl for as long as he could remember. He began to cross-dress at age five and continued to do so into junior high school. He associated mostly with girls, although he reported being attracted to a boy friend in the first grade. He reported that he had had his first sexual fantasies at about the age of twelve, picturing himself as a woman having intercourse with a male. These fantasies continued to the time at which he was treated, and although the client engaged in masturbation during the fantasies, he reported having neither orgasm nor ejaculation. "Upon referral he was moderately depressed, withdrawn, and attending secretarial school where he was the only boy in the class. He reported a strong desire to change his sex. Since surgery was not possible at his age, he agreed to enter a treatment program designed to change his gender identity on the premise that it might at least make him more comfortable and that surgery was always possible at a later date" (Barlow, 1974, p. 137).

The first intervention effort was devoted toward increasing heterosexual arousal through fading, a procedure in which heterosexual stimuli are gradually introduced while the client is sexually aroused (see the discussion of homosexuality earlier in this chapter). No change in sexual arousal, as measured by penile circumference changes, by six slides of nude men and women occurred over eight sessions nor did the client report any change in sexual fantasies. He was asked to record each sexual urge felt toward another person, each sexual fantasy in the absence of any person, and to indicate the sex of the person involved in the urge or fantasy.

Aversion therapy was then introduced to decrease arousal value of transsexual fantasies, to which he often masturbated. Electrical shock delivered to his forearm was paired with his transsexual fantasy until he indicated that the fantasy had ended. No changes occurred over forty-eight daily half-hour sessions in patterns of sexual arousal, in reports of urges and fantasies, or in the transsexual attitude scale. This scale was based on ten statements made by the client at the first interview. Each was written on a card, and the client sorted these into one of five envelopes, twice a week. Envelopes were marked from zero (no desirability) to four (much desirability). He placed each index card, which described a state of affairs, such as "I want to have female genitals," or an activity, such as "I want to have intercourse with a man," into one of the envelopes.

An effort was then made to alter his effeminate motor behavior. The first step in this procedure was to develop a "behavioral checklist of gender-specific motor behaviors" (Barlow, 1974, p. 138). On the basis of observation of men and women in the natural environment, three male characteristics and three female characteristics of sitting, walking, and standing were selected. The client's behavior in these three areas had elicited the most ridicule and caused him much discomfort. An example of one of the behavioral components selected as being characteristic of sitting in males was crossing the legs with one ankle resting on the opposite knee, whereas in the characteristic female behavior the legs were crossed and were closely together, with one knee on top of the other. This scale was validated on groups of five men and women selected as being normal for their sex. The scale clearly distinguished between male and female motor behavior and interrater reliability was .96.

Videotape feedback and model presentation were employed to attempt to modify sitting, standing, and walking patterns of the client. Intervention was applied to one behavior at a time within a multiple baseline design across behaviors (see Chapter Eight for further description of this design). Measures of gender-specific motor behaviors were gathered by an observer as the client came into the waiting room to attend daily half-hour sessions. Following five days of baseline observation, intervention was initiated with sitting behavior. Sitting was broken down into its components; each component was modeled by a male counselor and then practiced by the client. Praise and feedback were provided after each practice attempt. The client's last rehearsal of the day was replayed for him at the beginning of the next session. When appropriate sitting behavior had increased, intervention was then initiated for walking. Graphing of male and female behavior in relation to the three areas of sitting, walking, and standing revealed that the program was successful in increasing male behaviors and decreasing female behaviors in these areas. Although the client reported that he was pleased with the alteration in his behavior, because people did not stare at him as much, there were no changes in his pattern of sexual arousal, urges, or fantasies, and no changes on the transsexual attitude scale. Additional attention was then devoted to the alteration of other feminine sex role behaviors, such as vocal characteristics and sexual fantasies.

Additional behaviors were identified, and model presentation, rehearsal, and feedback employed to increase masculine behaviors. Situations included asking a girl out; being on a date; talking to his classmates (he had enrolled in a small high school, part-time) about his classes or other academic topics; and talking about football, dates, or girlfriends with a group of boys. Specific behaviors selected for increase in these situations included eye contact, duration of response, initiations of conversations, appropriate affect, and appropriate conversational content. Training also concentrated on decreasing the pitch of his voice, decreasing feminine inflections in his speech pattern, and increasing a relaxed speech pattern to replace his clipped manner of speaking. Daily sessions, for three weeks, were held for voice retraining. The suggestion that the client try to keep his thyroid cartilage low when speaking was helpful in regulating his speech. After this training, both the client and counselor felt there were positive changes, although no objective measures were made of these behaviors. In addition, the client reported several occasions on which a friend had not recognized his voice over the phone. Although the client now reported that he liked his new masculine behavior and that it was easier to look and act like a boy, he said that he still felt like a girl and that if he had the choice he would alter his sex.

The next component of the intervention program focused directly on altering his transsexual fantasies and thoughts. The object of this fantasy training was to develop competing gender-appropriate fantasies in which he, as a male, had intercourse with a female. Training involved trying to imagine sexual involvement with women depicted in a series of four pictures. He was also encouraged to fantasize sexual interactions with women whom he encountered. Duration of heterosexual fantasies increased over sessions, and for the first time transsexual attitude decreased and reports of sexual fantasies showed some change. Reported fantasies concerning women increased to five and then to nine a day from their zero baseline level. This phase of intervention lasted two months, during which thirty-four sessions were held. At the end of this program, although he now not only acted like a man, but also thought more like a man, the client still experienced sexual arousal to male stimuli and continued to feel attracted to men he met, on an average of about five times a day. One difference, however, was that his fantasies no longer involved gender role reversal. He still showed no arousal to women.

Slides of nude women were then paired with slides of nude men that elicited strong arousal, in order to alter his sexual arousal pattern. As a result of this procedure, arousal to female slides rose from zero to 40 percent of a full erection. This was accompanied by client reports of sexual attraction to and fantasies about girls he met. Aversion therapy was then introduced to decrease arousal to men, using both electrical aversion and covert sensitization. This time, aversive conditioning was effective. Sessions were held over a two-month period for a total of twenty sessions. Arousal to men decreased from 45 percent of a full erection to 5 percent, and fantasies decreased from eight per day to three per day, whereas arousal to female slides increased to 50 percent. Interestingly, although no further direct efforts had been made to alter patterns of sitting, walking, and standing behavior, there was an increase in masculine behavior in these areas after the program of heterosexual arousal via classical conditioning. Isolate and depressive tendencies had disappeared and he had started going full-time to high school. He said that he was comfortable on most social occasions and that he would like to date and have sexual exchanges with women. He reported orgasm and ejaculation for the first time, five months after intervention ended, as a result of masturbation while imagining sexual intercourse with a girl. Contacts with the client were gradually tapered off, being held once a week at first, then once a month and so on. Nine months following the end of the formal program, the transsexual card sort was zero, masculine behavior as recorded during observation was high, and he reported an absence of homosexual arousal and fantasies. He had begun to date and reported that he was doing well in school. Contact at the end of a year indicated that he now had a steady girlfriend and engaged in light petting with her. Heterosexual arousal remained at about 55 percent, and homosexual arousal remained low, at 15 percent.

Decreasing Deviant Sex-Role Behaviors in Children

There is increasing evidence that childhood cross-gender behaviors are indicative of later sexual variations, including transvestism, transsexualism and some forms of homosexuality (see, for example, Stoller, 1968; Green, 1968). Male children who are anatomically normal, but who have pronounced feminine characteristics, are now diagnosed as having childhood "cross-gender identity problems" (see, for example, Green, 1968). In the literature, a few reports have appeared in which an attempt has been made to normalize sex role behaviors of such children. For example, Rekers and Lovaas (1974) employed reinforcement procedures to increase appropriate gender behaviors of a boy aged four years, eleven months, who displayed a clinical history paralleling retrospective reports of adult transsexuals that included cross-gender clothing preference, actual or imaginal use of cosmetic items, feminine mannerisms, an aversion to masculine activities and a preference for girl playmates and feminine activities, preference for the female role, feminine voice inflection, and feminine speech content and verbal statements concerning a desire to be a girl (Rekers and Lovaas, 1974). Why would one wish to alter the behavior of such a child? Rekers and Lovaas (1974) offer four reasons. First, the feminine behavior on the part of this young male child was resulting in ridicule and isolation from peers. The authors point out that although perhaps society should become more tolerant of such behavior, it is not, at the present time, "and, realistically speaking, it is potentially more difficult to modify society's behavior than Kraig's in order to relieve Kraig's suffering" (Rekers and Lovaal, 1974, p. 174). Secondly, such deviation from appropriate sex-role behaviors at this early age seems to be associated with severe adjustment problems in adulthood. For example, substantial gender problems may occur in adulthood (Green and Money, 1969). Autocastration or autopenectomy was attempted by 18 percent of a sample of adult transsexuals and accomplished in 9 percent (Pauly, 1965). Moreover, arrest and imprisonment often occurs in adulthood (Money, 1968). Rekers and Lovaas (1974) also suggest that altering deviant sex-role development in childhood may be the only effective way to prevent "serious forms of sexual deviance" in the future. Sex reassignment surgery is often employed with transsexuals, involving a long series of painful operations. Until recently, other methods have failed to alter transsexual behaviors (see Barlow, Reynolds, and Agras, 1973). A last reason given by Rekers and Lovaas is the strong preference for treatment expressed by Kraig's parents. (The ethical questions involved in intervention efforts are discussed further in Chapter Twenty-Two.)

Given the lack of available information as to how to normalize deviant sex-role behavior, Rekers and Lovaas considered this study to be one of exploring possible environmental changes that might be effective. Several gender-related behaviors were selected for change, including playing with female dolls; playing with girls; feminine gestures, including limp wrist, "swishy" hand, arm, and torso movements, and swaying of hips; and female role play, which included pretending to be a female such as an actress, a mother, or a teacher. A sample of the frequency of the behaviors was gathered by Kraig's mother, who recorded his behavior for ten minutes four times each day. She checked each behavior observed during each time period. During clinic sessions, the mother was trained to differentially reinforce appropriate gender-related behaviors. Kraig and his mother visited the clinic three times a week and were involved in three ten-minute therapy sessions spread over an hour. "For each therapy session the following conditions were in effect: the mother was instructed to wear her earphones and to sit with a large book in her lap. She was told to attend selectively to masculine verbal and play behavior by smiling at Kraig and complimenting him on his play, and to ignore feminine behavior by picking up the book to 'read.' She was told that more specific instructions would be delivered over the earphones, to enable her to carry out these general instructions effectively" (Rekers and Lovaas, 1974, p. 179).

Observation of interaction between the mother and Kraig during clinic sessions revealed that sex-typed behaviors were greatly controlled by his mother's attention. The prompts given over the earphones were faded out in about four sessions, and over sessions the reinforcement schedule for appropriate behavior was thinned. The time-sampling information collected by Kraig's mother at home indicated that the changes observed during treatment sessions in the clinic did not generalize to the home situation, and therefore a treatment program was initiated in that setting. Both parents were first asked to read *Living with Children* (Patterson and Gullion, 1968), which describes the application of social learning principles to the behavior problems of children. A token program was established first, for nongender-associated behaviors, to see if the mother could apply contingencies in a consistent fashion; to establish a clear distinction between blue tokens, which could be exchanged for backup reinforcers, and red tokens, which were to become discriminative for response cost; and to test out how effective the response-cost component would be. Thus tokens were first awarded for brushing the teeth, washing hands before eating, chores and so forth and red tokens were given for slamming doors, cursing at mother, disturbing his baby sister, and breaking household objects. Instructions were given to the mother to be sure to verbally describe the contingencies to Kraig and to record desirable and undesirable behaviors each day. Use of red tokens for behaviors to be decreased did not result in any change until red tokens were backed up by spankings. "Kraig was told that he would get one 'swat' from his father for each red token he collected. After receiving two swats in this manner for red tokens he had received while engaged in non-gender-related behaviors, Kraig carefully avoided receiving but a few red tokens from that time on, even though the treatment was to persist for more than half a year" (Rekers and Lovaas, 1974, p. 185). Reliability of the mother's records were checked by a research assistant who visited the home two times a week. "The mother was required to sign a written contract with the investigators that specified that continued treatment was contingent upon the mother's success in carrying out two instructions: to take reliable observational data in the home, and to gain control over the non-gender-related behavior" (Rekers and Lovaas, 1974, p. 181).

The token program was applied to gender-related behaviors after it had been successful in altering non-gender-related behavior. It should be noted that considerable help was given to the mother in learning to employ the token program. A research assistant visited the home for forty-five-minute sessions at least three times a week for four months. This person not only collected observational information, but also answered questions concerning the operations of the token system. A multiple-baseline design across behaviors was employed, in which a response-cost condition was applied to only one feminine behavior at a time. As a result of the token system at home applied to gender-related behaviors, play with dolls decreased from zero to 15 percent during baseline to zero, and feminine gestures, which varied between zero and 50 percent during baseline, also decreased to zero. Rekers and Lovaas note that there was limited response and stimulus generalization. That is, intervention was largely related only to the specific behavior to which it was applied and there was little generalization from one stimulus situation to another. They also note the considerable time investment both by the parents and the counselor, and that it cannot be known at this time whether this intervention will have any effect on selection of sex mates in adulthood. As they note, preference for sex mate may be independent of the behaviors with which they were concerned.

Summary

The sexual response is viewed as primarily a learned behavioral pattern that is affected not only by physical factors but also by psychological and social factors. It is the interference of the latter with the natural sexual reaction that leads to such difficulties in sexual functioning as are displayed in erectile failure, premature ejaculation, and primary and secondary orgasmic problems in women. It has been especially within recent years that behavioral methods have been increasingly applied to the enhancement of sexual functioning through a procedure drawing on the Masters and Johnson (1970) programs and supplemented by a variety of other procedures. An important characteristic of these programs is an educational approach to enhancing sexual functioning in which the sexual response is returned to its natural context. A series of graduated homework assignments enables the gradual decrease of anxiety and inhibitions in the sexual area and the development of more functional communication patterns. Although the success of these programs is mainly attested to by uncontrolled case studies, the results so far appear most promising. Behavioral procedures have also been employed with a variety of sexual variations, including those involving nonvoluntary participants, such as rape, exhibitionism, voyeurism, and child molestation, and sexual variations in which voluntary participants interact, such as homosexuality. Many recent studies display a more informed approach to assessment and intervention compared to the earlier naive application of aversive conditioning, in which efforts are made to increase sexual arousal to appropriate stimuli and to develop needed heterosexual and heterosocial skills without the use of aversive conditioning. Promising results have also been achieved with modifying transsexual behavior.

21

Some clients are unable to manage by themselves in the community and require care in a twenty-four-hour residential facility, halfway house, or a day-care facility. This is true of many individuals discussed in Chapter Nineteen, which presented an overview of behavioral programs designed to affect severely disordered behavior. Management problems may be of concern to the community at large, such as with potentially assaultive clients. It is often necessary to refer a client to an appropriate setting: perhaps to find a nursing home for someone leaving a medical hospital, to locate a residential care home for a client returning from a mental hospital, or to find a halfway house for a teenager. This chapter directs attention to areas of concern in viewing residential care facilities and introduces the reader to some of the behavioral programs that have been carried out in

Residential Settings

these settings. Behavioral programs are in their infancy in some contexts, such as nursing and old-age homes whereas for others, including mental hospitals, institutions for the mentally retarded and halfway houses for delinquents, many years of accumulated information already exist.

Transitional Facilities

Transitional facilities are way stations between one setting and another (Keller and Alper, 1970). It is assumed that time spent there will provide for successful entry into the natural environment, and/or prevention of future breakdown of functioning. Thus, the overall objectives may be rehabilitative and/or preventative (Lamb, Heath, and Downing, 1969). They

995

may, for example, be employed when a client moves from residential care in a mental hospital as a first step toward reentry into the open community. Halfway houses, group homes, and day-care centers have been employed in this fashion (Lamb, Heath, and Downing, 1969). Now that care in the open community has become more popular, the use of such facilities has expanded.

The concept of transitional contexts is very reasonable, in that, if there is a careful matching between the repertoires of the residents, the objectives established for each, and the contingency systems in operation both inside and outside the setting, such contexts offer the opportunity to locate change efforts closer to the natural environment. Residents can remain in contact with situations in which problems occur and so work on them directly. For example, in Achievement Place, which is a halfway house for court-adjudicated delinquent, predelinquent, and dependent neglected boys in Lawrence, Kansas, rather than removing a boy from his problems with teachers, parents, and peer group, contact is maintained while seeking solutions (Phillips, 1968).

Even though a great many people reside in transitional facilities of various sorts, and such facilities are being developed at an increasing rate, there are few reports that describe the contingency systems operating within them, other than on an anecdotal basis. Exceptions include those run along behavioral lines, such as Achievement Place, and the group living environments created by Fairweather and his colleagues (see Fairweather, Sanders, Cressler, and Maynard, 1969).

Guidelines for Viewing Transitional Facilities. There are two major areas of concern in viewing the effectiveness of transitional settings: (1) the conditions provided within the facility, and (2) bridging arrangements with the natural environment. The contingencies arranged in either area may be, and often are, ineffective in relation to desired objectives. One problem often found is a failure to identify specific objectives for each resident. Rather, objectives are stated in global, general terms. Unless these are specified for each resident, one cannot, with any precision, examine the conditions provided by a program and assess their adequacy. Some attempts have been made to assess the quality of care in residential settings (see, for example, Whatmore, Durward, and Kushlick, 1975). The few careful studies that do exist, in addition to anecdotal material available, suggest additional sources of deficiency, as described in the following list.

1. Many reinforcers are available on a noncontingent basis that could be employed contingently to facilitate acquisition of appropriate behaviors, such as television, radio, access to staff, and work assignments.
2. Potential mediators are overlooked. Service staff, such as cooks, or the residents themselves, could be trained and employed as mediators of change for other residents, but typically are not.
3. Staff provides inconsistent or no reinforcement for appropriate behaviors, in addition to punishing some of these behaviors. In many settings, particularly for the elderly, residents are permitted and sometimes encouraged to just sit or sleep all day.
4. Staff provides reinforcement for inappropriate behaviors, so maintaining a repertoire that will make transition to the open community difficult. This kind of situation can have particularly unfortunate effects, in that not only may maintenance of an inappropriate behavior make life in the outside community a slim possibility, but in addition, if the behavior is unpleasant to staff, volunteers, or relatives who may visit, the resident may experience an increasing state of isolation. Rather than taking advantage of the unique possibilities offered by transitional settings (being close to the natural environment and taking advantage of the protection of the facility to develop acceptable behaviors) some facilities not only forgo these, but even utilize protection for just the opposite purpose—to create, or allow to be maintained, a repertoire that would not be tolerated in the open community and that prohibits entry there.
5. Little use is made of setting events to prompt appropriate behaviors and to decrease inappropriate behaviors.

6. Approximations to desirable behaviors are often over-looked and so not reinforced.
7. Little is done to encourage the use of some reinforcers through, for example, reinforcer sampling (Ayllon and Azrin, 1968b). Thus, behavior that might be strength-ened if supported by these may remain at low levels.
8. The setting includes only an impoverished selection of reinforcers. Even relatively inexpensive items that could be obtained are not available; for example, maga-zines and games.

There are, of course, exceptions in which these deficien-cies do not exist and some of these programs will be described in this chapter. For example, Spruce House in Philadelphia was the site of a demonstration project in which patients who would typically have been hospitalized were placed instead in a town house in Center City (Henderson, 1971). A token program was established and resident behavior was gradually shaped toward more effective behavior. Residents first received tokens contin-gent on performance of a number of tasks per day and per week. When behavior was maintained on a weekly schedule, the resident was then promoted to an outside workshop or to a regular job. Resources within the setting were used in a contin-gent fashion. Depending on the resident's token earnings, rooms of various degrees of privacy and pleasantness were available, and certain preferred jobs had to be earned.

Deficiencies in Links Between the Facility and the Com-munity. Location of the setting in the community should pro-vide the possibility for a variety of contacts with the natural environment that would otherwise not be possible. However, facilities differ in the extent to which they make use of avail-able outside resources. Thus, the degree of match between those both relevant and available, and those employed, is an impor-tant area to assess. Resources might include vocational training possibilities, jobs, recreational sources, social groups, and hobby groups.

Some facilities, such as Spruce House, have utilized out-side resources creatively. Facilities of the YWCA were used and the outside community was also taken advantage of by bringing portions of it inside for given purposes. Once a week, a group of college girls came to a dance held in the house. This provided an opportunity to establish social skills. The men received tokens for asking a girl to dance, for conversing with her, or initiating a conversation. Location in the community also permits community assignments, which increase skills required for reentry.

Preparation for Transition to the Community. Transitional facilities may be deficient in relation to the preparation of the resident, as well as the environment to which he or she will be moved. Lack of facilitative after-care is perhaps the main reason for the large recidivism rates. A decision must be made as to where the client should be located next. Available sites, including the home environment, should be scanned to determine the degree of match between conditions they could or do provide, and the desired and current repertoire of the client. If possible, the site selected should be maximally designed to maintain and establish adaptive behaviors and eliminate unadaptive ones, and should provide contingencies most closely approximating those in the natural environment.

If a resident is to be returned home, significant others should be involved prior to his return, so that they can learn to facilitate adaptive behavior. Prior to return home of children from the Children's Treatment Center, which is a residential facility for disturbed children in Madison, Wisconsin, parents are trained how to maintain and further goals already achieved. This program has been very successful (Browning and Stover, 1971). Also, to the degree possible, the client should be trained how to occasion and reinforce behaviors of significant others that will maintain adaptive behavior, and should also be trained in relevant self-management skills. In addition, programs can be established by the agency that facilitate and maintain behavior. The Huntsville-Madison County Mental Health Center has established some innovative programs for accomplishing this, including home visits by an agency person who, depending on available behaviors of the client that are identified prior to discharge (for example, being out of bed, shaving, dressing, and reading the newspaper), awards points to the client that can immediately be traded for a variety of reinforcers, such as candy, gum, or cigarettes. These visits are moved from a regular to an intermittent schedule, so that the client cannot predict when his behavior will be checked and so possibly reinforced (Rinn, Tapp, and Petrella, 1973). Intermittent schedules of reinforcement are effective in maintaining a high and consistent rate of behavior (Ferster, Culbertson, and Boren, 1975). If the client is to be located in another transitional facility—for example, moved from a residential hospital to a halfway house—this move should be accompanied by a list of behavioral objectives to be achieved. Such continuity of care is often talked about in the literature (see, for example, Lamb, Heath, and Downing, 1969), but is seldom carried out.

It may be decided that more than one transitional facility will be employed prior to the client's return to the natural environment. A client may move from a residential hospital, to a halfway house, and from there to an apartment maintained by an agency. The move into an agency-maintained apartment moves the client one step closer to the open community without requiring him to find and furnish an apartment of his own. With each move, both the client and the new setting should be carefully prepared, so as to facilitate and maintain positive change. Important information about the client should be provided to the new caretakers, including any special medical or income maintenance needs. Caretakers are often hampered by a lack of such information. Clients may be delivered to a setting not only with no information provided as to objectives, or recommended change programs, but also without important information as to medical needs (Stein and Young, 1968).

Two examples of transitional settings are described in the following sections: a halfway house for youth and a day-care center for psychiatric clients.

Home-Style Residential Programs for Predelinquent Boys. The dissatisfaction with the results of sending delinquent youth to reformatories has encouraged the development of other possibilities such as halfway houses, which provide closer ties with the natural environment and avoid the well-known negative effects of incarceration. Achievement Place, a small group home setting for six to eight predelinquent boys, was established to determine the effectiveness of a token program coordinating the behavior in the home and community, as well as behavior in school (Phillips, 1968). The program was managed by professionally trained live-in staff called *teaching parents*. The emphasis of the program is to teach youth behaviors required for successful participation in their community. The age range of the residents was from twelve to sixteen. All had been declared dependent and neglected by the court. They were from low-income families and had committed a variety of offenses such as stealing and fighting, were generally disruptive, and had a history of truancy and academic failure. Most boys were about three or four years below their grade level on achievement tests.

The point program was carefully described to each youth on entering the home and he was introduced to the other boys. He was given a 3- X 5-inch index card on which to record his behavior and points earned and lost. Cheating was not been found to be a problem, possibly because of the high fine if caught (Phillips, 1968). Boys could earn points in three areas: social, self-care, and academic (see Table 25). Behaviors were selected that would be of value to the residents both now and in their future lives. Points could be lost for certain behaviors (see Table 25). Natural reinforcers were employed that would usually be available at home and that were valued by the boys (see Table 26). Initially, points were exchanged for privileges each day. This was then extended to a weekly point system in which points were exchanged for privileges only once a week. In this way, privileges could be used over and over again as reinforcers, because they could only be purchased one week at a time (Phillips, 1968). A merit system was finally introduced in which no points were awarded or removed and all privileges were available free. The usual stay at Achievement Place was about nine to twelve months and most residents were on the point system for most of this stay (Fixsen, Phillips, Phillips, and Wolf, 1976). A routine was established in the home, including rising at 6:30 A.M., washing faces and brushing teeth, and cleaning bedrooms and bathroom. A manager elected by his peers assigned specific tasks to each boy and monitored their completion. Managers were elected each week. Some of the boys helped the teaching parent make breakfast. Appearance was checked after breakfast by the manager, who noted whether hair was properly combed, shirt tucked in, buttons fastened, and hands clean. Each boy

Table 25. Behaviors and Number of Points Earned or Lost

Behaviors That Earned Points	Points
1. Watching news on television or reading the news-paper	300 per day
2. Cleaning and maintaining neatness in one's room	500 per day
3. Keeping one's person neat and clean	500 per day
4. Reading books	5 to 10 per page
5. Aiding houseparents in various household tasks	20 to 1000 per task
6. Doing dishes	500 to 1000 per meal
7. Being well dressed for an evening meal	100 to 500 per meal
8. Performing homework	500 per day
9. Obtaining desirable grades on school report cards	500 to 1000 per grade
10. Turning out lights when not in use	25 per light
Behaviors That Lost Points	Points
1. Failing grades on the report card	500 to 1000 per grade
2. Speaking aggressively	20 to 50 per response
3. Forgetting to wash hands before meals	100 to 300 per meal
4. Arguing	300 per response
5. Disobeying	100 to 1000 per response
6. Being late	10 per min
7. Displaying poor manners	50 to 100 per response
8. Engaging in poor posture	50 to 100 per response
9. Using poor grammar	20 to 50 per response
10. Stealing, lying, or cheating	10,000 per response

Source: Phillips (1968), p. 215).

Table 26. Privileges That Could be Earned Each Week with Points

Privileges for the Week	Price in Points
Allowance	1000
Bicycle	1000
Television	1000
Games	500
Tools	1000
Snacks	500
Permission to go downtown	1000
Permission to stay up past bedtime	1000
Permission to come home late after school	1000

Source: Phillips (1968, p. 214).

also received a daily school note on which his teacher at public school recorded information about his daily behavior. She simply checked yes or no to a series of questions. Boys progressed from daily feedback from their teachers to weekly feedback. These completed report cards were returned by the boys to the teaching parents and points were awarded or lost, depending on the teacher's judgment of their performance.

Return home was followed by an afternoon snack prior to initiating homework or other activities by which they could earn points. Boys who earned the privilege of going into town could do so. A family conference was held either during or right after dinner (Fixsen, Phillips, and Wolf, 1973). Topics discussed during these conferences included events of the day, performance by the manager, rules that youth or the teaching parents think should be established or altered, and consequences for infractions. There was an emphasis on teaching the youth self-government behaviors. After completion of the family conference, the boys were free to watch television or listen to records. They then tallied up their points for the day and retired about half past ten. Prior to their return home, a program was initiated with the boy's parents, to offer them skills that would help to maintain appropriate behavior. Detailed descriptions of this home-style setting are now available in *The Teaching-Family Handbook* (Phillips, Phillips, Fixsen, and Wolf, 1975).

In many programs, there is a lack of opportunity for youths to take part in decision making concerning the rules they live by (Fixsen, Phillips, and Wolf, 1973). A program designed to enhance self-governing skills was developed at Achievement Place. Complaints by the boys were employed as an opportunity to teach them how to make reasonable rules. They were given the opportunity to establish consequences for rule infractions during family conferences. The consequences involved were initially quite harsh, until the rule makers quickly learned that their own behavior as well as the behavior of the boy who had originally committed the infraction was affected by their rule. They gradually learned to establish rules that were fair. Discussions provided an opportunity to identify the components involved in discussing rule infractions, including obtaining a description of the circumstance surrounding the incident (who saw it, what happened, and so forth) and how a given infraction would affect relations between Achievement Place and other agencies, such as the school, court, and neighborhood. At first, boys were reinforced for participating in discussions. Participation was defined as suggesting alternatives, adding information, or making a statement that was directly related to the discussion taking place.

A preliminary evaluation of the results of Achievement Place is very encouraging. Whereas boys who had been sent to Kansas Boys School (an institution for delinquent youth) returned to a high number of police and court contacts during the first year of release, the youth from Achievement Place maintained a low number of such contacts (Fixsen, and others, 1976). Of those boys on probation or in Boys School, 54 and 53 percent respectively had an incidence of recidivism, compared to only 19 percent of the youth from Achievement Place. It should be noted that it is not clear whether this result is caused by the differences in assignment of boys to one site or the other, because this was not carried out on a random basis.

As Fixsen and his colleagues point out, recidivism is a measure of failure, not of success, and thus other measures were also viewed, such as attendance at public school. Of the boys from Achievement Place, 90 percent were still in school by the third semester after treatment, compared to 37 percent of youth placed on probation and 9 percent placed in the Kansas Boys School. Positive comparative changes were also found in grades and in days absent from school. As the authors note, even if these results are due to a "population effect" caused by nonrandom distribution to groups, there are policy implications, because the cost of placing a boy in an institution (a capital investment per youth of $20,000 to $30,000 and a yearly operating cost of $6,000 to $12,000) is so much higher than the costs involved in running a halfway house (a capital investment per boy of $6,000 and a yearly operating expense of $4,000).

Day-Care Centers for Psychiatric Patients. It has been established that token economies can be effective in increasing a range of self-care, social, and work-related behaviors of psychiatric patients (Kazdin and Bootzin, 1972). Self-care behaviors have included self-feeding and continence, and behaviors related to personal appearance, such as shaving, keeping clothes clean, and getting out of bed on time. The necessary ingredients for a token economy have been described by Ayllon and Azrin (1968b), and a number of sources are available that describe token programs in detail (see, for example, Schaefer and Martin, 1969; Atthowe and Krasner, 1968). The number of token programs in residential settings for psychiatric patients has increased greatly over the past few years.

The use of token programs in day-care facilities is quite recent (Liberman, King, and DeRisi, 1976). Results achieved in terms of increasing participation are so far promising. In the day-care program at the Oxnard Community Mental Health Center, each resident receives a credit card, on which credits earned and spent can be recorded. When credits are earned, the card is punched with a small heart or diamond. As credits, are spent, they are punched over with a large circular die. This system permits easy keeping of records; weekly cards are simply collected and information graphed. This information is employed during feedback sessions with clients. Credits can be earned for attending and participating in workshop activities and completion of workshop assignments, for cooking or preparing lunch, for washing, drying and putting away dishes, for completing an occupational therapy project, and for assisting staff. Credits awarded for these tasks ranged from five to ten. Fifty credits are awarded for being menu-planning chairperson for a one-week period and fifteen each day for being credit system monitor. Credits can be spent on a number of items, including coffee, lunch, a weekly banquet, bowling, bus trips, private therapy (five for each 15 minutes), time off (five credits per hour), a prescription from the doctor (ten credits), and doing your own thing. A cost of one credit for each 10 minutes a patient is late is enforced. Credits not spent at the end of the week can be bid for bonuses (such as two free dinners at a local restaurant) at weekly auctions. The program is designed to increase patient participation, as well as to help the staff get daily chores completed. The patients participate in running the system. Weekly meetings are held where they decide if any prices require change, and a client monitor is elected, whose responsibility it is to dispense, collect, and record credits. Liberal use is made of staff social reinforcement for appropriate client behavior.

Center activities include workshops designed to offer skills in community living such as personal finance and consumerism; grooming; conversational skills; recreational, social and educational activities; and use of public agencies. Clients participate in social skill training sessions three times each week. Inclusion of an educational workshop format substantially increased clients' social participation in the center.

Personal effectiveness training, in which clients learn needed social skills, is given special emphasis. This workshop was designed to increase a range of basic verbal and social behaviors, including conversational skills, job interviewing skills, and interactions with personnel at social agencies (Liberman, King, and De Risi, 1976). A variety of problem behaviors have been addressed in this program, including depression, suicide threats, destruction of property, high rate of sick-role talk, muteness, social withdrawal, apathy, aggression toward others, unstable work history, delusions, and anxiety. Behavioral goals are established and progress monitored for each client. For example, one client had a high frequency of complaints about tension. After three months of intervention, complaints of tension decreased to once a week and after six months decreased to once every other week (Austin, Liberman, King, and De Risi, undated). Another patient never attended church and avoided contact with friends. After three months, he had one social contact per month and attended church every other week. After six months, he attended church every three or four weekends and had a social contact twice a month. In another case, appropriate speech increased from a base rate of 50 percent to 60 percent at three months, and to 85 percent at six months.

A comparison of the results attained with the behavioral-educative day-care program with an eclectic program based on the concepts of a therapeutic community showed that the former was more effective in establishing and maintaining positive changes (Austin and others, undated).

Facilitating Successful Transition
from the Hospital to the Community

The existence of strong family and social relationships increases the probability of successful discharge of long-term mental patients (Paul, 1969a). During long-term hospitalization, such relationships usually erode. The effectiveness of response priming and reinforcer sampling was compared to the normal visiting procedure and an invitation-only procedure. The normal visiting policy allowed any relative or friend, on request, to visit the client at any time, either on or off the ward. Under it, the families of three clients involved in this study visited an average of one minute per week. In the invitation-only procedure, each family received a letter each week explaining the importance of visiting, describing the hospital's normal open visiting policy and requesting each family to designate dates on an enclosed card when they would visit. A stamped self-addressed envelope was enclosed. "One of the listed dates was circled in red and the families were informed that if they did not return the card or check one of the alternative dates, they would be expected to visit the hospital on the date circled" (O'Brien and Azrin, 1973, p. 133). No visiting occurred under this condition. In the response-priming procedure, in addition to the described letter and postcard, each family was informed that the hospital would provide transportation home for a short visit, that a staff member would accompany the client and that the length of the visit would be up to the family members. The staff member was instructed to say, at fifteen-minute intervals, "We should return to the hospital now," to ensure that visits would not be overextended. Unless a family member objected, the visit would then end. Each family was telephoned two days before the visit to set up details of the visit. Under this condition, each family averaged 80 minutes per week visiting with the clients. The mean time spent visiting per week increased from 99 minutes during the first six week period, to 171 minutes during the last response-priming period. The reinforcer development and sampling procedure is described as follows. "During visits to the home, the staff member evaluated the setting as it related to the behavioral needs of the patient. (Four different staff members served in this capacity throughout the study.) The ward program then developed those skills that were seen to be useful or required in the home. For example, a patient was trained to speak louder, since her relative was hard of hearing. Another patient practiced washing and ironing of clothing, since her mother earned money by doing so for neighbors. Similarly, a patient was taught to shop for groceries and to cook family meals since her husband suggested such assistance would be welcomed. During visits, the staff arranged for the patients to perform skills that would be useful to the family especially during an extended home visit. Examples of such useful activities were: dusting furniture, cooking meals, and washing dishes. The performance of the patient was assessed during the visit and the hospital program was modified on the basis of these assessments to assure greater satisfaction on the subsequent visits. Particular value was placed on the families' solicited assessment of the patient's performance" (O'Brien and Azrin, 1973, p. 134). Each family requested that the client return home to live with them in the community. The results with one client are described in the following quote: "During the thirty consecutive years Mary had been hospitalized, neither her husband nor other family members had ever visited her. During the Invitation-Plus-Transportation procedure, several different family members visited with her, but she most enjoyed visiting with her husband, who was retired but continued working his farm. At his and her requests, Mary was discharged to live with him. Weekly staff visits occurred for two months after discharge to provide them with assistance in helping her readjust. Weekly reports from a nearby relative revealed no major problems. At the time of this writing, over two years since she was discharged, the patient has not returned to the hospital nor reported any problems" (O'Brien and Azrin, 1973, p. 134).

Increasing and Maintaining Grooming Skills. Successful community placement requires minimal grooming skills on the part of patients exiting from residential settings for the retarded or for psychiatric patients. A lack of such skills can also be a major barrier to employment or to the establishment of social contacts. "Undeniable standards of acceptable grooming do exist in the social and employment community. If a client is not acquainted with these standards and if he is not helped to meet them, he is likely to fail to achieve larger goals in the areas of competitive employment and socialization. Many professionals fail to realize that 'common knowledge' about basic hygiene and grooming which has been part of their own upbringing, is not necessarily 'common' to all people. Many individuals who are poorly groomed or unclean simply lack basic information about how to care for their bodies and their appearance" (Prazak and Birch, 1976, p. 325). An innovative program designed to teach clients grooming skills has been developed at the Minneapolis Rehabilitation Center, which is a private nonprofit vocational rehabilitation agency that receives clients with a variety of problems, including mental retardation, drug dependence, delinquency, physical handicaps, and emotional maladjustment (Prazak and Birch, 1976). Staff at this center estimated that as many as 40 percent of the clients who sought their help had grooming problems of such an extent that they would have difficulty being hired.

This program, which is conducted by nonprofessionals, consists of a series of training modules for a variety of areas related to grooming considered necessary by current community standards (Prazak and Birch, 1976). The client selects modules of interest to him, and ones not checked but felt to be essential by staff are also included. Material is presented by cassette tapes synchronized with color slides illustrating various procedures. Mirrors, a sink, and grooming aids are present as needed. The final objective is for the client to display appropriate presentation of self for a job interview. Learning is broken down into small steps to permit frequent reinforcement and consistent success experiences for clients. Social reinforcement is offered by staff participating in the program and from peers (other clients involved in the program), and staff in other settings were sent daily notes that indicated the area of grooming currently being focused on, so they could also offer reinforcement. Additional reinforcers, such as increased conversation time with staff, were employed as incentives as needed.

Increasing Attendance at Self-Help Classes. It is not infrequent that clients refuse to participate in training programs designed to help them reenter the community. One procedure that has been employed to increase attendance at training classes is overcorrection (Foxx, 1976). This procedure is best described by referring to a case example. "Kathy was a thirty-one-year-old mildly retarded female (IQ = 59) who had been institutionalized for twenty years. Her retardation was diagnosed as the result of a prenatal syphilitic infection. Kathy resided on a token economy exit ward that prepared residents for community placements by teaching them independent living skills. These skills included personal grooming, clothing care, and classroom studies at the institutional school. Kathy was paid tokens for attending and successfully completing each daily training and educational activity. Yet Kathy often refused to attend, or if in attendance, to participate in activities, even when other reinforcers—such as coffee, cigarettes, and snacks—in addition to tokens, were delivered. She was chronically absent from her grooming and special education classes. The exit-ward staff was very interested in motivating Kathy to attend these two activities, because if she did not learn behavior commensurate with community placement, there was little hope she would ever leave the hospital" (Foxx, 1976, p. 391). The grooming class met for two hours each weekday afternoon and a special education class, designed to teach residents how to use money, obey traffic signals, and to shop wisely, met one hour a day four days a week. Prior to use of the overcorrection procedure, the teachers had used a time-out period for absence at classes. They would notify ward staff of Kathy's absence and she would be placed in a time-out room. This procedure was not effective. Two different overcorrection procedures were employed, one for the grooming class and one for the special education class. The overcorrection procedure designed to increase attendance at grooming classes consisted of escorting Kathy to a room that contained a table and chair and grooming supplies, contingent on her absence from class.

A profoundly retarded female from an adjacent ward was brought into the room and seated at the table. Kathy was required to groom the resi-

dent for thirty minutes. The overcorrective grooming consisted of Kathy giving the resident a manicure, combing her hair, and applying cosmetics.
Several steps were involved for each grooming act.
For example, when Kathy gave a manicure she was
required to fill a shallow basin with water, soak the
resident's nails, clean them, dry them, file them,
and then apply fingernail polish. A special trainer,
one of the teachers or the author, instructed Kathy
in each phase of the grooming. Whenever Kathy
failed to follow an instruction, she was manually
guided through the desired responses. This graduated guidance (Foxx and Azrin, 1972; 1973[b])
was faded gradually as Kathy voluntarily began the
desired response. The trainer shadowed Kathy's
hands with his in order to reapply the guidance if
necessary.

    After thirty minutes, the resident was es-
corted to the ward and Kathy was asked whether
she wished to attend grooming class or groom another resident. If she stated that she wished to
attend grooming class, she was escorted to the
class. If she chose not to attend class, another resident was brought into the overcorrection room.
Each half hour, Kathy was offered her choice until
the regular grooming class ended. Since the grooming class was two hours in duration, Kathy could
groom from one to a maximum of four residents
during the overcorrection period.

    *Overcorrection for failure to attend special
education class.* If Kathy did not attend the special
education class, the treatment plan called for her
to tutor a lower functioning student for one half
hour. At the end of the tutoring session, Kathy
would be asked whether she wished to attend class
or tutor another student. Because the class met for
one hour, Kathy would be required to tutor a maximum of two students. [Foxx, 1976, p. 392]

Kathy attended 70 percent of the grooming classes during the
first week of intervention, compared to 22 percent during baseline. Attendance was defined as being present and taking part in
classroom activity. Attendance then increased to 95 percent the
second week and 100 percent during twelve of the next thirteen
weeks. During baseline, Kathy attended only 32 percent of spe-

cial education classes. A few weeks after initiation of the first overcorrection procedure she was informed that she would have to tutor lower functioning residents from another class if she did not attend her special education class. Her attendance increased to and remained at 100 percent, even though the overcorrection procedure for this class was never experienced!

Lest the reader think that this all progressed smoothly, it should be noted that it was also necessary to employ an overcorrection procedure for combative behavior, which was displayed the first time overcorrection was used. This procedure consisted in escorting Kathy to her bed where she received "Quiet Training For Agitation" (Foxx and Azrin, 1972, p. 18) for her agitation. This required her to lie down in her bed for fifteen minutes. She proceeded to kick the counselor, which resulted in fifteen minutes of "Medical Assistance Training" (Foxx and Azrin, 1972, p. 17), in which she was required to "clean and medicate the counselor's contused and lacerated shin." She was then escorted back to the overcorrection room where she was required to groom a resident for thirty minutes. The first day, she groomed four residents rather than participate in her grooming class, but was calm during the remaining two-hour overcorrection period. On only two other occasions during the first week did she become agitated during overcorrection training, and in both instances complied with instructions after she received "Quiet Training." Once during the second week, she was found sitting in the classroom five minutes before the class was to begin and after this was usually present before the arrival of the teachers.

As Foxx points out, grooming others required a great deal more physical effort than grooming herself, because she performed all grooming tasks for the resident in thirty minutes rather than the two-hour grooming period for herself entailed in her class. Another important aspect of this program was the overcorrection procedure employed for combative behavior. This prohibited escape from the procedure. The previous use of time out actually provided Kathy a desired period of inactivity or of solitude. Foxx was sensitive to the possible negative attitude that might have developed in Kathy in relation to other retarded residents and, to prohibit this, after she began attending class regularly, he established a program in which she received reinforcement for helping residents she had been grooming during the overcorrection procedure.

Increasing Social Interaction. Many clients fail to share their problems and possible solutions with staff. One procedure employed to increase suggestions made by clients during group meetings has been response priming, in which hospitalized clients were required, rather than invited, to attend a group meeting where suggestions were reinforced (O'Brien, Azrin, and Henson, 1969). It was hypothesized that the presence of the client in the suggestion situation would prime communications that otherwise would not have been made. Suggestions were defined as direct and unequivocal requests for an addition to or change in the ward treatment procedure. Clients were prompted by three questions from the group leader, one of which was, "Is there anything about the program that you would like changed? The mean number of suggestions increased from 0.4 to 3.0 for seven of the thirteen clients. The frequency of suggestions was a direct function of the likelihood that a staff member would implement the suggestion. This response-priming procedure (which was initially considered superfluous by clients and staff, who said that clients would attend the meetings if they had anything to suggest) did, in fact, result in an increase in suggestions. Increased participation of clients in their treatment is important as a step toward independent behavior.

Tokens have been employed to increase appropriate verbalizations of patients in small groups. For example, Pierce and Drasgow (1969) gave patients a list of common feelings such as depression, joy, and anger. They were also offered sentences referring to a feeling. Tokens were given first for using one-word descriptions, and when these increased, they were given for entire sentences, such as "You feel happy." Through this process, interaction between residents increased substantially.

Ward-wide token programs in psychiatric settings usually arrange for reinforcement of social and work behaviors and increased activity (see Kazdin and Bootzin, 1972). Even extremely withdrawn patients have increased their activity when the Premack Principle has been employed—for example, in using sitting as a reinforcer for activity (Mitchell and Stoffelmayr,

1973). Offering clients a certain number of tokens that are transferable (that can be given to other patients and that cannot otherwise be spent) was found to increase social interaction between patients (Abrams, Hines, Pollack, Ross, Stubbs, and Polyot, 1974). Speech has been increased by prompting and reinforcing imitative responses (Thomson, Fraser, and McDougall, 1974). Training procedures for increasing the social skills of psychiatric patients is discussed in detail in Chapter Thirteen.

Public display of behavior ratings for retarded adults living in a halfway house was effective in increasing a range of appropriate behaviors, including getting along with others (not fighting), acceptable heterosexual interaction, grooming, appropriate language, completion of assignments, punctuality, accepting criticism, and keeping one's own area neat (Slavin, 1972). Each resident was rated at the end of the day as to whether he or she had met the criterion in each area. The ratings were left on the diningroom table for anyone to examine. The mean daily rating for all ten residents increased from 1.8 during baseline (out of a possible total of eight) to 4.1 during the public display procedure.

Behavioral procedures have been applied to the alleviation of depressive behaviors among hospitalized patients (see, for example, Schaefer and Martin, 1969). For example, in a study by Hersen, Eisler, Alford, and Agras (1973) four patients were given tokens on the completion of behaviors classified as work, occupational therapy, responsibility, and personal hygiene. Client behaviors, rated by ward nurses on sixteen occasions each day, included talking, smiling, and motor activity. The token system resulted in a large increase in the target behaviors. As Hersen and others point out, the increase in work behavior resulted in greater social interaction, which resulted in more natural reinforcement for smiling and talking. Smiling and crying of a twenty-year-old female patient was altered by offering her tokens whenever she was observed to be smiling. These tokens were tradeable for social reinforcers. The patient was fined when she was found to be crying (Reisinger, 1972). A marked increase occurred in the frequency of smiling and a decrease in crying responses. The client was discharged twenty weeks after the initiation of intervention. A fourteen-month follow-up indicated that she had not been rehospitalized nor had she received treatment; however we do not know what other treatment was offered during her hospital stay. These studies indicate that concomitants of depressed behavior are responsive to reinforcement contingencies.

Prosthetic Environments

Because of certain physical and/or cognitive deficits, some individuals may require residential care for the duration of their lives, or may require permanent changes in aspects of their natural environment in order to remain in the open community, such as provision of meals to elderly people who live by themselves, thus enabling them to remain in their homes, or the provision of day-care centers for the elderly. Services such as these permit many people to continue living in the community rather than requiring them to enter residential care.

Prosthetic environments may be ineffectively employed in two major ways. First, many people who are sent to full-time residential care do not require such a radical change in their environment. Such a change would not be objectionable if the conditions provided in the new facility were pleasing to the residents; however, this is not necessarily so, and in many instances the person would prefer to remain in his or her home. A more diligent search for ways to compensate for deficits in the community would prevent the necessity of removing many people from their homes. Maintenance in the open community can be facilitated by the provision of home-care services, such as the delivery of meals when a person is unable to fix them himself; the offering of roles that he would find reinforcing and so would maintain adaptive behavior, such as employing people as mediators of change for others; and the addition of needed prosthetic devices, including simple response amplifiers in case of physical weakness or sensory deficits (Lindsley, 1964), and prompting devices, which, for example, can be employed to cue an individual to take required medication (Azrin and Powell, 1969). A search for and creation of prosthetic additions that allow people to maintain themselves partially in the natural environment would pay off handsomely, not only in the provi-

sion of a richer environment for those involved, but also in providing more available mediators. Ideal alternatives offer supportive conditions, not only for the mediator but also for those
with whom he interacts, such as having elderly people who
attend day-care centers function as mediators for children attending a nearby child day-care center. Another example
includes expanded use of the elderly in foster home situations,
where they are given a home in the community and also fulfill a
useful role in functioning as a mediator for children in the
family. The use of group settings, in which a number of people
live together in a mutually supportive way, may obviate the requirement for institutionalization (Fairweather and others,
1969). Buddy systems (Paul, 1969a) could be established in any
of these environments. Such systems make one individual responsible for the well-being of another, to provide needed support. In addition, more attention should be devoted to training
individuals such as relatives of elderly people to reinforce those
who can support existence in the community. Provision of
training in how to maintain a pleasing appearance may also
make it easier for some, such as the elderly, to remain in the
community (Lindsley, 1964).

The second major way in which prosthetic environments
may be ineffectively employed is in relation to the conditions
offered within the facility. It is assumed here that residential
care of some type is a requisite. Descriptions are available of the
interaction between staff and residents in a variety of institutional settings, including reformatories (Buehler, Patterson, and
Furniss, 1966), mental hospitals (Gelfand, Gelfand, and Dobson, 1967), prisons (Milan and McKee, 1976), detention centers
(Gambrill, 1974), and institutions for children (see, for example, Daily, Allen, Chinsky, and Veit, 1974). These have not
yielded a very positive picture. Peers have been found to be
more consistent in offering reinforcement for inappropriate behavior than are staff in offering positive events for appropriate
behavior (Buehler, Patterson, and Furniss, 1966). In some instances, desirable interactions accounted for less than 1 percent
of staff time. A majority of staff time may entail no interaction
between staff and residents, as in detention settings (Gambrill,
1974) and in after-care facilities for mentally retarded and emo-

tionally disturbed adults (Paulus, 1976). Thus, rather than providing contingency systems that maintain and facilitate adaptive behaviors, conditions are offered that bring about an unnecessary erosion of repertoires.

The Use of Behavioral Methods in Nursing Homes and Homes for the Aged. Only recently have behavioral programs been introduced in nursing homes. That such settings do not always provide the most happy conditions has been attested to in many reports, although, as with any residential setting, there are always exceptions where positive conditions are offered. General objectives within such facilities include maintaining available skills, making the living situation a positive one, and, if possible, helping residents to regain skills (see, for example, MacDonald and Butler, 1974; Sachs, 1975).

The goal of one recent study was to increase personal mail and number of correspondents for nursing home residents (Goldstein and Baer, 1976). It is widely recognized that isolation and loneliness are two important problems of residents in nursing homes, and, over time, as friends and relatives visit less frequently, these problems usually becomes more pronounced. Three residents took part in the correspondence project: Ed, a sixty-one-year-old retired farmer; Martha, a forty-eight-year-old former secretary who had multiple sclerosis and was unable to write; and Bill, a seventy-two-year-old retired teacher who had suffered a stroke and could not write. All three volunteered to participate in the project and said they would like to receive more mail. Their families lived considerable distances away from the residence. Personal mail was defined as letters and cards from nonbusiness correspondents. The baseline number of letters (taken over an eight- to twelve-week period) per two-week period was 0.6 for Martha, 1.8 for Bill, and 1.5 for Ed. The procedure employed (the R.S.V.P. procedure) consisted of prompting, in which residents were requested to write (or dictate) letters to people with whom they wished to correspond; reminders to answer mail quickly; and the inclusion of a stamped, addressed envelope with each letter sent. They were also coached as to what type of content to include in their letters to increase the possibility of a reply, such as asking at least one question, asking for a reply, an omission of reprimands for not writing, and, if a letter had been received, a thank you. Residents were also asked not to write again to a person they had not heard from, but to wait until at least a month had elapsed. They were encouraged to write to people who had never written them before or who had not written them for a long time. An undergraduate student was responsible for handling details of the program and for establishing rapport with the residents. He met with the residents twice a week for the first few weeks to prompt appropriate behaviors and to collect data and then only once a week thereafter. Weekly visits averaged about twenty-two minutes.

The prompting procedure increased the frequency of letters received to 3.0 per two-week period for Martha, 3.6 for Bill, and 2.7 for Ed. The rate of letters returned was also calculated and it was found that Martha sent 10 letters and received 21 (a return rate of 210 percent). Bill's return rate was 58 percent (71 sent and 41 received) and Ed's rate was 104 percent (27 sent and 28 received). Martha acquired nine new correspondents during the training program. New correspondents for the other two residents also increased but not as much (two and one). All participants said that they were pleased with the procedure and positively anticipated the weekly meetings.

Increasing participation in recreational and social activities. Although the literature on nursing homes stresses the need for recreational and group activities for residents, many facilities do not provide such opportunities (McClannahan and Risley, 1975). Remaining active is especially important for the institutionalized elderly, in order to prevent or at least slow down the degenerative effects associated with aging (Bonner, 1969). Inactivity appears to encourage the loss of verbal and self-care skills and facilitate the need for total nursing care of elderly people. One example of a program to increase resident participation in activities was carried out in a one-hundred-bed proprietary nursing home. The age of the residents varied from twenty-five to one hundred, with a modal age of eighty. Residents under fifty were mentally retarded or physically disabled. Only 20 percent of the residents were confined to their beds; 56 percent were ambulatory, 17 percent were confined to wheelchairs, and 7 percent employed walkers. A first step was to describe the activity of the residents. This is important, because we have all too little carefully gathered information as to what actually occurs in various types of settings. This also provides a baseline against which to assess the effects of any change efforts made. The location of the residents was noted, as well as their position, motion, speech, and participation. Participation was defined as appropriate engagement with equipment, materials, or other persons.

An activity check data sheet was employed to gather information (see Figure 44). Observation for one day a week for

Figure 44. Sample Activity Check Data Sheet

Time	Location	Position/Motion						Speech							Participation
		sitting	*standing*	*lying*	*walking*	*wheeling*	*other*	*no speech*	*to self*	*to resident*	*to staff*	*to visitor*	*to observer*	*other*	*none*	
10:00	Lounge	X						X							X	
		X									X					talking to aide
					X			X							X	
		X						X								eating candy

Source: McClannahan and Risley (1975, p. 263).

eight weeks indicated that most residents were located in their room (54 percent). Most were sitting (63 percent) or lying (23 percent), 87 percent were not engaged in social interaction, and only 36 percent were engaged in any appropriate activity. Determination of the percent of residents participating in various activities during one day indicated that 34 percent were occupied in food-related activities, 24 percent were occupied in social interaction, 14 percent were watching television, 8 percent were listening to the radio, and 8 percent were reading or writing (McClannahan and Risley, 1975). These initial data supported the need for programs that would increase appropriate participation by residents.

An area was created in the lounge and equipment and materials such as games were made available to residents. When residents entered the lounge, they were first given an opportunity to approach the display shelves and select a puzzle or game. Most residents who entered the area did not request or select a game. The activity leader would then approach the resident, place a piece of recreational equipment in the resident's hands and verbally prompt him to participate. These prompts included inviting the resident to use the equipment ("Would you like to use this?"), demonstrating how to use it ("Let me show you"), and, if necessary, helping the resident to use it appropriately. Interactions were limited to prompts; praise was not offered. Only when a resident stopped using a game or puzzle or asked for something else to do were further prompts offered.

Level of attendance in the lounge was very similar with or without the presence of equipment (about 18 percent). However, participation increased from 20 percent to 74 percent when prompts were employed. Thus placing materials in the residents' hands and prompting them to use them more than tripled the mean percent of residents in the lounge who were engaged with their environment. Prompting of initial participation seems to be an essential component of recreational programs for the institutionalized elderly.

Increasing the number of questions asked by a group leader has been found to increase appropriate verbalizations of elderly residents in activity groups (Linsk, Howe, and Pinkston, 1975). Not only did the number of appropriate verbalizations increase, but the percentage of residents offering such statements also increased. Attendance at the activity group meetings increased and the meetings were longer-lasting. "During later treatment conditions, meetings were attended by residents who had previously never participated in a group activity, and residents spoke appropriately who had previously remained silent" (Linsk, Howe, and Pinkston, 1975, p. 460).

Establishing and Maintaining Appropriate Staff Behavior

For residents in institutional settings, significant others include staff and other residents. Client behavior is integrally related to whether or not contingencies provided within the institution by staff and peers support appropriate or inappropriate behaviors, and, as we have mentioned, staff behavior often helps to support deviant behavior. Arranging more positive contingencies within institutional settings typically involves working with staff. The resistances encountered, as well as the new views that are necessary to cultivate, are very similar to those involved in working with parents or teachers. One alternative is to work directly with the residents, that is, to teach them how to cue more positive staff behaviors. For example, Seymour and Stokes (1976) used self-recording to train girls in a maximum security institution for offenders to increase work and to cue staff praise.

It is easy to identify staff behaviors to increase and decrease, if objectives for resident behavior are clearly identified. The most difficult part is in deciding on the most effective and efficient way to create and maintain changes in staff behavior. This decision, like any other, should be informed by a careful assessment of the situation. What are current patterns of staff behavior? Substantial changes may be required in these patterns. Are there attitudes that will interfere with changes in staff behavior? Even though the setting is supposedly transitional, it may be viewed by staff as custodial, as a repository for residents with little or no concern with maintaining and establishing adaptive behaviors, other than those that may be adaptive in that they make it easier for staff. If bringing about desirable changes in resident behavior is not a positive event for staff members, then incentives will have to be provided to encourage them to modify their behavior in ways that would facilitate client progress (see, for example, Loeber, 1971). Dramatic increases in the rate of daily training sessions conducted by attendants working with retarded clients occurred when small amounts of money were made contingent on job performance (Patterson, Griffin, and Panyan, 1976). A performance-based lottery was employed to improve care offered by staff at a residential center for the multiply handicapped retarded (Iwata, Bailey, Brown, Foshee, and Alpern, 1976). Weekly criteria were determined for appropriate staff behavior, for example, being observed changing at least one resident's clothing during daily checks; and, at the end of the week, slips of paper containing the names of attendants who met the criteria were placed in a container. The winner's name was drawn from this container and he or she received the opportunity to rearrange days off from work for the following week. The lottery resulted in several positive changes, including a decrease in off-task staff behavior and in residents found in soiled clothing when daily checks were made. Staff spent more time interacting with residents and better unit supervision was provided. In addition, a greater number of residents received daily toothbrushings and more participated in out-of-bed activities. It should be noted that individual performance varied considerably, with only one third of the staff being eligible to participate in the lottery in a given week. Feedback concerning staff behavior has also been employed to try to increase appropriate on-task behavior; however, this has not been found to be effective (see, for example, Pommer and Streedbeck, 1974).

There may be hidden agendas (or not so hidden, as the case may be) between staff and administration that will interfere with change. If so, these may have to be addressed, or they may completely block the effectiveness of a program. For example, in a program established in four units in a short-term detention facility, one unit felt that it was not receiving the same staff privileges as were the other units (Gambrill, 1976). This was discovered when the staff on this unit showed a drop in the consistency with which they implemented their token program. When asked about this, they voiced their dissatisfaction with the administration. They knew of the administration's interest in the success of the program, and this was their way of putting pressure on higher staff. It is important to ask the following questions: How are outside consultants viewed? Will they be welcomed for the knowledge that they may bring, or will they be looked on as more of those people who think they know it all but in fact have little to offer? What kind of training format will be employed? Will a low-key incremental approach, in which the consultant offers his or her services and waits to be called on by a staff member, be the best strategy? It is hoped, of course, that when the consultant *is* called on, success will be achieved with the problem of concern. Some examples have been reported in which dramatic positive changes were achieved, which then encouraged other staff members to call on the consultant for problems with residents.

If training is to be carried out on a more formal basis, decisions must be made as to how many staff members to include at first, and what kind of training procedures to use. Many training programs have included a mixture of didactic presentations, reading material, observation of models, and skills rehearsal. Requiring staff to rehearse new skills is more effective than didactic presentation alone (Gardner, 1972). Simply having staff respond to written material, although gains may be shown in their understanding of procedural components, does not necessarily result in use of new skills on the job or the ability to use them correctly.

Summary

Behavioral programs have been employed in a range of transitional and residential settings, including halfway houses for youth, day-care centers for psychiatric patients, institutional settings for the retarded and the mentally ill, and nursing homes. There is an extensive literature on the use of token programs in many of these settings, and a small but increasing literature describing means of facilitating transition from residential environments to the community so that positive changes are maintained. There is also a growing body of literature comparing divergent methods of staff training and ways to maintain positive staff behavior. Beginning attempts are being made to develop measures of the quality of care provided in a residential setting.

22

Perhaps in no other area in interpersonal helping is there more rhetoric and less identification of behaviors-in-situations as in the ethics of interpersonal helping. Let us take a look at the Code of Ethics of the National Association of Social Workers, amended in 1967 ("Profession of Social Work: Code of Ethics," 1971, p. 959).

> • I regard as my primary obligation the welfare of the individual or group served which includes action for improving social conditions.
> • I will not discriminate because of race, color, religion, age, sex, or national ancestry, and in my job capacity will work to prevent and eliminate such discrimination in rendering service, in work assignments, and in employment practices.

Ethics of
Interpersonal Helping

- I give precedence to my professional responsibility over my personal interests.
- I hold myself responsible for the quality and extent of the service I perform.
- I respect the privacy of the people I serve.
- I use in a responsible manner information gained in professional relationships.
- I treat with respect the findings, views and actions of colleagues and use appropriate channels to express judgment on these matters.
- I practice social work within the recognized knowledge and competence of the profession.
- I recognize my professional responsibility to add my ideas and findings to the body of social work knowledge and practice.

  ● I accept responsibility to help protect the
community against unethical practice by any individuals or organizations engaged in social welfare
activities.
  ● I stand ready to give appropriate professional service in public emergencies.
  ● I distinguish clearly, in public, between my
statements and actions as an individual and as a
representative of an organization.
  ● I support the principle that professional
practice requires professional education.
  ● I accept responsibility for working toward
the creation and maintenance of conditions within
agencies that enable social workers to conduct
themselves in keeping with this code.
  ● I contribute my knowledge, skills, and support to programs of human welfare.

Most social workers would probably agree that they should uphold the intent of these statements. But, exactly what would
this entail in each instance? How would standards of behavior
be applied in different situations? Let us say that the client
wishes to learn how to handle his concern that he is homosexual
and wishes to develop skills to meet more homosexually oriented people. Is acceptance of these goals as desired outcomes
"regarding the welfare of the client"? Or would their acceptance encourage the client in a direction that would only make
him more pathological in his behavior (as some [for example,
see Bieber, 1976] would argue, who would counsel against
acceptance of such outcomes)? Is the practitioner who selects a method that is relatively ineffective in relation to
achieving desired outcomes "regarding the welfare of the
client"? And what about giving precedence to personal value
systems over professional responsibilities? Is the counselor
who feels personally repelled at the thought of homosexuality,
and who tries to encourage the client to assume heterosexual
behaviors and responses (even though he knows there is no evidence showing that problems homosexuals may have are related
to their homosexuality per se), fulfilling this standard of behavior? Interestingly, the code says nothing concerning the client's
right of self-determination.

These vague ethical standards are not benign. They provide a false reassurance to professionals and clients—a false reassurance that everybody agrees about what should be done in diverse situations, and does it, and that client rights will be protected. These vague standards obscure areas of profound disagreement among practitioners and thus allow the continued practice of a multitude of value systems, some of which have been and are still to the distinct disadvantage of clients. Many professionals are probably well aware, as are an increasing number of laymen, about the atrocities that have occurred and still do occur in the name of helping the client, and about the social control functions of mental health agencies (see, for example, Szasz, 1970a, 1970b; Scheff, 1975). Many of these atrocities have been so severe, especially in institutional settings, that one wonders how they can be ignored. Of course, concerned citizens or concerned professionals often protest publicly and take legal action to try to alter the situation. All too often, however, the plight of children as well as adults is forgotten—out of sight, out of mind. The recognition that the ethical code proposed by various professional organizations, together with attempts to implement it—feeble, in most cases—does not protect clients has resulted in greater activity by other groups, such as clients' rights groups, and the judicial system. Also, some professional organizations are now trying to identify more specific guidelines for ethical practice (see, for example, the *AABT* [Association for Advancement of Behavior Therapy] *Newsletter* and guidelines for conduct of research with human participants by the American Psychological Association, 1973). The federal government has written guidelines protecting human subjects (U.S. Department of Health, Education and Welfare, 1973). Ethical concerns arise in all forms of interpersonal helping. "One important benefit of the public attention to and criticism of behavior modification has been increasing sensitivity on the part of all mental health workers to issues that were formerly often neglected. For example, many therapists are only recently becoming aware of the need to involve the client or his representative more realistically in the planning of the treatment programs, including the selection of both goals and methods. In the past, the mental health worker often used simply his own clinical judgment and experience as the basis for determining treatment goals and methods" (Brown, Wienckowski, and Stolz, 1975, p. 15).

Why haven't more specific guidelines been proposed and implemented? Any discussion of the ethics of interpersonal helping is hampered, because, unlike other areas, such as parent-child or marital interaction, professional practice typically does not create an opportunity to witness many relevant behaviors. Visibility, of course, largely depends on the setting in which a professional works. For example, a psychiatric nurse working in an institutional setting for children is readily observable in a number of situations. This type of setting differs considerably from the less observable interaction between client and counselors in open settings such as community mental health centers and family service centers. Many practitioners have never been observed while interacting with a client. Their behavior with clients is mainly known by what they care to report as narrative descriptions in staff meetings and case records. Thus the range of practiced behaviors that may be encompassed in relation to a particular area of ethical concern is unknown. (There are, however, ways in which counselor behavior can be made more visible. See the section on increasing accountability in Chapter Twenty-Three.)

One hindrance to the identification and implementation of clear ethical guidelines is the assumption that professionals will automatically adhere to ethical behavior. After all, we assume, isn't ethical behavior part of being a professional? To suggest that ethical behavior is not automatic is to question one of the mainstays of professional identity. The general failure of educational institutions to offer courses in the ethics of inter-personal helping indicates that most professions assume that budding professionals will develop appropriate standards of be-havior through osmosis during their classes and field experi-ences. Offering a course on the ethics of interpersonal change would undoubtedly reveal differences of opinion among profes-sionals themselves and thus would fracture the cohesive front that must be presented to the public and to professionals them-selves so that clients will be maximally responsive to suggestions by professionals. Thus, in addition to borrowing some useful characteristics from other professions such as law and medicine, the interpersonal helping professions also borrowed others that are distinctly disadvantageous to their clientele, such as the lack of commitment to specifically identifying the referents of the term *ethical practice* and arranging an effective monitoring and incentive system to support ethical behaviors.

No doubt the range of uncertainty in these fields breeds a temptation to deny this uncertainty, fearing that its recognition would stifle needed action. This appears to be the case, for example, when child welfare workers put off making a decision concerning a child's fate who is in foster care, because of the seriousness of consequences associated with possible alternatives and the risks involved in each, such as restoration of a child to a family in which the child has been abused, or moving toward termination of parental rights. The repercussions of a failure to act are often underestimated. Decisions must be made every day in the face of incomplete information. In some, if not many, instances, it is likely that additional information could have been gathered to inform decisions. Clients are often misinformed of the degree of uncertainty that is related to given counselor decisions. Uncertainty seems to breed overconfidence by professionals in their decisions, and perhaps interferes with their own recognition of how much uncertainty has been involved. In such a situation, of course, the client will not be privy to the base on which decisions critical to his life are made.

The emphasis on the sanctity of opinion of the individual professional is another hindrance to the identification of professional standards of behavior and to the arrangement of an incentive and monitoring system to support these. If a code of ethics existed, it might not match the behavior of a number of professionals—and professionals often object to being told what to do. Fortunately, clients' rights groups and the judicial system have finally lost some awe of professionals, have become more concerned with what they see as ethical lapses, and are leading efforts to design and legislate protections for clients.

There is certainly no lack of verbal protestations in support of ethical practice, such as statements by professionals that "Clients have a right to self-determination" or "Yes, I uphold and believe in my profession's code of ethics." However, verbal reports can be maintained by consequences very different from consequences that may maintain actual behavior related to these reports. The term *hypocrisy* refers to this disjunction between verbal statements and overt behavior, and, as Scott (1971) has pointed out, it is often in the interests of social control for the person to act in a hypocritical manner. "Insofar, therefore, as the hypocrite deviates in his private conduct, but pays public homage to virtue verbally and in public, he serves the interests of social control better (as well as his own) than if he were to advertise his deviation" (Scott, 1971, p. 120). Since the referents of the term *ethical practice* are not identified, let alone monitored, the deviations from ethical practice that actually occur are often not known. To the extent to which there would be public protestations against the actions of professionals if these were more visible in terms of actual objectives and procedures employed, it is in the interests of these professionals not to be fully honest in terms of their goals or procedures used. "Most institutions protect themselves by assuring a lack of information. In virtually any public institution, the goals are too imprecise to serve as a safeguard against which to judge the workings of the institution. It is impossible to tell by whom important decisions will be made, when they will be made, and what factors will be weighed in the process. Once a decision is made, it is impossible to trace its impact, good or bad. There is not only no feedback within the institution, but also no communication of objective data to the public" (Martin, 1975, pp. 97-98). This vagueness, which until recently has been completely tolerated by the courts, has resulted in thousands of people being denied their constitutional rights under the supposedly helpful and benign conditions of receiving mental health services. The public is more ready to accept institutionalization of a person publicly rationalized as necessary because of mental illness and the need for a supportive environment than to accept the rationale that she is being deprived of her freedom because she has telephoned the principal of her sons' school twice a day for the past three months and is becoming a bother. "There has been a growing sensitivity to the ambiguity that can underlie diagnosis and choice of treatment goals for these populations [hospitalized mental patients and institutionalized delinquents and criminals]. According to this view, a thin line sepa-, rates social deviance from a mental illness that requires hospital-ization. Society can often find it more convenient to institu-tionalize the deviant individual than to deal with the problem he represents. The hospitalization or incarceration thus may be more in the interest of social control than in the interest of the person's welfare. . . . The growing distrust of the exercise of control over the helpless and the disadvantaged even challenges the legitimacy of the authority of those who attempt to treat these persons" (Brown, Wienckowski, and Stolz, 1975, p. 12). Szasz (1961) would also argue that countless thousands of peo-ple have literally gotten away with murder and thus escaped responsibility for their actions on the grounds of being mentally ill. The change in what has been considered a mental illness over time reflects the consensual nature of psychiatric diagnosis. That is, psychiatric diagnoses are maintained by consensus ra-ther than by validation (Rosenhan, 1975). Rosenhan points out that the consensual nature of psychiatric disorders is empha-sized by the recent decision taken by the American Psychiatric Association to remove homosexuality from the *Diagnostic Manual on Mental Disorders* (1968). "Whatever one's opinion regarding the nature of homosexuality, the fact that a profes-sional association could vote on whether or not homosexuality should be considered a disorder surely underscores both the dif-ference between psychiatric/mental disorders and the context-susceptibility of psychiatric ones. Changes in informed public attitudes toward homosexuality have brought about correspond-ing changes in the psychiatric perception of it" (Rosenhan, 1975, pp. 464-465). The contextual nature of psychiatric diagnoses is demonstrated by many studies (see, for example, Rosenhan, 1973).

The possibility of abuse of the power invested in mental health professionals and the courts who often support the state-ments of such professionals makes it essential that regulations be established that require a clear statement of exactly why a person must have any part of his or her freedom curtailed and strict limitations of the grounds for doing so. The potential for abuse is, of course, not limited to the mental health field but is also seen in relation to the educational system and the juvenile court system. Great strides have already been made in some areas. For example, no longer can a child be denied a right to education by being suspended from school because of vague complaints that he is a management problem. The exact nature of the behavior of concern must be specified in writing and the parents and the child have a right to know what it is. It is now recognized that the educational system, the mental health system, and even the juvenile court system, may well be adversary systems in which the rights of the clients must be protected. The potential for abuse makes the distinction between verbal statements regarding ethical behavior and actual behavior an essential one. It is the latter that is of greatest concern. Too often contingencies are arranged only for the former. The failure to identify the referents of ethical practice and to arrange contingencies in support of these behaviors permit the unethical professional conduct we see around us.

It is always easy to criticize existing conditions and often difficult to make specific recommendations for change. However, in the area of ethics involved in interpersonal helping, there are indeed guidelines for starting to developing specific standards for practice, some of which are already written into the law and which are discussed in a later section on judicial rulings. In fact, some available guidelines are so clear, and have been so readily available, that one is forced to ask why they have not been implemented and to identify factors related to this failure as the major impediment to ensuring ethical practice. The presence of a social influence process in all interpersonal helping endeavors is assumed, as it is now well documented (Bandura, 1969). As Kanfer (1965) has pointed out, a first step in dealing with ethical issues is recognition of this influence. Practitioners influence not only problem behaviors, but also the client's value system. The use of positive incentives in helping efforts renders willing and even unaware acceptance of influence more likely. People tend to recognize aversive control and to rebel against it; however, this is not as true when positive incentives are employed (Skinner, 1971). Other factors that make such helping situations ideally suited for influence over behavior are the distress of the client and the sharing of private information (Kanfer, 1965).

Selection of Outcomes

Ethical issues are frequently raised in relation to selection of objectives. For example, some programs within institutional settings have been justifiably criticized for increasing participation of clients in work that benefits the institution rather than the residents of such institutions. Another example: Davison (1976) argues that counselors should not accept the goal of a homosexual person to become heterosexual, because the client has probably selected that desired outcome as a result of negative sanctions by society in relation to being a homosexual (see replies by Halleck, 1976, and Bieber, 1976). Similarly, Bem and Bem (1971) have argued that a high school counselor has no right to accept a teen-age girl's goal of being a nurse, because many years of socialization lie behind her selection and thus she is not exercising free choice. They contend that the counselor should encourage her to consider being a doctor. A client's goals may be strongly influenced by society, which imposes limits on freedom of choice. Each counselor must help clients to recognize the extent to which societal standards may intrude unnecessarily on their behavior, to help them consider whether and under what conditions these limits should be accepted, and to help clients expand their range of alternatives, keeping in mind the immediate and future interests of the client as well as those of society. An interest in expansion of freedom for clients is here accepted as a key criterion against which to judge selection of any objective of intervention (Bandura, 1969). This expansion includes freedom from restrictions imposed by behavior deficits and response inhibitions; freedom to pursue positive events that do not harm others; and freedom to avoid negative events that are unfairly imposed. Individual or group counseling are appropriate vehicles to help remove behavior deficits and response inhibitions and to offer the client a broader range of alternative emotional, cognitive and behavioral options. Broader efforts along a number of fronts will be required to alter inappropriate reactions of society.

Key factors in this issue of goal selection include keeping in mind both the immediate and future interests of the client and society and being forthright concerning the rationale for any disagreement or biasing tendencies. A counselor cannot ethically accept an objective that might entail harmful consequences to the client or society, now or in the future. This restriction may entail initially disagreeing with the client concerning the selection of goals, posing alternative outcomes, explaining the rationale for introducing them, and listing their advantages and disadvantages. It is then up to the client to make a final decision. Situation in which disagreement may occur include (1) when the counselor feels the client has stated an objective because of unnecessary and unfair societal pressure; (2) when achievement of an objective would be harmful to others; and (3) when achievement of an objective would constrict the freedom of action of the client. Disagreement concerning objectives may take place between a client and a significant other, or between the client, counselor, and some other change agent, such as the court. Both short- and long-term effects must be considered. A teacher's request to improve the classroom behavior of a student so that he completes more work and is more manageable, may not be considered to be within the short-term interests of a student. However, unless the school system can be changed so that conditions more beneficial to the student can immediately be offered, the alternatives to pursuit of this objective may be suspension from school and failing to learn a repertoire of behavior that would permit the student to complete school successfully and thus to be prepared for a range of career alternatives. Thus, the long-term effect of not attempting to alter the behavior of the student might be to restrict the child's freedom. Of course, in such a situation efforts should be made to alter the teacher's behavior and to renegotiate selected objectives.

When a counselor cannot accept a client's goals, the client must be so informed and offered an explanation. A mother may wish her teen-age daughter to take all responsibility for chores around the house, and the counselor may think that this would be unfair. There may be other children in the family among whom chores can be divided, thus providing each with an equal amount of free time. An open attempt may be made to influence the mother to change her goal, to settle for what the counselor considers to be a more equitable distribution of chores.

The key word here is *open*. Disagreement on goals should be clearly stated and a rationale for it offered. Sometimes a client may deny his or her own responsibility in a problem, and may request the counselor to alter the behavior of some significant other. A wife may say that her husband is insensitive and that he is to blame for all their marital difficulties and request the counselor to change his behavior. This goal may be denied both on ethical and practical grounds. It may be considered unethical not to involve the husband in a process that intimately concerns him. Also, achievement of change may be limited, if not impossible, without his involvement. Thus, it is clear that goals acceptable to the counselor and those desired by a client may at times clash. A counselor cannot pursue goals that he or she finds objectionable. There *is* an obligation to help the client obtain desired goals, within the limits of the counselor's personal value system and theoretical orientation and the likely short- and long-term effects on the client and society. However, both the counselor's personal value system and his theoretical orientation may place unethical restrictions on the help that he or she can offer the client. In such instances, the counselor has an ethical obligation to refer the client to someone else who can view the client's desired outcomes more objectively. Counselors differ in their personal values and it is unfortunate that we do not know more about their values systems, especially about how these are exercised in practice. We certainly do know that personal values and theoretical assumptions with no empirical basis have caused profound distress to many clients over the years, as witnessed, for example, by the involuntary treatment of homosexual persons to alter their sexual preferences (see, for example, Szasz, 1970b).

Differences of opinion about objectives may also relate to *who* is to be the target of change, in addition to *what* is to be altered. A mother may ask the counselor to "make my daughter listen to me when I tell her to do something," assuming that only the daughter will be involved in change efforts. Within a behavioral framework, in which significant others, such as the mother, are considered to be involved in the maintenance of behaviors, an effort would have to be made to enhance her recognition as to how she herself must participate in the change process. The same must be done with a teacher who complains about a student's classroom behavior and assumes that work will occur only with the student, and outside of class. A major effort may have to be made to increase the recognition of the teacher concerning the relationship between her own behavior and the behavior about which she complains.

Contingency matrices (see Kunkel, 1970) may be helpful in describing alternative courses and their potential benefits and risks both to involved parties and to society. Weighting benefits and risks in terms of importance as well as probability may be added when necessary, although these can only be estimates. Sometimes available data may help the counselor assess the probability of a given outcome. For example, once a child has been in the foster care system for three years, there is a higher probability that he or she will remain there until maturity (see, for example, Stein and Gambrill, 1976a). Another dimension that is of import is short- versus long-term consequences.

Whenever conflicting interests are involved, ethical practice calls for helping clients identify the range of alternatives that are open to each involved party, as well as the possible advantages and disadvantages of each. Counseling may offer new behaviors and the removal of emotional constraints that previously interfered with pursuit of one or more alternatives, thus making selection of one alternative easier for involved parties. The final decision must be the client's or clients'—that is, each person who has an interest in the situation. Helping the client identify alternatives and their respective potential benefits and risks in the course of assessment is helpful when clients present vaguely defined problems. This additional clarity can then be utilized by the client in making a decision concerning desired outcomes. The counselor may have emotional biases in relation to one of the involved parties, which may lead him to favor one party over another. If this interferes with offering fair services, the clients should be referred to someone who will not show such a differential preference.

Let us say that relatives of an elderly person seek consultation because they are finding it increasingly difficult to get along with their elderly mother who lives with them, and that they especially complain that she talks too much, is getting sloppy in her dress and that she always seems to be underfoot. She, in turn, feels that she is being picked on and is fine the way she is. Let us suppose that assessment reveals that she does not seem to be underfoot any more than any other family member in terms of the time she spends sitting with or talking to family members, and that her dressing habits could indeed be called sloppy. Doesn't she have a right to dress in any way she chooses and doesn't she have a right to interact with other family members as much as any other person in the family? And what about the rights of her significant others to arrange their own environment? Although we may all agree with these rights, the fact is, her current behavior is unpleasant to her significant others and unless these individuals change their response to her behavior and/or unless she changes her behavior, the situation will probably become more stressful, until perhaps the family decides that they no longer have room for grandmother at home and start the process of finding an institutional setting for her. The rights of the elderly have often been ignored, as have the rights of children—for example, not having them take part in counseling sessions and not having them sign contracts that will entail effects on their behavior. Acceptance of the guideline that anyone whose behavior will be affected by a change program should take part in the selection of desired outcomes and procedures to attain these, unless it is impossible or would have negative consequences for involved parties, should constrain the counselor to see that these arrangements are carried out. As in marriage counseling and sex counseling, where the counselor insists on interviewing both the partners to stress their mutual interaction, insisting on joint interviews of all involved parties when a child or older person is concerned can serve the same highlighting functions. (This is not to say that individual interviews might not also be held with different clients.)

A careful behavioral assessment may indicate that it is not the duration of the grandmother's talking (which is very similar to other family members), but the content of her conversation. Let us say we find that she is a poor listener and that she tells the same stories over and over again, and the family members find this irksome. Assessment may also reveal ways in which grandmother may desire significant others to alter their behavior. She may say, "I wish they would listen to me; they just seem to look bored when I talk." This, of course, provides a perfect opportunity to point out the relationship between her goals and those of the family. Family members may have unrealistic expectations of grandmother and be, in the counselor's opinion, unduly intolerant of grandmother. Let us assume, in our example, that they are not open to altering their views. They are adamant that grandmother is a bother. Is it the counselor's responsibility to bring to her attention the options she may have, meaning that if she does not alter her behavior, her significant others will eject her from their household? If she refuses to change, should the counselor simply accept this? It is the counselor's responsibility to point out the likely consequences of given courses of action and if possible, to offer additional behaviors that will broaden a client's range of possibilities (given, of course, in this situation, that the grandmother wishes to remain with her family). New possibilities may include a program focusing on alternative modes of dress. Lindsley (1964) points out the influence that this change may offer an older person over those with whom he or she interacts. In addition, her conversational skills may be enhanced by teaching her to ask more questions of others. Pleasant events that she may offer the family, so more positively disposing them toward her, may also facilitate pleasurable interaction between involved parties; for example, she may be able to babysit more frequently, thus allowing the adults more free time for themselves.

What are the consequences to the grandmother of not engaging in a change program? Short-term effects might include avoiding the time and effort necessary to alter her behavior, and failing to alter negative reactions of her significant others to her talking. Distinctly negative consequences would accrue to her family members, because the unpleasant situation they complain about would continue, although failure to initiate intervention would for them, too, remove the time, effort, and cost involved in a change program. (It is, however, the counselor's responsibility to select procedures, with the approval of the clients, that are effective and efficient and that may even be fun to carry out.) Not participating in a change program would also remove the necessity for each involved person to take a look at their own behavior and how they may affect those they live with. The short-term consequences can be mapped as follows:

Grandmother	*Significant Others*
Family members would still not listen to her	No change in grandmother's annoying behavior
Not have to bother changing	Not having to bother changing

The long-term consequences of failure to participate in a change program may be more serious. For the grandmother, these may entail being ejected from the household into an unknown environment. Perhaps the most difficult part of estimating costs and benefits in this situation is assessing how she might like this new environment if this came to pass.

Information could be obtained by exploring possible settings for the grandmother, perhaps having her take a look at these, and trying to help her make a judgment concerning how each one might match her own assets. Although her involvement in this endeavor may be painful for her, it does provide her with information necessary to make an informed decision concerning participation in a change effort. For example, she may visit one setting that she really likes and prefer pursuit of this option. Such a setting might provide her more pleasure than living at home. Let us assume that the settings available are quite dismal and that the cost of having to move to one would be very high. Related to this outcome is the likely deterioration of interactions between grandmother and her significant others. This, too, would be an unpleasant outcome. A final negative outcome may be the deterioration of the grandmother if she is moved to a setting that is not supportive of her independent behavior, so that her life span may be decreased. She may also feel abandoned by her significant others. Thus the long-term consequences for the grandmother, given our hypothesized outcomes, are distinctly negative. For her significant others, the long-term consequences are more mixed. For them, too, we can expect the negative consequence of continued deterioration in the quality of interaction with the grandmother if she remains at home with no attempt to alter behaviors of involved parties, although as this continues to become more unpleasant, it may have the positive effect of making it easier for them to make a decision to place the grandmother in another setting. (It is assumed here that the grandmother has no additional options, such as going to live with a friend, that she can pursue on her own.) The possible long-term consequences of failure to engage in a change program are described as follows:

Grandmother	*Significant Others*
Earlier movement to a disliked residential setting	Further deterioration of interaction with grandmother
Decreased life span	Earlier ejection of grandmother from the household
Perception and feeling of being rejected by her family	Guilt over action taken
	Possible avoidance of visiting grandmother, because of guilt

Consideration of possible short- and long-term consequences of a failure to engage in an intervention attempt indicates that these consequences may include cognitive and emotional components as well as behavioral components.

The short- and long-term consequences of participating in a change effort would be identified in the same manner. An example of a positive consequence of participation, for the grandmother, would be that the new skills she learns would enhance her interaction not only with family members, but also with friends she may have. When the possible consequences associated with engaging in a change effort are compared with those for not engaging in a program to enhance the quality of interaction between family members, the comparison may help involved parties to make a decision as to what they wish to do. It is the clients who will make the decision, not the counselor although he or she has certainly influenced involved parties by helping them to elaborate potential consequences of various options.

An important ethical question is whether or not the counselor should have a special interest in protecting clients in low power positions. For example, it could be argued that the grandmother in the example just described does not have as much outcome control over her fate as do her family members. The same situation occurs with children and with residents of institutional settings. (Ethical standards related to the latter group are discussed later in a separate section.) It would seem that the counselor does have a responsibility to be especially vigilant concerning the rights of individuals in such positions. Given that someone in a low power position is helped to alter the behavior of significant others, should these significant others be informed of this attempt? For example, when children are trained to alter the behavior of their teachers, should the teachers be informed of their attempts? The answer would clearly seem to be yes. However, what if sharing this information would mean that the children's attempt would not be effective? Given that there would be no short- or long-term adverse consequences for the teacher, why shouldn't the children be offered skills to alter the teacher's behavior, given the likely adverse consequences that would accrue for the children if they do not engage in such a change effort? The presence of possible adverse consequences to the uninformed significant other in such a situation makes a decision more difficult. Questions such as this are hard to answer because of possible competing interests of involved parties. A contingency analysis of the long- and short-term consequences for each involved person and the rule to involve all parties unless there are compelling reasons not to (such as increased punitive conditions for those in a low power position) may help to offer some guidelines in such situations.

The question of who is to be the target of change is also raised where behavior considered deviant by society is at issue. The example of homosexuality provides a good example. Changing homosexual orientation to a heterosexual one has until recently been readily accepted as a desired outcome by most professionals. Now, however, some are raising strong arguments against such ready acceptance. Some contend that continuing to offer intervention under any circumstances supports the societal belief that homosexuality is bad (Begelman, 1975). The impact of wider societal forces on individual problems further raises the question as to what the proper locus of intervention efforts is. The position assumed here is that one must work on multiple levels for societal change in relation to discriminatory practices, while maintaining the opportunity for clients to pursue individual desired outcomes. However, it is considered the ethical responsibility of each counselor to bring to the client's attention the possible role of societal restrictions on selection of a desired outcome. Furthermore, in the absence of any evidence that problems are caused by a particular characteristic, such as the person having problems because he is a homosexual, the counselor should cultivate a normalizing view of the client's behavior, and should be guided by Begelman's (1975) distinction between homosexual problem behaviors and problem behaviors of homosexuals.

Are there circumstances that ethically warrant change attempts that are not desired by the involved clients? What should be the relationship, if any, between acts proscribed by law and behaviors accepted as targets of change by professionals? People diverge considerably in their answers to these questions. Robinson (1974) accepts the position that "individuals presented for treatment . . . for reasons of having physically harmed others can lay no moral claim on the right not to be changed. It is my view . . . that proof of physical harm, intentionally perpetrated on one's self or on another, constitutes a forfeiture of . . . the right to be different" (Robinson, 1974, p. 236). (The right to be different in terms of physically harming others is a separate issue from the question as to whether society has a right to force such individuals to accept treatment.) Many, of course, would strongly disagree with this position. Szasz (1961), for example, would disagree with the position that society has a right to intervene when someone wishes to commit suicide or to use addictive substances such as heroin. He would, however, be more sympathetic to protection of society from those individuals who may commit violent actions such as physical assault on others, and feels, in fact, that these individuals have often been allowed to escape responsibility for their actions under the guise of being mentally ill. Certainly the interests of others must be balanced against the rights of individuals and often there may be conflicting interests. It is over how to best balance these conflicting interests that disagreement arises. Over the past years, there has been a growing concern that society has overstepped its legitimate interests at the expense of individual liberties, has used the mental health system for unwarranted social control purposes, that is, where physical harm is not at issue (see, for example, Scheff, 1975; Szasz, 1961).

Robinson goes on to propose that behaviors resulting in public harm, actions that are considered harmful to the government, such as stealing and selling state secrets, as well as behaviors that present an offense or a nuisance to others, do not justify coercive intervention. Robinson (1974), as well as others (Szasz, 1961), suggests that society has sufficient powers of persuasion to take care of offensive actions (excluding physical harm) and that "in instances of victimless crime, there would seem to be no ethical or principled basis on which the therapist must foist his treatment on an unwilling client" (Robinson, 1974, p. 237). He points to the unfortunate confusion that has been made between legally punishable acts, such as homosexuality, and acts considered to be a justifiable basis for therapeutic intervention, and notes that "Transferring moral paternalism from the legislature to the counseling room (or surgical theater) can have only monstrous consequences" (Robinson, 1974, p. 237).

The discussion thus far has emphasized selection of goals that encourage self-actualization whenever possible and that expand the freedom of the client. A stress on the identification of specific objectives and on the formulation of an agreement signed by the involved parties clarifies the goals of change efforts. This agreement concretizes the counselor's responsibility to work toward the explicit objectives described in it. The counselor is not free to redefine these goals in a unilateral fashion. "The less directly the persons are involved in the initial determination of means and goals, the more protections of those persons should be built into the system" (Brown, Wienckowski, and Stolz, 1975, p. 21). (See later section on consent.)

Selection of Procedures

The selection of objectives primarily involves value judgments, while the selection of procedures to alter behavior involves empirical issues to a much greater extent. The client has a "right to the best possible validated treatment" (Davison and Stuart, 1975, p. 760). The counselor should be well informed as to what procedures are most effective and efficient with a given problem. The word *best* implies that the procedure selected should be the least intrusive. The concept of intrusiveness of a therapy or a program may involve a number of criteria, including: "(1) the extent to which the effects of a therapy upon mentation are reversible; (2) the extent to which the resulting psychic state is 'foreign,' 'abnormal,' or 'unnatural' for the person in question, rather than simply a restoration of his prior psychic state (this is closely related to the 'magnitude' or 'intensity' of the change); (3) the rapidity with which the effects occur; (4) the scope of the change in the total 'ecology' of the mind's functions; (5) the extent to which one can resist acting in ways impelled by the psychic effects of the therapy; and (6) the duration of the change" (Shapiro, 1974, p. 262). Shapiro (1974) notes that no one item by itself may be sufficient to say that a therapy is intrusive, and no particular item is necessary. "These criteria of intrusiveness may be roughly captured in part by some notion of voluntariness or self-help in altering thought and behavior patterns. If such alterations seem to be more the joint product of the therapy and the person's voluntary efforts in changing himself rather than the product mainly of mentational effects over which the person has no control [such as when a drug is administered], then a conclusion that the regime (forcibly imposed though it may be) is beyond the First Amendment's protection seems justified. Something was done for the person with his help, and not to him, or to his mind or personality" (Shapiro, 1974, p. 267). Acceptance of this point would be influenced by whether or not the conditions required for informed consent were present.

All involved clients, whenever possible, should be involved in the agreement to employ selected procedures. For example, in a project that offers intensive intervention in an attempt to return children to their natural parents, both the parents and the counselor sign a written contract that describes the overall goal that the parents have selected as well as possible consequences of goal attainment or failure to bring about desired outcomes (Stein, Gambrill, and Wiltse, 1974). Time limits are also specified. Later contracts describe specific objectives related to each problem area as well as change procedures and who will be involved. Depending on the age of the children, they too sign the contract. Incentives and significant others involved in the change effort are described, and all must agree to their participation in the program. Dispensement of harmful reinforcers in change programs, such as stolen property, should obviously be avoided, as should arrangements that might upset other people or behavior systems—for example, paying such great amounts of money to a child that parental attention dwindles as reinforcer (Tharp and Wetzel, 1969). (Guidelines for assuring selection of the "best" procedure in relation to institutionalized residents are discussed in a later section.)

It would be unethical to employ a very weak procedure at the insistence of the client if empirical data indicate that other procedures would be much more effective, given that procedures do not differ in terms of potential discomfort. If a counselor finds himself in this position, his dilemma must be explained to the client and the client referred to someone who can offer the procedure desired by the client. A client, for example, may insist that she would like to employ exploration of her past history with her parents in order to develop insight into and alter current discord with her husband. A behavioral counselor could not accept this means of altering marital discord as the only procedure.

Davison and Stuart (1975) emphasize the relationship between ongoing evaluation of intervention programs and the client's right to the "best possible validated treatment." Only if such information is collected is it possible to identify effective, efficient, least intrusive intervention methods related to specific behaviors. Evaluation is also related to accountability. Should counselors be accountable to their clients? Surely one must offer an unwavering yes. However, to what extent are counselors indeed accountable? The answer requires a definition of the word *accountable*. First, the results of intervention "must be carefully monitored to insure that the goals agreed upon by the advisory committee or by the client and therapist are being achieved. If they are not, sound practice requires a reevaluation and revision of the methods being used . . . . Information on the effectiveness of the program should be made available to the consumers on a regular basis" (Stolz, Wienckowski, and Brown, 1975, p. 1045). This quote illustrates the close connection between accountability and tracking of change efforts. In order for the counselor to be accountable to the client, the effects of intervention must be carefully assessed and shared with the client or his representatives on an ongoing basis, so that the client is free to determine whether he wishes to continue participating in treatment procedures or to discontinue participation (one of the requirement of informed consent). Not all practitioners would agree with this definition of accountability. They might say that accountability is having the client's best interests at heart and acting accordingly, in allowing client self-determination, and in having respect for the client. The problem with these undefined terms is that they allow enormous leeway in the behaviors to which they refer, "In ethics, abstractions become dangerous and euphemisms poisonous whenever they mask the basic unit of concern, the individual human being, or when they describe things in ways too far removed from the palpable, sensory experience of the listener to be meaningful" (London, 1969, p. 203).

Recently suggested guidelines for the description of treatment plans are as follows (*Law and Behavior,* 1976a, p. 8).

> First, it [the treatment plan] must begin with a detailed description of the patient's condition and needs. This should be in the most behaviorally specific language possible. Subjective, vague statements will not suffice: only concrete, objective descriptions will provide the baseline necessary for evaluation and aid in prescribing treatment.
>
> Second, you [the counselor] must state the treatment goals and a projected timetable for attaining them. Again the language must be behaviorally specific so that all concerned can agree as to what the goal means. For example, "to function to the best of his ability" would communicate different things to different people, but "feed himself with a spoon" is sufficiently clear.
>
> The goal statement must include subgoals or interim objectives, not just one global final goal. Otherwise you could not know if the approach was working until the very end. And by requiring a

timetable for attaining interim objectives you will have sufficient periodic feedback on your efforts that you can change approaches that are not performing.

Third, the individual development plan must include a detailed description of the recommended treatment. The description should provide all the information needed for informed consent: for example, statement of risks, benefits, possible side effects and third-party sources of information which might aid in deciding whether to consent. By requiring this specificity, the court is also assuring that an actual treatment will be pursued. If it can't be described concretely, you should not attempt it.

Fourth, you must describe the relationship between each element of the treatment plan and each of the treatment goals. This will assure the obvious—that you have a plan to meet each change objective—but equally important it protects against overtreatment. For example, if there is no need for medication, or work therapy, then they should not exist.

Fifth, you must detail how persons from the client's normal environment will be involved in treatment. One goal of any public program should be to get the individual functioning again in his natural environment and representatives from that environment are vital keys. There is also a need for individuals to be transferred into less restrictive approaches as they become suitable, and peers and family members should be involved in treatment responsibilities increasingly until they eventually take over. Finally, any therapist should be concerned about maintenance of successful behavior changes and the most logical hope for maintenance is to involve individuals who will be able to reinforce the client's changed behavior as he returns to his former environment.

Sixth, you must name the persons responsible for implementing each element of the treatment. This should provide an internal check for the program since no individual should be in charge of a particular treatment phase if he is not fully qualified specifically for it. And it should provide more accountability to family and friends.

Seventh, the plan must be reviewed and up-

dated monthly. Any real behavioral program would
be revised constantly as feedback is received but
the monthly requirement means that the whole institution's effort must be reviewed at least that
often and, hopefully, will be moved away from
failures and toward success for the client.

Any decisions made concerning continuation or termination of
an intervention program should be based on performance criteria rather than on opinions (Martin, 1975).

The Issue of Consent

The issues surrounding the area of informed consent differ for different populations in different settings. "Informed
consent, for example, is clearly meaningful when a normal adult
voluntarily goes to an outpatient clinic to obtain guidance in
altering a specific behavior that he wants to change. However,
when prisoners are offered the opportunity of participating in
behavior modification, it is by no means clear that they can give
truly voluntary consent" (Brown, Wienckowski, and Stolz,
1975, p. 20). There are a number of factors that relate to the
issue of consent, including a judgment of the person's competence to offer consent, the extent to which consent is offered
voluntarily, and the extent to which this consent is informed. A
variety of definitions of competency have been proposed, including capacity to reach a reasonable result (that is, the decision made by the client is one that a reasonable man or woman
would also make); the capacity to reach a decision based on
rational reasons (can the client understand the nature of the
procedure to be employed and weigh possible costs and benefits?); and the capacity to make a decision (see Friedman,
1975). If the client is not competent to give his consent, the
question must be asked, as to whether use of a procedure being
considered would be in his best interests. One could argue, for
example, that the short-term use of painful events such as shock
to decrease severe self-destructive behavior is warranted by the
negative effects that would accrue if this self-injurious behavior
continued. However, prior to using this very intrusive procedure, it would have to be demonstrated that other less intrusive

procedures had failed or would be likely to be ineffective. Use of this punitive procedure, moreover, should be accompanied by the positive reinforcement of appropriate behaviors. The "best interest" standard has been sharply criticized on a number of grounds in its use in child welfare (Mnookin, 1973). This standard not only ignores the interests of the parents, but also is too vague—it is impossible to determine what is in the best interests of the child, because one would have to contrast the likely consequences if the child would stay at home with those that might occur if the child entered foster care, and the multiple likelihoods associated with each. Adequate information is simply not available, and even if it were, "our knowledge about human behavior provides no basis for the predictions called for by the 'best interests of' standard" (Mnookin, 1973, p. 616). This inability to predict future outcomes is strikingly demonstrated by the study completed at Berkeley in which 166 infants born in 1929 were followed over a thirty-year period, with the objective of studying the growth of normal people (MacFarlane, 1964). The predictions made by the researchers were wrong in two thirds of the cases. They had tended to overestimate the possible negative effects of early difficulties. Even if it were possible to make predictions, what value would be selected to optimize—happiness, productivity, stability and security, or intellectual stimulation? Thus this standard, in application, necessitates a reliance on individual values. Because "best interests" cannot be defined with any degree of consensus, unnecessary removal of children from their natural parents may occur, as well as the drift of children in and out of home or institutional care, since the state that would have to be achieved by the parents to gain their child back is poorly defined. Acceptance of a criterion of minimally effective parenting skills is recommended, because it is more likely that agreement can be reached on these, and it is more fair to require parents to achieve these than to achieve what many families might not have anyway. The critical question appears to be, Are "best interests" definable?

The issue of voluntariness relates to the absence of coercion. "Two examples of institutional coercion often occur. In one, the overwhelmingly impressive professional staff make the prospective consenter feel as if he would be dumb not to defer to the professional and accept his judgment. . . . In a second example, the client, probably a resident of a program, is deprived of the normal day-to-day contacts of the outside community, such as a next-door neighbor, which might offer a counterbalance to the sole source of information offered to elicit consent" (*Law and Behavior,* 1976c, p. 5). A third example concerns the withdrawal of privileges contingent on participation in a program. The third example represents a blatant failure to assure voluntariness criterion, whereas the first two are more subtle. In order to guard against the first two sources of subtle coercion, "as much as possible of the information can be presented in an impartial written manner rather than subjectively by a highly persuasive professional. Second, a former client can be consulted so that someone can introduce a perspective different from the professional. Third, there can be a delay of, for example, forty-eight hours between the professional's presentation and the client's consent, so there is time to think things over" (*Law and Behavior,* 1976c, p. 5).

Requirements for informed consent include "A fair explanation of the procedures to be followed, and their purposes, including identification of experimental procedures; a description of any expected discomforts and risks; a description of expected benefits; a disclosure of appropriate alternative procedures that would be advantageous for the subject; an offer to answer any inquiry concerning the procedures; and an instruction that the subject is free to withdraw his consent and discontinue participation in the project or activity at any time without prejudice to himself" (Stolz, Wienckowski, and Brown, 1975, p. 1045). Information that must be presented for informed consent is described in more detail in a later section dealing with institutional settings. These elements have also been discussed in Chapter Five in the section on the use of contracts, which provide one way to ensure that some of these elements have been carried out. A client can be requested to read and sign a written description of the procedure and possible risks and benefits can be written down, as well as the other elements described by Stolz, Wienckowski, and Brown. In order to conserve time and to preserve objectivity, descriptions of commonly used procedures and the benefits and risks associated with each could be written down and employed as attachments to a main contract, thus saving time in writing them down each time. Any variations in expected costs and benefits in a particular case could be duly noted on the contract. Procedural descriptions are necessary for other aspects of practice and thus should be written down anyway, so that the services offered the client will be clearly defined. Careful description of procedures enable the assessment of their quality and the informed continuation of intervention by another person who may assume responsibility for the case, as well as add information as to what works with what type of client. This written description must, of course, be supplemented by a description of exactly how the procedure is implemented or altered.

Disclosure of appropriate alternative procedures that would be advantageous to the subject will be limited by the boundaries of the counselor's knowledge. People cannot disclose what they do not know. Thus the knowledge of the counselor places a limitation on the degree to which this element of informed consent can actually be implemented. This is a particularly serious problem in professions where counselors often do not keep up with the published findings related to their area of clinical practice. Should the client be deprived of this element of informed consent because of the limitations of the counselor? And, if the answer is no, how can the possibility of providing compliance with this aspect of informed consent be encouraged? One is through a review panel monitoring the selection of intervention procedures and the alternatives posed to the client as written in the consent form. (See the later section on ensuring ethical standards in institutional settings.) A second is the provision of incentives for this aspect of counselor behavior. (See section in Chapter Twenty-Three on increasing accountability.) Over time, the selection of more effective intervention procedures hopefully would bring about changes in procedures selected by the counselors themselves, because they would have personal experience that one procedure was more effective and/or efficient than another. This topic, of course, relates directly to the issue of how much leeway practitioners should have over selection of intervention procedures (see later discussion on the limits of individual discretion).

Aspects of client-counselor interaction to which one does

not usually have access are closely related to how the client reacts to counselor-offered information concerning (for example) different procedures. Let us take the situation concerning the relative effectiveness of play therapy and behavioral methods with autistic children. Counselor A may say: "There is some evidence showing that behavioral methods are more effective than play therapy and you should consider this information in deciding which method you would like us to pursue." Counselor B might say: "A study has been done comparing the effectiveness of play therapy and behavioral methods in this area, however, it was not well designed and no one can tell anything from one study anyway." (Let us say that in fact the study was well designed.) The second counselor might say: "Mr. X. decided on play therapy even though I told him about the greater effectiveness of behavioral methods." Thus the way the counselor shares information concerning alternative procedures will influence client decisions. The client should be informed about alternative methods and their likely outcomes in an objective way, without intent to sway the client in one direction or another. At the same time, consideration must also be given to make client expectations at least moderately positive, because, as discussed in Chapter Three, positive expectations appear to facilitate change efforts.

What if the counselor does not have the skills to assess the adequacy of studies describing the effects of various procedures? Or what if no time is available for this task? The answers to these questions are easier to find if the counselor is part of an agency, in which case continuing education for staff could be arranged and monitoring systems designed to determine whether new information is being employed appropriately—for example, by reviewing interventions employed to attain specific outcomes (see Chapter Twenty-Three for further detail).

A second troublesome aspect of assuring informed consent concerns the phrase, "A description of any expected discomforts and risks, and a description of expected benefits." It is appropriate to consider both of these together, because only in weighing the two together can an informed decision be made. The expected benefits are perhaps easier to consider. These should be achievement of desired client outcomes. The expected benefit of social skill training program may be to increase the frequency of and pleasure experienced in social contacts with people. The expected benefits of offering a mother more positive child management skills may be to enhance the interaction between her and her children and to increase the positive feelings shared between them. What are the risks in these situations? Achievement of the desired outcome will require cost to the client in time and usually money, so one risk is that these may be expended with no commensurate return, that is, intervention might not work. Some discomfort may also be involved; for example, the client who tries out new social skills, may experience some initial discomfort at first when trying out his new skills, although if he experiences a great deal this is an indication that something is wrong with the intervention procedure (perhaps tasks have not been sufficiently graduated in accord with his skill and comfort levels). What about risks that are a slim possibility? Should the client be informed about these and given a rough percentage indication of the probability that they will occur? The policy of informed consent would require an affirmative answer. Contingency matrices may be useful in viewing possible consequences, their importance, and probability of occurrence (see previous section on ethical issues concerning selection of desired outcomes).

Another criterion for informed consent is the instruction that the client is free to withdraw his consent and discontinue participation in a program at any time without prejudice to himself. Fulfillment of this condition requires monitoring of intervention effects. If the counselor has not arranged for accountability—if changes that may be occurring in relation to desired outcomes are not being monitored—the client is not in an informed position to decide whether to continue or not. An explanation should be included in the counselor-client contract identifying exactly how progress will be evaluated and what criteria will be employed. There should be an offer to answer any inquiries the client may have and these "should be written in the client's hand on the consent form or in an attachment. On the same document should be a written response to each inquiry" (*Law and Behavior*, 1976c, p. 6). Information written down on the consent form should be at a level of comprehension that is appropriate for the client and instructions should be included "that the client is free to withdraw his consent and challenge his involvement in the approach at any time without unpleasant consequences and an assurance [given] that the client's need will still be met in some other way" (*Law and Behavior,* 1976c, p. 6). Other stipulations include an indication of the time at which the information will be shared with the client. The client should be allowed a forty-eight-hour period to think about the information presented in the consent form and whether he wishes to sign it. As a check on the degree to which the consent is informed, the client could be asked questions concerning what it would mean to him if he did consent. "A few multiple choice questions, correctly answered, would add more to the informing stage of the consent process and would more clearly manifest knowledge" (*Law and Behavior,* 1976c, p. 6). Ideally, there would also be a signature of a third person who was a witness to the consenting process and could indicate that that consent was obtained in accord with the requirements described in the document. If any of the procedures proposed in the contract are experimental, this must be clearly indicated and the client offered alternative procedures. In such situations, the client or his representatives "should be given access to a group of persons who have experienced this approach and might discuss freely its benefits and disadvantages. If not actual contact, the client [can be] given an article to read which argues both sides of the proposed approach" (*Law and Behavior,* 1976c, p. 6). Very detailed guidelines for the protection of subjects in experimental work have been outlined by the federal government.

Both the client as well as the counselor should sign the contract to indicate their mutual acceptance of negotiated agreements concerning desired outcomes and procedures. It is important to define who "the client" is. Goldiamond (1974) assumes the position that the client should be the person subject to change, that is, who agrees to alter his or her behavior. But does this definition protect other involved parties? If a mother, for example, wishes to learn more effective child management methods, then she would contract to alter her behavior and the counselor would contract to help her. As Goldiamond

(1974) states, "I do not contract with them to change their child's behavior. If we do see the child, we contract with him separately" (p. 44). As Feldman (1976) points out, this fails to protect and inform the person who will be affected by the change in behavior of a significant other, such as a parent, or a resident in an institutional setting where a contract has been made to alter behavior of the staff. Obviously, such a change will affect the behavior of the other residents. A more difficult question arises when one person who will be affected, such as a child, refuses to give his consent. Should nothing be done then? How can the multiple and sometimes conflicting interests of involved parties be handled most fairly? Contracting only with the person or persons who agree to alter their behavior is not sufficient. Refusing to help if an involved party does not sign a contract or verbally agree to it is also not sufficient, because inaction may allow an intolerable or unpleasant situation to continue or worsen. Let us say this mother is on the verge of requesting placement for her child in out-of-home care, because she finds him unmanageable. Should training in more effective and more positive child management methods be withheld from her because her child refuses to sign a contract for change, or verbally agree to such an attempt? They should not, and the guideline that makes this decision possible and even perhaps an easy one to make in this situation is an assessment of the current and future risks and benefits from failure to intervene against those that would probably accrue if successful intervention occurred, for all involved parties, including the client who did not agree to a change effort. Failure to act in the face of a client's refusal to participate does not allow evasion of the consequences of decisions. The consequences of a failure to act must be as carefully weighed as the consequence of acting.

    Ethical issues come to the fore when clients are not capable of giving informed consent and when vague problems are presented. That is, the client may be unsure of the benefits he or she hopes to derive from intervention. As Bandura (1969) points out, the decision can remain in the client's hands to the greatest extent possible by having the initial focus of interpersonal helping be the identification the client's current behavior patterns and the conditions that affect these, to point out the range of behavioral and situational changes likely to promote desired changes, and to identify various alternatives and their likely outcomes. At this point, the client can participate in an informed manner in selection of objectives.

A child may be too young to give informed consent. In such cases, the guidelines offered earlier can be employed, such as whether achievement of an objective would expand his range of freedom, both now and in the long run, without harming others. There will be individual differences in how such questions are answered in specific cases. What if parents ask to arrange for their son to practice the piano one hour a day? Is this objective an infringement on his freedom or a possible expansion both now and in the long run? The rights of parents in relation to making decisions for their children are being scrutinized more closely lately and these rights are being decreased in breadth. For example, in the past, under Pennsylvania law, children could be admitted to mental hospitals on application of their parents, even if the child protested. Children were being committed for actions that were unrelated either to mental illness or to mental retardation, such as truancy and delinquent acts. In one instance, a child was committed over a two-week period to allow his family to go on a vacation (*Law and Behavior,* 1976a). In a recent case in Pennsylvania, "The court found that parents or others acting in loco parentis, may at times be acting against the interests of their children and thus they cannot be allowed to waive their children's personal constitutional rights" (*Law and Behavior,* 1976c, p. 1).

A resident in a mental hospital may be in such a state of confusion that informed consent is not possible. Special safeguards are required in such situations to ensure that objectives pursued and procedures employed are in the client's interest while also protecting society's interests in terms of decreasing the possibility of physical harm to others. Procedures developed have not always succeeded in protecting clients. One of the best examples of such a lapse is the juvenile court system, which in fact stripped juveniles of basic rights available to adults and, as in the Gault case (In re Gault, 387 U.S. 1, 87 S.Ct. 1428, 18 L.Ed. and 527 1967), resulted in many years of incarceration for an offense that, if Gault had been eighteen, would have resulted in two months' imprisonment and a fifty-dollar fine. One safeguard that has been recommended for residents in institutional settings is approval and ongoing surveillance of all change programs by a board, composed of a concerned representative of the client, lay people not associated with the hospital, expert(s) in the application of behavioral methods, and a representative of the institution (Brown, Wienckowski, and Stolz, 1975). Such a board hopefully would assure that change efforts were for the benefit of the residents. (See later section on ensuring ethical standards in institutional settings.) The possibility of voluntary consent has been questioned for residents of prisons (see Shapiro, 1974). Inmates may believe that their chances of release will be better if they participate in programs and such activity may provide a welcome relief from the tedium of prison life. However, to say that prisoners should not have a right to choose whether they will participate in a program may also violate their rights. A reasonable alternative is to offer them a choice, provided that nonparticipation will not result in decreased privileges or punishment and with the stipulation that programs be reviewed by and continually monitored by a panel similar to that described for residents of mental hospitals. "This committee should be kept continually informed of the results of the programs including short- and long-term evaluations, and of any changes in goals or procedures. A meaningful proportion of the members of this committee should be prisoner representatives and the committee should also include persons with appropriate legal backgrounds. The person conducting the behavior modification program should be accountable to this committee and ultimately, to all the individuals participating in the program" (Stolz, Wienckowski, and Brown, 1975, p. 1041). As these authors point out, it is clear that in no setting should intervention methods of any type be employed simply to enhance institutionalization of the resident or to make him adjust to inhumane living conditions.

The Impact of Recent Legal Decisions

Recent years have witnessed increasing concern of the courts regarding client rights, especially with clients who are institutionalized. Rulings have been made, for example, concerning what patients are entitled to as basic rights. "According to the Wyatt court [*Wyatt* v. *Stickney*] a residence unit with screens or curtains to insure privacy, together with 'a comfortable bed . . . a closet or locker for [the patient's] personal belongings, a chair, and a bedside table are all constitutionally required.' (Under Wyatt [*Wyatt* v. *Stickney*] patients are also ensured nutritionally adequate meals with a diet that will provide 'at a minimum, the Recommended Daily Dietary Allowances as developed by the National Academy of Sciences.' Wyatt further enunciates a general right to have visitors, to attend religious services, to wear one's own clothes, (or, for those without adequate clothes, to be provided with a selection of suitable clothes), and to have clothing laundered. With respect to recreation, Wyatt speaks of a right to exercise physically several times weekly and to be outdoors regularly and frequently, a right to interact with members of the other sex, and a right to have a television set in the day room. Finally, Wyatt recognized that 'patients have a right to the least restrictive conditions necessary to achieve the purposes of commitment'—presumably including, if clinically acceptable, ground privileges and an open ward" (Wexler, 1973, p. 94). It should be noted that the right to treatment in the least restrictive alternative favors community settings and arguments are currently being voiced for a "right to normalization" (*Law and Behavior*, 1976b, p. 3). A program cannot legally be carried out in which these items are only available if the client earns them. Clients are entitled to these items and conditions under all circumstances. In the *Wyatt* v. *Stickey* decision, all involuntary work by patients concerning operations of the hospital and hospital maintenance functions was forbidden. This ruling also stipulated that clients should be reimbursed for work at minimum wage standards. As Wexler (1973) noted, only work that could be considered therapeutic for the client and that is unrelated to hospital functioning is exempt from this minimum wage ruling.

Does the client have a right to treatment? The *Wyatt* v. *Stickney* decision (344 F.Supp. 387 [M.D. Ala. 1972]) stated that clients had a right to adequate staff and a right to an individualized intervention program with a timetable for the achievement of specific objectives, as well as identification of criteria for release of clients to less restrictive environments and clear criteria for discharge. Another decision in which the client's right to treatment was upheld was in the *Donaldson* v. *O'Conner* case (493 F.2d. 507 [5th Cir. 1974]) in which an adult was committed to a Florida mental institution. "For religious reasons he refused the first two therapies offered him, electroshock and tranquilizing drugs. He was offered virtually no other therapy for the next fifteen years. Donaldson sued for his release, claiming he had a right either to be treated or released. The Federal Court of Appeals for the Fifth Circuit held that there is a constitutional right to such individual treatment as will help the patient to be cured or to improve his mental condition. Where the justification for commitment is treatment, it violates due process if the treatment is not provided. [Due process states that if a citizen is deprived of his liberty or his property through some governmental activity, it must do so with due process of law (Martin, 1975, p. 2).] If the justification for commitment is dangerousness to self or others, treatment is the quid pro quo society must pay as the price of the extra safety it derives from the denial of the individual's liberty. . . . Donaldson was awarded $38,000 from the two doctors in charge of his care" (Martin, 1975, p. 170). The right to treatment of juveniles was upheld in the *Morales* v. *Turman* case (383 F. Supp. 53 [E. D. Tex. 1974]). This court, as well as others (*Wyatt* and *Donaldson*), stipulated that there must be periodic progress reviews. However, as noted by Brown, Wienckowski, and Stolz (1975), there are inconsistencies in the rulings, especially in those related to voluntary hospitalization.

If it is accepted that the client does have right to treatment, does he have a right to the "best possible validated treatment" (a term from Davison and Stuart, 1975)? Would anyone disagree with such an assertion? Probably not. Why then do we look around us and see time and time again a failure to offer the best validated treatment? Is this because people differ in their definition of the term *validated*? Or does part of the answer lie in failure to arrange the conditions and incentives for offering the best treatment? Is it ignorance or lack of motivation that is related to this failure? Both factors would appear to be responsible. Many professionals do not accept a definition of validation in terms of empirically demonstrated effectiveness.

Rather, procedures are accepted and employed that fit the personal value system of the counselor. Davison and Stuart (1975) argue that not only do administrators of institutions have the obligation to monitor client progress within the institution as well as to gather follow-up data concerning how well residents do after leaving the setting, but are also obligated to compare the effectiveness of alternative programs. They contend that "positive results offer no assurance that a particular program is the most effective, least drastic alternative, nor do negative results suggest alternative strategies. . . . it is our judgment that rather than regarding institutional evaluative research as a potential violation of resident rights, these descriptive and evaluative and comparative research efforts should be *mandatory* aspects of responsible institutional management. Thus, contrary to public opinion we regard the monitoring of existing programs and the search for more beneficial alternatives as activities necessary to insure the basic rights of patients and inmates" (Davison and Stuart, 1975, p. 760). The reader is referred to *Law and Behavior* as a helpful source to keep one abreast of legal developments related to interpersonal helping.

Ensuring Ethical Standards in Institutional Settings

It is quite clear that professionals have not looked after their own ethical standards, even in contexts where abuse of power is most possible, namely institutional settings. A blatant example of this is the reaction of the Ethics Committee of the American Psychiatric Association to a complaint concerning the use of Anectine, a neuromuscular blocking agent that in sufficient dosage can produce paralysis of the muscles, including those of the respiratory system, causing feelings of suffocation and even causing death. This was employed, between 1966 and 1969, without consent, by Reimringer, Morgan, and Bramwell, with over ninety male patients at Atascadero State Hospital in California. This institution is a maximum security hospital for mentally disordered criminals. The criteria employed for selection of residents were vague, referring to residents who displayed persistent violence, deviant sexual behavior and who did not become involved in recommended treatment programs.

What happened following this complaint has been described by Serber, Hiller, Keith, and Taylor (1975). The investigators were contacted by representatives of the American Psychiatric Association. They concluded that there had been no unethical behavior. This decision was reached even though these representatives had not spoken to any of the residents who had experienced this procedure, did not review any charts, and totally ignored the entire issue of consent. According to Serber and others (1975), as of 1975, the American Psychiatric Association had no procedure of any systematic nature for reviewing complaints and allowed no money for investigations.

What can be done to ensure that clients' rights are protected? One of the most detailed statements is the *Guidelines for the Use of Behavioral Procedures in State Programs for the Retarded* (1976). An overview of guidelines for assuring ethical practice within institutional settings is offered in this section, drawing on a recent article by Friedman (1975). These are based on regulations described in the Florida regulations as well as on proposed regulations for the state of California (Shapiro, 1974). It is recommended that institutions embrace a policy in which all residents who are involuntarily confined have a right to refuse any procedures that may intrude on constitutional rights provided for in the First, Eighth and Fourteenth Amendments. This implies that if a person were able to give informed consent, he could not be compelled to undergo procedures. If the resident did not have the capacity to give informed consent, it would have to be shown that the use of procedures was in the best interests of the client and that all less intrusive procedures that might be effective had been tried and did not work. Before carrying out the procedure, a statewide peer review committee and a human rights committee would have to approve the procedure. It is recommended that the peer review committee be composed of two people who have demonstrated competence in applied behavior analysis and who are appointed by the governor of the state, and of three individuals approved by an organization representing the interests of the residents of the population within the residential setting—for example, the National Association for Retarded Citizens. This committee would review all new programs as well as make any reviews requested

by the human rights committee. Only if the committee ruled
that the procedure was in fact effective for altering specific behaviors and that the manner in which the procedure would be
carried out was sound, would permission be given. Possible risks
of the procedure would have to be described, as well as the likelihood of each. This committee would also state whether there
were less dangerous or less intrusive procedures available. A
human rights committee would consist of five members, including an applied behavior analyst, a lawyer with experience in
representing the population of concern and familiar with legislation related to civil liberties, a representative of the consumers
of the service, and members of the community specially concerned with the area. A number of such committees would be
set up in different geographic locations within each state. This
type of committee would investigate complaints as well as make
visits to institutions, both inspecting their facilities and examining their programs. It would also be responsible for categorizing
procedures used to alter given behaviors, in terms of the degree
of hazard and intrusiveness associated with each. Some procedures used to alter some behaviors would not require review of
the panel, such as the use of positive reinforcers (other than
those items guaranteed by law, such as meals) to increase self-
help skills or the use of operant extinction to decrease self-
destructive behaviors. A second group of procedures would
concern those where there was some hazard or intrusion, such
as the use of time out to decrease tantrums. The committee
would have to be notified of the use of any of the procedures in
the second group to alter specific behaviors not more than seven
days after their use. For behaviors not covered by the first two
provisions or for procedures not described there, additional constraints would be imposed. A procedure falling into this third
category would be the use of shock to decrease head banging.
The client would either have to give informed consent for use of
the procedure or be declared legally incompetent as described in
provisions presented earlier. Informed consent will require
provision to the client or to his parent or guardian a substantial
amount of information, including the following items (from
Friedman, 1975, p. 98).

1. The nature and seriousness of the client's behavioral problem and the proposed specific objectives for the client.
2. The nature of the proposed procedure to accomplish these objectives, its probable duration, and intensity.
3. The likelihood of improvement or deterioration, temporary or permanent, without the administration of the proposed procedure.
4. The likelihood and degree of improvement, remission, or control resulting from the administration of such procedure; the likelihood, nature, and extent of changes in and intrusions upon the person's personality and patterns of behavior and thought resulting from such procedure; and the degree to which these changes may be irreversible.
5. The likelihood, nature, extent, and duration of side effects of the proposed procedure and how and to what extent they may be controlled, if at all.
6. The uncertainty of the benefits and hazards of the proposed procedure.
7. The reasonable alternative therapies or procedures available and an explanation why the specific procedure recommended has been chosen. These alternatives shall be described and explained to the client/resident in the same manner as the recommended procedure.
8. Whether the proposed procedure is generally regarded as established procedure by applied behavior analysts or is considered experimental.
9. A description of the procedure for termination of the treatment program prior to completion and clear notification whether consent or waiver may be withdrawn at any time.
10. The data gathering procedures which will be used to evaluate the program.

The client would also have to be informed that special benefits or penalties were not contingent on whether or not he participated in the program. It would be the obligation of any staff person who knew about the use of coercion to inform the human rights committee. If knowledge of coercion were withheld, the party involved in this would be liable to punishment by law. No person would be considered unable to give informed consent simply because he was a resident in an institution. "One of the major difficulties in explicating the concept of capacity is that there seems to be a strong tendency on the part of both psychiatrists and the public generally to assume that mental disorder—or at least mental disorder requiring hospitalization (voluntary or involuntary)—entails a general lack of capacity for making decisions, including specifically a lack of capacity for making decisions concerning therapy or medication. But as a matter of empirical observation, it seems far too simplistic to regard someone who is mentally ill or disordered as being wholly unable to make rational decisions about the conduct of his life. The mind is just too complex to permit such an inference; it is a non sequitur to infer from a lack of aptitude or a dysfunction in one kind of mentation a similar lack or dysfunction in another" (Shapiro, 1974, pp. 308-309). A resident would be considered to be incapable of giving informed consent if he were unable to understand and knowingly act on the required information, or if his consent was not voluntary, as in the presence of coercion. The human rights committee would, in each case, review the documentation to be submitted by the director of the facility, which would have to describe the steps taken to inform the resident about the procedure, and which would have to present an evaluation as to whether he is able to give informed consent. Additional guidelines and recommendations relating to circumstances in which a client would be considered not competent to make his own decision would be as follows:

> If the client/resident has been determined to be legally incompetent by a court of competent jurisdiction, or if the director or his designated representative cannot certify without reservation that the client/resident understands the nature and consequences of the proposed procedure, the procedure may not be used unless the parents, in the case of a minor, or the guardian, in the case of an adult incompetent, of the client/resident have given informed consent and the HRC [human

rights committee] is persuaded that: the procedure complies with generally accepted professional standards; less intrusive alternatives either have been exhausted without success or would be clearly ineffective; the benefits of the procedure clearly outweigh the harms; and, the procedure would be in the best interest of the client/resident. If in rendering a decision under this paragraph the HRC finds that a less restrictive alternative is insufficient only because of the lack of staff or funds, it shall immediately notify the director, the governor, the attorney general, and the chairmen of the appropriate legislative committees, including health and appropriations. [Friedman, 1975, p. 99]

Prior to approval of the procedure, the human rights committee would review all appropriate information concerning the resident, including social, medical, and psychological records, and would interview the client or others as described below.

Prior to approving procedures [in this third category] the HRC shall review appropriate medical, social, and psychological information concerning the client/resident and shall interview the client/resident and others who in its judgment have information pertinent to its determination. The HRC shall maintain written records of its determinations and the reasons therefor, with supporting documentation. The HRC shall file a written report in the office of the state attorney general at least bimonthly indicating the number and nature of procedures approved and disapproved, the reasons for approval or disapproval, and other relevant information, including follow-up evaluations of the success of the procedures utilized. The identity of the client/resident involved shall not be disclosed in these reports. The reports shall be available to the public if they are released by a competent client/resident or by the parent or guardian and the legal representative of an incompetent client/resident. [Friedman, 1975, pp. 99-100]

The proposal also suggests that legal counsel of a lay advocate recommended by a concerned consumer group help and represent the client throughout the decision-making process. "Such counsel shall assist competent clients/residents in deciding whether to undergo proposed procedures and shall ensure for minor and incompetent clients/residents that all considerations militating against the proposed procedure have been fully explored and resolved. No such counsel shall be an officer, employee, or agent of the treating facility or have any other conflict of interest which would impair adequate representation. If such counsel believes the HRC has made a biased or mistaken decision based on all the evidence, he shall appeal the decision to a state court of competent jurisdiction, and the procedure shall not be utilized until and unless the court has given its approval" (Friedman, 1975, p. 100).

It has been recommended that the most intrusive, irreversible, and questionable procedures, such as psychosurgery and electroconvulsive therapy, be banned altogether for those individuals who lack the capacity for informed consent (see Shapiro, 1974). Recent court rulings have supported this recommendation. For example, in *Kaimowitz* v. *Michigan Department of Mental Health* (42 U. S. L Week 2063, Michigan Circuit Court, Wayne County, July 10, 1973), the court held that an involuntarily committed mental patient who volunteered to undergo psychosurgery to reduce his uncontrollable aggression was not in a position to offer informed consent. These guidelines place strict constraints on the use of aversion therapy, as they should. Use of such procedures must be preceded by showing that the client would undergo greater harm if they are not used than he would if they were, and that less intrusive methods have been tried and failed. Accumulated information has narrowed the range of situations under which such intrusive methods as shock are indicated. Overcorrection, for example, has now been successfully employed to decrease severe self-injurious behavior. Aversion therapy is not necessary to alter the sexual orientation of those with sexual variations, such as pedophiliacs, and, in fact, is often ineffective in the absence of other nonpunitive procedures. Programs have been designed and carried out that employ positive methods alone and that satisfy requirements for informed consent within prisons (Milan and McKee, 1976) and mental hospitals (see, for example, Fairweather and others, 1969).

Furthermore, attempted change of behavior is facilitated by the client's involvement and cooperation. In fact, it is difficult, if not impossible, to alter behavior without such cooperation. Aversive methods often result in countercontrol attempts —in resistance to the controlling efforts. This provides another compelling reason why the use of aversive procedures, in the absence of client consent, is of limited potential usefulness (Dirks, 1974).

It is probably impossible to prevent the misuse of aversive methods within institutional settings unless there is a meaningful review process of all procedures. "In the past courts have been too hesitant in their questioning of mental health professionals. Courts should not be reluctant to take corrective action against institutions and individual government employees who fail to provide promised treatment or who force inappropriate or punitive treatment on inmates. Mandatory periodic legal review, including the right to an annual hearing for all judicially-committed persons, may be one mechanism to expedite this process. However, the vagueness of traditional mental health jargon makes it difficult for an inmate to contest his prescribed treatment in court. Terms like 'psychopath,' 'deeper relationship,' and 'cured' offer little information into the institution's or individual practitioner's assessment of the inmate and the specific criteria used to make that assessment. Behavior modification can make important contributions to the process of court evaluation of inmate treatment" (Serber and others, 1975, p. 70). It is assumed that Serber and others are referring to the specification of desired outcomes and identification of criteria for their assessment, more precise procedural descriptions, monitoring of progress, and use of counselor-client contracts which are all characteristic of the behavioral model. The use of counselor-client contracts within child welfare settings has had a facilitating effect on the ability of the court to arrive at decisions concerning the fate of children in out-of-home placement (Stein and Gambrill, 1976a).

Ethical Practice Guidelines

The Association for Advancement of Behavior Therapy has recently formulated a series of questions that will hopefully function as a guide for counselors in assessing issues of ethical import (*AABT Newsletter,* 1976, p. 2). A semifinal version is described in the following outline.*

A. **Have the goals of treatment been adequately considered?**
   1. Have the therapist and client agreed on the goals of therapy?
   2. Has the client's understanding of the goals been assured by writing out the goals or by having the client restate them in his or her own words?
   3. Will serving the client's interests be contrary to the interests of other persons?
   4. Will serving the client's immediate interests be contrary to the client's long term interest?
B. **Has the choice of treatment methods been adequately considered?**
   1. Does the published literature show the procedure to be the best one for that problem?
   2. If no literature exists regarding the treatment method, is the method justified as being a standard practice?
   3. Has the client been told of alternative procedures that might be preferred by the client on the basis of significant differences in discomfort, treatment time, cost *or* degree of demonstrated effectiveness?
   4. If a treatment procedure is publically, legally or professionally controversial has formal professional consultation been obtained, has the reaction of the affected segment of the public been formally ascertained and have the alternative treatment methods been more closely reexamined and reconsidered?
C. **Is the patient's participation voluntary?**
   1. Has the client freely entered into treatment?
   2. If treatment is legally mandated, has a range of treatments and therapists been offered?
   3. Is the client's withdrawal from treatment being discouraged by a penalty or financial loss that exceeds actual clinical costs?

---

*A copy of the final version can be obtained from the Association for Advancement of Behavior Therapy, 420 Lexington Avenue, New York, N.Y. 10017.

D. **Does the therapist refer the patients to other therapists when necessary?**
  1. If the therapist is not qualified to deliver the best treatment is the client referred to other therapists?
  2. If treatment is partially or totally unsuccessful is the client freely referred to other therapists?
  3. If the client is dissatisfied with treatment, is referral freely made?

E. **Has the adequacy of treatment been evaluated?**
  1. Has a quantitative measure of the problem been obtained?
  2. Have the measures of the client's problem been made available to him during treatment?

F. **Has the confidentiality of the treatment relationship been protected?**
  1. Are records available only to authorized persons?
  2. Does the client know who has access to the records and agreed?

G. **Is the therapist qualified to provide treatment?**
  1. Has the therapist had training and/or experience in treating the client's problem?
  2. If deficits exist in the therapist's qualifications, has the client been informed?
  3. If the therapist is not adequately qualified is adequate supervision by a qualified therapist provided and the client informed of this relation?

H. **When another person or an agency is impowered to arrange for therapy have the personal interests of the subordinated client been sufficiently considered?**
  1. Has the subordinated client been informed of the treatment objectives and participated in choice of treatment procedures?
  2. Where the subordinated client's abilities are impaired (retardation, mental illness, child) has the client participated in the treatment discussions to the extent permitted by his or her abilities?
  3. Are the benefits to the superordinate agency or person contrary to the interests of the subordinated person?
  4. If the interests of the subordinated and superordinate persons conflict, have attempts been made to reduce the conflict by dealing with both interests?

The Limits of Individual Discretion

Clearly, more is known today concerning how to help clients alter their behavior in order to attain more satisfying lives than has ever been known before. On the other hand, it is also clear that we are just beginning to tap the surface in terms of developing a clear, teachable, technology, especially one that can be placed more and more in the hands of clients themselves in terms of self-help manuals and programs, peer counseling groups, and so forth. We still have relatively little information in relation to what works with what client under what circumstances, but on the other hand, we have enough to start formulating some standards for practice in certain settings. As more effective methods are developed, lack of knowledge concerning their existence becomes more problematic. In the past, when nobody knew too much about changing behavior, there was not much new work to keep up with and little information as to what worked best. How could one judge whether one procedure worked better than another except perhaps through the often incorrect appraisal based on the gradual accumulation of personal experience over one's career?

The existence of more information, as well as the historical incidence of ethical lapses, raises questions about the limits of personal discretion. For example, how much variance should be permitted individual counselors in the selection of intervention procedures related to given behaviors? Such discretion is so broad today that viewing current practice in the mental health field is like viewing a geological formation in which the traces of past years can be readily seen. So little sharing of helpful knowledge takes place, even between professionals in the same agency, that even a counselor sitting next to another one may not know that his peer knows about a more effective procedure with a given behavior.

The history of the interpersonal helping professions clearly indicates the need for greater influence over individual discretion of counselors in the selection of objectives (making sure that these are in the client's interests), in the selection of procedures (in terms of choosing those that, while least intrusive and restrictive, are most effective and efficient, given that information is available related to these characteristics) and assuring accountability of counselors to their clients or their concerned representatives by designing and implementing an effective monitoring procedure to assess degree of change.

Who is to exert this greater influence? Within a social learning theory, it is assumed that ethical behavior, if it is to occur, must be reinforced. It can only be reinforced if it in fact occurs, and thus training programs may be required to offer counselors the skills to engage in the components of this class of counselor behavior. Cueing and incentive systems will also be necessary, as well as effective monitoring systems. Supervisors, being much closer to the work of individual counselors, can monitor cases of those counselors for whom they are responsible, to ensure that counselor-client contracts with the necessary components exist; that the client has been an informed participant in the selection of desired outcomes and procedures; that a monitoring procedure has been designed and implemented; that strong rather than weak procedures have been selected to achieve given outcomes (with the client's consent); that the least intrusive and restrictive procedure has been selected (with the client's consent); and that the outcomes selected are in the client's interests and protect society's interests. Administrators could employ a probe procedure in relation to the work of counselors and supervisors, in which randomly selected cases are reviewed in terms of satisfying requirements (see the section on accountability in Chapter Twenty-Three). It is also clear that, in order to ensure ethical practice, agencies, institutions, and individual practitioners will have to be subject to periodic mandatory review either by the court or by a government-appointed review panel. Ideally, practitioner incentives such as salaries should be contingent in part on demonstrated use of the best validated assessment and intervention procedures and other aspects of ethical practice. Feldman (1976) recommends the creation of consumer interest groups that would be responsible for offering potential clients factual information concerning such factors as the efficiency, effectiveness, and intrusiveness of various assessment and intervention procedures. Such agencies should be staffed by disinterested parties to increase the probability of accurate information. The activity of the courts in assuring clients greater protection is indeed encouraging. Professional organizations are also making attempts to encourage competent and ethical behavior on the part of their constituencies. The effort on the part of the Association for Advancement of Behavior Therapy (AABT) to offer guidelines for ethical practice is one such effort, as is their offer of consultative aid to individuals who may have concerns about behavioral programs. Such persons can make request the president of AABT "to appoint a committee of persons to go to the site, investigate, and make an advisory report. These reports are compiled into a casebook of standards of practice" (Brown, Wienckowski, and Stolz, 1975, p. 22). And, of course, each counselor should be commited to providing the conditions necessary for ethical practice. Free telephone consultation is available if needed.

Are Special Ethical Guidelines
Required for Behavioral Methods?

Anyone who has been in touch with descriptions of behavioral methods in popular sources cannot but wonder whether ethical issues are more at issue with behavioral methods than with other methods of interpersonal helping. Is this true? Let us first consider the data, which indicate that interpersonal helping contains a social influence process in which it is probably impossible not to bias the actions of the client in some way (see the previous discussion in Chapter Three). Recognition of interpersonal helping as involving an inescapable influence process, which occurs within social learning theory, is likely to make the practioner more aware of possible biasing influences that may be exerted and more able to share these with clients. And what about the concern with the power of behavioral methods? As mentioned in the first chapter, this power has been considerably overestimated. Alteration of behavior without the cooperation of the client is usually not possible, and, if tried, often leads to countercontrol efforts. It is within social learning theory itself that evidence has accumulated showing the disadvantages of aversive methods. The emphasis on identification of specific desired outcomes and on use of a negotiated written contract between client and counselor, in which the method of assessing degree of progress is also described, helps protect clients against unwarranted intrusions, and from continued participation in ineffective treatment regimes.

Some assume that the technology of behavior modification implies a position in relation to selection of desired outcomes. Although there is some disagreement on this issue, even within the behavioral ranks (see, for example, Mahoney, 1974a), most assume the position that the technology does not imply how it is to be employed; that is, it can be used either for the advantage or for the disadvantage of clients. Certainly the information accumulated within the behavioral area is based on an acceptance of the scientific method as being of value in the collection of information, and the values of scientists influence their behavior. The model of man one holds also influences what one views as the potentialities for change and the methods that will be employed to create change. The point at issue here, however, is whether behavioral principles inform the selection of desired outcomes. Do they indicate what is good? The influence that is exerted in alternative intervention modes in choosing objectives is often obscured by the vagueness with which they are stated. In fact, Bandura (1969) proposes that objectives are often not specified to avoid the recognition of the value judgments that are involved in interpersonal helping, and that often relabeling of the client's problem is employed to minimize ethical decisions. For example, if a person is considered mentally ill, this may legitimize (in the eyes of the counselor) use of intrusive intervention methods that would not be considered ethical in other circumstances. People often do not object as much to change that is brought about in an unplanned way as they do to change brought about by carefully selected methods designed to achieve a clear objective. That is, change brought about accidentally seems more acceptable, especially when it is accompanied by verbal statements of good intentions. This view poses the disadvantage of allowing behavior to be influenced accidentally, which may be as much to a client's disadvantage as may deliberately working toward objectives that he has not selected. Good intentions work to the disadvantage of clients when such intentions are considered sufficient in and of themselves.

All interpersonal helping methods are in need of supervision within specific ethical guidelines, and, in some ways, behavioral procedures will be more amenable to satisfying such requirements. The failure of many to distinguish between use of the term *behavior modification* as referring to a particular model of practice and the use of this term to refer to an outcome is no doubt partially responsible for some of the concern about behavior modification, as is clear identification of objectives (Krasner, 1969). The overselling of the possibilities of behavioral influence without the consent of the involved parties probably also contributes to this greater concern, as does the unwillingness to attribute any influence over behavior to the environment—that is, the assumption that one is completely ruler of one's fate, rather than a recognition of the interaction between behavior, cognition, feelings, and environmental events. Increasing people's understanding of the way in which behavior is influenced by environmental events, including those events offered by the advertisers, government, and religious organizations, and offering people knowledge concerning behavioral principles, will allow them to exercise greater influence over their environment (Skinner, 1953; London, 1969). Behavioral methods can be employed for the advantage or disadvantage of clients, as can other methods. This necessitates implementation of a procedure that will monitor the use of *all* interpersonal helping methods to ensure that these methods are indeed being employed for the advantage of the client, with due concern for the interests of society. Specification of exactly what "due concern" relates to is critical, because people's rights have often been trampled on for behaviors that hurt no one else but that have been considered bad for society as well as bad for the person, such as smoking marihuana.

The Importance of Training Programs and Supervision

Only if appropriate counselor behaviors occur can they be reinforced. To this end, we have stressed, in this chapter, the need to identify specific ethical behaviors-in-situations in interpersonal helping. Ethically questionable practices may sometimes occur because the counselor does not discriminate the ethical issues involved in a certain situation. One function of training programs should be to facilitate identification by counselors of ethical issues that arise in practice. Another should be to increase counselor identification of interested parties involved in such critical areas as selection of goals, and to offer ways to roughly estimate potential benefits and costs to each. The range of possible factors has been elaborated by Feldman (1976), who includes the legal consequences associated with given outcomes, the ethical code of professions, personal evaluations, political and other pressure groups, the agency or institution within which the counselor works, and significant others of the client, such as friends, family members, or perhaps victims. In addition, goals may be limited by the state of knowledge that exists or by available resources. It is important that such training programs concentrate on specific behaviors-in-situations in which a determination can be made as to what is desirable for whom and under what circumstances. Such training programs may alter counselors' perception of problems. One of the first decisions that must be made during assessment is whether there is a problem. An example of this was offered in Chapter Twenty, in the discussion of permission giving—the counselor gives permission to the client to continue engaging in a behavior that the client had perceived as a problem, because it is not perceived as a problem by the counselor and in fact is normalized.

The casebook of ethical questions being put together by the Association for Advancement of Behavior Therapy can provide one source of situations of ethical concern. As a first step, questionnaires can be established to ascertain whether professionals can identify appropriate ethical behavior in specific situations. Such questionnaires should also tap knowledge of current legislation protecting client rights, so that this source of support for such rights can be employed (Sulzer-Azaroff, Thaw, and Thomas, 1975). Let us say, for example, that a counselor finds that his agency or institution is violating some court-mandated regulation of concern to client rights. If he voices a concern, it will probably bear greater weight if it is bolstered by legislation. Many aspects of counselor behavior can be monitored through records, which will reveal, for example, whether a viable procedure for monitoring progress has been designed and is being carried out (see the section on increasing accountability in Chapter Twenty-Three).

Training programs are critically important to assure ongoing staff education. "Training is where the problems of poor job creation, poor recruitment and poor selection come together. The expectation of most behavior change programs with which I am familiar is that, through training, the staff will learn what they need and will change. That training, however, often comes too late, for there are really several stages to staff training: orientation, preservice, unplanned inservice, and planned inservice" (Martin, 1975, pp. 110-111). Evaluation of staff is often completely unrelated to any changes that are desired through training programs. This may lead to two phenomena: "A staff member's behavior will be totally unchanged by training but he will receive high evaluation, or a staff member will perform very well in the new program, but will be evaluated just the same" (Martin, 1975, p. 112). Some recent legal decisions bear directly on competency of staff. "The court in *Morales* [v. *Turman* (383 F. Supp. 53; E. D. Tex. 1974)] suggested that placing a program in the hands of poorly trained staff violated constitutional requirements. It cited five problems in particular. The first problem is having insufficient staff to actually deal with the problem so that there is in reality no program, and things might actually get worse. Second, staff members must be properly screened to assure that they are not psychologically unfit for the job they must perform. Third, staff members cannot be allowed to make decisions beyond their level of competence. . . . Fourth, training cannot be insufficient preparation for the job. And fifth, there must be follow-up on training in the form of on-the-job supervision" (Martin, 1975, pp. 107-108).

Ethical Considerations Concerning Records

Clients may be hurt through a lack of care in handling records. Regulations for handling records are described in professional codes of ethics and the need to ensure confidentiality of the client is stressed. Martin (1975) identifies a number of concerns in relation to record keeping, including the following: that records should relate to overt behavior that justifies a change program; that the privacy of the client is not violated in obtaining information; that information in records is objective and can be verified; that files are periodically reviewed and extraneous items removed; that clients be permitted access to their files; that clients have a right to challenge items recorded and to have them removed from the record or to include a statement regarding the information; that files be kept in such a manner that a record could be completely removed; and that permission be gained from the clients before their records are made available to someone else. The importance of records was highlighted by the case of *Whitree* v. *New York State* (290 N.Y. S.2d. 486 [Ct. Claims] 1968), where the inadequacy of records was cited as the reason a client was held in a mental hospital for twelve years. The court held that inadequate records would hinder the development of treatment plans (Martin, 1975).

Actualities and Possibilities

This brief overview of the ethics of interpersonal helping has indicated that provisions protecting client rights have been legislatively mandated in many states and that this trend is likely to continue and is a much needed one. It has also indicated that some professional associations are taking steps to try to identify more specific ethical guidelines and to offer counsel to people establishing programs. The key item that is needed is the creation of meaningful incentive systems that will support ethical standards of practice, and this lags behind legislation. Where important incentives such as salaries are not contingent on appropriate behavior, as is the case in the civil service system, additional incentives will have to be located. One cannot expect change without alterations in the contingency systems that support inappropriate behavior. The past has proven that good intentions and verbal protestations are not enough. These must be legislated regulations in relation to ethical standards and a contingency system to support these.

How active should professionals be in relation to trying to alter social conditions that may be responsible for individual

problems? Should professionals be politically active? For example, Halleck (1971) states that "There is no reason why psychiatrists, both as private citizens and as professionals, should not
try to change some of our social conditions that produce so
much misery among large groups of people" (p. 241) and he
goes on to mention wars, overpopulation, poverty, and "any
form of oppression based on skin color, age, sex, or harmless
social deviation" (p. 241). He urges professional organizations
to take formal stands on important social issues. Unfortunately,
such recommendations imply that professionals are far more
powerful than they really are. Even if all professionals banded
together and took a stand on social issues, this would not necessarily change anything. Change will require the concerted efforts and continued vigilance of the public, the legal system and
governmental agencies as well as of professionals. Again, we
must consider the contingency system that maintains current
practice and, after understanding this, we must have access to
important variables within this system. Professionals simply do
not have access to many of the important variables such as the
power to make certain actions legally mandatory. To say that
any one professional group alone can ever have a large effect on
such problems as poverty or overpopulation offers false hopes
and poses the danger of deflecting professionals from areas
where they really could have an impact on assuring ethical standards of practice, namely in their own agencies, institutions,
and with their own clients in individual practice. This is not to
say that professionals should not take public stands on issues. It
is to say, let not this be an excuse for failing to attend to one's
own agency, institution, or practice. Some very specific ways in
which such attending can be carried out have been described in
this chapter (see also section on increasing accountability in
Chapter Twenty-Three).

Summary

Responsible practice requires the identification of the
specific behaviors-in-situations involved in ethical interpersonal
helping, as well as implementation of procedures to ensure compliance with these ethical standards. There is no doubt that con-

ditions previously thought to be sufficient to ensure the rights of clients, such as professional codes of ethics, have in too many instances failed miserably. The factors responsible for this state of affairs are more speculated about than known, and include the unwillingness of professionals to question their own behavior, the low power of clients' groups (now changing), and the unfortunate confusion among professionals concerning their own personal value system, legally prescribed behavior, and professional practice. Areas emphasized as of special import to ethical practice concern selection of objectives, ensuring that the elements of informed consent have been satisfied, or appropriate substitute arrangements made, selecting the least intrusive and most effective and efficient intervention procedures and being truly accountable to clients through careful monitoring of progress. It is strongly suggested that only if mandatory court or governmental review of agencies, institutions, and individual practitioners is carried out, will the client be assured of ethically responsible counseling. In view of the trespasses on client rights in the past, one cannot exercise too much vigilance in relation to the ethical concerns involved in interpersonal helping.

23

If the future holds as rapid an output of empirical studies on helping people to change their behavior as has the recent past, we should be blessed with increasingly effective change methods. Some trends and needs are discussed here as food for thought (self-stimulatory behavior).

Toward Increased Recognition of Individual Differences

In that behavioral theory holds that each of us has a unique learning history and stresses the need for individually tailored assessment and intervention, a behavioral framework is concerned with individual differences. However, individual differences are often overlooked in practice. This is reflected in the use of only one procedure with a group of individuals (as has

1080

Needs and Prospects of Behavior Modification

been done in weight reduction programs, treatment for problem drinkers, and clients with anxiety reactions), rather than individually tailoring particular interventions for particular clients. Failure to conduct an individual behavioral analysis in each case and to select intervention procedures in accord with this analysis allows a major source of uncontrolled variation that confounds attempts to compare the effectiveness of one procedure with those of another or with untreated control groups. If one intervention method appears to be more effective than another, part of this difference could be caused by a fortuitously better match between initial client characteristics and intervention components. One trend in the field is to give clients greater choice between various intervention methods (see, for example, Meichenbaum and Turk, 1976). Some attention has been given to individual differences that may be revealed by assessment tests, as these may relate to the relative effectiveness of procedures with given clients. For example, clients who scored high on a self-reinforcement test lost more weight under a self-control program than under a counselor-controlled program (Rozensky and Bellack, 1976). Often, however, there has been a failure to locate any relationship between client characteristics as revealed on assessment tests and outcome. As further information emerges concerning the relationship of individual differences to the achievement of given outcomes with given procedures, this should be incorporated into the helping endeavors.

The Relationship of Research and Practice

The history of interpersonal helping reflects a separation between clinical research and practice. This separation has impeded the accumulation of information relevant to practice and created a gap in understanding and appreciation of the relationship that should exist between research and practice. Such a division is not as severe in the behavioral model of practice, which draws on empirical literature to inform selection of assessment and intervention procedures and emphasizes the monitoring of change efforts and, if possible, showing that intervention was indeed responsible for the effects achieved (Risley, 1968). Ongoing evaluation of intervention effects is considered to be an essential ingredient. Often these evaluation efforts will allow more than an indication that the intervention was effective within the methodologically weak but clinically relevant AB designs. That is, often a methodologically strong design will be required for clinical reasons, such as making sure that a behavior that might have a physical basis is in fact really maintained by attention from significant others. Or, such a design may be just as easy to carry out as an AB design. Data resulting from these more informative single-organism designs will be valuable to others in terms of what intervention seems to work with what behavior. As more counselors are impressed by the advantages of carefully monitoring degree of progress, and view themselves as having meaningful contributions to make that are based on data, hopefully a closer interaction will occur between practitioners and researchers. The helping domain offers a natural arena in which procedures are continually tested in terms of their effectiveness. Case studies in which effects are carefully monitored may make many contributions, such as exploring the effectiveness of principles applied to a new area (see Lazarus and Davison, 1971).

Increasing Client Self-Determination

One of the attractions to many of those interested in a behavioral framework relates to the potential of offering the individual more influence over his or her environment. This environment includes the individual's own feelings, beliefs, and behaviors as well as the behavior of significant others and other external events. This area of self-management has always posed and still does pose a challenge to anyone who has tried to alter his or her own behavior—witness the high failure rates of New Year's resolutions! The problems of self-management pose unique difficulties in that the person himself must either pre-plan environmental events so that certain behaviors will be facilitated (for example, by bringing to a bar only enough money for one beer) or learn additional skills that will enable him to behave in desired ways when in the environment, such as stress management skills for use in social situations so that he can approach and initiate conversations with people he finds interesting. It is quite clear with many behaviors that cause later problems, such as failure to study, smoking, overeating, and drinking to excess, that an important part of the technology already exists in relation to altering the behavior. We know, for example, ways to effectively decrease eating behavior. However, getting people to carry out the program is another matter, and we still have a long way to go in developing a technology to accomplish this.

Self-determination is also increased by offering people greater influence over their social environment, and a number of examples have been presented in this book of offering those in a low power position, such as students, skills to alter the behavior of significant others who are in high power positions. This area offers a ripe one for use with other populations, such as the elderly, and in other situations, such as institutional settings.

Encouraging an Actualizing Model of Change

One dimension of difference between models of change is in terms of the degree to which they focus on the construction of repertoires employing available client assets and the degree to which they focus on the pathology of the client, mainly on locating his behavior deficits. Social learning theory presents an example of a constructional approach to change (Goldiamond, 1974), in which the development of repertoires is emphasized, building on available client assets. This emphasis can be highlighted even in the names given to agencies. For example, The Adult Development Center at the University of Washington uses neither the term *counselor* or the term *client*. Instead, "students" attend this school and participate in an "advisory relationship" with a person at the center to guide the student toward those programs that might be most helpful to him. This "is a 'college of behavioral change' with a 'curriculum' of courses, seminars, laboratory experiences, and some individual 'study,' all geared toward providing students with the opportunity to learn new behaviors, unlearn old ones, and develop their thinking with regard to the kind of specific behavioral goals they wish to achieve for themselves. . . . Requirements for enrollment in this school have to do primarily with an individual's personal desire to do so toward the end of gaining some behavioral change" (Armstrong and Bakker, 1971, p. 12). The students are encouraged to be helpful to other students, in order to increase their own feelings of self-worth. Those individuals who are unmotivated or, in the opinion of the staff, need medical care are screened out. "Self-assessment is a full week of intense orientation meetings, didactic presentations, workshops and self-examination sessions, interspersed with 'mini-labs' which are brief trial sessions of each of the classes that exist in the curriculum" (p. 13). Through this process, the student helps to define his or her goals, becomes familiar with the center and is encouraged to view active participation and practice as necessary for the achievement of goals.

Classes are offered in four different areas. Within the interpersonal area, courses are offered in "Parent Effectiveness," "Couples Communication," and "Interpersonal Relations." Courses in the personal curriculum include "Precision Behavior Change," "Mood-Thought Alteration," "Relaxation Training," "Basic Movement," and "Decision Making" (Armstrong and Bakker, 1971, p. 15). "Vocational Development," "Home Management," and "Time Management" are offered in the vocational curriculum, and in the last area, two courses are offered, "Leisure Time" and "Creativity." Students are introduced to a social learning view of their behavior and discouraged from applying labels to themselves that connote sickness. A background for staff in the area of mental health is considered a "mixed blessing," because of the difficulty that often occurs in relinquishing a pathological view of behavior. The advisory relationship created between staff and the student is characteristic of the behavioral model in which the client is helped to identify clear desired outcomes and is held responsible for making final decisions on aims to be pursued.

Availability of such a center allows consumers to pursue desired outcomes without the stigmatization that often accompanies this pursuit when professional help is sought. How different is going to classes at an Adult Development Center from attending therapy sessions at the local community mental health center! A report written at the end of a year of operation of this center indicated that "The evidence so far is that consumers will support a facility for behavior change which demands as its ticket of admission not the acknowledgement of personal illness but instead the assumption of personal responsibilities. The evidence is that this ticket of admission not only allows for involvement of the less seriously disturbed individuals . . . but also is a face-saving opportunity for persons with more imminent and critical needs to change behavior. Indeed, in the latter group it seems that there are many individuals quite capable of change if it is of their own volition and in the direction that their own initiative takes them rather than at the behest, direction, and manipulation of others" (Armstrong and Bakker, 1971, pp. 19-20). The range of skills present in diverse groups of people who come together seems to have a facilitating effect in that one can learn and teach at the same time. This is one promising model of service delivery system that conveys a constructional approach even in its very name.

Counseling for Prevention

Often the emphasis of programs seems to be on erasing problems once they occur rather than on preventing their occurrence. One example of a preventive approach is offering normal families more help in child rearing. The increased isolation of families removes potential models who have experience in child management methods. Parent training programs are helpful with "well-educated parents or to desperate parents willing to undergo reeducation in order to remediate child-rearing problems" (Risley, Clark, and Cataldo, 1976, p. 50). However, "society has not yet found a way to replace the most common child-rearing assistance once provided by the extended family: advice on solving chronic, everyday child-learning problems. . . . A substantial portion of child-rearing problems can be accounted for in a relatively small number of specific times and places in a family's daily life [such as family shopping trips]" (Risley, Clark, and Cataldo, 1976, pp. 50-51). Provision of programs in how to handle such situations would provide a useful preventive function.

One such program has been developed concerning family shopping trips (Clark, Greene, Macrae, McNees, Davis, and Risley, 1976). A survey indicated that this was a problem area and also provided indications of target behaviors, such as staying within conversational distance of one another, not touching merchandise unless intending to purchase it, not distracting people with comments such as "Will you buy me a doll?" or "I want to go to the candy store" (Clark and others, 1976, p. 5), avoiding fighting, running, yelling, and talking about items for which the adults were shopping. Seventy-six percent of one sample of parents interviewed ($N = 25$) said they would like advice about how to make shopping trips more fun and educational. The program developed trained parents how to use the natural reinforcers available contingent on appropriate child behaviors. Discourteous behaviors were followed by response cost, whereas appropriate behavior was followed by parental attention and conversation. "Remarkable changes in each family's conversation then occurred simply as a result of the instructions provided by the advice package that the parents use certain stimuli (the products on the shopping list) as prompts for initiating conversation. The children eagerly reciprocated and the family became 'trapped' (Baer and Wolf, 1970) in mutually reinforcing conversations" (Clark and others, 1976, p. 33). Two- and eight-week follow-ups showed that positive changes were maintained. Favorable comments were made regarding the program by the children as well as by the adults. (The authors note that after the development of such programs, programs must then be designed to disseminate them.)

The continually lessened time that parents spend with their children and the consequent need for more careful design of child care environments in which an increasing number of children spend their daytime hours have been noted by some authors and a number of studies to ascertain helpful dimensions of such environments have been carried out (see Risley, Clark, and Cataldo, 1976). Preventive programs have also been developed for older children. "As children grow older they no longer need care; instead they need guidance in establishing the skills necessary for successful and appropriate adult behavior and protection from being seriously affected by official consequences for their occasional acts of social deviance. We have considered two technologies for these goals. One, suitable for preadolescents who are more readily amenable to adult direction than are teen-agers, is 'survival training' in academic, achievement, and job-related skills. The second is a 'safe passage' program to provide older youth with an alternative to the activities of the street and/or irresponsible peers and to increase adolescents' contacts with and socialization to responsible adults. The focus for both programs is recreation which can provide both consequences for youths' activity, and maximum contact with responsible adults" (Risley, Clark, and Cataldo, 1976, p. 47). Procedures have been developed to evaluate toys and activities, to make sure that the programs offered at the recreation centers engage youth. Recreational activities are used as reinforcers. It has been found that new members can be attracted to the program by offering additional access to recreational activities for youth who bring them to the center (Pierce and Risley, 1974b). A response cost procedure in which the center is closed down for one to fifteen minutes earlier contingent on rule infractions is effective in decreasing infractions (Pierce and Risley, 1974b). Methods have also been developed for ensuring that helpful technology is actually employed by staff (Pierce and Risley, 1974a). Workers are credited with working time proportional to their rating on a simple checklist of job performance. Under these conditions, job performance was maintained at near-perfect levels. As the authors note, this changed the emphasis from clocked hours to hours worked.

Training clients in skills useful under many situations, such as general problem-solving skills and stress management procedures, also serves a preventive function. Future work should continue to explore their utility. Preventive efforts of clients in relation to health may be encouraged by appropriate prompting and incentive procedures, as illustrated by a recent study in which low-income parents were encouraged to attain dental care for their children (Reiss, Piotrowski, and Bailey, 1976). Offering community members more effective skills for participating in decision making in relation to issues that affect them may also serve a preventive function in that it should increase involvement in what happens in their community. In one recent study, nine adults of lower socioeconomic status, who were board members of a federally funded community project, were offered improved skills in problem solving to increase their effective participation during board meetings (Briscoe, Hoffman, and Baily, 1975). Behavioral procedures have also been employed to try to decrease pollution (see, for example, Chapman and Risley, 1974).

The emphasis within the behavioral approach on involving significant others and on identifying environmental factors related to given behaviors encourages attention to factors outside the individual. Such attention often reveals a lack of incentives for appropriate behavior. The negative interaction between the police and teen-agers that often occurs can be viewed in terms of the vigilance of the police for inappropriate rather than appropriate behaviors. In one program designed to alter this pattern gift certificates were solicited from shop owners and given to the police (James, 1973). They in turn were to award them to youth they caught doing something good, such as obeying the speed limit or helping someone across the street. All too often, appropriate behavior is ignored. Is it any wonder that it does not occur more frequently in areas often complained about, such as the prevalence of violence and the infrequency of Good Samaritanism? Greater recognition of appropriate behavior would hopefully serve to increase it, and there are many media within which this could occur. Why not, for example, have a good deed of the day award on each night's newscast, best deed of the year, and so forth?

Using Available Information

Why aren't programs that have shown themselves to be effective employed on a broader basis? That is, why isn't available information concerning effective programs employed more extensively? One example is the Fairweather Community Lodge Program, designed to maintain psychiatric patients in the community following release from the hospital (Fairweather and others, 1969). This was designed so that clients would have a social support system and would have a means of financial support following their release. Skills in problem solving and in decision making were developed within small task groups within the hospital prior to client release. Each task group was responsible for the behavior of its individual members. It should be noted that this program was carried out without any use of deprivation of privileges. Why hasn't this program been employed in other hospitals, since it showed itself to be effective in maintaining clients in the community for a much longer time compared to a control group that received the usual program offered by the hospital, was far more effective in maintaining employment in the community, and had a mean daily cost per person that was much lower than that in private psychiatric hospitals, local government psychiatric hospitals, or federal government hospitals?

The problems of introducing effective innovative programs into settings where less effective procedures are employed remains a major issue (see, for example, Fairweather, Sanders, Tornatzky, and Harns, 1974). It is the clients who lose in this failure to use effective programs, as well as the taxpayers, who must support more costly, less effective programs. A major need is the development of procedural review systems to ensure that methods employed by agencies are in fact the best validated procedures as well as the least intrusive and to find incentives for employing effective programs. Procedures for arranging quality control are available, as described in the next section.

Increasing Accountability

The term *accountability* is growing in popularity, but there is a discouraging lack of concordance between verbal statements that accountability is a good thing and actual behavior. Yet procedures to assure accountability are available, as illustrated by the program in effect at the Huntsville Community Mental Health Center (Rinn and Vernon, 1975). The center has succeeded in implementing process evaluation as well as outcome evaluation (the former term refers to the quality control of procedures implemented by staff). In order to determine whether staff is indeed employing validated procedures in an appropriate manner, one must monitor not only the results of intervention—for example, by use of goal attainment scaling—but also the process of service delivery. Inservice training for staff is provided at the Huntsville-Madison County Mental Health Center to keep staff informed about new procedures. These programs are evaluated both by objectively scored pre- and posttests and by presenting a contrived case study before and after training. "The therapist is required to show, step-by-step, how he/she would conduct treatment, including pinpointing, measuring, intervening, trouble shooting, and so forth" (Rinn and Vernon, 1975, p. 9). Answers are objectively scored. Here the counselor's ability to write about and talk about his skills is evaluated. Counselor behavior when with clients is evaluated via monthly monitoring of performance by the service coordinator acting as cotherapist or by this person reviewing an audiotape of a counseling session. Prior written permission is gained from the client. In this evaluation, the coordinator should "(1) pinpoint the therapist's behaviors to be altered, (2) measure the frequency of such behaviors, (3) develop a program to alter the therapist's behavior, and (4) provide the therapist with behavioral feedback" (Rinn and Vernon, 1975, p. 9).

The consistency with which appropriate procedures are employed is monitored by requiring each counselor to complete a Therapist Evaluation Data Sheet (TEDS) for each client. It is assumed that if a counselor sets behavioral goals and collects behavioral information that he will also employ behavioral methods.

> The TEDS measures, indirectly, eight specific aspects of treatment. It determines whether the therapist has: (1) enacted a client-therapist contract . . . ; (2) set behavioral goals and made plans based on behavioral techniques . . . ; (3) maintained a multiple baseline data graph . . . ; (4) dictated an initial therapy note concerning the therapist's clinical impression of the client and a diagnosis (in compliance with state regulations); (5) described each therapy session, including the presence or absence of client data; (6) informed the referring professional concerning the client's goals and plans before therapy . . . ; (7) informed the referring professional concerning the client's progress after therapy . . . ; and (8) entered a termination note including innovations, problems in treatment, and so forth. The first six steps earn the therapist 5, 5, 5, 5, 10, and 4 points per client respectively. If either of the last two steps is not completed, 3 and 5 points, respectively, are subtracted from the therapist's total score for the particular client [Rinn and Vernon, 1975, p. 9]

In each case, counselor behavior can be checked by the presence or absence of an appropriate record; thus, essentially, his record-keeping skills are assessed. Each month, five client files are randomly selected from each counselor's case load and the TEDS score calculated for each. This can vary from 0 to 34 points for each file. Annual salary increments are partially determined by the scores on the TEDS. The median monthly scores on counselor evaluation data sheets increased substantially, and there was a marked decrease in their variance under this salary contingent procedure. As the authors point out, the short-term nature of the service that is to be offered can be monitored by reviewing the average number of counselor sessions.

Developing a Coherent Terminology

Compared with most other therapeutic modes, behavior modification is in its infancy. Still, it is old enough, now stretching over twenty years, for new names to be applied to old procedures. For example, Hall and Dietz (1975) titled an article "Systematic Organismic Desensitization," but in fact they employed the familiar technique known as *systematic desensitization*. And, as Mahoney (1974a) points out, some procedures employed in behavior modification were written about long before the term *behavior modification* was ever heard of. Failure to point out the continuities between old procedures and variations or relabeling accepted procedures with new names is a hindrance to the field.

Summary

The added information we now have at hand to alleviate client problems is indeed encouraging. Perhaps the most difficult task is making use of this technology in such a way that the client's as well as societal interests are protected, that individual differences are recognized, that self-determination is enhanced, and that preventive efforts are augmented. A greater commitment to accountability will not only protect clients, but will also help to generate more useful information concerning what procedures are helpful with what problems. In the best spirit of the behavioral model, no matter what the behavior of concern, the emphasis should be on catching people doing something good and letting them know this, rather than, as so often happens now, trying to catch them doing something bad.

References

AABT [Association for the Advancement of Behavior Therapy] *Newsletter,* 1976, *3* (whole issue, No. 4).

Abel, G. G. "Assessment of Sexual Deviation in the Male." In M. Hersen and A. S. Bellack (Eds.), *Behavioral Assessment: A Practical Handbook.* New York: Pergamon, 1976.

Abel, G. G., and Blanchard, E. B. "The Role of Fantasy in the Treatment of Sexual Deviation." *Archives of General Psychiatry,* 1974, *30,* 467-475.

Abel, G. G., Blanchard, E. B., Barlow, D. H., and Mavissakalian, M. "Identifying Specific Erotic Cues in Sexual Deviations by Audio-Taped Descriptions." *Journal of Applied Behavior Analysis,* 1975, *8,* 247-260.

Abel, G. G., Blanchard, E. B., and Becker, J. V. "Psychological Treatment of Rapists." In M. Walker and S. Brodsky (Eds.), *Rape: Research, Prevention, Action.* Lexington, Mass.: Lexington, in press.

Abel, G. G., Levis, D., and Clancy, J. "Aversion Therapy Applied to Taped Sequences of Deviant Behavior in Exhibitionism and Other Sexual Deviations: A Preliminary Report." *Journal of Behavior Therapy and Experimental Psychiatry,* 1970, *1,* 59-66.

Abraham, K. "Notes on the Psycho-Analytical Investigation and Treatment of Manic-Depressive Insanity and Allied Conditions (1911)." In E. Jones (Ed.), *Selected Papers of Karl Abraham, M.D.* (D. Bryan and J. Strachey, Trans.) London: Hogarth, 1927.

Abrams, L., Hines, D., Pollack, D., Ross, M., Stubbs, D. A., and Polyot, C. J. "Transferable Tokens: Increasing Social Interaction in Token Economies." *Psychological Record,* 1974, *35,* 447-452.

Adams, K. A. "Behavioral Treatment of Reflex or Sensory Evoked Seizures." *Journal of Behavior Therapy and Experimental Psychiatry,* 1976, *7,* 123-127.

Addison, R. M., and Homme, L. E. "The Reinforcing Event (RE) Menu." *National Society for Programmed Instruction Journal,* 1966, *5,* 8-9.

Agras, W. S., Barlow, T. H., Chapin, H. N., Abel, G. G., and Leitenberg, H. "Behavior Modification of Anorexia Nervosa." *Archives of General Psychiatry,* 1974, *30,* 279-286.

Aitken, A. C. B. "Measures of Feeling Using Analogue Scales." *Proceedings of the Royal Society of Medicine,* 1969, *62,* 989-993.

Akiskal, H. S., and McKinney, W. T. "Depressive Disorders: Toward a Unified Hypothesis." *Science,* 1973, *182,* 20-29.

Alban, L. S., and Nay, W. R. "Reduction of Ritual Checking by a Relaxation-Delay Treatment." *Journal of Behavior Therapy and Experimental Psychiatry,* 1976, *7,* 151-154.

Alberti, R. E., and Emmons, M. L. *Your Perfect Right.* San Luis Obispo, Calif.: Impact, 1974.

Alden, S. E., Pettigrew, L. E., and Skiba, E. A. "The Effect of Individual-Contingent Group Reinforcement on Popularity." *Child Development,* 1970, *41,* 1191-1196.

Alexander, A. B., Chai, H., Creer, T. L., Micklich, D. R., Renne, C. M., and Cardoso, R. A. "The Elimination of Chronic Cough by Response Suppression Shaping." *Journal of Behavior Therapy and Experimental Psychiatry,* 1973, *4,* 75-80.

Alexander, A. B., Miklich, D. R., and Hershkoff, H. "The Immediate Effects of Systematic Relaxation Training on Peak Expiratory Flow Rates in Asthmatic Children." *Psychosomatic Medicine,* 1972, *34,* 388-394.

Alexander, J. F. "Defensive and Supportive Communications in Normal and Deviant Families." *Journal of Consulting and Clinical Psychology,* 1973, *40,* 223-231.

Alexander, J. F. "Behavior Modification and Delinquent Youth." In R. E. Hardy and J. L. Cull (Eds.), *Behavior Modification in Rehabilitation Settings.* Springfield, Ill.: Thomas, 1974.

Alexander, J. F., Barton, C., Schiavo, R. S., and Parsons, B. V. "Systems-Behavioral Intervention with Families of Delinquents: Therapist Characteristics, Family Behavior and Outcome." *Journal of Consulting and Clinical Psychology,* 1976, *44,* 656-664.

Allen, G. J. "The Behavioral Treatment of Test Anxiety." *Behavior Therapy,* 1972, *3,* 253-262.

Allen, K. E., and Harris, F. R. "Eliminating a Child's Excessive Scratching by Training the Mother in Reinforcement Procedures." *Behaviour Research and Therapy,* 1966, *4,* 79-84.

Allen, K. E., Hart, B. M., Buell, J. S., Harris, F. R., and Wolf, M. M. "Effects of Social Reinforcement on Isolate Behavior of a Nursery School Child." *Child Development,* 1964, *35,* 511-518.

American Cancer Society. *Cancer Facts and Figures '74.* New York: American Cancer Society, 1974.

American Psychiatric Association. *Diagnostic and Statistical Manual of Mental Disorders.* (2nd ed.) Washington, D.C.: American Psychiatric Association, 1968.

American Psychological Association, Ad Hoc Committee on Ethical Standards in Psychological Research. "Ethical Principles in the Conduct of Research with Human Participants." *American Psychologist,* 1973, *28,* 79-80.

Anant, S. S. "Treatment of Alcoholics and Drug Addicts by Verbal Aversion Techniques." *International Journal of the Addictions,* 1968, *3,* 381-388.

Anderson, G. S., and Nutter, R. W. "Clients and Outcomes of a Methadone Treatment Program." *International Journal of the Addictions,* 1975, *10,* 937-948.

Andrews, J. D. "Psychotherapy of Phobias." *Psychological Bulletin,* 1966, *66,* 455-480.

Annon, J. S. *The Behavioral Treatment of Sexual Problems. Vol. 1: Brief Therapy.* Honolulu: Enabling Systems, 1974.

Annon, J. S. *The Behavioral Treatment of Sexual Problems. Vol. 2: Intensive Therapy.* Honolulu: Enabling Systems, 1975a.

Annon, J. S. *The Sexual Fear Inventory—Female Form.* Honolulu: Enabling Systems, 1975b.

Annon, J. S. *The Sexual Fear Inventory—Male Form.* Honolulu: Enabling Systems, 1975c.

Annon, J. S. *The Sexual Pleasure Inventory—Female Form.* Honolulu: Enabling Systems, 1975d.

Annon, J. S. *The Sexual Pleasure Inventory—Male Form.* Honolulu: Enabling Systems, 1975e.

Anton, J. L., Dunbar, J., and Friedman, L. "Anticipation Training in the Treatment of Depression." In J. D. Krumboltz and C. E. Thoresen (Eds.), *Counseling Methods.* New York: Holt, 1976.

Aragona, J., Cassady, J., and Drabman, R. S. "Treating Overweight Children Through Parental Training and Contingency Contracting." *Journal of Applied Behavior Analysis,* 1975, *8*, 269-278.

Arkowitz, H., Lichtenstein, E., McGovern, K., and Hines, P. "The Behavioral Assessment of Social Competence in Males." *Behavior Therapy,* 1975, *6*, 3-13.

Armstrong, H. E., Jr., and Bakker, C. B. "Day Hospitals or Night Schools?" Unpublished manuscript available from author at Department of Psychiatry and Behavioral Sciences, University of Washington, Seattle, WA 98195, 1971.

Arnold, J. E., Levine, A. G., and Patterson, G. R. "Changes in Sibling Behavior Following Family Intervention." *Journal of Consulting and Clinical Psychology,* 1975, *43*, 683-688.

Ashkenazi, Z. "The Treatment of Encopresis Using a Discriminative Stimulus and Positive Reinforcement." *Journal of Behavior Therapy and Experimental Psychiatry,* 1975, *6*, 155-157.

Atthowe, J. "Controlling Noctural Enuresis in Severely Disabled and Chronic Patients." *Behavior Therapy,* 1972, *3*, 232-239.

Atthowe, J. M., Jr., and Krasner, L. "A Preliminary Report on the Application of Contingent Reinforcement Procedures (Token Economy) on a 'Chronic' Psychiatric Ward." *Journal of Abnormal Psychology,* 1968, *73,* 37-43.

Austin, N. K., Liberman, R. P., King, L. W., and DeRisi, W. J. "Comparative Evaluation of Two-Day Treatment Programs: Goal Attainment Scaling in Behavior Therapy vs. Milieu Therapy." *Journal of Nervous and Mental Diseases,* 1976, *163,* 253-262.

Averill, J. R. "Personal Control over Aversive Stimulus and Its Relationship to Stress." *Psychological Bulletin,* 1973, *80,* 286-303.

Ayllon, T., and Azrin, N. H. "Reinforcement and Instructions with Mental Patients." *Journal of the Experimental Analysis of Behavior,* 1964, *7,* 327-332.

Ayllon, T., and Azrin, N. H. "The Measurement and Reinforcement of Behavior of Psychotics." *Journal of the Experimental Analysis of Behavior,* 1965, *8,* 353-383.

Ayllon, T., and Azrin, N. H. "Reinforcer Sampling: A Technique for Increasing the Behavior of Mental Patients." *Journal of Applied Behavior Analysis,* 1968a, *1,* 13-20.

Ayllon, T., and Azrin, N. H. *The Token Economy: A Motivational System for Therapy and Rehabilitation.* New York: Appleton-Century-Crofts, 1968b.

Ayllon, T., Garber, S., and Pisor, K. "The Elimination of Discipline Problems Through a Combined School-Home Motivational System." *Behavior Therapy,* 1975, *6,* 616-626.

Ayllon, T., Layman, D., and Burke, S. "Disruptive Behavior and Reinforcement of Academic Performance." *Psychological Record,* 1972, *22,* 315-323.

Ayllon, T., Layman, D., and Kandel, H. J. "A Behavioral-Educational Alternative to Drug Control of Hyperactive Children." *Journal of Applied Behavior Analysis,* 1975, *8,* 137-146.

Ayllon, T., and Roberts, M. D. "Eliminating Discipline Problems by Strengthening Academic Performance." *Journal of Applied Behavior Analysis,* 1974, *7,* 71-76.

Ayllon, T., and Roberts, M. D. "Mothers as Educators for Their Children." In T. Travis and W. S. Dockens (Eds.), *Applications of Behavior Modification.* New York: Academic, 1975.

Ayllon, T., and Skuban, W. "Accountability in Psychotherapy:

A Case Test." *Journal of Behavior Therapy and Experimental Psychiatry,* 1973, *4,* 19-30.

Azrin, N. H. "Improvements in the Community-Reinforcement Approach to Alcoholism." *Behaviour Research and Therapy,* 1976, *5,* 339-348.

Azrin, N. H., Flores, T., and Kaplan, S. J. "Job-Finding Club: A Group-Assisted Program for Obtaining Employment." *Behaviour Research and Therapy,* 1975, *13,* 17-27.

Azrin, N. H., and Foxx, R. M. *Toilet Training in Less Than a Day.* New York: Simon & Schuster, 1974.

Azrin, N. H., Gottlieb, L., Hughart, L., Wesolowski, M. D., and Rahn, T. "Eliminating Self-Injurious Behavior by Educative Procedures." *Behaviour Research and Therapy,* 1975, *13,* 101-111.

Azrin, N. H., and Holz, W. C. "Punishment." In W. K. Honig (Ed.), *Operant Behavior: Areas of Research and Application.* New York: Appleton-Century-Crofts, 1966.

Azrin, N. H., Naster, J., and Jones, R. "Reciprocity Counseling: A Rapid Learning-Based Procedure for Marital Counseling." *Behaviour Research and Therapy,* 1973, *11,* 365-382.

Azrin, N. H., and Nunn, R. G. "Habit Reversal: A Method of Eliminating Nervous Habits and Tics." *Behaviour Research and Therapy,* 1973, *11,* 619-628.

Azrin, N. H., and Powell, J. "Behavioral Engineering: The Reduction of Smoking Behavior by a Conditioning Apparatus and Procedure." *Journal of Applied Behavior Analysis,* 1968, *1,* 193-200.

Azrin, N. H., and Powell, J. "Behavioral Engineering: The Use of Response Priming to Improve Prescribed Self-Medication." *Journal of Applied Behavior Analysis,* 1969, *2,* 39-42.

Azrin, N. H., and Wesolowski, M. D. "Theft Reversal: An Overcorrection Procedure For Eliminating Stealing by Retarded Persons." *Journal of Applied Behavior Analysis,* 1974, *7,* 577-582.

Azrin, N. H., and Wesolowski, M. D. "Eliminating Habitual Vomiting in a Retarded Adult by Positive Practice and Self-Correction." *Journal of Behavior Therapy and Experimental Psychiatry,* 1975, *6,* 145-148.

Bach, R., and Moylan, J. J. "Parents Administer Behavior Therapy for Inappropriate Urination and Encopresis: A Case

Study." *Journal of Behavior Therapy and Experimental Psychiatry,* 1975, *6,* 239-241.

Bachrach, A. J., Erwin, W. J., and Mohr, J. P. "The Control of Eating Behavior in an Anorexic by Operant Conditioning Techniques." In L. P. Ullmann and L. Krasner (Eds.), *Case Studies in Behavior Modification.* New York: Holt, Rinehart and Winston, 1965.

Baekeland, F., and Lundwall, L. "Dropping Out of Treatment: A Critical Review." *Psychological Bulletin,* 1975, *82,* 738-783.

Baer, D., and Wolf, M. "The Entry into Natural Communities of Reinforcement." In R. Ulrich, T. Stachnick, and J. Mabry (Eds.), *Control of Human Behavior.* Glenview, Ill.: Scott Foresman, 1970.

Bailey, J. S., Timbers, G. D., Phillips, E. L., and Wolf, M. M. "Modification of Articulation Errors of Pre-Delinquents by Their Peers." *Journal of Applied Behavior Analysis,* 1971, *4,* 265-282.

Baker, B. L. "Symptom Treatment and Symptom Substitution in Enuresis." *Journal of Abnormal Psychology,* 1969, *74,* 42-49.

Baker, B. L., Cohen, D. C., and Saunders, J. T. "Self-Directed Desensitization for Acrophobia." *Behaviour Research and Therapy,* 1973, *11,* 79-89.

Ball, J. C. "The Reliability and Validity of Interview Data Obtained from 59 Narcotic Drug Addicts." *American Journal of Sociology,* 1967, *72,* 650-654.

Bancroft, J. *Deviant Sexual Behavior: Modification and Assessment.* Oxford, England: Clarendon, 1974.

Bandura, A. *Principles of Behavior Modification.* New York: Holt, Rinehart and Winston, 1969.

Bandura, A. "Psychotherapy Based upon Modeling Principles." In A. E. Bergin and S. L. Garfield (Eds.), *Handbook of Psychotherapy and Behavior Change.* New York: Wiley, 1971a.

Bandura, A. *Social Learning Theory.* Morristown, N.J.: General Learning Press, 1971b.

Bandura, A. "Vicarious- and Self-Reinforcement Processes." In R. Glasser (Ed.), *The Nature of Reinforcement.* New York: Academic, 1971c.

Bandura, A. "Self-Efficacy: Towards a Unifying Theory of Behavioral Change." *Psychological Bulletin,* in press (page citations from this source refer to advance copy of manuscript made available to author of this book).

Bandura, A., Blanchard, E. B., and Ritter, B. "Relative Efficacy of Desensitization and Modeling Approaches for Inducing Behavioral, Affective, and Attitudinal Changes." *Journal of Personality and Social Psychology*, 1969, *13*, 173-199.

Bandura, A., Grusec, J. E., and Menlove, F. L. "Observational Learning as a Function of Symbolization and Incentive Set." *Child Development*, 1966, *37*, 499-506.

Bandura, A., Jeffery, R. W., and Gajdos, E. "Generalizing Change Through Participant Modeling with Self-Directed Mastery." *Behaviour Research and Therapy*, 1975, *13*, 141-152.

Bandura, A., Jeffery, R. W., and Wright, C. L. "Efficacy of Participant Modeling as a Function of Response Induction Aids." *Journal of Abnormal Psychology*, 1974, *83*, 56-64.

Barabasz, A. F. "Quantifying Hierarchy Stimuli in Systematic Desensitization via GSR: A Preliminary Investigation." *Child Study Journal*, 1974, *4*, 207-211.

Barlow, D. H. "Increasing Hetero-Sexual Responsiveness in the Treatment of Sexual Deviation: A Review of the Clinical and Experimental Literature." *Behavior Therapy*, 1973, *4*, 655-671.

Barlow, D. H. "The Treatment of Sexual Deviation: Toward a Comprehensive Behavioral Approach." In K. S. Calhoun, H. E. Adams, and K. M. Mitchell (Eds.), *Innovative Treatment Methods in Psychopathology*. New York: Wiley, 1974.

Barlow, D. H., and Agras, W. S. "Fading to Increase Heterosexual Responsiveness in Homosexuals." *Journal of Applied Behavior Analysis*, 1973, *6*, 355-366.

Barlow, D. H., Agras, W. S., and Reynolds, E. J. "Direct and Indirect Modification of Gender Specific Motor Behavior in a Transsexual." Paper presented at the annual meeting of the American Psychological Association, Honolulu, September 1972.

Barlow, D. H., Becker, R., Leitenberg, H., and Agras, W. S. "A Mechanical Strain Gauge for Recording Penile Circumference Change." *Journal of Applied Behavior Analysis*, 1970, *3*, 73-76.

Barlow, D. H., Leitenberg, H., and Agras, W. S. "Experimental

Control of Sexual Deviation Through Manipulation of the Noxious Scene in Covert Sensitization." *Journal of Abnormal Psychology*, 1969, *74*, 596-601.

Barlow, D. H., Leitenberg, H., Agras, W. S., and Wincze, J. P. "The Transfer Gap in Systematic Desensitization: An Analogue Study." *Behaviour Research and Therapy*, 1969, *7*, 191-196.

Barlow, D. H., Reynolds, E. J., and Agras, W. S. "Gender Identity Change in a Transsexual." *Archives of General Psychiatry*, 1973, *28*, 569-579.

Barnes, M. R. "Token Economy Control of Fluid Overload in a Patient Receiving Hemodialysis." *Journal of Behavior Therapy and Experimental Psychiatry*, 1976, *7*, 305-306.

Barrish, H. H., Saunders, M., and Wolf, M. M. "Good Behavior Game: Effects of Individual Contingencies for Group Consequences on Disruptive Behavior in a Classroom." *Journal of Applied Behavior Analysis*, 1969, *2*, 119-124.

Baum, W. M. "The Correlation-Based Law of Effect." *Journal of the Experimental Analysis of Behavior*, 1973, *20*, 137-153.

Beck, A. T. *Depression: Clinical, Experimental and Theoretical Aspects.* New York: Harper & Row, 1967.

Beck, A. T. "Cognitive Therapy: Nature and Relation to Behavior Therapy." *Behavior Therapy*, 1970, *1*, 184-200.

Beck, A. T. *Depression: Causes and Treatment.* Philadelphia: University of Pennsylvania Press, 1972.

Becker, H. S. *Outsiders: Studies in The Sociology of Deviance.* New York: Free Press, 1963.

Becker, W. C. *Parents Are Teachers.* Champaign, Ill.: Research Press, 1971.

Becker, W. C., Madsen, C. H., Jr., Arnold, C. R., and Thomas, D. R. "The Contingent Use of Teacher Attention and Praise in Reducing Classroom Behavior Problems." *The Journal of Special Education*, 1967, *1*, 287-307.

Becker, W. C., Thomas, D. R., and Carnine, D. "Reducing Behavior Problems: An Operant Conditioning Guide for Teachers." In W. C. Becker (Ed.), *An Empirical Basis for Change in Education.* Chicago: Science Research Associates, 1971.

Beech, H. R., Watts, F., and Poole, A. D. "Classical Conditioning of Sexual Deviation: A Preliminary Note." *Behavior Therapy*, 1971, *2*, 400-402.

Begelman, D. "Ethical and Legal Issues of Behavior Modification." In N. Hersen, R. Eisler, and P. Miller (Eds.), *Progress in Behavior Modification*. Vol. 1. New York: Academic, 1975.

Beisser, A. R., and Glasser, N. "The Precipitating Stress Leading to Psychiatric Hospitalization." *Comprehensive Psychiatry*, 1968, *9*, 50-61.

Bem, S. L., and Bem, D. J. "Training the Woman to Know Her Place: The Social Antecedents of Women in the World of Work." Unpublished manuscript available from author at Department of Psychology, Stanford University, Stanford, CA 94305, 1971.

Bennett, P. S., and Maley, R. F. "Modification of Interactive Behaviors in Chronic Mental Patients." *Journal of Applied Behavior Analysis*, 1973, *6*, 609-20.

Bentler, P. M. "An Infant's Phobia Treated with Reciprocal Inhibition Therapy." *Journal of Child Psychology and Psychiatry*, 1962, *3*, 185-189.

Berger, R. M., and Rose, S. D. "Interpersonal Skill Training with Institutionalized Elderly Patients." Unpublished paper available from author at School of Social Work, University of Wisconsin, Madison, WI 53706, 1976.

Bergin, A. E., and Suinn, R. M. "Individual Psychotherapy and Behavior Therapy." *Annual Review of Psychology*, 1975, *26*, 509-556.

Bergman, R. L. "Behavioral Contracting with Chronic Schizophrenics." *Journal of Behavior Therapy and Experimental Psychiatry*, 1975, *6*, 355-356.

Bernal, M. E. "Comparison of Behavioral and Nondirective Parent Counseling." Paper presented at the Annual Convention of the Association for the Advancement of Behavior Therapy, San Francisco, December 1975.

Bernal, M. E., Duryee, J. S., Pruett, H. L., and Burns, B. J. "Behavior Modification and the Brat Syndrome." *Journal of Consulting and Clinical Psychology*, 1968, *32*, 447-455.

Bernstein, D. A., and Borkovec, T. D. *Progressive Relaxation Training: A Manual for the Helping Professions*. Champaign, Ill.: Research Press, 1973.

Bibring, E. "The Mechanism of Depression." In P. Greenacre (Ed.), *Affective Disorders*. New York: International Universities Press, 1953.

Bieber, I. "A Discussion of Homosexuality: The Ethical Challenge." *Journal of Consulting and Clinical Psychology,* 1976, *44,* 163-166.

Bigelow, G., Strickler, D., Liebson, I., and Griffiths, R. "Maintaining Disulfiram Ingestion Among Outpatient Alcoholics: A Security Deposit Contingency Contracting Procedure." *Behaviour Research and Therapy,* 1976, *14,* 378-380.

Bijou, S. W. "Development in the Preschool Years: A Functional Analysis." *American Psychologist,* 1975, *30,* 829-837.

Bijou, S. W., Peterson, R. F., and Ault, M. H. "A Method to Integrate Descriptive and Experimental Field Studies at the Level of Data and Empirical Concepts." *Journal of Applied Behavior Analysis,* 1968, *1,* 175-191.

Bijou, S. W., Peterson, R. F., Harris, F. R., Allen, K. E., and Johnston, M. S. "Methodology for Experimental Studies of Young Children in Natural Settings." *Psychological Record,* 1969, *19,* 177-210.

Birchler, G. R., Weiss, R. L., and Vincent, J. P. "A Multimethod Analysis of Social Reinforcement Exchange Between Maritally Distressed and Nondistressed Spouse and Stranger Dyads." *Journal of Personality and Social Psychology,* 1975, *31,* 349-360.

Birchler, G. R., Weiss, R. L., and Wampler, L. D. "Differential Patterns of Social Reinforcement as a Function of Degree of Marital Distress and Level of Intimacy." Paper presented at the annual meeting of the Western Psychological Association, Portland, Oregon, April 1972.

Birnbrauer, J. S. "Mental Retardation." In H. Leitenberg (Ed.), *Handbook of Behavior Modification and Behavior Therapy.* Englewood Cliffs, N.J.: Prentice-Hall, 1976.

Blanchard, E. B., and Young, L. D. "Self-Control of Cardiac Functioning: A Promise as Yet Unfulfilled." *Psychological Bulletin,* 1973, *79,* 145-163.

Blanchard, E. B., and Young, L. D. "Clinical Applications of Biofeedback." *Archives of General Psychiatry,* 1974, *30,* 573-589.

Blechman, E. A., and Olson, D. H. L. "The Family Contract Game: 1." In D. H. L. Olson (Ed.), *Treating Relationships.* Lake Mills, Iowa: Graphic Publishing, 1976.

1104 References

Blechman, E. A., Olson, D. H. L., and Hellman, I. D. "Stimulus Control Over Family Problem-Solving Behavior: The Family Contract Game." *Behavior Therapy,* 1976, *7,* 686-692.

Blechman, E. A., Olson, D. H. L., and Turner, A. J. "The Family Contract Game: Technique and Case Study." *Journal of Consulting and Clinical Psychology,* 1976, *44,* 449-455.

Blinder, B. J., Freeman, D. M., and Stunkard, A. J. "Behavior Therapy of Anorexia Nervosa: Effectiveness of Activity as a Reinforcer of Weight Gain." *American Journal of Psychiatry,* 1970, *126,* 1093-1098.

Boland, T. B. "A Social Skills Assessment of Non-Dating College Males." Unpublished doctoral dissertation, University of Wisconsin at Madison, 1973.

Bolin, D. C., and Kivens, L. "Evaluation in a Community Mental Health Center, Huntsville, Alabama." *Evaluation,* 1974, *2,* 26-35.

Bonner, C. D. "Rehabilitation Instead of Bed Rest?" *Geriatrics,* 1969, *24,* 109-118.

Bootzin, R. "Treatment of Sleep Disorders." Paper presented at the annual meeting of the American Psychological Association in Montreal, August 1973.

Borkovec, T. D. "The Role of Expectancy and Physiological Feedback in Fear Research: A Review with Special Reference to Subject Characteristics." *Behavior Therapy,* 1973, *4,* 491-505.

Borkovec, T. D., and Boudewyns, P. A. "Treatment of Insomnia with Stimulus Control and Progressive Relaxation Procedures." In J. D. Krumboltz and C. E. Thoresen (Eds.), *Counseling Methods.* New York: Holt, 1976.

Borkovec, T. D., and Fowles, D. E. "Controlled Investigation of the Effects of Progressive and Hypnotic Relaxation on Insomnia." *Journal of Abnormal Psychology,* 1973, *82,* 153-158.

Borkovec, T. D., Stone, N. M., O'Brian, G. T., and Kaloupek, D. G. "Evaluation of a Clinically Relevant Target Behavior for Analogue Outcome Research." *Behavior Therapy,* 1974, *5,* 503-513.

Boudin, H. M. "Contingency Contracting as a Therapeutic Tool in the Deceleration of Amphetamine Use." *Behavior Therapy,* 1972, *3,* 604-608.

Boudin, H., and Valentine, V. E. "Behavioral Techniques as an Alternative to Methadone Maintenance." Unpublished manuscript available from author at 308 SW 40th Terrace, Gainesville, FLA 32601, 1973.

Boudin, H. M., Valentine, V. E., III, Inghram, R. D., Jr., Brantley, J. M., Ruiz, M. R., Smith, G. G., Catlin, R. P., III, and Regan, E. J., Jr. "Contingency Contracting with Drug Users in the Natural Environment." *International Journal of the Addictions,* in press.

Boyer, J. L. "Coronary Heart Disease as a Pediatric Problem." *American Journal of Cardiology,* 1974, *33,* 784-786.

Brady, J. P. "Brevital-Aided Systematic Desensitization." In R. D. Rubin, H. Fensterheim, A. A. Lazarus, and C. M. Franks (Eds.), *Advances in Behavior Therapy.* New York: Academic, 1971a.

Brady, J. P. "Metronome-Conditioned Speech Retraining for Stuttering." *Behavior Therapy,* 1971b, *2,* 129-150.

Brady, J. P., and Lind, D. L. "Experimental Analysis of Hysterical Blindness." *Archives of General Psychiatry,* 1961, *4,* 331-339.

Brady, J. P., and Rieger, W. "Behavioral Treatment of Anorexia Nervosa." Paper presented at the International Symposium on Behavior Modification, Minneapolis, October 1972.

Brammer, L. *The Helping Relationship: Process and Skills.* Englewood Cliffs, N.J.: Prentice-Hall, 1973.

Breyer, N. L., and Allen, G. J. "Effects of Implementing a Token Economy on Teacher Attending Behavior." *Journal of Applied Behavior Analysis,* 1975, *8,* 373-380.

Briscoe, R. V., Hoffman, D. B., and Bailey, J. S. "Behavioral Community Psychology: Training a Community Board to Problem Solve." *Journal of Applied Behavior Analysis,* 1975, *8,* 157-168.

Brison, D. W. "A Nontalking Child in Kindergarten." *Journal of School Psychology,* 1966, *4,* 65-69.

Brockway, B. S. "Assertive Training for Professional Women." *Social Work,* 1976, *21,* 498-505.

Broden, M., Bruce, C., Mitchell, M. A., Carter, V., and Hall, R. V. "Effects of Teacher Attention on Attending Behavior of Two Boys at Adjacent Desks." *Journal of Applied Behavior Analysis,* 1970, *3,* 199-203.

Broden, M., Hall, R. V., and Mitts, B. "The Effect of Self-

Recording on the Classroom Behavior of Two Eighth-Grade Students." *Journal of Applied Behavior Analysis,* 1971, *4,* 191-199.

Bronfenbrenner, U. *Two Worlds of Childhood: U.S. and U.S.S.R.* New York: Russell Sage Foundation, 1970.

Brown, B. S., Wienckowski, L. A., and Stolz, S. B. *Behavior Modification: Perspective on a Current Issue.* Pub. No. (ADM) 75-202. Washington, D.C.: U.S. Department of Health, Education and Welfare, National Institute of Mental Health, 1975.

Brown, G. W., Harris, T. O., and Petro, J. "Life Events and Psychiatric Disorders. Part 2: Nature and Causal Link." *Psychological Medicine,* 1973, *3,* 159-176.

Browning, R. M., and Stover, D. O. *Behavior Modification in Child Treatment: An Experimental and Clinical Approach.* Chicago: Aldine-Atherton, 1971.

Bucher, B., and Hawkins, J. "Comparison of Response Cost and Token Reinforcement Systems in a Class for Academic Underachievers." In R. D. Rubin and J. P. Brady (Eds.), *Advances in Behavior Therapy.* Vol. 4. New York: Academic, 1973.

Bucher, B., and Lovaas, O. I. "Use of Aversive Stimulation in Behavior Modification." In M. R. Jones (Ed.), *Miami Symposium on the Prediction of Behavior, 1967: Aversive Stimulation.* Coral Gables, Fla.: University of Miami Press, 1968.

Buckley, N. K., and Walker, H. M. *Modifying Classroom Behavior: A Manual of Procedure for Classroom Teachers.* Champaign, Ill.: Research Press, 1970.

Buehler, R. E., Patterson, G. R., and Furniss, J. M. "The Reinforcement of Behaviour in Institutional Settings." *Behaviour Research and Therapy,* 1966, *4,* 157-167.

Burgess, E. P. "The Modification of Depressive Disorders." In R. D. Rubin and C. M. Franks (Eds.), *Advances in Behavior Therapy, 1968.* New York: Academic, 1969.

Burgess, E. W., Locke, J. J., and Thomas, M. M. *The Family.* New York: Van Nostrand Reinhold, 1971.

Butler, J. F. "The Toilet Training Success of Parents After Reading *Toilet Training* in Less Than a Day." *Behavior Therapy,* 1976, *7,* 185-191.

Butler, P. E., and Salamy, A. "Eliminating a Conditioned Muscle Spasm by External Exhibition by an Electric Vibrator." *Journal of Behavior Therapy and Experimental Psychiatry,* 1975, *6,* 159-161.

Caddy, G. R., and Lovibond, S. H. "Self-Regulation and Discriminated Aversive Conditioning in the Modification of Alcoholics' Drinking Behavior." *Behavior Therapy,* 1976, *7,* 223-230.

Cahalan, D. *Problem Drinkers: A National Survey.* San Francisco: Jossey-Bass, 1970.

Cahalan, D., Cisin, I. H., and Crossley, H. M. *American Drinking Practices: A National Study of Drinking Behavior and Attitudes.* Monograph No. 6. New Brunswick: Rutgers Center of Alcohol Studies, 1969.

Caird, W. K., and Wincze, J. P. "Videotaped Desensitization of Frigidity." *Journal of Behavior Therapy and Experimental Psychiatry,* 1974, *5,* 175-178.

Callner, D. A. "Behavioral Treatment Approaches to Drug Abuse: A Critical Review of the Research." *Psychological Bulletin,* 1975, *82,* 143-164.

Callner, D. A., and Ross, S. M. "The Reliability and Validity of Three Measures of Assertion in a Drug Addict Population." *Behavior Therapy,* 1976, *7,* 659-667.

Camp, B., Blom, G., Herbert, F., and Van Doorninck, W. J. " 'Think Aloud': A Program for Developing Self-Control in Young Aggressive Boys." An unpublished manuscript, University of Colorado, Medical Center, Pediatrics and Psychiatry, 4200 E 9th Ave., Denver, CO 80220, 1976.

Campbell, D. T., and Stanley, J. C. *Experimental and Quasi-Experimental Designs for Research.* Chicago: Rand McNally, 1966.

Campbell, L. M. "A Variation of Thought Stopping in a Twelve-Year-Old Boy: A Case Report." *Journal of Behavior Therapy and Experimental Psychiatry,* 1973, *4,* 69-70.

Cappell, H., and Herman, C. P. "Alcohol and Tension Reduction: A Review." *Quarterly Journal of Studies on Alcohol,* 1972, *33,* 33-64.

Carr, J. E. "Behavior Therapy in a Case of Multiple Sexual Disorders." *Journal of Behavior Therapy and Experimental Psychiatry,* 1974, *5,* 171-178.

Carter, R. D. "Outline for Procedural Guide to Behavioral Case Management." Unpublished manuscript available from author at School of Social Work, University of Michigan, Ann Arbor, MI 48104, 1973.

Carter, R., and Thomas, E. J. "Modification of Problematic Marital Communication Using Corrective Feedback and Instruction." *Behavior Therapy*, 1973, *4*, 100-109.

Cash, W. M., and Evans, I. M. "Training Pre-School Children to Modify Their Retarded Siblings' Behavior." *Journal of Behavior Therapy and Experimental Psychiatry*, 1975, *6*, 13-16.

Caudill, B. D., and Marlatt, G. A. "Modeling Influences in Social Drinking: An Experimental Analogue." *Journal of Consulting and Clinical Psychology*, 1975, *43*, 405-415.

Cautela, J. R. "Treatment of Compulsive Behavior by Covert Sensitization." *Psychological Record*, 1966, *16*, 33-41.

Cautela, J. R. "Covert Sensitization." *Psychological Record*, 1967, *20*, 459-68.

Cautela, J. R. "Covert Negative Reinforcement." *Journal of Behavior Therapy and Experimental Psychiatry*, 1970a, *1*, 273-278.

Cautela, J. R. "Covert Reinforcement." *Behavior Therapy*, 1970b, *1*, 33-50.

Cautela, J. R. "The Treatment of Alcoholism by Covert Sensitization." *Psychotherapy*, 1970c, *7*, 86-90.

Cautela, J. R. "Covert Extinction." *Behavior Therapy*, 1971a, *2*, 192-200.

Cautela, J. R. "Covert Modeling." Paper presented at the fifth annual meeting of the Association for the Advancement of Behavior Therapy, Washington, D.C., September, 1971b.

Cautela, J. R., and Wisocki, P. A. "The Use of Male and Female Therapists in the Treatment of Homosexual Behavior." In R. Rubin and C. Franks (Eds.), *Advances in Behavior Therapy, 1968*. New York: Academic, 1969.

Cautela, J. R., and Wisocki, P. A. "Covert Sensitization for the Treatment of Sexual Deviations." *Psychological Record*, 1971, *21*, 37-48.

Chapman, C., and Risley, T. R. "Anti-litter Procedures in an Urban High-Density Area." *Journal of Applied Behavior Analysis*, 1974, *7*, 377-384.

Charlesworth, R., and Hartup, W. W. "Positive Social Reinforcement in the Nursery School Peer Group." *Child Development*, 1967, *38*, 993-1003.

Chesney, M. A., and Shelton, J. L. "A Comparison of Muscle Relaxation and Electromyogram Biofeedback Treatments for Muscle Contracting Headache." *Journal of Behavior Therapy and Experimental Psychiatry,* 1976, *7,* 221-225.

Chesney, M., and Tasto, D. L. "The Effectiveness of Behavior Modification with Spasmodic and Congestive Dysmenorrhea." *Behaviour Research and Therapy,* 1975, *13,* 245-253.

Christensen, A., Arkowitz, H., and Anderson, J. "Practice Dating as Treatment for College Dating Inhibitions." *Behaviour Research and Therapy,* 1975, *13,* 321-332.

Christopherson, E. R., Arnold, C. M., Hill, D. W., and Quilitch, H. R. "The Home Point System: Token Reinforcement Procedures for Application by Parents of Children with Behavior Problems." *Journal of Applied Behavior Analysis,* 1972, *5,* 485-497.

Clark, H. B., Boyd, S. B., and Macrae, J. W. "A Classroom Program Teaching Disadvantaged Youths to Write Biographic Information." *Journal of Applied Behavior Analysis,* 1975, *8,* 67-76.

Clark, H. B., Greene, B. F., Macrae, J. W., McNees, M. P., Davis, J. L., and Risley, T. R. "A Parent Advice Package for Family Shopping Trips: Development and Evaluation." Unpublished manuscript, available from author at Department of Human Development, University of Kansas, Lawrence, KAN 66044, 1976.

Clark, H. B., Rowbury, T., Baer, A. M., and Baer, D. M. "Time Out as a Punishing Stimulus in Continuous and Intermittent Schedules." *Journal of Applied Behavior Analysis,* 1973, *6,* 443-455.

Coché, E., and Flick, A. "Problem-Solving Training Groups for Hospitalized Psychiatric Patients." *Journal of Psychology,* 1975, *91,* 19-29.

Cochrane, C. L. "The Improvement of Social Interaction Skills in Cerebral Palsied Children Through Observational Learning." Unpublished doctoral dissertation, University of Washington, 1974.

Coghlan, A. J., Gold, S. R., Dohrenwend, E. F., and Zimmerman, R. S. "A Psychobehavioral Residential Drug Abuse Program: A New Adventure in Adolescent Psychiatry." *International Journal of the Addictions,* 1973, *8,* 767-777.

Cohen, H. L., and Filipczak, J. *A New Learning Environment.* San Francisco: Jossey-Bass, 1971.

Cohen, M., Liebson, I., and Faillace, L. A. "Controlled Drinking in Chronic Alcoholics over Extended Periods of Free Access." *Psychological Reports,* 1973, *32,* 1107-1110.

Cohen, S., Keyworth, J., Kleiner, R., and Libert, J. "The Support of School Behaviors by Home-Based Reinforcement via Parent-Child Contingency Contracts." In E. Ramp and B. Hopkins (Eds.), *A New Direction for Education: Behavior Analysis.* Lawrence: University of Kansas, 1971.

Coleman, R. E. "Manipulation of Self-Esteem as a Determinant of Mood of Elated and Depressed Women." *Journal of Abnormal Psychology,* 1975, *84,* 693-700.

Coleman, R. E., and Miller, A. G. "The Relationship Between Depression and Marital Maladjustment in a Clinic Population: A Multitrait-Multimethod Study." *Journal of Consulting and Clinical Psychology,* 1975, *43,* 647-651.

Conger, J. C. "The Treatment of Encopresis by the Management of Social Consequences." *Behavior Therapy,* 1970, *1,* 386-390.

Cooper, M. L., Thomson, C. L., and Baer, D. M. "The Experimental Modification of Teacher Attending Behavior." *Journal of Applied Behavior Analysis,* 1970, *3,* 153-157.

Copeman, C. D. "Aversive Counterconditioning and Social Retraining: A Learning Theory Approach to Drug Rehabilitation." Unpublished doctoral dissertation, State University of New York at Stony Brook, 1973.

Cossairt, A., Hall, R. V., and Hopkins, B. L. "The Effects of Experimenter's Instructions, Feedback, and Praise on Teacher Praise and Student Attending Behavior." *Journal of Applied Behavior Analysis,* 1973, *6,* 89-100.

Coursey, R. D. "Electromyograph Feedback as a Relaxation Technique." *Journal of Consulting and Clinical Psychology,* 1975, *43,* 825-834.

Cowen, E. L., Pederson, A., Babijian, H., Izzo, L. D., and Trost, M. A. "Long-Term Follow-Up of Early Detected Vulnerable Children." *Journal of Consulting and Clinical Psychology,* 1973, *41,* 438-446.

Craighead, W. E., Mercatoris, M., and Bellack, B. "A Brief Report on Mentally Retarded Residents as Behavioral Observers." *Journal of Applied Behavior Analysis,* 1974, *7,* 333-340.

Creer, T. "The Use of a Time-Out from Positive Reinforcement Procedure with Asthmatic Children." *Journal of Psychosomatic Research,* 1970, *14,* 117-120.

Crisp, A. H. "Anorexia Nervosa: Feeding Disorders, Nervous Malnutrition, or Weight Phobia." *World Review of Nutrition and Dietetics,* 1970, *12,* 452-504.

Croghan, L., and Musante, G. J. "The Elimination of a Boy's High Building Phobia by In-Vivo Desensitization and Game Playing." *Journal of Behavior Therapy and Experimental Psychiatry,* 1975, *6,* 87-88.

Crowe, M. J., Marks, I. M., Agras, W. J., and Leitenberg, H. "Time-Limited Desensitization, Implosion and Shaping for Phobic Patients: A Crossover Study." *Behaviour Research and Therapy,* 1972, *10,* 319-328.

Curlee, J. "Alcoholism and the 'Empty Nest.' " *Bulletin of the Menninger Clinic,* 1969, *33,* 165-171.

Daily, W. F., Allen, G. J., Chinsky, J. M., and Veit, S. W. "Attendant Behavior and Attitudes Toward Institutionalized Children." *American Journal of Mental Deficiency,* 1974, *78,* 586-591.

Danaher, B. G. "Theoretical Foundations and Clinical Applications of the Premack Principle: Review and Critique." *Behavior Therapy,* 1974, *5,* 307-324.

Danaher, B. G., and Thoresen, C. E. "Imagery Assessment by Self-Report and Behavioral Measures." *Behaviour Research and Therapy,* 1972, *10,* 131-138.

Daniels, L. K. "Treatment of Urticaria and Severe Headache by Behavior Therapy." *Psychosomatics,* 1973, *14,* 347-351.

Davidson, W. S. "Studies of Aversive Conditioning for Alcoholics: A Critical Review of Theory and Research Methodology." *Psychological Bulletin,* 1974, *81,* 571-581.

Davis, J. R., Wallace, C. J., Liberman, R. P., and Finch, B. E. "The Use of Brief Isolation to Suppress Delusional and Hallucinatory Speech." *Journal of Behavior Therapy and Experimental Psychiatry,* 1976, *7,* 269-275.

Davis, M. "Effects of Having One Remedial Student Tutor Another Remedial Student." In G. Semb, R. P. Hawkins, J. Michael, E. L. Phillips, J. A. Sherman, H. Sloane, and D. R. Thomas (Eds.), *Behavior Analysis and Education, 1972.* Lawrence: University of Kansas, Department of Human Development, 1972.

Davison, G. C. "Differential Relaxation and Cognitive Restructuring in Therapy with a 'Paranoid Schizophrenic' or Paranoid State." In *Proceedings of the 74th Annual Convention of the American Psychological Association, 1966.* Washington, D.C.: American Psychological Association, 1966.

Davison, G. C. "Elimination of a Sadistic Fantasy by a Client-Controlled Counterconditioning Technique." *Journal of Abnormal Psychology*, 1968, *73*, 84-90.

Davison, G. C. "Appraisal of Behavior Modification Techniques with Adults in Institutional Settings." In C. M. Franks (Ed.), *Behavior Therapy: Appraisal and Status*. New York: McGraw-Hill, 1969.

Davison, G. C. "Homosexuality: The Ethical Challenge." *Journal of Consulting and Clinical Psychology*, 1976, *44*, 157-162.

Davison, G. C., and Stuart, R. B. "Behavior Therapy and Civil Liberties." *American Psychologist*, 1975, *30*, 755-763.

Davison, G. C., and Wilson, G. T. "Goals and Strategies in Behavioral Treatment of Homosexual Pedophilia." *Journal of Abnormal Psychology*, 1974, *83*, 196-198.

Dawley, H. H., and Guidry, L. S. "Self-Administered Desensitization on a Psychiatric Ward: A Case Report." *Journal of Behavior Therapy and Experimental Psychiatry*, 1973, *4*, 301-303.

Deffenbacher, J. L. "Relaxation in vivo in the Treatment of Test Anxiety." *Journal of Behavior Therapy and Experimental Psychiatry*, 1976, *7*, 289-292.

Denney, N. W., and Connors, G. J. "Altering the Questioning Strategies of Preschool Children." *Child Development*, 1974, *45*, 1108-1112.

Dirks, S. J. "Aversion Therapy: Its Limited Potential for Use in the Correctional Setting." *Stanford Law Review*, 1974, *26*, 1327-1341.

Doke, L. A. "Assessment of Children's Behavioral Deficits." In M. Hersen and A. S. Bellack (Eds.), *Behavioral Assessment: A Practical Handbook*. New York: Pergamon, 1976.

Doke, L. A., and Risley, T. R. "The Organization of Daycare Environments: Required vs. Optional Activities." *Journal of Applied Behavior Analysis*, 1972, *5*, 405-420.

Donner, L., and Guerney, B. G., Jr. "Automated Group Desensitization for Test Anxiety." *Behaviour Research and Therapy*, 1969, *7*, 1-13.

Drabman, R. S., and Spitalnik, R. "Social Isolation as a Punishment Procedure: A Controlled Study." *Journal of Experimental Child Psychology*, 1973, *16*, 236-249.

Drabman, R. S., Spitalnik, R., and O'Leary, K. D. "Teaching Self-Control to Disruptive Children." *Journal of Abnormal Psychology*, 1973, *82*, 10-16.

Droppa, D. C. "Behavioral Treatment of Drug Addiction: A Review and Analysis." *International Journal of the Addictions,* 1973, *8,* 143-161.

Droppa, D. C. "Covert Conditioning in the Treatment of Drug Addiction." Unpublished doctoral dissertation, University of California at Berkeley, 1976.

Duehn, W. D., and Mayadas, N. S. "Assertive Training for Coming Out: A Structured Videotape Format for Counseling Gays." Paper presented at the tenth annual convention of the Association for Advancement of Behavior Therapy, New York, December 1976.

Duehn, W. D., and Shannon, C. "Covert Sensitization in the Public High School: Short-Term Group Treatment of Male Adolescent Drug Abusers." Unpublished manuscript available from authors at School of Social Work, University of Texas at Arlington, Arlington, TX 76019, 1973.

Dulany, D. E. "Awareness, Rules, and Propositional Control: A Confrontation with S-R Behavior Theory." In T. R. Dixon and D. L. Horton (Eds.), *Verbal Behavior and General Behavior Theory.* Englewood Cliffs, N.J.: Prentice-Hall, 1968.

Duster, T. *The Legislation of Morality.* New York: Free Press, 1970.

Duvall, H. J., Locke, B. Z., and Brill, L. "Follow-Up Study of Narcotic Drug Addicts Five Years After Hospitalization." *Public Health Reports,* 1963, *78,* 185-193.

D'Zurilla, T. J. "Reducing Heterosexual Anxiety." In J. D. Krumboltz and C. E. Thoresen (Eds.), *Behavioral Counseling: Cases and Techniques.* New York: Holt, Rinehart and Winston, 1969.

D'Zurilla, T., and Goldfried, M. "Problem Solving and Behavior Modification." *Journal of Abnormal Psychology,* 1971, *78,* 107-126.

D'Zurilla, T. J., Wilson, G. T., and Nelson, R. "A Preliminary Study of the Effectiveness of Graduated Prolonged Exposure in the Treatment of Irrational Fear." *Behavior Therapy,* 1973, *4,* 672-685.

Edwards, N. B. "Case Conference: Assertive Training in a Case of Homosexual Pedophilia." *Journal of Behavior Therapy and Experimental Psychiatry,* 1972, *3,* 55-63.

Efron, R. "The Effect of Olfactory Stimuli in Arresting Uncinate Fits." *Brain,* 1956, *79,* 267-281.

Egan, G. *The Skilled Helper: A Model for Systematic Helping*

and Interpersonal Relating. Monterey, Calif.: Brooks/
Cole, 1975.

Eisler, R. M. "Assertive Training in the Work Situation." In
J. D. Krumboltz and C. E. Thoresen (Eds.), *Counseling
Methods* (New York: Holt, Rinehart and Winston, 1976).

Eisler, R. M., Hersen, M., and Agras, W. S. "Effects of Videotape and Instructional Feedback on Nonverbal Marital
Interaction: An Analogue Study." *Behavior Therapy,*
1973, *4*, 551-558.

Eisler, R. M., Hersen, M., and Miller, P. M. "Effects of Modeling
on Components of Assertive Behavior." *Journal of Behavior Therapy and Experimental Psychiatry,* 1973, *4*, 1-6.

Eisler, R. M., Hersen, M., and Miller, P. M. "Shaping Components of Assertive Behavior with Instructions and Feedback." *American Journal of Psychiatry,* 1974, *131*,
1344-1347.

Eisler, R. M., Hersen, M., Miller, P. M., and Blanchard, E. F.
"Situational Determinants of Assertive Behaviors." *Journal of Consulting and Clinical Psychology,* 1975, *43*,
330-340.

Eisler, R. M., Miller, P. M., and Hersen, M. "Components of Assertive Behavior." *Journal of Clinical Psychology,* 1973,
29, 295-299.

Eisler, R. M., Miller, P. M., Hersen, M., and Alford, H. "Effects
of Assertive Training on Marital Interaction." *Archives of
General Psychiatry,* 1974, *30*, 643-649.

Elliot, C. H., and Denney, D. R. "Weight Control Through Covert Sensitization and False Feedback." *Journal of Consulting and Clinical Psychology,* 1975, *43*, 842-850.

Elliott, R., and Tighe, T. "Breaking the Cigarette Habit: Effects
of a Technique Involving Threatened Loss of Money."
Psychological Record, 1968, *18*, 503-513.

Ellis, A. A. "A Homosexual Treated with Rational Psychotherapy." *Journal of Clinical Psychology,* 1959, *15*, 338-343.

Ellis, A. *Reason and Emotion in Psychotherapy.* New York:
Stuart, 1962.

Ellis, A. *The Art and Science of Love.* New York: Bantam,
1966.

Ellis, A., and Harper, R. A. *A New Guide to Rational Living.*
Englewood Cliffs, N.J.: Prentice-Hall, 1975.

Emmelkamp, P. M. "Self-Observation Versus Flooding in the
Treatment of Agoraphobia." *Behaviour Research and
Therapy,* 1974, *12*, 229-237.

Emmelkamp, P. M. G., and Wessels, H. "Flooding in Imagination vs. Flooding In Vivo: A Comparison with Agoraphobics." *Behaviour Research and Therapy,* 1975, *13,* 7-15.

Engel, B. T., Nikoomanesh, P., and Shuster, M. M. "Operant Conditioning of Rectosphincteric Responses in the Treatment of Fecal Incontinence." *New England Journal of Medicine,* 1974, *290,* 646-649.

Epstein, L. H. "Psychophysiological Measurement In Assessment." In M. Hersen and A. S. Bellack (Eds.), *Behavioral Assessment: A Practical Handbook.* New York: Pergamon, 1976.

Epstein, L. H., Doke, L. A., Sajwaj, T. E., Sorrell, S., and Rimmer, B. "Generality and Side Effects of Overcorrection." *Journal of Applied Behavior Analysis,* 1974, *7,* 385-390.

Epstein, L., and Hersen, M. "A Multiple Baseline Analysis of Coverant Control." *Journal of Behavior Therapy and Experimental Psychiatry,* 1974, *5,* 7-12.

Eyberg, S. M., and Johnson, S. M. "Multiple Assessment of Behavior Modification with Families: Effects of Contingency Contracting and Order of Treated Problems." *Journal of Consulting and Clinical Psychology,* 1974, *42,* 594-606.

Eysenck, H. J. "Personality and the Maintenance of the Smoking Habit." In W. L. Dunn, Jr. (Ed.), *Smoking Behavior: Motives and Incentives.* New York: Wiley, 1973.

Fairweather, G., Sanders, D., Cressler, D., and Maynard, H. *Community Life for the Mentally Ill.* Chicago: Aldine, 1969.

Fairweather, G. W., Sanders, D. H., Tornatzky, L. G., and Harns, R. M., Jr. *Creating Change in Mental Health Organizations.* New York: Pergamon, 1974.

Farmer, R. G., and Wright, J. M. C. "Muscular Reactivity and Systematic Desensitization." *Behavior Therapy,* 1971, *2,* 1-10.

Fawcett, S. B., and Miller, L. K. "Training Public Speaking Behavior: An Experimental Analysis and Social Validation." *Journal of Applied Behavior Analysis,* 1975, *8,* 125-135.

Fazio, A. F. "Use of Behavioral Techniques in Bladder Training with a Flaccid Neurogenic Bladder Condition: A Case Study." Paper presented at the 82nd Annual Convention of the American Psychological Association, New Orleans, August-September 1974.

Feather, N. T., and Saville, M. R. "Effects of Amount of Prior Success and Failure on Expectations of Success and Subsequent Task Performance." *Journal of Personality and Social Psychology,* 1967, *5,* 226-232.

Fedoravicius, A. S. "The Patient as Shaper of Required Parental Behavior: A Case Study." *Journal of Behavior Therapy and Experimental Psychiatry,* 1973, *4,* 395-396.

Feingold, B. D., and Mahoney, M. J. "Reinforcement Effects on Intrinsic Interest: Undermining the Overjustification Hypothesis." *Behavior Therapy,* 1975, *6,* 367-377.

Feldman, H. W. "Ideological Supports to Becoming and Remaining a Heroin Addict." *Journal of Health and Social Behavior,* 1968, *9,* 131-139.

Feldman, M. P. "The Behaviour Therapies and Society." In M. P. Feldman and A. Broadhurst (Eds.), *Theoretical and Experimental Bases of the Behaviour Therapies.* New York: Wiley, 1976.

Feldman, M. P., and MacCullough, M. J. "The Application of Anticipatory Avoidance Learning to the Treatment of Homosexuality. Part 1: Theory, Technique, and Preliminary Results." *Behaviour Research and Therapy,* 1965, *2,* 165-183.

Feldman, M. P., and MacCulloch, M. J. *Homosexual Behaviour: Theory and Assessment.* Oxford, England: Pergamon, 1971.

Feldman, R., Wodarski, J., Flax, N., and Goodman, M. "Treating Delinquents in Traditional Agencies." *Social Work,* 1972, *17,* 72-79.

Felixbrod, J. J., and O'Leary, K. D. "Effects of Reinforcement on Children's Academic Behavior as a Function of Self-Determined and Externally-Imposed Contingencies." *Journal of Applied Behavior Analysis,* 1973, *6,* 241-250.

Fensterheim, H., and Baer, J. *Don't Say Yes When You Want to Say No.* New York: McKay, 1975.

Ferguson, J. M. *Learning to Eat: Behavior Modification for Weight Control.* Palo Alto, Calif.: Bull, 1975.

Ferritor, D. E., Buckholdt, D., Hamblin, R. L., and Smith, L. "The Noneffects of Contingent Reinforcement for Attending Behavior on Work Accomplished." *Journal of Applied Behavior Analysis,* 1972, *5,* 7-17.

Ferster, C. B. "Positive Reinforcement and Behavior Deficits of Autistic Children." *Child Development,* 1961, *32,* 437-456.

Ferster, C. B. "Classification of Behavioral Pathology." In L. Krasner and L. P. Ullman (Eds.), *Research in Behavior Modification.* New York: Holt, Rinehart and Winston, 1965.

Ferster, C. B. "Animal Behavior and Mental Illness." *Psychological Record,* 1966, *16,* 345-356.

Ferster, C. B. "An Experimental Analysis of a Clinical Phenomenon." In S. W. Bijou and E. Ribes-Inesta (Eds.), *Behavior Modification: Issues and Extensions.* New York: Academic, 1972.

Ferster, C. B. "A Functional Analysis of Depression." *American Psychologist,* 1973, *28,* 857-870.

Ferster, C. B., Culbertson, S., and Boren, M. C. *Behavior Principles.* (2nd ed.) Englewood Cliffs, N.J.: Prentice-Hall, 1975.

Ferster, C. B., Nurnberger, J. I., and Levitt, E. B. "The Control of Eating." *Journal of Mathetics,* 1962, *1,* 87-109.

Ferster, C. B., and Skinner, B. F. *Schedules of Reinforcement.* New York: Appleton-Century-Crofts, 1957.

Field, G. D., and Test, M. A. "Group Assertive Training for Severely Disturbed Patients." *Journal of Behavior Therapy and Experimental Psychiatry,* 1975, *6,* 129-134.

Fink, W. T., and Carnine, D. W. "Control of Arithmetic Errors Using Information Feedback and Graphing." *Journal of Applied Behavior Analysis,* 1975, *8,* 461.

Fisher, E. B., and Winkler, R. C. "Self-Control over Intrusive Experiences: Case Study." *Journal of Consulting and Clinical Psychology,* 1975, *43,* 911-916.

Fisher, S., and Cleveland, S. E. *Body Image And Personality.* Princeton, N.J.: Van Nostrand, 1958.

Fixsen, D. L., Phillips, E. L., and Wolf, M. M. "Achievement Place: The Reliability of Self-Reporting and Peer-Reporting and Their Effects on Behavior." *Journal of Applied Behavior Analysis,* 1972, *5,* 19-30.

Fixsen, D. L., Phillips, E. L., and Wolf, M. M. "Achievement Place: Experiments in Self-Government with Pre-Delinquents." *Journal of Applied Behavior Analysis,* 1973, *6,* 31-47.

Fixsen, D. L., Phillips, E. L., Phillips, E. A., and Wolf, M. M. "The Teaching Family Model of Group Home Treatment." In W. E. Craighead, A. E. Kazdin, and M. J. Mahoney (Eds.), *Behavior Modification: Principles, Issues and Applications.* Boston: Houghton Mifflin, 1976.

Fjellstedt, N., and Sulzer-Azaroff, B. "Reducing the Latency of a Child's Responding to Instructions by Means of a Token System." *Journal of Applied Behavior Analysis*, 1973, *6*, 125-130.

Flannery, R. B. "Use of Covert Conditioning in the Behavioral Treatment of a Drug-Dependent College Dropout." *Journal of Counseling Psychology*, 1972, *19*, 547-550.

Flaxman, J. "Smoking Cessation: Gradual vs. Abrupt Quitting." Paper presented at the meeting of the Association for Advancement of Behavior Therapy, Chicago, November 1974.

Flaxman, J. "Quitting Smoking." In W. E. Craighead, A. E. Kazdin, and M. J. Mahoney (Eds.), *Behavior Modification: Principles, Issues and Applications*. Boston: Houghton Mifflin, 1976.

Flowers, J. V., Booraem, C. D., Brown, T. R., and Harris, D. E. "An Investigation of a Technique for Facilitating Patient to Patient Therapeutic Interactions in Group Therapy." *Journal of Community Psychiatry*, 1974, *2*, 39-42.

Fodor, I. G. "The Phobic Syndrome in Women: Implications for Treatment." In V. Franks and V. Burtle (Eds.), *Women In Therapy: New Psychotherapies for a Changing Society*. New York: Brunner/Mazel, 1974.

Fordyce, W. E. "Behavioral Concepts in Chronic Pain and Illness." In P. O. Davison (Ed.), *The Behavioral Management of Anxiety, Depression and Pain*. New York: Brunner/Mazel, 1976a.

Fordyce, W. *Behavioral Methods for Chronic Pain and Illness*. St. Louis: Mosby, 1976b.

Forgione, A. G. "The Use of Mannequins in the Behavioral Assessment of Child Molesters: Two Case Reports." *Behavior Therapy*, 1976, *7*, 678-685.

Fowler, R. S., Fordyce, W. E., and Berni, R. "Operant Conditioning in Chronic Illness." *American Journal of Nursing*, 1969, *69*, 1226-1228.

Fox, L. "Effecting the Use of Efficient Study Habits." *Journal of Mathetics*, 1962, *1*, 76-86.

Foxx, R. M. "Increasing a Mildly Retarded Woman's Attendance at Self-Help Classes by Overcorrection and Instruction." *Behavior Therapy*, 1976, *7*, 390-396.

Foxx, R. M., and Azrin, N. H. "Restitution: A Method of Eliminating Aggressive-Disruptive Behavior of Retarded and

Brain-Damaged Patients." *Behaviour Research and Therapy,* 1972, *10,* 15-27.

Foxx, R. M., and Azrin, N. H. "Dry Pants: A Rapid Method for Toilet Training Children." *Behaviour Research and Therapy,* 1973a, *11,* 435-442.

Foxx, R. M., and Azrin, N. H. "The Elimination of Autistic Self-Stimulatory Behavior by Overcorrection." *Journal of Applied Behavior Analysis,* 1973b, *6,* 1-14.

Foxx, R. M., and Azrin, N. H. *Toilet Training the Retarded: A Rapid Program for Day and Nighttime Independent Training.* Champaign, Ill.: Research Press, 1973c.

Foxx, R. M., and Martin, P. L. "A Useful Portable Timer." *Journal of Applied Behavior Analysis,* 1971, *4,* 60.

Foy, D. W., Eisler, R. M., and Pinkston, S. "Modeled Assertion in a Case of Explosive Rages." *Journal of Behavior Therapy and Experimental Psychiatry,* 1975, *6,* 135-137.

Frank, J. *Persuasion and Healing: A Comparative Study of Psychotherapy.* Baltimore, Md.: Johns Hopkins University Press, 1961.

Franks, C. M. "Reflections Upon the Treatment of Sexual Disorders by the Behavioral Clinician: An Historical Comparison with the Treatment of the Alcoholic." *Journal of Sex Research,* 1967, *3,* 212-222.

Franks, C. M., and Wilson, G. T. (Eds.) *Annual Review of Behavior Therapy, Theory and Practice, 1974.* New York: Brunner/Mazel, 1974.

Franks, C. M., and Wilson, G. T. (Eds.) *Annual Review of Behavior Therapy, Theory, and Practice, 1975.* New York: Brunner/Mazel, 1975.

Frazier, J. R., and Schneider, H. "Parental Management of Inappropriate Hyperactivity in a Young Retarded Child." *Journal of Behavior Therapy and Experimental Psychiatry,* 1975, *6,* 246-247.

Freedman, J. L., and Fraser, S. "Compliance Without Pressure: The Foot-in-the-Door Technique." *Journal of Personality and Social Psychology,* 1966, *4,* 195-202.

Freedman, B. J. "An Analysis of Social-Behavioral Skill Deficits in Delinquent and Non-Delinquent Adolescent Boys." Unpublished doctoral dissertation, University of Wisconsin, 1974.

Freeman, B. J., Roy, R. R., and Hemmick, S. "Extinction of a Phobia of Physical Examinations in a 7-Year-Old Mentally Retarded Boy." Paper presented at the 82nd Annual Meeting of the American Psychological Association, New Orleans, August-September 1974.

French, J. R. P., and Raven, B. "The Bases of Social Power." In D. Cartwright and A. Zander (Eds.), *Group Dynamics Research and Theory*. Evanston, Ill.: Row Peterson, 1960.

Freud, S. "Mourning and Melancholia." In J. Strachey (Ed.), *The Complete Psychological Works of Sigmund Freud*. (J. Strachey, Trans.) London: Hogarth, 1955. Originally published 1917.

Friedman, P. R. "Legal Regulation of Applied Behavior Analysis in Mental Institutions and Prisons." *Arizona Law Review*, 1975, *17*, 75-104.

Fuchs, C., and Rehm, L. P. "A Self-Control Behavior Therapy Program for Depression." Unpublished manuscript available from author at Department of Psychology, University of Pittsburgh, Pittsburgh, PA 15232, 1975.

Galassi, J. P., and Galassi, M. D. "Session by Session Assertive Training Procedures." Unpublished manuscript available from author at School of Education, Peabody Hall, University of North Carolina, Chapel Hill, NC 27514, 1974.

Galassi, J. P., Galassi, M. D., and Litz, M. C. "Assertive Training in Groups Using Video Feedback." *Journal of Counseling Psychology*, 1974, *21*, 390-394.

Gambrill, E. D. "A Behavioral Program for Increasing Social Interaction." Paper presented at the 7th annual convention of the Association for the Advancement of Behavior Therapy, Chicago, 1973. Expanded version available from author at School of Social Welfare, University of California, Berkeley, CA 94720.

Gambrill, E. D. "A Descriptive Study of Staff-Detainee Interaction in a Short-Term Detention Facility." Paper presented at the eighth annual meeting of the Association for Advancement of Behavior Therapy, Chicago, November 1974.

Gambrill, E. D. "The Use of Behavioral Methods in a Short-Term Detention Setting." *Criminal Justice and Behavior*, 1976, *3*, 53-66.

Gambrill, E. D., and Richey, C. A. "An Assertion Inventory for Use in Assessment and Research." *Behavior Therapy*, 1975, *6*, 547-549.

Gambrill, E. D., and Richey, C. A. *It's Up To You: Developing Assertive Social Skills.* Millbrae, Calif.: Les Femmes, 1976.

Gambrill, E. D., Thomas, E. J., and Carter, R. D. "Procedure for Socio-Behavioral Practice in Open Settings." *Social Work,* 1971, *16,* 51-62.

Gambrill, E. D., and Wiltse, K. D. "Foster Care: Prescriptions for Change." *Public Welfare,* 1974, *32,* 39-47.

Gardner, J. "Behavior Therapy Treatment Approach to a Psychogenic Seizure Case." *Journal of Consulting Psychology,* 1967, *31,* 209-212.

Gardner, J. "Teaching Behavior Modification to Nonprofessionals." *Journal of Applied Behavior Analysis,* 1972, *5,* 517-521.

Gardner, J. M., Brust, D. J., and Watson, L. S. "A Scale to Measure Proficiency in Applying Behavior Modification Techniques to the Mentally Retarded." *American Journal of Mental Deficiency,* 1970, *74,* 633-636.

Gardner, W. I. *Behavior Modification in Mental Retardation.* Chicago: Aldine-Atherton, 1971.

Garfield, S. L. "Values: An Issue in Psychotherapy: Comments on a Case Study." *Journal of Abnormal Psychology,* 1974, *83,* 202-203.

Garvey, W., and Hegrenes, J. "Desensitization Techniques in the Treatment of School Phobia." *American Journal of Orthopsychiatry,* 1966, *36,* 147-152.

Geer, J. H., and Katkin, E. S. "Treatment of Insomnia Using a Variant of Systematic Desensitization: A Case Report." *Journal of Abnormal Psychology,* 1966, *71,* 161-164.

Gelfand, D. M., Elton, R. H., and Harman, R. E. "A Videotape-Feedback Training Method to Teach Behavior Modification Skills to Non-Professionals." *Research in Education.* ERIC Document ED 056 314. Washington, D.C.: U.S. Office of Education, 1972.

Gelfand, D. M., Gelfand, S., and Dobson, W. R. "Unprogrammed Reinforcement of Patients' Behavior in a Mental Hospital." *Behaviour Research and Therapy,* 1967, *5,* 201-207.

Gelfand, D. M., and Hartmann, D. P. *Child Behavior Analysis and Therapy.* New York: Pergamon, 1975.

Gershman, L., and Clouser, R. A. "Treating Insomnia with Relaxation and Desensitization in a Group Setting by an Automated Approach." *Journal of Behavior Therapy and Experimental Psychiatry,* 1974, *5,* 31-35.

Gertz, H. O. "Paradoxical Intention in Obsessives." *American Journal of Psychiatry,* 1966, *23,* 548-553.

Gittleman, M. "Behavior Rehearsal as a Technique in Child Treatment." *Journal of Child Psychology and Psychiatry,* 1965, *6,* 251-255.

Glahn, T. J. "Effects of Modeling Techniques Versus Instruction in Operant Principles for Teaching Behavior Modification Procedures to Parents." Unpublished master's thesis, University of California at Santa Barbara, 1975.

Glasgow, R. E., and Arkowitz, H. "The Behavioral Assessment of Male and Female Social Competence in Dyadic Heterosexual Interactions." *Behavior Therapy,* 1975, *6,* 488-498.

Glass, C., Gottman, J., and Shmurak, S. "Response Acquisition and Cognitive Self-Statement Modification Approaches to Dating Skills Training." *Journal of Counseling Psychology,* 1976, *23,* 520-526.

Glogower, F., and Sloop, E. W. "Two Strategies of Group Training of Parents As Effective Behavior Modifiers." *Behavior Therapy,* 1976, *7,* 177-184.

Gold, M. W. "Research on the Vocational Habilitation of the Retarded: The Present, the Future." *International Review of Research in Mental Retardation,* 1973, *6,* 97-147.

Goldblatt, M., and Munitz, H. "Behavioral Treatment of Hysterical Leg Paralysis." *Journal of Behavior Therapy and Experimental Psychiatry,* 1976, *7,* 259-263.

Goldfried, M. R. "Systematic Desensitization as Training in Self-Control." *Journal of Consulting and Clinical Psychology,* 1971, *37,* 228-234.

Goldfried, M. R., Decenteceo, E. T., and Weinberg, L. "Systematic Rational Restructuring as a Self-Control Technique." *Behavior Therapy,* 1974, *5,* 247-254.

Goldfried, M. R., and D'Zurilla, T. J. "A Behavior-Analytic Model for Assessing Competence." In C. D. Spielberger (Ed.), *Current Topics in Clinical and Community Psychology.* Vol. 1. New York: Academic, 1969.

Goldfried, M. R., and Goldfried, A. P. "Cognitive Change Methods." In F. H. Kanfer and A. P. Goldstein (Eds.), *Helping*

People Change: A Textbook of Methods. New York: Pergamon, 1975.

Goldiamond, I. "Self-Control Procedures in Personal Behavior Problems." *Psychological Reports,* Monograph Supplement 3-V17, 1965, *17,* 851-68.

Goldiamond, I. "Towards a Constructional Approach to Social Problems." *Behaviorism,* 1974, *2,* 1-85.

Goldiamond, I., and Dyrud, J. E. "Some Applications and Implications of Behavioral Analysis for Psychotherapy." In J. Schlein (Ed.), *Research in Psychotherapy.* Vol. 3. Washington, D.C.: American Psychological Association, 1967.

Goldman, R., Jaffa, M., and Schachter, S. "Yom Kippur, Air France, Dormitory Food, and the Eating Behavior of Obese and Normal Persons." *Journal of Personality and Social Psychology,* 1968, *10,* 117-123.

Goldsmith, J. B., and McFall, R. M. "Development and Evaluation of an Interpersonal Skill-Training Program for Psychiatric Patients." *Journal of Abnormal Psychology,* 1975, *84,* 51-58.

Goldstein, A. P. *Therapist-Patient Expectancies in Psychotherapy.* New York: Pergamon, 1962.

Goldstein, R. S., and Baer, D. M. "R.S.V.P.: A Procedure to Increase the Personal Mail and Number of Correspondents for Nursing Home Residents." *Behavior Therapy,* 1976, *17,* 348-354.

Goodwin, D. L., and Coates, T. J. "The Teacher-Pupil Interaction Scale." *Journal of Applied Behavior Analysis,* 1976, *9,* 114.

Goodwin, S. E., and Mahoney, M. J. "Modification of Aggression Through Modeling: An Experimental Probe." *Journal of Behavior Therapy and Experimental Psychiatry,* 1975, *6,* 200-202.

Götestam, K. G., and Melin, L. "Covert Extinction of Amphetamine Addiction." *Behavior Therapy,* 1974, *5,* 90-92.

Gottheil, E., Caddy, G. R., and Austin, D. L. "Clinical Significance of Urine Drug Screens." Paper presented at the Canadian Psychiatric Association Annual Meeting, Banff, Canada, September 1975.

Gottman, J. "The Topography of Marital Conflict." Unpublished manuscript available from author at Department of

Psychology, University of Illinois, Urbana-Champaign, IL 61801, 1975.

Gottman, J. M., and McFall, R. M. "Self-Monitoring Effects in a Program for Potential High School Dropouts: A Time Series Analysis." *Journal of Consulting and Clinical Psychology*, 1972, *39*, 273-281.

Gottman, J., Notarius, C., Gonso, J., and Markman, H. *A Couple's Guide to Communication.* Champaign, Ill.: Research Press, 1976.

Graubard, P. S., Rosenberg, H., and Miller, M. B. "Student Applications of Behavior Modification to Teachers and Environments or Ecological Approaches to Social Deviancy." In E. A. Ramp and B. L. Hopkins (Eds.), *A New Direction for Education: Behavior Analysis, 1971.* Vol. 1. Lawrence: University of Kansas, Department of Human Development, 1971.

Gray, B., England, G., and Mahoney, J. "Treatment of Benign Vocal Nodules by Reciprocal Inhibition." *Behaviour Research and Therapy*, 1965, *3*, 187-193.

Graziano, A. M., and Kean, J. E. "Programmed Relaxation and Reciprocal Inhibition with Psychotic Children." *Behaviour Research and Therapy*, 1968, *6*, 433-437.

Green, R. "Childhood Cross-Gender Identification." *Journal of Nervous and Mental Disease*, 1968, *147*, 500-509.

Green, R., and Money, J. *Transsexualism and Sex Reassignment.* Baltimore, Md.: Johns Hopkins University Press, 1969.

Greenleigh Associates. *An Evaluation of the Foster Grandparent Program.* New York: Greenleigh Associates, 1966.

Greenwood, C. R., Sloane, H. N., Jr., and Baskin, A. "Training Elementary-Aged Peer Behavior Managers to Control Small Group Programmed Mathematics." *Journal of Applied Behavior Analysis*, 1974, *7*, 103-114.

Griffiths, R., Bigelow, G., and Liebson, I. "Alcohol Self-Administration and Social Interactions in Alcoholics." In *Proceedings, 81st Annual Convention,* American Psychological Association. Washington, D.C.: American Psychological Association, 1973.

Grossberg, J. M., and Wilson, H. K. "Physiological Changes Accompanying the Visualization of Fearful and Neutral Situations." *Journal of Personality and Social Psychology*, 1968, *10*, 124-133.

Groveman, A. M., Richards, C. S., and Caple, R. B. "Literature Review, Treatment Manuals, and Bibliography for Study Skills Counseling and Behavioral Self-Control Approaches to Improving Study Behavior." Journal Supplement Abstract Service, MS. No. 1128. American Psychological Association, 1200 17th St. N.W. Washington, D.C. 20036, 1975.

Guidelines for the Use of Behavioral Procedures in State Programs for the Retarded. Mental Retardation Research Monograph Series, Vol. 1, No. 1. Arlington, Tex.: National Association for Retarded Citizens, Research Advisory Committee, 1976.

Gurman, A. S. "Treatment of a Case of Public Speaking Anxiety by In Vivo Desensitization and Cue Controlled Relaxation." Journal of Behavior Therapy and Experimental Psychiatry, 1973, 4, 51-54.

Guthrie, E. R. The Psychology of Human Learning. New York: Harper, 1935.

Gutride, M. E., and Goldstein, A. P., and Hunter, G. F. "The Use of Modeling and Role Playing to Increase Social Interaction Among Asocial Psychiatric Patients." Journal of Consulting and Clinical Psychology, 1973, 40, 408-415.

Gutride, M. E., Goldstein, A. P., Hunter, G. F., Carrol, S., Clark, L., Furia, R., and Lower, W. "Structured Learning Therapy with Transfer Training for Chronic Inpatients." Journal of Clinical Psychology, 1974, 30, 277-279.

Hagen, R. L. "Group Therapy Versus Bibliotherapy in Weight Reduction." Behavior Therapy, 1974, 5, 222-234.

Hagen, R. L., Foreyt, J. P., and Durham, T. W. "The Dropout Problem: Reducing Attrition in Obesity Research." Behavior Therapy, 1976, 7, 463-471.

Haley, J. Uncommon Therapy: The Psychiatric Techniques of Milton H. Erickson, M.D. New York: Norton, 1973.

Hall, R. A., and Dietz, A. J. "Systematic Organismic Desensitization." Psychotherapy: Theory, Research and Practice, 1975, 12, 388-390.

Hall, R. V., Axelrod, S., Tyler, L. F., Grief, E., Jones, F. C., and Robertson, R. "Modification of Behavior Problems in the Home with a Parent as Observer and Experimentor." Journal of Applied Behavior Analysis, 1972, 5, 53-64.

Hall, R. V., Cristler, C., Cranston, S. S., and Tucker, B. "Teachers and Parents as Researchers Using Multiple-Baseline

Designs." *Journal of Applied Behavior Analysis,* 1970, *3,* 247-255.

Hall, R. V., Lund, D., and Jackson, D. "Effects of Teacher Attention on Study Behavior." *Journal of Applied Behavior Analysis,* 1968, *1,* 1-12.

Hall, R. V., Panyan, M., Rabon, D., and Broden, M. "Instructing Beginning Teachers in Reinforcement Procedures Which Improve Classroom Control." *Journal of Applied Behavior Analysis,* 1968, *1,* 315-322.

Halleck, S. L. *The Politics of Therapy.* New York: Science House, 1971.

Halleck, S. L. "Another Response to 'Homosexuality: The Ethical Challenge'." *Journal of Consulting and Clinical Psychology,* 1976, *44,* 167-170.

Hamblin, R. L., Hathaway, C., and Wodarski, J. S. "Group Contingencies, Peer Tutoring and Accelerating Academic Achievement." In E. A. Ramp and B. I. Hopkins (Eds.), *A New Direction for Education: Behavior Analysis, 1971.* Vol. 1. Lawrence, Kan.: Department of Human Development, University of Kansas, 1971.

Harbert, T. L., Barlow, D. H., Hersen, M., and Austin, J. B. "Measurement and Modification of Incestuous Behavior: A Case Study." *Psychological Reports,* 1974, *34,* 79-86.

Harris, V. W., Bushell, D., Sherman, J. A., and Kane, J. F. "Instructions, Feedback, Praise, Bonus Payments and Teacher Behavior." *Journal of Applied Behavior Analysis,* 1975, *8,* 462.

Harris, F. R., Johnston, M. K., Kelley, C. S., and Wolf, M. M. "Effects of Positive Social Reinforcement on Regressed Crawling of a Nursery School Child." *Journal of Educational Psychology,* 1964, *55,* 35-41.

Hart, B. M., Allen, K. E., Buell, J. S., Harris, F. R., and Wolf, M. M. "Effects of Social Reinforcement on Operant Crying." *Journal of Experimental Child Psychology,* 1964, *1,* 145-153.

Hartmann, D. P., and Hall, R. V. "The Changing Criterion Design." *Journal of Applied Behavior Analysis,* 1976, *9,* 527-532.

Hawkins, R. P., and Dobes, R. W. "Behavioral Definitions in Applied Behavior Analysis: Explicit or Implicit." In B. C. Etzel, J. M. LeBlanc, and D. M. Baer (Eds.), *New Developments in Behavioral Research: Theory, Methods and*

Applications. In Honor of Sidney W. Bijou. Hillsdale, N.J.: Lawrence Erlbaum Associates, in press.

Hawkins, R. P., Peterson, R. F., Schweid, E., and Bijou, S. W. "Behavior Therapy in the Home: Amelioration of Problem Parent-Child Relations with the Parent in a Therapeutic Role." *Journal of Experimental Child Psychology,* 1966, *4,* 99-107.

Hay, W. M., Hay, L. R., and Nelson, P. O. "The Adaptation of Covert Modeling Procedures to the Treatment of Chronic Alcoholism and Obsessive Compulsive Behavior." *Behavior Therapy,* 1977, *8,* 70-76.

Hayes, L. A. "The Use of Group Contingencies for Behavioral Control: A Review." *Psychological Bulletin,* 1976, *83,* 628-648.

Hays, V., and Waddell, K. J. "A Self-Reinforcing Procedure for Thought Stopping." *Behavior Therapy,* 1976, *7,* 559.

Hedberg, A. G. "The Treatment of Chronic Diarrhea by Systematic Desensitization: A Case Report." *Journal of Behavior Therapy and Experimental Psychiatry,* 1973, *4,* 67-68.

Heiman, J., LoPiccolo, L., and LoPiccolo, J. *Becoming Orgasmic: A Sexual Growth Program For Women.* Englewood Cliffs, N.J.: Prentice-Hall, 1976.

Henderson, J. "A Community Based Operant Learning Environment. Part 1: Overview." In R. Rubin, H. Fensterheim, A. Lazarus, and C. Franks (Eds.), *Advances in Behavior Therapy.* New York: Academic, 1971.

Henson, D. E., and Rubin, H. H. "Voluntary Control of Eroticism." *Journal of Applied Behavior Analysis,* 1971, *4,* 37-44.

Herbert, E. W., and Baer, D. M. "Training Parents as Behavior Modifiers: Self-Recording of Contingent Attention." *Journal of Applied Behavior Analysis,* 1972, *5,* 139-149.

Herbert, E., Pinkston, E., Hayden, M., Sajwaj, T., Pinkston, S., Cordua, G., and Jackson, C. "Adverse Effects of Differential Parental Attention." *Journal of Applied Behavior Analysis,* 1973, *6,* 15-30.

Hersen, M., and Barlow, D. H. *Single Case Experimental Designs: Strategies for Studying Behavior Change.* New York: Pergamon, 1976.

Hersen, M., and Bellack, A. S. "A Multiple Baseline Analysis of Social-Skills Training in Chronic Schizophrenics." *Journal of Applied Behavior Analysis,* 1976, *9,* 239-246.

Hersen, M., and Bellack, A. S. "Social Skills Training for Chronic Psychiatric Patients: Rationale, Research Findings and Future Directions." *Comprehensive Psychiatry*, in press.

Hersen, M., Eisler, R. M., Alford, G. S., and Agras, W. S. "Effects of Token Economy on Neurotic Depression: An Experimental Analysis." *Behavior Therapy*, 1973, *4*, 392-97.

Hersen, M., Eisler, R. M., Miller, P. M., Johnson, M. D., and Pinkston, J. G. "Effects of Practice, Instructions and Modeling on Components of Assertive Behavior." *Behavior Research and Therapy*, 1973, *11*, 443-451.

Higgins, R. L., and Marlatt, G. A. "The Effects of Anxiety Arousal on the Consumption of Alcohol by Alcoholics and Social Drinkers." *Journal of Consulting and Clinical Psychology*, 1973, *41*, 426-433.

Higgins, R. L., and Marlatt, G. A. "Fear of Interpersonal Evaluation as a Determinant of Alcohol Consumption in Male Social Drinkers." *Journal of Abnormal Psychology*, 1975, *84*, 644-651.

Hirsch, J., and Knittle, J. L. "Cellularity of Obese and Nonobese Human Adipose Tissue." *Federation Proceedings*, 1971, *29*, 1516-1521.

Hodgson, R. J., and Rachman, S. "The Effects of Contamination and Washing in Obsessional Patients." *Behaviour Research and Therapy*, 1972, *10*, 111-117.

Hogan, R. A. "Implosive Therapy in the Short-Term Treatment of Psychotics." *Psychotherapy: Theory, Research and Practice*, 1966, *3*, 25-32.

Holland, J. G., and Skinner, B. F. *The Analysis of Behavior.* New York: McGraw-Hill, 1961.

Homans, G. C. *The Human Group.* New York: Harcourt Brace, 1950.

Homme, L. E. "Perspectives in Psychology. Part 24: Control of Coverants, the Operants of the Mind." *Psychological Record*, 1965, *15*, 501-511.

Homme, L. E., Csanyi, A., Gonzales, M., and Rechs, J. *How to Use Contingency Contracting in the Classroom.* Champaign, Ill.: Research Press, 1969.

Homme, L. E., deBaca, P., Cottingham, L., and Homme, A. "What Behavioral Engineering Is." *Psychological Record*, 1968, *18*, 425-434.

Homme, L. E., deBaca, P. C., Devine, J. V., Steinhorst, R., and Rickert, E. J. "Use of the Premack Principle in Controlling the Behavior of Nursery School Children." *Journal of the Experimental Analysis of Behavior,* 1963, *6,* 544.

Homme, L., and Tosti, D. *Behavior Technology: Motivation and Contingency Management.* San Rafael, Calif.: Individual Learning Systems, 1971.

Hopkins, B. L., Schutte, R. C., and Garton, K. L. "The Effects of Access to a Playroom on the Rate and Quality of Printing and Writing of First and Second Grade Students." *Journal of Applied Behavior Analysis,* 1971, *4,* 77-87.

Hops, H. "Behavioral Treatment of Marital Problems." In W. E. Craighead, A. E. Kazdin, and M. J. Mahoney (Eds.), *Behavior Modification: Principles, Issues and Applications.* Boston: Houghton Mifflin, 1976.

Horn, J. L., Wanberg, K. W., Adams, G., Wright, S., and Foster, F. M. *The Alcohol Use Questionnaire.* Denver, Colo.: Fort Logan Mental Health Center, 1973. (Available from the Center for Alcohol Abuse Research and Evaluation, P.O. Box 26528, Denver, CO 80226.)

Horner, R. D., and Keilitz, I. "Training Mentally Retarded Adolescents to Brush Their Teeth." *Journal of Applied Behavior Analysis,* 1975, *8,* 301-310.

Horton, G. O. "Generalization of Teacher Behavior as a Function of Subject Matter Specific Discrimination Training." *Journal of Applied Behavior Analysis,* 1975, *8,* 311-319.

Hoyt, M. F., and Janis, I. L. "Increasing Adherence to a Stressful Decision via a Motivational Balance-Sheet Procedure: A Field Experiment." *Journal of Personality and Social Psychology,* 1975, *31,* 833-839.

Human Development Institute. *Improving Communication in Marriage.* Chicago: Human Development Institute, 1969.

Humphreys, L., and Beiman, I. "The Application of Multiple Behavioral Techniques to Multiple Problems of a Complex Case." *Journal of Behavior Therapy and Experimental Psychiatry,* 1975, *6,* 311-315.

Hunt, G. M., and Azrin, N. H. "The Community Reinforcement Approach to Alcoholism." *Behaviour Research and Therapy,* 1973, *11,* 91-104.

Huntington, J. "DWI Arrests Increase." In [Montana] State Department of Health and Environmental Science, *Treasure State Health.* Helena, Mont.: State Department of Health and Environmental Science, 1972.

Hurvitz, N. "Interaction Hypotheses in Marriage Counseling." *The Family Coordinator,* 1970, *19,* 64-75.

Ince, L. P. "The Use of Relaxation Training and a Conditioned Stimulus in the Elimination of Epileptic Seizures in a Child: A Case Study." *Journal of Behavior Therapy and Experimental Psychiatry,* 1976, *7,* 39-42.

Iwata, B. A., Bailey, J. S., Brown, K. M., Foshee, T. J., and Alpern, M. "A Performance Based Lottery to Improve Residential Care and Training of Institutional Staff." *Journal of Applied Behavior Analysis,* 1976, *9,* 417-431.

Jackson, B. "Treatment of Depression by Self-Reinforcement." *Behavior Therapy,* 1972, *3,* 298-307.

Jacobs, A., and Felton, G. S. "Visual Feedback of Myoelectric Output to Facilitate Muscle Relaxation in Normal Persons and Patients with Neck Injuries." *Archives of Physical Medicine and Rehabilitation,* 1969, *50,* 34-39.

Jacobs, J. L., and Sharma, K. N. "Taste Versus Calories: Sensory and Metabolic Signals in the Control of Food Intake." *Annals of the New York Academy of Science,* 1969, *157,* 1084-1125.

Jacobson, E. *Progressive Relaxation.* Chicago: University of Chicago Press, 1938.

Jacobson, N. S., and Martin, B. "Behavioral Marriage Therapy: Current Status." *Psychological Bulletin,* 1976, *83,* 540-556.

Jakubowski-Spector, P., Pearlman, J., and Coburn, K. *Assertive Training for Women: Stimulus Films.* Washington, D.C.: American Personnel and Guidance Association, 1973.

James, R. Presentation made at the Sixth Annual Conference in Behavior Modification, Tuscaloosa, Alabama, April 1973.

Jarvik, M. E. "The Role of Nicotine in the Smoking Habit." In W. A. Hunt (Ed.), *Learning Mechanisms in Smoking.* Chicago: Aldine, 1970.

Jeffrey, D. B. "A Comparison of the Effects of External Control and Self-Control on the Modification and Maintenance of Weight." *Journal of Abnormal Psychology,* 1974, *83,* 404-410.

Jeffrey, D. B. "Behavioral Management of Obesity." In W. E. Craighead, A. E. Kazdin, and M. J. Mahoney (Eds.), *Behavior Modification: Principles, Issues and Applications.* Boston: Houghton Mifflin, 1976.

Jellinek, S. M. *The Disease Concept of Alcoholism.* New Haven, Conn.: Hillhouse, 1960.

Johnson, S. M., and Alevizos, P. N. "Strategic Therapy: A

Systematic Outline of Procedures." Paper presented at the Ninth Annual Conference of the Association for the Advancement of Behavior Therapy, San Francisco, December 1975.

Johnson, S. M., and Bolstad, O. D. "Methodological Issues in Naturalistic Observation: Some Problems and Solutions for Field Research." In L. A. Hamerlynck, L. C. Handy, and E. J. Mash (Eds.), *Behavior Change: Methodology, Concepts and Practice.* Champaign, Ill.: Research Press, 1973.

Johnson, S. M., Bolstad, O. D., and Lobitz, G. K. "Generalization and Contrast Phenomena in Behavior Modification with Children." In E. J. Mash, L. A. Hamerlynck, and L. C. Handy (Eds.), *Behavior Modification and Families.* New York: Brunner/Mazel, 1976.

Johnson, S. M., Christensen, A., and Bellamy, G. T. "Evaluation of Family Intervention Through Unobtrusive Audio Recordings: Experiences in 'Bugging Children'." *Journal of Applied Behavior Analysis,* 1976, *9,* 213-219.

Johnson, S., and Lobitz, G. "The Personal and Marital Adjustment of Parents as Related to Observed Child Deviance and Parenting Behaviors." *Journal of Abnormal Child Psychiatry,* 1974, *2,* 192-207.

Johnson, S. M., and White, G. "Self-Observation as an Agent of Behavioral Change." *Behavior Therapy,* 1971, *2,* 488-497.

Johnston, J. M. "Generalization and its Relation to Generality." Paper presented at the Ninth Annual Convention of the Association for Advancement of Behavior Therapy, San Francisco, December 1975.

Jones, F. H., and Eimers, R. C. "Role Playing to Train Elementary Teachers to Use a Classroom Management 'Skill Package.'" *Journal of Applied Behavior Analysis,* 1975, *8,* 421-433.

Jones, H. G. "The Application of Conditioning and Learning Techniques to the Treatment of a Psychiatric Patient." *Journal of Abnormal and Social Psychology,* 1956, *52,* 414-420.

Jones, M. C. "The Elimination of Children's Fears." *Journal of Experimental Psychology,* 1924, *7,* 383-390.

Jones, R. J., and Azrin, N. H. "An Experimental Application of a Social Reinforcement Approach to the Problem of Job

Finding." *Journal of Applied Behavior Analysis,* 1973, *6,* 345-354.

Jones, R. R., Vaught, R. S., and Reid, J. B. "Time Series Analysis as a Substitute for Single Analysis of Variance Designs." Paper presented at the symposium on "Methodological Issues in Applied Behavior Analysis," at the meeting of the American Psychological Association, Montreal, August 1973.

Jones, R. T., and Kazdin, A. E. "Programming Response Maintenance After Withdrawing Token Reinforcement." *Behavior Therapy,* 1975, *6,* 153-164.

Kadushin, A. *The Social Work Interview.* New York: Columbia University Press, 1972.

Kales, A., Preston, T. A., Tan, T. L., and Allen, C. "Hypnotics and Altered Sleep-Dream Patterns: Part 1. All-Night EEG Studies of Glutethimide, Methprylon, and Pentobarbital." *Archives of General Psychiatry,* 1970, *23,* 211-218.

Kanfer, F. H. "Issues and Ethics in Behavior Manipulation." *Psychological Reports,* 1965, *16,* 187-196.

Kanfer, F. H. "Self-Monitoring Methodological Limitations and Clinical Applications." *Journal of Consulting and Clinical Psychology,* 1970, *35,* 148-152.

Kanfer, F. H. "The Maintenance of Behavior by Self-Generated Stimuli and Reinforcement." In A. Jacobs and L. B. Sachs (Eds.), *The Psychology of Private Events: Perspectives on Covert Response Systems.* New York: Academic, 1971.

Kanfer, F. H., and Duerfeldt, P. H. "Comparison of Self-Reward and Self-Criticism as a Function of Types of Prior External Reinforcement." *Journal of Personality and Social Psychology,* 1968, *8,* 261-268.

Kanfer, F. H., Karoly, P., and Newman, A. "Reduction of Children's Fear of the Dark by Competence-Related and Situational Threat-Related Verbal Cues." *Journal of Consulting and Clinical Psychology,* 1975, *43,* 251-258.

Kanfer, F. H., and Phillips, J. S. "A Survey of Current Behavior Therapies and a Proposal for Classification." In C. M. Franks (Ed.), *Behavior Therapy: Appraisal and Status.* New York: McGraw-Hill, 1969.

Kanfer, F. H., and Saslow, G. "Behavioral Diagnosis." In C. H. Franks (Ed.), *Behavior Therapy: Appraisal and Status.* New York: McGraw-Hill, 1969.

Kanhouse, D. E., Hanson, L., and Reid, W. J. *Negativity in Evaluations.* Morristown, N.J.: General Learning Press, 1972.

Kaplan, H. S. *The New Sex Therapy.* New York: Brunner/Mazel, 1974.

Karacan, I., and Williams, R. L. "Insomnia: Old Wine in a New Bottle." *Psychiatric Quarterly,* 1971, *45,* 274-288.

Katkin, E. S. "Electrodermal Lability: A Psychophysiological Analysis of Individual Differences in Response to Stress." In I. G. Sarason and C. D. Spielberger (Eds.), *Stress and Anxiety.* Washington, D.C.: Hemisphere Publishing, 1975.

Katz, R. C. "Single Session Recovery from a Hemodialysis Phobia: A Case Study." *Journal of Behavior Therapy and Experimental Psychiatry,* 1974, *5,* 205-206.

Katz, R. C., and Zlutnick, S. *Behavioral Therapy and Health Care: Principles and Applications.* New York: Pergamon, 1975.

Katzenberg, A. *How To Draw Graphs.* Kalamazoo, Mich.: Behaviordelia, 1975.

Kaufman, K. F., and O'Leary, K. D. "Reward, Cost, and Self-Evaluation Procedures for Disruptive Adolescents in a Psychiatric Hospital School." *Journal of Applied Behavior Analysis,* 1972, *5,* 293-309.

Kaufman, L. M., and Wagner, B. R. "Barb: A Systematic Treatment Technology for Temper Control Disorders." *Behavior Therapy,* 1972, *3,* 84-90.

Kaul, T. J., and Parker, C. A. "Suggestibility and Expectancy in a Counseling Analogue." *Journal of Counseling Psychology,* 1971, *18,* 536-541.

Kazdin, A. E. "The Effect of Vicarious Reinforcement on Attentive Behavior in the Classroom." *Journal of Applied Behavior Analysis,* 1973a, *6,* 71-78.

Kazdin, A. E. "Methodological Assessment Considerations in Evaluating Reinforcement Programs in Applied Settings." *Journal of Applied Behavior Analysis,* 1973b, 517-531.

Kazdin, A. E. "Covert Modeling and the Reduction of Avoidance Behavior." *Journal of Abnormal Psychology,* 1973c, *81,* 87-95.

Kazdin, A. E. "Covert Modeling, Model Similarity and Reduction of Avoidance Behavior." *Behavior Therapy,* 1974a, *5,* 325-340.

Kazdin, A. E. "Self-Monitoring and Behavior Change." In M. J.

Mahoney and C. E. Thoresen (Eds.), *Self-Control: Power to the Person.* Monterey, Calif.: Brooks/Cole, 1974b.

Kazdin, A. E. "Covert Modeling, Imagery Assessment and Assertive Behavior." *Journal of Consulting and Clinical Psychology,* 1975, *43,* 716-724.

Kazdin, A. E. "Assessment of Imagery During Covert Modeling of Assertive Behavior." *Journal of Behavior Therapy and Experimental Psychiatry,* 1976, *7,* 213-220.

Kazdin, A. E., and Bootzin, R. R. "The Token Economy: An Evaluative Review." *Journal of Applied Behavior Analysis,* 1972, *5,* 343-372.

Kazdin, A. E., and Kopel, S. A. "On Resolving Ambiguities of the Multiple Base-Line Design: Problems and Recommendations." *Behavior Therapy,* 1975, *6,* 601-608.

Keat, D. B. "Survey Schedule of Rewards for Children." *Psychological Reports,* 1974, *35,* 287-293.

Keller, M. F., and Carlson, P. M. "The Use of Symbolic Modeling to Promote Social Skills in Preschool Children with Low Levels of Social Responsiveness." *Child Development,* 1974, *45,* 912-919.

Keller, O., and Alper, B. *Halfway Houses: Community Centered Correction and Treatment.* Lexington, Mass.: Heath Lexington, 1970.

Kennedy, W. A. "School Phobia: Rapid Treatment of 50 Cases." *Journal of Abnormal Psychology,* 1965, *70,* 285-289.

Kessler, M., and Gomberg, C. "Observations of Barroom Drinking: Methodology and Preliminary Results." *Quarterly Journal of Studies on Alcohol,* 1974, *35,* 1392-1396.

Kiesler, D. J. "Some Myths of Psychotherapy Research and the Search for a Paradigm." *Psychological Bulletin,* 1966, *65,* 110-136.

Kifer, R. E., Lewis, M. A., Green, D. R., and Phillips, E. L. "Training Predelinquent Youths and Their Parents to Negotiate Conflict Situations." *Journal of Applied Behavior Analysis,* 1974, *7,* 357-364.

Kimmel, D., and Van Der Veen, F. "Factors of Marital Adjustment in Locke's Marital Adjustment Test." *Journal of Marriage and the Family,* 1974, *36,* 57-63.

King, L. W., and Turner, R. D. "Teaching a Profoundly Retarded Adult at Home by Non-Professionals." *Journal of Behavior Therapy and Experimental Psychiatry,* 1975, *6,* 117-121.

Kinsey, A. C., Pomeroy, W. B., and Martin, C. E. *Sexual Behavior in the Male.* Philadelphia: Saunders, 1948.

Kinsey, A. C., Pomeroy, W. B., and Martin, C. E. *Sexual Behavior in the Female.* Philadelphia: Saunders, 1953.

Kiresuk, T. J., and Sherman, R. E. "Goal Attainment Scaling: A General Method for Evaluating Comprehensive Mental Health Programs." *Community Mental Health Journal,* 1968, *4,* 443-453.

Kirsch, I., Wolpin, M., and Knutson, J. L. "A Comparison of In Vivo Methods for Rapid Reduction of 'Stage-Fright' in the College Classroom: A Field Experiment." *Behavior Therapy,* 1975, *6,* 165-171.

Klein, M., Paluck, R. J., and Beresford, P. "The Modification of Disruptive Behaviors by a Group of Trainable Mentally Retarded Adults." *Journal of Behavior Therapy and Experimental Psychiatry,* 1976, *7,* 299-300.

Klepac, R. K. "Successful Treatment of Avoidance of Dentistry by Desensitization or by Increasing Pain Tolerance." *Journal of Behavior Therapy and Experimental Psychiatry,* 1975, *6,* 307-310.

Klerman, G. L. "Depression in Adaptation." In R. J. Friedman and M. M. Katz (Eds.), *The Psychology of Depression: Contemporary Theory and Research.* New York: Wiley, 1974.

Knox, D. *Marital Happiness: A Behavioral Approach to Counseling.* Champaign, Ill.: Research Press, 1971.

Knupfer, G. "Ex-Problem Drinkers." In M. Roff, L. N. Robins, and M. Pollack (Eds.), *Life History Research in Psychopathology.* Minneapolis: University of Minnesota Press, 1972.

Koegel, R., and Rincover, A. "Treatment of Psychotic Children in a Classroom Environment. Part 1: Learning in a Large Group." *Journal of Applied Behavior Analysis,* 1974, *7,* 45-59.

Koegel, R. L., and Rincover, A. "The Generalization and Maintenance of Treatment Gains." *Journal of Applied Behavior Analysis,* in press.

Kohlenberg, R. J. "Directed Masturbation and the Treatment of Primary Orgasmic Dysfunction." *Archives of Sexual Behavior,* 1974a, *3,* 349-356.

Kohlenberg, R. J. "Treatment of a Homosexual Pedophiliac Using In Vivo Desensitization: A Case Study." *Journal of Abnormal Psychology,* 1974b, *83,* 192-195.

Kondas, O., and Scetnicka, B. "Systematic Desensitization as a Method of Preparation for Childbirth." *Journal of Behavior Therapy and Experimental Psychiatry*, 1972, *3*, 51-54.

Kopel, S., and Arkowitz, H. "The Role of Attribution and Self-perception in Behavior Change: Implications for Behavior Therapy." *Genetic Psychology Monographs*, 1975, *92*, 175-212.

Kozloff, M. A. *Reaching the Autistic Child: A Parent Training Program.* Champaign, Ill.: Research Press, 1973.

Kraft, T. "Case of Homosexuality Treated by Systematic Desensitization." *American Journal of Psychotherapy*, 1967, *21*, 815-821.

Kraft, T. "Treatment of Drinamyl Addiction." *International Journal of Addictions*, 1969, *4*, 59-64.

Kraft, T. "Successful Treatment of 'Drinamyl' Addicts and Associated Personality Changes." *Canadian Psychiatric Association Journal*, 1970, *15*, 223-227.

Kraft, T., and Al-Issa, I. "Alcoholism Treated by Desensitization: A Case Report." *Behaviour Research and Therapy*, 1967, *5*, 69-70.

Krapfl, J. E., Bry, P., and Nawas, M. "Use of the 'Bug in the Ear' in the Modification of Parents' Behavior." In R. R. Rubin and C. M. Franks (Eds.), *Advances in Behavior Therapy, 1968.* New York: Academic, 1969.

Krasner, L. "Behavior Modification—Values and Training: The Perspective of a Psychologist." In C. M. Franks (Ed.), *Behavior Therapy: Appraisal and Status.* New York: McGraw-Hill, 1969.

Krasner, L., and Ullman, L. P. *Behavior Influence and Personality: The Social Matrix of Human Action.* New York: Holt, Rinehart and Winston, 1973.

Krumboltz, J. D., and Krumboltz, H. B. *Changing Children's Behavior.* Englewood Cliffs, N.J.: Prentice-Hall, 1972.

Krumboltz, J. D., and Thoresen, C. E. (Eds.) *Counseling Methods.* New York: Holt, Rinehart and Winston, 1976.

Kubany, E. S., and Sloggett, B. B. "Coding Procedure for Teachers." *Journal of Applied Behavior Analysis*, 1973, *6*, 339-344.

Kubany, E. S., Weiss, L. E., and Sloggett, B. B. "The Good Behavior Clock: A Reinforcement/Time-Out Procedure for Reducing Disruptive Classroom Behavior." *Journal of*

Behavior Therapy and Experimental Psychiatry, 1971, *2*, 173-179.

Kunkel, J. H. *Social and Economic Growth: A Behavioral Perspective of Social Change.* New York: Oxford University Press, 1970.

Lacey, J. I. "Somatic Response Patterning and Stress: Some Revisions of Activation Theory." In M. H. Appley and R. Trumbull (Eds.), *Psychological Stress: Issues in Research.* New York: Appleton-Century-Crofts, 1967.

Lamb, R., Heath, D., and Downing, J. (Eds.) *Handbook of Community Mental Health Practice.* San Francisco: Jossey-Bass, 1969.

Lambley, P. "Treatment of Transvestism and Subsequent Coital Problems." *Journal of Behavior Therapy and Experimental Psychiatry*, 1974, *5*, 101-102.

Lamontagne, Y., and Marks, I. M. "Psychogenic Urinary Retention: Treatment by Prolonged Exposure." *Behavior Therapy*, 1973, *4*, 581-585.

Lang, P. J. "Fear Reduction and Fear Behavior: Problems in Treating a Construct." In J. M. Shlien (Ed.), *Research in Psychotherapy.* Vol. 3. Washington, D.C.: American Psychological Association, 1968.

Lang, P. J. "The Mechanisms of Desensitization and Laboratory Studies of Human Fear." In C. M. Franks (Ed.), *Behavior Therapy: Appraisal and Status.* New York: McGraw-Hill, 1969.

Lang, P. J., and Lazovik, A. D. "Experimental Desensitization of a Phobia." *Journal of Abnormal and Social Psychology*, 1963, *66*, 519-525.

Lang, P. J., Melamed, B. G., and Hart, J. A. "A Psychophysiological Analysis for Fear Modification Using an Automated Desensitization Procedure." *Journal of Abnormal Psychology*, 1970, *76*, 220-234.

Lange, A. J., and Jakubowski, P. *Responsible Assertive Behavior: Cognitive/Behavioral Procedures for Trainers.* Champaign, Ill.: Research Press, 1976.

Langer, E. J., Janis, I. L., and Wolfer, J. A. "Reduction of Psychological Stress in Surgical Patients." *Journal of Experimental Social Psychology*, 1975, *11*, 155-165.

Lanyon, R. I., and Barocas, V. S. "Effects of Contingent Events on Stuttering and Fluency." *Journal of Consulting and Clinical Psychology*, 1975, *43*, 786-793.

Lavigueur, H. "The Use of Siblings as an Adjunct to the Behavioral Treatment of Children in the Home with Parents as Therapists." *Behavior Therapy,* 1976, *7,* 602-613.

Law and Behavior, Quarterly Analysis of Legal Developments Affecting Professionals in Human Services, 1976a, *1* (whole issue No. 1).

Law and Behavior, Quarterly Analysis of Legal Developments Affecting Professionals in Human Services, 1976b, *1* (whole issue No. 3).

Law and Behavior, Quarterly Analysis of Legal Developments Affecting Professionals in Human Services, 1976c, *1* (whole issue No. 4).

Lawrence, P. S. "The Assessment and Modification of Assertive Behavior." Doctoral dissertation, Arizona State University, 1970. (University Microfilms, 396-B, No. 70-11, 888)

Laws, D. R., and Serber, M. "Measurement and Evaluation of Assertive Training with Sexual Offenders." In R. E. Hosford and S. Moss (Eds.), *The Crumbling Walls: Treatment and Counseling of the Youthful Offender.* Champaign: University of Illinois Press, 1974.

Laws, J. L. "A Feminist View of Marital Adjustment." In A. S. Gurman and D. G. Rice (Eds.), *Couples in Conflict: New Directions in Marital Therapy.* New York: Aronson, 1975.

Lazarus, A. A. "A Preliminary Report on the Use of Directed Muscular Activity in Counterconditioning." *Behaviour Research and Therapy,* 1965a, *2,* 301-303.

Lazarus, A. A. "Towards the Understanding and Effective Treatment of Alcoholism." *South African Medical Journal,* 1965b, *39,* 736-741.

Lazarus, A. A. "Broad Spectrum Behavior Therapy and the Treatment of Agoraphobia." *Behaviour Research and Therapy,* 1966, *4,* 95-97.

Lazarus, A. A. "Learning Theory and the Treatment of Depression." *Behaviour Research and Therapy,* 1968, *6,* 83-89.

Lazarus, A. A. *Behavior Therapy and Beyond.* New York: McGraw-Hill, 1971.

Lazarus, A. A. "Multimodal Behavior Therapy: Treating The Basic ID." *Journal of Nervous and Mental Disease,* 1973a,

156, 404-411.

Lazarus, A. A. "On Assertive Behavior: A Brief Note." *Behavior Therapy,* 1973b, *4,* 697-699.

Lazarus, A. A. "Women in Behavior Therapy." In V. Franks and V. Burtle (Eds.), *Women in Therapy: New Perspectives for a Changing Society.* New York: Brunner/Mazel, 1974.

Lazarus, A. A., and Abramowitz, A. "The Use of 'Emotive Imagery' in the Treatment of Children's Phobias." *Journal of Mental Science,* 1962, *108,* 191-195.

Lazarus, A. A., and Davison, G. C. "Clinical Innovation in Research and Practice." In A. E. Bergin and S. L. Garfield (Eds.), *Handbook of Psychotherapy and Behavior Change: An Empirical Analysis.* New York: Wiley, 1971.

Lazarus, A. A., Davison, G. C., and Polefka, D. A. "Classical and Operant Factors in the Treatment of a School Phobia." *Journal of Abnormal Psychology,* 1965, *70,* 225-229.

Lazarus, A. A., and Fay, A. *I Can If I Want To.* New York: Morrow, 1975.

Lazarus, A. A., and Serber, M. "Is Systematic Desensitization Being Misapplied?" *Psychological Reports,* 1968, *23,* 215-218.

Lederer, W. J., and Jackson, D. D. *The Mirages of Marriage.* New York: Norton, 1968.

Leitenberg, H. "Behavioral Approaches to Treatment of Neuroses." In H. Leitenberg (Ed.), *Handbook of Behavior Modification and Behavior Therapy.* Englewood Cliffs, N.J.: Prentice-Hall, 1976.

Leitenberg, H., Agras, W. S., Allen, R., Butz, R. R., and Edwards, J. "Feedback and Therapist Praise During Treatment of Phobia." *Journal of Consulting and Clinical Psychology,* 1975, *43,* 396-404.

Leitenberg, H., Agras, W. S., Thompson, L. E., and Wright, D. E. "Feedback in Behavior Modification: An Experimental Analysis in Two Phobic Cases." *Journal of Applied Behavior Analysis,* 1968, *1,* 131-137.

Leitenberg, H., and Callahan, E. J. "Reinforced Practice and Reduction of Different Kinds of Fears in Adults and Children." *Behaviour Research and Therapy,* 1973, *11,* 19-30.

Lemere, F., and Voetglin, W. "An Evaluation of the Aversion

Treatment of Alcoholism." *Quarterly Journal of Studies on Alcohol,* 1950, *11,* 199-204.

Leon, G. R. "Current Dimensions in the Treatment of Obesity." *Psychological Bulletin,* 1976, *83,* 557-578.

Lepper, M. R., Greene, D., and Nisbett, R. E. "Undermining Children's Intrinsic Interest with Extrinsic Reward: A Test of the 'Overjustification' Hypothesis." *Journal of Personality and Social Psychology,* 1973, *28,* 129-137.

Lesser, E. "Behavior Therapy with a Narcotics User: A Case Report." *Behaviour Research and Therapy,* 1967, *5,* 252-253.

Lettieri, D. J. "Research Issues in Developing Prediction Scales." In C. Neuringer (Ed.), *Psychological Assessment in Assessment of Suicidal Risk.* Springfield, Ill.: Thomas, 1974.

Levendusky, P., and Pankrantz, L. "Self-Control Techniques as an Alternative to Pain Medication." *Journal of Abnormal Psychology,* 1975, *84,* 165-168.

Levinger, G. "Marital Cohesiveness and Dissolution: An Integrative Review." *Journal of Marriage and the Family,* 1965, *27,* 19-28.

Levinger, G., and Senn, D. J. "Disclosure of Feelings in Marriage." *Merrill-Palmer Quarterly of Behavior and Development,* 1967, *13,* 252-258.

Levitz, L. S., and Stunkard, A. J. "A Therapeutic Coalition for Obesity: Behavior Modification and Patient Self-Help." *American Journal of Psychiatry,* 1974, *131,* 423-427.

Levy, L. H. "Facts and Choice in Counseling and Counselor Education: A Cognitive Viewpoint." In C. A. Parker (Ed.), *Counseling Theories and Counselor Education.* Boston: Houghton Mifflin, 1968.

Lewinsohn, P. M. "Clinical and Theoretical Aspects of Depression." In K. S. Calhoun, H. E. Adams, and K. M. Mitchell (Eds.), *Innovative Treatment Methods in Psychopathology.* New York: Wiley, 1974.

Lewinsohn, P. M. "The Behavioral Study and Treatment of Depression." In M. Hersen, R. M. Eisler, and P. M. Miller (Eds.), *Progress in Behavior Modification.* Vol. 1. New York: Academic, 1975.

Lewinsohn, P. M., Biglan, A., and Zeiss, A. M. "Behavioral Treatment of Depression." In P.O. Davidson (Ed.), *Behavioral Management of Anxiety, Depression and Pain.* New York: Brunner/Mazel, 1976.

Lewinsohn, P. M., and Graf, M. "Pleasant Activities and Depression." *Journal of Consulting and Clinical Psychology,* 1973, *41,* 261-268.

Lewinsohn, P. M., and Libet, J. "Pleasant Events, Activity Schedules and Depression." *Journal of Abnormal Psychology,* 1972, *79,* 291-295.

Lewinsohn, P. M., and Schaffer, M. "The Use of Home Observation as an Integral Part of the Treatment of Depression: Preliminary Report and Case Studies." *Journal of Consulting and Clinical Psychology,* 1971, *37,* 87-94.

Lewinsohn, P. M., Weinstein, M. S., and Alper, T. "A Behaviorally Oriented Approach to the Group Treatment of Depressed Persons: A Methodological Contribution." *Journal of Clinical Psychology,* 1970, *26,* 525-532.

Lewinsohn, P. M., Weinstein, M. S., and Shaw, D. "Depression: A Clinical-Research Approach." In R. D. Rubin and C. M. Franks (Eds.), *Advances in Behavior Therapy, 1968.* New York: Academic, 1969.

Lewis, S. "A Comparison of Behavior Therapy Techniques in the Reduction of Fearful Avoidance Behavior." *Behavior Therapy,* 1974, *5,* 648-655.

Liberman, R. P. *Behavioral Marital Therapy: Group Leaders Guide.* Oxnard, Calif.: Behavior Analysis and Modification Project, 1975.

Liberman, R. P., De Risi, W. J., King, L. W., Eckman, T. A., and Wood, D. "Behavioral Measurement in a Community Mental Health Center." In P. O. Davidson, F. W. Clark, and L. A. Hamerlynck (Eds.), *Evaluation of Behavioral Programs in Community, Residential and School Settings.* Champaign, Ill.: Research Press, 1974.

Liberman, R. P., King, L. W., and De Risi, W. J. "Behavior Analysis and Therapy in Community Mental Health." In H. Leitenberg (Ed.), *Handbook of Behavior Modification and Behavior Therapy.* Englewood Cliffs, N.J.: Prentice-Hall, 1976.

Liberman, R. P., King, L. W., De Risi, W. J., and McCann, M. *Personal Effectiveness: Guiding People to Assert Themselves and Improve Their Social Skills.* Champaign, Ill.: Research Press, 1975.

Liberman, R. P., and Raskin, D. E. "Depression: A Behavioral Formulation." *Archives of General Psychiatry,* 1971, *24,* 515-523.

Liberman, R. P., and Roberts, J. "Contingency Management of

Neurotic Depression and Marital Disharmony." In H. J. Eysenck (Ed.), *Case Histories in Behavior Therapy.* London: Routledge & Kegan Paul, 1976.

Liberman, R. P., Teigen, J., Patterson, R., and Baker, V. "Reducing Delusional Speech in Chronic Paranoid Schizophrenics." *Journal of Applied Behavior Analysis,* 1973, *6,* 57-64.

Libet, J., and Lewinsohn, P. M. "The Concept of Social Skill with Special References to the Behavior of Depressed Persons." *Journal of Consulting and Clinical Psychology,* 1973, *40,* 304-312.

Libet, J. M., Lewinsohn, P. M., and Javorek, F. "The Construct of Social Skill: An Empirical Study of Several Measures on Temporal Stability, Internal Structure, Validity, and Situational Generalizability." Unpublished manuscript, available from second author, Department of Psychology, University of Oregon, Eugene, OR 97403, 1973.

Lichtenberg, P. "A Definition and Analysis of Depression." *Archives of Neurology and Psychiatry,* 1957, *77,* 519-527.

Lichtenstein, E., Harris, D. E., Birchler, G. R., Wahl, J. M., and Schmahl, D. P. "Comparison of Rapid Smoking, Warm, Smoky Air, and Attention Placebo in the Modification of Smoking Behavior." *Journal of Consulting and Clinical Psychology,* 1973, *40,* 92-98.

Lick, J., and Bootzin, R. "Expectancy Factors in the Treatment of Fear: Methodological and Theoretical Issues." *Psychological Bulletin,* 1975, *82,* 917-931.

Lick, J. R., and Katkin, E. S. "Assessment of Anxiety and Fear." In M. Hersen and A. S. Bellack (Eds.), *Behavioral Assessment: A Practical Handbook.* New York: Pergamon, 1976.

Lindsley, O. R. "Geriatric Prosthetics." In R. Kastenbaum (Ed.), *New Thoughts on Old Age.* New York: Springer, 1964. (Also in R. Ulrich, T. Stachnik, and J. Mabry (Eds.), *Control of Human Behavior.* Glenview, Ill.: Scott, Foresman, 1966.)

Lindsley, O. R. "An Experiment with Parents Handling Behavior at Home." *Johnstone Bulletin,* 1966, *9,* 27-36.

Lindsley, O. R. "A Reliable Wrist Counter for Recording Behavior Rates." *Journal of Applied Behavior Analysis,* 1968a, *1,* 77-78.

Lindsley, O. R. "Training Parents and Teachers to Precisely

Manage Children's Behavior." Unpublished manuscript, available from author at School of Education, University of Kansas Medical Center, Lawrence, KAN 66044, 1968b.

Linsk, N., Howe, M. W., Pinkston, E. M. "Behavioral Group Work in a Home for The Aged." *Social Work*, 1975, *20*, 454-463.

Lipinski, E., and Lipinski, B. G. "Motivational Factors in Psychedelic Drug Use by Male College Students." *Journal of the American Health Association*, 1967, *16*, 145-149.

Liversedge, L. A., and Sylvester, J. D. "Conditioning Techniques in the Treatment of Writer's Cramp." *Lancet*, 1955, *2*, 1147-1149.

Lloyd, R. W., and Salzberg, H. C. "Controlled Social Drinking: An Alternative to Abstinence as a Treatment Goal for Some Alcohol Abusers." *Psychological Bulletin*, 1975, *82*, 815-842.

Lobitz, G., and Johnson, S. "Normal vs. Deviant Children: A Multimethod Comparison." Paper presented at the Western Psychological Association Convention, San Francisco, April 1974.

Lobitz, W. C., and LoPiccolo, J. "New Methods in the Behavioral Treatment of Sexual Dysfunction." *Journal of Behavior Therapy and Experimental Psychiatry*, 1972, *3*, 265-271.

Lobitz, W. C., LoPiccolo, J., Lobitz, G. K., and Brockway, J. "A Closer Look at 'Simplistic' Behaviour Therapy for Sexual Dysfunction: Two Case Studies." In H. J. Eysenck (Ed.), *Case Studies in Behavior Therapy*. London: Routledge & Kegan Paul, 1976.

Locke, H. J., and Wallace, K. M. "Short-Term Marital Adjustment and Prediction Tests: Their Reliability and Validity." *Journal of Marriage and Family Living*, 1959, *21*, 251-255.

Loeber, R. "Engineering the Behavioral Engineer." *Journal of Applied Behavior Analysis*, 1971, *4*, 321-326.

Lofland, J. *Deviance and Identity*. Englewood, Cliffs, N.J.: Prentice-Hall, 1969.

Logan, F. "Self-Control as Habit, Drive, and Incentive." *Journal of Abnormal Psychology*, 1973, *81*, 127-136.

London, P. *Behavior Control*. New York: Harper & Row, 1969.

LoPiccolo, J., and Lobitz, W. C. "Behavior Therapy of Sexual

Dysfunction." In L. A. Hammerlynck, L. C. Handy, and E. J. Mash (Eds.), *Behavior Change: Methodology Concepts and Practice*. Champaign, Ill.: Research Press, 1973.

LoPiccolo, J., and Steger, J. C. "The Sexual Interaction Inventory: A New Instrument For Assessment of Sexual Dysfunction." *Archives of Sexual Behavior,* 1974, *2,* 163-171.

Lovaas, O. I. *Language Acquisition Programs for Nonlinguistic Children*. New York: Irvington, 1976.

Lovaas, O. I., and Newsom, C. D. "Behavior Modification with Psychotic Children." In H. Leitenberg (Ed.), *Handbook of Behavior Modification and Behavior Therapy*. Englewood Cliffs, N.J.: Prentice-Hall, 1976.

Lovaas, O. I., Schaeffer, B., and Simmons, J. Q. "Building Social Behavior in Autistic Children by Use of Electric Shock." *Journal of Experimental Research in Personality,* 1965, *1,* 99-109.

Lovitt, P., Lovitt, T. C., Eaton, M., and Kirkwood, M. "The Deceleration of Inappropriate Comments by a Natural Consequence." *Journal of School Psychology,* 1973, *11,* 149-156.

Lowe, J. C. "Excitatory Response to Music as a Reciprocal Inhibitor." *Journal of Behavior Therapy and Experimental Psychiatry,* 1973, *4,* 297-299.

Lubin, B. "Adjective Checklists for the Measurement of Depression." *Archives of General Psychiatry,* 1965, *12,* 57-62.

Lubin, B. *Manual for the Depression Adjective Check Lists*. San Diego, Calif.: Education and Industrial Testing Service, 1967.

Lutker, E. R. "Treatment of Migraine Headache by Conditioned Relaxation: A Case Study." *Behavior Therapy,* 1971, *2,* 592-593.

MacDonald, M. "A Behavioral Assessment Methodology as Applied to the Measurement of Assertion." Unpublished doctoral dissertation, University of Illinois, 1974.

MacDonald, M. L. "Multiple Impact: Behavior Therapy in a Child's Dog Phobia." *Journal of Behavior Therapy and Experimental Psychiatry,* 1975a, *6,* 317-322.

MacDonald, M. L. "Teaching Assertion: A Paradigm for Therapeutic Intervention." *Psychotherapy: Theory, Research, and Practice,* 1975b, *12,* 60-67.

MacDonald, M. L., and Butler, A. K. "Reversal of Helplessness:

Producing Walking Behavior in Nursing Home Wheelchair Residents Using Behavior Modification Procedures." *Journal of Gerontology,* 1974, *29,* 97-101.

MacFarlane, J. W. "Perspectives on Personality Consistency and Change from the Guidance Study." *Vita Humana,* 1964, *7,* 115-126.

MacPherson, E. L. R. "Control of Involuntary Movement." *Behaviour Research and Therapy,* 1967, *5,* 143-145.

MacPhillamy, D., and Lewinsohn, P. "Measurement of Reinforcing Events." *Proceedings of the 80th Annual Convention, American Psychological Association, 1972.* Washington, D.C.: American Psychological Association, 1972.

MacPhillamy, D. J., and Lewinsohn, P. M. "Manual for the Pleasant Events Schedule." Available from Lewinsohn at Psychology Department, University of Oregon, Eugene, OR 97403, 1975. Mimeographed.

Madsen, C. H., Becker, W. C., and Thomas, D. R. "Rules, Praise and Ignoring: Elements of Elementary Classroom Control." *Journal of Applied Behavior Analysis,* 1968, *1,* 139-50.

Madsen, C. H., Becker, W. C., Thomas, D. R., Koser, L., and Plager, E. "An Analysis of the Reinforcing Function of 'Sit Down' Commands." In R. K. Parker (Ed.), *Readings in Educational Psychology.* Boston: Allyn & Bacon, 1970.

Madsen, C. H., and Madsen, C. K. *Teaching Discipline: Behavioral Principles Toward a Positive Approach.* Boston: Allyn & Bacon, 1970.

Madsen, C. H., Jr., Madsen, C. K., and Thompson, F. "Increasing Rural Head Start Children's Consumption of Middle-Class Meals." *Journal of Applied Behavior Analysis,* 1974, *7,* 257-62.

Madsen, C. H., Madsen, C. K., Saudargas, R. A., Hammond, W. R., and Egar, D. E. "Classroom RAID (Rules, Approval, Ignore, Disapproval): A Cooperative Approach for Professionals and Volunteers." Unpublished manuscript available from first author at Department of Psychology, University of Florida, Tallahassee, FL 32306, 1970.

Madsen, C. H., and Ullman, L. P. "Innovations in the Desensitization of Frigidity." *Behaviour Research and Therapy,* 1967, *5,* 67-68.

Mahler, M. S., and Luke, J. A. "Outcome of the Tic Syndrome." *Journal of Nervous and Mental Diseases,* 1946, *103,* 433-445.

Mahoney, K., and Mahoney, M. J. "Cognitive Factors in Weight Reduction." In J. D. Krumboltz and C. E. Thoresen (Eds.), *Counseling Methods.* New York: Holt, Rinehart and Winston, 1976.

Mahoney, M. J. "The Self-Management of Covert Behavior: A Case Study." *Behavior Therapy,* 1971, *2,* 575-578.

Mahoney, M. J. *Cognition and Behavior Modification.* Cambridge, Mass.: Ballinger, 1974a.

Mahoney, M. J. "Self-Reward and Self-Monitoring Techniques for Weight Control." *Behavior Therapy,* 1974b, *5,* 48-57.

Mahoney, M. J. "Fat Fiction." *Behavior Therapy,* 1975, *6,* 416-418.

Mahoney, M. J., and Mahoney, K. *Permanent Weight Control.* New York: Norton, 1976a.

Mahoney, M. J., and Mahoney, K. "Treatment of Obesity: A Clinical Exploration." In B. J. Williams, S. Martin, and J. P. Foreyt (Eds.), *Obesity: Behavioral Approaches to Dietary Management.* New York: Brunner/Mazel, 1976b.

Mahoney, M. J., Moura, N. G. M., and Wade, T. C. "The Relative Efficacy of Self-Reward, Self-Punishment, and Self-Monitoring Techniques for Weight Loss." *Journal of Consulting and Clinical Psychology,* 1973, *40,* 404-407.

Mahoney, M. J., and Thoresen, C. E. *Self-Control: Power To The Person.* Monterey, Calif.: Brooks/Cole, 1974.

Malament, I. B., Dunn, M. E., and Davis, R. "Pressure Sores: An Operant Conditioning Approach." *Archives of Physical Medicine and Rehabilitation,* 1975, *56,* 161-165.

Maletzky, B. M. " 'Assisted' Covert Sensitization in the Treatment of Exhibitionism." *Journal of Consulting and Clinical Psychology,* 1974, *42,* 34-40.

Maletzky, B. M. "Behavior Recording as Treatment: A Brief Note." *Behavior Therapy,* 1974, *5,* 107-111.

Maloney, K. B., and Hopkins, B. L. "The Modification of Sentence Structure and its Relationship to Subjective Judgments of Creativity in Writing." *Journal of Applied Behavior Analysis,* 1973, *6,* 425-434.

Mandler, G., and Watson, D. "Anxiety and the Interruption of Behavior." In C. Speilberger (Ed.), *Anxiety and Behavior.* New York: Academic, 1966.

Manson, M. P., and Lerner, A. *The Marriage Adjustment Inventory.* Los Angeles: Western Psychological Services, 1962.

Margolis, R. B., and Shemberg, K. M. "Cognitive Self-Instruction in Process and Reactive Schizophrenics: A Failure to Replicate." *Behavior Therapy*, 1976, 7, 668-671.

Marks, F. M. *Fears and Phobias.* New York: Academic, 1969.

Marks, I. M. "Management of Sexual Disorders." In H. Leitenberg (Ed.), *Handbook of Behavior Modification and Behavior Therapy.* Englewood Cliffs, N.J.: Prentice-Hall, 1976.

Marlatt, G. A. "Behavioral Assessment of Social Drinking and Alcoholism." In G. A. Marlatt and P. E. Nathan (Eds.), *Behavioral Approaches to the Assessment and Treatment of Alcoholism.* New Brunswick, N.J.: Rutgers University, Center of Alcohol Studies, 1976a.

Marlatt, G. A. "The Drinking Profile: A Questionnaire for the Behavior Assessment of Alcoholism." In E. J. Mash and L. G. Terdal (Eds.), *Behavior Therapy Assessment: Diagnosis, Design and Evaluation.* New York: Springer, 1976b.

Marlatt, G. A., Demming, B., and Reid, J. B. "Loss of Control Drinking in Alcoholics: An Experimental Analogue." *Journal of Abnormal Psychology*, 1973, 81, 233-241.

Marlatt, A., Kosturn, C. F., and Lang, A. R. "Provocation to Anger and Opportunity for Retaliation as Determinants of Alcohol Consumption in Social Drinkers." *Journal of Abnormal Psychology*, 1975, 84, 652-659.

Marquis, J. N. "Orgasmic Reconditioning: Changing Sexual Object Choice Through Controlling Masturbation Fantasies." *Journal of Behavior Therapy and Experimental Psychiatry*, 1970, 1, 263-272.

Marquis, J. N., and Morgan, W. G. "A Guidebook for Systematic Desensitization." Palo Alto, Calif.: Veterans Workshop, Veterans Administration Hospital, 1969.

Marshall, W. L. "A Combined Treatment Approach to the Reduction of Multiple Fetish-Related Behaviors." *Journal of Consulting and Clinical Psychology*, 1974, 42, 613-616.

Marshall, W. L. "Reducing Masturbatory Guilt." *Journal of Behavior Therapy and Experimental Psychiatry*, 1975, 6, 260-261.

Marshall, W. L., Boutilier, J., and Minnes, P. "The Modification of Phobic Behavior by Covert Reinforcement." *Behavior Therapy*, 1974, 5, 469-480.

Martin, R. *Legal Challenges to Behavior Modification: Trends in*

Schools, Corrections, and Mental Health. Champaign, Ill.:
    Research Press, 1975.
Martin, S., Johnson, S. M., Johansson, S., and Wahl, G. "The
    Comparability of Behavioral Data in Laboratory and
    Natural Settings." In E. J. Marsh, L. A. Hamerlynck, and
    L. C. Handy (Eds.), *Behavior Modification in Families.*
    New York: Brunner/Mazel, 1976.
Masters, W. H., and Johnson, V. E. *Human Sexual Response.*
    Boston: Little, Brown, 1966.
Masters, W. H., and Johnson, V. E. *Human Sexual Inadequacy.*
    Boston: Little, Brown, 1970.
Mavissakalian, M., Blanchard, E. B., Abel, G. G., and Barlow,
    D. H. "Responses to Complex Stimuli in Homosexual and
    Heterosexual Males." *British Journal of Psychiatry,* 1975,
    126, 252-257.
Mayer, J. E., and Timms, N. *The Client Speaks: Working Class
    Impressions of Casework.* London: Routledge & Kegan
    Paul, 1970.
McClannahan, L. E., and Risley, T. R. "Design of Living Envi-
    ronments for Nursing Home Residents: Increasing Partici-
    pation in Recreational Activities." *Journal of Applied
    Behavior Analysis,* 1975, *8,* 261-268.
McClelland, D. C., Davis, W. N., Kalin, R., and Wanner, E. *The
    Drinking Man: Alcohol and Human Motivation.* New
    York: Free Press, 1972.
McCullough, J. P., Cornell, J. E., McDaniel, M. H., and Mueller,
    R. K. "Utilization of the Simultaneous Treatment Design
    to Improve Student Behavior in a First-Grade Class-
    room." *Journal of Consulting and Clinical Psychology,*
    1974, *42,* 288-292.
McFall, R. M. "The Effects of Self-Monitoring on Normal
    Smoking Behavior." *Journal of Consulting and Clinical
    Psychology,* 1970, *35,* 135-142.
McFall, R. M. "Analogue Methods in Behavioral Assessment."
    In J. D. Cone and R. P. Hawkins (Eds.), *Behavioral As-
    sessment: New Directions in Clinical Psychology.* New
    York: Brunner/Mazel, in press.
McFall, R. M., and Bridges, D. V. "Behavior Rehearsal with
    Modeling and Coaching in Assertive Training: Assessment
    and Training Stimuli." Unpublished manuscript available
    from author at Department of Psychology, University of
    Wisconsin, Charter and Johnson Streets, Madison, WI
    53706, 1970.

McFall, R. M., and Lillesand, D. B. "Behavior Rehearsal with Modeling and Coaching in Assertive Training." *Journal of Abnormal Psychology*, 1971, *77*, 313-323.

McFall, R. M., and Marston, A. R. "An Experimental Investigation of Behavioral Rehearsal in Assertive Training." *Journal of Abnormal Psychology*, 1970, *76*, 295-303.

McFall, R. M., and Twentyman, C. T. "Four Experiments on the Relative Contributions of Rehearsal, Modeling, and Coaching to Assertion Training." *Journal of Abnormal Psychology*, 1973, *81*, 199-218.

McGhie, A., and Russell, S. M. "The Subjective Assessment of Normal Sleep Patterns." *Journal of Mental Science,* 1962, *108*, 642-654.

McGovern, K. B., and Burkhard, J. "Initiating Social Contact with the Opposite Sex." In J. D. Krumboltz and C. E. Thoresen (Eds.), *Counseling Methods.* New York: Holt, Rinehart and Winston, 1976.

McGuire, R. J., Carlisle, J. M., and Young, B. G. "Sexual Deviation as Conditioned Behavior: A Hypothesis." *Behaviour Research and Therapy,* 1965, *2,* 185-190.

McKeown, D., Jr., Adams, H. E., and Forehand, R. "Generalization to the Classroom of Principles of Behavior Modification Taught to Teachers." *Behaviour Research and Therapy,* 1975, *13,* 85-92.

McLaughlin, T. F., and Malaby, J. "Intrinsic Reinforcers in a Classroom Token Economy." *Journal of Applied Behavior Analysis,* 1972, *5,* 263-270.

McLean, P. "Therapeutic Decision-Making in the Behavioral Treatment of Depression." In P. O. Davidson (Ed.), *The Behavioral Management of Anxiety, Depression and Pain.* New York: Brunner/Mazel, 1976.

McLean, P. D., Ogston, K., and Grauer, L. "A Behavioral Approach to the Treatment of Depression." *Journal of Behavior Therapy and Experimental Psychiatry,* 1973, *4,* 323-330.

McMullin, R., and Casey, B. *Talk Sense to Yourself.* Lakewood, Colo.: Jefferson County Mental Health Center, 1975.

Medland, M. B., and Stachnik, T. J. "Good Behavior Game: A Replication and Systematic Analysis." *Journal of Applied Behavior Analysis,* 1972, *5,* 45-51.

Mehrabian, A. *Nonverbal Communication.* Chicago: Aldine, 1972.

Meichenbaum, D. "Examination of Model Characteristics in

Reducing Avoidance Behavior." *Journal of Personality and Social Psychology,* 1971, *17,* 298-307.

Meichenbaum, D. "Cognitive Modification of Test Anxious College Students." *Journal of Consulting and Clinical Psychology,* 1972, *39,* 370-380.

Meichenbaum, D. H. "Therapist Manual for Cognitive Behavior Modification." Unpublished manuscript available from author at Psychology Department, University of Waterloo, Waterloo, Ontario, Canada, 1974.

Meichenbaum, D. "Enhancing Creativity by Modifying What Subjects Say to Themselves." *American Educational Research Journal,* 1975a, *12,* 129-145.

Meichenbaum, D. "Self-Instructional Methods." In F. H. Kanfer and A. P. Goldstein (Eds.), *Helping People Change: A Textbook of Methods.* New York: Pergamon, 1975b.

Meichenbaum, D. "A Cognitive-Behavior Modification Approach to Assessment." In M. Hersen and A. Bellack (Eds.), *Behavioral Assessment: A Practical Handbook.* New York: Pergamon, 1976.

Meichenbaum, D. H., and Cameron, R. "Training Schizophrenics to Talk to Themselves: A Means of Developing Attentional Controls." *Behavior Therapy,* 1973, *4,* 515-534.

Meichenbaum, D. H., Gilmore, B., and Fedoravicius, A. "Group Insight vs. Group Desensitization in Treating Speech Anxiety." *Journal of Abnormal Psychology,* 1971, *77,* 115-126.

Meichenbaum, D. H., and Goodman, J. "Training Impulsive Children to Talk to Themselves: A Means for Developing Self-Control." *Journal of Abnormal Psychology,* 1971, *77,* 115-126.

Meichenbaum, D., and Turk, D. "The Cognitive-Behavioral Management of Anxiety, Anger and Pain. In P. O. Davidson (Ed.), *The Behavioral Management of Anxiety, Depression and Pain.* New York: Brunner/Mazel, 1976.

Melamed, B. G., and Siegel, L. J. "Reduction of Anxiety in Children Facing Hospitalization and Surgery by the Use of Filmed Models." *Journal of Consulting and Clinical Psychology,* 1975a, *43,* 511-521.

Melamed, B. G., and Siegel, L. J. "Self-Directed In Vivo Treatment of an Obsessive-Compulsive Checking Ritual." *Journal of Behavior Therapy and Experimental Psychiatry,* 1975b, *6,* 31-36.

Mellstrom, M. "Contingency Management of an Adult's Inappropriate Urination and Masturbation in a Family Context." *Journal of Behavior Therapy and Experimental Psychiatry*, 1976, 7, 89-90.

Mendels, J. *Concepts of Depression*. New York: Wiley, 1970.

Meyer, V., Robertson, J., and Tatlow, A. "Home Treatment of an Obsessive-Compulsive Disorder by Response Prevention." *Journal of Behavior Therapy and Experimental Psychiatry*, 1975, 6, 37-38.

Meyers, A., Mercatorius, M., and Artz, L. "On the Development of a Cognitive Self-Monitoring Skill." *Behavior Therapy*, 1976, 7, 128-129.

Meyers, A., Mercatorius, M., and Sirota, A. "Use of Covert Self-Instructions for the Elimination of Psychotic Speech." *Journal of Consulting and Clinical Psychology*, 1976, 44, 480-482.

Meyerson, L., Kerr, N., and Michael, J. L. "Behavior Modification in Rehabilitation." In S. W. Bijou and D. M. Baer (Eds.), *Child Development: Readings in Experimental Analysis*. New York: Appleton-Century-Crofts, 1967.

Michael, J. "Management of Behavioral Consequences in Education." Paper presented at the 80th Annual convention of the American Psychological Association, Honolulu, September 1972.

Miklich, D. R. "Operant Conditioning Procedures with Systematic Desensitization in a Hyperkinetic Asthmatic Boy." *Journal of Behavior Therapy and Experimental Psychiatry*, 1973, 4, 177-182.

Milan, M. A., and McKee, J. M. "The Cellblock Token Economy: Token Reinforcement Procedures in a Maximum Security Correctional Institution for Adult Male Felons." *Journal of Applied Behavior Analysis*, 1976, 9, 253-277.

Milich, R. S. "A Critical Analysis of Schachter's Theory of Obesity." *Journal of Abnormal Psychology*, 1975, 84, 586-588.

Millenson, J. R. *Principles of Behavioral Analysis*. New York: Macmillan, 1967.

Miller, L. K. "Behavioral Principles and Experimental Communities." In W. E. Craighead, A. E. Kazdin, and M. J. Mahoney (Eds.), *Behavior Modification: Principles, Issues and Applications*. Boston: Houghton Mifflin, 1976.

Miller, L. K., and Miller, O. L. "Reinforcing Self-Help Group

Activities of Welfare Recipients." *Journal of Applied Behavior Analysis,* 1970, *3,* 57-64.

Miller, N. E. "Learning of Visceral and Glandular Responses." *Science,* 1969, *163,* 434-453.

Miller, P. M. "The Use of Behavioral Contracting in the Treatment of Alcoholism: A Case Report." *Behavior Therapy,* 1972, *3,* 593-596.

Miller, P. M. "A Behavioral Intervention Program for Chronic Public Drunkenness Offenders." *Archives of General Psychiatry,* 1975, *32,* 915-918.

Miller, P. M., Hersen, M., Eisler, R. M., and Elkin, T. E. "A Retrospective Analysis of Alcohol Consumption on Laboratory Tasks as Related to Therapeutic Outcome." *Behaviour Research and Therapy,* 1974, *12,* 73-76.

Miller, P. M., Hersen, M., Eisler, R., Epstein, L. H., and Wooten, L. S. "Relationship of Alcohol Cues to the Drinking Behavior of Alcoholics and Social Drinkers: An Analogue Study." *Psychological Records,* 1974, *24,* 61-66.

Miller, P. M., Hersen, M., Eisler, R. M., and Hillsman, G. "Effects of Social Stress on Operant Drinking of Alcoholics and Social Drinkers." *Behaviour Research and Therapy,* 1974, *12,* 67-72.

Miller, W. R. "Alcoholism Scales and Objective Assessment Methods: A Review." *Psychological Bulletin,* 1976, *83,* 649-674.

Miller, W. R., and Muñoz, R. F. *How to Control Your Drinking.* Englewood Cliffs, N.J.: Prentice-Hall, 1976.

Miller, W. R., and Selegman, M. E. P. "Depression and the Perception of Reinforcement." *Journal of Abnormal Psychology,* 1973, *82,* 62-73.

Mills, H. L., Agras, S., Barlow, D. H., and Mills, J. R. "Compulsive Rituals Treated by Response Prevention." *Archives of General Psychiatry,* 1973, *28,* 524-529.

Minuchin, S., Chamberlain, P., and Graubard, P. "A Project to Teach Learning Skills to Disturbed Delinquent Children." *American Journal of Orthopsychiatry,* 1967, *37,* 558-567.

Mischel, W. *Personality and Assessment.* New York: Wiley, 1968.

Mischel, W. "Toward a Cognitive Social Learning Reconceptualization of Personality." *Psychological Review,* 1973, *80,* 252-283.

Mischel, W., and Baker, N. "Cognitive Appraisals and Transformations in Delay Behavior." Unpublished manuscript available from author at Psychology Department, Stanford University, Stanford CA 94305, 1973.

Mishler, E., and Waxler, N. *Interaction in Families.* New York: Wiley, 1968.

Mitchell, K. R. "The Treatment of Migraine: An Exploratory Application of Time-Limited Behavior Therapy." *Technology,* 1969, *14,* 50.

Mitchell, K. R., Hall, R. F., and Piatkowska, O. E. "A Group Program for the Treatment of Failing College Students." *Behavior Therapy,* 1975, *6,* 324-336.

Mitchell, K. R., and Mitchell, D. M. "Migraine: An Exploratory Treatment Application of Programmed Behavior Therapy Techniques." *Journal of Psychosomatic Research,* 1971, *15,* 137-157.

Mitchell, W. S., and Stoffelmayr, B. E. "Application of the Premack Principle to the Behavioral Control of Extremely Inactive Schizophrenics." *Journal of Applied Behavior Analysis,* 1973, *6,* 419-423.

Mnookin, R. H. "Foster Care—In Whose Best Interest?" *Harvard Educational Review,* 1973, *43,* 599-638.

Moed, G., and Muhich, P. "Some Problems and Parameters of Mental Health Consultation." *Community Mental Health Journal,* 1972, *8,* 232-239.

Money, J. *Sex Errors of the Body: Dilemmas, Education, Counseling.* Baltimore, Md.: Johns Hopkins University Press, 1968.

Moore, B. L., and Bailey, J. S. "Social Punishment in the Modification of a Pre-School Child's 'Autistic-Like' Behavior with a Mother as Therapist." *Journal of Applied Behavior Analysis,* 1973, *6,* 497-507.

Moore, N. "Behavior Therapy in Bronchial Asthma: A Controlled Study." *Journal of Psychosomatic Research,* 1965, *9,* 257-276.

Morganstern, K. P. "Implosive Therapy and Flooding Procedures: A Critical Review." *Psychological Bulletin,* 1973, *79,* 318-334.

Morris, R. J. *Behavior Modification with Children: A Systematic Guide.* Cambridge, Mass.: Winthrop, 1976.

Moser, A. J. "Covert Punishment of Hallucinatory Behavior in a Psychotic Male." *Journal of Behavior Therapy and Experimental Psychiatry,* 1974, *5,* 297-299.

Moss, G. R., and Boren, J. J. "Depression as a Model for Behavioral Analysis." *Comprehensive Psychiatry,* 1972, *13,* 581-590.

Moss, G. R., Rada, R. T., and Appel, J. B. "Positive Control as an Alternative to Aversion Therapy." *Journal of Behavior Therapy and Experimental Psychiatry,* 1970, *1,* 291-294.

Mowrer, O. H., and Mowrer, W. M. "Enuresis: A Method for Its Study and Treatment." *American Journal of Orthopsychiatry,* 1938, *8,* 436-459.

Nathan, P. E. "Alcoholism." In H. Leitenberg (Ed.), *Handbook of Behavior Modification and Behavior Therapy.* Englewood Cliffs, N.J.: Prentice-Hall, 1976.

Nathan, P. E., and O'Brian, J. S. "An Experimental Analysis of the Behavior of Alcoholics and Non-Alcoholics During Prolonged Experimental Drinking." *Behavior Therapy,* 1971, *2,* 455-476.

National Center for Health Statistics. *Monthly Vital Statistics Report* [No.] 3 (whole issue), March 1, 1973.

Neisworth, J. T., and Moore, F. "Operant Treatment of Asthmatic Responding with the Parent as Therapist." *Behavior Therapy,* 1972, *3,* 95-99.

Newell, A. G. "A Case of Ejaculatory Incompetence Treated with a Mechanical Aid." *Journal of Behavior Therapy and Experimental Psychiatry,* 1976, *7,* 193-194.

Newton, J. R. "Considerations for the Psychotherapeutic Technique of Symptom Scheduling." *Psychotherapy: Theory, Research and Practice,* 1968, *2,* 95-103.

Ney, P. G., Palvesky, A. E., and Markely, J. "Relative Effectiveness of Operant Conditioning and Play Therapy in Childhood Schizophrenia." *Journal of Autism and Childhood Schizophrenia,* 1971, *1,* 337-349.

Nicholis, F. B., and Silvestri, L. G. "Hypnotic Activity of Placebo in Relation to Severity of Insomnia: A Qualitative Evaluation." *Clinical Pharmacological Therapies,* 1967, *8,* 841-847.

Nimmer, W. H., and Kapp, R. A. "A Multiple Impact Program for the Treatment of Injection Phobias." *Journal of Behavior Therapy and Experimental Psychiatry,* 1974, *5,* 257-258.

Novaco, R. W. *Anger Control: The Development and Evaluation of an Experimental Treatment.* Lexington, Mass.: Heath, 1975.

Novaco, R. W. "Treatment of Chronic Anger Through Cognitive

and Relaxation Controls." *Journal of Consulting and Clinical Psychology,* 1976, *44,* 681.

Nydegger, R. V. "The Elimination of Hallucinatory and Delusional Behavior by Verbal Conditioning and Assertive Training: A Case Study." *Journal of Behavior Therapy and Experimental Psychiatry,* 1972, *3,* 225-227.

O'Banion, K., and Arkowitz, H. "Social Anxiety and Selective Memory for Affective Information about the Self." Unpublished manuscript available from author at Department of Psychology, University of Oregon, Eugene, OR 97403, 1974.

O'Brien, F., and Azrin, N. H. "Interaction-Priming: A Method of Reinstating Patient-Family Relationships." *Behaviour Research and Therapy,* 1973, *11,* 133-136.

O'Brien, F., Azrin, N. H., and Henson, K. "Increased Communications in Chronic Mental Patients by Reinforcement and Response Priming." *Journal of Applied Behavior Analysis,* 1969, *2,* 23-29.

O'Brien, J. S., Raynes, A. E., and Patch, V. D. "Treatment of Heroin Addiction with Aversion Therapy, Relaxation Training and Systematic Desensitization." *Behaviour Research and Therapy,* 1972, *10,* 77-80.

O'Connor, R. D. "Modification of Social Withdrawal Through Symbolic Modeling." *Journal of Applied Behavior Analysis,* 1969, *2,* 15-22.

O'Dell, S. "Training Parents in Behavior Modification." *Psychological Bulletin,* 1974, *81,* 418-433.

Oden, S. L., and Asher, S. R. "Coaching Children in Social Skills for Friendship Making." Unpublished manuscript, available from author at College of Education, Center For Development, Learning, and Instruction, University of Rochester, Rochester, NY 14627, 1975.

O'Donnell, J. "Lifetime Patterns of Narcotic Addiction." In M. Ruff, L. N. Robbins, and M. Pollack (Eds.), *Life History Research in Psychopathology.* Vol. 2. Minneapolis: University of Minnesota Press, 1972.

O'Leary, K. D., and Becker, W. C. "Behavior Modification of an Adjustment Class: A Token Reinforcement Program." *Exceptional Children,* 1967, *33,* 637-642.

O'Leary, K. D., and Drabman, R. S. "Token Reinforcement Programs in the Classroom: A Review." *Psychological Bulletin,* 1971, *75,* 379-398.

O'Leary, K. D., O'Leary, S., and Becker, W. C. "Modification of a Deviant Sibling Interaction Pattern in the Home." *Behaviour Research and Therapy,* 1967, *5,* 113-120.

O'Leary, K. D., and Wilson, G. T. *Behavior Therapy: Application and Outcome.* Englewood Cliffs, N.J.: Prentice-Hall, 1975.

O'Leary, S. G., and O'Leary, K. D. "Behavior Modification in the School." In H. Leitenberg (Ed.), *Handbook of Behavior Modification and Behavior Therapy.* Englewood Cliffs, N.J.: Prentice-Hall, 1976.

O'Neil, S. "The Application and Methodological Implications of Behavior Modification in Nursing Research." In M. Batey (Ed.), *Communicating Nursing Research: The Many Sources of Nursing Knowledge.* Boulder, Colo.: Western Interstate Commission for Higher Education, 1972.

Orne, M. "On the Social Psychology of the Psychological Experiment, with Particular Reference to Demand Characteristics and Their Implications." *American Psychologist,* 1962, *17,* 776-783.

Orne, M. T., and Wender, P. H. "Anticipatory Socialization for Psychotherapy: Method and Rationale." *American Journal of Psychiatry,* 1968, *124,* 1202-1212.

Oswald, I., and Priest, R. G. "Five Weeks to Escape the Sleeping-Pill Habit." *British Medical Journal,* 1965, *2,* 1093-1095.

Panyan, M., Boozer, H., and Morris, N. "Feedback to Attendants as a Reinforcer for Applying Operant Techniques." *Journal of Applied Behavior Analysis,* 1970, *3,* 1-4.

Park, P., and Whitehead, P. C. "Developmental Sequence and Dimensions of Alcoholism." *Quarterly Journal of Studies on Alcohol,* 1973, *34,* 887-904.

Parke, R. D. "Effectiveness of Punishment as an Interaction of Intensity, Timing, Agent Nurturance and Cognitive Structuring." *Child Development,* 1969, *40,* 213-235.

Parrino, J. "Reduction of Seizures by Desensitization." *Journal of Behavior Therapy and Experimental Psychiatry,* 1971, *2,* 215-218.

Paschalis, A. P. H., Kimmel, H. D., and Kimmel, E. "Further Study of Diurnal Instrumental Conditioning in the Treatment of Enuresis Nocturna." *Journal of Behavior Therapy and Experimental Psychiatry,* 1972, *3,* 253-256.

Passman, R. H. "A Procedure for Eliminating Writer's Block in a College Student." *Journal of Behavior Therapy and Experimental Psychiatry,* 1976, *7,* 297-298.

Passmore, R., Strong, A., Swindells, Y. E., and El Din, N. "The

Effect of Overfeeding on Two Fat Young Women." *British Journal of Nutrition,* 1963, *17,* 373.

Patterson, C. J., and Mischel, W. "Effects of Temptation-Inhibiting and Task-Facilitating Plans on Self-Control." *Journal of Personality and Social Psychology,* 1976, *33,* 209-217.

Patterson, E. T., Griffin, J. C., and Panyan, M. C. "Incentive Maintenance of Self-Help Skill Training Programs for Non-Professional Personnel." *Journal of Behavior Therapy and Experimental Psychiatry,* 1976, 7, 249-253.

Patterson, G. R. "An Application of Conditioning Techniques to the Control of a Hyperactive Child." In L. P. Ullman and L. Krasner (Eds.), *Case Studies in Behavior Modification.* New York: Holt, Rinehart and Winston, 1965.

Patterson, G. R. "The Mother as a Social Engineer in the Classroom." In J. D. Krumboltz and C. E. Thoresen (Eds.), *Behavioral Counseling: Cases and Techniques.* New York: Holt, Rinehart and Winston, 1969.

Patterson, G. R. "Behavioral Intervention Procedures in the Classroom and in the Home." In A. E. Bergin and S. L. Garfield (Eds.), *Handbook of Psychotherapy and Behavior Change: An Empirical Analysis.* New York: Wiley, 1971a.

Patterson, G. R. *Families: Applications of Social Learning to Family Life.* Champaign, Ill.: Research Press, 1971b.

Patterson, G. R. "Intervention for Boys with Conduct Problems: Multiple Settings, Treatments and Criteria." *Journal of Consulting and Clinical Psychology,* 1974, *42,* 471-481.

Patterson, G. R. "The Aggressive Child: Victim and Architect of a Coercive System." In E. J. Mash, L. A. Hamerlynck, and L. C. Handy (Eds.), *Behavior Modification and Families.* New York: Brunner/Mazel, 1976.

Patterson, G. R., and Brodsky, G. "Behavior Modification for a Child with Multiple Problem Behaviors." *Journal of Child Psychology and Psychiatry,* 1966, 7, 277-295.

Patterson, G., Cobb, J. A, and Ray, R. "A Social Engineering Technology for Retraining the Families of Aggressive Boys." In H. Adams and L. Unikel (Eds.), *Issues and Trends in Behaviour Therapy.* Springfield, Ill.: Thomas, 1973.

Patterson, G. R., and Gullion, E. *Living with Children: New Methods for Parents and Teachers.* Champaign, Ill.: Research Press, 1968.

Patterson, G. R., and Hops, H. "Coercion, A Game for Two:

Intervention Techniques for Marital Conflict." In R. E. Ulrich and P. Mountjoy (Eds.), *The Experimental Analysis of Social Behavior*. New York: Appleton-Century-Crofts, 1972.

Patterson, G. R., and Reid, J. B. "Reciprocity and Coercion: Two Facets of Social Systems." In C. Neuringer and J. L. Michael (Eds.), *Behavior Modification in Clinical Psychology*. New York: Appleton-Century-Crofts, 1970.

Patterson, G. R., Littman, R. A., and Bricker, W. "Assertive Behavior in Children: A Step Toward a Theory of Aggression." *Monographs of the Society for Research in Child Development*, 1967, *32*, (whole issue No. 5).

Patterson, G. R., McNeal, S., Hawkins, N., and Phelps, R. "Reprogramming the Social Environment." *Journal of Child Psychology and Psychiatry*, 1967, *8*, 181-195.

Patterson, G. R., Ray, R. S., Shaw, D. A., and Cobb, J. A. *Manual for Coding of Family Interactions*. Rev. ed., 1969. Document No. 01234. Order from ASIS/NAPS, c/o Microfiche Publications, 440 Park Ave. S., New York, NY 10016.

Patterson, G. R., Reid, J. B., Jones, R. R., and Conger, R. E. *A Social Learning Approach to Family Intervention. Vol. 1: Families with Aggressive Children*. Eugene, Ore.: Castalia, 1975.

Patterson, G. R., Shaw, D. A., and Ebner, M. J. "Teachers, Peers, and Parents as Agents of Change in the Classroom." In F. A. M. Benson (Ed.), *Modifying Deviant Social Behavior in Various Classroom Settings*. Monograph No. 1. Eugene, Ore.: Department of Special Education, College of Education, University of Oregon, 1969.

Patterson, R. L. "Time-Out and Assertive Training for a Dependent Child." *Behavior Therapy*, 1972, *3*, 466-468.

Paul, G. L. *Insight Versus Desensitization in Psychotherapy: An Experiment in Anxiety Reduction*. Stanford, Calif.: Stanford University Press, 1966.

Paul, G. L. "Two-Year Follow-Up of Systematic Desensitization in Therapy Groups." *Journal of Abnormal Psychology*, 1968, *73*, 119-130.

Paul, G. L. "Chronic Mental Patient: Current Status—Future Directions." *Psychological Bulletin*, 1969a, *71*, 81-94.

Paul, G. L. "Outcome of Systematic Desensitization. Part 2: Background and Procedures, and Uncontrolled Reports of Individual Treatments." In C. M. Franks (Ed.), *Behavior Therapy: Appraisal and Status*. New York: McGraw-

Hill, 1969b.

Paul, G. L., and Shannon, D. T. "Treatment of Anxiety Through Systematic Desensitization in Therapy Groups." *Journal of Abnormal Psychology,* 1966, *71,* 124-135.

Paulus, M. J. "Systematized Observation of Environmental Contingencies in Residential Care Homes." Unpublished manuscript, School of Social Welfare, University of California, Berkeley, 1976.

Pauly, I. "Male Psychosexual Inversion: Transsexualism, a Review of 100 Cases." *Archives of General Psychiatry,* 1965, *13,* 172-181.

Pavlov, I. P. *Conditioned Reflexes.* (G. V. Anrip, Trans.) New York: Liveright, 1927.

Paykel, E. S., Meyers, J. K., Dienelt, M. N., Klerman, G. L., Lindenthal, J. J., and Pepper, M. P. "Life Events and Depression: A Controlled Study." *Archives of General Psychiatry,* 1969, *21,* 753-760.

Pendergrass, V. E. "Timeout from Positive Reinforcement Following Persistent High Rate Behavior in Retardates." *Journal of Applied Behavior Analysis,* 1972, *5,* 85-91.

Perkins, W. H. "Replacement of Stuttering with Normal Speech. Part 2: Clinical Procedures." *Journal of Speech and Hearing Disorders,* 1973, *38,* 295-303.

Perzan, R. S., Boulanger, F., and Fischer, D. G. "Complex Factors in Inhibition of Defecation: Review and Case Study." *Journal of Behavior Therapy and Experimental Psychiatry,* 1972, *3,* 129-133.

Phelps, S., and Austin, N. *The Assertive Woman.* San Luis Obispo, Calif.: Impact Press, 1975.

Phillips, E. L. "Achievement Place: Token Reinforcement Procedures in a Home-Style Rehabilitation Setting for 'Pre-Delinquent' Boys." *Journal of Applied Behavior Analysis,* 1968, *1,* 213-223.

Phillips, E. L., Phillips, E. A., Fixsen, D. L., and Wolf, M. M. *The Teaching-Family Handbook.* Lawrence: University of Kansas Printing Service, 1975.

Phillips, E. L., Wolf, M. M., and Fixsen, D. L. "Achievement Place: Development of the Elected Manager System." *Journal of Applied Behavior Analysis,* 1973, *6,* 541-561.

Pierce, C. H., and Risley, T. R. "Improving Job Performance of Neighborhood Youth Corps Aides in an Urban Recreation Program." *Journal of Applied Behavior Analysis,* 1974a, *7,* 207-215.

Pierce, C. H., and Risley, T. R. "Recreation as a Reinforcer:

Increasing Membership and Decreasing Disruptions in an Urban Recreational Center." *Journal of Applied Behavior Analysis,* 1974b, *7,* 403-411.

Pierce, R. M., and Drasgow, J. "Teaching Facilitative Interpersonal Functioning to Neuropsychiatric Patients." *Journal of Counseling Psychology,* 1969, *16,* 295-298.

Pion, R. J. *The Sexual Response Profile.* Honolulu: Enabling Systems, 1975.

Platt, J. J., Siegel, J. M., and Spivack, G. "Do Psychiatric Patients and Normals See the Same Solutions as Effective in Solving Interpersonal Problems?" *Journal of Consulting and Clinical Psychology,* 1975, *43,* 279.

Platt, J. J., and Spivack, G. "Problem-Solving Thinking of Psychiatric Patients." *Journal of Consulting and Clinical Psychology,* 1972, *39,* 148-151.

Platt, J. J., and Spivack, G. "Means of Solving Real-Life Problems. Part 1: Psychiatric Patients Versus Controls, and Cross-Cultural Comparisons of Normal Females." *Journal of Community Psychology,* 1974, *2,* 45-48.

Plummer, K. *Sexual Stigma: An Interactionist Account.* London: Routledge & Kegan Paul, 1975.

Polakow, R. L. "Covert Sensitization Treatment of a Probationed Barbiturate Addict." *Journal of Behavior Therapy and Experimental Psychiatry,* 1975, *6,* 53-54.

Polakow, R. L., and Doctor, R. M. "Treatment of Marijuana and Barbiturate Dependency by Contingency Contracting." *Journal of Behavior Therapy and Experimental Psychiatry,* 1973, *4,* 375-377.

Polivy, J. "Perception of Calories and Regulation of Intake in Man and Animals." Unpublished manuscript, available from author at Loyola University of Chicago, 1975.

Pomerleau, O. F., and Brady, J. P. "Behavior Modification in Medical Practice." *Pennsylvania Medicine,* 1975, *78,* 49-53.

Pommer, D. A., and Streedbeck, D. "Motivating Staff Performance in an Operant Learning Program for Children." *Journal of Applied Behavior Analysis,* 1974, *7,* 217-222.

Porteus, B. D. *Training the Elderly to Administer Mental Health Services.* Paper presented at the 80th Annual Convention of the American Psychological Association, Honolulu, September 1972.

Prazak, J. A. "Learning Job-Seeking Interview Skills." In J. D. Krumboltz and C. E. Thoresen (Eds.), *Behavioral Counseling: Cases and Techniques*. New York: Holt, Rinehart and Winston, 1969.

Prazak, J. A., and Birch, K. S. "Improving Clients' Grooming." In J. D. Krumboltz and C. E. Thoresen (Eds.), *Counseling Methods*. New York: Holt, Rinehart and Winston, 1976.

Premack, D. "Toward Empirical Behavior Laws. Part 1: Positive Reinforcement." *Psychological Review*, 1959, *66*, 219-233.

Premack, D. "Reinforcement Theory." In D. Levine (Ed.), *Nebraska Symposium on Motivation: 1965*. Lincoln: University of Nebraska Press, 1965.

Premack, D. "Mechanisms of Self-Control." In W. A. Hunt (Ed.), *Learning and Mechanisms of Control of Smoking*. Chicago: Aldine-Atherton, 1970.

Prochaska, J., Smith, N., Marzilli, R. "Remote-Control Aversive Stimulation in the Treatment of Head-Banging in a Retarded Child." *Journal of Behavior Therapy and Experimental Psychiatry*, 1974, *5*, 285-289.

"Profession of Social Work: Code of Ethics." In *The Encyclopedia of Social Work*. Vol. 2. Albany, N.Y.: National Association of Social Workers, 1971.

Quay, H. C. "Patterns of Aggressions, Withdrawal and Immaturity." In H. C. Quay and J. S. Werry (Eds.), *Psychopathological Disorders of Children*. New York: Wiley, 1972.

Quilitch, H. R. "A Portable Programmed Audible Timer." *Journal of Applied Behavior Analysis*, 1972, *5*, 18.

Rachman, S. "Sexual Fetishism: An Experimental Analogue." *Psychological Record*, 1966, *16*, 293-296.

Rachman, S. "The Role of Muscular Relaxation in Desensitization Therapy." *Behaviour Research and Therapy*, 1968, *6*, 159-166.

Rafi, A. "Learning Theory and the Treatment of Tics." *Journal of Psychosomatic Research*, 1962, *6*, 71-76.

Rappaport, A. F., and Harrell, J. "A Behavioral-Exchange Model for Marital Counseling." *Family Coordinator*, 1972, *21*, 203-213.

Raskin, D. E., and Klein, Z. E. "Losing a Symptom Through Keeping It." *Archives of General Psychiatry*, 1976, *33*, 548-555.

Rathus, S. A. "Motoric, Autonomic and Cognitive Reciprocal Inhibition of a Case of Hysterical Bronchial Asthma." *Adolescence,* 1973, *8,* 29-32.

Raymond, M. J. "Case of Fetishism Treated by Aversion Therapy." *British Medical Journal,* 1956, *2,* 854-857.

Rehm, L. P., and Marston, A. R. "Reduction of Social Anxiety Through Modification of Self-Reinforcement." *Journal of Consulting and Clinical Psychology,* 1968, *32,* 565-574.

Rehm, L. P., and Rozensky, R. H. "Multiple Therapy Techniques with a Homosexual Client: A Case Study." *Journal of Behavior Therapy and Experimental Psychiatry,* 1974, *5,* 53-58.

Reid, W. J., and Shyne, A. W. *Brief and Extended Casework.* New York: Columbia University Press, 1969.

Reisinger, J. J. "The Treatment of 'Anxiety-Depression' via Positive Reinforcement and Response Cost." *Journal of Applied Behavior Analysis,* 1972, *5,* 125-130.

Reiss, M. L., Piotrowski, W. D., and Bailey, J. S. "Behavioral Community Psychology: Encouraging Low-Income Parents to Seek Dental Care for Their Children." *Journal of Applied Behavior Analysis,* 1976, *9,* 387-398.

Reitz, W. E., and Keil, W. E. "Behavioral Treatment of an Exhibitionist." *Journal of Behavior Therapy and Experimental Psychiatry,* 1971, *2,* 67-69.

Rekers, G. A., and Lovaas, O. I. "Behavioral Treatment of Deviant Sex-Role Behaviors in a Male Child." *Journal of Applied Behavior Analysis,* 1974, *7,* 173-190.

Renne, K. S. "Correlates of Dissatisfaction in Marriage." *Journal of Marriage and the Family,* 1970, *32,* 54-67.

Repp, A. C., Roberts, D. M., Slack, D. J., Repp, C. F., and Berkler, M. S. "A Comparison of Frequency, Interval, and Time-Sampling Methods of Data Collection." *Journal of Applied Behavior Analysis,* 1976, *9,* 501-508.

Research Rehabilitation Foundation. *Correctional Officer Training Program* (conducted by the Experimental Manpower Laboratory for Corrections for the U.S. Department of Labor, 1972). P.O. Box 3587, Montgomery, AL 36109, 1972.

Retka, R. L., and Fenker, R. M. "Self-Perception Among Narcotic Addicts: An Exploratory Study Employing Multi-Dimensional Scaling Techniques." *International Journal of the Addictions,* 1975, *10,* 1-12.

Reynolds, N. J., and Risley, T. R. "The Role of Social and Maternal Reinforcers in Increasing Talking of a Disadvantaged Preschool Child." *Journal of Applied Behavior Analysis,* 1968, *1,* 253-262.

Richey, C. A. "Increased Female Assertiveness Through Self-Reinforcement." Unpublished doctoral dissertation, University of California at Berkeley, 1974.

Rimm, D. C., deGroot, J. C., Boord, P., Heiman, J., and Dillow, P. V. "Systematic Desensitization of an Anger Response." *Behaviour Research and Therapy,* 1971, *9,* 273-280.

Rimm, D. C., and Masters, J. C. *Behavior Therapy: Techniques and Empirical Findings.* New York: Wiley, 1974.

Rincover, A., and Koegel, R. L. "Setting Generality and Stimulus Control in Autistic Children." *Journal of Applied Behavior Analysis,* 1975, *8,* 235-246.

Ringer, V. M. J. "The Use of a 'Token Helper' in the Management of Classroom Behavior Problems and in Teacher Training." *Journal of Applied Behavior Analysis,* 1973, *6,* 671-677.

Rinn, R. C., Tapp, L., and Petrella, R. "Behavior Modification with Outpatients in a Community Mental Health Center." *Journal of Behavior Therapy and Experimental Psychiatry,* 1973, *4,* 243-248.

Rinn, R. C., and Vernon, J. C. "Process Evaluation of Outpatient Treatment in a Community Mental Health Center." *Journal of Behavior Therapy and Experimental Psychiatry,* 1975, *6,* 5-12.

Risley, T. R. "The Effects and Side Effects of the Use of Punishment with an Autistic Child." *Journal of Applied Behavior Analysis,* 1968, *1,* 21-34.

Risley, T. R. "Behavior Modification: An Experimental-Therapeutic Endeavor." In L. A. Hamerlynck, P.O. Davidson, and L. E. Acker (Eds.), *Behavior Modification and Ideal Mental Health Services.* (First Banff International Conference on Behavior Modification.) Calgary, Alberta, Canada: University of Calgary, 1969.

Risley, T. R., Clark, H. B., and Cataldo, M. F. "Behavioral Technology for the Normal Middle Class Family." In E. J. Mash, L. A. Hamerlynck, and L. C. Handy (Eds.), *Behavior Modification and Families.* New York: Brunner/Mazel, 1976.

Risley, T., Reynolds, N., and Hart, B. "Behavior Modification With Disadvantaged Children." In R. Bradfield (Ed.), *Behavior Modification: The Human Effort.* Palo Alto, Calif.: Science and Behavior Books, 1970.

Ritter, B. "The Use of Contact Desensitization, Demonstration-Plus-Participation, and Demonstration Alone in the Treatment of Acrophobia." *Behaviour Research and Therapy,* 1969, *7,* 157-164.

Robinson, D. N. "Harm, Offense, and Nuisance: Some First Steps in the Establishment of an Ethics of Treatment." *American Psychologist,* 1974, *29,* 233-238.

Robinson, C. H., and Annon, J. S. *The Heterosexual Attitude Scale—Female Form.* Honolulu: Enabling Systems, 1975a.

Robinson, C. H., and Annon, J. S. *The Heterosexual Attitude Scale—Male Form.* Honolulu: Enabling Systems, 1975b.

Robinson, C. H., and Annon, J. S. *The Heterosexual Behavior Inventory—Female Form.* Honolulu: Enabling Systems, 1975c.

Robinson, C. H., and Annon, J. S. *The Heterosexual Behavior Inventory—Male Form.* Honolulu: Enabling Systems, 1975d.

Robinson, E. A., and Price, M. G. "Behavioral and Self-Report Correlates of Marital Satisfaction." Unpublished manuscript available from author at Veterans Administration Hospital, 3801 Miranda Ave, Palo Alto, CA 94304, 1976.

Roosa, J. B. "SOCS: Situations, Options, Consequences, Simulation: A Technique for Teaching Social Interaction." Unpublished paper presented at 81st Annual Convention of the American Psychological Association, Montreal, August 1973.

Rooth, F. G., and Marks, I. M. "Persistent Exhibitionism: Short-Term Response to Aversion, Self-Regulation and Relaxation Treatments." *Archives of Sexual Behavior,* 1974, *3,* 227-248.

Rose, S. D. "A Behavioral Approach to the Group Treatment of Parents." *Social Work,* 1969, *14,* 21-29.

Rose, S. D. *Group Therapy: A Behavioral Approach.* Englewood Cliffs, N.J.: Prentice-Hall, 1977.

Rosen, M. "A Dual Model of Obsessional Neurosis." *Journal of Consulting and Clinical Psychology,* 1975, *43,* 453-459.

Rosen, G. M., Glasgow, R. E., and Barrera, M. A. "Controlled Study to Assess the Clinical Efficacy of Totally Self-Administered Systematic Desensitization." *Journal of Consulting and Clinical Psychology,* 1976, *44,* 208-217.

Rosenhan, D. L. "On Being Sane in Insane Places." *Science,* 1973, *180,* 365-369.

Rosenhan, D. L. "The Contextual Nature of Psychiatric Diagnosis." *Journal of Abnormal Psychology*, 1975, *84*, 462-474.

Ross, S. A. "Effects of Intentional Training in Social Behavior on Retarded Children." *American Journal of Mental Deficiency*, 1969, *73*, 912-919.

Ross, S. M., and Proctor, S. "Frequency and Duration of Hierarchy Item Exposure in a Systematic Desensitization Dialogue." *Behaviour Research and Therapy*, 1973, *11*, 303-312.

Ross, S. M., and Ross, S. A. "Cognitive Training for the EMR Child: Situational Problem Solving and Planning." *American Journal of Mental Deficiency*, 1973, *78*, 20-26.

Roth, D., Rehm, L. P., and Rozensky, R. A. "Depression and Self-Reinforcement." Unpublished manuscript available from author at Department of Psychology, University of Pittsburgh, Pittsburgh, PA 15232, 1975.

Rotter, J. B. "Generalized Expectancies for Internal vs. External Control of Reinforcement." *Psychological Monographs: General and Applied*, 1966, *80* (Whole No. 609).

Rozensky, R. H., and Bellack, A. S. "Individual Differences in Self-Reinforcement Style and Performance in Self- and Therapist-Controlled Weight Reduction Programs." *Behaviour Research and Therapy*, 1976, *14*, 357-364.

Rugh, C. D., and Solberg, W. K. "The Identification of Stressful Stimuli in Natural Environments Using a Portable Biofeedback Unit." *Proceedings of the Biofeedback Research Society*, 1974, *54* (abstract).

Rush, A. J., Khatani, M., and Beck, A. T. "Cognitive and Behavior Therapy in Chronic Depression." *Behavior Therapy*, 1975, *6*, 398-404.

Russel, R. K., and Sipich, J. F. "Treatment of Test Anxiety by Cue-Controlled Relaxation." *Behavior Therapy*, 1974, *5*, 389-397.

Rutner, I. T., and Bugle, C. "An Experimental Procedure for the Modification of Psychotic Behavior." *Journal of Consulting and Clinical Psychology*, 1969, *33*, 651.

Sachs, D. A. "Behavioral Techniques Within a Residential Nursing Home Facility." *Journal of Behavior Therapy and Experimental Psychiatry*, 1975, *6*, 123-127.

Sachs, L. B., Bean, H., and Morrow, J. E. "Comparison of Smoking Treatments." *Behavior Therapy*, 1970, *1*, 465-472.

Sailor, W., and Mix, B. *The TARC Assessment System.* Lawrence, Kan.: H & H Enterprises, 1975.

Sajwaj, T., Twardosz, S., and Burke, M. "Side Effects of Extinction Procedures in a Remedial Preschool." *Journal of Applied Behavior Analysis,* 1972, *5,* 163-175.

Sallows, G. "Comparative Responsiveness of Normal and Deviant Children to Naturally Occurring Consequences." Unpublished doctoral dissertation, University of Oregon, 1972.

Salter, A. *Conditioned Reflex Therapy.* New York: Farrar, Straus, & Giroux, 1949.

Sand, P. L., Fordyce, W. E., and Fowler, R. S. "Fluid Intake Behavior in Patients with Spinal-Cord Injury: Prediction and Modification." *Archives of Physical Medicine Rehabilitation,* 1973, *54,* 254-262.

Sank, L. I., and Biglan, A. "Operant Treatment of a Case of Recurrent Abdominal Pain in a 10-Year-Old Boy." *Behavior Therapy,* 1974, *5,* 677-681.

Santogrossi, D. A., O'Leary, K. D., Romanczyk, R. G., and Kaufman, K. F. "Self-Evaluation by Adolescents in a Psychiatric Hospital School Token Program." *Journal of Applied Behavior Analysis,* 1973, *6,* 277-87.

Sarason, I. G. "Test Anxiety and the Self-Disclosing Coping Model." *Journal of Consulting and Clinical Psychology,* 1975, *43,* 148-153.

Sarason, I. G. "Using Modeling to Strengthen the Behavioral Repertory of the Juvenile Delinquent." In J. D. Krumboltz and C. E. Thoresen (Eds.), *Counseling Methods.* New York: Holt, Rinehart and Winston, 1976.

Sarason, I. G., and Ganzer, V. J. *Modeling: An Approach to the Rehabilitation of Juvenile Offenders (Final Report to the Social and Rehabilitation Service of the [U.S.] Department of Health, Education and Welfare).* Washington, D.C.: U.S. Department of Health, Education and Welfare, 1971.

Sarason, I. G., and Ganzer, V. J. "Modeling and Group Discussion in the Rehabilitation of Juvenile Delinquents." *Journal of Counseling Psychology,* 1973, *20,* 442-449.

Sarbin, T. R. "On the Futility of the Proposition That Some People be Labeled 'Mentally Ill.' " *Journal of Consulting Psychology,* 1967, *31,* 447-453.

Schachter, S. "The Interaction of Cognitive and Physiological

Determinants of Emotional State." In C. Spielberger (Ed.), *Anxiety and Behavior.* New York: Academic, 1966.

Schaefer, H. H., and Martin, P. L. *Behavioral Therapy.* New York: McGraw-Hill, 1969.

Scheff, T. J. *Labeling Madness.* Englewood Cliffs, N.J.: Prentice-Hall, 1975.

Scheiderer, E. G., and Bernstein, D. A. "A Case of Chronic Back Pain and the 'Unilateral' Treatment of Marital Problems." *Journal of Behavior Therapy and Experimental Psychiatry,* 1976, *7,* 47-50.

Schneider, M., and Robin, A. "The Turtle Technique: A Method for the Self-Control of Impulsive Behavior." In J. D. Krumboltz and C. E. Thoresen (Eds.), *Counseling Methods.* New York: Holt, Rinehart and Winston, 1976.

Schumacher, S., and Lloyd, C. W. "Assessment of Sexual Dysfunction." In M. Hersen and A. S. Bellack (Eds.), *Behavioral Assessment: A Practical Handbook.* New York: Pergamon, 1976.

Schwab, J. J., Brown, J. M., Holzer, C. E., and Sokolof, M. "Current Concepts of Depression: The Sociocultural." *International Journal of Social Psychiatry,* 1968, *14,* 226-234.

Schwartz, A., and Goldiamond, I. *Social Casework: A Behavioral Approach.* New York: Columbia University Press, 1975.

Schwartz, R. M., and Gottman, J. M. "Toward a Task Analysis of Assertive Behavior." *Journal of Consulting and Clinical Psychology,* 1976, *44,* 910-920.

Schwartz, W. "Private Troubles and Public Issues: One Social Work Job or Two." In M. Branscombe (Ed.), *Social Welfare Forum.* New York: Columbia University Press, 1969.

Schwitzgebel, R. K. "A Contractual Model for the Protection of the Rights of Institutionalized Mental Patients." *American Psychologist,* 1975, *30,* 815-820.

Sclare, A. B. "The Female Alcoholic." *British Journal of Addiction,* 1970, *65,* 99-107.

Scott, J. F. *Internalization of Norms: A Sociological Theory of Moral Commitment.* Englewood Cliffs, N.J.: Prentice-Hall, 1971.

Seligman, M. E. P. *Helplessness: On Depression, Development and Death.* San Francisco: Freeman, 1975.

Seligman, M. E. P., Klein, D. C., and Miller, W. R. "Depression." In H. Leitenberg (Ed.), *Handbook of Behavior Modification and Behavior Therapy*. Englewood Cliffs, N.J.: Prentice-Hall, 1976.

Semans, J. H. "Premature Ejaculation: A New Approach." *Southern Medical Journal*, 1956, *49*, 353-361.

Serber, M. "Shame Aversion Therapy." *Journal of Behavior Therapy and Experimental Psychiatry*, 1970, *1*, 213-215.

Serber, M. "Teaching the Nonverbal Components of Assertive Training." *Journal of Behavior Therapy and Experimental Psychiatry*, 1972, *3*, 179-183.

Serber, M., Hiller, C., Keith, C., and Taylor, J. "Behavior Modification in Maximum Security Settings: One Hospital's Experience." *The American Criminal Law Review*, 1975, *13*, 85-99.

Serber, M., and Keith, C. G. "The Atascadero Project: Model of a Sexual Retraining Program for Incarcerated Homosexual Pedophiles." *Journal of Homosexuality*, 1974, *1*, 87-97.

Seymour, F. W., and Stokes, T. F. "Self-Recording in Training Girls to Increase Work and Evoke Staff Praise in an Institution for Offenders." *Journal of Applied Behavior Analysis*, 1976, *9*, 41-54.

Shaffer, M., and Lewinsohn, P. M. "Interpersonal Behaviors in the Home of Depressed Versus Nondepressed Psychiatric and Normal Controls: A Test of Several Hypotheses." Paper presented at the Annual Convention of the Western Psychological Association, San Francisco, April 1971.

Shapiro, D., and Surwit, R. S. "Learned Control of Physiological Function and Disease." In H. Leitenberg (Ed.), *Handbook of Behavior Therapy and Behavior Modification*. Englewood Cliffs, N.J.: Prentice-Hall, 1976.

Shapiro, M. H. "Legislating the Control of Behavior Control: Autonomy and the Coercive Use of Organic Therapies." *Southern California Law Review*, 1974, *47*, 237-356.

Sherman, J. A., and Baer, D. M. "Appraisal of Operant Therapy Techniques with Children and Adults." In C. M. Franks (Ed.), *Behavior Therapy: Appraisal and Status*. New York: McGraw-Hill, 1969.

Sherman, T. M., and Cormier, W. H. "The Use of Subjective Scales for Measuring Interpersonal Reactions." *Journal of Behavior Therapy and Experimental Psychiatry*, 1972, *3*, 279-280.

Shorkey, C., and Taylor, J. "Management of Maladaptive Behavior of a Severely Burned Child." *Child Welfare,* 1973, *52,* 543-547.

Sidman, M. *Tactics of Scientific Research.* New York: Basic Books, 1960.

Silber, L. D., and Howard, J. "Systematic Desensitization with a Cerebral Palsied Student." *Psychotherapy Theory, Research and Practice,* 1972, *9,* 17.

Simmons, M., and Camp, B. "Great Expectations Program Manual." Unpublished manuscript, available from Camp at University of Colorado Medical Center, Pediatrics and Psychiatry, 4200 E. 9th Ave., Denver, CO 80220, 1975.

Sintchak, G., and Geer, J. H. "A Vaginal Plethysmograph System." *Psychophysiology,* in press.

Sirota, A. D., and Mahoney, M. J. "Relaxing on Cue: The Self-Regulation of Asthma." *Journal of Behavior Therapy and Experimental Psychiatry,* 1974, *5,* 65-66.

Skiba, E., Pettigrew, L. E., and Alden, S. E. "A Behavioral Approach to the Control of Thumbsucking in the Classroom." *Journal of Applied Behavior Analysis,* 1971, *4,* 121-128.

Skindrud, K. "Training Mothers of Disruptive Non-Readers in Remedial Skills: A Home Tutoring Program." Unpublished manuscript available from author at Department of Psychology, University of Oregon, Eugene, OR 97403, undated.

Skinner, B. F. *Science and Human Behavior.* New York: Macmillan, 1953.

Skinner, B. F. *Beyond Freedom and Dignity.* New York: Knopf, 1971.

Skolada, T. E., Alterman, A., Cornelison, F. S., and Gottheil, E. "Treatment Outcome in a Drinking Decisions Program." *Journal of Studies on Alcohol,* 1975, *36,* 365-380.

Slade, P. D. "The Effects of Systematic Desensitization on Auditory Hallucinations." *Behaviour Research and Therapy,* 1972, *10,* 85-92.

Slavin, D. R. "Behavior Ratings as an Accelerator for Retardates in a Halfway House." In R. Rubin, H. Fensterheim, J. D. Henderson, and L. P. Ullman (Eds.), *Advances in Behavior Therapy.* New York: Academic, 1972.

Sloane, R. B., Staples, F. R., Cristol, A. H., Yorkston, N. J., and Whipple, K. *Psychotherapy Versus Behavior Therapy.* Cambridge, Mass.: Harvard University Press, 1975.

Smith, M. J. *When I Say No I Feel Guilty.* New York: Dial, 1975.

Smith, R. E. "The Use of Humor in the Counter Conditioning of Anger Responses: A Case Study." *Behavior Therapy,* 1973, *4,* 576-580.

Smith, R. E., and Sarason, I. G. "Social Anxiety and the Evaluation of Negative Interpersonal Feedback." *Journal of Consulting and Clinical Psychology,* 1975, *43,* 429.

Snyder, A., LoPiccolo, L., and LoPiccolo, J. "Secondary Orgasmic Dysfunction. Part 2. Case Study." *Archives of Sexual Behavior,* 1975, *4,* 277-283.

Sobell, M. B., Schaefer, H. H., and Mills, K. C. "Differences in Baseline Drinking Behavior Between Alcoholics and Normal Drinkers." *Behaviour Research and Therapy,* 1972, *10,* 257-267.

Sobell, M. B., and Sobell, L. C. *Individualized Behavior Therapy for Alcoholics: Rationale, Procedures, Preliminary Results and Appendix.* California Mental Health Research Monograph No. 13. Sacramento, Calif.: Bureau of Research, Calif. Dept. of Mental Hygiene, 1972.

Sobell, M. B., and Sobell, L. C. "Alcoholics Treated by Individualized Behavior Therapy: One-Year Treatment Outcome." *Behaviour Research and Therapy,* 1973, *2,* 599-618.

Sobell, M. B., and Sobell, L. C. "A Brief Technical Report on the MOBAT: An Inexpensive Portable Test for Determining Blood Alcohol Concentrations." *Journal of Applied Behavior Analysis,* 1975, *8,* 117-120.

Sobell, M. B., and Sobell, L. C. "Second Year-Treatment Outcome of Alcoholics Treated by Individualized Behaviour Therapy: Results." *Behaviour Research and Therapy,* 1976, *14,* 195-216.

Sobell, M. B., Sobell, L. C., and Samuels, F. H. "Validity of Self-Reports of Alcohol-Related Arrests by Alcoholics." *Quarterly Journal of Studies on Alcohol,* 1974, *35,* 276-280.

Sobell, M. B., Sobell, L. C., and Sheahan, D. B. "Contingency Diagramming: An Aid in Developing Optimal Behavior Therapy Programs for Problem Drinkers." Paper presented at the Seventh Annual Meeting of the Association for Advancement of Behavior Therapy, Miami, Florida, December, 1973.

Solomon, R. W., and Wahler, R. G. "Peer Reinforcement Control of Classroom Problem Behavior." *Journal of Applied Behavior Analysis*, 1973, *6*, 49-56.

Spivak, G., and Shure, M. B. *Social Adjustment of Young Children: A Cognitive Approach to Solving Real Life Problems*. San Francisco: Jossey-Bass, 1974.

Staats, A. W., and Butterfield, W. H. "Treatment of Non-Reading in a Culturally Deprived Juvenile Delinquent: An Application of Reinforcement Principles." *Child Development*, 1965, *36*, 925-942.

Staats, A. W., and Staats, C. K. *Complex Human Behaviors: A Systematic Extension of Learning Principles*. New York: Holt, Rinehart and Winston, 1963.

Stamm, J. M. "An Analysis of the Effects of a Continuous Counter on Response Rate Under Fixed-Ratio and Reinforcement of Retarded Adolescents and Young Adults." Unpublished doctoral dissertation, University of Wisconsin, 1970.

Stampfl, T. G., and Levis, D. J. "Essentials of Implosive Therapy: A Learning Theory Based Psychodynamic Behavioral Therapy." *Journal of Abnormal Psychology*, 1967, *72*, 496-503.

Starfield, B. "Enuresis: Its Pathogenesis and Management." *Clinical Pediatrics*, 1972, *11*, 343-349.

Steel, C., and Hochmann, J. *Improving Personal Relationships: Assertive Training for High School Women, Stimulus Films*. Washington, D.C.: American Personnel and Guidance Association, in press.

Steffy, R. A. "Service Applications: Psychotic Adolescents and Adults Treatment of Aggression." Unpublished paper presented at the annual convention of the American Psychological Association, San Francisco, September 1968.

Stein, H., and Young, M. *Aftercare Services to Mentally Ill Convalescent Leave Patients*. Sacramento, Calif.: Department of Mental Hygiene, Office of Program Review, 1968.

Stein, T. J., and Gambrill, E. D. "The Alameda Project: A Two-Year Report." Paper presented at the tenth annual meeting of the Association for Advancement of Behavior Therapy Convention, New York, December 1976a.

Stein, T. J., and Gambrill, E. D. *Decision Making in Foster Care: A Training Manual*. Berkeley, Calif.: University Extension Publications, University Extension, University of California, Berkeley, 1976b.

Stein, T. J., Gambrill, E. D., and Wiltse, K. T. "Foster Care: The Use of Contracts." *Public Welfare,* 1974, *32,* 20-25.

Sterman, M. B. "Neurophysiologic and Clinical Studies of Sensorimotor EEG Biofeedback Training: Some Effects on Epilepsy." *Seminars in Psychiatry,* 1973, *5,* 507-525.

Stern, R., and Marks, I. "Brief and Prolonged Flooding: A Comparison in Agoraphobic Patients." *Archives of General Psychiatry,* 1973, *28,* 270-276.

Stevenson, I., and Wolpe, J. "Recovery from Sexual Deviations Through Overcoming Nonsexual Neurotic Responses." *American Journal of Psychiatry,* 1960, *116,* 737-742.

Stewart, R. C. "The Differential Effects of Positive and Negative Social Reinforcement Upon Depressed and Non-Depressed Subjects." Unpublished master's thesis, University of Oregon, 1968.

Stokes, T. F., Baer, D. M., and Jackson, R. L. "Programming the Generalization of a Greeting Response in Four Retarded Children." *Journal of Applied Behavior Analysis,* 1974, *7,* 599-610.

Stoller, R. J. "Parental Influences in Male Transsexualism." In R. Green and J. Money (Eds.), *Transsexualism and Sex Reassignment.* Baltimore, Md.: Johns Hopkins University Press, 1969.

Stolz, S. B., Wienckowski, L. A., and Brown, B. S. "Behavior Modification: A Perspective on Critical Issues." *American Psychologist,* 1975, *30,* 1027-1048.

Stone, G. L., Hinds, W. C., and Schmidt, G. W. "Teaching Mental Health Behaviors to Elementary School Children." *Professional Psychology,* 1975, *6,* 34-40.

Stoudenmire, J. "Behavioral Treatment of Voyeurism and Possible Symptom Substitution." *Psychotherapy: Theory, Research, and Practice,* 1973, *10,* 328-333.

Straits, B. C. "Sociological and Psychological Correlates of Adoption and Discontinuation of Cigarette Smoking." University of Chicago, 1965. Mimeographed.

Strong, S. R. "Counseling: An Interpersonal Influence Process." *Journal of Counseling Psychology,* 1968, *15,* 215-224.

Strong, S. R. "Causal Attribution in Counseling and Psychotherapy." *Journal of Counseling Psychology,* 1970, *17,* 388-399.

Stuart, F., Stuart, R. B., Maurice, W. D., and Szasz, G. *Sexual Adjustment Inventory.* Champaign, Ill.: Research Press, 1975.

Stuart, R. B. "Behavioral Control of Overeating." *Behaviour Research and Therapy,* 1967a, *5,* 357-365.

Stuart, R. B. "Casework Treatment of Depression Viewed as an Interpersonal Disturbance." *Social Work,* 1967b, *12,* 27-36.

Stuart, R. B. "Operant-Interpersonal Treatment for Marital Discord." *Journal of Consulting and Clinical Psychology,* 1969, *33,* 675-82.

Stuart, R. B. "Assessment and Change of the Communication Patterns of Juvenile Delinquents and Their Parents." In R. D. Rubin, Fensterheim, H., Lazarus, A. A. and C. M. Franks (Eds.), *Advances in Behavior Therapy.* New York: Academic, 1971a.

Stuart, R. B. "Behavioral Contracting with the Families of Delinquents." *Journal of Behavior Therapy and Experimental Psychiatry,* 1971b, *2,* 1-11.

Stuart, R. B. "Behavioral Remedies for Marital Ills: A Guide to the Use of Operant-Interpersonal Techniques." In A. S. Gurman and D. G. Rice (Eds.), *Couples in Conflict: New Directions in Marital Therapy.* New York: Aronson, 1975.

Stuart, R. B., and Davis, B. *Slim Chance in a Fat World: Behavioral Control of Obesity.* Champaign, Ill.: Research Press, 1972.

Stuart, R. B., and Lederer, W. J. *Caring Days: Techniques for Marriage Improvement.* New York: Norton, in press.

Stuart, R. B., and Lott, L. A. "Behavioral Contracting with Delinquents: A Cautionary Note." *Journal of Behavior Therapy and Experimental Psychiatry,* 1972, *3,* 161-169.

Stuart, R. B., and Stuart, F. M. *Marriage Pre-Counseling Inventory and Guide.* Champaign, Ill.: Research Press, 1972.

Stuart, R. B., and Stuart, F. M. *Family Counseling Inventory and Guide.* Champaign, Ill.: Research Press, 1975.

Stuart, R. B., and Tripodi, T. "Experimental Evaluation of Three Time-Constrained Behavioral Treatments for Predelinquents and Delinquents." In R. D. Rubin, J. P. Brady, and J. D. Henderson (Eds.), *Advances in Behavior Therapy.* Vol. 4. New York: Academic, 1973.

Stunkard, A. J. "The Management of Obesity." *New York Journal of Medicine,* 1958, *58,* 79-87.

Stunkard, A. J. "Anorexia Nervosa." In J. P. Sanford (Ed.), *The Science and Practice of Clinical Medicine.* New York: Grune & Stratton, 1975.

Stunkard, A. J., and Burt, V. "Obesity and the Body Image. Part 2: Age of Onset of Disturbances in the Body Image." *American Journal of Psychiatry,* 1967, *123,* 1443-1447.

Stunkard, A. J., and Mahoney, M. J. "Behavioral Treatment of the Eating Disorders." In H. Leitenberg (Ed.), *Handbook of Behavior Modification and Behavior Therapy.* Englewood Cliffs, N.J.: Prentice-Hall, 1976.

Suinn, R. M. "Short-Term Desensitization Therapy." *Behaviour Research and Therapy,* 1970, *8,* 383-384.

Suinn, R. M. "Behavior Rehearsal for Ski Racers." *Behavior Therapy,* 1972, *3,* 519-520.

Suinn, R. M. "Behavior Therapy for Cardiac Patients." *Behavior Therapy,* 1974, *5,* 569-571.

Suinn, R., Edie, C., and Spinelli, P. "Accelerated Massed Desensitization: Innovation in Short-Term Treatment." *Behavior Therapy,* 1970, *1,* 303-311.

Suinn, R. M., and Richardson, I. "Anxiety Management Training: A Non-Specific Behavior Therapy Program for Anxiety Control." *Behavior Therapy,* 1971, *2,* 498-510.

Sulzer-Azaroff, B., Thaw, J., and Thomas, C. "Behavioral Competencies for the Evaluation of Behavior Modifiers." In W. S. Wood (Ed.), *Issues in Evaluating Behavior Modification.* Champaign, Ill.: Research Press, 1975.

Surratt, P. R., Ulrich, R. E., and Hawkins, R. P. "An Elementary Student as a Behavioral Engineer." *Journal of Applied Behavior Analysis,* 1969, *2,* 85-92.

Szasz, T. S. *The Myth of Mental Illness.* New York: Harper & Row, 1961.

Szasz, T. S. *Ideology and Insanity: Essays on The Psychiatric Dehumanization of Man.* New York: Doubleday, 1970a.

Szasz, T. S. *The Manufacture of Madness: A Comparative Study of the Inquisition and the Mental Health Movement.* New York: Harper & Row, 1970b.

Taplin, P. S., and Reid, J. B. "Effects of Instructional Set and Experimenter Influence on Observer Reliability." *Child Development,* 1973, *44,* 547-554.

Taylor, D. W. "Treatment of Excessive Frequency of Urination by Desensitization." *Journal of Behavior Therapy and Experimental Psychiatry,* 1972, *3,* 311-313.

Tharp, R. G., Watson, D., and Kaya, J. "Self-Modification of Depression." *Journal of Consulting and Clinical Psychology,* 1974, *42,* 624.

Tharp, R. G., and Wetzel, R. J. *Behavior Modification in the Natural Environment.* New York: Academic, 1969.

Thase, M. E., and Moss, M. K. "The Relative Efficacy of Covert Modeling Procedures and Guided Participant Modeling in the Reduction of Avoidance Behavior." *Journal of Behavior Therapy and Experimental Psychiatry,* 1976, *7,* 7-12.

Thelan, M. H., Fry, R. A., Dollinger, S. J., and Paul, S. C. "Use of Videotaped Models to Improve the Interpersonal Adjustment of Delinquents." *Journal of Consulting and Clinical Psychology,* 1976, *44,* 492.

Thibaut, J., and Kelley, H. H. *The Social Psychology of Groups.* New York: Wiley, 1959.

Thomas, E. J. *Marital Communication and Decision Making.* New York: Free Press, 1976.

Thomas, E. J., Abrams, K. S., and Johnson, J. B. "Self-Monitoring and Reciprocal Inhibition in the Modification of Multiple Tics of Giles de la Tourette's Syndrome." *Journal of Behavior Therapy and Experimental Psychiatry,* 1971, *2,* 159-171.

Thomas, E. J., and Carter, R. D. "Instigative Modification with a Multi-Problem Family." *Social Casework,* 1971, *52,* 444-455.

Thomas, E. J., Carter, R., and Gambrill, E. D. "Some Possibilities of Behavioral Modification with Marital Problems Using 'Sam' (Signal System for the Assessment and Modification of Behavior)." In R. H. Rubin, H. Fensterheim, A. A. Lazarus, and E. M. Franks (Eds.), *Advances in Behavior Therapy.* New York: Academic, 1971.

Thomas, E. J., O'Flaherty, K., and Borkin, J. "Coaching Marital Partners in Family Decision Making." In J. D. Krumboltz and C. E. Thoresen (Eds.), *Counseling Methods.* New York: Holt, Rinehart and Winston, 1976.

Thomas, E. J., Walter, C. L., and O'Flaherty, K. "A Verbal Problem Checklist for Use in Assessing Family Verbal Behavior." *Behavior Therapy,* 1974, *5,* 235-246.

Thomson, N., Fraser, D., and McDougall, A. "The Reinstatement of Speech in Near-Mute Chronic Schizophrenics by

Instructions, Imitative Prompts and Reinforcement." *Journal of Behavior Therapy and Experimental Psychiatry,* 1974, *5,* 83-89.

Thoresen, C. E., and Mahoney, M. J. *Behavioral Self-Control.* New York: Holt, Rinehart and Winston, 1974.

Thorndike, E. L. *The Fundamentals of Learning.* New York: Teachers College, Columbia University, 1932.

Todd, F. J. "Coverant Control of Self-Evaluative Responses in the Treatment of Depression: A New Use for an Old Principle." *Behavior Therapy,* 1972, *3,* 91-94.

Tokarz, T. P., and Lawrence, P. S. "An Analysis of Temporal and Stimulus Factors in the Treatment of Insomnia." Unpublished manuscript available from Lawrence at Department of Psychology, University of North Carolina, 1000 Spring Garden St., Greensboro, NC 27412, 1974.

Tomlinson, J. R. "The Treatment of Bowel Retention by Operant Procedures: A Case Study." *Journal of Behavior Therapy and Experimental Psychiatry,* 1970, *1,* 83-85.

Tracey, D. A., Karlin, R., and Nathan, P. E. "A Behavioral Analysis of Chronic Alcoholism in Four Women." *Journal of Consulting and Clinical Psychology,* 1976, *44,* 832-842.

Truax, C. "Reinforcement and Nonreinforcement in Rogerian Psychotherapy." *Journal of Abnormal Psychology,* 1966, *71,* 1-9.

Truax, C. B., and Carkhuff, R. R. *Toward Effective Counseling and Psychotherapy: Training and Practice.* Chicago: Aldine, 1967.

Truax, C. B., and Mitchell, K. M. "Research on Certain Therapist Interpersonal Skills in Relation to Process and Outcome." In A. E. Bergin and S. L. Garfield (Eds.), *Handbook of Psychotherapy and Behavior Change.* New York: Wiley, 1971.

Twentyman, C., and McFall, R. "Behavioral Training of Social Skills in Shy Males." *Journal of Consulting and Clinical Psychology,* 1975, *43,* 384-395.

Ullman, C. A. "Teachers, Peers and Tests as Predictors of Adjustment." *Journal of Educational Psychology,* 1957, *48,* 257-267.

Ullman, L. P., and Krasner, L. *A Psychological Approach to Abnormal Behavior.* Englewood Cliffs, N.J.: Prentice-Hall, 1969.

U.S. Bureau of the Census. *U.S. Department of Commerce, Mar-*

riage, Divorce and Remarriage by Year of Birth: June 1971. Washington, D.C.: U.S. Bureau of the Census, Social and Economic Statistics Administration, 1972.

U.S. Department of Health, Education and Welfare. "Protection of Human Subjects: Policies and Procedures." *Federal Register,* 1973, *39,* 18914-18920.

Valentine, J., and Arkowitz, H. "Social Anxiety and the Self-Evaluation of Interpersonal Performance." *Psychological Reports,* 1975, *36,* 211-221.

Van Houten, R., Hill, S., and Parsons, M. "An Analysis of a Performance Feedback System: The Effects of Timing and Feedback, Public Posting and Praise Upon Academic Performance and Peer Interaction." *Journal of Applied Behavior Analysis,* 1975, *8,* 449-457.

Van Houten, R., and Sullivan, K. "Effects of an Audio Cueing System on the Rate of Teacher Praise." *Journal of Applied Behavior Analysis,* 1975, *8,* 197-201.

Vasta, R. "Coverant Control of Self-Evaluations Through Temporal Cueing." *Journal of Behavior Therapy and Experimental Psychiatry,* 1976, *7,* 35-37.

Velten, E. "A Laboratory Task for Induction of Mood States." *Behaviour Research and Therapy,* 1968, *6,* 473-482.

Ventis, W. L. "Case History: The Use of Laughter as an Alternative Response in Systematic Desensitization." *Behavior Therapy,* 1973, *4,* 120-122.

Vincent, J. P. "Problem-Solving Behavior in Distressed and Non-Distressed Married and Stranger Dyads." Unpublished doctoral dissertation, University of Oregon, 1972.

Vincent, J. P., Weiss, R. L., and Birchler, G. R. "A Behavioral Analysis of Problem Solving in Distressed and Non-Distressed Married and Stranger Dyads." *Behavior Therapy,* 1975, *6,* 475-480.

Voegtlin, W. L., Lemere, F., and Broz, W. R. "Conditional Reflex Therapy of Alcoholic Addiction. Part 3: An Evaluation of Present Results in Light of Previous Experience with this Method." *Quarterly Journal of Studies on Alcohol,* 1940, *1,* 501-515.

Voegtlin, W. L., Lemere, F., Broz, W. R., and O'Hallaren, P. "Conditioned Reflex Therapy of Chronic Alcoholics. Part 4: A Preliminary Report on the Value of Reinforcement." *Quarterly Journal of Studies on Alcohol,* 1942, *2,* 505-511.

Vogler, R. E., Compton, J. V., and Weissbach, T. A. "Integrated Behavior Change Techniques for Alcoholics." *Journal of Consulting and Clinical Psychology,* 1975, *43,* 233-243.

Vogler, R. E., Ferstl, R., Kraemer, S., and Brengelmann, J. C. "Electrical Aversion Conditioning of Alcoholics: One-Year Follow-Up." *Journal of Behavior Therapy and Experimental Psychiatry,* 1975, *6,* 171-173.

Wahler, R. G. "Oppositional Children: A Quest for Parental Reinforcement Control." *Journal of Applied Behavior Analysis,* 1969a, *2,* 159-170.

Wahler, R. G. "Setting Generality: Some Specific and General Effects of Child Behavior Therapy." *Journal of Applied Behavior Analysis,* 1969b, *2,* 239-246.

Wahler, R. G. "Some Structural Aspects of Deviant Child Behavior." *Journal of Applied Behavior Analysis,* 1975, *8,* 27-42.

Wahler, R., and Cormier, W. "The Ecological Interview: A First Step in Out-Patient Child Behavior Therapy." *Journal of Behavior Therapy and Experimental Psychiatry,* 1970, *1,* 279-289.

Wahler, R. G., and Leske, G. "Accurate Observers Summary Reports." Unpublished paper available from author at University of Tennessee, Department of Psychology, 4115 Forest Glen Dr., Knoxville, TENN 37919, 1972.

Wahler, R. G., and Pollio, H. R. "Behavior and Insight: A Case Study in Behavior Therapy." *Journal of Experimental Research in Personality,* 1968, *3,* 45-56.

Wahler, R. G., Sperling, K. A., Thomas, M. R., Teeter, N. C., and Luper, H. L. "The Modification of Childhood Stuttering: Some Response-Response Relationships." *Journal of Experimental Child Psychology,* 1970, *9,* 411-428.

Wahler, R. G., Winkel, G. H., Peterson, R. F., and Morrison, D. C. "Mothers as Behavior Therapists for Their Own Children." *Behaviour Research and Therapy,* 1965, *3,* 113-124.

Walk, R. D. "Self-Ratings of Fear in a Fear-Invoking Situation." *Journal of Abnormal and Social Psychology,* 1956, *52,* 171-178.

Wallace, C. J., Teigen, J. R., Liberman, R. P., and Baker, V. "Destructive Behavior Treated by Contingency Contracts and Assertive Training: A Case Study." *Journal of Behavior Therapy and Experimental Psychiatry,* 1973, *4,* 273-274.

Walsh, W. B. "Validity of Self-Report." *Journal of Counseling Psychology,* 1967, *14,* 18-23.

Walter, H., and Gilmore, S. K. "Placebo versus Social Learning Effects in Parent Training Procedures Designed to Alter the Behaviors of Aggressive Boys." *Behavior Therapy,* 1973, *4,* 361-377.

Walter, T., and Siebert, A. *Student Success: How to be a Better Student and Still Have Time for Your Friends.* New York: Holt, Rinehart and Winston, 1976.

Walton, D. "The Application of Learning Theory to the Treatment of a Case of Neurodermatitis." In H. J. Eysenck (Ed.), *Behavior Therapy and the Neuroses.* New York: Pergamon, 1960.

Walton, D., and Mather, M. D. "The Application of Learning Principles to the Treatment of Obsessive Compulsive States in the Acute and Chronic Phases of Illness." *Behaviour Research and Therapy,* 1963, *1,* 163-174.

Wanberg, K. W., and Knapp, J. "Differences in Drinking Symptoms and Behavior of Men and Women Alcoholics." *British Journal of Addictions,* 1970, *64,* 347-355.

Watson, D., and Tharp, R. *Self-Directed Behavior: Self-Modification for Personal Adjustment.* Monterey, Calif.: Brooks/Cole, 1972.

Watson, D. L., Tharp, R. G., and Krisberg, J. "Case Study in Self-Modification: Suppression of Inflammatory Scratching While Awake and Asleep." *Journal of Behavior Therapy and Experimental Psychiatry,* 1972, *3,* 213-215.

Watzlawick, P., Beavin, J. H., and Jackson, D. D. *Pragmatics of Human Communication—A Study of Interactional Patterns, Pathologies, and Paradoxes.* New York: Norton, 1967.

Watzlawick, P., Weakland, J., and Fisch, R. *Change: Principles of Problem Formation and Problem Resolution.* New York: Norton, 1974.

Weathers, L., and Liberman, R. "The Porta-Prompter—A New Electronic Prompting and Feedback Device: A Technical Note." *Behavior Therapy,* 1973, *4,* 703-705.

Weathers, L., and Liberman, R. P. "Contingency Contracting with Families of Delinquent Adolescents." *Behavior Therapy,* 1975a, *6,* 356-366.

Weathers, L., and Liberman, R. P. "The Family Contracting Exercise." *Journal of Behavior Therapy and Experimental Psychiatry,* 1975b, *6,* 208-214.

Webster, D. R., and Azrin, N. H. "Required Relaxation: A Method of Inhibiting Agitative Disruptive Behavior of Retardates." *Behaviour Research and Therapy,* 1973, *11,* 67-78.

Weight, T. "A Portable Audible-Interval Signal Device." *Behavior Research and Instrumentation,* 1969, *1,* 228.

Weil, G., and Goldfried, M. G. "Treatment of Insomnia in an Eleven-Year-Old Child Through Self-Relaxation." *Behavior Therapy,* 1973, *4,* 282-294.

Wein, K. S., Nelson, R. O., and Odom, J. V. "The Relative Contributions of Reattribution and Verbal Extinction to the Effectiveness of Cognitive Restructing." *Behavior Therapy,* 1975, *6,* 459-474.

Weiss, R. L. "Contracts, Cognition and Change: A Behavioral Approach to Marriage Therapy." *The Counseling Psychologist,* 1975, *5,* 15-26.

Weiss, R. L., Birchler, G. R., and Vincent, J. P. "Contractual Models for Negotiation Training in Marital Dyads." *Journal of Marriage and the Family,* 1974, *36,* 321-331.

Weiss, R. L., and Cerreto, M. "Marital Status Inventory: Steps to Divorce." Unpublished manuscript available from author at Department of Psychology, University of Oregon, Eugene, OR 97403, 1975.

Weiss, R. L., Hops, H., and Patterson, G. R. "A Framework for Conceptualizing Marital Conflict, A Technology for Altering It, Some Data for Evaluating It." In L. A. Hamerlynck, L. C. Handy, and E. J. Mash (Eds.), *Behavior Change: Methodology, Concepts and Practice.* Champaign, Ill.: Research Press, 1973.

Weiss, R. L., and Margolin, G. "Marital Conflict and Accord." In A. R. Ciminero, K. S. Calhoun, and H. E. Adams (Eds.), *Handbook for Behavioral Assessment.* New York: Wiley, in press.

Weiss, T., and Engel, B. "Operant Conditioning of Heart Rate in Patients with Premature Ventricular Contractions." *Psychosomatic Medicine,* 1971, *33,* 301-321.

Weitzman, L. J. "Legal Regulation of Marriage: Tradition and Change." *California Law Review,* 1974, *62,* 11.

Wetzel, R. "Use of Behavioral Techniques in a Case of Compulsive Stealing." *Journal of Consulting Psychology,* 1966, *30,* 367-374.

Wetzel, R. J., Baker, J., Roney, M., and Martin, M. "Outpatient Treatment of Autistic Children." *Behaviour Research and Therapy,* 1966, *4,* 169-177.

Wexler, D. B. "Token and Taboo: Behavior Modification, Token Economics and the Law." *California Law Review,* 1973, *61,* 81-109.

Whatmore, R., Durward, L., and Kushlick, A. "Measuring the Quality of Residential Care." *Behaviour Research and Therapy,* 1975, *13,* 227-236.

Wheeler, M. E., and Hess, K. W. "Treatment of Juvenile Obesity by Successive Approximation Control of Eating." *Journal of Behavior Therapy and Experimental Psychiatry,* 1976, *7,* 235-241.

Whelan, P. "Reliability of Human Observers." Unpublished doctoral dissertation, University of Utah, 1974.

White, M. A. "Natural Rates of Teacher Approval and Disapproval in the Classroom." *Journal of Applied Behavior Analysis,* 1975, *8,* 367-372.

Wickramasekera, I. "Aversive Behavior Rehearsal for Sexual Exhibitionism." *Behavior Therapy,* 1976, *7,* 167-176.

Wikler, A. "Conditioning Factors in Opiate Addiction and Relapse." In D. Wilner and G. Kassebaum (Eds.), *Narcotics.* New York: McGraw-Hill, 1965.

Williams, G. D. "The Elimination of Tantrum Behavior by Extinction Procedures." *Journal of Abnormal and Social Psychology,* 1959, *59,* 269.

Williams, H. L., and Salamy, A. "Alcohol and Sleep." In B. Kissin and H. Begleiter (Eds.), *The Biology of Alcoholism.* Vol. 2. New York: Plenum, 1972.

Williams, J. G., Barlow, D. H., and Agras, W. S. "Behavioral Measurement of Severe Depression." *Archives of General Psychiatry,* 1975, *84,* 221-227.

Willis, J., Crowder, J., and Morris, B. "A Behavioral Approach to Remedial Reading Using Students as Behavioral Engineers." In G. Semb, D. R. Green, R. P. Hawkins, J. Michael, E. L. Phillips, J. A. Sherman, H. Sloane, and D. R. Thomas (Eds.), *Behavior Analysis & Education— 1972.* Lawrence: University of Kansas, Department of Human Development, Support and Development Center for Follow Through, 1972.

Wills, T. A., Weiss, R. L., and Patterson, G. R. "A Behavioral

Analysis of the Determinants of Marital Satisfaction." *Journal of Consulting and Clinical Psychology,* 1974, *42,* 802-811.

Wilson, G. T. "Innovation in the Modification of Phobic Behaviors in Two Clinical Cases." *Behavior Therapy,* 1973, *4,* 426-430.

Wilson, G. T., and Davison, G. C. "Aversion Techniques in Behavior Therapy: Some Theoretical and Metatheoretical Considerations." *Journal of Consulting and Clinical Psychology,* 1969, *33,* 327-329.

Wilson, G. T.. and Davison, G. C. "Process of Fear Reduction in Systematic Desensitization: Animal Studies." *Psychological Bulletin,* 1971, *76,* 1-14.

Wilson, G. T., and Davison, G. C. "Behavior Therapy and Homosexuality: A Critical Perspective." *Behavior Therapy,* 1974, *5,* 16-28.

Wincze, J. P., and Caird, W. K. "The Effects of Systematic Desensitization and Video Desensitization in the Treatment of Essential Sexual Dysfunction in Women." *Behavior Therapy,* 1976, *7,* 335-342.

Winter, W. D., and Ferreira, A. J. "Talking Time as an Index of Intrafamilial Similarity in Normal and Abnormal Families." *Journal of Abnormal Psychology,* 1969, *74,* 574-575.

Wisocki, P. "The Successful Treatment of a Heroin Addict by Covert Conditioning Techniques." *Journal of Behavior Therapy and Experimental Psychiatry,* 1973, *4,* 55-61.

Wolf, M., Birnbrauer, J. S., Williams, T., and Lawler, J. "A Note on Apparent Extinction of the Vomiting Behavior of a Retarded Child." In L. P. Ullman and L. Krasner (Eds.), *Case Studies in Behavior Modification.* New York: Holt, Rinehart and Winston, 1965.

Wolf, M., Risley, T., Johnston, M., Harris, F., and Allen, E. "Application of Operant Conditioning Procedures to Behavior Problems of an Autistic Child: A Follow-Up and Extension." *Behaviour Research and Therapy,* 1967, *5,* 103-111.

Wolf, M., Risley, T., and Mees, H. "Application of Operant Conditioning Procedures to the Behavior Problems of an Autistic Child." *Behavioral Research Therapy,* 1964, *1,* 305-312.

Wolpe, J. *Psychotherapy by Reciprocal Inhibition.* Stanford, Calif.: Stanford University Press, 1958.

Wolpe, J. "Conditioned Inhibition of Craving in Drug Addiction: A Pilot Experiment." *Behaviour Research and Therapy,* 1965, *2,* 285-288.

Wolpe, J. *The Practice of Behavior Therapy.* (2nd ed.) New York: Pergamon, 1973a.

Wolpe, J. "Supervision Transcript. Part 5: Mainly About Assertive Training." *Journal of Behavior Therapy and Experimental Psychiatry,* 1973b, *2,* 141-148.

Wolpe, J. "Supervision Transcript. Part 7: Neglecting the Case History and Other Elementary Errors." *Journal of Behavior Therapy and Experimental Psychiatry,* 1973c, *4,* 365-370.

Wolpe, J., and Lang, P. J. "A Fear Survey Schedule for Use in Behavior Modification." *Behaviour Research and Therapy,* 1964, *2,* 27-30.

Wolpe, J., and Lazarus, A. *Behavior Therapy Techniques.* New York: Pergamon, 1966.

Wood, H. P., and Duffy, E. L. "Psychological Factors in Alcoholic Women." *American Journal of Psychiatry,* 1966, *123,* 341-345.

Wright, J. C. "A Comparison of Systematic Desensitization and Social Skill Acquisition in the Modification of a Social Fear." *Behavior Therapy,* 1976, *7,* 205-210.

Wright, L., Nunnery, A., Eichel, B., and Scott, R. "Behavioral Tactics for Reinstating Natural Breathing in Infants with Tracheostomy." *Pediatrics Research,* 1969, *3,* 275-278.

Youell, K. J., and McCullough, J. P. "Behavioral Treatment of Mucous Colitis." *Journal of Consulting and Clinical Psychology,* 1975, *43,* 740-745.

Young, G. C., and Morgan, R. T. "Overlearning in the Conditioning Treatment of Enuresis: A Long-Term Follow-Up Study." *Behaviour Research and Therapy,* 1972, *10,* 419-420.

Zeilberger, J., Sampen, S. E., and Sloane, H. N., Jr. "Modification of a Child's Problem Behaviors in the Home with the Mother as Therapist." *Journal of Applied Behavior Analysis,* 1968, *1,* 47-58.

Zigler, E., and Phillips, L. "Social Competence and Outcome in

Psychiatric Disorder." *Journal of Abnormal and Social Psychology,* 1961, *63,* 264-271.

Zimbardo, P., Pilkonis, P. A., and Norwood, R. M. "The Social Disease Called Shyness." *Psychology Today,* 1975, *8,* 69-72.

Zlutnick, S., Mayville, W., and Moffat, S. "Behavioral Control of Seizure Disorders: The Interruption of Chained Behavior." In R. C. Katz and S. Zlutnick (Eds.), *Behavior Therapy and Health Care: Principles and Applications.* New York: Pergamon, 1975.

Name Index

1185

Subject Index